This image for the role of accounting in society is also integrated into the REAL WORLD logo. The logo, also based on the Chrysler Building, appears beside discussions of actual companies in the text, the Analytical Application sections, and the Analytical Application Cases.

 Another aspect of the accountant's role in society emphasized in this book is the ethical dimension. Each chapter contains an Ethics Case, marked by an ETHICS logo using a compass to indicate a means for providing direction. The ethical issues raised illustrate the potential complexities of working within the accounting environment.

 An additional function of the accountant is the communication of accounting information. This can take various forms, primary among which is written communication. End-of-chapter assignment materials requiring written communication skills are identified by a WRITING SHILLS logo consisting of a pen and paper.

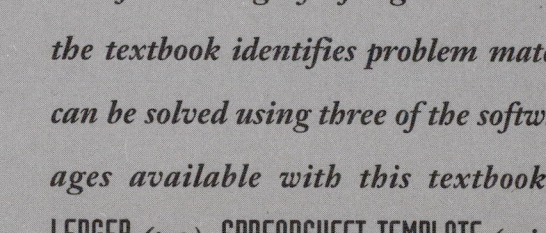 The final category of logos used throughout the textbook identifies problem material that can be solved using three of the software packages available with this textbook: GENERAL LEDGER (top), SPREADSHEET TEMPLATE (middle), and the Computer Resource Guide [CRG] (bottom).

SIXTH EDITION

PRINCIPLES OF ACCOUNTING

SIXTH EDITION

THE DRYDEN PRESS SERIES IN ACCOUNTING

INTRODUCTORY

BISCHOFF
Introduction to College Accounting
Second Edition

PRINCIPLES

HANSON, HAMRE, AND WALGENBACH
Principles of Accounting
Sixth Edition

HILLMAN, KOCHANEK, AND NORGAARD
Principles of Accounting
Sixth Edition

COMPUTERIZED

BISCHOFF AND WANLASS
The Computer Connection
Second Edition

BRIGHAM AND KNECHEL
Financial Accounting Using Lotus 1-2-3

WANLASS
Computer Resource Guide: Principles of Accounting
Fourth Edition

YASUDA AND WANLASS
The Real Time Advantage

FINANCIAL

BACKER, ELGERS, AND ASEBROOK
Financial Accounting: Concepts and Practices

BEIRNE AND DAUDERIS
Financial Accounting: An Introduction to Decision Making

HANSON, HAMRE, AND WALGENBACH
Financial Accounting
Seventh Edition

HOSKIN AND HUGHES
Financial Accounting Cases

KOCHANEK, HILLMAN, AND NORGAARD
Financial Accounting
Second Edition

STICKNEY, WEIL, AND DAVIDSON
*Financial Accounting: An Introduction to Concepts,
Methods, and Uses*
Sixth Edition

MANAGERIAL

KETZ, CAMPBELL, AND BAXENDALE
Management Accounting

MAHER, STICKNEY, WEIL, AND DAVIDSON
*Managerial Accounting: An Introduction to Concepts,
Methods, and Uses*
Fourth Edition

INTERMEDIATE

WILLIAMS, STANGA, AND HOLDER
Intermediate Accounting
Fourth Edition

ADVANCED

HUEFNER AND LARGAY
Advanced Financial Accounting
Third Edition

PAHLER AND MORI
Advanced Accounting
Fourth Edition

FINANCIAL STATEMENT ANALYSIS

STICKNEY
Financial Statement Analysis: A Strategic Perspective
Second Edition

AUDITING

GUY, ALDERMAN, AND WINTERS
Auditing
Third Edition

THEORY

BELKAOUI
Accounting Theory
Third Edition

BLOOM AND ELGERS
Accounting Theory and Policy: A Reader
Second Edition

TAXATION

EVERETT, RAABE, AND FORTIN
Income Tax Fundamentals

SOMMERFELD, MADEO, ANDERSON, AND JACKSON
Concepts of Taxation

REFERENCE

WILLIAMS AND MILLER
HBJ Miller GAAP Guide
College Edition

MILLER AND BAILEY
HBJ Miller GAAS Guide
College Edition

THE HBJ COLLEGE OUTLINE SERIES INCLUDES
THESE FINE STUDY AIDS:

CAMPBELL, GRIERSON, AND TAYLOR: *Principles of
Accounting I*, Revised Edition   EMERY: *Principles of
Accounting II*   EMERY: *Intermediate Accounting I*,
Second Edition   EMERY: *Intermediate Accounting II*
FRIGO: *Cost Accounting*

SIXTH EDITION

PRINCIPLES OF ACCOUNTING

ERNEST I. HANSON
University of Wisconsin—Madison

JAMES C. HAMRE
University of Wisconsin—Madison

PAUL H. WALGENBACH
University of Wisconsin—Madison

THE DRYDEN PRESS

Harcourt Brace Jovanovich College Publishers

Fort Worth   Philadelphia   San Diego   New York   Orlando   Austin   San Antonio
Toronto   Montreal   London   Sydney   Tokyo

Editor in Chief	*Robert A. Pawlik*
Acquisitions Editor	*Tim Vertovec*
Developmental Editor	*Craig Avery*
Project Editor	*Cheryl Hauser*
Production Manager	*Diane Southworth*
Designer	*Linda Wooton Miller*
Photo/Permissions Editors	*Mark Brelsford and Sheila Shutter*

Cover Photo: Copyright © 1992 Stock Yard. Architectural models courtesy of Roger Walcker.

Address for Editorial Correspondence
The Dryden Press, 301 Commerce Street, Suite 3700, Fort Worth, TX 76102

Address for Orders
The Dryden Press, 6277 Sea Harbor Drive, Orlando, FL 32887
1-800-782-4479, or 1-800-433-0001 (in Florida)

ISBN: 0-03-096197-1
         0-03-097431-3 (A.I.E.)

Library of Congress Catalog Number: 92-71286
Printed in the United States of America

3 4 5 6 7 8 9 0 1 2   048   9 8 7 6 5 4 3 2 1

The Dryden Press
Harcourt Brace Jovanovich

Photo Credits: **Chapter 1** Copyright 1988 Comstock. **Chapter 2** Courtesy of SkyWest Airlines. **Chapter 3** John McDonough/Sports Illustrated. **Chapter 4** Courtesy of Georgia Pacific. **Chapter 5** Michael A. Keller/Third Coast Stock. **Chapter 6** Courtesy of Chrysler Financial; Photography by Arnold Zann/Blackstar. **Chapter 7** Michael Newman/Photo Edit. **Chapter 8** Tony Freeman/Photo Edit. **Chapter 9** Courtesy of Electronic Data Systems. **Chapter 10** Charles Beck Studios. **Chapter 11** Courtesy of Georgia Pacific. **Chapter 12** Tony Freeman/Photo Edit. **Chapter 13** Courtesy of NCR Corporation. **Chapter 14** Buck Miller/Third Coast Stock. **Chapter 15** Courtesy of General Cinema Corporation. **Chapter 16** Courtesy of Phillips Petroleum. **Chapter 17** Courtesy of Southwestern Bell Telephone. **Chapter 18** Courtesy of American Brands, Inc. **Chapter 19** Courtesy of Norfolk Southern Corporation. **Chapter 20** Courtesy of Stride Rite Corporation. **Chapter 21** Courtesy of Saturn. **Chapter 22** Courtesy of John Deere. **Chapter 23** Courtesy of American Petroleum Institute. **Chapter 24** Lee Gregory. **Chapter 25** Bill Varie/The Image Bank. **Chapter 26** Courtesy of Giddings & Lewis. **Chapter 27** Walter Bibikow/The Image Bank. **Chapter 28** Courtesy of International Business Machines Corporation. Back Cover: Loeb Photographics, Madison, Wisconsin.

Change is all around us. Change in business. Change in government. Universal changes are everywhere, and the discipline of accounting is no exception. Not content to simply respond to change in the discipline, *Principles of Accounting*, Sixth Edition, has taken bold steps to be in the forefront of accounting education.

Like its predecessors, *Principles of Accounting*, Sixth Edition, provides a comprehensive introduction to accounting concepts and procedures for both external users (financial accounting) and internal users (managerial accounting). Because a proper understanding of fundamental accounting principles is critical to success in business, this textbook has been written to meet the needs of both accounting majors and general business majors.

RESPONDING TO THE CALL FOR CHANGE IN ACCOUNTING EDUCATION

The reality of change in accounting education became evident in 1989, with the creation of the Accounting Education Change Commission by the American Accounting Association and the nation's largest public accounting firms. In an effort to improve the academic preparation of accountants, they have suggested a variety of goals of accounting education that are mirrored in this textbook.

- **PROVIDE A BROAD VIEW OF THE ROLE OF ACCOUNTING IN SOCIETY** Every business function has a relationship to accounting. Incentive plans for marketing, performance measurements for management, internal control systems for business computing, profitability analysis in economics, and capital budgeting in finance are a few examples. The pervasive need for accounting information in the business world is one of the themes of this revision. Beginning with cover images of the Chrysler and Empire State buildings, the importance of the business world is emphasized, and this same theme is carried through as the backdrop for every chapter. Each chapter begins with a chapter overview photo, question, and response that identify accounting concepts in practice for actual companies. And it doesn't stop there. Interwoven into the text are more than 160 references to real-world companies.

- **PROVIDE AN OVERVIEW OF THE ETHICAL RESPONSIBILITIES OF THE ACCOUNTANT** Introduced in Chapter 1, a new section on ethics and the accounting environment sets the foundation for ethics cases in each chapter. These cases focus not on general matters of right and wrong, but on how the accountant's particular responsibilities may require him or her to confront ethical dilemmas.

- **ENHANCE STUDENTS' ANALYTICAL SKILLS** A key to sucess in business is the ability to solve unstructured problems. Multiple opportunities to gain such experience are presented in end-of-chapter Analytical Application Cases and Business Decision Cases.

- **DEVELOP COMMUNICATION SKILLS** For accounting information to be effective, it must be communicated. Through writing requirements integrated into the end-of-chapter assignment material, written communication skills are developed. Through group projects identified in the instructor's materials, improvements in interpersonal communication skills are encouraged.

- **GAIN AN UNDERSTANDING OF THE BUSINESS PRACTICES OF OTHER CULTURES** The effective business person must see beyond his or her own environment and understand the world beyond. To encourage this, international accounting issues have now been integrated into the text wherever appropriate.

LEARNING FEATURES FOR THE TEXT

- **CHAPTER OVERVIEW QUESTION, PHOTO, AND RESPONSE** bring the real world into the text by illustrating accounting concepts in practice for actual companies.

- **CHAPTER OBJECTIVES,** with page references, are stated at the beginning of each chapter and indicate what students should understand when they complete the chapter. So that students will be encouraged to take an active learning approach, action words appear in boldface. All teaching and learning aids are tied to chapter objectives.

- **A CHAPTER QUOTATION** begins each chapter, exposing the student to a broader perspective.

- **CHAPTER OBJECTIVES,** repeated in the margins of the text, help the students to better structure their learning strategy.

- **BOXED INSERTS** (one per chapter) feature excerpts from a variety of business publications that illustrate the real-life complexities of accounting. A majority are new to this edition.

- **ANALYTICAL APPLICATION SECTION** (in the first 19 chapters) identifies a specific financial ratio or other analytical tool related to the chapter and illustrates how it can be used to interpret accounting data. The section is placed at the end of the chapter to permit convenient exclusion by instructors who want to defer coverage of this material until Chapter 20.

- **KEY POINTS FOR CHAPTER OBJECTIVES,** with chapter objectives repeated, clearly summarize each chapter.

- **SELF-TEST QUESTIONS FOR REVIEW** present five multiple-choice questions per chapter. Answers, with page numbers referring to the relevant discussion in the text, appear after the Solution to Demonstration Problem and give students immediate feedback.

- **DEMONSTRATION PROBLEM FOR REVIEW,** with complete solution, gives the students another opportunity to assess their comprehension of the material.

- **GLOSSARY OF KEY TERMS USED IN THIS CHAPTER,** with page references to their introduction in the chapter, provides a convenient opportunity for vocabulary review.

- **QUESTIONS,** approximately 20 per chapter, provide an opportunity for class discussion or single-concept review. Many questions feature a written requirement.

- **EXERCISES,** approximately 8 per chapter, are identified by both topic and chapter objective.

- **PROBLEMS** are also identified by topic and chapter objective. Problems that can be solved using three of the four software packages available with this textbook are identified with special logos.

- **ALTERNATE EXERCISES,** new to this edition, provide an even wider variety of assignment material.

- **ALTERNATE PROBLEMS** cover the same concepts as the problems with new data to ensure comprehension.

- **BUSINESS DECISION CASE** (one per chapter) requires the student to analyze a business situation and make a judgment. Several cases have a written requirement.

- **ANALYTICAL APPLICATION CASE** (Chapters 1–20) allows students to apply newly learned financial ratios to evaluate financial statement data of real-world companies.

- **ETHICS CASE,** one per chapter, challenges the students to make an ethical judgment concerning a businesss situation related to the material in the chapter.

- **MINI PRACTICE SETS I** and **II,** following Chapter 4, constitute an extensive accounting cycle assignment. Set I covers one accounting period and Set II covers two accounting periods.

- **CHECKLIST OF KEY FIGURES,** provided as an appendix to the book, gives students feedback when solving the assignment material.

- **ACETATE OVERLAYS** in Chapter 4 explain how to prepare a worksheet in a step-by-step process.

- **FINANCIAL STATEMENTS AND RELATED DISCLOSURES FROM THE 1991 ANNUAL REPORT OF DONNELLY CORPORATION** appear at the end of the textbook as Appendix L to provide an example of the accounting principles discussed throughout the textbook.

MAJOR CONTENT CHANGES IN THIS REVISION

■ **PRESENTATION OF ANALYTICAL APPLICATIONS**

To demonstrate the usefulness of accounting data and to encourage critical thinking by students, each of the first 19 chapters introduces a financial ratio or other analytical tool that relates to the chapter content. The end-of-chapter assignment material includes an Analytical Application Case that uses financial data from real-world companies. Chapter 20 provides a comprehensive and integrative summary of these ratios and analytical tools.

■ **EXPANDED COVERAGE OF PERPETUAL INVENTORY**

Consistent with the increased use of the perpetual inventory system in the business world, the textbook devotes increased attention to this topic. The Sixth Edition features a new section in Chapter 5 introducing perpetual inventory techniques, an expanded discussion of perpetual inventory pricing methods in Chapter 9, and the use of perpetual inventory as the basis for the introduction of manufacturing accounting in Chapter 21.

■ **INTEGRATED COVERAGE OF CASH FLOWS**

Consistent with its status as one of the basic financial statements, the textbook improves its integration of the statement of cash flows. The statement of cash flows is introduced as one of the basic financial statements in Chapter 1 and 2; financial ratios using cash flow data are presented in Chapters 2, 12, and 13; the statement of cash flows and related ratios are added to Chapter 20; and a budgeted statement of cash flows is presented in Chapter 26. In addition, Chapter 19, Statement of Cash Flows, has been rewritten to permit complete segregation of the direct and indirect methods of reporting net cash flow from operations. The instructor can now present either method or both, with or without a worksheet, as desired.

■ **EXPANDED COVERAGE OF INTERNATIONAL ACCOUNTING**

The need for increased attention to international issues led to the movement of the topic of import and export accounting into Chapter 9, a new section on international accounting principles in Chapter 13, exclusive devotion of Appendix F to the topic of conversion of foreign currency financial statements, and coverage of international transfer pricing in Appendix I.

■ **EXPANDED COVERAGE OF PLANNING, BUDGETING, AND FLEXIBLE BUDGETING**

Chapter 26 from the Fifth Edition has been expanded into two chapters and now includes coverage of strategic planning and operational planning as well as static and flexible budgets and their impact on performance reports.

■ **COVERAGE OF TIMELY TOPICS IN MANAGERIAL ACCOUNTING**

Coverage of just-in-time inventory (Chapters 21 and 26) and activity-based costing and cost drivers (Chapter 22) reflect the modern manufacturing environment. Transfer pricing, a topic that is receiving increased attention from both business and government, is discussed in Appendix I.

■ **NEW APPENDIXES ON TAXES**

Appendix J, new to this edition, brings into proper focus the relationship of taxes to the business environment by discussing the effect of various taxes on decision making. Appendix K, also new to this edition, presents updated material on income taxation of individuals that was previously contained in Chapter 28.

CHAPTER-BY-CHAPTER CHANGES FOR THE SIXTH EDITION

CHAPTER 1

- A new section on ethics and the accounting environment is included.
- The introduction of the matching concept has been moved into the chapter from Chapter 3.
- The statement of cash flows is introduced along with an exhibit (1-3) that integrates the statement of cash flows with other basic financial statements.
- A boxed insert on ethics is introduced.
- The accounting equation is used to analyze transactions (earlier editions used balance sheets to analyze transactions).
- The chapter content is simplified by eliminating all references to adjustments, which are now introduced in Chapter 3. The chapter illustration is revised to continue the text's tradition of always presenting accurate financial statements.

CHAPTER 2

- Exhibit 2-1 is a new exhibit showing a blank account.
- A new section on permanent and temporary accounts is included, along with an expanded Exhibit 2-3 to distinguish between permanent owners' equity and owners' withdrawals.
- Exhibit 2-5 is revised to place the general ledger and trial balance in the same exhibit; the exhibit is sized so that the student does not have to turn the page sideways to view it.
- A new section on the relationships among financial statements includes an exhibit (2-6) showing these relationships.
- Number slides are added to the section on errors in transaction analysis.

CHAPTER 3

- Material on prepayments recorded as revenue and expense is expanded and moved to Appendix A.
- All references to special journals have been eliminated; special journals are now introduced in Chapter 6.
- Exhibit 3-5 on posting is divided into two parts.
- Exhibit 3-6 from the Fifth Edition is divided into two exhibits (3-6 and 3-7) and reduced considerably in length.

CHAPTER 4

- An acetate overlay, which gives a step-by-step illustration of worksheet preparation, is added (Exhibits 4-2 through 4-6).
- A section that covers the classified balance sheet is moved into the chapter from Chapter 5.
- New diagrams showing the operating cycle for a service firm and merchandising firm are included.

- The discussion of closing entries is expanded to cover partnerships as well as sole proprietorships and corporations.

CHAPTER 5

- A new exhibit (5-4) is included on the treatment of freight costs.
- A new section on perpetual inventory techniques and a comparison to periodic inventory techniques has been added as well as a new section on a perpetual inventory worksheet.
- The order of closing entries has changed to be consistent with coverage in other chapters.
- A new boxed insert on bar codes is included.
- In Appendix B, adjusting entries are changed to use the Cost of Goods Sold account.

CHAPTER 6

- Special journals for perpetual inventory are added to the examples of special journals for periodic inventory.
- The graphic design of exhibits that contain examples of special journals has been improved.
- A new boxed insert on fault-tolerant computers has been included.

CHAPTER 8

- The chapter has been reorganized to present the allowance method before the direct write-off method.
- The coverage of credit card sales is expanded.
- Terminology has been changed to address clearly add-on interest and borrowing at a discount.
- A new boxed insert on granting credit is added.

CHAPTER 9

- The discussion of perpetual inventory pricing methods is expanded, and new illustrations of perpetual specific identification, perpetual moving average, and perpetual LIFO to go with the previous illustration of perpetual FIFO are included.
- The discussion and exhibit (9-3) of comparative analysis of pricing methods is revised so that it now applies to both periodic and perpetual methods.
- Accounting for imports and exports is moved into the chapter from the appendix on international accounting.
- Payment methods for international trade is a new boxed insert.

CHAPTER 10

- The section on original measurement of plant assets includes resequenced material.
- Graphs comparing straight-line, sum-of-the-years'-digits, and double-declining balance depreciation methods are added.

CHAPTER 11

- The section on exchange of plant assets has been revised to reflect consensus positions of the FASB Emerging Issues Task Force.

- A new exhibit (11-1) is included that summarizes plant asset disposals.
- The discussion of financial statement reporting of depletion charge is expanded.
- A new boxed insert is featured on selecting consumer product names.

CHAPTER 12

- A new Exhibit 12-1, Liabilities: Criteria and Financial Statement Treatment, is included to clarify accounting treatment of liabilities.
- The coverage of contingent liabilities, including environmental cleanup costs, is expanded.
- The discussion on payroll calculations is updated to include current rates.
- A boxed insert on accounting for environmental cleanup costs is new.

CHAPTER 13

- There is a new section on international accounting principles.
- Most material on inflation accounting is moved to Appendix C, Reporting the Impact of Changing Prices.
- The discussion of basic accounting principles is resequenced.
- New real-world examples of various types of disclosures are provided.
- A new boxed insert is included on variation in international accounting principles.

CHAPTER 14

- A new boxed insert explains how to achieve a productive partnership.

CHAPTER 15

- Sections on the advantages and disadvantages of the corporate form of organization are included.
- A new exhibit (15-1) is provided on corporate organizational structure.
- Discussion of cumulative versus noncumulative preferred stock features a new illustration.
- A new boxed insert on the phasing out of stock certificates is added.

CHAPTER 16

- Separate Cash Dividends and Stock Dividends accounts are introduced for the declaration of dividends.
- Material dealing with income statement sections is resequenced, and the section on tax allocation within a period is rewritten.
- The section on appropriations of retained earnings (with journal entries) is replaced with a section on restrictions on retained earnings (disclosed in notes to the financial statements).
- The section on earnings per share is rewritten.
- A new boxed insert is featured on basics of dividend reinvestment plans.

CHAPTER 17

- A new section is added on the advantages and disadvantages of issuing bonds.
- New discussion as well as a new exhibit (17-1) target trading on the equity (topic was in Chapter 20 in the Fifth Edition).

- Discussion of bond pricing is expanded, and a new exhibit (17-2) is introduced on the topic.

- Discussion of mortgage notes payable is expanded, and a new exhibit (17-6) is featured.

- Example and end-of-chapter assignments dealing with bond issuance between interest dates are revised to occur at some point other than exactly halfway between interest dates.

- Illustration and end-of-chapter assignments on early retirement of bonds are simplified by having retirements occur on an interest payment date.

- A brief discussion of liability associated with retirement benefits other than pensions is added.

- A new boxed insert features bond redemptions and call features.

- Coverage of long-term bond investments is moved to Chapter 18.

- Appendix D now includes an example of installment payment computation.

CHAPTER 18

- A section is added on long-term bond investments (in Chapter 17 in the Fifth Edition).

- The section on the consolidated retained earnings statement is eliminated.

- A section on unrealized profit on intercompany sales is also eliminated.

- Material on intercompany receivables and payables is moved to appear earlier in the chapter.

- The Demonstration Problem is changed to illustrate a consolidation that has both a minority interest and goodwill from consolidation.

- Appendix F is revised to deal only with conversion of foreign currency financial statements.

CHAPTER 19

- The direct method and the indirect method for preparing the statement of cash flows are discussed and illustrated separately.

- Sections are added to both direct and indirect methods for preparing the statement of cash flows without using a worksheet.

- Two Demonstration Problems are provided, one for the direct method and another for the indirect method. Both demonstration problems are changed to be non-worksheet illustrations.

- End-of-chapter problems are identified as whether the direct method or indirect method should be used and whether a worksheet is required.

CHAPTER 20

- Extensively revised, Chapter 20 reviews and integrates all of the analytical applications from Chapters 1–19. As such, the chapter may be used as an integrative supplement to these applications. Because all applications are reviewed in the chapter, it may also be used as the initial exposure to any, or all, of these analytical tools.

- The following ratios have been *added:* gross profit percentage; asset turnover; operating cash flow to current liabilities ratio; accounts receivable turnover; days' sales in inventory; operating cash flow to total liabilities ratio; and operating cash flow to capital expenditures ratio.

- All ratios are now grouped into the following categories: analyzing profitability; analyzing short-term liquidity; analyzing long-term solvency; and analyses for common stock investors.

- A statement of cash flows is added to the chapter (Exhibit 20-3), and three cash flow ratios are integrated into the material.

- The topic of trading on the equity has been moved to Chapter 17.

- Industry averages are added to the illustrations of various ratios in the chapter.

- A new boxed insert on measuring a company's earnings potential is featured.

CHAPTER 21

- Periodic manufacturing inventories are eliminated and perpetual manufacturing inventories are used to be consistent with subsequent chapters and actual practice.

- Exhibit 21-1 on manufacturing product cost flows is improved.

- The schedule of cost of goods manufactured and sold replaces the cost of goods manufactured statement.

- The perpetual inventory manufacturing worksheet is used to prepare financial statements.

- An illustration of product cost accumulation (journal entries and T accounts) is added.

- A section on major trends in manufacturing is added, including manufacturing cells, automation, and flexible manufacturing systems.

- Problems and a boxed insert on just-in-time inventories are included.

CHAPTER 22

- The exhibits related to product cost accumulation are improved and expanded.

- A section is added on dispostion of underapplied or overapplied overhead by allocating it to Work in Process Inventory, Finished Goods Inventory, and Cost of Goods Sold.

- A section on *activity-based costing* with a comparison to plantwide overhead rates and departmental overhead rates is added.

- Problems are added on activity-based costing.

- A boxed insert on cost drivers in an activity-based costing system is introduced.

CHAPTER 23

- A boxed insert on productivity and technology is added.

CHAPTER 25

- Appendix I on domestic and international transfer pricing is added.

- Appendix J on tax considerations in business decision making is introduced.

CHAPTER 26

- A section on planning, including strategic planning and operational planning, is added.

- The format of the cash budget has been changed to the more traditional format of beginning balance plus cash receipts minus cash disbursements equals ending cash balance.

- The following are all new exhibits featured in the chapter: Exhibit 26-1, Sequence for Preparing Plans and Budgets; Exhibit 26-2, Budgets and Data Flows Comprising the Master Budget; Exhibit 26-9, Selling and Administrative Expense Budget; Exhibit 26-12, Schedule of Estimated Product Cost per Unit; Exhibit 26-13, Budgeted Income Statement; Exhibit 26-14, Budgeted Balance Sheet; Exhibit 26-15, Budgeted Statement of Cash Flows.

- The boxed insert on zero-base budgeting is improved.

CHAPTER 27

- A section on static budgets, flexible budgets, and performance reports using both types of budgets is expanded and improved.

- The following are new exhibits introduced in the chapter: Exhibit 27-1, Static Budget for Product Costs; Exhibit 27-2, Static Budget Performance Report; Exhibit 27-3, Flexible Budget for Product Costs; Exhibit 27-4, Flexible Budget Performance Report.

- There is a new boxed insert on variance analysis for a thoroughbred horse boarding farm ("Old Rosebud").

CHAPTER 28

- Chapter 28 in the Sixth Edition was Chapter 27 in the Fifth Edition.

- A new boxed insert is featured on capital investments.

APPENDIX K

- Appendix K in the Sixth Edition replaces the coverage of income taxation of individuals that was included in Chapter 28 in the Fifth Edition.

- Material is updated for changes in the income tax law.

APPENDIX L

- The financial statements and related disclosures from the 1991 annual report of Donnelly Corporation are included.

APPENDIX M

- Appendix M covers how to use the Sixth Edition's MICROSTUDY+, the improved and expanded version of the MicroStudy self-paced computerized tutorial.

THE TEACHING PACKAGE
For the Instructor

In addition to the textbook, the teaching package includes a wide-ranging set of teaching tools for the instructor and learning tools for the student.

- **ANNOTATED INSTRUCTOR'S EDITION**, with annotations by Shirley Glass (Macomb Community College), includes annotations throughout. These include lecture notes, discussion questions, and many suggestions for illustrating concepts with real-world examples.

■ **INSTRUCTOR'S MANUAL**, by Sandra Bitenc, CPA (Texas Christian University), includes key Teaching Points; Lecture Notes and Illustrations; Suggested Assignment Sequences for light, moderate, and heavy amounts of homework; Expanded Requirements for selected exercises; Writing Requirements for Selected Exercises; Self-Study Problems with worked solutions; and two Ten-minute Quizzes (with solutions in the back) per chapter.

■ **INSTRUCTOR'S MANUAL ON DISK** contains the entire Manual in ASCII format for use with virtually any word processing program. The instructor can customize by adding personal lecture outlines and making modifications as necessary.

■ **SOLUTIONS MANUAL**, prepared by the textbook authors, includes answers to all questions, exercises, alternate exercises, problems, alternate problems, and cases. For all exercises, alternate exercises, problems and alternate problems, the topic and chapter objective number(s) are identified. It is available in two volumes.

■ **SOLUTIONS TRANSPARENCIES**, available in two volumes, are easy-to-read, large-type transparencies that provide solutions to all exercises, problems, alternate exercises, alternate problems, and cases.

■ **INSTRUCTOR'S MANUAL FOR MONOPOLY GAME PRACTICE SET**, by Richard S. Rand (Tennessee Technological University) includes grading procedures, alternate assignments, and substitute procedures for the Monopoly Game Practice Set.

■ **SOLUTIONS TO PRACTICE SETS** contains solutions to Practice Set A and Computerized Practice Set A, Practice Set B and Computerized Practice Set B, and Practice Set with Business Papers. It does not contain solutions to the Monopoly Game Practice Set.

■ **INSTRUCTOR'S MANUAL AND SOLUTIONS DISK FOR THE COMPUTER RESOURCE GUIDE**, by John W. Wanlass (DeAnza College).

■ **INSTRUCTOR'S VERSION OF THE ANALYTICAL APPLICATION SOFTWARE**, by Thomas L. Barton and Dilip D. Kare (both of University of North Florida), consists of an open-ended, easy to use financial statement analysis tool that is pre-programmed to include formulas and financial data from the Analytical Applications Cases in the textbook.

■ **TEACHING TRANSPARENCIES**, by Shirley Glass (Macomb Community College) and Sharyll A. B. Plato (University of Central Oklahoma), are 100 color transparencies that include additional instructional material and exhibits from the textbook.

■ **PRESENTATION SOFTWARE** contains all the teaching transparencies on disk, as well as additional interactive displays for the electronic classroom.

■ **INSTRUCTIONAL VIDEOS**, produced by Pennsylvania State University, provide additional instruction for students who missed a class or are confused by a certain point.

- **TEST RESOURCE MANUAL,** prepared by the textbook authors, contains more than 2,500 items keyed to chapter objectives. They include true/false and multiple-choice questions and several problems for both chapters and appendixes. The Test Resource Manual also contains the **ACHIEVEMENT TESTS,** which are available in two parallel sets. Tests are ready for duplication and distribution to students. These provide a quick alternative to constructing a customized test.

- **EXAMASTER COMPUTERIZED TEST BANK** also contains editable Achievement Test files for more customized testing.

- **REQUESTEST.** Call a toll-free number to order test masters through the HBJ RequesTest service. Allow 48 hours for compiling the test in addition to first-class mail delivery. RequesTest service and software support are available Monday through Friday, 9 A.M. to 4 P.M. (Central Time) for questions, guidance, or other help.

Ancillaries Provided as Master to Instructor for Duplication and Distribution—Free upon Adoption

- **TEMPLATE SOFTWARE,** by Kent Finkle, contains data for use in solving identified problems in the text. This template can be used with Lotus 1-2-3 or a compatible spreadsheet program. A master disk will be provided to instructors upon adoption for duplication and distribution to students.

- **GENERAL LEDGER SOFTWARE,** by Leon Hanouille (Syracuse University) and John Jay Cappy, allows students to solve identified problems in the text. This closed-ended package will demonstrate for students the potential applications of general ledger software. A master disk will be provided to instructors upon adoption for duplication and distribution to students.

- **MICROSTUDY +,** the computerized study guide, is an interactive tutorial program that reinforces concepts learned in the text and allows students to identify areas requiring additional study. A variety of question types is included.

For the Student

- **STUDY GUIDE,** by Imogene A. Posey (The University of Tennessee), includes a brief chapter summary highlighting key concepts, a more detailed chapter review organized by chapter objectives, and a wide variety of questions and exercises. Every chapter includes 10–15 true/false questions, 10–15 multiple-choice questions, 10–15 completion items, 10–12 matching items, and exercises, with working papers, keyed to chapter objectives. Answers to exercises also show in step-by-step fashion how to solve similar exercises and problems. It is available in two volumes.

- **WORKING PAPERS,** in two volumes, are available for all exercises, alternate exercises, problems, alternate problems, and cases. Often an exercise and its alternate exercise can use the same working paper; in these situations, only one set of forms is provided.

- **PRACTICE SET WITH BUSINESS PAPERS.** "Travis Apparel Shop," addresses the basic accounting steps using a sole proprietorship. This revised practice set includes source documents such as invoices, checks, and receipts. Working papers are included as well. Approximately 18–20 hours are required for completion.

- **COMPUTERIZED PRACTICE SET A** and **COMPUTERIZED PRACTICE SET B,** by Leon Hanouille (Syracuse University) and John Jay Cappy, contain general ledger software designed to allow students to concentrate on accounting principles rather than clerical work, allowing faster and easier solution of the manual practice sets.

- **PRACTICE SET A,** "Let There Be Light," by Ron Burnette (Macomb Community College) and the textbook authors, covers the basic steps in the accounting cycle using a sole proprietorship business that sells light fixtures. Approximately 15–18 hours are required for completion.

- **PRACTICE SET B,** "'In' Frequencies, Inc.," by Ron Burnette (Macomb Community College) and the textbook authors, addresses the basic accounting cycle for a corporation. Approximately 15–18 hours are required for completion.

- **MONOPOLY GAME PRACTICE SET,** by W. Robert Knechel (University of Florida), requires students to work in groups using a Monopoly game (not included). Various assignments address the accounting cycle, cash flow analysis, and financial statement analysis.

- **COMPUTER RESOURCE GUIDE,** by John W. Wanlass (DeAnza College), reinforces student understanding of accounting procedures and the benefits of a computerized general ledger accounting system. The guide contains problems and a practice set, in addition to a general ledger system and spreadsheets in one package. The general ledger software is powerful enough to handle the practice set in the student manual as well as other practice sets. The section on electronic spreadsheets includes an introduction to Lotus 1-2-3. Spreadsheet templates allow students to work selected problems, with alternate problems suggested for further work. No prior computer training is required. Instantaneous menu accessing, logical menu structure, and on-line help ease student use.

- **ANALYTICAL APPLICATION SOFTWARE,** by Thomas L. Barton and Dilip D. Kare (both of the University of North Florida), can be used to analyze financial data using the 20 financial ratios and other analytical tools presented in the textbook. It is especially useful in solving the Analytical Application Cases in Chapters 1–19. Ratio analysis and "what if" calculations can be performed and results can be displayed and printed both graphically and numerically to show change over time or comparison between companies. A complete help screen is included in each module. This software is available as an option packaged with the textbook.

ACKNOWLEDGMENTS

We are especially grateful to the following for their contributions to the supplements for the Sixth Edition: Thomas L. Barton (University of North Florida); Sandra Bitenc (Texas Christian University); Ronald Burnette (Macomb Community College); John Jay Cappy (Cappy Corporation); Kent Finkle; Shirley Glass (Macomb Community College); Leon Hanouille (Syracuse University); W. Robert Knechel (University of Florida) Dilip D. Kare (University of North Florida); Richard Metcalf (University of South Dakota); Sharyll A. B. Plato (University of Central Oklahoma); Imogene Posey (The University of Tennessee); Richard S. Rand (Tennessee Technological University); and John W. Wanlass (DeAnza College). We give a special thanks to Katherine Terrell (University of Central Oklahoma) for her work on Appendix J; Lynn Mazzola Paluska (Nassau Community College) for her assistance with the ethics cases, and to David Ravetch (University of California, Los Angeles) for his work on Appendix G. We owe a large debt of gratitude to the many reviewers whose suggestions have contributed to the improvements contained in the Sixth Edition. Among the dedicated teachers and educators whose advice made this revision possible are

John Alcorn, Morehead State University

Marilyn Allan, Central Michigan University

John Arnsparger, Red Rocks Community College

Melody Ashenfelter, Southwestern Oklahoma State University

Eddy Birrer, Gonzaga University

Sarah Brown, University of North Alabama

Nancy Boyd, Middle Tennessee State University

Judity Cook, Grossmont College

Clifford Cox, University of Alaska—Fairbanks

Rosemary Daniels, Utah State University

Larry Davis, Southwest Virginia Community College

Charles Erickson, Carroll College

Clyde Galbraith, West Chester University

Daniel Galvin, Diablo Valley College

Susan Garr, Wayne State University

Shirley Glass, Macomb Community College

Gloria Grayless, Sam Houston State University

Connie Hall, East Central Oklahoma State University

Marcia L. Halvorsen, University of Cincinnati

Marie Hardink, Anne Arundel Community College

Sara Harris, Arapahoe Community College

Nabil Hassan, Wright State University

Sue Haygood, Auburn University

Thomas Hilgeman, St. Louis Community College at Meramec

Anita Hope, Tarrant County Junior College

Jean Marie Hudson, Lamar University

Harry Huges, University of Tennessee

Rhonda Hulkonen, University of South Dakota

Fred Jex, Macomb Community College

Stephen Johnson, Griffin College

Nancy Kegelman, Brookdale Community College

Joyce Lockman, Jackson Community College

Al McKinnie, Northeast State Technical Community College

Frank Minter, Samford University

Marilyn Okleshen, Mankato State University

Kay Pitt, Northern Arizona University

Olga Quintana, University of Miami

David Ravetch, University of California, Los Angeles

Diane Roberts, California State University at Fullerton

E. Thomas Robinson, University of Alaska at Fairbanks

Louis Rosamilia, Hudson Valley Community College

Fabiola Rubio, El Paso Community College

David Sayers, Auburn University at Montgomery

Edward Scott, Olympic College

Margaret Shelton, University of Houston

David Skougstad, Metropolitan State College of Denver

Jane Stockard, Georgia College

J. B. Stroud, Nicholls State University

Larry Sundby, St. Cloud State University

Richard Sweet, University of South Alabama

Katherine Terrell, University of Central Oklahoma

Robert Terrell, University of Central Oklahoma

Dennis Tiger, Indiana University of Pennsylvania

Brad Trettin, Truckee Meadows Community College

Gerald Unruh, Arapahoe Community College

Ronald Walters, Aurora Community College

Karen Walton, John Carroll University

Paul Wheaton, University of Michigan, Dearborn

L. K. Williams, Morehead State University

Roger Woods, Northwest Missouri State University

Marilyn Young, Tulsa Junior College

The authors wish to thank the following persons who supplied helpful information and insights by responding to a survey on the Fifth Edition of Principles of Accounting:

Stuart Arends, Madonna University

Tom Bartlett, University of Alaska—Fairbanks

Martin Bartel, St. Vincent College

Carie Bamberg, Birmingham Southern College

William H. Barnett II, Walters State Community College

J. W. Bilsborrow, Principia College

Kenneth Block, Macomb Community College

Frank Bucci, Ursinus College

C. Chanter, Grand Rapids Community College

Richard Czarnecki, University of Michigan, Dearborn

Elvis Davis, Lamar University

Robert J. DePasquale, St. Vincent College

Greg Ellis, Keller Graduate School

Baruch Englard, College of Staten Island

Pat Evens, Auburn University

M. A. Fink, University of Alaska—Fairbanks

R. K. Fleischman, John Carroll University

Thomas Grant, Kutztown University

Peter Grierson, Slippery Rock University

R. Hardcastle, Pacific Union College

Thomas C. Holowaty, St. Vincent College

Jean Marie Hudson, Lamar University

Fred R. Jex, Macomb Community College

R. W. Jones, Lamar University

Royal E. Knight, University of North Alabama

G. D. Lorenzo, Gloucester County College

J. Thomas Love, Walters State Community College

William Mayfield, Northwest Oklahoma State University

Florence McGovern, Bergen Community College

Heidi Meier, Cleveland State University

Janet E. Mercincavage, King's College

Susan Murphy, Aquinas College

Jon Nitschke, Great Falls Vo-Tech Center

Ruth O'Keefe, Jacksonville University

Sharyll Plato, University of Central Oklahoma

Dennis Ratliff, Jacksonville University

E. Thomas Robinson, University of Alaska—Fairbanks

James Skidmore, Grand Rapids Community College

Jeff Spoelman, Grand Rapids Community College

William Stevens, University of South Alabama

LaVerne Summiel, St. Paul's College

Richard Sweet, University of South Alabama

Forrest Thompson, Florida A&M University

Leon Trekell, West Texas State University

Brad Trettin, Truckee Meadows Community College

Marilyn Uecker, Fox Valley Technical College

Gerald Unruh, Arapahoe Community College

Gerald Weinstein, John Carroll University

Harold Wente, Iowa Lakes Community College

Paul Wheaton, University of Michigan, Dearborn

Sam Wilson, Keller Graduate School

Jerry L. Wood, Northern Montana College

Peggy Wright, Averett College

We wish to thank the members of the book team at The Dryden Press for their tireless efforts on behalf of the project: Tim Vertovec, acquisitions editor; Craig Avery, developmental editor; Cheryl Hauser, project editor; Diane Southworth, production manager; Linda Wooton Miller, designer; Mark Brelsford and Sheila Shutter, permissions editors; Tim Westmoreland, ancillary project editor; Eddie Dawson, production coordinator; and Traci Keller, assistant editor.

ERNEST I. HANSON

JAMES C. HAMRE

PAUL H. WALGENBACH

How is a company's working capital determined?

CHAPTER OPENING OVERVIEW

The chapter overview question, photo, and response bring the real world into the text by illustrating accounting concepts in practice for actual companies.

A company's financial statements, prepared in the part of the accounting cycle covered in this chapter, will show the firm's current assets and current liabilities. ■ *Working capital is the current assets minus the current liabilities.* ■ *In some respects, working capital represents a firm's lifeblood.* ■ *Without adequate working capital, a firm like Georgia-Pacific Corporation would have difficulty meeting the current expenses of manufacturing and distributing its various pulp, paper, and building products.*

4 THE ACCOUNTING CYCLE CONCLUDED

CHAPTER OBJECTIVES

Chapter objectives, with page references, are listed at the beginning of each chapter. All teaching and study aids are tied to these objectives.

ACTIVE LEARNING

For each objective, action words appear in boldface to encourage an active learning approach.

Everything ends that has a beginning.
QUINTILIAN

OPENING QUOTATION

A quotation begins each chapter, exposing the student to a broader perspective.

he first five steps in the accounting cycle—analyzing and journalizing transactions, posting to accounts, preparing a trial balance, and adjusting the accounts—are essential to the process of classifying financial data and, when necessary, aligning the data with appropriate periods. The goal of these procedures is to prepare the data so that they can be summarized in a set of meaningful financial statements.

Accountants typically use a *worksheet* to compile the information needed for financial statements. A worksheet is incorporated into steps 4 and 5 of the accounting cycle (preparing a trial balance and adjusting the accounts). In this chapter, we will explain the preparation of a worksheet and its integration into steps 4 and 5 of the accounting cycle. Then we will discuss steps 6 through 9 of the accounting cycle. Our discussion continues to use the December 1993 financial data given in the preceding chapter for Landen TV Service.

THE NINE STEPS IN THE ACCOUNTING CYCLE

OBJECTIVE ❶ IDENTIFY *a worksheet's place in the accounting cycle and* EXPLAIN *the procedures for preparing a worksheet.*

CHAPTER OBJECTIVES

Chapter objectives, repeated in the margin, help the student structure the learning strategy.

Utilizing a worksheet creates a nine-step accounting cycle. These nine steps are listed below. The steps in the boxed area will be discussed in this chapter.

1. Analyze transactions from source documents.
2. Record transactions in journals.
3. Post journal entries to general ledger accounts.
4. Prepare a trial balance to start a worksheet.
5. Adjust the general ledger accounts on the worksheet and complete the worksheet.
6. Prepare financial statements.
7. Journal and post adjusting entries.
8. Journalize and post closing entries.
9. Prepare a post-closing trial balance.

PREPARING A WORKSHEET

The **worksheet** is a tool of the accountant, not part of a company's formal accounting records. The accountant prepares a worksheet at that stage of the accounting cycle when it is time to adjust the accounts and prepare financial statements.

The basic structure of the worksheet is presented in Exhibit 4-1, which includes an explanation of the format used. The worksheet is prepared in the order indicated by the boxed numbers in the exhibit. As we discuss the procedures for preparing a worksheet, we will illustrate them by preparing the worksheet for Landen TV Service for the month ended December 31, 1993, using a series of acetate overlays. Exhibits 4-2 to 4-6 (on page 118) present the step-by-step process used in preparing the worksheet.

❶ HEADING The worksheet *heading* should include (a) the name of the accounting entity involved, (b) the term *Worksheet* to indicate the type of analysis performed, and (c) a date describing the period covered. The worksheet includes both income statement data (for the period described) and balance sheet data (for the end of the period described). Exhibit 4-2 illustrates the heading for Landen TV Service's worksheet.

116

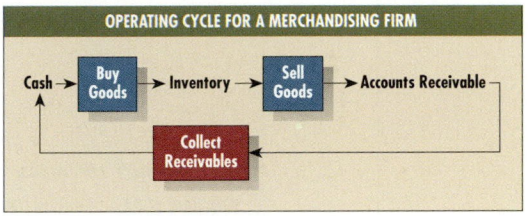

OPERATING CYCLE FOR A MERCHANDISING FIRM

ILLUSTRATIONS

Enhanced graphics improve the appearance of exhibits and illustrations.

For many businesses, the normal operating cycle is less than one year. Certain industries, however, may have an operating cycle of more than one year. For example, a company may be in the inventory stage for an extended period of time—a winery aging wine or a nursery growing trees—so its normal operating cycle may extend several years.

Current assets are usually listed in the order of their *liquidity*, that is, their convertibility into cash. Prepaid expenses such as rent, insurance, and supplies are normally consumed during the operating cycle rather than converted into cash. These items are considered current assets, however, because the prepayments make cash outlays for services unnecessary during the current period. Examples of current assets other than those shown in Exhibit 4-9 are notes receivable, temporary investments, and inventory.

PLANT ASSETS **Plant assets** are the land, buildings, equipment, vehicles, furniture, and fixtures that a firm uses in its operations. This section of the balance sheet may also be labeled *property and equipment*, or *property, plant, and equipment*. Landen TV Service has only one type of plant asset in its balance sheet at December 31, 1993. Note that the presentation in Exhibit 4-9 shows the truck's original cost and separately deducts the related accumulated depreciation.

OTHER ASSET CATEGORIES Other categories of assets include investments (for long-term investments), natural resources, and intangible assets. Landen TV Service has no assets in any of these categories. We will discuss these types of assets in more detail in later chapters.

KEY TERMS

Key terms appear in boldface at their first introduction in the text. They are again defined in the chapter glossary.

CURRENT LIABILITIES **Current liabilities** are liabilities that must be settled within the normal operating cycle or one year, whichever is longer. Examples of current liabilities are accounts payable, short-term notes payable, wages payable, interest payable, utilities payable, income tax payable, and property taxes payable. Also included in current liabilities are any advance payments received from customers that

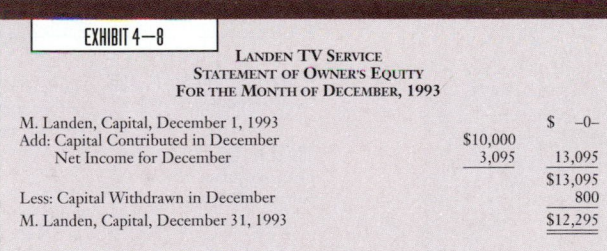

EXHIBIT 4—8

LANDEN TV SERVICE
STATEMENT OF OWNER'S EQUITY
FOR THE MONTH OF DECEMBER, 1993

M. Landen, Capital, December 1, 1993		$ –0–
Add: Capital Contributed in December	$10,000	
Net Income for December	3,095	13,095
		$13,095
Less: Capital Withdrawn in December		800
M. Landen, Capital, December 31, 1993		$12,295

BOXED INSERTS

Boxed inserts feature excerpts from well-known business publications such as **Forbes** *and* **The Wall Street Journal.**

REPORTS TO STOCKHOLDERS

Corporations include their financial statements in periodic reports to stockholders. The annual report to stockholders for large corporations may be quite extensive, often running 20–50 pages or more. In addition to financial statements, the annual report may include a message from the chair of the board of directors and the chief executive officer, a review of the year's operations, a financial review, the accountants' report, and selected financial statistics for several years. A variety of charts, graphs, and photographs of the company's products and facilities may supplement these items.

Reports to stockholders covering less than one year (interim reports) are much less extensive. They are intended to provide owners and potential investors with timely information on the corporation's progress and may include summarized financial information rather than a complete set of financial statements.

Comprehensive annual reports to stockholders are a relatively recent development in the United States. Before the 1900s, corporate management generally disclosed little, if any, financial information to stockholders. The first corporations were usually small and obtained much of their funding through short-term bank loans rather than from the public sale of stocks. Bankers who needed to assess the borrower's ability to repay short-term loans considered the balance sheet the primary financial statement because it revealed the total short-term obligations and the assets that would likely be converted to cash

in the near future. By the late 1920s, however, corporate expansion led to increased financing through stock issuances and long-term debt. Owners and creditors used the income statement to judge earning power. Corporate reporting, then, evolved from providing balance sheets for bankers to providing income statements and balance sheets for stockholders and creditors.[*]

The first modern annual report was issued in 1902 by U.S. Steel Corporation. The report was lengthy and detailed, revealing so much about the corporation's operations that the directors were practically scandalized.[†] The extensive disclosures broke with tradition, and most corporations did not follow U.S. Steel's lead for many years.

Considerable variety exists in the length and detail of reports to stockholders. Remarks by the president of Diamond Match Company used 100 pages of the company's 1942 annual

report.[‡] In contrast, a 1972 semiannual report from North American Publishing of Philadelphia was more to the point. The report was poster size (three feet long) and featured letters eight inches high and six inches wide that stated: "We Had a BIG IMPROVEMENT for the First Six Months."[§]

Many corporations view the annual report, in part, as a public relations document. Imagine the chagrin, then, at Citizens Valley Bank in Albany, Oregon, a number of years ago. Half of the copies of the bank's 1973 annual report had been mailed before a particular omission was noted—the bank's name had been dropped from the report's cover and did not appear anywhere in the report.[‖]

At about the same time, Mott's Super Markets was reprinting 5,000 copies of its annual report. The corporation discovered the asset and liability figures on its balance sheet had been inadvertently reversed.[#]

[*]A. C. Littleton and V. K. Zimmerman, *Accounting Theory: Continuity and Change* (Englewood Cliffs, NJ: Prentice-Hall, Inc., 1962), pp. 92–97.
[†]"Annual Reports—No Longer Dry," *Fortune*, February 1944, p. 62.
[‡]*Ibid.*
[§]"The Numbers Game: A Few (Fairly) Kind Words," *Forbes*, May 1, 1973, p. 36.
[‖]"Business Bulletin," *The Wall Street Journal*, February 14, 1974, p. 1.
[#]"Business Bulletin," *The Wall Street Journal*, May 2, 1974, p. 1.

Step 7: Journalize and Post Adjusting Entries

OBJECTIVE 3 ILLUSTRATE *the process of journalizing and posting adjusting entries.*

At the close of the fiscal year, the adjusting entries on the worksheet must be recorded in the general journal and posted to the general ledger accounts in order to accomplish the proper closing procedures described in the next section. Although Landen TV Service has been in business only for December, its accounting year ends on December 31. Therefore, the adjusting entries are entered in the records and closing procedures are followed. The adjusting entries appear in the general journal as shown in Exhibit 4-10.

These journal entries are posted to the general ledger accounts of Landen TV Service shown in Exhibit 4-13. The entries are identified by the parenthetical notation (adjusting).

The debit balance in Commissions Earned is eliminated when Landen TV Service receives its three-month commission payment of $150 on February 28, 1994. This receipt is recorded as follows:

Feb. 28	Cash	150	
	Commissions Earned		150
	To record receipt of quarterly commission.		

This entry leaves a credit balance of $100 in the Commissions Earned revenue account, reflecting the proper amount of revenue for commission work performed in January and February 1994.

Although the use of reversing entries is optional, it does permit us to analyze certain transactions the same way all the time. For example, if reversals are used, an accountant may be instructed (or a computer programmed) to debit Wages Expense and credit Cash every time wages are paid. Similarly, every interest payment may be analyzed as a debit to Interest Expense and a credit to Cash, and every receipt of commissions may be recorded as a debit to Cash and a credit to Commissions Earned. Reversals eliminate the need to remember the effects of previous accruals and, therefore, contribute to the more efficient processing of data.

Reversals normally are not appropriate for adjustments involving prepayments of expense or advance receipts of revenues. Only if a company's policy is to record expense prepayments in expense accounts and advance revenue receipts in revenue accounts might adjustments involving these items be reversed. In these cases, the reversals reestablish the remaining expense prepayments and advance revenue receipts in the appropriate expense and revenue accounts. These types of situations, however, are not common and will not be illustrated here.

ANALYTICAL APPLICATION

OBJECTIVE **8** DEFINE *the current ratio and* EXPLAIN *its use.*

CURRENT RATIO

The **working capital** of a firm is the difference between its current assets and current liabilities. Landen TV Service's working capital at December 31, 1993, is $12,445 ($14,120 current assets − $1,675 current liabilities). Adequate working capital permits a firm to meet its current obligations and carry on its normal operating activities without having to borrow money or issue stock (if a corporation) at inopportune times.

In analyzing the adequacy of a firm's working capital, the current ratio is a widely used financial statistic. The **current ratio** is computed as follows:

$$\text{Current Ratio} = \frac{\text{Current Assets}}{\text{Current Liabilities}}$$

The current ratio for Landen TV Service at December 31, 1993 is 8.43 ($14,120/$1,675), or 8.43:1. This ratio means that current assets are more than eight times current liabilities. This is a high current ratio and indicates that Landen TV Service should have little difficulty meeting its current obligations. Historically, a current ratio of 2.00 has often been considered a minimum acceptable current ratio. This is a general guide only. Successful operation with a current ratio below 2.00 is possible for some companies, particularly service firms, because they do not have large amounts of inventory among their current assets. In evaluating a specific firm's current ratio, one should consider such things as the nature of the business, the industry average, the composition of the current assets, and the recent trend in the current ratio. Indeed, one might even conclude that a firm's current ratio is too high; that is, the firm may have far more current assets than are needed to provide adequate coverage of current liabilities. The excess resources might better be directed to more profitable uses.

Following are examples of recent current ratios for several companies in different industries.

CIS TECHNOLOGIES, INC. (health-care claims management services)	9.57
OVERSEAS SHIPHOLDING GROUP, INC. (overseas cargo transportation)	2.71
PFIZER INC. (manufacturer of pharmaceuticals and drugs)	1.42
GEORGIA-PACIFIC CORPORATION (manufacturer of pulp, paper, and building products)	0.70

REAL-WORLD EXAMPLES

Actual companies are used throughout the text to increase student interest and move accounting principles from the abstract to the world of the student. Examples from the real world are identified by a special logo.

HEY POINTS

As a summary device, key points highlight the important concepts for each chapter objective.

KEY POINTS FOR CHAPTER OBJECTIVES

1 IDENTIFY a worksheet's place in the accounting cycle and EXPLAIN the procedures for preparing a worksheet (pp. 116–21).
 ■ The worksheet begins with the unadjusted trial balance, step 4 in the accounting cycle.
 ■ The worksheet facilitates the preparation of financial statements.
 ■ Adjusted account balances, which are extended into the income statement and balance sheet columns of the worksheet, provide the data for the formal financial statements.

2 ILLUSTRATE the financial statements prepared from a worksheet and DESCRIBE a classified balance sheet (pp. 121–24).
 ■ An income statement, statement of owner's equity, and balance sheet may be prepared from data on the worksheet. The owner's capital account may also need to be reviewed to obtain information on owner capital contributions during the period for the statement of owner's equity.
 ■ Assets in the balance sheet are classified as current assets, investments, plant assets, natural resources, or intangible assets. Liabilities are classified as current or long-term liabilities.
 ■ Current assets are cash and other assets that will be converted into cash or used up during the normal operating cycle of the business or one year, whichever is longer. Current liabilities are amounts due within the normal operating cycle or one year, whichever is longer.

3 ILLUSTRATE the process of journalizing and posting adjusting entries (pp. 125–26).
 ■ End-of-year adjustments are recorded in the general journal and posted to the general ledger. Adjustments for interim financial statements are usually made only on the worksheet.

4 DESCRIBE the process of closing the temporary accounts (pp. 127–32).
 ■ *Closing the books* means closing the revenue, expense, and other temporary accounts. Revenue and expense account balances are transferred to the Income Summary account. The balances of the Income Summary account and the owners' drawing accounts are closed to the owners' capital accounts. For corporations, the Income Summary account and Cash Dividends account are closed to Retained Earnings.

5 EXPLAIN the nature of a post-closing trial balance (p. 132).
 ■ A post-closing trial balance contains only balance sheet accounts.

6 SUMMARIZE the complete accounting cycle (pp. 132).
 ■ The first three steps in the accounting cycle—analyzing transactions, recording transactions, and posting the transaction journal entries—occur daily.
 ■ The next three steps in the accounting cycle—preparing a trial balance, adjusting the accounts on a worksheet, and preparing financial statements—occur whenever financial statements are desired.
 ■ The last three steps in the accounting cycle—journalizing and posting adjusting entries, journalizing and posting closing entries, and preparing a post-closing trial balance—occur at the end of the accounting period.

7 DISCUSS the purpose of reversing entries (pp. 132–36).
 ■ The reversal of adjustments made for *accrued* items permits the normal recording of subsequent transactions. It safeguards against reflecting the same revenue or expense in successive periods.

8 ANALYTICAL APPLICATION: DEFINE the current ratio and EXPLAIN its use (pp. 136–37).
 ■ The current ratio is computed by dividing current assets by current liabilities.

2. Unpaid wages earned by employees in December are $950.
3. Prepaid insurance at December 31 is $2,080.
4. Unearned service fees at December 31 are $1,000.
5. Rental income of $800 owed by a tenant is not recorded at December 31.

b. Assume the company makes reversing entries. Which of the adjustments in part (a) should be reversed? Make the proper reversing entries on January 1, 1994.

c. Assume reversing entries have been made. Prepare the journal entries on January 4, 1994, to record (1) the payment of $1,600 in wages and (2) the receipt from the tenant of the $800 rental income.

d. Assume reversing entries have not been made. Prepare the journal entries on January 4, 1994, to record (1) the payment of $1,600 in wages and (2) the receipt from the tenant of the $800 rental income.

ALTERNATE EXERCISES

ALTERNATE EXERCISES

ALTERNATE EXERCISES

In addition to the self-test questions for review, the glossary of key terms, the questions, exercises, problems, alternate problems, and business decision case, the end-of-chapter assignment material now also includes alternate exercises, providing an even wider variety of review material.

PROBLEM IDENTIFIERS

Exercises and problems are identified by both topic and chapter objective.

4-20A The adjusted trial balance columns of a worksheet for Bonn Corporation are shown below. The worksheet is prepared for the year ended December 31, 1993.

WORKSHEET, CORPORATION
— OBJ. 1 —

	Adjusted Trial Balance	
	Debit	Credit
Cash	3,000	
Accounts Receivable	5,500	
Equipment	75,000	
Accumulated Depreciation		15,000
Notes Payable		2,300
Capital Stock		40,000
Retained Earnings		17,600
Cash Dividends	5,000	
Service Fees Earned		61,700
Rent Expense	13,000	
Salaries Expense	27,100	
Depreciation Expense	8,000	
	136,600	136,600

Complete the worksheet by (a) entering the adjusted trial balance on paper, (b) putting in the worksheet income statement and balance sheet columns, (c) extending the adjusted trial balance to the income statement and balance sheet columns, and (d) balancing the worksheet.

CLASSIFIED BALANCE SHEET, CORPORATION
— OBJ. 2 —

4-21A The income statement and balance sheet columns of a worksheet for Baxter Corporation are shown below. The worksheet is prepared as of December 31, 1993.

	Income Statement		Balance Sheet	
	Debit	Credit	Debit	Credit
Cash			2,500	
Accounts Receivable			5,400	
Office Equipment			50,000	
Accumulated Depreciation				6,000
Accounts Payable				1,100
Long-term Notes Payable				5,000
Capital Stock				14,000
Retained Earnings				10,400
Service Fees Earned		47,000		
Wages Expense	14,400			
Rent Expense	7,200			
Depreciation Expense	4,000			
Income Tax Expense	3,200			
Income Tax Payable				3,200
	28,800	47,000	57,900	39,700
Net Income	18,200			18,200
	47,000	47,900	57,900	57,900

4. A ball-throwing machine, purchased used, turned out to be quite temperamental. With a complete breakdown shortly after it was purchased, it was junked. (*Note:* Debit Equipment Loss.)

5. Supplies consisted of cans of tennis balls. Lori gave away a free can of tennis balls for each five hours of court time rented by an individual. Supplies amounting to $120 were on hand at August 31; these may be returned for a full refund. Lori estimates that each month during the summer, she took home $15 worth of supplies for personal use.

6. All lease payments due the city were paid except for the final amount of $180.

7. Lori estimates that the utility bill for August, when received, will be $100.

8. The insurance premiums represent coverage for the months of June, July, and August.

REQUIRED

Prepare financial statements for Lori's tennis concession (a sole proprietorship). You should formulate general journal entries summarizing the cash receipts and the cash disbursements and incorporating the additional data. After posting these to T accounts, you will be able to prepare the financial statements.

In further talks with Lori, you learn that the amount she contributed had been in a savings account earning 6% interest and that she worked an average of 60 hours in each of the 13 weeks the tennis concession was operated. What observations might you offer Lori regarding the financial success of the summer venture? What nonfinancial considerations are involved?

ANALYTICAL APPLICATION CASES

Analytical Application Cases in Chapters 1–20 allow students to apply newly learned financial ratios to evaluate the financial statements of actual companies. Specialized computer software is available to aid the student.

Analytical Application Case

METRO AIRLINES, INC., headquartered at the Dallas/Fort Worth International Airport, operated several airline passenger systems and an air cargo system during the years 1988 to 1990. One of the passenger systems operated as EASTERN METRO EXPRESS in Atlanta, Georgia. In that location, the company had a service agreement with EASTERN AIR LINES and provided connecting service between small and medium-sized cities and Eastern Air Lines' Atlanta hub. Following are data on the company's current assets and current liabilities at the end of its 1988, 1989, and 1990 fiscal years (the company's fiscal year ends on April 30; amounts are in thousands):

	April 30, 1990	April 30, 1989	April 30, 1988
Current Assets			
Cash	$ 3,862	$ 8,656	$ 9,330
Trade Accounts Receivable	6,147	5,068	1,207
Other Receivables	1,526	1,809	3,155
Expendable Parts and Supplies	7,299	6,646	3,509
Prepayments and other	1,010	1,970	1,560
Flight Equipment Held for Sale	–0–	1,197	–0–
Total Current Assets	$19,844	$25,346	$18,761
Current Liabilities			
Current maturities of long-term debt	$10,951	$ 6,586	$ 3,144
Notes Payable	–0–	4,000	–0–
Accounts Payable	16,411	10,102	10,314
Accrued Payroll Costs	3,233	2,923	2,108
Accrued Lease Payments	3,448	3,118	1,565
Other Accrued Liabilities	5,124	4,583	1,135
Total Current Liabilities	$39,167	$31,312	$18,266

In fiscal 1988, passengers boarded by the Atlanta hub represented more than 25% of Metro Airlines' passengers. Passengers boarded by the Atlanta hub dropped more than 20% in fiscal 1989 because of labor conflicts and unfavorable publicity experienced by Eastern Air Lines. Late in fiscal 1989, Eastern Air Lines filed for protection under Chapter 11 of the U.S. Bankruptcy Code. Passengers boarded in Atlanta by Metro Airlines dropped another 5% in fiscal 1990.

a. Compute Metro Airlines' working capital at the end of fiscal years 1988, 1989, and 1990. Comment on the trend of working capital from April 30, 1988, to April 30, 1990.

b. Compute Metro Airlines' current ratio at the end of fiscal years 1988, 1989, and 1990. Has

ETHICS CASE

Identified by a special logo, each chapter contains an end-of-chapter case that brings an ethical dimension to the chapter content.

WRITING REQUIREMENTS

Wherever appropriate, expository writing is encouraged. Most writing requirements are highlighted by a special logo.

MINI PRACTICE SETS

Chapter 4 now concludes with two Mini Practice Sets covering the accounting cycle. Set I covers one accounting period and Set II covers two accounting periods.

Metro Airlines' ability to meet its current obligations improved or worsened from April 30, 1988, to April 30, 1990?

Ethics Case

Ed Finlay is controller for ServiceView, Inc., a corporation that provides cable television service throughout the Midwest. His son-in-law, Bryan Foote, owns and manages a printing company, Total Print. Foote has plans to develop a specialty for Total Print in printing corporate annual reports for stockholders. Foote has asked Finlay many questions about this possible specialty, including questions about ServiceView's cost of using an outside company to do the printing of its annual reports. Finlay has been quite candid and helpful in answering Foote's questions and providing prices of the current supplier and has encouraged his son-in-law to pursue this line of business.

This morning, Finlay received a call from ServiceView's president. "I need your help, Ed," stated the president. "I am reviewing a recommendation from the purchasing department for the printing of this year's annual report. The purchasing department recommends that we continue to use Excelprint, which has been printing our annual report for the last decade and with which we have a very good relationship. However, Excelprint is not the low bidder this year; an outfit called Total Print has bid $15,000 less to do the job. Total Print's sample of its work looks very good, and I am inclined to go with the lowest bid. What do you recommend, Ed?"

REQUIRED

What are the ethical considerations that Finlay faces in answering the president's question?

MINI PRACTICE SET

Complete Accounting Cycle

Keith Howe, tax consultant, began business on December 1, 1993. December transactions were as follows.

Dec. 1   Howe invested $15,000 in the business.
    2   Paid rent for December to Star Realty, $800.
    2   Purchased various supplies on account, $720.
    3   Purchased $7,500 of office equipment, paying $3,700 down with the balance due in 30 days.
    8   Paid $720 on account for supplies purchased December 2.
    14 Paid assistant's wages for two weeks, $600.
    20 Performed consulting services for cash, $2,000.
    28 Paid assistant's wages for two weeks, $600.
    30 Billed clients for December consulting services, $4,800.
    31 Howe withdrew $1,200 from the business.

REQUIRED

a. Open the following general ledger accounts, using the account numbers shown: Cash (11); Accounts Receivable (12); Fees Receivable (13); Supplies (14); Office Equipment (15); Accumulated Depreciation (16); Accounts Payable (21); Wages Payable (22); K. Howe, Capital (31); K. Howe, Drawing (32); Income Summary (33); Consulting Revenue (41); Supplies Expense (51); Wages Expense (52); Rent Expense (53); and Depreciation Expense (54).
b. Journalize the December transactions, and post to the ledger.
c. Prepare a trial balance directly on a worksheet, and complete the worksheet using the following information:
   1. Supplies on hand at December 31 are $470.
   2. Accrued wages payable at December 31 are $180.
   3. Depreciation for December is $80.
   4. Howe has spent 20 hours on an involved tax fraud case during December. When completed in January, his work will be billed at $50 per hour. (*Note:* The firm uses the account Fees Receivable to reflect amounts earned but not yet billed.)
d. Prepare a December income statement and statement of owner's equity and a December 31, 1993, classified balance sheet.
e. Journalize and post adjusting and closing entries.
f. Prepare a post-closing trial balance.
g. Journal and post the appropriate reversing entries.

CONTENTS

2

THE DOUBLE-ENTRY ACCOUNTING SYSTEM 41

VIDEO LESSONS 2, 3, AND 4

3

THE ACCOUNTING CYCLE 73

VIDEO LESSONS 4, 5, AND 6

6

ACCOUNTING SYSTEMS 215

VIDEO LESSONS 11 AND 12

PRACTICE SET A (OR COMPUTERIZED PRACTICE SET A), "LET THERE BE LIGHT," OR PRACTICE SET WITH BUSINESS PAPERS, "TRAVIS APPAREL SHOP," MAY BE USED AFTER CHAPTER 6.

7

INTERNAL CONTROL, CASH, AND SHORT-TERM INVESTMENTS 253

VIDEO LESSONS 11, 14, AND 29

8

TRADE ACCOUNTS AND NOTES 291

VIDEO LESSONS 15 AND 17

9

INVENTORIES 325

VIDEO LESSONS 18 AND 19

10

PLANT ASSETS: MEASUREMENT AND DEPRECIATION 361

VIDEO LESSONS 20 AND 21

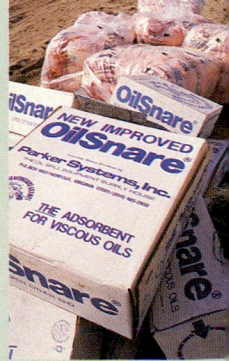

13

ACCOUNTING PRINCIPLES AND FINANCIAL STATEMENT DISCLOSURES 461

VIDEO LESSON 23

16

CORPORATIONS: DIVIDENDS, RETAINED EARNINGS, AND EARNINGS DISCLOSURE 569

VIDEO LESSON 26

PRACTICE SET B, "'IN' FREQUENCIES," MAY BE USED AFTER CHAPTER 16.

17

LONG-TERM LIABILITIES 601

VIDEO LESSONS 27 AND 28

18

LONG-TERM INVESTMENTS AND CONSOLIDATED FINANCIAL STATEMENTS 647

VIDEO LESSON 29

19

STATEMENT OF CASH FLOWS 697

VIDEO LESSON 30

20

ANALYSIS AND INTERPRETATION OF FINANCIAL STATEMENTS 751

26

PLANNING AND BUDGETING 993

**MANAGEMENT CASE
VIDEO 6**

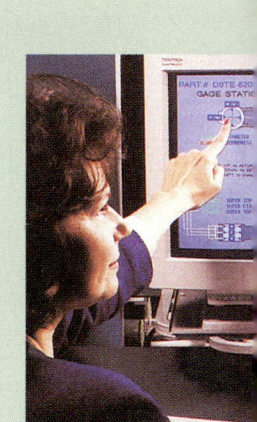

27

FLEXIBLE BUDGETS, STANDARD COSTS, AND COST VARIANCES 1027

28

CAPITAL BUDGETING
1061

MANAGEMENT CASE
VIDEO 8

*W*hat is the basic purpose of accounting?

*T*he basic purpose of accounting is to provide *financial information* useful in making economic decisions. ■ From large firms like IBM to small entrepreneurs, the need for such information exists. ■ The information generated by the accounting process includes a set of financial statements that show a firm's financial position, cash flows, and results of operations. ■ Creditors or investors use the financial statements to help evaluate whether they should establish, maintain, or terminate a financial relationship with the firm.

ACCOUNTING: AN INFORMATION SYSTEM

CHAPTER OBJECTIVES

1 **PROVIDE** a basis for understanding the goals of the accounting process and flows of accounting information (pp. 1–8).

2 **DESCRIBE** the various fields of accounting activity (pp. 8–9).

3 **IDENTIFY** ethical dimensions related to the accounting environment (pp. 9–10).

4 **DEFINE** the accounting equation (pp. 10–11).

5 **INTRODUCE** basic principles that underlie financial accounting (pp. 12–13).

6 **EXPLAIN** and **ILLUSTRATE** the effects of transactions on the accounting equation (pp. 13–20).

7 **INTRODUCE** the basic financial statements (pp. 20–22).

8 **EXPLAIN** the forms of business organization (pp. 22–24).

9 **ANALYTICAL APPLICATION: DEFINE** the *debt-to-equity ratio* and **EXPLAIN** its use (p. 24).

he need for financial information leads to a process for creating that information. On a personal level, for example, we need to know how much cash we have available to spend, so we keep a record of our personal checking account. Or we may need to evaluate whether we can afford to attend a particular school, so we prepare a budget showing the expected costs of that school to compare with our expected financial resources. Or we need to determine how much income tax we owe the government, so we prepare an income tax return. In all of these cases, we are engaged in an accounting activity because *the basic purpose of accounting is to provide financial information that is useful in making economic decisions.*

Economic decisions need to be made for organizations as well as individuals. Accounting is the means by which managers and others are informed of the financial status and progress of their organizations. The ability to use the accounting data helps managers and others accomplish their economic objectives. Our study of accounting will emphasize the accounting for organizations, particularly businesses. You will discover the types of economic activities that can be accounted for usefully, the methods used to collect accounting data, and the implications of the resulting information. Furthermore—and often just as important—you will become aware of the limitations of accounting reports.

ACCOUNTING AS AN INFORMATION SYSTEM

OBJECTIVE ❶ PROVIDE *a basis for understanding the goals of the accounting process and flows of accounting information.*

Virtually all profit-seeking organizations and most nonprofit organizations maintain extensive accounting records. One reason is that these records are often required by law. A more basic reason is that, even in a very small organization, a manager is confronted with a multitude of complex variables. Not even the most brilliant manager can be sufficiently informed just by observing daily operations. Instead, he or she must depend on the accounting process to convert the organization's economic activity into useful statistical data that can be abstracted and summarized in accounting reports. In every sense, this process is essential to the coordinated and rational management of most organizations—regardless of their size. Thus, accounting is an *information system* necessitated by the great complexity of modern organizations.

In today's society, many persons and agencies outside of management are involved in the economic life of an organization. These persons frequently require financial data. For example, owners must have financial information in order to measure management's performance and to evaluate their own holdings. Potential investors need financial data in order to compare prospective investments. Creditors must consider the financial strength of an organization before lending it funds. Also, labor unions, financial analysts, and economists often expect a considerable amount of reliable financial data. Finally, many laws require that extensive financial information be reported to the various levels of government. As an information system, the accounting process serves persons both inside and outside an organization.

THE ACCOUNTING PROCESS

Accounting can be defined as the process of (1) *recording*, (2) *classifying*, (3) *reporting*, and (4) *interpreting* the financial data of an organization. Once an accounting system has been designed and installed, recording and classifying data may become somewhat routine and repetitive. While it is important for accountants to have a sound knowledge of this phase of the accounting process, it is often a relatively minor part.

of their total responsibility. Accountants direct most of their attention to the reporting and interpretation of the meaningful implications of the data.

Except in small organizations, much routine accounting work has become highly mechanized and automatic. Microcomputers and related software programs enable even small firms to process accounting data electronically. The emergence of electronic data processing has freed accountants from the routine aspects of recording and classifying data, enabling them to concentrate more on the analytical and interpretive aspects of the accounting function—the areas most affected by increased demands for accounting information.

Whether the accounting records for a given organization should be maintained manually or electronically will depend on several things, such as the size of the organization, the amount of data to be processed, the amount of information required, and the need for prompt access to stored data. Regardless of the method used, the underlying accounting concepts are essentially the same. Because a manually maintained system is most easily handled in the classroom and in problem situations, we use this type of system throughout this book. Where appropriate, however, we include comments relating to computer systems. Also, certain of the exercises and problems in the text, identified by computer-related logos, may be worked using computer supplements available with this text.

THE REPORTING PROCESS

Channel A: Managerial Data and Reports

The reporting process comprises four main channels of information flow. They are graphically represented in Exhibit 1-1.

A major function of accounting is to provide management with the data needed for decision making and for efficient operation of the firm. Although managers routinely receive the financial reports, tax returns, and special reports prepared for outsiders, they also require various other information, such as the unit cost of a product, estimates of the profit earned from a specific sales campaign, cost comparisons of alternative courses of action, and long-range budgets. Because of the strategic nature of some of this information, it may be available only to the firm's high-level management. The process of generating and analyzing such data is referred to as **managerial accounting.**

Channel B: Tax Returns

Taxes provide the funds to operate various levels of government. There are many kinds of taxes and, consequently, many kinds of tax returns. Most organizations must file one or more tax returns. A business, for example, may be required to file returns for federal, state, and municipal income taxes, sales and excise taxes, and payroll taxes. The preparation of these returns is governed by the rulings and special reporting requirements of the taxing agencies involved. Proper compliance is generally a matter of law and can be quite complicated.

Channel C: Special Reports

Some companies, by the nature of their activities, are required to report periodically to regulatory agencies. For example, most banks must report to the Comptroller of the Currency, and most public utility companies must report to a public utility commission. The regulatory agency may use the reported information to monitor solvency (as in the case of the banks) or the rate of income to be earned (as in the case of public utilities). Although these reports are based primarily on accounting data, often they must be prepared in accordance with additional conditions, rules, and definitions. Some agencies, such as stock exchanges and the Securities and Exchange Commission, do require reports prepared in accordance with the generally accepted accounting principles that we shall discuss later. We have therefore shown regulatory agencies in both channels C and D of Exhibit 1-1.

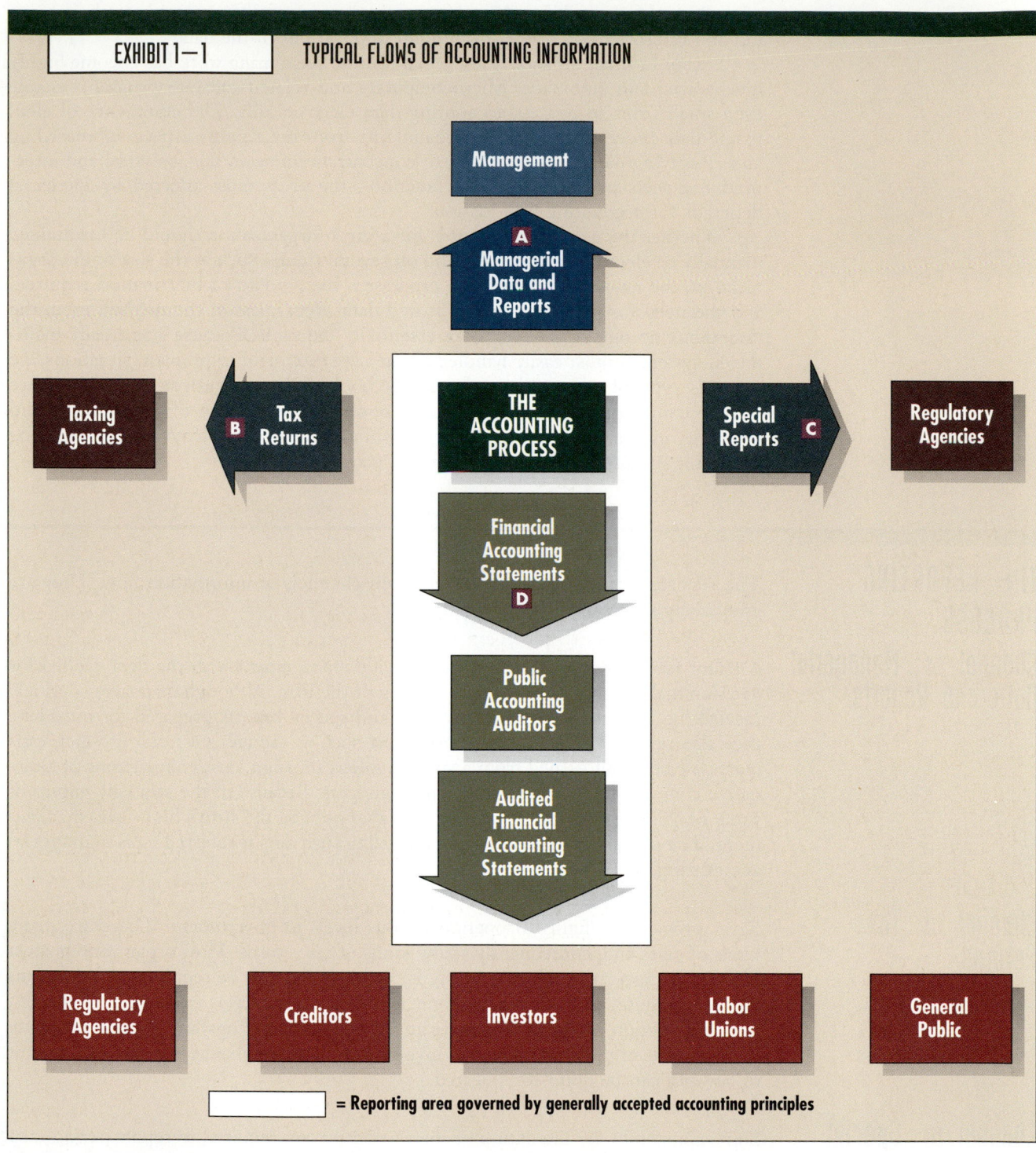

EXHIBIT 1–1   TYPICAL FLOWS OF ACCOUNTING INFORMATION

Management

A Managerial Data and Reports

Taxing Agencies   **B** Tax Returns   THE ACCOUNTING PROCESS   Special Reports **C**   Regulatory Agencies

Financial Accounting Statements **D**

Public Accounting Auditors

Audited Financial Accounting Statements

Regulatory Agencies   Creditors   Investors   Labor Unions   General Public

☐ = Reporting area governed by generally accepted accounting principles

Channel D: Financial Accounting Statements

One of the most important functions of the accounting process is to accumulate and report accounting information that shows an organization's financial position, cash flows, and the results of its operations. Many businesses publish such financial statements at least annually. The subdivision of the accounting process that produces these general-purpose reports is referred to as **financial accounting.** Financial accounting is essentially retrospective, because it deals primarily with historical information, or events that have already happened.

Although financial accounting data are primarily historical, they are also useful for planning and control. Indeed, a considerable amount of planning must be based on what has happened in the recent past. In addition, historical financial information is inherently a control mechanism, since it can be used to measure the success of past planning. We should also emphasize that, although financial accounting is primarily historical, it is not merely a process of "filling in the numbers." As you study further, you will discover that determining the financial position and profitability of an enterprise is a complex job that requires professional judgment.

Financial accounting statements are the main source of information for parties— other than governmental agencies—outside the business. Because these reports will often be used to evaluate management, their objectivity could be subject to question. To establish the validity of their financial statements, most firms have them audited by independent public accountants. The independent auditor examines the statements and suggests any changes that may be warranted. He or she then expresses a professional opinion that the financial statements are fairly stated "in conformity with generally accepted accounting principles" or indicates any reservations about the statements. Usually, outside parties have greater faith in financial statements that have been audited. Both the role of the professional public accountant and the nature of "generally accepted accounting principles" are complex. Therefore, each is treated separately in later sections of this chapter.

As Exhibit 1-1 indicates, generally accepted accounting principles are primarily relevant to financial accounting. In managerial accounting, the main objective is to assist management in making decisions and in operating effectively, and in such cases it is frequently useful to depart from concepts utilized in financial accounting. On many occasions, financial accounting data must be reassembled or altered to be most useful in solving internal business problems.

GENERALLY ACCEPTED ACCOUNTING PRINCIPLES

To be useful, financial accounting information must be assembled and reported objectively. Those who must rely on such information have a right to be assured that the data are free from bias and inconsistency, whether deliberate or not. For this reason, financial accounting relies on certain standards or guides that have proved useful over the years in imparting economic data. These standards are called **generally accepted accounting principles (GAAP).** Because accounting is more an art than a science, these principles are not immutable laws like those in the physical sciences. Instead, they are *guides to action* and may change over time. Sometimes specific principles must be altered or new principles must be formulated to fit changed economic circumstances or changes in business practices.

A number of organizations are concerned with the formulation of accounting principles. The most prominent among these is the Financial Accounting Standards Board (FASB). The FASB, organized in 1973, is a nongovernmental body whose pronouncements have the force of setting authoritative rules for the general practice of financial accounting. Before the creation of the FASB, the Accounting Principles Board (APB) of the American Institute of Certified Public Accountants fulfilled the function of formulating accounting principles. If the *attest* function (auditing and independent reporting) of the independent certified public accountant is to be meaningful, the businesses of this country must generally observe substantially comparable accounting principles.

Various regulatory bodies—such as the Securities and Exchange Commission and the Internal Revenue Service—also prescribe rules to be used in financial reporting. Because these rules often touch on accounting principles and may conflict with the rules and practices specified by other agencies, compromises sometimes have to be made in financial reporting. This has been especially true when the rules of a regulatory body have conflicted with those considered "generally accepted" by accounting practitioners.

Often, income determined by income tax regulations differs from that determined by generally accepted accounting principles. When rules or methods prescribed by the Internal Revenue Service for the determination of taxable income conflict with those acceptable for business reporting, an enterprise may keep more than one set of records to satisfy both reporting requirements.

The accounting principles we discuss are generally accepted in the United States. Accounting principles, however, differ in various ways among countries. Energized by the continuing growth of international business, efforts are under way to create more uniformity in worldwide accounting principles.

FIELDS OF ACCOUNTING ACTIVITY

OBJECTIVE ② DESCRIBE *the various fields of accounting activity.*

Accountants perform many diverse services and are engaged in various types of employment. The three major fields of accounting activity are *private accounting*, *public accounting*, and *governmental accounting*. Because each of these may comprise many aspects of accounting activity, it is possible to give only a broad description for each type of accounting employment.

Private Accounting

More accountants are employed in private accounting than in any other field. Private employers of accountants include manufacturers, wholesalers, retailers, and service firms. Depending on the size and complexity of the business, the private accountant's duties may vary from routine reporting to the design and implementation of computerized accounting systems. The major objective of the private accountant, however, is to assist management in planning and controlling the firm's operations. In many large businesses, the head of the accounting department is called the **controller** and is a key executive who works closely with other management personnel.

Frequently, a large company will have an **internal auditing** staff that reports to a high-ranking management officer or to an audit committee of the board of directors. Internal auditing is an appraisal activity conducted within the business to determine if management's financial and operating controls are effective and are being used properly. An internal auditor investigates policies and procedures designed to safeguard assets, promote operational efficiency, and provide reliable information.

Public Accounting

The field of public accounting is composed of firms that render independent audit reports on financial statements of businesses. Public accounting firms also perform a wide variety of accounting and managerial services, acting as consultants to their clients. Most accountants in public accounting firms are *certified public accountants* (CPAs), holding certificates from the particular states in which they work. To be certified, a person must pass a rigorous examination and meet the requirements for education and experience set by the state to ensure high standards of performance.

The professional responsibility of the certified public accountant is unique. While the attorney and the physician are responsible only to their clients and patients, the certified public accountant may be professionally responsible to third parties who rely on the financial statements the CPA has audited. This is true even though the third party in no way contributes to the fee paid for the audit and has no contractual relationship whatsoever with the accountant.

Governmental Accounting

A large number of accountants are employed by federal, state, and local governmental agencies. The services performed by these accountants parallel those of private and public accountants and may cover the entire spectrum of financial and managerial accounting. For example, the General Accounting Office of the federal government and the audit agencies in the various state governments engage in auditing activities similar to those of public accountants. Audits may be conducted not only of governmental agencies but also of private firms doing business with a governmental unit. Accounting personnel of the Internal Revenue Service and the corresponding state agencies conduct accounting investigations of firms and individuals in connection with their tax liabilities. Among the many other governmental agencies and regulatory bodies that employ accountants are the Securities and Exchange Commission, the Department of Defense, the Federal Power Commission, the Interstate Commerce Commission, and state utility commissions and agencies.

ETHICS AND THE ACCOUNTING ENVIRONMENT

OBJECTIVE ❸ IDENTIFY *ethical dimensions related to the accounting environment.*

Ethics deals with the values, rules, and justifications that govern one's way of life. Although fundamental ethical concepts like right and wrong, good and evil, justice, and morality tend to be abstract, many of the issues we face in our daily lives have ethical dimensions. The way we respond to these issues defines our ethical profile. In both our personal and professional lives, our goal should be to act ethically and responsibly.

Ethical behavior has not always been the case in the business world. Business history reveals such unethical activities as price gouging customers, using inside information for personal gain, paying bribes to government officials, ignoring safety regulations, selling arms to aggressor governments, polluting the environment, and issuing misleading financial information.

Increasingly, however, business managements recognize the importance of ethical behavior from their employees. It is now common for businesses to develop written codes of ethics to guide their employees. About 75% of the top 1,200 U.S. companies have written ethical codes. Similarly, professional organizations of accountants have written ethical codes. The American Institute of Certified Public Accountants (AICPA) has a professional code of ethics to guide the conduct of member CPAs. The Institute of Management Accountants (IMA) has formulated written standards of ethical conduct for accountants employed in private accounting.

Accountants face several unique ethical dimensions as a result of their work. These dimensions include the following:

1. The output produced by accountants may have significant financial implications for one or more persons. These situations may generate pressures on the accountant to "improve" the outcome. The amount of income taxes to be paid by an individual or organization, the amount of a bonus to be received by an employee, the price to be paid by a customer, and the amount of money to be distributed to owners are examples of situations in which the financial implications may lead to efforts to influence the outcome. *Ethical behavior mandates that accountants should ignore these pressures.*

2. Accountants have access to confidential and sensitive information. Tax returns, salary data, details of financial arrangements, planned acquisitions, and proposed price changes illustrate these types of information. *Ethically, accountants must respect the confidentiality of the data used in their work.*

3. An emphasis on short-term profits may contribute to ethical breakdowns within businesses. One of the criticisms of U.S. business practices is that they are too "bottom line" (that is, short-term profit) oriented. This orientation may lead to unethical actions by management to increase reported short-term profits. Because accountants compute and report firms' profits, they should be particularly concerned about these ethical breakdowns. *Both accountants and managements must recognize the importance of a long-run perspective.* Indeed, studies indicate that, over the long term, successful companies and ethical practices go hand in hand.

ETHICS

Ethics is definitely in. *The subject has even made its way into the pages of* The New Yorker: *A recent cartoon depicts an executive at a meeting saying, "This might not be ethical. Is that a problem for anyone?"* ■ *This question, if asked of many executives today, would undoubtedly elicit a resounding yes. "Ethical awareness is definitely growing," says Gary Edwards, director of the Washington, D.C.–based Ethics Resource Center. Managers have begun to realize that ethics is not only a legitimate business concern, but also a management responsibility. "I would estimate*

that about one of three of the largest companies today provide some kind of management education on ethics. This training usually takes the form of case studies rather than moralistic exhortations."

No one is predicting the demise of our basic Christian-Judaic code of values—indeed, it is generally agreed that the inquiry into ethics will only serve to validate traditional distinctions as to what is right and what is wrong. But as the world grows more complex, it is clear, so do questions of behavior. The field of ethics has, accordingly, begun to concern itself not only with what is legal versus illegal, but with the elusive nature and measurable benefits of ethical behavior itself. A report on this phenomenon cannot pretend to find "answers"

to the myriad of questions that are being asked these days—it can only hope to explore and define some of the key issues. Business ethics is currently receiving most of the attention, but the questions that are being explored apply to every profession. "Most executives are disgusted by illegal or unethical activities that have come to light in business," comments W. Michael Hoffman, director of the Center for Business Ethics at Bentley College in Waltham, Mass. "It's naive to claim that businesspeople are inherently any more or less ethical than others."

In the view of Edwards, the preoccupation with ethics is the outgrowth of a succession of contributing events. "In the sixties," he says, "to the extent that ethics was on any-

body's mind, the focus was external. Companies were beginning to come to terms with what they felt they owed to others besides shareholders. These groups included local communities, charities, and educational organizations. Today we call this 'corporate social responsibility.' Then about ten years ago, the focus shifted dramatically to the inside of the organization, to the proper conduct of the individuals who make up the organization."

Edwards credits this shift to the atmosphere surrounding Watergate as well as to a number of foreign bribery scandals that pointed up the shortcomings of certain corporate managers. Laws such as the 1977 Foreign Corrupt Practices Act appear to have signaled the beginning of the current period of corporate introspection. And the recent scandals in insider trading have given it new momentum.

When academia begins to take something seriously, then one can assume that it has "arrived," and business ethics has increasingly become a subject fit for classroom discussion.

SOURCE: Warren Kalbacker, "Digging for Direction," *World*, Winter 1988, p. 20. This article appeared in the Winter 1988 issue of *World* magazine, which is published by KPMG Peat Marwick.

THE ACCOUNTING EQUATION

OBJECTIVE ④ DEFINE *the accounting equation.*

Accounting analysis takes place within a framework identified as the *accounting equation*. The **accounting equation** states that the economic resources of a specific entity are equal to the claims on those resources. Another term used to refer to the claims on resources is *equities*. For a business, equities may represent the claims of creditors or of owners. In its basic form, then, the accounting equation appears as follows:

Economic Resources = Claims of Creditors + Claims of Owners

In stating the accounting equation, accountants use the technical terms *assets, liabilities,* and *owners' equity* to refer, respectively, to a company's economic resources, claims of creditors, and claims of owners. In its technical formulation, then, the accounting equation appears as follows:

Assets = Liabilities + Owners' Equity

This equation states that an entity's assets will equal the sum of its liabilities and owners' equity. *Throughout our accounting analysis, this accounting equation will (and must) remain in balance.*

Accounting Equation for a Business Entity			
Technical Terms:	Assets	= Liabilities	+ Owners' Equity
Basic Meanings:	Economic Resources	= Claims of Creditors	+ Claims of Owners

We now briefly explain each of the three elements in the accounting equation.

Assets

Assets are the economic resources of an entity that can be usefully expressed in money terms. Assets may take many forms. Cash is an asset, as are claims to receive cash payments from customers for services or goods provided (accounts receivable). Some assets—such as supplies, land, buildings, and equipment—may have readily identifiable physical characteristics. Others may simply represent prepayments for future services (for example, prepaid advertising) or nonphysical rights (for example, patents and copyrights).

The key characteristic of an asset is that it represents a probable future economic benefit owned or controlled by the entity. Although most items reported as assets are owned by the entity, ownership is not an essential test for an asset. To illustrate, assume that a business with a temporary need for storage space rents warehouse space for one year and prepays the year's rent. Although it does not own the storage space, the firm has paid for the right to use the warehouse for one year. This is a future economic benefit for the firm, which will report the prepaid rent as one of its assets.

Liabilities

Liabilities are the obligations, or debts, that an entity must pay in money or services at some time in the future because of past transactions or events. For example, a firm may borrow money and sign a promissory note agreeing to pay it back six months in the future. The firm will report this obligation as a liability called *notes payable*. Similarly, the firm may owe amounts to various suppliers for goods or services already provided (*accounts payable*), or it may owe wages to employees for work already performed (*wages payable*). Notes payable, accounts payable, and wages payable are obligations that will be settled in the relatively near future. Other liabilities may take long periods to settle. For example, a business may borrow funds to finance the construction of a building and agree to pay them back over the next 15 years, with the building serving as collateral for the loan. This transaction results in a liability called *mortgage payable*.

Although most liabilities are payable in cash, some may involve the performance of services. A magazine publisher, for example, may receive advance cash payments for three-year subscriptions. The receipt of these payments creates an obligation for the publisher to provide subscribers with issues of the magazine. The publisher will report a liability (subscriptions received in advance) that will be reduced as the magazines are sent to subscribers.

Owners' Equity

Owners' equity is the interest of the owners in the assets of an entity. The owners' interest is a *residual claim* on the entity's assets; that is, it is a claim to the assets remaining after the liabilities to creditors have been discharged. For this reason, owners' equity may also be defined as the **net assets** of an entity; net assets is the difference between the assets and the liabilities. Thus,

$$\text{Assets} - \text{Liabilities} = \text{Owners' Equity}$$
$$\text{Net Assets} = \text{Owners' Equity}$$

AN INTRODUCTION TO BASIC PRINCIPLES

OBJECTIVE 5 INTRODUCE *basic principles that underlie financial accounting.*

Certain fundamental principles underlie the recording and reporting of an entity's economic activity. These principles have been developed over time to provide general guides to making financial reports as useful as possible. Although various terms—such as principles, concepts, assumptions, conventions, and standards—are often used to describe such guides, a distinction among these terms is not essential to understand the guides. At this point, a brief discussion of some of these guides will be helpful in understanding the structure of the accounting process.

Accounting Entity Concept

Before any accounting analysis may begin, the boundaries of the unit to be accounted for must be identified. This unit of focus for the accumulation and reporting of accounting data is the **accounting entity.** In financial accounting, the accounting entity is usually an entire enterprise. A business enterprise is typically organized as either a sole proprietorship, a partnership, or a corporation. Each such firm is an accounting entity that is distinct and separate from the activities and affairs of its owners. The information presented in a firm's financial statements reflects the economic activity of only that firm; it does not reflect the economic activity of its owners or other firms.

For certain managerial accounting uses, the accounting entity may be smaller than the entire organization. Management, for example, may want financial information about a certain department or division within the company. The particular department or division becomes the accounting entity for the purpose of gathering and reporting the desired information.

Cost Principle

The **cost principle** states that assets are initially recorded at the amounts paid to acquire the assets. Land, for example, may be purchased for $75,000 cash. The land will be recorded at its $75,000 cost. Cost is considered the proper initial measure because, at the time an asset is acquired, cost represents the fair value of the asset as agreed to by both the buyer and seller.

In general, cost also is the basis used to report an asset at subsequent times while it is still held by a firm. A year later, for example, the land purchased above may be appraised at $90,000. The firm will continue to report the land at $75,000, because that amount was verified by engaging in an exchange transaction with another entity; the $90,000 amount has not been verified by an exchange transaction. In this context, the cost measure is often referred to as *historical cost* (a cost measure that continues to be utilized through time). Accountants have long recognized that historical cost is probably the most objective and verifiable basis for reporting assets. As you will learn, historical costs are often *reduced* over time to reflect asset expirations, and, in some cases, they may be reduced to market values; upward revaluations, however, are not permitted in conventional financial statements.

Objectivity Principle

The usefulness of accounting reports is enhanced when the underlying data are objective and verifiable. The **objectivity principle** dictates that the recording of transactions should be based on reliable and verifiable evidence. Amounts recorded should be supported by actual invoices, physical counts, and other relatively bias-free evidence whenever possible. Undocumented opinions of management or others do not provide a good basis for accounting determinations. As we shall see throughout our discussion of accounting, however, it is often necessary to incorporate estimates into our analyses. Even when a certain amount of subjectivity cannot be avoided, it is important that such estimates be supported by some type of objective analysis if possible.

Going Concern Concept

The **going concern concept** assumes that an entity will continue to operate indefinitely and will not be sold or liquidated. This assumption supports the use of historical cost to measure assets, such as supplies and equipment, that will be used in operating the business. The going concern concept implies that the firm will operate long enough to use up the supplies and equipment. As they are used up, their costs will be reflected as costs of operations. Information about the current market values or liquidation values of assets that are going to be used in operations rather than sold is not considered to be particularly relevant information.

Sometimes accountants have strong evidence that the entity is not going to operate indefinitely into the future. If this is the case, the going concern assumption is not used, and amounts other than historical cost may become useful data. For example, a firm that is bankrupt and in the process of liquidating will find estimated liquidation values for its assets to be more useful information than historical costs. Throughout this book, however, we will use the going concern concept.

Measuring Unit Concept

The economic activity that accountants record must be expressed in a common unit of measure so that the data may be easily classified, summarized, and reported. The **measuring unit concept** specifies that a monetary unit (the dollar in the United States) is to be used to measure and record an entity's economic activity. When all assets, liabilities, and owners' equity are stated in monetary terms, they may be easily added or subtracted, as necessary, to prepare financial statements. Also, various relationships among financial statement components may be easily calculated and presented to help interpret the statements.

Recording and reporting in monetary terms creates two limitations to the financial accounting process. First, only items that may be expressed in monetary terms are brought into the information system. Some economic resources and obligations may be excluded from the accounting information system because there is no agreement as to how to express them monetarily. For example, the human resource (that is, a firm's employees) is not recorded and reported as an asset in conventional financial statements. Accountants recognize that a firm's work force is an economic resource, but accountants have not yet determined an appropriate way to measure this resource in monetary terms. Until this measurement issue is resolved, the human resource will not be reported among a firm's assets.

The second limitation is that the U.S. dollar (as well as the currencies of other countries) is not a stable unit of measure. Inflation causes a currency's purchasing power to decline through time. Failure to adjust for this may cause some distortion in a firm's financial statements because the amounts appearing in the statements are expressed in dollars of different vintages. For example, in computing total assets at December 31, 1993, supplies purchased in 1993 may be added to land purchased in 1970; both supplies and land are measured in U.S. dollars, but they are dollars from two quite different points in time (1993 and 1970) and, thus, represent quite different units of purchasing power. Some persons believe that using dollars with different purchasing powers limits the usefulness of financial data. However, no adjustments are made to U.S. basic financial statements to reflect the impact of purchasing power changes in the unit of measure. The measuring unit concept specifies that the U.S. dollar's purchasing power, while not completely stable, is stable enough so that no adjustments are necessary. The Financial Accounting Standards Board, however, does encourage firms to make supplementary disclosures concerning the effects of inflation on their operations.

EFFECT OF TRANSACTIONS ON THE ACCOUNTING EQUATION

An *accounting transaction* is an economic event that requires accounting recognition. Therefore, an event that affects any of the elements in the accounting equation (assets, liabilities, or owners' equity) must be recorded. Some activities—for example, ordering supplies, bidding for an engagement or contract, and negotiating for the acquisition of assets—may represent economic activities, but an accounting transaction does not occur until such activities result in a change in the firm's assets, liabilities, or owners' equity.

OBJECTIVE ⑥ EXPLAIN *and* ILLUSTRATE *the effects of transactions on the accounting equation.*

Earlier, we observed that the accounting equation (Assets = Liabilities + Owners' Equity) will always remain in balance. An accounting transaction may affect the components of this equation in various ways, but the equation stays in balance. If assets, liabilities, and owners' equity are computed after each accounting transaction is recorded, the equality of assets and equities will always be confirmed.

Transactions Not Affecting Owners' Equity

Certain transactions may change the character and amounts of assets or liabilities, or both, but have no effect on owners' equity. For example, if a firm purchases equipment for $1,000 cash, the asset Equipment will increase by $1,000, but the asset Cash will decrease by $1,000. This transaction causes only a shift in the composition of individual assets; it does not change total assets. In the same way, collection of accounts receivable causes a shift of assets. Collection of $500 of Accounts Receivable would result in a decrease in this asset and an increase in Cash of $500.

If the $1,000 worth of equipment had been purchased on credit rather than for cash, the result would have been a $1,000 increase in Equipment and an equal increase in the liability Accounts Payable. On the other hand, payment of liabilities reduces both assets and liabilities. If $800 is paid to creditors, both Cash and Accounts Payable would decrease by $800.

Transactions Affecting Owners' Equity

The following four types of transactions change the amount of owners' equity:

Transaction	Effect on Owners' Equity
1. Owner contributions	Increase
2. Owner withdrawals	Decrease
3. Revenues	Increase
4. Expenses	Decrease

When an owner contributes cash or other assets to a business firm, the firm's accounting records show an increase in assets and an increase in owners' equity. Conversely, when an owner withdraws assets from the firm, both assets and owners' equity decrease. The primary goal of any business, however, is to increase the owners' equity by earning profits, or **net income.** The net income of a firm is determined by subtracting *expenses incurred* from *revenues earned.*

$$\text{Net Income} = \text{Revenues} - \text{Expenses}$$

Owners' equity is increased by revenues and decreased by expenses. Let us examine the nature of revenues and expenses.

Revenues

Revenues are the increases in owners' equity that a firm earns by providing goods or services for its customers. The revenue earned typically is measured by the assets received in exchange for the goods or services. Sometimes the earning of revenue decreases a liability rather than causing assets to increase. It is important to recognize that *revenue is created at the time that goods or services are provided.* The asset initially received may be cash, but often it is a different asset, such as accounts receivable. For example, if a firm sells goods for $1,500 cash, it has earned $1,500 of revenue and the asset received is $1,500 Cash. If the firm sells other goods for $1,000 on credit (with payment due in 30 days), it has earned another $1,000 of revenue and the asset received is $1,000 Accounts Receivable.

The following example illustrates when the earning of revenue decreases a liability. Suppose a magazine publisher receives $3,600 cash representing 100 one-year subscriptions to its monthly magazine. This event increases Cash by $3,600 and creates a $3,600 Subscriptions Received in Advance liability. When the publisher sends out the magazine each month to the 100 subscribers, it earns $300 of Subscription Revenue ($\frac{1}{12}$ of $3,600) and the Subscriptions Received in Advance liability is decreased by $300.

Receipt of cash by a firm does not necessarily mean that revenue has been earned. As previously noted, the subsequent collection of an account receivable merely results in a shift of assets from Accounts Receivable to Cash—it does not increase revenue. Also as previously noted, payments received in advance for goods or services create a liability because no revenue has yet been earned. Neither is revenue earned when a business borrows money or when the owners contribute cash. Such increases in assets are not earned because the firm has provided no goods or services.

Expenses

Expenses are the decreases in owners' equity that a firm incurs in the process of earning revenues. Generally, expenses are measured by the assets that are used up or flow out of a firm as a result of its operating activities. Expenses may also cause an increase in liabilities. For example, if a firm pays $2,000 to an employee as one month's salary, it has incurred $2,000 of Salaries Expense and the asset given up (that is, flowing out of the firm) is $2,000 Cash. If a firm obtains legal services and receives a $500 invoice from the attorney, the firm has incurred $500 of Legal Expense and has increased its liabilities by $500 Accounts Payable. Rent, supplies, advertising, and the costs of heat, light, and telephone are other examples of expenses incurred in producing revenues.

Payments of cash by a firm do not necessarily mean that an expense has been incurred. Cash expenditures made to acquire assets do not represent expenses. Cash expenditures made to pay liabilities, such as the payment of an account payable, also do not represent expenses and do not affect owners' equity. Withdrawals of cash by owners, although they do reduce owners' equity, do not represent expenses. Expenses are directly related to the earning of revenues; owner withdrawals are not part of a firm's efforts to generate revenues.

Accrual-Basis Accounting and the Matching Concept

The foregoing concepts of revenues and expenses apply to firms that employ **accrual-basis accounting.** In accrual accounting, revenues are recorded when they are earned and expenses are recorded in the period they help to generate revenues. There is a linkage, therefore, between expenses and revenues—expenses are incurred to generate revenues. In accrual accounting, the process of determining net income uses this linkage through a basic principle known as the *matching concept.*

The **matching concept** states that net income is determined by linking, or matching, expenses incurred with the related revenues earned. As mentioned earlier, revenues and expenses for determining net income do not depend on when cash is actually received or paid. For example, store rent for March helps a firm generate revenues during March and, under the matching concept, the rent is an expense for March regardless of when it is actually paid. Similarly, supplies help a firm in its operations (that is, help in the process of generating revenues) when the supplies are used, which may be a different period than when the supplies are actually purchased and paid for. Under the matching concept, the supplies are an expense in the period they are used.

Cash-Basis Accounting

Cash-basis accounting contrasts with accrual-basis accounting. Under cash-basis accounting, revenues are recorded when cash is received from operating activities and expenses are recorded when cash payments related to operating activities are made. Net income, therefore, becomes the difference between operating cash receipts and cash payments. Cash-basis accounting is a relatively simple system for determining net income. There is no attempt, however, to match expenses with revenues; thus, cash-basis accounting is not consistent with generally accepted accounting principles for determining net income.

Although cash-basis accounting is unacceptable for net income computations, information about cash flows is useful because cash is a particularly important asset. As we will see, a financial statement reporting cash flows is prepared as is another financial statement that reports net income computed under accrual-basis accounting.

TRANSACTIONS AND THE ACCOUNTING EQUATION: AN ILLUSTRATION

Now that we have described the effects of transactions on the accounting equation, let us illustrate the effects with an example.

Experienced driver education instructor John King established a private driving school called Westgate Driving School. King intends to buy a lot for vehicle storage and driver instruction, but to lease training vehicles. The transactions for June, the first month of operations, are analyzed below. The accounting equation for Westgate Driving School is presented after each transaction so that the effect on the equation may be examined. When a transaction affects owner's equity, the specific type of change will also be shown.

Initial Investment

TRANSACTION 1   On June 1, King invested $40,000 of his personal funds in the school. This first business transaction increased the asset Cash and increased King's equity (J. King, Capital).

	Assets	=	Liabilities	+	Owner's Equity	
	Cash	=			J. King, Capital	Type of Change
1	+$40,000	=			+$40,000	Investment

Purchase of Land

TRANSACTION 2   On June 2, Westgate Driving School paid $26,000 cash for a lot to be used for storing vehicles and for some driving instruction. This transaction reduced the asset Cash and created another asset, Land, for an equivalent amount. This transaction was merely the conversion of one asset to another.

	Assets			=	Liabilities	+	Owner's Equity	
	Cash	+	Land	=			J. King, Capital	Type of Change
Balance	$40,000			=			$40,000	
2	−26,000		+$26,000					
Balance	$14,000	+	$26,000	=			$40,000	

Payment of Rent

TRANSACTION 3   On June 3, the school paid $800 to rent a furnished office (including utilities) near the parking lot for June. This expenditure is a June expense, representing the cost of using office space for the month. The transaction reduced assets (Cash) and owner's equity (J. King, Capital) by $800.

	Assets			=	Liabilities	+	Owner's Equity	
	Cash	+	Land	=			J. King, Capital	Type of Change
Balance	$14,000	+	$26,000	=			$40,000	
3	−800						−800	Expense: Rent
Balance	$13,200	+	$26,000	=			$39,200	

Payment of Lease

TRANSACTION 4 On June 3, the school paid $3,500 to lease cars for the month of June. This payment permits the driving school to use the automobiles during June and is an expense for June. The transaction reduced assets (Cash) and owner's equity (J. King, Capital) by $3,500.

	Assets			=	Liabilities	+	Owner's Equity	
	Cash	+	Land	=			J. King, Capital	Type of Change
Balance	$13,200	+	$26,000	=			$39,200	
4	**−3,500**						**−3,500**	**Expense: Car Lease**
Balance	$ 9,700	+	$26,000	=			$35,700	

Purchase of Advertising on Account

TRANSACTION 5 On June 10, the school received a $300 invoice from the local newspaper for a driving school advertisement that will run in the newspaper four times during June. The invoice will be paid on June 30. The cost of advertising services is an expense incurred to generate revenues, and this $300 is an expense for June. As a result of this transaction, liabilities (Accounts Payable) are increased and owner's equity (J. King, Capital) is decreased by $300.

	Assets			=	Liabilities	+	Owner's Equity	
	Cash	+	Land	=	Accounts Payable	+	J. King, Capital	Type of Change
Balance	$9,700	+	$26,000	=			$35,700	
5					**+$300**		**−300**	**Expense: Advertising**
Balance	$9,700	+	$26,000	=	$300	+	$35,400	

Billing for Fee Revenue

TRANSACTION 6 On June 26, students were billed $16,000 for June instructional fees. Providing instruction during the month generated an asset, Accounts Receivable, and revenue, which increased owner's equity (J. King, Capital), even though payment will not be received until later.

	Assets					=	Liabilities	+	Owner's Equity	
	Cash	+	Accounts Receivable	+	Land	=	Accounts Payable	+	J. King, Capital	Type of Change
Balance	$9,700			+	$26,000	=	$300	+	$35,400	
6			**+$16,000**						**+16,000**	**Revenue: Instructional Fees Earned**
Balance	$9,700	+	$16,000	+	$26,000	=	$300	+	$51,400	

Payment of Salaries

TRANSACTION 7 On June 30, the school paid instructors' salaries of $9,000 for June. This amount was June expense, because it represented the cost of employees' services used during June. Therefore, Cash and J. King, Capital were both reduced by $9,000.

		Assets			=	Liabilities	+	Owner's Equity	
	Cash	+ Accounts Receivable	+	Land	=	Accounts Payable	+	J. King, Capital	Type of Change
Balance	$9,700	+ $16,000	+	$26,000	=	$300	+	$51,400	
7	−9,000							−9,000	Expense: Salaries
Balance	$ 700	+ $16,000	+	$26,000	=	$300	+	$42,400	

Collection of Accounts Receivable

TRANSACTION 8 On June 30, the school collected $10,000 on account from students billed in transaction 6. This transaction increased Cash and decreased Accounts Receivable—merely a shift in assets. Note that the revenue, which increased owner's equity, had already been reflected when the month's billings were made on June 26.

		Assets			=	Liabilities	+	Owner's Equity	
	Cash	+ Accounts Receivable	+	Land	=	Accounts Payable	+	J. King, Capital	Type of Change
Balance	$ 700	+ $16,000	+	$26,000	=	$300	+	$42,400	
8	+10,000	−10,000							
Balance	$10,700	+ $ 6,000	+	$26,000	=	$300	+	$42,400	

Receipt of Invoice for Gas and Oil

TRANSACTION 9 On June 30, the school received a $400 invoice from the local service station for gas and oil charged to the school's account during June. The invoice will be paid in July. Gas and oil used during the month represent a June expense. Consequently, liabilities (Accounts Payable) are increased and owner's equity (J. King, Capital) is decreased by $400.

		Assets			=	Liabilities	+	Owner's Equity	
	Cash	+ Accounts Receivable	+	Land	=	Accounts Payable	+	J. King, Capital	Type of Change
Balance	$10,700	+ $6,000	+	$26,000	=	$300	+	$42,400	
9						+400		−400	Expense: Gas and Oil
Balance	$10,700	+ $6,000	+	$26,000	=	$700	+	$42,000	

Payment of Accounts Payable

TRANSACTION 10 On June 30, the school paid the $300 invoice for advertising that was received on June 10. This transaction reduced assets (Cash) and liabilities (Accounts Payable) by $300.

		Assets			=	Liabilities	+	Owner's Equity	
	Cash	+	Accounts Receivable	+	Land	=	Accounts Payable	+	J. King, Capital	Type of Change
Balance	$10,700	+	$6,000	+	$26,000	=	$700	+	$42,000	
10	−300					=	−300			
Balance	$10,400	+	$6,000	+	$26,000	=	$400	+	$42,000	

Borrowing of Cash

TRANSACTION 11 On June 30, the school borrowed $3,000 from a bank and King, as owner of Westgate Driving School, signed a promissory note agreeing to pay it back in six months. (The school will use the money to buy a video projection unit so that instructional video-tapes may be shown to students.) This borrowing transaction increased both assets (Cash) and liabilities (Notes Payable) by $3,000.

		Assets			=	Liabilities		+	Owner's Equity	
	Cash	+	Accounts Receivable	+	Land	=	Notes Payable	+ Accounts Payable	+	J. King, Capital	Type of Change
Balance	$10,400	+	$6,000	+	$26,000	=		$400	+	$42,000	
11	+3,000						+$3,000				
Balance	$13,400	+	$6,000	+	$26,000	=	$3,000 +	$400	+	$42,000	

Withdrawal by Owner

TRANSACTION 12 On June 30, King withdrew $1,400 from the firm for personal use. This withdrawal reduced Cash and J. King, Capital by $1,400. Note that the effect of this transaction was the reverse of transaction **1**, in which King invested personal funds in the school.

		Assets			=	Liabilities		+	Owner's Equity	
	Cash	+	Accounts Receivable	+	Land	=	Notes Payable	+ Accounts Payable	+	J. King, Capital	Type of Change
Balance	$13,400	+	$6,000	+	$26,000	=	$3,000	+ $400	+	$42,000	
12	−1,400									−1,400	Withdrawal
Balance	$12,000	+	$6,000	+	$26,000	=	$3,000	+ $400	+	$40,600	

Summary of June Activities

Exhibit 1-2 summarizes the June activities of the Westgate Driving School. At the end of June, total assets of $44,000 are equaled by a $44,000 total for liabilities plus owner's equity. As a result of the driving school's June activities, John King's capital

EXHIBIT 1—2	SUMMARY OF JUNE ACTIVITIES AND THEIR EFFECT ON THE ACCOUNTING EQUATION

	Assets			=	Liabilities		+	Owner's Equity	
Transaction	Cash	+ Accounts Receivable +	Land	=	Notes Payable +	Accounts Payable	+	J. King, Capital	Type of Change
1	+$40,000							+$40,000	Investment
2	−26,000		+$26,000						
3	−800							−800	Rent Expense
4	−3,500							−3,500	Car Lease Expense
5						+$300		−300	Advertising Expense
6		+$16,000						+16,000	Instructional Fees Earned
7	−9,000							−9,000	Salaries Expense
8	+10,000	−10,000							
9						+400		−400	Gas and Oil Expense
10	−300					−300			
11	+3,000				+$3,000				
12	−1,400							−1,400	Withdrawal
	$12,000 +	$ 6,000 +	$26,000	=	$3,000 +	$400	+	$40,600	
		$44,000				$44,000			

increased from his original investment of $40,000 to $40,600, an increase of $600. Had King not withdrawn $1,400 for personal use, the increase would have been $2,000, which represents the net income, or net earnings, for June.

BASIC FINANCIAL STATEMENTS

OBJECTIVE ⑦ INTRODUCE *the basic financial statements.*

The basic set of statements that are communicated to interested parties comprise four financial statements. They are the income statement, the statement of owners' equity, the balance sheet, and the statement of cash flows. Exhibit 1-3 shows these financial statements for Westgate Driving School.

Note that each financial statement begins with a heading. The heading gives the name of the company and the name of the financial statement. In addition, the balance sheet heading identifies the specific date of the balance sheet, while the headings for the other three financial statements identify the time period that they cover. Note also that the totals in the various financial statements have been double ruled. Accountants do this principally to signify that all necessary calculations have been performed and to emphasize final amounts for the benefit of readers.

Although financial statements are the end result of the financial accounting process, we introduce them in simplified form here, early in our study. Having some knowledge of the ultimate objective of financial accounting will help you understand the various steps in the accounting process.

Income Statement

The **income statement** reports the results of operations for a period. The income statement lists the revenues and expenses of the firm. Accrual-basis accounting is used to determine the revenues and expenses. When total revenues exceed total expenses, the resulting amount is net income; when expenses exceed revenues, the resulting amount is a net loss. Westgate Driving School reports a net income of $2,000 for June because its revenues exceed its expenses by that amount.

| EXHIBIT 1—3 | FINANCIAL STATEMENTS FOR WESTGATE DRIVING SCHOOL |

WESTGATE DRIVING SCHOOL
INCOME STATEMENT
FOR THE MONTH OF JUNE, 1993

Revenue

Instructional Fees Earned		$16,000
Expenses		
Rent Expense	$ 800	
Car Lease Expense	3,500	
Advertising Expense	300	
Salaries Expense	9,000	
Gas and Oil Expense	400	
Total Expenses		14,000
Net Income		$ 2,000

WESTGATE DRIVING SCHOOL
STATEMENT OF OWNER'S EQUITY
FOR THE MONTH OF JUNE, 1993

J. King, Capital, June 1, 1993		$ –0–
Add: Capital Contributed in June		40,000
Net Income for June		2,000
		$42,000
Less: Capital Withdrawn in June		1,400
J. King, Capital, June 30, 1993		$40,600

WESTGATE DRIVING SCHOOL
BALANCE SHEET
JUNE 30, 1993

Assets		**Liabilities**	
Cash	$12,000	Notes Payable	$ 3,000
Accounts Receivable	6,000	Accounts Payable	400
Land	26,000	Total Liabilities	$ 3,400
		Owner's Equity	
		J. King, Capital	40,600
		Total Liabilities and	
Total Assets	$44,000	Owner's Equity	$44,000

WESTGATE DRIVING SCHOOL
STATEMENT OF CASH FLOWS
FOR THE MONTH OF JUNE, 1993

Cash Flows from Operating Activities

Cash Received from Clients		$10,000
Cash Paid to Employees and Suppliers		(13,600)
Net Cash Used by Operating Activities		($ 3,600)
Cash Flows from Investing Activities		
Purchase of Land		(26,000)
Cash Flows from Financing Activities		
Investment by J. King	$40,000	
Borrowing from Bank	3,000	
Withdrawal by J. King	(1,400)	
Net Cash Provided by Financing Activities		41,600
Net Increase in Cash		$12,000
Cash at June 1, 1993		–0–
Cash at June 30, 1993		$12,000

Statement of Owners' Equity

The **statement of owners' equity** presents information on the events causing a change in owners' equity during a period. The statement starts with owners' equity at the beginning of the period, then reports the events causing increases and decreases in the owners' equity, and ends with owners' equity at the end of the period. Owners' equity is increased when owners make investments in the firm and when operations achieve a net income. Owners' equity is decreased when owners make withdrawals from the firm and when operations result in a net loss. During June, the owner's equity of Westgate Driving School increased by $40,000 from owner investments and $2,000 from net income. Withdrawals of $1,400 decreased owner's equity. At the end of June, owner's equity was $40,600.

Balance Sheet

The **balance sheet,** sometimes called the **statement of financial position,** is a listing of a firm's assets, liabilities, and owners' equity on a given date. Each of these categories represents a section in a balance sheet. The balance sheet for Westgate Driving School illustrates the typical format for a balance sheet—total assets ($44,000) are shown to be equal to the sum of liabilities and owner's equity ($44,000). This equality, of course, is the equality presented by the accounting equation. For this reason, the accounting equation is sometimes called the *balance sheet equation*.

Statement of Cash Flows

The **statement of cash flows** reports information about cash inflows and outflows during a period of time. The cash flows are grouped into three categories of activities —operating, investing, and financing. The cash flows from operating activities are the same cash flows that develop when cash basis accounting is used to compute net income. The cash flows from investing activities include the cash payments and receipts that occur when a firm buys and sells assets that it uses in its operations, such as land, buildings, and equipment. The cash flows from financing activities identify owner investments and withdrawals of cash, as well as cash borrowed and repaid.

The Westgate Driving School financial statements in Exhibit 1-3 illustrate the difference between accrual-basis accounting and cash-basis accounting (a topic discussed earlier in this chapter). The company reports a net income of $2,000 in its income statement when accrual-basis accounting is used. In the statement of cash flows, cash-basis accounting is used in the operating activities section, and that section reports a net cash *outflow* of $3,600. There is a $5,600 difference between these two results. What explains this difference? The income statement includes (1) $6,000 of revenue (instructional fees earned) that has been earned but not yet received in cash and (2) $400 of expense (gas and oil expense) that has been incurred but not yet paid in cash.

FORMS OF BUSINESS ORGANIZATION

OBJECTIVE **8** EXPLAIN *the forms of business organization.*

The principal forms of business organization are the sole proprietorship, the partnership, and the corporation. Although each of these organizational units is treated as an accounting entity, only the corporation is viewed under the law as a legal entity separate from its owners. A **sole proprietorship** is a business owned by one person; it is the most numerous of the three forms of business organization. A **partnership** is a voluntary association of two or more persons for the purpose of conducting a business. A **corporation** is a separate legal entity created under the laws of a state or the federal government. Owners of a corporation receive shares of stock as evidence of their ownership and, consequently, the owners are referred to as *stockholders*, or *shareholders*. The corporation is the most dominant organizational form in terms of the volume of business activity conducted.

The principal differences in the financial statements for the three types of business organizations just described appear in the owners' equity section of the balance sheet. State corporation laws require that corporations segregate, in their balance sheets, the owners' investment (the amount paid for their stock) and any accumulated earnings. Because there are no comparable legal restrictions on sole proprietorships and partnerships, these types of businesses do not have to distinguish between amounts invested by owners and undistributed earnings.

The following illustrations demonstrate the variations in the balance sheet presentation of owners' equity for the three forms of business organization.

Case I: Sole Proprietorship

George Taylor originally invested $50,000 in a graphics business. Subsequent earnings left in the business amounted to $30,000. The owner's equity section of the firm's balance sheet would appear at follows:

Owner's Equity

G. Taylor, Capital	$80,000

Case II: Partnership

George Taylor, Eva Williams, and John Young invested $25,000, $15,000, and $10,000, respectively, in a graphics business. Each partner's share of the subsequent earnings of $30,000 not withdrawn from the business was $10,000. The owners' equity section of this firm's balance sheet would appear as follows:

Owners' Equity

G. Taylor, Capital	$35,000
E. Williams, Capital	25,000
J. Young, Capital	20,000
Total Owners' Equity	$80,000

Case III: Corporation

George Taylor, Eva Williams, and John Young began a corporation investing $25,000, $15,000, and $10,000, respectively, and receiving shares of stock for those amounts, totaling $50,000. This amount, called Capital Stock, is not available for distribution to the owners (stockholders). Unlike sole proprietorships and partnerships, in which owners are personally liable for the firm's debts, corporate stockholders' liability is usually limited to their investment. Therefore, the capital stock amount is kept intact to protect the firm's creditors. Because there may be many shareholders and because the shares of stock are freely transferable, the identity of the stockholders is not shown in the balance sheet. Corporate earnings, amounting to $30,000, that have not been distributed are identified as *retained earnings* in the corporate balance sheet. Ordinarily, this is the maximum amount that can be distributed to the shareholders. The stockholders' equity section of the firm's balance sheet would appear as follows:

Stockholders' Equity

Capital Stock	$50,000
Retained Earnings	30,000
Total Stockholders' Equity	$80,000

In sole proprietorships and partnerships, the owners may make withdrawals at their own discretion. A withdrawal results in a decrease in cash and a decrease in the owner's capital. In a corporation, a formal procedure is needed. The board of directors, elected by the stockholders, must meet and "declare a dividend" before the distribution can be made to the stockholders. If the firm in our illustration declared and paid a dividend of $5,000, both cash and retained earnings would be reduced by that amount, and the retained earnings balance would be $25,000.

DEBT-TO-EQUITY RATIO

OBJECTIVE ❾ DEFINE *the* **debt-to-equity ratio** *and* EXPLAIN *its use.*

Financial statements provide the basis for the financial analysis done by and for the various external users. In this and subsequent chapters, we will introduce appropriate analytical applications.

The relationship between a firm's liabilities and its owners' equity is one important indicator of the firm's financial strength. The debt-to-equity ratio measures this relationship. In practice, there are several variations in the computation of this ratio. In its most fundamental form, the **debt-to-equity ratio** is computed as follows:

$$\text{Debt-to-Equity Ratio} = \frac{\text{Total Liabilities}}{\text{Total Owners' Equity}}$$

A debt-to-equity ratio of 1.0 means a firm has equal amounts of liabilities and owners' equity. A ratio below 1.0 indicates that liabilities are less than owners' equity, and a ratio greater than 1.0 means that liabilities exceed owners' equity. The debt-to-equity ratio for Westgate Driving School at June 30, 1993, is $3,400/$40,600 = 0.08.

The debt-to-equity ratio gives potential creditors an indication of the margin of protection available to them (creditors' claims to assets have priority over owners' claims). The lower the ratio, the better a creditor would feel about extending additional credit. As the ratio increases, creditors may charge higher interest rates to compensate for the decreased margin of protection. At some point, the ratio may become so large that it signals creditors that extending additional credit may be unwise.

The interpretation of a firm's debt-to-equity ratio is aided by looking at its trend in recent years (whether it is going up or down) and by comparing it to industry averages. Certain stable industries, such as utilities, tend to have higher debt-to-equity ratios than other industries whose operating results are more volatile. Following are examples of debt-to-equity ratios at a similar point in time for several companies in different industries.

BOB EVANS FARMS, INC. (food services)	0.19
KELLY SERVICES, INC. (temporary help)	0.31
PPG INDUSTRIES, INC. (glass, paint, chemicals)	1.40
SOUTHERN NEW ENGLAND TELECOMMUNICATIONS CORPORATION (telecommunications)	2.04
PHILLIPS PETROLEUM COMPANY (petroleum, chemicals)	3.46

KEY POINTS FOR CHAPTER OBJECTIVES

❶ PROVIDE a basis for understanding the goals of the accounting process and flows of accounting information (pp. 1–8).
- Accounting is the process of (1) recording, (2) classifying, (3) reporting, and (4) interpreting financial data.
- The basic purpose of accounting is to provide financial information that is useful in making economic decisions.
- Reporting to management, taxing agencies, and regulatory agencies is in accordance with their directives or regulations; reporting to most other users is in accordance with generally accepted accounting principles.

❷ DESCRIBE the various fields of accounting activity (pp. 8–9).
- Private accountants assist their employers (manufacturing, wholesale, retail, and service firms) in planning, controlling, and reporting operations.

- Public accountants render independent audit reports and provide other services for client firms.
- Government accountants are employed by federal, state, and local government agencies.

3 IDENTIFY ethical dimensions related to the accounting environment (pp. 9–10).
- Certain accounting data may have significant financial implications for individuals.
- Accountants have access to confidential and sensitive information.
- An emphasis on short-term profits may contribute to ethical breakdowns within business firms.

4 DEFINE the accounting equation (pp. 10–11).
- The accounting equation, Assets = Liabilities + Owners' Equity, is the basic framework within which accounting analysis takes place.
- Assets are the economic resources of an entity that can be usefully expressed in money terms.
- Liabilities are the obligations that an entity must pay in money or services in the future because of past transactions or events.
- Owners' equity is the interest of owners in the assets of an entity.

5 INTRODUCE basic principles that underlie financial accounting (pp. 12–13).
- *Accounting entity:* The economic unit for which accounting information is gathered and reported.
- *Cost:* Assets are initially recorded at acquisition price and are not subsequently adjusted upward.
- *Objectivity:* When possible, recording of transactions should be supported by reliable and verifiable evidence.
- *Going concern:* The assumption is made that a business entity will continue indefinitely.
- *Measuring unit:* A monetary unit is used to measure and record an entity's economic activity.

6 EXPLAIN and ILLUSTRATE the effects of transactions on the accounting equation (pp. 13–20).
- Certain transactions may change the character and amount of assets and liabilities, but have no effect on owners' equity.
- Owners' equity is increased by contributions from owners and by revenues. It is decreased by owner withdrawals and expenses.
- Net income (or loss) is the difference between revenues and expenses. The computation of net income using accrual-basis accounting matches expenses incurred with revenues earned.

7 INTRODUCE the basic financial statements (pp. 20–22).
- *Income statement:* Presents revenues and expenses for a period of time.
- *Statement of owners' equity:* Reports events causing a change in owners' equity during a period of time.
- *Balance sheet:* Presents the assets, liabilities, and owners' equity on a given date.
- *Statement of cash flows:* Reports information about cash inflows and outflows during a period of time.

8 EXPLAIN the forms of business organization (pp. 22–24).
- Sole proprietorships, partnerships, and corporations are the major forms of business organization.
- In sole proprietorships and partnerships, the balance sheet reports a single amount of equity for each owner.
- For a corporation, state laws require the owners' investment to be shown separately, as capital stock, and the undistributed net income shown separately as retained earnings.

9 ANALYTICAL APPLICATION: DEFINE the *debt-to-equity ratio* and EXPLAIN its use (p. 24).
- The debt-to-equity ratio is computed as (Total Liabilities)/(Total Owners' Equity). It is an indicator of the extent to which a firm is using debt for financing purposes.

SELF-TEST QUESTIONS FOR REVIEW

(Answers follow the Solution to Demonstration Problem.)

1. To which area of accounting are generally accepted accounting principles primarily relevant?
   a. Managerial accounting
   b. Financial accounting

    c. Tax accounting

    d. Financial reporting to all regulatory agencies

2. Net assets are equal to

    a. Assets minus liabilities

    b. Assets plus liabilities

    c. Assets minus owners' equity

    d. Assets plus owners' equity

3. A sole proprietor decided to use the same bank account for his personal affairs as for his business. Which of the following accounting concepts is violated?

    a. Going concern

    b. Accounting entity

    c. Measuring unit

    d. Objectivity

4. Which of the following transactions does not affect the balance sheet totals?

    a. Purchasing $500 supplies on account.

    b. Paying a $3,000 note payable.

    c. Collecting $4,000 from customers on account.

    d. Withdrawal of $800 by the firm's owner.

5. The beginning and ending balances of owner's equity for the year were $30,000 and $35,000, respectively. If owner's withdrawals exceeded contributions during the year by $3,000, what was the net income or net loss for the year?

    a. $8,000 net loss

    b. $14,000 net income

    c. $2,000 net income

    d. $8,000 net income

DEMONSTRATION PROBLEM FOR REVIEW

Lisa D. Ford operates Ford Aerobics Studio, a sole proprietorship. The firm rents studio space (including a sound system) and specializes in offering aerobics classes to various groups. On January 1, 1993, the assets and liabilities of the business were as follows: Cash, $5,000; Accounts Receivable, $5,200; Notes Payable, $2,500; and Accounts Payable, $1,000. The January business activities were as follows:

  (1) Paid $600 on accounts payable.

  (2) Paid January rent, $3,600.

  (3) Billed clients for January classes, $11,500.

  (4) Received $500 invoice from supplier for T-shirts given to January class members as an advertising promotion.

  (5) Collected $10,000 on account from clients.

  (6) Paid employees' wages, $2,400.

  (7) Received $680 invoice for January utilities.

  (8) Paid $20 to bank as January interest on note payable.

  (9) Ford withdrew $900 cash for personal use.

(10) Paid $4,000 on January 31 to purchase sound system equipment that will replace the rental system.

REQUIRED

a. Set up an accounting equation in columnar form with the following individual assets, liabilities, and owner's equity: Cash, Accounts Receivable, Equipment, Notes Payable, Accounts Payable, and L. D. Ford, Capital. Enter January 1 amounts below each item. (*Note:* Equipment amount is $0.)

b. Show the impact (increase or decrease) of transactions (1)–(10) on the beginning amounts, and total the columns to prove that total assets equal liabilities plus owner's equity at January 31.

c. Prepare an income statement for January.

d. Prepare a statement of owner's equity for January.

e. Prepare a balance sheet at January 31, 1993.

SOLUTION TO DEMONSTRATION PROBLEM

		Cash	+	Accounts Receivable	+	Equipment	=	Notes Payable	+	Accounts Payable	+	L. D. Ford, Capital
a.		$ 5,000	+	$ 5,200	+	$ –0–	=	$2,500	+	$1,000	+	$ 6,700
b.	(1)	−600								−600		
	(2)	−3,600										−3,600
	(3)			+11,500									+11,500
	(4)										+500		−500
	(5)	+10,000		−10,000									
	(6)	−2,400											−2,400
	(7)										+680		−680
	(8)	−20											−20
	(9)	−900											−900
	(10)	−4,000				+4,000							
		$ 3,480	+	$ 6,700	+	$4,000	=	$2,500	+	$1,580	+	$10,100

$14,180 = $14,180

c.

FORD AEROBICS STUDIO
INCOME STATEMENT
FOR THE MONTH OF JANUARY, 1993

Revenue		
Aerobics Fees Earned		$11,500
Expenses		
Rent Expense	$3,600	
Advertising Expense	500	
Wages Expense	2,400	
Utilities Expense	680	
Interest Expense	20	
Total Expenses		7,200
Net Income		$ 4,300

d.

FORD AEROBICS STUDIO
STATEMENT OF OWNER'S EQUITY
FOR THE MONTH OF JANUARY, 1993

L. D. Ford, Capital, January 1, 1993	$ 6,700
Add: Net Income for January	4,300
	$11,000
Less: Capital Withdrawn in January	900
L. D. Ford, Capital, January 31, 1993	$10,100

e.

FORD AEROBICS STUDIO
BALANCE SHEET
JANUARY 31, 1993

Assets		Liabilities	
Cash	$ 3,480	Notes Payable	$ 2,500
Accounts Receivable	6,700	Accounts Payable	1,580
Equipment	4,000	Total Liabilities	$ 4,080
		Owner's Equity	
		L. D. Ford, Capital	10,100
		Total Liabilities and	
Total Assets	$14,180	Owner's Equity	$14,180

GLOSSARY OF KEY TERMS USED IN THIS CHAPTER

accounting   The process of recording, classifying, reporting, and interpreting the financial data of an organization. The purpose is to provide financial information that is useful in making economic decisions (p. 4).

accounting entity   The unit of focus for the accumulation and reporting of accounting data (p. 12).

accounting equation   An expression of the equivalency of the economic resources and the claims upon those resources of a specific entity; often stated as Assets = Liabilities + Owners' Equity (p. 10).

accrual-basis accounting   Accounting procedures whereby revenues are recorded when they are earned and expenses are recorded in the period in which they help to generate revenues (p. 15).

assets   The economic resources of an entity that can be usefully expressed in money terms (p. 11).

balance sheet   A financial statement showing an entity's assets, liabilities, and owner's equity at a specific date; sometimes called a *statement of financial position* (p. 22).

cash-basis accounting   Accounting procedures whereby revenues are recorded when cash is received from operating activities and expenses are recorded when cash payments related to operating activities are made (p. 15).

controller   Usually the highest ranking accounting officer in a firm (p. 8).

corporation   A legal entity created under the laws of a state or the federal government. Owners of a corporation receive shares of stock as evidence of their ownership (p. 22).

cost principle   An accounting guideline stating that assets are initially recorded at the amounts paid to acquire the assets (p. 12).

debt-to-equity ratio   A ratio measuring the relationship between a firm's liabilities and its owners' equity; computed as (Total Liabilities)/(Total Owners' Equity) (p. 24).

ethics   An area of inquiry dealing with the values, rules, and justifications that govern one's way of life (p. 9).

expenses   Decreases in owners' equity incurred by a firm in the process of earning revenues (p. 15).

financial accounting   The area of accounting activities dealing with the preparation of publishable, general-purpose financial statements (p. 6).

generally accepted accounting principles (GAAP)   A group of standards or guides that are used in preparing financial accounting reports (p. 7).

going concern concept   An accounting guideline that assumes, in the absence of evidence to the contrary, that a business entity will continue to operate indefinitely and will not be sold or liquidated (p. 12).

income statement   A financial statement reporting an entity's revenues and expenses for a period of time (p. 20).

internal auditing   An appraisal activity of a firm's operations conducted by a firm's own internal audit staff to determine whether management's financial and operating policies are being properly implemented (p. 8).

liabilities   The obligations, or debts, that an entity must pay in money or services at some time in the future because of past transactions or events (p. 11).

managerial accounting   The accounting activities carried out by a firm's accounting staff primarily to furnish management with accounting data needed for decisions related to the firm's operations (p. 5).

matching concept   An accounting guideline stating that net income is determined by linking, or matching, expenses incurred with related revenues earned (p. 15).

measuring unit concept   An accounting guideline specifying that a monetary unit (the dollar in the United States) is to be used to measure and record an entity's economic activity (p. 13).

net assets   The difference between an entity's assets and liabilities. Net assets are equal to owners' equity (p. 11).

net income   The excess of a firm's revenues over its expenses (p. 14).

objectivity principle   An accounting guideline stating that the recording of transactions should be based on reliable and verifiable evidence (p. 12).

owners' equity   The interest of owners in the assets of an entity; equal to the difference between the entity's assets and liabilities (p. 11).

partnership   A voluntary association of two or more persons for the purpose of conducting a business (p. 22).

revenues   Increases in owners' equity a firm earns by providing goods or services for its customers (p. 14).

sole proprietorship   A form of business organization in which one person owns the business (p. 22).

statement of cash flows   A financial statement showing a firm's cash inflows and outflows for a specific period, classified into operating, investing, and financing categories (p. 22).

statement of financial position   A financial statement showing a firm's assets, liabilities, and owners' equity at a specific date; also called a *balance sheet* (p. 22).

statement of owners' equity   A financial statement presenting information on the events causing a change in owners' equity during a period. The statement presents the beginning balance, additions to, deductions from, and the ending balance of owners' equity for the period (p. 22).

QUESTIONS

1-1   Define *accounting*. What is the basic purpose of accounting?

1-2   Distinguish between *financial* and *managerial* accounting.

1-3   Name some outside groups that may be interested in a company's financial data and state their particular interests.

1-4   What are *generally accepted accounting principles* and by whom are they established?

1-5   Why do business firms frequently keep more than one set of records on certain aspects of their financial activities?

1-6   How do the functions of private accountants and public accountants differ?

1-7   Identify three aspects of the accounting environment that may create ethical pressure on accountants.

1-8   State the accounting equation and define *assets*, *liabilities*, and *owners' equity*.

1-9   What is meant by the *accounting entity*?

1-10   Baylor Company pays $6,000 for a new computer and records the asset at this amount. What basic principle governs this recording?

1-11   What is meant by the *objectivity principle?* the *going concern concept?*

1-12   What are two limitations of using the U.S. dollar as the unit of measure in accounting?

1-13   Describe a transaction that would
   a. Increase one asset but not change the amount of total assets.
   b. Decrease an asset and a liability.
   c. Decrease an asset and owners' equity.
   d. Increase an asset and a liability.

1-14   Indicate whether each of the following would increase, decrease, or have no effect on owners' equity:
   a. Purchased supplies for cash.
   b. Withdrew supplies for personal use.
   c. Paid salaries.
   d. Purchased equipment for cash.
   e. Invested cash in business.
   f. Rendered service to customers, on account.
   g. Rendered service to customers, for cash.

1-15   Define *revenues* and *expenses*.

1-16   How do the accrual basis and the cash basis of accounting differ? To which of these accounting approaches does the matching concept relate?

1-17 What is the purpose of an income statement? a statement of owners' equity? a balance sheet? a statement of cash flows?

1-18 The owner's capital on a particular balance sheet is $60,000. Without seeing the rest of this financial statement, can you say that the owner should be able to withdraw $60,000 cash from the business? Justify your answer.

1-19 Explain how the presentation of owners' equity in the balance sheet of a corporation differs from that of a sole proprietorship.

1-20 On December 31, 1993, Miller Company had $600,000 in total assets and owed $210,000 to creditors. If this corporation's capital stock amounted to $300,000, what amount of retained earnings should appear on a December 31, 1993, balance sheet?

1-21 At year-end, Layden Company had total liabilities of $300,000 and a debt-to-equity ratio of 0.75. What is Layden Company's total owner's equity at year-end?

EXERCISES

ETHICS
— OBJ. 3 —

1-22 In each of the following cases, (a) identify the aspect of the accounting environment primarily responsible for the ethical pressure on the accountant and (b) indicate the appropriate response for the accountant.

1. James Jehring, tax accountant, is preparing an income tax return for a client. The client wants Jehring to take a sizable deduction on the return for business-related travel, even though the client states that he has no documentation to support the deduction. "I don't think the IRS will audit my return," declares the client.

2. Willa English, accountant for Dome Construction Company, has just finished putting the numbers together for a construction project on which the firm is going to submit a bid next month. At a social gathering that evening, a friend casually asks English what Dome's bid is going to be. English knows the friend's brother works for a competitor.

3. The manager of Cross Department Store is ending his first year with the firm. December's business was slower than expected, and the firm's annual results are trailing last year's results. The manager instructs Kyle Tarpley, store accountant, to include revenues from the first week of January in the December data. "This way, we'll show an increase over last year," declares the manager.

ACCOUNTING EQUATION
— OBJ. 4 —

1-23 Determine the missing amount in each of the following cases.

	Assets	Liabilities	Owners' Equity
a.	$100,000	$35,000	?
b.	?	$12,000	$26,000
c.	$68,000	?	$44,000

TRANSACTION ANALYSIS
— OBJ. 6 —

1-24 Following the example shown in (a) below, indicate the effects of the listed transactions on the assets, liabilities, and owner's equity of Joyce Martin, certified public accountant, a sole proprietorship.

(a) Purchased, for cash, a typewriter for use in office.
   ANSWER: Increase assets (Office Equipment)
            Decrease assets (Cash)

(b) Rendered accounting services and billed client.

(c) Paid rent for month.

(d) Rendered tax services to client for cash.

(e) Received amount due from client in (b).

(f) Purchased an office desk on account.

(g) Paid employees' salaries for month.

(h) Paid for desk purchased in (f).

(i) Withdrew cash for personal use.

TRANSACTION ANALYSIS
— OBJ. 6 —

1-25 The accounting equation of Liang Chen, attorney, at the beginning of an accounting period is given below, followed by seven transactions whose effects on the equation are shown. Describe each transaction that occurred. Of the transactions affecting L. Chen, Capital, transaction (e) had no effect on net income for the period.

	Cash	+	Accounts Receivable	+	Supplies	=	Notes Payable	+	Accounts Payable	+	L. Chen, Capital
Balance	$3,300	+	$9,800	+	$900	=	$2,000	+	$500	+	$11,500
(a)	+5,500		−5,500								
(b)					+800				+800		
(c)			+8,000								+8,000
(d)	−900								−900		
(e)	−4,600										−4,600
(f)	−100				+100						
(g)	+1,000						+1,000				

BALANCE SHEET AND NET INCOME DETERMINATION — OBJ. 6, 7 —

1-26 At the beginning of 1993, Flynn's Parking Lots had the following balance sheet:

Assets		Liabilities	
Cash	$ 3,200	Accounts Payable	$ 8,000
Accounts Receivable	9,800		
Land	40,000	**Owner's Equity**	
		A. Flynn, Capital	45,000
		Total Liabilities and	
Total Assets	$53,000	Owner's Equity	$53,000

a. At the end of 1993, Flynn had the following assets and liabilities: Cash, $5,900; Accounts Receivable, $11,600; Land, $40,000; and Accounts Payable, $5,000. Prepare a year-end balance sheet for Flynn's Parking Lots.

b. Assuming that Flynn did not invest any money in the business during the year, but withdrew $8,000 for personal use, what was the net income or net loss for 1993?

c. Assuming that Flynn invested an additional $9,000 early in the year, but withdrew $14,000 before the end of the year, what was the net income or net loss for 1993?

DETERMINATION OF RETAINED EARNINGS AND NET INCOME — OBJ. 6, 8 —

1-27 The following information appears in the records of Bock Corporation at the end of 1993:

Accounts Receivable	$ 21,000	Retained Earnings	$?
Accounts Payable	14,000	Supplies	7,000
Cash	5,000	Equipment	128,000
Capital Stock	100,000		

a. Calculate the amount of retained earnings at the end of 1993.

b. If the amount of the retained earnings at the beginning of 1993 was $26,000, and $9,000 in dividends were declared and paid during 1993, what was the net income for 1993?

FINANCIAL STATEMENTS — OBJ. 7 —

1-28 Heather Meier operates The Print Shop as a sole proprietorship. For each of the following financial items related to her business, indicate the financial statement (or statements) in which the item would be reported.

a. Cash (at year-end).

b. Advertising expense.

c. H. Meier, capital (at year-end).

d. Printing fees, earned.

e. Cash withdrawn by H. Meier for personal use.

f. Accounts payable.

g. Cash paid to purchase equipment.

h. Equipment.

PROBLEMS

TRANSACTION ANALYSIS — OBJ. 6 —

1-29 An analysis of the transactions of Hewit Detective Agency for the month of May appears below. Line 1 summarizes Hewit's accounting equation data on May 1; lines 2–10 represent the transactions for May.

	Cash	+	Accounts Receivable	+	Supplies	+	Equipment	=	Notes Payable	+	Accounts Payable	+	P. Hewit, Capital
(1)	$3,400	+	$8,600	+	$840	+	$5,000	=	$4,000	+	$340	+	$13,500
(2)	+1,000								+1,000				
(3)	+6,300		−6,300										
(4)					+780						+780		
(5)			+9,800										+9,800
(6)	−300										−300		
(7)	+2,000												+2,000
(8)	−500												−500
(9)	−600						+600						
(10)	−1,500								−1,500				

REQUIRED

a. Prove that assets equal liabilities plus owner's equity at May 1.

b. Describe the apparent transaction indicated by each line. (For example, line 2: Borrowed $1,000, giving a note payable.) If any line could reasonably represent more than one type of transaction, describe each type of transaction.

c. Prove that assets equal liabilities plus owner's equity at May 31.

TRANSACTION ANALYSIS, INCOME STATEMENT, OWNER'S EQUITY STATEMENT, AND BALANCE SHEET
— Obj. 6, 7 —

1-30   Grant Appraisal Service is a sole proprietorship providing commercial and industrial appraisals and feasibility studies. On January 1, 1993, assets and liabilities of the business were the following: Cash, $6,600; Accounts Receivable, $14,500; Notes Payable, $1,500; and Accounts Payable, $800. The following transactions occurred during January:

(1) Paid rent for January, $900.   *RENT EXPENSE*

(2) Received $8,300 on customers' accounts.

(3) Paid $700 on accounts payable.

(4) Received $1,400 for services performed for cash customers.

(5) Borrowed $4,500 from bank and signed note payable for that amount.

(6) Billed the city for a feasibility study performed, $5,200, and various other credit customers, $2,800.

(7) Paid salary of assistant, $3,000.

(8) Received invoice for January utilities, $360.

(9) Lindsey Grant withdrew $4,000 cash for personal use.

(10) Purchased van (on January 31) for business use, $9,500.

(11) Paid $40 to bank as January interest on notes payable.

REQUIRED

a. Set up an accounting equation in columnar form with the following individual assets, liabilities, and owner's equity: Cash, Accounts Receivable, Van, Notes Payable, Accounts Payable, and L. Grant, Capital. Enter January 1 amounts below each item. (*Note:* Van amount is $0.)

b. Show the impact (increase or decrease) of transactions 1–11 on the beginning amounts, and total the columns to prove that assets equal liabilities plus owner's equity at January 31, 1993.

c. Prepare an income statement for the month of January 1993.

d. Prepare a statement of owner's equity for the month of January 1993.

e. Prepare a balance sheet at January 31, 1993.

TRANSACTION ANALYSIS AND INCOME STATEMENT FOR A CORPORATION
— Obj. 6, 7, 8 —

1-31   On June 1, 1993, a group of bush pilots in Thunder Bay, Ontario, formed the Outpost Fly-In Service, Inc., by selling $60,000 capital stock for cash. The group then leased several amphibious aircraft and docking facilities, equipping them to transport campers and hunters to outpost camps owned by various resorts. The following transactions occurred during June 1993:

(1) Sold capital stock for cash, $60,000.

(2) Paid June rent for aircraft, dockage, and dockside office, $4,500.   *EXP*

(3) Received invoice for the cost of a dinner and reception the firm gave to entertain resort owners, $1,000.   *CHARGE*   *exp*

(4) Paid for June advertising in various sport magazines, $600.   *EXP*

(5) Paid insurance premium for January, $1,600.   *EXP*

(6) Rendered fly-in services for various groups for cash, $19,500.   *REV*

*R*cv

(7) Billed the Ministry of Natural Resources for transporting mapping personnel, $3,200, and also billed various firms for fly-in services, $11,000.

(8) Paid $800 on accounts payable.

(9) Received $10,300 on account from clients. *Acc. Rec.*

Exd **(10)** Paid June wages, $12,000.

Exp **(11)** Received invoice for the cost of fuel used during June, $2,400.

(12) Declared and paid a cash dividend, $2,000.

REQUIRED

a. Set up an accounting equation in columnar form with the following column headings: Cash, Accounts Receivable, Accounts Payable, Capital Stock, and Retained Earnings.

b. Show how the June transactions affect the items in the accounting equation, and total all columns to prove that assets equal liabilities plus stockholders' equity at June 30. (*Note:* Revenues, expenses, and dividends affect Retained Earnings.)

c. Prepare an income statement for June.

INCOME STATEMENT, OWNER'S EQUITY STATEMENT, AND BALANCE SHEET — OBJ. 7 —

1-32 On March 1, 1993, Amy Dart began Dart Delivery Service, which provides delivery of bulk mailings to the post office, neighborhood delivery of weekly papers, data delivery to computer service centers, and various other delivery services via leased vans. On February 28, Dart invested $15,000 of her own funds in the firm and borrowed $5,000 from her father on a six-month, noninterest-bearing note payable. The following information is available at March 31 (*Note:* Owner's capital reflects March 1, 1993, amount):

Accounts Receivable	$9,400	Delivery Fees Earned	$18,400
Rent Expense	1,200	Cash	13,900
Advertising Expense	500	Supplies	2,500
Supplies Expense	1,700	Notes Payable	5,000
Accounts Payable	1,400	Insurance Expense	300
Salaries Expense	6,100	A. Dart, Capital (March 1)	15,000
Miscellaneous Expense	200		

Dart made a $2,000 additional investment during March, but withdrew $6,000 during the month.

REQUIRED

a. Prepare an income statement for the month of March 1993.

b. Prepare a statement of owner's equity for the month of March 1993.

c. Prepare a balance sheet at March 31, 1993.

BALANCE SHEETS AND INCOME DETERMINATION — OBJ. 6, 7 —

1-33 Balance sheet information for Jordan Packaging Service at the end of 1992 and 1993 is as follows:

	December 31, 1993	December 31, 1992
Accounts Receivable	$20,500	$16,000
Accounts Payable	1,300	1,600
Cash	12,000	9,000
Equipment	28,000	21,000
Supplies	3,800	3,400
Notes Payable	20,000	20,000
N. Jordan, Capital	?	?

REQUIRED

a. Prepare balance sheets for December 31 of each year.

b. Noel Jordan contributed $6,000 to the business early in 1993 but withdrew $15,000 in December 1993. Calculate the net income for 1993.

BALANCE SHEETS FOR A CORPORATION — OBJ. 6, 7, 8 —

1-34 The following balance sheet data are given for Normandy Catering Service, a corporation, at May 31, 1993:

Accounts Receivable	$16,300	Accounts Payable	$ 3,300
Notes Payable	10,000	Cash	11,200
Equipment	48,000	Capital Stock	40,000
Supplies	10,400	Retained Earnings	?

Assume that on June 1, 1993, only the following transactions occurred:

June 1   Purchased additional equipment costing $10,000, giving $2,000 cash and an $8,000 note payable.
    1   Declared and paid a cash dividend of $5,000.

REQUIRED

a. Prepare a balance sheet at May 31, 1993.
b. Prepare a balance sheet at June 1, 1993.

ALTERNATE EXERCISES

ETHICS
— OBJ. 3 —

1-22A In each of the following cases, (a) identify the aspect of the accounting environment primarily responsible for the ethical pressure on the accountant and (b) indicate the appropriate response for the accountant.

1. Patricia Kelly, accountant for Wooden Company, is reviewing the costs charged to a government contract that Wooden worked on this year. Wooden is manufacturing special parts for the government and is allowed to charge the government for the actual manufacturing costs plus a fixed fee. Kelly notes that $60,000 worth of art objects purchased for the president's office is buried among the miscellaneous costs charged to the contract. Upon inquiry, the firm's vice president replies, "This sort of thing is done all the time."

2. Barry Marklin, accountant for Smith & Wesson partnership, is working on the 1993 year-end financial data. The partnership agreement calls for Smith and Wesson to share the firm's 1993 net income equally. In 1994, the partners will share the net income 60% to Smith and 40% to Wesson (Wesson plans to cut back his involvement in the firm). Smith wants Marklin to delay recording revenue from work done at the end of 1993 until January 1994. "We haven't received the cash yet from these services," declares Smith.

3. The St. Louis Wheelers, a new professional football franchise, has just signed its first-round draft pick to a multiyear contract that is reported in the newspapers as a four-year, $18 million contract. Johanna Factor, Wheelers' accountant, receives a call from the agent of another team's first-round pick. "Just calling to confirm the terms reported in the papers," states the agent, "My client should receive a similar contract, and I'm sure you don't want him to get shortchanged."

ACCOUNTING EQUATION
— OBJ. 4, 8 —

1-23A Determine the following:
a. The owner's equity of a sole proprietorship that has assets of $225,000 and liabilities of $163,000.
b. The equity of partner Fisk in the Fisk & Blake partnership that has assets of $412,000, liabilities of $150,000, and Y. Blake, Capital of $110,000.
c. The assets of a corporation that has liabilities of $300,000, capital stock of $200,000, and retained earnings of $40,000.

TRANSACTION ANALYSIS
— OBJ. 6 —

1-24A Following the example shown in (a) below, indicate the effects of the listed transactions on the assets, liabilities, and owner's equity of Martin Andrews, attorney, a sole proprietorship.
(a) Rendered legal services to clients for cash.
    ANSWER: Increase assets (Cash)
                    Increase owner's equity (M. Andrews, Capital)
(b) Purchased office supplies on account.
(c) Andrews invested cash into the firm.
(d) Paid amount due on account for office supplies purchased in (b).
(e) Borrowed cash (and signed a six-month note) from bank.
(f) Rendered legal services and billed clients.
(g) Purchased, for cash, a desk lamp for the office.
(h) Paid interest on note payable to bank.
(i) Received invoice for month's utilities.

**TRANSACTION ANALYSIS
— OBJ. 6 —**

1-25A On October 1, Alice Bloom started a consulting firm. The asset, liability, and owner's equity amounts after each of her first six transactions are shown below. Describe each of these six transactions.

Amounts after Transaction:	Cash	+	Accounts Receivable	+	Supplies	+	Equipment	=	Notes Payable	+	A. Bloom, Capital
(a)	$5,000	+	$ –0–	+	$ –0–	+	$ –0–	=	$ –0–	+	$5,000
(b)	4,000	+	–0–	+	1,000	+	–0–	=	–0–	+	5,000
(c)	8,000	+	–0–	+	1,000	+	–0–	=	4,000	+	5,000
(d)	5,000	+	–0–	+	1,000	+	3,000	=	4,000	+	5,000
(e)	5,000	+	1,500	+	1,000	+	3,000	=	4,000	+	6,500
(f)	6,000	+	500	+	1,000	+	3,000	=	4,000	+	6,500

**DETERMINATION OF NET INCOME AND ENDING CAPITAL
— OBJ. 6, 7 —**

1-26A The following income statement and balance sheet information is available for Lloyd Appraisers at the end of the current month:

Supplies	$ 4,500	Accounts Payable	$ 8,000
Accounts Receivable	19,000	Salaries Expense	12,000
Utilities Expense	800	Appraisal Fees Earned	28,000
Supplies Expense	1,100	C. Lloyd, Capital (at	
Rent Expense	2,000	beginning of month)	15,000
Cash	5,600		

a. Calculate the net income or net loss for the month.
b. If C. Lloyd made no additional investment during the month, but withdrew $6,000, what is the amount of his capital at the end of the month?

**DETERMINATION OF OMITTED FINANCIAL STATEMENT DATA
— OBJ. 6, 7 —**

1-27A For the four unrelated situations A–D below, compute the unknown amounts indicated by the letters appearing in each column.

	A	B	C	D
Beginning				
Assets	$18,000	$10,000	$28,000	$ (d)
Liabilities	8,600	4,000	16,000	9,000
Ending				
Assets	20,000	25,000	38,000	40,000
Liabilities	9,300	(b)	18,000	15,000
During Year				
Capital Contributed	2,000	2,500	(c)	2,500
Revenues	(a)	18,000	13,000	24,000
Capital Withdrawn	6,000	500	1,000	8,500
Expenses	7,500	11,000	10,000	15,000

**FINANCIAL STATEMENTS
— OBJ. 7 —**

1-28A Karl Flury operates a golf driving range as a sole proprietorship. For each of the following financial items related to his business, indicate the financial statement (or statements) in which the item would be reported.
a. Accounts receivable.
b. Cash received from sale of land.
c. Net income.
d. Cash invested in business by Flury.
e. Notes payable.
f. Supplies expense.
g. Land.
h. Supplies.

ALTERNATE PROBLEMS

**TRANSACTION ANALYSIS
— OBJ. 6 —**

1-29A Appearing below is an analysis of the June transactions for Gary Rhode, consulting engineer. Line 1 summarizes Rhode's accounting equation data on June 1; lines 2–10 are the transactions for June.

	Cash	+	Accounts Receivable	+	Supplies	+	Equipment	=	Notes Payable	+	Accounts Payable	+	G. Rhode, Capital
(1)	$4,500	+	$6,200	+	$920	+	$8,000	=	$2,000	+	$500	+	$17,120
(2)					+570						+570		
(3)							+3,000		+3,000				
(4)	+5,700		−5,700										
(5)			+7,300										+7,300
(6)	−500										−500		
(7)	−100				+100								
(8)	−3,600												−3,600
(9)	+1,000								+1,000				
(10)							+900						+900

REQUIRED

a. Prove that assets equal liabilities plus owner's equity at June 1.

b. Describe the apparent transaction indicated by each line. For example, line 2: Purchased supplies on account, $570. If any line could reasonably represent more than one type of transaction, describe each type of transaction.

c. Prove that assets equal liabilities plus owner's equity on June 30.

TRANSACTION ANALYSIS, INCOME STATEMENT, OWNER'S EQUITY STATEMENT, AND BALANCE SHEET
— OBJ. 6, 7 —

1-30A Grace Main began the Main Answering Service, a sole proprietorship, during December 1992. The firm provides services for professional people and is currently operating with leased equipment. On January 1, 1993, the assets and liabilities of the business were: Cash, $3,400; Accounts Receivable, $6,500; Notes Payable, $1,000; and Accounts Payable, $500. The following transactions occurred during January.

(1) Paid rent on office and equipment for January, $750.
(2) Collected $4,200 on account from clients.
(3) Borrowed $1,500 from bank and signed note payable for that amount.
(4) Billed clients for work performed on account, $8,800.
(5) Paid $400 on accounts payable.
(6) Received invoice for January advertising, $350.
(7) Paid January salaries, $3,500.
(8) Paid January utilities, $280.
(9) Main withdrew $1,600 cash for personal use.
(10) Purchased fax machine (on January 31) for business use, $1,100.
(11) Paid $20 to bank as January interest on notes payable.

REQUIRED

a. Set up an accounting equation in columnar form with the following individual assets, liabilities, and owner's equity: Cash, Accounts Receivable, Equipment, Notes Payable, Accounts Payable, and G. Main, Capital. Enter January 1 amounts below each item. (*Note:* Equipment amount is $0.)

b. Show the impact (increase or decrease) of the January transactions on the beginning amounts, and total all columns to prove that assets equal liabilities plus owner's equity at January 31.

c. Prepare an income statement for the month of January 1993.

d. Prepare a statement of owner's equity for the month of January 1993.

e. Prepare a balance sheet at January 31, 1993.

TRANSACTION ANALYSIS AND INCOME STATEMENT
— OBJ. 6, 7 —

1-31A On December 1, 1993, Peter Allen started Career Services, a sole proprietorship furnishing career and vocational counseling services. The following transactions took place during December:

(1) Allen invested $5,000 in the business.
(2) Paid rent for December on furnished office space, $600.
(3) Received invoice for December advertising, $450.
(4) Borrowed $20,000 from bank and signed note payable for that amount.
(5) Received $950 for counseling services rendered for cash.
(6) Billed certain governmental agencies and other clients for counseling services, $5,800.
(7) Paid secretary's salary, $1,900.
(8) Paid December utilities, $240.
(9) Allen withdrew $800 cash for personal use.
(10) Purchased land for cash to use as a site for own facility, $18,000.
(11) Paid $150 to bank as December interest on note payable.

REQUIRED

a. Set up an accounting equation in columnar form with the following column headings: Cash, Accounts Receivable, Land, Notes Payable, Accounts Payable, and P. Allen, Capital.

b. Show how the December transactions affect the items in the accounting equation, and total all columns to prove that assets equal liabilities plus owner's equity at December 31.

c. Prepare an income statement for the month of December 1993.

INCOME STATEMENT, OWNER'S EQUITY STATEMENT, AND BALANCE SHEET — OBJ. 7 —

1-32A After all transactions have been reflected for 1993, the records of R. Levy, interior decorator, show the following information (*Note:* Owner's capital reflects January 1, 1993, amount):

Notes Payable	$ 3,000	Supplies	$ 8,100
Decorating Fees Earned	55,600	Cash	4,900
Supplies Expense	6,600	Accounts Receivable	9,500
Insurance Expense	800	Advertising Expense	1,200
Miscellaneous Expense	100	Salaries Expense	27,000
R. Levy, Capital		Rent Expense	6,900
(January 1)	11,900	Accounts Payable	1,600

Levy made an additional investment of $2,000 in the business during the year and withdrew $9,000 near the end of the year.

REQUIRED

a. Prepare an income statement for 1993.

b. Prepare a statement of owner's equity for 1993.

c. Prepare a balance sheet at December 31, 1993.

BALANCE SHEETS AND INCOME DETERMINATION FOR A CORPORATION — OBJ. 6, 7, 8 —

1-33A Following is balance sheet information for Lynch Janitorial Service, Inc., at the end of 1992 and 1993:

	December 31, 1993	December 31, 1992
Accounts Payable	$ 5,000	$ 7,000
Cash	13,000	10,000
Accounts Receivable	21,000	16,000
Land	20,000	20,000
Building	150,000	160,000
Equipment	36,000	38,000
Mortgage Payable	70,000	75,000
Supplies	19,000	13,000
Capital Stock	120,000	120,000
Retained Earnings	?	?

REQUIRED

a. Prepare balance sheets at December 31 of each year.

b. The firm declared and paid a dividend of $9,000 in December 1993. Calculate the net income for 1993. (*Hint:* The net increase in retained earnings is equal to the net income less the dividend.)

BALANCE SHEETS FOR A CORPORATION — OBJ. 6, 7, 8 —

1-34A The following balance sheet data are given for Bettis Plumbing Contractors, Inc., at June 30, 1993.

Accounts Payable	$ 8,700	Capital Stock	$105,000
Cash	18,600	Retained Earnings	?
Supplies	26,200	Notes Payable	20,000
Equipment	95,000	Accounts Receivable	9,100
Land	30,000		

Assume that, during the next two days, only the following transactions occurred:

July 1 Paid noninterest-bearing note due today, $5,000.

   2 Purchased equipment for $10,000, paying $1,000 cash and giving a note payable for the balance.

   2 Declared and paid a cash dividend, $9,000.

REQUIRED

a. Prepare a balance sheet at June 30, 1993.
b. Prepare a balance sheet at July 2, 1993.

CASES

Business Decision Case

Paul Seale, a friend of yours, is negotiating the purchase of an extermination firm called Total Pest Control. Seale has been employed by a national pest control service and knows the technical side of the business. However, he knows little about accounting, so he asks for your assistance. The sole owner of the firm, Greg Krey, has provided Seale with income statements for the past three years, which show an average net income of $56,000 per year. The latest balance sheet shows total assets of $185,000 and liabilities of $25,000. Included among the assets is land listed at $15,000. Seale brings the following matters to your attention:

1. Krey is asking $200,000 for the firm. He has told Seale that, because the firm has been earning 35% on the owner's investment, the price should be higher than the net assets on the balance sheet.

2. Seale has noticed no salary for Krey on the income statements, even though he worked half-time in the business. Krey explained that because he had other income, he withdrew only $15,000 each year from the firm for personal use. If he purchases the firm, Seale will hire a full-time manager for the firm at an annual salary of $30,000.

3. Seale wonders whether the land is really worth $15,000, the amount shown on the balance sheet.

4. Krey's tax returns for the past three years report a lower net income for the firm than the amounts shown in the financial statements. Seale is skeptical about the accounting principles used in preparing the financial statements.

REQUIRED

a. How did Krey arrive at the 35% return figure given in point 1? If Seale accepts Krey's average annual income figure of $56,000, what would Seale's percentage return be, assuming that the net income remained at the same level and that the firm was purchased for $200,000?

b. Should Krey's withdrawals affect the net income reported in the financial statements? What will Seale's percentage return be if he takes into consideration the $30,000 salary he plans to pay a full-time manager?

c. What explanation would you give Seale with respect to the value of the land?

d. Could there be legitimate reasons for the difference between net income shown in the financial statements and net income reported on the tax returns, as mentioned in point 4? How might Seale obtain additional assurance about the propriety of the financial statements?

Analytical Application Case

FANSTEEL INC., with headquarters in North Chicago, Illinois, is a specialty metals manufacturer that fabricates precision metal products. The firm's assets, liabilities, and stockholders' equity (to the nearest thousand dollars) for three recent consecutive years are given below (Year 3 is the most recent year).

	Year 3	Year 2	Year 1
Assets	$94,520,000	$107,965,000	$143,500,000
Liabilities	25,180,000	39,059,000	75,061,000
Stockholders' Equity	69,340,000	68,906,000	68,439,000

REQUIRED

a. Compute the debt-to-equity ratio for each of the three years.

b. Assume you are a potential creditor of Fansteel. Does the information revealed by the debt-to-equity ratio over the three years influence your credit decision positively or negatively? Comment.

Ethics Case

Jack Hardy, CPA, has a brother, Ted, in the retail clothing business. Ted ran the business as a sole proprietor for ten years. During this ten-year period, Jack helped Ted with various accounting matters. For example, Jack designed the accounting system for the company, prepared Ted's personal income tax returns (which included financial data about the clothing business), and recommended various cost control procedures. Ted paid Jack for all these services. A year ago, Ted expanded the business and incorporated. Ted is president of the corporation and also chairs the corporation's board of directors. The board of directors has overall responsibility for corporate affairs. When the corporation was formed, Ted asked Jack to serve on its board of directors. Jack accepted. In addition, Jack now prepares the corporation's income tax returns and continues to advise his brother on accounting matters.

Recently, the corporation applied for a large bank loan. The bank wants audited financial statements for the corporation before it will decide on the loan request. Ted asked Jack to perform the audit. Jack replied that he cannot do the audit because the code of ethics for CPAs requires that he be independent when providing audit services.

REQUIRED

Why is it important that a CPA be independent when providing audit services? Which of Jack's activities or relationships impair his independence?

What is an account?

An account is a record of changes maintained for each asset, liability, and owners' equity component. ▪ A corporation like SkyWest, Inc., engages in a variety of activities related to air transportation. ▪ SkyWest must maintain a sufficient number of accounts to provide the financial detail that management needs to operate and that outside parties need to evaluate the firm's financial status.

2

THE DOUBLE-ENTRY ACCOUNTING SYSTEM

CHAPTER OBJECTIVES

1 **EXPLAIN** the nature and format of an account (pp. 42–45).

2 **DEFINE** permanent and temporary accounts (p. 45).

3 **DESCRIBE** the system of debits and credits (pp. 45–47).

4 **ILLUSTRATE** debit and credit analysis of transactions (pp. 47–52).

5 **EXPLAIN** the nature and format of a general ledger and trial balance (pp. 52–53).

6 **DISCUSS** common types of errors in transaction analysis (pp. 52–54).

7 **DESCRIBE** and **ILLUSTRATE** the relationships among financial statements (pp. 54, 55).

8 **ANALYTICAL APPLICATION: DEFINE** the *operating cash flow to total liabilities ratio* and **EXPLAIN** its use (pp. 54, 56).

What advantages does the Merchant derive by Bookkeeping by double-entry? It is amongst the finest inventions of the human mind.

JOHANN WOLFGANG

VON GOETHE

nalyzing and recording transactions in columnar fashion within the accounting equation framework is useful in conveying a basic understanding of how transactions affect a firm's financial data. It is not a feasible approach, however, once the total number of individual assets, liabilities, and owners' equity becomes large. Therefore, an efficient, formal system of classification and recording is required so that financial data may be gathered for day-to-day management requirements and timely accounting reports. In this chapter, we will examine the classification and recording system commonly called *double-entry* accounting.

THE ACCOUNT

OBJECTIVE ❶ EXPLAIN *the nature and format of an account.*

The basic component of the formal accounting system is the **account,** which is an individual record of increases and decreases in specific assets, liabilities, and owners' equity. An account is created for each individual asset, liability, and owners' equity.

Most transactions of business firms involve the earning of revenues or the incurrence of expenses. The income statement reports information about revenues and expenses for a specific time period. Because of the importance of revenues and expenses, individual accounts are created for each type of revenue and expense. As discussed earlier, revenues increase owners' equity and expenses decrease owners' equity. Revenue and expense accounts, therefore, are considered temporary subdivisions within the owners' equity category.

In sole proprietorships and partnerships, each owner's equity is reflected in an owner's capital account. Investments by an owner increase the owner's capital and will be immediately shown in the owner's capital account. Withdrawals by an owner decrease the owner's equity. Generally, owner withdrawals occur often enough that a separate account, called a **drawing account,** is created for each owner to accumulate information about withdrawals for a period of time. Drawing accounts are considered temporary subdivisions within owners' equity. Information about withdrawals appears in the statement of owners' equity.

The stockholders' equity of a corporation is represented by its capital stock and retained earnings. A corporation will open an account for each type of capital stock and for retained earnings. Corporation revenue and expense accounts are considered temporary subdivisions of the corporation's retained earnings. Cash dividends declared and paid to stockholders decrease retained earnings and cash. When dividends are declared and paid several times a year (each quarter, for example), a *Cash Dividends* account is used to accumulate information about dividends for the year. The Cash Dividends account is a temporary subdivision of retained earnings. The Cash Dividends account serves the same role in corporation accounting as that provided by drawing accounts in sole proprietorships and partnerships.

Exhibit 2-1 shows the form of a *two-column* account, a form often used in a manual record-keeping system. The form is called a two-column account because it has two money columns. Another popular form, called a *running balance* (or *three-column*) account, is illustrated later in this chapter.

Most account forms facilitate recording the following information:

1. The account title and number.
2. Amounts reflecting increases and decreases.

EXHIBIT 2—1	FORM FOR TWO-COLUMN ACCOUNT

(ACCOUNT TITLE)   ACCOUNT NO. _____

Date	Description	Post. Ref.	Amount	Date	Description	Post. Ref.	Amount

3. Cross-references to other accounting records.

4. Dates and descriptive notations.

Each account has a short account title that describes the item whose data are being recorded in that account. Some common account titles are Cash, Accounts Receivable, Notes Payable, Professional Fees Earned, and Rent Expense. Increases and decreases are recorded in the appropriate money columns. These amounts are referred to as *entries*. In other words, making an entry in an account consists of recording an amount in a particular place to represent either an increase or a decrease in the account. Accounts also contain space for presentation of other types of information—for example, the date of any entry, a description section to record any memoranda explaining a particular entry, and a posting reference column (indicated by Post. Ref.). The posting reference column is used for noting the records from which entries into this account have been taken. This practice will be explained more fully in the next chapter.

A two-column Cash account for Westgate Driving School is presented in Exhibit 2-2. In our example, there is no beginning amount (balance) because June was the first month of business. Increases in cash from the June transactions have been placed on the left side of the Cash account and the decreases on the right side. Periodically, the balance of the account is determined and shown in the account.

An account balance is determined by totaling the left side and right side money columns and entering the difference on the side with the largest total. At June 30, 1993, Westgate Driving School's Cash account shows a $12,000 balance on the left side of the account. This amount is the difference between the $53,000 left side column total and the $41,000 right side column total.

The account is an extremely simple record that can be summarized in terms of four money elements:

1. Beginning balance.
2. Additions.
3. Deductions.
4. Ending balance.

If any three elements are known, the fourth can easily be computed. Normally, after transactions have been recorded, only the ending balance needs to be computed. Accountants, however, are sometimes confronted with situations in which available

EXHIBIT 2—2	TWO-COLUMN CASH ACCOUNT FOR WESTGATE DRIVING SCHOOL

CASH   ACCOUNT NO. 11

Date	Description	Post. Ref.	Amount	Date	Description	Post. Ref.	Amount
1993 June 1			40,000	1993 June 2			26,000
30			10,000	3			800
30			3,000	3			3,500
				30			9,000
				30			300
				30			1,400
	Total		53,000		Total		41,000
30	Balance		12,000				

data are incomplete and reconstruction of accounts is necessary. Let us demonstrate such an analysis with the following example:

	A	B	C	D
Beginning balance	$10	$70	$ 40	$?
Additions	40	30	?	100
Deductions	20	?	160	120
Ending balance	?	10	0	40

In column A, the ending balance must be $20 greater than the beginning balance, because the additions exceed the deductions by $20. The ending balance is therefore $30. In B, the account balance decreased by $60, so the deductions must exceed the additions by $60. Therefore, total deductions are $90. Show that the unknown variable in column C is $120 and in column D is $60.

A simplified form often used to represent the account in accounting textbooks and in the classroom is referred to as the **T account** (because it resembles the letter *T*). This is merely a skeleton version of the account illustrated for actual record keeping. A T-account form with the June changes in Cash entered for Westgate Driving School follows:

CASH

(1)	40,000	(2)	26,000
(8)	10,000	(3)	800
(11)	3,000	(4)	3,500
		(7)	9,000
		(10)	300
		(12)	1,400
Total	53,000	Total	41,000
Bal.	12,000		

Because dates and other related data are usually omitted in T accounts, it is customary to "key" the entries with a number or a letter to identify the transactions or entry. This permits a systematic review of the entries in the event that an error has been made. It also enables anyone to review a set of such accounts and match related entries. The numerical keys in this T account are the ones used to identify the June transactions for the Westgate Driving School example in the previous chapter.

The printed account form in Exhibit 2-1 is appropriate for classifying accounting data in manual record-keeping systems. In accounting systems using computers, the account form may not be obvious because the actual data might be stored on media such as magnetic tapes or discs. Every accounting system, however, whether manual or automated, must provide for the retrieval and printing out of the types of information shown in the manual form.

PERMANENT AND TEMPORARY ACCOUNTS

OBJECTIVE ❷ DEFINE *permanent and temporary accounts.*

All accounts may be classified as either permanent accounts or temporary accounts. The **permanent accounts** are the accounts presented in the balance sheet. They consist of the accounts for assets, liabilities, owners' capital (for sole proprietorships and partnerships), and capital stock and retained earnings (for corporations). The distinguishing feature of a permanent account is that any balance in the account at the end of an accounting period is carried forward to the next accounting period.

As discussed earlier, accounts for revenues, expenses, owners' drawings (for sole proprietorships and partnerships), and cash dividends (for corporations) are temporary subdivisions of owners' equity. These accounts compose a firm's temporary accounts. **Temporary accounts** are used to gather information for a particular accounting period; at the end of the accounting period, temporary account balances are transferred to a permanent owners' equity account. The specific procedures used to transfer temporary account balances to a permanent owners' equity account are explained in a later chapter.

The following schedule summarizes the classification of permanent and temporary accounts.

Permanent Accounts	Temporary Accounts
Assets	Revenues
Liabilities	Expenses
Owners' Capital*	Owners' Drawings*
Capital Stock†	Cash Dividends†
Retained Earnings†	

* Accounts unique to sole proprietorships and partnerships.
† Accounts unique to corporations.

THE SYSTEM OF DEBITS AND CREDITS

OBJECTIVE ❸ DESCRIBE *the system of debits and credits.*

One basic characteristic of all account forms is that entries recording increases and decreases are separated. In some accounts, such as the Cash account illustrated in Exhibit 2-2, increases are recorded on the left side of the account and decreases on the right side; in other accounts the reverse is true. The method used in different types of accounts is a matter of convention; that is, a simple set of rules is followed. We will now discuss and illustrate these rules.

The terms **debit** and **credit** are used to refer to the left side and the right side of an account, as shown below.

(Any type of account)

Debit	**Credit**
Always the left side	Always the right side

Regardless of what is recorded in an account, an entry made on the left side is a debit to the account; an entry recorded on the right side is a credit to the account. The words *debit* and *credit* are abbreviated *dr.* (from the Latin *debere*) and *cr.* (from the Latin *credere*), respectively.

| EXHIBIT 2—3 | PATTERN OF INCREASES AND DECREASES, DEBITS AND CREDITS, AND NORMAL BALANCES |

Categories of Accounts

	Assets		Liabilities		Permanent Owners' Equity*		Owner Withdrawals†		Revenues		Expenses	
	Debit	Credit	Debit	Credit	Debit	Credit	Debit	Credit	Debit	Credit	Debit	Credit
1 Always true												
2 Increases	+			+		+	+			+	+	
3 Decreases		−	−		−			−	−			−
4 Normal balance	★			★		★	★			★	★	

*Owners' Capital accounts for sole proprietorships and partnerships; Capital Stock and Retained Earnings accounts for corporations.
†Owners' Drawing accounts for sole proprietorships and partnerships; Cash Dividends account for corporations.

The rules of debit and credit identify which accounts are increased by debits and reduced by credits, and which accounts are increased by credits and reduced by debits. Exhibit 2-3 summarizes these rules for each of six categories of accounts—assets, liabilities, permanent owners' equity, owner withdrawals, revenues, and expenses.

Observe the following relationships in Exhibit 2-3:

1 *Debit* always refers to the left side of any account; *credit* refers to the right side.

2 Increases in asset, owner withdrawal, and expense accounts are debit entries, while increases in liability, permanent owners' equity, and revenue accounts are credit entries.

3 Decreases are logically recorded on the side opposite increases.

4 The normal balance of any account is on the side on which increases are recorded—asset, owner withdrawal, and expense accounts normally have debit balances; the other three groups normally have credit balances. This result occurs because increases in an account are usually greater than or equal to decreases.

Note that the pattern for assets is opposite that for liabilities and permanent owners' equity. Also observe that the pattern for revenues is the same as for permanent owners' equity. This is to be expected, because revenues are a temporary subdivision of owners' equity and increase owners' equity. Following the same logic, the pattern for owner withdrawals and expenses is opposite that of permanent owners' equity, because owner withdrawals and expenses are temporary subdivisions of owners' equity and reduce owners' equity.

The system of debits and credits illustrated here is known as the **double-entry system,** so called because at least two entries, a debit and a credit, are made for each transaction. For the accounting equation to remain in balance (and it must), the dollar amount of debits must equal the dollar amount of credits for each transaction.

THE RUNNING BALANCE ACCOUNT

A different account form, the **running balance,** or three-column, account is often used rather than the symmetrical two-column form illustrated in Exhibit 2-1. The Cash account for Westgate Driving School in running balance form is shown in Exhibit 2-4. Notice that the account contains all the information shown in the two-column account but also provides a balance after each transaction.

EXHIBIT 2—4	RUNNING BALANCE CASH ACCOUNT FOR WESTGATE DRIVING SCHOOL

CASH ACCOUNT NO. 11

Date		Description	Post. Ref.	Debit*	Credit	Balance
1993 June	1			40,000		40,000
	2				26,000	14,000
	3				800	13,200
	3				3,500	9,700
	30				9,000	700
	30			10,000		10,700
	30				300	10,400
	30			3,000		13,400
	30				1,400	12,000

*Designates normal balance.

The major advantage of this type of account over the two-column account is that the account balance is apparent for any date during the period. A slight disadvantage is that one must be careful to note whether the account has a normal balance or not. An abnormal account balance should be placed in parentheses. For example, if we overdrew our bank balance, the Cash account balance would be abnormal (a credit balance).

We will use the running balance account in our formal illustrations throughout the succeeding chapters. *To assist you in the earlier chapters, we have placed an asterisk (*) in the column of the account that designates its normal balance.* In illustrations in which detail is not needed and concepts are emphasized, we will use T accounts.

ILLUSTRATION OF DEBIT AND CREDIT ANALYSIS

OBJECTIVE 4 ILLUSTRATE *debit and credit analysis of transactions.*

The following illustration of debit and credit analysis uses the transactions given in the previous chapter for the first month's operations of Westgate Driving School. Each transaction is stated, analyzed, and followed by an illustration of the appropriate debit and credit entries in the various accounts, using T accounts for simplicity. We have numbered each transaction for reference. In the transaction analysis and the resulting debits and credits, each entry resulting from a particular transaction is parenthetically keyed to the transaction number. Refer to Exhibit 2-3 for an explanation of the use of debits and credits in the analysis.

TRANSACTION 1

On June 1, John King deposited $40,000 of his personal funds in a special checking account for the Westgate Driving School.

ANALYSIS In the first transaction of Westgate Driving School, King's contribution of capital increases both the assets and the equities of the firm. Specifically, Cash increases by $40,000, and the permanent owner's equity account, J. King, Capital, increases by the same amount. The entries are

Debit Cash $40,000   **Credit** J. King, Capital $40,000

The related accounts would appear as shown on the following page:

THE ORIGINS OF RECORD KEEPING

Double-entry bookkeeping is simply a specialized form of keeping accounts. It is neither a discovery of science nor the inspiration of a happy moment, but the outcome of continued efforts to meet the changing necessities of trade.* ■ *The origin of keeping accounts has been traced as far back as 8500 B.C., the date archaeologists have established for certain clay tokens—cones, disks, spheres, and pellets—found in Mesopotamia (modern Iraq). These tokens represented such commodities as sheep, jugs of oil, bread, or clothing and were used in the Middle East to keep*

records. The tokens were often sealed in clay balls, called *bullae*, which were broken on delivery so the shipment could be checked against the invoice; *bullae*, in effect, were the first bills of lading. Later, symbols impressed on wet clay tablets replaced the tokens. Some experts consider this stage of record keeping the beginning of the art of writing, which spread rapidly along the trade routes and took hold throughout the known civilized world.†

Development of more formal account-keeping methods is attrib-uted to the merchants and bankers of Florence, Venice, and Genoa during the thirteenth to fifteenth centuries. The earliest of these methods con-sisted of accounts kept by a Floren-tine banker in 1211 A.D. The system was fairly primitive; accounts were not related in any special way (in terms of equality for entries), and bal-ancing of the accounts was lacking. Systematic bookkeeping evolved from these methods, however, and double-entry records first appeared in Genoa in 1340 A.D.‡

The first treatise on the art of sys-tematic bookkeeping appeared in 1494, in Venice. "Everything about Arithmetic, Geometry, Proportions, and Proportionality" (*Summa de Arithmetica, Geometria, Proportioni et Proportionalita*) was written by the Franciscan monk, Fra Luca Pacioli, one of the most celebrated mathe-maticians of his day. The work was intended to summarize the existing knowledge of mathematics. Included in the arithmetical part of the work was a section that explained in detail the double-entry system of bookkeep-ing. Although Pacioli made no claim to developing the art of bookkeeping, he has been regarded as the father of double-entry accounting. All of today's accounting textbooks have their foundation in this system described 500 years ago by Pacioli.

* Richard Brown, ed., *A History of Account-ing and Accountants* (New York: Augustus M. Kelly Publishers, 1968), p. 93.

† "The Roots of Writing," *Time*, August 1, 1977, p. 76.

‡ Richard Brown, p. 99.

CASH				J. KING, CAPITAL		
(1)	40,000				(1)	40,000

TRANSACTION 2 On June 2, Westgate Driving School paid $26,000 for a lot to be used for storing vehicles and for some driving instruction.

ANALYSIS This transaction represents the conversion of one asset to another, causing an increase in the asset Land and a decrease in the asset Cash. The entries are

Debit Land $26,000 **Credit** Cash $26,000

The related accounts would appear as follows:

LAND				CASH		
(2)	26,000		(1)	40,000	(2)	26,000

TRANSACTION 3   On June 3, the school paid $800 to rent a furnished office near the parking lot for June.

ANALYSIS   The cost of using the office is a June operating expense. When financial statements are prepared at the end of June, the month's rent will appear on the income statement as an expense. The transaction increases Rent Expense and reduces Cash. The entries are

Debit Rent Expense $800   **Credit** Cash $800

The related accounts would appear as follows:

RENT EXPENSE			CASH			
(3)	800		(1)	40,000	(2)	26,000
					(3)	800

TRANSACTION 4   On June 3, the school paid $3,500 to lease cars for the month of June.

ANALYSIS   This payment permits the driving school to use the automobiles during June and, therefore, is a June operating expense. The transaction increases Car Lease Expense and reduces Cash. The entries are

Debit Car Lease Expense $3,500   **Credit** Cash $3,500

The related accounts would appear as follows:

CAR LEASE EXPENSE			CASH			
(4)	3,500		(1)	40,000	(2)	26,000
					(3)	800
					(4)	3,500

TRANSACTION 5   On June 10, the school received a $300 invoice from the local newspaper for a driving school advertisement that will run in the newspaper four times during June. The invoice will be paid on June 30.

ANALYSIS   Advertising for the month of June is a June operating expense. Receipt of the invoice indicates that an amount is owed to the newspaper for this advertising. Therefore, this transaction increases an expense, Advertising Expense, and increases a liability, Accounts Payable. The entries are

Debit Advertising Expense $300   **Credit** Accounts Payable $300

The related accounts would appear as follows:

ADVERTISING EXPENSE			ACCOUNTS PAYABLE	
(5)	300		(5)	300

TRANSACTION 6   On June 26, the school's students were billed $16,000 for June instructional fees.

ANALYSIS   Providing instruction during the month generates an asset, Accounts Receivable, and revenue, Instructional Fees Earned. Note that the revenue is reflected in the month that instruction is given, even though the students may not pay the fees until a later period. The entries are

Debit Accounts Receivable $16,000   **Credit** Instructional Fees Earned $16,000

The related accounts would appear as follows:

ACCOUNTS RECEIVABLE		INSTRUCTIONAL FEES EARNED	
(6)　　16,000			(6)　　16,000

TRANSACTION 7　On June 30, the school paid instructors' salaries for June of $9,000.

ANALYSIS　The services received from driving instructors during the month represent an expense that will be shown on the June income statement. Therefore, this transaction increases an expense, Salaries Expense, and decreases an asset, Cash. The entries are

Debit Salaries Expense $9,000　　**Credit** Cash $9,000

The related accounts would appear as follows:

SALARIES EXPENSE		CASH		
(7)　　9,000		(1)　　40,000	(2)　　26,000	
			(3)　　　　800	
			(4)　　3,500	
			(7)　　9,000	

TRANSACTION 8　On June 30, the school collected $10,000 on account from students billed in transaction 6.

ANALYSIS　Receipt of this amount represents the collection of students' accounts, not new revenue. Recall that the related revenue was recorded in transaction 6, when the claims against students were recognized as the asset Accounts Receivable. This transaction converts one asset (accounts receivable) into another asset (cash). Cash increases by $10,000 and Accounts Receivable decreases by the same amount. The entries are

Debit Cash $10,000　　**Credit** Accounts Receivable $10,000

The related accounts would appear as follows:

CASH			ACCOUNTS RECEIVABLE	
(1)　　40,000	(2)　　26,000		(6)　　16,000	(8)　　10,000
(8)　　10,000	(3)　　　　800			
	(4)　　3,500			
	(7)　　9,000			

TRANSACTION 9　On June 30, the school received a $400 invoice from the local service station for gas and oil charged to the school's account during June. The invoice will be paid in July.

ANALYSIS　Under accrual-basis accounting, expenses are recorded in the period they help to generate revenues, regardless of when payment is made. The gas and oil were used in the school's activities during June and their cost is a June expense. This transaction increases Gas and Oil Expense and also increases the liability Accounts Payable. The entries are

Debit Gas and Oil Expense $400　　**Credit** Accounts Payable $400

The related accounts would appear as follows:

GAS AND OIL EXPENSE			ACCOUNTS PAYABLE		
(9)	400			(5)	300
				(9)	**400**

TRANSACTION 10

On June 30, the school paid the $300 invoice for advertising that was received on June 10.

ANALYSIS This payment settles a previously recorded obligation. Therefore, this transaction reduces both a liability, Accounts Payable, and an asset, Cash, by $300. The entries are

Debit Accounts Payable $300   **Credit** Cash $300

The related accounts would appear as follows:

ACCOUNTS PAYABLE			CASH			
(10)	300	(5)	300	(1)	40,000	(2)	26,000
		(9)	400	(8)	10,000	(3)	800
						(4)	3,500
						(7)	9,000
						(10)	300

TRANSACTION 11

On June 30, the school borrowed $3,000 from a bank and King, as owner of Westgate Driving School, signed a promissory note agreeing to pay it back in six months.

ANALYSIS Borrowing $3,000 in exchange for a promissory note increases both the asset Cash and the liability Notes Payable by $3,000. The entries are

Debit Cash $3,000   **Credit** Notes Payable $3,000

The related accounts would appear as follows:

CASH				NOTES PAYABLE	
(1)	40,000	(2)	26,000	(11)	**3,000**
(8)	10,000	(3)	800		
(11)	**3,000**	(4)	3,500		
		(7)	9,000		
		(10)	300		

TRANSACTION 12

On June 30, King withdrew $1,400 from the firm for personal use.

ANALYSIS The withdrawal of cash by King reduces King's equity in Westgate Driving School. King will use a drawing account to accumulate information about his withdrawals from the firm. Recall that a drawing account is a temporary subdivision of owner's equity. Because the drawing account accumulates information about a type of event (owner asset withdrawals) that reduces owner's equity, the account is increased by debit entries. King's withdrawal of $1,400 cash, therefore, increases the drawing account, J. King, Drawing, and reduces Cash by $1,400. The entries are

Debit J. King, Drawing $1,400   **Credit** Cash $1,400

The related accounts would appear as follows:

J. KING, DRAWING			CASH			
(12)	1,400		(1)	40,000	(2)	26,000
			(8)	10,000	(3)	800
			(11)	3,000	(4)	3,500
					(7)	9,000
					(10)	300
					(12)	1,400

The entries for each of the foregoing transactions have total debits equal to total credits. This equality of debits and credits is the distinguishing characteristic of the double-entry system of accounting.

THE GENERAL LEDGER AND THE TRIAL BALANCE

OBJECTIVE 5 EXPLAIN *the nature and format of a general ledger and trial balance.*

A grouping of a firm's accounts is referred to as a *ledger*. Although firms may use various ledgers to accumulate certain detailed information, all firms have a general ledger. A **general ledger** is the grouping of all of the accounts that are used to prepare the basic financial statements. In a manual system, the general ledger would consist of a loose-leaf binder or a tray of cards, with each page or card representing an account. The general ledger in a computerized accounting system is maintained on magnetic tapes or disks.

The left portion of Exhibit 2-5 shows the general ledger of Westgate Driving School. The accounts in the general ledger usually are grouped by category in the following order: (1) assets, (2) liabilities, (3) permanent owners' equity, (4) owner withdrawals, (5) revenues, and (6) expenses.

The **trial balance** is a list of the account titles in the general ledger with their respective debit or credit balances. It is prepared at the close of an accounting period after transactions have been recorded. The right side of Exhibit 2-5 illustrates a trial balance for Westgate Driving School at the end of June 1993. Note that the sequence of accounts and the dollar amounts are taken directly from the general ledger. The debit and credit columns balance; that is, each column totals to the same amount ($59,400).

The two main reasons for preparing a trial balance are

1. To serve as an interim mechanical check to determine if the debits and credits in the general ledger are equal.
2. To show all general ledger account balances on one concise record. This is often convenient when preparing financial statements. The trial balance itself, though, is not a financial statement.

Note that a trial balance should be dated; the trial balance of Westgate Driving School was taken at June 30, 1993.

ERRORS IN TRANSACTION ANALYSIS

OBJECTIVE 6 DISCUSS *common types of errors in transaction analysis.*

Several types of errors will cause a trial balance to be out of balance. If only one of these is present, it may be identified and located by one of the approaches suggested below. If several errors exist, however, often the only way to find them is to retrace each entry, check the arithmetic performed in balancing the accounts, and make certain that no error has occurred in transcribing amounts or in adding the trial balance. To search for errors, one should systematically follow certain procedures so that all steps are retraced only once and no steps are overlooked.

When there is a mistake in a trial balance, the first step is to determine the amount by which the total debits and credits disagree. Certain characteristics of this

| EXHIBIT 2—5 | WESTGATE DRIVING SCHOOL GENERAL LEDGER AND TRIAL BALANCE |

General Ledger

CASH

(1) 40,000	(2) 26,000
(8) 10,000	(3) 800
(11) 3,000	(4) 3,500
	(7) 9,000
	(10) 300
	(12) 1,400
Tot. 53,000	Tot. 41,000
Bal. 12,000	

ACCOUNTS RECEIVABLE

| (6) 16,000 | (8) 10,000 |
| Bal. 6,000 | |

LAND

| (2) 26,000 | |

NOTES PAYABLE

| | (11) 3,000 |

ACCOUNTS PAYABLE

(10) 300	(5) 300
	(9) 400
Tot. 300	Tot. 700
	Bal. 400

J. KING, CAPITAL

| | (1) 40,000 |

J. KING, DRAWING

| (12) 1,400 | |

INSTRUCTIONAL FEES EARNED

| | (6) 16,000 |

RENT EXPENSE

| (3) 800 | |

CAR LEASE EXPENSE

| (4) 3,500 | |

ADVERTISING EXPENSE

| (5) 300 | |

SALARIES EXPENSE

| (7) 9,000 | |

GAS AND OIL EXPENSE

| (9) 400 | |

WESTGATE DRIVING SCHOOL
TRIAL BALANCE
JUNE 30, 1993

	Debit	Credit
Cash	$12,000	
Accounts Receivable	6,000	
Land	26,000	
Notes Payable		$ 3,000
Accounts Payable		400
J. King, Capital		40,000
J. King, Drawing	1,400	
Instructional Fees Earned		16,000
Rent Expense	800	
Car Lease Expense	3,500	
Advertising Expense	300	
Salaries Expense	9,000	
Gas and Oil Expense	400	
	$59,400	$59,400

amount may provide a clue to identifying the type of error and finding where it was made.

DEBITS AND CREDITS INTERCHANGED

When a debit is entered as a credit (or vice versa), the trial balance totals will differ by twice the amount involved. For example, if the credits exceed the debits by $246, one should first look for a $123 debit that has been treated as a credit. With this type of error, the amount of the discrepancy in the trial balance totals is divisible by two. If this is not the case, either another type of error or a number of errors are involved.

TRANSPOSITION OR SLIDE OF NUMBERS

Transposing numbers means simply reversing their order. For example, transposing the first two digits in $360 would result in $630. This type of error usually occurs when amounts are transcribed from one record to another. The resulting discrepancy is always evenly divisible by nine ($630 − $360 = $270, and $270/9 = $30). A *number slide* means that the decimal point is moved when recording an amount. Recording a $5,700 account balance as $570 in the trial balance illustrates a number slide. The resulting discrepancy also always divides evenly by nine ($5,700 − $570 = $5,130, and $5,130/9 = $570). Therefore, if a discrepancy between trial balance totals is evenly divisible by nine, one would suspect either a transposition error or a number slide.

AMOUNTS OMITTED

An amount can be omitted if one enters only part of an entry, fails to include an entry when balancing an account, or leaves out an account balance in a trial balance. The resulting discrepancy is equal in amount to the omitted item. Of course, the omission of a debit amount will cause an excess of credits by that amount, and vice versa.

It is always reassuring when a trial balance does balance. However, even when a trial balance is in balance, the accounting records may still contain errors. A balanced trial balance simply proves that, *as recorded*, debits equal credits. The following errors, for example, are *not detected* by taking a trial balance:

1. Failing to record or enter a particular transaction.
2. Entering a transaction more than once.
3. Entering one or more amounts in the wrong accounts.
4. Making an error that exactly offsets the effect of another error.

RELATIONSHIPS AMONG FINANCIAL STATEMENTS

OBJECTIVE **7** DESCRIBE *and* ILLUSTRATE *the relationships among financial statements.*

The income statement, the statement of owners' equity, the balance sheet, and the statement of cash flows complement one another. To illustrate, refer to the financial statements of Westgate Driving School in Exhibit 2-6. Observe that **A** the net income (or net loss) for a period is an input into the statement of owner's equity; and **B** the ending owner's equity is an input into the balance sheet. Further, the statement of cash flows explains the reasons for a change in cash for a period, and **C** its ending cash amount agrees with the cash amount in the balance sheet. When financial statements are prepared, the sequence suggested by these relationships is customarily followed; that is, the income statement is prepared first, then the statement of owners' equity, then the balance sheet, and then the statement of cash flows.

Three of the basic financial statements present information covering a specific period of time. They are the income statement, the statement of owners' equity, and the statement of cash flows. For this reason, these financial statements are referred to as **period statements.** In contrast, the balance sheet shows information as of a specific date. The balance sheet, therefore, is referred to as a **position statement.**

ANALYTICAL APPLICATION

OBJECTIVE **8** DEFINE *the* **operating cash flow to total liabilities ratio** *and* EXPLAIN *its use.*

OPERATING CASH FLOW TO TOTAL LIABILITIES RATIO

The ability of a company's operating activities to provide cash to pay off liabilities as they become due is one sign of a financially strong company. A ratio that examines this particular dimension is the operating cash flow to total liabilities ratio. The **operating cash flow to total liabilities ratio** is computed as follows:

$$\text{Operating Cash Flow to Total Liabilities Ratio} = \frac{\text{Net Cash Flow from Operating Activities}}{\text{Average Total Liabilities}}$$

The numerator in this ratio comes from the first section of the statement of cash flows—the section reporting the cash flow from operating activities. The denominator takes data from the balance sheet. As noted earlier, the statement of cash flows is a period statement; the balance sheet is a position statement. Because this ratio relates period data to position data, it is best to average the balance sheet data (total liabilities) over the time period covered by the numerator. This average is computed by summing the total liabilities at the beginning and end of the period and dividing

EXHIBIT 2—6 | **FINANCIAL STATEMENTS FOR WESTGATE DRIVING SCHOOL**

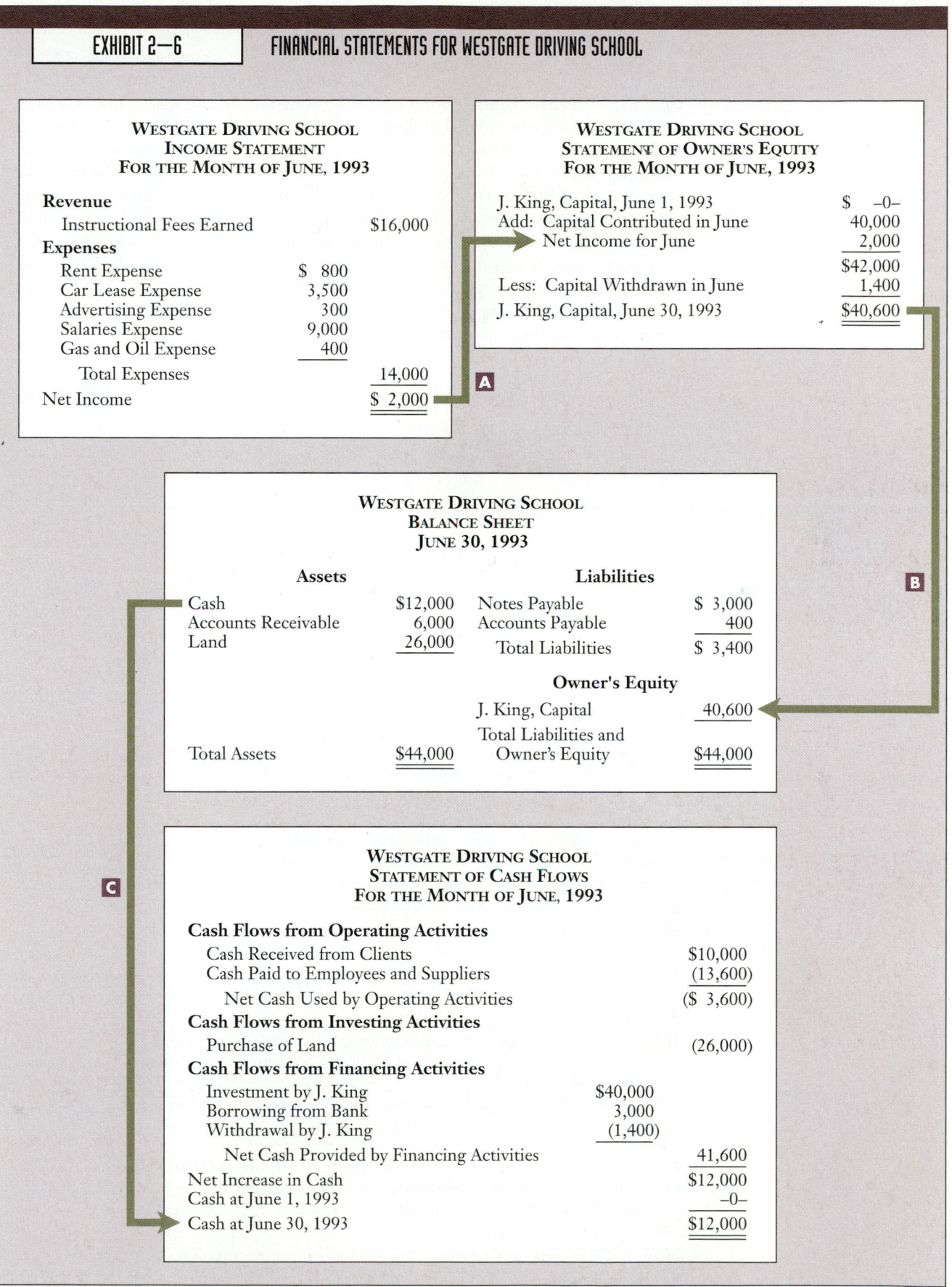

WESTGATE DRIVING SCHOOL
INCOME STATEMENT
FOR THE MONTH OF JUNE, 1993

Revenue

Instructional Fees Earned		$16,000
Expenses		
Rent Expense	$ 800	
Car Lease Expense	3,500	
Advertising Expense	300	
Salaries Expense	9,000	
Gas and Oil Expense	400	
Total Expenses		14,000
Net Income		$ 2,000

A

WESTGATE DRIVING SCHOOL
STATEMENT OF OWNER'S EQUITY
FOR THE MONTH OF JUNE, 1993

J. King, Capital, June 1, 1993	$ –0–
Add: Capital Contributed in June	40,000
Net Income for June	2,000
	$42,000
Less: Capital Withdrawn in June	1,400
J. King, Capital, June 30, 1993	$40,600

B

WESTGATE DRIVING SCHOOL
BALANCE SHEET
JUNE 30, 1993

Assets		**Liabilities**	
Cash	$12,000	Notes Payable	$ 3,000
Accounts Receivable	6,000	Accounts Payable	400
Land	26,000	Total Liabilities	$ 3,400
		Owner's Equity	
		J. King, Capital	40,600
		Total Liabilities and	
Total Assets	$44,000	Owner's Equity	$44,000

C

WESTGATE DRIVING SCHOOL
STATEMENT OF CASH FLOWS
FOR THE MONTH OF JUNE, 1993

Cash Flows from Operating Activities

Cash Received from Clients	$10,000	
Cash Paid to Employees and Suppliers	(13,600)	
Net Cash Used by Operating Activities		($ 3,600)
Cash Flows from Investing Activities		
Purchase of Land		(26,000)
Cash Flows from Financing Activities		
Investment by J. King	$40,000	
Borrowing from Bank	3,000	
Withdrawal by J. King	(1,400)	
Net Cash Provided by Financing Activities		41,600
Net Increase in Cash		$12,000
Cash at June 1, 1993		–0–
Cash at June 30, 1993		$12,000

by 2. An operating cash flow to total liabilities ratio of at least 0.20 is usually interpreted as an indicator of financial soundness.[1]

Computing this ratio for Westgate Driving School, we get a negative 2.12, computed as follows: $-\$3,600/[(\$0 + \$3,400)/2] = -\$3,600/\$1,700 = -2.12$. The company had a net cash outflow from operating activities, so the numerator is a negative number. Also, there were no liabilities at the beginning of the month, so a zero shows in the computation for beginning total liabilities. By itself, a negative 2.12 ratio of operating cash flow to total liabilities would be considered a sign of financial weakness. Any ratio, however, must be evaluated in the context of the firm being analyzed. June is Westgate Driving School's first month of operations, and it is not at all unusual to experience operating cash outflows when just starting a business. A negative ratio, therefore, is not unexpected for Westgate Driving School. What happens to this ratio in the future is much more significant than this initial negative ratio.

Following are recent operating cash flow to total liabilities ratios for several companies that have been operating for many years:

DEERE & COMPANY (farm and industrial equipment)	0.06
EATON CORPORATION (diversified manufacturing)	0.20
SkyWest, INC. (airline)	0.28
FREDERICK'S OF HOLLYWOOD (women's apparel retailer)	0.41

KEY POINTS FOR CHAPTER OBJECTIVES

1 **EXPLAIN** the nature and format of an account (pp. 42–45).
- An account is an individual record of increases and decreases in specific assets, liabilities, permanent owners' equity, owner withdrawals, revenues, and expenses.
- Information provided by the account includes title, amounts reflecting increases and decreases, cross-references to other accounting records, and dates and descriptive notations.

2 **DEFINE** permanent and temporary accounts (p. 45).
- Permanent accounts are the balance sheet accounts — assets, liabilities, and permanent owners' equity; any balance in a permanent account at the end of an accounting period is carried forward to the next period.
- Temporary accounts consist of revenue, expense, and owner withdrawal accounts; they gather information for an accounting period and at the end of the period, their balances are transferred to a permanent owners' equity account.

3 **DESCRIBE** the system of debits and credits (pp. 45–47).
- The left side of an account is always the debit side; the right side is always the credit side.
- Increases in assets, owner withdrawals, and expenses are debit entries; increases in liabilities, permanent owners' equity, and revenues are credit entries. Decreases are the opposite.
- The normal balance of any account appears on the side for recording increases.

4 **ILLUSTRATE** debit and credit analysis of transactions (pp. 47–52).
- Each accounting transaction should be analyzed into equal debits and credits.
- All accounting transactions are analyzed using one or more of the basic account categories: (1) assets, (2) liabilities, (3) permanent owners' equity, (4) owner withdrawals, (5) revenues, and (6) expenses.

5 **EXPLAIN** the nature and format of a general ledger and trial balance (pp. 52–53).
- A general ledger is the grouping of all of the accounts that are used to prepare the basic financial statements.
- A trial balance is a list of the accounts in the general ledger with their respective debit or credit balances; it is prepared after transactions have been recorded for an accounting period.
- A trial balance serves as a check to determine the equality of debits and credits.
- Showing all the account balances on one concise record (that is, a trial balance) facilitates preparation of the financial statements.

---

[1]Clyde P. Stickney, *Financial Statement Analysis: A Strategic Perspective* (San Diego: Harcourt Brace Jovanovich, 1990), p. 243.

6 DISCUSS common types of errors in transaction analysis (pp. 52–54).
- Common errors that cause the trial balance not to balance include entering a debit as a credit (or vice versa), transposition errors, number slides, and omitted amounts.
- Errors that are not detected by a trial balance include failing to record a transaction, recording a transaction more than once, entering amounts in the wrong accounts but on the correct side, and offsetting errors.

7 DESCRIBE and ILLUSTRATE the relationships among financial statements (pp. 54, 55).
- The net income (or net loss) from the income statement flows into the statement of owner's equity; the ending owner's capital from the statement of owner's equity flows into the balance sheet, and the ending cash from the balance sheet agrees with the ending cash shown in the statement of cash flows.

8 ANALYTICAL APPLICATION: DEFINE the *operating cash flow to total liabilities ratio* and EXPLAIN its use (pp. 54, 56).
- The operating cash flow to total liabilities ratio is computed as (Net Cash Flow from Operating Activities)/(Average Total Liabilities) and is an indicator of the availability of cash from operations to settle liabilities as they become due.

SELF-TEST QUESTIONS FOR REVIEW

(Answers follow the Solution to Demonstration Problem.)

1. The ending balance of the Accounts Receivable account was $12,000. Services billed to customers for the period were $21,500, and collections on account from customers were $23,600. The beginning balance of Accounts Receivable was
   a. $33,500   b. $14,100   c. $9,900   d. $33,100

2. Which of the following accounts is a temporary account?
   a. Accounts Receivable
   b. Notes Payable
   c. P. Reilly, Capital
   d. Advertising Expense

3. In applying the rules of debit and credit
   a. The word *debit* means to increase and the word *credit* means to decrease.
   b. Asset, expense, and owner drawing accounts are debited for increases.
   c. Liability, revenue, and owner drawing accounts are debited for increases.
   d. Asset, expense, and owner capital accounts are debited for increases.

4. Which of the following is not true of a general ledger trial balance?
   a. It proves that the total debits equal total credits, if it balances.
   b. It helps in preparing financial statements.
   c. It proves that no errors have been made in recording transactions, if it balances.
   d. It will not detect an error where the accounts debited and credited are reversed in recording a particular transaction.

5. Which of the following combinations of trial balance totals suggests the presence of either a transposition error or a number slide?
   a. $65,470 debit and $68,170 credit
   b. $33,220 debit and $35,420 credit
   c. $25,670 debit and $26,670 credit
   d. $14,517 debit and $15,477 credit

DEMONSTRATION PROBLEM FOR REVIEW

For each of the transactions listed below for Thomas Company, a sole proprietorship, fill in the blank spaces to answer the following questions:
1. Which specific accounts are affected by the transaction?
2. What type of account is each account affected (that is, is it an asset, liability, owner capital, owner drawing, revenue, or expense account)?
3. Should the account be increased or decreased?
4. Should the account be debited or credited?

Transactions:
(A) The company received $1,300 cash from clients for services rendered.
(B) The company paid $2,400 of salaries to employees.
(C) The company collected $600 from clients on account.
(D) The owner, F. Thomas, withdrew $400 cash for personal use.
(E) The company purchased $700 of supplies on account.
(F) The company billed clients $900 for services rendered.
(G) The company paid $500 to suppliers on account.

Transaction	Accounts Affected	Type of Account	Increase or Decrease	Debit or Credit
(A)	1. _____	1. _____	1. _____	1. _____
	2. _____	2. _____	2. _____	2. _____
(B)	1. _____	1. _____	1. _____	1. _____
	2. _____	2. _____	2. _____	2. _____
(C)	1. _____	1. _____	1. _____	1. _____
	2. _____	2. _____	2. _____	2. _____
(D)	1. _____	1. _____	1. _____	1. _____
	2. _____	2. _____	2. _____	2. _____
(E)	1. _____	1. _____	1. _____	1. _____
	2. _____	2. _____	2. _____	2. _____
(F)	1. _____	1. _____	1. _____	1. _____
	2. _____	2. _____	2. _____	2. _____
(G)	1. _____	1. _____	1. _____	1. _____
	2. _____	2. _____	2. _____	2. _____

SOLUTION TO DEMONSTRATION PROBLEM

Transaction	Accounts Affected	Type of Account	Increase or Decrease	Debit or Credit
(A)	1. Cash	1. Asset	1. Increase	1. Debit
	2. Service Fees Earned	2. Revenue	2. Increase	2. Credit
(B)	1. Salaries Expense	1. Expense	1. Increase	1. Debit
	2. Cash	2. Asset	2. Decrease	2. Credit
(C)	1. Cash	1. Asset	1. Increase	1. Debit
	2. Accounts Receivable	2. Asset	2. Decrease	2. Credit
(D)	1. F. Thomas, Drawing	1. Owner Drawing	1. Increase	1. Debit
	2. Cash	2. Asset	2. Decrease	2. Credit
(E)	1. Supplies	1. Asset	1. Increase	1. Debit
	2. Accounts Payable	2. Liability	2. Increase	2. Credit
(F)	1. Accounts Receivable	1. Asset	1. Increase	1. Debit
	2. Service Fees Earned	2. Revenue	2. Increase	2. Credit
(G)	1. Accounts Payable	1. Liability	1. Decrease	1. Debit
	2. Cash	2. Asset	2. Decrease	2. Credit

ANSWERS TO SELF-TEST QUESTIONS

1. b, p. 43　**2.** d, p. 45　**3.** b, p. 46　**4.** c, p. 54　**5.** a, p. 53

GLOSSARY OF KEY TERMS USED IN THIS CHAPTER

account　A record of the additions, deductions, and balances of individual assets, liabilities, permanent owners' equity, owner drawings, revenues, and expenses (p. 42).

credit (entry)　An entry on the right side (or in the credit column) of any account (p. 45).

debit (entry)　An entry on the left side (or in the debit column) of any account (p. 45).

double-entry system　A method of accounting that recognizes the duality of a transaction such that the analysis results in a recording of equal amounts of debits and credits (p. 46).

drawing account　A temporary owners' equity account used to accumulate owner withdrawals from the business (p. 42).

general ledger　A grouping of all of an entity's accounts that are used to prepare the basic financial statements (p. 52).

operating cash flow to total liabilities ratio A ratio measuring the relationship between a firm's cash flow from operating activities and its average total liabilities; computed as (Net Cash Flow from Operating Activities)/(Average Total Liabilities) (p. 54).

period statement A financial statement accumulating information for a specific period of time; examples are the income statement, the statement of owners' equity, and the statement of cash flows (p. 54).

permanent account An account used to prepare the balance sheet; that is, asset, liability, and owner capital (or, for a corporation, capital stock and retained earnings) accounts. Any balance in a permanent account at the end of an accounting period is carried forward to the next period (p. 45).

position statement A financial statement presenting information as of a particular date; the balance sheet is a position statement (p. 54).

running balance account An account form having money columns for debit entries, credit entries, and the account balance. Sometimes called the *three-column account* (p. 46).

T account An abbreviated form of the formal account in the shape of a *T*; use is usually limited to illustrations of accounting techniques and analysis (p. 44).

temporary account An account used to gather information for an accounting period; at the end of the period, the balance is transferred to a permanent owners' equity account. Revenue, expense, and owners' drawing accounts are temporary accounts (p. 45).

trial balance A list of the account titles in the general ledger, their respective debit or credit balances, and the totals of the debit and credit amounts (p. 52).

QUESTIONS

2-1 What is an *account?*

2-2 What information is recorded in an account?

2-3 What is the justification for using a separate owner's drawing account?

2-4 Define and give an example of a *permanent account.*

2-5 Identify the type of permanent owners' equity account used in sole proprietorships and partnerships. Identify the types used in corporations.

2-6 Define and give an example of a *temporary account.*

2-7 What does the term *debit* mean? What does the term *credit* mean?

2-8 Identify the following as an asset, liability, permanent owner's equity, owner withdrawal, revenue, or expense account and indicate whether a debit entry or a credit entry increases the balance of the account.

Professional Fees Earned	S. Adams, Capital
Accounts Receivable	Advertising Expense
Accounts Payable	Supplies
Cash	S. Adams, Drawing

2-9 How is the normal side of an account determined?

2-10 Indicate the normal balance (debit or credit) of each account in Question 2–8.

2-11 Identify one advantage and one disadvantage of the running balance, or three-column, account form compared with the two-column form.

2-12 Present three common business transactions that would not affect the amount of owners' equity.

2-13 Explain the terms *general ledger* and *trial balance.* What are the reasons for preparing a trial balance?

2-14 Describe three distinct types of errors that may be present even when a trial balance is in balance.

2-15 "A trial balance is a list showing all account titles in the general ledger and the total debits and total credits in each account." Do you agree with this statement? Why or why not?

2-16 The assistant accountant of Laird Sports prepared a trial balance that had total debits of $72,850 and total credits of $78,050. Compute the correct trial balance totals by assuming that only the following errors were involved:

1. Accounts Payable with a normal balance of $2,850 was listed as a debit.

  2. During the current period, a $500 check for Utilities Expense was debited to Office Expense.
  3. Supplies with a normal balance of $1,900 had been omitted.
  4. R. Laird, Drawing, with a normal balance of $4,500 was included as a credit.

2-17 What is the usual sequence for the preparation of financial statements?

2-18 Define and give an example of a *period statement; a position statement.*

2-19 "During the year, the total owner's equity of Wanda's Gift Shop increased from $58,000 to $80,000. Therefore, the annual net income must have been $22,000." Is this statement necessarily true? Explain.

2-20 Which financial statements provide the data for computing the ratio of operating cash flow to total liabilities?

2-21 Leyden Company had total liabilities of $6,200,000 at December 31, 1993, and $7,400,000 at December 31, 1994. For 1994, Leyden Company's cash provided by operating activities was $1,564,000. What is Leyden Company's 1994 ratio of operating cash flow to total liabilities?

EXERCISES

**ANALYSIS OF ACCOUNTS
— OBJ. 1 —**

2-22 Compute the unknown amount required in each of the following five independent situations. The answer to situation (a) is given as an example.

	Account	Beginning Balance	Ending Balance	Other Information
(a)	Cash	$ 6,100	$ 5,250	Total cash disbursed, $5,400.
(b)	Accounts Receivable	8,500	9,700	Services on account, $26,400.
(c)	Notes Payable	5,000	20,000	Funds borrowed by notes, $30,000.
(d)	Accounts Payable	2,180	1,720	Payments on account, $1,900.
(e)	M. Ventura, Capital	32,000	40,000	Capital contributions, $2,000.

Unknown Amounts Required

  a. Total cash received   __$4,550__

  b. Total amount collected from credit customers   _____

  c. Notes payable repaid during the period   _____

  d. Amount received from suppliers on account   _____

  e. Net income, if no withdrawals were made   _____

**NATURE OF ACCOUNTS,
DEBIT AND CREDIT RULES
— OBJ. 2, 3 —**

2-23 For each of the accounts listed below, indicate whether the account (1) is increased by a debit or a credit and (2) is a permanent or a temporary account.

Accounts Payable	G. Frankel, Capital
Advertising Expense	G. Frankel, Drawing
Cash	Land
Equipment	Service Fees Earned

**TRANSACTION ANALYSIS
— OBJ. 4 —**

2-24 Match each of the following transactions of L. Boyd, a printer, with the appropriate letters (given on the following page), indicating the debits and credits to be made. The correct answer for transaction 1 is given.

	Answer
(1) The owner contributed cash to the business.	__a, f__
(2) Purchased equipment on account.	_____
(3) Received and immediately paid advertising bill.	_____
(4) Purchased supplies for cash.	_____
(5) Borrowed money from bank, giving a note payable.	_____
(6) Billed customers for services rendered.	_____
(7) Made partial payment on account for equipment.	_____
(8) Paid employee's salary.	_____
(9) Collected amounts due from customers billed in transaction 6.	_____

Effect of Transaction

a. Debit an asset	f. Credit owner's capital
b. Credit an asset	g. Debit a revenue
c. Debit a liability	h. Credit a revenue
d. Credit a liability	i. Debit an expense
e. Debit owner's capital	j. Credit an expense

TRANSACTION ANALYSIS — OBJ. 4 —

2-25 The accounts below are from the general ledger of Tiffany Bast, an architect. For each letter given in the T accounts, describe the type of business transaction(s) or event(s) that would most probably be reflected by entries on that side of the account. For example, the answer to (a) is Amounts of services performed for clients on account.

ACCOUNTS RECEIVABLE		NOTES PAYABLE	
(a)	(b)		(c)

OFFICE EQUIPMENT		ACCOUNTS PAYABLE	
(d)		(e)	(f)

PROFESSIONAL FEES EARNED		T. BAST, DRAWING	
	(g)	(h)	

T. BAST, CAPITAL		SALARIES EXPENSE	
	(i)	(j)	

TRANSACTION ANALYSIS AND TRIAL BALANCE — OBJ. 4, 5 —

2-26 Make T accounts for the following accounts that appear in the general ledger of R. Mead, a veterinarian: Cash; Accounts Receivable; Supplies; Office Equipment; Accounts Payable; R. Mead, Capital; R. Mead, Drawing; Professional Fees Earned; Salaries Expense; and Rent Expense. Record the following December, 1993, transactions in the T accounts and key all entries with the number identifying the transaction. Finally, determine the balance in each account and prepare a trial balance at December 31, 1993.

(1) Mead opened a checking account on December 1 at United Bank in the name of Pet Hospital and deposited $25,000 cash.

(2) Paid rent for December, $950.

(3) Purchased office equipment on account, $3,400.

(4) Purchased supplies for cash, $1,400.

(5) Billed clients for services rendered, $7,100.

(6) Paid secretary's salary, $1,750.

(7) Paid $2,000 on account for the equipment purchased in transaction 3.

(8) Collected $5,500 from clients previously billed for services.

(9) Mead withdrew $1,800 cash for personal use.

EFFECT OF ERRORS ON TRIAL BALANCE — OBJ. 6 —

2-27 Indicate how each of the following errors would affect the trial balance totals. For each error, specify whether the debit or credit totals would be overstated, understated, or whether both totals would be unaffected.

a. The Accounts Receivable normal balance of $35,900 was listed in the trial balance as $39,500.

b. A $900 payment for rent was debited to Utilities Expense during the accounting period.

c. The Accounts Payable normal balance of $17,200 was omitted from the trial balance.

d. Salaries Expense of $7,800 was listed in the trial balance as a credit.

e. The owner's Drawing account, with a debit balance of $8,500, was listed as a credit in the trial balance.

FINANCIAL STATEMENTS — OBJ. 7 —

2-28 Listed below are four financial statements and two columns with unfilled blanks. In the column headed Sequence, place the numbers 1–4 to indicate the sequence in which the financial statements are usually prepared. In the column headed Period or Position, write *period* if the financial statement is a period statement and *position* if the financial statement is a position statement.

	Sequence	Period or Position
Balance Sheet	_____	_____
Income Statement	_____	_____
Statement of Cash Flows	_____	_____
Statement of Owners' Equity	_____	_____

PROBLEMS

**TRANSACTION ANALYSIS
AND TRIAL BALANCE
— OBJ. 4, 5 —**

2-29 James Behm, electrical contractor, began business on May 1, 1993. The following transactions occurred during May:

  (1) Behm invested $20,000 of his personal funds in the business.
  (2) Purchased equipment on account, $3,500.
  (3) Returned $200 of equipment that was not satisfactory. The return reduced the amount owed to the supplier.
  (4) Purchased supplies on account, $920.
  (5) Purchased a truck for $10,500. Behm paid $4,500 cash and gave a note payable for the balance.
  (6) Paid rent for May, $825.
  (7) Paid fuel cost for truck, $80.
  (8) Billed customers for services rendered, $12,400.
  (9) Paid $2,000 on account for equipment purchased in transaction 2.
  (10) Paid cost of utilities for May, $180.
  (11) Received invoice for May advertising, to be paid in June, $250.
  (12) Paid employees' wages, $3,150.
  (13) Collected $7,200 on accounts receivable.
  (14) Behm withdrew $900 for personal expenses.
  (15) Paid interest for May on note payable, $50.

REQUIRED

  a. Record the above transactions in T accounts, and key entries with the numbers of the transactions. The following accounts will be needed to record the transactions for May: Cash; Accounts Receivable; Supplies; Equipment; Truck; Notes Payable; Accounts Payable; J. Behm, Capital; J. Behm, Drawing; Service Revenue; Rent Expense; Wages Expense; Utilities Expense; Truck Expense; Advertising Expense; and Interest Expense.
  b. Prepare a trial balance of the general ledger as of May 31, 1993.

**TRIAL BALANCE AND
FINANCIAL STATEMENTS
— OBJ. 5, 7 —**

2-30 The following account balances, in alphabetical order, are from the general ledger of Morgan's Waterproofing Service at January 31, 1993. The firm's accounting year began on January 1. All accounts have normal balances.

Accounts Payable	$ 1,300	Notes Payable	$ 3,000
Accounts Receivable	15,500	Rent Expense	850
Advertising Expense	210	Salaries Expense	4,000
Cash	5,200	Service Fees Earned	12,880
Interest Expense	25	Supplies	4,480
K. Morgan, Capital (January 1)	19,870	Supplies Expense	5,125
K. Morgan, Drawing	1,500	Utilities Expense	160

REQUIRED

  a. Prepare a trial balance in good form from the given data.
  b. Prepare an income statement for the month of January 1993.
  c. Prepare a statement of owner's equity for the month of January 1993.
  d. Prepare a balance sheet at January 31, 1993.

**TRANSACTION ANALYSIS
AND THE EFFECT OF
ERRORS ON TRIAL BALANCE
— OBJ. 4, 5, 6 —**

2-31 The following T accounts contain numbered entries for the May transactions of Carol Marsh, a market analyst, who opened her offices on May 1, 1993:

	CASH				C. MARSH, CAPITAL	
(1)	15,000	(2)	4,600		(1)	15,000
(9)	3,300	(4)	860			
		(6)	950			
		(8)	1,000			

ACCOUNTS RECEIVABLE					C. MARSH, DRAWING		
(5)	5,400	(9)	3,300	(8)	1,000		

OFFICE SUPPLIES					PROFESSIONAL FEES EARNED		
(3)	1,800					(5)	5,400

OFFICE EQUIPMENT					RENT EXPENSE		
(2)	4,600			(4)	860		

ACCOUNTS PAYABLE					UTILITIES EXPENSE		
(6)	950	(3)	1,800	(7)	170		
		(7)	170				

REQUIRED

a. Give a reasonable description of each of the nine numbered transactions entered in the above accounts. Example: (1) Carol Marsh invested $15,000 of her personal funds in her business.

b. The following trial balance, taken for Marsh's firm on May 31, contains several errors. Itemize the errors and indicate the correct totals for the trial balance.

CAROL MARSH, MARKET ANALYST
TRIAL BALANCE
MAY 31, 1993

	Debit	Credit
Cash	$10,980	
Accounts Receivable	1,900	
Office Supplies	1,800	
Office Equipment	4,600	
Accounts Payable		$ 1,020
C. Marsh, Capital		15,000
C. Marsh, Drawing		1,000
Professional Fees Earned		5,400
Rent Expense	860	
	$20,140	$22,420

TRANSACTION ANALYSIS, TRIAL BALANCE, AND FINANCIAL STATEMENTS — OBJ. 4, 5, 7 —

2-32 Pam Brown owns Art Graphics, a firm providing designs for advertisers, market analysts, and others. On July 1 1993, her general ledger showed the following normal account balances:

Cash	$ 9,500	Notes Payable	$ 4,000
Accounts Receivable	8,200	Accounts Payable	1,800
		P. Brown, Capital	11,900
	$17,700		$17,700

The following transactions occurred in July:

July 2 Paid July rent, $580.

2 Collected $6,500 on account from customers.

5 Paid $2,000 installment due on the $4,000 noninterest-bearing note payable to a relative.

9 Billed customers for design services rendered on account, $14,750.

12 Rendered design services and collected from cash customers, $950.

15 Paid $1,200 to creditors on account.

18 Collected $10,800 on account from customers.

21 Paid a delivery service for delivery of graphics to commercial firms, $280.

30 Paid July salaries, $3,200.

30 Received invoice for July advertising expense, to be paid in August, $500.

31 Paid cost of utilities for July, $190.

July 31   Brown withdrew $700 for personal use.

31   Received invoice for supplies used in July, to be paid in August, $2,760.

31   Purchased computer for $5,000 cash to be used in the business starting next month.

REQUIRED

a. Set up running balance accounts for the general ledger accounts with July 1 balances and enter the beginning balances. Also provide the following running balance accounts: Equipment; P. Brown, Drawing; Service Fees Earned; Rent Expense; Salaries Expense; Delivery Expense; Advertising Expense; Utilities Expense; and Supplies Expense. Record the listed transactions in the accounts.

b. Prepare a trial balance at July 31, 1993.

c. Prepare an income statement for the month of July 1993.

d. Prepare a statement of owner's equity for the month of July 1993.

e. Prepare a balance sheet at July 31, 1993.

Transaction Analysis, Trial Balance, and Financial Statements — Obj. 4, 5, 7 —

2-33   Outpost Fly-In Service, Inc., operates leased amphibious aircraft and docking facilities, equipping the firm to transport campers and hunters from Thunder Bay, Ontario, to outpost camps owned by various resorts in Ontario. On August 1, 1993, the firm's trial balance was as follows:

OUTPOST FLY-IN SERVICE, INC.
TRIAL BALANCE
AUGUST 1, 1993

	Debit	Credit
Cash	$59,300	
Accounts Receivable	25,800	
Notes Payable		$ 2,500
Accounts Payable		1,400
Capital Stock		60,000
Retained Earnings		21,200
	$85,100	$85,100

During August the following transactions occurred:

Aug. 1   Paid August rental cost for aircraft, dockage, and dockside office, $4,500.

3   Paid insurance premium for August, $1,600.

5   Paid for August advertising in various sports magazines, $600.

6   Rendered fly-in services for various groups for cash, $15,650.

8   Billed the Ministry of Natural Resources for services in transporting mapping personnel, $2,900.

13   Received $19,500 on account from clients.

16   Paid $1,200 on accounts payable.

24   Billed various clients for services, $17,600.

31   Paid interest on note payable for August, $20.

31   Paid August wages, $12,000.

31   Received invoice for the cost of fuel used during August, $3,600.

31   Declared and paid a cash dividend, $5,000 (debit Retained Earnings).

REQUIRED

a. Set up running balance accounts for each item in the August 1 trial balance and enter the beginning balances. Also provide similar accounts for the following items: Service Fees Earned, Wages Expense, Advertising Expense, Rent Expense, Fuel Expense, Insurance Expense, and Interest Expense. Record the transactions for August in the accounts, using the dates given.

b. Prepare a trial balance at August 31, 1993.

c. Prepare an income statement for the month of August 1993.

d. Prepare a balance sheet at August 31, 1993. (*Note:* The month's net income increases Retained Earnings.)

EFFECT OF ERRORS ON TRIAL BALANCE
— OBJ. 6 —

2-34 The following trial balance for Ryan Janitorial Service, prepared after its first month of operations on January 31, 1993, does not balance because of a number of errors.

RYAN JANITORIAL SERVICE
TRIAL BALANCE
JANUARY 31, 1993

	Debit	Credit
Cash	$ 9,540	
Accounts Receivable	8,370	
Supplies	12,530	
Equipment	27,000	
Accounts Payable		$ 8,310
E. Ryan, Capital		36,650
E. Ryan, Drawing		1,800
Service Fees Earned		27,750
Wages Expense	9,500	
Insurance Expense	180	
Advertising Expense	840	
Rent Expense	1,200	
	$69,160	$74,510

1. Utilities Expense, with a $240 balance, was omitted from the trial balance.
2. Supplies, listed in the trial balance as $12,530, should be $12,350.
3. During the period, a cash payment of $170 was recorded as a $1,700 credit to Cash.
4. A debit of $210 to Accounts Payable was erroneously recorded as a credit to the account.
5. In determining the Accounts Receivable balance, a credit of $360 was overlooked.
6. The $1,800 balance of the E. Ryan, Drawing account is listed as a credit in the trial balance.
7. The balance of the Service Fees Earned account was overfooted (overadded) by $100.

REQUIRED

Prepare a corrected trial balance as of January 31, 1993.

ALTERNATE EXERCISES

NATURE OF ACCOUNTS, DEBIT AND CREDIT RULES
— OBJ. 2, 3 —

2-22A Refer to the schedule of account categories below. In the first blank column, enter *permanent* or *temporary* to describe the nature of an account in the category shown to the left. In the last three blank columns, enter *debit* or *credit* to describe the entry necessary to increase and decrease an account in the category shown to the left, and which side of the account represents the normal balance.

	Permanent or Temporary	Increase	Decrease	Normal Balance
Asset	_____	_____	_____	_____
Liability	_____	_____	_____	_____
Owner, Capital	_____	_____	_____	_____
Owner, Drawing	_____	_____	_____	_____
Revenue	_____	_____	_____	_____
Expense	_____	_____	_____	_____

NATURE OF ACCOUNTS, DEBIT AND CREDIT RULES
— OBJ. 2, 3 —

2-23A For each of the accounts listed below, indicate whether the account (1) is increased by a debit or a credit, and (2) is a permanent or temporary account.

Accounts Receivable	Notes Payable
Advertising Revenue	Retained Earnings
Building	Supplies
Capital Stock	Utilities Expense

TRANSACTION ANALYSIS
— OBJ. 4 —

2-24A   Match each of the following transactions of S. Lesch, a landscape architect, with the appropriate letters, indicating the debits and credits to be made. The correct answer for transaction 1 is given.

		Answer
(1)	Purchased supplies on account.	a, d
(2)	Paid interest on note payable.	
(3)	The owner withdrew cash from the business for personal use.	
(4)	Returned some defective supplies and received a reduction in the amount owed.	
(5)	Made payment to settle note payable.	
(6)	Received an invoice for monthly utilities used.	
(7)	Received payment in advance from client for work to be done next month.	
(8)	The owner contributed a number of landscape design books to the business.	

Effect of Transaction

a. Debit an asset	g. Debit owner's drawing
b. Credit an asset	h. Credit owner's drawing
c. Debit a liability	i. Debit a revenue
d. Credit a liability	j. Credit a revenue
e. Debit owner's capital	k. Debit an expense
f. Credit owner's capital	l. Credit an expense

TRANSACTION ANALYSIS
— OBJ. 4 —

2-25A   Make T accounts for the following accounts that appear in the general ledger of Daniel Kelly, an attorney: Cash; Accounts Receivable; Law Library; Office Equipment; Accounts Payable; D. Kelly, Capital; D. Kelly, Drawing; Legal Fees Earned; Salaries Expense; Rent Expense; and Utilities Expense. Record the following October transactions in the T accounts and key all entries with the number identifying the transaction. Determine the balance in each account.

(1) Kelly started his law practice by contributing $22,000 cash to the business on October 1, 1993.
(2) Purchased legal books on account, $9,200.
(3) Paid office rent for October, $600.
(4) Purchased office equipment for cash, $6,300.
(5) Billed clients for services rendered, $10,550.
(6) Made $5,000 payment on account for the books purchased in transaction 2.
(7) Paid legal assistant's salary, $2,400.
(8) Collected $7,400 from clients previously billed for services.
(9) Received invoice for October utilities, $150; it will be paid in November.
(10) Kelly withdrew $1,000 cash for personal use.

TRIAL BALANCE
— OBJ. 5 —

2-26A   After recording the transactions in the previous exercise, prepare a trial balance for Daniel Kelly, attorney, at October 31, 1993.

EFFECT OF ERRORS ON
TRIAL BALANCE
— OBJ. 6 —

2-27A   Indicate how each of the following errors would affect the trial balance totals. For each error, specify whether the debit or credit totals would be overstated, understated, or whether both totals would be unaffected (that is, they would remain in balance).

a. A $500 collection of an account receivable during the period was recorded as a $5,000 debit to Cash and a $5,000 credit to Accounts Receivable.
b. The normal balance of $7,600 in Supplies was listed in the trial balance at $6,700.

c. A $240 payment of an account payable during the period was recorded as a $240 debit to Accounts Receivable and a $240 credit to Cash.
d. The Notes Payable normal balance of $10,000 was listed in the trial balance at $1,000.
e. The Service Fees Earned normal balance of $38,000 was listed in both the debit and credit columns of the trial balance.

DETERMINATION OF OMITTED FINANCIAL STATEMENT DATA — OBJ. 7 —

2-28A In the five independent situations below, replace the question marks with the amounts that should appear in the statement of owner's equity.

Owner's Equity	A	B	C	D	E
Beginning Balance	$29,000	$63,000	$77,000	$?	$45,000
Capital Contributions	8,000	9,000	?	7,000	6,000
Net Income (Loss)	?	15,000	28,000	(8,000)	?
Capital Withdrawals	11,000	?	24,000	12,000	2,000
Ending Balance	$42,000	$80,000	$91,000	$54,000	$48,000

ALTERNATE PROBLEMS

TRANSACTION ANALYSIS AND TRIAL BALANCE — OBJ. 4, 5 —

2-29A Mary Aker opened a tax practice on June 1, 1993. The following accounts will be needed to record her transactions for June: Cash; Accounts Receivable; Office Supplies; Tax Library; Office Furniture and Fixtures; Notes Payable; Accounts Payable; M. Aker, Capital; M. Aker, Drawing; Professional Fees Earned; Rent Expense; Salaries Expense; Advertising Expense; Utilities Expense; and Interest Expense. The following transactions occurred in June:

(1) Aker opened a special checking account at the bank for the business, investing $15,000 in her practice.
(2) Purchased office furniture and fixtures for $8,800, paid $1,800 cash and gave a note payable for the balance.
(3) Purchased books and software for tax library on account, $4,500.
(4) Purchased office supplies for cash, $640.
(5) Paid rent for June, $700.
(6) Returned $500 of books with defective bindings. The return reduced the amount owed to the supplier.
(7) Billed clients for professional services rendered, $7,500.
(8) Paid $2,500 on account for the library items purchased in transaction 3.
(9) Collected $4,800 on account from clients billed in transaction 7.
(10) Paid June salaries, $2,700.
(11) Received invoice for June advertising, to be paid in July, $200.
(12) Aker withdrew $500 cash for personal use.
(13) Paid utilities for June, $190.
(14) Paid interest for June on note payable, $60.

REQUIRED

a. Record the above transactions in T accounts, and key entries with the numbers of the transactions.
b. Prepare a trial balance of the general ledger as of June 30, 1993.

TRIAL BALANCE AND FINANCIAL STATEMENTS — OBJ. 5, 7 —

2-30A The following account balances were taken (out of order) from the general ledger of R. Ladd, dog trainer, at January 31, 1993. Ladd trains dogs for competitive championship field trials. The firm's accounting year began on January 1. All accounts have normal balances.

Land	$10,500	Office Rent Expense	$ 400
Maintenance Expense	230	Supplies Expense	380
Supplies	820	Utilities Expense	100
Advertising Expense	180	Fees Earned	8,240
R. Ladd, Capital (January 1)	14,500	Accounts Receivable	4,100
Cash	3,650	Salaries Expense	2,240
Accounts Payable	460	R. Ladd, Drawing	600

REQUIRED

a. Prepare a trial balance in good form from the given data.
b. Prepare an income statement for the month of January 1993.
c. Prepare a statement of owner's equity for the month of January 1993.
d. Prepare a balance sheet at January 31, 1993.

Transaction Analysis and the Effect of Errors on Trial Balance
— Obj. 4, 5, 6 —

2-31A The following T accounts contain numbered entries for the May transactions of Flores Corporation, an architectural firm, which opened its offices on May 1, 1993:

CASH					ACCOUNTS PAYABLE			
(1)	30,000	(4)	1,000		(5)	240	(3)	1,840
(10)	4,200	(7)	5,050		(8)	1,400	(9)	190
		(8)	1,400					

ACCOUNTS RECEIVABLE					CAPITAL STOCK			
(6)	6,750	(10)	4,200				(1)	30,000

SUPPLIES					PROFESSIONAL FEES EARNED			
(3)	1,840	(5)	240				(6)	6,750

OFFICE EQUIPMENT			RENT EXPENSE		
(2)	6,000		(4)	1,000	

NOTES PAYABLE			UTILITIES EXPENSE		
	(2)	6,000	(9)	190	

SALARIES EXPENSE		
(7)	5,050	

REQUIRED

a. Give a reasonable description of each of the 10 numbered transactions entered in the above accounts. Example: (1) Flores Corporation issued capital stock for cash, $30,000.

b. The following trial balance, taken for Flores Corporation on May 31, contains several errors. Itemize the errors, and indicate the correct totals for the trial balance.

FLORES CORPORATION
TRIAL BALANCE
MAY 31, 1993

	Debit	Credit
Cash	$62,750	
Accounts Receivable	2,550	
Supplies	1,600	
Office Equipment		$ 6,000
Notes Payable		60,000
Accounts Payable		390
Capital Stock		3,000
Professional Fees Earned		6,570
Rent Expense	1,000	
Utilities Expense	190	
Salaries Expense	5,050	
	$73,140	$75,960

Transaction Analysis, Trial Balance, and Financial Statements
— Obj. 4, 5, 7 —

2-32A Angela Mehl operates the Mehl Dance Studio. On June 1, 1993, her general ledger contained the following information:

Cash	$ 5,600	Notes Payable	$ 2,000
Accounts Receivable	4,420	Accounts Payable	450
		A. Mehl, Capital	7,570
	$10,020		$10,020

The following transactions occurred in June:

June   2   Paid June rent for practice and performance studio, $925.
        3   Paid June piano rental, $85 (Rent Expense).
        6   Collected $3,820 from students on account.
       10   Borrowed $1,000 and signed a promissory note payable due in six months.
       15   Billed students for June instructional fees, $4,600.
       18   Paid interest for June on notes payable, $20.
       20   Paid $225 for advertising ballet performances.
       21   Paid costume rental, $300 (Rent Expense).
       25   Collected $2,300 admission fees from ballet performances given today.
       27   Paid $450 owed on account.
       30   Received invoice for June utilities, to be paid in July, $230.
       30   Mehl withdrew $550 for personal expenses.
       30   Purchased piano for $4,700 cash, to be used in business starting in July.

REQUIRED

a. Set up running balance accounts for the general ledger accounts with June 1 balances and enter the beginning balances. Also provide the following accounts: Piano; A. Mehl, Drawing; Instructional Fees Earned; Performance Revenue; Rent Expense; Utilities Expense; Advertising Expense; and Interest Expense. Record the listed transactions in the accounts.
b. Prepare a trial balance at June 30, 1993.
c. Prepare an income statement for the month of June 1993.
d. Prepare a statement of owner's equity for the month of June 1993.
e. Prepare a balance sheet as of June 30, 1993.

TRANSACTION ANALYSIS, TRIAL BALANCE, AND FINANCIAL STATEMENTS — OBJ. 4, 5, 7 —

2-33A   On December 1, 1993, a group of individuals formed a corporation to establish the *Beeper*, a neighborhood weekly newspaper featuring want ads of individuals and advertising of local firms. The free paper will be mailed to about 8,000 local residents; revenue will be generated from advertising and want ads. The December transactions are summarized below:

Dec.   1   Sold capital stock of Beeper, Inc., for cash, $35,000.
        2   Paid December rent on furnished office, $950.
        3   Purchased for $800, on account, T-shirts displaying company logo. The T-shirts were distributed at a grand opening held today.
        5   Paid to creditor on account, $800.
        8   Collected want ad revenue in cash, $2,300.
       12   Paid post office for cost of bulk mailing, $820.
       14   Billed various firms for advertising in first two issues of the newspaper, $5,600.
       15   Paid Acme Courier Service for transporting newspapers to post office, $70.
       16   Paid for printing newspaper, $2,850.
       18   Collected want ad revenue in cash, $2,420.
       31   Received invoice for December utilities, to be paid in January, $250.
       31   Paid for printing newspaper, $2,850.
       31   Paid December salaries, $3,800.
       31   Billed various firms for advertising in two issues of the newspaper, $6,670.
       31   Paid post office for cost of bulk mailing, $860.
       31   Paid Acme Courier Service for transporting newspapers to post office, $70.
       31   Collected $5,200 on accounts receivable.
       31   Purchased fax machine for office in exchange for a six-month note payable, $1,200.

REQUIRED

a. Set up running balance accounts for the following: Cash, Accounts Receivable, Office Equipment, Notes Payable, Accounts Payable, Capital Stock, Advertising Revenue, Want Ad Revenue, Printing Expense, Advertising Expense, Utilities Expense, Salaries Expense, Rent Expense, and Delivery Expense. Record the foregoing transactions in the accounts.

b. Take a trial balance at December 31, 1993.

c. Prepare an income statement for the month of December 1993.

d. Prepare a balance sheet as of December 31, 1993. (*Note:* In this problem, the net income for December becomes the amount of retained earnings at December 31, 1993.)

EFFECT OF ERRORS ON TRIAL BALANCE — OBJ. 6 —

2-34A The following trial balance for Allen Tree Service, prepared after its first month of operations on May 31, 1993, does not balance.

ALLEN TREE SERVICE
TRIAL BALANCE
MAY 31, 1993

	Debit	Credit
Cash	$ 3,110	
Accounts Receivable	9,100	
Supplies	7,620	
Trucks	14,800	
Equipment	10,350	
Accounts Payable		$ 4,380
D. Allen, Capital		20,000
D. Allen, Drawing		1,000
Service Fees Earned		19,470
Wages Expense		6,100
Rent Expense	700	
Advertising Expense	600	
Utilities Expense	220	
	$46,500	$50,950

In reviewing the general ledger, you discover the following:

1. All general ledger accounts have normal balances.

2. The Cash account was underfooted (underadded) by $100.

3. There were no transpositions, slides, or other arithmetic errors in transferring numbers from the general ledger to the trial balance.

4. Two accounts—Fuel Expense with a $150 balance and Notes Payable with a $10,000 balance—were omitted from the trial balance.

REQUIRED

Prepare a corrected trial balance as of May 31, 1993.

CASES

Business Decision Case

Sarah Penney operates the Wildlife Picture Gallery, selling original art and signed prints received on consignment (rather than purchased) from recognized wildlife artists throughout the country. The firm receives a 30% commission on all art sold and remits 70% of the sales price to the artists. All art is sold on a strictly cash basis.

Sarah began the business on March 1, 1993. She received a $10,000 loan from a relative to help her get started in business. Sarah signed a note agreeing to pay the loan back in one year. No interest is being charged on the loan, but the relative does want to receive a set of financial statements each month. On April 1, 1993, Sarah asks for your help in preparing the statements for the first month.

Sarah has carefully kept the firm's checking account up to date and provides you with the following complete listing of the cash receipts and disbursements for March 1993:

Cash Receipts

Original investment by Sarah Penney	$ 7,500	
Loan from relative	10,000	
Sales of art	90,000	
Total cash receipts		$107,500

Cash Disbursements

Payments to artists for sales made	$52,500	
Payment of March rent for gallery space	800	
Payment of March wages to staff	5,400	
Payment of airfare for personal vacation of Sarah Penney (vacation will be taken in April)	600	
Total cash disbursements		59,300
Cash balance, March 31, 1993		$ 48,200

Sarah also gives you the following documents she has received:

1. A $310 invoice for March utilities; payment is due by April 15, 1993.

2. A $1,000 invoice from Careful Express for the shipping of the artwork sold during March; payment is due by April 10, 1993.

3. The one-year lease she signed for the gallery space; as an incentive to sign the lease, the landlord reduced the first month's rent by 50%; the monthly rent starting in April is $1,600.

In your discussions with Sarah, she tells you that she has been so busy that she is behind in sending artists their share of the sales proceeds. She plans to catch up within the next week.

REQUIRED

From the above information, prepare the following financial statements for Wildlife Picture Gallery: (a) income statement for the month of March 1993; (b) statement of owner's equity for the month of March 1993; and (c) balance sheet as of March 31, 1993. To obtain the data needed, you may wish to use T accounts to construct the company's accounts.

Analytical Application Case

PEPSICO, INC., is in the business of soft drinks, snack foods, and restaurants. Among its well-known products and restaurants are Pepsi-Cola, FRITO-LAY, PIZZA HUT, and TACO BELL. Selected financial data for PepsiCo, Inc., for four recent years are shown below (amounts in millions; Year 4 is the most recent year).

	Year 4	Year 3	Year 2	Year 1
Year-end Data				
Assets	$17,143.4	$15,126.7	$11,135.3	$9,022.7
Liabilities	12,239.2	11,235.6	7,974.3	6,514.1
Stockholders' Equity	4,904.2	3,891.1	3,161.0	2,508.6
Annual Data				
Cash Provided by Operating Activities	2,110.0	1,885.9	1,894.5	1,334.5

REQUIRED

a. Compute the operating cash flow to total liabilities ratio for years 2, 3, and 4.
b. Has this ratio improved, worsened, or remained about the same over the three-year period (years 2–4)? Assume you are evaluating whether or not to lend PepsiCo, Inc. money. Does the information revealed by the operating cash flow to total liabilities ratio over the three-year period influence your decision positively or negatively?

Ethics Case

Andy Frame and his supervisor are sent on an out-of-town assignment by their employer. At the supervisor's suggestion, they stay at the Spartan Inn (across the street from the Luxury Inn). After three days of work, they settle their lodging bills and leave. On the return trip, the supervisor gives Andy what appears to be a copy of a receipt from the Luxury Inn for three nights of lodging. Actually, the supervisor indicates that he prepared the Luxury Inn receipt on his office computer and plans to complete his expense reimbursement request using the higher lodging costs from the Luxury Inn.

REQUIRED

What are the ethical considerations that Andy faces when he prepares his expense reimbursement request?

Why do firms make end-of-period accounting adjustments?

Accrual accounting records revenues when earned and expenses when incurred. ■ Because these amounts are not necessarily tied to cash receipts and payments, adjustments to revenues and expenses may be necessary at year-end so that they reflect the proper amounts for the period. ■ Adjustments apply to all types of entities, whether it be a service firm, a retailer, a manufacturer, or a professional sports organization like the Chicago Bulls.

3

THE ACCOUNTING CYCLE

he double-entry accounting system provides a basic framework for the analysis of business activities. Now we wish to go into greater detail about the accounting procedures used to account for the operations of a business during a specific period. The accounting procedures of most businesses involve certain basic steps that are accomplished in a given order. This sequence of operations is known as the **accounting cycle.** We will divide the accounting cycle into nine steps. In this chapter we will explain the first five steps and in the next chapter we will discuss the remaining four steps.

THE FIRST FIVE STEPS IN THE ACCOUNTING CYCLE

OBJECTIVE ❶ IDENTIFY *the first five steps in the accounting cycle.*

The first five steps in the accounting cycle are listed below.

1. Analyze transactions from source documents.
2. Record transactions in a journal.
3. Post journal entries to general ledger accounts.
4. Prepare a trial balance.
5. Adjust the general ledger accounts.

These initial steps in the accounting cycle do not occur with equal frequency. Usually, analyzing, journalizing, and posting (steps 1–3) take place regularly throughout each operating period. At a minimum, a trial balance is prepared (step 4) whenever the accounts are to be adjusted (step 5). The adjustments occur only when management requires financial statements, usually at monthly or quarterly intervals, but at least annually.

The annual accounting period adopted by a business firm is known as its **fiscal year.** Business firms whose fiscal year ends on December 31 are said to be on a **calendar-year** basis. Many firms prefer to have their accounting year coincide with their "natural" business year; that is, the fiscal year ends when business is slow and inventory quantities are small and easy to count. Year-end accounting procedures are most efficiently accomplished at this time. For example, most department stores choose a fiscal year ending on the last day of January or February, when their inventories are depleted from the normally heavy holiday sales and from post-holiday clearance sales.

Exhibit 3-1 shows the percentage of companies (of 600 industrial and merchandising firms recently surveyed) having fiscal years ending during the various months of the year. Note that ending the fiscal year in December is clearly most popular, but 40% of the companies have fiscal years ending in some month other than December.

We will use an example to help explain the various steps in the accounting cycle. Our example will be the December 1993 transactions of Landen TV Service, a repair business begun by Mark Landen on December 1, 1993. Landen TV Service's fiscal year-end will be December 31, so the first accounting period will be only one month long.

ANALYZING TRANSACTIONS FROM SOURCE DOCUMENTS

Source documents are printed or written forms that are generated when the firm engages in business transactions. Even a brief source document usually specifies the dollar amounts involved, the date of the transaction, and possibly the party dealing with the firm. Some examples of source documents are (1) a sales invoice showing evidence of a purchase of supplies on account, (2) a bank check indicating payment

ABOUT THOSE SOURCE DOCUMENTS...?

Source documents underlie the recording of accounting transactions and, thus, are an integral part of the accounting process. The significance of source documents has not been overlooked by various embezzlers and swindlers who try to cover up their schemes with false accounting entries. Fictitious source documents are created to support the fake entries. A prominent example is the fraud perpetrated upon McKesson & Robbins, a pharmaceutical company, by Philip Musica and his three brothers during the period 1927–1938.

Philip Musica, alias William Johnson alias Frank D. Costa alias Dr. F. Donald Coster, bought control of McKesson & Robbins in 1926 and immediately assumed the presidency. Although convicted twice in earlier years (on charges of bribery and embezzlement), Musica had successfully managed to hide his unsavory past by 1926. In 1927, Musica organized McKesson & Robbins, Ltd., a Canadian subsidiary that ostensibly would buy and sell crude drugs outside the United States—*ostensibly*, because the entire operation was fictitious.

Musica put himself in charge of the Canadian subsidiary's activities. Within McKesson & Robbins, he was aided by his brothers George (assistant treasurer) and Robert (shipping department head). Both brothers used aliases. Another brother, Arthur (alias George Vernard), headed up two fictitious outside firms—W. W. Smith & Co., a trading agent for the Canadian subsidiary, and Manning & Co., a private banking firm. With this arrangement, Musica was ready to siphon funds from the parent McKesson & Robbins company to pay for the "purchase" of crude drugs by the Canadian subsidiary and to pay fees to W. W. Smith & Co.

According to the accounting records and source documents, the Canadian subsidiary traded millions of dollars' worth of crude drugs throughout the world. Yet no crude drugs were actually traded. About all that really existed in the subsidiary's Montreal location were a rented office, five rented (and empty) warehouses, and a vacant lot.

An elaborate facade of false documents concealed the fraud. Musica hired a printer to print letterheads, invoices, and receipts bearing the names of corporations all over the world. A secretary working with seven different typewriters typed all correspondence, trading orders, and inventory statements (she believed she was doing important work for an international business network). The Montreal locations were essentially mail drops—secretaries there received large envelopes sent by Arthur and remailed the smaller envelopes they contained to W. W. Smith & Co. The smaller envelopes, of course, contained forged documents. W. W. Smith & Co. provided McKesson & Robbins with documentation showing sales made, deliveries completed, payments received from customers, and deposits made in the Manning bank. Each month Manning & Co. sent the accounting department a detailed statement showing bills paid, deposits received from sales, and itemized inventories of the crude drugs in the warehouses.

By the end of 1937, the Canadian subsidiary showed accounts receivable and inventories of crude drugs totaling $18,000,000—all fictitious. Through the years, McKesson & Robbins' auditors did not detect the fraud. They never visited the Canadian warehouses, relying instead on statements of drugs on hand provided by the warehouses and carefully checking these statements against the source documents in McKesson & Robbins' headquarters. These forged documents, however, did contain some strange data that went unnoticed by the auditors. Some drug quantities on hand, for example, would supply the entire United States for years, and some shipping orders moved drugs from South America to Australia by truck.

The fraud was finally uncovered in 1938 by a company officer who became suspicious when he noted that the Canadian crude drug inventories were not insured. This fraud had a significant impact on auditing procedures. Shortly after the fraud was detected, the physical observation of inventory counts and the direct confirmation of receivables with customers became standard audit techniques—techniques that continue to this day.*

*For a complete story of Philip Musica and the McKesson & Robbins fraud, see Charles Keats, *Magnificent Masquerade: The Strange Case of Dr. Coster and Mr. Musica* (New York: Funk & Wagnalls Company, Inc., 1964).

EXHIBIT 3—1	FREQUENCY OF FISCAL YEAR-END FOR 600 COMPANIES

Month of Fiscal Year-End	Percentage of Companies
January	4%
February	2
March	3
April	1
May	2
June	10
July	3
August	3
September	6
October	3
November	3
December	60
Total	100%

SOURCE: Based on data in American Institute of Certified Public Accountants, *Accounting Trends and Techniques—1990.*

Step 1: Analyze Transactions from Source Documents

OBJECTIVE ② EXPLAIN *the role of source documents in transaction analysis.*

of an obligation, (3) a deposit slip showing the amount of funds turned over to the bank, (4) a cash receipt indicating funds received from a customer, and (5) a cash register tape listing a day's over-the-counter sales to customers.

Exhibit 3-2 lists the December transactions of Landen TV Service, together with their related source documents. Ordinarily, source documents or business papers such as those listed in Exhibit 3-2 will alert the accountant to the need for an entry in the records. Usually the accountant is able to analyze the transaction by examining the documents to determine the appropriate accounts to be debited and credited. For example, in transaction 2, the seller's invoice or bill of sale would probably indicate both the cost of the supplies and parts and the down payment. The check copy (most businesses keep a copy of checks issued) would further confirm the amount paid, and the accountant would debit Supplies and Parts for $950, credit Cash for $250, and credit Accounts Payable for $700.

Many transactions affect several accounting periods, and the accounting for these transactions after their initial occurrence may require the accountant to refer back to previously received documents and the accounting records themselves. Examples from Exhibit 3-2 include transaction 3, where the rent payment covers six months; transaction 4, where the truck will be useful for several years and the note payable extends two years; transaction 5, where the contract runs for four months; and transaction 6, where the contract runs for one year. To ensure the proper analysis in accounting for these transactions later on, the accountant may refer back to the original source documents or review the entry made at the time of the initial transaction. We illustrate the subsequent accounting for the above transactions later in this chapter.

JOURNALIZING

Step 2: Record Transactions in a Journal

For simplicity, the entries used to this point have been made directly in the general ledger accounts. This method would not prove feasible, however, for even a modest-sized business. For instance, suppose an owner wished to investigate a $1,000 credit in the Cash account. If entries were actually recorded directly in the general ledger, the purpose of the $1,000 expenditure could be difficult to determine. The owner might be forced to search through the entire general ledger to discover the offsetting

	EXHIBIT 3—2		DECEMBER, 1993, TRANSACTIONS OF LANDEN TV SERVICE

Transaction	Date	Brief Description	Related Source Documents
(1)	Dec. 1	Mark Landen deposited $10,000 in the firm's bank account to start the business.	Bank deposit slip
(2)	1	Purchased supplies and parts for $950; paid $250 down; remainder to be paid in 60 days.	Seller's invoice, bank check
(3)	1	Paid rent for six months, December–May, $3,600.	Bank check, lease contract
(4)	1	Purchased truck for $10,800 and signed two-year note payable for $10,800. Annual interest at 10% is due each November 30.	Seller's invoice, promissory note
(5)	2	Signed contract to perform service work for a local TV dealer for four months, December–March, at $250 per month. Received $1,000 in advance.	Contract, dealer's check
(6)	2	Signed one-year contract with cable TV company to provide Landen TV's customers with cable TV promotional literature. For distributing the literature, Landen TV will receive a $50 monthly commission, payable at the end of every three months. The first $150 commission will be paid February 28, 1994.	Contract
(7)	10	Performed TV service for various customers and received $650 cash.	Duplicates of cash receipt forms
(8)	13	Billed various customers for TV service rendered on account, $1,580.	Bills to customers
(9)	13	Paid employee's wages for first two weeks of December, $540.	Bank check
(10)	19	Received $800 on account from customers.	Customers' checks
(11)	21	Performed TV service for various customers and received $520 cash.	Duplicates of cash receipt forms
(12)	27	Paid employee's wages for second two weeks of December, $540.	Bank check
(13)	29	Withdrew $800 cash for personal use.	Bank check
(14)	30	Paid December truck expenses (gas and oil), $160.	Seller's invoice, bank check
(15)	31	Billed various customers for TV service rendered on account, $2,700.	Bills to customers

OBJECTIVE ❸ DESCRIBE *the general journal and the process of journalizing transactions.*

debit of $1,000. Consequently, accounting records include a journal, which shows the total effect of a business transaction in one location.

A **journal**, or *book of original entry*, is a tabular record in which business activities are analyzed in terms of debits and credits and recorded in chronological order before they are entered in the general ledger. A journal, therefore, organizes information by date rather than by account. The complete analysis for one transaction is shown in a journal before the next transaction analysis is recorded. The word *journalize* means to record a transaction in a journal.

CHART OF ACCOUNTS

A chart of accounts is usually prepared in order to facilitate the analysis of activities and the formulation of journal entries. The **chart of accounts** is a list of the titles and numbers of all accounts found in the general ledger. The account titles should be grouped by, and in order of, the five major sections of the general ledger (assets, liabilities, owners' equity, revenues, and expenses). Exhibit 3-3 shows a chart of accounts for the Landen TV Service, indicating the account numbers that will now be used.

The method of assigning account numbers usually ensures that the numbers of all the accounts in a major section of the general ledger start with the same digit. In

EXHIBIT 3—3	LANDEN TV SERVICE CHART OF ACCOUNTS

Assets

11 Cash
12 Accounts Receivable
13 Commissions Receivable
14 Supplies and Parts
15 Prepaid Rent
18 Truck
19 Accumulated Depreciation—Truck

Liabilities

21 Accounts Payable
22 Interest Payable
23 Wages Payable
24 Unearned Service Fees
25 Long-term Notes Payable

Owner's Equity

31 M. Landen, Capital
32 M. Landen, Drawing
33 Income Summary

Revenues

41 Service Fees Earned
42 Commissions Earned

Expenses

51 Rent Expense
52 Wages Expense
53 Supplies and Parts Expense
54 Truck Expense
55 Depreciation Expense—Truck
56 Interest Expense

Exhibit 3-3, all asset accounts begin with 1, liabilities with 2, and so on. Complicated accounting systems may use three- or four-digit account numbers and may even employ suffixes to designate various branches, departments, or divisions. A numbering system permits easy reference to accounts even if the account title contains several words. For example, the account Supplies and Parts Expense might be referred to simply as account No. 53.

GENERAL JOURNAL   The **general journal** is a journal with enough flexibility so that any type of business transaction may be recorded in it. (We discuss other journals later in the text.) Exhibit 3-4 shows the first two transactions from Exhibit 3-2 as they would be recorded in Landen TV Service's general journal. Most journal entries are based on information appearing on a source document resulting from a transaction between the business and an outside party.

The procedure for recording entries in the general journal is as follows:

1 Indicate the year, month, and date of the entry. Usually the year and month are rewritten only at the top of each page of the journal or at the point where they change.

2 Enter titles of the accounts affected in the description column. Accounts to receive debits are entered close to the left margin and are traditionally recorded first. Accounts to receive credits are then recorded, indented slightly.

3 Place the appropriate money amounts in the left (debit) and right (credit) money columns.

4 Write an explanation of the transaction below the account titles. The explanation should be as brief as possible, disclosing all the information necessary to understand the event being recorded.

Each transaction entered in the journal should be stated in terms of equal dollar amounts of debits and credits. The account titles cited in the description column should correspond to those used for the related general ledger accounts. To separate clearly the various entries, we leave a line blank between entries. We explain the use

EXHIBIT 3—4	GENERAL JOURNAL				PAGE 1

Date	Description	Post. Ref.	Debit	Credit
1993 Dec. 1 **1**	Cash **2**		10,000	**3**
	M. Landen, Capital			10,000
	Owner invested cash to start business. **4**			
1	Supplies and Parts		950	
	Cash			250
	Accounts Payable			700
	Purchased supplies and parts for $950.			
	Terms: $250 down, remainder due in 60 days.			

of the column headed Post.Ref. (posting reference) later in step 3 of the accounting cycle.

COMPOUND JOURNAL ENTRIES

A journal entry that involves more than just two accounts is called a **compound journal entry.** The second journal entry in Exhibit 3-4 is an example of a compound journal entry involving three accounts. The debit of $950 to Supplies and Parts is offset by credits of $250 to Cash and $700 to Accounts Payable. Any number of accounts may appear in a compound entry; but, regardless of how many accounts are used, the total of the debit amounts must always equal the total of the credit amounts.

CORRECTION OF JOURNAL ERRORS

Certain procedures should be followed when errors are found in journal entries. Errors should not be erased, because erasures completely remove the original recording. As you might imagine, the acceptance of erasures might allow someone to falsify accounting records; consequently, other procedures are used.

If an erroneous journal entry has not been transferred to the general ledger, a single line is drawn through the erroneous amount or account title, and the correction is entered on the same line just above the error. Often the person correcting the entry must place his or her initials near the correction. This facilitates any subsequent inquiry about the nature of or reason for the correction. Once an erroneous journal entry has been transferred to the ledger accounts, both records contain the error. The recommended procedures for correcting this situation are discussed in step 3.

POSTING

Step 3: Post Journal Entries to General Ledger Accounts

OBJECTIVE 4 EXPLAIN *the process of posting information from the general journal to the general ledger accounts.*

After transactions have been journalized, the next step in the accounting cycle is to transcribe the debits and credits in each journal entry to the appropriate general ledger accounts. This transcribing process is called **posting** to the general ledger. Thus, data from a journal that stresses the total effect of particular transactions (such as the collection of accounts receivable) are transcribed to a ledger that stresses the total effect of many business transactions on a particular business variable (such as cash, accounts receivable, and so on). This latter type of data is specifically needed for the preparation of financial statements.

When records are kept by hand, posting from the general journal may be done daily, every few days, or at the end of each month. Journalizing and posting often occur simultaneously when the record-keeping process is automated.

POSTING REFERENCES   It is important to be able to trace any entry appearing in a ledger account to the journal location from which it was posted. Consequently, accounting records use a system of references. Both the general journal and ledger accounts have **posting reference** columns. Entries in the posting reference column of the general journal indicate the account to which the related debit or credit has been posted. Posting references appearing in ledger accounts identify the journal location from which the related entry was posted. The posting references in the general journal and ledger accounts are entered when the journal entries are posted to the ledger accounts.

To keep accounting records uncluttered, we make posting references simple. For example, the posting reference of the general journal might be GJ or simply J. Thus, a posting reference of J9 appearing on the line with a $1,000 debit entry in the Cash account means that the ninth page of the general journal contains the entire entry in which the $1,000 debit to Cash appears. Every entry appearing in a ledger account should have a related posting reference. Posting references appearing in the journal are usually the numbers that have been assigned to the general ledger accounts.

ILLUSTRATION OF POSTING   Exhibit 3-5 diagrams the posting of Landen TV Service's first transaction from the general journal to the ledger accounts. Each debit entry and each credit entry are posted as follows:

1 The date (year, month, and day) is entered in the appropriate account. Note that this is the date of the journal entry, not necessarily the date of the actual posting. As with journals, the year and month are restated only at the top of a new account page or at the point where they change.

2 The amount is entered in the account as a debit or a credit, as indicated in the journal's money columns, and the new balance is calculated.

3 The posting reference from the journal (both symbol and page number) is placed in the posting reference column of the ledger account.

4 The account number is placed in the posting reference column of the journal.

Exhibit 3-6 (on pages 82–83) shows the general journal for Landen TV Service with all of the December transactions from Exhibit 3-2 journalized and posted. Bear in mind that the account numbers in the posting reference column are not entered when the journal entry is recorded; they are inserted when the entry is posted. You should review each transaction in the illustration for (1) the nature of the transaction and (2) the related journal entry. We comment on transactions 3, 5, and 6 below.

Transaction 3 is the payment of rent for six months; the journal entry debits Prepaid Rent for $3,600 and credits Cash for $3,600. Prepaid Rent is an asset account; it is debited because the time period covered by the rental payment extends beyond the current accounting period (which is the month of December). Asset accounts should be debited when payments are made in advance for services to be received over more than just the current accounting period. Other examples include the payment in advance of insurance premiums for coverage that extends beyond the current accounting period (debit Prepaid Insurance) and the payment in advance for advertising services that extend beyond the current period (debit Prepaid Advertising).

Transactions 5 and 6 relate to contracts entered into by Landen TV Service. The mere signing of a contract does not normally require a journal entry, because a contract is just an agreement by each party to do something, and neither party has performed yet. This is the case in transaction 6; no entry is made in the general journal because the cable TV company has not paid anything yet, and Landen TV Service has not yet distributed any promotional literature. In transaction 5, however, Landen TV Service receives payment in advance for four months of services. The receipt of this payment requires a journal entry debiting Cash for $1,000 and crediting Unearned Service Fees for $1,000. Unearned Service Fees is a liability account and represents the obligation of Landen TV Service to provide four months of service for which payment has already been received.

EXHIBIT 3—5	DIAGRAMS OF POSTING TO LEDGER ACCOUNTS

Step 1: Posting the Debit Entry

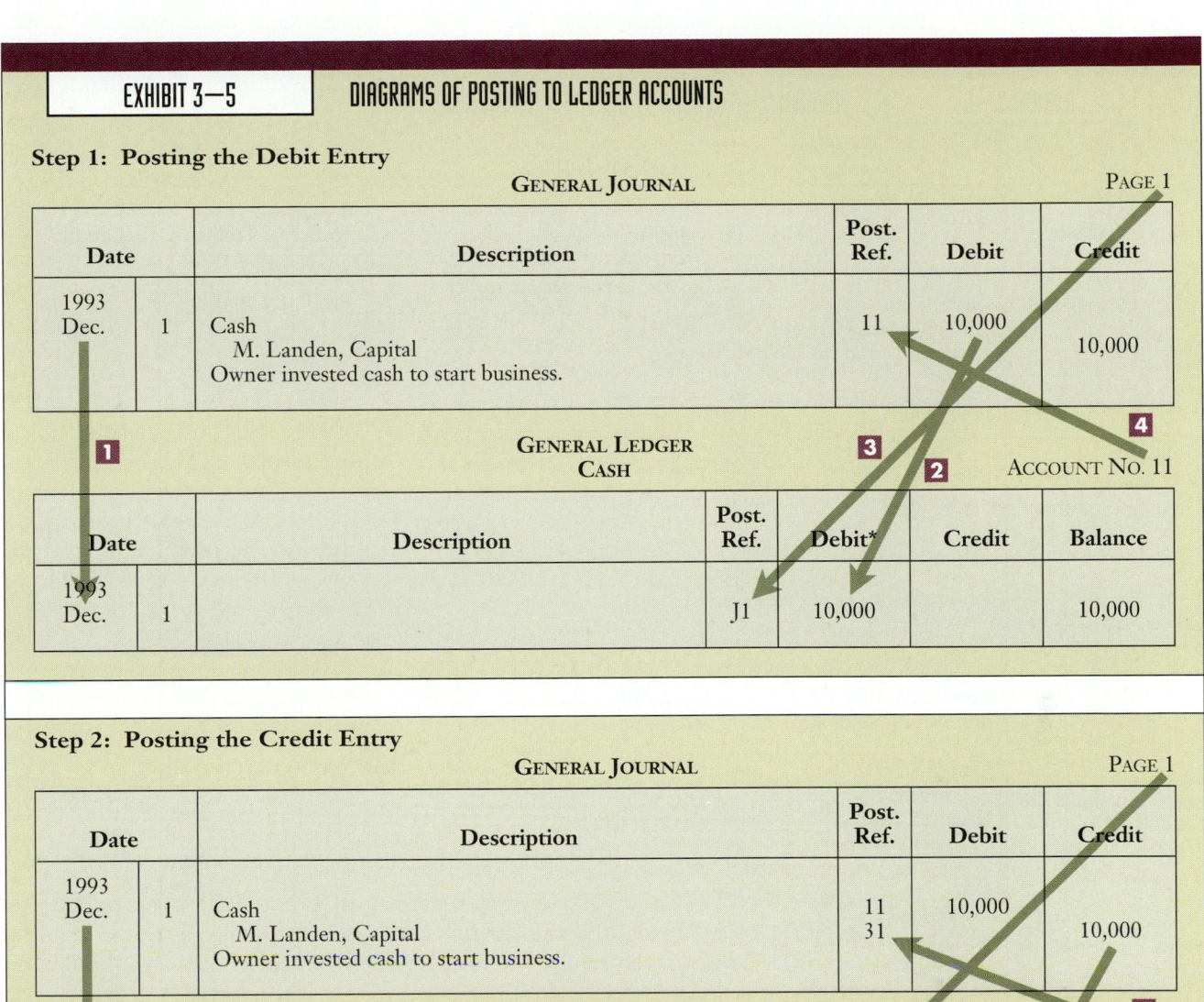

GENERAL JOURNAL   PAGE 1

Date	Description	Post. Ref.	Debit	Credit
1993 Dec. 1	Cash	11	10,000	
	M. Landen, Capital			10,000
	Owner invested cash to start business.			

GENERAL LEDGER
CASH   ACCOUNT No. 11

Date	Description	Post. Ref.	Debit*	Credit	Balance
1993 Dec. 1		J1	10,000		10,000

Step 2: Posting the Credit Entry

GENERAL JOURNAL   PAGE 1

Date	Description	Post. Ref.	Debit	Credit
1993 Dec. 1	Cash	11	10,000	
	M. Landen, Capital	31		10,000
	Owner invested cash to start business.			

GENERAL LEDGER
M. LANDEN, CAPITAL   ACCOUNT No. 31

Date	Description	Post. Ref.	Debit	Credit*	Balance
1993 Dec. 1		J1		10,000	10,000

*Throughout this chapter, the asterisk indicates the column that designates the normal balance.

Exhibit 3-7 (on page 84) presents the general ledger accounts of Landen TV Service that have received the postings from the journal entries in Exhibit 3-6. You should trace several of the postings from the general journal to these ledger accounts. Note the references J1 and J2 in the posting reference columns of the ledger accounts. These refer to the page numbers used in the general journal illustrated in Exhibit 3-6.

CORRECTING ERRONEOUS POSTINGS

Even the most carefully kept accounts will occasionally contain posting errors. An error involving only the wrong amount being posted may be corrected by drawing a line through the incorrect amount, entering the correct amount above, and initialing the correction. When an amount has been posted to the wrong account, however,

EXHIBIT 3—6	JOURNALIZING LANDEN TV SERVICE TRANSACTIONS

GENERAL JOURNAL   PAGE 1

Date		Description	Post. Ref.	Debit	Credit
1993 Dec.	1	Cash	11	10,000	
		M. Landen, Capital	31		10,000
		Owner invested cash to start business.			
	1	Supplies and Parts	14	950	
		Cash	11		250
		Accounts Payable	21		700
		Purchased supplies and parts for $950.			
		Terms: $250 down, remainder due in 60 days.			
	1	Prepaid Rent	15	3,600	
		Cash	11		3,600
		Paid rent for December–May.			
	1	Truck	18	10,800	
		Long-term Notes Payable	25		10,800
		Purchased truck for two-year note payable; annual interest rate is 10%.			
	2	Cash	11	1,000	
		Unearned Service Fees	24		1,000
		Received advance on four-month contract at $250 per month.			
	10	Cash	11	650	
		Service Fees Earned	41		650
		Services rendered for cash.			
	13	Accounts Receivable	12	1,580	
		Service Fees Earned	41		1,580
		Services rendered on account.			
	13	Wages Expense	52	540	
		Cash	11		540
		Paid wages for first two weeks of December.			
	19	Cash	11	800	
		Accounts Receivable	12		800
		Received $800 on account from credit customers.			

the correction should be made with a journal entry. Let us assume that Landen TV Service paid $100 cash for gas and oil used in the truck and that the accountant erroneously debited the amount to Supplies and Parts instead of to Truck Expense. The following entry in the general journal corrects the error by transferring the debit to the correct account:

Truck Expense	100	
Supplies and Parts		100
To correct entry for gas and oil payment.		

EXHIBIT 3–6 [Continued]

GENERAL JOURNAL   PAGE 2

Date		Description	Post. Ref.	Debit	Credit
1993 Dec.	21	Cash	11	520	
		Service Fees Earned	41		520
		Services rendered for cash.			
	27	Wages Expense	52	540	
		Cash	11		540
		Paid wages for second two weeks of December.			
	29	M. Landen, Drawing	32	800	
		Cash	11		800
		Withdrew $800 for personal use.			
	30	Truck Expense	54	160	
		Cash	11		160
		Gas and oil for December.			
	31	Accounts Receivable	12	2,700	
		Service Fees Earned	41		2,700
		Services rendered on account.			

TRIAL BALANCE

Step 4: Prepare a Trial Balance

OBJECTIVE 5 REVIEW *the nature and format of a trial balance.*

After the journal entries have been posted to the general ledger accounts, a trial balance is prepared of all the general ledger accounts that show a balance. As noted earlier, the trial balance lists the general ledger accounts with their respective debit or credit balances. The debit balances and credit balances are each totaled to confirm their equality (that is, to confirm that the general ledger is "in balance"). We want to be sure the general ledger is in balance before we start to adjust the accounts (the next step in the accounting cycle). Because this trial balance shows the account balances before any adjustments have been made, it is sometimes called an **unadjusted trial balance.**

Because the trial balance is prepared as of a particular date, the heading for the trial balance should show that date. The trial balance of the Landen TV Service at December 31 is shown in Exhibit 3-8 (on page 85). Showing all the general ledger account balances in one place, as is done in this trial balance, makes it easier to review the accounts and determine which account balances need to be adjusted.

ADJUSTMENTS

Step 5: Adjust the General Ledger Accounts

It is important that amounts appearing in financial statements be properly stated. As introduced in an earlier chapter, the *matching concept* used in accrual accounting states that net income is determined by linking, or matching, expenses incurred with the related revenues earned. Clearly, if the income statement is to portray net income based on accrual accounting, all revenues *earned* and all expenses *incurred* during the period must be shown. Many of the transactions reflected in the accounting records through the first four steps in the accounting cycle affect the net income of more than one period. Other events, not yet recorded in the accounts, affect the current

EXHIBIT 3—7   **GENERAL LEDGER FOR LANDEN TV SERVICE**

CASH   ACCOUNT NO. 11

Date	Description	Post. Ref.	Debit*	Credit	Balance
1993 Dec. 1		J1	10,000		10,000
1		J1		250	9,750
1		J1		3,600	6,150
2		J1	1,000		7,150
10		J1	650		7,800
13		J1		540	7,260
19		J1	800		8,060
21		J2	520		8,580
27		J2		540	8,040
29		J2		800	7,240
30		J2		160	7,080

ACCOUNTS RECEIVABLE   ACCOUNT NO. 12

Date	Description	Post. Ref.	Debit*	Credit	Balance
1993 Dec. 13		J1	1,580		1,580
19		J1		800	780
31		J2	2,700		3,480

SUPPLIES AND PARTS   ACCOUNT NO. 14

Date	Description	Post. Ref.	Debit*	Credit	Balance
1993 Dec. 1		J1	950		950

PREPAID RENT   ACCOUNT NO. 15

Date	Description	Post. Ref.	Debit*	Credit	Balance
1993 Dec. 1		J1	3,600		3,600

TRUCK   ACCOUNT NO. 18

Date	Description	Post. Ref.	Debit*	Credit	Balance
1993 Dec. 1		J1	10,800		10,800

ACCOUNTS PAYABLE   ACCOUNT NO. 21

Date	Description	Post. Ref.	Debit	Credit*	Balance
1993 Dec. 1		J1		700	700

UNEARNED SERVICE FEES   ACCOUNT NO. 24

Date	Description	Post. Ref.	Debit	Credit*	Balance
1993 Dec. 2		J1		1,000	1,000

LONG-TERM NOTES PAYABLE   ACCOUNT NO. 25

Date	Description	Post. Ref.	Debit	Credit*	Balance
1993 Dec. 1		J1		10,800	10,800

M. LANDEN, CAPITAL   ACCOUNT NO. 31

Date	Description	Post. Ref.	Debit	Credit*	Balance
1993 Dec. 1		J1		10,000	10,000

M. LANDEN, DRAWING   ACCOUNT NO. 32

Date	Description	Post. Ref.	Debit*	Credit	Balance
1993 Dec. 29		J2	800		800

SERVICE FEES EARNED   ACCOUNT NO. 41

Date	Description	Post. Ref.	Debit	Credit*	Balance
1993 Dec. 10		J1		650	650
13		J1		1,580	2,230
21		J2		520	2,750
31		J2		2,700	5,450

WAGES EXPENSE   ACCOUNT NO. 52

Date	Description	Post. Ref.	Debit*	Credit	Balance
1993 Dec. 13		J1	540		540
27		J2	540		1,080

TRUCK EXPENSE   ACCOUNT NO. 54

Date	Description	Post. Ref.	Debit*	Credit	Balance
1993 Dec. 30		J2	160		160

EXHIBIT 3—8				

LANDEN TV SERVICE
TRIAL BALANCE
DECEMBER 31, 1993

	Debit	Credit
Cash	$ 7,080	
Accounts Receivable	3,480	
Supplies and Parts	950	
Prepaid Rent	3,600	
Truck	10,800	
Accounts Payable		$ 700
Unearned Service Fees		1,000
Long-term Notes Payable		10,800
M. Landen, Capital		10,000
M. Landen, Drawing	800	
Service Fees Earned		5,450
Wages Expense	1,080	
Truck Expense	160	
	$27,950	$27,950

OBJECTIVE 6 DESCRIBE *the adjusting process and* ILLUSTRATE *typical adjusting entries.*

period's accrual basis net income. Therefore, to achieve a proper matching of expenses with revenues, we must adjust the account balances at the end of each accounting period.

Four general types of adjustments are made at the end of an accounting period:

1. Allocating various assets to expense to reflect expenses incurred during the accounting period.
2. Allocating revenues received in advance to revenue to reflect revenues earned during the accounting period.
3. Accruing expenses to reflect expenses incurred during the accounting period that are not yet paid or recorded.
4. Accruing revenues to reflect revenues earned during the accounting period that are not yet received or recorded.

The journal entries made to give effect to these various adjustments are known as **adjusting entries.** Each adjusting entry affects a balance sheet account (an asset or liability account) and an income statement account (an expense or revenue account). Adjustments in the first two categories—allocating various assets to expense and allocating revenues received in advance to revenue—are often referred to as **deferrals.** The distinguishing characteristic of a deferral is that the adjustment deals with an amount that has previously been recorded in a balance sheet account; the adjusting entry, in effect, decreases the balance sheet account and increases an income statement account. Adjustments in the last two categories—accruing expenses and accruing revenues—are often referred to as **accruals.** The unique characteristic of an accrual is that the adjustment deals with an amount that has not previously been recorded in any account; the adjusting entry, therefore, increases both a balance sheet account and an income statement account.

ALLOCATING ASSETS TO EXPENSE

Many business outlays may benefit a number of accounting periods. Some common examples are purchases of buildings, equipment, and supplies; prepayments of rent and advertising; and payments of insurance premiums covering a period of years. Ordinarily, these outlays are debited to an asset account at the time of expenditure. Then, at the end of each accounting period, the estimated portion of the outlay that has expired during the period or that has benefited the period is transferred to an expense account.

Under most circumstances, we can discover when adjustments of this type are needed by inspecting the trial balance for costs that benefit several periods. By looking at the December 31 trial balance of Landen TV Service (Exhibit 3-8), for example, we would find that adjustments are required to apportion the costs of the supplies and parts, the prepaid rent, and the truck between December and subsequent periods.

SUPPLIES AND PARTS During December, Landen TV Service purchased supplies and parts and recorded the outlay in an asset account, Supplies and Parts, as follows:

Dec. 1	Supplies and Parts	950
	Cash	250
	Accounts Payable	700
	Purchased supplies and parts for $950.	
	Terms: $250 down, remainder due in 60 days.	

During December, supplies and parts were used up as repair services were provided. The cost of supplies and parts used is an expense for December that reduces the amount of supplies and parts on hand. It is not necessary, however, to record the expense as each individual supply item or part is used. Instead, at the end of December, the firm would count the items still on hand. Suppose the count shows $510 worth of supplies and parts on hand at the end of the month, indicating that $440 ($950 − $510) worth of supplies and parts have been used in service work during the month. Therefore, at the end of the period, an adjusting entry will transfer this amount to an expense account, Supplies and Parts Expense, as follows:

Dec. 31	Supplies and Parts Expense	440
	Supplies and Parts	440
	To record expense of supplies and parts used in December.	

When this adjusting entry is posted, it will properly reflect the December expense for supplies and parts and will reduce the asset account Supplies and Parts to $510, the actual amount of the asset remaining at December 31. After the entry is posted, the related ledger accounts appear as follows:

SUPPLIES AND PARTS   ACCOUNT NO. 14

Date		Description	Post. Ref.	Debit*	Credit	Balance
1993 Dec.	1		J1	950		950
	31		J3		440	510

SUPPLIES AND PARTS EXPENSE   ACCOUNT NO. 53

Date		Description	Post. Ref.	Debit*	Credit	Balance
1993 Dec.	31		J3	440		440

If financial statements were prepared without this adjustment, the December income statement would omit an important expense and would overstate net income by $440. Similarly, the balance sheet would overstate assets by $440, because the Supplies and Parts balance would remain at $950. As a result of overstating net income, owner's equity in the balance sheet would also be overstated by $440.

PREPAID RENT On December 1, Landen TV Service paid six months' rent in advance and debited the $3,600 payment to Prepaid Rent, an asset account. As each day passes and the rented space is occupied, rent expense is being incurred, and the prepaid rent is decreasing. It is not necessary to record rent expense on a daily basis because financial statements are not prepared daily. At the end of an accounting period, however, an adjustment must be made to recognize the proper amount of rent expense for the period just ended and to decrease the prepaid rent.

On December 31, one month's rent has been used up, so Landen TV Service will transfer $600 ($3,600/6) from Prepaid Rent to Rent Expense, as follows:

```
Dec. 31   Rent Expense                              600
              Prepaid Rent                                    600
          To record rent expense for December.
```

The posting of this adjusting entry will create the proper rent expense for December in the Rent Expense ledger account and will reduce the Prepaid Rent balance to the amount that is prepaid as of December 31 ($3,000). After the entry is posted, these ledger accounts appear as follows:

PREPAID RENT   ACCOUNT NO. 15

Date		Description	Post. Ref.	Debit*	Credit	Balance
1993 Dec.	1		J1	3,600		3,600
	31		J3		600	3,000

RENT EXPENSE   ACCOUNT NO. 51

Date		Description	Post. Ref.	Debit*	Credit	Balance
1993 Dec.	31		J3	600		600

If financial statements were prepared without this adjustment, the December income statement would not show any rent expense and net income would be overstated by $600. This net income overstatement means that owner's equity in the December 31 balance sheet would be $600 too high. Also, Prepaid Rent in the balance sheet would remain at its initial amount of $3,600, which is $600 more than the proper amount of prepaid rent at December 31.

Examples of other prepaid expenses for which similar adjustments are made include prepaid insurance and prepaid advertising. When insurance premiums are paid, the amount is debited to Prepaid Insurance. At the end of an accounting period, the adjusting entry to record the portion of the insurance coverage that expired during the period debits Insurance Expense and credits Prepaid Insurance. Similarly, when advertising services are purchased in advance, the payment is debited to Prepaid Advertising. At the end of an accounting period, an adjustment is needed to recognize the cost of any of the prepaid advertising that was used during the period. The adjusting entry debits Advertising Expense and credits Prepaid Advertising.

DEPRECIATION The process of allocating the costs of a firm's equipment, vehicles, and buildings to the periods benefiting from their use is called **depreciation accounting.** Because these long-lived assets help generate revenue in a company's operations, each accounting period in which the assets are used should reflect a portion of their cost as expense. This periodic expense is known as depreciation expense.

Periodic depreciation expense must be estimated by accountants. The procedure we use here estimates the annual amount of depreciation expense by dividing the cost of the asset by its estimated useful life in years. This method is called **straight-line depreciation.** (We will explore other methods in a later chapter.)

When recording depreciation expense, the asset amount is not reduced directly. Instead, the reduction is recorded in a contra account called *Accumulated Depreciation.* **Contra accounts** are so named because they are used to record reductions in or offsets against a related account. The Accumulated Depreciation account will normally have a credit balance and appears in the balance sheet as a deduction from the related asset amount. Use of the contra account Accumulated Depreciation will allow the original cost of the related asset to be shown in the balance sheet, followed by the accumulated amount of depreciation.

Let us assume that the truck purchased by Landen TV Service for $10,800 is expected to last six years. Straight-line depreciation recorded on the truck is therefore $1,800 ($10,800/6) per year, or $150 ($1,800/12) per month. At the end of December, we would make the following adjusting entry:

Dec. 31	Depreciation Expense—Truck	150	
	Accumulated Depreciation—Truck		150
	To record December depreciation on truck.		

When the preceding entry is posted, it will properly reflect the cost of using this asset during December, and the correct expense will appear in the December income statement. After the adjusting entry has been posted, the asset account, accumulated depreciation account, and depreciation expense account appear as follows:

TRUCK   ACCOUNT NO. 18

Date		Description	Post. Ref.	Debit*	Credit	Balance
1993 Dec.	1		J1	10,800		10,800

ACCUMULATED DEPRECIATION—TRUCK   ACCOUNT NO. 19

Date		Description	Post. Ref.	Debit	Credit*	Balance
1993 Dec.	31		J3		150	150

DEPRECIATION EXPENSE—TRUCK   ACCOUNT NO. 55

Date		Description	Post. Ref.	Debit*	Credit	Balance
1993 Dec.	31		J3	150		150

If the firm failed to record the adjusting entry for depreciation, an expense would be omitted from the income statement. In the above situation, such an omission would result in an overstatement of net income by $150. Furthermore, assets and owner's equity would be overstated by the same amount on the balance sheet.

On the balance sheet, the accumulated depreciation amount is subtracted from the related asset amount. The resulting balance (cost less accumulated depreciation), which is the asset's **book value,** represents the unexpired asset cost to be applied as an expense against future operating periods. For example, the December 31, 1993, balance sheet would show the truck with a book value of $10,650, presented as follows:

Truck	$10,800	
Less: Accumulated Depreciation	150	$10,650

ALLOCATING REVENUES RECEIVED IN ADVANCE TO REVENUE

Sometimes a business receives fees for services before service is rendered. Such transactions are ordinarily recorded by debiting Cash and crediting a liability account for the **unearned revenue.** The liability account in this situation may also be referred to as **deferred revenue** and shows the obligation for performing future service. As the service is performed, the revenue is earned by the firm. When it is time to make adjustments, an entry will be made to record the revenue that was earned in the current accounting period and to reduce the liability account.

DEFERRED SERVICE REVENUE During December, Landen TV Service entered one transaction that generated an advance receipt of revenues. On December 2, the firm signed a four-month contract to perform service for a local TV dealer at $250 per month, with the entire contract price of $1,000 received in advance. The entry made on December 2 was as follows:

Dec.	2	Cash	1,000	
		Unearned Service Fees		1,000
		Received advance on four-month contract		
		at $250 per month.		

On December 31, the following adjusting entry would be made to transfer $250, the revenue earned in December, to Service Fees Earned and reduce the liability Unearned Service Fees by the same amount:

Dec.	31	Unearned Service Fees	250	
		Service Fees Earned		250
		To record portion of advance earned in December.		

After the entry is posted, the liability account will show a balance of $750, the amount of future services still owing, and the Service Fees Earned account will reflect the $250 earned in December.

UNEARNED SERVICE FEES   ACCOUNT NO. 24

Date		Description	Post. Ref.	Debit	Credit*	Balance
1993 Dec.	2		J1		1,000	1,000
	31		J3	250		750

SERVICE FEES EARNED   ACCOUNT NO. 41

Date		Description	Post. Ref.	Debit	Credit*	Balance
1993 Dec.	10		J1		650	650
	13		J1		1,580	2,230
	21		J2		520	2,750
	27		J2		2,700	5,450
	31		J3		250	5,700

Even though Landen TV Service received the cash on December 2, it is important to make the adjusting entry on December 31. If the adjusting entry is ignored, the December income statement fails to report $250 of revenue that has been earned, and the December 31 balance sheet overstates liabilities by $250.

Other examples of revenues received in advance include rental payments received in advance by real estate management companies, insurance premiums received in advance by insurance companies, subscription revenues received in advance by magazine and newspaper publishers, and membership fees received in advance by health clubs. In each case, a liability account should be established when the advance payment is received. Later, an adjusting entry will be made to reflect the revenues earned from the services provided or products delivered during the period.

ACCRUING EXPENSES

A firm will often incur expenses before paying for them. Wages, salaries, interest, utilities, and taxes are examples of expenses that are incurred before payment is made. Usually the cash payments are made at regular intervals of time, such as weekly, monthly, quarterly, or annually. If the accounting period ends on a date that does not coincide with a scheduled cash payment date, an adjusting entry is needed to reflect the expense incurred since the last cash payment. Such an expense is often referred to as an **accrued expense.** Landen TV Service has two such adjustments to make at December 31—wages and interest.

ACCRUED WAGES

A Landen TV Service employee is paid every two weeks at the rate of $270 for each six-day work week. The employee was paid $540 on December 13 and December 27. Let us assume that both these dates fell on Saturday and that Sunday is the employee's day off. At the close of business on Wednesday, December 31, the employee will have worked three days (Monday, Tuesday, and Wednesday) during December for which wages will not be paid until January. Because the employee's wages are $45 per day ($270/6 days), additional wages expense of $135 should be reflected in the income statement for December. The adjusting entry at the end of December would be as follows:

Dec. 31	Wages Expense	135	
	Wages Payable		135
	To record accrued wages for December 29, 30, and 31.		

After posting, the Wages Expense and Wages Payable accounts would appear as follows:

WAGES EXPENSE   ACCOUNT NO. 52

Date		Description	Post. Ref.	Debit*	Credit	Balance
1993 Dec.	13		J1	540		540
	27		J2	540		1,080
	31		J3	135		1,215

WAGES PAYABLE   ACCOUNT NO. 23

Date		Description	Post. Ref.	Debit	Credit*	Balance
1993 Dec.	31		J3		135	135

This adjustment enables the firm to reflect as December expense all wages *earned* by the employee during the period rather than just the wages *paid*. In addition, the balance sheet will show the liability for unpaid wages at the end of the period. Omitting this adjustment would cause a $135 overstatement of net income in the December income statement, with a concurrent $135 overstatement of owner's equity and a $135 understatement of liabilities in the December 31 balance sheet.

When the employee is paid on the next regular payday in January, the accountant must make sure that the three days' pay accrued at the end of December is not again charged to expense. If we assume that the employee is paid $540 on Saturday, January 10, the following entry can be made:

Jan. 10	Wages Payable		135	
	Wages Expense		405	
	Cash			540
	To record wages paid.			

This entry eliminates the liability recorded in Wages Payable at the end of December and debits January Wages Expense for only those wages earned by the employee in January. Another method of avoiding dual charges, that of reversing entries, will be explained in the next chapter.

ACCRUED INTEREST On December 1, 1993, Landen TV Service signed a two-year note payable for $10,800 to finance the purchase of its truck. The annual interest rate on the note is 10%, with interest payable each November 30. The first year's interest of $1,080 ($10,800 × 10%) is due on November 30, 1994. Because interest accumulates as time passes, an adjusting entry is needed at December 31, 1993, to reflect the interest expense for December. December's interest is $90 ($1,080/12), and the adjusting entry at December 31 is as follows:

Dec. 31	Interest Expense	90	
	Interest Payable		90
	To record interest expense for December.		

When this entry is posted to the general ledger, the accounts show the correct interest expense for December as well as a liability for the one month's interest that has accrued by December 31. The general ledger accounts appear as follows after the posting of the adjusting entry:

INTEREST EXPENSE ACCOUNT NO. 56

Date		Description	Post. Ref.	Debit*	Credit	Balance
1993 Dec.	31		J3	90		90

INTEREST PAYABLE ACCOUNT NO. 22

Date		Description	Post. Ref.	Debit	Credit*	Balance
1993 Dec.	31		J3		90	90

When the first year's interest of $1,080 is paid on November 30, 1994, the accountant must not forget that $90 of that amount relates to 1993. Assume, for example, that Landen TV Service is going to prepare only annual financial statements in 1994 and makes no 1994 adjustments for interest through the end of November. On November 30, 1994, the following entry to record the interest payment on that date can be made:

Nov. 30	Interest Payable	90	
	Interest Expense	990	
	Cash		1,080
	To record payment of annual interest.		

This entry eliminates the interest payable that was accrued on December 31, 1993, and debits Interest Expense for $990, the correct interest expense for the first 11 months of 1994. Another way to handle the accounting for interest in 1994, using reversing entries, is discussed in the next chapter.

Should the adjustment to accrue interest at December 31 not be recorded, the December income statement would not show any interest expense, and net income would be overstated by $90. This means that owner's equity in the December 31 balance sheet would also be overstated by $90. No interest payable would be shown among the liabilities in the balance sheet, so total liabilities would be understated by $90.

ACCRUING REVENUES A company may provide services during a period that are neither paid for by clients or customers nor billed at the end of the period. Yet the value of these services represents revenue earned by the firm and should be included in its accrual basis income statement. To accomplish this, end-of-period adjusting entries are made to reflect any revenues for the period that have been earned, but are not yet paid for or billed. Such accumulated revenue is often called **accrued revenue.**

ACCRUED COMMISSIONS Landen TV Service entered into a contract with a cable TV company on December 2 that requires a December 31 adjusting entry to accrue earned revenue. Under the one-year contract, Landen TV Service agreed to distribute cable TV promotional literature to customers in exchange for a monthly commission of $50, payable at the end of every three months. (A commission represents a payment to an employee or agent for specific services rendered and usually is a percentage of the amounts involved in the related transaction, such as a commission to a real estate broker for selling a home; a commission may be a fixed amount, as is true for Landen TV Service's contract with the cable TV company.) By December 31, Landen TV Service has earned one month's commission, and the following adjusting entry would be made:

Dec. 31	Commissions Receivable	50	
	Commissions Earned		50
	To record commissions earned for December.		

After this entry is posted, a $50 normal balance is created in a new asset account, Commissions Receivable, to reflect Landen TV Service's claim to receive revenues already earned. A new revenue account, Commissions Earned, also has a $50 normal balance created. A different revenue account is used because a different activity generates the revenue—distributing promotional literature as contrasted with repairing television sets. These two ledger accounts are shown below.

COMMISSIONS RECEIVABLE   ACCOUNT NO. 13

Date		Description	Post. Ref.	Debit*	Credit	Balance
1993 Dec.	31		J3	50		50

COMMISSIONS EARNED   ACCOUNT NO. 42

Date		Description	Post. Ref.	Debit	Credit*	Balance
1993 Dec.	31		J3		50	50

When Landen TV Service receives the first $150 commission payment on February 28, 1994, the accountant must be alert to the fact that $50 was earned and recorded in 1993. Assuming Landen TV Service accrues no more commissions before

February 28, 1994, the following entry can be made to record the commissions received on that date.

Feb. 28	Cash	150	
	Commissions Receivable		50
	Commissions Earned		100
	To record receipt of quarterly commission.		

This entry eliminates the Commissions Receivable that was established on December 31, 1993, and records $100 of commissions earned, the proper amount of revenue from commissions for the first two months of 1994. Another way to account for the commissions earned in 1994, using reversing entries, is discussed in the next chapter.

If we did not make the December 31, 1993, adjustment to accrue $50 of commissions earned, neither the Commissions Receivable nor Commissions Earned accounts would have a balance at December 31. Consequently, the December net income would be understated by $50, and both assets and owner's equity would also be understated by $50 in the December 31 balance sheet.

Another example of an adjusting entry to accrue revenue involves a firm that has loaned money on which interest has been earned that is not collected by the end of the period. The amount of the interest should be reflected in the net income of the period in which it is earned. In this situation, an adjusting entry would be made debiting Interest Receivable and crediting Interest Income for the amount of interest earned.

Exhibit 3-9 summarizes our discussion about the various types of adjustments.

EXHIBIT 3—9	SUMMARY OF ADJUSTMENTS		

Adjustment Category	Nature of Adjusting Entry	Examples from Chapter	
		Entry	
1. Allocating various assets to expense	Increase expense Decrease asset	Supplies and Parts Expense	440
		Supplies and Parts	440
		Rent Expense	600
		Prepaid Rent	600
	Increase expense Increase contra asset (which decreases asset's book value)	Depreciation Expense—Truck	150
		Accumulated Depreciation—Truck	150
2. Allocating revenues received in advance to revenue	Decrease liability Increase revenue	Unearned Service Fees	250
		Service Fees Earned	250
3. Accruing expenses	Increase expense Increase liability	Wages Expense	135
		Wages Payable	135
		Interest Expense	90
		Interest Payable	90
4. Accruing revenues	Increase asset Increase revenue	Commissions Receivable	50
		Commissions Earned	50

TREND PERCENTAGES

A single accounting number or financial statistic by itself is not particularly useful in understanding a company's financial performance or financial strength. The interpretation of financial data is enhanced by comparing the data with other relevant data. The data might be compared, for example, with data from a similar company or with industry averages or with some broad economic indicators. Another very helpful comparison is to compare the data with the same firm's results from other years. One procedure for comparing a firm's data through several years is to compute trend percentages.

Trend percentages are calculated by choosing a base year and stating the amounts of subsequent years as percentages of that base year. To do trend percentages, of course, a firm must have a financial history. The firm illustrated in this chapter has operated only one month, so we cannot do trend percentages for Landen TV Service. Our illustration, therefore, will use KELLY SERVICES, INC., a service organization headquartered in Troy, Michigan. Kelly Services, Inc., provides temporary help services to a variety of customers.

In a recent year, Kelly Services, Inc., reported revenues of $1,470,524,000 from the sales of services to customers. To aid in interpreting this number, we relate it to revenues from earlier years. Three years of revenues are as follows (Year 3 is the most recent year):

	Year 3	Year 2	Year 1
Revenues	$1,470,524,000	$1,377,453,000	$1,269,427,000

This comparison shows us that revenues increased each year, which is desirable. It is easier to identify the significance of the increases by computing trend percentages over the three-year period. We will set Year 1 as the base year (its revenues will represent 100 percent) and report Years 2 and 3 as percentages of the Year 1 revenues. The trend percentages for revenues follow:

	Year 3	Year 2	Year 1
Revenues	115.8	108.5	100.0

These trend percentages show that Year 3 and Year 2 revenues exceeded Year 1 revenues by 15.8% and 8.5%, respectively. This appears to be fairly reasonable growth.

Now look at the trend percentages for net earnings over this same three-year period.

	Year 3	Year 2	Year 1
Net Earnings	113.7	113.7	100.0

Comparing these trend percentages with the trend percentages for revenues, we may somewhat change our interpretation of Year 3's performance. What we see is that the growth in earnings compared with the growth in the revenues has reversed from Year 2 to Year 3. In Year 3, earnings are only 13.7% larger than base-year earnings while revenues are 15.8% greater than base-year revenues. Also, earnings show no growth from Year 2 to Year 3 while revenues exhibit reasonable growth. This comparison of trend percentages should cause us to look more carefully at the income statement data to try to determine why these changes in relationships occurred from Year 2 to Year 3.

A further examination of income statement data and management's discussion reveals that in Year 3, Kelly Services, Inc., had increases in employee payroll and benefit costs that, due to competitive pressures, it was not able to fully pass on to customers.

KEY POINTS FOR CHAPTER OBJECTIVES

❶ IDENTIFY the first five steps in the accounting cycle (pp. 74, 76).
- The first five steps in the accounting cycle are
  a. Analyze transactions from source documents.
  b. Record transactions in a journal.
  c. Post journal entries to general ledger accounts.
  d. Prepare a trial balance.
  e. Adjust the general ledger accounts.

❷ EXPLAIN the role of source documents in transaction analysis (pp. 74–76).
- Source documents usually provide the basis for analyzing business transactions.
- Source documents are printed or written forms that are generated when a transaction occurs.

❸ DESCRIBE the general journal and the process of journalizing transactions (pp. 76–79).
- Accounting entries are initially recorded in a journal; the entries are in chronological order, and the journal shows the total effect of each transaction or adjustment.

❹ EXPLAIN the process of posting information from the general journal to the general ledger accounts (pp. 79–84).
- Posting is the transfer of information from a journal to the general ledger accounts.
- Posting references are used to cross-reference the information in journals and the general ledger accounts.

❺ REVIEW the nature and format of a trial balance (pp. 83, 85).
- A trial balance lists the general ledger accounts with their respective debit or credit balances.

❻ DESCRIBE the adjusting process and **ILLUSTRATE** typical adjusting entries (pp. 83, 85–93).
- Adjusting entries made to achieve the appropriate matching of expenses and revenue consist of the following four types:
  a. Allocating various assets to expense to reflect expenses incurred during the accounting period.
  b. Allocating revenues received in advance to revenue to reflect revenues earned during the accounting period.
  c. Accruing expenses to reflect expenses incurred during the accounting period that are not yet paid or recorded.
  d. Accruing revenues to reflect revenues earned during the accounting period that are not yet received or recorded.

❼ ANALYTICAL APPLICATION: **DEFINE** *trend percentages* and **EXPLAIN** their use (p. 94).
- Trend percentages relate financial data for several periods by choosing a base year and stating the amounts of subsequent years as percentages of that base year.

SELF-TEST QUESTIONS FOR REVIEW

(Answers follow the Solution to Demonstration Problem.)

1. The first step in the accounting cycle is to
   a. Record transactions in a journal.
   b. Analyze transactions from source documents.
   c. Post journal entries to general ledger accounts.
   d. Adjust the general ledger accounts.

2. A journal entry that contains more than just two accounts is called
   a. A posted journal entry.
   b. An adjusting journal entry.
   c. An erroneous journal entry.
   d. A compound journal entry.

3. *Posting* refers to the process of transferring information from
   a. A journal to general ledger accounts.
   b. General ledger accounts to a journal.
   c. Source documents to a journal.
   d. A journal to source documents.

4. Which of the following is an example of an adjusting entry?
   a. Recording the purchase of supplies on account.
   b. Recording depreciation expense on a truck.
   c. Recording the billing of customers for services rendered.
   d. Recording the payment of wages to employees.

5. An adjusting entry to accrue utilities used during a month for which no bill has yet been received is an example of
   a. Allocating various assets to expense to reflect expenses incurred during the accounting period.
   b. Allocating revenues received in advance to revenue to reflect revenues earned during the accounting period.
   c. Accruing expenses to reflect expenses incurred during the accounting period that are not yet paid or recorded.
   d. Accruing revenues to reflect revenues earned during the accounting period that are not yet received or recorded.

DEMONSTRATION PROBLEM FOR REVIEW

Balke Laboratory began operations on July 1, 1991, and provides various diagnostic services for physicians and clinics. Its fiscal year ends on June 30 and the accounts are adjusted annually on this date. Its unadjusted trial balance at June 30, 1994, is as follows:

BALKE LABORATORY
TRIAL BALANCE
JUNE 30, 1994

	Debit	Credit
Cash	$ 1,000	
Accounts Receivable	9,200	
Prepaid Insurance	6,000	
Supplies	31,300	
Laboratory Equipment	270,000	
Accumulated Depreciation—Laboratory Equipment		$ 60,000
Accounts Payable		3,100
Diagnostic Fees Received in Advance		4,000
P. Balke, Capital		110,000
Diagnostic Fees Revenue		220,400
Wages Expense	58,000	
Rent Expense	22,000	
	$397,500	$397,500

The following information is also available:
1. The Prepaid Insurance account balance represents a premium paid on January 1, 1994, for two years of fire and casualty insurance coverage. Before 1994, Balke Laboratory had no insurance protection.
2. The supplies on hand were counted at June 30, 1994. The total count was $6,300.
3. All laboratory equipment was purchased on July 1, 1991. It is expected to last nine years.
4. Balke Laboratory received a $4,000 cash payment on April 1, 1994, from Boll Clinic for diagnostic services to be provided uniformly over the four months beginning April 1, 1994. Balke credited the payment to Diagnostic Fees Received in Advance. The services for April, May, and June have been provided to Boll Clinic.
5. Unpaid wages at June 30 were $600.
6. Balke Laboratory rents facilities for $2,000 per month. Because of cash flow problems, Balke was unable to pay the rent for June 1994. The landlord gave Balke permission to delay the payment until July.

REQUIRED

Make the adjusting entries, in general journal form, needed at June 30.

SOLUTION TO DEMONSTRATION PROBLEM

June 30	Insurance Expense	1,500	
	Prepaid Insurance		1,500
	To record 6 months' insurance expense ($6,000/4 = $1,500).		

30	Supplies Expense	25,000	
	Supplies		25,000
	To record supplies expense for the year		
	($31,300 − $6,300 = $25,000).		
30	Depreciation Expense—Laboratory Equipment	30,000	
	Accumulated Depreciation—Laboratory Equipment		30,000
	To record depreciation for the year		
	($270,000/9 years = $30,000).		
30	Diagnostic Fees Received in Advance	3,000	
	Diagnostic Fees Revenue		3,000
	To record portion of advance payment that has		
	been earned ($4,000 × $\frac{3}{4}$ = $3,000).		
30	Wages Expense	600	
	Wages Payable		600
	To record unpaid wages at June 30.		
30	Rent Expense	2,000	
	Rent Payable		2,000
	To record rent expense for June.		

ANSWERS TO SELF-TEST QUESTIONS

1. b, p. 74   **2.** d, p. 79   **3.** a, p. 79   **4.** b, p. 87   **5.** c, p. 90

Expenditures made to benefit future periods and amounts received for services yet to be performed are usually first recorded in balance sheet accounts. Then the adjusting procedure consists of transferring the expired portion of prepaid expenses to expense accounts and transferring the earned portion of unearned revenues to revenue accounts. We have just described these procedures in the preceding chapter.

Some companies may debit an outlay benefiting future periods to an expense account rather than to prepaid expense, or credit an amount received for future services to a revenue account rather than to unearned revenue. In such situations, the adjusting procedure consists of transferring the unexpired or unearned portion of the recorded amount to the appropriate balance sheet account. We will present two examples—a prepaid expense recorded initially in an expense account and revenue received in advance recorded initially in a revenue account—and compare the accounting with the analysis used when the amounts are first taken to balance sheet accounts.

PREPAID EXPENSE

Suppose that on December 1, 1993, a one-year insurance premium of $1,200 is paid by a firm. The insurance coverage begins on December 1, 1993, and is the firm's only insurance coverage. The journal entry to record the payment of the premium under the two alternatives being considered is as follows:

Payment Recorded as Expense			**Payment Recorded as Asset**		
Dec. 1 Insurance Expense	1,200		Prepaid Insurance	1,200	
Cash		1,200	Cash		1,200
To record payment of insurance premium.			To record payment of insurance premium.		

At the end of the firm's fiscal year on December 31, an adjusting entry is needed to establish the proper balances in the Insurance Expense and Prepaid Insurance accounts. At December 31, one month's insurance coverage has expired, and 11 months' coverage remains prepaid. The adjusting entry when the initial payment went to Insurance Expense transfers $1,100 (11 months' cost) from Insurance Expense to Prepaid Insurance. The adjusting entry when the initial payment went to Prepaid Insurance transfers $100 (one month's cost) from Prepaid Insurance to Insurance Expense. These adjusting entries are as follows:

Payment Recorded as Expense			**Payment Recorded as Asset**		
Dec. 31 Prepaid Insurance	1,100		Insurance Expense	100	
Insurance Expense		1,100	Prepaid Insurance		100
To establish year-end asset for prepaid insurance.			To record insurance expense for December.		

After the adjusting entry is posted, the balances in the Prepaid Insurance and Insurance Expense accounts are the same under each method, as shown below.

Payment Recorded as Expense	**Payment Recorded as Asset**
December 31 account balances:	December 31 account balances:
Prepaid Insurance $1,100 debit	Prepaid Insurance $1,100 debit
Insurance Expense 100 debit	Insurance Expense 100 debit

REVENUE RECEIVED IN ADVANCE

Now suppose that on December 1, the firm decides to rent some excess warehouse space to a tenant for six months (starting December 1) and receives an advance payment of $1,800 covering all six months. The firm has no other rental agreements. The journal entry to record the receipt of the rent payment under the two alternatives being considered is as follows:

Receipt Recorded as Revenue				Receipt Recorded as Liability		
Dec. 1	Cash	1,800		Cash	1,800	
	Rent Revenue		1,800	Unearned Rent Revenue		1,800
	To record receipt of			To record receipt of		
	advance rent payment.			advance rent payment.		

At December 31, the end of the firm's fiscal year, an adjusting entry must be made to establish the proper balances in the Rent Revenue and Unearned Rent Revenue accounts. At December 31, one month's rental fees have been earned and five months' rent remains collected in advance. The adjusting entry when the initial cash receipt was credited to a revenue account transfers $1,500 (five months' rent) from Rent Revenue to Unearned Rent Revenue. The adjusting entry when the initial cash receipt was credited to a liability account transfers $300 (one month's rent) from Unearned Rent Revenue to Rent Revenue. These adjusting entries follow.

Receipt Recorded as Revenue				Receipt Recorded as Liability		
Dec. 31	Rent Revenue	1,500		Unearned Rent Revenue	300	
	Unearned Rent Revenue		1,500	Rent Revenue		300
	To establish year-end liability			To record rent revenue		
	for unearned rent revenue.			earned in December.		

After the adjusting entry is posted, the year-end balances in the Unearned Rent Revenue and Rent Revenue accounts are the same under both methods, as shown below.

Receipt Recorded as Revenue		Receipt Recorded as Liability	
December 31 account balances:		December 31 account balances:	
Unearned Rent Revenue	$1,500 credit	Unearned Rent Revenue	$1,500 credit
Rent Revenue	300 credit	Rent Revenue	300 credit

It is important to note that the nature of the adjusting entry depends on how the transaction was recorded initially (a prepayment debited to either an asset or expense account and an advance receipt credited to either a liability or revenue account). *After* the adjusting entry has been made and posted, however, the balances in the affected accounts will be the same regardless of how the transaction was initially recorded.

Exhibit A-1 summarizes our discussion in the chapter and this appendix about the various types of adjustments.

GLOSSARY OF KEY TERMS USED IN THIS CHAPTER

accounting cycle A series of basic steps followed to process accounting transactions during a fiscal year (p. 74).

accruals Adjustments that reflect revenues earned but not received or recorded and expenses incurred but not paid or recorded (p. 85).

accrued expense An expense incurred but not yet paid; recognized with an adjusting entry (p. 90).

accrued revenue Revenue earned but not yet billed or received; recognized with an adjusting entry (p. 92).

adjusting entries Entries made at the end of an accounting period under accrual basis accounting to ensure the proper matching of expenses incurred with revenues earned for the period (p. 85).

book value The dollar amount carried in the accounts for a particular item. The book value of a depreciable asset is derived by deducting the contra account Accumulated Depreciation from the balance in the depreciable asset account (p. 88).

calendar year A fiscal year that ends on December 31 (p. 74).

chart of accounts A list of all the general ledger account titles and their numerical code (p. 77).

compound journal entry A journal entry containing more than just one debit and one credit (p. 79).

EXHIBIT A–1	SUMMARY OF ADJUSTMENTS	

		Examples from Chapter and Appendix
Adjustment Category	**Nature of Adjusting Entry**	**Entry**

1. Allocating various prepayments
  a. Initially recorded as an asset
	Increase expense
	Decrease asset
		Supplies and Parts Expense 440
		   Supplies and Parts 440
		Rent Expense 600
		   Prepaid Rent 600
		Insurance Expense 100
		   Prepaid Insurance 100

	Increase expense Increase contra asset	Depreciation Expense—Truck 150 Accumulated Depreciation—Truck 150
b. Initially recorded as an expense	Increase asset Decrease expense	Prepaid Insurance 1,100 Insurance Expense 1,100

2. Allocating revenues received in advance
  a. Initially recorded as a liability
	Decrease liability
	Increase revenue
		Unearned Service Fees 250
		   Service Fees Earned 250
		Unearned Rent Revenue 300
		   Rent Revenue 300

b. Initially recorded as revenue	Decrease revenue Increase liability	Rent Revenue 1,500 Unearned Rent Revenue 1,500

3. Accruing expenses	Increase expense
	Increase liability
		Wages Expense 135
		   Wages Payable 135
		Interest Expense 90
		   Interest Payable 90

4. Accruing revenues	Increase asset Increase revenue	Commissions Receivable 50 Commissions Earned 50

contra account An account related to, and deducted from, another account when financial statements are prepared or when book values are computed (p. 88).

deferrals Adjustments that allocate various assets and revenues received in advance to the proper accounting periods as expenses and revenues (p. 85).

deferred revenue A liability representing revenues received in advance. Also called *unearned revenue* (p. 89).

depreciation accounting The process of allocating the cost of equipment, vehicles, and buildings to expense over the time period benefiting from their use (p. 87).

fiscal year The annual accounting period used by a business firm (p. 74).

general journal A journal with enough flexibility so that any type of business transaction may be recorded in it (p. 78).

journal A tabular record in which business transactions are analyzed in debit and credit terms and recorded in chronological order (p. 77).

posting The transfer of information from the journal to the ledger accounts (p. 79).

posting references A series of abbreviations used in posting to indicate to where or from where a journal entry is posted (p. 80).

source document Any written document evidencing an account transaction, such as a bank check or deposit slip, sales invoice, or cash register tape (p. 74).

straight-line depreciation A depreciation procedure that allocates uniform amounts of depreciation expense to each full period of a depreciable asset's useful life (p. 87).

trend percentages   A comparison of the same financial item over two or more years stated as percentages of a base-year amount (p. 94).

unadjusted trial balance   A trial balance of the general ledger accounts taken before the adjusting step of the accounting cycle (p. 83).

unearned revenue   A liability representing revenues received in advance. Also called *deferred revenue* (p. 89).

QUESTIONS

3-1   List in their proper order the first five steps in the accounting cycle.

3-2   Define the term *fiscal year.*

3-3   Give three examples of source documents that underlie business transactions.

3-4   Explain the nature and purpose of a general journal.

3-5   What is a compound journal entry?

3-6   What is the appropriate procedure for correcting an erroneous general journal entry (a) before it has been posted and (b) after it has been posted?

3-7   Explain the technique of posting references. What is the justification for their use?

3-8   Describe a chart of accounts, and give an example of a coding system for identifying different types of accounts.

3-9   Why is the adjusting step of the accounting cycle necessary?

3-10   What four different types of adjustments are frequently necessary at the close of an accounting period? Give examples of each type.

3-11   On January 1, Prepaid Insurance was debited with the cost of a two-year premium, $1,368. What adjusting entry should be made on January 31 before financial statements are prepared for the month?

3-12   What is a contra account? What contra account is used in reporting the book value of a depreciable asset?

3-13   At the beginning of January, the first month of the accounting year, the Supplies account had a debit balance of $640. During January, purchases of $390 worth of supplies were debited to the account. Although only $430 worth of supplies were on hand at the end of January, the necessary adjusting entry was omitted. How will the omission affect (a) the income statement for January and (b) the balance sheet prepared at January 31?

3-14   The publisher of *International View*, a monthly magazine, received two-year subscriptions totaling $9,840 on January 1. (a) What entry should be made to record the receipt of the $9,840? (b) What entry should be made at the end of January before financial statements are prepared for the month?

3-15   Globe Travel Agency pays an employee $450 in wages each Friday for the five-day work week ending on that day. The last Friday of January falls on January 27. What adjusting entry should be made on January 31, the fiscal year-end?

3-16   The Bayou Company earns interest amounting to $270 per month on its investments. The company receives the interest every six months, on December 31 and June 30. Monthly financial statements are prepared. What adjusting entry should be made on January 31?

3-17   What are trend percentages and how are they calculated?

EXERCISES

TRANSACTION ENTRIES
— OBJ. 3 —

3-18   Creative Designs, a firm providing art services for advertisers, began business on June 1, 1993. The following accounts in its general ledger are needed to record the transactions for June: Cash; Accounts Receivable; Supplies; Office Equipment; Accounts Payable; L. Ryan, Capital; L. Ryan, Drawing; Service Fees Earned; Rent Expense; Utilities Expense; and Salaries Expense. Record the following transactions for June in a general journal:

June   1   Lisa Ryan invested $11,000 cash to begin the business.

      2   Paid rent for June, $850.

      3   Purchased office equipment on account, $6,600.

June   6   Purchased art materials and other supplies costing $3,500; paid $1,800 down with the remainder due within 30 days.
     11   Billed clients for services, $4,400.
     17   Collected $3,150 from clients on account.
     19   Paid $3,300 on account to office equipment firm (see June 3).
     25   Lisa Ryan withdrew $1,000 cash for personal use.
     30   Paid utilities bill for June, $310.
     30   Paid salaries for June, $2,600.

SOURCE DOCUMENTS
— OBJ. 2 —

3-19   For each transaction in Exercise 3-18, indicate the related source document or documents that evidence the transaction.

ERROR CORRECTIONS
— OBJ. 4 —

3-20   The following erroneous journal entries have been posted to the general ledger. Prepare the journal entries to correct the errors.
a.   A $400 cash collection of an account receivable was recorded as a debit to Cash and as a credit to Service Fees Earned.
b.   A $700 purchase of supplies on account was recorded as a debit to Supplies and as a credit to Cash.
c.   A $600 billing of customers for services rendered was recorded as a debit to Accounts Payable and as a credit to Service Fees Earned.
d.   A $425 cash payment for the current month's newspaper advertising was recorded as a debit to Rent Expense and as a credit to Cash.
e.   A $1,300 cash payment for office equipment purchased was recorded as a debit to Cash and as a credit to Office Equipment.

TRANSACTION ENTRY AND
ADJUSTING ENTRIES
— OBJ. 3, 6 —

3-21   Deluxe Building Services offers janitorial services on both a contract basis and an hourly basis. On January 1, 1993, Deluxe collected $18,900 in advance on six-month contracts for work to be performed evenly during the next six months.
a.   Give the general journal entry on January 1 to record the receipt of $18,900 for contract work.
b.   Give the adjusting entry to be made on January 31, 1993, for the contract work done during January.
c.   At January 31, a total of 30 hours of hourly rate janitor work was unbilled. The billing rate is $17 per hour. Give the adjusting entry needed on January 31, 1993. (*Note:* The firm uses the account Fees Receivable to reflect amounts due but not yet billed.)

ADJUSTING ENTRIES
— OBJ. 6 —

3-22   Selected accounts of Ideal Properties, a real estate management firm, are shown below as of January 31, 1993, before any adjusting entries have been made.

	Debit	**Credit**
Prepaid Insurance	$5,940	
Supplies	1,620	
Office Equipment	5,376	
Unearned Rent Revenue		$ 5,100
Salaries Expense	3,200	
Rent Revenue		14,000

Monthly financial statements are prepared. Using the following information, record in a general journal the adjusting entries necessary on January 31:
a.   Prepaid Insurance represents a three-year premium paid on January 1, 1993.
b.   Supplies of $550 were on hand January 31.
c.   Office equipment is expected to last eight years.
d.   On January 1, 1993, the firm collected six months' rent in advance from a tenant renting space for $850 per month.
e.   Accrued salaries not recorded as of January 31 are $470.

OMISSION OF ADJUSTING
ENTRIES
— OBJ. 6 —

3-23   Refer to Exercise 3-22. Assume the adjusting entries for items (a)–(e) were not made. For each item, indicate the effect on the January 1993 income statement and the January 31, 1993, balance sheet from the failure to make the necessary adjusting entry.

ADJUSTING ENTRIES
— OBJ. 6 —

3-24   For each of the following unrelated situations, prepare the necessary adjusting entry in general journal form.
a.   Unrecorded depreciation on equipment is $730.
b.   The Supplies account has a balance of $1,990. Supplies on hand at the end of the period total $860.

c. On the date for preparing financial statements, an estimated utilities expense of $275 has been incurred, but no utility bill has yet been received.

d. On the first day of the current month, rent for four months was paid and recorded as a $2,600 debit to Prepaid Rent and a $2,600 credit to Cash. Monthly statements are now being prepared.

e. Nine months ago, Solid Insurance Company sold a one-year policy to a customer and recorded the receipt of the premium by debiting Cash for $720 and crediting Unearned Premium Revenue for $720. No adjusting entries have been prepared during the nine-month period. Annual statements are now being prepared.

f. At the end of the accounting period, employee wages of $920 have been incurred but not paid.

g. At the end of the accounting period, $200 of interest has been earned but not yet received on notes receivable that are held.

PREPAYMENTS RECORDED AS REVENUE AND EXPENSE — APPENDIX A —

3-25 Rattenbury Associates, a legal firm, has a policy of initially recording prepayments in expense and revenue accounts (see Appendix discussion). The firm's fiscal year ends on December 31 and adjusting entries are made once a year on December 31. On September 1, 1993, the firm paid $8,400 for a one-year professional liability insurance policy starting on October 1, 1993. On November 1, 1993, the firm was retained on a monthly basis ($500 per month) by a local corporation and received $3,000 as the retainer fee for November 1993 through April 1994.

a. Prepare a general journal entry to record the September 1, 1993, cash payment.

b. Prepare a general journal entry to record the November 1, 1993, cash receipt.

c. Prepare the adjusting entry for insurance needed at December 31, 1993.

d. Prepare the adjusting entry for legal fees needed at December 31, 1993.

PROBLEMS

SOURCE DOCUMENTS, TRANSACTION ENTRIES, POSTING, TRIAL BALANCE, AND ADJUSTING ENTRIES — OBJ. 2, 3, 4, 5, 6 —

3-26 Mark Ladd opened Ladd Roofing Service on April 1, 1993. Transactions for April are as follows:

Apr. 1 Ladd contributed $9,000 of his personal funds to begin the business.

2 Purchased a used truck for $5,100 cash.

2 Purchased ladders and other equipment for a total of $2,800, paid $1,000 cash, with the balance due in 30 days.

3 Paid three-year premium on liability insurance, $2,700.

5 Purchased supplies on account, $1,300.

5 Received an advance payment of $1,600 from a customer for roof repair work to be done during April and May.

12 Billed customers for roofing services, $3,500.

18 Collected $2,900 on account from customers.

29 Paid bill for truck fuel used in April, $60.

30 Paid April newspaper advertising, $80.

30 Paid assistants' wages, $2,000.

30 Billed customers for roofing services, $3,000.

REQUIRED

a. For each transaction, indicate the related source document or documents that evidence the transaction.

b. Set up a general ledger with the following accounts, using the account numbers shown: Cash (11); Accounts Receivable (12); Supplies (13); Prepaid Insurance (14); Trucks (15); Accumulated Depreciation—Trucks (16); Equipment (17); Accumulated Depreciation—Equipment (18); Accounts Payable (21); Unearned Roofing Fees (22); M. Ladd, Capital (31); Roofing Fees Earned (41); Fuel Expense (51); Advertising Expense (52); Wages Expense (53); Insurance Expense (54); Supplies Expense (55); Depreciation Expense—Trucks (56); and Depreciation Expense—Equipment (57).

c. Record these transactions in general journal form and post to the ledger accounts.

d. Take a trial balance.

e. Make the journal entries to adjust the books for insurance expense, supplies expense, depreciation expense on the truck, depreciation expense on the equipment, and roofing fees earned. Supplies on hand on April 30 amounted to $400. Depreciation for April was $120 on the truck and $30 on the equipment. One-fourth of the roofing fee received in advance was earned by April 30. Post the adjusting entries.

Transaction Entries, Posting, Trial Balance, and Adjusting Entries — Obj. 3, 4, 5, 6 —

3-27 The Wellness Catering Service had the following transactions in July 1993, its first month of operations:

July 1 Kelly Foster contributed $10,000 of personal funds to the business.

1 Purchased the following items for cash from a catering firm that was going out of business (make a compound entry): delivery van, $3,600; equipment, $2,160; and supplies, $1,500.

2 Paid premium on a one-year liability insurance policy, $960.

2 Entered into a contract with a local service club to cater weekly luncheon meetings for one year at a fee of $600 per month. Received six months' fees in advance.

3 Paid rent for July, August, and September, $1,950.

12 Paid employee's two weeks' wages (five-day week), $1,400.

15 Billed customers for services rendered, $3,500.

18 Purchased supplies on account, $2,200.

26 Paid employee's two weeks' wages, $1,400.

30 Paid July bill for gas, oil, and repairs on delivery van, $570.

30 Collected $2,900 from customers on account.

31 Billed customers for services rendered, $3,800.

31 Foster withdrew $1,000 cash for personal use.

REQUIRED

a. Set up a general ledger that includes the following accounts, using the account numbers shown: Cash (11); Accounts Receivable (12); Supplies (13); Prepaid Rent (14); Prepaid Insurance (15); Delivery Van (16); Accumulated Depreciation—Delivery Van (17); Equipment (18); Accumulated Depreciation—Equipment (19); Accounts Payable (21); Wages Payable (22); Unearned Catering Fees (23); K. Foster, Capital (31); K. Foster, Drawing (32); Catering Fees Revenue (41); Wages Expense (51); Rent Expense (52); Supplies Expense (53); Insurance Expense (54); Delivery Van Expense (55); Depreciation Expense—Delivery Van (56); and Depreciation Expense—Equipment (57).

b. Record July transactions in general journal form and post to the ledger accounts.

c. Take a trial balance at July 31, 1993.

d. Record adjusting journal entries in the general journal and post to the ledger accounts. The following information is available on July 31, 1993:

> Supplies on hand, $1,200
> Accrued wages, $420
> Estimated life of delivery van, three years
> Estimated life of equipment, six years

Also, make any necessary adjusting entries for insurance, rent, and catering fees indicated by the July transactions.

Trial Balance and Adjusting Entries — Obj. 5, 6 —

3-28 Photomake, Inc., a commercial photography studio, has just completed its first full year of operations on December 31, 1993. The general ledger account balances before year-end adjustments follow. No adjusting entries have been made to the accounts at any time during the year. Assume that all balances are normal.

Cash	$ 1,150	Accounts Payable	$ 1,850
Accounts Receivable	2,800	Unearned Photography Fees	1,600
Prepaid Rent	10,200	Capital Stock	15,000
Prepaid Insurance	2,910	Photography Fees Earned	26,480
Supplies	4,150	Wages Expense	9,000
Equipment	12,300	Utilities Expense	2,420

An analysis of the firm's records discloses the following items:

1. Photography services of $860 have been rendered, but customers have not yet been billed. The firm uses the account Fees Receivable to reflect amounts due but not yet billed.

2. The equipment, purchased January 1, 1993, has an estimated life of ten years.

3. Utilities expense for December is estimated to be $310, but the bill will not arrive until January of next year.
4. The balance in Prepaid Rent represents the amount paid on January 1, 1993, for a two-year lease on the studio.
5. In November, customers paid $1,600 in advance for pictures to be taken for the holiday season. When received, these fees were credited to Unearned Photography Fees. By December 31, all these fees are earned.
6. A three-year insurance premium paid on January 1, 1993, was debited to Prepaid Insurance.
7. Supplies on hand at December 31 are $1,220.
8. At December 31, wages expense of $300 has been incurred but not paid.

REQUIRED

a. Prove that debits equal credits for the unadjusted account balances shown above by preparing a trial balance at December 31, 1993.
b. Record adjusting entries in general journal form.

ADJUSTING ENTRIES
— OBJ. 6 —

3-29 Dole Carpet Cleaners ended its first month of operations on June 30, 1993. Monthly financial statements will be prepared. The unadjusted account balances are as follows:

DOLE CARPET CLEANERS
TRIAL BALANCE
JUNE 30, 1993

	Debit	Credit
Cash	$ 980	
Accounts Receivable	450	
Prepaid Rent	2,700	
Supplies	1,900	
Equipment	4,200	
Accounts Payable		$ 530
T. Dole, Capital		7,000
T. Dole, Drawing	200	
Service Fees Earned		3,850
Wages Expense	950	
	$11,380	$11,380

The following information is also available:
1. The balance in Prepaid Rent was the amount paid on June 1 for the first four months' rent.
2. Supplies on hand at June 30 were $740.
3. The equipment, purchased June 1, has an estimated life of five years.
4. Unpaid wages at June 30 were $180.
5. Utility services used during June were estimated at $200. A bill is expected early in July.
6. Fees earned for services performed but not yet billed on June 30 were $350. The firm uses the account Fees Receivable to reflect amounts due but not yet billed.

REQUIRED

In general journal form, make the adjusting entries needed at June 30, 1993.

ADJUSTING ENTRIES
— OBJ. 6 —

3-30 The following information relates to December 31 adjustments for Finest Print, a printing company. The firm's fiscal year ends on December 31.
1. Weekly salaries for a five-day week total $1,300, payable on Fridays. December 31 of the current year is a Tuesday.
2. Finest Print has $10,000 of notes payable outstanding at December 31. Interest of $100 has accrued on these notes by December 31, but will not be paid until the notes mature next year.
3. During December, Finest Print provided $750 of printing services to clients who will be billed on January 2. The firm uses the account Fees Receivable to reflect amounts due but not yet billed.
4. Starting December 1, all maintenance work on Finest Print's equipment is handled by Prompt Repair Company under an agreement whereby Finest Print pays a fixed monthly charge of $85. Finest Print paid six months' service charge in advance on December 1, debiting Prepaid Maintenance for $510.
5. The firm paid $600 on December 15 for a series of radio commercials to run during

December and January. One-third of the commercials have aired by December 31. The $600 payment was debited to Prepaid Advertising.

6. Starting December 16, Finest Print rented 400 square feet of storage space from a neighboring business. The monthly rent of $0.60 per square foot is due in advance on the first of each month. Nothing was paid in December, however, because the neighbor agreed to add the rent for one-half of December to the January 1 payment.

7. Finest Print invested $5,000 in securities on December 1 and earned interest of $45 on these securities by December 31. No interest will be received until January.

8. The annual depreciation on the firm's equipment is $2,160. No depreciation has been recorded during the year.

REQUIRED

Prepare the required December 31 adjusting entries in general journal form.

PREPAYMENTS RECORDED AS REVENUE AND EXPENSE
— APPENDIX A —

3-31 Every summer the Classical Music Society sponsors a series of six classical music concerts. For 1993, two concerts monthly are scheduled for June, July, and August.

Season tickets are on sale June 1–16, 1993 (the first concert is June 16), and cost $54 for the six concerts. Tickets for individual concerts cost $10 each and go on sale June 15, 1993. The society sold 500 season tickets during June 1–16 and credited the $27,000 proceeds to the Ticket Revenue account.

The concerts are given in a pavilion located in a city park. The society rents the facility from the city for $500 per concert. The city requires advance payment for all concerts by June 5. On June 3, 1993, the society mailed a $3,000 check to the city and debited the amount to the Rent Expense account. The society incurs no other rent costs.

The two concerts for June were presented as scheduled. Individual tickets sold for the June concerts totaled $4,600 and were credited to the Ticket Revenue account. Other than the season tickets sold during June 1–16, no advance tickets have been sold by June 30 for the July and August concerts.

REQUIRED [See Appendix discussion.]

a. Prepare the necessary adjusting entries at June 30, 1993, for rent expense and ticket revenue.

b. After the adjustments made in (a) have been posted, what are the June 30, 1993, balances in the following accounts: Prepaid Rent, Unearned Ticket Revenue, Ticket Revenue, and Rent Expense?

c. Assume the society credited the $27,000 season ticket sales amount to the Unearned Ticket Revenue account rather than to the Ticket Revenue account. Also assume the society debited Prepaid Rent rather than Rent Expense for the $3,000 payment on June 3, 1993. Given these assumptions, prepare the necessary adjusting entries at June 30, 1993, for rent expense and ticket revenue.

d. After the adjustments made in (c) have been posted, what are the June 30, 1993, balances in the following accounts: Prepaid Rent, Unearned Ticket Revenue, Ticket Revenue, and Rent Expense?

ALTERNATE EXERCISES

TRANSACTION ENTRIES
— OBJ. 3 —

3-18A Thoro Clean, a firm providing house cleaning services, began business on April 1, 1993. The following accounts in its general ledger are needed to record the transactions for April: Cash; Accounts Receivable; Supplies; Prepaid Van Lease; Equipment; Notes Payable; Accounts Payable; R. Storm, Capital; R. Storm, Drawing; Cleaning Fees Earned; Wages Expense; Advertising Expense; and Van Fuel Expense. Record the following transactions for April in a general journal:

April 1 Randy Storm invested $8,000 cash to begin the business.
       2 Paid six months' lease on van, $2,700.
       3 Borrowed $5,000 from bank and signed note payable agreeing to repay the $5,000 in one year plus 10% interest.
       3 Purchased $4,500 of cleaning equipment; paid $1,500 down with the remainder due within 30 days.
       4 Purchased cleaning supplies for $2,300 cash.
       7 Paid $150 for advertisements to run in newspaper during April.
      21 Billed customers for services, $2,900.

April 23 Paid $2,000 on account to cleaning equipment firm (see April 3).
     28 Collected $1,300 from customers on account.
     29 Randy Storm withdrew $500 cash from the firm.
     30 Paid wages for April, $1,200.
     30 Paid service station for gasoline used during April, $65.

SOURCE DOCUMENTS
— OBJ. 2 —

3-19A For each transaction in Exercise 3-18A, indicate the related source document or documents that evidence the transaction.

ERROR CORRECTIONS
— OBJ. 4 —

3-20A The following erroneous journal entries have been posted to the general ledger. Prepare the journal entries to correct the errors.

a. A $2,500 borrowing from the bank, evidenced by a note payable, was recorded as a debit to Cash and a credit to Accounts Payable.

b. A $9,000 cash payment for the purchase of a truck was recorded as a debit to Truck Expense and a credit to Accounts Payable.

c. A $500 cash payment on account was recorded as a debit to Accounts Receivable and a credit to Cash.

d. A $1,000 cash collection representing two month's rent in advance from a tenant was recorded as a debit to Unearned Rental Fees and a credit to Cash.

e. A $250 purchase of office supplies on account was recorded as a debit to Office Equipment and a credit to Accounts Payable.

ANALYSIS OF ADJUSTED
DATA
— OBJ. 6 —

3-21A Selected T-account balances for Coyle Company are shown below as of January 31, 1993; adjusting entries have already been posted. The firm uses a calendar-year accounting period and makes monthly adjustments.

SUPPLIES	SUPPLIES EXPENSE
Jan. 31 Bal. 600	Jan. 31 Bal. 850

PREPAID INSURANCE	INSURANCE EXPENSE
Jan. 31 Bal. 624	Jan. 31 Bal. 78

WAGES PAYABLE	WAGES EXPENSE
Jan. 31 Bal. 300	Jan. 31 Bal. 3,700

TRUCK	ACCUMULATED DEPRECIATION—TRUCK
Jan. 31 Bal. 8,700	Jan. 31 Bal. 2,465

a. If the amount in Supplies Expense represents the January 31 adjustment for the supplies used in January, and $750 worth of supplies were purchased during January, what was the January 1 balance of Supplies?

b. The amount in the Insurance Expense account represents the adjustment made at January 31 for January insurance expense. If the original premium was for one year, what was the amount of the premium and on what date did the insurance policy start?

c. If we assume no balance existed in Wages Payable or Wages Expense on January 1, how much cash was paid as wages during January?

d. If the truck has a useful life of five years, what is the monthly amount of depreciation expense and how many months has Coyle owned the truck?

ADJUSTING ENTRIES
— OBJ. 6 —

3-22A Judy Brock began Brock Refinishing Service on July 1, 1993. Selected accounts are shown below as of July 31, before any adjusting entries have been made.

	Debit	Credit
Prepaid Rent	$5,520	
Prepaid Advertising	540	
Supplies	2,000	
Unearned Refinishing Fees		$ 500
Refinishing Fees Revenue		1,500

Using the following information, record in a general journal the adjusting entries necessary on July 31:
a. On July 1, the firm paid one year's rent of $5,520.
b. On July 1, $540 was paid to the local newspaper for an advertisement to run daily for the months of July, August, and September.
c. Supplies on hand at July 31 total $700.
d. At July 31, refinishing services of $600 have been performed but not yet billed to customers. The firm uses the account Fees Receivable to reflect amounts due but not yet billed.
e. One customer paid $500 in advance for a refinishing project. At July 31, the project is one-half complete.

ANALYSIS OF THE IMPACT OF ADJUSTMENTS ON FINANCIAL STATEMENTS
— OBJ. 6 —

3-23A At the end of the first month of operations, Bradley Company's accountant prepared financial statements that showed the following amounts:

Assets	$50,000
Liabilities	20,000
Owners' Equity	30,000
Net Income	8,000

In preparing the statements, the accountant overlooked the following items:
a. Depreciation for the month, $800.
b. Service revenue earned but unbilled at month-end, $1,000.
c. Employee wages earned but unpaid at month-end, $300.

Determine the correct amounts of assets, liabilities, and owners' equity at month-end and net income for the month.

ADJUSTING ENTRIES
— OBJ. 6 —

3-24A For each of the following unrelated situations, prepare the necessary adjusting entry in general journal form.
a. At the end of the accounting period, $160 of interest on notes payable has been incurred but not paid.
b. In addition to a base salary, sales personnel receive a commission of 6% of the sales value of merchandise sold. At the end of the accounting period, commissions on $100,000 of merchandise sold during the period have not been paid or recorded.
c. Unrecorded depreciation on company automobiles is $1,150.
d. At the end of the accounting period, the company has earned two-thirds of a payment for services that was received in advance. When received, the $3,900 advance payment was credited to Unearned Service Fees. No adjusting entry has been prepared since the payment was received.
e. Two months ago, the company paid $4,200 in advance for a six-month advertising campaign starting on the payment date. The payment was debited to Prepaid Advertising. No adjusting entry has been prepared since the payment was made, and the company is now at the end of an accounting period.

PREPAYMENTS RECORDED AS REVENUE AND EXPENSE
— APPENDIX A —

3-25A Ziegler Company, a food catering firm, has a policy of initially recording prepayments in expense and revenue accounts (see Appendix discussion). The company's fiscal year ends on December 31, and adjusting entries are made once a year on December 31. On October 1, 1993, the company paid $15,000 for a one-year advertising campaign that started on October 1. On December 1, 1993, the company received $12,000 from a local university to cater a training table for the basketball team during December, January, and February.
a. Prepare a general journal entry to record the October 1, 1993, cash payment.
b. Prepare a general journal entry to record the December 1, 1993, cash receipt.
c. Prepare the adjusting entry for advertising needed at December 31, 1993.
d. Prepare the adjusting entry for catering fees needed at December 31, 1993.

ALTERNATE PROBLEMS

SOURCE DOCUMENTS, TRANSACTION ENTRIES, POSTING, TRIAL BALANCE, AND ADJUSTING ENTRIES
— OBJ. 2, 3, 4, 5, 6 —

3-26A Huang Karate School began business on June 1, 1993. Transactions for June were as follows:

June 1 Po Huang contributed $7,000 of his personal funds to begin the business.
2 Purchased equipment for $2,250, paying $750 cash, with the balance due in 30 days.

June 2 Paid six months' rent, $3,300.

3 Paid one-year premium on liability insurance, $852.

8 Paid June newspaper advertising, $125.

15 Billed participants for karate lessons to date, $1,900.

20 Received $525 from a local company to conduct a special three-session class on self-defense for its employees. The three sessions will be held on June 29, July 6, and July 13, at $175 per session.

21 Collected $1,500 on account from participants.

25 Paid $255 to repair damage to wall caused by an errant kick.

30 Billed participants for karate lessons to date, $2,000.

30 Paid assistant's wages, $600.

REQUIRED

a. For each transaction, indicate the related source document or documents that evidence the transaction.

b. Set up a general ledger with the following accounts, using the account numbers shown: Cash (11); Accounts Receivable (12); Prepaid Rent (13); Prepaid Insurance (14); Equipment (15); Accumulated Depreciation—Equipment (16); Accounts Payable (21); Utilities Payable (22); Unearned Karate Fees (23); P. Huang, Capital (31); Karate Fees Earned (41); Advertising Expense (51); Repairs Expense (52); Wages Expense (53); Rent Expense (54); Insurance Expense (55); Depreciation Expense—Equipment (56); and Utilities Expense (57).

c. Record these transactions in general journal form and post to the ledger accounts.

d. Take a trial balance.

e. Make the adjusting entries for rent expense, insurance expense, depreciation expense, utilities expense, and karate fees earned. Depreciation expense for June is $30, and estimated utilities expense for June is $110. Post the adjusting entries.

TRANSACTION ENTRIES, POSTING, TRIAL BALANCE, AND ADJUSTING ENTRIES — OBJ. 3, 4, 5, 6 —

3-27A Market-Probe, a market research firm, had the following transactions in June 1993, its first month of operations.

June 1 J. Witson invested $20,000 of personal funds in the firm.

1 The firm purchased the following from an office supply company: office equipment, $10,560; office supplies, $1,840. Terms called for a cash payment of $3,000, with the remainder due in 60 days. (Make a compound entry.)

2 Paid June rent, $800.

2 Contracted for three months' advertising in a local newspaper at $240 per month and paid for the advertising in advance.

2 Signed a six-month contract with an electronics firm to provide research consulting services at a rate of $2,700 per month. Received two months' fees in advance. Work on the contract started immediately.

10 Billed various customers for services rendered, $3,800.

12 Paid two weeks' salaries (five-day week) to employees, $3,200.

15 Paid J. Witson's travel expenses to business conference, $1,130.

18 Paid post office for bulk mailing of survey research questionnaire, $520 (postage expense).

26 Paid two weeks' salaries to employees, $3,200.

28 Billed various customers for services rendered, $5,100.

30 Collected $7,300 from customers on account.

30 J. Witson withdrew $1,200 for personal use.

REQUIRED

a. Set up a general ledger that includes the following accounts, using the account numbers shown: Cash (11); Accounts Receivable (12); Office Supplies (14); Prepaid Advertising (15); Office Equipment (16); Accumulated Depreciation—Office Equipment (17); Accounts Payable (21); Salaries Payable (22); Unearned Service Fees (23); J. Witson, Capital (31); J. Witson, Drawing (32); Service Fees Earned (41); Salaries Expense (51); Advertising Expense (52); Supplies Expense (53); Rent Expense (54); Travel Expense (55); Depreciation Expense—Office Equipment (56); and Postage Expense (57).

b. Record June transactions in general journal form and post to the ledger accounts.

c. Take a trial balance at June 30, 1993.

d. Record adjusting journal entries in general journal form, and post to the ledger accounts. The following information is available on June 30, 1993:

> Office supplies on hand, $790
> Accrued salaries, $640
> Estimated life of office equipment, eight years

Also, make any necessary adjusting entries for advertising and for service fees indicated by the June transactions.

TRIAL BALANCE AND ADJUSTING ENTRIES — OBJ. 5, 6 —

3-28A Deliverall, a mailing service, has just completed its first full year of operations on December 31, 1993. The firm's general ledger account balances before year-end adjustments are given below. No adjusting entries have been made to the accounts at any time during the year. Assume that all balances are normal.

Cash	$ 1,900	Accounts Payable	$ 1,700
Accounts Receivable	4,860	V. Pryor, Capital	9,550
Prepaid Advertising	1,620	Mailing Fees Earned	80,000
Supplies	5,270	Wages Expense	36,300
Equipment	40,320	Rent Expense	6,120
Notes Payable	8,000	Utilities Expense	2,860

An analysis of the firm's records reveals the following:

1. The balance in Prepaid Advertising represents the amount paid for newspaper advertising for one year. The agreement, which calls for the same amount of space each month, covers the period from February 1, 1993, to January 31, 1994. Deliverall did not advertise during its first month of operations.
2. The equipment, purchased January 1, has an estimated life of eight years.
3. Utilities expense does not include expense for December, estimated at $320. The bill will not arrive until January 1994.
4. At year-end, employees have earned $800 in wages that will not be paid until January.
5. Supplies on hand at year-end amounted to $740.
6. At year-end, unpaid interest of $480 has accrued on the notes payable.
7. The firm's lease calls for rent of $510 per month payable on the first of each month, plus an amount equal to $\frac{1}{2}$% of annual mailing fees earned. The rental percentage is payable within 15 days after the end of the year.

REQUIRED

a. Prove that debits equal credits for the unadjusted account balances shown above by preparing a trial balance.
b. Record adjusting entries in general journal form.

ADJUSTING ENTRIES — OBJ. 6 —

3-29A The Wheel Place, Inc., began operations on March 1, 1993 to provide automotive wheel alignment and balancing services. On March 31, 1993, the unadjusted balances of the firm's accounts are as follows:

THE WHEEL PLACE, INC.
TRIAL BALANCE
MARCH 31, 1993

	Debit	Credit
Cash	$ 1,400	
Accounts Receivable	3,810	
Prepaid Rent	4,650	
Supplies	2,700	
Equipment	35,100	
Accounts Payable		$ 1,500
Unearned Service Revenue		900
Capital Stock		38,000
Service Revenue		11,160
Wages Expense	3,900	
	$51,560	$51,560

The following information is also available:

1. The balance in Prepaid Rent was the amount paid on March 1 to cover the first six months' rent.

2. Supplies on hand on March 31 amounted to $1,120.
3. The equipment has an estimated life of nine years.
4. Unpaid wages at March 31 were $400.
5. Utility services used during March were estimated at $350. A bill is expected early in April.
6. The balance in Unearned Service Revenue was the amount received on March 1 from a new car dealer to cover alignment and balancing services on all new cars sold by the dealer in March and April. The Wheel Place agreed to provide the services at a fixed fee of $450 each month.

REQUIRED

In general journal form, make the adjusting entries needed at March 31, 1993.

ADJUSTING ENTRIES — OBJ. 6 —

3-30A

The following information relates to the December 31, 1993, adjustments for Water Barrier, a firm providing waterproofing services for commercial and residential customers. The firm's fiscal year ends December 31; no adjusting entries have been made during 1993.

1. The firm paid a $2,160 premium for a three-year insurance policy, coverage to begin October 1, 1993. The premium payment was debited to Prepaid Insurance.
2. Weekly wages for a five-day work week total $1,150, payable on Fridays. December 31, 1993, is a Thursday.
3. Water Barrier received $2,400 in November 1993 for services to be performed during December 1993 through February 1994. When received, this amount was credited to Unearned Service Fees. By December 31, one-third of this amount was earned.
4. Water Barrier receives a 5% commission from the manufacturer on sales of a waterproofing agent to Water Barrier's customers. By December 31, 1993, Water Barrier had sales of $7,000 (during November and December) for which no commissions had yet been received.
5. During December, fuel oil costs of $395 were incurred to heat the firm's buildings. Because the monthly bill from the oil company has not yet arrived, no entry has been made for this amount (fuel oil costs are charged to Utilities Expense).
6. The Supplies account has a balance of $15,900 on December 31. A count of supplies on December 31 indicates that $2,800 worth of supplies are still on hand.
7. On December 1, 1993, Water Barrier borrowed $9,000 from the bank, giving a note payable. Interest is not payable until the note is due near the end of January, 1994. However, the interest for December is $70.
8. Water Barrier rents parking spaces in its lot to firms in the office building next door. On December 1, 1993, Water Barrier received $8,000 as advance payments to cover parking privileges in the lot for December 1993 through March 1994. When received, the $8,000 was credited to Unearned Parking Fees.

REQUIRED

Prepare the necessary December 31, 1993, adjusting entries in general journal form.

PREPAYMENTS RECORDED AS REVENUE AND EXPENSE — APPENDIX A —

3-31A

Real Tee Company was organized on January 1, 1993, to manage apartment buildings. The firm will prepare monthly financial statements.

On January 2, the company entered into a maintenance contract with a repair service to maintain the laundry equipment in the various apartment buildings for a fixed monthly fee of $90. The contract is for one year, and Real Tee paid the full year's fee of $1,080 in advance. The company debited the payment to Maintenance Expense. The company had no other maintenance costs during January.

For six deluxe apartments, the lease requires quarterly rent payments in advance. These apartments rent for $750 per month. On January 3, Real Tee received the $13,500 quarterly (January–March) rent payments on these six apartments. The company credited the receipt to Rent Revenue. Other apartments require monthly payments, and the company received $30,000 for January rentals of these apartments. The $30,000 was credited to Rent Revenue.

REQUIRED [See Appendix discussion.]

a. Prepare the necessary adjusting entries at January 31, 1993, for maintenance expense and rent revenue.
b. After the adjustments made in (a) have been posted, what are the January 31, 1993, balances in the following accounts: Prepaid Maintenance, Unearned Rent Revenue, Rent Revenue, and Maintenance Expense?

c. Assume Real Tee Company debited the $1,080 prepayment of maintenance to Prepaid Maintenance rather than to Maintenance Expense. Also assume the firm credited the $13,500 advance quarterly rent payments to Unearned Rent Revenue rather than to Rent Revenue. Given these assumptions, prepare the necessary adjusting entries at January 31, 1993, for maintenance expense and rent revenue.

d. After the adjustments made in (c) have been posted, what are the January 31, 1993, balances in the following accounts: Prepaid Maintenance, Unearned Rent Revenue, Rent Revenue, and Maintenance Expense?

CASES

Business Decision Case

Wyland Consulting Services, a firm started three years ago by Bruce Wyland, offers consulting services for material handling and plant layout. The balance sheet prepared by the firm's accountant at the close of 1993 is shown below:

WYLAND CONSULTING SERVICES
BALANCE SHEET
DECEMBER 31, 1993

Assets			Liabilities		
Cash		$ 2,300	Notes Payable	$20,000	
Accounts Receivable		15,000	Accounts Payable	2,800	
Supplies		9,450	Unearned Consulting Fees	7,500	
Prepaid Insurance		3,000	Wages Payable	300	
Equipment	$45,000		Total Liabilities		$30,600
Less: Accumulated			**Owner's Equity**		
Depreciation	15,750	29,250	B. Wyland, Capital		28,400
			Total Liabilities and		
Total Assets		$59,000	Owner's Equity		$59,000

Earlier in the year, Wyland obtained a bank loan of $20,000 for the firm. One of the provisions of the loan is that the year-end debt-to-equity ratio (ratio of total liabilities to total owner's equity) shall not exceed 1.0. Based on the above balance sheet, the ratio at the end of 1993 is 1.08.

Wyland is concerned about being in violation of the loan agreement and asks your assistance in reviewing the situation. Wyland believes that his rather inexperienced accountant may have overlooked some items at year-end.

In discussions with Wyland and the accountant, you learn the following:

1. On January 1, 1993, the firm paid a $3,000 insurance premium for two years of coverage. The amount in Prepaid Insurance has not been adjusted.

2. Depreciation on the equipment should be 10% of cost per year. The accountant inadvertently recorded 15% for 1993.

3. Interest on the bank loan has been paid through the end of 1993.

4. The firm concluded a major consulting engagement in December, doing a plant layout analysis for a new factory. The $4,000 fee has not been billed or recorded in the accounts.

5. On December 1, 1993, the firm received a $7,500 advance payment from Croy Corporation for consulting services to be rendered over a two-month period. This payment was credited to the Unearned Consulting Fees account. One-half of this fee was earned by December 31, 1993.

6. Supplies costing $3,200 were on hand on December 31. The accountant filed the record of the count but made no entry in the accounts.

REQUIRED

What is the correct debt-to-equity ratio at December 31, 1993? Is the firm in violation of the loan agreement? Prepare a schedule to support your computation of the correct total liabilities and total owner's equity at December 31, 1993.

Analytical Application Case

HEALTH IMAGES, INC., headquartered in Atlanta, Georgia, provides fixed-site outpatient magnetic resonance imaging (MRI) services. In addition to developing and operating imaging centers, Health Images, Inc., services MRI equipment and oversees the construction of clinical facilities. Following are selected financial data for Health Images, Inc., over a three-year period (Year 3 is the most recent year; amounts are in thousands):

	Year 3	Year 2	Year 1
Gross Patient Service Revenue	$48,630	$31,274	$22,243
Contractual Adjustments	6,895	3,907	2,556
Operating Costs	31,742	21,237	15,609
Net Income	3,024	2,266	1,906

Some patients at Health Images' imaging centers (and one radiation oncology center) have their costs borne by third-party payors, such as health maintenance organizations and Medicare. Health Images has frequently entered into arrangements with these third-party payors to provide services at reduced rates. The amounts of these adjustments are identified as contractual adjustments in the above schedule of financial data and are subtracted from gross patient service revenue in the income statement.

REQUIRED

a. Using Year 1 as a base, calculate the trend percentages for each category of financial data given.

b. Looking at the Year 3 trend percentages, which category has shown the greatest percentage growth relative to Year 1? the smallest percentage growth?

c. Have the contractual adjustments grown at a faster, slower, or the same rate as gross patient service revenue? What are some possible explanations for the growth pattern of the contractual adjustments relative to gross patient service revenue?

d. During Years 2 and 3, Health Images opened 15 new imaging centers and one radiation oncology center—6 centers one year and 10 centers the other year. During which year do the trend percentages suggest that the 10 new centers were opened? Briefly explain.

Ethics Case

It is the end of an accounting year for Juliet Kravetz, controller of a medium-sized, publicly held corporation specializing in toxic waste cleanup. Within the corporation, only Kravetz and the president know that the firm has been negotiating for several months to land a very large contract for waste cleanup in Western Europe. The president has hired another firm with excellent contacts in Western Europe to help with the negotiations. The outside firm will charge an hourly fee plus expenses, but has agreed not to submit a bill until the negotiations are in their final stages (expected to occur in another three to four months). Even if the contract falls through, the outside firm is entitled to receive payment for its services. Based upon her discussion with a member of the outside firm, Kravetz knows that their charge for services provided to date will be $150,000. This is a material amount for the company.

Kravetz knows that the president wants the negotiations to remain as secret as possible so that competitors will not learn of the contract the company is pursuing in Europe. Indeed, the president recently stated to her, "This is not the time to reveal our actions in Western Europe to other staff members, our auditors, or readers of our financial statements; securing this contract is crucial to our future growth." No entry has been made in the accounting records for the cost of the contract negotiations. Kravetz now faces an uncomfortable situation. The company's outside auditor has just asked her if she knows of any year-end adjustments that have not yet been recorded.

REQUIRED

What are the ethical considerations that Kravetz faces in answering the auditor's question? How should she respond to the question?

How is a company's working capital determined?

A company's financial statements, prepared in the part of the accounting cycle covered in this chapter, will show the firm's current assets and current liabilities. ■ Working capital is the current assets minus the current liabilities. ■ In some respects, working capital represents a firm's lifeblood ■ Without adequate working capital, a firm like Georgia-Pacific Corporation would have difficulty meeting the current expenses of manufacturing and distributing its various pulp, paper, and building products.

4 THE ACCOUNTING CYCLE CONCLUDED

Everything ends that has a beginning.

QUINTILIAN

he first five steps in the accounting cycle—analyzing and journalizing transactions, posting to accounts, preparing a trial balance, and adjusting the accounts—are essential to the process of classifying financial data and, when necessary, aligning the data with appropriate periods. The goal of these procedures is to prepare the data so that they can be summarized in a set of meaningful financial statements.

Accountants typically use a *worksheet* to compile the information needed for financial statements. A worksheet is incorporated into steps 4 and 5 of the accounting cycle (preparing a trial balance and adjusting the accounts). In this chapter, we will explain the preparation of a worksheet and its integration into steps 4 and 5 of the accounting cycle. Then we will discuss steps 6 through 9 of the accounting cycle. Our discussion continues to use the December 1993 financial data given in the preceding chapter for Landen TV Service.

THE NINE STEPS IN THE ACCOUNTING CYCLE

OBJECTIVE ❶ IDENTIFY *a worksheet's place in the accounting cycle and* EXPLAIN *the procedures for preparing a worksheet.*

Utilizing a worksheet creates a nine-step accounting cycle. These nine steps are listed below. The steps in the boxed area will be discussed in this chapter.

1. Analyze transactions from source documents.
2. Record transactions in journals.
3. Post journal entries to general ledger accounts.
4. Prepare a trial balance to start a worksheet.
5. Adjust the general ledger accounts on the worksheet and complete the worksheet.
6. Prepare financial statements.
7. Journal and post adjusting entries.
8. Journalize and post closing entries.
9. Prepare a post-closing trial balance.

PREPARING A WORKSHEET

The **worksheet** is a tool of the accountant, not part of a company's formal accounting records. The accountant prepares a worksheet at that stage of the accounting cycle when it is time to adjust the accounts and prepare financial statements.

The basic structure of the worksheet is presented in Exhibit 4-1, which includes an explanation of the format used. The worksheet is prepared in the order indicated by the boxed numbers in the exhibit. As we discuss the procedures for preparing a worksheet, we will illustrate them by preparing the worksheet for Landen TV Service for the month ended December 31, 1993, using a series of acetate overlays. Exhibits 4-2 to 4-6 (on page 118) present the step-by-step process used in preparing the worksheet.

❶ HEADING The worksheet *heading* should include (a) the name of the accounting entity involved, (b) the term *Worksheet* to indicate the type of analysis performed, and (c) a date describing the period covered. The worksheet includes both income statement data (for the period described) and balance sheet data (for the end of the period described). Exhibit 4-2 illustrates the heading for Landen TV Service's worksheet.

EXHIBIT 4—1	BASIC STRUCTURE OF A WORKSHEET

1
(HEADING FOR WORKSHEET)

Description	Trial Balance		Adjustments		Adjusted Trial Balance		Income Statement		Balance Sheet	
	Debit	Credit	Debit	Credit	Debit	Credit	Debit	Credit	Debit	Credit
2 The unadjusted trial balance			**3** Amounts of adjustments		**4** Amounts of all account balances		**5** Extension of adjusted trial balance			
							Income statement accounts		Balance sheet accounts	
Titles of accounts not in unadjusted trial balance, added as needed							**6** Balancing of columns for each statement			

The worksheet form we have illustrated has a description column and 10 amount (money) columns. A set of debit and credit columns is provided for each of the five headings, Trial Balance, Adjustments, Adjusted Trial Balance, Income Statement, and Balance Sheet.

2 TRIAL BALANCE Recall that the *trial balance* taken as step 4 of the accounting cycle is an unadjusted trial balance. This unadjusted trial balance becomes the starting point for the accounting analysis on the worksheet. The trial balance is entered in the worksheet's description column and the first pair of money columns. Once the trial balance is placed on the worksheet and double ruled, it reflects the state of the general ledger at the time the worksheet is prepared. Exhibit 4-2 shows the worksheet placement of Landen TV Service's unadjusted trial balance at December 31, 1993.

3 ADJUSTMENTS *When a worksheet is used, all adjustments are first entered on the worksheet.* This procedure permits the adjustment to be reviewed for completeness and accuracy. To adjust accounts already appearing in the unadjusted trial balance, we simply enter the amounts in the appropriate side (debit or credit) of the adjustments columns on the lines containing the accounts. When accounts not appearing in the unadjusted trial balance require adjustment, their titles are listed as needed in the description column below the accounts already listed. Note that adjustments entered on the worksheet are not yet journalized; journalizing the adjustments occurs later in the accounting cycle (step 7).

The adjustments recorded on Landen TV Service's worksheet in Exhibit 4-3 are identical to those illustrated earlier in general journal form in step 5 of the accounting cycle (see the preceding chapter). It is common practice to "key" the amounts of each adjusting entry with the same letter or number. Note that the numbers (1) through (7) are used in Exhibit 4-3. This procedure makes it easy to check the equality of debits and credits in each entry and to identify all the amounts related to a particular adjustment.

We repeat the adjusting entries made at the end of December for Landen TV Service and explain their placement on the worksheet (Exhibit 4-3). Remember,

EXHIBIT 4—2	HEADING AND TRIAL BALANCE ENTERED ON WORKSHEET

Enter the heading. **1**

LANDEN TV SERVICE
WORKSHEET
FOR THE MONTH ENDED DECEMBER 31, 1993

Description	Trial Balance		Adjustments		Adjusted Trial Balance		Income Statement		Balance Sheet	
	Debit	Credit	Debit	Credit	Debit	Credit	Debit	Credit	Debit	Credit
Cash	7,080									
Accounts Receivable	3,480									
Supplies and Parts	950									
Prepaid Rent	3,600									
Truck	10,800									
Accounts Payable		700								
Unearned Service Fees		1,000								
Long-term Notes Payable		10,800								
M. Landen, Capital		10,000								
M. Landen, Drawing	800									
Service Fees Earned		5,450								
Wages Expense	1,080									
Truck Expense	160									
	27,950	27,950								

2

Enter the trial balance
in the worksheet's
description and trial
balance amount
columns.

because we are preparing a worksheet, these adjustments are entered on the worksheet first; they are not yet recorded in the general journal.

(1)	Supplies and Parts Expense	440	
	Supplies and Parts		440

Because $510 worth of supplies were on hand at December 31, we reduce the asset Supplies and Parts from $950 to $510 and record the $440 difference as expense. Note that the expense account, Supplies and Parts Expense, does not appear in the unadjusted trial balance and must be added below the accounts already listed on the worksheet.

(2)	Rent Expense	600	
	Prepaid Rent		600

This adjustment records the rent expense for December ($600) and reduces the prepaid rent to an amount representing five months' prepayment ($3,000). The Rent Expense account is not in the unadjusted trial balance and, therefore, must be added below the Supplies and Parts Expense account on the worksheet.

(3)	Depreciation Expense—Truck	150	
	Accumulated Depreciation—Truck		150

The truck depreciation for December is reflected by this adjustment. The two accounts used in the adjustment, Depreciation Expense—Truck and Accumulated Depreciation—Truck, do not appear in the unadjusted trial balance. Therefore, these two accounts must be listed in the worksheet's description column below the Rent Expense account.

(4)	Unearned Service Fees	250	
	Service Fees Earned		250

This adjustment is made to reflect the portion of a $1,000 advance earned in December. The liability account Unearned Service Fees, originally credited for the $1,000 advance, is reduced by a $250 debit, and a corresponding credit is made to the revenue account Service Fees Earned. Since both accounts appear in the unadjusted trial balance, we record this adjustment on the lines already provided for these accounts.

(5)	Wages Expense	135	
	Wages Payable		135
(6)	Interest Expense	90	
	Interest Payable		90

These adjustments reflect expenses incurred in December 1993 that will not be paid until 1994. Wages are accrued for the last three days in December, and interest is accrued for the month of December. The accounts Wages Payable, Interest Expense, and Interest Payable do not appear in the unadjusted trial balance; they are added beneath the Accumulated Depreciation—Truck account on the worksheet.

(7)	Commissions Receivable	50	
	Commissions Earned		50

This adjustment reflects the commission earned during December 1993 that will not be received until 1994. Neither of the accounts in this adjustment appears in the unadjusted trial balance, so both the Commissions Receivable and Commissions Earned accounts are added to the worksheet below the Interest Payable account.

After recording all the adjusting entries on the worksheet, we total the adjustments columns to prove that debits equal credits.

4 ADJUSTED TRIAL BALANCE

A trial balance of all account balances after adjustments is called an **adjusted trial balance.** Once the adjustments have been entered on the worksheet, there is sufficient information available to compile an adjusted trial balance. The adjusted figures are determined by combining horizontally, line by line, the amounts in the first four money columns—that is, the unadjusted trial balance and the adjustments.

We review the calculations for three lines of Exhibit 4-4 to illustrate this process. The first line shows Cash with a debit amount of $7,080 in the trial balance. Because Cash is not affected by any adjustments, the $7,080 appears in the debit column of the adjusted trial balance. On the third line, Supplies and Parts begins with a debit of $950 in the trial balance and then shows a credit of $440 in the adjustments columns. The $440 credit is subtracted from the $950 debit, and the remaining $510 is shown as a debit in the adjusted trial balance. Service Fees Earned, on the eleventh line, shows a $5,450 credit balance in the trial balance and a $250 credit in the adjustments columns. These two credit amounts are added, and the $5,700 sum is shown in the credit column of the adjusted trial balance.

After computing the adjusted trial balance amounts for all the accounts on the worksheet, we total the two columns of the adjusted trial balance to confirm that they are equal and that, therefore, our worksheet still balances.

5 EXTENSION OF ADJUSTED TRIAL BALANCE

The amounts in the adjusted trial balance columns are extended into the two remaining pairs of columns as follows:

Expenses	$\longrightarrow$ Debit column of income statement
Revenues	$\longrightarrow$ Credit column of income statement
Assets, owner's drawing, and cash dividends	$\longrightarrow$ Debit column of balance sheet
Liabilities, owner's capital, capital stock, retained earnings, and contra assets, such as accumulated depreciation	$\longrightarrow$ Credit column of balance sheet

Expense and revenue account balances are extended to the income statement columns because these accounts will be used to prepare the income statement. Similarly, asset, contra asset, liability, and owner's capital accounts are balance sheet accounts, so their balances are extended to the balance sheet columns. Although not a balance sheet account, an owner's drawing account debit balance is also extended to the appropriate balance sheet column (the debit column). We will use the owner's drawing account balance in deriving the proper end-of-period owner's capital amount.

If the worksheet is for a corporation, a cash dividends debit balance is extended to the balance sheet debit column. Credit balances in the capital stock and retained earnings accounts are extended to the balance sheet credit column.

Exhibit 4-5 shows the extension of Landen TV Service's adjusted trial balance to the worksheet's income statement and balance sheet columns. Once the proper extensions are made, the worksheet is complete except for the balancing of the two pairs of statement columns containing the adjusted balances.

6 BALANCING THE WORKSHEET

The first step in balancing is to add each of the income statement and balance sheet columns and record their respective totals on the same line as the totals of the adjusted trial balance columns. The difference between the total debits and total credits in the income statement columns will be the difference between total revenues and total expenses—that is, the net income or net loss for the period. The net income or net loss should also be the amount by which the debit and credit columns for the balance sheet differ. This is true because the owner's capital account balance, as extended, does not yet reflect the net income or net loss for the current period.

When revenues exceed expenses, we balance the two pairs of statement columns by adding the net income figure to both the debit column of the income statement and the credit column of the balance sheet. Exhibit 4-6 illustrates this balancing situation with Landen TV Service's net income for December of $3,095. If expenses exceed revenues, we add the amount of net loss to the credit column of the income statement and to the debit column of the balance sheet. After we have added the net income (or loss) to the proper columns, we total and double rule the four columns. The worksheet is now complete and ready for the next step in the accounting cycle—the preparation of financial statements.

A careful study of a worksheet's preparation shows the following advantages of the worksheet:

1. The balances of all general ledger accounts appear in one location and may be easily reviewed to determine whether any of them need adjusting.
2. The total effect of any adjustment—whether contemplated or actually made on the worksheet—can be readily determined. Because these adjustments are reviewed before adjusting entries are journalized and posted, the likelihood of incorrect adjustments appearing in the formal accounting records is reduced.
3. Once all the adjustments have been made, the adjusted account balances can be determined and separated into a group for the income statement and a group for the balance sheet, simplifying the preparation of these statements.

COMPLETION OF THE ACCOUNTING CYCLE

Once the worksheet is prepared, we proceed to the remaining steps in the accounting cycle. These steps are as follows:

6. Prepare financial statements.
7. Journalize and post adjusting entries.
8. Journalize and post closing entries.
9. Prepare a post-closing trial balance.

Step 6: Prepare Financial Statements

A basic set of financial statements includes an income statement, a statement of owner's equity, a balance sheet, and a statement of cash flows. We will illustrate the preparation of the first three of these financial statements using the completed worksheet for Landen TV Service shown in Exhibit 4-5. The statement of cash flows is not prepared from this worksheet. We discuss and illustrate the preparation of the statement of cash flows in a later chapter.

INCOME STATEMENT

OBJECTIVE 2 ILLUSTRATE *the financial statements prepared from a worksheet and* **DESCRIBE** *a classified balance sheet.*

Exhibit 4-7 presents the income statement for Landen TV Service for December 1993. The income statement is prepared directly from the income statement columns of the worksheet shown in Exhibit 4-5.

EXHIBIT 4—7		

LANDEN TV SERVICE
INCOME STATEMENT
FOR THE MONTH OF DECEMBER, 1993

Revenues		
Service Fees Earned	$5,700	
Commissions Earned	50	
Total Revenues		$5,750
Expenses		
Wages Expense	$1,215	
Truck Expense	160	
Supplies and Parts Expense	440	
Rent Expense	600	
Depreciation Expense—Truck	150	
Interest Expense	90	
Total Expenses		2,655
Net Income		$3,095

STATEMENT OF OWNER'S EQUITY

Normally, we use both the worksheet and the owner's capital account in the general ledger to prepare the statement of owner's equity. We cannot determine from the worksheet alone the beginning of the period balance of owner's capital and the amount of capital contributions, if any, during the period. Consequently, we must examine the owner's capital account in the general ledger to determine these amounts. The worksheet reveals the owner's drawings during a period and the period's net income or net loss.

Exhibit 4-8 shows Landen TV Service's statement of owner's equity for December 1993. Because December is the first month of operations, we know that the $10,000 balance showing for M. Landen, Capital in the worksheet (Exhibit 4-5) must be from investments made during December. In this special case, therefore, we can prepare the statement of owner's equity without reviewing the M. Landen, Capital account in the general ledger.

CLASSIFIED BALANCE SHEET

The balance sheet for Landen TV Service at December 31, 1993, is shown in Exhibit 4-9 (on page 124). This balance sheet is prepared from the balance sheet columns of the worksheet shown in Exhibit 4-5, with the exception of Mark Landen's capital balance, which at December 31, 1993, is taken from the statement of owner's equity shown in Exhibit 4-8.

Note that the balance sheet presented is a *classified* balance sheet; that is, the assets and liabilities are separated into various categories. Assets are divided between current assets and plant assets; liabilities are separated into current liabilities and long-term liabilities. Classifying a balance sheet aids in the analysis of financial statement data.

CURRENT ASSETS

Current assets are cash and other assets that will be converted into cash or used up during the normal operating cycle of the business or one year, whichever is longer. The **normal operating cycle** of a business is the average period of time between the use of cash in its typical operating activity and the subsequent collection of cash from customers. In a service business, for example, the firm uses cash to provide services, which create accounts receivable from customers, which are then collected in cash. A service firm's operating cycle, then, may be portrayed as follows:

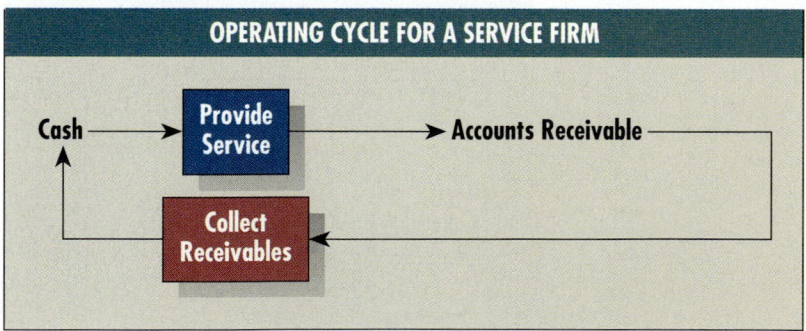

The operating cycle for a firm that buys and sells goods (a merchandising firm) starts when cash is used to buy goods (an asset called *inventory*), which are then sold, which create accounts receivable from customers, which are then collected in cash. The operating cycle for a merchandising firm, then, may be portrayed as shown in the box at the top of the following page. For many businesses, the normal operating cycle is less than one year. Certain industries, however, may have an operating cycle of more than one year. For example, a company may be in the inventory stage for an

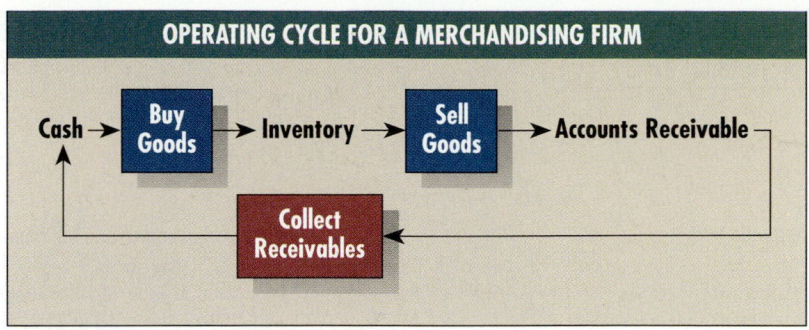

extended period of time—a winery aging wine or a nursery growing trees—so its normal operating cycle may extend several years.

Current assets are usually listed in the order of their *liquidity*, that is, their convertibility into cash. Prepaid expenses such as rent, insurance, and supplies are normally consumed during the operating cycle rather than converted into cash. These items are considered current assets, however, because the prepayments make cash outlays for services unnecessary during the current period. Examples of current assets other than those shown in Exhibit 4-9 are notes receivable, temporary investments, and inventory.

PLANT ASSETS   **Plant assets** are the land, buildings, equipment, vehicles, furniture, and fixtures that a firm uses in its operations. This section of the balance sheet may also be labeled *property and equipment*, or *property, plant, and equipment*. Landen TV Service has only one type of plant asset in its balance sheet at December 31, 1993. Note that the presentation in Exhibit 4-9 shows the truck's original cost and separately deducts the related accumulated depreciation.

OTHER ASSET CATEGORIES   Other categories of assets include investments (for long-term investments), natural resources, and intangible assets. Landen TV Service has no assets in any of these categories. We will discuss these types of assets in more detail in later chapters.

CURRENT LIABILITIES   **Current liabilities** are liabilities that must be settled within the normal operating cycle or one year, whichever is longer. Examples of current liabilities are accounts payable, short-term notes payable, wages payable, interest payable, utilities payable, income tax payable, and property taxes payable. Also included in current liabilities are any advance payments received from customers that

EXHIBIT 4—8		
LANDEN TV SERVICE		
STATEMENT OF OWNER'S EQUITY		
FOR THE MONTH OF DECEMBER, 1993		
M. Landen, Capital, December 1, 1993		$ –0–
Add: Capital Contributed in December	$10,000	
Net Income for December	3,095	13,095
		$13,095
Less: Capital Withdrawn in December		800
M. Landen, Capital, December 31, 1993		$12,295

EXHIBIT 4—9

LANDEN TV SERVICE
BALANCE SHEET
DECEMBER 31, 1993

Assets			Liabilities		
Current Assets			**Current Liabilities**		
Cash	$ 7,080		Accounts Payable	$700	
Accounts Receivable	3,480		Unearned Service Fees	750	
Commissions Receivable	50		Wages Payable	135	
Supplies and Parts	510		Interest Payable	90	
Prepaid Rent	3,000		Total Current Liabilities		$ 1,675
Total Current Assets		$14,120	**Long-term Liabilities**		
Plant Assets			Long-term Notes Payable		10,800
Truck	$10,800		Total Liabilities		$12,475
Less: Accumulated Depreciation	150	10,650	**Owner's Equity**		
			M. Landen, Capital		12,295
Total Assets		$24,770	Total Liabilities and Owner's Equity		$24,770

will be earned as revenue within the normal operating cycle or one year, whichever is longer. The unearned service fees shown in Landen TV Service's December 31, 1993, balance sheet are classified within current liabilities because they will be earned within the next year (Landen TV Service's normal operating cycle is less than one year).

LONG-TERM LIABILITIES **Long-term liabilities** are obligations not due to be settled within the normal operating cycle or one year, whichever is longer. Long-term notes payable and bonds payable are two examples of long-term liabilities. Landen TV Service's two-year note payable was entered into on December 1, 1993, and, thus, matures on November 30, 1995. As of December 31, 1993, it should be classified as a long-term liability. The balance sheet prepared at the end of the next year (December 31, 1994), however, will classify this note payable as a current liability because, at that point, it will mature within the next year.

OWNERS' EQUITY The owners' interest in the assets of a firm appears in the owners' equity section of the balance sheet. For sole proprietorships and partnerships, the interest is reflected in a capital account for each owner. A corporation labels its owners' equity as *stockholders' equity* or *shareholders' equity* and divides the equity into two main categories—amounts invested by owners and cumulative net incomes (less net losses) not yet distributed to owners as dividends. Identified as capital stock and retained earnings, each of these two categories will be examined in more detail in later chapters.

Landen TV Service is a sole proprietorship. The interest of owner Mark Landen in the firm's assets at December 31, 1993, is shown by his capital account balance of $12,295 in the balance sheet presented in Exhibit 4-9.

BALANCE SHEET FORMAT There are two acceptable formats for reporting balance sheets—an account form and a report form. Exhibit 4-9 illustrates the account form. In the *account form*, assets are displayed on the left side and liabilities and owners' equity are displayed on the right side. The *report form* stacks the presentation of balance sheet data—assets are reported first and beneath the assets are reported the liabilities and owners' equity. The demonstration problem at the end of this chapter presents the balance sheet in report form.

REPORTS TO STOCKHOLDERS

Corporations include their financial statements in periodic reports to stockholders. The annual report to stockholders for large corporations may be quite extensive, often running 20–50 pages or more. In addition to financial statements, the annual report may include a message from the chair of the board of directors and the chief executive officer, a review of the year's operations, a financial review, the accountants' report, and selected financial statistics for several years. A variety of charts, graphs, and photographs of the company's products and facilities may supplement these items.

Reports to stockholders covering less than one year (interim reports) are much less extensive. They are intended to provide owners and potential investors with timely information on the corporation's progress and may include summarized financial information rather than a complete set of financial statements.

Comprehensive annual reports to stockholders are a relatively recent development in the United States. Before the 1900s, corporate management generally disclosed little, if any, financial information to stockholders. The first corporations were usually small and obtained much of their funding through short-term bank loans rather than from the public sale of stocks. Bankers who needed to assess the borrower's ability to repay short-term loans considered the balance sheet the primary financial statement because it revealed the total short-term obligations and the assets that would likely be converted to cash

in the near future. By the late 1920s, however, corporate expansion led to increased financing through stock issuances and long-term debt. Owners and creditors used the income statement to judge earning power. Corporate reporting, then, evolved from providing balance sheets for bankers to providing income statements and balance sheets for stockholders and creditors.*

The first modern annual report was issued in 1902 by U.S. Steel Corporation. The report was lengthy and detailed, revealing so much about the corporation's operations that the directors were practically scandalized.[†] The extensive disclosures broke with tradition, and most corporations did not follow U.S. Steel's lead for many years.

Considerable variety exists in the length and detail of reports to stockholders. Remarks by the president of Diamond Match Company used 100 pages of the company's 1942 annual

report.[‡] In contrast, a 1972 semiannual report from North American Publishing of Philadelphia was more to the point. The report was poster size (three feet long) and featured letters eight inches high and six inches wide that stated: "We Had a BIG IMPROVEMENT for the First Six Months."[§]

Many corporations view the annual report, in part, as a public relations document. Imagine the chagrin, then, at Citizens Valley Bank in Albany, Oregon, a number of years ago. Half of the copies of the bank's 1973 annual report had been mailed before a particular omission was noted—the bank's name had been dropped from the report's cover and did not appear anywhere in the report.[‖]

At about the same time, Mott's Super Markets was reprinting 5,000 copies of its annual report. The corporation discovered the asset and liability figures on its balance sheet had been inadvertently reversed.[#]

---

*A. C. Littleton and V. K. Zimmerman, *Accounting Theory: Continuity and Change* (Englewood Cliffs, NJ: Prentice-Hall, Inc., 1962), pp. 92–97.

[†]"Annual Reports—No Longer Dry," *Fortune*, February 1944, p. 62.

[‡]*Ibid.*

[§]"The Numbers Game: A Few (Fairly) Kind Words," *Forbes*, May 1, 1973, p. 36.

[‖]"Business Bulletin," *The Wall Street Journal*, February 14, 1974, p. 1.

[#]"Business Bulletin," *The Wall Street Journal*, May 2, 1974, p. 1.

Step 7: Journalize and Post Adjusting Entries

OBJECTIVE 3 ILLUSTRATE *the process of journalizing and posting adjusting entries.*

At the close of the fiscal year, the adjusting entries on the worksheet must be recorded in the general journal and posted to the general ledger accounts in order to accomplish the proper closing procedures described in the next section. Although Landen TV Service has been in business only for December, its accounting year ends on December 31. Therefore, the adjusting entries are entered in the records and closing procedures are followed. The adjusting entries appear in the general journal as shown in Exhibit 4-10.

These journal entries are posted to the general ledger accounts of Landen TV Service shown in Exhibit 4-13 (pages 130–131). The entries are identified by the parenthetical notation (adjusting).

EXHIBIT 4—10	ADJUSTING ENTRIES

GENERAL JOURNAL   PAGE 3

Date		Description	Post. Ref.	Debit	Credit
1993 Dec.	31	Supplies and Parts Expense	53	440	
		Supplies and Parts	14		440
		To record expense of supplies and parts used in December.			
	31	Rent Expense	51	600	
		Prepaid Rent	15		600
		To record rent expense for December.			
	31	Depreciation Expense—Truck	55	150	
		Accumulated Depreciation—Truck	19		150
		To record December depreciation on truck.			
	31	Unearned Service Fees	24	250	
		Service Fees Earned	41		250
		To record portion of advance earned in December.			
	31	Wages Expense	52	135	
		Wages Payable	23		135
		To record accrued wages for December 29, 30, and 31.			
	31	Interest Expense	56	90	
		Interest Payable	22		90
		To record interest expense for December.			
	31	Commissions Receivable	13	50	
		Commissions Earned	42		50
		To record commissions earned for December.			

INTERIM FINANCIAL STATEMENTS

Financial statements covering periods within a company's fiscal year or prepared at a date other than the fiscal year-end are called **interim financial statements.** Financial statements prepared monthly or quarterly, for example, are interim financial statements. Most companies prepare interim financial statements from worksheet data, but they do not journalize and post the interim adjustments (they prefer to journalize and post adjusting entries only at year-end). Interim adjustments, then, are reflected only on the worksheet. When making interim adjusting entries on the worksheet, the accountant must consider the period for which the adjustments are made. Some adjustment amounts will accumulate; others will not. For example, in writing off a $1,200 one-year prepaid insurance premium paid on January 1 and debited to the asset account, the accountant would debit Insurance Expense and credit Prepaid Insurance for $100 on the worksheet at January 31. The amount of the adjustment would be $200 at the end of February, $300 at the end of March, and so on. Similarly, the amount of the worksheet adjusting entry for depreciation will increase each month. On the other hand, an adjusting entry to accrue salaries at the end of any month will consist only of unpaid salaries at the date of adjustment, because salaries accrued at the end of each month are ordinarily paid during the ensuing month.

When the year-end worksheet is prepared, the adjusting data will pertain to the entire year. Therefore, the adjusting entries to be journalized and posted to the ledger accounts can be taken directly from this worksheet.

Step 8: Journalize and Post Closing Entries

OBJECTIVE **4** **DESCRIBE** *the process of closing the temporary accounts.*

Revenue, expense, and drawing accounts are temporary accounts that accumulate data related to a specific accounting year. These temporary accounts facilitate preparation of the income statement and provide additional information. At the end of each accounting year, the balances of these temporary accounts are transferred to the capital account (the Retained Earnings account for corporations). Therefore, the balance of the owner's capital account includes on a cumulative basis the net result of all revenue, expense, and drawing transactions. This phase in the accounting cycle is referred to as the **closing procedures.**

A temporary account is said to be *closed* when an entry is made that changes its balance to zero—that is, an entry that is equal in amount to the account's balance but is opposite to the balance as a debit or credit. An account that is closed is said to be closed *to* the account that receives the offsetting debit or credit. Thus, a closing entry simply transfers the balance of one account to another account. In this manner, closing procedures transfer the balances of temporary accounts to the capital account.

A summary account is traditionally used to close the temporary revenue and expense accounts. For our illustration, we will use an account titled Income Summary, although a variety of titles are found in practice (Revenue and Expense Summary, Income and Expense Summary, or Profit and Loss Summary, for example). The entries for opening and closing Income Summary are quite simple and occur only during the closing procedures. The entries that close the temporary accounts are as follows:

1 **Close the revenue accounts.** Debit each revenue account for an amount equal to its balance, and credit Income Summary for the total amount of revenues.

2 **Close the expense accounts.** Credit each expense account for an amount equal to its balance, and debit Income Summary for the total amount of expenses.

After these temporary accounts have been closed, the balance of the Income Summary account is equal to the period's net income (if a credit balance) or net loss (if a debit balance). The remaining closing steps depend on the form of business organization and are as follows:

3 **Close the Income Summary account.**
   a. *For sole proprietorships:* In the case of a net income, debit Income Summary and credit the owner's capital account for the net income amount. In the case of a net loss, debit the owner's capital account and credit Income Summary for the net loss amount.
   b. *For partnerships:* Partners should have an agreement as to how they are to share net incomes and losses of the partnership. In the case of a net income, debit Income Summary for the net income amount and credit each partner's capital account for the partner's proper share of the net income. In the case of a net loss, debit each partner's capital account for the partner's proper share of the net loss and credit Income Summary for the net loss amount.
   c. *For corporations:* In the case of a net income, debit Income Summary and credit Retained Earnings for the net income amount. In the case of a net loss, debit Retained Earnings and credit Income Summary for the net loss amount.

4 **Close the owner drawing accounts (sole proprietorships and partnerships) or close the dividends account (corporations).**
   a. *For sole proprietorships:* Debit the owner's capital account and credit the owner's drawing account for an amount equal to the debit balance in the owner's drawing account.
   b. *For partnerships:* For each partner, debit the partner's capital account and credit the partner's drawing account for an amount equal to the debit balance in the partner's drawing account.
   c. *For corporations:* Debit Retained Earnings and credit Cash Dividends for the debit balance in the Cash Dividends account.

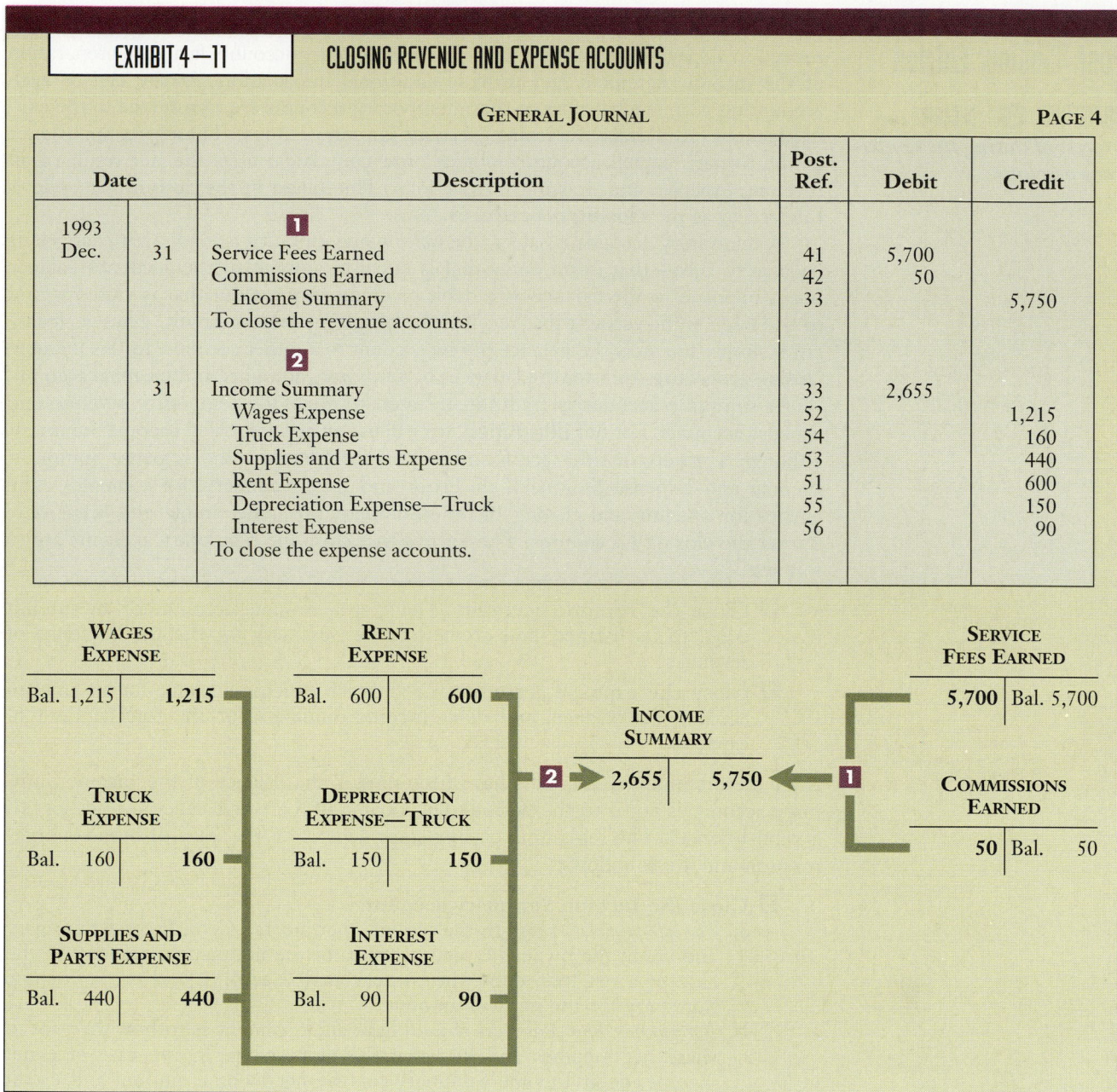

EXHIBIT 4—11   CLOSING REVENUE AND EXPENSE ACCOUNTS

GENERAL JOURNAL   PAGE 4

Date		Description	Post. Ref.	Debit	Credit
1993 Dec.	31	**1** Service Fees Earned	41	5,700	
		Commissions Earned	42	50	
		Income Summary	33		5,750
		To close the revenue accounts.			
	31	**2** Income Summary	33	2,655	
		Wages Expense	52		1,215
		Truck Expense	54		160
		Supplies and Parts Expense	53		440
		Rent Expense	51		600
		Depreciation Expense—Truck	55		150
		Interest Expense	56		90
		To close the expense accounts.			

SOLE PROPRIETORSHIP CLOSING   In Exhibit 4-11, we illustrate the entries for closing the revenue and expense accounts to the Income Summary account of Landen TV Service as they would be recorded in the general journal. The effect of these two entries is shown using T accounts.

At this point, the balance of the Income Summary is a credit equal to the net income of $3,095. The closing procedure is completed by closing the Income Summary and M. Landen, Drawing accounts to the M. Landen, Capital account. These two entries are recorded in the general journal as shown in Exhibit 4-12. The effect of these entries on the general ledger is also diagrammed.

It is probably most convenient to take the data necessary for formulating the closing entries from the worksheet, although the information can also be derived from the ledger. After the closing entries for Landen TV Service have been recorded and posted to the firm's general ledger, all temporary accounts have zero balances and the owner's capital account has a balance equal to the amount shown on Landen TV Service's balance sheet (see Exhibit 4-9). Exhibit 4-13 illustrates the general

| EXHIBIT 4—12 | CLOSING THE INCOME SUMMARY AND DRAWING ACCOUNTS |

GENERAL JOURNAL   PAGE 4

Date		Description	Post. Ref.	Debit	Credit
1993 Dec.	31	**3** Income Summary	33	3,095	
		M. Landen, Capital	31		3,095
		To close the Income Summary account.			
	31	**4** M. Landen, Capital	31	800	
		M. Landen, Drawing	32		800
		To close the drawing account.			

M. LANDEN, DRAWING	M. LANDEN, CAPITAL	INCOME SUMMARY
Bal. 800 | 800 ▬ **4** ➔	800 | Bal. 10,000	2,655 | 5,750
	3,095 ⬅ **3** ▬ 3,095	

ledger of Landen TV Service after all the closing procedures have been followed. Closing entries are identified by the parenthetical notation (closing).

PARTNERSHIP CLOSING

To illustrate the unique aspects of a partnership closing, assume the partnership of partners Coy and Day has the same revenues and expenses as Landen TV Service. The partners have agreed to share net incomes and losses 60% to Coy and 40% to Day. During the period, Coy had $600 of withdrawals and Day had $200 of withdrawals. After closing the revenue and expense accounts (exactly as shown in Exhibit 4-11), the final two closing entries are as follows:

Income Summary	3,095	
E. Coy, Capital		1,857
P. Day, Capital		1,238
To close the Income Summary account, 60% to Coy and 40% to Day.		
E. Coy, Capital	600	
P. Day, Capital	200	
E. Coy, Drawing		600
P. Day, Drawing		200
To close the drawing accounts.		

CORPORATION CLOSING

To illustrate the unique aspects of a corporation closing, assume a corporation has exactly the same revenues and expenses as Landen TV Service. (Because a corporation is subject to an income tax, it would have an additional expense account called Income Tax Expense; we will disregard income taxes for this illustration.) During the period, cash dividends of $800 were declared and paid (creating a Cash Dividends account with an $800 debit balance). After closing the revenue and expense accounts (exactly as shown in Exhibit 4-11), the final two closing entries are as follows:

Income Summary	3,095	
Retained Earnings		3,095
To close the Income Summary account.		
Retained Earnings	800	
Cash Dividends		800
To close the Cash Dividends account.		

EXHIBIT 4—13	GENERAL LEDGER FOR LANDEN TV SERVICE

CASH — ACCOUNT NO. 11

Date		Description	Post. Ref.	Debit*	Credit	Balance
1993						
Dec.	1		J1	10,000		10,000
	1		J1		250	9,750
	1		J1		3,600	6,150
	2		J1	1,000		7,150
	10		J1	650		7,800
	13		J1		540	7,260
	19		J1	800		8,060
	21		J2	520		8,580
	27		J2		540	8,040
	29		J2		800	7,240
	30		J2		160	7,080

ACCOUNTS RECEIVABLE — ACCOUNT NO. 12

Date		Description	Post. Ref.	Debit*	Credit	Balance
1993						
Dec.	13		J1	1,580		1,580
	19		J1		800	780
	31		J2	2,700		3,480

COMMISSIONS RECEIVABLE — ACCOUNT NO. 13

Date		Description	Post. Ref.	Debit*	Credit	Balance
1993						
Dec.	31	(adjusting)	J3	50		50

SUPPLIES AND PARTS — ACCOUNT NO. 14

Date		Description	Post. Ref.	Debit*	Credit	Balance
1993						
Dec.	1		J1	950		950
	31	(adjusting)	J3		440	510

PREPAID RENT — ACCOUNT NO. 15

Date		Description	Post. Ref.	Debit*	Credit	Balance
1993						
Dec.	1		J1	3,600		3,600
	31	(adjusting)	J3		600	3,000

TRUCK — ACCOUNT NO. 18

Date		Description	Post. Ref.	Debit*	Credit	Balance
1993						
Dec.	1		J1	10,800		10,800

ACCUMULATED DEPRECIATION— TRUCK — ACCOUNT NO. 19

Date		Description	Post. Ref.	Debit	Credit*	Balance
1993						
Dec.	31	(adjusting)	J3		150	150

ACCOUNTS PAYABLE — ACCOUNT NO. 21

Date		Description	Post. Ref.	Debit	Credit*	Balance
1993						
Dec.	1		J1		700	700

INTEREST PAYABLE — ACCOUNT NO. 22

Date		Description	Post. Ref.	Debit	Credit*	Balance
1993						
Dec.	31	(adjusting)	J3		90	90

WAGES PAYABLE — ACCOUNT NO. 23

Date		Description	Post. Ref.	Debit	Credit*	Balance
1993						
Dec.	31	(adjusting)	J3		135	135

UNEARNED SERVICE FEES — ACCOUNT NO. 24

Date		Description	Post. Ref.	Debit	Credit*	Balance
1993						
Dec.	2		J1		1,000	1,000
	31	(adjusting)	J3	250		750

EXHIBIT 4—13 [Continued]

LONG-TERM NOTES PAYABLE   ACCOUNT NO. 25

Date		Description	Post. Ref.	Debit	Credit*	Balance
1993 Dec.	1		J1		10,800	10,800

M. LANDEN, CAPITAL   ACCOUNT NO. 31

Date		Description	Post. Ref.	Debit	Credit*	Balance
1993 Dec.	1		J1		10,000	10,000
	31	(closing)	J4		3,095	13,095
	31	(closing)	J4	800		12,295

M. LANDEN, DRAWING   ACCOUNT NO. 32

Date		Description	Post. Ref.	Debit*	Credit	Balance
1993 Dec.	29		J2	800		800
	31	(closing)	J4		800	–0–

INCOME SUMMARY   ACCOUNT NO. 33

Date		Description	Post. Ref.	Debit	Credit*	Balance
1993 Dec.	31	(closing)	J4		5,750	5,750
	31	(closing)	J4	2,655		3,095
	31	(closing)	J4	3,095		–0–

SERVICE FEES EARNED   ACCOUNT NO. 41

Date		Description	Post. Ref.	Debit	Credit*	Balance
1993 Dec.	10		J1		650	650
	13		J1		1,580	2,230
	21		J2		520	2,750
	31		J2		2,700	5,450
	31	(adjusting)	J3		250	5,700
	31	(closing)	J4	5,700		–0–

COMMISSIONS EARNED   ACCOUNT NO. 42

Date		Description	Post. Ref.	Debit	Credit*	Balance
1993 Dec.	31	(adjusting)	J3		50	50
	31	(closing)	J4	50		–0–

RENT EXPENSE   ACCOUNT NO. 51

Date		Description	Post. Ref.	Debit*	Credit	Balance
1993 Dec.	31	(adjusting)	J3	600		600
	31	(closing)	J4		600	–0–

WAGES EXPENSE   ACCOUNT NO. 52

Date		Description	Post. Ref.	Debit*	Credit	Balance
1993 Dec.	13		J1	540		540
	27		J2	540		1,080
	31	(adjusting)	J3	135		1,215
	31	(closing)	J4		1,215	–0–

SUPPLIES AND PARTS EXPENSE   ACCOUNT NO. 53

Date		Description	Post. Ref.	Debit*	Credit	Balance
1993 Dec.	31	(adjusting)	J3	440		440
	31	(closing)	J4		440	–0–

TRUCK EXPENSE   ACCOUNT NO. 54

Date		Description	Post. Ref.	Debit*	Credit	Balance
1993 Dec.	30		J2	160		160
	31	(closing)	J4		160	–0–

DEPRECIATION EXPENSE—TRUCK   ACCOUNT NO. 55

Date		Description	Post. Ref.	Debit*	Credit	Balance
1993 Dec.	31	(adjusting)	J3	150		150
	31	(closing)	J4		150	–0–

INTEREST EXPENSE   ACCOUNT NO. 56

Date		Description	Post. Ref.	Debit*	Credit	Balance
1993 Dec.	31	(adjusting)	J3	90		90
	31	(closing)	J4		90	–0–

	EXHIBIT 4—14		

LANDEN TV SERVICE
POST-CLOSING TRIAL BALANCE
DECEMBER 31, 1993

	Debit	Credit
Cash	$ 7,080	
Accounts Receivable	3,480	
Commissions Receivable	50	
Supplies and Parts	510	
Prepaid Rent	3,000	
Truck	10,800	
Accumulated Depreciation—Truck		$ 150
Accounts Payable		700
Interest Payable		90
Wages Payable		135
Unearned Service Fees		750
Long-term Notes Payable		10,800
M. Landen, Capital		12,295
	$24,920	$24,920

Step 9: Prepare a Post-closing Trial Balance

OBJECTIVE 5 EXPLAIN *the nature of a post-closing trial balance.*

A **post-closing trial balance** is taken after the completion of the closing process. The balancing of this trial balance is evidence that an equality of debits and credits has been maintained in the general ledger throughout the adjusting and closing process and that the general ledger is in balance to start the next accounting period. Because the temporary accounts have been closed, only balance sheet accounts appear in a post-closing trial balance. Exhibit 4-14 presents the post-closing trial balance for Landen TV Service.

SUMMARY OF THE ACCOUNTING CYCLE

OBJECTIVE 6 SUMMARIZE *the complete accounting cycle.*

The sequence of accounting procedures known as the *accounting cycle* occurs each fiscal year and represents a systematic process for analyzing, accumulating, classifying, and reporting the financial data of a business entity. Exhibit 4-15 summarizes the actions taken in the accounting cycle and notes their frequency of occurrence and the related document or accounting record.

REVERSING ENTRIES: OPTIONAL FIRST STEP IN NEXT ACCOUNTING PERIOD

In our discussion of adjusting entries for accrued items in the previous chapter, we pointed out that certain precautions are necessary to avoid reflecting the same expense or revenue in two successive periods. We now review two alternative procedures for recording the settlement of accrued items in the period after their accrual. We illustrate these procedures using wages expense for Landen TV Service.

Wages Expense in December

Recall that the Landen TV Service employee received wages of $270 for each six-day work week ($45 per day) and that the employee was paid every other Saturday. We assumed that the two paydays in December 1993 fell on December 13 and 27. Wages expense of $135 was accrued for December 29, 30, and 31. We made the following adjusting entry to reflect the proper expense for December:

EXHIBIT 4—15	THE ACCOUNTING CYCLE	
Frequency	**Action Taken**	**Related Document or Record**
Daily	**1.** Analyze transactions	Source documents
	2. Record transactions	Journal
	3. Post journal entries	General ledger
Whenever financial statements are desired	**4.** Prepare trial balance	Worksheet
	5. Adjust general ledger accounts	
	6. Prepare financial statements*	Income statement Statement of owner's equity Balance sheet
End of period	**7.** Journalize and post adjusting entries	Journal and General ledger
	8. Journalize and post closing entries	
	9. Prepare post-closing trial balance	Post-closing trial balance

*The preparation of the statement of cash flows is discussed in a later chapter.

OBJECTIVE 7 DISCUSS *the purpose of reversing entries.*

```
1993
Dec. 31   Wages Expense                                  135
              Wages Payable                                     135
          To record accrued wages for December 29, 30, and 31.
```

After this adjusting entry was posted, the Wages Expense account had a debit balance of $1,215. This consisted of two debits of $540 made on December 13 and 27 and the $135 accrual on December 31. Along with other expenses, the Wages Expense account was closed to Income Summary on December 31. After the closing procedures, the Wages Expense and Wages Payable accounts appeared in the ledger as follows:

WAGES EXPENSE   ACCOUNT NO. 52

Date		Description	Post. Ref.	Debit*	Credit	Balance
1993 Dec.	13		J1	540		540
	27		J2	540		1,080
	31	(adjusting)	J3	135		1,215
	31	(closing)	J4		1,215	–0–

WAGES PAYABLE   ACCOUNT NO. 23

Date		Description	Post. Ref.	Debit	Credit*	Balance
1993 Dec.	31	(adjusting)	J3		135	135

January Accounting without Using Reversals

On January 10, 1994, the employee will receive another $540 wage payment. Of this amount, only $405 should be reflected as January expense since only nine days were worked in January (the other three days were worked in December and accrued as December wages expense). We may record the wage payment and the correct January wages expense by making the following entry:

```
1994
Jan. 10   Wages Payable              135
          Wages Expense              405
              Cash                              540
          To record wages paid.
```

This procedure, however, requires extreme vigilance in recording routine transactions on the part of the accountant, who must keep in mind previously made accruals in order to record subsequent payments correctly. Many accountants find this a nuisance and avoid the problem by reversing adjustments made for accruals.

January Accounting Using Reversals

As an alternative to the preceding procedure, then, an accountant may use **reversing entries.** Reversing entries are made after all closing procedures have been completed and the post-closing trial balance has been prepared. Reversing entries are dated the first day of the following period and, therefore, are the first journal entries in that period. A reversing entry is so named because the entry exactly reverses the debits and credits of an adjusting entry. For example, the reversing entry for the accrual of wages would be

```
1994
Jan. 1    Wages Payable              135
              Wages Expense                     135
          To reverse accrual made December 31.
```

This entry reduces the liability Wages Payable to zero and results in a $135 abnormal credit balance in the Wages Expense account at the start of the new accounting period. On the next payday, however, the wage payment of $540 is recorded as all wage payments are recorded, as follows:

```
Jan. 10   Wages Expense              540
              Cash                              540
          Paid wages for two weeks ended January 10.
```

When this entry is posted to the Wages Expense account, the $540 debit is combined with the $135 credit balance created by the reversing entry. As a result, the account balance is the proper wages expense for January 1–10 ($405). After the January 1 reversing entry and the January 10 payment have been posted, the Wages Expense and Wages Payable accounts appear as shown below. Note that the $135 abnormal balance is placed in parentheses.

WAGES EXPENSE   ACCOUNT NO. 52

Date		Description	Post. Ref.	Debit*	Credit	Balance
1993 Dec.	13		J1	540		540
	27		J2	540		1,080
	31	(adjusting)	J3	135		1,215
	31	(closing)	J4		1,215	–0–
1994 Jan.	1	(reversing)	J5		135	(135)
	10		J6	540		405

WAGES PAYABLE   ACCOUNT NO. 23

Date		Description	Post. Ref.	Debit	Credit*	Balance
1993 Dec.	31	(adjusting)	J3		135	135
1994 Jan.	1	(reversing)	J5	135		–0–

Both of the alternative procedures for handling the December accrued wages in January give the same result—the elimination of the $135 wages payable and the portrayal of $405 of wages expense for the first 10 days in January. By using reversals, however, the accountant can record the first January payroll without having to consider the amount of wages accrued at December 31.

Other Reversals

A reversing entry simplifies the recording of a transaction that relates to an earlier adjusting entry. The appropriate adjustments to reverse are *accruals* of revenues and expenses. Of the adjustments made by Landen TV Service (in addition to the accrual of wages), reversing entries would be employed for the two other accruals—the $90 interest expense and the $50 commissions earned. The accountant would therefore make two additional reversing entries after the books are closed:

1994			
Jan. 1	Interest Payable	90	
	Interest Expense		90
	To reverse accrual made December 31.		
Jan. 1	Commissions Earned	50	
	Commissions Receivable		50
	To reverse accrual made December 31.		

These entries eliminate the accrued amounts from the liability and asset accounts and create an abnormal credit balance of $90 in Interest Expense and an abnormal debit balance of $50 in Commissions Earned.

The credit balance in Interest Expense will be eliminated when the annual interest of $1,080 on the note payable is paid on November 30, 1994. The entry to record this interest payment is as follows:

Nov. 30	Interest Expense	1,080	
	Cash		1,080
	To record payment of annual interest.		

After the entry for payment is posted, Interest Expense will have a $990 debit balance, the proper amount of interest expense on the note payable for the first 11 months of 1994.

The debit balance in Commissions Earned is eliminated when Landen TV Service receives its three-month commission payment of $150 on February 28, 1994. This receipt is recorded as follows:

Feb. 28   Cash   150
           Commissions Earned   150
           To record receipt of quarterly commission.

This entry leaves a credit balance of $100 in the Commissions Earned revenue account, reflecting the proper amount of revenue for commission work performed in January and February 1994.

Although the use of reversing entries is optional, it does permit us to analyze certain transactions the same way all the time. For example, if reversals are used, an accountant may be instructed (or a computer programmed) to debit Wages Expense and credit Cash every time wages are paid. Similarly, every interest payment may be analyzed as a debit to Interest Expense and a credit to Cash, and every receipt of commissions may be recorded as a debit to Cash and a credit to Commissions Earned. Reversals eliminate the need to remember the effects of previous accruals and, therefore, contribute to the more efficient processing of data.

Reversals normally are not appropriate for adjustments involving prepayments of expense or advance receipts of revenues. Only if a company's policy is to record expense prepayments in expense accounts and advance revenue receipts in revenue accounts might adjustments involving these items be reversed. In these cases, the reversals reestablish the remaining expense prepayments and advance revenue receipts in the appropriate expense and revenue accounts. Adjustments leading to reversals of this sort are discussed in the appendix to the previous chapter.

ANALYTICAL APPLICATION

CURRENT RATIO

OBJECTIVE 8 DEFINE *the* **current ratio** *and* EXPLAIN *its use.*

The **working capital** of a firm is the difference between its current assets and current liabilities. Landen TV Service's working capital at December 31, 1993, is $12,445 ($14,120 current assets − $1,675 current liabilities). Adequate working capital permits a firm to meet its current obligations and carry on its normal operating activities without having to borrow money or issue stock (if a corporation) at inopportune times.

In analyzing the adequacy of a firm's working capital, the current ratio is a widely used financial statistic. The **current ratio** is computed as follows:

$$\text{Current Ratio} = \frac{\text{Current Assets}}{\text{Current Liabilities}}$$

The current ratio for Landen TV Service at December 31, 1993 is 8.43 ($14,120/$1,675), or 8.43:1. This ratio means that current assets are more than eight times current liabilities. This is a high current ratio and indicates that Landen TV Service should have little difficulty meeting its current obligations. Historically, a current ratio of 2.00 has often been considered a minimum acceptable current ratio. This is a general guide only. Successful operation with a current ratio below 2.00 is possible for some companies, particularly service firms, because they do not have large amounts of inventory among their current assets. In evaluating a specific firm's current ratio, one should consider such things as the nature of the business, the industry average, the composition of the current assets, and the recent trend in the current ratio. Indeed, one might even conclude that a firm's current ratio is too high; that is, the firm may have far more current assets than are needed to provide adequate coverage of current liabilities. The excess resources might better be directed to more profitable uses.

Following are examples of recent current ratios for several companies in different industries.

CIS TECHNOLOGIES, INC. (health-care claims management services)	9.57
OVERSEAS SHIPHOLDING GROUP, INC. (overseas cargo transportation)	2.71
PFIZER INC. (manufacturer of pharmaceuticals and drugs)	1.42
GEORGIA-PACIFIC CORPORATION (manufacturer of pulp, paper, and building products)	0.70

KEY POINTS FOR CHAPTER OBJECTIVES

1 IDENTIFY a worksheet's place in the accounting cycle and EXPLAIN the procedures for preparing a worksheet (pp. 116–121).
- The worksheet begins with the unadjusted trial balance, step 4 in the accounting cycle.
- The worksheet facilitates the preparation of financial statements.
- Adjusted account balances, which are extended into the income statement and balance sheet columns of the worksheet, provide the data for the formal financial statements.

2 ILLUSTRATE the financial statements prepared from a worksheet and DESCRIBE a classified balance sheet (pp. 121–124).
- An income statement, statement of owner's equity, and balance sheet may be prepared from data on the worksheet. The owner's capital account may also need to be reviewed to obtain information on owner capital contributions during the period for the statement of owner's equity.
- Assets in the balance sheet are classified as current assets, investments, plant assets, natural resources, or intangible assets. Liabilities are classified as current or long-term liabilities.
- Current assets are cash and other assets that will be converted into cash or used up during the normal operating cycle of the business or one year, whichever is longer. Current liabilities are amounts due within the normal operating cycle or one year, whichever is longer.

3 ILLUSTRATE the process of journalizing and posting adjusting entries (pp. 125–126).
- End-of-year adjustments are recorded in the general journal and posted to the general ledger. Adjustments for interim financial statements are usually made only on the worksheet.

4 DESCRIBE the process of closing the temporary accounts (pp. 127–131).
- *Closing the books* means closing the revenue, expense, and other temporary accounts. Revenue and expense account balances are transferred to the Income Summary account. The balances of the Income Summary account and the owners' drawing accounts are closed to the owners' capital accounts. For corporations, the Income Summary account and Cash Dividends account are closed to Retained Earnings.

5 EXPLAIN the nature of a post-closing trial balance (p. 132).
- A post-closing trial balance contains only balance sheet accounts.

6 SUMMARIZE the complete accounting cycle (pp. 132–133).
- The first three steps in the accounting cycle—analyzing transactions, recording transactions, and posting the transaction journal entries—occur daily.
- The next three steps in the accounting cycle—preparing a trial balance, adjusting the accounts on a worksheet, and preparing financial statements—occur whenever financial statements are desired.
- The last three steps in the accounting cycle—journalizing and posting adjusting entries, journalizing and posting closing entries, and preparing a post-closing trial balance—occur at the end of the accounting period.

7 DISCUSS the purpose of reversing entries (pp. 132–136).
- The reversal of adjustments made for *accrued* items permits the normal recording of subsequent transactions. It safeguards against reflecting the same revenue or expense in successive periods.

8 ANALYTICAL APPLICATION: DEFINE the *current ratio* and EXPLAIN its use (pp. 136–137).
- The current ratio is computed by dividing current assets by current liabilities.

SELF-TEST QUESTIONS FOR REVIEW

(Answers follow the Solution to Demonstration Problem.)

1. Which trial balance begins a worksheet?
   a. Post-closing trial balance.
   b. Adjusted trial balance.
   c. Unadjusted trial balance.
   d. Beginning-of-year trial balance.

2. In preparing a worksheet, you have just extended the adjusted account balances to the income statement and balance sheet columns and totaled these columns. If the company is profitable this period, the total of the income statement credit column will be
   a. Larger than the balance sheet debit column total.
   b. Larger than the income statement debit column total.
   c. Smaller than the income statement debit column total.
   d. Larger than the balance sheet credit column total.

3. Closing entries
   a. Are an optional step in the accounting cycle.
   b. Affect only balance sheet accounts.
   c. Permit a company to analyze routine, repetitive transactions the same way all the time.
   d. Remove the balances from a firm's temporary accounts.

4. Which of the following closing procedures is unique to a corporation?
   a. Close each revenue account to the Income Summary account.
   b. Close each expense account to the Income Summary account.
   c. Close the Income Summary account to the Retained Earnings account.
   d. Close the owner's drawing account to the owner's capital account.

5. Assume Zee Company initially records prepayments in balance sheet accounts and makes reversing entries when appropriate. Which of the following year-end adjusting entries by Zee Company should be reversed?
   a. The entry to record depreciation expense for the period.
   b. The entry to record the portion of service fees received in advance that is earned by year-end.
   c. The entry to record supplies used during the period.
   d. The entry to record interest earned by year-end but not yet received.

DEMONSTRATION PROBLEM FOR REVIEW

The unadjusted trial balance of Gibbons Repair Service, Inc., at the end of 1993 is shown below. The firm provides repair services on a cash-only basis and operates on a calendar-year basis.

GIBBONS REPAIR SERVICE, INC.
TRIAL BALANCE
DECEMBER 31, 1993

	Debit	Credit
Cash	$ 2,200	
Supplies	6,200	
Equipment	19,600	
Accumulated Depreciation—Equipment		$ 1,800
Accounts Payable		800
Long-term Notes Payable		4,000
Capital Stock		8,000
Retained Earnings		2,400
Service Fees Earned		28,000
Rent Expense	6,000	
Wages Expense	11,000	
	$45,000	$45,000

The following additional information is available at December 31, 1993:
1. Supplies on hand at December 31 are $3,300.
2. Annual depreciation on the equipment is $1,800.

3. Interest accrued on the note payable at December 31 is $100.

4. Income tax expense for 1993 is estimated to be $900.

REQUIRED

a. Prepare a 10-column worksheet for the year ended December 31, 1993.

b. Prepare closing entries in general journal form.

c. Prepare an income statement for 1993 and a classified balance sheet at December 31, 1993.

d. Compute the current ratio at December 31, 1993.

SOLUTION TO DEMONSTRATION PROBLEM

a.

GIBBONS REPAIR SERVICE, INC.
WORKSHEET
FOR THE YEAR ENDED DECEMBER 31, 1993

Description	Trial Balance Debit	Trial Balance Credit	Adjustments Debit	Adjustments Credit	Adjusted Trial Balance Debit	Adjusted Trial Balance Credit	Income Statement Debit	Income Statement Credit	Balance Sheet Debit	Balance Sheet Credit
Cash	2,200				2,200				2,200	
Supplies	6,200			(1)2,900	3,300				3,300	
Equipment	19,600				19,600				19,600	
Accumulated Depreciation—Equipment		1,800		(2)1,800		3,600				3,600
Accounts Payable		800				800				800
Long-term Notes Payable		4,000				4,000				4,000
Capital Stock		8,000				8,000				8,000
Retained Earnings		2,400				2,400				2,400
Service Fees Earned		28,000				28,000		28,000		
Rent Expense	6,000				6,000		6,000			
Wages Expense	11,000				11,000		11,000			
	45,000	45,000								
Supplies Expense			(1)2,900		2,900		2,900			
Depreciation Expense			(2)1,800		1,800		1,800			
Interest Expense			(3) 100		100		100			
Interest Payable				(3) 100		100				100
Income Tax Expense			(4) 900		900		900			
Income Tax Payable				(4) 900		900				900
			5,700	5,700	47,800	47,800	22,700	28,000	25,100	19,800
Net Income							5,300			5,300
							28,000	28,000	25,100	25,100

b.

Dec. 31	Service Fees Earned		28,000	
	Income Summary			28,000
	To close the revenue account.			
31	Income Summary		22,700	
	Rent Expense			6,000
	Wages Expense			11,000
	Supplies Expense			2,900
	Depreciation Expense			1,800
	Interest Expense			100
	Income Tax Expense			900
	To close the expense accounts.			
31	Income Summary		5,300	
	Retained Earnings			5,300
	To close the Income Summary account.			

GIBBONS REPAIR SERVICE, INC.
INCOME STATEMENT
FOR THE YEAR ENDED DECEMBER 31, 1993

Revenue		
Service Fees Earned		$28,000
Expenses		
Rent Expense	$ 6,000	
Wages Expense	11,000	
Supplies Expense	2,900	
Depreciation Expense	1,800	
Interest Expense	100	
Income Tax Expense	900	
Total Expenses		22,700
Net Income		$ 5,300

GIBBONS REPAIR SERVICE, INC.
BALANCE SHEET
DECEMBER 31, 1993

Assets

Current Assets		
Cash	$ 2,200	
Supplies	3,300	
Total Current Assets		$ 5,500
Plant Assets		
Equipment	$19,600	
Less: Accumulated Depreciation	3,600	16,000
Total Assets		$21,500

Liabilities

Current Liabilities		
Accounts Payable	$ 800	
Interest Payable	100	
Income Tax Payable	900	
Total Current Liabilites		$ 1,800
Long-term Liabilities		
Long-term Notes Payable		4,000
Total Liabilities		$ 5,800

Stockholders' Equity

Capital Stock	$ 8,000	
Retained Earnings	7,700*	
Total Stockholders' Equity		15,700
Total Liabilities and Stockholders' Equity		$21,500

*$2,400 + $5,300 net income = $7,700.

d. Current Ratio: $5,500/$1,800 = 3.06

GLOSSARY OF KEY TERMS USED IN THIS CHAPTER

adjusted trial balance   A list of general ledger accounts and their balances taken after adjustments have been made (p. 119).

closing procedures   A step in the accounting cycle in which the balances of all temporary accounts are transferred to the owner's capital account or the Retained Earnings account, leaving the temporary accounts with zero balances (p. 127).

current assets Cash and other assets that will be converted into cash or used up within the normal operating cycle of the business or one year, whichever is longer (p. 122).

current liabilities Liabilities that must be settled within the normal operating cycle of the business or one year, whichever is longer (p. 123).

current ratio A firm's current assets divided by its current liabilities (p. 136).

interim financial statements Financial statements covering periods within a firm's fiscal year or prepared at a date other than the fiscal year-end (p. 126).

long-term liabilities Obligations not due to be settled within the normal operating cycle or one year, whichever is longer (p. 124).

normal operating cycle The average period of time between a firm's use of cash in its typical operating activities and the subsequent collection of cash from customers (p. 122).

plant assets The land, buildings, equipment, vehicles, furniture, and fixtures that a firm uses in its operations (p. 123).

post-closing trial balance A list of general ledger accounts and their balances after closing entries have been recorded and posted (p. 132).

reversing entries Journal entries made the first day of an accounting period that reverse the debits and credits of accrual adjusting entries made at the end of the preceding period (p. 134).

working capital The difference between a firm's current assets and current liabilities (p. 136).

worksheet An informal accounting document used to facilitate the preparation of financial statements (p. 116).

QUESTIONS

4-1 At what point in the accounting cycle is a worksheet used? What is the first accounting information placed on the worksheet?

4-2 After a worksheet is completed at the end of the accounting year, what steps remain to complete the accounting cycle?

4-3 What are the advantages of preparing a worksheet?

4-4 Identify each of the 10 amount columns of the worksheet and indicate to which column the adjusted balance of the following accounts would be extended:
   - **a.** Accounts Receivable
   - **b.** Accumulated Depreciation
   - **c.** W. Biggs, Drawing
   - **d.** Wages Payable
   - **e.** Depreciation Expense
   - **f.** Rent Receivable
   - **g.** Prepaid Insurance
   - **h.** Service Fees Earned
   - **i.** Capital Stock
   - **j.** Retained Earnings

4-5 Suppose the total adjusted revenue of a business is $87,000 and total adjusted expense is $68,000. (a) When the worksheet is completed, in which columns would the $19,000 difference appear? (b) If total adjusted expense amounted to $95,000, in which columns of the completed worksheet would the $8,000 difference appear?

4-6 What is the reason that the total of the balance sheet debit column of the worksheet may differ from the total asset amount on the formal balance sheet?

4-7 When adjusted balances are extended on the worksheet, Unearned Service Fees of $3,000 is extended as a credit in the income statement columns and Accounts Receivable of $1,200 is extended as a debit in the income statement columns. All other extensions are properly made. (a) Does the worksheet balance? (b) How do these incorrect extensions affect the calculation of net income shown on the worksheet?

4-8 Define (a) *current assets* and (b) *current liabilities.*

4-9 Identify the asset categories that may appear in a classified balance sheet.

4-10 Define *interim financial statements.* Give an example of an interim financial statement.

4-11 A firm on a calendar-year basis prepares cumulative statements monthly, using a worksheet. Adjusting and closing entries are entered in journals and posted only on December 31. On January 1, the firm paid $2,016 for a two-year insurance policy and debited Prepaid Insurance. What worksheet adjustments for insurance should be made on (a) January 31, (b) February 28, and (c) May 31?

4-12 Which groups of accounts are closed at the end of the accounting year?

4-13 How do closing entries for a corporation differ from closing entries for a proprietorship?

4-14 What is the purpose of a post-closing trial balance? Which of the following accounts should not appear in the post-closing trial balance: Cash; Unearned Revenue; R. Davis, Drawing; Depreciation Expense; Utilities Payable; Supplies Expense; and Retained Earnings?

4-15 Why are reversing entries made? If reversals are made, which entries would normally be reversed?

4-16 A firm accrued wages of $1,800 on December 31. On January 8, the next payday, the firm paid $4,000 in wages. The company does not make reversing entries. On January 8, the company debited Wages Expense and credited Cash for $4,000. (a) How will this procedure affect January net income? (b) What entry should the firm have made to record the January 8 payment of wages?

4-17 A firm accrued wages of $1,800 on December 31. On January 8, the next payday, the firm paid $4,000 in wages. The firm makes reversing entries. (a) What reversing entry should the firm make on January 1? (b) What entry should the firm make to record the January 8 payment of wages?

4-18 Define *working capital*. How is the *current ratio* computed?

4-19 Nectar Company has current assets of $316,000 and current liabilities of $162,000. What is Nectar Company's working capital? Current ratio?

EXERCISES

WORKSHEET
— OBJ. 1 —

4-20 The adjusted trial balance columns of a worksheet for Martha Pick, consultant, are shown below. The worksheet is prepared for the year ended December 31, 1993.

	Adjusted Trial Balance	
	Debit	**Credit**
Cash	3,500	
Supplies	7,000	
Equipment	60,000	
Accumulated Depreciation		24,000
Accounts Payable		2,300
M. Pick, Capital		33,600
M. Pick, Drawing	12,000	
Service Fees Earned		49,900
Rent Expense	13,200	
Supplies Expense	8,100	
Depreciation Expense	6,000	
	109,800	109,800

Complete the worksheet by (a) entering the adjusted trial balance on paper, (b) adding the worksheet income statement and balance sheet columns, (c) extending the adjusted trial balance to the income statement and balance sheet columns, and (d) balancing the worksheet.

CLASSIFIED BALANCE SHEET
— OBJ. 2 —

4-21 Blier Company's completed worksheet shows the following accounts with normal balances in the balance sheet columns: Accounts Payable; Accounts Receivable; Accumulated Depreciation—Building; Accumulated Depreciation—Equipment; S. Blair, Capital; S. Blair, Drawing; Building; Cash; Equipment; Interest Payable; Land; Long-term Notes Payable; Office Supplies; Prepaid Insurance; and Wages Payable. Identify the category in which each account would be reported in a classified balance sheet.

STATEMENT OF OWNER'S
EQUITY
— OBJ. 2 —

4-22 On January 1, 1993, the credit balance of the M. Strife, Capital account was $28,000, and on December 31, 1993, the credit balance before closing was $33,000. The M. Strife, Drawing account had a debit balance of $8,700 on December 31, 1993. After revenue and expense accounts were closed, the Income Summary account had a credit balance of $19,900. Prepare a 1993 statement of owner's equity for Mark Strife, architect.

PREPARING ADJUSTING ENTRIES FROM WORKSHEET — OBJ. 3 —

4-23 Listed below are the items from the Adjustments columns of a December 31, 1993, worksheet for Bay Company. Use this information to prepare the adjusting journal entries in general journal form at December 31. Explanations may be omitted.

	Adjustments	
	Debit	**Credit**
Supplies		(2) 1,300
Prepaid Advertising		(3) 200
Accumulated Depreciation—Building		(4) 8,100
Service Fees Earned		(1) 500
Salaries Expense	(5) 800	
Fees Receivable	(1) 500	
Supplies Expense	(2) 1,300	
Advertising Expense	(3) 200	
Depreciation Expense—Building	(4) 8,100	
Salaries Payable		(5) 800

CLOSING ENTRIES FOR SOLE PROPRIETORSHIP — OBJ. 4 —

4-24 The income statement columns of a worksheet prepared December 31, 1993, for Phil Howell, consultant, contain only the following accounts:

	Debit	**Credit**
Service Fees Earned		60,300
Rent Expense	14,800	
Salaries Expense	36,700	
Supplies Expense	4,600	
Depreciation Expense	6,100	

Included among the accounts in the balance sheet columns of the worksheet are P. Howell, Capital, $57,000 (credit) and P. Howell, Drawing, $8,000 (debit). Prepare entries to close the accounts. After these entries are posted, what is the balance of the P. Howell, Capital account?

CLOSING ENTRIES FOR PARTNERSHIP — OBJ. 4 —

4-25 The income statement columns of a December 31, 1993, worksheet prepared for the Brim and Stone partnership contain only the following accounts:

	Debit	**Credit**
Professional Fees Earned		90,000
Rent Expense	18,000	
Supplies Expense	14,000	
Advertising Expense	5,000	
Depreciation Expense	9,000	

Included among the accounts in the balance sheet columns of the worksheet are F. Brim, Capital, $32,000 (credit); K. Stone, Capital, $43,000 (credit); F. Brim, Drawing, $6,000 (debit); and K. Stone, Drawing, $9,000 (debit). Brim and Stone have agreed to share net incomes (and losses) equally. Prepare journal entries to close the accounts of the partnership.

CLOSING ENTRIES FOR CORPORATION — OBJ. 4 —

4-26 In the midst of closing procedures, Echo Corporation's accountant became ill and was hospitalized. You have volunteered to complete the closing of the books, and you find that all revenue and expense accounts have zero balances and that the Income Summary account has a single debit entry for $208,800 and a single credit entry for $257,400. The Cash Dividends account has a debit balance of $12,000, and the Retained Earnings account has a credit balance of $106,000. Prepare journal entries to complete the closing procedures at December 31, 1993.

REVERSING ENTRIES — OBJ. 7 —

4-27 Fibre Company closes its accounts on December 31 each year. The company works a five-day work week and pays its employees every two weeks. On December 31, 1993, Fibre accrued $2,700 of salaries payable. On January 9, 1994, the company paid salaries of $9,000 to employees. Prepare journal entries to (a) accrue the salaries payable on December 31; (b) close the Salaries Expense account on December 31 (the account has a year-end balance of $230,000 after adjustments); (c) reverse the December 31 salary accrual on January 1; and (d) record the salary payment on January 9.

PROBLEMS

**WORKSHEET AND CLOSING
ENTRIES
— OBJ. 1, 4 —**

4-28 Love Cleaning Service will prepare financial statements on December 31, 1993. The trial balance and adjustments columns of the firm's worksheet at December 31 follow.

	Trial Balance		Adjustments		
	Debit	**Credit**	**Debit**		**Credit**
Cash	2,800				
Accounts Receivable	5,100				
Supplies	9,000			(1)	6,500
Prepaid Insurance	1,560			(2)	520
Equipment	36,000				
Accumulated Depreciation		7,200		(3)	3,600
Accounts Payable		1,900			
R. Love, Capital		19,800			
R. Love, Drawing	1,600				
Cleaning Revenue		49,480			
Salaries Expense	15,400		(4)	480	
Rent Expense	5,900				
Miscellaneous Expense	1,020				
	78,380	78,380			
Supplies Expense			(1)	6,500	
Insurance Expense			(2)	520	
Depreciation Expense			(3)	3,600	
Salaries Payable				(4)	480
				11,100	11,100

REQUIRED

a. Complete the worksheet.

b. Prepare the closing entries at December 31 in general journal form.

**WORKSHEET AND
FINANCIAL STATEMENTS
— OBJ. 1, 2 —**

4-29 The following unadjusted trial balance was taken at March 31, 1993:

**FOCUS TRAVEL AGENCY
TRIAL BALANCE
MARCH 31, 1993**

	Debit	Credit
Cash	$ 2,400	
Commissions Receivable	5,000	
Supplies	1,750	
Prepaid Insurance	1,800	
Equipment	13,000	
Accumulated Depreciation		$ 2,600
Accounts Payable		550
Unearned Commissions		600
G. Owen, Capital		10,000
G. Owen, Drawing	900	
Commissions Earned		18,990
Salaries Expense	4,500	
Rent Expense	1,770	
Advertising Expense	1,000	
Utilities Expense	620	
	$32,740	$32,740

The trial balance data are cumulative for the first three months of 1993. No adjusting entries have been made in the accounts, and Grace Owen has not made any capital contributions during this period. The following additional information is available:

1. Depreciation for the first quarter is $325.

2. Supplies on hand at March 31 amount to $520.

3. During the quarter, $200 of the unearned commissions were earned. The remainder will be earned in the next quarter.

4. Insurance expense for the quarter is $450.
5. Accrued salaries payable total $500 at March 31.

REQUIRED

a. Enter the trial balance on a worksheet and complete the worksheet using the adjustment data given above.
b. Prepare an income statement and a statement of owner's equity for the first quarter of the year and a classified balance sheet at March 31, 1993.

ADJUSTING ENTRIES AND ACCOUNT CLASSIFICATION — OBJ. 1, 2 —

4-30 The first six columns of a worksheet for Complete Upholstery Service, Inc., are given below. However, only the totals of the adjustments columns are given.

COMPLETE UPHOLSTERY SERVICE, INC.
WORKSHEET
FOR THE YEAR ENDED DECEMBER 31, 1993

	Trial Balance		Adjustments		Adjusted Trial Balance	
	Debit	Credit	Debit	Credit	Debit	Credit
Cash	1,900				1,900	
Accounts Receivable	3,720				3,720	
Prepaid Rent	2,100				1,400	
Supplies	12,380				4,140	
Equipment	24,000				24,000	
Accumulated Depreciation		5,720				8,580
Accounts Payable		1,600				1,600
Unearned Service Fees		800				300
Capital Stock		12,000				12,000
Retained Earnings		9,670				9,670
Service Fees Earned		33,050				33,550
Wages Expense	8,500				9,030	
Utilities Expense	2,540				2,820	
Rent Expense	7,700				8,400	
	62,840	62,840				
Supplies Expense					8,240	
Depreciation Expense					2,860	
Wages Payable						530
Utilities Payable						280
			13,110	13,110	66,510	66,510

REQUIRED

a. Determine the adjusting entries for Complete Upholstery Service, Inc., and prepare these entries in general journal form.
b. For each account in the adjusted trial balance, indicate whether it will appear in an income statement or in a balance sheet. For each balance sheet account, indicate where the account will appear in a classified balance sheet.

WORKSHEET, FINANCIAL STATEMENTS, AND CLOSING ENTRIES — OBJ. 1, 2, 4 —

4-31 The unadjusted trial balance shown below is for Fine Freight Service at December 31, 1993. Byran Fine made no capital contributions during 1993. The following data for adjustments are also available at December 31, 1993:
1. Supplies on hand amount to $1,070.
2. Prepaid insurance is $500.
3. Depreciation for the year is as follows: Equipment, $720; Trucks, $2,750.
4. Accrued wages payable are $820.
5. Estimated December utilities expense is $460; the bill has not arrived.

	Debit	Credit
Cash	$ 2,700	
Accounts Receivable	3,270	
Supplies	3,060	
Prepaid Insurance	1,500	
Equipment	6,400	
Accumulated Depreciation—Equipment		$ 1,080

(CONTINUED)

Trucks	22,000	
Accumulated Depreciation—Trucks		4,125
Accounts Payable		845
Long-term Notes Payable		7,000
B. Fine, Capital		11,140
B. Fine, Drawing	2,900	
Service Fees Earned		85,620
Rent Expense	12,000	
Salaries and Wages Expense	43,400	
Fuel Expense	8,700	
Utilities Expense	3,250	
Interest Expense	630	
	$109,810	$109,810

REQUIRED

a. Prepare a 10-column worksheet for the year ended December 31, 1993. Set up any additional accounts needed.

b. Prepare an income statement and a statement of owner's equity for 1993 and a classified balance sheet at December 31, 1993.

c. Prepare closing entries in general journal form.

CLOSING ENTRIES AND CORPORATION ACCOUNTS
— OBJ. 4 —

4-32 The last 4 columns of a 10-column worksheet prepared at December 31, 1993, for Bayou, Inc., are reproduced below.

	Income Statement		Balance Sheet	
	Debit	**Credit**	**Debit**	**Credit**
Cash			3,200	
Accounts Receivable			9,000	
Prepaid Insurance			3,600	
Equipment			62,000	
Accumulated Depreciation				10,000
Accounts Payable				500
Capital Stock				30,000
Retained Earnings				12,000
Cash Dividends			3,000	
Service Fees Earned		86,200		
Miscellaneous Income		4,100		
Salaries Expense	41,300			
Rent Expense	11,400			
Insurance Expense	1,800			
Depreciation Expense	7,500			
Income Tax Expense	4,200			
Income Tax Payable				4,200
	66,200	90,300	80,800	56,700
Net Income	24,100			24,100
	90,300	90,300	80,800	80,800

REQUIRED

a. From the given information, prepare closing entries in general journal form.

b. After the closing entries are posted, what is the balance in the Retained Earnings account?

c. Which accounts in the worksheet would not appear if the company were organized as a sole proprietorship rather than as a corporation?

ADJUSTING AND REVERSING ENTRIES
— OBJ. 3, 7 —

4-33 The following selected accounts appear in Shaw Company's unadjusted trial balance at December 31, 1993, the end of the fiscal year (all accounts have normal balances):

Prepaid Advertising	$ 1,200	Unearned Service Fees	$ 5,400
Wages Expense	43,800	Service Fees Earned	87,000
Prepaid Insurance	3,120	Rental Income	4,900

REQUIRED

a. Make the necessary adjusting entries in general journal form at December 31, 1993, assuming the following:

1. Prepaid advertising at December 31 is $900.

2. Unpaid wages earned by employees in December are $950.
3. Prepaid insurance at December 31 is $2,080.
4. Unearned service fees at December 31 are $1,000.
5. Rent revenue of $800 owed by a tenant is not recorded at December 31.

b. Assume the company makes reversing entries. Which of the adjustments in part (a) should be reversed? Make the proper reversing entries on January 1, 1994.

c. Assume reversing entries have been made. Prepare the journal entries on January 4, 1994, to record (1) the payment of $1,600 in wages and (2) the receipt from the tenant of the $800 rent revenue.

d. Assume reversing entries have not been made. Prepare the journal entries on January 4, 1994, to record (1) the payment of $1,600 in wages and (2) the receipt from the tenant of the $800 rent revenue.

ALTERNATE EXERCISES

WORKSHEET, CORPORATION — OBJ. 1 —

4-20A The adjusted trial balance columns of a worksheet for Bonn Corporation are shown below. The worksheet is prepared for the year ended December 31, 1993.

	Adjusted Trial Balance	
	Debit	Credit
Cash	3,000	
Accounts Receivable	5,500	
Equipment	75,000	
Accumulated Depreciation		15,000
Notes Payable		2,300
Capital Stock		40,000
Retained Earnings		17,600
Cash Dividends	5,000	
Service Fees Earned		61,700
Rent Expense	13,000	
Salaries Expense	27,100	
Depreciation Expense	8,000	
	136,600	136,600

Complete the worksheet by (a) entering the adjusted trial balance on paper, (b) putting in the worksheet income statement and balance sheet columns, (c) extending the adjusted trial balance to the income statement and balance sheet columns, and (d) balancing the worksheet.

CLASSIFIED BALANCE SHEET, CORPORATION — OBJ. 2 —

4-21A The income statement and balance sheet columns of a worksheet for Baxter Corporation are shown below. The worksheet is prepared as of December 31, 1993.

	Income Statement		Balance Sheet	
	Debit	Credit	Debit	Credit
Cash			2,500	
Accounts Receivable			5,400	
Office Equipment			50,000	
Accumulated Depreciation				6,000
Accounts Payable				1,100
Long-term Notes Payable				5,000
Capital Stock				14,000
Retained Earnings				10,400
Service Fees Earned		47,000		
Wages Expense	14,400			
Rent Expense	7,200			
Depreciation Expense	4,000			
Income Tax Expense	3,200			
Income Tax Payable				3,200
	28,800	47,000	57,900	39,700
Net Income	18,200			18,200
	47,000	47,000	57,900	57,900

Prepare a classified balance sheet for Baxter Corporation.

STEPS IN ACCOUNTING CYCLE
— OBJ. 6 —

4-22A Listed below, out of order, are the steps in the accounting cycle.
1. Prepare a trial balance to start a worksheet.
2. Post journal entries to general ledger accounts.
3. Analyze transactions from source documents.
4. Journalize and post adjusting entries.
5. Prepare financial statements.
6. Record transactions in journals.
7. Prepare a post-closing trial balance.
8. Adjust the general ledger accounts on the worksheet and finish the worksheet.
9. Journalize and post closing entries.

(a) Place the numbers from the above list in the order in which the steps in the accounting cycle are performed, and (b) identify the steps in the accounting cycle that occur daily.

PREPARING ADJUSTING ENTRIES FROM WORKSHEET
— OBJ. 3 —

4-23A Listed below are the items from the Adjustments columns of a December 31, 1993, worksheet for Tusk Company. Use this information to prepare the adjusting entries in general journal form at December 31. Explanations may be omitted.

	Adjustments			
	Debit		**Credit**	
Prepaid Rent			(1)	900
Accumulated Depreciation—Trucks			(2)	6,200
Unearned Professional Fees	(3)	500		
Professional Fees Earned			(3)	500
Utilities Expense	(5)	190		
Rent Expense	(1)	900		
Depreciation Expense—Trucks	(2)	6,200		
Interest Receivable	(4)	350		
Interest Income			(4)	350
Utilities Payable			(5)	190

CLOSING ENTRIES FOR SOLE PROPRIETORSHIP
— OBJ. 4 —

4-24A The income statement columns of a worksheet prepared December 31, 1993, for Cheryl Fontaine, agent, contain only the following accounts:

	Debit	**Credit**
Commissions Earned		74,900
Wages Expense	35,000	
Insurance Expense	1,700	
Utilities Expense	8,200	
Depreciation Expense	9,300	

Included among the accounts in the balance sheet columns of the worksheet are C. Fontaine, Capital, $63,400 (credit) and C. Fontaine, Drawing, $10,000 (debit). Prepare entries to close the accounts. After these entries are posted, what is the balance of the C. Fontaine, Capital account?

CLOSING ENTRIES FOR PARTNERSHIP
— OBJ. 4 —

4-25A The income statement columns of a December 31, 1993, worksheet prepared for the Avon, Cleary, and Moon partnership contain only the following accounts:

	Debit	**Credit**
Delivery Fees Earned		49,000
Rent Expense	24,000	
Supplies Expense	8,000	
Fuel Expense	15,000	
Depreciation Expense	11,000	

Included among the accounts in the balance sheet columns of the worksheet are G. Avon, Capital, $13,000 (credit); S. Cleary, Capital, $22,000 (credit); N. Moon, Capital, $20,000 (credit); and N. Moon, Drawing, $3,000 (debit). Avon, Cleary, and Moon have agreed to share net incomes (and losses) 20% to Avon, 30% to Cleary, and 50% to Moon. Prepare journal entries to close the accounts of the partnership.

CLOSING ENTRIES FOR CORPORATION
— OBJ. 4 —

4-26A The income statement columns of Rose Corporation's worksheet prepared December 31, 1993, contain only the following accounts:

	Debit	Credit
Service Fees Earned		88,400
Interest Income		1,200
Salaries Expense	41,500	
Advertising Expense	4,200	
Depreciation Expense	6,700	
Income Tax Expense	5,600	

Included among the accounts in the balance sheet columns of the worksheet are Capital Stock, $100,000 (credit); Retained Earnings, $58,300 (credit); and Cash Dividends, $11,000 (debit). Prepare journal entries to close the accounts. After these entries are posted, what is the balance of the Retained Earnings account?

REVERSING ENTRIES
— OBJ. 7 —

4-27A Lewis Company closes its accounts on December 31 each year. On December 31, 1993, Lewis accrued $500 of interest income that was earned on an investment but not yet received or recorded (the investment will pay interest of $600 on January 31, 1994). On January 31, 1994, the company received the $600 cash as interest on the investment. Prepare journal entries to (a) accrue the interest earned on December 31; (b) close the Interest Income account on December 31 (the account has a year-end balance of $1,900 after adjustments); (c) reverse the December 31 interest accrual on January 1; and (d) record the cash receipt of interest on January 31.

ALTERNATE PROBLEMS

4-28A The trial balance and adjustments columns of the worksheet for Okay Moving Service at December 31, 1993, are shown below.

WORKSHEET AND CLOSING ENTRIES
— OBJ. 1, 4 —

	Trial Balance		Adjustments	
	Debit	Credit	Debit	Credit
Cash	3,800			
Accounts Receivable	5,250			
Supplies	4,100			(1) 2,300
Prepaid Advertising	3,000			(2) 2,000
Trucks	28,300			
Accumulated Depreciation— Trucks		7,500		(3) 3,000
Equipment	7,600			
Accumulated Depreciation— Equipment		2,100		(4) 700
Accounts Payable		1,200		
Unearned Service Fees		2,700	(5) 1,800	
S. Warner, Capital		13,550		
S. Warner, Drawing	5,500			
Service Fees Earned		72,200		(5) 1,800
Wages Expense	29,600			
Rent Expense	10,200			
Insurance Expense	1,900			
	99,250	99,250		
Supplies Expense			(1) 2,300	
Advertising Expense			(2) 2,000	
Depreciation Expense— Trucks			(3) 3,000	
Depreciation Expense— Equipment			(4) 700	
			9,800	9,800

REQUIRED

a. Complete the worksheet.

b. Prepare the closing entries at December 31 in general journal form.

WORKSHEET AND FINANCIAL STATEMENTS — OBJ. 1, 2 —

4-29A The July 31, 1994, unadjusted trial balance of Sharp Outfitters, a firm renting various types of equipment to canoeists and campers, is shown below.

SHARP OUTFITTERS
TRIAL BALANCE
JULY 31, 1994

	Debit	Credit
Cash	$ 3,750	
Supplies	8,600	
Prepaid Insurance	2,800	
Equipment	90,000	
Accumulated Depreciation		$ 16,500
Accounts Payable		3,100
Unearned Rental Fees		3,850
C. Sharp, Capital		39,000
C. Sharp, Drawing	1,200	
Rental Fees Earned		78,150
Wages Expense	27,800	
Rent Expense	3,300	
Advertising Expense	2,300	
Travel Expense	850	
	$140,600	$140,600

The trial balance data are cumulative for the first three months of the firm's fiscal year, which begins May 1. No adjusting entries have been made in the accounts during the quarter. The general ledger account for C. Sharp, Capital reveals Casey Sharp made a $9,000 capital contribution on July 1, 1994. The following additional information is available:

1. Supplies on hand at July 31 amount to $5,300.

2. Insurance expense for the first quarter is $700.

3. Depreciation for the first quarter is $2,600.

4. The unearned rental fees consist of deposits received from customers in advance when reservations are made. During the quarter, $2,850 of the unearned rental fees were earned. The remaining deposits apply to rentals for August and September 1994.

5. At July 31, revenue from rental services earned during July but not yet billed or received amounts to $2,500. (*Note:* Debit Fees Receivable.)

6. Accrued wages payable for equipment handlers and guides amounts to $750 at July 31.

REQUIRED

a. Enter the trial balance in a worksheet and complete the worksheet using the adjustment data given above.

b. Prepare an income statement and a statement of owner's equity for the first quarter of the fiscal year and a classified balance sheet at July 31, 1994.

WORKSHEET ERROR CORRECTIONS — OBJ. 1 —

4-30A Michele Hill, owner of Hill Refinishing Service, has completed a worksheet for her business at the end of its first year of operations. She is unsure of her accounting skills, however, and asks you to review the worksheet before she prepares financial statements from it. You have reviewed the unadjusted trial balance, the adjustments, and the compilation of the adjusted trial balance columns and have found no errors. The last six columns of the worksheet are shown on the next page (as noted, the adjusted trial balance columns are correct).

HILL REFINISHING SERVICE
WORKSHEET
FOR THE YEAR ENDED DECEMBER 31, 1993

	Adjusted Trial Balance		Income Statement		Balance Sheet	
	Debit	Credit	Debit	Credit	Debit	Credit
Cash	1,300				1,300	
Accounts Receivable	860				860	
Prepaid Rent	930				930	
Supplies	1,400				1,400	
Equipment	5,000				5,000	
Accounts Payable		450				450
M. Hill, Capital		6,000				6,000
M. Hill, Drawing	2,200				2,200	
Service Revenue		18,650		18,560		
Wages Expense	6,220		6,220			
Utilities Expense	940		490			
Rent Expense	4,800		4,800			
Supplies Expense	1,860		1,860			
Depreciation Expense	480		840			
Accumulated Depreciation		520		520		
Wages Payable		200		200		
Utilities Payable		170		170		
	25,990	25,990	14,210	19,450	11,690	6,450
Net Income			5,240			5,240
			19,450	19,450	11,690	11,690

REQUIRED

a. Identify the errors contained in this partial worksheet.
b. Prepare a correct partial worksheet (the last six columns).

WORKSHEET, FINANCIAL STATEMENTS, AND CLOSING ENTRIES FOR CORPORATION — OBJ. 1, 2, 4 —

4-31A Trails, Inc., publishes magazines for skiers and hikers. The firm has the following unadjusted trial balance at December 31, 1993.

TRAILS, INC.
TRIAL BALANCE
DECEMBER 31, 1993

	Debit	Credit
Cash	$ 5,400	
Accounts Receivable	8,600	
Supplies	10,100	
Prepaid Insurance	1,860	
Office Equipment	56,000	
Accumulated Depreciation		$ 4,000
Accounts Payable		2,100
Unearned Subscription Revenue		10,000
Long-term Notes Payable		15,000
Capital Stock		25,000
Retained Earnings		10,290
Subscription Revenue		165,100
Advertising Revenue		57,600
Salaries Expense	100,130	
Printing and Mailing Expense	95,600	
Rent Expense	8,800	
Interest Expense	1,000	
Income Tax Expense	1,600	
	$289,090	$289,090

The following information for adjusting the accounts is available at December 31:
1. Supplies on hand amount to $3,800.
2. Prepaid insurance at December 31 is $930.
3. Accrued salaries at December 31 are $1,900.

4. Of the unearned subscription revenue shown in the trial balance, $6,000 was earned during the year. The remainder will be earned next year.
5. Depreciation on office equipment for the year is $4,000.
6. Interest accrued on notes payable at December 31 is $500.

REQUIRED

a. Prepare a 10-column worksheet for the year ended December 31, 1993. Set up any additional accounts needed.
b. Prepare an income statement for 1993 and a classified balance sheet at December 31, 1993.
c. Prepare closing entries in general journal form.

WORKSHEET AND FINANCIAL STATEMENTS FOR CORPORATION
— OBJ. 1, 2 —

4-32A Central Engineering Services, Inc., prepares a year-to-date income statement each month. Also, a balance sheet is prepared at the end of each month. The firm makes adjusting and closing entries in its accounts only at December 31 each year. The firm's unadjusted trial balance at April 30, 1994, is given below.

CENTRAL ENGINEERING SERVICES, INC.
TRIAL BALANCE
APRIL 30, 1994

	Debit	Credit
Cash	$ 5,400	
Supplies	8,800	
Prepaid Insurance	2,745	
Equipment	150,000	
Accumulated Depreciation		$ 36,000
Accounts Payable		2,800
Capital Stock		50,000
Retained Earnings		42,500
Service Revenue		75,200
Salaries Expense	26,000	
Legal Fees Expense	4,500	
Rent Expense	3,560	
Utilities Expense	1,495	
Income Tax Expense	4,000	
	$206,500	$206,500

The following data for adjustments are available at April 30, 1994:
1. Three years of insurance coverage was purchased January 1, 1994.
2. Supplies on hand at April 30 are $5,200.
3. Monthly depreciation on equipment is $1,500.
4. Accrued salaries at April 30 are $800.
5. The firm is involved in a lawsuit with a former client. Legal fees incurred in April but not yet billed by legal counsel are estimated at $1,800 (credit Legal Fees Payable).

REQUIRED

a. Record the April 30 trial balance on a 10-column worksheet. Enter the necessary adjusting entries and complete the worksheet for the four months ended April 30, 1994.
b. Prepare an income statement for the four months ended April 30, 1994.
c. Prepare a classified balance sheet at April 30, 1994.

ADJUSTING AND REVERSING ENTRIES
— OBJ. 7 —

4-33A The following selected accounts appear in Birch Company's unadjusted trial balance at December 31, 1993, the end of the fiscal year (all accounts have normal balances):

Prepaid Maintenance	$2,100	Commission Fees Earned	$84,000
Supplies	6,400	Rent Expense	7,200
Unearned Commission Fees	8,500		

REQUIRED

a. Make the necessary adjusting entries in general journal form at December 31, assuming the following:
1. On September 1, 1993, the company entered into a prepaid equipment maintenance contract. Birch Company paid $2,100 to cover maintenance service for

six months, beginning September 1, 1993. The $2,100 payment was debited to Prepaid Maintenance.

2. Supplies on hand at December 31 are $3,700.
3. Unearned commission fees at December 31 are $5,000.
4. Commission fees earned but not yet billed at December 31 are $2,500. (*Note:* Debit Fees Receivable.)
5. Birch Company's lease calls for rent of $600 per month payable on the first of each month, plus an annual amount equal to 1% of annual commissions earned. This additional rent is payable on January 10 of the following year. (*Note:* Be sure to use the adjusted amount of commissions earned in computing the additional rent.)

b. Assume the company makes reversing entries. Which of the adjustments in (a) should be reversed? Make the proper reversing entries on January 1, 1994.

c. Assume reversing entries have been made. Prepare the journal entries on January 10, 1994, to record (1) the billing of $4,500 of commissions earned (an amount which includes the $2,500 of commissions earned but not billed at December 31) and (2) the payment of the additional rent owed for 1993.

d. Assume reversing entries have not been made. Prepare the journal entries on January 10, 1994, to record (1) the billing of $4,500 of commissions earned (an amount which includes the $2,500 of commissions earned but not billed at December 31) and (2) the payment of the additional rent owed for 1993.

CASES

Business Decision Case

As an alternative to a summer job paying $6 per hour between her junior and senior years in college, Lori Hart accepted an opportunity to lease and operate the tennis court concession in a local city recreational complex during June, July, and August, 1993. Although she kept no accounting records, Lori was careful to handle all funds related to the tennis concession through a special bank account opened for that purpose. An analysis of those deposit slips and check stubs for the three months is summarized below.

Receipts:	
Hart's investment of personal funds	$ 1,400
Court rental fees	7,375
Tennis lesson fees	1,975
Tennis lesson fees received in advance	150
Proceeds of short-term loan from bank	900
Total receipts	$11,800
Disbursements:	
Purchase of ball-throwing machine	$ 140
Supplies purchased	960
Utilities	175
Lease payments to city	990
Wages to part-time assistant	1,500
Liability insurance premiums	210
Repayment of bank loan, including interest	920
Withdrawals of cash for personal expenses	750
Total disbursements	$ 5,645
Cash balance, August 31, 1993	$ 6,155

Lori confides in you, a personal friend who happens to be studying accounting, that she is pleased with her apparent profit of $6,155 for the summer. Eager to practice your newly acquired skills, you offer to review her records and prepare an income statement for the three months and a classified balance sheet at the end of August. In discussions with Lori, you learn that

1. Some tennis lessons, paid for in advance, could not be scheduled during the summer. Lori plans to refund these fees, which total $150.
2. Repayment to the bank included $20 of interest expense on the loan.
3. Rental receipts include all revenue earned except for $500 due from a company that rented the entire set of courts for a weekend late in August.

4. A ball-throwing machine, purchased used, turned out to be quite temperamental. With a complete breakdown shortly after it was purchased, it was junked. (*Note:* Debit Equipment Loss.)

5. Supplies consisted of cans of tennis balls. Lori gave away a free can of tennis balls for each five hours of court time rented by an individual. Supplies amounting to $120 were on hand at August 31; these may be returned for a full refund. Lori estimates that each month during the summer, she took home $15 worth of supplies for personal use.

6. All lease payments due the city were paid except for the final amount of $180.

7. Lori estimates that the utility bill for August, when received, will be $100.

8. The insurance premiums represent coverage for the months of June, July, and August.

REQUIRED

Prepare financial statements for Lori's tennis concession (a sole proprietorship). You should formulate general journal entries summarizing the cash receipts and the cash disbursements and incorporating the additional data. After posting these to T accounts, you will be able to prepare the financial statements.

In further talks with Lori, you learn that the amount she contributed had been in a savings account earning 6% interest and that she worked an average of 60 hours in each of the 13 weeks the tennis concession was operated. What observations might you offer Lori regarding the financial success of the summer venture? What nonfinancial considerations are involved?

Analytical Application Case

METRO AIRLINES, INC., headquartered at the Dallas/Fort Worth International Airport, operated several airline passenger systems and an air cargo system during the years 1988 to 1990. One of the passenger systems operated as EASTERN METRO EXPRESS in Atlanta, Georgia. In that location, the company had a service agreement with EASTERN AIR LINES and provided connecting service between small and medium-sized cities and Eastern Air Lines' Atlanta hub. Following are data on the company's current assets and current liabilities at the end of its 1988, 1989, and 1990 fiscal years (the company's fiscal year ends on April 30; amounts are in thousands):

	April 30, 1990	April 30, 1989	April 30, 1988
Current Assets			
Cash	$ 3,862	$ 8,656	$ 9,330
Trade Accounts Receivable	6,147	5,068	1,207
Other Receivables	1,526	1,809	3,155
Expendable Parts and Supplies	7,299	6,646	3,509
Prepayments and other	1,010	1,970	1,560
Flight Equipment Held for Sale	–0–	1,197	–0–
Total Current Assets	$19,844	$25,346	$18,761
Current Liabilities			
Current maturities of long-term debt	$10,951	$ 6,586	$ 3,144
Notes Payable	–0–	4,000	–0–
Accounts Payable	16,411	10,102	10,314
Accrued Payroll Costs	3,233	2,923	2,108
Accrued Lease Payments	3,448	3,118	1,565
Other Accrued Liabilities	5,124	4,583	1,135
Total Current Liabilities	$39,167	$31,312	$18,266

In fiscal 1988, passengers boarded by the Atlanta hub represented more than 25% of Metro Airlines' passengers. Passengers boarded by the Atlanta hub dropped more than 20% in fiscal 1989 because of labor conflicts and unfavorable publicity experienced by Eastern Air Lines. Late in fiscal 1989, Eastern Air Lines filed for protection under Chapter 11 of the U.S. Bankruptcy Code. Passengers boarded in Atlanta by Metro Airlines dropped another 5% in fiscal 1990.

a. Compute Metro Airlines' working capital at the end of fiscal years 1988, 1989, and 1990. Comment on the trend of working capital from April 30, 1988, to April 30, 1990.

b. Compute Metro Airlines' current ratio at the end of fiscal years 1988, 1989, and 1990. Has

Metro Airlines' ability to meet its current obligations improved or worsened from April 30, 1988, to April 30, 1990?

Ethics Case

Ed Finlay is controller for ServiceView, Inc., a corporation that provides cable television service throughout the Midwest. His son-in-law, Bryan Foote, owns and manages a printing company, Total Print. Foote has plans to develop a specialty for Total Print in printing corporate annual reports for stockholders. Foote has asked Finlay many questions about this possible specialty, including questions about ServiceView's cost of using an outside company to do the printing of its annual reports. Finlay has been quite candid and helpful in answering Foote's questions and providing prices of the current supplier and has encouraged his son-in-law to pursue this line of business.

This morning, Finlay received a call from ServiceView's president. "I need your help, Ed," stated the president. "I am reviewing a recommendation from the purchasing department for the printing of this year's annual report. The purchasing department recommends that we continue to use Excelprint, which has been printing our annual report for the last decade and with which we have a very good relationship. However, Excelprint is not the low bidder this year; an outfit called Total Print has bid $15,000 less to do the job. Total Print's sample of its work looks very good, and I am inclined to go with the lowest bid. What do you recommend, Ed?"

REQUIRED

What are the ethical considerations that Finlay faces in answering the president's question?

MINI PRACTICE SET 1

Complete Accounting Cycle

Keith Howe, tax consultant, began business on December 1, 1993. December transactions were as follows.

Dec. 1   Howe invested $15,000 in the business.
  2   Paid rent for December to Star Realty, $800.
  2   Purchased various supplies on account, $720.
  3   Purchased $7,500 of office equipment, paying $3,700 down with the balance due in 30 days.
  8   Paid $720 on account for supplies purchased December 2.
 14   Paid assistant's wages for two weeks, $600.
 20   Performed consulting services for cash, $2,000.
 28   Paid assistant's wages for two weeks, $600.
 30   Billed clients for December consulting services, $4,800.
 31   Howe withdrew $1,200 from the business.

REQUIRED

a. Open the following general ledger accounts, using the account numbers shown: Cash (11); Accounts Receivable (12); Fees Receivable (13); Supplies (14); Office Equipment (15); Accumulated Depreciation (16); Accounts Payable (21); Wages Payable (22); K. Howe, Capital (31); K. Howe, Drawing (32); Income Summary (33); Consulting Revenue (41); Supplies Expense (51); Wages Expense (52); Rent Expense (53); and Depreciation Expense (54).
b. Journalize the December transactions, and post to the ledger.
c. Prepare a trial balance directly on a worksheet, and complete the worksheet using the following information:
   1. Supplies on hand at December 31 are $470.
   2. Accrued wages payable at December 31 are $180.
   3. Depreciation for December is $80.
   4. Howe has spent 20 hours on an involved tax fraud case during December. When completed in January, his work will be billed at $50 per hour. (*Note:* The firm uses the account Fees Receivable to reflect amounts earned but not yet billed.)
d. Prepare a December income statement and statement of owner's equity and a December 31, 1993, classified balance sheet.
e. Journalize and post adjusting and closing entries.
f. Prepare a post-closing trial balance.
g. Journal and post the appropriate reversing entries.

MINI PRACTICE SET II

Two Consecutive Accounting Cycles

Karen Fero, attorney, opened her practice on December 1, 1993. December 1993 transactions were as follows:

Dec. 1   Fero invested $7,000 in the firm.
  1   Paid one-year premium on professional liability insurance policy, $1,080.
  2   Paid December rent, $900.
  2   Purchased various supplies for cash, $680.
  3   Purchased office furniture and fixtures on account, $5,700.
  8   Paid $3,000 on account for furniture and fixtures purchased December 3.
  12   Paid assistant's salary for two weeks, $700.
  19   Performed legal services for cash, $1,200.
  26   Paid assistant's salary for two weeks, $700.
  30   Billed clients for legal work completed during the month, $3,600.
  31   Fero withdrew $500 from the business.

REQUIRED

a. Open the following general ledger accounts, using the account numbers shown: Cash (11); Accounts Receivable (12); Fees Receivable (13); Supplies (14); Prepaid Insurance (15); Furniture and Fixtures (16); Accumulated Depreciation (17); Accounts Payable (21); Salary Payable (22); Unearned Legal Fees (23); Long-term Notes Payable (25); K. Fero, Capital (31); K. Fero, Drawing (32); Income Summary (33); Legal Fees Earned (41); Supplies Expense (51); Salary Expense (52); Rent Expense (53); Depreciation Expense (54); and Insurance Expense (55).

b. Journalize the December transactions, and post to the ledger.

c. Prepare a trial balance directly on a worksheet, and complete the worksheet using the following information:
  1. Supplies on hand at December 31 are $560.
  2. Accrued salary payable at December 31 is $210.
  3. Depreciation for December is $40.
  4. Fero has spent 25 hours on an involved estate planning case during December. When completed in January, her work will be billed at $60 per hour. (*Note:* The firm uses the account Fees Receivable to reflect amounts earned but not yet billed.)
  5. Prepaid insurance at December 31 is $990.

d. Prepare a December income statement and statement of owner's equity and a December 31, 1993, classified balance sheet.

e. Journalize and post adjusting and closing entries.

f. Prepare a post-closing trial balance.

g. Journalize and post the appropriate reversing entries as of January 1, 1994.

The January 1994 transactions were as follows:

Jan. 2   Borrowed $5,000 from a relative on a two-year note payable. The relative is not charging interest on the loan, but does want to see financial statements each month.
  2   Paid January rent, $900.
  2   Paid $2,700 on account for furniture and fixtures purchased December 3, 1993.
  5   Purchased various supplies on account, $290.
  9   Paid assistant's salary for two weeks, $700.
  13   Collected $3,000 on account from clients.
  15   Increased the limits on professional liability insurance and paid an additional premium of $420 for the remaining term ($10\frac{1}{2}$ months) of the policy. (See December 1, 1993, transaction.)
  15   Received $1,500 cash as advance payment from a client for legal work to be done over the next three months.
  20   Purchased additional office furniture for cash, $2,300.
  23   Paid assistant's salary for two weeks, $700.
  30   Billed clients for legal work completed during the month, $6,100. (This billing includes the estate planning work that was started in December 1993 and finished in January 1994.)

REQUIRED

h. Journalize the January transactions and post to the ledger that you provided in part a.

i. Prepare a trial balance directly on a worksheet and complete the worksheet using the following information:

  1. Supplies on hand at January 31 are $630.

  2. Accrued salary payable at January 31 is $350.

  3. Depreciation for January is $50.

  4. Prepaid insurance at January 31 is $1,300.

  5. Unearned legal fees at January 31 are $1,250.

j. Prepare a January income statement and statement of owner's equity and a January 31, 1994, classified balance sheet.

k. Journalize and post adjusting and closing entries. (Fero has decided to close the books monthly in 1994.)

l. Prepare a post-closing trial balance.

m. Journalize and post the appropriate reversing entries as of February 1, 1994.

How do merchandising companies account for their stock of merchandise and what effect does the merchandise have on the financial statements?

A merchandising firm acquires products and offers them for sale to other businesses or the general public. ■ *Best Buy, for example, is a store that sells appliances and electronics by manufacturers such as General Electric, Toshiba, and Sharp.* ■ *As with most merchandising firms, the largest expense item on the income statement for Best Buy is cost of goods sold.* ■ *The cost of merchandise on hand is one of the largest assets on the balance sheet.*

5

MERCHANDISING OPERATIONS

Everyone lives by selling something.

ROBERT LOUIS STEVENSON

n previous chapters, we used as examples firms providing services rather than those selling products. Revenue for small service enterprises consisted of fees earned for the services performed. In these firms, net income is determined simply by deducting total expenses incurred from total fees earned during a period.

Revenue for firms that sell products consists of the total amount for which the products are sold. To determine net income for such firms, we deduct from the revenue (called *sales*) for the period not only the operating expenses incurred, but also the costs of acquiring the products sold. In this chapter, we present the procedures followed in accounting for the costs of acquiring and selling products.

THE NATURE OF MERCHANDISING OPERATIONS

OBJECTIVE ❶ DESCRIBE *the nature of merchandising operations and* INTRODUCE *the income statement for a merchandising firm.*

The business segment of society is often classified into three broad types of enterprises: (1) service, (2) manufacturing, and (3) merchandising. Commercial airlines, physicians, lawyers, insurance companies, and banks are examples of service enterprises. Manufacturing enterprises convert raw materials into finished products through the application of skilled labor and machine operations. Merchandising enterprises buy and sell finished products and include both wholesalers and retailers. Exhibit 5-1 illustrates the position of merchandising enterprises in the manufacturing and distribution process.

The accounting records of a merchandising firm must accommodate many transactions for the purchase of products and payment of the related accounts. Moreover, the accounting reports should indicate whether the difference between the acquisition

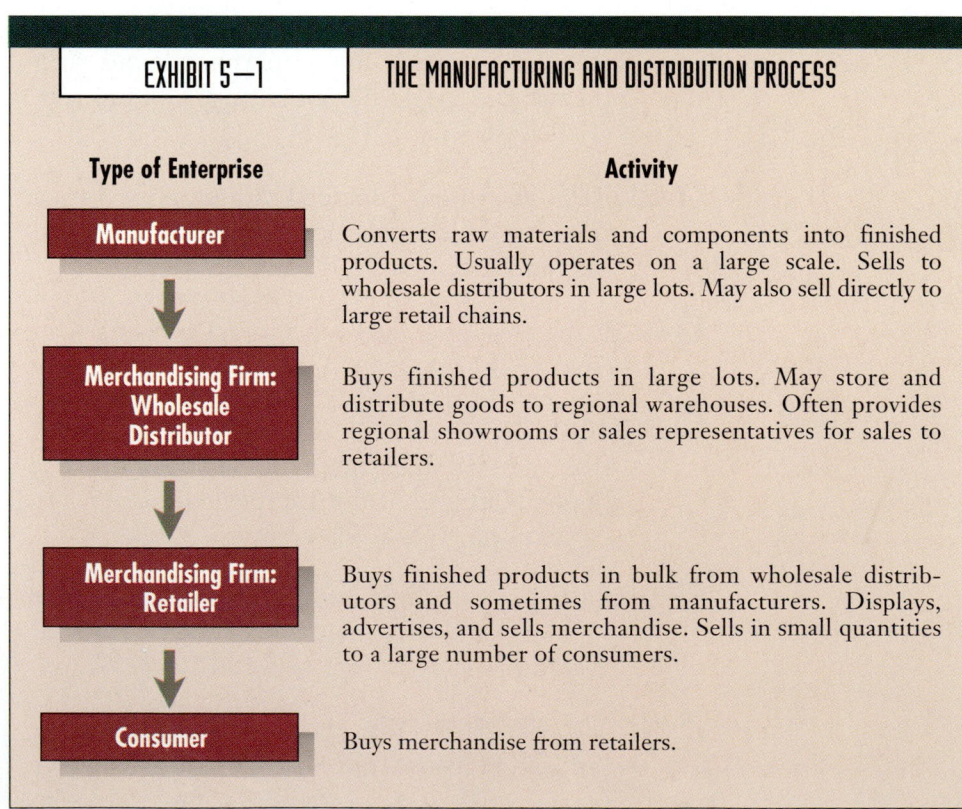

EXHIBIT 5—1	THE MANUFACTURING AND DISTRIBUTION PROCESS
Type of Enterprise	**Activity**
Manufacturer	Converts raw materials and components into finished products. Usually operates on a large scale. Sells to wholesale distributors in large lots. May also sell directly to large retail chains.
Merchandising Firm: Wholesale Distributor	Buys finished products in large lots. May store and distribute goods to regional warehouses. Often provides regional showrooms or sales representatives for sales to retailers.
Merchandising Firm: Retailer	Buys finished products in bulk from wholesale distributors and sometimes from manufacturers. Displays, advertises, and sells merchandise. Sells in small quantities to a large number of consumers.
Consumer	Buys merchandise from retailers.

price and the sales price to customers covers the costs of storing, displaying, advertising, selling, delivering, and collecting for the merchandise. Finally, the accounting records must reflect not only cash sales but also individual accounts receivable for a large number of customers.

INCOME STATEMENT FOR A MERCHANDISING FIRM

Exhibit 5-2 is an income statement for a merchandising firm, Madison Electronics Company. For simplicity, the expenses are condensed into three amounts—selling expenses, administrative expenses, and interest expense.

The major difference between the income statement of a merchandising firm and that of a service business is the inclusion of an amount for the **cost of goods sold** to customers in the merchandising firm's statement. Ordinarily, this amount is deducted from the revenue figure (sales) to arrive at an intermediate amount called **gross profit on sales.** The operating expenses are then deducted from the gross profit on sales to obtain net income.

STEPS IN A MERCHANDISE TRANSACTION

OBJECTIVE ❷ IDENTIFY *and* **DISCUSS** *the steps in a merchandise transaction.*

Whenever a transaction for the purchase or sale of merchandise occurs, the buyer and the seller should agree on the price of the merchandise, the terms of payment, and the party to bear the cost of transportation. Owners or managers of small merchandising firms may settle the terms of the transaction informally by telephone or by discussion with the supplier's sales representative. Most large businesses, however, fill out a purchase order when ordering merchandise. A typical sequence of events for a large firm is as follows:

1. When certain items are needed or when quantities of certain merchandise fall below established reorder points, a request for a purchase, called a **purchase requisition,** is sent to the purchasing department by the person in charge of merchandise stock records. These requisitions may also be initiated by other authorized personnel, such as department heads.

2. The purchasing department then prepares a **purchase order** after consulting price lists, quotations, or suppliers' catalogs. The purchase order, addressed to the selected vendor, indicates the quantity, description, and price of the merchandise ordered. It may also indicate expected terms of payment and arrangements for transportation, including payment of freight costs.

3. After receiving the purchase order, the seller forwards an **invoice** to the purchaser after shipment of the merchandise. The invoice—called a **sales invoice**

EXHIBIT 5—2

MADISON ELECTRONICS COMPANY
INCOME STATEMENT
FOR THE YEAR ENDED DECEMBER 31, 1993

Net Sales		$425,000
Cost of Goods Sold		255,000
Gross Profit on Sales		$170,000
Expenses:		
Selling Expenses	$96,200	
Administrative Expenses	46,200	
Interest Expense	2,100	
Total Expenses		144,500
Net Income		$ 25,500

| EXHIBIT 5—3 | SAMPLE INVOICE |

INVOICE
MADISON ELECTRONICS COMPANY
1400 South Park St.
Madison, Wisconsin 53705

| | | | FOR CUSTOMER'S USE ONLY |

Customer's
Order No. & Date 1503
Requisition No.
Contract No.

Refer to
Invoice No. 12015
Invoice Date Nov. 20, 1993
Vendor's Nos.

Register No.   Voucher No.

F.O.B. Checked

Terms Approved   Price Approved *LNJ*

Calculations Checked *RSD*

SOLD   Video Magic Company
TO   120 Weston Street
        Lansing, Michigan 48835

Transportation

Freight Bill No.   Amount

Material Received

Shipped to
  and
Destination Same
Date Shipped Nov. 20, 1993   From Madison   Prepaid or Collect
Car Initials and No.
How Shipped and   F.O.B. Madison   Collect
  Route
Terms 2/10, n/30

Date   Signature   Title

Satisfactory and Approved

Adjustments

Accounting Distribution

Audited   Final Approval

QUANTITY	DESCRIPTION	UNIT PRICE	AMOUNT
7	Model E Voicemaster Tape Recorders	$70	$490

by the seller and a **purchase invoice** by the buyer—defines the terms of the transaction. A sample invoice is shown in Exhibit 5-3.

4. Upon receiving the shipment of merchandise, the purchaser's receiving department counts and inspects the items in the shipment and completes a **receiving report** detailing the quantities received.

5. Before approving the invoice for payment, the accounts payable department compares copies of the purchase order, invoice, and receiving report to ensure that quantities, descriptions, and prices are in agreement.

Although all of the above forms—purchase requisition, purchase order, invoice, and receiving report—are source documents, only the invoice provides the basis for recording the purchase. The other three documents are merely supporting documents. The purchaser makes no entries in the accounts until the invoice is approved for payment. The seller enters the transaction in the records when the invoice is prepared, usually after shipment of the merchandise.

TERMS OF TRANSACTIONS

Merchandise may be purchased and sold either on credit terms or for cash on delivery. Most merchandise transactions today are made on account rather than for cash. When goods are sold on account, a period of time called the **credit period** is allowed for payment. The length of the credit period varies among business firms and may

OBJECTIVE ❸ DESCRIBE *the cash payment terms, trade discount terms, and shipping terms of merchandise transactions.*

even vary within a firm, depending on the type of product. A typical credit period for wholesalers is 30 days. Payment is expected within 30 days of the invoice date, after which the purchaser is considered delinquent. The credit period is frequently described as the *net* credit period, or *net* terms, and the notation commonly used to designate this period is "n/" followed by the length of the period in days; for example, n/30 indicates that the credit period is 30 days.

Cash Discounts

To encourage early payment of bills, many firms designate a **discount period** that is shorter than the credit period. Purchasers who remit payment during this period are entitled to deduct a **cash discount** from the total payment. Ostensibly, this discount is for prompt payment. The discount is designated by such notation as "2/10," which means that 2% may be deducted if payment is made within 10 days. For example, if a November 10 invoice for $800 carries terms of 2/10, n/30, the purchaser may deduct 2% from the invoice price if the bill is paid by November 20. The cash discount would be $16 (2% of $800), and the amount of the remittance would be $784. The full amount of the invoice, $800, would be expected if the purchaser paid after November 20 and by December 10. After December 10, the amount would be overdue.

Businesses try to maintain a good cash position so they can take advantage of cash discounts. For example, assume that a firm purchased $800 worth of merchandise on terms of 2/10, n/30. The firm has a choice of paying $784 within 10 days of the invoice date or the full amount before the end of another 20 days. Passing up the discount is essentially the same as paying 2% interest for the use of $800 for 20 days, which is equivalent to a 36% annual interest rate (360 days/20 days × 2%). Clearly, the firm would be wiser to borrow from a bank at an annual interest rate of 9–12% rather than lose a discount that amounts to a much higher rate.

Trade Discounts

Many businesses furnish customers with price lists or catalogs showing suggested retail prices for their products. These firms, however, also include a schedule of **trade discounts** from the listed prices that enable a customer to determine the invoice price to be paid. Suppose that Madison Electronics Company quoted a list price of $100 for each Model E tape recorder, less a trade discount of 30% if purchased in lots of 10 items or less and 40% if purchased in lots of more than 10. If Video Magic Company ordered seven tape recorders from Madison Electronics Company, Video Magic would calculate the invoice price as follows:

List Price ($100 × 7)	$700
Less 30% Trade Discount	210
Invoice Price	$490

Trade discounts enable a supplier to vary prices for small and large purchasers and, by changing the discount schedule, to alter prices periodically without the inconvenience and expense of revising catalogs and price lists.

Trade discounts are simply a means of determining invoice prices and should not be confused with cash discounts. Trade discounts and list prices are not reflected in the accounts of either the purchaser or the seller of merchandise. In the foregoing example, both the purchaser and the seller would record only the $490 invoice amount.

Shipping Costs

When merchandise is shipped by a common carrier—a railroad, a trucking company, or an airline—the carrier prepares a *freight bill* in accordance with the instructions of the party making the transportation arrangements. The freight bill designates which party bears the shipping costs and whether the shipment is *freight prepaid* or *freight collect*.

		EXHIBIT 5—4		TREATMENT OF FREIGHT COSTS

Freight Terms	Pays Shipper	Bears Freight Cost
F.O.B. Shipping Point, Freight Collect	Buyer	Buyer
F.O.B. Destination, Freight Prepaid	Seller	Seller
F.O.B. Shipping Point, Freight Prepaid	Seller	Buyer
F.O.B. Destination, Freight Collect	Buyer	Seller

Freight bills usually show whether the shipping terms are F.O.B. shipping point or F.O.B. destination. F.O.B. is an abbreviation for "free on board." When the freight terms are F.O.B. shipping point, the purchaser bears the shipping costs; when the terms are F.O.B. destination, the seller bears the shipping costs. Usually, the party bearing the freight cost pays the carrier. Thus, goods are typically shipped *freight collect* when the terms are F.O.B. shipping point and *freight prepaid* when the terms are F.O.B. destination. Sometimes, as a matter of convenience, the firm not bearing the freight cost pays the carrier. When this situation occurs, the seller and buyer simply adjust the amount of the payment for the merchandise.

Exhibit 5-4 shows which party—the buyer or the seller—pays the shipper and bears the freight cost for various freight terms. Demonstration Problem 2 at the end of this chapter provides numerical illustrations of the different freight arrangements.

INVENTORY SYSTEMS

OBJECTIVE 4 INTRODUCE *the periodic inventory system and* ILLUSTRATE *the treatment of merchandise accounts using the periodic inventory system.*

The inventory of a merchandising firm consists of a stock of merchandise that the firm owns and has available for sale to customers. The dollar amount of this merchandise is carried in an asset account called **Merchandise Inventory,** or **Inventory.**

Two systems are available to merchandising firms to record events related to the inventory—the periodic inventory system and the perpetual inventory system. The *periodic inventory system* is introduced in the following sections; the perpetual inventory system is presented at the end of this chapter.

The **periodic inventory system** is primarily used by businesses that sell large quantities of low-priced items and are not yet using computerized scanning systems to analyze their goods sold. In these situations, it generally is not feasible to determine the cost of the merchandise sold at the time of sale. For example, consider a hardware store that sells a customer one roll of masking tape, a small packet of brass screws, and a hammer. The selling prices are marked on price tags on the items and are quickly determinable. Their costs, however, are not so easily and quickly determined. Thus, the hardware store makes no entry at the time of each sale to record the cost of goods sold and to reduce the inventory. Periodically, the store will count its inventory and determine the cost of all goods sold during the period using the procedure we describe in this chapter.

A characteristic of the periodic inventory system is that no entries are made to the Inventory account during the period as merchandise is bought and sold. As just noted, the Inventory account is not reduced when goods are sold. Similarly, when goods are purchased, a separate set of accounts other than Inventory is used to accumulate information on the net cost of the purchases. Only at the end of the period, when the inventory is counted, will entries be made to the Inventory account to establish its proper balance at that time.

MERCHANDISE SALES: PERIODIC INVENTORY SYSTEM

After a vendor has processed a customer's purchase order and prepared the goods for shipment, a sales invoice is prepared in several copies. The original copy is sent to the customer, and duplicate copies are retained by the seller. The duplicates may be distributed to the shipping department to support its shipping records; to the sales department so it can analyze sales by product, territory, or sales representative; and to the accounting department so that the transaction can be recorded in the accounts.

Suppose the accounting department of Madison Electronics Company receives its copy of the November 20 invoice for the sale of the tape recorders described in the previous section. The general journal entry to record the sale would be

Nov. 20	Accounts Receivable	490	
	Sales		490
	To record the sale of seven Model E tape recorders to Video Magic Company. Terms 2/10, n/30; F.O.B. shipping point, freight collect.		

The **Sales** account is used by almost all manufacturing and merchandising companies to record revenue transactions. As a revenue account, Sales is credited whenever credit or cash sales are made, and invariably it has a credit balance at the end of the accounting period. Only sales of merchandise held for resale are recorded in the Sales account. If a merchandising firm sold one of its delivery trucks, the credit would be made to the Delivery Equipment account, not to the Sales account. At the end of the accounting period, the Sales account is closed to the Income Summary account in the same way other revenue accounts are closed. Sales is debited and Income Summary is credited for the accumulated credit balance in the Sales account. Because Madison Electronics is using the periodic inventory system, no entry is made to reflect any reduction in the Inventory account at the time the goods are sold.

As we mentioned earlier, the sales invoice is the document used to record credit sales. For cash sales, however, the procedure is different. For a large volume of cash sales, as in a retail merchandising establishment, cash sales are recorded and accumulated on a cash register tape as they are made.[1] At the end of each day, the amount of sales shown on the tape is recorded on a summary sheet or report. The totals on these reports are usually recorded in the Sales account for the week. Shorter or longer recording intervals may be used, depending on management's reporting needs. In general journal form, the entry to record a week's cash sales of $3,200 would be

Nov. 27	Cash	3,200	
	Sales		3,200
	To record cash sales for week of November 23–27.		

MERCHANDISE PURCHASES: PERIODIC INVENTORY SYSTEM

When a business using the periodic inventory system purchases merchandise for resale to customers, the amount is debited to the **Purchases** account. The credit is made to Accounts Payable or to Cash, depending on whether the purchase was on credit or cash terms. Assume that on November 23, Video Magic Company received its shipment of seven tape recorders from Madison Electronics Company, along with

---

[1] Some retail firms may record sales by electronic means at the time of sale, updating computerized records with each transaction.

2/10 , N

the vendor's invoice for $490. To record the credit purchase, Video Magic Company makes the following entry:

```
Nov. 23   Purchases                                      490
              Accounts Payable                                     490
          To record the purchase of seven Model E tape recorders
          from Madison Electronics Company. Terms 2/10, n/30;
          F.O.B. shipping point, freight collect.
```

Only merchandise purchased for resale is recorded in the Purchases account. Acquisitions of such things as equipment, supplies, and investments are entered in the corresponding asset accounts rather than in Purchases. Recording merchandise purchases at invoice price is known as the **gross price method of recording purchases.**

SHIPPING COSTS: PERIODIC INVENTORY SYSTEM

The shipping costs borne by a purchaser using the periodic inventory system are debited to an account called **Transportation In.** On the firm's income statement, the balance in this account is added to Purchases in computing the net cost of purchases for the period. Shipping costs borne by a seller are debited to an account called **Transportation Out.** This account—sometimes called *Delivery Expense*—is listed with expenses on the income statement.

The tape recorders purchased by Video Magic Company were shipped F.O.B. shipping point, freight collect. These terms indicate that Video Magic Company bears the cost of shipping and will also pay the shipping company. Assume that on November 24, Video Magic Company issued a $20 check to the freight company to pay for the cost of shipping the tape recorders. The following journal entry would be made:

```
Nov. 24   Transportation In                              20
              Cash                                              20
          To record payment of shipping costs.
```

The Transportation In account has a normal debit balance. It is a temporary account and will be closed at the end of the accounting period along with the other temporary accounts.

RETURNS AND ALLOWANCES: PERIODIC INVENTORY SYSTEM

Sometimes a customer returns merchandise to the seller because of defects, damage in transit, or because the wrong merchandise was shipped. Upon returning merchandise, the customer requests an appropriate reduction in the original amount billed. Similar requests are made when an invoicing error has occurred. Upon receiving notification that the buyer has returned goods or has requested an allowance, the seller usually issues the customer a **credit memorandum.**

The credit memorandum (sometimes called *credit memo*) is a formal acknowledgment that the seller has reduced the amount owed by the customer. When the seller issues a credit memo, the accounting department retains a duplicate copy, which is the source document for an entry crediting the customer's account. For example, suppose two of the seven tape recorders sold to Video Magic Company were returned for credit. Upon issuing a credit memo to Video Magic Company, Madison Electronics Company would make the following entry:

```
Nov. 25   Sales Returns and Allowances                   140
              Accounts Receivable                               140
          To record the issuance of credit memo No. 23 for two
          Model E tape recorders returned by Video Magic
          Company.
```

Upon receipt of the credit memo, Video Magic Company would make the following entry:

Nov. 27	Accounts Payable	140	
	Purchases Returns and Allowances		140
	To record the receipt of credit memo No. 23 for two Model E tape recorders returned to Madison Electronics Company.		

In the first entry above, Madison Electronics Company could have debited the Sales account rather than Sales Returns and Allowances. If Sales were debited, however, the account balance at the end of the accounting period would not reveal total sales made but total sales less all returns and allowances. Most companies prefer to record sales returns and allowances in a separate contra account in order to determine the aggregate amount of such items. If the amount is abnormally large, an investigation should be made to determine the reason. Returns and allowances may be caused by defective products, faulty packing or shipping, or improper billing procedures. The additional handling of goods and the additional clerical work of making adjustments can be costly, and customers may be lost in the process.

For similar reasons, the purchaser ordinarily credits the Purchases Returns and Allowances account rather than the Purchases account when a credit memo is received. The separate accounting permits a company to determine whether its purchasing procedures should be reviewed. The company may discover, for instance, that not enough care is exercised in filling out requisitions and purchase orders or in selecting reliable suppliers.

The Sales Returns and Allowances account typically has a debit balance at the end of the accounting period. On the income statement, the amount is a deduction from the Sales amount. The Purchases Returns and Allowances account usually has a credit balance at the end of the accounting period, and the balance is subtracted from the Purchases amount on the income statement. Both the Sales Returns and Allowances and the Purchases Returns and Allowances accounts are closed at the end of the accounting year.

Many companies record all credit memos in the returns and allowances accounts. When the memos are issued as a result of mere clerical or arithmetical errors, however, the adjustment should be recorded in the Sales or Purchases accounts.

RECEIPTS AND PAYMENTS: PERIODIC INVENTORY SYSTEM

A set of merchandise transactions concludes when the seller receives the proper remittance from the purchaser and each firm makes the appropriate entries for the settlement of accounts. To illustrate, let us review the entries made thus far for Madison Electronics Company's sale of the tape recorders to Video Magic Company.

Seller (Madison Electronics Company)				**Buyer (Video Magic Company)**			
To Record Sale				**To Record Purchase**			
Nov. 20	Accounts Receivable	490		Nov. 23	Purchases	490	
	Sales		490		Accounts Payable		490
	To record the sale of seven Model E tape recorders to Video Magic Company. Terms 2/10, n/30; F.O.B. shipping point, freight collect.				To record the purchase of seven Model E tape recorders from Madison Electronics Company. Terms 2/10, n/30; F.O.B. shipping point, freight collect.		
				To Record Shipping Costs			
				Nov. 24	Transportation In	20	
					Cash		20
					To record payment of shipping costs.		

To Record Return of Merchandise

Nov. 25   Sales Returns and
                Allowances   140
                    Accounts Receivable   140
           To record the issuance of
           credit memo No. 23 for
           two Model E tape record-
           ers returned by Video
           Magic Company.

To Record Return of Merchandise

Nov. 27   Accounts Payable   140
                Purchases Returns and
                    Allowances   140
           To record the receipt of
           credit memo No. 23 for
           two Model E tape record-
           ers returned to Madison
           Electronics Company.

After these transactions have been posted, the seller's Accounts Receivable account and the buyer's Accounts Payable account appear as follows:

Seller (Madison Electronics Company)		**Buyer** (Video Magic Company)	
ACCOUNTS RECEIVABLE		**ACCOUNTS PAYABLE**	
1993	1993	1993	1993
Nov. 20 490	Nov. 25 140	Nov. 27 140	Nov. 23 490

If Video Magic Company takes advantage of the 2% discount, its remittance must be made within 10 days of the November 20 invoice date. Usually, the discount is granted if the payment is mailed and postmarked on the last day of the discount period. The amount that Video Magic Company should remit by November 30 is $343 ($350 balance owed less 2% discount of $7). Note that the discount is calculated only on the cost of the merchandise kept by the purchaser, not on the invoice price of the goods originally shipped. The entries made on the books of the seller and buyer are as follows:

Seller (Madison Electronics Company)

Dec. 2   Cash   343
            Sales Discounts   7
                Accounts Receivable   350
         To record remittance in
         full of account.

Buyer (Video Magic Company)

Nov. 30   Accounts Payable   350
                Purchases Discounts   7
                Cash   343
           To record payment of
           account.

After this entry is posted, the seller's Accounts Receivable and the purchaser's Accounts Payable appear as follows:

Seller (Madison Electronics Company)		**Buyer** (Video Magic Company)	
ACCOUNTS RECEIVABLE		**ACCOUNTS PAYABLE**	
1993	1993	1993	1993
Nov. 20 490	Nov. 25 140	Nov. 27 140	Nov. 23 490
	Dec. 2 350	30 350	

Note that the discount taken in this transaction is not revealed in either the seller's Accounts Receivable account or the buyer's Accounts Payable account. Discounts are accumulated in Sales Discounts on the seller's books and Purchases Discounts on the buyer's books.

The other accounts relevant to the set of transactions for the tape recorders are shown below in T-account form, after the appropriate postings have been made.

Seller (Madison Electronics Company)		**Buyer** (Video Magic Company)	
SALES		**PURCHASES**	
	1993	1993	
	Nov. 20 490	Nov. 23 490	

SALES RETURNS AND ALLOWANCES			PURCHASES RETURNS AND ALLOWANCES	
1993 Nov. 25	140		1993 Nov. 27	140

SALES DISCOUNTS			PURCHASES DISCOUNTS	
1993 Dec. 2	7		1993 Nov. 30	7

			TRANSPORTATION IN	
			1993 Nov. 24	20

From this illustration, we see that both Sales Returns and Allowances and Sales Discounts have debit balances, and the Sales account has a credit balance. At the close of the accounting period, the net sales for the period can be calculated by subtracting the balances of the Sales Returns and Allowances account and the Sales Discounts account from the Sales account. The revenue section of the seller's income statement for the year will show this calculation as follows:

Revenue			
Sales			$433,000
Less: Sales Returns and Allowances		$2,500	
Sales Discounts		5,500	8,000
Net Sales			$425,000

COST OF GOODS SOLD: PERIODIC INVENTORY SYSTEM

The cost of goods sold for a firm using the periodic inventory system is calculated in the following manner:

$$\begin{matrix} \text{Beginning} \\ \text{Inventory} \end{matrix} + \begin{matrix} \text{Net Cost} \\ \text{of Purchases} \end{matrix} = \begin{matrix} \text{Cost of Goods} \\ \text{Available} \\ \text{for Sale} \end{matrix}$$

$$\begin{matrix} \text{Cost of Goods} \\ \text{Available} \\ \text{for Sale} \end{matrix} - \begin{matrix} \text{Ending} \\ \text{Inventory} \end{matrix} = \begin{matrix} \text{Cost of} \\ \text{Goods Sold} \end{matrix}$$

These calculations are included in the cost of goods sold section in the firm's income statement.

At year-end, the company determines the amount of its ending inventory by taking a physical inventory. Taking the inventory usually consists of the following steps:

1. Count the quantity of each individual item of merchandise in stock at year-end.

2. Determine the unit cost of each individual item and multiply its quantity times the unit cost to obtain the total cost for each individual item of merchandise.

3. Add together the total costs of all individual items to obtain the total cost of the complete inventory.

Year-end journal entries (which we illustrate later) will establish the ending inventory amount in the Inventory account and remove the beginning inventory from the account.

Balances contained in the Purchases, Purchases Returns and Allowances, Purchases Discounts, and Transportation In accounts are combined to compute the net cost of purchases. Purchases and Transportation In have debit balances; Purchases

Returns and Allowances and Purchases Discounts have credit balances. Thus, to compute the net cost of purchases, we start with the Purchases amount, deduct the sum of Purchases Returns and Allowances and Purchases Discounts and add Transportation In.

Assuming Madison Electronics Company determines that its year-end inventory is $120,000, cost of goods sold will be computed in its income statement as follows:

Inventory, January 1, 1993			$115,000
Add: Net Cost of Purchases:			
Purchases		$256,500	
Less: Purchases Returns and Allowances	$1,800		
Purchases Discounts	4,400	6,200	
		$250,300	
Add: Transportation In		9,700	260,000
Cost of Goods Available for Sale			$375,000
Less: Inventory, December 31, 1993			120,000
Cost of Goods Sold			$255,000

NET PRICE METHOD OF RECORDING PURCHASES: PERIODIC INVENTORY SYSTEM

Some firms anticipate the cash discounts they expect to take on merchandise purchases and initially record such purchases net of the discounts. For example, if a firm purchased merchandise for $500 on terms of 2/10, n/30, the 2% cash discount ($10) would be deducted from the invoice cost, and the entry to record the transaction would debit Purchases and credit Accounts Payable for $490. When this amount is paid during the discount period, the debit to Accounts Payable and the credit to Cash would be for the net amount, $490. No purchase discount would be recorded. When the **net price method** is used, returns and allowances are also recorded net of the related cash discount.

If a firm delays payment beyond the discount period, the amount of the cash discount not taken is debited to an account called **Discounts Lost** when the remittance is made. If the firm in our example failed to remit within the discount period, it would record the payment as a $490 debit to Accounts Payable, $10 debit to Discounts Lost, and a $500 credit to Cash.

The Discounts Lost account balance is normally added to the cost of purchases in the cost of goods sold section of the income statement. However, some firms include it with operating expenses. The principal advantage of the net price method is that it focuses attention on discounts not taken, so that management can take immediate corrective action when the aggregate amount of lost cash discounts becomes significant.

Illustrations of the types of entries used in the net price method are given below:

Purchase of merchandise for $500 on terms of 2/10, n/30

Purchases	490	
Accounts Payable		490
($500 purchase, less 2% cash discount)		

Return of $200 merchandise

Accounts Payable	196	
Purchases Returns and Allowances		196
($200 return, less 2% cash discount)		

Payment within discount period

Accounts Payable	294	
Cash		294
($300 merchandise, less 2% cash discount)		

Payment after discount period

Accounts Payable	294	
Discounts Lost	6	
Cash		300
($300 merchandise, less 2% cash discount lost)		

WORKSHEET FOR A MERCHANDISING FIRM: PERIODIC INVENTORY SYSTEM

A worksheet is prepared at the close of an accounting period to facilitate preparation of the financial statements. The structure of a worksheet for a merchandising firm is the same 10-column form used for a service firm, with pairs of columns for the trial balance, adjustments, adjusted trial balance, income statement, and balance sheet. Madison Electronics Company's worksheet in Exhibit 5-5 is prepared after all transactions for the year are recorded and posted to the accounts. Assume that Madison Electronics Company uses the periodic inventory system. The first step in preparing the worksheet is to take a trial balance of the general ledger at December 31 and record the account balances in the first two columns of the worksheet.

Adjustments in the Worksheet

OBJECTIVE 5 **ILLUSTRATE** *the preparation of a worksheet and the year-end entries for a merchandising firm using the periodic inventory system.*

The second step in preparing the worksheet is to record the year-end adjusting entries in the adjustments columns. These entries, with explanations, are as follows:

1.	Dec. 31	Insurance Expense	280	
		Prepaid Insurance		280
		To charge one year's premium to expense (three-year premium, $840, paid January 1).		
2.	31	Supplies Expense	1,200	
		Supplies		1,200
		To charge to expense the supplies used during year. (Inventory of supplies is $1,600 on December 31.)		
3.	31	Depreciation Expense	6,000	
		Accumulated Depreciation		6,000
		To charge to expense one year's depreciation on delivery equipment.		
4.	31	Sales Salaries Expense	500	
		Salaries Payable		500
		To reflect the salaries earned by salespersons but not paid at December 31.		

To reflect the adjusting entries, we add the accounts not included in the trial balance to the bottom of the worksheet. After making these entries, we total the adjustments columns to confirm that debits equal credits. The trial balance amounts are combined with the adjustments to obtain the adjusted trial balance amounts; these amounts are also summed to determine the equality of the totals. We then extend the adjusted trial balance amounts into the income statement and balance sheet columns. We can see in Exhibit 5-5 that Sales, Purchases, related returns and allowances, discounts, transportation in, and expense accounts are extended into the income statement columns. Assets, liabilities, and owners' equity accounts are extended into the balance sheet columns.

Inventories in the Worksheet

Because the periodic inventory system is used, the inventory amount that appears in the unadjusted trial balance columns in Exhibit 5-5 is that for the January 1 inventory. This amount still appears in the account because additions and deductions during the year have not been reflected in the Inventory account. The beginning inventory of $115,000 is extended as a debit in the income statement columns because it is combined with Purchases (less returns and allowances and discounts) and Transportation In to determine the cost of goods available for sale. The $120,000 ending inventory, recorded at the bottom of the worksheet, is a credit in the income statement columns because it is deducted from cost of goods available for sale in the calculation of cost of goods sold. In Exhibit 5-5, all the amounts included in cost of goods sold appear in bold type to emphasize how cost of goods sold is reflected in the income statement columns of the worksheet. The ending inventory of $120,000 is also entered as a debit in the balance sheet columns because it is an asset at December 31.

EXHIBIT 5—5

MADISON ELECTRONICS COMPANY
WORKSHEET (PERIODIC INVENTORY SYSTEM)
FOR THE YEAR ENDED DECEMBER 31, 1993

Description	Trial Balance Debit	Trial Balance Credit	Adjustments Debit	Adjustments Credit	Adjusted Trial Balance Debit	Adjusted Trial Balance Credit	Income Statement Debit	Income Statement Credit	Balance Sheet Debit	Balance Sheet Credit
Cash	18,240				18,240				18,240	
Accounts Receivable	32,000				32,000				32,000	
Inventory (January 1)	115,000				115,000		115,000			
Prepaid Insurance	840			(1) 280	560				560	
Supplies	2,800			(2)1,200	1,600				1,600	
Delivery Equipment	30,000				30,000				30,000	
Accumulated Depreciation		4,300		(3)6,000		10,300				10,300
Accounts Payable		17,500				17,500				17,500
Long-term Notes Payable		20,000				20,000				20,000
J. Madison, Capital		134,000				134,000				134,000
J. Madison, Drawing	5,400				5,400				5,400	
Sales		433,000				433,000		433,000		
Sales Returns and Allowances	2,500				2,500		2,500			
Sales Discounts	5,500				5,500		5,500			
Purchases	256,500				256,500		256,500			
Purchases Returns and Allowances		1,800				1,800		1,800		
Purchases Discounts		4,400				4,400		4,400		
Transportation In	9,700				9,700		9,700			
Sales Salaries Expense	64,000		(4) 500		64,500		64,500			
Advertising Expense	6,170				6,170		6,170			
Delivery Expense	19,250				19,250		19,250			
Office Salaries Expense	28,500				28,500		28,500			
Rent Expense	16,500				16,500		16,500			
Interest Expense	2,100				2,100		2,100			
	615,000	615,000								
Insurance Expense			(1) 280		280		280			
Supplies Expense			(2)1,200		1,200		1,200			
Depreciation Expense			(3)6,000		6,000		6,000			
Salaries Payable				(4) 500		500				500
			7,980	7,980	621,500	621,500				
Inventory (December 31)								120,000	120,000	
							533,700	559,200	207,800	182,300
Net Income							25,500			25,500
							559,200	559,200	207,800	207,800

The last step in completing the worksheet is to total the income statement and balance sheet columns and insert the balancing amount—the $25,500 net income for the year. A net income amount results in a debit in the income statement columns and a credit in the balance sheet columns. A net loss would result in a credit in the income statement columns and a debit in the balance sheet columns.

An alternative method of dealing with periodic inventories in the worksheet and the adjusting and closing process is preferred by some accountants. This method, which removes the beginning inventory and records the ending inventory by means of adjusting entries, is explained in Appendix B.

FINANCIAL STATEMENTS OF A MERCHANDISING FIRM

Once the worksheet is completed, preparing the **classified financial statements** is a simple matter. The income statement is the first financial statement to be prepared. Exhibit 5-6 presents the income statement for the year for Madison Electronics Company. This income statement is *classified*, meaning that accounts are separated into various categories. The income statements in previous illustrations were not classified because only a few accounts were used. A business with many accounts, however, classifies the items on the income statement to facilitate analysis and interpretation of the data.

EXHIBIT 5—6

MADISON ELECTRONICS COMPANY
INCOME STATEMENT
FOR THE YEAR ENDED DECEMBER 31, 1993

Sales				$433,000
Less: Sales Returns and Allowances			$ 2,500	
Sales Discounts			5,500	8,000
Net Sales				$425,000
Cost of Goods Sold:				
Inventory, January 1, 1993			$115,000	
Add: Net Cost of Purchases				
Purchases		$256,500		
Less: Purchases Returns and Allowances	$1,800			
Purchases Discounts	4,400	6,200		
		$250,300		
Add: Transportation In		9,700	260,000	
Cost of Goods Available for Sale			$375,000	
Less: Inventory, December 31, 1993			120,000	
Cost of Goods Sold				255,000
Gross Profit on Sales				$170,000
Operating Expenses:				
Selling Expenses				
Sales Salaries Expense		$ 64,500		
Delivery Expense		19,250		
Advertising Expense		6,170		
Depreciation Expense		6,000		
Insurance Expense		280		
Total Selling Expenses			$ 96,200	
Administrative Expenses				
Rent Expense		$ 16,500		
Office Salaries Expense		28,500		
Supplies Expense		1,200		
Total Administrative Expenses			46,200	
Total Operating Expenses				142,400
Income from Operations				$ 27,600
Other Income and Expense:				
Interest Expense				2,100
Net Income				$ 25,500

Classified Income Statement

OBJECTIVE 6 ILLUSTRATE *classified financial statements for a merchandising firm and* DESCRIBE *the classified income statement.*

The major categories of the income statement for a merchandising firm are revenues, cost of goods sold, and operating expenses. The major revenue source is sales of goods to customers. In the revenue section, sales returns and allowances and sales discounts are deducted from gross sales to yield net sales.

We noted earlier that the cost of goods sold amount is obtained by adding the beginning inventory and net cost of purchases and deducting the ending inventory. To calculate net cost of purchases, we deduct purchases returns and allowances and purchases discounts from the purchases amount and add transportation costs of purchased goods.

A firm's *operating expenses* are the expenses that relate to its primary operating functions. The operating expenses of a merchandising business are typically classified as selling or administrative expenses. Therefore, in our illustration, expenses resulting from sales efforts—such as sales salaries, advertising, and delivery—are classified separately from administrative expenses such as office salaries and supplies. Certain types of expenses may appear under both categories. For example, the insurance expense in Exhibit 5-6 is apparently on merchandise or delivery equipment, because it appears as a selling expense. Insurance on a company-owned office building, on the other hand, would appear with the administrative expenses. Similarly, the rent expense in Exhibit 5-6 must relate only to administrative space because it is classified as an administrative expense.

Some business items affecting the final net income amount may not relate to the primary operating activity of the business. Interest income and interest expense, for example, may relate more to financing and investing activities than to merchandising efforts. For this reason, such items are often shown in a separate category called *Other Income and Expense* at the bottom of the income statement. In Exhibit 5-6, Madison Electronics Company reports its interest expense in this category.

Statement of Owner's Equity

Exhibit 5-7 presents the statement of owner's equity for Madison Electronics Company. J. Madison's capital balance increased during the year because the firm's net income exceeded J. Madison's withdrawals of assets from the firm.

Classified Balance Sheet

The balance sheet for Madison Electronics Company at December 31, 1993, is shown in Exhibit 5-8 on page 176. Note that the balance sheet is classified, with assets classified as either current assets or plant assets and liabilities segregated into current liabilities and long-term liabilities.

ADJUSTING AND CLOSING ENTRIES

As explained previously, a company often will prepare monthly or quarterly financial statements directly from worksheets and not record adjusting and closing entries in the general ledger until the end of the year. Let us examine year-end procedures for Madison Electronics Company.

Adjusting Entries

After financial statements have been prepared from the worksheet, the adjusting entries shown on the worksheet are recorded in the general journal and posted to the accounts. These entries, given in general journal form earlier in this chapter, will not be repeated here.

Closing Entries

OBJECTIVE 7 OUTLINE *the closing entries for a merchandising firm.*

The closing entries follow the adjusting entries in the general journal. The procedure consists of the following steps:

1 Record the ending inventory, close all income statement accounts with *credit* balances, and credit the total to the Income Summary account.

2 Remove the beginning inventory, close all income statement accounts with *debit* balances, and debit the total to the Income Summary account.

EXHIBIT 5—7

MADISON ELECTRONICS COMPANY
STATEMENT OF OWNER'S EQUITY
FOR THE YEAR ENDED DECEMBER 31, 1993

J. Madison, Capital, January 1, 1993	$134,000
Add: Net Income for 1993	25,500
	$159,500
Less: Capital Withdrawn in 1993	5,400
J. Madison, Capital, December 31, 1993	$154,100

---

3 Transfer the balance of the Income Summary account to the owner's capital account (the Retained Earnings account in a corporation).

4 Transfer the balance of the owner's drawing account to the owner's capital account.

Closing entries for Madison Electronics Company are given below:

1	Dec. 31	Inventory	120,000	
		Sales	433,000	
		Purchases Returns and Allowances	1,800	
		Purchases Discounts	4,400	
		Income Summary		559,200
		To record the ending inventory and to close income statement accounts with credit balances.		
2	31	Income Summary	533,700	
		Inventory		115,000
		Sales Returns and Allowances		2,500
		Sales Discounts		5,500
		Purchases		256,500
		Transportation In		9,700
		Sales Salaries Expense		64,500
		Advertising Expense		6,170
		Delivery Expense		19,250
		Office Salaries Expense		28,500
		Rent Expense		16,500
		Interest Expense		2,100
		Insurance Expense		280
		Supplies Expense		1,200
		Depreciation Expense		6,000
		To remove the beginning inventory and close income statement accounts with debit balances.		
3	31	Income Summary	25,500	
		J. Madison, Capital		25,500
		To close the Income Summary account and transfer net income to the owner's capital account.		
4	31	J. Madison, Capital	5,400	
		J. Madison, Drawing		5,400
		To close the owner's drawing account to the capital account.		

After the adjusting and closing entries have been recorded and posted, the Income Summary and J. Madison, Capital accounts appear as shown below. (J. Madison's withdrawal was made on October 10.) Although we have labeled these entries for illustrative purposes, Income Summary would ordinarily not be so completely labeled in the actual accounts.

EXHIBIT 5—8

MADISON ELECTRONICS COMPANY
BALANCE SHEET
DECEMBER 31, 1993

Assets			Liabilities		
Current Assets			**Current Liabilities**		
Cash	$ 18,240		Accounts Payable	$17,500	
Accounts Receivable	32,000		Salaries Payable	500	
Inventory	120,000		Total Current Liabilities		$ 18,000
Supplies	1,600		**Long-term Liabilities**		
Prepaid Insurance	560		Long-term Notes Payable		20,000
Total Current Assets		$172,400	Total Liabilities		$ 38,000
Plant Assets					
Delivery Equipment	$ 30,000		**Owner's Equity**		
Less: Accumulated Depreciation	10,300	19,700	J. Madison, Capital		154,100
Total Assets		$192,100	Total Liabilities and Owner's Equity		$192,100

INCOME SUMMARY   ACCOUNT NO. 33

Date		Description	Post. Ref.	Debit	Credit	Balance
1993						
Dec.	31	Ending Inventory, Sales, and Other Credits			559,200	559,200
	31	Beginning Inventory, Purchases, Expenses, and Other Debits		533,700		25,500
	31	Net Income		25,500		-0-

J. MADISON, CAPITAL   ACCOUNT NO. 31

Date		Description	Post. Ref.	Debit	Credit	Balance
1993						
Jan.	1	Balance				134,000
Oct.	10	Withdrawal		5,400		128,600
Dec.	31	Net Income			25,500	154,100

PERPETUAL INVENTORY SYSTEM

OBJECTIVE 8 PRESENT *the perpetual inventory system and* CONTRAST *the merchandise transaction entries using it and the entries using the periodic inventory system.*

The perpetual inventory system is an alternative to the periodic inventory system. Under the **perpetual inventory system,** the Inventory account is perpetually, or continually (as opposed to periodically), updated. Perpetually updating the Inventory account requires that (1) at the time of purchase, merchandise acquisitions be recorded as debits to the Inventory account and (2) at the time of sale, the cost of goods sold be determined and recorded by a debit to the Cost of Goods Sold account and a credit to the Inventory account. With a perpetual inventory system, both the Inventory and Cost of Goods Sold accounts receive entries throughout the accounting period.

Many merchandising firms are now using the perpetual inventory system with point-of-sale equipment. Supermarkets use point-of-sale scanners built into checkout counters to collect transactional data for the cash register and to update their perpetual inventory system. Department stores use point-of-sale wand scanners to collect inventory data to update their perpetual inventory system. The perpetual inventory system is also appropriate for firms that sell low-volume, high-priced goods such as automobiles.

When a company uses a perpetual inventory system, the Inventory account at the end of the year shows the amount of inventory that should be on hand at the end of the period—assuming that no theft, spoilage, or error has occurred. However, even if there is little chance for or suspicion of inventory discrepancy, most companies take a physical inventory count at the end of the year. At that time, the account is adjusted for any inaccuracies discovered.

The following example demonstrates the entries typically used with the perpetual inventory system, contrasted with the entries used with the periodic inventory system. For this example, assume that the beginning inventory for the year is $25,000.

Periodic Inventory System			Perpetual Inventory System		

1. Sold merchandise on account costing $8,000 for $10,000; terms were 2/10, n/30:

Accounts Receivable	10,000		Accounts Receivable	10,000	
Sales		10,000	Sales		10,000
			Cost of Goods Sold	8,000	
			Inventory		8,000

2. Customer returned merchandise costing $400 that had been sold on account for $500 (part of the $10,000 sale):

Sales Returns and Allowances	500		Sales Returns and Allowances	500	
Accounts Receivable		500	Accounts Receivable		500
			Inventory	400	
			Cost of Goods Sold		400

3. Received payment from customer for merchandise sold above [cash discount taken: ($10,000 − $500) × 0.02 = $190]:

Cash	9,310		Cash	9,310	
Sales Discounts	190		Sales Discounts	190	
Accounts Receivable		9,500	Accounts Receivable		9,500

4. Purchased on account merchandise for resale for $6,000; terms were 2/10, n/30 (purchases recorded at invoice price):[2]

Purchases	6,000		Inventory	6,000	
Accounts Payable		6,000	Accounts Payable		6,000

5. Paid $200 freight on the $6,000 purchase; terms were F.O.B. shipping point, freight collect:

Transportation In	200		Inventory	200	
Cash		200	Cash		200

6. Returned merchandise costing $300 (part of $6,000 purchase):

Accounts Payable	300		Accounts Payable	300	
Purchases Returns and Allowances		300	Inventory		300

7. Paid for merchandise purchased above [cash discount taken: ($6,000 − $300) × 0.02 = $114]:

Accounts Payable	5,700		Accounts Payable	5,700	
Purchases Discounts		114	Inventory		114
Cash		5,586	Cash		5,586

Assuming the previous seven transactions were the only transactions for the entire year, the balance in the Inventory account at year-end under the periodic inventory system is $25,000 (the beginning inventory). The year-end balance in the Inventory account under the perpetual inventory system is $23,186. Note that under

---

[2] The net price method described earlier may also be used with a perpetual inventory system.

BIGGER JOBS AWAITING BAR CODES

After years of playing an important bit part in the information revolution, the bar code is being groomed for a more demanding role. ■ Several companies that make scanning and printing equipment have designed new codes, the most sophisticated of which can actually work as if they were miniature printouts from computer data files. ■ The new codes are expected to replace lengthy typewritten shipping documents, allow manufacturers to individually label small items like microchips, and help prevent the mishandling of hazardous waste, among other applications.

Most of the ubiquitous black and white stripes printed on the sides of cereal boxes represent short sequences of numbers, letters, or both.

Somewhat like figures on license plates, each bar code is really a label for files of information that are stored elsewhere in a computer. When a laser at the checkout counter scans the bar code on a box of grits, for instance, the store's computer instantly tells the cash register the price and how to describe it on the receipt.

The new bar codes allow lines of code to be stacked up, storing information in two dimensions instead of in one line.

Symbol Technologies Inc., which is based in Bohemia, N.Y., and is the nation's largest bar-code equipment supplier, has developed the most sophisticated of the new so-called two-dimensional, or 2D, codes.

The code can pack several hundred characters into a square inch of space, serving, in essence, as a portable data file on paper instead of a floppy disk.

"You could call it a non-technical form of electronic data interchange," said Robert Moore, director of technical publications for Automatic Identification Manufacturers Inc., a trade group based in Pittsburgh.

Backers of the 2D codes say they could substitute for papers about a shipment. Instead of typing out lists of the contents of the shipment and its routing, a small textile company could print the information in bar code form and fax it to shippers and retailers, who would scan it to put the data into their computer files.

The same bar symbol would be attached to the shipment. From then on, all parties involved in the stream of trade would have a much easier time tracking the goods, leading to fewer distribution errors, better scheduling of trucks and warehouse space, quicker recording of transfers and smoother reordering.

The new codes might also help manufacturers track production of complex machines, like tractors, without stuffing a plant with computer terminals and support equipment.

A 2D bar symbol could be scanned to tell workers, or a robot, where a part came from, what needed to be done, where it had to go next, and when.

An updated symbol reflecting completion of the work could be printed out for less than half a cent and attached to the part before sending it on. The complete record could be put in the plant's main computer system at the end of the day.

Two-dimensional codes might also be a useful way to keep production records and maintenance schedules with military equipment that is suddenly sent to remote areas beyond the reach of the Defense Department's computer networks.

The Energy Department is considering using them to attach detailed handling instructions and other information to hazardous waste shipments.

Two-dimensional bar code labels might also be used to post repair records on leased equipment.

And direct mailers might use them to build new information files limited to people who respond to their junk mail.

SOURCE: Barnaby J. Feder, "Bigger Jobs Awaiting Bar Codes," *New York Times*, May 5, 1991, p. 2C. Copyright © 1991 by The New York Times Company. Reprinted by permission.

the perpetual inventory system, the Inventory account is increased by purchases, transportation in, and sales returns and is decreased by the cost of goods sold, purchases returns and allowances, and purchases discounts. At year-end, the physical inventory is taken, and it reveals that the actual inventory on hand is $23,150. The following year-end journal entries are then made to bring the Inventory account balance into agreement with the amount of the physical inventory.

Periodic Inventory System		Perpetual Inventory System	

8. To transfer the beginning inventory balance to the Income Summary account (part of the closing entries under the periodic inventory system):[3]

Income Summary	25,000		(No entry required)	
Inventory		25,000		

9. To record the ending inventory balance (part of the closing entries under the periodic inventory system)[4] *or* to adjust the ending perpetual inventory balance for the shrinkage during the year:

Inventory	23,150		Cost of Goods Sold[5]	36	
Income Summary		23,150	Inventory		36

When posted to the general ledger, both the periodic and perpetual inventory systems result in the same ending inventory amount, $23,150.

WORKSHEET FOR A MERCHANDISING FIRM: PERPETUAL INVENTORY SYSTEM

OBJECTIVE 9 ILLUSTRATE *the worksheet and income statement for a merchandising firm using the perpetual inventory system.*

Earlier in this chapter, we presented the worksheet for Madison Electronics Company under the periodic inventory system. Exhibit 5-9 presents the worksheet for Madison Electronics Company, assuming the perpetual inventory system is used. The worksheet in Exhibit 5-9 is prepared after all transactions for the year have been journalized and posted, using the perpetual inventory system. The following items on the worksheet should be noted:

1. The inventory amount in the trial balance is the December 31, 1993, balance because the Inventory account has been perpetually updated.
2. The Cost of Goods Sold account appears on the worksheet. There are no accounts for Purchases, Purchases Returns and Allowances, Purchases Discounts, and Transportation In because information related to these items is recorded directly in the Inventory account under the perpetual inventory system. When closing entries are made, Cost of Goods Sold is closed with the other debit-balanced income statement accounts.
3. The adjustments are handled exactly the same way as they were handled in the periodic worksheet.
4. No entry is necessary to the Inventory account because Madison Electronics Company had no inventory shrinkage or other discrepancy during 1993; that is, the year-end account balance agreed with the physical inventory amount.

INCOME STATEMENT FOR A MERCHANDISING FIRM: PERPETUAL INVENTORY SYSTEM

Exhibit 5-10 (on page 181) shows the classified income statement prepared from the worksheet for Madison Electronics Company in Exhibit 5-9. Because Madison Electronics Company is using the perpetual inventory system, the cost of goods sold amount is available in the Cost of Goods Sold ledger account shown in the worksheet. Thus, there is no need to present an extensive cost of goods sold section in the income statement. As shown in Exhibit 5-10, cost of goods sold is presented on a single line. The rest of the income statement is similar to that prepared for a company using a periodic inventory system.

There are no differences in the statement of owner's equity and classified balance sheet prepared for a firm on a perpetual inventory system compared with a periodic inventory system. The statement of owner's equity and classified balance sheet prepared from the worksheet in Exhibit 5-9, therefore, will be the same statements as presented earlier in Exhibits 5-7 and 5-8.

---

[3] As discussed in Appendix B, an alternative method of recording inventories under the periodic method treats this entry as a year-end adjusting entry rather than a closing entry.
[4] See note 3 above.
[5] Some firms may use a special Loss on Inventory Shrinkage account.

EXHIBIT 5—9

MADISON ELECTRONICS COMPANY
WORKSHEET (PERPETUAL INVENTORY SYSTEM)
FOR THE YEAR ENDED DECEMBER 31, 1993

Description	Trial Balance		Adjustments		Adjusted Trial Balance		Income Statement		Balance Sheet	
	Debit	Credit	Debit	Credit	Debit	Credit	Debit	Credit	Debit	Credit
Cash	18,240				18,240				18,240	
Accounts Receivable	32,000				32,000				32,000	
Inventory (December 31)	120,000				120,000				120,000	
Prepaid Insurance	840			(1) 280	560				560	
Supplies	2,800			(2)1,200	1,600				1,600	
Delivery Equipment	30,000				30,000				30,000	
Accumulated Depreciation		4,300		(3)6,000		10,300				10,300
Accounts Payable		17,500				17,500				17,500
Long-term Notes Payable		20,000				20,000				20,000
J. Madison, Capital		134,000				134,000				134,000
J. Madison, Drawing	5,400				5,400				5,400	
Sales		433,000				433,000		433,000		
Sales Returns and Allowances	2,500				2,500		2,500			
Sales Discounts	5,500				5,500		5,500			
Cost of Goods Sold	255,000				255,000		255,000			
Sales Salaries Expense	64,000		(4) 500		64,500		64,500			
Advertising Expense	6,170				6,170		6,170			
Delivery Expense	19,250				19,250		19,250			
Office Salaries Expense	28,500				28,500		28,500			
Rent Expense	16,500				16,500		16,500			
Interest Expense	2,100				2,100		2,100			
	608,800	608,800								
Insurance Expense			(1) 280		280		280			
Supplies Expense			(2)1,200		1,200		1,200			
Depreciation Expense			(3)6,000		6,000		6,000			
Salaries Payable				(4) 500		500				500
			7,980	7,980	615,300	615,300	407,500	433,000	207,800	182,300
Net Income							25,500			25,500
							433,000	433,000	207,800	207,800

ANALYTICAL APPLICATION

GROSS PROFIT PERCENTAGE

OBJECTIVE 10 DEFINE *the gross profit percentage and explain its use.*

Gross profit on sales is an amount that management, investors, and outsiders monitor very closely. In addition, these same groups are very interested in the **gross profit percentage,** which is calculated as follows:

EXHIBIT 5—10

MADISON ELECTRONICS COMPANY
INCOME STATEMENT
FOR THE YEAR ENDED DECEMBER 31, 1993

Sales			$433,000
Less: Sales Returns and Allowances		$ 2,500	
Sales Discounts		5,500	8,000
Net Sales			$425,000
Cost of Goods Sold			255,000
Gross Profit on Sales			$170,000
Operating Expenses:			
Selling Expenses			
Sales Salaries Expense	$ 64,500		
Delivery Expense	19,250		
Advertising Expense	6,170		
Depreciation Expense	6,000		
Insurance Expense	280		
Total Selling Expenses		$ 96,200	
Administrative Expenses			
Rent Expense	$ 16,500		
Office Salaries Expense	28,500		
Supplies Expense	1,200		
Total Administrative Expenses		46,200	
Total Operating Expenses			142,400
Income from Operations			$ 27,600
Other Income and Expense:			
Interest Expense			2,100
Net Income			$ 25,500

$$\text{Gross Profit Percentage} = \frac{\text{Gross Profit on Sales}}{\text{Net Sales}}$$

The income statement for the year ended December 31, 1993, for Madison Electronics Company in Exhibit 5-2 included the following amounts:

Net Sales	$425,000
Cost of Goods Sold	255,000
Gross Profit on Sales	$170,000

The gross profit percentage for Madison Electronics Company for 1993 was $170,000/$425,000 = 0.40, or 40%. This figure means that after 60 cents was deducted from each sales dollar to cover the cost of goods sold, 40 cents remained to cover operating expenses as well as provide a net income.

The gross profit percentage for a particular company for a particular year (40% for Madison Electronics Company for 1993) is frequently compared to the gross profit percentage for prior years and to the gross profit percentage for companies in the same industry. For example, if Madison's percentage for 1992 had been 43%, then the rate of gross profit decreased from 1992 to 1993. This decrease alerts management to analyze carefully product prices, purchasing policies, and cost controls to determine why the percentage has decreased. Further, if the industry average for similar-sized firms is 45%, it appears that Madison's pricing and purchasing policies and cost controls may be less effective than those of other companies in the industry.

KEY POINTS FOR CHAPTER OBJECTIVES

❶ DESCRIBE the nature of merchandising operations and **INTRODUCE** the income statement for a merchandising firm (pp. 160–161).

■ Merchandising enterprises are characterized by buying and selling finished products and include both wholesalers and retailers.

■ The income statement for a merchandising firm includes amounts that reveal cost of goods sold and gross profit on sales.

❷ IDENTIFY and **DISCUSS** the steps in a merchandise transaction (pp. 161–162).

■ When merchandise is needed, a purchase requisition is forwarded to the purchasing department, which sends a purchase order to the vendor. The vendor sends an invoice to the purchaser after the goods are shipped.

■ The invoice, called a *purchase invoice* by the buyer and a *sales invoice* by the seller, is the basic document initiating entries for merchandise transactions.

❸ DESCRIBE the cash payment terms, trade discount terms, and shipping terms of merchandise transactions (pp. 162–164).

■ A cash discount is a reduction of the sales price for paying the invoice amount less cash discount within the discount period, which is less than the credit period.

■ The invoice price of merchandise is determined by subtracting the trade discount from the list price.

■ When freight terms are F.O.B. shipping point, the buyer bears the freight cost; when freight terms are F.O.B. destination, the seller bears the shipping cost.

■ The firm bearing the freight costs usually pays for them. Sometimes, as a convenience, the firm not bearing the freight costs pays for them. When this happens, the buyer and seller adjust the amount of the payment for the merchandise.

❹ INTRODUCE the periodic inventory system and **ILLUSTRATE** the treatment of merchandise accounts using the periodic inventory system (pp. 164–170).

■ When a credit sale occurs, the seller debits Accounts Receivable and credits Sales.

■ When a credit purchase of merchandise takes place, the buyer debits Purchases (not Inventory) and credits Accounts Payable. Purchases becomes part of cost of goods sold.

■ Freight cost borne by the purchaser is debited to Transportation In, a component of net cost of purchases in the income statement. Freight cost borne by the seller is debited to Transportation Out, an operating expense account.

■ When goods are returned to the seller, the buyer credits Purchases Returns and Allowances (a contra account to Purchases); the seller debits Sales Returns and Allowances (a contra account to Sales).

■ When goods are paid for within the cash discount period, the buyer credits Purchases Discounts (a contra account to Purchases); the seller debits Sales Discounts (a contra account to Sales).

■ Cost of goods sold is determined as follows: beginning inventory plus net cost of purchases less ending inventory.

■ When the net price method of recording purchases is used, purchases and purchases returns and allowances are recorded net of the related purchase discount.

❺ ILLUSTRATE the preparation of a worksheet and the year-end entries for a merchandising firm using the periodic inventory system (pp. 171–173).

■ Sales, purchases, related returns and allowances, discounts, and expense accounts are extended into the income statement columns of the worksheet, with the same debit and credit positions shown in the adjusted trial balance.

■ The beginning inventory balance is extended as a debit in the income statement columns, and, on the bottom of the worksheet, a line is added for the ending inventory. This amount is placed as a credit in the income statement columns and a debit in the balance sheet columns.

❻ ILLUSTRATE classified financial statements for a merchandising firm and **DESCRIBE** the classified income statement (p. 174).

■ The classified income statement for a merchandising firm has three major sections: revenue, cost of goods sold, and operating expenses.

■ The revenue section shows sales less related returns and allowances and discounts.

■ Operating expenses are classified functionally as selling expenses or administrative expenses.

■ The statement of owners' equity shows beginning capital balance plus net income less capital withdrawn.

■ In the balance sheet, assets are classified as current or plant; liabilities are classified as current or long term.

7 OUTLINE the closing entries for a merchandising firm (pp. 174–176).
- ■ The adjusting entries for a merchandising firm are similar to those of a service firm.
- ■ Closing procedures are as follows:
  - **a.** Record the ending inventory, close all income statement accounts with credit balances, and credit the total to the Income Summary account.
  - **b.** Remove the beginning inventory, close all income statement accounts with debit balances, and debit the total to the Income Summary account.
  - **c.** Transfer the balance of the Income Summary account to the owners' capital account (Retained Earnings account for a corporation).
  - **d.** Transfer the balance of the owners' drawing account to the owners' capital account.

8 PRESENT the perpetual inventory system and CONTRAST the merchandise transaction entries using it and the entries using the periodic inventory system (pp. 176–179).
- ■ When a credit sale of merchandise is recorded using the perpetual inventory system, one entry is made to debit Accounts Receivable and to credit Sales, and another entry is made to debit Cost of Goods Sold and credit Inventory.
- ■ Purchases and related returns and allowances, discounts, and expenses are perpetually recorded directly into the Inventory account.
- ■ The only year-end entry needed is one to adjust the perpetual inventory balance for shrinkage.

9 ILLUSTRATE the worksheet and income statement for a merchandising firm using the perpetual inventory system (pp. 179–180).
- ■ The inventory amount in the trial balance is the year-end balance of the Inventory account. As a result, the amount can be extended as a debit into the balance sheet columns.
- ■ The Cost of Goods Sold account summarizes the merchandise transactions related to inventory that was sold during the year.

10 ANALYTICAL APPLICATION: DEFINE the *gross profit percentage* and EXPLAIN its use (pp. 180–181).
- ■ The gross profit percentage is determined by dividing the gross profit on sales amount by the net sales amount.
- ■ This percentage is compared to percentages for prior years and to industry ranges and averages.

SELF-TEST QUESTIONS FOR REVIEW

(Answers follow the Solution to Demonstration Problem 2 for Review.)

1. Which of the following documents does *not* initiate an entry to be made in the accounts?
   - **a.** Sales invoice.
   - **b.** Purchase invoice.
   - **c.** Purchase order.
   - **d.** Credit memorandum.

2. Troy, Inc., purchased merchandise from Athens, Inc., for $3,600 list price, subject to a trade discount of 25%. The goods were purchased on terms of 2/10, n/30, F.O.B. destination. Troy paid $100 transportation costs. Troy returned $400 (list price) of the merchandise to Athens and later paid the amount due Athens within the discount period. The amount paid is
   - **a.** $2,254   **b.** $2,252   **c.** $2,246   **d.** $2,352

3. Bennett, Inc., which uses the net price method of recording purchases, and the periodic inventory system, bought merchandise for $800, terms 2/10, n/30. If Bennett returns $200 of the goods to the vendor, the entry to record the return should include a
   - **a.** Debit to Accounts Payable of $200.
   - **b.** Debit to Discounts Lost of $4.
   - **c.** Credit to Purchases Returns and Allowances of $196.
   - **d.** Debit to Purchases Returns and Allowances of $196.

4. The December 31, 1993, trial balance for Sabre, Inc., included the following amounts: Purchases, $40,000; Purchases Returns and Allowances, $2,000; Transportation In, $3,000; Transportation Out, $4,000; Sales Discounts, $5,000. Beginning inventory was $6,000 and ending inventory was $8,000. What was the cost of goods sold for 1993?
   - **a.** $39,000   **b.** $43,000   **c.** $38,000   **d.** $46,000

5. In preparing a 10-column worksheet for a merchandising firm that uses the periodic inventory system
   a. The beginning inventory is extended as a credit in the income statement columns.
   b. The beginning inventory is extended as a credit in the balance sheet columns.
   c. The ending inventory is shown as a debit in the income statement columns and as a credit in the balance sheet columns.
   d. The ending inventory is shown as a credit in the income statement columns and as a debit in the balance sheet columns.

DEMONSTRATION PROBLEM 1 FOR REVIEW

Sportcraft, a wholesaler of sporting goods that uses the periodic inventory system, had the following trial balance at December 31, 1993:

SPORTCRAFT
TRIAL BALANCE
DECEMBER 31, 1993

	Debit	Credit
Cash	$ 6,200	
Accounts Receivable	28,000	
Inventory (January 1)	45,000	
Office Supplies	800	
Prepaid Insurance	2,100	
Land	34,000	
Building	82,000	
Accumulated Depreciation—Building		$ 16,000
Office Equipment	21,300	
Accumulated Depreciation—Office Equipment		5,300
Accounts Payable		19,000
J. Moran, Capital		161,200
J. Moran, Drawing	10,000	
Sales		252,000
Sales Discounts	3,500	
Purchases	151,000	
Purchases Returns and Allowances		2,400
Transportation In	8,200	
Sales Salaries Expense	27,600	
Transportation Out	7,800	
Advertising Expense	6,100	
Office Salaries Expense	22,300	
	$455,900	$455,900

The following information is available at December 31, 1993:
1. Office supplies at December 31 are $250.
2. Prepaid insurance at December 31 is $1,500.
3. Depreciation for the year is building, $2,000; office equipment, $2,400.
4. Salaries payable at December 31 are sales salaries, $300; office salaries, $200.
5. Inventory at December 31 is $43,500.

REQUIRED

a. Prepare a 10-column worksheet for the year.
b. Prepare a classified income statement for 1993. Of the insurance expense and depreciation expense on the building, 75% is treated as selling expense and 25% is treated as administrative expense.
c. Prepare a statement of owner's equity for 1993.
d. Prepare a classified balance sheet at December 31, 1993.
e. Prepare adjusting entries in general journal form.
f. Prepare closing entries in general journal form.

SOLUTION TO DEMONSTRATION   a.
        PROBLEM 1

SPORTCRAFT
WORKSHEET (PERIODIC INVENTORY SYSTEM)
FOR THE YEAR ENDED DECEMBER 31, 1993

Description	Trial Balance Debit	Trial Balance Credit	Adjustments Debit	Adjustments Credit	Adjusted Trial Balance Debit	Adjusted Trial Balance Credit	Income Statement Debit	Income Statement Credit	Balance Sheet Debit	Balance Sheet Credit
Cash	6,200				6,200				6,200	
Accounts Receivable	28,000				28,000				28,000	
Inventory (January 1)	45,000				45,000		45,000			
Office Supplies	800			(1) 550	250				250	
Prepaid Insurance	2,100			(2) 600	1,500				1,500	
Land	34,000				34,000				34,000	
Building	82,000				82,000				82,000	
Accumulated Depreciation—Building		16,000		(3)2,000		18,000				18,000
Office Equipment	21,300				21,300				21,300	
Accumulated Depreciation— Office Equipment		5,300		(3)2,400		7,700				7,700
Accounts Payable		19,000				19,000				19,000
J. Moran, Capital		161,200				161,200				161,200
J. Moran, Drawing	10,000				10,000				10,000	
Sales		252,000				252,000		252,000		
Sales Discounts	3,500				3,500		3,500			
Purchases	151,000				151,000		151,000			
Purchases Returns and Allowances		2,400				2,400		2,400		
Transportation In	8,200				8,200		8,200			
Sales Salaries Expense	27,600		(4) 300		27,900		27,900			
Transportation Out	7,800				7,800		7,800			
Advertising Expense	6,100				6,100		6,100			
Office Salaries Expense	22,300		(4) 200		22,500		22,500			
	455,900	455,900								
Office Supplies Expense			(1) 550		550		550			
Insurance Expense			(2) 600		600		600			
Depreciation Expense—Building			(3)2,000		2,000		2,000			
Depreciation Expense— Office Equipment			(3)2,400		2,400		2,400			
Salaries Payable				(4) 500		500				500
			6,050	6,050	460,800	460,800				
Inventory (December 31)								43,500	43,500	
							277,550	297,900	226,750	206,400
Net Income							20,350			20,350
							297,900	297,900	226,750	226,750

b.

SPORTCRAFT
INCOME STATEMENT
FOR THE YEAR ENDED DECEMBER 31, 1993

Sales		$252,000	
Less: Sales Discounts		3,500	
Net Sales			$248,500
Cost of Goods Sold:			
Inventory, January 1		$ 45,000	
Add: Net Cost of Purchases			
Purchases	$151,000		
Less: Purchases Returns and Allowances	2,400		
	$148,600		
Add: Transportation In	8,200	156,800	
Cost of Goods Available for Sale		$201,800	
Less: Inventory, December 31		43,500	
Cost of Goods Sold			158,300
Gross Profit on Sales			$ 90,200
Operating Expenses:			
Selling Expenses			
Sales Salaries Expense	$ 27,900		
Transportation Out	7,800		
Advertising Expense	6,100		
Insurance Expense	450		
Depreciation Expense—Building	1,500		
Total Selling Expenses		$ 43,750	
Administrative Expenses			
Office Salaries Expense	$ 22,500		
Office Supplies Expense	550		
Insurance Expense	150		
Depreciation Expense—Building	500		
Depreciation Expense—Office Equipment	2,400		
Total Administrative Expenses		26,100	
Total Operating Expenses			69,850
Net Income			$ 20,350

c.

SPORTCRAFT
STATEMENT OF OWNER'S EQUITY
FOR THE YEAR ENDED DECEMBER 31, 1993

J. Moran, Capital, January 1, 1993	$161,200
Add: Net Income for 1993	20,350
	181,550
Less: Capital Withdrawn in 1993	10,000
J. Moran, Capital, December 31, 1993	$171,550

d.

SPORTCRAFT
BALANCE SHEET
DECEMBER 31, 1993

Assets

Current Assets		
Cash	$ 6,200	
Accounts Receivable	28,000	
Inventory	43,500	
Office Supplies	250	
Prepaid Insurance	1,500	
Total Current Assets		$ 79,450

Plant Assets

Land		$34,000	
Building	$82,000		
Less: Accumulated Depreciation	18,000	64,000	
Office Equipment	$21,300		
Less: Accumulated Depreciation	7,700	13,600	
Total Long-term Assets			111,600
Total Assets			$191,050

Liabilities

Current Liabilities

Accounts Payable	$19,000	
Salaries Payable	500	
Total Current Liabilities		$ 19,500

Owner's Equity

J. Moran, Capital	171,550
Total Liabilities and Owner's Equity	$191,050

e. Adjusting entries:

Dec. 31	Office Supplies Expense		550	
	Office Supplies			550
	To reflect as expense supplies used during the year.			
31	Insurance Expense		600	
	Prepaid Insurance			600
	To reflect as expense insurance expired during the year.			
31	Depreciation Expense—Building		2,000	
	Depreciation Expense—Office Equipment		2,400	
	Accumulated Depreciation—Building			2,000
	Accumulated Depreciation—Office Equipment			2,400
	To record depreciation on building and office equipment.			
31	Sales Salaries Expense		300	
	Office Salaries Expense		200	
	Salaries Payable			500
	To reflect salaries earned by employees but unpaid at December 31.			

f. Closing entries:

Dec. 31	Inventory		43,500	
	Sales		252,000	
	Purchases Returns and Allowances		2,400	
	Income Summary			297,900
	To record the ending inventory and close income statement accounts with credit balances.			
31	Income Summary		277,550	
	Inventory			45,000
	Sales Discounts			3,500
	Purchases			151,000
	Transportation In			8,200
	Sales Salaries Expense			27,900
	Transportation Out			7,800
	Advertising Expense			6,100
	Office Salaries Expense			22,500
	Office Supplies Expense			550
	Insurance Expense			600
	Depreciation Expense—Building			2,000
	Depreciation Expense—Office Equipment			2,400
	To remove the beginning inventory and close income statement accounts with debit balances.			

Dec. 31	Income Summary	20,350	
	J. Moran, Capital		20,350
	To close the Income Summary account and transfer net income to the owner's capital account.		
31	J. Moran, Capital	10,000	
	J. Moran, Drawing		10,000
	To close the owner's drawing account to the capital account.		

DEMONSTRATION PROBLEM 2 FOR REVIEW

On June 16, 1993, Wolf Company sold merchandise to Bolt Company for $600, terms 2/10, n/30. Shipping costs were $60. Bolt Company received the goods (and Wolf Company's invoice) on June 17. On June 24, Bolt Company sent the proper payment to Wolf Company, which Wolf Company received on June 25. Both Wolf Company and Bolt Company use the periodic inventory system, and Bolt Company records goods purchased at invoice price.

The following are several alternative arrangements regarding the shipping costs.

a. Shipping terms are F.O.B. shipping point, freight collect. Bolt Company pays the shipping costs on June 17 and remits $588 on June 24.

    1. Prepare journal entries for Wolf Company to record the June 16 sale and the June 25 cash receipt.

    2. Prepare journal entries for Bolt Company to record the June 17 purchase, the June 17 payment of shipping costs, and the June 24 cash remittance.

b. Shipping terms are F.O.B. destination, freight prepaid. Wolf Company pays the shipping costs on June 16. Bolt Company remits $588 on June 24.

    1. Prepare journal entries for Wolf Company to record the June 16 sale, the June 16 payment of shipping costs, and the June 25 cash receipt.

    2. Prepare journal entries for Bolt Company to record the June 17 purchase and the June 24 cash remittance.

c. Shipping terms are F.O.B. shipping point, freight prepaid. Wolf Company pays the shipping costs on June 16 and adds the $60 cost to the invoice sent to Bolt Company. Bolt Company remits $648 on June 24.

    1. Prepare journal entries for Wolf Company to record the June 16 sale and freight payment (a compound journal entry) and the June 25 cash receipt.

    2. Prepare journal entries for Bolt Company to record the June 17 purchase (with shipping costs added to the invoice from Wolf Company) and the June 24 cash remittance.

d. Shipping terms are F.O.B. destination, freight collect. Bolt Company pays the shipping costs on June 17 and deducts the $60 from the amount owed to Wolf Company (and provides a copy of the freight bill to Wolf Company with the June 24 cash remittance). Bolt Company remits $528 on June 24.

    1. Prepare journal entries for Wolf Company to record the June 16 sale and the June 25 cash receipt.

    2. Prepare journal entries for Bolt Company to record the June 17 purchase, the June 17 freight payment, and the June 24 cash remittance.

SOLUTION TO DEMONSTRATION PROBLEM 2

a. **1.** Wolf Company (Seller): The amount of the cash discount is 2% × $600 = $12.

June 16	Accounts Receivable	600	
	Sales		600
	To record sale on account.		
25	Cash	588	
	Sales Discounts	12	
	Accounts Receivable		600
	To record collection on account, 2% cash discount taken.		

2. Bolt Company (Buyer): The amount of the cash discount is 2% × $600 = $12.

June 17	Purchases	600	
	Accounts Payable		600
	To record purchase on account.		

June 17	Transportation In	60	
	Cash		60
	To record payment of shipping costs.		
24	Accounts Payable	600	
	Purchases Discounts		12
	Cash		588
	To record payment on account, 2% cash discount taken.		

b. 1. Wolf Company (Seller): The amount of the cash discount is 2% × $600 = $12.

June 16	Accounts Receivable	600	
	Sales		600
	To record sale on account.		
16	Transportation Out	60	
	Cash		60
	To record payment of shipping costs.		
25	Cash	588	
	Sales Discounts	12	
	Accounts Receivable		600
	To record collection on account, 2% cash discount taken.		

2. Bolt Company (Buyer): The amount of the cash discount is 2% × $600 = $12.

June 17	Purchases	600	
	Accounts Payable		600
	To record purchase on account.		
24	Accounts Payable	600	
	Purchases Discounts		12
	Cash		588
	To record payment on account, 2% cash discount taken.		

c. 1. Wolf Company (Seller): The amount of the cash discount is 2% × $600 = $12. Bolt Company is not entitled to a cash discount on the shipping costs.

June 16	Accounts Receivable	660	
	Sales		600
	Cash		60
	To record sale on account and payment of shipping costs, terms F.O.B. shipping point.		
25	Cash	648	
	Sales Discounts	12	
	Accounts Receivable		660
	To record collection on account, 2% cash discount taken.		

2. Bolt Company (Buyer): The amount of the cash discount is 2% × $600 = $12. Bolt Company is not entitled to a cash discount on the shipping costs.

June 17	Purchases	600	
	Transportation In	60	
	Accounts Payable		660
	To record purchase on account and shipping costs paid by seller, terms F.O.B. shipping point.		
24	Accounts Payable	660	
	Purchases Discounts		12
	Cash		648
	To record payment on account, 2% cash discount taken.		

d. 1. Wolf Company (Seller): The cash discount is 2% × $600 = $12. The shipping costs of $60 are borne by Wolf Company even though paid by Bolt Company because the shipping terms are F.O.B. destination.

June 16	Accounts Receivable	600	
	Sales		600
	To record sale on account.		
25	Cash	528	
	Transportation Out	60	
	Sales Discounts	12	
	Accounts Receivable		600
	To record collection on account, 2% cash discount taken, and delivery expense paid by buyer.		

2. Bolt Company (Buyer): The cash discount is 2% × $600 = $12. Bolt Company is entitled to a cash discount on the $600 invoice price of goods purchased even though the $60 freight payment is applied against the amount owed to Wolf Company.

June 17	Purchases	600	
	Accounts Payable		600
	To record purchase on account.		
17	Accounts Payable	60	
	Cash		60
	To record payment of shipping costs, terms F.O.B. destination.		
24	Accounts Payable	540	
	Purchases Discounts		12
	Cash		528
	To record payment on account, 2% cash discount taken.		

ANSWERS TO SELF-TEST QUESTIONS

1. c, p. 161 **2.** b, pp. 163–164 **3.** c, p. 170 **4.** a, pp. 169–170 **5.** d, pp. 171–173

APPENDIX B

In Chapter 5, a worksheet was prepared for Madison Electronics Company using the periodic inventory system (see Exhibit 5-5). In that example, the ending inventory was recorded and the beginning inventory was removed as a part of the year-end closing entries, and the computation of cost of goods sold was shown in the income statement. An alternative method, presented in this appendix, handles the beginning and ending inventories and the determination of cost of goods sold in the adjusting entries. This alternative approach uses a separate Cost of Goods Sold account in the adjusting entries. Under both approaches (chapter and appendix), the Income Summary account is used only for closing entries. To illustrate the alternative method, we use the same data for Madison Electronics Company shown in Chapter 5 and again assume that Madison Electronics Company is using the periodic inventory system.

ADJUSTING ENTRIES

We repeat below the four year-end adjusting entries for Madison Electronics Company shown in Chapter 5. In addition, we add a fifth adjusting entry that removes the beginning inventory, records the ending inventory, and determines and sets up cost of goods sold. These five adjusting entries would be recorded in the general journal and posted to the related general ledger accounts. They would also be entered in the Adjustments columns of the worksheet prepared at year-end.

1. Dec. 31	Insurance Expense		280	
	Prepaid Insurance			280
	To charge one year's premium to expense (three-year premium, $840, paid January 1.)			
2.	31	Supplies Expense	1,200	
	Supplies			1,200
	To charge to expense the supplies used during the year. (Supplies on hand on December 31 is $1,600.)			
3.	31	Depreciation Expense	6,000	
	Accumulated Depreciation			6,000
	To charge to expense one year's depreciation on delivery equipment.			
4.	31	Sales Salaries Expense	500	
	Salaries Payable			500
	To reflect the salaries earned by salespeople but not paid at December 31.			
5.	31	Cost of Goods Sold	255,000	
	Purchases Returns and Allowances	1,800	
	Purchases Discounts	4,400	
	Inventory	120,000	
	Purchases			256,500
	Transportation In			9,700
	Inventory			115,000
	To remove the beginning inventory ($115,000), to record the ending inventory ($120,000), and to determine and set up cost of goods sold.			

WORKSHEET

After the adjusting entries have been entered in the worksheet (Exhibit B-1), the adjusted amounts are extended to the Adjusted Trial Balance columns. Note that the cost of goods sold entry removed the $115,000 beginning inventory balance and established the $120,000 ending inventory balance to be extended to the Adjusted

EXHIBIT B–1

MADISON ELECTRONICS COMPANY
WORKSHEET (PERIODIC INVENTORY SYSTEM)
FOR THE YEAR ENDED DECEMBER 31, 1993

Description	Trial Balance Debit	Trial Balance Credit	Adjustments Debit	Adjustments Credit	Adjusted Trial Balance Debit	Adjusted Trial Balance Credit	Income Statement Debit	Income Statement Credit	Balance Sheet Debit	Balance Sheet Credit
Cash	18,240				18,240				18,240	
Accounts Receivable	32,000				32,000				32,000	
Inventory	115,000		(5) 120,000	(5) 115,000	120,000				120,000	
Prepaid Insurance	840			(1) 280	560				560	
Supplies	2,800			(2) 1,200	1,600				1,600	
Delivery Equipment	30,000				30,000				30,000	
Accumulated Depreciation		4,300		(3) 6,000		10,300				10,300
Accounts Payable		17,500				17,500				17,500
Long-term Notes Payable		20,000				20,000				20,000
J. Madison, Capital		134,000				134,000				134,000
J. Madison, Drawing	5,400				5,400				5,400	
Sales		433,000				433,000		433,000		
Sales Returns and Allowances	2,500				2,500		2,500			
Sales Discounts	5,500				5,500		5,500			
Purchases	256,500			(5) 256,500						
Purchases Returns and Allowances		1,800	(5) 1,800							
Purchases Discounts		4,400	(5) 4,400							
Transportation In	9,700			(5) 9,700						
Sales Salaries Expense	64,000		(4) 500		64,500		64,500			
Advertising Expense	6,170				6,170		6,170			
Delivery Expense	19,250				19,250		19,250			
Office Salaries Expense	28,500				28,500		28,500			
Rent Expense	16,500				16,500		16,500			
Interest Expense	2,100				2,100		2,100			
	615,000	615,000								
Insurance Expense			(1) 280		280		280			
Supplies Expense			(2) 1,200		1,200		1,200			
Depreciation Expense			(3) 6,000		6,000		6,000			
Salaries Payable				(4) 500		500				500
Cost of Goods Sold			(5) 255,000		255,000		255,000			
			389,180	389,180	615,300	615,300	407,500	433,000	207,800	182,300
Net Income							25,500			25,500
							433,000	433,000	207,800	207,800

Trial Balance columns. This amount is next extended as a debit in the Balance Sheet columns.

A single cost of goods sold amount will appear in the Adjusted Trial Balance Debit column and will be extended as a debit in the Income Statement columns. The cost of goods sold amount incorporates purchases, purchases returns and allowances, purchases discounts, and transportation in, as well as the change in inventory during the period.

Although the alternative method yields different totals for the Adjustments, Adjusted Trial Balance, and Income Statement columns, the totals of the Balance Sheet columns are the same as shown in Exhibit 5-5.

The alternative method produces the same financial statements as the method in the chapter. The income statement is the same as shown in Exhibit 5-10, the statement of owner's equity is the same as Exhibit 5-7, and the balance sheet is the same as shown in Exhibit 5-8.

CLOSING ENTRIES

The closing entries using the alternative method of dealing with periodic inventories are shown below. There are no entries for inventory, purchases, purchases returns and allowances, purchases discounts, and transportation in since these have already been transferred to the Cost of Goods Sold account by means of an adjusting entry. The Cost of Goods Sold account is closed in the closing entries.

Dec. 31	Sales		433,000	
		Income Summary		433,000
		To close income statement accounts with credit balances.		
	31	Income Summary	407,500	
		Sales Returns and Allowances		2,500
		Sales Discounts		5,500
		Cost of Goods Sold		255,000
		Sales Salaries Expense		64,500
		Advertising Expense		6,170
		Delivery Expense		19,250
		Office Salaries Expense		28,500
		Rent Expense		16,500
		Interest Expense		2,100
		Insurance Expense		280
		Supplies Expense		1,200
		Depreciation Expense		6,000
		To close income statement accounts with debit balances.		
	31	Income Summary	25,500	
		J. Madison, Capital		25,500
		To close the Income Summary account and transfer net income to the owner's capital account.		
	31	J. Madison, Capital	5,400	
		J. Madison, Drawing		5,400
		To close the owner's drawing account to the capital account.		

GLOSSARY OF KEY TERMS USED IN THIS CHAPTER

cash discount   An amount, often 2% of the purchase price, that a buyer may deduct from the purchase price for paying within the discount period (p. 163).

classified financial statements   Financial statements that separate accounts into various categories to aid in the interpretation of the financial data (p. 173).

cost of goods sold   The cost of merchandise sold to customers during the accounting period. It is calculated by adding the beginning inventory and net cost of purchases and deducting the ending inventory (p. 169).

credit memorandum   A form used by a seller to notify a customer of a reduction in the amount owed by the customer (p. 166).

credit period   The period of time a buyer has to pay for goods or services received on account (p. 162).

discount period   The number of days beyond the related sales invoice date during which payment entitles the buyer to deduct any cash discount offered (p. 163).

Discounts Lost   An account reflecting the amount of cash discounts available but not taken. This account is used with the net price method (p. 170).

gross price method of recording purchases   An accounting procedure by which purchases are recorded at invoice price. When discounts are taken, the amount of the discount is recorded in the Purchases Discounts account (p. 166).

gross profit on sales   The excess of the sales price over the net delivered cost of the product sold (sometimes called *gross margin*) (p. 161).

gross profit percentage   Gross profit divided by net sales (p. 180).

inventory   A significant current asset for merchandisers and manufacturers representing goods for resale or goods to be used in the manufacturing process (p. 164).

invoice   A document used in business transactions that sets forth the precise terms regarding date, customer, vendor, quantities, prices, and freight and credit terms of a transaction (p. 161).

Merchandise Inventory   An asset account in which is recorded the purchase price of merchandise held for resale; sometimes referred to as *Inventory* (p. 164).

net price method of recording purchases   An accounting procedure by which purchases are recorded at amounts that anticipate taking any cash discounts available. When discounts are not taken, the amounts paid in excess of the recorded purchase price are charged to the Discounts Lost account (p. 170).

periodic inventory system   A system of accounting for inventories by which no record is made in the Inventory account for the purchase or sale of merchandise at the time of such transactions (p. 164).

perpetual inventory system   A system of accounting for inventories by which both purchases and sales of merchandise are reflected in the Inventory account at the time such transactions occur (p. 176).

purchase invoice   An invoice received by the buyer of merchandise (p. 162).

purchase order   A document completed by the purchasing firm setting forth the quantities, descriptions, prices, and vendor for merchandise to be purchased (p. 161).

purchase requisition   A form that a firm uses to start the procedures leading to the purchase of needed items (p. 161).

Purchases   The title of the account in which is recorded the acquisition price of merchandise purchased by companies using the periodic inventory system (p. 165).

receiving report   A document that a firm uses to record formally the quantities and descriptions of merchandise and other items received (p. 162).

Sales   In merchandising and manufacturing firms, the account in which revenue from the sale of goods held for resale is recorded (p. 165).

sales invoice   An invoice issued by a seller of merchandise (p. 161).

trade discounts   The differences between suggested retail prices and the prices at which wholesale purchasers are able to buy merchandise (p. 163).

Transportation In   An account for recording the freight charges on merchandise purchased and held for resale (p. 166).

Transportation Out   An account for recording the freight charges incurred in the delivery of merchandise sold to customers (p. 166).

QUESTIONS

5-1   What is the most significant difference between the income statement of a service firm and that of a merchandising firm?

5-2   What is meant by *gross profit on sales*?

5-3   Explain the nature, purpose, and key information appearing on each of the following forms:
  a. Purchase requisition.
  b. Purchase order.
  c. Sales invoice.
  d. Receiving report.
  e. Credit memo.

5-4   Differentiate between (a) credit period and discount period and (b) cash discounts and trade discounts.

5-5   For the accounts titled Sales Returns and Allowances and Purchases Returns and Allowances, indicate (a) the justification for their use and (b) their normal balances (debit or credit) and their position in the financial statements.

5-6   Explain the appropriate treatment in the income statement of the accounts Transportation In and Transportation Out.

5-7 Under each of the following selling terms, who (buyer or seller) would bear the freight cost and who would pay the freight company?
   a. F.O.B. shipping point, freight collect.
   b. F.O.B. destination, freight prepaid.
   c. F.O.B. shipping point, freight prepaid.
   d. F.O.B. destination, freight collect.

5-8 On April 2, Sprague Company purchased $1,500 worth of merchandise from Jones Company, F.O.B. shipping point, freight collect, terms 2/10, n/30. On April 4, Sprague Company returned $200 of the goods for credit. On April 5, Sprague paid $100 freight on the shipment. If Sprague settles its account with Jones Company on April 11, how much would Sprague remit?

5-9 How much does Sprague remit in Question 5-8 if the terms are F.O.B. destination rather than F.O.B. shipping point?

5-10 Krane Wholesale Company's gross purchases during an accounting period totaled $120,000, and Transportation In was $5,000. If the firm returned goods amounting to $2,000 and took $1,000 in purchases discounts during the period, what was the net delivered purchases cost for the period?

5-11 When an unadjusted trial balance of the general ledger is prepared for a merchandising firm using the periodic inventory system, does the beginning inventory or the ending inventory appear in the trial balance? Explain.

5-12 The beginning inventory for a merchandising firm was $70,000 and the ending inventory is $60,000. If the net cost of purchases was $220,000 and net sales were $400,000, what was the gross profit?

5-13 A portion of a worksheet for a merchandising firm follows. Identify the columns—A, B, C, or D—into which the balance of any of the listed accounts should be extended. The periodic inventory system is being used.

Account	Income Statement		Balance Sheet	
	Debit (A)	Credit (B)	Debit (C)	Credit (D)
Inventory (Beginning)				
Sales				
Sales Returns and Allowances				
Purchases				
Purchases Returns and Allowances				
Purchases Discounts				
Transportation In				
Salaries Payable				
Inventory (Ending)				

5-14 A firm using the net price method of recording merchandise purchases and the periodic inventory system bought goods with a price of $700, terms 2/10, n/30. What amount would be debited to the Purchases account?

5-15 Contrast the entry or entries that would be required to record a credit sale under the periodic inventory system and under the perpetual inventory system.

5-16 Contrast the entry or entries that would be required at the end of the year under the periodic inventory system and under the perpetual inventory system.

5-17 Define the *gross profit percentage* and explain its use.

EXERCISES

**TRADE AND CASH
DISCOUNT CALCULATIONS
— OBJ. 3 —**

5-18 On June 1, Forest Company sold merchandise with a list price of $12,000. For each of the sales terms below, determine (a) the amount recorded as a sale and (b) the proper amount of cash received.

	Applicable Trade Discount (%)	Credit Terms	Date Paid
1.	30	2/10, n/30	June 8
2.	40	1/10, n/30	June 15
3.	—	2/10, n/30	June 11
4.	20	1/15, n/30	June 14
5.	40	n/30	June 28

Cash Discount and Remittance Calculations — Obj. 3 —

5-19 For each of the following Columbus Company purchases, assume that credit terms are 2/10, n/30 and that any credit memorandum was issued and known before Columbus Company made the payments.

	Purchases Amount	Shipping Terms	Prepaid Freight (by seller)	Credit Memorandum
1.	$1,200	F.O.B. shipping point	$100	$300
2.	2,400	F.O.B. destination	240	200
3.	2,800	F.O.B. shipping point	—	400
4.	4,000	F.O.B. shipping point	300	—

In each case, determine (a) the appropriate cash discount available and (b) the cash remitted if the payment is made within the discount period.

Entries for Sale, Return, and Remittance—Periodic — Obj. 3, 4 —

5-20 On June 8, 1993, Stevens Company sold merchandise listing for $1,600 to Dalton Company, terms 2/10, n/30. On June 12, $400 worth of the merchandise was returned because it was the wrong color. On June 18, Stevens Company received a check for the amount due.

Record the general journal entries made by Stevens Company for the above transactions. Stevens uses the periodic inventory system.

Entries for Purchase, Return, and Remittance—Periodic — Obj. 4 —

5-21 On March 10, 1993, Horton Company purchased $18,000 worth of merchandise from James Company, terms 1/10, n/30, F.O.B. shipping point. On March 12, Horton paid $160 freight on the shipment. On March 15, Horton returned $200 of merchandise for credit. Final payment was made to James on March 19. Horton Company uses the gross price method of recording purchases and uses the periodic inventory system.
  a. Prepare the general journal entries that Horton should make on March 12, March 15, and March 19.
  b. Prepare the entries that Horton should make on these three dates if the terms are F.O.B. destination.

Entries for Merchandise Transactions on Seller's and Buyer's Records—Periodic — Obj. 3, 4 —

5-22 The following are selected transactions of Franklin, Inc., during 1993:

April 20 Sold and shipped on account to Lind Stores merchandise listing for $2,400, terms 2/10, n/30.
  27 Lind Stores returned defective merchandise billed at $200 on April 20.
  29 Received from Lind Stores a check for full settlement of the April 20 transaction.

Record, in general journal form, the above transactions as they would appear on the books of (a) Franklin, Inc., and (b) Lind Stores. Lind Stores records purchases using the gross price method. Both companies use the periodic inventory system.

Net Price Method of Recording Purchases — Obj. 4 —

5-23 Alvarez, Inc., uses the net price method of recording purchases. On July 1, 1993, the firm purchased merchandise for $1,800, terms 2/10, n/30. On July 5, the firm returned $600 of the merchandise to the seller. Payment of the account occurred on July 8. Alvarez uses the periodic inventory system.
  a. Give the general journal entries for July 1, July 5, and July 8.
  b. Assuming that the account was settled on July 14, give the entry for payment on that date.

Determination of Omitted Income Statement Data — Obj. 4 —

5-24 The box on the next page contains portions of the income statements of four different companies, each with certain data omitted. Replace the lettered blanks with the appropriate amounts.

	1	2	3	4
Net Sales	$100,000	$ d	$200,000	$240,000
Beginning Inventory	15,000	12,000	g	30,000
Net Cost of Purchases	55,000	e	125,000	95,000
Cost of Goods Available for Sale	a	f	145,000	j
Ending Inventory	10,000	25,000	h	k
Cost of Goods Sold	b	40,000	i	l
Gross Profit	c	90,000	85,000	130,000

EFFECTS OF INVENTORY ERRORS
— OBJ. 4 —

5-25 Jordan Company's operating figures for four consecutive periods are given below.

	Period			
	(1)	(2)	(3)	(4)
Beginning Inventory	$ 50,000	$ 40,000	$ 30,000	$ 46,000
Net Cost of Purchases	90,000	110,000	100,000	90,000
Cost of Goods Available for Sale	$140,000	$150,000	$130,000	$136,000
Ending Inventory	40,000	30,000	46,000	32,000
Cost of Goods Sold	$100,000	$120,000	$ 84,000	$104,000

Assuming that the following errors were made, compute the correct cost of goods sold for each period:

Period	Error in Ending Inventory
1	Overstated $4,000
2	Understated $6,000
3	Overstated $2,000

CLOSING ENTRIES—
PERIODIC
— OBJ. 7 —

5-26 A portion of the December 31, 1993, worksheet for Karlman Distributors is shown below. For simplicity, all operating expenses have been combined. The periodic inventory system is used.

	Income Statement		Balance Sheet	
	Debit	Credit	Debit	Credit
Inventory (January 1)	128,000			
T. Karlman, Capital				280,000
T. Karlman, Drawing			24,000	
Sales		1,000,000		
Sales Returns and Allowances	3,000			
Sales Discounts	9,000			
Purchases	660,000			
Purchases Returns and Allowances		6,000		
Purchases Discounts		13,200		
Transportation In	16,000			
Operating Expenses	250,000			
Inventory (December 31)		118,000	118,000	

Using the given information, prepare the general journal entries to close the books.

CLASSIFIED BALANCE SHEET
— OBJ. 6 —

5-27 From the following accounts, listed in alphabetical order, prepare a classified balance sheet for Berkly Wholesalers at December 31, 1993. All accounts have normal balances.

Accounts Receivable	44,000	Inventory	$117,000
Accounts Payable	43,000	Land	45,000
Accumulated Depreciation—		Mortgage Payable	
Building	23,000	(long term)	78,000
Accumulated Depreciation—		Office Equipment	21,000
Office Equipment	5,000	Office Supplies	2,000
Building	90,000	Salaries Payable	7,000
Cash	22,000	T. Berkly, Capital	185,000

**ENTRIES FOR SALE,
RETURN, AND
REMITTANCE—PERPETUAL
— OBJ. 8 —**

5-28 On September 13, 1993, Brady Company sold merchandise with an invoice price of $900 ($600 cost), terms 2/10, n/30, to Dalton Company. On September 17, $150 of the merchandise ($100 cost) was returned because it was the wrong model. On September 23, Brady Company received a check for the amount due from Dalton Company.

Record the journal entries made by Brady Company for the above transactions. Brady uses the perpetual inventory system.

**ENTRIES FOR PURCHASE,
RETURN, AND
REMITTANCE—PERPETUAL
— OBJ. 8 —**

5-29 On April 13, 1993, Kesselman Company purchased $22,000 of merchandise from Krausman Company, terms 1/10, n/30, F.O.B. shipping point. On April 15, Kesselman paid $300 to Ace Trucking Company for freight on the shipment. On April 18, Kesselman Company returned $1,000 of merchandise for credit. Final payment was made to Krausman on April 22. Kesselman Company records purchases using the gross price method and uses the perpetual inventory system.

a. Prepare the journal entries that Kesselman Company should make on April 13, 15, 18, and 22.

b. Prepare the entries that Kesselman should make on these four dates if the terms are F.O.B. destination.

**ENTRIES FOR MERCHANDISE
TRANSACTIONS ON SELLER'S
AND BUYER'S RECORDS—
PERPETUAL
— OBJ. 8 —**

5-30 The following are selected transactions of Lamont, Inc., during 1993:

June 21 Sold and shipped on account to Lowery Company $2,880 ($2,000 cost) of merchandise, terms 2/10, n/30.

28 Lowery Company returned defective merchandise billed at $280 on June 21 ($210 cost).

30 Received from Lowery Company a check for full settlement of the June 21 transaction.

Record, in general journal form, the above transactions as they would appear on the books of (a) Lamont, Inc., and (b) Lowery Company. Both companies use the perpetual inventory system and Lowery records purchases using the gross price method.

PROBLEMS

**ENTRIES FOR MERCHANDISE
TRANSACTIONS ON SELLER'S
AND BUYER'S RECORDS—
PERIODIC
— OBJ. 3, 4 —**

5-31 The following transactions occurred between Southwick Company and Mann Stores, Inc., during March, 1993.

Mar. 8 Southwick sold $6,600 worth of merchandise to Mann Stores, terms 2/10, n/30, F.O.B. shipping point.

10 Mann Stores paid freight charges on the shipment from Southwick Company, $100.

12 Mann Stores returned $600 of the merchandise shipped on March 8. Southwick issued a credit memo for this amount.

17 Southwick received full payment for the net amount due from the March 8 sale.

20 Mann Stores returned goods that had been billed originally at $200. Southwick issued a check for $196.

REQUIRED

Record the above transactions in general journal form as they would appear on (a) the books of Southwick Company and (b) the books of Mann Stores, Inc. Mann Stores, Inc., records purchases using the gross price method. Assume both companies use the periodic inventory system.

**ENTRIES FOR MERCHANDISE
TRANSACTIONS—PERIODIC
— OBJ. 3, 4 —**

5-32 Malvado Corporation, which began business on August 1, 1993, sells on terms of 2/10, n/30, F.O.B. shipping point. Credit terms and freight terms for its purchases vary with the supplier. Selected transactions for August are given below. Unless noted, all transactions are on account and involve merchandise held for resale. All purchases are recorded using the gross price method; the periodic inventory system is used.

Aug. 1 Purchased merchandise from Norris, Inc., $1,700, terms 2/10, n/30, F.O.B. shipping point, freight collect.

5 Paid freight on shipment from Norris, Inc., $80.

7 Sold merchandise to Denton Corporation, $2,400.

7 Paid freight on shipment to Denton Corporation, $120, and billed Denton for the charges.

Aug. 9 Returned $300 worth of the merchandise purchased August 1 from Norris, Inc., because it was defective. Norris approved the return.

9 Issued a credit memorandum to Denton Corporation for $400 worth of merchandise returned by Denton.

10 Paid Norris, Inc., the amount due.

14 Purchased from Chambers, Inc., goods with a list price of $4,000. Malvado Corporation was entitled to a 25% trade discount; terms 1/10, n/30, F.O.B. shipping point, freight collect.

15 Paid freight on shipment from Chambers, Inc., $140.

17 Received the amount due from Denton Corporation.

18 Sold merchandise to Weber, Inc., $4,800.

20 Paid freight on August 18 shipment to Weber, Inc., $160.

24 Paid Chambers, Inc., the amount due.

28 Received the amount due from Weber, Inc.

REQUIRED

Record the transactions for Malvado Corporation in general journal form.

PREPARATION OF A WORKSHEET—PERIODIC — OBJ. 5 —

5-33 The unadjusted trial balance of Wong Distributors on December 31, 1993, is shown below; the periodic inventory system has been used.

WONG DISTRIBUTORS
TRIAL BALANCE
DECEMBER 31, 1993

	Debit	Credit
Cash	$ 15,200	
Accounts Receivable	80,200	
Inventory	138,000	
Prepaid Insurance	7,200	
Supplies	6,400	
Delivery Equipment	80,000	
Accumulated Depreciation		$ 19,000
Accounts Payable		69,600
T. Wong, Capital		168,000
T. Wong, Drawing	26,000	
Sales		812,000
Sales Returns and Allowances	11,600	
Sales Discounts	14,600	
Purchases	522,000	
Purchases Returns and Allowances		5,200
Purchases Discounts		10,200
Transportation In	12,800	
Salaries Expense	108,000	
Rent Expense	40,000	
Gas, Oil, and Repairs Expense	18,400	
Utilities Expense	3,600	
	$1,084,000	$1,084,000

The following data are available at December 31, 1993:

1. Prepaid insurance at December 31 is $2,400.
2. Supplies at December 31 amount to $4,200.
3. Depreciation on the delivery equipment is 20% per year.
4. At December 31, the company owes its employees $1,200 in salaries.
5. At December 31, the company estimates unbilled utilities at $280.
6. Inventory at December 31 is $144,000.

REQUIRED

Prepare a 10-column worksheet for Wong Distributors for 1993.

INCOME STATEMENT AND CALCULATION OF GROSS PROFIT PERCENTAGE — OBJ. 6, 10 —

5-34 The following selected information is available for the Boston Wholesale Company for March 1993.

Purchases	$ 86,000
Sales	197,000
Transportation In	4,000

(CONTINUED)

Purchases Discounts	1,600
Inventory (March 1)	74,000
Inventory (March 31)	44,000
Purchases Returns and Allowances	1,400
Sales Returns and Allowances	3,000
Transportation Out	900
Rent Expense (an administrative expense)	3,200
Sales Salaries Expense	38,400
Sales Discounts	2,400
Depreciation Expense—Office Equipment	200
Office Supplies Expense	480
Office Salaries Expense	13,100
Advertising Expense	3,000
Insurance Expense (a selling expense)	320

REQUIRED

a. Prepare the March classified income statement for Boston Wholesale Company.

b. Calculate the gross profit percentage.

WORKSHEET, FINANCIAL STATEMENTS, AND ADJUSTING AND CLOSING ENTRIES—PERIODIC — OBJ. 5, 6, 7 —

5-35 Apache Trading Company, whose accounting year ends on December 31, had the following normal balances in its general ledger at December 31, 1993:

Cash	13,000	Sales	$640,000
Accounts Receivable	25,600	Sales Returns and	
Inventory	104,000	Allowances	4,400
Prepaid Insurance	6,000	Sales Discounts	5,600
Office Supplies	4,200	Purchases	412,000
Furniture and Fixtures	21,000	Purchases Returns and	
Accumulated Depreciation—		Allowances	3,800
Furniture and Fixtures	5,000	Purchases Discounts	4,200
Delivery Equipment	84,000	Transportation In	9,000
Accumulated Depreciation—		Sales Salaries Expense	82,000
Delivery Equipment	12,000	Delivery Expense	10,800
Accounts Payable	41,000	Advertising Expense	5,600
Long-term Notes Payable	30,000	Rent Expense	14,400
J. Apache, Capital	136,000	Office Salaries Expense	56,000
J. Apache, Drawing	9,600	Utilities Expense	4,800

Rent expense and utilities expense are administrative expenses. During the year, the accounting department prepared monthly statements using worksheets, but no adjusting entries were made in the journals and ledgers. Data for the year-end procedures are as follows:

1. Prepaid insurance, December 31, 1993 (75% of insurance expense is classified as selling expense, and 25% is classified as administrative expense)	$ 1,200
2. Office supplies on hand, December 31, 1993	1,400
3. Depreciation expense on furniture and fixtures for 1993 (an administrative expense)	1,800
4. Depreciation expense on delivery equipment for 1993	13,000
5. Salaries payable, December 31, 1993 ($1,800 sales salaries and $1,200 office salaries)	3,000
6. Inventory, December 31, 1993 (periodic inventory system)	113,000

REQUIRED

a. Prepare a worksheet for 1993.

b. Prepare a classified income statement for 1993.

c. Prepare a classified balance sheet at December 31, 1993.

d. Record the necessary adjusting entries in general journal form.

e. Record the closing entries in general journal form.

PREPARATION OF INCOME STATEMENT FROM INCOMPLETE DATA — OBJ. 6 —

5-36 While on her way to the bank to negotiate a loan, Linda Evans, the treasurer of Silcon, Inc., realizes that the income statement for the current year is missing from her papers. She has a December 31 balance sheet, however, and after searching through her papers, locates an unadjusted trial balance taken at December 31. She arrives at your office shortly before her appointment at the bank and asks your assistance in preparing an income statement for the year. The available data at December 31, 1993, are listed on the following page:

	Unadjusted Trial Balance		Balance Sheet Data
	Debit	**Credit**	
Cash	$ 78,000		$ 78,000
Accounts Receivable	91,000		91,000
Inventory	152,000		160,000
Office Supplies	6,200		2,800
Prepaid Insurance	6,400		4,000
Delivery Equipment	104,000		104,000
Accumulated Depreciation		$ 33,000	(49,000)
			$390,800
Accounts Payable		78,000	$ 78,000
Salaries Payable			800
Capital Stock		200,000	200,000
Retained Earnings		64,000	112,000
Sales		500,000	
Purchases	328,000		
Rent Expense	16,400		
Salaries Expense	68,000		
Advertising Expense	8,400		
Delivery Expense	16,600		
	$875,000	$875,000	$390,800

REQUIRED

Use the given data to prepare the year's income statement for Silcon, Inc., for Linda Evans. She informs you that the amounts shown in the unadjusted trial balance for Inventory, Office Supplies, Prepaid Insurance, and Accumulated Depreciation are the account balances at January 1, 1993. No dividends were declared or paid during the year.

EFFECT OF WORKSHEET ERRORS—PERIODIC — OBJ. 5 —

5-37 The first six columns of a 10-column worksheet prepared for the Magnum Sport Shop are as follows (the periodic inventory system is being used):

	Trial Balance		Adjustments		Adjusted Trial Balance	
	Debit	**Credit**	**Debit**	**Credit**	**Debit**	**Credit**
Cash	18,000				18,000	
Inventory (January 1)	72,000				72,000	
Office Supplies	2,000			1,200	800	
Prepaid Insurance	2,400				2,400	
Equipment	60,000				60,000	
Accumulated Depreciation		12,000		6,000		18,000
Accounts Payable		16,000				16,000
W. Magnum, Capital		96,000				96,000
W. Magnum, Drawing	10,000				10,000	
Sales		240,000				240,000
Purchases	130,000				130,000	
Transportation In	3,600				3,600	
Rent Expense	6,000				6,000	
Salaries Expense	60,000		600		60,600	
	364,000	364,000				
Depreciation Expense			6,000		6,000	
Salaries Payable				600		600
Office Supplies Expense			1,200		1,200	
			7,800	7,800	370,600	370,600
Inventory (December 31)						
Net Income						

In completing the worksheet, Magnum's accountant made the following errors:

1. The adjustment for expired insurance was omitted; premiums amounting to $1,800 expired during the year.
2. The $10,000 balance of Magnum's drawing account was extended as a debit in the income statement columns.
3. The $600 credit to Salaries Payable was extended as a credit in the income statement columns.
4. The January 1, 1993, Inventory balance of $72,000 was extended as a credit in the income statement columns.
5. The December 31, 1993, Inventory balance of $80,000 was recorded as a debit in the income statement columns and as a credit in the balance sheet columns.

REQUIRED

a. Which of the errors would cause the worksheet not to balance?
b. Without completing the worksheet, calculate the net income for 1993. Assume that the accountant made no other errors and that the worksheet totals, before adding net income or net loss, were

	Debit	Credit
Income statement	$297,400	$312,600
Balance sheet	81,200	210,000

ENTRIES FOR MERCHANDISE TRANSACTIONS ON SELLER'S AND BUYER'S RECORDS— PERPETUAL — OBJ. 8 —

5-38 The following transactions occurred between Decker Company and Mann Stores, Inc., during March 1993:

Mar. 8 Decker sold $6,600 worth of merchandise ($4,400 cost) to Mann Stores, terms 2/10, n/30, F.O.B. shipping point.
10 Mann Stores paid freight charges on the shipment from Decker Company, $100.
12 Mann Stores returned $600 of the merchandise ($400 cost) shipped on March 8. Decker issued a credit memorandum for this amount.
17 Decker received full payment for the net amount due from the March 8 sale.
20 Mann Stores returned goods that had been billed originally at $300 ($200 cost). Decker issued a check for $294.

REQUIRED

Record the above transactions in general journal form as they would appear on (a) the books of Decker Company and (b) the books of Mann Stores, Inc. Mann Stores, Inc., records purchases at invoice price. Assume both companies use the perpetual inventory system.

ENTRIES FOR MERCHANDISE TRANSACTIONS— PERPETUAL — OBJ. 8 —

5-39 Rockford Corporation, which began business on August 1, 1993, sells on terms of 2/10, n/30, F.O.B. shipping point. Credit terms and freight terms for its purchases vary with the supplier. Selected transactions for August are given below. Unless noted, all transactions are on account and involve merchandise held for resale. All purchases are recorded using the gross price method, and the perpetual inventory system is used.

Aug. 1 Purchased merchandise from Norris, Inc., $1,700, terms 2/10, n/30, F.O.B. shipping point, freight collect.
5 Paid freight on shipment from Norris, Inc., $80.
7 Sold merchandise to Denton Corporation, $2,400 ($1,700 cost).
7 Paid freight on shipment to Denton Corporation, $120, and billed Denton for the charges.
9 Returned $300 worth of the merchandise purchased August 1 from Norris, Inc., because it was defective. Norris approved the return.
9 Issued a credit memorandum to Denton Corporation for $400 ($300 cost) worth of merchandise returned by Denton.
10 Paid Norris, Inc., the amount due.
14 Purchased from Chambers, Inc., goods with a list price of $4,000. Rockford Corporation was entitled to a 25% trade discount; terms 1/10, n/30, F.O.B. shipping point, freight collect.

Aug. 15 Paid freight on shipment from Chambers, Inc., $140.

17 Received the amount due from Denton Corporation.

18 Sold merchandise to Weber, Inc., $4,800 ($3,300 cost).

20 Paid freight on August 18 shipment to Weber, Inc., $160.

24 Paid Chambers, Inc., the amount due.

28 Received the amount due from Weber, Inc.

REQUIRED

Record the transactions for Rockford Corporation in general journal form.

PREPARATION OF A WORKSHEET—PERPETUAL — OBJ. 9 —

5-40 The unadjusted trial balance of Crane Distributors on December 31, 1993, is shown below; the perpetual inventory system has been used.

CRANE DISTRIBUTORS
TRIAL BALANCE
DECEMBER 31, 1993

	Debit	Credit
Cash	$ 15,200	
Accounts Receivable	80,200	
Inventory	144,000	
Prepaid Insurance	7,200	
Supplies	6,400	
Delivery Equipment	80,000	
Accumulated Depreciation		$ 19,000
Accounts Payable		69,600
H. Crane, Capital		168,000
H. Crane, Drawing	26,000	
Sales		812,000
Sales Returns and Allowances	11,600	
Sales Discounts	14,600	
Cost of Goods Sold	513,400	
Salaries Expense	108,000	
Rent Expense	40,000	
Gas, Oil, and Repairs Expense	18,400	
Utilities Expense	3,600	
	$1,068,600	$1,068,600

The following data are available at December 31, 1993:

1. Prepaid insurance at December 31 is $2,400.
2. Supplies at December 31 amount to $4,200.
3. Depreciation on the delivery equipment is 20% per year.
4. At December 31, the company owes its employees $1,200 in salaries.
5. At December 31, the company estimated unbilled utilities at $280.

REQUIRED

Prepare a 10-column worksheet for Crane Distributors for 1993.

PREPARATION OF A WORKSHEET—PERIODIC — APPENDIX B —

5-41 Follow the requirements in Problem 5-33, using the method described in Appendix B.

WORKSHEET, FINANCIAL STATEMENTS, AND ADJUSTING AND CLOSING ENTRIES—PERIODIC — APPENDIX B —

5-42 Follow the requirements in Problem 5-35, using the method described in Appendix B.

ALTERNATE EXERCISES

5-18A On April 1, Fitzgerald Company sold merchandise with a list price of $20,000. For each of the sales terms below, determine (a) the amount recorded as a sale and (b) the proper amount of cash received.

TRADE AND CASH
DISCOUNT CALCULATIONS
— OBJ. 3 —

	Applicable Trade Discount (%)	Credit Terms	Date Paid
1.	20	1/15, n/30	April 14
2.	40	n/30	April 28
3.	—	2/10, n/30	April 11
4.	30	2/10, n/30	April 8
5.	40	1/10, n/30	April 15

CASH DISCOUNT AND
REMITTANCE
CALCULATIONS
— OBJ. 3 —

5-19A For each of the following Clarenden Company purchases, assume that credit terms are 2/10, n/30 and that any credit memo was issued and known before Clarenden Company made the payments.

	Amount	Shipping Terms	Prepaid Freight (by seller)	Credit Memorandum
1.	$3,000	F.O.B. shipping point	—	$400
2.	4,500	F.O.B. shipping point	$400	—
3.	2,500	F.O.B. destination	300	400
4.	1,500	F.O.B. shipping point	100	300

In each case, determine (a) the appropriate cash discount available and (b) the cash remitted if the payment is made within the discount period.

ENTRIES FOR SALE,
RETURN, AND
REMITTANCE—PERIODIC
— OBJ. 3 —

5-20A On March 10, 1993, Sharon Company sold merchandise listing for $2,000 to Dillard Company, terms 2/10, n/30. On March 14, $500 of merchandise was returned because it was the wrong size. On March 20, Sharon Company received a check for the amount due.

Record the general journal entries made by Sharon Company for the above transactions. Sharon uses the periodic inventory system.

ENTRIES FOR PURCHASE,
RETURN, AND
REMITTANCE—PERIODIC
— OBJ. 3, 4 —

5-21A On August 15, 1993, Harris Company purchased $20,000 of merchandise from Jason Company, terms 2/10, n/30, F.O.B. shipping point. On August 17, Harris paid $200 freight on the shipment. On August 20, Harris returned $300 worth of the merchandise for credit. Final payment was made to Jason on August 24. Harris Company records purchases using the gross price method, and it uses the periodic inventory system.

a. Give the general journal entries that Harris should make on August 17, August 20, and August 24.

b. Give the entries that Harris should make on these three dates if the terms are F.O.B. destination.

ENTRIES FOR MERCHANDISE
TRANSACTIONS ON SELLER'S
AND BUYER'S RECORDS—
PERIODIC
— OBJ. 3, 4 —

5-22A The following are selected transactions of Fenton, Inc., during 1993:

Jan. 18 Sold and shipped on account to Lawrence Stores merchandise listing for $1,500, terms 2/10, n/30.

25 Lawrence Stores was granted a $200 allowance on goods shipped January 18.

27 Received from Lawrence Stores a check for full settlement of the January 18 transaction.

Record, in general journal form, the above transactions as they would appear on the books of (a) Fenton, Inc., and (b) Lawrence Stores. Lawrence Stores records purchases using the gross price method. Both companies use the periodic inventory system.

NET PRICE METHOD OF
RECORDING PURCHASES
— OBJ. 4 —

5-23A Evans, Inc., uses the net price method of recording purchases. On September 12, 1993, the firm purchased merchandise for $3,000, terms 2/10, n/30. On September 16, the firm returned $900 of the merchandise to the seller. Payment of the account occurred on September 19. Evans uses the periodic inventory system.

a. Give the general journal entries for September 12, September 16, and September 19.

b. Assuming that the account was settled on September 25, give the entry for payment on that date.

DETERMINATION OF
OMITTED INCOME
STATEMENT DATA
— OBJ. 4 —

5-24A The box on the following page contains portions of four unrelated income statements, each with certain data omitted. Fill in the lettered blanks with the appropriate amounts.

	1	2	3	4
Net Sales	$220,000	$120,000	$260,000	$ j
Beginning Inventory	a	14,000	23,000	25,000
Net Cost of Purchases	126,000	70,000	106,000	k
Cost of Goods Available for Sale	148,000	d	g	l
Ending Inventory	b	12,000	h	20,000
Cost of Goods Sold	c	e	i	108,000
Gross Profit	120,000	f	155,000	72,000

EFFECTS OF INVENTORY ERRORS
— OBJ. 4 —

5-25A Moore Company's operating figures for four consecutive periods are given below.

	Period			
	(1)	**(2)**	**(3)**	**(4)**
Beginning Inventory	$30,000	$25,000	$20,000	$28,000
Net Cost of Purchases	55,000	65,000	60,000	70,000
Cost of Goods Available for Sale	$85,000	$90,000	$80,000	$98,000
Ending Inventory	25,000	20,000	28,000	22,000
Cost of Goods Sold	$60,000	$70,000	$52,000	$76,000

Assuming that the following errors were made, compute the correct cost of goods sold for each period:

Period	Error in Ending Inventory
1	Understated $3,000
2	Overstated $5,000
3	Overstated $4,000

CLOSING ENTRIES— PERPETUAL
— OBJ. 9 —

5-26A A portion of the December 31, 1993, worksheet for Kokomo Distributors is shown below. Kokomo uses the perpetual inventory system.

	Income Statement		Balance Sheet	
	Debit	**Credit**	**Debit**	**Credit**
Inventory (December 31)			88,500	
K. Kokomo, Capital				210,000
K. Kokomo, Drawing			18,000	
Sales		750,000		
Sales Returns and Allowances	2,200			
Sales Discounts	6,800			
Cost of Goods Sold	495,000			
Advertising Expense	6,000			
Delivery Expense	9,000			
Depreciation Expense	12,000			
Salaries Expense	187,500			
Interest Expense	2,000			

Using the given information, prepare the general journal entries to close the books.

CLASSIFIED BALANCE SHEET
— OBJ. 6 —

5-27A From the following accounts, listed in alphabetical order, prepare a classified balance sheet for Balford Wholesalers at December 31, 1993. All accounts have normal balances.

Accounts Receivable	$ 54,000	Inventory	$142,000
Accounts Payable	52,000	Land	58,000
Accumulated Depreciation— Building	28,000	Mortgage Payable (long-term)	100,000
Accumulated Depreciation— Office Equipment	7,000	Office Equipment	26,000
		Office Supplies	2,000
Building	110,000	Salaries Payable	8,000
Cash	30,000	V. Balford, Capital	227,000

ENTRIES FOR SALE,
RETURN, AND
REMITTANCE—PERPETUAL
— OBJ. 8 —

5-28A On October 14, 1993, Patrick Company sold merchandise with an invoice price of $1,000 ($750 cost), terms 2/10, n/30, to Baxter Company. On October 18, $200 of merchandise ($150 cost) was returned because it was the wrong size. On October 24, Patrick Company received a check for the amount due from Baxter Company.

Record the journal entries made by Patrick Company for the above transactions. Patrick uses the perpetual inventory system.

ENTRIES FOR PURCHASE,
RETURN, AND
REMITTANCE—PERPETUAL
— OBJ. 8 —

5-29A On May 15, 1993, Monique Company purchased $25,000 of merchandise from Terrell Company, terms 1/10, n/30, F.O.B. shipping point. On May 17, Monique paid $260 to Swift Trucking Company for freight on the shipment. On May 20, Monique Company returned $500 of merchandise for credit. Final payment was made to Terrell on May 24. Monique Company records purchases using the gross price method and uses the perpetual inventory system.

a. Prepare the journal entries that Monique Company should make on May 15, 17, 20, and 24.

b. Prepare the entries that Monique should make on these four dates if the terms are F.O.B. destination.

ENTRIES FOR MERCHANDISE
TRANSACTIONS ON SELLER'S
AND BUYER'S RECORDS—
PERPETUAL
— OBJ. 8 —

5-30A The following are selected transactions of Candello, Inc., during 1993:

June 18   Sold and shipped on account to Dante Company $4,000 ($3,000 cost) of merchandise, terms 2/10, n/30.

    25   Dante Company returned defective merchandise billed at $400 on June 18 ($300 cost).

    27   Received from Dante Company a check for full settlement of the June 18 transaction.

Record, in general journal form, the above transactions as they would appear on the books of (a) Candello, Inc., and (b) Dante Company. Both companies use the perpetual inventory system and Dante records purchases using the gross price method.

ALTERNATE PROBLEMS

ENTRIES FOR MERCHANDISE
TRANSACTIONS ON SELLER'S
AND BUYER'S RECORDS—
PERIODIC
— OBJ. 3, 4 —

5-31A Fortune Distributing Company had the following transactions with Arlington, Inc. during 1993:

Nov. 10   Fortune sold and shipped $6,000 worth of merchandise to Arlington, terms 2/10, n/30, F.O.B. shipping point.

    12   Arlington, Inc., paid freight charges on the shipment from Fortune Company, $360.

    14   Fortune issued a credit memo for $600 for merchandise returned by Arlington.

    19   Fortune received payment in full for the net amount due on the November 10 sale.

    24   Arlington returned goods that had originally been billed at $500. Fortune issued a check for $490.

REQUIRED

Record the above transactions in general journal form as they would appear (a) on the books of Fortune Distributing Company and (b) on the books of Arlington, Inc. Arlington, Inc., records purchases using the gross price method. Assume both companies use the periodic inventory system.

COMPLEX ENTRIES FOR
MERCHANDISE
TRANSACTIONS—PERIODIC
— OBJ. 3, 4 —

5-32A Polidor Company was established on July 1, 1993. Its sales terms are 2/10, n/30, F.O.B. destination. Credit terms for its purchases vary with the supplier. Selected transactions for the first month of operations are given below. Unless noted, all transactions are on account and involve merchandise held for resale. All purchases are recorded using the gross price method and the periodic inventory system is used.

July 1   Purchased goods from Dawson, Inc., $1,900; terms 1/10, n/30, F.O.B. shipping point, freight collect.

    2   Purchased goods from Penn Company, $4,200, terms 2/10, n/30, F.O.B. destination. Freight charges of $160 were prepaid by Penn.

July 3   Paid freight on shipment from Dawson, $80.

5   Sold merchandise to Ward, Inc., $1,300.

5   Paid freight on shipment to Ward, Inc., $60.

8   Returned $300 worth of the goods purchased July 1 from Dawson, Inc., because some goods were damaged. Dawson approved the return.

9   Issued credit memorandum to Ward, Inc., for $200 worth of merchandise returned.

10   Paid Dawson, Inc., the amount due.

10   Purchased goods from Dorn Company with a list price of $2,400. Polidor was entitled to a $33\frac{1}{3}$% trade discount; terms 2/10, n/30, F.O.B. destination, freight collect.

11   Paid freight on shipment from Dorn Company, $130.

15   Received the amount due from Ward, Inc.

15   Sold merchandise to Colby Corporation, $3,200.

16   Mailed a check to Penn Company for the amount due on its July 2 invoice.

17   Received a notice from Colby Corporation stating that it had paid freight of $120 on the July 15 shipment.

18   Received a credit memorandum of $100 from Dorn Company, as an allowance for defective merchandise purchased on July 10.

19   Paid Dorn Company the amount due.

25   Received the amount due from Colby Corporation.

REQUIRED

Record the transactions for Polidor Company in general journal form.

PREPARATION OF A
WORKSHEET—PERIODIC
— OBJ. 5 —

5-33A   The unadjusted trial balance of Lincoln Corporation on December 31, 1993, is shown below; the periodic inventory system has been used.

LINCOLN CORPORATION
TRIAL BALANCE
DECEMBER 31, 1993

	Debit	Credit
Cash	$ 43,000	
Accounts Receivable	65,200	
Inventory	112,000	
Prepaid Insurance	1,800	
Supplies	3,400	
Furniture and Fixtures	32,000	
Accumulated Depreciation—Furniture and Fixtures		$ 3,600
Delivery Equipment	65,000	
Accumulated Depreciation—Delivery Equipment		19,000
Accounts Payable		17,400
Capital Stock		200,000
Retained Earnings		76,000
Sales		374,000
Sales Returns and Allowances	4,800	
Sales Discounts	4,000	
Purchases	220,000	
Purchases Returns and Allowances		5,600
Purchases Discounts		2,800
Transportation In	11,200	
Salaries Expense	92,000	
Rent Expense	20,800	
Delivery Expense	16,400	
Utilities Expense	6,800	
	$698,400	$698,400

The following data are available at December 31, 1993:

1. Prepaid insurance at December 31 is $360.
2. Supplies on hand at December 31 amount to $1,600.
3. Depreciation on the furniture and fixtures is 10% per year.

4. Depreciation on the delivery equipment is 20% per year.
5. At December 31, accrued salaries total $1,400.
6. Inventory at December 31 is $120,000.

REQUIRED

Prepare a 10-column worksheet for Lincoln Corporation for 1993.

INCOME STATEMENT AND CALCULATION OF GROSS PROFIT PERCENTAGE
— OBJ. 6, 10 —

5-34A The following selected information is available for Steinberg Distributing Company for February, 1993.

Purchases	$164,000
Sales	290,000
Transportation In	3,600
Purchases Discounts	2,800
Inventory, February 1	63,000
Inventory, February 28	56,000
Purchases Returns and Allowances	3,200
Sales Returns and Allowances	1,800
Transportation Out	7,600
Rent Expense	12,000
Salaries Expense	61,000
Sales Discounts	2,200
Depreciation Expense	5,600

REQUIRED

a. Prepare a February income statement for Steinberg Distributing Company. Operating expenses should be shown in one category.
b. Calculate the gross profit percentage.

WORKSHEET, FINANCIAL STATEMENTS, AND ADJUSTING AND CLOSING ENTRIES—PERIODIC
— OBJ. 5, 6, 7 —

5-35A Oregon Distributors, whose accounting year ends on December 31, had the following normal balances in its ledger accounts at December 31, 1993:

Cash	$ 32,800	Sales	$1,180,000
Accounts Receivable	53,000	Sales Returns and	
Inventory	140,000	Allowances	9,600
Prepaid Insurance	7,200	Sales Discounts	16,400
Office Supplies	4,800	Purchases	790,000
Furniture and Fixtures	28,000	Purchases Returns and	
Accumulated Depreciation—		Allowances	3,200
Furniture and Fixtures	10,800	Purchases Discounts	8,400
Delivery Equipment	70,000	Transportation In	34,800
Accumulated Depreciation—		Sales Salaries Expense	108,000
Delivery Equipment	24,400	Delivery Expense	36,800
Accounts Payable	69,400	Advertising Expense	26,200
Long-term Notes Payable	30,000	Rent Expense	30,000
W. Oregon, Capital	150,000	Office Salaries Expense	72,000
W. Oregon, Drawing	8,000	Utilities Expense	8,600

Rent expense and utilities expense are administrative expenses. During the year, the accounting department prepared monthly statements using worksheets, but no adjusting entries were made in the journals and ledgers. Data for the year-end procedures are as follows:

1. Prepaid insurance, December 31, 1993 (insurance expense is classified as a selling expense) — $ 2,400
2. Office supplies on hand, December 31, 1993 — 1,800
3. Depreciation expense on furniture and fixtures for the year (an administrative expense) — 2,000
4. Depreciation expense on delivery equipment for the year — 10,000
5. Salaries payable, December 31, 1993 ($1,000 sales salaries and $600 office salaries) — 1,600
6. Inventory, December 31, 1993 (periodic inventory system) — 132,000

REQUIRED

a. Prepare a worksheet for 1993.
b. Prepare a classified income statement for 1993.
c. Prepare a classified balance sheet at December 31, 1993.
d. Make the necessary adjusting entries in general journal form.
e. Make the closing entries in general journal form.

PREPARATION OF INCOME STATEMENT FROM INCOMPLETE DATA — OBJ. 6 —

5-36A Your neighbor, James Lennon, treasurer of Nelson, Inc., has misplaced the firm's income statement for the current year. He needs this statement to complete a report due the next day. He comes to you with a December 31 balance sheet and an unadjusted trial balance taken at December 31 and asks if you can develop an income statement for 1993. The available data at December 31, 1993, are given below.

	Unadjusted Trial Balance		Balance Sheet Data
	Debit	**Credit**	
Cash	$ 56,000		$ 56,000
Accounts Receivable	84,000		84,000
Inventory	128,000		96,000
Office Supplies	1,800		1,200
Prepaid Insurance	3,000		2,000
Delivery Equipment	92,000		92,000
Accumulated Depreciation		$ 18,000	(24,000)
			$307,200
Accounts Payable		64,000	$ 64,000
Salaries Payable			2,400
Capital Stock		180,000	180,000
Retained Earnings		32,000	60,800
Sales		432,000	
Purchases	288,000		
Rent Expense	7,200		
Salaries Expense	50,000		
Advertising Expense	6,000		
Delivery Expense	10,000		
	$726,000	$726,000	$307,200

REQUIRED

Use the given data to prepare the year's income statement for Nelson, Inc. Operating expenses should be shown as one category. Lennon informs you that the amounts shown in the unadjusted trial balance for Inventory, Office Supplies, Prepaid Insurance, and Accumulated Depreciation are the account balances at January 1, 1993. No dividends were declared or paid during the year.

EFFECT OF WORKSHEET ERRORS—PERIODIC — OBJ. 5 —

5-37A The first six columns of a 10-column worksheet prepared for Humphrey Specialty Shop are as follows (the periodic inventory system is being used):

	Trial Balance		Adjustments		Adjusted Trial Balance	
	Debit	**Credit**	**Debit**	**Credit**	**Debit**	**Credit**
Cash	11,200				11,200	
Inventory (January 1)	60,000				60,000	
Office Supplies	2,800				2,800	
Prepaid Insurance	1,200			600	600	
Equipment	50,000				50,000	
Accumulated Depreciation		8,000		4,000		12,000
Accounts Payable		20,000				20,000
M. Humphrey, Capital		72,000				72,000
M. Humphrey, Drawing	6,000				6,000	
Sales		180,000				180,000
Purchases	96,000				96,000	
Transportation In	800				800	
Rent Expense	4,000				4,000	
Salaries Expense	48,000		1,000		49,000	
	280,000	280,000				
Depreciation Expense			4,000		4,000	
Salaries Payable				1,000		1,000
Insurance Expense			600		600	
			5,600	5,600	285,000	285,000
Inventory (December 31)						
Net Income						

In completing the worksheet, Humphrey's accountant made the following errors:

1. The adjustment for Office Supplies Expense was omitted; office supplies at December 31 amounted to $1,200.
2. The $4,000 amount for Depreciation Expense was extended as a debit in the balance sheet columns.
3. The $1,000 credit to Salaries Payable was extended as a credit in the income statement columns.
4. The January 1, 1993, Inventory balance of $60,000 was extended as a credit in the income statement columns.
5. The December 31, 1993, Inventory balance of $70,000 was recorded as a debit in the income statement columns and as a credit in the balance sheet columns.

REQUIRED

a. Which of the errors would cause the worksheet not to balance?
b. Without completing the worksheet, calculate the net income for 1993. Assume that the accountant made no other errors and that the worksheet totals, before adding net income or net loss, were

	Debit	Credit
Income statement	$220,400	$241,000
Balance sheet	74,600	174,000

ENTRIES FOR MERCHANDISE TRANSACTIONS ON SELLER'S AND BUYER'S RECORDS— PERPETUAL
— OBJ. 8 —

5-38A Riggs Distributing Company had the following transactions with Arlington, Inc. during 1993:

Nov. 10 Riggs sold and shipped $6,000 worth of merchandise ($4,200 cost) to Arlington, terms 2/10, n/30, F.O.B. shipping point.

12 Arlington, Inc., paid freight charges on the shipment from Riggs Company, $360.

14 Riggs issued a credit memo for $600 for merchandise returned by Arlington ($420 cost).

19 Riggs received payment in full for the net amount due on the November 10 sale.

24 Arlington returned goods that had originally been billed at $300 ($210 cost). Riggs issued a check for $294.

REQUIRED

Record the above transactions in general journal form as they would appear (a) on the books of Riggs Distributing Company and (b) on the books of Arlington, Inc. Arlington, Inc., records purchases at invoice price. Assume both companies use the perpetual inventory system.

COMPLEX ENTRIES FOR MERCHANDISE TRANSACTIONS— PERPETUAL
— OBJ. 8 —

5-39A Webster Company was established on July 1, 1993. Its sales terms are 2/10, n/30, F.O.B. destination. Credit terms for its purchases vary with the supplier. Selected transactions for the first month of operations are given below. Unless noted, all transactions are on account and involve merchandise held for resale. All purchases are recorded using the gross price method and the perpetual inventory system is used.

July 1 Purchased goods from Dawson, Inc., $1,900; terms 1/10, n/30, F.O.B. shipping point, freight collect.

2 Purchased goods from Penn Company, $4,200, terms 2/10, n/30, F.O.B. destination. Freight charges of $160 were prepaid by Penn.

3 Paid freight on shipment from Dawson, $80.

5 Sold merchandise to Ward, Inc., $1,300 ($975 cost).

5 Paid freight on shipment to Ward, Inc., $60.

8 Returned $300 worth of the goods purchased July 1 from Dawson, Inc., because some goods were damaged. Dawson approved the return.

July 9 Issued credit memorandum to Ward, Inc., for $200 ($150 cost) worth of merchandise returned.

10 Paid Dawson, Inc., the amount due.

10 Purchased goods from Dorn Company with a list price of $2,400. Webster was entitled to a $33\frac{1}{3}$% trade discount; terms 2/10, n/30, F.O.B. destination, freight collect.

11 Paid freight on shipment from Dorn Company, $130.

15 Received the amount due from Ward, Inc.

15 Sold merchandise to Colby Corporation, $3,200 ($2,400 cost).

16 Mailed a check to Penn Company for the amount due on its July 2 invoice.

17 Received a notice from Colby Corporation stating that it had paid freight of $120 on the July 15 shipment.

18 Received a credit memorandum of $100 from Dorn Company, as an allowance for defective merchandise purchased on July 10.

19 Paid Dorn Company the amount due.

25 Received the amount due from Colby Corporation.

REQUIRED

Record the transactions for Webster Company in general journal form.

PREPARATION OF A WORKSHEET—PERPETUAL — OBJ. 9 —

5-40A The unadjusted trial balance of Marshall Corporation on December 31, 1993, is shown below; the perpetual inventory system has been used.

MARSHALL CORPORATION
TRIAL BALANCE
DECEMBER 31, 1993

	Debit	Credit
Cash	$ 43,000	
Accounts Receivable	65,200	
Inventory	120,000	
Prepaid Insurance	1,800	
Supplies	3,400	
Furniture and Fixtures	32,000	
Accumulated Depreciation—Furniture and Fixtures		$ 3,600
Delivery Equipment	65,000	
Accumulated Depreciation—Delivery Equipment		19,000
Accounts Payable		17,400
Capital Stock		200,000
Retained Earnings		76,000
Sales		374,000
Sales Returns and Allowances	4,800	
Sales Discounts	4,000	
Cost of Goods Sold	214,800	
Salaries Expense	92,000	
Rent Expense	20,800	
Delivery Expense	16,400	
Utilities Expense	6,800	
	$690,000	$690,000

The following data are available at December 31, 1993:

1. Prepaid insurance at December 31 is $360.
2. Supplies on hand at December 31 amount to $1,600.
3. Depreciation on the furniture and fixtures is 10% per year.
4. Depreciation on the delivery equipment is 20% per year.
5. At December 31, accrued salaries total $1,400.

REQUIRED

Prepare a 10-column worksheet for Marshall Corporation for 1993.

PREPARATION OF A WORKSHEET—PERIODIC — APPENDIX B —

5-41A Follow the requirements given in Problem 5-33A, using the method described in Appendix B.

WORKSHEET, FINANCIAL STATEMENTS, AND ADJUSTING AND CLOSING ENTRIES—PERIODIC — APPENDIX B —

5-42A Follow the requirements given in Problem 5-35A, using the method described in Appendix B.

CASES

Business Decision Case

Northwestern Corporation started a retail clothing business on July 1, 1993. During 1993, Northwestern Corporation had the following summary transactions related to merchandise inventory:

	Purchases	Sales
July	$200,000	$ 300,000
August	320,000	580,000
September	260,000	480,000
October	300,000	550,000
November	750,000	850,000
December	220,000	1,120,000

On average, Northwestern's cost of goods sold is 50% of sales. Assume there were no sales returns and allowances or purchases returns and allowances during this six-month time period.

REQUIRED

a. Calculate the ending merchandise inventory for each of the six months.
b. Northwestern's purchases peaked during November; its sales peaked during December. Did Northwestern plan its purchases wisely? Should Northwestern expect a similar pattern in future years?

Analytical Application Case

THE SHERWIN-WILLIAMS COMPANY reported the following results (in millions of dollars) for three recent years (Year 3 is the most recent):

	Year 3	Year 2	Year 1
Net Sales	$2,123	$1,950	$1,801
Cost of Goods Sold	1,275	1,187	1,067

Assume that similar-sized companies in the same basic industries have experienced the following average gross profit percentages:

Year 3:	39.5
Year 2:	39.0
Year 1:	40.5

REQUIRED

a. Calculate the gross profit percentage for The Sherwin-Williams Company for the three years.
b. Compare the three-year trend in gross profit percentage for The Sherwin-Williams Company to the assumed industry averages for the same three-year period. Analyze the trend and evaluate the performance of The Sherwin-Williams Company compared to the assumed industry averages.

Ethics Case

During the last week of 1993, George Connors, controller for We 'R' Appliances, received a memorandum from the firm's president, John Anderson. The memorandum stated that Anderson had negotiated a very large sale with a new customer and directed Connors to see that the order was processed and the goods shipped before the end of the year. Anderson noted he had to depart from the usual credit terms of n/30 and allow terms of n/60 to clinch the sale. Although the credit terms were unusual for the company, Connors was particularly pleased with the news because business had been somewhat slow. The goods were shipped on December 29 and the sale was incorporated into the 1993 financial data.

It is now mid-February 1994, and two events have occurred recently that, together, cause concern for Connors. First, he was inadvertently copied on a letter from the firm's bank to Anderson. The letter stated that the bank had reconsidered its decision to deny a loan to the company and is now granting the loan based on the new, and favorable, sales data supplied by the president. The bank was "particularly impressed with the sales improvement shown in December." Although Connors had been involved in the initial loan application that was denied, he had been unaware that the president had reapplied for the loan.

The second event was that all of the goods shipped on December 29 to the new customer had just been returned.

REQUIRED

What are the ethical considerations George Connors faces as a result of the recent events?

What changes are required in the accounting system as a company increases its size and complexity of operation?

As a company grows, it increases the number of customers, suppliers, products, and employees that it deals with. ■ *Smaller companies may use special journals and voucher systems.* ■ *For large companies such as Chrysler Credit Corporation, computerized accounting systems are essential.* ■ *Through a branch information system, Chrysler Credit Corporation has instant access to dealer inventory records, retail and lease account histories, payoff quotations, and automated credit applications.*

ACCOUNTING SYSTEMS

n previous chapters, we limited our discussion of the processing of accounting transactions to recording in a general journal and posting to a general ledger. This type of accounting system is satisfactory for introducing basic accounting procedures. However, this system would be inadequate for a business having even a moderate volume of transactions for two reasons.

First, recording all transactions in the general journal would seriously limit the number of transactions that could be processed in a day, simply because only one person at a time could make entries. Second, transactions recorded in a general journal must be posted individually in the general ledger, resulting in a great deal of posting labor. To overcome these shortcomings, firms adopt an accounting system that incorporates either special journals or a voucher procedure. These two approaches are discussed in later sections of this chapter.

Further, our previous illustrations contained only a single Accounts Receivable account and a single Accounts Payable account. Firms that keep accounts with individual customers and creditors find it quite burdensome to work with a general ledger containing a large number of customer and creditor accounts. Therefore, firms adopt an accounting system that uses control accounts in the general ledger and separate subsidiary ledgers to record and control the accounts of individual customers and creditors. The next section discusses this approach.

CONTROL ACCOUNTS AND SUBSIDIARY LEDGERS

OBJECTIVE ❶ EXPLAIN *the characteristics of and interrelationships between control accounts and subsidiary ledgers.*

When a business firm keeps charges to and payments from all customers in a single Accounts Receivable account in the general ledger, the account in T-account form would appear as follows:

ACCOUNTS RECEIVABLE

3,000	900
300	400
800	

The firm cannot easily bill or mail statements to customers, answer inquiries about individual customer balances, or make any collection efforts if it has only a single record showing total claims against all customers. The company needs to know each customer's name and address, transaction dates, amounts billed, and amounts received on account for each account receivable.

We could solve this problem by maintaining in the general ledger an individual Account Receivable for each customer. The trial balance of such a general ledger might appear as follows:

	Trial Balance	
	Debit	**Credit**
Cash	$13,130	
Accounts Receivable—Customer A	300	
Accounts Receivable—Customer B	700	
Accounts Receivable—Customer C	800	
Accounts Receivable—Customer D	1,000	
(All other assets)	15,350	
(All liabilities)		$ 3,550
Owner's Capital		25,000
Owner's Drawing	800	
Revenue		5,450
(All expenses)	1,920	
	$34,000	$34,000

We can see the limitations of this approach. The general ledger becomes unreasonably large when hundreds of customers' accounts are involved. With thousands of customers, it becomes unworkable. Alternatively, we might use one **control account** titled Accounts Receivable in the general ledger and maintain individual customer accounts in a **subsidiary ledger**. Under this approach, the general ledger is kept to a manageable size, and a detailed record of transactions with individual customers exists in the subsidiary ledger.

The accounts receivable subsidiary ledger, like the general ledger, may be simply a group of accounts in a binder, or it may be a file card arrangement.[1] In either case, the order is either alphabetical by customer name or numerical by customer number. Exhibit 6-1 shows a typical form for an accounts receivable subsidiary ledger. When the three-column form is used, abnormal balances are enclosed in parentheses or shown in red. The information placed at the top of the account varies with the needs of the business and the type of customer. Often, such information concerns the granting of credit.

The following diagram shows the relationships between the Accounts Receivable control account in the general ledger and the accounts receivable subsidiary ledger.

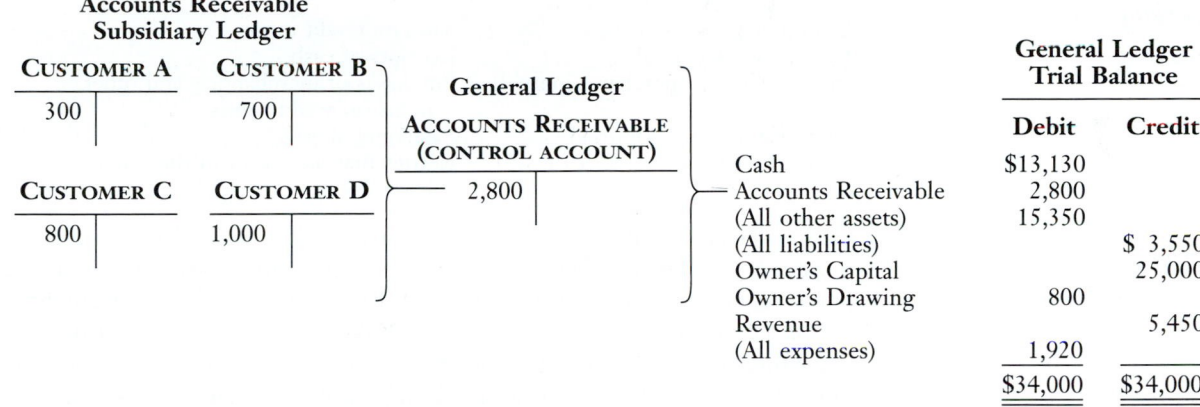

Accounts Receivable Subsidiary Ledger

CUSTOMER A	CUSTOMER B
300	700

CUSTOMER C	CUSTOMER D
800	1,000

General Ledger
ACCOUNTS RECEIVABLE (CONTROL ACCOUNT)
2,800

General Ledger Trial Balance

	Debit	Credit
Cash	$13,130	
Accounts Receivable	2,800	
(All other assets)	15,350	
(All liabilities)		$ 3,550
Owner's Capital		25,000
Owner's Drawing	800	
Revenue		5,450
(All expenses)	1,920	
	$34,000	$34,000

EXHIBIT 6—1	CUSTOMER ACCOUNT FORM IN SUBSIDIARY LEDGER

Name _____

Address _____   Phone _____

Employed at _____   Position _____

Special terms _____   Maximum credit $ _____

Date	Remarks	Post. Ref.	Debit	Credit	Balance

---

[1]In electronic data processing systems, the customers' ledger would be stored on magnetic tape or disk.

Because the total of all the balances in the accounts receivable subsidiary ledger must equal the balance in the Accounts Receivable control account in the general ledger, it follows that for every amount posted to the Accounts Receivable control account, an equal amount must be posted to one or more of the customers' accounts in the accounts receivable subsidiary ledger. We will consider the specific posting procedures later in this chapter.

The control account–subsidiary ledger technique can be used to yield a detailed breakdown of many general ledger accounts, not just Accounts Receivable. Subsidiary ledgers are often used for Accounts Payable, Inventory, Buildings, and Equipment.

SPECIAL JOURNALS

OBJECTIVE ❷ DESCRIBE *the recording process in an accounting system that uses special journals.*

Journals specifically designed in a tabular fashion to accommodate the recording of one type of transaction are called **special journals**. Most firms adopting special journals use the following journals:

Journal	Specific Transactions Recorded	Posting Abbreviation
Sales journal	Sales on credit terms	S
Cash receipts journal	Receipts of cash	CR
Invoice register (purchases journal)	Purchases of merchandise and other items on credit terms	IR
Cash disbursements journal	Payments of cash	CD
General journal	Entries that do not fit in the other journals	J

Cash sales are usually recorded in the cash receipts journal rather than in the sales journal because cash is best controlled when *all* routine cash receipts are recorded in one journal. Similarly, a firm can increase control over cash disbursements by recording purchases of merchandise or other items for cash in the cash disbursements journal rather than in the purchases journal. When special journals are used, the general journal is used only for adjusting, closing, and reversing entries, and for recording transactions that do not "fit" well in any special journal. Examples of the latter include the recording of purchases returns and allowances and sales returns and allowances.

Posting references from the special journals are identified in the general and subsidiary ledger accounts by the letters shown above. For example, postings from page one of the Sales Journal to the general ledger and the accounts receivable subsidiary ledger are identified as "S1" (see Exhibit 6-2).

Advantages of Special Journals

A major advantage of special journals is that their use permits a division of labor. When special journals are used, the recording step in the accounting cycle can be divided among several persons, each of whom is responsible for particular types of transactions. Persons making entries in special journals do not have to be highly skilled or have a thorough knowledge of the entire accounting system.

The use of special journals often reduces recording time. Special journal transactions of a given type need no routine explanations for each entry. Also, because special column headings are used, account titles need not be repeated as is necessary in the general journal.

Probably the most significant advantage of using special journals is the time saved in posting from the journals to the ledgers. When a general journal is used, each entry must be posted separately to the general ledger. The tabular arrangement of special journals, however, often permits all entries to a given account to be added and posted as a single aggregate posting. For instance, if we entered 1,000 sales transactions in a general journal, we would make 1,000 separate credit postings to the Sales account. If we use a sales journal, however, the amounts of the 1,000 sales will appear in one money column. Therefore, we may easily obtain a total and post it as one

EXHIBIT 6—2

SALES JOURNAL   PAGE 1

Date	Invoice No.	Account	Post. Ref.	Accts Rec Debit/Sales Credit
1993 June				
1	101	J. Norton	✓	200
5	102	L. Ross	✓	100
12	103	B. Travis	✓	1,000
22	104	R. Douglas	✓	400
29	105	M. Holton	✓	300
30	106	E. Knight	✓	500
				2,500
				(12/40)

GENERAL LEDGER

ACCOUNTS RECEIVABLE (12)			SALES (40)		
6/30 S1 2,500				6/30 S1 2,500	

ACCOUNTS RECEIVABLE SUBSIDIARY LEDGER

R. DOUGLAS		J. NORTON	
6/22 S1 400		6/1 S1 200	

M. HOLTON		L. ROSS	
6/29 S1 300		6/5 S1 100	

E. KNIGHT		B. TRAVIS	
6/30 S1 500		6/12 S1 1,000	

credit to the Sales account. The sales journal has saved us the time necessary for 999 postings to the Sales account. Clearly, as more transactions are involved, more posting time is saved.

SALES JOURNAL

Periodic Inventory System

The **sales journal** of the Excel Company, shown in Exhibit 6-2, is designed for a company using the periodic inventory system. This journal lists all credit sales for June. The information for each sale comes from a copy of the related sales invoice. Note that the tabular form of the journal is specifically designed to record sales on account.

OBJECTIVE 3 OUTLINE *and* ILLUSTRATE *the use of the special journal system.*

If the same credit terms are extended to all customers, as we assume in our illustration, we need not describe them in the sales journal. When credit terms vary from customer to customer, a column can be added to the sales journal to explain the terms of each sale.

As we might expect, the posting of any journal to the general ledger must result in equal debits and credits. Also, for any posting to a control account in the general ledger, the same total amount must be posted to one or more related subsidiary ledger accounts. Exhibit 6-2 illustrates how to post the amounts in Excel Company's sales journal.

Usually, as entries are recorded in the sales journal throughout each month, they are also posted to the accounts receivable subsidiary ledger. A customer's account then reflects a transaction within a day or two of its occurrence. Consequently, the credit office can review and monitor a customer's account balance at times other than a billing date. Daily postings to the accounts receivable subsidiary ledger also allow for cycle billings (for example, billing customers whose names begin with different letters at different times of the month). The advantage of cycle billings is that statements of account can be mailed throughout the month rather than in one large group at the end of the month.

A check mark is placed in the posting reference column of the sales journal to indicate that the amount has been posted to the customer's account in the subsidiary ledger. At the end of the month, when all sales have been recorded and the sales journal has been totaled and ruled, the total sales figure is posted to the general ledger as a debit to the Accounts Receivable control account and as a credit to the Sales account. Note the double posting reference at the bottom of the posting reference column in the illustration; this indicates that Accounts Receivable is account No. 12 in the ledger and Sales is account No. 40. Posting of the sales journal is now complete.

Sales journals may accommodate additional information. For example, columns could be included for sales by department or by product, so that a breakdown of sales is available to management. Columns may also be provided for sales tax information, where necessary.

Perpetual Inventory System

A sales journal for a firm using the perpetual inventory system would include a column to record a debit to Cost of Goods Sold and a credit to Inventory for each sale. The column headings for such a sales journal are shown below.

Date	Invoice Number	Account	Accounts Receivable Debit and Sales Credit		Cost of Goods Sold Debit and Inventory Credit	
			Amount	Post. Ref.	Amount	Post. Ref.

The posting reference under Accounts Receivable Debit and Sales Credit would be used for debit postings to the individual accounts in the accounts receivable subsidiary ledger. The posting reference under Cost of Goods Sold Debit and Inventory Credit would be used for credit postings in the individual accounts in the Inventory subsidiary ledger.

CASH RECEIPTS JOURNAL

Periodic Inventory System

All transactions involving cash receipts are recorded in a **cash receipts journal**. Exhibit 6-3 shows a cash receipts journal for a firm using the periodic inventory system. Because cash sales and collections from credit customers occur most often, this journal provides special columns for recording debits to Cash and to Sales Discounts and credits to Sales and Accounts Receivable. In addition, the columns on the right-hand side of the journal can be used for debits and credits to any other account.

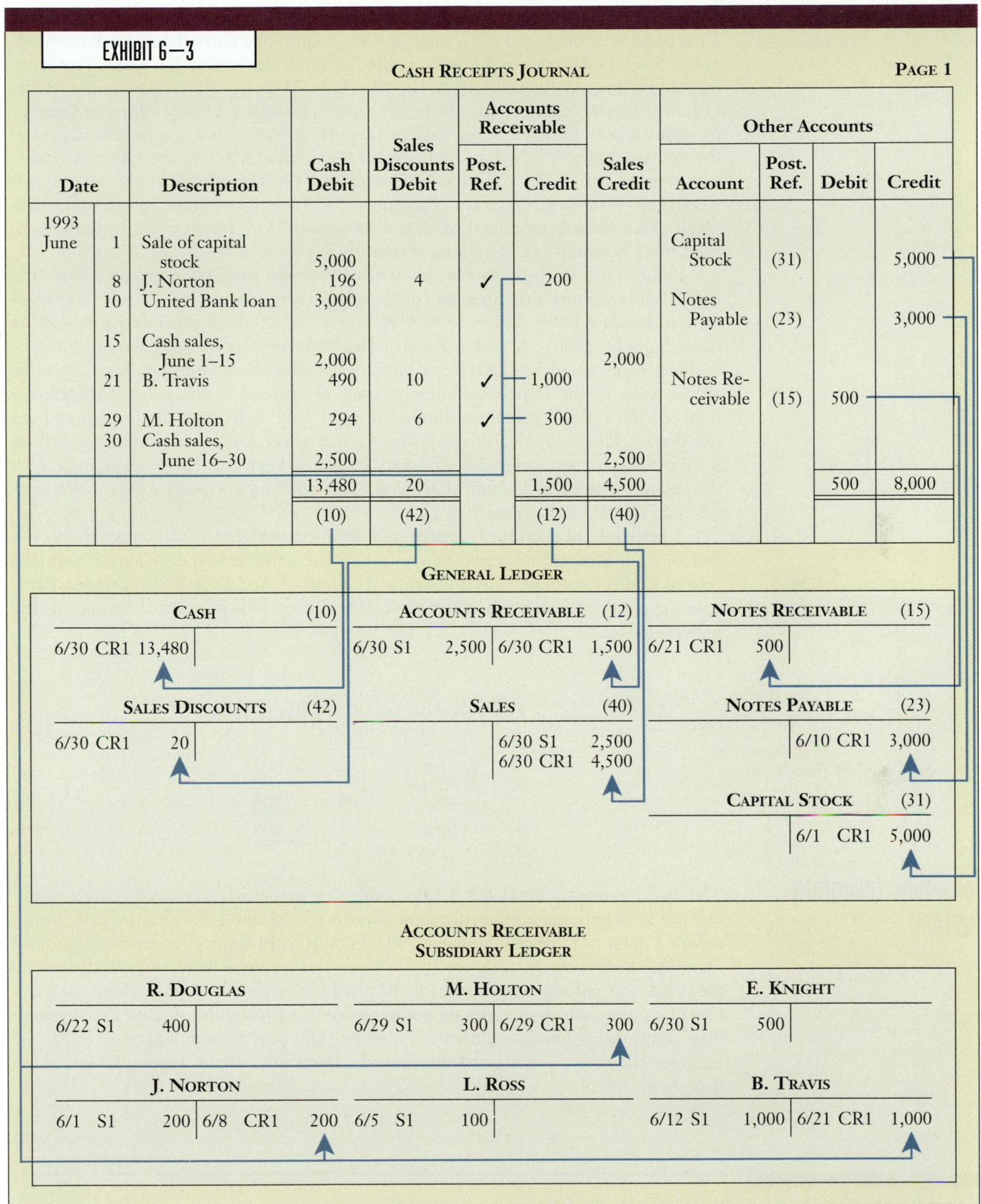

EXHIBIT 6—3

CASH RECEIPTS JOURNAL — PAGE 1

Note that the entries on June 15 and June 30, debiting Cash and crediting Sales, record cash sales for a certain period. Actually, cash sales would be recorded daily rather than semimonthly, but we have recorded them only twice here for simplicity.

The entry on June 8 records $196 received from J. Norton in payment of his June 1 purchase of $200, less the 2% cash discount taken. The entry debits Cash for $196, debits Sales Discounts for $4, and credits Accounts Receivable for $200. The entry for M. Holton on June 29 is similar. The June 21 entry illustrates the use of the Other Accounts debit column. Here, B. Travis settles her $1,000 billing of June 12 by giving a note for $500 of the debt and remitting $490 ($500 less the 2% discount) for the remainder. The debits are to Notes Receivable, $500, in the Other Accounts column; to Cash, $490; and to Sales Discounts, $10. The $1,000 credit to Accounts Receivable completes the entry. The entries on June 1 and June 10 represent cash received for the sale of capital stock and for a bank loan, respectively. In both cases, the Other Accounts credit column is used.

Before posting the cash receipts journal, we add each column and *balance* the journal to make sure that aggregate debits equal aggregate credits. (Note in our illustration that $13,480 + $20 + $500 = $1,500 + $4,500 + $8,000.) The totals of the Cash, Sales Discounts, Accounts Receivable, and Sales columns are posted to the general ledger, as noted by the posting references below these columns. Also, the individual items in the Other Accounts columns are posted to the general ledger; the totals of the Other Accounts columns are used only to balance the journal and are not posted. The individual items in the Accounts Receivable column are posted on a daily basis to the customers' subsidiary ledger to keep this ledger in balance with the Accounts Receivable control account. The postings to the customers' accounts are indicated by a check mark ($\checkmark$).

A **schedule of account balances** in a subsidiary ledger is usually prepared at the end of each accounting period to verify that the subsidiary ledger agrees with the related control account. The following schedule of Accounts Receivable for Excel Company indicates that the subsidiary ledger agrees with its control account in the general ledger.

EXCEL COMPANY
SCHEDULE OF ACCOUNTS RECEIVABLE
JUNE 30, 1993

R. Douglas	$ 400
E. Knight	500
L. Ross	100
Total	$1,000

Perpetual Inventory System

The cash receipts journal for a firm using the perpetual inventory system would include an additional column to those shown in Exhibit 6-3. This column would record a debit to Cost of Goods Sold and a credit to Inventory for merchandise sold on a cash basis. The amount recorded in this column would be the cost of the inventory sold. The column would probably be placed immediately to the right of the Sales Credit column (which includes the selling price of merchandise sold on a cash basis). The additional column would have a posting reference column adjacent to it to be used for the credit postings to the individual accounts in the Inventory subsidiary ledger.

INVOICE REGISTER (PURCHASES JOURNAL)

To record purchases of merchandise on account, we can use a single-column journal similar to the sales journal considered earlier (see Exhibit 6-2). The single money column would debit Purchases and credit Accounts Payable for each purchase transaction. We would post each entry in the journal to the individual creditors' accounts in the accounts payable subsidiary ledger. At the end of the month, we would post

Periodic Inventory System

the total of the amount column to the general ledger as a debit to the Purchases account and as a credit to the Accounts Payable control account.

Most businesses, however, keep a multicolumn journal to record all acquisitions on account, including such items as supplies and equipment, as well as merchandise. This journal may be called a *purchases journal*, but it is more properly called an **invoice register**. Exhibit 6-4 illustrates an invoice register for a firm using the periodic inventory system.

The illustration shows special columns for debits to Purchases, Office Supplies, and Store Supplies, as well as for credits to Accounts Payable. A column is also provided for debits to accounts for which no special column is available.

The amounts in the Accounts Payable column are posted to the accounts payable subsidiary ledger on a daily basis. A check mark in the posting reference column indicates that this has been done. At the end of the month, the columns of the register are totaled and the journal is balanced to ensure that total debits equal total credits. (In the example, $4,000 + $500 + $200 + $1,200 = $5,900.) The posting pattern for the invoice register is diagrammed in Exhibit 6-4.

Perpetual Inventory System

An invoice register for a firm using the perpetual inventory system would have the same basic structure as the invoice register of the firm using the periodic inventory system, with the heading on the Purchases Debit column changed to Inventory Debit. In addition, a posting reference column would be inserted to the right of the Inventory Debit column for debits to the individual accounts in the Inventory subsidiary ledger.

CASH DISBURSEMENTS JOURNAL

Periodic Inventory System

All cash payments are recorded in a **cash disbursements journal**. Exhibit 6-5 shows the June cash disbursements journal for Excel Company (which uses the periodic inventory system) after the related transactions have been recorded and the journal balanced and posted. Note the special columns for credits to Cash and Purchases Discounts, and for debits to Accounts Payable. Ordinarily these accounts will have the most entries. Also observe that, as in the cash receipts journal, the Other Accounts columns are available for recording debits or credits to any other accounts.

The June 2 entry in Exhibit 6-5 recorded a check for $2,800, which provided the cash needed to pay employees for the last part of May. The entries on June 12 and June 19 paid the accounts payable balances due Able, Inc., and Barr Company, less 2% and 1% cash discounts, respectively. Note that $1,000 of equipment was purchased on June 15 by giving $500 cash and a note payable for $500; the latter amount was recorded in the Other Accounts credit column. Also observe that the cash purchase of merchandise for $150 is recorded in the cash disbursements journal rather than in the purchases journal. The other entries in the journal are self-explanatory. Again, we have diagrammed the posting format for the journal.

After both the invoice register and the cash disbursements journal have been posted, the Accounts Payable control account has a $3,300 balance ($5,900 − $2,600). This total agrees with the following schedule of creditors' accounts:

EXCEL COMPANY
SCHEDULE OF ACCOUNTS PAYABLE
JUNE 30, 1993

Echo Distributors	$ 400
Holt, Inc.	300
Stix Supply Company	1,200
Ward Company	1,400
Total	$3,300

EXHIBIT 6—4

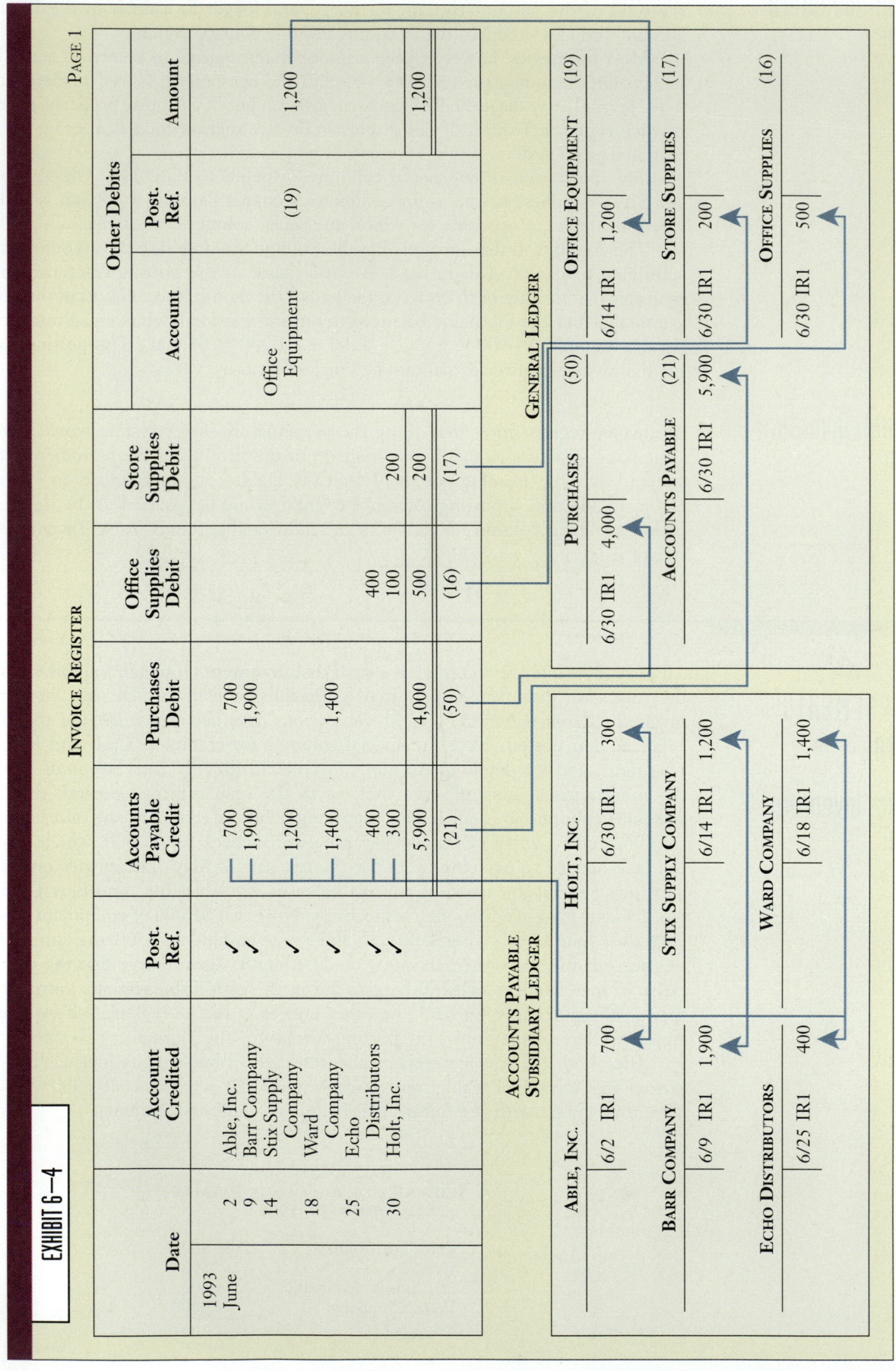

INVOICE REGISTER

PAGE 1

Date	Account Credited	Post. Ref.	Accounts Payable Credit	Purchases Debit	Office Supplies Debit	Store Supplies Debit	Other Debits Account	Other Debits Post. Ref.	Other Debits Amount
1993 June 2	Able, Inc.	✓	700	700					
9	Barr Company	✓	1,900	1,900					
14	Stix Supply Company	✓	1,200				Office Equipment	(19)	1,200
18	Ward Company	✓	1,400	1,400					
25	Echo Distributors	✓	400		400				
30	Holt, Inc.	✓	300		100	200			
			5,900	4,000	500	200			1,200
			(21)	(50)	(16)	(17)			

GENERAL LEDGER

PURCHASES (50)
6/30 IR1 4,000

OFFICE SUPPLIES (16)
6/30 IR1 500

STORE SUPPLIES (17)
6/30 IR1 200

OFFICE EQUIPMENT (19)
6/14 IR1 1,200

ACCOUNTS PAYABLE (21)
6/30 IR1 5,900

ACCOUNTS PAYABLE SUBSIDIARY LEDGER

ABLE, INC.
6/2 IR1 700

BARR COMPANY
6/9 IR1 1,900

ECHO DISTRIBUTORS
6/25 IR1 400

HOLT, INC.
6/30 IR1 300

STIX SUPPLY COMPANY
6/14 IR1 1,200

WARD COMPANY
6/18 IR1 1,400

EXHIBIT 6—5

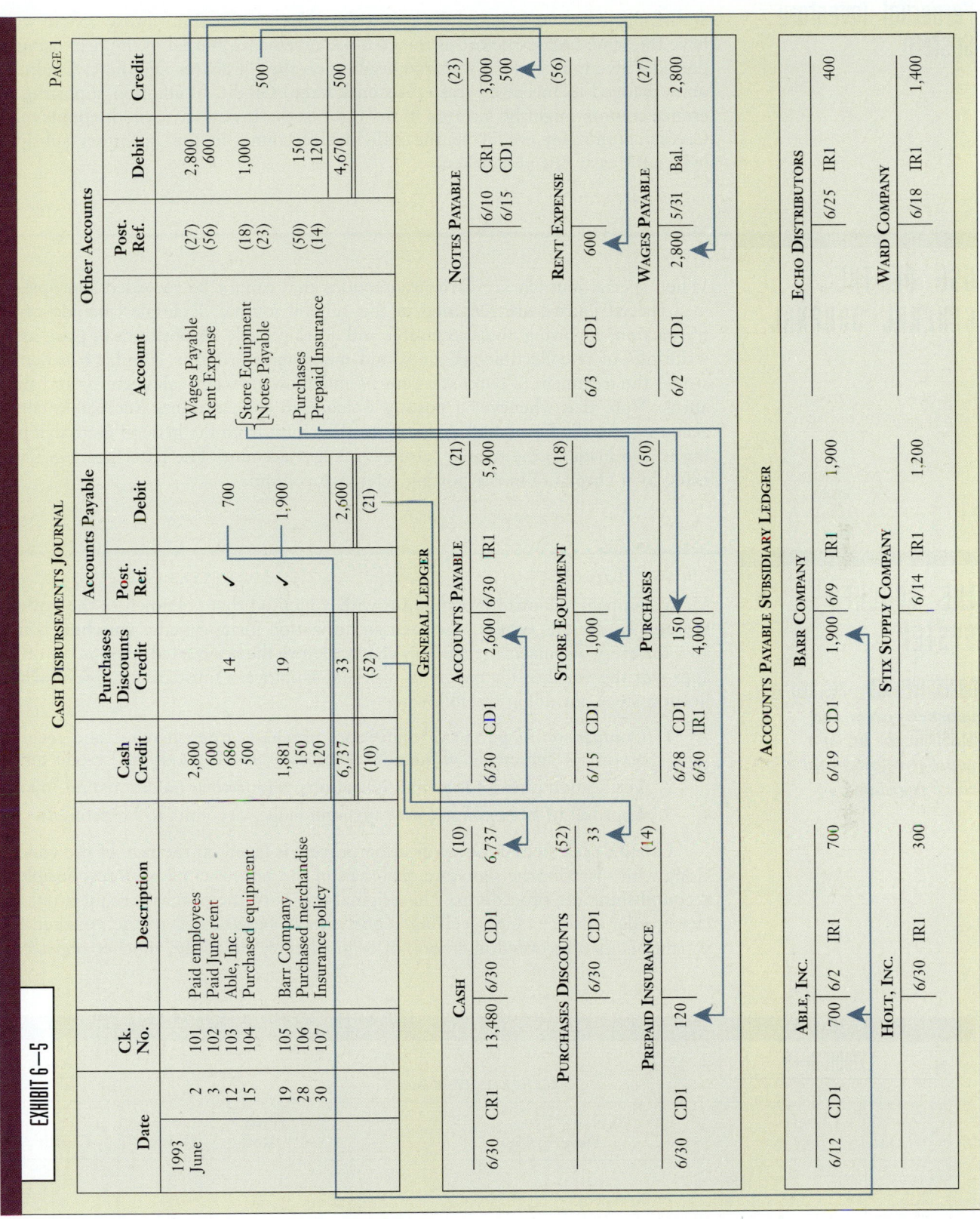

CASH DISBURSEMENTS JOURNAL

Perpetual Inventory System

A cash disbursements journal for a firm using the perpetual inventory system would have the same basic structure as the cash disbursements journal of the firm using the periodic inventory system, with the heading on the Purchases Discounts Credit column changed to Inventory (cash discounts taken) Credit. In addition, a posting reference column might be inserted to the right of the Inventory (cash discounts taken) Credit column for credits to the individual accounts in the Inventory subsidiary ledger for cash discounts taken.

USE OF THE GENERAL JOURNAL

When special journals are used, transactions that cannot be recorded appropriately in a special journal are recorded in the general journal. Examples include certain transactions involving notes receivable and notes payable, dispositions of plant assets, write-offs of uncollectible accounts, and merchandise returns. Exhibit 6-6 demonstrates the treatment of purchases returns and allowances and sales returns and allowances. Note that whenever a posting is made to the Accounts Receivable control account or to the Accounts Payable control account from the general journal, a posting is also made to the related subsidiary ledger account. The latter posting is indicated by a check ($\checkmark$) in the posting reference column.

THE VOUCHER SYSTEM

OBJECTIVE **4** **DESCRIBE** *the voucher system and* **ILLUSTRATE** *the use of a voucher register and a check register.*

Many companies control expenditures with a method that is known as the **voucher system**. Under this system, a written authorization form, called a **voucher**, is initiated for every disbursement the firm makes. Before the designated responsible official approves the voucher for payment, different employees must perform several verification steps, including the following:

1. Comparison of purchase requisition, purchase order, invoice, and receiving report for agreement of quantities, prices, types of goods, and credit terms.
2. Verification of *extensions* (multiplications) and *footings* (additions) on invoice.
3. Approval of *account distribution* (general ledger accounts to be debited).

Usually, each step in the verification process is listed on the face of the voucher, along with space for the signature or initials of the various employees responsible for accomplishing the procedures. The original copies of the purchase requisition, purchase order, invoice, and receiving report should be attached to the voucher. The voucher is then recorded in a book of original entry called the voucher register.

EXHIBIT 6—6

GENERAL JOURNAL   PAGE 1

Date		Description	Post. Ref.	Debit	Credit
1993 July	2	Sales Returns and Allowances	41	100	
		Accounts Receivable—R. Douglas	12/$\checkmark$		100
		R. Douglas returned $100 merchandise for credit.			
	5	Accounts Payable—Ward Company	21/$\checkmark$	70	
		Purchases Returns and Allowances	51		70
		Returned $70 merchandise to Ward Company for credit.			

The Voucher Register

When a voucher system is used, the **voucher register** replaces the invoice register (or purchases journal) we discussed earlier. The voucher register provides columns for all items—merchandise, other assets, and services—for which payment must be made. Because all such items are recorded in the voucher register whether the transaction is for cash or on account, the voucher register also substitutes for part of the cash disbursements journal. Exhibit 6-7 shows one form of a simple voucher register.

Vouchers are entered in the voucher register in sequence. The vouchers should be prenumbered so they can be accounted for and referred to easily. All entries result in a credit to Vouchers Payable, which replaces the Accounts Payable control account for the company. The register has columns for those expense and asset accounts most frequently debited, such as Purchases, Transportation In, Office Supplies, and Delivery Expense. Debits to accounts for which columns are not provided are made in the Other Accounts section. A credit column also included in this section may be used for adjustments to vouchers and for recording purchases returns and allowances.

After vouchers have been entered in the voucher register, they are filed in an unpaid vouchers file in the order of required date of payment. In this way, the company will not miss discounts, and its credit standing will not be impaired. When a voucher is processed, the due date is usually written on the face of the voucher for filing convenience.

On the due date, the voucher is removed from the unpaid file and forwarded to the firm's disbursing officer for final approval of payment. After signing the voucher, the disbursing officer has a check drawn and mailed to the payee. The check number and payment date are recorded on the voucher, which is then returned to the accounting department. To safeguard against irregularities, the voucher should not be handled again by those who prepared it, and the underlying documents should be canceled or perforated by the disbursing officer before the voucher is returned to the accounting department.

After a voucher is paid, the check number and payment date are entered in the appropriate columns of the voucher register. The total unpaid ("open") vouchers at any time may be determined by adding the items in the Vouchers Payable column for which the date paid and check number columns contain no entries. This total should, of course, agree with the total of vouchers in the unpaid file and, at the end of the month, with the amount in the Vouchers Payable account.

After these procedures have been followed, the payment is recorded in a book of original entry called the *check register*. Finally, the vouchers are filed in numerical sequence in a paid vouchers file.

The Check Register

In a voucher system, the **check register** replaces the cash disbursements journal. Because debits to asset, expense, and other accounts are made in the voucher register, only a few columns are required in the check register. We can see in Exhibit 6-8 that these consist of a debit column for vouchers payable and credit columns for purchases discounts and cash in bank. In addition, the check register has columns for the check number, date, and voucher number.

The check register is a company's chronological record of all check payments. Since checks are entered in the check register in numerical sequence, this record provides a convenient reference for payments when either the date or check number is known.

Under the voucher system, discounts may cause the amount of the check to differ from the gross amount of this voucher. For example, the entries for recording and paying the liability to Olson Company for merchandise (voucher No. 121, dated December 1; see Exhibit 6-7) are summarized in general journal form as follows:

Voucher Register			Check Register		
Dec. 1 Purchases	350		Dec. 9 Vouchers Payable	350	
Vouchers Payable		350	Purchases Discounts		7
			Cash in Bank		343

EXHIBIT 6—7		VOUCHER REGISTER				

Voucher No.	Date	Name	Date Paid	Check No.	Vouchers Payable Credit	Purchases Debit
121	12/1	Olson Company	12/9	528	350	350
122	12/3	Tempo Freight	12/5	527	30	
123	12/5	Horder, Inc.	12/15	531	120	
...						
146	12/21	Jones Company	12/31	539	1,200	
147	12/27	Green Company			250	250
148	12/30	Dee Delivery			25	
					18,500	12,200
					(32)	(55)

Because both the gross and the net amounts of the liability are indicated on the voucher, this system should create no difficulty. Some companies, however, anticipate taking all discounts and prepare vouchers at the net amount. When this procedure is followed, only two money columns are needed in the check register—one for a debit to Vouchers Payable and one for a credit to Cash in Bank. If the company should miss a discount, an adjustment must be made in the voucher (or the original voucher must be canceled and a new one prepared). The accountant must also record discounts lost in the general journal. An alternative solution for handling lost discounts when the net price method is used is to provide a Discounts Lost column in the check register.

Recording Purchases Returns and Allowances

Companies usually handle purchases returns and allowances by canceling the original voucher and issuing a new one for the lower amount. Consider the following example.

Voucher No. 147 for $250, prepared for a merchandise purchase from Green Company, is recorded in the voucher register on December 27. Assume that merchandise costing $50 is returned for credit and that a credit memo arrives on Decem-

EXHIBIT 6—8		CHECK REGISTER				

Check No.	Date	Payee	Voucher No.	Vouchers Payable Debit	Purchases Discounts Credit	Cash in Bank Credit
525	12/2	Able Corporation	120	250		250
526	12/4	Smith Company	119	500	10	490
527	12/5	Tempo Freight	122	30		30
528	12/9	Olson Company	121	350	7	343
...						
539	12/31	Jones Company	146	1,200		1,200
				16,700	120	16,580
				(32)	(57)	(11)

Trans-portation in Debit	Office Supplies Debit	Delivery Expense Debit	Other Accounts			
			Account	Post. Ref.	Debit	Credit
30	120		Office Equipment	(15)	1,200	
		25				
850	460	320			4,670	
(56)	(16)	(68)				

ber 30. The original voucher for $250 is canceled and a reference made on it to a new voucher for $200. Furthermore, a note about the new voucher (No. 149) is made in the Date Paid column of the voucher register beside the entry for the original voucher. In recording the new voucher, the bookkeeper credits $200 in the Vouchers Payable column. In the Other Accounts columns, Vouchers Payable is debited for $250 and Purchases Returns and Allowances is credited for $50. The net effect of these recording procedures is a debit of $250 to Purchases, a credit of $200 to Vouchers Payable, and a credit of $50 to Purchases Returns and Allowances (see Exhibit 6-9).

Recording Partial Payments

When installment or partial payments are made on invoices, a separate voucher is prepared for the amount of each check issued. If a single voucher has been prepared for an invoice and the firm later decides to pay in installments, the original voucher is canceled and new vouchers are prepared. The cancelation of the original voucher and the issuance of new vouchers can be recorded in the same way that purchases returns are recorded.

EXHIBIT 6-9   **VOUCHER REGISTER**

Voucher No.	Date	Name	Date Paid	Check No.	Vouchers Payable Credit	Purchases Debit	. . .	Other Accounts		
								Account	Debit	Credit
147	12/27	Green Company	Canceled, see #149		250	250				
. . . 149	12/30	Green Company			200		. . .	Vouchers Payable Purchases Returns and Allowances	250	50

MANUAL AND COMPUTER PROCESSING COMPARED

Manual Processing

We have described the manner in which data-processing functions are accomplished in a manual accounting system. Source documents are prepared and entered manually; classification and sorting are accomplished through columnar arrangements such as journals and ledgers; computations are often done manually; and storage is achieved by manual filing. Storage is in the form of ledger accounts, subsidiary ledgers, and various files. Retrieval and summarization are entirely manual.

Exhibit 6-10 summarizes the main procedures in the processing of accounting data for a manual accounting system. This exhibit does not contain all the detailed steps of the accounting process. It is presented as a basis for comparison with the processing of accounting data in a computer system.

The first step of the manual system involves the processing of source documents. This includes the manual preparation of documents generated by the firm, and the accumulation of documents from external sources. Examples of primary source documents generated by the firm are the sales invoice that is sent to a customer to request payment, the payment check that is sent to a vendor to pay for products or services acquired, and the payroll check that is given to employees to compensate

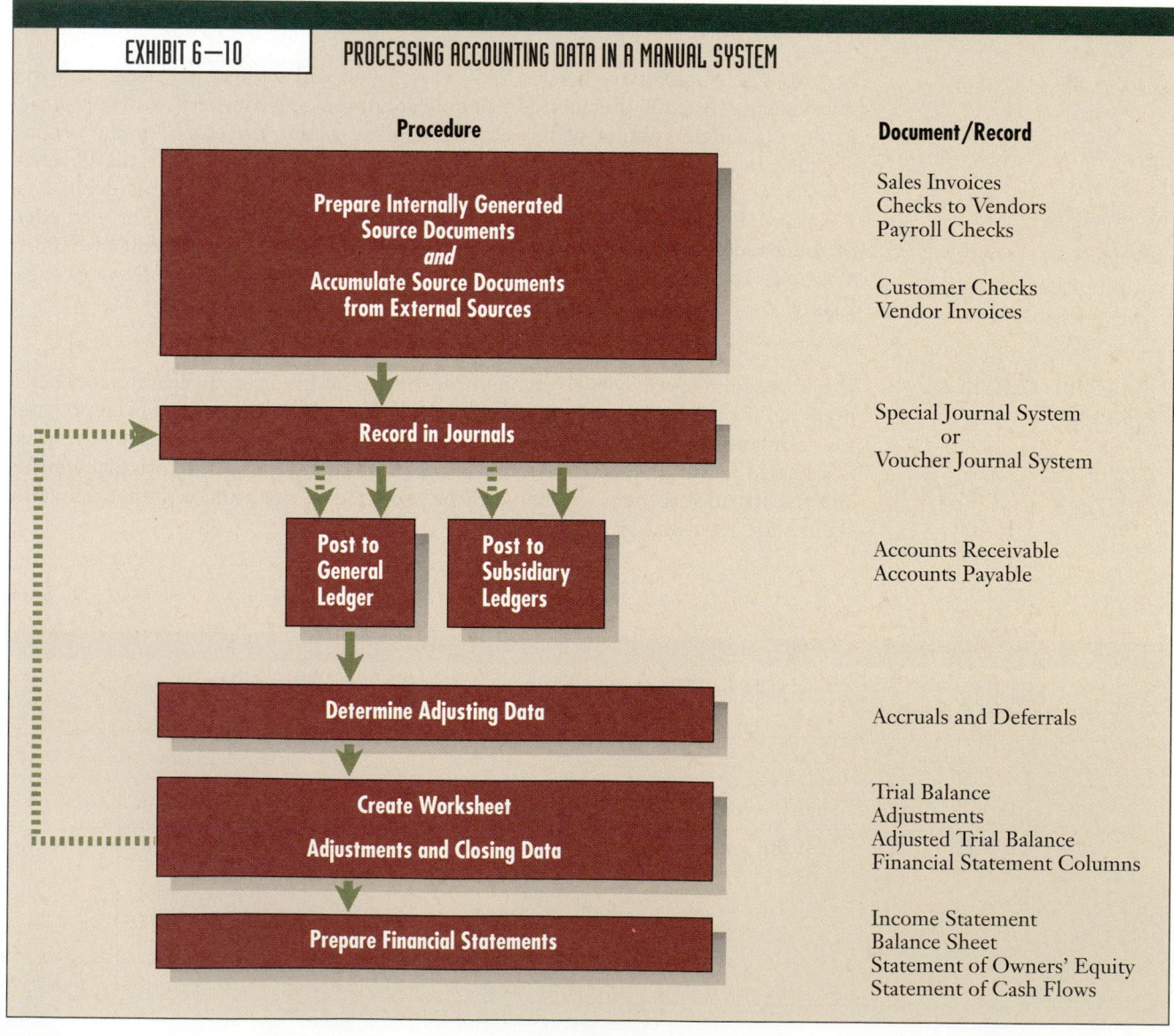

EXHIBIT 6—10   PROCESSING ACCOUNTING DATA IN A MANUAL SYSTEM

Procedure	Document/Record
Prepare Internally Generated Source Documents *and* **Accumulate Source Documents from External Sources**	Sales Invoices / Checks to Vendors / Payroll Checks / Customer Checks / Vendor Invoices
Record in Journals	Special Journal System or Voucher Journal System
Post to General Ledger / **Post to Subsidiary Ledgers**	Accounts Receivable / Accounts Payable
Determine Adjusting Data	Accruals and Deferrals
Create Worksheet Adjustments and Closing Data	Trial Balance / Adjustments / Adjusted Trial Balance / Financial Statement Columns
Prepare Financial Statements	Income Statement / Balance Sheet / Statement of Owners' Equity / Statement of Cash Flows

FAIL-SAFE COMPUTERS

Computers, like humans, err. But if computers are expected to fail once in a while, it's nice to know that there are ways to make those failures invisible to people who depend on machines—for instance, people waiting in line at an airline counter. That's the gist of so-called fault-tolerant computers—machines that can suffer failures while continuing to function. ■ For companies like banks and airlines that rely on computers for service, having a fault-tolerant computer can mean the difference between being open for business and being closed. After the 1989 San Francisco

earthquake a Bay area bank was able to keep its automatic teller network up and running, even though the bank's Tandem fault-tolerant computer had been knocked onto the floor. American Airlines wasn't so lucky. In 1989, when its reservation system crashed for 12 hours, American could have lost up to $50 million of revenue. American didn't then have a fault-tolerant computer; it still doesn't, relying on eight mainframes.

The two leading makers of fault-tolerant machines have grown very rich by marketing catastrophe prevention to companies that require on-line transaction processing to provide services like ATMs, electronic mail, wire transfers and airline reservations. Tandem Computers, of Cupertino, California, invented fault-tolerant computing and then became famous for its folksy management. . . . The challenger in the market is Stratus Computer. . . . It focuses on mini-computers where Tandem leans to mainframes. . . .

Putting redundant hardware into a box is no big deal. The trick, rather, is how to handle a failure that occurs in mid-transaction. If the transaction is a wire transfer, how can you be certain that your customer has been paid, but paid only once? Tandem's Guardian operating system keeps close watch over the workings of two computers linked together. Each computer works on different problems, but the Guardian constantly watches for failures, and keeps a separate record of every calculation. When processor A fails, the Guardian can switch its task over to processor B by referring to the last error-free calculation on the electronic trail. Then both tasks run at once on the remaining processor.

Stratus handles failure without the complicated housekeeping by hard-wiring computer components together. The Stratus system works on one job at a time, but gives the job to two pairs of independent Motorola microprocessors so it can compare results. Let's say the job at hand is adding $2 to $3. Each microprocessor crunches the numbers, and then the paired microprocessors compare results. If the results from one pair of microprocessors are $5 and $6, then those processors are shut down momentarily, while the computer simply uses the result from the other pair.

Both schemes have their relative advantages, but as computer power keeps getting cheaper and more potent, the hard-wired approach is gaining converts. Tandem's new line of Integrity S2 machines eliminates the need to run the bulky Guardian operating system by using a hardware-only approach to fault tolerance.

There is no shortage of customers willing to pay a 30% premium over the price of an ordinary computer to get fault tolerance. Stratus and Tandem have moved into the new world of computers using the Unix operating system on reduced instruction set microprocessors. This enables fault tolerance to move from mainframe customers like banks into more mundane users with network file servers. Unix has also opened up the virtually untapped market of selling computers to switchboard makers. In some companies, having the phone system go dead is even worse than having the computer go down.

SOURCE: David Churbuck, "Fail-Safe," *Forbes*, April 1, 1991, p. 116. Reprinted by permission of *Forbes* Magazine, April 1, 1991. © Forbes Inc. 1991.

them for services rendered. Examples of primary documents received from external sources are customer checks and vendor invoices.

After the source documents are prepared by the firm or received from outsiders, they are analyzed and recorded in journals. Many firms using a manual accounting system use a special journal system or a voucher system. Next, the data recorded in the various journals are manually posted to the general ledger, and, when needed, to a subsidiary ledger, such as accounts receivable or accounts payable.

At the end of an accounting period, we determine the adjustments needed and manually create a worksheet. The worksheet has the familiar pairs of columns—trial balance, adjustments, adjusted trial balance, income statement, and balance sheet. If it is the end of the accounting year, the adjusting and closing data shown on the worksheet can be recorded in the journals and then posted to the ledger (see dashed arrows in Exhibit 6-10). The financial statements are prepared using the information contained in the worksheet.

Computer Processing

OBJECTIVE 5 DISCUSS *the use of computers for processing accounting data.*

Many businesses today use computers to process accounting data so that large volumes of data can be handled quickly. **Computer systems** used to process accounting data follow the logic of manual systems, but the procedures are very different.

Exhibit 6-11 outlines the processing of accounting data using a computer system. Similar to that of the manual system, the first step involves gathering data to be processed through the system. Internally generated data are identified, but primary

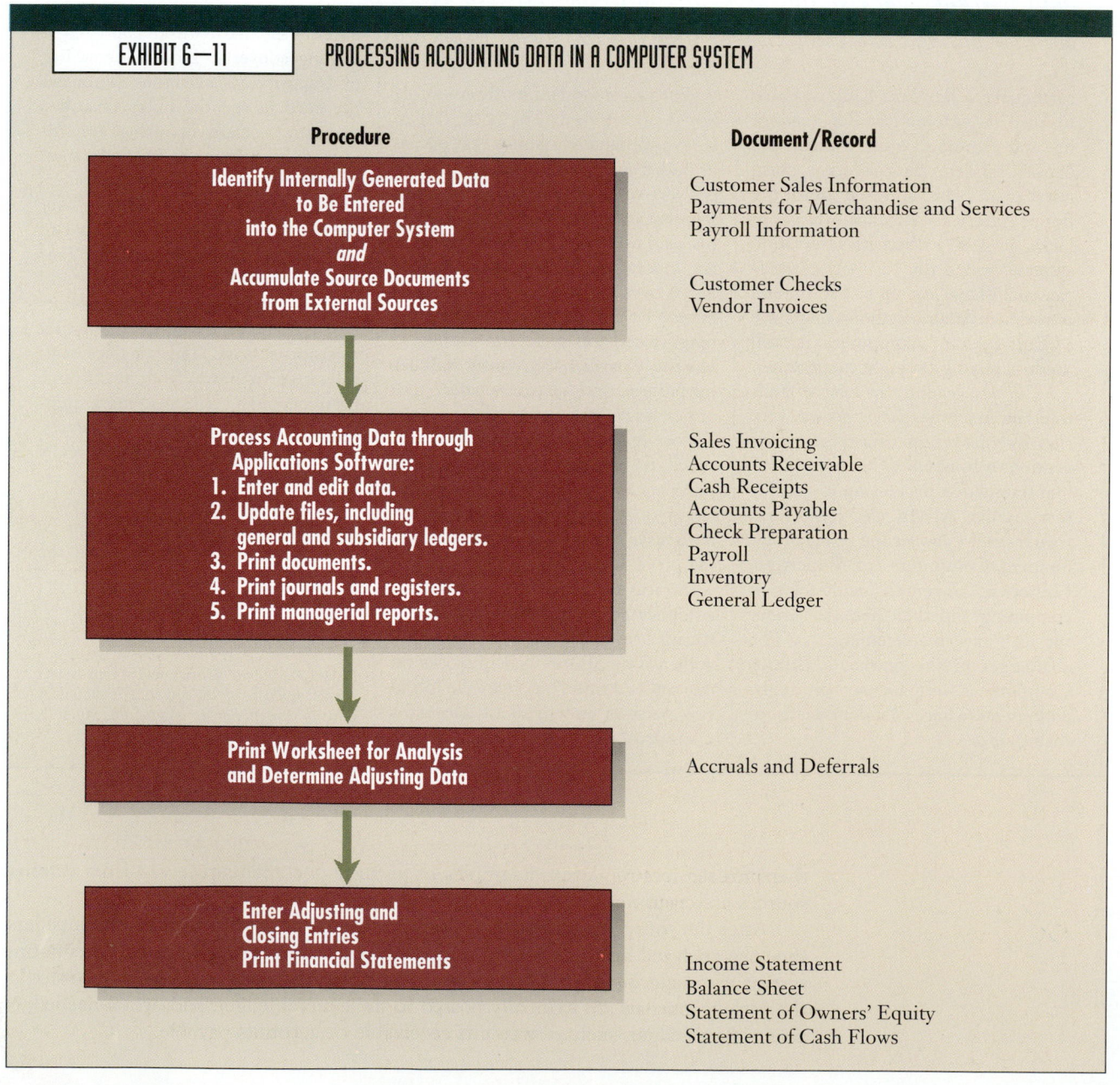

| EXHIBIT 6—11 | PROCESSING ACCOUNTING DATA IN A COMPUTER SYSTEM |

Procedure

Document/Record

Identify Internally Generated Data to Be Entered into the Computer System *and* **Accumulate Source Documents from External Sources**

Customer Sales Information
Payments for Merchandise and Services
Payroll Information

Customer Checks
Vendor Invoices

Process Accounting Data through Applications Software:
1. Enter and edit data.
2. Update files, including general and subsidiary ledgers.
3. Print documents.
4. Print journals and registers.
5. Print managerial reports.

Sales Invoicing
Accounts Receivable
Cash Receipts
Accounts Payable
Check Preparation
Payroll
Inventory
General Ledger

Print Worksheet for Analysis and Determine Adjusting Data

Accruals and Deferrals

Enter Adjusting and Closing Entries Print Financial Statements

Income Statement
Balance Sheet
Statement of Owners' Equity
Statement of Cash Flows

source documents are usually not manually prepared. Instead, they are prepared as part of the computer processing. Both the internally generated data and the data from external source documents are entered in the computer.

Next, the accounting data are processed using **applications programs**. Usually there are separate programs for sales invoicing, accounts receivable, cash receipts, accounts payable, check preparation, payroll, inventory, and general ledger.

Each applications program incorporates five primary functions:

1. Data are entered and processed through edit controls to ensure that the data are valid and reasonable.
2. Files maintained by the computer system on either disk or magnetic tape, including the general ledger and subsidiary ledgers, are updated.
3. Documents such as sales invoices, payment checks to vendors, and employee payroll checks are printed.
4. Journals and registers such as the sales journal or the check register are printed.
5. Various managerial reports are printed.

Many of the steps that are undertaken separately in the manual system are concentrated into this step in the computer system.

After the data have been processed, a worksheet is printed so that a staff member can analyze the trial balance and prepare the necessary adjusting entries. After the worksheet has been completed, the adjusting and closing entries are entered in the computer system and the files updated and made ready for future processing; this is often done only at the end of the accounting year. Finally, the computer prints the financial statements using formats stored in the applications programs.

Alternative Approaches in Computer Processing

Computers can be incorporated into an accounting system in a number of ways. Companies can select among computer service bureaus, timeshare arrangements, and application of their own in-house computers to process accounting data.

A **computer service bureau** is usually an economical approach to processing accounting data. Service bureaus specialize in taking data from clients, entering the data into their computer, processing it, and printing the desired documents, journals, and reports, which are returned to the clients along with the data. Typically this approach results in rather slow processing of accounting data.

Timesharing facilities involve the use of a remote computer that is accessed through a terminal using telephone lines. Several companies can use the same computer with this approach. Each company using the system usually has its own staff members to enter data into the system, initiate the processing, and request printing through instructions entered on the terminal. Processing is significantly faster using this approach, but the cost is usually higher than that of a computer service bureau.

In-house computers are becoming increasingly popular with businesses of all sizes. Large companies, which invariably process accounting data with computers, typically use the main computer that all departments of the company use. Their accounting applications software resides in the computer system along with the applications of the other departments. The main computer can be either a mainframe computer (such as the IBM 3090) or a mid-range computer (such as the IBM AS/400). Data can be entered either in batches (*batch processing*) or as each transaction is encountered (*interactive processing*). Many companies, such as banks and airlines, require that each transaction be entered immediately so that their files are always up to date.

The personal computer, also known as a **microcomputer**, is now being used by many smaller companies to process accounting data. A full range of applications software is available for virtually every type and brand of personal computer. Typically, there are no other users of the microcomputer when accounting data are being processed.

The various computer systems can be quite powerful and complex. The discussion above is intended only as an introduction to the use of computers for processing accounting data. A fuller discussion of manual versus computer systems can be found in *Computer Resource Guide: Principles of Accounting*, Fourth Edition, by John W. Wanlass, CPA, an ancillary to this textbook.

ANALYTICAL APPLICATION

OBJECTIVE **6** DEFINE return on sales *and* EXPLAIN *its use.*

RETURN ON SALES

Many people view the income statement as the most important financial statement, primarily because the income statement determines net income, frequently referred to as *the bottom line*. Most companies share the goal of generating a profit—that is, a positive net income. In addition to looking at the net income amount, managers and investors also look at **return on sales,** or percent profit, in an attempt to understand the rate of profitability. Return on sales is calculated as follows:

$$\text{Return on Sales} = \frac{\text{Net Income}}{\text{Net Sales}}$$

The consolidated income statements for E. I. DU PONT DE NEMOURS AND COMPANY (Du Pont) for three recent years (Year 3 is the most recent) reveal the following information (in millions of dollars):

	Year 3	Year 2	Year 1
Net Sales	$40,047	$35,534	$32,360
Net Income	$ 2,310	$ 2,480	$ 2,190

The return on sales for Year 3 would be calculated as follows:

$$\text{Return on Sales} = \$2,310/\$40,047 = 0.058 \text{ or } 5.8\%$$

This amount means that for each dollar of net sales, 5.8 cents remained after deducting cost of goods sold, operating expenses, and income taxes.

The return on sales for each of the years would be:

	Year 3	Year 2	Year 1
Return on Sales	5.8%	7.0%	6.8%

Although both the net sales and net income of Du Pont have increased from Year 1 to Year 3, the return on sales has decreased from 6.8% to 5.8%, a difference of 1%. If the return on sales for Year 3 had been at the same level as it had been in Year 1, the net income for Year 3 would have been approximately $400 million higher ($40,047,000,000 × 1%)!

There could be a number of reasons for the decrease in return on sales from Year 1 to Year 3. Du Pont operates in a number of industries, including chemicals, fibers, pigments, and polymers. Their operations and customers span the globe. As a result, many different factors affect earnings. During Year 3, some of their worldwide operations may have experienced a recession, unusual price competition, or new competitors. Any of these factors could have caused a reduction in Du Pont's return on sales.

HEY POINTS FOR CHAPTER OBJECTIVES

1 EXPLAIN the characteristics of and interrelationship between control accounts and subsidiary ledgers (pp. 216–218).

- Subsidiary ledgers for accounts receivable and accounts payable enable a firm to keep track of amounts owed from customers and owed to creditors.
- Control accounts reveal totals of amounts owing from customers and to creditors.

2 DESCRIBE the recording process in an accounting system that uses special journals (pp. 218–219).

- Using special journals for recording different classes of transactions permits a division of labor, reduces recording time, and reduces the number of postings to the general ledger.
- The general journal is used for adjusting, closing, and reversing entries, and for transactions that do not "fit" in the special journals.

3 OUTLINE and ILLUSTRATE the use of the special journal system (pp. 219–226).

- The sales journal is used to record credit sales.
- The cash receipts journal is used to record all cash receipts.
- The invoice register is used to record all credit purchases.
- The cash disbursements journal is used to record all cash payments.

4 DESCRIBE the voucher system and ILLUSTRATE the use of a voucher register and a check register (pp. 226–229).

- The voucher system is used to control cash disbursements. All requests for cash disbursements must be verified and approved.
- A voucher register replaces the invoice register, and a check register replaces the cash disbursements journal.

5 DISCUSS the use of computers for processing accounting data (pp. 229–234).

- Data entered in computer processing include data from external source documents as well as the firm's own data, which enable the computer to produce the firm's primary source documents.
- Applications software programs edit entered data, update files and ledgers, print documents, print journals and registers, and print reports.

6 ANALYTICAL APPLICATION: DEFINE *return on sales* and EXPLAIN its use (p. 234).

- Return on sales is determined by dividing net income by net sales.
- The return on sales percentage is compared to percentages for prior years and to industry averages and ranges.

SELF-TEST QUESTIONS FOR REVIEW

(Answers follow the Solution to Demonstration Problem for Review.)

1. If a firm uses special journals, in which journal would the sale of merchandise for cash be recorded?
   - **a.** Sales journal.
   - **b.** Cash receipts journal.
   - **c.** General journal.
   - **d.** Cash disbursements journal.

2. A firm that uses special journals acquires merchandise for $500, giving a $500 note payable. In which journal would the transaction be recorded?
   - **a.** Invoice register.
   - **b.** Sales journal.
   - **c.** Cash disbursements journal.
   - **d.** General journal.

3. A special journal contains columns for Cash, Purchases Discounts, and Accounts Payable. This journal is a(n)
   - **a.** Invoice register.
   - **b.** Sales journal.
   - **c.** Cash receipts journal.
   - **d.** Cash disbursements journal.

4. Which of the following is true of a voucher system?
   - **a.** All major expenditures, including cash transactions for payment of rent and utilities expense, would first be credited to Vouchers Payable before payment is made.
   - **b.** Transactions are first entered in the check register, and later, when payment is made, in the voucher register.

c. The check register replaces the cash receipts journal.

d. The voucher register contains a debit column for Vouchers Payable.

5. When a computer is used to process accounting data with applications software,

a. The general and subsidiary ledgers can be automatically updated, but related documents must always be manually prepared.

b. The general and subsidiary ledgers can be automatically updated and documents automatically prepared, but journals must always be prepared manually.

c. The general and subsidiary ledgers can be automatically updated, documents and journals automatically prepared, but managerial reports must always be prepared manually.

d. The general and subsidiary ledgers can be automatically updated, and documents, journals, and managerial reports can be automatically prepared.

DEMONSTRATION PROBLEM FOR REVIEW

The post-closing trial balance for Harper Distributors at December 31, 1992, is given below:

HARPER DISTRIBUTORS
POST-CLOSING TRIAL BALANCE
DECEMBER 31, 1992

	Debit	Credit
Cash	$ 13,250	
Accounts Receivable	24,500	
Inventory	56,200	
Office Supplies	350	
Office Equipment	14,000	
Accumulated Depreciation		$ 3,600
Accounts Payable		21,700
K. Harper, Capital		83,000
	$108,300	$108,300

At the end of January 1993, the totals of the firm's special journals, before posting, are as follows:

Invoice register:

Accounts Payable	$79,200
Purchases	74,100
Office Supplies	400
Other accounts:	
Office Equipment (Dr.)	4,700

Cash disbursements journal:

Cash	$71,540
Purchases Discounts	960
Accounts Payable	66,400
Other accounts:	
Rent Expense (Dr.)	1,600
Salaries Expense (Dr.)	4,500

Sales journal	$93,500

Cash receipts journal:

Cash	$88,300
Sales Discounts	1,400
Accounts Receivable	79,300
Sales	6,400
Other accounts:	
K. Harper, Capital (Cr.)	4,000

REQUIRED

Prepare an unadjusted trial balance for Harper Distributors at January 31, 1993. *Note:* A convenient method is to use a six-column worksheet, placing the post-closing trial balance in the first two columns after the account description and listing the account titles of the other accounts needed below the post-closing balance totals. The next two columns are used to record the debits and credits from the special journals, and the last two columns are used for the unadjusted trial balance at January 31.

SOLUTION TO DEMONSTRATION PROBLEM

	HARPER DISTRIBUTORS WORKSHEET JANUARY 31, 19X1					
	Post-closing Trial Balance December 31, 1992		January, 1993 Transactions		Trial Balance January 31, 1993	
	Debit	**Credit**	**Debit**	**Credit**	**Debit**	**Credit**
Cash	13,250		(CR) 88,300	(CD) 71,540	30,010	
Accounts Receivable	24,500		(S) 93,500	(CR) 79,300	38,700	
Inventory	56,200				56,200	
Office Supplies	350		(IR) 400		750	
Office Equipment	14,000		(IR) 4,700		18,700	
Accumulated Depreciation		3,600				3,600
Accounts Payable		21,700	(CD) 66,400	(IR) 79,200		34,500
K. Harper, Capital		83,000		(CR) 4,000		87,000
	108,300	108,300				
Sales				(S) 93,500		99,900
				(CR) 6,400		
Sales Discounts			(CR) 1,400		1,400	
Purchases			(IR) 74,100		74,100	
Purchases Discounts				(CD) 960		960
Rent Expense			(CD) 1,600		1,600	
Salaries Expense			(CD) 4,500		4,500	
			334,900	334,900	225,960	225,960

ANSWERS TO SELF-TEST QUESTIONS   **1.** b, p. 220   **2.** d, p. 226   **3.** d, p. 225   **4.** a, p. 227   **5.** d, p. 233

GLOSSARY OF KEY TERMS USED IN THIS CHAPTER

applications programs   Computer software that directs the processing of data, including accounting data, through a computer system (p. 233).

cash disbursements journal   A special journal used to record all transactions involving payment of cash (p. 223).

cash receipts journal   A special journal used to record all transactions involving receipt of cash (p. 220).

check register   A special journal used in place of a cash disbursements journal when the voucher system is used; a record of all checks written in payment of vouchers (p. 227).

computer service bureau   A company that provides various computing services to clients (p. 233).

computer systems   A system that utilizes computers to process data (p. 232).

control account   A general ledger account, the balance of which reflects the aggregate balance of many related subsidiary accounts. Most firms maintain such records for credit customers, creditors, and inventory (p. 217).

in-house computer   A computer operated on site for a single company (p. 233).

invoice register   A special journal, sometimes called a *purchases journal*, in which all acquisitions on account are chronologically recorded (p. 223).

microcomputer   A personal computer used by individuals and business firms (p. 233).

return on sales   Net income divided by net sales (p. 234).

sales journal   A special journal for recording sales transactions (p. 219).

schedule of account balances   A list of the account balances in the accounts receivable or accounts payable subsidiary ledger (p. 222).

special journals   The records of original entry that are designed for recording specific types of transactions such as cash receipts, credit sales, purchases on account, and cash disbursements (p. 218).

subsidiary ledger   A group of accounts, not part of the general ledger, that explain or reflect the detail (such as individual customer balances) underlying the balance in a related control account (such as Accounts Receivable) in the general ledger (p. 217).

timesharing facilities   A remote computer facility that is shared by various users and is accessed through a terminal via a telecommunication link, such as a telephone line (p. 233).

voucher   A written authorization form for a cash disbursement (p. 226).

voucher register   A special journal used in place of the invoice register when the voucher system is used; a record of all vouchers issued (p. 227).

voucher system   A system for controlling expenditures requiring the preparation and approval of individual vouchers for each contemplated expenditure (p. 226).

QUESTIONS

6-1   What is a control account? What is a subsidiary ledger?

6-2   Criticize the following statement: "When a debit entry is made to a control account, one or more credit entries of the same aggregate total must be posted to the related subsidiary ledger."

6-3   Compare the benefits of using special journals with using only a general journal.

6-4   Explain why transactions should be posted to the subsidiary ledgers more frequently than to the general ledger.

6-5   How would you prove that a special journal "balances"?

6-6   Identify the type of transaction that would be entered in the following:
   a. A sales journal.   **d.** A cash receipts journal.
   b. A (single-column) purchases journal.   **e.** A cash disbursements journal.
   c. An invoice register.

6-7   A sale made on account to Stefan Nordquist for $900 was recorded in a single-column sales journal on April 7. On April 9, Nordquist returned $100 worth of merchandise for credit. Where should the seller record the entry for the sales return? What entry would be made and how would it be posted?

6-8   A $760 purchase of merchandise on account from L. Rau was properly recorded in the invoice register, but was posted as $670 to Rau's subsidiary ledger account. How might this error be discovered?

6-9   Indicate how the following errors might be discovered:
   a. The total of the Accounts Payable column of the invoice register was understated by $85.
   b. The total of the single-column sales journal was understated by $45.

6-10   A retail merchandising firm recorded the sale of one of its delivery trucks in the sales journal. Why is this procedure incorrect?

6-11   Bill Yates keeps an invoice register and employs the net method of recording merchandise purchases. Assume that he makes an $800 purchase from Dane Company, terms 2/10, n/30. Which journal columns would he use to record the purchase, and what debits and credits would be made? The periodic inventory system is used.

6-12   Suppose that, in Question 6-11, Yates made his remittance 20 days after the date of purchase. State the amounts involved, and describe how the payment would be recorded in a multicolumn cash disbursements journal.

6-13   What supporting documents are reviewed before a voucher for the purchase of merchandise is approved?

6-14   When a voucher system is used, what special journals are replaced by the voucher register and the check register?

6-15   Name three primary source documents that are manually prepared by a firm with manual processing and that could be automatically printed with computer processing.

6-16   What five primary functions are incorporated into most computer application programs?

6-17   Name and describe three alternative approaches to processing accounting data on computers.

6-18   Define the term *return on sales* and explain its use.

EXERCISES

POSTING SPECIAL JOURNALS
AND GENERAL JOURNAL
— OBJ. 2 —

6-19 Listed below are headings for the columns into which dollar amounts are entered for four special journals and a general journal for a firm that uses the periodic inventory system. (For the sales journal, the accounts to which the single column relates are shown.) For each column heading, show where the amounts in that column should be posted, using the space provided. Use the appropriate letter (or letters) from the following key.

Key
a. Column total posted to general ledger
b. Column detail posted to subsidiary ledger
c. Column detail posted to general ledger

The correct answer for the first item is given.

Sales Journal
1. Accounts Receivable   <u>a, b</u>
2. Sales   _____

Invoice Register
3. Accounts Payable   _____
4. Purchases   _____
5. Office Supplies   _____
6. Store Supplies   _____
7. Other Debits   _____

Cash Receipts Journal
8. Cash   _____
9. Sales Discounts   _____
10. Accounts Receivable   _____
11. Sales   _____
12. Other Accounts—Debit   _____
13. Other Accounts—Credit   _____

Cash Disbursements Journal
14. Cash   _____
15. Purchases Discounts   _____
16. Accounts Payable   _____
17. Other Accounts—Debit   _____
18. Other Accounts—Credit   _____

General Journal
19. Debit column   _____
20. Credit column   _____

**DESIGNING SALES AND
PURCHASES JOURNALS
— OBJ. 2 —**

6-20 Heather Durant is a wholesaler of office supplies, vending equipment, and commercial cleaning supplies. Her income statement shows sales, cost of goods sold, and gross profit amounts for each of her three product lines. She takes periodic inventories separately for each of these three departments and uses the periodic inventory system. Design multicolumn sales and purchases journals to provide the information that Durant wants.

**RECORDING TRANSACTIONS
IN JOURNALS
— OBJ. 3 —**

6-21 Describe how the following transactions would be recorded, indicating the journals used, the columns of each journal involved, and the way in which posting procedures are accomplished. Assume the four special journals illustrated in the chapter are available, together with a general journal, and that the periodic inventory system is used.
a. Purchased equipment for $5,000, giving $3,000 cash and a note payable for $2,000.
b. Returned to a creditor merchandise purchased on account for $600.
c. Owner contributed $1,500 cash and $12,000 of delivery equipment to the business.
d. The business sold the delivery equipment in part (c) for $12,000 cash.
e. Sent check for $100 to a customer, L. Burns, who had overpaid his account by this amount.
f. Paid $80 freight to Ross Express Company on sale to a customer, C. Lundy. Terms were F.O.B. shipping point, and customer was obligated to bear the freight cost.

**ERRORS IN RECORDING AND
POSTING
— OBJ. 3 —**

6-22 In recording transactions and posting from various journals, the bookkeeper made the following errors while using the periodic inventory system. In each case, state how the error might be discovered or whether discovery is unlikely.
a. In the single-column sales journal, this month's total was underfooted (underadded) by $200.
b. The total of the purchases column in the multicolumn invoice (purchases) register, correctly footed as $8,370, was posted to the Purchases account as $8,730.
c. In the single-column sales journal, a sale to T. Rostad was correctly recorded at $790, but posted to T. Roston's account as $970.
d. A $500 remittance from E. Gann was correctly recorded in the cash receipts journal, but the amount was inadvertently posted to M. Gunn's account in the customers' ledger.
e. A $580 payment to a creditor, S. Conway, was recorded in the cash disbursements journal as $480.

**RECORDING IN A VOUCHER
REGISTER
— OBJ. 4 —**

6-23 Describe how the following transactions would be recorded in a voucher register, stating which columns would be used and the dollar amount placed in each column. For items in the Other Accounts columns, state the account name and whether the amount would appear in the Debit column or the Credit column. Refer to the voucher register in Exhibit 6-7 in the chapter. Assume that the periodic inventory system is used and that purchases are recorded at invoice price.

a. Purchased $500 of merchandise from Ambrose Company on account, F.O.B. shipping point.

b. Received a $40 freight bill from Deakin Trucking for the merchandise purchased from Ambrose Company.

c. Purchased $1,000 of office equipment on account from Wiggins Office Supply Company.

d. Paid the $275 utility bill from Platte River Electric Company. This bill had not been previously recorded in the voucher register.

PROBLEMS

RECORDING IN THE SALES, CASH RECEIPTS, AND GENERAL JOURNALS — OBJ. 3 —

Note: In the following problems, the journal forms used should correspond to those illustrated in the chapter.

6-24 Monroe Company makes all sales on terms of 2/10, n/30. Transactions for May 1993, involving sales, related returns and allowances, and cash receipts are shown below. Monroe uses the periodic inventory system.

May 1 Sold merchandise on account to Lund, Inc., $900. Invoice No. 901.

2 Collected $392 from Grady, Inc., on account. A discount was taken by Grady.

3 Sold merchandise for cash to D. Harris, $200.

4 Issued credit memorandum to Lund, Inc., for return of $150 worth of merchandise purchased May 1.

7 Sold merchandise on account to Smart Company, $1,000. Invoice No. 902.

8 Received remittance from Lund, Inc., for the amount owed, less discount.

11 Sold merchandise for cash to B. Nelson, $175.

16 Sold merchandise to G. Little, receiving a note receivable for $800. Invoice No. 903.

21 Collected a non-interest-bearing note receivable from J. Boyd, $700.

22 Sold merchandise on account to Tull Company, $750. Invoice No. 904.

25 Owner S. Monroe contributed cash to the business, $6,000.

28 Smart Company paid for merchandise purchased May 7.

29 Issued credit memorandum to Tull Company for $100 worth of merchandise purchased on May 22.

30 Sold merchandise on account to Young Company, $600. Invoice No. 905.

REQUIRED

a. Record the given transactions in a single-column sales journal, a general journal, and a cash receipts journal.

b. Open the following general ledger accounts and insert balances, when given: Cash (11) $9,000; Notes Receivable (15) $700; Accounts Receivable (16) $400; S. Monroe, Capital (31) $18,000; Sales (41); Sales Returns and Allowances (42); and Sales Discounts (43). Also open a subsidiary ledger with the following customer accounts: Grady, Inc., $400; Lund, Inc.; Smart, Inc.; Tull Company; and Young Company. Only Grady's account had a beginning balance.

c. Post all necessary amounts to the general and subsidiary ledger accounts.

d. Prove that the Accounts Receivable control account agrees with the subsidiary ledger.

RECORDING IN INVOICE REGISTER, CASH DISBURSEMENTS JOURNAL, AND GENERAL JOURNAL — OBJ. 3 —

6-25 Brookfield Company had the following transactions involving purchases, purchases returns and allowances, and cash payments during August 1993. Brookfield records purchases at gross invoice price. The periodic inventory system is used.

Aug. 1 Purchased merchandise on account from Vine Company, $1,000, terms 2/10, n/30, F.O.B. shipping point.

2 Paid Wynn Trucking, Inc., freight bill for August 1 purchase, $80. Check No. 100.

5 Paid Travis, Inc., on account, $400. Check No. 101.

8 Purchased store supplies on account from Gem Supply Company, $450, terms n/30.

Aug. 9 Owner J. Brookfield withdrew $900 cash from the business. Check No. 102.

11 Paid Vine Company for August 1 purchase. Check No. 103.

12 Returned $50 worth of the store supplies purchased from Gem Supply Company on August 8.

15 Purchased store supplies for cash from Rowley Wholesalers, $250. Check No. 104.

17 Purchased merchandise on account from Ford, Inc., $750, terms 2/10, n/30.

18 Paid Gem Supply Company in full of account. Check No. 105.

19 Returned $250 worth of merchandise to Ford, Inc., for credit.

22 Paid Ford, Inc., for August 17 purchase. Check No. 106.

24 Purchased office supplies on account from Travis, Inc., $120, terms n/30.

26 Purchased delivery equipment from Long, Inc., $12,000, giving $5,000 cash and a note payable for $7,000. Check No. 107.

29 Purchased office equipment on account from Travis, Inc., $650, terms n/30.

31 Purchased merchandise on account from Vine Company, $1,600, terms 2/10, n/30, F.O.B. shipping point.

REQUIRED

a. Record these transactions in an invoice register (purchases journal), a cash disbursements journal, and a general journal.

b. Open the following general ledger accounts and insert balances, when given: Cash (11) $15,000; Office Supplies (15) $450; Store Supplies (16) $320; Delivery Equipment (17) $9,000; Office Equipment (18) $6,500; Notes Payable (21); Accounts Payable (22) $400; J. Brookfield, Drawing (32); Purchases (51); Purchases Returns and Allowances (52); Purchases Discounts (53); and Transportation In (54). Also open a subsidiary ledger with the following creditor accounts: Ford, Inc.; Travis, Inc., $400; Gem Supply Company; and Vine Company. Only the Travis account had a beginning balance.

c. Post all necessary amounts to the general and subsidiary ledger accounts.

d. Prove that the Accounts Payable control account agrees with the subsidiary ledger.

RECORDING IN CASH RECEIPTS AND CASH DISBURSEMENTS JOURNALS — OBJ. 3 —

6-26 Ardox Company began business on April 1, 1993. The purchases and sales made on account during April have been recorded in the sales and purchases journals below. Purchases are recorded at gross invoice price; the periodic inventory system is used.

SALES JOURNAL PAGE 1

Date		Customer	Terms	Post. Ref.	Amount
1993 Apr.	5	Lane, Inc.	2/10, n/30		700
	10	Baker Wholesalers	2/10, n/30		600
	18	Martin, Inc.	2/10, n/30		920
	21	Arden Wholesalers	2/10, n/30		650
	28	B. Hayden	2/10, n/30		815

PURCHASES JOURNAL PAGE 1

Date		Creditor	Terms	Post. Ref.	Amount
1993 Apr.	2	Foster Company	2/15, n/30		1,500
	4	Whelan Corporation	n/30		950
	12	Rowe, Inc.	2/10, n/30		500
	22	Foster Company	2/15, n/30		650
	29	Slade, Inc.	1/10, n/30		480

The April transactions to be recorded in the cash receipts and cash disbursements journals are the following:

Apr. 1 Laura Ardox invested $20,000 cash and $15,000 worth of office equipment in the firm, a sole proprietorship. (Use two lines for entry.)

Apr. 2   Paid April rent, $800. Check No. 101.

5   Received rental income for space sublet to Mann Realty, $350.

7   Purchased office supplies for cash, $280. Check No. 102.

14   Paid Foster Company for April 2 purchase. Check No. 103.

15   Cash sales were $1,200.

15   Received $686 from Lane, Inc., on account (April 5 sale).

18   Received $588 from Baker Wholesalers on account (April 10 sale).

21   Paid Rowe, Inc., for April 12 purchase. Check No. 104.

30   Paid office clerk's salary, $2,000. Check No. 105.

30   Cash sales were $1,400.

REQUIRED

a. Record the April transactions in cash receipts and cash disbursements journals.

b. Total and balance the cash receipts and cash disbursements journals.

RECORDING IN SPECIAL JOURNALS, POSTING, AND TAKING A TRIAL BALANCE — OBJ. 3 —

6-27   Lincoln Distributors, which sells on terms of 2/10, n/30, and uses the periodic inventory system, had the following transactions during January 1993.

Jan. 1   Paid January rent, $600. Check No. 200.

2   Paid Sprague, Inc., $686 for merchandise purchased December 28, 1992. A 2% discount was taken. Check No. 201.

3   Issued checks of $450 to Davis Company and $950 to Lenz Suppliers, both creditors. No discount was taken on these amounts. Checks No. 202 and No. 203.

7   Sold merchandise on account to Lyons, Inc., $620. Invoice No. 470.

8   Received checks in payment of accounts as follows: Lyons, Inc., $392; Thomas Company, $900; and White Company, $294. Discounts had been taken by Lyons, Inc., and White Company.

9   Sold merchandise on account to Thomas Company, $780. Invoice No. 471.

10   Issued check for freight to Ruan Freight, Inc., on Thomas Company shipment, $55, terms F.O.B. destination. Check No. 204.

11   Issued credit memorandum to Thomas Company for merchandise returned, $180.

14   Purchased merchandise on account from Davis Company, $900, terms 1/10, n/60.

15   Issued check for freight to Arrow Transport on purchase from Davis Company, $40, terms F.O.B. shipping point. Check No. 205.

15   Paid office salaries, $1,800. Checks No. 206 and No. 207 for $900 each for L. Voss and C. Downs.

16   Received check in payment of Cooper Company account, $650.

18   Received check from Lyons, Inc., in payment of January 7 shipment, $620.

18   Purchased store supplies, $120; equipment, $600; and office supplies, $70, on account from Lenz Suppliers, terms n/30.

21   Paid Davis Company for January 14 purchase, $891. Check No. 208.

22   Paid miscellaneous expenses, $50. Check No. 209.

24   Issued check to R. Lincoln for a personal withdrawal, $500. Check No. 210.

28   Purchased merchandise on account from Sprague, Inc., $1,500, terms 2/15, n/60.

29   Returned $300 worth of merchandise to Sprague, Inc., for credit.

30   Sold merchandise on account to White Company, $1,400. Invoice No. 472.

31   Sold merchandise for cash to R. Nolan, $250.

31   Collected miscellaneous income from Dunn Advertising for use of billboard space, $405.

REQUIRED

a. Open the following general ledger accounts, and enter the indicated January 1, 1993, balances. Number the accounts as shown.

Cash (11)	$ 6,000	Sales Discounts (43)
Accounts Receivable (12)	2,250	Miscellaneous Income (44)
Inventory (14)	30,000	Purchases (51)
Store Supplies (15)	800	Purchases Returns and
Office Supplies (16)	700	Allowances (52)

Equipment (17)	$24,000
Accumulated Depreciation (18)	(6,000)
Accounts Payable (21)	(2,000)
R. Lincoln, Capital (31)	(55,650)
R. Lincoln, Drawing (32)	
Sales (41)	
Sales Returns and Allowances (42)	

Purchases Discounts (53)
Transportation In (54)
Rent Expense (61)
Salaries Expense (62)
Transportation Out (63)
Miscellaneous Expense (64)

b. Open the following accounts in the subsidiary ledgers and enter the January 1, 1993, balances:

Customers		Creditors	
Cooper Company	$ 650	Davis Company	$ 450
Lyons, Inc.	400	Lenz Suppliers	950
Thomas Company	900	Sprague, Inc.	700
White Company	300		$2,100
	$2,250		

c. Record the January transactions in the four special journals (sales, invoice register, cash receipts, and cash disbursements) and in the general journal. Lincoln records purchases at gross invoice price.

d. Using the forms prepared in parts (a) and (b), post all necessary amounts to the general ledger and subsidiary ledgers from the journals. Postings should be made to the subsidiary ledgers throughout the month.

e. Prepare a trial balance of the general ledger.

f. Prepare a schedule of accounts receivable and a schedule of accounts payable to prove control account balances.

POSTING SPECIAL JOURNALS AND PREPARING A TRIAL BALANCE
— OBJ. 3 —

6-28 The post-closing trial balance at December 31, 1992, for Rindt Distributors is given below:

RINDT DISTRIBUTORS
POST-CLOSING TRIAL BALANCE
DECEMBER 31, 1992

	Debit	Credit
Cash	$ 12,200	
Accounts Receivable	22,000	
Inventory	66,300	
Office Supplies	740	
Store Supplies	410	
Office Equipment	13,000	
Accumulated Depreciation		$ 4,800
Accounts Payable		31,200
L. Rindt, Capital		78,650
	$114,650	$114,650

At the end of January, 1993, the totals of the firm's special journals, before posting, are as follows:

Invoice register:		Sales journal	$98,900
Accounts Payable	$87,800		
Purchases	82,300	Cash receipts journal:	
Office Supplies	600	Cash	$95,830
Store Supplies	900	Sales Discounts	1,420
Other accounts:		Accounts Receivable	77,400
Office Equipment (Dr.)	4,000	Sales	11,850
		Other accounts:	
		L. Rindt, Capital (Cr.)	8,000

Cash disbursements journal:	
Cash	$80,240
Purchases Discounts	960
Accounts Payable	75,200
Other accounts:	
Rent Expense (Dr.)	1,900
Advertising Expense (Dr.)	900
Salaries Expense (Dr.)	3,200

REQUIRED

Prepare an unadjusted trial balance for Rindt Distributors at January 31, 1993. *Note:* A convenient method is to use a six-column worksheet, placing the post-closing trial balance in the first two columns after the account descriptions and listing the account titles of the temporary accounts below the post-closing balance totals. The next two columns are used to record the debits and credits from the special journals, while the last two columns are used for the unadjusted trial balance at January 31, 1993. (See the demonstration problem at the end of this chapter.)

RECORDING IN A VOUCHER REGISTER AND CHECK REGISTER
— OBJ. 4 —

6-29   Lakeland, Inc., controls its disbursements through a voucher system. The following transactions occurred during January 1993. The firm records merchandise purchases at gross invoice price and uses the periodic inventory system.

Jan. 1   Issued check No. 701 in payment of voucher No. 600 to Wells Company, $931. The voucher was recorded December 31, 1992, for $950. A 2% discount was taken.

   1   Recorded voucher No. 601 payable to Dane Realty for January rent, $925.

   2   Recorded voucher No. 602 payable to Noble Supply, Inc., for $800 worth of merchandise purchased, terms 2/10, n/30.

   3   Issued check No. 702 in payment of voucher No. 601.

   5   Recorded voucher No. 603 payable to Marshall Sales, Inc., for $600 worth of office supplies, terms 2/10, n/30. (Make voucher for net amount.)

   7   Recorded voucher No. 604 payable to Nash Freight Company for transportation in on merchandise purchased, $70, terms F.O.B. shipping point.

   10   Issued check No. 703 in payment of voucher No. 602, less discount.

   12   Issued check No. 704 in payment of voucher No. 603.

   15   Recorded voucher No. 605 payable to Ladd, Inc., for store equipment, $1,500, terms 2/20, n/60. (Make voucher for net amount.)

   18   Issued check No. 705 in payment of voucher No. 604.

   22   Recorded voucher No. 606 payable to Strang, Inc., for merchandise purchased, $850, terms 2/10, n/30.

   26   Recorded voucher No. 607 payable to Union Gas and Light Company for utilities expense, $256.

   26   Issued check No. 706 in payment of voucher No. 607.

   28   Received credit memo for $150 from Strang, Inc., for merchandise returned to it. Canceled original voucher (No. 606) and issued voucher No. 608.

   28   Issued check No. 707 in payment of voucher No. 605.

   31   Recorded voucher No. 609 payable to Reeves, Inc., for merchandise purchased, $735, terms 2/10, n/30.

REQUIRED

a. Open the following accounts and insert balances when given: Cash in Bank (11), $13,400; Office Supplies (17), $230; Store Equipment (18), $9,500; Vouchers Payable (21), $950; Purchases (51); Purchases Returns and Allowances (52); Purchases Discounts (53); Transportation In (54); Rent Expense (61); and Utilities Expense (62).

b. Record Lakeland's transactions in a voucher register and check register and post amounts to the accounts.

c. List the unpaid vouchers, and compare the total with the balance of the Vouchers Payable account.

RECORDING IN A VOUCHER REGISTER AND CHECK REGISTER
— OBJ. 4 —

6-30   Sloan Company, which employs a voucher system, had the following transactions during July 1993 (the periodic inventory system is used):

July 1   Recorded voucher No. 701 payable to L. Barr for $950 worth of merchandise purchased, terms 2/10, n/30.

   2   Recorded voucher No. 702 payable to Colby Rentals for July rent, $725.

   3   Issued check No. 803 in payment of voucher No. 702.

   9   Recorded voucher No. 703 payable to Daly Express, Inc., for transportation in, $52, terms F.O.B. shipping point.

   10   Issued check No. 804 in payment of voucher No. 701, less discount.

   11   Issued check No. 805 in payment of voucher No. 703.

   15   Recorded voucher No. 704 payable to Mason Company for $800 worth of merchandise, terms 2/10, n/30.

July 20   Received credit memo from Mason Company for $200 worth of the merchandise recorded on voucher No. 704. Canceled voucher No. 704 and issued voucher No. 705.

24   Recorded voucher No. 706 payable to Harris Company for $1,250 worth of merchandise, terms 2/10, n/30.

25   Issued check No. 806 in payment of voucher No. 705, less discount.

REQUIRED

Prepare a voucher register and check register, and record the transactions for Sloan Company. The firm records merchandise purchases at gross invoice price.

ALTERNATE EXERCISES

RECORDING TRANSACTIONS IN JOURNALS — OBJ. 2 —

6-19A   Simpson Suppliers uses the four special journals illustrated in this chapter and a general journal. In which journal(s) would each of the following kinds of transactions be recorded?

a. Owner's cash investment in business.
b. Sale of merchandise for cash.
c. Sale of merchandise on account.
d. Return of merchandise sold on account.
e. Owner's withdrawal of cash.
f. Owner's withdrawal of merchandise for personal use.
g. Collections from customers on account.
h. Purchase of merchandise for cash.
i. Purchase of merchandise on account.
j. Return of merchandise purchased on account.
k. Purchase of office supplies on account.
l. Purchase of equipment for cash and a note payable.

DESIGNING A SALES JOURNAL—PERPETUAL — OBJ. 2 —

6-20A   William Bradford Company is a manufacturer of garden products. The company has two major product lines, commercial and home. William Bradford Company wants to be able to determine gross profit by product line. The company uses perpetual inventory procedures, maintaining separate inventories and Cost of Goods Sold accounts for the two product lines. Design a multicolumn sales journal that would collect the data needed to prepare the desired financial statements.

RECORDING TRANSACTIONS IN JOURNALS—PERPETUAL — OBJ. 3 —

6-21A   Describe how the following transactions would be recorded, indicating the journals used, the columns of each journal involved, and the way in which posting procedures are accomplished. Assume the four special journals discussed in the chapter are available, together with a general journal. The perpetual inventory system is used.

a. Returned to a creditor merchandise purchased on account for $575.
b. Sold merchandise costing $800 for $1,000; terms F.O.B. shipping point.
c. Received payment on account from customer, $350.
d. Paid $100 freight to Acme Express Company on sale to a customer, W. Hardy. Terms were F.O.B. shipping point, and customer was obligated to bear the freight cost.
e. Purchased merchandise, $500; terms 2/10, n/30 (use gross price method).
f. Paid for merchandise purchased in (e) within discount period.

ERRORS IN RECORDING AND POSTING—PERPETUAL — OBJ. 3 —

6-22A   In recording transactions and posting from various journals, the accountant made the following errors. In each case, state how the error might be discovered or whether discovery is unlikely. The company uses the perpetual inventory system.

a. In posting the invoice register, the $1,300 column total for Office Supplies was posted to the Store Supplies account and the $2,200 column total for Store Supplies was posted to the Office Supplies account.
b. In the sales journal, this month's total in the Cost of Goods Sold Debit and Inventory Credit column was overfooted (overadded) by $100.
c. A $620 receipt from a customer, B. Patrick, as payment on account was incorrectly recorded in the cash receipts journal as $520.
d. The total of the Inventory column in the invoice register, correctly footed as $9,670, was posted to the Inventory account as $9,760.
e. A $600 cash sale of goods costing $350 was recorded in the cash receipts journal using $600 as the sale amount and $530 as the cost of goods sold amount.

RECORDING IN A VOUCHER
REGISTER
— OBJ. 4 —

6-23A Describe how the following transactions would be recorded in a voucher register, stating which columns would be used and the dollar amount placed in each column. For items in the Other Accounts columns, state the account name and whether the amount would appear in the Debit column or the Credit column. Refer to the voucher register in Exhibit 6-7 in the chapter. Assume that the periodic inventory system is used and that all vouchers are prepared net of any discount.

a. Purchased $450 of merchandise from Norman Company on account, 2/10, n/30, F.O.B. shipping point.

b. Received a $35 freight bill from Flowers Trucking for the merchandise purchased from Norman Company.

c. Purchased $200 of office supplies on account from Anderson Office Supply Company at 1/10, n/30.

d. Received a $105 invoice from National Express for overnight deliveries to customers; the goods were sent F.O.B. destination.

ALTERNATE PROBLEMS

Note: In the following problems, the journal forms used should correspond to those illustrated in the chapter.

RECORDING IN THE SALES,
CASH RECEIPTS, AND
GENERAL JOURNALS
— OBJ. 3 —

6-24A Oakdale Sales Company makes all sales on terms of 2/10, n/30. Transactions for May 1993 involving sales, related returns and allowances, and cash receipts are shown below. The periodic inventory system is used.

May 1 Collected $588 from J. Winslow on account. A discount was taken.

1 Sold merchandise on account to Carr, Inc., $600. Invoice No. 201.

4 Sold merchandise for cash to L. Chang, $150.

5 Issued credit memorandum to Carr, Inc., for return of $100 worth of merchandise purchased May 1.

8 Sold merchandise on account to Lynch Company, $800. Invoice No. 202.

10 Received remittance from Carr, Inc., for the amount owed, less discount.

12 Sold merchandise for cash to T. Lowe, $250.

15 Sold merchandise to S. Macklin, receiving a note receivable for $900. Invoice No. 203.

18 Collected a non-interest-bearing note receivable from R. Bond, $850.

20 Owner J. Oakdale contributed cash to the business, $3,500.

24 Sold merchandise on account to Pearson Company, $500. Invoice No. 204.

25 Lynch Company paid for merchandise purchased on May 8.

26 Issued credit memorandum to Pearson Company for $40 worth of merchandise purchased on May 24.

30 Sold merchandise on account to M. Stone, Inc., $1,000. Invoice No. 205.

REQUIRED

a. Record the given transactions in a single-column sales journal, a general journal, and a cash receipts journal.

b. Open the following general ledger accounts and insert balances, when given: Cash (11) $7,600; Notes Receivable (15) $850; Accounts Receivable (16) $600; J. Oakdale, Capital (31) $32,500; Sales (41); Sales Returns and Allowances (42); Sales Discounts (43). Also open a subsidiary ledger with the following customer accounts: Carr, Inc.; Lynch Company; Pearson Company; M. Stone, Inc.; and J. Winslow, $600. Only J. Winslow's account had a beginning balance.

c. Post all necessary amounts to the general ledger and subsidiary ledger accounts.

d. Prove that the Accounts Receivable control account agrees with the subsidiary ledger.

RECORDING IN INVOICE
REGISTER, CASH
DISBURSEMENTS JOURNAL,
AND GENERAL JOURNAL
— OBJ. 3 —

6-25A Diamond Distributors had the following transactions involving purchases, purchases returns and allowances, and cash payments during June 1993. Diamond records purchases at gross invoice price and uses the periodic inventory system.

June 1 Paid Beyer, Inc., on account, $520. Check No. 100.

1 Purchased merchandise on account from Gibson Company, $950, terms 2/10, n/30, F.O.B. shipping point.

2 Paid freight bill to Omaha Delivery for June 1 purchase, $50. Check No. 101.

June 5 Purchased store supplies on account from Cole Supply Company, $410, terms n/30.

   7 Owner D. Diamond withdrew cash from the business, $1,000. Check No. 102.

   8 Purchased store supplies for cash from Wynn Wholesalers, $120. Check No. 103.

  10 Paid Gibson Company amount due for June 1 purchase. Check No. 104.

  11 Returned $40 worth of the store supplies purchased from Cole Supply Company on June 5.

  15 Purchased merchandise on account from Ryan, Inc., $800, terms 1/10, n/30.

  16 Paid Cole Supply Company in full of account. Check No. 105.

  18 Returned $100 worth of merchandise to Ryan, Inc., for credit.

  20 Paid Ryan, Inc., for June 15 purchase. Check No. 106.

  21 Purchased office supplies on account from Beyer, Inc., $235, terms n/30.

  25 Purchased delivery equipment from Austin, Inc., $8,000, giving $3,000 cash and a note payable for $5,000. Check No. 107.

  30 Purchased office equipment on account from Beyer, Inc., $525, terms n/30.

  30 Purchased merchandise on account from Gibson Company, $765, terms 2/10, n/30, F.O.B. shipping point.

REQUIRED

a. Record these transactions in an invoice register (purchases journal), a cash disbursements journal, and a general journal.

b. Open the following general ledger accounts and insert balances, when given: Cash (11) $9,500; Office Supplies (15) $340; Store Supplies (16) $460; Delivery Equipment (17) $9,000; Office Equipment (18) $3,600; Notes Payable (21); Accounts Payable (22) $520; D. Diamond, Drawing (32); Purchases (51); Purchases Returns and Allowances (52); Purchases Discounts (53); and Transportation-In (54). Also open a subsidiary ledger with the following creditor accounts: Beyer, Inc., $520; Cole Supply Company; Gibson Company; and Ryan, Inc. Only the Beyer, Inc., account had a beginning balance.

c. Post all necessary amounts to the general ledger and subsidiary ledger accounts.

d. Prove that the Accounts Payable control account agrees with the subsidiary creditors' ledger.

RECORDING IN CASH RECEIPTS AND CASH DISBURSEMENTS JOURNALS — OBJ. 3 —

6-26A Chandler Wholesalers began business on May 1, 1993. The purchases and sales made on account during May have been recorded in the sales and purchases journals below. Purchases are recorded at gross invoice price, and the periodic inventory system is used.

		SALES JOURNAL			PAGE 1
Date		**Customer**	**Terms**	**Post. Ref.**	**Amount**
1993 May	6	Temple, Inc.	2/10, n/30		750
	9	Gray and Company	2/10, n/30		500
	17	R. D. Holmes	2/10, n/30		600
	22	Gray and Company	2/10, n/30		475
	25	F. Sanchez	2/10, n/30		230

		PURCHASES JOURNAL			PAGE 1
Date		**Creditor**	**Terms**	**Post. Ref.**	**Amount**
1993 May	3	L. Gregg	2/10, n/30		850
	5	Carter Corporation	n/30		430
	16	Alpine, Inc.	2/10, n/30		700
	25	L. Gregg	2/10, n/30		375
	30	G. Moss	1/10, n/30		800

The May transactions to be recorded in the cash receipts and cash disbursements journals are the following:

May 1 R. Chandler invested $30,000 cash and $8,000 worth of office equipment in the firm, a sole proprietorship. (Use two lines for entry.)

2 Paid May rent, $1,200. Check No. 101.

3 Received rental income for space sublet to Greenleaf, Inc., $400.

4 Purchased office supplies for cash, $525. Check No. 102.

10 Paid L. Gregg for May 3 purchase. Check No. 103.

15 Cash sales were $695.

16 Received $735 from Temple, Inc., in payment of account.

19 Received $490 from Gray and Company in payment of account.

26 Paid Alpine, Inc., for May 16 purchase. Check No. 104.

31 Paid office clerk's salary, $1,800. Check No. 105.

31 Cash sales were $915.

REQUIRED

a. Record the May transactions in cash receipts and cash disbursements journals.

b. Total and balance the cash receipts and cash disbursements journals.

Recording in Special Journals, Posting, and Taking a Trial Balance — Obj. 3 —

6-27A Sterling Wholesalers, which sells on terms of 2/10, n/30, had the following transactions during January 1993. The periodic inventory system has been used.

Jan. 2 Paid Simon, Inc., for merchandise purchased December 28, $588. Check No. 125. Reed took a 2% discount.

3 Paid January rent, $875. Check No. 126.

5 Issued checks of $320 to Blair Company and $530 to Gabriel Suppliers, both creditors. No discount was taken on these amounts. Checks No. 127 and No. 128.

5 Sold merchandise on account to Judd, Inc., $1,500. Invoice No. 251.

6 Received checks in payment of accounts as follows: Judd, Inc., $294; Murray Company, $630; and Rodgers Distributors, $490. Discounts had been taken by Judd, Inc., and Rodgers Distributors.

7 Sold merchandise on account to Murray Company, $2,300. Invoice No. 252.

8 Issued check for freight to Interstate, Inc., on Murray Company shipment, $70, terms F.O.B. destination. Check No. 129.

9 Issued credit memorandum to Murray Company for merchandise returned, $200.

12 Purchased merchandise on account from Blair Company, $1,400, terms 1/10, n/60.

13 Issued check for freight to Fry Freightways on purchase from Blair Company, $50, terms F.O.B. shipping point. Check No. 130.

14 Received check in payment of Birch Company account, $480.

15 Received check from Judd, Inc., in payment of January 5 shipment, $1,470.

15 Paid office salaries, $2,400. Checks No. 131 and No. 132 for $1,200 each for M. Sims and D. Ricco.

19 Purchased store supplies, $360; equipment, $950; and office supplies, $180, on account from Gabriel Suppliers, terms n/30.

20 Paid Blair Company for January 12 purchase, $1,386. Check No. 133.

21 Paid miscellaneous expense, $60. Check No. 134.

22 Owner J. Sterling made a personal withdrawal, $800. Check No. 135.

26 Purchased merchandise on account from Simon, Inc., $580, terms, 2/15, n/60.

27 Returned $50 worth of merchandise to Simon, Inc., for credit.

28 Sold merchandise on account to Rodgers Distributors, $3,100. Invoice No. 253.

30 Sold merchandise for cash to R. Mills, $120.

30 Collected miscellaneous income from Ward Advertising for use of billboard space, $180.

REQUIRED

a. Open the following general ledger accounts, and enter the indicated January 1, 1993, balances. Number the accounts as shown.

Cash (11)	$12,800	Sales Discounts (43)
Accounts Receivable (12)	1,910	Miscellaneous Income (44)
Inventory (14)	32,500	Purchases (51)
Store Supplies (15)	520	Purchases Returns and
Office Supplies (16)	360	Allowances (52)
Equipment (17)	24,000	Purchases Discounts (53)
Accumulated Depreciation (18)	(4,500)	Transportation In (54)
Accounts Payable (21)	(1,450)	Rent Expense (61)
J. Sterling, Capital (31)	(66,140)	Salaries Expense (62)
J. Sterling, Drawing (32)		Transportation Out (63)
Sales (41)		Miscellaneous Expense (64)
Sales Returns and Allowances (42)		

b. Open the following accounts in the subsidiary ledgers and enter the January 1, 1993, balances:

Customers		**Creditors**	
Birch Company	$ 480	Blair Company	$ 320
Judd, Inc.	300	Gabriel Suppliers	530
Murray Company	630	Simon, Inc.	600
Rodgers Distributors	500		$1,450
	$1,910		

c. Record the January transactions in the four special journals (sales, invoice register, cash receipts, and cash disbursements) and in the general journal. Sterling records purchases at gross invoice price.

d. Using the forms prepared in parts (a) and (b), post all necessary amounts to the general ledger and subsidiary ledgers from the journals. Postings should be made to the subsidiary ledgers throughout the month.

e. Prepare a trial balance of the general ledger.

f. Prepare a schedule of accounts receivable and a schedule of accounts payable to prove control account balances.

POSTING SPECIAL JOURNALS AND PREPARING A TRIAL BALANCE
— **OBJ. 3** —

6-28A The post-closing trial balance at December 31, 1992, for Brown Distributors is given below:

BROWN DISTRIBUTORS
POST-CLOSING TRIAL BALANCE
DECEMBER 31, 1992

	Debit	Credit
Cash	$ 15,300	
Accounts Receivable	25,000	
Inventory	63,400	
Office Supplies	630	
Store Supplies	770	
Office Equipment	14,000	
Accumulated Depreciation		$ 5,200
Accounts Payable		24,100
M. Brown, Capital		89,800
	$119,100	$119,100

At the end of January 1993, the totals of the firm's special journals, before posting, are as follows:

Invoice register:		Sales journal	$108,600
Accounts Payable	$98,130		
Purchases	92,300	Cash receipts journal:	
Office Supplies	450	Cash	$98,390
Store Supplies	580	Sales Discounts	1,510
Other accounts:		Accounts Receivable	89,500
Office Equipment (Dr.)	4,800	Sales	7,400
		Other accounts:	
		M. Brown, Capital (Cr.)	3,000

Cash disbursements journal:

Cash	$89,800
Purchases Discounts	1,300
Accounts Payable	86,200
Other accounts:	
Rent Expense (Dr.)	1,200
Advertising Expense (Dr.)	900
Salaries Expense (Dr.)	2,800

REQUIRED

Prepare an unadjusted trial balance for Brown Distributors at January 31, 1993. *Note:* A convenient method is to use a six-column worksheet, placing the post-closing trial balance in the first two columns after the account descriptions and listing the account titles of the temporary accounts below the post-closing balance totals. The next two columns are used to record the debits and credits from the special journals, and the last two columns are used for the unadjusted trial balance at January 31. (See the demonstration problem at the end of this chapter.)

RECORDING IN A VOUCHER REGISTER AND CHECK REGISTER
— OBJ. 4 —

6-29A   Meridian, Inc., controls its disbursements through a voucher system. The following transactions occurred during January 1993. The firm records merchandise purchases at gross invoice price and uses the periodic inventory system.

Jan. 1   Issued check No. 505 in payment of voucher No. 400 to Ellis Company, $1,372. The voucher was recorded December 31, 1992, for $1,400. A 2% discount was taken.

1   Recorded voucher No. 401 payable to Moon Realty for January rent, $1,350.

2   Recorded voucher No. 402 payable to Spartan Service Corporation for $900 worth of merchandise purchased, terms 2/10, n/30.

2   Issued check No. 506 in payment of voucher No. 401.

5   Recorded voucher No. 403 payable to Allied Sales, Inc., for $400 worth of office supplies.

7   Recorded voucher No. 404 payable to Hill Freight Lines, Inc., for freight in on merchandise purchased, $62, terms F.O.B. shipping point.

10   Issued check No. 507 in payment of voucher No. 402, less discount.

12   Issued check No. 508 in payment of voucher No. 403.

14   Recorded voucher No. 405 payable to Verona Equipment Sales, Inc., for equipment, $3,000, terms 2/15, n/60. (Make voucher for net amount.)

18   Issued check No. 509 in payment of voucher No. 404.

21   Recorded voucher No. 406 payable to Diaz, Inc., for merchandise purchased, $700, terms 2/10, n/30.

25   Recorded voucher No. 407 payable to Capitol Gas and Light Company for utilities expense, $245.

26   Issued check No. 510 in payment of voucher No. 407.

28   Received credit memo for $100 from Diaz, Inc., for merchandise returned to it. Canceled original voucher (No. 406) and issued voucher No. 408.

28   Issued check No. 511 in payment of voucher No. 405.

31   Recorded voucher No. 409 payable to Fisher, Inc., for merchandise, $750, terms 2/10, n/30.

REQUIRED

a.   Open the following accounts and insert balances when given: Cash in Bank (11), $16,300; Office Supplies (17), $430; Equipment (18), $8,600; Vouchers Payable (21), $1,400; Purchases (51); Purchases Returns and Allowances (52); Purchases Discounts (53); Transportation In (54); Rent Expense (61); and Utilities Expense (62).

b.   Record Meridian's transactions in a voucher register and check register and post amounts to the accounts.

c.   List the unpaid vouchers and compare the total with the balance of the Vouchers Payable account.

RECORDING IN A VOUCHER REGISTER AND CHECK REGISTER
— OBJ. 4 —

6-30A   Gilroy Company, which uses a voucher system, had the following transactions during June 1993 (the periodic inventory system is used):

June 1   Recorded voucher No. 601 payable to R. Long for $1,100 worth of merchandise purchased, terms 2/10, n/30.

2   Recorded voucher No. 602 payable to Anchor Rentals for June rent, $975.

June 3 Issued check No. 903 in payment of voucher No. 602.

    9 Recorded voucher No. 603 payable to Drew Freightways for transportation in, $67, terms F.O.B. shipping point.

  10 Issued check No. 904 in payment of voucher 601, less discount.

  11 Issued check No. 905 in payment of voucher No. 603.

  15 Recorded voucher No. 604 payable to Field Company for $850 worth of merchandise, terms 2/10, n/30.

  20 Received credit memo from Field Company for $150 worth of the merchandise recorded on voucher No. 604. Canceled voucher No. 604 and issued voucher No. 605.

  24 Recorded voucher No. 606 payable to Downey Company for $1,480 worth of merchandise, terms 2/10, n/30.

  25 Issued check No. 906 in payment of voucher No. 605, less discount.

REQUIRED

Prepare a voucher register and check register, and record the transactions for Gilroy Company. The firm records merchandise purchases at gross invoice price.

CASES

Business Decision Case

Caltronec, Inc., sells a variety of office products and supplies, including word processing equipment, desks, chairs, filing systems, and various office supplies. Most sales are on account; however, small equipment items and supplies are also sold over the counter for cash.

Manager R. Sullivan asks you to provide special journals for the firm's accounting system. After discussing the matter with Sullivan, you decide to design journals for three departments: Equipment, Furniture, and Supplies. Sullivan wants the income statement to show sales, cost of goods sold, and gross profit for each of the three departments. Merchandise inventory for the three departments will be taken separately.

Practically all the firm's purchases are merchandise for resale. Most cash disbursements are payments on account to suppliers, freight on purchases (most purchases are F.O.B. shipping point), and for advertising expense. Spot advertising in local newspapers and on television is paid when bills are received; no accounts payable are kept for these expenses. Employees are paid monthly.

REQUIRED

List the column headings (from left to right) that you would provide in the (a) sales journal, (b) invoice register, (c) cash receipts journal, and (d) cash disbursements journal for the three departments of Caltronec, Inc. Assume that Caltronec uses the periodic inventory system.

Analytical Application Case

The consolidated income statements for W. R. GRACE AND COMPANY for three recent years (Year 3 is the most recent) reveal the following information (in millions of dollars):

	Year 3	Year 2	Year 1
Net Sales	$6,114.6	$5,786.1	$4,515.4
Cost of Goods Sold	4,176.0	3,956.3	3,091.9
Income Taxes	128.8	124.6	105.8
Net Income	253.2	233.6	173.1

REQUIRED

a. Calculate the return on sales for each of the three years.

b. What trend is evident in the three years?

Ethics Case

Donald Keane is an employee in the central purchasing department of Home Centers, a large retail hardware chain. His job includes recommending suppliers to the purchasing supervisor. This recommendation is only one of the many factors the supervisor considers when making the final decision for a supplier.

Donald is offered an all-expenses-paid weekend at a resort by Tools & Stuff, a new supplier that wants to increase the amount of business it does with Home Centers. Tools & Stuff owns a condo at this resort and frequently offers customers all-expenses-paid weekends. Donald Keane does not know what Home Centers' policy, if any, is on the acceptance of gratuities.

REQUIRED

What are the ethical considerations facing Donald Keane? What are his alternatives?

What factors should be considered in evaluating the financial stability of a company?

A number of factors contribute to the financial stability of a company, including a sound internal control structure and sufficient cash available to pay outstanding debts on a timely basis. ■ In recent years, a number of banks and savings and loans have been forced to close. ■ These closures often resulted from poor internal control and inadequate cash management. ■ In this chapter we discuss procedures that are essential to proper cash management and good internal control.

7

INTERNAL CONTROL, CASH, AND SHORT-TERM INVESTMENTS

CHAPTER OBJECTIVES

1 DESCRIBE the internal control features of an accounting system (pp. 254–257).

2 IDENTIFY key controls over cash and **EXPLAIN** the procedures for preparing a bank reconciliation (pp. 257–265).

3 DISCUSS the accounting for a petty cash fund (pp. 265–267).

4 OUTLINE the accounting for short-term investments in stocks and bonds (pp. 267–272).

5 ANALYTICAL APPLICATION: DEFINE the *quick ratio* and **EXPLAIN** its use (p. 272).

The use of money is all the advantage there is in having money.

BENJAMIN FRANKLIN

anagement must plan, direct, and control the operations of a firm. The elements of control are important to all aspects of a firm's operations, but they are critical in establishing methods of handling and accounting for monetary assets. In this chapter, we consider the features that are desirable in an accounting control system and examine procedures that are especially important in accounting for and controlling cash transactions. The latter procedures include bank reconciliations and petty cash procedures.[1] We conclude the chapter by examining accounting for short-term investments in stocks and bonds.

INTERNAL CONTROL STRUCTURE

OBJECTIVE ① DESCRIBE *the internal control features of an accounting system.*

A firm's **internal control structure** is defined as

> the policies and procedures established to provide reasonable assurance that specific entity objectives will be achieved.[2]

Establishing an effective internal control structure is an important management responsibility. First, a firm's management is expected to provide a good *control environment*—that is, the firm's organizational structure, the functioning of the board of directors and its committees, personnel policies, and various other policies for monitoring performance. These should all be designed to foster good internal control. Second, management should provide an effective *accounting system* that will furnish complete, accurate, and timely financial data. Finally, *control procedures* should be integrated into the components of the control environment and accounting system.

The control procedures of particular concern to the accountant are those that help (1) produce accurate and reliable financial data about the firm and (2) safeguard the firm's assets. We use the term **accounting controls** to refer to the policies and procedures designed to promote achievement of these two objectives.

FEATURES OF AN ACCOUNTING CONTROL SYSTEM

Good internal accounting control includes the following requirements:

1. Competent personnel.
2. Assignment of responsibility.
3. Division of work.
4. Separation of accountability from custodianship.
5. Adequate records and equipment.
6. Rotation of personnel.
7. Internal auditing.
8. Physical protection of assets.

Accounting controls may interrelate with controls in other areas. For example, hiring procedures used to identify competent accounting personnel may also be used to hire capable employees for other areas in the firm.

Competent Personnel

Employees should be carefully selected and their talents used intelligently in the operation of the accounting information system. Each person should thoroughly understand his or her function and its relationship to other functions in the system.

---

[1] The voucher system discussed in a prior chapter is a system of controls over cash disbursements.

[2] *Statement on Auditing Standards No. 55*, "Consideration of the Internal Control Structure in a Financial Statement Audit" (New York: American Institute of Certified Public Accountants, 1988), p. 4.

Above all, an employee must realize the importance of following the procedures prescribed by management and should be in sympathy with the system. A well-formulated system of internal control can be destroyed by employees' lack of confidence or cooperation.

Employee cooperation is enhanced by paying employees a fair salary or wage. Poorly paid employees may feel justified in stealing from their employer or being indifferent toward their work.

Assignment of Responsibility

The plan of organization should fix responsibility for functions and confer the authority necessary to perform them. Responsibility and authority for a given function should not be shared, because this may result in duplication of effort and in jobs going undone if individuals think that another is performing the assignment. When one person is responsible for a function, praise or blame can be clearly assigned for specific results. Thus, if a plant supervisor is responsible for staying within budgeted amounts for labor costs, he or she should be given the authority to assign personnel to jobs, control overtime, and so on.

Division of Work

Division of work is one of the most important facets of a good system of controls. The duties of individuals should be defined so that no single individual has complete control over a sequence of related transactions. For example, the person who authorizes a purchase order should not also confirm receipt of the merchandise or authorize payment for the merchandise. Likewise, the person handling bank deposits and the person keeping the cash books should not receive bank statements or make bank reconciliations. Improper division of work, or segregation of duties, increases the possibility of fraud, carelessness, and unreliable record keeping. With a proper division of duties, the work of one person or group can act as a check on work performed by another person or group. For example, when purchase orders and receiving reports are processed by different individuals, a third person can compare the order, receiving report, and vendor's invoice before approving payment. This practice reduces the likelihood of errors from carelessness as well as the possibility of fictitious purchases or fraudulent conversion of goods.

Work division is valuable not only in preventing errors and fraud, but also in providing the advantages of specialization—better performance and easier employee training.

Separation of Accountability from Custodianship

Employees who are responsible for keeping records of a firm's assets should not have custody of the assets or access to them. Separating the custody of assets from the maintenance of records is another safeguard against fraud. An employee should not be able to convert assets for personal use and cover up the conversion by falsifying the records. Periodically, an independent comparison should be made of the recorded amounts with the actual assets to determine whether there is agreement between the two amounts.

When custody of assets is adequately separated from record keeping, collusion among employees is usually necessary to perpetrate fraud. If collusion does exist, embezzlement can go undetected for a long time.

The separation feature, which should be incorporated in the system to protect all assets, is especially important in handling cash and negotiable items. For example, cash remittances from customers should be listed by personnel who have no access to accounting records. These lists can then be forwarded to the accounts receivable department for posting to customer accounts in the subsidiary ledger, while the cash receipts themselves are sent to the cashier for deposit. A duplicate list of cash receipts should also be given to the person who makes the cash receipts journal entries. This method provides several cross-checks—bank deposits must agree with the recorded cash receipts, and the Accounts Receivable control account must agree with subsidiary ledger totals. Finally, the bank should send its monthly statement to someone other than the cashier or those keeping cash-related records, so that an independent

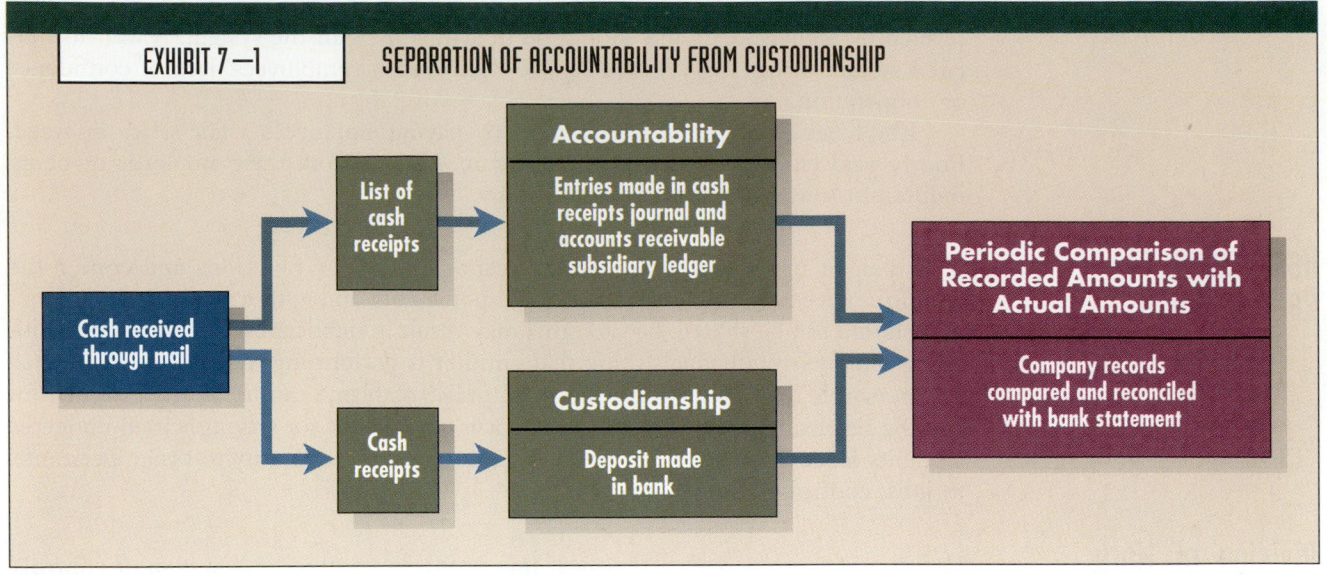

EXHIBIT 7—1   SEPARATION OF ACCOUNTABILITY FROM CUSTODIANSHIP

comparison of the bank statement and the company's records can be made. Exhibit 7-1 illustrates this example of separating accountability from custodianship.

Adequate Records and Equipment

Adequate records are important not only in accounting for a company's resources but also in providing management with accurate and reliable information. One of the most important features in a satisfactory record-keeping system is a comprehensive chart of accounts that classifies information in a manner best suited to management's needs. Control accounts and subsidiary records should be used when appropriate, so that work can be subdivided, and cross-checks may be made when the two types of accounts are reconciled. Control and subsidiary accounts can be used for such areas as accounts and notes receivable, accounts and notes payable, plant assets, and the major expense classifications of selling expense and administrative expense.

The forms used with the accounting records should promote accuracy and efficiency. If possible, individual forms should be prenumbered so that the sequence of forms used can be accounted for. Moreover, prenumbering helps a firm trace its transactions and reduces the possibility of failing to record a transaction. For example, suppose a firm issues prenumbered sales slips for each sale. A check of the number sequence would disclose any diversion of sales proceeds accomplished by destruction of the sales slip. Likewise, accounting for the sequence of prenumbered checks can detect whether unrecorded checks have been issued for unauthorized purchases.

Various types of equipment can be used with the record-keeping system to provide helpful controls. The cash registers used in retail operations, for example, have several important control features—a bell or other sound signals that the register has been opened, and a receipt allows the customer to check the transaction. Most cash registers have a locked-in tape that accumulates and classifies transactions that have been registered. A responsible employee controlling the key can reconcile amounts shown on the tape with daily cash counts. Some registers contain multiple cash drawers so that several clerks can use the same cash register and each be accountable for his or her own cash drawer. Check protectors, which perforate checks with indelible ink, are another example of a protective device for cash transactions. Checks written with such a machine cannot be altered without the change being obvious.

An electronic cash register tied in to a computer may improve control over the extension of credit to a customer using a credit card. Quick point-of-sale credit verification is possible. In a few seconds, the computer can ensure that the customer has not exceeded his or her credit limit and has been prompt with payments. The computer can also determine if the card has been reported lost or stolen. The computer either authorizes or disapproves the use of the credit card, depending on the status of the customer's account.

Rotation of Personnel

Some companies rotate the positions of certain operating personnel. For example, accounts receivable clerks, each responsible for a certain alphabetical segment of the accounts, might be rotated periodically to other segments. This procedure may disclose errors and irregularities caused by carelessness or dishonesty. Requiring employees to take vacations may also reveal lapses, carelessness, and dishonesty on the part of employees. Misappropriations of funds—especially in financial institutions such as banks—have often been discovered during an employee's absence, when the perpetrator could no longer control or manipulate records.

Internal Auditing

An important feature of the internal control structure of large companies is the internal audit function. The internal auditing department independently appraises the firm's financial and operational activities. In addition to reviewing activities for errors and irregularities, the internal audit staff determines whether prescribed policies and procedures are being followed and attempts to uncover wasteful and inefficient situations. Internal auditing is a *staff*, or advisory, function that consists of reviewing activities and making written recommendations to management. To be effective, the internal audit staff must be independent of operating (line) functions and should report to a high-ranking executive or to the firm's board of directors.

Physical Protection of Assets

Frequently, management initiates a number of physical controls to protect company property. Although some of these controls may not be closely related to the accounting system, they are almost invariably discussed in the context of internal control.

Only minimal amounts of cash or negotiable assets should be kept on the company premises, and these should be stored in a vault. A firm should keep its inventory in a secure area and maintain strict controls over issuances and physical counts of inventory. Security personnel are often engaged to protect inventories and other physical property. A company may employ outside protection services to safeguard against burglary and arson and might post gatekeepers at plant entrances and exits to observe employees and others entering and leaving the plant.

A business must be adequately insured against losses from fire, outside theft, and similar events. In addition to insuring its physical assets, employees having access to cash, securities, and other easily diverted assets should be bonded. For a fee, a bonding company guarantees to pay for any loss from theft or embezzlement by the bonded person, up to some specified maximum amount. The bonding company investigates employees to be bonded, and anyone with a record of questionable integrity is not likely to qualify.

CASH AND CASH CONTROLS

In accounting, the term **cash** means paper money, coins, checks, and money orders—all items that are acceptable for deposit in a bank—as well as money already on deposit with a bank. IOUs, postdated checks (checks dated in the future), and uncollected customers' checks returned by the bank stamped NSF (not sufficient funds) are not considered cash but are normally classified as receivables. Notes sent to the bank for collection remain classified as notes receivable until notification of collection is received from the bank.

Cash in the Balance Sheet

Various ledger accounts are used to record cash transactions; some common examples are Cash on Hand, Petty Cash, and Cash in Bank. The Cash on Hand account reflects cash receipts not yet deposited in the bank, and Petty Cash represents a fund

---

EXTERNAL EXPROPRIATIONS

A business is vulnerable to fraud not only by its employees, but also by its customers and suppliers. The following hypothetical examples show how a company can unwittingly fall prey to outside purloiners. ■ Red flag: Open-ended contracts with suppliers. *The nature of contractual or other agreements for the supply of goods or services to a business may provide opportunities for fraud. A case in point: Central Fuel won a three-year contract to provide oil to the local school board. The contract was based on a fixed price per gallon for fuel oil delivered, but did not require* an estimate of, nor place a limit on, the quantity of oil to be provided.

The meter in the truck that delivered the fuel was fixed so that it continued to run, even if the fuel hose had been shut off. Thus, Central Fuel was able to inflate the quantity of fuel alleged to have been delivered.

When the owner of Central Fuel was finally brought to trial, the prosecution revealed the results of an engineering study that showed that the amount of fuel that had been invoiced and allegedly delivered was considerably more than would have been required to maintain the heating system during the winter with all windows in the building wide open.

An open-ended contract also enabled Super Disposal Services, which was in the business of waste disposal, to defraud numerous customers. While SDS charged a flat fee for removal of waste bins, it also charged its customers for the cost, by weight, of the waste it disposed at local dump sites for them. Because none of the customers bothered to determine the weight of the waste removed by SDS, the company was able to defraud them by charging for inflated waste amounts. The heaviest weighbill on a given day was photocopied, and distributed to all customers, regardless of the amount of waste that each of them had had carted away.

Even when open-ended contracts are used, a business can forestall fraud by anticipating the amount of goods and services it is likely to require and comparing this with the charges. Any discrepancies will then be obvious, and will warrant immediate investigation.

■ *Red flag: An unusual increase in purchases by a customer during a brief period.* It's easy for customers to take unfair advantage of a longstanding business relationship; in fact, this often happens before a planned bankruptcy.

For example, Brittany Antiques, a company that had experienced a change in ownership and had established relationships with suppliers, was able to increase the volume of its purchases and delay payment for goods received before a planned bankruptcy. As a result it was able to acquire and dispose of large amounts of inventory without making payment—and to leave its suppliers empty-handed when the business went bankrupt.

To prevent a business from falling victim to a planned bankruptcy, it's essential to monitor customer orders on an ongoing basis and check into any sudden or unusual increases.

There are no simple, foolproof solutions to the problem of fraud. But you can provide optimum protection for your business by being alert to any red flags that exist.

SOURCE: Robert J. Lindquist and James E. Baskerville, "To Catch a Thief," *World*, July–August 1985, p. 35. This article appeared in the July–August issue of *World* magazine, which is published by KPMG Peat Marwick.

OBJECTIVE ② IDENTIFY *key controls over cash and* **EXPLAIN** *the procedures for preparing a bank reconciliation.*

used for small disbursements. Cash in Bank usually refers to demand deposits in a checking account.

When a business firm has several checking accounts, a separate ledger account should be maintained for each account rather than one overall Cash in Bank account. Although a balance sheet prepared for management may show all individual cash accounts, a balance sheet prepared for outsiders normally shows the combined balances of all cash accounts under a single heading, Cash. Management is interested in the detail because it must establish policies on balances to be maintained in various bank accounts and on hand. Most outsiders, on the other hand, are interested only in the total cash balance and its relationship to other items on the financial statements.

Cash amounts subject to use or withdrawal without restriction are current assets and are normally shown first in the balance sheet listing of assets. Sometimes the cash account may include an amount, called a **compensating balance,** that is not readily available for use. A compensating balance is a minimum amount that a financial institution requires a firm to maintain in its account as part of a borrowing arrangement. Compensating balances related to short-term borrowings are current assets but, if significant, should be reported separately from cash available for use without restriction. Compensating balances related to long-term borrowings should be classified among a firm's long-term assets.

Certain short-term, highly liquid investments may be combined with cash and presented in the balance sheet as one amount called *cash and cash equivalents*. Examples of such investments are Treasury bills and money market funds. These items are combined in one amount to tie the balance sheet to the statement of cash flows. The statement of cash flows explains the changes during a period in a firm's cash and cash equivalents.

Cash Control Procedures

A firm must control the handling and recording of cash because it is so susceptible to misappropriation. An adequate system of internal control over cash would include the following features:

1. Cash is handled separately from the recording of cash transactions.
2. The work and responsibilities of cash handling and recording are divided in such a way that errors are readily disclosed and the possibility of irregularities is reduced.
3. All cash receipts are deposited intact in the bank each day.
4. All major disbursements are made by check, and an imprest (fixed amount) petty cash fund is used for small cash disbursements.

In our earlier discussion of internal control, we described and explained the desirability of the first two features. By observing the last two—depositing all receipts intact daily at the bank and making disbursements by check—a company establishes a double record of cash transactions. One record is generated by the firm's record-keeping procedures, and the other is furnished by the bank. Comparing the two records and accounting for any differences provides control. This important procedure is called *reconciling the bank statement with the book record of cash transactions* or, simply, making a *bank reconciliation* (discussed later).

The Bank Account

When a firm opens a checking account at a bank, the members of the firm who are authorized to draw checks sign signature cards that the bank files. Occasionally, bank employees may check the signatures on these cards against the signatures on the checks.

The bank submits monthly statements to the depositor showing the beginning cash balance, all additions and deductions for the month, and the ending cash balance. In addition, the bank usually returns the paid (or canceled) checks for the month, together with "advice" slips indicating other charges and credits made to the account. The bank may also send copies of such advice slips individually during the month to the depositor.

To reduce handling costs, some banks do not return canceled checks to the depositor, but use a procedure called *check truncation*. The bank retains the canceled checks for a period of time (typically 90 days) and a microfilm copy of the checks for a longer period (at least one year). Should the depositor need to review a canceled check within these periods, the bank provides the check or a photocopy of it for a small fee. A bank's monthly statements to a depositor usually list paid checks in numerical sequence, so check truncation does not affect the preparation of a bank reconciliation.

Exhibit 7-2 is an example of a bank statement. The left-hand section of the statement lists deposits and other credits in sequence by date. The middle section lists checks paid and other charges to the account. The checks are listed in numerical sequence, and the payment date for each check is shown in the date column. Listing checks in numerical sequence helps the depositor identify checks written but not yet paid by the bank. The right-hand section shows the checking account balance as of the date shown in the date column.

Code letters on a bank statement identify debits and credits not related to paying checks or making deposits. A list of codes usually appears at the bottom of the statement explaining the code letters. Although such codes are not standard from bank to bank, they are easy to understand. As mentioned before, the depositor also receives an advice slip from the bank explaining nonroutine entries. The statement illustrated in Exhibit 7-2 uses the following codes:

EC —Error correction. Identifies transcription, arithmetic, and similar errors and corrections made by the bank.

DM —Debit memo. Identifies collection charges, repayment of bank loans, and other special charges made by the bank against the depositor's account.

CM —Credit memo. Identifies amounts collected by the bank for the depositor, such as a note receivable left at the bank by the depositor, or a loan from the bank to the depositor that is credited to the depositor's checking account.

SC —Service charge. Identifies the amount charged by the bank for servicing the account. The amount is normally based on the average balance maintained and the number of items processed during the month. Service charges are usually made on small accounts that are not otherwise profitable for the bank to handle.

OD —Overdraft. Indicates a negative balance in the account.

RT —Returned item. Indicates items such as postdated checks or checks without proper endorsement received from customers and deposited. Sometimes NSF (not sufficient funds) checks charged back to the account are identified with these letters in the statement. NSF checks may also be identified with the letters DM (debit memo).

LS —List of checks. Identifies the total of a batch of checks too numerous to list separately on the statement. An adding machine tape listing the individual check amounts usually accompanies each batch of checks listed.

IN —Interest. Indicates the amount of interest added to the account.

The Bank Reconciliation

The ending balance on the bank statement usually differs from the balance in the company's Cash in Bank account. Some reasons for the differences follow:

1. **Outstanding checks**—checks written and deducted in arriving at the book balance but not yet presented to the bank for payment.

2. Deposits not yet credited by the bank—deposits made near the end of the month and processed by the bank *after* the monthly statement has been prepared. These **deposits in transit** will appear on next month's statement.

3. Charges made by the bank but not yet reflected on the depositor's books—for example, service and collection charges, NSF checks, and repayments of the depositor's bank loans charged against the checking account.

4. Credits made by the bank but not yet reflected on the depositor's books—for example, collections of notes and drafts by the bank for the depositor and interest earned by the depositor on the checking account balance.

5. Accounting errors—errors made either by the depositor or by the bank.

The **bank reconciliation** is a schedule that accounts for any of the above differences between the bank statement balance and the company's book balance. Although we could reconcile either of these figures to the other, it is more convenient

EXHIBIT 7—2	BANK STATEMENT

First National Bank • Madison

123 MAIN STREET
MADISON, WISCONSIN 53701

STATEMENT OF ACCOUNT

Beta Company
2683 Beltline Highway
Madison, Wisconsin 53715

ACCOUNT NUMBER
313111386

STATEMENT DATE: December 31, 1993

Deposits/Credits		Checks/Debits			Balance	
Date	*Amount*	*No.*	*Date*	*Amount*	*Date*	*Amount*
12/01	420.00 ✓	149	12/02	125.00 ✓	12/01	6,060.30
12/02	630.00 ✓	154	12/03	56.25 ✓	12/02	6,565.30
12/07	560.80 ✓	155	12/10	135.00 ✓	12/03	6,509.05
12/10	480.25 ✓	156	12/08	315.10	12/07	6,801.19
12/14	525.00 ✓	157	12/07	233.26	12/08	6,486.09
12/17	270.25 ✓	158	12/11	27.14	12/10	6,831.34
12/21	640.20 ✓	159	12/18	275.00	12/11	6,804.20
12/26	300.00CM	160	12/15	315.37	12/14	7,329.20
12/26	475.00 ✓	161	12/17	76.40	12/15	7,013.83
12/30	440.00 ✓	162	12/21	325.60	12/17	7,207.68
		163	12/21	450.00	12/18	6,932.68
		164	12/23	239.00	12/21	6,731.58
		165	12/21	65.70	12/23	6,492.58
		166	12/28	482.43	12/26	7,262.58
		169	12/28	260.00	12/28	6,520.15
		170	12/31	122.50	12/30	6,590.04
		171	12/30	370.11	12/31	6,457.54
		RT	12/07	35.40		
		DM	12/26	5.00		
		SC	12/31	10.00		

Beginning Balance	Deposits/Credits		Checks/Debits		Ending Balance
11/30/93 5,640.30	*No.*	*Amount*	*No.*	*Amount*	12/31/93 6,457.54
	10	4,741.50	20	3,924.26	

Item Codes:	EC—Error Correction	DM—Debit Memo	CM—Credit Memo
	SC—Service Charge	OD—Overdraft	RT—Returned Item
	LS—List of Checks	IN—Interest	

to reconcile both figures to an adjusted balance, which is the cash balance that will appear on the balance sheet. This amount could be withdrawn from the bank after all outstanding items have cleared. A convenient reconciliation form is illustrated on the following page.

Balance per bank statement		$XXX
Add: Deposits not yet credited by bank		<u>XXX</u>
		$XXX
Less: Outstanding checks: (list)	$XXX	
	XXX	
	<u>XXX</u>	<u>XXX</u>
Adjusted balance		$XXX

Balance per books		$XXX
Add: Items credited by bank, not yet entered on books (e.g., notes collected)		<u>XXX</u>
		$XXX
Less: Items charged by bank, not yet entered on books (e.g., service and collection charges, NSF checks)		<u>XXX</u>
Adjusted balance		$XXX

THESE FINAL AMOUNTS SHOULD AGREE

After the reconciliation is prepared, the adjusted balance per bank statement should agree with the adjusted book balance. If these amounts do not agree, we should look carefully for reconciling items omitted from the schedule or for possible errors in record keeping. The bank reconciliation may not only bring to light transactions that must be recorded, but may also detect errors or irregularities.

BANK RECONCILIATION PROCEDURE

Assume that a December 31, 1993, bank reconciliation is to be prepared for Beta Company, whose bank statement is illustrated in Exhibit 7-2. Exhibits 7-3 and 7-4 show the company's December cash receipts and cash disbursements journals, respectively, in abbreviated form. Cash receipts journals may have a column for bank deposits, as shown in Exhibit 7-3.

After the cash journals have been posted, the Cash in Bank account of the Beta Company appears as follows:

CASH IN BANK (FIRST NATIONAL BANK)   ACCOUNT NO. 11

Date		Description	Post. Ref.	Debit	Credit	Balance
1993						
Nov.	30	Balance				5,744.05
Dec.	31		CR	4,246.50		9,990.55
	31		CD		4,699.27	5,291.28

The procedures for reconciling the December 31, 1993, bank statement balance of $6,457.54 with the $5,291.28 balance on the company's books are these:

1. Trace outstanding items on the previous (November 1993) bank reconciliation to this period's statement. The November reconciliation for Beta Company appears in Exhibit 7-5. The items identified with the √ mark, which were outstanding at the end of November 1993, were all processed in December 1993; these amounts are identified by the same mark (√) on the bank statement in Exhibit 7-2. Any checks that have still not cleared in December should appear again on the December reconciliation.

2. Compare the record of deposits in the cash receipts journal (Exhibit 7-3) with the list of deposits on the bank statement. A check mark (√) has been placed next to the amounts that appear in both records. Note that the $225 deposit made on December 31, 1993, does not appear on the bank statement. Enter this item in the December bank reconciliation as a deposit not yet credited by the bank.

3. Arrange in numerical sequence the paid checks that have been returned by the bank. Compare the record of checks written from the cash disbursements journal (Exhibit 7-4) with the checks paid by the bank and returned with the bank statement. A check mark (√) has been placed in the cash disbursements journal next to the amount of each check paid by the bank. Because checks numbered 167, 168, 172, and 173 have not cleared the bank, enter them in

EXHIBIT 7—3

BETA COMPANY
[PARTIAL] CASH RECEIPTS JOURNAL
DECEMBER, 1993

Date		Description	Cash Receipts	Bank Deposits
1993 Dec.	1	Hickman, Inc.	$ 230.00	
	2	Cash sales	400.00	$ 630.00 ✓
	4	Denton Company	410.80	
	7	Jewel and Son	150.00	560.80 ✓
	8	Benson Company (note)	300.00	
	10	Cash sales	180.25	480.25 ✓
	14	Taylor Brothers	525.00	525.00 ✓
	17	Cash sales	270.25	270.25 ✓
	18	Johnson Company	250.15	
	21	Bates Company	390.05	640.20 ✓
	26	Jordan Brothers	475.00	475.00 ✓
	30	Cash sales	440.00	440.00 ✓
	31	Johnson Company	225.00	225.00
			$4,246.50	$4,246.50

EXHIBIT 7—4

BETA COMPANY
[PARTIAL] CASH DISBURSEMENTS JOURNAL
DECEMBER, 1993

Date		Description	Check No.	Cash Payments
1993 Dec.	1	Boynton Company	156	$ 315.10 ✓
	2	Meyer, Inc.	157	233.26 ✓
	4	Rapid Transit, Transportation In	158	27.14 ✓
	7	Acme Realty, December rent	159	275.00 ✓
	8	Stanton Company	160	315.37 ✓
	10	Horder, Inc., Office supplies	161	76.40 ✓
	14	A. L. Smith Company	162	325.60 ✓
	17	J. B. Adams, Office salary	163	450.00 ✓
	17	O. L. Holmes, Office salary	164	239.00 ✓
	18	Abbot Van Lines, Transportation In	165	65.70 ✓
	21	Millston, Inc.	166	482.43 ✓
	21	Odana Corporation	167	301.66
	22	R. W. Knight, Cash purchase	168	149.50
	26	W. A. Sutton	169	260.00 ✓
	29	Border and Son, Cash purchase	170	122.50 ✓
	30	R. L. Olson	171	370.11 ✓
	31	J. B. Adams, Office salary	172	450.00
	31	O. L. Holmes, Office salary	173	240.50
				$4,699.27

EXHIBIT 7—5	BETA COMPANY BANK RECONCILIATION NOVEMBER 30, 1993			

			Balance per books	$5,754.05
Balance per bank statement		$5,640.30		
Add: Deposit not credited by bank		420.00 ✓		
		$6,060.30		
Less: Outstanding checks:			Less: Bank service charge	10.00
No. 149	$125.00 ✓			
No. 154	56.25 ✓			
No. 155	135.00 ✓	316.25		
Adjusted balance		$5,744.05	Adjusted balance	$5,744.05

the December bank reconciliation as outstanding checks. (If paid checks are not returned with the bank statement, compare the record of checks written from the cash disbursements journal with the numerical listing of paid checks on the bank statement.)

4. Scan the bank statement for charges and credits not yet reflected in the company's records. Note that the statement contains a charge of $35.40 for a returned item, a debit memo of $5.00, and a service charge of $10.00. Also, a credit for $300.00 appears in the deposits column on December 26. Bank advices indicate that an NSF check for $35.40 was charged against the company's account; that a $300.00 note receivable was collected on the company's behalf and a $5.00 collection charge was made; and that a $10.00 service charge was made for the month. Enter these items also in the December bank reconciliation.

After the preceding procedures have been completed, the December 31, 1993, bank reconciliation for Beta Company appears as shown in Exhibit 7-6.

Before financial statements are prepared for the period ended December 31, 1993, journal entries should be made to bring the Cash account balance into agreement with the adjusted balance shown on the reconciliation. The entries for Beta Company would reflect the collection of the note receivable and the related collection

EXHIBIT 7—6	BETA COMPANY BANK RECONCILIATION DECEMBER 31, 1993				

			Balance per books		$5,291.28
Balance per bank statement		$6,457.54	Add: Collection of note	$300.00	
Add: Deposit not credited by bank		225.00	Less: Collection charge	5.00	295.00
		$6,682.54			$5,586.28
Less: Outstanding checks:			Less: NSF check	$ 35.40	
No. 167	$301.66		Bank service charge	10.00	45.40
No. 168	149.50				
No. 172	450.00				
No. 173	240.50	1,141.66			
Adjusted balance		$5,540.88	Adjusted balance		$5,540.88

expense, reclassification of the NSF check as an account receivable, and the bank service charge for the month.

Cash	295.00	
Miscellaneous Expense	5.00	
Notes Receivable		300.00
To record note collected by bank, less service charge.		
Accounts Receivable	35.40	
Cash		35.40
To reclassify NSF check as an account receivable.		
Miscellaneous Expense	10.00	
Cash		10.00
To record bank service charge for December.		

Electronic Funds Transfer

Billions of paper checks are written each year by businesses and individuals. The costs of processing this large volume of checks have motivated financial institutions to develop systems for transferring funds among parties electronically, without the need for paper checks. The exchange of cash through such a system is called **electronic funds transfer (EFT).**

A typical example of EFT is the payment of a payroll. An employer firm obtains authorizations from its employees to deposit their payroll checks directly to their checking accounts. The firm then sends to the bank a magnetic tape coded with the appropriate payroll data. The bank's computer processes the magnetic tape, deducts the total payroll amount from the firm's checking account, and adds each employee's payroll amount to his or her checking account.

EFT may also be useful for retailers in situations in which customers typically pay for goods with a check at the time of purchase. Some grocery stores, for example, now use EFT. At the check-out counter, the customer uses a plastic card to activate a computer terminal connected with the bank. Funds to pay for the groceries are immediately transferred from the customer's checking account to the grocery store's account at the bank. This procedure not only eliminates the cost of processing the paper checks for the bank, but also eliminates the risk of bad checks for the grocery store.

The use of EFT will increase with the development of expanded computer networks capable of handling electronic funds transfers. The specific controls over cash transactions handled through EFT, of course, may vary from the internal control procedures under a paper check system. However, adequate controls are no less important in an electronic funds transfer system.

THE PETTY CASH FUND

OBJECTIVE ③ DISCUSS *the accounting for a petty cash fund.*

Most business firms find it inconvenient and expensive to write checks for small expenditures. Therefore, small amounts of cash needed for items such as postage, delivery service, and minor purchases of supplies are most conveniently handled by establishing a **petty cash fund.**

The size of the petty cash fund depends on the number and the amounts of minor expenditures. Of course, it is unwise to have a large amount of cash on hand because of the risk of theft or misuse. Yet, too frequent replenishment can be a nuisance. Many firms maintain funds that will last three or four weeks. The size of expenditures made from the fund is also usually limited.

Although the use of a petty cash fund technically violates the control maxim of making all expenditures by check, control can be maintained by handling the fund on an *imprest* basis and by following certain well-established procedures. In accounting, an imprest fund contains a fixed amount of cash.

Although expenditures from an imprest petty cash fund are made in currency and coin, the fund is established by writing a check against the general bank account.

Replenishments are also accomplished by issuing checks—after a review of expenditures. Therefore, in the final analysis, all expenditures are actually controlled by check.

Establishing the Fund

Assume that Beta Company establishes a petty cash fund of $100. It draws a check payable to Cash and exchanges it at the bank for currency and coin in denominations that are convenient for small expenditures. The entry reflecting establishment of the fund is:

Petty Cash	100	
Cash in Bank		100
To establish imprest petty cash fund.		

As evidence of a disbursement from the fund, the person in charge should place a prenumbered petty cash receipt in the petty cash box. At any time, the total cash on hand plus the total of the receipts should equal $100. Each receipt should give the date, amount, and nature of the expenditure and should be signed by the recipient of the cash. Such documents as cash register tapes and copies of invoices should be attached to the receipts.

Replenishing the Fund

When the fund must be replenished, a check is drawn to Cash in an amount that will bring the cash value of the fund back to $100. Expenditures from the fund are analyzed according to expense or other account category and recorded in the books. For example, assume that Beta Company's fund has been drawn down to $28 and that analysis of the $72 in receipts reveals the following expenditures: Office Expense, $40; Transportation In, $27; and Postage Expense, $5. The following entry would be made in the cash disbursements journal (shown in general journal form):

Office Expense	40	
Transportation In	27	
Postage Expense	5	
Cash in Bank		72
To replenish petty cash fund.		

The fund cashier cashes the replenishment check at the bank and places the cash in the petty cash box.

If the imprest amount is adequate, no further entries are made to the Petty Cash account itself. Notice that replenishment results in an entry to the Cash in Bank account. Only when the prescribed amount of the imprest fund is changed will entries be made to the Petty Cash account, increasing or decreasing the amount of the fund.

One person in the firm's office should be solely responsible for custody of the fund and expenditures made from it. The replenishment checks, however, should be written by another authorized person, after review of the petty cash receipts and the expense distribution. Furthermore, this person should stamp, perforate, or otherwise cancel the supporting receipts and documents to prevent them from being used again as a basis for reimbursement.

Cash Short and Over

Errors in making change from cash funds result in less or more cash than can be accounted for. Usually, such shortages or overages are not material in amount. An account called **Cash Short and Over** is commonly used to record these discrepancies; shortages are debited to the account, and overages are credited. For example, suppose a $100 petty cash fund contains $80 in receipts for office expense and only $16 in currency and coins. The entry to replenish the fund and to record the $4 shortage would be:

Office Expense	80	
Cash Short and Over	4	
Cash in Bank		84
To replenish petty cash fund and record the cash shortage.		

If the fund had contained $23 in cash together with the $80 in expense receipts, the $3 overage would be credited to the Cash Short and Over account. The credit to Cash in Bank for replenishment would be $77.

The Cash Short and Over account may also be used to record cash short or over from sales when cash register tape totals do not agree with the count of cash receipts. Large discrepancies, particularly recurring shortages, should always be investigated to determine appropriate corrective steps.

A Cash Short and Over account with a debit balance at the close of an accounting period is classified as Miscellaneous Expense on the income statement. A credit balance can be classified as Other Income.

INTERNAL CONTROL IN OTHER AREAS

While it is vitally important to establish effective controls over the handling of and accounting for cash, control should also be provided for a firm's other activities. As with cash, most controls separate the authorization of a transaction, the accounting for the transaction, and the custody of any related assets. For example, the purchase and sale of securities normally require authorization by a company's board of directors, and officers who have access to the securities should not have access to the accounting records. Other personnel should record security transactions and keep a record of security certificates by certificate number and amount.

Similarly, employees handling inventory items should not have access to inventory records, and their duties should be separated from the receiving department and the processing of accounts payable. Similar controls should be exercised over receivables, plant assets, payroll transactions, and every other facet of business activity.

The subject of internal control is quite complex. Both external and internal auditors devote a great deal of attention to internal control when analyzing an accounting system and preparing audits. The importance of internal control is underscored by the Foreign Corrupt Practices Act. Among other provisions, this law requires all corporations registering with the Securities and Exchange Commission to devise and maintain an adequate system of internal accounting controls.

SHORT-TERM INVESTMENTS

OBJECTIVE **4** **OUTLINE** *the accounting for short-term investments in stocks and bonds.*

Corporate stocks and bonds may be acquired by a variety of investors, including individuals, partnerships, corporations, mutual funds, pension funds, foundations, and trusts. Shares of stock, of course, represent ownership interests in a corporation. Investors holding a corporation's **common stock** have the most basic ownership rights. **Bonds** are long-term debt securities issued by corporations and various governmental agencies. Our discussion here focuses on short-term investments in stocks and bonds made by corporations.

A firm issuing stocks or bonds may sell directly to investors, or the securities may be sold through an underwriter. Most investments, however, do not involve original issues. In the typical investment, one investor purchases from another investor who happens to be selling at that time. Stocks and bonds are bought and sold on organized exchanges—such as the New York Stock Exchange—and through a less formal *over-the-counter market*. Both the buyer and the seller of a security normally use the services of a broker to acquire or dispose of their investments.

Many firms make temporary investments in highly marketable securities using seasonal excesses of cash. Furthermore, some firms invest in high-quality stocks and bonds as "back-up" cash. Management could convert these securities to cash, if needed, without interfering with the company's normal operations. In the meantime, the investments produce dividend and interest income for the company. Both of these types of investments (investments of seasonal excesses of cash and for back-up cash) are considered **short-term investments** and are classified as current assets on the balance sheet. They may be identified as either short-term investments or **marketable securities** on the balance sheet.

When a firm makes numerous short-term stock investments and short-term bond investments, a separate control account is established in the general ledger for each investment category. A subsidiary ledger maintained for each control account will show the detailed information about each investment—purchase date, number of shares of stock or bonds purchased, total cost, and cost per share of stock or bond acquired.

Short-term Investments in Stocks

When stock is purchased as a short-term investment, the amount initially recorded in the investment account is the stock's cost—that is, its total purchase price. The purchase price may include charges for such items as broker's commissions and transfer taxes. Suppose 100 shares of United Pride common stock are acquired as a short-term investment on October 1 at a cost of $4,290, including commissions and taxes. The investment is recorded as follows:

Oct. 1	Short-term Stock Investment—United Pride	4,290	
	Cash		4,290
	To record purchase of 100 shares of United Pride common stock for $4,290.		

DIVIDENDS

A corporation's board of directors may declare a **dividend,** which is a distribution of the corporation's assets. The asset distributed is usually cash. A corporation also may distribute a **stock dividend**—shares of its own stock. For example, if a board of directors declares a 5% stock dividend, then additional shares of stock equal to 5% of the corporation's outstanding stock are distributed to the current stockholders in proportion to their current stock holdings.

Dividends do not accrue on shares of stock. A corporation has no legal obligation to pay a dividend until it is declared by the board of directors. A company holding stock may record a cash dividend after it has been declared by debiting Dividends Receivable and crediting Dividend Income, but ordinarily no entry is made until the dividend is received. Assuming the United Pride board of directors declares a cash dividend of $1 per share and dividend income is recorded when received, the entry to record the receipt of the cash dividend on December 29 would be

Dec. 29	Cash	100	
	Dividend Income		100
	To record receipt of $100 dividend on investment in United Pride stock.		

The receipt of a stock dividend does not constitute income and requires no formal journal entry. A memorandum of the number of shares received, however, should be recorded in the general ledger and the investment subsidiary ledger. The recipient of the stock dividend now holds more stock without further investment, so the average cost of each share held has been reduced. If United Pride declares a 10% common stock dividend, the company holding 100 shares of United Pride would make the following notation on receipt of 10 additional shares:

(Memorandum) Received 10 shares of United Pride common stock as stock dividend. Average cost per share of 110 shares held is now $39 ($4,290/110).

LOWER OF COST OR MARKET FOR PORTFOLIO

A corporation's **stock portfolio** refers to its investment in several different stocks. At the end of an accounting period, short-term stock investments are reported on the balance sheet at the lower of the total cost or market value of the portfolio. A portfolio valuation is used because firms typically view (and manage) their stock investments as collective assets (a portfolio). Should the total market value drop below total cost, an unrealized loss[3] is recorded, and a contra asset account (to offset short-term

---

[3] Unrealized losses are losses on securities still owned by the firm. For details, see *Statement of Financial Accounting Standards No. 12,* "Accounting for Certain Marketable Securities" (Stamford, CT: Financial Accounting Standards Board, 1975).

stock investments) is credited. To illustrate, let us assume a company has the following portfolio of short-term stock investments at the end of its first year of operations:

Stock	Cost	Market Value
United Pride Common	$ 4,290	$ 3,800
Bayou Oil Common	17,000	17,500
Swan, Inc., Common	16,500	15,200
Total	$37,790	$36,500

Because the total market value ($36,500) is less than total cost ($37,790), the following journal entry is made:

Dec. 31	Unrealized Loss on Short-term Stock Investments	1,290	
	Allowance to Reduce Short-term Stock Investments to Market		1,290
	To record unrealized loss on portfolio of short-term stock investments.		

The unrealized loss is reported in the current year's income statement. The credit to the contra asset account (1) permits original cost to remain in the short-term stock investment control and subsidiary ledger accounts and (2) reduces the total book value of the investments to market value on the balance sheet. The short-term stock investments would appear on the balance sheet as follows:

Short-term Stock Investments (Cost)	$37,790	
Less: Allowance to Reduce Short-term Stock Investments to Market	1,290	$36,500

Or, the investments may be reported in condensed form:

Short-term Stock Investments, at market (cost $37,790)	$36,500

Of course, if the portfolio's market value exceeds its total cost, the investments are reported at cost and no allowance account is created.

SALE OF SHORT-TERM STOCK INVESTMENTS

When a short-term stock investment is sold, a gain or loss is recorded equal to the difference between the proceeds of the sale and the stock's original cost (or the original cost adjusted for the effect of a stock dividend). For example, if all 110 shares of the United Pride stock discussed above were sold on February 1 of the next year for $3,800, the following entry would be made:

Feb. 1	Cash	3,800	
	Loss on Sale of Stock Investments	490	
	Short-term Stock Investment—United Pride		4,290
	To record sale of United Pride stock for $3,800.		

The $490 loss is a realized loss because it relates to securities sold by the firm. Realized losses and realized gains from the sale of investments are included in the income statement in the year the securities are sold.

In general, the gain or loss calculation noted above (sales proceeds minus original cost) is the way the sale of a firm's non-inventory items is analyzed and recorded. Note the contrast with the accounting for sales of inventory. When inventory is sold, the sales proceeds are recorded as revenue, and the cost of goods sold is shown separately as an expense. When something other than inventory is sold (such as a stock investment), the sales proceeds and cost of the item sold are offset and only the difference—a gain or a loss from the sale—is recorded. Gains and losses from sales of investments are normally reported in the other income and expense section of a classified income statement.

RECOVERY OF UNREALIZED LOSS

The difference between the total cost and the market value of a short-term stock portfolio will likely change from one year-end to the next because of changes in market values or in the portfolio's composition. Thus, the contra asset account will be increased or decreased each year-end to reflect the net unrealized portfolio loss at that time. If the net unrealized loss at year-end is smaller than it was the year before, the adjusting entry records a recovery of an unrealized loss. To illustrate, let us assume that the company whose investments we have been analyzing has the following portfolio of short-term stock investments at the end of its second year of operations:

Stock	Cost	Market Value
Bayou Oil Common	$17,000	$17,600
Swan, Inc., Common	16,500	15,700
Total	$33,500	$33,300

The net unrealized loss is now $200 ($33,500 − $33,300); at the end of the preceding year, it had been $1,290. The following entry would adjust the allowance account:

Dec. 31	Allowance to Reduce Short-term Stock Investments to Market	1,090	
	Recovery of Unrealized Loss on Short-term Stock Investments		1,090
	To record decrease in net unrealized loss on short-term stock investments.		

The recovery of the unrealized loss is included in the other income and expense section of the current year's income statement. The $200 credit balance now in the allowance account offsets the cost of short-term investments in the year-end balance sheet. The balance sheet presentation is as follows:

Short-term Stock Investments (Cost)		$33,500	
Less: Allowance to Reduce Short-term Stock Investments to Market		200	$33,300

Short-term Investments in Bonds

A short-term bond investment is initially recorded at its acquisition cost, which includes any broker's commissions and transfer taxes. Because a bond is a debt security, the bondholder receives periodic interest payments from the bond issuer. Interest accrues daily on a bond and usually is paid semiannually. On an interest payment date, a bondholder receives the full amount of interest accrued since the last payment date, regardless of when the bond was purchased. As a result, the purchase price of a bond that is sold between interest payment dates includes not only the current market price but also any interest accrued since the last interest payment date. The bond seller, therefore, receives the interest income earned up to the date of sale. The bond investor debits the accrued interest purchased to a Bond Interest Receivable account. Because the accrued interest is received with the first interest payment, it is not treated as part of the initial cost of the investment.

The **face value,** or **maturity value,** of a bond is the amount of principal to be repaid at the maturity date. The annual rate of interest payable on a bond—often called the *coupon* or *nominal* rate of interest—is stated in the bond agreement. To determine the amount of interest paid semiannually on such bonds, we multiply the face value by one-half the coupon rate of interest.

Purchasing a bond at **par value** means paying an amount equal to its face value. A bond purchased at a *discount* costs less than its face value, and a bond purchased at a *premium* costs more than its face value. An investor discounts a bond when the current market rate of interest exceeds the bond's coupon interest rate; a bond sells at a premium when its coupon rate exceeds the current market interest rate. Bond prices are usually stated as a percentage of face value—for example, a bond selling at 98 costs 98% of its face value, and a bond quoted at 101 sells for 101% of its face value.

Let us assume that $10,000 face value of Anko Company 12% bonds are bought on May 1 at 97 plus accrued interest. The brokerage commission is $40. Semiannual interest is paid on January 1 and July 1. The accrued interest from January 1 to May 1 is $400 ($10,000 × 0.12 × $\frac{4}{12}$), which is recorded separately in a Bond Interest Receivable account. The cost entered in the bond investment account is $9,740, including the brokerage commission. The following entry records the acquisition:

May 1	Short-term Bond Investment—Anko Company	9,740	
	Bond Interest Receivable	400	
	Cash		10,140
	To record purchase of Anko Company bonds at 97 plus commission of $40 plus four months' accrued interest.		

The entry to record the receipt of the semiannual interest payment on July 1 would be:

July 1	Cash	600	
	Bond Interest Receivable		400
	Bond Interest Income		200
	To record receipt of semiannual interest on Anko Company bonds.		

The $200 credit to interest income reflects the interest earned for the two months the bonds have been held. The other $400 is the accrued interest purchased when the bonds were acquired.

Short-term bond investments are usually sold at a gain or loss. Such gain or loss is computed by comparing the proceeds of the sale, net of any accrued interest received, to the carrying value of the investment. If the proceeds from the sale of Anko Company bonds on October 1 were $9,800 plus accrued interest of $300 for three months, the following entry would be made:

Oct. 1	Cash	10,100	
	Short-term Bond Investment—Anko Company		9,740
	Bond Interest Income		300
	Gain on Sale of Bond Investments		60
	To record sale of Anko Company bonds for $9,800 plus interest of $300.		

Certificates of Deposit

In addition to marketable stocks and bonds, a corporation may invest excess cash in another type of security—a **certificate of deposit (CD).** These certificates may be purchased at banks and other financial institutions. They offer fixed rates of return on investments for specified periods (such as 90 days, six months, or one year). Generally, the fixed interest rate increases with the amount or the duration of the investment. CDs are recorded at cost and reported on the balance sheet as a current asset immediately below cash. Interest income from CDs is recorded in the period in which it is earned. These accounting guidelines apply also to short-term investments in other forms of savings certificates. The investment is recorded at its cost, and interest income is recorded in the period in which it is earned.

Disclosure of Fair Value

Firms must disclose the fair value of most financial instruments in their financial statements, either in the body of the balance sheet or in the notes to the financial statements.[4] Thus, the fair values of short-term investments in stocks, bonds, and certificates of deposit must be disclosed in the financial statements. Sometimes the carrying value in the balance sheet already approximates fair value, such as a portfolio of short-term stock investments reported at a market value lower than cost. Some firms carry their short-term bond investments at the lower of cost or market, so a similar result would occur for these investments when market is below cost. Also, the carrying values of most short-term certificates of deposit usually approximate their current fair values. In cases where carrying value does not approximate fair value,

---

[4]*Statement of Financial Accounting Standards No. 107,* "Disclosures about Fair Value of Financial Instruments" (Norwalk, CT: Financial Accounting Standards Board, 1991).

management must estimate and disclose the fair value. Quoted market prices, when available, are usually good evidence of fair value.

ANALYTICAL APPLICATION

QUICK RATIO

OBJECTIVE ⑤ DEFINE *the* **quick ratio** *and* **EXPLAIN** *its use.*

The **quick ratio** is one of the ratios used to analyze a company's working capital position. The quick ratio (sometimes called the *acid test ratio*) is calculated using the following formula:

$$\text{Quick Ratio} = \frac{\text{Cash and Cash Equivalents} + \text{Short-term Investments} + \text{Current Receivables}}{\text{Current Liabilities}}$$

Cash and cash equivalents, short-term investments, and current receivables (notes, accounts, and others) are known as *quick assets*. Quick assets are converted to cash more quickly than inventory and prepaid assets.

Comparing the quick ratio to the current ratio, the main items omitted from the numerator when calculating the quick ratio are inventory and prepaid assets. The quick ratio is used because it may give a better picture than the current ratio of a company's ability to pay current liabilities and take advantage of cash discounts. When the quick ratio is 1.00 (or 1:1), the quick assets available are equal to the current liabilities.

W. R. GRACE & COMPANY, a specialty chemicals firm based in Boca Raton, Florida, reported the following information (in millions of dollars) for three recent years (Year 3 is the most recent year):

	Year 3	Year 2	Year 1
Cash and Cash Equivalents	$ 108.7	$ 132.7	$ 151.4
Notes and Accounts Receivable, Net	1,163.2	1,068.9	826.5
Quick Assets	$1,271.9	$1,201.6	$ 977.9
Inventory and Other Current Assets	894.4	826.5	744.8
Current Assets	$2,166.3	$2,028.1	$1,722.7
Current Liabilities	$1,589.1	$1,498.1	$1,164.6

The quick ratio for W. R. Grace & Company for each of the years would be

Year 3: $1,271.9/$1,589.1 = 0.80

Year 2: $1,201.6/$1,498.1 = 0.80

Year 1: $ 977.9/$1,164.6 = 0.84

These ratios indicate that the quick assets available are consistently less than the current liabilities. This company has a fairly high level of inventory as part of its current assets. How soon Grace's inventory will sell and be converted into cash will determine whether the quick ratio should be a concern.

KEY POINTS FOR CHAPTER OBJECTIVES

❶ **DESCRIBE** the internal control features of an accounting system (pp. 254–257).
- An internal control structure consists of the policies and procedures established to help ensure that specific entity objectives are achieved.
- Accounting controls relate to the reliability of accounting data and the protection of assets.
- Accounting controls include competent personnel, assignment of responsibility, division of work, separation of accountability from custodianship, adequate records and equipment, rotation of personnel, internal auditing, and physical protection of assets.

❷ IDENTIFY key controls over cash and EXPLAIN the procedures for preparing a bank reconciliation (pp. 257–265).

■ Depositing all receipts intact at the bank and making all major cash disbursements by check are important cash controls. These procedures provide a double record of cash—the firm's record and the bank's record.

■ Neither the book balance nor the bank statement balance of cash usually represents the cash balance shown on the balance sheet. Both amounts are reconciled to a third figure—the adjusted balance—that appears on the balance sheet and is the amount that could be withdrawn after all outstanding items have cleared.

❸ DISCUSS the accounting for a petty cash fund (pp. 265–267).

■ Petty Cash is debited when an imprest fund for small expenditures is established or increased. When the fund is replenished, the individual accounts for which expenditures have been made are debited.

❹ OUTLINE the accounting for short-term investments in stocks and bonds (pp. 267–272).

■ Short-term investments in stock are normally carried at the lower of cost or market value of the portfolio. Unrealized losses or recoveries of unrealized losses are included in the income statement, as are realized gains and losses from the sale of investments.

■ Short-term investments in bonds are recorded at their acquisition cost. When sold, the difference between the sales proceeds (net of accrued interest) and the bond's carrying value is shown as a gain (when proceeds exceed carrying value) or as a loss (when carrying value exceeds proceeds).

❺ **ANALYTICAL APPLICATION:** DEFINE the *quick ratio* and EXPLAIN its use (p. 272).

■ The quick ratio is determined by dividing quick assets by current liabilities.

■ The quick ratio is a measure of a firm's ability to pay current liabilities and take advantage of cash discounts.

SELF-TEST QUESTIONS FOR REVIEW

(Answers follow the Solution to Demonstration Problem.)

1. A system of good internal accounting controls includes
   a. Sharing the responsibility and authority for a given function among competent employees.
   b. Placing one person in complete control over a sequence of related transactions.
   c. Using checks and sales invoices that are prenumbered.
   d. Keeping large amounts of cash on the company premises.

2. A bank reconciliation is
   a. A formal financial statement that lists all of a firm's bank account balances.
   b. A merger of two banks that previously were competitors.
   c. A statement sent monthly by a bank to a depositor that lists all deposits, checks paid, and other credits and charges to the depositor's account for the month.
   d. A schedule that accounts for differences between a firm's cash balance as shown on its bank statement and the balance shown in its general ledger Cash account.

3. An entry to debit Petty Cash is made when
   a. A petty cash fund is established.
   b. A petty cash fund is replenished.
   c. A petty cash fund is established *and* when it is replenished.
   d. A shortage in the petty cash fund is recorded.

4. Which of the following is a contra asset account?
   a. Recovery of Unrealized Loss on Short-term Stock Investments.
   b. Unrealized Loss on Short-term Stock Investments.
   c. Loss on Sale of Bond Investments.
   d. Allowance to Reduce Short-term Stock Investments to Market.

5. Emerson Company purchased bonds with a face value of $50,000 and a 10% coupon rate at 99 plus three months' accrued interest. The brokerage commission is $50. What amount should be debited to the bond investment account?
   a. $50,000   c. $49,500
   b. $49,550   d. $50,800

DEMONSTRATION PROBLEM FOR REVIEW

At December 31, 1993, the Cash account in Tyler Company's general ledger had a debit balance of $18,434.27. The December 31, 1993, bank statement showed a balance of $19,726.40. In reconciling the two amounts, you discover the following:

1. Bank deposits made by Tyler on December 31, 1993, amounting to $2,145.40 do not appear on the bank statement.
2. A non-interest-bearing note receivable for $2,000, left with the bank for collection, was collected by the bank near the end of December. The bank credited the proceeds, less a $5 collection charge, on the bank statement. Tyler Company has not recorded the collection.
3. Accompanying the bank statement is a debit memorandum indicating that John Miller's check for $450 was charged against Tyler's bank account on December 30 because of insufficient funds.
4. Check No. 586, written for advertising expense of $869.10, was recorded as $896.10 in Tyler Company's cash disbursements journal.
5. A comparison of the paid checks returned by the bank with the cash disbursements journal revealed the following checks still outstanding at December 31, 1993:

No. 561	$306.63	No. 591	$190.00
No. 585	440.00	No. 592	282.50
No. 588	476.40	No. 593	243.00

6. The bank mistakenly charged Tyler Company's account for check printing costs of $30.50, which should have been charged to Taylor Company.
7. The bank charged Tyler Company's account $42.50 for rental of a safe deposit box. No entry has been made in Tyler's records for this expense.

REQUIRED

a. Prepare a bank reconciliation at December 31, 1993.
b. Prepare any necessary journal entries at December 31, 1993.

SOLUTION TO DEMONSTRATION PROBLEM

a.

TYLER COMPANY
BANK RECONCILIATION
DECEMBER 31, 1993

Balance per bank statement	$19,726.40	Balance per books		$18,434.27
Add: Deposits not credited by bank	2,145.40	Add: Collection of note	$2,000.00	
		Less: Collection charge	5.00	1,995.00
Error by bank (Check printing charge of Taylor Co.)	30.50	Error in recording check No. 586		27.00
	$21,902.30			$20,456.27
Less: Outstanding checks:		Less:		
No. 561	$306.63	NSF check	$450.00	
No. 585	440.00	Charge for safe deposit box	42.50	492.50
No. 588	476.40			
No. 591	190.00			
No. 592	282.50			
No. 593	243.00	1,938.53		
Adjusted balance	$19,963.77	Adjusted balance		$19,963.77

b.

Dec. 31	Cash	1,995.00	
	Miscellaneous Expense	5.00	
	Notes Receivable		2,000.00
	To record collection of note by bank, less collection charge.		
31	Cash	27.00	
	Advertising Expense		27.00
	To correct error in recording advertising expense.		
31	Accounts Receivable	450.00	
	Cash		450.00
	To reclassify NSF check as an account receivable.		
31	Miscellaneous Expense	42.50	
	Cash		42.50
	To record rental expense of safe deposit box.		

ANSWERS TO SELF-TEST
QUESTIONS

1. c, pp. 254–257   **2.** d, pp. 260–265   **3.** a, p. 266   **4.** d, p. 269
5. b, p. 271

GLOSSARY OF KEY TERMS USED IN THIS CHAPTER

accounting controls   Internal control procedures that help (1) produce accurate and reliable financial data and (2) safeguard assets (p. 254).

bank reconciliation   A procedure or analysis explaining the various items—such as deposits in transit, checks outstanding, bank charges, and errors—that lead to differences between the balance shown on a bank statement and the related Cash account in the general ledger (p. 260).

bond   A form of interest-bearing note payable, usually issued by the borrower for a relatively long period, to a group of lenders. Bonds may incorporate a wide variety of special provisions related to security for the debt involved, methods of paying the periodic interest payments, and maturity and retirement provisions (p. 267).

cash   An asset category representing the amount of a firm's paper money, coins, checks, money orders, and demand deposits with financial institutions (p. 257).

Cash Short and Over   An account that contains the amounts by which actual daily cash collections differ from the amounts recorded as being collected (p. 266).

certificate of deposit (CD)   An investment security available at financial institutions generally offering a fixed rate of return for a specified period of time (p. 271).

common stock   Basic ownership class of corporate capital stock, carrying the rights to vote, share in earnings, participate in future stock issues, and share in liquidation proceeds after prior claims have been settled (p. 267).

compensating balance   A minimum amount that a financial institution requires a firm to maintain in its account as part of a borrowing arrangement (p. 259).

deposits in transit   Cash deposits made to a bank account near the end of a month that do not appear on that month's bank statement (p. 260).

dividend   A distribution of a corporation's assets to its stockholders (p. 268).

electronic funds transfer (EFT)   A system for transferring funds among parties electronically, without the need for paper checks (p. 265).

face value   The amount of principal to be repaid at maturity. Also called *par value* (p. 270).

internal control structure   The policies and procedures established by a firm to provide reasonable assurance that specific entity objectives will be achieved (p. 254).

marketable securities   An asset classification representing temporary investments in highly marketable stocks, notes, and bonds; may also be called *short-term investments* (p. 268).

maturity value (bond)   The amount of bond principal to be paid at maturity (p. 270).

outstanding checks   Checks issued by a firm that have not yet been presented to its bank for payment (p. 260).

par value (bond)   The face value of a bond (p. 270).

petty cash fund   A special, relatively small cash fund established for making minor cash disbursements in the operation of a business (p. 265).

quick ratio   Quick assets (cash and cash equivalents, short-term investments, and current receivables) divided by current liabilities (p. 272).

short-term investments   An asset classification representing temporary investments in highly marketable stocks, notes, and bonds; may also be called *marketable securities* (p. 267).

stock dividend   Additional shares of its own stock issued by a corporation to its current stockholders in proportion to their ownership interests (p. 268).

stock portfolio   A firm's investment in several different stocks. For accounting purposes, stock investments are divided into a current portfolio and a noncurrent portfolio; the portfolios are reported on the balance sheet at the lower of the portfolio's total cost or market value (p. 268).

QUESTIONS

7-1   Define *internal control structure*; define *accounting controls*.

7-2   Name several specific features of a good system of internal accounting controls.

7-3   Why is work division an important feature of good internal accounting controls?

7-4   What internal control procedures are especially important in handling cash transactions?

7-5 Indicate whether the following statements relating to internal control structures are true or false:

a. Under the principle of separating accountability and physical custodianship, the accounts receivable bookkeeper should not make bank deposits.

b. When possible, the general ledger bookkeeper should also keep subsidiary records.

c. Rotation of personnel in record-keeping duties violates the rule that responsibility should not be shared.

d. Even with careful attention to good internal controls, guarding against embezzlements and irregularities involving collusion among employees is difficult.

e. Internal auditing departments eliminate the need for audits by independent public accountants.

7-6 Accounting controls have two objectives. What objective is served by (a) keeping the petty cash fund in a locked desk drawer and (b) having a comprehensive chart of accounts?

7-7 What is the purpose of a bank reconciliation?

7-8 In preparing a bank reconciliation, how should you determine (a) deposits not recorded in the bank statement and (b) outstanding checks?

7-9 Indicate whether the following bank reconciliation items should be (1) added to the bank statement balance, (2) deducted from the bank statement balance, (3) added to the ledger account balance, or (4) deducted from the ledger account balance:

a. Bank service charge.

b. NSF check.

c. Deposit in transit.

d. Outstanding check.

e. Bank error charging company's account with another company's check.

f. Difference of $270 in amount of check written for $410 but recorded in the cash disbursements journal for $140.

7-10 Which of the items listed in Question 7-9 require a journal entry on the company's books?

7-11 What is an imprest petty cash fund? How is such a fund established and replenished? Describe the accounting entries involved.

7-12 In preparing to replenish the $200 petty cash fund, the cashier discovers that the fund contains $178 in petty cash vouchers for office expenses and $18 in currency and coins. (a) What should be the amount of the replenishment check? (b) How should the $4 discrepancy be recorded?

7-13 Why do companies make short-term investments in securities? Where should short-term investments be classified in the balance sheet?

7-14 Interest on bond investments is accrued, but dividends on stock investments are not accrued. Why?

7-15 What entry, if any, should be made when a corporation receives a stock dividend on a short-term stock investment? What entry should be made when a cash dividend is received on a short-term stock investment?

7-16 At what amount are short-term stock investments reported in the balance sheet? Where are unrealized losses on the short-term stock investments portfolio reported?

7-17 Wallace Corporation purchased Brian Company bonds with a face value of $90,000 and a 10% coupon rate at 102 plus two months' accrued interest. Calculate the total cash outlay for the bonds. What amount should be debited to Short-term Bond Investment—Brian Company?

 7-18 What is a certificate of deposit? When should interest income on a certificate of deposit be recorded?

7-19 Define the *quick ratio* and explain its use.

EXERCISES

 7-20 The following four situations occurred in Regent Corporation:

a. The mail opener converted a check payable to Regent Corporation to his personal use. The check was included in the list of remittances sent to the accounting depart-

INTERNAL CONTROL
— OBJ. 1 —

ment. He treated the missing amount as a deposit in transit while doing the bank reconciliation.

b. The purchasing agent used the company's purchase order form to order building materials. Later, she instructed the building supply company by telephone to deliver the materials to her home and to charge Regent Corporation's account. At month-end, she approved the invoice for payment.

c. A vendor was paid twice for the same shipment. One payment was made on receipt of the invoice and a second payment on receipt of the monthly statement—the first remittance had arrived too late to appear on the monthly statement.

d. The cashier pocketed cash received over the counter from certain customers paying their accounts. He then wrote off the receivables by recording a sales allowance for a billing error.

For each situation, indicate any violations of good internal control procedures, and describe the steps you would take to safeguard the system against this type of occurrence.

INTERNAL CONTROL
— OBJ. 1 —

7-21 Explain how each of the following unrelated procedures strengthens internal control:

a. After preparing a check for a cash disbursement, Travis Lumber Company's treasurer cancels the supporting documentation (purchase requisition, receiving report, and invoice) with a perforator.

b. The clerks of Davis Department Store give each customer a cash register receipt along with the proper change.

c. The ticket-taker of the Esquire movie theater tears each admission ticket in half and gives each patron one-half.

d. John Rapp's restaurant provides servers with prenumbered customer's checks. The servers are to void checks with mistakes on them and issue new ones rather than make alterations or corrections on them. Voided checks must be given to the manager every day.

BANK RECONCILIATION
— OBJ. 2 —

7-22 Use the following information to prepare a bank reconciliation for Young Company at June 30, 1993.

1. Balance per Cash account, June 30, $7,055.80.
2. Balance per bank statement, June 30, $7,300.25.
3. Deposits not reflected on bank statement, $675.
4. Outstanding checks, June 30, $1,210.45.
5. Service charge on bank statement not recorded in books, $11.
6. Error by bank—Yertel Company check charged on Young Company's bank statement, $550.
7. Check for advertising expense, $250, incorrectly recorded in books as $520.

BANK RECONCILIATION
COMPONENTS
— OBJ. 2 —

7-23 Identify the amount asked for in each of the following situations.

a. Munsing Company's May 31 bank reconciliation shows deposits in transit of $1,400. The general ledger Cash in Bank account shows total cash receipts during June of $57,300. The June bank statement shows total cash deposits of $55,900 (and no credit memos). What amount of deposits in transit should appear in the June 30 bank reconciliation?

b. Sandusky Company's August 31 bank reconciliation shows outstanding checks of $2,100. The general ledger Cash in Bank account shows total cash disbursements (all by check) during September of $51,500. The September bank statement shows $49,200 of checks clearing the bank. What amount of outstanding checks should appear in the September 30 bank reconciliation?

c. Fremont Corporation's March 31 bank reconciliation shows deposits in transit of $800. The general ledger Cash in Bank account shows total cash receipts during April of $36,000. The April bank statement shows total cash deposits of $37,100 (including a credit memo for $1,300 from the collection of a note; the note collection has not yet been recorded by Fremont). What amount of deposits in transit should appear in the April 30 bank reconciliation?

PETTY CASH
— OBJ. 3 —

7-24 Record the following Eaton Company April 1993 activities in general journal form:

Apr. 1 Established a $250 petty cash fund by writing a check on the First National Bank.

17 Replenished the petty cash fund by writing a check on the First National Bank. The fund contains the following:

Currency and coins	$ 32
Bills and receipts:	
Delivery Expense	85
Contributions Expense	62
Office Expense	71
	$250

Apr. 30   Replenished the petty cash fund and increased it to $300 by writing a check on the First National Bank. The fund contains the following:

Currency and coins	$ 37
Bills and receipts:	
Transportation In	114
Delivery Expense	23
Office Expense	76
	$250

**SHORT-TERM STOCK
INVESTMENTS
— OBJ. 4 —**

7-25   During its first year of operations, Hudson, Inc., made two purchases of common stock as short-term investments. On May 20, 1993, the firm acquired 300 shares of Amherst Company at $30 per share plus a $150 broker's fee, and on July 16, 1993, it purchased 200 shares of Niles Company at $20 per share plus a $100 broker's fee. On December 27, Hudson, Inc., received a cash dividend of $1.10 per share from Amherst Company (Hudson records dividend income when received). The December 31 quoted market prices per share for the stock were Amherst Company, $25, and Niles Company, $22. On January 26, 1994, Hudson sold the Niles Company stock for $24 per share. Present journal entries to reflect (a) the stock purchases, (b) the receipt of the Amherst Company dividend, (c) the reduction of the stock portfolio to the lower of cost or market at December 31, 1993, and (d) the sale of the Niles Company stock.

**SHORT-TERM STOCK
INVESTMENTS
— OBJ. 4 —**

7-26   At December 31, 1993, Midland Company had the following short-term stock portfolio:

Stock	Cost	Market Value
Cline, Inc., Common	$ 9,200	$ 9,700
Dwyer, Inc., Common	6,000	6,600
Total	$15,200	$16,300

On March 18, 1994, Midland sold the Cline, Inc., stock for $9,400. On September 8, 1994, Midland purchased Newman, Inc., common stock for $10,200. At December 31, 1994, the common stock market values were Dwyer, Inc., $6,200; Newman, Inc., $9,650. Prepare journal entries to reflect (a) the March 18 stock sale, (b) the September 8 stock purchase, and (c) the reduction of the stock portfolio to the lower of cost or market at December 31, 1994.

**SHORT-TERM BOND
INVESTMENT
— OBJ. 4 —**

7-27   As a short-term investment, Edwards Company purchased eighteen $1,000, 10% bonds of Kyle, Inc. at 98 plus three months' accrued interest on April 1, 1993. The brokerage commission was $100. The bonds pay interest on June 30 and December 31. Present journal entries to reflect: (a) the purchase of the bonds for cash on April 1, 1993; (b) the receipt of the semiannual interest payment on June 30, 1993; and (c) the receipt of the semiannual interest payment on December 31, 1993.

PROBLEMS

**INTERNAL CONTROL
— OBJ. 1 —**

7-28   The western branch of Rettinger Distributors, Inc., handles a significant amount of credit sales, over-the-counter cash sales, and C.O.D. (cash on delivery) sales. The sales-clerk prepares two copies of a sales ticket for all cash sales. One copy is given to the customer. The cashier keeps the other copy and stamps it "paid" when cash is received from an over-the-counter customer or from the delivery service. Because the sales tickets are not prenumbered, the cashier files them by the date of sale. At the end of each day, the cashier summarizes the over-the-counter cash sales and the amounts received from the delivery service for C.O.D. sales and sends the total to the accountant for recording.

The branch does its own billings and collects receivables from credit customers. Mail remittances from credit customers are opened in the mailroom. Mailroom personnel make one copy of a list of remittances, which they forward to the accountant together with the customers' checks. The accountant verifies the cash discounts (credit sales are 2/10, n/30), records the remittances, and then sends the checks to the cashier. The cashier makes up the daily deposits for the bank, including both cash sales and remittances received on account. At the end of the month, the cashier receives the bank statement and makes the bank reconciliation. Also at month-end, the accountant mails monthly statements of account to customers with outstanding balances.

REQUIRED

a. List the irregularities that might occur with this system.

b. Suggest improvements in the system of internal control.

c. What feature of internal control in the current system would likely reveal that a mail clerk has converted checks received through the mail to personal use (that is, the mail clerk steals the check and does not record it on the list of cash receipts)?

INTERNAL CONTROL
— OBJ. 1 —

7-29 Each of the following lettered paragraphs (a)–(d) briefly describes an independent situation involving some aspect of internal control.

REQUIRED

Answer the questions at the end of each paragraph or numbered section.

a. As the office manager of a small business, Robert Flynn opens all incoming mail, makes bank deposits, and keeps both the general ledger and the customers' subsidiary ledger. Two assistants write up the special journals (cash, purchases, and sales) and prepare the customers' monthly statements.

    1. If Flynn pocketed Customer A's $200 check (payment in full) and made no effort to conceal his embezzlement in the books, how would the misappropriation probably be discovered?

    2. What routine accounting procedure would disclose Flynn's $200 embezzlement in part (1), even if he destroyed Customer A's subsidiary ledger card?

    3. What circumstances might disclose Flynn's $200 embezzlement if he marked Customer A's account "paid in full" and set up a $200 account for fictitious Customer B with a fictitious address?

    4. In part (3), why might Flynn be anxious to open the mail himself each morning?

    5. In part (3), why might Flynn want to have the authority to write off accounts considered uncollectible?

b. A doughnut shop uses a cash register with a locked-in tape that accumulates registered transactions. A prominently displayed sign announces a free doughnut for every customer who is not given the cash register receipt with his or her purchase. How is this procedure an internal control device for the doughnut shop?

c. Jason Miller, a swindler, sent several business firms invoices requesting payment for office supplies that had never been delivered to the firm. A 5% discount was offered for prompt payment. What internal control procedures should prevent this swindle from being successful?

d. Customers of Downtown Cafeteria encounter the cashier at the end of the food line. At this point, the cashier rings up the food costs, and the customer pays the bill. The customer line frequently backs up while the person paying searches for the correct amount of cash. To speed things up, the cashier often collects money from the next customer or two who have the correct change without ringing up their food costs. After the first customer finally pays, the cashier rings up the costs for those customers who have already paid.

    1. What is the internal control weakness in this procedure?

    2. How might the internal control over the collection of cash from the cafeteria customers be strengthened?

BANK RECONCILIATION
— OBJ. 2 —

7-30 On July 31, 1993, Sullivan Company's Cash in Bank account had a balance of $7,216.60. On that date, the bank statement indicated a balance of $9,534.75. Comparison of returned checks and bank advices revealed the following:

1. Deposits in transit July 31 amounted to $3,140.75.

2. Outstanding checks July 31 totaled $1,467.90.

3. The bank erroneously charged a $325 check of Solomon Company against the Sullivan bank account.

4. A $25 bank service charge has not yet been recorded on the books.

5. Sullivan neglected to record $4,000 borrowed from the bank on a 10% six-month note. The bank statement shows the $4,000 as a deposit.

6. Included with the returned checks is a memo indicating that J. Martin's check for $640 had been returned NSF. Martin, a customer, had sent the check to pay an account of $660 less a $20 discount.

7. Sullivan Company recorded a $109 payment for repairs as $1,090.

REQUIRED

a. Prepare a bank reconciliation for Sullivan Company at July 31.

b. Prepare the general journal entry or entries necessary to bring the Cash in Bank account into agreement with the adjusted balance on the bank reconciliation.

BANK RECONCILIATION
— OBJ. 2 —

7-31   The bank reconciliation made by Winton, Inc., on August 31, 1993, showed a deposit in transit of $1,280 and two outstanding checks, No. 597 for $830 and No. 603 for $640. The adjusted balance per books on August 31 was $14,110.

The following bank statement is available for September:

BANK STATEMENT

TO Winton, Inc. St. Louis, MO					September 30, 1993 STATE BANK	
Date	**Deposits**	**No.**	**Date**	**Charges**	**Date**	**Balance**
					Aug. 31	$14,300
Sept. 1	$1,280	597	Sept. 1	$ 830	Sept. 1	14,750
2	1,120	607	5	1,850	2	15,870
5	850	608	5	1,100	5	13,770
9	744	609	9	552	8	13,130
15	1,360	610	8	640	9	13,322
17	1,540	611	17	488	15	14,008
25	1,028	612	15	674	17	15,060
30	680	614	25	920	25	15,168
		NSF	29	1,028	29	14,140
		SC	30	36	30	14,784

A list of deposits made and checks written during September, taken from the cash receipts journal and cash disbursements journal, respectively, is shown below:

Deposits Made		Checks Written	
Sept. 1	$1,120	No. 607	$1,850
4	850	608	1,100
8	744	609	552
12	1,360	610	640
16	1,540	611	488
24	1,028	612	746
29	680	613	310
30	980	614	920
	$8,302	615	386
		616	420
			$7,412

The Cash in Bank account balance on September 30 was $15,000. In reviewing checks returned by the bank, the bookkeeper discovered that check No. 612, written for $674 for advertising expense, was recorded in the cash disbursements journal as $746. The NSF check for $1,028, which Winton deposited on September 24, was a payment on account from customer D. Walker.

REQUIRED

a. Prepare a bank reconciliation for Winton, Inc., at September 30, 1993.

b. Prepare the necessary journal entries to bring the Cash in Bank account into agreement with the adjusted balance on the bank reconciliation.

PETTY CASH
— OBJ. 3 —

7-32 Cameron, Inc., established an imprest petty cash fund on July 1, 1993. The following transactions took place during July:

July 1 Wrote check against United Bank account to establish the petty cash fund, $300.

15 Replenished the fund by check against the United Bank account for $251. The following bills and receipts were on hand:

Freight on C.O.D. purchase of merchandise	$ 65
Postage	50
Computer repair	90
Lunch with client (entertainment expense)	46
	$251

July 29 Replenished the fund and increased it to $400 by writing a check against the United Bank account. On this date, the fund contained $29 in currency and coins. Bills and receipts on hand were for postage, $56; office supplies expense, $71; charitable contributions, $60; and freight on C.O.D. purchase of merchandise, $82.

REQUIRED

Record the July petty cash transactions for Cameron, Inc., in general journal form.

SHORT-TERM INVESTMENTS
— OBJ. 4 —

7-33 The following selected transactions relate to Bennett Corporation during 1992 and 1993, its first two years of operations. The company closes its books on December 31.

1992

Mar. 26 Purchased 2,000 common shares of Tower, Inc., as a short-term investment at a total cost of $22,748.

July 1 Invested $12,000 in a one-year certificate of deposit at State Bank. The annual interest rate on the certificate is 8%.

1 Purchased, as a short-term investment, twenty $1,000, 10% Garcia Company bonds at 102 plus $150 of commissions and taxes. The bonds pay interest on June 30 and December 31.

Sept. 7 Purchased 3,000 common shares of Adair, Inc., as a short-term investment at a total cost of $81,750.

Dec. 2 Adair, Inc., declared a cash dividend of 40 cents per common share, payable on December 29. Bennett Corporation records dividend income when dividends are received.

3 Received 200 shares of Tower, Inc., common stock as a 10% stock dividend. The stock's current market price per share was $12.

29 Received cash dividend, declared December 2, from Adair, Inc.

31 Received semiannual interest payment on Garcia Company bonds.

31 Accrued interest receivable for six months on certificate of deposit. (Bennett Corporation does not use reversing entries.)

31 Adjusted portfolio of short-term stock investments to lower of cost or market. Current market prices per share were Tower, Inc., $11, and Adair, Inc., $24.

1993

June 30 Received $12,960 when the one-year certificate of deposit (purchased July 1, 1992) was cashed in.

30 Received semiannual interest payment on Garcia Company bonds.

REQUIRED

a. Record these transactions in general journal form.
b. Assume that holdings of short-term stock investments did not change during 1993. What entry would be made at December 31, 1993, to adjust the portfolio to the lower of cost or market if the per share market prices at that date were $12 for Tower, Inc., and $25 for Adair, Inc.?

SHORT-TERM STOCK INVESTMENTS
— OBJ. 4 —

7-34   Carlton Corporation began operations on January 1, 1992. The following transactions relate to Carlton Corporation's short-term investments in stocks during 1992 and 1993:

1992

Feb. 15   Purchased 3,000 common shares of Leyden, Inc., at a total cost of $66,000.

April 20   Purchased 1,300 common shares of Gold Corporation at a total cost of $60,060.

June 25   Received 65 shares of Gold Corporation common stock as a 5% stock dividend. The stock's current market price per share was $46.

Aug. 6   Purchased 2,500 common shares of Archer, Inc., at a total cost of $42,500.

Sept. 3   Sold 365 Gold Corporation common shares at a price of $46 per share.

Dec. 15   Received a cash dividend of $1 per common share from Leyden, Inc. Leyden declared the dividend on November 20. Carlton Corporation records dividend income when dividends are received.

     30   Received a cash dividend of 60 cents per common share from Archer, Inc.

     31   Adjusted portfolio of short-term stock investments to lower of cost or market. Current market prices per share were Leyden, Inc., $20; Gold Corporation, $46; and Archer, Inc., $15.

1993

Mar. 11   Sold remaining 1,000 Gold Corporation common shares at a price of $42 per share.

Dec. 15   Received a cash dividend of $1.20 per common share from Leyden, Inc.

     30   Received a cash dividend of 60 cents per common share from Archer, Inc.

     31   Adjusted portfolio of short-term stock investments to lower of cost or market. Current market prices per share were Leyden, Inc., $22; and Archer, Inc., $16.

REQUIRED

Record these transactions in general journal form.

ALTERNATE EXERCISES

INTERNAL CONTROL
— OBJ. 1 —

7-20A   The following three situations occurred in Kaplan Corporation:

a. J. Farrell, head of the receiving department, created a fictitious company called Forms Consulting and used it to bill Kaplan for forms it never ordered or received. When Kaplan received a bill, Farrell would confirm (wrongly) that the forms had been received and Kaplan's treasurer would then issue a check to Forms Consulting.

b. The company lost one day's cash receipts at the local bank. The employee took the cash receipts to the bank, after bank closing hours, to deposit them in the bank's night depository slot. A creative thief had placed a sign on the depository slot saying it was out of order and the deposits should be placed in the metal cannister placed next to the building. The cannister was chained and padlocked to a light pole. The employee placed the cash receipts through the slot in the cannister. After several employees from different companies had done the same thing, the thief came, unlocked the cannister, and left with it.

c. The company does not use prenumbered sales invoices for over-the-counter sales. A cashier pocketed cash receipts and destroyed the related sales invoice.

For each situation, indicate any violations of good internal control procedures, and describe the steps you would take to safeguard the system against this type of occurrence.

INTERNAL CONTROL
— OBJ. 1 —

7-21A   Explain how each of the following unrelated procedures strengthens internal control:

a. Western Corporation's copy machines are activated by keying a code number; each employee is assigned a different number. Each copy machine keeps track of the number of copies run by employee code number.

b. Palace Company's bank requires a signature card on file for each officer that is authorized to sign company checks.

c. Fast 'N Convenient Stores have programmed their cash registers to imprint a blue star on the cash register receipt of every 500th receipt issued. A sign by each cash register states that the customer receives $2 if his or her receipt has a blue star on it.

d. Wisdom Corporation has a policy that every employee must take two weeks of vacation each year.

**BANK RECONCILIATION
— OBJ. 2 —**

7-22A Use the following information to prepare a bank reconciliation for Dillon Company at April 30, 1993.
1. Balance per Cash account, April 30, $6,042.10.
2. Balance per bank statement, April 30, $6,300.28.
3. Deposits not reflected on bank statement, $525.
4. Outstanding checks, April 30, $1,015.18.
5. Service charge on bank statement not recorded in books, $12.
6. Error by bank—Dillard Company check charged on Dillon Company's bank statement, $400.
7. Check for advertising expense, $130, incorrectly recorded in books at $310.

**BANK RECONCILIATION
COMPONENTS
— OBJ. 2 —**

7-23A Identify the amount asked for in each of the following situations.
a. Howell Company's August 31 bank reconciliation shows deposits in transit of $2,400. The general ledger Cash in Bank account shows total cash receipts during September of $89,900. The September bank statement shows total cash deposits of $88,000 (and no credit memos). What amount of deposits in transit should appear in the September 30 bank reconciliation?
b. Wright Corporation's March 31 bank reconciliation shows deposits in transit of $1,600. The general ledger Cash in Bank account shows total cash receipts during April of $63,100. The April bank statement shows total cash deposits of $66,200 (including a credit memo for $2,000 from the collection of a note; the note collection has not yet been recorded by Wright). What amount of deposits in transit should appear in the April 30 bank reconciliation?
c. Braddock Company's October 31 bank reconciliation shows outstanding checks of $2,600. The general ledger Cash in Bank account shows total cash disbursements (all by check) during November of $69,500. The November bank statement shows $67,200 of checks clearing the bank. What amount of outstanding checks should appear in the November 30 bank reconciliation?

**PETTY CASH
— OBJ. 3 —**

7-24A Record the following Evans Corporation 1993 activities in general journal form:

July 1 Established a $300 petty cash fund by writing a check on First National Bank.
  18 Replenished the petty cash fund by writing a check on First National Bank. The fund contains the following:

Currency and coins	$ 37
Bills and receipts:	
Delivery Expense	102
Contributions Expense	74
Office Expense	87
	$300

  30 Replenished the petty cash fund and increased it to $350 by writing a check on First National Bank. The fund contains the following:

Currency and coins	$ 43
Bills and receipts:	
Transportation In	138
Delivery Expense	26
Office Expense	93
	$300

**SHORT-TERM STOCK
INVESTMENTS
— OBJ. 4 —**

7-25A During its first year of operations, Benton Corporation made two purchases of common stock as short-term investments. On June 15, 1992, the firm acquired 300 shares of Dale Company at $42 per share plus a $200 broker's fee, and on August 10, 1992, it purchased 200 shares of Chester Company at $25 per share plus a $100 broker's fee. On December 27, Benton received a cash dividend of $1.20 per share from Dale Company (Benton records dividend income when received). The December 31 quoted market prices per share for the stock were Dale Company, $36, and Chester Company, $27. On January 26, 1993, Benton sold the Chester Company stock for $28 per share. Present journal entries to reflect (a) the stock purchases, (b) the receipt of the Dale Company dividend, (c) the reduction of the stock portfolio to the lower of cost or market at December 31, 1992, and (d) the sale of the Chester Company stock.

Short-term Stock Investments — Obj. 4 —

7-26A At December 31, 1992, Howard Company had the following short-term stock portfolio:

Stock	Cost	Market Value
Oxford, Inc., Common	$14,000	$14,600
Elkhart, Inc., Common	9,200	10,000
Total	$23,200	$24,600

On March 10, 1993, Howard sold the Oxford, Inc., stock for $14,500. On August 15, 1993, Howard purchased Perry, Inc., common stock for $15,300. At December 31, 1993, the common stock market values were: Elkhart, Inc., $9,400; Perry, Inc., $14,500. Prepare journal entries to reflect (a) the March 10 stock sale, (b) the August 15 stock purchase, and (c) the reduction of the stock portfolio to the lower of cost or market at December 31, 1993.

Short-term Bond Investment — Obj. 4 —

7-27A As a short-term investment, Larkin Company purchased sixteen $1,000, 10% bonds of Shurr, Inc. at 99 plus three months' accrued interest on April 1, 1993. The brokerage commission was $100. The bonds pay interest on June 30 and December 31. Present journal entries to reflect (a) the purchase of the bonds for cash on April 1, 1993; (b) the receipt of the semiannual interest payment on June 30, 1993; and (c) the receipt of the semiannual interest payment on December 31, 1993.

ALTERNATE PROBLEMS

Internal Control — Obj. 1 —

7-28A Zastro Company has three clerical employees who must perform the following functions:
1. Maintain general ledger.
2. Maintain accounts payable ledger.
3. Maintain accounts receivable ledger.
4. Prepare checks for signature.
5. Maintain cash disbursements journal.
6. Issue credits on returns and allowances.
7. Reconcile the bank account.
8. Handle and deposit cash receipts.

The office manager of Zastro Company wishes to assign the above functions to the three employees in the manner that achieves the highest degree of internal control.

REQUIRED

Distribute the functions among the employees in a manner compatible with good internal control.

Internal Control — Obj. 1 —

7-29A The Mountain Twister amusement ride has the following system of internal control over its cash receipts. All persons pay the same price for a ride. An individual taking the ride pays the cashier and receives a ticket. The individual then walks to the ride site, hands the ticket to a ticket taker (who controls the number of people getting on each ride), and passes through a turnstile. All tickets are prenumbered. At the end of each day, the beginning ticket number is subtracted from the ending ticket number to determine the number of admissions sold. The cash is counted and compared with the number of tickets sold. The turnstile records each person who passes through it. At the end of each day, the beginning turnstile number is subtracted from the ending turnstile number to determine the number of riders that day. The number of riders is compared with the number of tickets sold.

REQUIRED

Which internal control feature would reveal each of the following irregularities?
a. The ticket taker admits her friends without a ticket.
b. The cashier gives his friends tickets without receiving any cash.
c. The cashier gives too much change.
d. The ticket taker returns the tickets she has collected to the cashier. The cashier then resells these tickets and splits the proceeds with the ticket taker.
e. An individual sneaks into the ride line without paying the cashier.

BANK RECONCILIATION — OBJ. 2 —

7-30A On May 31, 1993, the Cash in Bank account of Wallace Company, a sole proprietorship, had a balance of $6,122.50. On that date, the bank statement indicated a balance of $8,180.40. Comparison of returned checks and bank advices revealed the following:
1. Deposits in transit May 31 totaled $2,585.60.
2. Outstanding checks May 31 totaled $3,211.70.
3. The bank added to the account $27.80 of interest income earned by Wallace during May.
4. The bank collected a $2,400 note receivable for Wallace and charged a $20 collection fee. Both items appear on the bank statement.
5. Bank service charges in addition to the collection fee, not yet recorded on the books, were $20.
6. Included with the returned checks is a memo indicating that L. Ryder's check for $686 had been returned NSF. Ryder, a customer, had sent the check to pay an account of $700 less a 2% discount.
7. Wallace Company recorded the payment of an account payable as $690; the check was for $960.

REQUIRED

a. Prepare a bank reconciliation for Wallace Company at May 31.
b. Prepare the general journal entry or entries necessary to bring the Cash in Bank account into agreement with the adjusted balance on the bank reconciliation.

BANK RECONCILIATION — OBJ. 2 —

7-31A The bank reconciliation made by Sandler Company, a sole proprietorship, on March 31, 1993, showed a deposit in transit of $1,100 and two outstanding checks, No. 797 for $450 and No. 804 for $890. The adjusted balance per books on March 31 was $11,720.

The following bank statement is available for April:

BANK STATEMENT

TO Sandler Company Fairbanks, AK			April 30, 1993 FAIRBANKS NATIONAL BANK				
Date	**Deposits**	**No.**	**Date**	**Charges**		**Date**	**Balance**
						March 31	$11,960
Apr. 1	$1,100	804	Apr. 2	$ 890		Apr. 1	13,060
3	1,680	807	3	730		2	12,170
7	1,250	808	7	1,140		3	13,120
13	1,020	809	7	838		7	12,392
18	840	810	16	1,040		13	13,086
23	790	811	13	326		16	12,046
27	1,340	813	27	540		18	12,386
30	1,160	814	23	600		23	12,576
30	60IN	NSF	18	500		27	13,376
		SC	30	40		30	14,556

A list of deposits made and checks written during April, taken from the cash receipts journal and cash disbursements journal, respectively, is shown below:

	Deposits Made		Checks Written	
Apr. 2	$1,680	No. 807	$730
6	1,250	808	1,140
10	1,020	809	838
17	840	810	1,040
22	790	811	272
24	1,340	812	948
29	1,160	813	540
30	1,580	814	600
	$9,660	815	372
		816	920
			$7,400

The Cash in Bank account balance on April 30 was $13,980. In reviewing checks returned by the bank, the bookkeeper discovered that check No. 811, written for $326 for delivery expense, was recorded in the cash disbursements journal as $272. The NSF check for $500 was that of customer R. Koppa, deposited in April. Interest for April added to the account by the bank was $60.

REQUIRED

a. Prepare a bank reconciliation for Sandler Company at April 30.
b. Prepare the necessary journal entries to bring the Cash in Bank account into agreement with the adjusted balance on the bank reconciliation.

PETTY CASH
— OBJ. 3 —

7-32A Wells, Inc., established an imprest petty cash fund on May 1, 1993. The following transactions took place during May:

May 1   Wrote check against American Bank account to establish the petty cash fund, $350.

12   Replenished the fund by check against the American Bank account for $309. The following bills and receipts were on hand:

Charge for rush delivery of packages across town	$ 57
Postage	64
Computer terminal repairs	76
Flowers sent to customer opening new office (advertising expense)	112
	$309

25   Replenished the fund and increased it to $400 by writing a check against the American Bank account. On this date, the fund contained $22 in currency and coins. Bills and receipts on hand were for postage, $90; office supplies expense, $117; and instant printing charges (advertising expense), $124.

REQUIRED

Record the May petty cash transactions for Wells, Inc., in general journal form.

SHORT-TERM INVESTMENTS
— OBJ. 4 —

7-33A The following selected transactions relate to Newell Corporation during 1991 and 1992, its first two years of operations. The company closes its books on December 31.

1991

Feb. 17   Purchased 1,500 common shares of Heath, Inc., as a short-term investment at a total cost of $43,500.

May 31   Purchased, as a short-term investment, sixteen $1,000, 9% Berk Company bonds at 98 plus five months' accrued interest. The brokerage commission was $100. The bonds pay interest on June 30 and December 31.

June 30   Received semiannual interest payment on Berk Company bonds.

July 1   Invested $30,000 in a one-year certificate of deposit at Hilldale Bank. The annual interest rate on the certificate is 7%.

Aug. 10   Purchased 1,200 common shares of Glade, Inc., as a short-term investment at a total cost of $25,200.

Dec. 1 Heath, Inc., declared a cash dividend of $1.15 per common share, payable on December 28. Newell Corporation records dividend income when dividends are received.

5 Received 60 shares of Glade, Inc., common stock as a 5% stock dividend. The stock's current market price per share was $19.

28 Received cash dividend, declared December 1, from Heath, Inc.

31 Received semiannual interest payment on Berk Company bonds.

31 Accrued interest receivable for six months on certificate of deposit. (Newell Corporation does not use reversing entries.)

31 Adjusted portfolio of short-term stock investments to lower of cost or market. Current market prices per share were Heath, Inc., $27, and Glade, Inc., $18.

1992

Feb. 1 Sold Berk Company bonds for $15,920 plus accrued interest for one month.

June 30 Received $32,100 when the one-year certificate of deposit (purchased July 1, 1991) was cashed in.

REQUIRED

a. Record these transactions in general journal form.

b. Assume that holdings of short-term stock investments did not change during 1992. What entry would be made at December 31, 1992, to adjust the portfolio to the lower of cost or market if the per-share market prices at that date were $28 for Heath, Inc., and $20 for Glade, Inc.?

SHORT-TERM INVESTMENTS — OBJ. 4 —

7-34A The following transactions relate to Muller Company's short-term investments in stocks and bonds during 1993:

1993

Jan. 10 Purchased 3,500 common shares of Pond Corporation at a total cost of $96,460.

Feb. 1 Purchased twelve $1,000, 12% Gammon Company bonds at 104 plus one month's accrued interest. The brokerage commission was $80. The bonds pay interest on January 1 and July 1.

May 28 Purchased 1,400 common shares of Edberg, Inc., at a total cost of $19,600.

June 30 Received a cash dividend of 40 cents per common share from Edberg, Inc.

July 1 Received semiannual interest payment on Gammon Company bonds.

1 Purchased fifteen $1,000, 10% Watson Company bonds at 97 plus a $100 brokerage commission. The bonds pay interest on January 1 and July 1.

Sept. 30 Received 210 shares of Pond Corporation common stock as a 6% stock dividend. The stock's current market price per share was $27.

Nov. 1 Sold the Gammon Company bonds for $12,140 plus accrued interest for four months.

17 Sold the Pond Corporation common stock for $29 per share.

Dec. 1 Sold the Watson Company bonds for $15,020 plus accrued interest for five months.

14 Sold the Edberg, Inc., common stock for $12 per share.

REQUIRED

Record these transactions in general journal form.

CASES

Business Decision Case

On December 15, 1993, Sharon Taylor, who owns Taylor Company, asks you to investigate the cash-handling activities in her firm. She believes that an employee might be stealing funds. "I have no proof," she says, "but I'm fairly certain that the November 30, 1993, undeposited receipts amounted to more than $12,000, although the November 30 bank reconciliation prepared by the cashier shows only $7,238.40. Also, the November bank reconciliation doesn't show several checks that have been outstanding for a long time. The cashier told me that these checks needn't appear on the reconciliation because he had notified the bank to stop payment on them and he had made the necessary adjustment on the books. Does that sound reasonable to you?"

At your request, Taylor shows you the following November 30, 1993, bank reconciliation prepared by the cashier:

TAYLOR COMPANY
BANK RECONCILIATION
NOVEMBER 30, 1993

Balance per bank statement		$ 4,720.24	Balance per books		$10,770.44
Add: Deposits in transit		7,238.40			
		$11,958.64			
Less:			Less:		
Outstanding checks:			Bank service charge	$ 60	
No. 2351	$1,100.20		Unrecorded credit	1,200	1,260.00
No. 2353	578.32				
No. 2354	969.68	2,448.20			
Adjusted balance		$ 9,510.44	Adjusted balance		$9,510.44

You discover that the $1,200 unrecorded bank credit represents a note collected by the bank on Taylor's behalf; it appears in the deposits column of the November bank statement. Your investigation also reveals that the October 31, 1993, bank reconciliation showed three checks that had been outstanding longer than 10 months: No. 1432 for $600, No. 1458 for $466.90; and No. 1512 for $253.10. You also discover that these items were never added back into the Cash account in the books. In confirming that the checks shown on the cashier's November 30 bank reconciliation were outstanding on that date, you discover that check No. 2353 was actually a payment of $1,658.32 and had been recorded on the books for that amount.

To confirm the amount of undeposited receipts at November 30, you request a bank statement for December 1–12 (called a *cut-off bank statement*). This indeed shows a December 1 deposit of $7,238.40.

REQUIRED

a. Calculate the amount of funds stolen by the cashier.
b. Describe how the cashier concealed the theft.
c. What sort of entry or entries should be made when a firm decides that checks outstanding for a long time should no longer be carried in the bank reconciliation?
d. What suggestions would you make to Sharon Taylor about cash control procedures?

Analytical Application Case

Balance sheet information (in millions of dollars) from a recent year is summarized below for three companies: PHILLIPS PETROLEUM COMPANY (Phillips), KNIGHT-RIDDER, INC. (Knight), and KELLY SERVICES, INC. (Kelly):

	Phillips	Knight	Kelly
Cash, Cash Equivalents, and Short-term Investments	$ 670	$ 26.2	$217.4
Notes and Accounts Receivable, Net	1,595	262.0	163.5
Inventory and Other Current Assets	1,057	100.7	12.3
Current Liabilities	2,910	313.5	106.0

REQUIRED

a. Calculate the quick ratio for all three companies.
b. Which company is the best able to pay its current liabilities? How is the asset structure of this company different from that of the other two?

Ethics Case

Gina Pullen is the petty cash cashier of a large family-owned restaurant. She has been presented on numerous occasions with properly approved receipts for reimbursement from petty cash that she believes are personal expenses of one of the five owners. She reports to the controller of the company. The controller is also a family member and is the person who approves the receipts for payment out of petty cash.

REQUIRED

What are the accounting implications if Gina is correct? What alternatives should she consider?

How does a company account for losses from uncollectible accounts that arise from credit sales?

When a company extends credit to customers as products or services are sold, the company incurs a risk that the amount owed by the customer will not be collected.

■ Many companies make most of their sales on an open account (accounts receivable) or a credit card basis, rather than a cash basis. ■ On January 25, 1992, J.C. Penney had approximately $3.5 billion total accounts receivable from customers. ■ Of that amount, they estimated that $79 million (approximately 2%) would not be collected.

8

TRADE ACCOUNTS AND NOTES

Business practice today is governed by credit. In recent years, the use of credit by businesses and individuals has expanded immensely. Millions of consumers possess and regularly use several credit cards.

The growth of credit has created a need for more sophisticated systems for processing transactions and gathering credit information. However, the basic accounting problems of keeping track of payables and receivables have remained essentially the same.

TRADE RECEIVABLES AND PAYABLES

OBJECTIVE ❶ INTRODUCE *trade receivables and trade payables and* **DESCRIBE** *installment accounts.*

The terms **trade receivable** and **trade payable** usually refer to receivables and payables that arise in the regular course of a company's transactions with customers and suppliers. Payments normally are made within 10 to 60 days. Therefore, the amount of a sale of merchandise sold on account is debited to the appropriate customer's account in the accounts receivable subsidiary ledger; this amount is also debited to the Accounts Receivable control account when credit sales are posted periodically to it. The subsidiary ledger and the control account should reflect only trade accounts. Advances to company employees or officers should not be included here, nor should advances to affiliated companies, such as subsidiaries, be included. Such receivables should be recorded in separate accounts. In many instances, such receivables are not current, and as a result, they often appear in the balance sheet under a noncurrent heading, such as Other Assets. Advances to subsidiary companies are frequently semipermanent, and they may be found in the balance sheet under the Investments caption.

Likewise, trade accounts payable consist only of open amounts owing for the purchase of merchandise and materials, or the acquisition of services from outsiders. Separate current liability accounts contain amounts that a firm owes for salaries, wages, taxes, and various accruals.

Occasionally, individual accounts within the accounts receivable or accounts payable subsidiary ledgers may show abnormal balances. A customer may have overpaid an account, paid an advance on goods not yet shipped, or returned goods already paid for. A substantial credit balance in a customer's Accounts Receivable account is reclassified as a current liability when a balance sheet is prepared. On the other hand, if the firm itself makes advances on purchases or overpays accounts, the resulting debit balances in Accounts Payable are reclassified as current assets in the balance sheet.

INSTALLMENT ACCOUNTS

Many business concerns—such as mail-order houses and appliance dealers—make many of their sales on the **installment** basis. Typically, a customer of such a firm purchases merchandise by signing an installment contract in which the customer agrees to a down payment plus installment payments of a fixed amount over a period such as 24 or 36 months. Normally, the total price of the merchandise sold includes an interest charge, and the contract allows the seller to repossess the merchandise if the installment payments are not made. If the installment contract conforms to the firm's normal trade practices and terms, the installment receivable is classified as a current asset.

LOSSES FROM UNCOLLECTIBLE ACCOUNTS

OBJECTIVE ❷ DEFINE *losses from uncollectible accounts,* **DISCUSS** *the allowance method, and* **ILLUSTRATE** *writing off specific accounts under the allowance method.*

Firms that extend credit to customers anticipate reasonable credit losses. The magnitude of such losses is usually related to the firm's credit policy. A company may deliberately liberalize its credit policy to obtain increased sales, fully anticipating an increase in credit losses.

Most large companies have credit departments to administer management's credit policies. Credit personnel may conduct investigations, establish credit limits, and follow up on unpaid accounts. They may also decide, following written collection procedures, when a debt is uncollectible.

Credit losses, considered operating expenses of the business, are debited to an appropriately titled account such as **Uncollectible Accounts Expense.** Other account titles frequently used are *Loss from Uncollectible Accounts, Loss from Doubtful Accounts,* or *Bad Debts Expense.* Normally, the expense is classified as a selling expense on the income statement, although some companies include it with administrative expenses.

Credit losses are incurred in the process of generating sales revenue. The matching concept used in accrual accounting states that expenses should be linked, or matched, with the revenues to which they relate in determining net income. Applied to credit losses, the matching concept dictates that uncollectible accounts expense be recorded in the same accounting period as the related credit sales are made. At the time a specific credit sale is made, however, the seller does not know whether the account receivable will be collected in full, in part, or not at all. Any loss from an uncollectible account may not be known for several months, or even a year or more. To accomplish the appropriate matching, therefore, accountants must estimate the uncollectible accounts expense to report in the income statement. The estimate is recorded in an end-of-period adjusting entry. The overall process of estimating uncollectible accounts expense is called the *allowance method.*

The **allowance method** receives its name because the adjusting entry credits a contra asset account called *Allowance for Uncollectible Accounts.* Consequently, the allowance method not only matches credit losses with the related sales, but also reports accounts receivable at their estimated realizable value in the end-of-period balance sheet. To illustrate, assume a firm estimates its uncollectible accounts expense for a period to be $4,000 and makes the following adjusting entry:

1992			
Dec. 31	Uncollectible Accounts Expense	4,000	
	Allowance for Uncollectible Accounts		4,000
	To record uncollectible accounts expense.		

The credit is made to the **Allowance for Uncollectible Accounts** account rather than to Accounts Receivable for two reasons. First, when the firm makes the adjusting entry, it does not know which accounts in the subsidiary accounts receivable ledger will be uncollectible. If the Accounts Receivable control account is credited and no entries are made in the subsidiary ledger, then the two records no longer agree in total. Second, because the amount involved is only an estimate, it is preferable not to reduce Accounts Receivable directly.

Allowance for Uncollectible Accounts is a contra asset account with a normal credit balance. To present the expected realizable value of Accounts Receivable, we deduct Allowance for Uncollectible Accounts from Accounts Receivable in the balance sheet. Assuming the firm had $100,000 of accounts receivable (and a zero balance in Allowance for Uncollectible Accounts before the December 31, 1992, adjusting entry), the year-end balance sheet presentation is as follows:

Current Assets		
Cash		$ 52,000
Accounts Receivable	$100,000	
Less: Allowance for Uncollectible Accounts	4,000	96,000
Inventory		125,000
Other Current Assets		31,000
Total Current Assets		$304,000

Writing Off Specific Accounts under the Allowance Method

The credit manager or other company official normally authorizes writing off a specific account. When the accounting department is notified of the action, it makes the following entry:

```
1993
Jan. 5    Allowance for Uncollectible Accounts          300
              Accounts Receivable—Monroe Company              300
          To write off Monroe Company's account.
```

The credit in the above entry is made to Monroe Company's account in the accounts receivable subsidiary ledger as well as to the Accounts Receivable control account; therefore, these two records remain in agreement.

The entry to write off an account does not affect net income or total assets. By means of the year-end adjusting entry, the expense is reflected in the period when the related revenue is recorded. Furthermore, because Allowance for Uncollectible Accounts is deducted from Accounts Receivable in the balance sheet, the *net* realizable value of accounts receivable is not changed by the write-off. After Monroe Company's account has been written off, the Accounts Receivable and Allowance for Uncollectible Accounts general ledger accounts appear as follows:

ACCOUNTS RECEIVABLE   ACCOUNT NO. 12

Date		Description	Post. Ref.	Debit	Credit	Balance
1993 Jan.	1	Balance				100,000
	5	Write-off, Monroe Company			300	99,700

ALLOWANCE FOR UNCOLLECTIBLE ACCOUNTS   ACCOUNT NO. 13

Date		Description	Post. Ref.	Debit	Credit	Balance
1993 Jan.	1	Balance				4,000
	5	Write-off, Monroe Company		300		3,700

In these accounts, the net realizable value of accounts receivable on January 1, 1993, is $96,000 ($100,000 − $4,000 allowance). After the January 5, 1993, write-off, the net realizable value of accounts receivable is still $96,000 ($99,700 − $3,700 allowance). Thus, the write-off of an account does not affect the net asset balance.

ESTIMATING CREDIT LOSSES UNDER THE ALLOWANCE METHOD

Estimates of credit losses are generally based on past experience, with consideration given to forecasts of sales activity, economic conditions, and planned changes in credit policy. The most commonly used calculations are related either to credit sales for the period or to the amount of accounts receivable at the close of the period.

Percentage of Net Sales Method

Through experience, many companies can determine the approximate percentage of credit sales that will be uncollectible. At the end of an accounting period, the amount of the adjusting entry is determined by multiplying the total credit sales by this per-

OBJECTIVE ③ DESCRIBE *and* ILLUSTRATE *two methods for estimating credit losses—the percentage of net sales method and the accounts receivable aging method—and* ILLUSTRATE *how to record recoveries of accounts written off.*

centage. Suppose that credit sales for 1993 amount to $500,000 and that past experience indicates a loss of 2%. The adjusting entry for expected losses for 1993 would appear as follows:

1993			
Dec. 31	Uncollectible Accounts Expense	10,000	
	Allowance for Uncollectible Accounts		10,000
	To record uncollectible accounts expense.		

Because the periodic estimates for uncollectible accounts under this procedure are related to sales, a firm should review its allowance account regularly to ensure a reasonable balance. Should the allowance account balance become too large or too small, the percentage used for the periodic estimates should be revised accordingly.

A company that uses the **percentage of net sales method** usually applies the uncollectible percentage only to credit sales, excluding cash sales, since only credit sales will be subject to credit losses. Further, sales discounts and sales returns and allowances should be deducted from the credit sales before applying the percentage.

Accounts Receivable Aging Method

A firm may estimate uncollectible accounts expense indirectly by determining the appropriate balance in the Allowance for Uncollectible Accounts account at the end of the year. The year-end balance in Allowance for Uncollectible Accounts represents the firm's estimate of the year-end accounts receivable that will prove uncollectible. The **accounts receivable aging method** uses this approach. When using the accounts receivable aging method, a company would determine the amount needed in the allowance account by analyzing the age structure of the account balances. An aging schedule similar to the one in Exhibit 8-1 would be used. An **aging schedule** is simply an analysis that shows how long customers' balances have remained unpaid. Assume that the firm whose aging schedule appears in Exhibit 8-1 sells on net terms of 30 days. Alton's account is current, which means that the $320 billing was made within the last 30 days. Bailey's account is 0–30 days *past due*, which means that the account is from 31 to 60 days old. Wall's balance consists of a $50 billing made from 91 to 150 days ago and a $100 billing made from 151 days to seven months ago, and so on.

Companies that analyze their bad accounts experience with the aged balances may develop percentages of each age group that are likely to prove uncollectible. At the end of each period, these percentages are applied to the totals of each age group to determine the allowance account balance. For our example, these percentages are shown below. Applying the percentages to the totals in our aging schedule, we calculate an allowance requirement of $1,560.

EXHIBIT 8—1	AGING SCHEDULE OF CUSTOMER BALANCES DECEMBER 31, 1993

			Past Due				
Customer	Account Balance	Current	0–30 Days	31–60 Days	61–120 Days	121 Days –6 Mos.	Over 6 Mos.
Alton, J.	$ 320	$ 320					
Bailey, C.	400		$ 400				
. . .	. . .	. . .	. . .	. . .	. . .	. . .	. . .
Wall, M.	150				50	100	
Zorn, W.	210			210			
	$50,000	$42,000	$4,000	$2,000	$1,000	$800	$200

	Amount	Percent Doubtful	Allowance Required
Current	$42,000	2	$ 840
0–30 days past due	4,000	3	120
31–60 days past due	2,000	5	100
61–120 days past due	1,000	20	200
121 days–6 months past due	800	25	200
Over 6 months past due	200	50	100
Total Allowance Required			$1,560

Suppose that the allowance account has a $400 credit balance before adjustment. The adjusting entry would be

1993
Dec. 31 Uncollectible Accounts Expense 1,160
   Allowance for Uncollectible Accounts 1,160
  To record uncollectible accounts expense.

This entry brings the credit balance in the allowance account to the required amount—$1,560, as shown below:

ALLOWANCE FOR UNCOLLECTIBLE ACCOUNTS   ACCOUNT NO. 13

Date		Description	Post. Ref.	Debit	Credit	Balance
1993 Dec.	31	Balance before adjusting entry				400
	31	Adjusting entry			1,160	1,560

It is possible to have a debit balance in the allowance account before adjustment. This would occur whenever the write-off of specific accounts during the year exceeded the credit balance in the account at the beginning of the year. Assume, for example, that the allowance account had a $350 debit balance before the December 31, 1993, adjusting entry and that the aging schedule showed that the allowance account should have a $1,560 credit balance. The adjusting entry would then be as follows:

1993
Dec. 31 Uncollectible Accounts Expense 1,910
   Allowance for Uncollectible Accounts 1,910
  To record uncollectible accounts expense.

The Allowance for Uncollectible Accounts ledger account below shows that this entry creates the desired year-end credit balance of $1,560.

ALLOWANCE FOR UNCOLLECTIBLE ACCOUNTS   ACCOUNT NO. 13

Date		Description	Post. Ref.	Debit	Credit	Balance
1993 Dec.	31	Balance before adjusting entry				(350)
	31	Adjusting entry			1,910	1,560

Recoveries of Accounts Written Off under the Allowance Method

Occasionally, accounts written off against Allowance for Uncollectible Accounts later prove to be wholly or partially collectible. In such situations, a firm should reinstate the customer's account for the amount recovered before recording the collection. Then the payment can be recorded in the customer's account. The entry made for the write-off is reversed to the extent of the recovery and the receipt is recorded in the usual manner. For example, assume that a company using the allowance method wrote off Monroe Company's $300 account on January 5, 1993, but received a $200 payment on April 20, 1993. The following entries (including write-off) illustrate the recovery procedure.

To write off the account

1993			
Jan. 5	Allowance for Uncollectible Accounts	300	
	Accounts Receivable—Monroe Company		300
	To write off Monroe Company's account.		

To reinstate the account

Apr. 20	Accounts Receivable—Monroe Company	200	
	Allowance for Uncollectible Accounts		200
	To reinstate Monroe Company's account to the extent of the recovery.		

To record remittance

Apr. 20	Cash	200	
	Accounts Receivable—Monroe Company		200
	To record collection of cash on account.		

These last two entries are prepared the same way even if the recovery occurs in a year subsequent to the year in which the account was written off.

DIRECT WRITE-OFF METHOD

OBJECTIVE 4 INTRODUCE *the direct write-off method and* CONTRAST *it to the allowance method.*

The direct write-off method of accounting for credit losses is an alternative to the allowance method. Under the **direct write-off method,** uncollectible accounts are charged to expense in the period in which they are determined to be uncollectible. There is no estimate of uncollectible accounts expense, no allowance account, and no year-end adjusting entry. For most companies, the direct write-off method is not an acceptable method of accounting for credit losses, because it does not properly match credit losses with sales. However, the direct write-off method is used by virtually all companies for income tax purposes. Only certain financial institutions are allowed to use the allowance method for income tax purposes in limited situations.

The entries that would be made when the direct write-off method is used are illustrated below, using the data from the previous example:

To write off the account

1993			
Jan. 5	Uncollectible Accounts Expense	300	
	Accounts Receivable—Monroe Company		300
	To write off Monroe Company's account.		

To reinstate the account

Apr. 20	Accounts Receivable—Monroe Company	200	
	Uncollectible Accounts Expense		200
	To reinstate Monroe Company's account to the extent of the recovery.		

To record remittance

Apr. 20	Cash	200	
	Accounts Receivable—Monroe Company		200
	To record collection of cash on account.		

If an account written off in a prior year is reinstated during the current year, and the Uncollectible Accounts Expense account has no balance from other write-offs (and no more write-offs are expected), then the account credited in the reinstatement entry would be Uncollectible Accounts Recovery, a revenue account.

The major shortcoming of the direct write-off method is that credit losses are not matched with related sales. The use of the direct write-off method also causes consistent overstatement of accounts receivable on the balance sheet. Because generally accepted accounting principles prescribe that accounts receivable be shown at the amount that the firm expects to collect, the direct write-off method is usually inappropriate except for income tax calculations.

THE CREDIT DECISION

Businesses and individuals become borrowers whenever they buy merchandise on credit or take out a loan from a financial institution. Before selling on credit or granting a loan, the potential lender (the seller or financial institution) must evaluate the credit-worthiness of the borrower. Lenders typically use one or both of two primary techniques to evaluate credit-worthiness—credit scoring and credit bureau checking. ■ *Many of the credit scoring systems in use today are computer-based, to facilitate the many calculations and comparisons necessary to score a*

credit application. These computerized systems were developed by analyzing profiles of past borrowers, both those who repaid their debt on a timely basis and those who did not. The results of the analysis are then formulated into a set of characteristics and variables with minimal values, used to predict whether a particular applicant is likely to be a good or bad borrower.

Prior to receiving the loan, a potential borrower completes a credit application that contains questions related to the characteristics and variables in the scoring system. The data on the credit application are then entered into the computerized scoring system, which grades the application. Each potential lender will

place slightly different emphasis on each factor. Most of the lenders' scoring systems focus on the applicant's ability to generate net income and cash flow, current level and planned repayment of existing borrowing, existing level of current assets, industry or occupation, and plans for the future.

If the result of the credit scoring falls within an acceptable range, the lender will continue the credit approval process by contacting a credit bureau or other credit references. A credit bureau is an organization that collects borrowing and repayment information about businesses and individuals, summarizes it over time, and adds other information that the credit bureau obtains from a

variety of sources. Lenders use *credit bureau checking* to quickly and conveniently obtain a prior borrowing and repayment profile of the applicant.

The three leading nationwide credit bureaus for information on individuals are TRW, Equifax, and Trans Union Credit Information. It is estimated that these organizations have 400 million records on 160 million individuals. In addition to providing information on credit history to lenders, these credit bureaus also provide their information in various forms to smaller credit bureaus as well as a number of other customers who use the information for telemarketing (selling by telephone) and direct sales solicitation (selling by mail).*

After receiving the credit score and a report from a credit bureau, the lender decides whether to extend credit to the applicant. Most lenders follow strict procedures in the granting of credit to make sure that they are not extending credit to applicants that are bad credit risks and to comply with federal, state, and local regulations concerning the granting of credit.

* For further information, see "Is Nothing Private?" *Business Week*, September 4, 1989, pp. 74–82.

CREDIT CARD SALES

OBJECTIVE 5 DISCUSS *the accounting treatment of credit card sales.*

Many businesses, especially retailers, allow their customers to use credit cards for credit sales. Popular credit cards include VISA, MasterCard, Discover, American Express, Carte Blanche, and Diners Club. When a purchaser uses a credit card to make a credit purchase, the seller collects cash from the credit card company, and the purchaser pays cash to the credit card company. To facilitate this process, the seller prepares a sales slip using the credit card. The seller will either imprint the card number on a slip using the card or will use an electronic device such as a cash register with a card reader to read the card number from the magnetic strip on the back of the card and print a sales slip with the card number on it. The second approach also allows for electronic accumulation of credit card sales data. In either case, the purchaser is usually asked to sign the sales slip.

The issuer of a credit card, frequently a financial institution or one of its subsidiaries, charges the seller a fee each time a card is used. This **credit card fee** usually ranges from 1% to 5% of credit card sales. Sellers are willing to incur this fee because credit cards provide benefits to the seller: the seller does not have to evaluate creditworthiness of customers using credit cards; the seller avoids all risks of noncollection of the account; and the seller typically receives the cash from the credit card issuer faster than if the customer were granted credit by the seller.

Depending on the type of credit card, there are two ways that the seller may collect from the credit card issuer: immediately upon deposit of the credit card sales slips or delayed until paid subsequently by the credit card company. For cards issued by a financial institution, cash is received immediately upon deposit of the sales slips at the financial institution. The entry to record a $1,000 credit card sale of this type on March 15, with a 3% credit card fee, follows:

Mar. 15	Cash	970	
	Credit Card Fee Expense	30	
	Sales		1,000
	To record credit card sales and collection, less a 3% fee.		

If, instead, sales slips are sent to a credit card company for subsequent cash settlement, the entries to record the $1,000 credit card sale with subsequent collection on March 23, would be as follows:

Mar. 15	Accounts Receivable—Credit Card Company	970	
	Credit Card Fee Expense	30	
	Sales		1,000
	To record credit card sales.		
Mar. 23	Cash	970	
	Accounts Receivable—Credit Card Company		970
	To record collection from credit card company.		

NOTES RECEIVABLE AND PAYABLE

OBJECTIVE 6 ILLUSTRATE *a promissory note, discuss the calculation of interest on promissory notes, and* PRESENT *journal entries to record notes and interest.*

Promissory notes are often used in transactions when the credit period is longer than the 30 or 60 days typical for open accounts. Although promissory notes are used frequently in sales of equipment and real property, a note is sometimes exchanged for merchandise. Occasionally, a note is substituted for an open account when an extension of the usual credit period is granted. Promissory notes are normally prepared when loans are obtained from financial institutions.

A **promissory note** is a written promise to pay a certain sum of money on demand or at a fixed and determinable future date. The note is signed by the **maker** and made payable to the order of either a specific **payee** or to the **bearer**. The interest rate specified on the note is typically an annual rate. A promissory note is illustrated in Exhibit 8-2.

A note from a debtor is called a **note receivable** by the holder and a **note payable** by the debtor. A note is usually regarded as a stronger claim against a debtor than an open account because the terms of payment are specified in writing. Although open accounts can be sold (*factored*), a note can be converted to cash more easily by discounting it at a bank.

Interest on Notes

Interest is a charge for the use of money. Interest incurred on a promissory note is interest income to the holder or payee of the note and interest expense to the maker of the note. Since business firms want to distinguish between operating and nonoperating items in their income statements, they place interest income and interest expense under the Other Income and Expense heading in the income statement.

The amount of interest on a promissory note is determined using one of two methods: the add-on interest method or the discount method.

EXHIBIT 8—2	A PROMISSORY NOTE

$2,000.00   Chicago, Illinois   May 3, 1993

Sixty days   after date   I   promise to pay to

the order of _____ Susan Robinson _____

Two Thousand and no/100---------------------------dollars

for value received with interest at   9%

payable at   First Bank of Chicago, Illinois

James Stone

Add-on Interest Method

Interest on a short-term promissory note using the *add-on interest method* is paid at the maturity date of the note. The formula for determining the amount of interest follows:

$$\text{Interest} = \text{Principal} \times \frac{\text{Interest}}{\text{Rate}} \times \frac{\text{Interest}}{\text{Time}}$$

The principal or face amount of a note with add-on interest is the amount borrowed. The interest rate is the annual rate of interest. Interest time is the fraction of a year that the note is outstanding.

When a note is written for a certain number of months, time is expressed in twelfths of a year. For example, interest on a six-month note for $2,000 with a 9% annual interest rate would be

$$\text{Interest} = \$2,000 \times 0.09 \times \frac{6}{12} = \$90$$

When a note's duration is given in days, time is expressed as a fraction of a year; the numerator is the number of days the note will be outstanding and the denominator is 360 days. (Some lenders use 360 days; others use 365 days; we will use 360 days in our examples, exercises, and problems). For example, interest on a 60-day note for $2,000 with a 9% annual interest rate would be

$$\text{Interest} = \$2,000 \times 0.09 \times \frac{60}{360} = \$30$$

DETERMINING MATURITY DATE

When a note's duration is expressed in days, we count the exact days in each calendar month to determine the **maturity date.** For example, a 90-day note dated July 21 would have an October 19 maturity date, which we determine as follows:

10 days in July (remainder of month—31 days minus 21 days)
31 days in August
30 days in September
19 days in October (number of days required to total 90)
90

If the duration of a note is expressed in months, we find the maturity date simply by counting the months from the date of issue. For example, a two-month note dated January 31 would mature on March 31, a three-month note of the same date would mature on April 30 (the last day of the month), and a four-month note would mature on May 31.

RECORDING NOTES AND INTEREST

When a note is exchanged to settle an open trade account, an entry is made to reflect the note receivable or payable and to reduce the balance of the related account receivable or payable. For example, suppose Jordon Company sold $12,000 of merchandise on account to Bowman Company. On October 1, after the regular credit period had elapsed, Bowman Company gave Jordon Company a 60-day, 9% note for $12,000. The following entries would be made by each of the parties:

Jordon Company

Oct. 1	Notes Receivable	12,000	
	Accounts Receivable—Bowman Company		12,000
	Received 60-day, 9% note in payment of account.		

Bowman Company

Oct. 1	Accounts Payable—Jordon Company	12,000	
	Notes Payable		12,000
	Gave 60-day, 9% note in payment of account.		

If Bowman Company pays the note on the November 30 maturity date, the following entries would be made by the parties involved:

Jordon Company

Nov. 30	Cash	12,180	
	Interest Income		180
	Notes Receivable		12,000
	Collected Bowman Company note		
	($12,000 × 0.09 × $\frac{60}{360}$ = $180).		

Bowman Company

Nov. 30	Notes Payable	12,000	
	Interest Expense	180	
	Cash		12,180
	Paid note to Jordon Company.		

RECORDING DISHONORED NOTES

The interest for 60 days at 9% is recorded by the respective parties on the maturity date of the note, even if the maker defaults on (dishonors) the note. When a note is dishonored at maturity, the amount of the combined principal plus interest is converted to an open account. This procedure leaves only the current, unmatured notes in the holder's Notes Receivable account and the maker's Notes Payable account. If Bowman Company did not pay the note on November 30, the following entries would be made:

Jordon Company

Nov. 30	Accounts Receivable—Bowman Company	12,180	
	Interest Income		180
	Notes Receivable		12,000
	To record the dishonoring of a note by Bowman Company.		

Bowman Company

Nov. 30	Notes Payable—Jordon Company	12,000	
	Interest Expense	180	
	Accounts Payable—Jordon Company		12,180
	To record the nonpayment of a note due to Jordon Company.		

Discount Method

The discount method of determining interest is used in two different situations—borrowing at a discount and discounting customers' notes receivable. In both situations, the party discounting the note will receive less than the note's maturity value.

BORROWING AT A DISCOUNT

When a company borrows money from a financial institution, such as a bank, the financial institution may require the company to sign a note and "borrow at a discount." In this case, the company is said to be "discounting its own note."

OBJECTIVE 7 DESCRIBE *the procedures and journal entries for borrowing at a discount and discounting customers' notes receivable.*

When a company **borrows at a discount,** the face amount of the note is equal to its maturity value. No additional amount will be required at the maturity date for interest since the interest is included in the maturity value. The cash proceeds of the borrowing will be determined using the following formula:

$$\text{Proceeds} = \frac{\text{Maturity}}{\text{Value}} - \text{Discount}$$

The formula for determining the amount of discount follows:

$$\text{Discount} = \frac{\text{Maturity}}{\text{Value}} \times \frac{\text{Discount}}{\text{Rate}} \times \frac{\text{Discount}}{\text{Time}}$$

Note the similarity to the add-on interest formula, which was previously explained:

$$\text{Interest} = \text{Principal} \times \frac{\text{Interest}}{\text{Rate}} \times \frac{\text{Interest}}{\text{Time}}$$

In the discount formula, the discount rate is the annual rate being charged by the financial institution on a discounted basis, and the discount time is the fraction of a year that the discounted note will be outstanding.

Suppose that Jordon Company agrees to borrow at a discount and signs a 12%, $8,000, 60-day note at Great American Bank. The note is dated December 16. The calculation of discount and proceeds are as follows:

$$\text{Discount} = \$8,000 \times 0.12 \times \frac{60}{360} = \$160$$

$$\text{Proceeds} = \$8,000 - \$160 = \$7,840$$

Jordon Company would make the following entry to record the signing of the note and the receipt of the $7,840 cash proceeds:

Dec. 16	Cash	7,840	
	Discount on Notes Payable	160	
	Notes Payable		8,000
	To record the note signed at Great American Bank and the receipt of the proceeds.		

Note that the $160 is debited to **Discount on Notes Payable** rather than Interest Expense. Discount on Notes Payable is a contra account that is subtracted from the Notes Payable amount on the balance sheet. As the life of the note elapses, the discount is reduced and charged to Interest Expense. We illustrate this adjustment procedure later in the chapter.

Because the proceeds of this type of note are less than the maturity value of the note, the **effective interest rate** for the loan is greater than the stated discount rate. The effective interest rate may be calculated by the following formula:

$$\text{Effective Interest Rate} = \frac{\text{Maturity Value of Note} \times \text{Stated Discount Rate}}{\text{Cash Proceeds from Note}}$$

Therefore, the effective interest rate on the Jordon Company note is computed as follows:

$$\frac{\$8,000 \times 12\%}{\$7,840} = 12.24\%$$

When a company receives a note receivable from a customer, the company may not want to wait until the maturity date of the note to receive cash. The company can endorse the note over to a financial institution, such as a bank, and receive cash from the institution. This process is known as **discounting** a customer's note receivable at the bank. The amount received will be the maturity value less a discount.

The financial institution will collect the maturity value of a discounted note from the maker on the maturity date of the note. If the discounting was done **with**

recourse, the company that discounted the note is liable if the maker of the note does not pay the financial institution. If the discounting was done **without recourse,** the company that discounted the note is not liable if the maker of the note does not pay the financial institution. In most instances, discounting is done with recourse.

When a company discounts a customer's note receivable at a financial institution with recourse, a contingent or potential liability is created (that is, the liability is contingent on the failure of the maker to pay). The **contingent liability** from a significant discounted notes receivable is disclosed in footnotes to the financial statements.

Three formulas are required to determine the proceeds received from discounting a customer's note receivable at a financial institution:

$$\text{Maturity Value} = \text{Principal} + \text{Interest to Maturity}$$

$$\text{Discount} = \text{Maturity Value} \times \text{Discount Rate} \times \text{Discount Time}$$

$$\text{Proceeds} = \text{Maturity Value} - \text{Discount}$$

The terms of these formulas are similar to the terms used in the formulas for borrowing at a discount. Maturity value includes the entire amount of interest that the maker of the note will eventually pay. Interest to maturity will be determined by multiplying the principal amount of the note times the interest stated on the face of the note times the fraction of a year that the note will be outstanding.

The discount rate is the annual rate charged by the financial institution when the discount is determined. The discount rate can be higher, the same, or lower than the interest rate of the note itself. Discount time is the amount of time, expressed in a fraction of a year, between the date the note is discounted and the maturity date of the note. Discount time is always less than or equal to interest time.

Suppose Jordon Company receives a $10,000 note from Langford Company on April 15. The note has an annual interest rate of 12% and is due in 90 days. Jordon holds the note for 50 days, then discounts it (on June 4) at Great American Bank at a discount rate of 9%. The calculation of the proceeds would be as follows:

$$\text{Maturity Value} = \text{Principal} + \text{Interest to Maturity}$$

$$= \$10,000 + \left(\$10,000 \times 0.12 \times \frac{90}{360}\right)$$

$$= \$10,300$$

$$\text{Discount} = \text{Maturity Value} \times \text{Discount Rate} \times \text{Discount Time}$$

$$= \$10,300 \times 0.09 \times \frac{40}{360}$$

$$= \$103$$

$$\text{Proceeds} = \text{Maturity Value} - \text{Discount}$$

$$= \$10,300 - \$103$$

$$= \$10,197$$

The journal entry that Jordon Company would make to record the discounting of the Langford Company note follows:

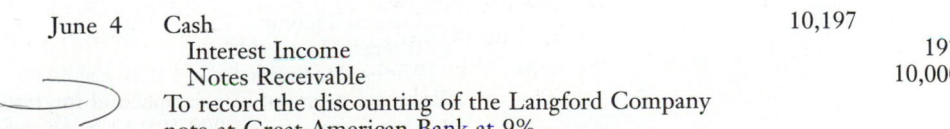

June 4	Cash	10,197	
	Interest Income		197
	Notes Receivable		10,000
	To record the discounting of the Langford Company note at Great American Bank at 9%.		

In the previous entry, the cash proceeds exceed the principal amount of the note. It is possible, when discounting another note, that the cash proceeds would be less than the principal amount of the note. In that case, the difference between the cash proceeds and the principal would be debited to Interest Expense.

DISCOUNTED NOTES RECEIVABLE DISHONORED

At the maturity date, the bank contacts the maker of a discounted note and attempts to collect the maturity value. If the maker refuses to pay, and if the note was discounted with recourse, the bank will contact the company that discounted the note and demand that it pay the maturity value. The bank communicates to the company that discounted the note by sending it a *notice of protest*. This notice will document the maturity value that is due and will also state the amount of *protest fee* that the bank is charging the company that discounted the note.

Jordon Company would make the following entry to record its payment after receiving a notice of protest on July 16 that Langford Company failed to pay its note to Great American Bank on July 14 (protest fee is $25):

July 16	Accounts Receivable—Langford Company	10,325	
	Cash		10,325
	Paid Langford Company's note plus a $25 protest fee to Great American Bank.		

Jordon Company would then attempt to collect the entire $10,325 from Langford Company. If Jordon fails to do so, then Jordon would write off the account as uncollectible, using the procedures described earlier in this chapter.

Adjusting Entries for Interest

When the terms of promissory notes extend beyond the end of an accounting period, adjusting entries are necessary to reflect interest in the proper accounting period. Year-end adjusting entries are made to record interest income on notes receivable and interest expense on notes payable. The adjustments apply to both notes with add-on interest and discount notes.

ADD-ON INTEREST

OBJECTIVE 8 PRESENT *the adjusting entries required for add-on interest and borrowing at a discount.*

Assume that Jordon Company has one note receivable outstanding at December 31, 1993. The note receivable from Garcia Company is dated December 21, 1993, has a principal amount of $6,000, an interest rate of 12%, and a maturity date of February 19, 1994. The adjusting entries that Jordon Company and Garcia Company would make at December 31, 1993, follow:

Jordon Company

1993			
Dec. 31	Interest Receivable	20	
	Interest Income		20
	To accrue interest income on the note from Garcia Company ($6,000 × 0.12 × $\frac{10}{360}$ = $20).		

Garcia Company

1993			
Dec. 31	Interest Expense	20	
	Interest Payable		20
	To accrue interest expense on the note to Jordon Company.		

When the note is subsequently paid on February 19, 1994, the two companies would make the following entries (assuming no reversing entries were made on January 1, 1994):

Jordon Company

1994			
Feb. 19	Cash	3,120	
	Interest Income		100
	Interest Receivable		20
	Notes Receivable		3,000
	Received payment of principal and interest from Garcia Company ($6,000 × 0.12 × $\frac{50}{360}$ = $100).		

Garcia Company

1994

Feb. 19	Notes Payable	3,000	
	Interest Expense	100	
	Interest Payable	20	
	Cash		3,120
	Paid principal and interest to Jordon Company.		

BORROWING AT A DISCOUNT

Earlier in this chapter, we illustrated borrowing at a discount by having Jordon Company sign an $8,000 note in exchange for $7,840 cash. The entry that Jordon Company made to record the note (assume that the date of the note was December 16, 1993) follows:

1993

Dec. 16	Cash	7,840	
	Discount on Notes Payable	160	
	Notes Payable		8,000
	To record the note signed at Great American Bank and the receipt of the proceeds.		

The following is the adjusting entry that Jordon Company would make at December 31, 1993:

1993

Dec. 31	Interest Expense	40	
	Discount on Notes Payable		40

To record interest expense on the note to Great American Bank ($160 $\times \dfrac{15 \text{ days}}{60 \text{ days}} =$ $40).

In its December 31, 1993 balance sheet, Jordon Company would show the $120 remaining Discount on Notes Payable as a contra liability account, subtracted from the Notes Payable amount.

When the note is paid off on February 14, 1994, Jordon Company would make the following entry (assuming no reversing entries were made on January 1, 1994):

1994

Feb. 14	Notes Payable	8,000	
	Interest Expense	120	
	Discount on Notes Payable		120
	Cash		8,000
	Payment of note to Great American Bank at maturity.		

Notes and Interest in Financial Statements

OBJECTIVE 9 ILLUSTRATE *the treatment of notes and interest in financial statements.*

A business shows short-term trade notes receivable as current assets in the balance sheet; because they can normally be converted to cash fairly easily, these notes usually are placed above trade accounts receivable. As with accounts receivable, trade notes receivable are separated from notes from officers and employees and notes representing advances to affiliated companies. If such notes are not truly short-term, they should not be classified as current assets. Interest Receivable is also a current asset.

Sometimes companies with a large volume of notes receivable must provide for possible losses on notes. Frequently, the provision for credit losses also covers losses on notes as well. In such cases, the Allowance for Uncollectible Accounts account is deducted from the sum of Accounts Receivable and Notes Receivable in the balance sheet.

Trade notes payable and notes payable to banks are usually shown separately in the current liabilities section of the balance sheet. Interest Payable is normally shown separately. Discount on Notes Payable is deducted from the related Notes Payable amount. The order in which current payables appear is less important than the sequence of current assets; however, Notes Payable customarily precedes Accounts Payable.

A current section of a balance sheet is shown in Exhibit 8-3 to illustrate the presentation of items discussed in this chapter.

EXHIBIT 8—3		

HURON COMPANY
PARTIAL BALANCE SHEET
DECEMBER 31, 1993

Current Assets

Cash		$ 2,000
Notes Receivable—Trade		24,000
Accounts Receivable—Trade	$50,000	
Less: Allowance for Uncollectible Accounts	1,500	48,500
Interest Receivable		300
Inventory		75,000
Prepaid Expenses		200
Total Current Assets		$150,000

Current Liabilities

Notes Payable—Banks	$ 8,000	
Less: Discount on Notes Payable	60	$ 7,940
Notes Payable—Trade		20,000
Accounts Payable—Trade		30,000
Interest Payable		400
Other Accrued Liabilities		11,660
Total Current Liabilities		$ 70,000

Because they are financial rather than operating items, we often separate Interest Expense and Interest Income from operating items in the income statement. They usually appear under the classification *Other Income and Expense*, as shown in Exhibit 8-4. With this type of presentation, readers can make intercompany comparisons of operating results that are not influenced by the financing patterns of the companies involved.

ANALYTICAL APPLICATION

OBJECTIVE 10 DEFINE accounts receivable turnover *and* average collection period *and* EXPLAIN *their use*.

ACCOUNTS RECEIVABLE TURNOVER AND AVERAGE COLLECTION PERIOD

Most companies make the majority of their sales on credit. Doing so creates trade accounts receivable. Management and financial analysts monitor trade accounts receivable using a variety of measures, including accounts receivable turnover and the average collection period. **Accounts receivable turnover** indicates how many times a year a firm collects its average accounts receivable and, thus, measures how fast accounts receivable are converted into cash. Accounts receivable turnover is computed as follows:

$$\text{Accounts Receivable Turnover} = \frac{\text{Net Sales}}{\text{Average Accounts Receivable}}$$

The numerator in this ratio is net sales. Ideally, the numerator should be net credit sales, but financial information available to analysts and other external users does not usually divide net sales into credit sales and cash sales. Average accounts receivable (net of the allowance for uncollectible accounts) is calculated by summing the beginning and ending accounts receivable (net) and dividing the sum by 2.

PFIZER INC., a diversified health care company with sales of pharmaceuticals and other products in more than 140 countries, reported the following results for two recent years (Year 2 is the more recent year; amounts in millions):

```
┌─────────────────────────────────────────────────────────────┐
│  ┌──────────────────────┐                                    │
│  │   EXHIBIT 8—4        │      HURON COMPANY                  │
│  └──────────────────────┘   PARTIAL INCOME STATEMENT         │
│                      FOR THE YEAR ENDED DECEMBER 31, 1993     │
│                                                               │
│   Sales                                          $200,000     │
│   Cost of Goods Sold                              140,000     │
│                                                               │
│   Gross Profit on Sales                          $ 60,000     │
│   Operating Expenses:                                         │
│      • • •                                          • • •     │
│      Total Operating Expenses                      40,000     │
│                                                               │
│   Income from Operations                         $ 20,000     │
│   Other Income and Expense:                                   │
│      Interest Income                  $1,400                  │
│      Interest Expense                    800          600     │
│                                                               │
│   Net Income                                     $ 20,600     │
└─────────────────────────────────────────────────────────────┘
```

	Year 2	Year 1
Net Sales	$6,406.0	$5,671.5
Beginning Accounts Receivable (net)	1,233.5	1,122.8
Ending Accounts Receivable (net)	1,377.2	1,233.5

Pfizer's accounts receivable turnover for Year 2 is $6,406.0/[($1,233.5 + $1,377.2)/2] = 4.91. The accounts receivable turnover for Year 1 is $5,671.5/[($1,122.8 + $1,233.5)/2] = 4.81. The higher the turnover ratio is, the faster accounts receivable are being converted into cash. The slight increase in Pfizer's ratio from Year 1 to Year 2, therefore, would be considered a positive sign.

A variation (or extension) of accounts receivable turnover is the **average collection period,** computed as follows:

$$\text{Average Collection Period} = \frac{365}{\text{Accounts Receivable Turnover}}$$

This ratio indicates how many days it takes on average to collect an account receivable. During Year 2, for example, Pfizer's average collection period was 365/4.91 = 74.3 days.

The average collection period may be used to evaluate the effectiveness of a firm's credit policies. To illustrate, assume Pfizer's credit terms require payment within 60 days from the date of sale. An average collection period of 74.3 days would be at the upper bound of acceptability with such a policy (one rule of thumb, for example, is that the average collection period should not exceed the credit period plus 15 days).

KEY POINTS FOR CHAPTER OBJECTIVES

❶ INTRODUCE trade receivables and trade payables and DESCRIBE installment accounts (p. 292).
  ■ Trade receivables and payables refer to receivables and payables that arise in the regular course of a firm's credit transactions with customers and suppliers.
  ■ Business concerns such as mail-order houses and appliance dealers make many of their sales on an installment basis, creating installment receivables.

❷ DEFINE losses from uncollectible accounts, DISCUSS the allowance method, and ILLUSTRATE writing off specific accounts under the allowance method (pp. 293–294).
  ■ The credit department of a company extending credit to its customers is responsible for conducting investigations, establishing credit limits, and following up on unpaid accounts.
  ■ The allowance method is designed to record uncollectible accounts expense in the same accounting period as the related credit sales are made.

- When the allowance method is used, specific accounts are written off by debiting Allowance for Uncollectible Accounts and crediting Accounts Receivable.

❸ DESCRIBE and **ILLUSTRATE** two methods for estimating credit losses—the percentage of net sales method and the accounts receivable aging method—and **ILLUSTRATE** how to record recoveries of accounts written off (pp. 294–297).

- The percentage of net sales method is used to determine estimated credit losses directly. Estimated credit losses are determined by multiplying credit sales (net of discounts and returns and allowances) times the estimated percentage of uncollectible credit sales.
- The accounts receivable aging method determines the estimated credit loss indirectly. The balance in Accounts Receivable is segmented into age categories. Then the balance of each category is multiplied times the estimated uncollectible percentage for that age category. The results are added to obtain the desired balance in Allowance for Uncollectible Accounts. The desired balance is then compared to the existing balance in Allowance for Uncollectible Accounts to determine the estimated credit losses.
- Occasionally, accounts written off against Allowance for Uncollectible Accounts later prove to be wholly or partially collectible. When this happens, the account is reinstated to the extent of the recovery (debit Accounts Receivable and credit Allowance for Uncollectible Accounts), and the collection is recorded (debit Cash and credit Accounts Receivable).

❹ INTRODUCE the direct write-off method and **CONTRAST** it with the allowance method (p. 297).

- Under the direct write-off method, uncollectible accounts are charged to expense in the period in which they are determined to be uncollectible.
- For most companies, the direct write-off method is not an acceptable method of accounting for credit losses; however, virtually all companies use the direct write-off method for income tax purposes.

❺ DISCUSS the accounting treatment of credit card sales (pp. 298–299).

- The issuer of the credit card can reimburse the merchant accepting the credit card immediately upon deposit or subsequently after processing the sales slip.
- In both situations, the credit card fee expense is recognized when the credit card sales slips are remitted to the credit card issuer.

❻ ILLUSTRATE a promissory note, **DISCUSS** the calculation of interest on promissory notes, and **PRESENT** journal entries to record notes and interest (pp. 299–301).

- Interest on a short-term promissory note using add-on interest is determined using the following formula:

$$\text{Interest} = \text{Principal} \times \frac{\text{Interest}}{\text{Rate}} \times \frac{\text{Interest}}{\text{Time}}$$

- When a note is received in payment of an account, Notes Receivable is debited and Accounts Receivable is credited. (The maker of the note debits Accounts Payable and credits Notes Payable.)
- The holder of the note recognizes interest income at the maturity date; the maker recognizes interest expense.

❼ DESCRIBE the procedures and journal entries for borrowing at a discount and discounting customers' notes receivable (pp. 301–304).

- The formulas used when borrowing money at a discount are

$$\text{Discount} = \frac{\text{Maturity}}{\text{Value}} \times \frac{\text{Discount}}{\text{Rate}} \times \frac{\text{Discount}}{\text{Time}}$$

$$\text{Proceeds} = \frac{\text{Maturity}}{\text{Value}} - \text{Discount}$$

where maturity value is the amount that will be paid at the maturity date of the note.

- The entry to record borrowing at a discount requires a debit to Cash for the proceeds, a credit to Notes Payable for the maturity value, and a debit to Discount on Notes Payable for the difference between the maturity value and the proceeds.
- The effective interest rate when borrowing at a discount, typically greater than the discount rate, is determined using the following formula:

$$\frac{\text{Effective}}{\text{Interest Rate}} = \frac{\text{Maturity Value} \times \text{Stated Discount Rate}}{\text{Cash Proceeds from the Note}}$$

■ The following formulas are used when discounting a customer's note receivable:

$$\frac{\text{Maturity}}{\text{Value}} = \text{Principal} + \frac{\text{Interest}}{\text{to Maturity}}$$

$$\text{Discount} = \frac{\text{Maturity}}{\text{Value}} \times \frac{\text{Discount}}{\text{Rate}} \times \frac{\text{Discount}}{\text{Time}}$$

$$\text{Proceeds} = \frac{\text{Maturity}}{\text{Value}} - \text{Discount}$$

■ The entry to record the discounting of a customer's note receivable requires a debit to Cash for the proceeds, a credit to Notes Receivable for the principal amount of the note, and either a debit to Interest Expense or a credit to Interest Income to make the entry balance.

⑧ PRESENT the adjusting entries required for add-on interest and borrowing at a discount (pp. 304–305).

■ At year-end, adjusting entries are required to accrue interest income and income expense on promissory notes with add-on interest.

■ At year-end, adjusting entries are required for all notes related to borrowing at a discount. These entries will debit Interest Expense and credit Discount on Notes Payable.

⑨ ILLUSTRATE the treatment of notes and interest in financial statements (pp. 305–306).

⑩ ANALYTICAL APPLICATION: **DEFINE** *accounts receivable turnover* and *average collection period* and **EXPLAIN** their use (pp. 306–307).

■ Accounts Receivable Turnover = $\dfrac{\text{Net Sales}}{\text{Average Accounts Receivable}}$

■ Average Collection Period = $\dfrac{365}{\text{Accounts Receivable Turnover}}$

■ *Accounts receivable turnover* indicates how many times a year a firm collects its average accounts receivable. *Average collection period* indicates how many days it takes to collect an account receivable.

SELF-TEST QUESTIONS FOR REVIEW

(Answers follow the Solution to Demonstration Problem.)

1. A firm using the allowance method of recording credit losses wrote off a customer's account of $500. Later, the customer paid the account. The firm reinstated the account by means of a journal entry, then recorded the collection. The result of these procedures
   a. Increased total assets by $500.
   b. Decreased total assets by $500.
   c. Decreased total assets by $1,000.
   d. Had no effect on total assets.

2. A firm has accounts receivable of $90,000 and a debit balance of $900 in Allowance for Uncollectible Accounts. Two-thirds of the accounts receivable are current and one-third is past due. The firm estimates that 2% of the current accounts and 5% of the past due accounts will prove to be uncollectible. The adjusting entry to provide for uncollectible accounts expense should be for
   a. $2,700   c. $1,800
   b. $3,600   d. $4,500

3. A firm borrowed money from a bank, signing a $12,000, 90-day note payable that the bank discounted at 10%. The effective interest rate for this transaction is
   a. 10%   c. 9.74%
   b. 8.33%   d. 10.26%

4. A firm held an $18,000, 10%, 120-day note receivable for 20 days, then discounted the note at the bank at 12%. The entry to record the discounting of the note will show
   a. Interest Income of $600.   c. Interest Expense of $20.
   b. Interest Income of $20.   d. Interest Expense of $620.

5. On December 1, 1993, a firm discounted its own $9,000, 120-day note payable at the bank at 12%. The adjusting entry for interest at December 31, 1993, will show a
   a. $90 credit to Discount on Notes Payable.
   b. $90 debit to Discount on Notes Payable.

c. $90 credit to Interest Expense.
d. $360 debit to Interest Expense.

DEMONSTRATION PROBLEM FOR REVIEW

At December 31, 1992, the following selected accounts appeared in Delta Company's unadjusted trial balance:

Accounts Receivable	$81,000
Allowance for Uncollectible Accounts	1,200 (credit)
Notes Receivable (Jason, Inc.)	12,000
Notes Payable (Ward, Inc.)	9,000

Net credit sales for 1992 were $250,000. The $12,000 note receivable was a 90-day, 8% note dated December 13, 1992, and the $9,000 note payable was a 60-day, 9% note dated December 7, 1992. The following adjusting entries and transactions occurred at the end of 1992 and during the following year, 1993:

1992

Dec. 31 Recorded the adjusting entry for uncollectible accounts expense, at $1\frac{1}{2}$% of net credit sales.

31 Recorded the adjusting entry for interest on the $12,000 note receivable.

31 Recorded the adjusting entry for interest on the $9,000 note payable.

1993

Feb. 5 Paid the $9,000 note payable to Ward, Inc., plus interest.

Mar. 13 Received payment on the $12,000 note receivable from Jason, Inc., plus interest.

Apr. 5 Wrote off the account of Abilene Company, $2,850.

July 9 Wrote off the account of Acme Suppliers, $1,450.

Sept. 5 Acme Suppliers, which is in bankruptcy proceedings, paid $450 in final settlement of the account written off on July 9.

Dec. 6 Wrote off the account of Jacobs, Inc., $1,300.

16 Negotiated a loan at the bank; signed a $7,500 60-day note, which the bank discounted at 8%.

31 Changed from the percent-of-net-sales method of providing for uncollectible accounts to an estimate based on aged accounts receivable. The firm's analysis indicated a desired credit balance of $4,500 in Allowance for Uncollectible Accounts.

31 Made the adjusting entry for interest on the note payable dated December 16.

REQUIRED

Prepare the journal entries for the foregoing adjustments, reversals, and transactions.

SOLUTION TO DEMONSTRATION PROBLEM

1992

Dec. 31	Uncollectible Accounts Expense		3,750	
	Allowance for Uncollectible Accounts			3,750
	To provide for uncollectible accounts expense at $1\frac{1}{2}$% of net credit sales, $250,000.			
31	Interest Receivable		48	
	Interest Income			48
	To accrue interest on note receivable ($12,000 $\times$ 0.08 $\times \frac{18}{360}$ = $48).			
31	Interest Expense		54	
	Interest Payable			54
	To accrue interest on note payable ($9,000 $\times$ 0.09 $\times \frac{24}{360}$ = $54).			

1993

Feb. 5	Notes Payable		9,000	
	Interest Expense		81	
	Interest Payable		54	
	Cash			9,135
	To record payment of Ward, Inc., note ($9,000 $\times$ 0.09 $\times \frac{36}{360}$ = $81).			

Mar. 13	Cash		12,240	
	Interest Income			192
	Interest Receivable			48
	Notes Receivable			12,000

To record receipt of payment of Jason, Inc., note ($12,000 × 0.08 × $\frac{72}{360}$ = $192).

Apr. 5	Allowance for Uncollectible Accounts		2,850	
	Accounts Receivable—Abilene Company			2,850

To write off the account of Abilene Company as uncollectible.

July 9	Allowance for Uncollectible Accounts		1,450	
	Accounts Receivable—Acme Suppliers			1,450

To write off the account of Acme Suppliers as uncollectible.

Sept. 5	Accounts Receivable—Acme Suppliers		450	
	Allowance for Uncollectible Accounts			450

To reinstate $450 of the account of Acme Suppliers that proved collectible.

5	Cash		450	
	Accounts Receivable—Acme Suppliers			450

To record payment of Acme Suppliers' account.

Dec. 6	Allowance for Uncollectible Accounts		1,300	
	Accounts Receivable—Jacobs, Inc.			1,300

To write off the account of Jacobs, Inc., as uncollectible.

16	Cash		7,400	
	Discount on Notes Payable		100	
	Notes Payable			7,500

Signed a $7,500 discounted note at bank ($7,500 × 0.08 × $\frac{60}{360}$ = $100).

31	Uncollectible Accounts Expense		4,700	
	Allowance for Uncollectible Accounts			4,700

To provide for uncollectible accounts expense ($4,500 desired balance + $200 existing debit balance = $4,700).

31	Interest Expense		25	
	Discount on Notes Payable			25

To record interest expense on discounted note ($7,500 × 0.08 × $\frac{15}{360}$ = $25).

ANSWERS TO SELF-TEST QUESTIONS   **1.** d, pp. 296–297   **2.** b, pp. 295–296   **3.** d, p. 302   **4.** c, pp. 302–303
5. a, p. 302

GLOSSARY OF KEY TERMS USED IN THIS CHAPTER

accounts receivable aging method   A procedure that uses an aging schedule to determine the year-end balance needed in the Allowance for Uncollectible Accounts account (p. 295).

accounts receivable turnover   Annual net sales divided by average accounts receivable (p. 306).

aging schedule   An analysis that shows how long customers' accounts receivable balances have remained unpaid (p. 295).

Allowance for Uncollectible Accounts   A contra asset account with a normal credit balance shown on the balance sheet as a deduction from accounts receivable to reflect the expected realizable amount of accounts receivable (p. 293).

allowance method   An accounting procedure whereby the amount of uncollectible accounts expense is estimated and recorded in the period in which the related credit sales occur (p. 293).

average collection period   Determined by dividing 365 days by accounts receivable turnover (p. 307).

bearer   One of the terms that may be used to designate the payee on a promissory note; means the note is payable to whoever holds the note (p. 299).

borrowing at a discount   When a firm borrows money from a financial institution at a discount, the firm signs a note payable to the financial institution. The face amount of the note equals its maturity value, and the cash proceeds equal the maturity value less the discount charged by the financial institution (p. 302).

contingent liability   A potential obligation, the eventual occurrence of which usually depends on some future event beyond the control of the firm. Contingent liabilities may originate with lawsuits, credit guarantees, and contested income tax assessments (p. 303).

credit card fee   A fee charged retailers for credit card services provided by financial institutions. The fee is usually stated as a percentage of credit card sales (p. 299).

direct write-off method   An accounting procedure whereby the amount of uncollectible accounts expense is not recorded until specific uncollectible accounts are identified (p. 297).

Discount on Notes Payable   A contra account to notes payable (p. 302).

discounting   The exchanging of notes receivable and notes payable for cash at a financial institution when the cash received (the proceeds) is less than the note's maturity value (p. 302).

effective interest rate (discounted note)   Maturity value of the note multiplied by the stated discount rate divided by the cash proceeds from the note (p. 302).

installment accounts   The accounts receivable or payable for which payments or collections are routinely scheduled over extended periods, such as 24 or 36 months (p. 292).

maker   The signer of a promissory note (p. 299).

maturity date   The date on which a note or bond matures (p. 300).

maturity value (note)   The amount of principal plus interest on the note to be paid at maturity (p. 302).

note payable   A promissory note owed by the maker of the note (p. 299).

note receivable   A promissory note held by the note's payee (p. 299).

payee   The company or individual to whom a promissory note is made payable (p. 299).

percentage of net sales method   A procedure that determines the uncollectible accounts expense for the year by multiplying net credit sales by the estimated uncollectible percentage (p. 295).

promissory note   A written promise to pay a certain sum of money on demand or at a determinable future time (p. 299).

trade payables   Liabilities arising from the ordinary open account transactions between a business and its regular trade suppliers (p. 292).

trade receivables   Assets arising from the ordinary open account transactions between a business and its regular trade customers (p. 292).

Uncollectible Accounts Expense   The expense stemming from the inability of a business to collect an amount previously recorded as a receivable. Sometimes called *bad debts expense*. Normally classified as a selling or administrative expense (p. 293).

with recourse   A customer's note receivable is discounted with recourse if the party discounting the note becomes liable for the note if the customer fails to pay the financial institution (p. 303).

without recourse   A customer's note receivable is discounted without recourse if the party discounting the note does not become liable for the note if the customer fails to pay the financial institution (p. 303).

QUESTIONS

8-1   What events might cause credit balances in customers' accounts and debit balances in creditors' accounts? How are such items classified in the balance sheet?

8-2   A mail-order firm regularly makes a large proportion of its sales on the installment basis, requiring a 20% down payment and monthly payments over a period of 6 to 24 months, depending on the type of item sold. Where should the installment receivables be classified in the balance sheet of this mail-order firm?

8-3   How do the allowance method and the direct write-off method of handling credit losses differ with respect to the timing of expense recognition?

8-4   When a firm provides for credit losses under the allowance method, why is Allowance for Uncollectible Accounts credited rather than Accounts Receivable?

8-5   Describe the two most commonly used methods of estimating uncollectible accounts expense when the allowance method is employed.

8-6   Murphy Company estimates its uncollectibles by aging its accounts and applying percentages to various age groups of the accounts. Murphy calculated a total of $2,100 in possible losses as of December 31, 1993. Accounts Receivable has a balance of $98,000, and Allowance for Uncollectible Accounts has a credit balance of $600 before adjustment at December 31, 1993. Give the December 31, 1993, adjusting entry to provide for credit losses. Determine the net amount of Accounts Receivable included in current assets.

8-7 On June 15, 1992, Rollins, Inc., sold $860 worth of merchandise to Dell Company. On November 20, 1992, Rollins, Inc., wrote off Dell's account. On March 10, 1993, Dell Company paid the account in full. Give the entries made by Rollins, Inc., for the write-off and the recovery, assuming that Rollins, Inc., uses (a) the allowance method of handling credit losses and (b) the direct write-off method.

8-8 Wood Company sold a $675 refrigerator to a customer who charged the sale with a VISA bank credit card. Wood Company deposits credit card sales slips daily; cash is deposited in Wood Company's checking account at the same time. Wood Company's bank charges a credit card fee of 4% of sales. What entry should Wood Company make to record the sale?

8-9 Volter, Inc., received a 60-day, 9% note for $12,000 on March 5, 1993, from a customer.
  a. What is the maturity date of the note?
  b. What is the maturity value of the note?
  c. Assuming Volter, Inc., discounted the note at 9% at the bank on March 25, 1993, calculate the proceeds from discounting the note.

8-10 On July 18, 1993, James Brown borrowed at a discount at the bank, signing a 90-day note for $8,000 at 9%.
  a. What is the maturity date of the note?
  b. What is the maturity value of the note?
  c. What are the proceeds from discounting the note?

8-11 Why is a discounted customer's note a contingent liability of the endorser?

8-12 The maturity value of a $7,500 customer's note discounted by Schoff Company is $7,810. The customer dishonored the note, and the bank charged the $7,810 plus a $15 protest fee to Schoff's bank account. What entries should Schoff make to record this event?

8-13 Stanley Company received a 150-day, 8% note for $15,000 on December 1, 1993. What adjusting entry is needed to accrue interest on December 31, 1993?

8-14 On December 10, 1993, Mary Reed discounted her own 90-day note for $12,000 at the bank at 8% and charged the discount to Discount on Notes Payable. What adjusting entry is necessary on December 31, 1993?

8-15 Shaun Jackson gave a creditor a 90-day, 8% note for $7,200 on December 16, 1993. What adjusting entry should Jackson make on December 31, 1993?

8-16 Define *accounts receivable turnover* and explain its use.

EXERCISES

CREDIT LOSSES BASED ON SALES
— OBJ. 3, 9 —

8-17 Lewis Company uses the allowance method of handling credit losses. It estimates losses at 1% of credit sales, which were $900,000 during 1993. On December 31, 1993, the Accounts Receivable balance was $150,000, and Allowance for Uncollectible Accounts had a credit balance of $800 before adjustment.
  a. Prepare the adjusting entry to record credit losses for 1993.
  b. Show how Accounts Receivable and Allowance for Uncollectible Accounts would appear in the December 31, 1993, balance sheet.

CREDIT LOSSES BASED ON ACCOUNTS RECEIVABLE
— OBJ. 3 —

8-18 Hunter, Inc., analyzed its Accounts Receivable balances at December 31, 1993, and arrived at the aged balances listed below, along with the percentage that is estimated to be uncollectible.

Age Group	Balance	Estimated Loss %
Current	$ 85,000	1
30–60 days past due	20,000	2
61–120 days past due	11,000	5
121 days–six months past due	6,000	10
Over six months past due	4,000	25
	$126,000	

The company handles credit losses with the allowance method. The credit balance of Allowance for Uncollectible Accounts is $520 on December 31, 1993, before any adjustments.

a. Prepare the adjusting entry for estimated credit losses on December 31, 1993.

b. Give the entry to write off Rose Company's account on April 10, 1994, $385.

ALLOWANCE VS. DIRECT WRITE-OFF METHODS — OBJ. 2, 4 —

8-19 On March 10, 1993, Gardner, Inc., declared a $750 account receivable from Gates Company uncollectible and wrote off the account. On November 18, 1993, Gardner received a $300 payment on the account from Gates.

a. Assume Gardner uses the allowance method of handling credit losses. Give the entries to record the write-off and the subsequent recovery of Gates' account.

b. Assume Gardner uses the direct write-off method of handling credit losses. Give the entries to record the write-off and the subsequent recovery of Gates' account.

c. Assume the payment from Gates arrives on February 5, 1994, rather than on November 18, 1993. (1) Give the entries to record the write-off and subsequent recovery of Gates' account under the allowance method. (2) Give the entries to record the write-off and subsequent recovery of Gates' account under the direct write-off method. Assume Gardner expects to write off several accounts in 1994.

CREDIT CARD SALES — OBJ. 5 —

8-20 Ruth Anne's Fabrics accepts cash, personal checks, and two credit cards when customers buy merchandise. With the Great American Bank Card, Ruth Anne's Fabrics receives an immediate deposit in its checking account when credit card sales slips are deposited at the bank. The bank charges a 4% fee. With the United Merchants card, Ruth Anne's Fabrics mails the credit card sales slips to United Merchants' regional processing center each day. United Merchants accumulates these slips for three days and then mails a check to Ruth Anne's Fabrics, after deducting a 3% fee. Prepare journal entries to record the following:

a. Sales for March 15, 1993, were as follows:

Cash and checks	$ 850
Great American Bank Card (Deposited at the end of the day)	1,100
United Merchants Card (Mailed at the end of the day)	700
	$2,650

b. Received a check for $4,753 from United Merchants on March 20, 1993.

MATURITY DATES OF NOTES — OBJ. 6 —

8-21 Determine the maturity date and compute the interest for each of the following notes:

	Date of Note	Principal	Interest Rate (%)	Term
a.	August 5	$ 6,000	8	120 days
b.	May 10	8,400	7	90 days
c.	October 20	12,000	9	45 days
d.	July 6	4,500	10	60 days
e.	September 15	9,000	8	75 days

DISCOUNTING NOTE RECEIVABLE — OBJ. 7 —

8-22 Record the following transactions on the books of both Mooney Company and Jacobs, Inc., for 1993:

Oct. 1 Jacobs, Inc., gave Mooney Company a $6,000, 90-day, 8% note in payment of account.

21 Mooney Company discounted the note at the bank at 10%.

Dec. 30 On the maturity date, Jacobs, Inc., paid the amount due to the bank.

DISHONORED NOTE — OBJ. 7 —

8-23 Suppose that, in Exercise 8-22, Jacobs, Inc., dishonored its note and the bank notified Mooney Company that it had charged the maturity value plus a $12 protest fee to Mooney Company's bank account. What entry should Mooney Company make on the maturity date?

DISCOUNTING NOTE PAYABLE — OBJ. 7 —

8-24 On November 21, 1993, Tilden Company signed an 8%, $7,200, 60-day note at the bank; Tilden borrowed at a discount.

a. What is the maturity date of the note?

b. What are the proceeds of the note?

c. What amount of interest expense should be recorded as an adjustment at December 31, 1993?

d. What will be the balance in the Discount on Notes Payable account at December 31, 1993?

e. What is the effective interest rate on the note?

ADJUSTING ENTRIES FOR INTEREST
— OBJ. 8 —

8-25 The following note transactions occurred during 1993 for Towell Company:

Nov. 25 Towell received a 90-day, 9% note for $8,000 from Hyatt Company.

Dec. 7 Towell discounted its own 120-day, $12,000 note at the bank at 10%, charging the discount to Discount on Notes Payable.

22 Towell gave Barr, Inc., a $6,000, 10%, 60-day note in payment of account.

Prepare the general journal entries necessary to adjust the interest accounts at December 31, 1993.

COMPUTING ACCRUED INTEREST
— OBJ. 8 —

8-26 Compute the interest accrued on each of the following notes receivable held by Northland, Inc., on December 31, 1993:

Maker	Date of Note	Principal	Interest Rate (%)	Term
Maple	11/21/93	$ 9,000	10	120 days
Wyman	12/13/93	14,000	9	90 days
Nahn	12/19/93	21,000	8	60 days

PROBLEMS

ALLOWANCE VS. DIRECT WRITE-OFF METHODS
— OBJ. 2, 3, 4 —

8-27 Fullerton Company, which has been in business for three years, makes all of its sales on account and does not offer cash discounts. The firm's credit sales, collections from customers, and write-offs of uncollectible accounts for the three-year period are summarized below:

Year	Sales	Collections	Accounts Written Off
1	$600,000	$574,000	$4,200
2	770,000	760,000	6,700
3	840,000	814,000	7,300

REQUIRED

a. If Fullerton Company had used the direct write-off method of recognizing credit losses during the three years, what amount of Accounts Receivable would appear on the firm's balance sheet at the end of the third year? What total amount of uncollectible accounts expense would have appeared on the firm's income statement during the three-year period?

b. If Fullerton Company had used an allowance method of recognizing credit losses and had provided for such losses at the rate of $1\frac{1}{4}$% of sales, what amounts in Accounts Receivable and Allowance for Uncollectible Accounts would appear on the firm's balance sheet at the end of the third year? What total amount of uncollectible accounts expense would have appeared on the firm's income statement during the three-year period?

c. Comment on the use of the $1\frac{1}{4}$% rate to provide for losses in part (b).

ENTRIES FOR CREDIT LOSSES
— OBJ. 2, 3 —

8-28 At the beginning of 1993, Whitney Company had the following accounts on its books:

Accounts Receivable	$122,000 (debit)
Allowance for Uncollectible Accounts	7,900 (credit)

During 1993, credit sales were $1,066,000 and collections on account were $1,045,000. The following transactions, among others, occurred during the year:

Feb. 17 Wrote off R. Lowell's account, $3,600.

May 28 Wrote off G. Boyd's account, $2,400.

Oct. 13 G. Boyd, who is in bankruptcy proceedings, paid $450 in final settlement of the account written off on May 28. This amount is not included in the $1,045,000 collections.

Dec. 15 Wrote off K. Marshall's account, $1,500.

  31 In an adjusting entry, recorded the provision for uncollectible accounts at ¾% of credit sales for the year.

REQUIRED

a. Prepare general journal entries to record the credit sales, the collections on account, and the above transactions and adjustment.

b. Show how Accounts Receivable and Allowance for Uncollectible Accounts would appear in the December 31, 1993, balance sheet.

CREDIT LOSSES BASED ON ACCOUNTS RECEIVABLE — OBJ. 2, 3 —

8-29 At December 31, 1993, Schuler Company had a balance of $360,000 in its Accounts Receivable account and a credit balance of $4,200 in the Allowance for Uncollectible Accounts account. The accounts receivable subsidiary ledger consisted of $365,000 in debit balances and $5,000 in credit balances. The company has aged its accounts as follows:

Current	$304,000
0–60 days past due	34,000
61–180 days past due	18,000
Over six months past due	9,000
	$365,000

In the past, the company has experienced losses as follows: 1% of current balances, 5% of balances 0–60 days past due, 15% of balances 61–180 days past due, and 40% of balances over six months past due. The company bases its provision for credit losses on the aging analysis.

REQUIRED

a. Prepare the adjusting journal entry to record the provision for credit losses for 1993.

b. Show how Accounts Receivable (including the credit balances) and Allowance for Uncollectible Accounts would appear in the December 31, 1993, balance sheet.

CREDIT CARD SALES — OBJ. 5 —

8-30 Valderi's Gallery sells quality art work, with prices for individual pieces ranging from $500 to $25,000. Sales are infrequent, typically three to five pieces per week. The following transactions occurred during the first week of June, 1993:

On June 1, sold an $800 framed print to Kerwin Antiques on open account, with 2/10, n/30 terms. Periodic inventory is used.

On June 2, sold three framed etchings totaling $2,400 to Maria Alvado, who used the United Merchants Card to charge the etchings. Valderi mailed the credit card sales slip to United Merchants the same day. United Merchants will send a check within seven days after deducting a 1% fee.

On June 4, sold an $1,800 oil painting to Shaun Chandler, who paid with a personal check.

On June 5, sold a $2,000 watercolor to Julie and John Malbie, who used their Great American Bank Card to charge the watercolor. Valderi deposited the credit card sales slip the same day and received immediate credit in the company's checking account. The bank charged a 2% fee.

On June 6, received payment from Kerwin Antiques for its June 1 purchase.

On June 7, received a check from United Merchants for the June 2 sale.

REQUIRED

Prepare journal entries to record these transactions.

BORROWING AT A DISCOUNT — OBJ. 7 —

8-31 Gordon Products, Inc., had the following transactions for 1993 and 1994:

1993

May 18 Discounted its own $24,000, 90-day note at the bank at 8%.

Aug. 16 Paid the bank the amount due from the May 18 note.

Oct. 2 Discounted its own $16,800, 120-day note at the bank at 9%.

Dec. 31 Made the appropriate adjusting entry for interest expense.

1994

Jan. 30 Paid the bank the amount due from the October 2, 1993, note.

REQUIRED

a. Record the above transactions and adjustment in general journal form.

b. Compute the effective interest rate on the loan of
   1. May 18, 1993.
   2. October 2, 1993.

VARIOUS ENTRIES FOR ACCOUNTS AND NOTES — OBJ. 2, 3, 7, 8 —

8-32 Logan Company had the following transactions during 1993:

Apr. 8 Received a $4,800, 75-day, 8% note from J. Dean in payment of account.
May 24 Wrote off customer P. Gunn's account against Allowance for Uncollectible Accounts, $1,240.
June 22 J. Dean paid note in full.
Sept. 10 Gave a $6,400, 90-day, 9% note to M. Bolton in payment of account.
   18 P. Gunn paid account written off on May 24.
Dec. 4 Discounted its own $12,000, 90-day note at the bank at 9%.
   9 Paid principal and interest due on note to M. Bolton.
   21 Received a $10,000, 60-day, 9% note from C. Lester on account.
   23 Gave a $14,000, 60-day, 9% note to L. Shaw in payment of account.

REQUIRED

a. Record the above transactions in general journal form.
b. Make any necessary adjusting entries for interest at December 31, 1993.

VARIOUS ENTRIES FOR ACCOUNTS AND NOTES — OBJ. 2, 3, 7, 8 —

8-33 Lancaster, Inc., began business on January 1, 1993. Certain transactions for 1993 are given below:

1993

May 1 Borrowed $17,000 from the bank on a six-month, 9% note, interest to be paid at maturity.
June 8 Received a $15,000, 60-day, 8% note on account from R. Elliot.
   28 Discounted Elliot's note at the bank at 9%.
Aug. 7 R. Elliot paid her note at the bank, with interest.
Sept. 1 Received an $18,000, 120-day, 9% note from B. Shore on account.
   21 Discounted Shore's note at the bank at 10%.
Nov. 1 Paid May 1 note, with interest.
   21 Discounted its own $10,800, 120-day note at the bank at 9%.
Dec. 16 Received a $14,400, 45-day, 10% note from C. Judd on account.
   30 The bank notified Lancaster, Inc., that B. Shore's note was dishonored. Maturity value of the note plus a $20 protest fee was charged against Lancaster's checking account at the bank.
   31 Wrote off Shore's account as uncollectible. Lancaster, Inc., uses the allowance method of providing for credit losses.
   31 Recorded expected credit losses for the year by an adjusting entry. Write-offs of accounts during this first year have created a debit balance in Allowance for Uncollectible Accounts of $21,400. Analysis of aged receivables indicates that the desired balance of the allowance account is $19,500.
   31 Made the appropriate adjusting entries for interest.

REQUIRED

Record the foregoing transactions and adjustments in general journal form.

ADJUSTING ENTRIES FOR INTEREST — OBJ. 8 —

8-34 At December 31, 1992, Hoffman Corporation held one note receivable and had one note payable outstanding. At December 31, 1993, Hoffman again held one note receivable and had outstanding one note payable. The notes are described below.

	Date of Note	Principal	Interest Rate (%)	Term
December 31, 1992				
Note receivable	11/16/92	$12,000	8%	120 days
Note payable (add-on)	12/4/92	$16,000	9%	60 days
December 31, 1993				
Note receivable	12/7/93	$ 9,000	9%	60 days
Note payable (add-on)	12/21/93	$18,000	10%	30 days

REQUIRED

a. Prepare the appropriate adjusting entries for interest at December 31, 1992.
b. Assume that the appropriate adjusting entries were made at December 31, 1992, but

that no reversing or adjusting entries were made in 1993. Give the journal entries during 1993 to record payment of the notes that were outstanding December 31, 1992.

c. Make the necessary adjusting entries for interest at December 31, 1993.

ALTERNATE EXERCISES

CREDIT LOSSES BASED ON SALES
— OBJ. 3, 9 —

8-17A Highland Company uses the allowance method of handling credit losses. It estimates losses at 1% of credit sales, which were $1,200,000 during 1993. On December 31, 1993, the Accounts Receivable balance was $280,000, and Allowance for Uncollectible Accounts had a credit balance of $1,800 before adjustment.

a. Prepare the adjusting entry to record credit losses for 1993.

b. Show how Accounts Receivable and Allowance for Uncollectible Accounts would appear in the December 31, 1993, balance sheet.

CREDIT LOSSES BASED ON ACCOUNTS RECEIVABLE
— OBJ. 3 —

8-18A Maxwell, Inc., analyzed its Accounts Receivable balances at December 31, 1993, and arrived at the aged balances listed below, along with the percentage that is estimated to be uncollectible.

Age Group	Balance	Estimated Loss %
Current	$100,000	1
30–60 days past due	15,000	3
61–120 days past due	20,000	6
121 days–six months past due	7,000	10
Over six months past due	2,000	20
	$144,000	

The company handles credit losses with the allowance method. The credit balance of Allowance for Uncollectible Accounts is $840 on December 31, 1993, before any adjustments.

a. Prepare the adjusting entry for estimated credit losses on December 31, 1993.

b. Give the entry to write off Porter Company's account on May 12, 1994, $480.

ALLOWANCE VS. DIRECT WRITE-OFF METHODS
— OBJ. 2, 4 —

8-19A On April 12, 1993, Maddox Company declared a $900 account receivable from Ward Company uncollectible and wrote off the account. On December 5, 1993, Maddox received a $700 payment on the account from Ward.

a. Assume Maddox uses the allowance method of handling credit losses. Give the entries to record the write-off and the subsequent recovery of Ward's account.

b. Assume Maddox uses the direct write-off method of handling credit losses. Give the entries to record the write-off and the subsequent recovery of Ward's account.

c. Assume the payment from Ward arrives on January 18, 1994, rather than on December 5, 1993. (1) Give the entries to record the write-off and subsequent recovery of Ward's account under the allowance method. (2) Give the entries to record the write-off and subsequent recovery of Ward's account under the direct write-off method. Assume Maddox expects to write off several accounts in 1994.

CREDIT CARD SALES
— OBJ. 5 —

8-20A Historically, 60% of customer bills at Andrews Supper Club are paid with cash or check, and 40% are charged using either the Great American Bank Card or the United Merchants Card. Andrews pays a 4% fee with both cards. Great American Bank deposits cash in Andrews' checking account when the credit card sales slips are deposited. United Merchants makes an electronic funds transfer three days after the sales slips are mailed. Prepare journal entries to record the following:

a. Sales for September 10, 1993, were as follows:

Cash and checks	$1,260
Great American Bank Card (Deposited at the end of the day)	500
United Merchants Card (Mailed at the end of the day)	300
	$2,060

b. On September 13, 1993, received an electronic funds transfer from United Merchants for the September 10, 1993, sales.

MATURITY DATES OF NOTES
— OBJ. 6 —

8-21A Determine the maturity date and compute the interest for each of the following notes:

	Date of Note	Principal	Interest Rate (%)	Term
a.	July 10	$ 7,200	9	90 days
b.	April 14	12,000	8	120 days
c.	May 19	5,600	$7\frac{1}{2}$	120 days
d.	June 10	5,400	8	45 days
e.	October 29	15,000	8	75 days

DISCOUNTING NOTE RECEIVABLE
— OBJ. 7 —

8-22A Record the following transactions on the books of both Jerome Company and Quinn, Inc., for 1993:

Mar. 5 Quinn, Inc., gave Jerome Company an $18,000, 90-day, 8% note in payment of account.

25 Jerome Company discounted the note at the bank at 10%.

June 3 On the maturity date, Quinn, Inc., paid the amount due to the bank.

DISHONORED NOTE
— OBJ. 7 —

8-23A Suppose that, in Exercise 8-22A, Quinn, Inc., dishonored its note and the bank notified Jerome Company that it had charged the maturity value plus a $20 protest fee to Jerome Company's bank account. What entry should Jerome Company make on the maturity date?

DISCOUNTING NOTE PAYABLE
— OBJ. 7 —

8-24A On April 21, 1993, Prospect Company discounted its own $9,000, 60-day note at the bank at 9%.
a. What is the maturity date of the note?
b. What are the proceeds of the note?
c. What is the effective interest rate on the note?

ADJUSTING ENTRIES FOR INTEREST
— OBJ. 8 —

8-25A The following note transactions occurred during 1993 for Zuber Company:

Nov. 25 Zuber received a 90-day, 9% note for $6,000 from Porter Company.

Dec. 10 Zuber discounted its own 120-day, $7,200 note at the bank at 10%, charging the discount to Discount on Notes Payable.

23 Zuber gave Dale, Inc., a $9,000, 10%, 60-day note in payment of account.

Prepare the general journal entries necessary to adjust the interest accounts at December 31, 1993.

COMPUTING ACCRUED INTEREST
— OBJ. 8 —

8-26A Compute the interest accrued on each of the following notes receivable held by Galloway, Inc., on December 31, 1993:

Maker	Date of Note	Principal	Interest Rate (%)	Term
Barton	12/4/93	$10,000	8	120 days
Lawson	12/13/93	12,000	9	90 days
Riley	12/19/93	9,000	10	60 days

ALTERNATE PROBLEMS

ALLOWANCE VS. DIRECT WRITE-OFF METHODS
— OBJ. 2, 3, 4 —

8-27A Steinbrook Company, which has been in business for three years, makes all of its sales on account and does not offer cash discounts. The firm's credit sales, collections from customers, and write-offs of uncollectible accounts for the three-year period are summarized below:

Year	Sales	Collections	Accounts Written Off
1	$744,000	$726,000	$5,300
2	876,000	864,000	5,500
3	972,000	938,000	6,500

REQUIRED

a. If Steinbrook Company had used the direct write-off method of recognizing credit losses during the three years, what amount of Accounts Receivable would appear on the firm's balance sheet at the end of the third year? What total amount of uncollectible accounts expense would have appeared on the firm's income statements during the three-year period?

b. If Steinbrook Company had used an allowance method of recognizing credit losses and had provided for such losses at the rate of 1% of sales, what amounts of Accounts Receivable and Allowance for Uncollectible Accounts would appear on the firm's balance sheet at the end of the third year? What total amount of uncollectible accounts expense would have appeared on the firm's income statement during the three-year period?

c. Comment on the use of the 1% rate to provide for losses in part (b).

ENTRIES FOR CREDIT LOSSES
— OBJ. 2, 3 —

8-28A At January 1, 1993, Griffin Company had the following accounts on its books:

Accounts Receivable	$126,000 (debit)
Allowance for Uncollectible Accounts	6,800 (credit)

During 1993, credit sales were $756,000 and collections on account were $740,000. The following transactions, among others, occurred during the year:

Jan. 11 Wrote off J. Wolf's account, $3,400.
Apr. 29 Wrote off B. Avery's account, $1,000.
Nov. 15 B. Avery paid debt of $1,000, written off April 29. This amount is not included in the $740,000 collections.
Dec. 5 Wrote off D. Wright's account, $2,150.
      31 In an adjusting entry, recorded the provision for uncollectible accounts at 1% of credit sales for the year.

REQUIRED

a. Prepare general journal entries to record the credit sales, the collections on account, and the above transactions and adjustment.

b. Show how Accounts Receivable and Allowance for Uncollectible Accounts would appear in the December 31, 1993, balance sheet.

CREDIT LOSSES BASED ON ACCOUNTS RECEIVABLE
— OBJ. 2, 3 —

8-29A At December 31, 1993, Rinehart Company had a balance of $304,000 in its Accounts Receivable account and a credit balance of $2,800 in the Allowance for Uncollectible Accounts account. The accounts receivable subsidiary ledger consisted of $309,600 in debit balances and $5,600 in credit balances. The company has aged its accounts as follows:

Current	$272,000
0–60 days past due	18,000
61–180 days past due	11,200
Over six months past due	8,400
	$309,600

In the past, the company has experienced losses as follows: 2% of current balances, 6% of balances 0–60 days past due, 15% of balances 61–180 days past due, and 30% of balances more than six months past due. The company bases its provision for credit losses on the aging analysis.

REQUIRED

a. Prepare the adjusting journal entry to record the provision for credit losses for 1993.

b. Show how Accounts Receivable (including the credit balances) and Allowance for Uncollectible Accounts would appear in the December 31, 1993, balance sheet.

CREDIT CARD SALES
— OBJ. 5 —

8-30A Captain Paul's Marina sells boats and other water recreational vehicles (approximately three vehicles are sold each week). The following transactions occurred during the third week of May, 1993:

On May 15, sold a $600 boat trailer to Sam and Myrna Marston, who paid using a personal check.

On May 16, sold a $10,000 boat to the Calumet Lake Patrol on open account, with 2/10, n/30 terms.

On May 18, sold a $1,200 water scooter to Kyle Bronson, who used the United Merchants Card to charge the water scooter. Captain Paul's mailed the credit card sales slip to United Merchants the same day. United Merchants will send a check within seven days, net of a 2% fee.

On May 19, sold a $1,600 fishing boat to Michael Ferguson, who used the Great American Bank Card to pay for the boat. Captain Paul's deposited the credit card sales slip the same day and received an immediate credit in the company's checking account, net of a 2% fee.

On May 20, received payment from Calumet Lake Patrol for the boat purchased on May 16.

On May 21, received payment from United Merchants for the May 19 transaction.

REQUIRED

Prepare journal entries to record these transactions.

DISCOUNTING NOTES RECEIVABLE — OBJ. 7 —

8-31A Peabody Corporation had the following transactions for 1993 and 1994:

1993

Mar.	6	Sold $9,000 worth of merchandise to E. Neal and received a $9,000, 60-day, 8% note.
	21	Discounted E. Neal's note at the bank at 10%.
May	5	Neal paid the bank the amount due on the March 6 note.
Dec.	11	Received an $8,000, 60-day, 9% note from J. Banning in settlement of an open account.
	31	Made the appropriate adjusting entry for interest income.

1994

Jan.	1	Reversed the December 31 adjustment for interest income.
Feb.	9	Received payment from J. Banning on the December 11 note.

REQUIRED

a. Record the above transactions, adjustment, and reversal in general journal form.

b. Assume Peabody Corporation does not make reversing entries. Give the entry to record the receipt of the note payment from J. Banning on February 9, 1994.

VARIOUS ENTRIES FOR ACCOUNTS AND NOTES — OBJ. 2, 3, 7, 8 —

8-32A Marion Company had the following transactions during 1993:

July	15	Received a $12,500, 90-day, 8% note from L. Dobbs in payment of account.
Sept.	5	Wrote off customer D. Simon's account against Allowance for Uncollectible Accounts, $925.
	9	Gave a $10,000, 90-day, 10% note to F. Sharp in payment of account.
Oct.	13	L. Dobbs paid note in full.
	21	D. Simon paid account written off on September 5.
Dec.	8	Paid principal and interest due on note to F. Sharp.
	13	Discounted its own $14,000, 90-day note at the bank at 10%.
	19	Received a $10,800, 60-day, 10% note from K. Brian on account.
	22	Gave a $16,000, 60-day, 9% note to R. Sinclair on account.

REQUIRED

a. Record the above transactions in general journal form.

b. Make any necessary adjusting entries for interest at December 31.

VARIOUS ENTRIES FOR ACCOUNTS AND NOTES — OBJ. 2, 3, 7, 8 —

8-33A Armstrong, Inc., began business on January 1, 1993. Several transactions for 1993 are given below:

Mar.	1	Borrowed $20,000 from the bank on a five-month, 9% note, interest to be paid at maturity.
May	2	Received a $14,400, 60-day, 10% note on account from G. Holt.
	17	Discounted G. Holt's note at the bank at 10%.
July	1	G. Holt paid his note at the bank, with interest.
	1	Received a $27,000, 120-day, 10% note from B. Rich on account.
	25	Discounted Rich's note at the bank at 10%.
Aug.	1	Paid March 1 note, with interest.
Oct.	30	The bank notified Armstrong, Inc., that B. Rich's note was dishonored. Maturity value of the note plus a $15 protest fee was charged against Armstrong's checking account at the bank.
Dec.	1	Discounted its own $18,000, 120-day note at bank at 9%.

Dec. 9 Wrote off Rich's account as uncollectible. Armstrong, Inc., uses the allowance method of providing for credit losses.

11 Received a $21,000, 90-day, 9% note from W. Maling on account.

31 Recorded expected credit losses for the year by an adjusting entry. Allowance for Uncollectible Accounts has a debit balance of $28,300 as a result of write-offs of accounts during this first year. Analysis of aged receivables indicates that the desired balance of the allowance account is $5,800.

31 Made the appropriate adjusting entries for interest.

REQUIRED

Record the foregoing transactions and adjustments in general journal form.

ADJUSTING ENTRIES FOR INTEREST
— OBJ. 8 —

8-34A At December 31, 1992, Portland Corporation held one note receivable and had one note payable outstanding. At December 31, 1993, Portland again held one note receivable and had outstanding one note payable. The notes are described below.

	Date of Note	Principal	Interest Rate (%)	Term
December 31, 1992				
Note receivable	11/25/92	$27,000	8%	90 days
Note payable (add-on)	12/16/92	16,800	9%	60 days
December 31, 1993				
Note receivable	12/11/93	$15,400	9%	120 days
Note payable (add-on)	12/7/93	18,000	10%	90 days

REQUIRED

a. Prepare the appropriate adjusting entries for interest at December 31, 1992.

b. Assume that the appropriate adjusting entries were made at December 31, 1992, but that no reversing or adjusting entries were made in 1993. Give the journal entries to record payment during 1993 of the notes that were outstanding December 31, 1992.

c. Make the necessary adjusting entries for interest at December 31, 1993.

CASES

Business Decision Case

The latest income statement for Greenwood Sales, Inc., a wholesaler of electronic parts and equipment, is shown below. Company president Mark Winslow has been dissatisfied with the firm's rate of growth for several years. He believes that increasing sales promotion and liberalizing credit policies would raise gross sales substantially. Specifically, Winslow is fairly confident that gross sales would increase by 30% if the firm adopted the following plan:

1. Increase certain of the firm's trade discounts. This change would reduce the average selling price of merchandise somewhat, but it would increase sales volume.

2. Extend credit to an additional number of less creditworthy customers.

GREENWOOD SALES, INC.
INCOME STATEMENT
FOR THE YEAR ENDED DECEMBER 31, 1993

Sales	$1,200,000	
Less: Sales Discounts	16,000	
Net Sales	$1,184,000	100%
Cost of Goods Sold	769,600	65
Gross Profit on Sales	$ 414,400	35%
Selling Expenses (Excluding Uncollectible Accounts Expense)	$ 296,000	25%
Uncollectible Accounts Expense	11,840	1
Administrative Expenses	60,000	5
Total Expenses	$ 367,840	31%
Net Income	$ 46,560	4%

The controller for Greenwood Sales, Inc., makes the following comments after analyzing Winslow's proposal for its likely impact on other income statement items:

1. Gross Profit on Sales—The slight decline in average selling prices of merchandise resulting from an increase in trade discounts will reduce the gross profit rate from 35% to $33\frac{1}{3}$%.

2. Sales Discounts—The firm has been selling to selected retailers on terms of 2/15, n/30, with about two-thirds of total sales subject to the discount. Even with an increased number of customers, two-thirds of total sales will still be subject to the discount.

3. Selling Expenses—Excluding uncollectible accounts expense, selling expenses will remain at 25% of net sales. Because of the expected 25% increase in sales, selling expenses, including promotion outlays, will rise accordingly.

4. Uncollectible Accounts Expense—Uncollectible accounts expense has been about 1% of net sales for several years. The proposed liberalization of credit policies will increase this expense to 2% of net sales.

5. Administrative Expenses—These expenses will remain constant even if gross sales increase.

REQUIRED

Prepare a projected income statement for 1994 based on Winslow's proposal and the controller's comments. Based on your results, should Greenwood Sales, Inc. adopt Winslow's proposal?

Analytical Application Case

SNAP-ON TOOLS CORPORATION, headquartered in Kenosha, Wisconsin, manufacturers hand and power tools, electronic equipment, and tool storage units. W. H. BRADY COMPANY, headquartered in Milwaukee, manufactures a variety of items including specialized adhesives and tapes, thin film products, and coated products. These two companies reported the following information in their financial statements for two recent years (Year 2 is the more recent year; amounts in thousands):

	Year 2	Year 1
Snap-on Tools Corporation		
Net Sales	$931,533	$890,792
Beginning Accounts Receivable (Net)	403,926	336,588
Ending Accounts Receivable (Net)	459,381	403,926
W. H. Brady Co.		
Net Sales	$191,161	$174,174
Beginning Accounts Receivable (Net)	22,874	21,307
Ending Accounts Receivable (Net)	25,185	22,874

REQUIRED

a. Calculate the accounts receivable turnover and the average collection period for Snap-on Tools Corporation and W. H. Brady Co. for Year 1 and Year 2.

b. Compare the average collection periods for the two companies and comment on possible reasons for the difference in average collection periods for the two companies.

Ethics Case

Tractor Motors' best salesperson is Marie Glazer. Glazer's largest sales have been to Farmers Cooperative, a customer she brought to the company. Another salesperson, Bryan Blanchard, has been told in confidence by his cousin (an employee of Farmers Cooperative) that Farmers Cooperative is experiencing financial difficulties and may not be able to pay Tractor Motors what is owed to them.

Both Glazer and Blanchard are being considered for promotion to a new sales manager position.

REQUIRED

What are the ethical considerations that face Bryan Blanchard? What alternatives does he have?

What options does a firm have in how it determines the dollar amount of its inventory?

Drug giant McKesson has reduced the chore of measuring physical inventories thanks to the 13-ounce Acumax computer, developed by EDS and Symbol Technologies. ■ The hand-held unit allows workers to take inventory by walking down aisles and scanning bar codes. ■ In addition to counting the inventory, firms must also select a method to measure the dollar amount of their inventory. ■ This chapter includes specific identification; average; first-in, first-out; and last-in, first-out.

9

INVENTORIES

Good merchandise finds a ready buyer.
PLAUTUS

nventories constitute the lifeblood of merchandising firms. For these firms, inventory is a significant asset, and the sale of inventory provides the major source of revenue. This chapter focuses on inventory accounting for merchandisers—firms that buy finished products to sell to their customers.

We have already introduced the special source documents, business transactions, and accounting techniques related to routine inventory transactions. Now we build on these facts by examining additional inventory topics such as alternative pricing methods, departures from cost, estimation procedures, and accounting for imports and exports.

REVIEW OF BASIC CONCEPTS

OBJECTIVE ❶ DISCUSS *basic inventory concepts, the need for inventories, and inventory counts.*

Before discussing new material, let us review some of the pertinent concepts covered earlier.

Inventory is all merchandise owned by a company and held for resale to customers in the ordinary course of business. Inventories are current assets because they typically will be sold within one year, or during a firm's normal operating cycle if it should be longer than a year. For retailing firms, inventories are often the largest or most valuable current asset.

Inventory costs are all costs necessary to acquire the merchandise and bring it to the site of sale. Inventory costs include the purchase price, plus any transportation or freight in, less purchases returns and allowances and purchases discounts.

Cost of goods sold is an expense reflecting the net acquisition cost of the merchandise sold to customers during an accounting period.

A firm using a **periodic inventory system** makes no entries to the Inventory account as merchandise is purchased and sold. Information on the net cost of purchases is recorded in separate accounts for purchases, purchases returns and allowances, purchases discounts, and transportation in. At year-end, the ending inventory is counted and established in the Inventory account. Cost of goods sold is determined at year-end by subtracting the ending inventory from the cost of goods available for sale.

A firm using a **perpetual inventory system** makes entries directly to the Inventory account when merchandise is purchased and sold. The balance in the Inventory account, therefore, is "perpetually" maintained and should continuously reflect the cost of merchandise on hand. A debit entry to the Cost of Goods Sold account is made each time merchandise is sold (with an equal credit amount recorded in the Inventory account).

THE NEED FOR INVENTORIES

Most well-managed merchandisers find it necessary and desirable to maintain large, varied inventories. As a consumer, you have probably experienced a favorable buyer reaction to the availability of a wide assortment of colors, sizes, qualities, and types of the goods for which you shop. Consumer preferences have probably made large, varied inventories an operating necessity for most retail firms.

Other business factors can justify the existence of relatively large inventories. A firm can sell more goods in a period than it can purchase only by having beginning inventories. Beginning inventories are particularly important for seasonal merchandise. Attractive quantity discounts may justify a firm's buying in excess of its current sales requirements and therefore creating additional inventories. Strategic purchases offer still another reason for carrying inventories. Many firms—especially those that sell in seasonal markets—buy in excess of their needs when supply prices are favorable. They store the goods and can then maintain sales during a period of unfavorable supply prices.

Progressive firms take into account customer preferences, competitors' merchandising patterns, and favorable market situations in determining inventory size and balance, but they must also consider the cost of carrying large inventories. Often, savings obtained by purchasing in large quantities or under favorable market conditions may be more than offset by increased carrying costs. Storage and handling costs for large inventories can increase substantially. In addition, the firm may suffer losses from inventory deterioration and obsolescence. Finally, inventories tie up working capital that might be used more profitably elsewhere.

As a result of the high cost of carrying inventories, retailers often work with manufacturers to find ways to shorten the lead time to obtain goods. Manufacturers also want to minimize inventory levels and generally prefer smooth production flows to variable production activity. Indeed, some manufacturers now offer discounts to retailers for steady, smaller purchases rather than volume purchases, because the former pattern contributes to the smooth flow of production activity and minimum inventory levels.

INVENTORY COUNTS

The dollar amount of an inventory depends on two variables—quantity and price. We usually express inventories as the aggregate dollar value (Quantity × Price) of the goods on hand at a specific time. "Taking" an inventory consists of (1) counting the items involved, (2) pricing each item, and (3) summing the amounts. Exhibit 9-1 illustrates these three steps.

Inventory counts can be extremely complicated and expensive. Even moderate-sized firms may have thousands of items, hundreds of types, sizes, and qualities, purchased at a variety of unit prices, and located in dozens of warehouses, stores, branches, and departments. Proper planning and coordination are imperative if all items are to be counted—only once—and properly priced. Although some firms "close" for inventory taking, many continue operations during the count. Firms that continue operations must know if counted or uncounted merchandise is sold during the inventory-taking period.

Another problem in inventory counts is deciding what goods should be counted. Often the proper inventory is not simply "all merchandise on site." By definition, the inventory should include—and be limited to—goods *owned* by the firm and *available* for resale. Ownership transfers when title to the goods passes from the seller to the buyer. Title may pass at any time expressly agreed to by these two parties. In the absence of a specific agreement, title generally passes when the seller completes performance with regard to delivery. Therefore, a firm purchasing merchandise on terms F.O.B. shipping point may acquire title to the goods before it physically receives

EXHIBIT 9—1	THE THREE STEPS OF TAKING AN INVENTORY

1. PHYSICAL COUNT		**2. PRICING**	**3. SUMMATION**
Merchandise Item	Unit Count	Unit Price	Extension
A	30	$6	$180
B	40	7	280
C	50	8	400
			$860

them. Such items (often called *goods in transit*) should be included in the inventory count.

Merchandise whose title has passed to customers does not belong in the inventory count, even if it has not been removed from the store or warehouse. A buyer, for example, may agree to pick up the goods at the seller's place of business. When the seller identifies the goods that fulfill the contract, title transfers to the buyer. These goods should be excluded from the seller's inventory count because they are no longer owned or available for resale. Similarly, goods held for resale on consignment from another firm are not included in the inventory count, because the goods are not owned by the firm holding them.

We see, therefore, that although a firm's ownership of merchandise often is indicated by the physical presence of goods, a firm can also own goods that it has not yet received and not own goods that it still possesses.

INVENTORY PRICING METHODS: PERIODIC INVENTORY SYSTEM

OBJECTIVE 2 DESCRIBE *inventory pricing under a periodic inventory system using the (1) specific identification method, (2) weighted average method, (3) FIFO method, and (4) LIFO method.*

In general, inventories are priced at their historical cost. Inventory pricing is quite simple when acquisition prices remain constant. When prices for like items change during the accounting period, however, it is not always apparent which price should be used to measure the ending inventory. Consequently, when cost prices fluctuate, we must either keep track of all costs for specific goods or make assumptions about which goods have been sold and which goods are on hand. The need for such assumptions has led to the commonly used methods of inventory pricing that we illustrate in this section. We illustrate a rising price pattern, which is the most prevalent in our economy.

Two terms are useful in considering the problems of pricing inventories under fluctuating prices. *Goods flow* describes the actual physical movement of goods in the firm's operations. Goods flow is a result of physical events. *Cost flow* is the real or *assumed* association of unit costs with goods either sold or on hand. The assumed cost flow does not always reflect the actual goods flow. Furthermore, generally accepted accounting principles permit the use of an assumed cost flow that does *not* reflect the real goods flow. There is nothing illicit about this practice; in fact, there are often compelling reasons for adopting it.

In this section, we introduce four generally accepted methods of pricing inventories under a periodic inventory system: (1) specific identification; (2) weighted average; (3) first-in, first-out; and (4) last-in, first-out. Each of the four methods illustrated uses historical costs. Initially, we will concentrate primarily on the computational technique of each method. A comparative evaluation is presented in a later section.

To compare more easily the four inventory methods, we illustrate all four with the following identical data:

Jan. 1	Beginning inventory	60 units @ $10	=	$	600
Mar. 27	Purchase	90 units @	11	=	990
Aug. 15	Purchase	100 units @	13	=	1,300
Nov. 6	Purchase	50 units @	16	=	800
	Goods available for sale	300 units			$3,690
	Sales	220 units			
Dec. 31	Ending inventory	80 units			

Therefore, in each illustration,

1. Beginning inventory is priced at $600.
2. Three purchases are made during the period, as listed above.
3. Goods available for sale during the period amount to 300 units at a total cost of $3,690.
4. During the period, 220 units are sold, leaving an ending inventory of 80 units.

The four inventory pricing methods differ in the way they assign costs to the units in the ending inventory. Under the periodic inventory system, once the total cost of the ending inventory is determined, the ending inventory amount is subtracted from the cost of goods available for sale to derive the period's total cost of goods sold.

Specific Identification Method

The **specific identification method** involves (1) keeping track of the purchase price of each specific unit available for sale and (2) pricing the ending inventory at the actual prices of the specific units not sold. Assume that the 80 unsold units consist of 10 units from beginning inventory, 20 units from the August 15 purchase, and all 50 of the units purchased on November 6. The costs assigned to the ending inventory and cost of goods sold are shown below. Note that the full $3,690 cost of the goods available for sale has been assigned as either ending inventory or as cost of goods sold.

SPECIFIC IDENTIFICATION METHOD
PERIODIC INVENTORY SYSTEM

	Goods Available			Ending Inventory		
	Units	Cost	Total	Units	Cost	Total
Jan. 1 Beginning inventory	60 @	$10 =	$ 600	10 @	$10 =	$ 100
Mar. 27 Purchase	90 @	11 =	990			
Aug. 15 Purchase	100 @	13 =	1,300	20 @	13 =	260
Nov. 6 Purchase	50 @	16 =	800	50 @	16 =	800
	300		$3,690	80		$1,160

Cost of goods available for sale $3,690
Less: Ending inventory   1,160
Cost of goods sold $2,530

Weighted Average Method

The **weighted average method** spreads the total dollar cost of the goods available for sale equally among all units. In our illustration, this figure is $3,690/300, or $12.30 per unit. The following schedule diagrams the assignment of costs under this method. Note again that the entire cost of goods available for sale has been divided between ending inventory and cost of goods sold.

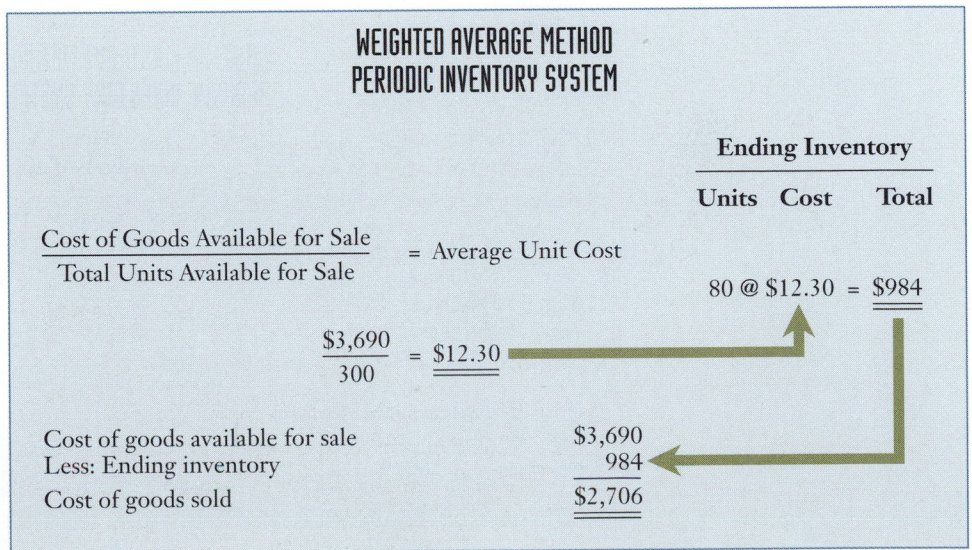

WEIGHTED AVERAGE METHOD
PERIODIC INVENTORY SYSTEM

	Ending Inventory		
	Units	Cost	Total

$$\frac{\text{Cost of Goods Available for Sale}}{\text{Total Units Available for Sale}} = \text{Average Unit Cost}$$

80 @ $12.30 = $984

$$\frac{\$3,690}{300} = \$12.30$$

Cost of goods available for sale $3,690
Less: Ending inventory   984
Cost of goods sold $2,706

It would be incorrect to use a *simple* average of the prices. The average price paid is ($10 + $11 + $13 + $16)/4 = $12.50; this figure fails to take into account the different numbers of units available at the various prices. The simple average yields the same figure as the weighted average only when the same number of units are purchased at each price.

First-in, First-out (FIFO) Method

First-in, first-out (FIFO) pricing assumes that the oldest goods on hand (or earliest purchased) are sold first. Thus, ending inventories are always made up of the most recent purchases. Under FIFO, goods in the beginning inventory can also be in the ending inventory only when the number of units sold is less than the number of units in the beginning inventory. A FIFO approach would result in the cost allocations as shown below. This method assumes the first 220 units acquired are sold and the last 80 units purchased are still on hand.

FIRST-IN, FIRST-OUT METHOD
PERIODIC INVENTORY SYSTEM

	Goods Available			Ending Inventory		
	Units	Cost	Total	Units	Cost	Total
Jan. 1 Beginning inventory	60 @	$10 =	$ 600			
Mar. 27 Purchase	90 @	11 =	990			
Aug. 15 Purchase	100 @	13 =	1,300	30 @	$13 =	$ 390
Nov. 6 Purchase	50 @	16 =	800	50 @	16 =	800
	300		$3,690	80		$1,190
Cost of goods available for sale			$3,690			
Less: Ending inventory			1,190			
Cost of goods sold			$2,500			

Last-in, First-out (LIFO) Method

The **last-in, first-out (LIFO)** approach assumes that the most recent purchases are sold first. Thus, unless sales exceed purchases, the beginning inventory remains on hand as part of the ending inventory. The following schedule shows how LIFO works. This method assumes the 220 units most recently purchased are sold, and the 80 oldest units available for sale (60 units from the beginning inventory and 20 units from the March 27 purchase) remain on hand at the end of the period.

LAST-IN, FIRST-OUT METHOD
PERIODIC INVENTORY SYSTEM

	Goods Available			Ending Inventory		
	Units	Cost	Total	Units	Cost	Total
Jan. 1 Beginning inventory	60 @	$10 =	$ 600	60 @	$10 =	$600
Mar. 27 Purchase	90 @	11 =	990	20 @	11 =	220
Aug. 15 Purchase	100 @	13 =	1,300			
Nov. 6 Purchase	50 @	16 =	800			
	300		$3,690	80		$820
Cost of goods available for sale			$3,690			
Less: Ending inventory			820			
Cost of goods sold			$2,870			

EXHIBIT 9—2	EFFECT OF INVENTORY ERROR ON TWO CONSECUTIVE PERIODS PERIODIC INVENTORY SYSTEM			
	Year 1		**Year 2**	
	Correct	Erroneous	Erroneous	Correct
Sales	$5,600	$5,600	$6,800	$6,800
Beginning inventory	$ 600	$ 600	**$1,290**	$1,190
Net cost of purchases	3,090	3,090	4,010	4,010
Cost of goods available for sale	$3,690	$3,690	$5,300	$5,200
Ending inventory	1,190	**1,290**	1,900	1,900
Cost of goods sold	$2,500	$2,400	$3,400	$3,300
Gross profit on sales	$3,100	$3,200	$3,400	$3,500
Overstatement or (understatement) of gross profit caused by error		$100		($100)

Effect of Inventory Errors

Errors may occur when an ending inventory is counted and priced. Errors result from miscounting the number of inventory units, incorrectly applying the inventory pricing method, or miscalculating the product of quantity times price.

One year's ending inventory is the next year's beginning inventory. Thus, an error in computing an ending inventory means that the same error exists in the next year's beginning inventory. Under the periodic inventory system, beginning and ending inventories are key components in the calculation of cost of goods sold. As a result, an ending inventory error causes cost of goods sold and gross profit to be incorrect for two consecutive periods. The misstatements in cost of goods sold and gross profit for each of the two periods will be equal in amount but opposite in direction; thus, the errors in the two periods offset each other.

Exhibit 9-2 illustrates the effect of an ending inventory error on cost of goods sold and gross profit for two consecutive years. We assume a $100 error is made in computing the inventory at the end of Year 1, causing the inventory to be overstated. This error causes Year 1's cost of goods sold to be understated by $100 and gross profit to be overstated by $100. Note, however, that the effects in Year 2 are equal in amount but opposite in direction. In Year 2, cost of goods sold is overstated by $100 and gross profit is understated by $100.

INVENTORY PRICING METHODS: PERPETUAL INVENTORY SYSTEM

OBJECTIVE ❸ DESCRIBE *inventory pricing under a perpetual inventory system using the (1) specific identification method, (2) moving average method, (3) FIFO method, and (4) LIFO method.*

We will illustrate four pricing methods for a perpetual inventory system: (1) specific identification; (2) moving average; (3) first in, first out; and (4) last in, first out. These methods parallel the four methods illustrated for a periodic inventory system. *The basic difference under a perpetual inventory system is that we compute cost of goods sold every time merchandise is sold.* Deducting the cost of goods sold from the Inventory account leaves a balance that should represent the cost of inventory on hand (the accuracy of the account balance will be verified when the physical inventory is taken). Under a periodic inventory system, in contrast, the cost of goods sold is not determined until the ending inventory is computed.

To illustrate the perpetual inventory pricing methods, we will use the same data as we used to calculate inventory under a periodic inventory system. The timing of merchandise sales is important under a perpetual inventory system, so we will add to the data specific dates and quantities for merchandise sold. Thus, the necessary information is as follows:

Jan.	1	Beginning inventory	60 units @ $10 = $ 600
Mar.	27	Purchase	90 units @ $11 = $ 990
May	2	Sell	(130) units
Aug.	15	Purchase	100 units @ $13 = $1,300
Nov.	6	Purchase	50 units @ $16 = $ 800
Dec.	10	Sell	(90) units
		Ending inventory	80 units

Under all four perpetual inventory pricing methods, the Inventory account is increased each time a purchase occurs (by the cost of the purchase) and decreased each time a sale occurs (by the cost of goods sold). The methods differ in the way the cost of goods sold amounts are computed. Each method will result in a year-end Inventory account balance that represents the cost of the 80 units on hand.

Specific Identification Method

When the **specific identification method** is used, the actual costs of the specific units sold are identified and used to compute the cost of goods sold. To illustrate, assume that (1) 50 of the units sold on May 2 came from the beginning inventory and 80 units came from the purchase on March 27 and (2) 10 of the units sold on December 10 came from the purchase on March 27 and 80 units came from the purchase on August 15. With these assumptions, the specific identification method gives the results shown below.

SPECIFIC IDENTIFICATION METHOD
PERPETUAL INVENTORY SYSTEM

	Received			Sold			Inventory Balance		
Date	Units	Unit Cost	Total	Units	Unit Cost	Total	Units	Unit Cost	Total
Jan. 1							60	$10	$ 600
Mar. 27	90	$11	$ 990				60	10	
							90	11	1,590
May 2				50	$10	$ 500	10	10	
				80	11	880	10	11	210
Aug. 15	100	13	1,300				10	10	
							10	11	
							100	13	1,510
Nov. 6	50	16	800				10	10	
							10	11	
							100	13	
							50	16	2,310
Dec. 10				10	11	110	10	10	
				80	13	1,040	20	13	
							50	16	1,160

The specific identification method gives the same results (total cost of goods sold and ending inventory) under both the perpetual and periodic inventory systems. The basic differences under a perpetual inventory system are that cost of goods sold is computed whenever a sale occurs and the Inventory account continuously shows the cost of goods on hand. Thus, the Inventory account shows what the ending balance should be before a physical inventory count is taken.

Moving Average Method

The average method under a perpetual inventory system is called the **moving average method.** Under this method, each time goods are purchased, a new average unit cost is computed for the goods on hand (total cost divided by total units on hand). Cost of goods sold for each sale is computed by multiplying the average unit cost at the time of sale by the number of units sold. The following schedule shows how the moving average method works.

MOVING AVERAGE METHOD
PERPETUAL INVENTORY SYSTEM

Date	Received Units	Received Unit Cost	Received Total	Sold Units	Sold Unit Cost	Sold Total	Inventory Balance Units	Inventory Balance Unit Cost	Inventory Balance Total
Jan. 1							60	$10.00	$ 600
Mar. 27	90	$11	$ 990				150	10.60	1,590
May 2				130	$10.60	$1,378	20	10.60	212
Aug. 15	100	13	1,300				120	12.60	1,512
Nov. 6	50	16	800				170	13.60	2,312
Dec. 10				90	13.60	1,224	80	13.60	1,088

Because unit average costs are recomputed each time a purchase occurs, the moving average method gives different answers from those obtained by using the weighted average method under a periodic inventory system.

First-in, First-out (FIFO) Method

Under the perpetual **first-in, first-out (FIFO) method,** each time a sale is made the costs of the oldest goods on hand are charged to cost of goods sold. Using the data from our illustration, perpetual FIFO gives the results shown below.

FIRST-IN, FIRST-OUT METHOD
PERPETUAL INVENTORY SYSTEM

Date	Received Units	Received Unit Cost	Received Total	Sold Units	Sold Unit Cost	Sold Total	Inventory Balance Units	Inventory Balance Unit Cost	Inventory Balance Total
Jan. 1							60	$10	$ 600
Mar. 27	90	$11	$ 990				60 / 90	10 / 11	1,590
May 2				60 / 70	$10 / 11	$600 / 770	20	11	220
Aug. 15	100	13	1,300				20 / 100	11 / 13	1,520
Nov. 6	50	16	800				20 / 100 / 50	11 / 13 / 16	2,320
Dec. 10				20 / 70	11 / 13	220 / 910	30 / 50	13 / 16	1,190

The perpetual FIFO method derives the same cost of goods sold for the period ($2,500) and the same ending inventory ($1,190) as those achieved under the periodic FIFO method. The differences between the two methods are the result of the basic differences between a perpetual and a periodic inventory system. Under perpetual FIFO, cost of goods sold is computed throughout the period as goods are sold, and the Inventory account balance reflects the cost of goods on hand at all times throughout the period.

Last-in, First-out (LIFO) Method

When perpetual **last-in, first-out (LIFO)** is used, each time a sale is made the costs of the most recent purchases are charged to cost of goods sold. The schedule below shows the results obtained using perpetual LIFO.

LAST-IN, FIRST-OUT METHOD
PERPETUAL INVENTORY SYSTEM

Date	Received Units	Received Unit Cost	Received Total	Sold Units	Sold Unit Cost	Sold Total	Inventory Balance Units	Inventory Balance Unit Cost	Inventory Balance Total
Jan. 1							60	$10	$ 600
Mar. 27	90	$11	$ 990				60 90	10 11	1,590
May 2				90 40	11 10	$990 400	20	10	200
Aug. 15	100	13	1,300				20 100	10 13	1,500
Nov. 6	50	16	800				20 100 50	10 13 16	2,300
Dec. 10				50 40	16 13	800 520	20 60	10 13	980

Because perpetual LIFO expenses the most recent purchases at the time of each sale, the total cost of goods sold ($2,710) and ending inventory ($980) will differ from the corresponding amounts computed under periodic LIFO. Periodic LIFO waits until year-end before assuming that the most recent purchases are sold first.

Perpetual Inventory Records

When a perpetual inventory system is used, a detailed perpetual inventory record must be maintained—manually or by computer—for each inventory item. The perpetual inventory records must provide for both the inflow and outflow of merchandise as well as disclose the quantities and prices of items at any time. The preceding illustrations of the four perpetual inventory pricing methods show the type of information kept in the perpetual inventory records. These inventory records constitute a subsidiary ledger to the Inventory control account in the general ledger. At year-end, the balances on all the perpetual inventory records are added, and their total dollar amount should agree with the amount in the Inventory control account.

Although the perpetual inventory records are continually maintained, their accuracy should be verified at least once each year by physical counts of the merchandise. If the actual count reveals a difference, the Inventory control account and subsidiary records are adjusted to agree with the actual count.

COMPARATIVE ANALYSIS OF INVENTORY PRICING METHODS

Cost Flows

OBJECTIVE **4** ANALYZE *the effects inventory pricing methods have on gross profits, matching of expenses with revenues, and income taxes.*

In this section, we consider the effects of and reasons for using the various inventory pricing methods just illustrated.

The specific identification method is most appropriate for operations that involve somewhat differentiated products of relatively high unit values. New automobiles and construction equipment are good examples of merchandise that would justify the cost of tracking the specific price of each inventory unit. Specific identification is usually not feasible when products have low unit values and involve large volumes.

Specific identification offers a limited potential for income manipulation. To the degree that like units of inventory are available at various cost figures, we can maximize reported income by "choosing" to sell the unit with the lowest cost. Income could be minimized by choosing to sell the unit with the highest cost.

The average approaches to inventory measurement are best suited to operations that store a large volume of undifferentiated goods in common areas. Liquid fuels, grains, and other commodities are good examples. To some degree, the average cost represents all the various costs of accumulating the goods currently on hand. Consequently, average costs typically fall between the extreme cost figures that can result from other methods.

As a matter of good business, most companies—especially those with perishable or style-affected goods—attempt to sell the oldest merchandise first. This is especially true of companies dealing in foods, certain chemicals, or drugs. In these cases, FIFO most nearly matches an assumed cost flow to the probable goods flow.

Finding an example of a business operation in which LIFO represents the natural flow of goods is difficult. Purchases of coal or a similar commodity may all be dumped onto one pile from an overhead trestle, and sales may be taken from the top of the pile by a crane. If beginning inventories have been maintained or increased, we conclude that the firm's original purchases are still in inventory. In this case, LIFO represents the actual goods flow. Although LIFO is not the goods flow for most businesses, an estimated 50% or more of major businesses use LIFO to price some of their inventories. We explore the reasons for this choice later in this chapter.

In summary,

1. In a physical sense, specific identification best presents actual cost of goods sold and ending inventory.
2. An average approach can best be associated with business operations in which like goods are commingled.
3. FIFO approximates the actual goods flow for most firms.
4. Although LIFO represents the least plausible goods flow for most businesses, many major firms use it.

Variations in Gross Profit

For comparative purposes, let us assume that the 220 units sold in our previous illustrations were sold for $20 each. Exhibit 9-3 shows the differences among gross profit figures resulting from each of the inventory pricing methods. Remember that these differences in reported gross profit result from assumptions made about cost flows, not from any difference in actual goods flows. Each of the inventory pricing methods is in accord with generally accepted accounting principles, yet one method's impact on income determination may be quite different from the impact of another method.

CONSISTENCY AND FULL DISCLOSURE PRINCIPLES

The area of inventory pricing permits the application of two basic principles of accounting: *consistency* and *full disclosure*. Because of the possible variation in income amounts from the use of different inventory pricing methods, it is important that a firm use the same inventory pricing method from one accounting period to the next. This adherence to the consistency principle enhances the comparability of a firm's financial data through time. Also, a firm should disclose the inventory pricing method

EXHIBIT 9—3	DIFFERENTIAL GROSS PROFIT ON SALES BASED ON VARIOUS INVENTORY PRICING METHODS

Periodic Inventory Pricing Method

	Sp. Id.	Average	FIFO	LIFO
Sales (220 units @ $20)	$4,400	$4,400	$4,400	$4,400
Cost of goods sold	2,530	2,706	2,500	2,870
Gross profit on sales	$1,870	$1,694	$1,900	$1,530
Increased gross profit compared with LIFO	$340	$164	$370	

Perpetual Inventory Pricing Method

	Sp. Id.	Average	FIFO	LIFO
Sales (220 units @ $20)	$4,400	$4,400	$4,400	$4,400
Cost of goods sold	2,530	2,602	2,500	2,710
Gross profit on sales	$1,870	$1,798	$1,900	$1,690
Increased gross profit compared with LIFO	$180	$108	$210	

it uses. This information—called for by the full disclosure principle—may be particularly helpful to users who compare financial data of two or more firms.

Matching Expenses with Revenues

As Exhibit 9-3 shows, LIFO results in the smallest gross profit among the alternative inventory pricing methods. This is because our illustration assumed that the purchase price of merchandise was increasing throughout the year. Most accountants agree that when prices are rising, FIFO tends to overstate gross profit (and income) because older, lower unit costs are included in the cost of goods sold and matched with current sales prices. In other words, in our example, all of the units sold are charged to costs of goods sold under FIFO at unit costs of $10, $11, and $13. If our latest purchases reflect current acquisition prices, the units sold must be replaced by units costing $16 (or more if prices continue to rise). Thus, we can argue that LIFO better matches current costs with current revenues, because the cost of the most recent purchases constitutes cost of goods sold.

However, while LIFO associates the current, most significant, unit prices with cost of goods sold, it consequently prices the ending inventory at the older, less realistic unit prices. Because of this, the LIFO inventory figure on the balance sheet is often meaningless in terms of current prices. As we noted earlier, when inventory quantities are maintained or increased, the LIFO method prevents the older prices from appearing in the cost of goods sold. No doubt, some firms still carry LIFO inventories at unit prices that prevailed more than 25 years ago. Under FIFO, in contrast, the ending inventory is measured at relatively recent prices.

Income Tax Advantage of LIFO

As just noted, during periods of rising prices, LIFO generally results in a lower gross profit than the alternative pricing methods. Lower gross profits (and incomes) mean lower amounts of income taxes to pay to the government. The desire to reduce current income tax payments is a major reason for the widespread usage of LIFO. (Corporations pay income taxes on their pretax incomes; although sole proprietorships and partnerships do not pay income taxes, the owners pay income taxes on their share of the entity's net income.)

| EXHIBIT 9—4 | FIFO-LIFO COMPARISON: PHANTOM PROFIT EFFECT AND TAX BENEFIT | | | |

	FIFO		LIFO	
	Income Statement	**Cash In (Out)**	**Income Statement**	**Cash In (Out)**
Sales (10 @ $700)	$ 7,000	$7,000	$ 7,000	$7,000
Cost of goods sold:				
Beginning inventory (10 @ $500)	$ 5,000		$ 5,000	
Purchases (10 @ $630)	6,300	(6,300)	6,300	(6,300)
Goods available (20 units)	$11,300		$11,300	
Ending inventory:				
10 @ FIFO	6,300			
10 @ LIFO			5,000	
Cost of goods sold	$ 5,000		$ 6,300	
Pretax income	$ 2,000		$ 700	
Income tax at 35%	700	(700)	245	(245)
Net income	$ 1,300		$ 455	
Net cash proceeds		$ 0		$ 455

A highly simplified example will compare FIFO with LIFO to illustrate the advantage of using LIFO during times of rising prices. Assume that a corporation using a periodic inventory system has an opening inventory of 10 units costing $500 each. The firm sells 10 units for $700 each and replaces its inventory by purchasing 10 more units costing $630 each. All transactions are for cash and, for simplicity, we also assume that operating expenses are zero and the applicable income tax rate is 35%. Exhibit 9-4 shows the income statements and cash flows under both FIFO and LIFO.

Note that under FIFO, $1,300 of net income is reported, but the amount of cash from sales is only enough to replace the inventory sold and pay the income tax on the $2,000 pretax income. Thus, the net income of $1,300 is not realized in cash that can be declared as dividends or reinvested in the business; it is considered *phantom* (or *inventory*) *profit*. We can easily imagine how the phantom profit element causes problems in the planning of corporate dividend policy and the use of net income as a funding source for capital investments.

As Exhibit 9-4 shows, LIFO results in a smaller ending inventory and larger cost of goods sold than FIFO. This translates directly into a smaller amount of income subject to tax and smaller cash outflows for income taxes under LIFO. The attractiveness of LIFO during periods of rising prices is evidenced by its more favorable cash flows compared with FIFO. Use of LIFO during times of *falling* prices, however, can have quite the opposite tax consequence.

DEPARTURES FROM COST

Inventories are generally measured at cost. The measurement may be reduced below cost, however, if there is evidence that the inventory's utility has fallen below cost. Such *inventory write-downs* may occur when (1) merchandise must be sold at reduced prices because it is damaged or otherwise not in normal salable condition or (2) the cost of replacing items in the ending inventory has declined below their recorded cost.

Net Realizable Value

OBJECTIVE **5** EXPLAIN *when inventories are measured at less than cost.*

Damaged, physically deteriorated, or obsolete merchandise should be measured and reported at **net realizable value** when this value is less than cost. Net realizable value is the estimated selling price less the expected cost of disposal. For example, assume that an inventory item cost $300 but can be sold for only $200 because it is damaged. Related selling costs are an estimated $20. We should write down the item to $180 ($200 estimated selling price less $20 estimated disposal cost) and reflect a $120 loss for this period.

Lower of Cost or Market

The **lower of cost or market (LCM)** rule provides for the recognition of a loss when prices decline on new inventory items. Under this rule, the loss is reported in the period when the prices decline, rather than during a subsequent period of sale. *Market* is defined as the current replacement cost of the merchandise. This procedure assumes that decreases in replacement costs will be accompanied by proportionate decreases in selling prices. If applicable, the LCM rule simply measures inventory at the lower (replacement) market figure. Consequently, reported income decreases by the amount that the ending inventory has been written down. When the ending inventory becomes part of the cost of goods sold in a future period of lower selling prices, its reduced carrying value helps maintain normal profit margins in the period of sale.

To illustrate, let us assume an inventory item that cost $80 has been selling for $100 during the year, yielding a gross profit of 20% on sales. At year-end, the item's replacement cost has dropped to $60—a 25% decline—and a proportionate reduction in the selling price to $75 is expected. In this case, the inventory would be written down to the $60 replacement cost, reducing the current period's net income by the $20 loss. When the item is sold in a subsequent period for $75, a normal gross profit of 20% on sales will be reported ($75 − $60 = $15 gross profit).[1]

We may apply the LCM rule to (1) each inventory item, (2) the totals of major inventory classes or categories, or (3) the total inventory. The following simple illustration shows the application of these alternatives and indicates that the inventory amount obtained depends on how the rule is applied.

		Per Unit		Total		Lower of Cost or Market by		
Inventory Item	Quantity	Cost	Market	Cost	Market	Indiv. Items	Major Categories	Total Inventory
Cameras								
Model V70	40	$80	$75	$3,200	$3,000	$3,000		
Model V85	30	60	64	1,800	1,920	1,800		
Subtotal				$5,000	$4,920		$4,920	
Calculators								
Model C20	90	13	15	$1,170	$1,350	1,170		
Model C40	50	20	17	1,000	850			
Subtotal				$2,170	$2,200	850	2,170	
Total				$7,170	$7,120	$6,820	$7,090	$7,120

If we apply LCM to the total inventory, our result is $7,120. Applied by item, however, the LCM amount is $6,820, and applied by major category, the LCM amount is $7,090. Although the item-by-item procedure is used most often, any of the three ways is acceptable. In any case, one method should be used consistently. Inventory market values appear in such sources as current price catalogs, purchase contracts with suppliers, and other forms of price quotations.

---

[1] Because of the scale and complexity of modern markets, not all decreases in replacement prices are followed by proportionate reductions in selling prices. In these cases, the application of the LCM rule is modified. These modifications are covered in more advanced accounting courses.

ESTIMATING INVENTORIES: PERIODIC INVENTORY SYSTEM

There are several good reasons for estimating inventories when firms use a periodic inventory system.[2] When taking physical inventory counts for interim financial statements is impractical, an estimate is sufficient. The adequacy of inventory insurance coverage may be determined on the basis of an inventory estimate. Finally, an estimate may be necessary to determine the loss from merchandise destroyed by fire or other disaster. Therefore, we should examine some methods for estimating inventories.

Gross Profit Method

OBJECTIVE 6 DESCRIBE *the gross profit and retail methods of estimating inventories.*

The **gross profit method** of estimating inventories merely rearranges the cost of goods sold section of the income statement: Estimated cost of goods sold is deducted from the cost of goods available for sale to derive the estimated ending inventory. Subtracting an estimated gross profit amount from sales provides the estimated cost of goods sold figure. For the gross profit method to be valid, the gross profit percentage (gross profit/net sales) used must be representative of the merchandising activities leading up to the date of the inventory estimate.

Suppose that over the past three years a company's gross profit averaged 30% of net sales. Assume also that the net sales for the current year's first interim period are $80,000; the inventory at the beginning of the period was $20,000; and net cost of purchases for the period is $50,000. Exhibit 9-5 shows how to estimate the ending inventory using the gross profit method.

EXHIBIT 9—5	GROSS PROFIT METHOD OF ESTIMATING INVENTORY	
Beginning inventory		$20,000
Net cost of purchases		50,000
Cost of goods available for sale		$70,000
Net sales	$80,000	
Estimated gross profit (30%)	24,000	
Estimated cost of goods sold		56,000
Estimated ending inventory		$14,000

Retail Method

The **retail method** represents another approach to estimating inventories. It is widely used by retail businesses, such as department stores, that keep periodic inventory records. Such firms typically mark each item of merchandise with the retail price and record purchases at both cost and retail price. The retail price information is kept as a supplemental record separate from the general ledger. A firm can estimate its ending inventory at *retail* price merely by subtracting sales from the retail price of merchandise available for sale. To determine the inventory *cost*, the firm applies a cost-to-retail price percentage, which is the ratio of cost to retail price of merchandise available for sale. In Exhibit 9-6 this ratio is 70%, which yields a cost amount of $21,000 when applied to the $30,000 estimated retail value of the ending inventory.

The cost-to-retail ratio can also be used to compute the cost of a physical inventory taken at retail prices. Thus, the firm saves the considerable effort and expense of determining cost prices for each inventory item. Suppose, for example, that sales clerks count their stock and determine that the ending inventory has an aggregate retail value of $40,000. If the cost-to-retail price ratio is 70%, management could

---

[2]There is no need to estimate inventories under a perpetual inventory system because the Inventory account continuously reflects the cost of goods on hand.

	EXHIBIT 9—6	RETAIL METHOD OF ESTIMATING INVENTORY	

	Cost	Retail Price
Beginning inventory	$14,000	$ 22,000
Net purchases	70,000	98,000
Total merchandise available for sale	$84,000	$120,000

Cost-to-retail percentage:
$$\frac{\$84,000}{\$120,000} = 70\%$$

		Retail Price
Less: Sales during period		90,000
Estimated ending inventory at retail prices		$ 30,000
Applicable cost percentage to convert to estimated cost		× 0.70
Estimated ending inventory at cost		$ 21,000

easily obtain the estimated cost of the inventory, $28,000, that is needed to prepare financial statements.

The accuracy of the retail method depends on the assumption that the ending inventory contains the same proportion of goods at the various mark-up percentages as did the original group of merchandise available for sale. To the extent that the mix of mark-up percentages does not remain constant, the accuracy of the estimate is impaired.

ACCOUNTING FOR IMPORTS AND EXPORTS

OBJECTIVE **7** EXPLAIN *the accounting for merchandise imports and exports.*

The market today for consumer and capital goods is truly a world market. An individual in the United States, for example, may drink Brazilian coffee, jog in German running shoes, drive a Japanese automobile, snack on a Swiss chocolate bar, and enjoy English records played on a stereo system with Danish components.

United States export and import levels indicate the extensive involvement of U.S. firms in international trade. Annual merchandise exports and imports each amount to several hundred billion dollars. The existence of world markets affects accounting because currencies other than the U.S. dollar may be involved in the transactions. Financial data stated in a foreign currency must be converted to U.S. dollars. Before examining these transactions, however, we consider foreign currency exchange rates.

Foreign Currency Exchange Rates

Exchange rates are used to convert one currency into a different currency. An **exchange rate** states the price, in terms of one currency, at which one unit of another currency may be bought or sold. Because our focus is on accounting in U.S. dollars, we express foreign currency exchange rates in terms of the U.S. dollar.

Exhibit 9-7 presents exchange rates for several foreign currencies. The exhibit shows, for example, that one Canadian dollar converts to $0.8446; that is, it takes $0.8446 to purchase one Canadian dollar. Similarly, one British pound converts to $1.7595, or it takes $1.7595 to purchase one British pound. Currencies are bought and sold like other goods. Thus, a currency's price (its exchange rate) is determined by the supply and demand for that currency. Exchange rates change frequently so the rates in Exhibit 9-7 (which are for a particular date) are illustrative only. Current exchange rates, no doubt, are different.

EXHIBIT 9–7	EXCHANGE RATES WITH THE U.S. DOLLAR	
Country	**Currency Unit**	**Price of One Unit in U.S. Dollars**
Brazil	Cruzeiro	$0.00046
Canada	Dollar	0.8446
Denmark	Kroner	0.1558
France	Franc	0.17840
Germany	Mark	0.6042
Great Britain	Pound	1.7595
Italy	Lira	0.0008001
Japan	Yen	0.007513
Netherlands	Guilder	0.5367
Switzerland	Franc	0.6564

SOURCE: *The Wall Street Journal*, April 14, 1992.

Imports and Exports Denominated in a Foreign Currency

Transactions a U.S. business may have with a foreign entity include the purchase (import) or sale (export) of goods. A transaction is a **foreign currency transaction** if it is *denominated* in a foreign currency; that is, if its terms are fixed in the amount of foreign currency to be paid or received. An import of television sets from a Japanese firm requiring payment of a fixed number of yen is a foreign currency transaction. Similarly, an export of computers to an English enterprise that requires settlement in a fixed number of British pounds is a foreign currency transaction.

ACCOUNTING AT TRANSACTION DATE

A U.S. firm keeps its financial records in U.S. dollars. All foreign currency transactions, therefore, must be translated into U.S. dollars so they may be properly recorded. When journalized, each transaction component is translated into U.S. dollars using the exchange rate at the transaction date.

IMPORTS To illustrate, assume a U.S. firm on a periodic inventory system purchases merchandise on account from a Canadian firm on June 1, 1993. The cost is 10,000 Canadian dollars (C$). Payment is due in 30 days. Assume the exchange rate for Canadian dollars on June 1 is $0.88 per Canadian dollar. Using the June 1 exchange rate, the U.S. firm translates the C$10,000 to $8,800 (C$10,000 × $0.88) and makes the following entry:

June 1	Purchases	8,800	
	Accounts Payable		8,800
	To record purchase of merchandise on account (C$10,000 × $0.88 = $8,800).		

EXPORTS Assume that on June 1, 1993, our U.S. firm also sells merchandise to a French firm on account, billing the firm 60,000 French francs (FF) due in 30 days. Assume the exchange rate for French francs on June 1 is $0.172 per franc. Using this exchange rate, the U.S. firm makes the following entry on June 1:

June 1	Accounts Receivable	10,320	
	Sales		10,320
	To record sale of merchandise on account (FF60,000 × $0.172 = $10,320).		

ACCOUNTING AT SETTLEMENT DATE

Exchange rates may change before the settlement date for a foreign currency payable or receivable. Should this occur, a **foreign exchange gain or loss** is recorded at the settlement date. The foreign exchange gain or loss measures the change in the U.S.

dollar equivalent required to settle the transaction. Foreign exchange gains and losses are reported in the income statement. A company experiencing both foreign exchange gains and foreign exchange losses during the same period may combine them and report a net foreign exchange gain or loss in its income statement.

SETTLEMENT OF ACCOUNTS PAYABLE

We continue our previous example. Assume that on July 1 the U.S. company settles its account payable with the Canadian firm, and the exchange rate on that date is $0.86 per Canadian dollar. On July 1, it costs the U.S. firm $8,600 to purchase the 10,000 Canadian dollars needed to settle the account. The exchange rate decline creates a $200 foreign exchange gain ($8,800 − $8,600) for the U.S. firm. The July 1 settlement is recorded as follows:

July 1	Accounts Payable	8,800	
	Cash		8,600
	Foreign Exchange Gain		200
	To record payment of account payable		
	(C$10,000 × $0.86 = $8,600) and		
	foreign exchange gain.		

SETTLEMENT OF ACCOUNTS RECEIVABLE

Assume that on July 1 the U.S. company also receives 60,000 French francs from the French firm as payment of its account receivable. Assume further the exchange rate with the French franc on July 1 has fallen to $0.168 per franc. This exchange rate decline creates a $240 foreign exchange loss for the U.S. firm. The July 1 receipt is recorded as follows:

July 1	Cash	10,080	
	Foreign Exchange Loss	240	
	Accounts Receivable		10,320
	To record collection of account receivable		
	(FF60,000 × $0.168 = $10,080) and foreign exchange		
	loss.		

UNSETTLED FOREIGN CURRENCY TRANSACTIONS

Foreign currency receivables and payables that are not settled at a balance sheet date are adjusted to reflect the exchange rate at that date. Such adjustments place foreign exchange gains and losses in the period when exchange rates change. Any foreign exchange gain or loss at the settlement date, then, relates only to exchange rate changes since the latest balance sheet date.

To illustrate, assume that on December 15, 1993, our U.S. firm purchases more merchandise on a 30-day account from the Canadian firm. The merchandise costs 15,000 Canadian dollars. The U.S. firm's accounting period ends on December 31, 1993. The account payable is settled on January 14, 1994. Exchange rates for the Canadian dollar are assumed to be as follows:

December 15	$0.82 per Canadian dollar
December 31	0.84
January 14	0.81

The U.S. firm accounts for this foreign currency transaction as follows:

1993

Dec. 15	Purchases	12,300	
	Accounts Payable		12,300
	To record purchase of merchandise on account		
	(C$15,000 × $0.82 = $12,300).		
31	Foreign Exchange Loss	300	
	Accounts Payable		300
	To adjust accounts payable to current exchange rate		
	(C$15,000 × $0.84 = $12,600; $12,600 − $12,300 =		
	$300) and record foreign exchange loss.		

PAYMENT METHODS FOR INTERNATIONAL TRADE

There are six basic methods of payment for international trade: ■ **CASH IN ADVANCE.** *This is simple. The importer sends the exporter a check, transfers money through banking channels, or actually hands over the currency. The importer bears all the risk. Some countries limit this payment method by restricting the amount of currency travelers can take in or out of the country.* ■ **LETTER OF CREDIT.** *This is a letter written by the importer's bank to the exporter, detailing when and how much he will be paid and what must be done to receive payment. To be*

paid, the exporter presents evidence that he has fulfilled the conditions to a branch or correspondent of the bank in this country.

■ **A BILL OF EXCHANGE.** This is a payment document initiated by the exporter through his own bank. It asks the importer to pay a certain amount of money for goods that have been, or are about to be, shipped. This is an inexpensive payment method commonly used for low-value shipments between non-related companies in developed countries.

■ **OPEN ACCOUNT.** The exporter simply ships and sends a bill; the importer pays by check or through banking channels. About half of all

international trade is conducted on open account, since much of this trade is conducted between large firms that know and trust each other or are affiliated.

■ **CONSIGNMENT.** The importer is given possession of the goods, but not title to them. If and when he sells them, he remits the proceeds to the exporter, less the selling commission and expenses.

■ **COUNTER TRADE.** These payment techniques include barter and switch trade, buy-back, and offset. Barter, perhaps the least common form of international trade, is a simple exchange of one commodity for another. A switch trade involves three or more parties to a transaction.

A buy-back allows the importer to pay for all or part of exported equipment with goods produced with that equipment. An offset refers to any other way in which an exporter helps an importer pay for its merchandise.

In general, counter trade is both risky and expensive. It is quite common, and many countries have laws that both facilitate and control its use.

Once products have been shipped, it may take months to receive payment. Many exporters are financially strong enough to wait to be paid, but some obtain commercial bank loans to cover their costs.

In the United States, exporters can use programs of the Small Business Administration, the Export/Import Bank, and state export credit agencies to guarantee bank loans. The U.S. government also has a variety of export-import programs for insuring account shipments. These change frequently.

SOURCE: William Zink, "Essential Steps to Building a Successful Export Business," *Manufacturing Issues* (Grant Thornton, Fall 1991). Used by permission.

1994

Jan. 14	Accounts Payable	12,600	
	Cash		12,150
	Foreign Exchange Gain		450

To record payment of account payable (C$15,000 × $0.81 = $12,150) and foreign exchange gain.

On December 31, 1993, a $300 foreign exchange loss is recorded to reflect the impact of the strengthening of the Canadian dollar between December 15 and December 31. Because the account payable is not settled on this date, the loss is unrealized. It is included, however, in the 1993 income statement. The account payable is settled on January 14, 1994. The Canadian dollar has weakened since December 31, 1993, so a $450 foreign exchange gain is recorded and included in the 1994 income statement.

Transactions Denominated in U.S. Currency

A U.S. firm's transactions with foreign entities that are denominated in U.S. dollars are *not* foreign currency transactions. No translation is required (the transaction is initially stated in U.S. dollars) and no foreign exchange gains or losses develop. For example, assume a U.S. firm sells merchandise to a Swiss firm on account. The sales price is $6,000 U.S. dollars, due in 30 days. Because the transaction is denominated in U.S. dollars, the U.S. firm accounts for the transaction no differently than if the customer was in the United States. The Swiss firm, in contrast, must translate its foreign currency transaction into Swiss francs and faces gains and losses from exchange rate changes.

ANALYTICAL APPLICATION

OBJECTIVE 8 DEFINE inventory turnover *and* days' sales in inventory *and* EXPLAIN *their use*.

INVENTORY TURNOVER AND DAYS' SALES IN INVENTORY

The inventory turnover ratio indicates how many times a year a firm sells its average inventory. **Inventory turnover** is computed as follows:

$$\text{Inventory Turnover} = \frac{\text{Cost of Goods Sold}}{\text{Average Inventory}}$$

This ratio relates data from two financial statements: the income statement and the balance sheet. Cost of goods sold is taken from the income statement. Average inventory is calculated from balance sheet data; the beginning and ending inventories are summed and the total is divided by 2.

In general, the faster a company can turn over its inventory, the better. The higher the inventory turnover ratio, the less time a firm has funds tied up in its inventory and the less risk the firm faces of trying to sell out-of-date merchandise. What is considered to be a satisfactory inventory turnover varies by industry; a grocery store, for example, should have a much higher inventory turnover than a jewelry shop.

WAL-MART STORES, INC., one of the nation's largest retail chains, reported the following financial data for three recent years (Year 3 is the most recent year; amounts in thousands):

	Year 3	Year 2	Year 1
Cost of goods sold	$25,499,834	$20,070,034	$16,056,856
Beginning inventory	4,428,073	3,351,367	2,651,760
Ending inventory	5,808,416	4,428,073	3,351,367

Wal-Mart's Year 3 inventory turnover is $25,499,834/[($4,428,073 + $5,808,416)/2] = 4.98. Similar computations reveal the inventory turnover is 5.16 for Year 2 and 5.35 for Year 1. Although a decline in inventory turnover is not a positive sign, there may be underlying economic causes. During this three-year period, for example, the country was entering a recession, so a decline in inventory turnover for a retail chain during this period would not be unexpected.

Inventory turnover is a ratio that is affected by a firm's inventory pricing method. Inventory amounts computed using LIFO will typically be smaller than the same inventory computed using FIFO. A person who is going to compare inventory turnover ratios among firms in the same industry needs to be alert to the inventory pricing method used by each firm.

A variation (or extension) of inventory turnover is **days' sales in inventory,** computed as follows:

$$\text{Days' Sales in Inventory} = \frac{365}{\text{Inventory Turnover}}$$

This ratio indicates how many days it takes a firm to sell its average inventory. During Year 3 for Wal-Mart Stores, Inc., for example, the days' sales in inventory were 365/4.98 = 73.3.

KEY POINTS FOR CHAPTER OBJECTIVES

❶ **DISCUSS** basic inventory concepts, the need for inventories, and inventory counts (pp. 326–328).
- Inventory represents goods owned by a firm and available for resale.

❷ **DESCRIBE** inventory pricing under a periodic inventory system using the (1) specific identification method, (2) weighted average method, (3) FIFO method, and (4) LIFO method (pp. 328–331).
- These methods differ in the way they assume inventory costs flow through a business.
- Uncorrected ending inventory errors cause the income of two periods to be misstated. The errors are equal in amount, opposite in direction, and therefore offsetting.

❸ **DESCRIBE** inventory pricing under a perpetual inventory system using the (1) specific identification method, (2) moving average method, (3) FIFO method, and (4) LIFO method (pp. 331–334).
- Perpetual specific identification and FIFO pricing methods give the same results as periodic specific identification and FIFO pricing methods.

❹ **ANALYZE** the effects inventory pricing methods have on gross profits, matching of expenses with revenues, and income taxes (pp. 335–337).
- Reported income can be influenced by choosing among different inventory pricing methods.
- When prices are rising, LIFO matches current costs with revenues and results in lower reported gross profit and income than FIFO does, and thus may provide a related tax benefit.

❺ **EXPLAIN** when inventories are measured at less than cost (pp. 337–338).
- The lower of cost or market rule provides for losses to be recorded in the period that replacement costs of inventory items decline.
- The lower of cost or market rule may be applied to (1) each inventory item, (2) major inventory categories, or (3) the total inventory.

❻ **DESCRIBE** the gross profit and retail methods of estimating inventories (pp. 339–340).
- The gross profit method subtracts the estimated cost of goods sold from the cost of goods available for sale. A representative gross profit percentage must be used in estimating the cost of goods sold.
- The retail method uses an appropriate cost-to-retail price percentage to reduce the ending inventory from a retail amount to a cost amount.

❼ **EXPLAIN** the accounting for merchandise imports and exports (pp. 340–344).
- Imports and exports denominated in a foreign currency result in foreign exchange gains and losses if the exchange rate changes from the transaction date to the settlement date.

❽ **ANALYTICAL APPLICATION:** **DEFINE** *inventory turnover* and *days' sales in inventory* and **EXPLAIN** their use (pp. 344–345).
- Inventory turnover and days' sales in inventory indicate, respectively, how many times a year a firm sells its average inventory and how many days it takes to sell the firm's average inventory.
- Inventory turnover and days' sales in inventory help in the evaluation of a firm's ability to sell its inventory.

SELF-TEST QUESTIONS FOR REVIEW

(Answers follow the Solution to Demonstration Problem.)

1. Which inventory pricing method assumes that the goods most recently purchased are sold first?
   - **a.** FIFO.
   - **b.** Specific identification.
   - **c.** Weighted average.
   - **d.** LIFO.

2. The average inventory pricing method under a perpetual inventory system is called the
   - **a.** Weighted average method.
   - **b.** Moving average method.
   - **c.** Composite average method.
   - **d.** Simple average method.

3. Which inventory pricing method results in the largest ending inventory amount during a period of rising prices?
   a. FIFO.
   b. LIFO.
   c. Moving average.
   d. Weighted average.

4. Boyer Company started 1993 with a $140,000 inventory. Purchases totaled $300,000 during the first three months of 1993. Sales during the same period were $500,000. Boyer's gross profit averages 45% of sales. Using the gross profit method, Boyer's March 31, 1993, inventory is estimated at
   a. $165,000
   b. $275,000
   c. $225,000
   d. $215,000

5. On April 1, 1993, Drew Company purchased goods from a French supplier for 100,000 French francs, payable in 60 days. On May 29, 1993, Drew's bank sent the supplier a bank draft for 100,000 francs and charged Drew's account for the cost of the francs. The exchange rate for the franc was $0.176 on April 1, 1993, and $0.169 on May 29, 1993. The purchase and settlement of this import results in Drew Company showing a
   a. $16,900 foreign exchange loss.
   b. $700 foreign exchange gain.
   c. $17,600 foreign exchange gain.
   d. $700 foreign exchange loss.

DEMONSTRATION PROBLEM FOR REVIEW

Mackenzie, Inc., began a new fiscal year on January 1, 1993. Sales revenue for 1993 totaled $90,000. The company uses the periodic inventory system. Its beginning inventory was $4,000, consisting of 2,000 units at $2 per unit. A summary of 1993 purchases appears below.

April 8	5,000 units @ $2.50 =	$12,500
August 19	10,000 units @ 3.00 =	30,000
December 29	6,000 units @ 3.50 =	21,000
	Total	$63,500

At December 31, 1993, 7,000 unit were on hand.

REQUIRED

a. How much gross profit on sales would Mackenzie, Inc., report for 1993 under (1) first-in, first-out inventory pricing and (2) last-in, first-out inventory pricing?

b. Calculate Mackenzie's gross profit on sales for 1993 under (1) first-in, first-out and (2) last-in, first-out if the December 29 purchase had been postponed until January 1994.

c. Calculate Mackenzie's gross profit on sales for 1993 under (1) first-in, first-out and (2) last-in, first-out if the December 29 purchase had been 9,000 units instead of 6,000 units.

d. Based on your answers to parts (a), (b), and (c), what can you conclude about the impact of the timing or amount of end-of-period purchases on the gross profit on sales computed under the (1) first-in, first-out and (2) last-in, first-out methods of inventory pricing?

SOLUTION TO DEMONSTRATION PROBLEM

a.

	FIFO	LIFO
Sales	$90,000	$90,000
Cost of goods sold:		
Beginning inventory	$ 4,000	$ 4,000
Add: Purchases	63,500	63,500
Cost of goods available for sale	$67,500	$67,500
Less: Ending inventory		
FIFO: 6,000 × $3.50 = $21,000		
1,000 × $3.00 = 3,000	24,000	
LIFO: 2,000 × $2.00 = $ 4,000		
5,000 × $2.50 = 12,500		16,500
Cost of goods sold	$43,500	$51,000
Gross profit on sales	$46,500	$39,000

b. If the December 29 purchase of 6,000 units was postponed until January, the ending inventory would have been 1,000 units and purchases for 1993 would have totaled $42,500 ($12,500 on April 8 + $30,000 on August 19). The gross profit on sales would then be computed as follows:

	FIFO	LIFO
Sales	$90,000	$90,000
Cost of goods sold:		
Beginning inventory	$ 4,000	$ 4,000
Add: Purchases	42,500	42,500
Cost of goods available for sale	$46,500	$46,500
Less: Ending inventory		
FIFO: 1,000 × $3.00	3,000	
LIFO: 1,000 × $2.00		2,000
Cost of goods sold	$43,500	$44,500
Gross profit on sales	$46,500	$45,500

c. If 9,000 units were purchased on December 29, then the ending inventory would have been 10,000 units and purchases for 1993 would have totaled $74,000 ($12,500 on April 8 + $30,000 on August 19 + $31,500 on December 29). The gross profit on sales would then be computed as follows:

	FIFO	LIFO
Sales	$90,000	$90,000
Cost of goods sold:		
Beginning inventory	$ 4,000	$ 4,000
Add: Purchases	74,000	74,000
Cost of goods available for sale	$78,000	$78,000
Less: Ending inventory		
FIFO: 9,000 × $3.50 = $31,500		
1,000 × $3.00 = 3,000	34,500	
LIFO: 2,000 × $2.00 = $ 4,000		
5,000 × $2.50 = 12,500		
3,000 × $3.00 = 9,000		25,500
Cost of goods sold	$43,500	$52,500
Gross profit on sales	$46,500	$37,500

d. Gross profit on sales under the FIFO method is the same in all three cases. The gross profit is unaffected by changes in the amount or timing of end-of-period purchases.

Gross profit on sales under the LIFO method is different in each case. Gross profit is affected by changes in the amount or timing of end-of-period purchases, because—under the periodic LIFO method—the costs of the most recently purchased goods are the first costs charged to cost of goods sold.

ANSWERS TO SELF-TEST QUESTIONS

1. d, p. 330   **2.** b, p. 333   **3.** a, p. 330   **4.** a, p. 339   **5.** b, p. 342

GLOSSARY OF KEY TERMS USED IN THIS CHAPTER

cost of goods sold An expense reflecting the cost of merchandise sold to customers during an accounting period (p. 326).

days' sales in inventory A ratio computed as 365/(Inventory Turnover) that indicates the number of days it takes to sell a firm's average inventory (p. 344).

exchange rate The price, in terms of one currency, at which one unit of another currency may be bought or sold (p. 340).

first-in, first-out (FIFO) method An inventory pricing method that assumes that the oldest (earliest purchased) goods on hand are sold first, resulting in an ending inventory priced at the most recent acquisition costs (p. 330, 333).

foreign currency transaction   A transaction whose terms are fixed in the amount of foreign currency to be paid or received (p. 341).

foreign exchange gain or loss   A gain or loss arising from a change in exchange rates before a foreign currency transaction is settled (p. 341).

gross profit method   A procedure for estimating the cost of an inventory by subtracting an estimated cost of goods sold amount from the cost of goods available for sale (p. 339).

inventory   Merchandise owned by a company and held for resale to customers in the ordinary course of business (p. 326).

inventory turnover   A ratio computed by dividing cost of goods sold by average inventory (p. 344).

last-in, first-out (LIFO) method   An inventory pricing method that assumes that the most recently purchased goods are sold first, resulting in an ending inventory priced at the earliest acquisition costs (p. 330, 334).

lower of cost or market (LCM)   A measurement guideline that, when applied to inventory, provides for inventory to be presented in the balance sheet at the lower of its acquisition cost or current replacement cost (p. 338).

moving average method   An inventory pricing method under a perpetual inventory system that recomputes an average unit cost each time a purchase occurs and uses that average unit cost to determine the cost of goods sold for each subsequent sale (p. 333).

net realizable value   An asset measure computed by subtracting expected disposal costs from the asset's expected selling price (p. 338).

periodic inventory system   An inventory system in which no entries are made to the Inventory account as merchandise is purchased and sold. At year-end, the ending inventory is counted and established in the Inventory account (p. 326).

perpetual inventory system   An inventory system in which both purchases and sales of merchandise are reflected in the Inventory account at the time such transactions occur (p. 326).

retail method   A procedure for estimating the cost of an inventory by multiplying the estimated retail value of the inventory by an appropriate cost percentage (p. 339).

specific identification method   An inventory pricing method involving the physical identification of goods sold and goods remaining on hand and pricing these amounts at their actual costs (p. 329, 332).

weighted average method   An inventory pricing method under a periodic inventory system that spreads the total dollar cost of goods available for sale equally among all units on hand and sold (p. 329).

QUESTIONS

9-1   Define *inventory* and identify the costs that should be included as inventory costs.

9-2   For a physical inventory count, explain (a) the three steps involved, (b) why firms maintaining perpetual inventory records still take physical counts, and (c) what merchandise should be included.

9-3   What is meant by *goods flow* and *cost flow*?

9-4   Briefly describe each of the following inventory pricing methods under a periodic inventory system: (a) specific identification; (b) weighted average; (c) first-in, first-out; and (d) last-in, first-out.

9-5   Thorp Company understated its 1993 periodic ending inventory by $18,000. Assuming the error was not discovered, what was the effect on gross profit for 1993? For 1994?

9-6   Which inventory pricing methods give the same results (ending inventory and total cost of goods sold) when applied under a perpetual inventory system and a periodic inventory system?

9-7   Describe an appropriate operating situation (that is, goods flow corresponds with cost flow) for each of the following approaches to inventory pricing: specific identification; average; first-in, first out; and last-in, first-out.

9-8   Why do relatively stable purchase prices reduce the significance of the choice of an inventory pricing method?

9-9   Briefly explain the nature of *phantom profits* during periods of rising merchandise purchase prices.

9-10 If prices have been rising, which periodic inventory pricing method—weighted average; first-in, first-out; or last-in, first-out—yields (a) the lowest inventory amount? (b) the lowest net income? (c) the largest inventory amount? (d) the largest net income?

9-11 Even though it does not represent their goods flow, why might firms adopt last-in, first-out inventory pricing during periods when prices are consistently rising?

9-12 Identify two situations in which merchandise may be inventoried at an amount less than cost.

9-13 In what way is the lower of cost or market rule applied to inventory more flexible than when it is applied to short-term stock investments?

9-14 At year-end, The Appliance Shop has a refrigerator on hand that has been used as a demonstration model. The refrigerator cost $350 and sells for $500 when new. In its present condition, the refrigerator will be sold for $325. Related selling costs are an estimated $15. At what amount should the refrigerator be carried in inventory?

9-15 Discuss the effect on reported income of applying the lower of cost or market rule to inventory.

9-16 Under what circumstances might firms estimate the dollar amount of their inventories rather than actually count them?

9-17 What event causes a foreign exchange loss to occur when accounting for an import, purchased on account, that is denominated in a foreign currency?

9-18 What is the likely effect on the inventory turnover ratio for a company that switches from FIFO to LIFO?

9-19 Moyer Company has a 1993 inventory turnover of 4.20. What is Moyer's 1993 days' sales in inventory?

EXERCISES

**ENDING INVENTORY
COUNT
— OBJ. 1 —**

9-20 The December 31, 1993, inventory of Loften Company was $76,000. In arriving at this amount, the following items were considered:
1. Included in the inventory count were goods on hand costing $3,000 owned by Hefty Company but on consignment to Loften Company.
2. Included in the inventory count were goods in transit at December 31 to Loften Company from Gier, Inc. These goods, costing $7,000, were shipped F.O.B. destination and arrived on January 3, 1994.
3. Excluded from the inventory count were goods sitting on Loften Company's shipping dock on December 31. These goods, costing $3,500, were sold to Vine, Inc., on December 31 and were picked up by a Vine truck on January 2, 1994.
4. Included in the inventory count were goods in transit at December 31 to Loften Company from Yukon, Inc. The goods, costing $4,000, were shipped F.O.B. shipping point and arrived on January 2, 1994.

Compute the correct December 31, 1993, inventory amount for Loften Company. Loften has no specific agreement with any party concerning the passage of title to goods bought or sold.

**INVENTORY PRICING
METHODS—PERIODIC
— OBJ. 2 —**

9-21 The following information is for Bloom Company for 1993. Bloom sells just one product.

	Units	Unit Cost
Beginning inventory	200	$ 5
Purchases: Feb. 11	500	7
May 18	400	8
Oct. 23	100	10

At December 31, 1993, there was an ending inventory of 360 units. Assume periodic inventory procedures and compute the ending inventory and the cost of goods sold using (a) first-in, first-out; (b) last-in, first-out; and (c) weighted average.

**INVENTORY ERROR
CORRECTIONS
— OBJ. 2 —**

9-22 The following information is available for Spangler Company during four consecutive operating periods:

	Amounts by Period			
	1	**2**	**3**	**4**
Beginning inventory	$14,000	$28,000	$21,000	$19,000
Net cost of purchases	82,000	57,000	67,000	58,000
Cost of goods available for sale	$96,000	$85,000	$88,000	$77,000
Ending inventory	28,000	21,000	19,000	18,000
Cost of goods sold	$68,000	$64,000	$69,000	$59,000

Assuming that the company used the periodic inventory system and made the following errors, compute the revised cost of goods sold figure for each period.

Period	Error in Ending Inventory	
1	Overstated	$3,000
2	Overstated	4,000
3	Understated	2,000

INVENTORY PRICING METHODS—PERPETUAL — OBJ. 3 —

9-23 The following are July inventory data for Lippin Company, which uses perpetual inventory procedures.

July 1 Beginning inventory, 30 units @ $16 per unit.
    10 Purchased 50 units @ $18 per unit.
    15 Sold 60 units.
    26 Purchased 15 units @ $19 per unit.

Compute the cost of goods sold for July 15 using (a) first-in, first-out; (b) last-in, first-out; and (c) moving average.

DEPARTURES FROM COST — OBJ. 5 —

9-24 Determine the proper total inventory amount for each of the following items in Viking Company's year-end inventory.
  a. Viking has 400 video games in stock. The games cost $36 each, but their year-end replacement cost is $30. Viking has been selling these games for $60, but competitors are now selling them for $50. Viking plans to drop its price to $50. Viking's normal gross profit rate on video games is 40%.
  b. Viking has 300 rolls of camera film that are past the expiration date marked on each film's box. The films cost $1.65 each and are normally sold for $3.30. New replacement films still cost $1.65. To clear out these old films, Viking will drop their selling price to $1.50. There are no related selling costs.
  c. Viking has five cameras in stock that have been used as demonstration models. The cameras cost $180 and normally sell for $270. Because these cameras are in used condition, Viking has set the selling price at $160 each. Expected selling costs are $10 per camera. New models of the camera (on order) will cost Viking $200 and will be priced to sell at $300.

GROSS PROFIT METHOD — OBJ. 6 —

9-25 Over the past several years Hartley Company's gross profit has averaged 48% of net sales. During the first six months of the current year, net sales are $850,000 and net cost of purchases totals $450,000. Inventory at the beginning of the period was $60,000. The company prepares quarterly interim financial statements. Use the gross profit method to determine the estimated cost of inventory at the end of the current six-month period.

RETAIL METHOD — OBJ. 6 —

9-26 Berger Company's April 1 inventory had a cost of $42,000 and a retail value of $75,000. During April, Berger's net merchandise purchases cost $35,000 and had a net retail value of $65,000. Net sales for April totaled $90,000.
  a. Compute the estimated cost of the April 30 inventory using the retail method.
  b. What key assumptions underlie the validity of this estimate of inventory cost?

IMPORTS AND EXPORTS — OBJ. 7 —

9-27 **a.** National Company, a U.S. firm, purchased merchandise on account from Soytan Company, a Japanese supplier, for 800,000 yen. On the purchase date, the exchange rate was $0.00765 per yen. On the payment date, the exchange rate was $0.00788 per yen. What are the (1) cost of the merchandise purchased, and (2) the foreign exchange gain or loss from the settlement?
  b. Starr Company, a U.S. firm, sold merchandise on account to Brinker Company, a Danish firm, for 50,000 kroner. On the sale date, the exchange rate was $0.1522

per kroner. On the settlement date, the exchange rate was $0.1548 per kroner. What are the (1) sales revenue, and (2) the foreign exchange gain or loss from the settlement?

PROBLEMS

INVENTORY PRICING METHODS—PERIODIC AND PERPETUAL
— OBJ. 2, 3, 4 —

9-28 Chen Sales, Inc., had a beginning inventory on January 1 of 500 units that cost $20 per unit. A summary of purchases and sales during the year follows:

	Unit Cost	Units Purchased	Units Sold
Feb. 2			200
Apr. 6	$22	900	
July 10			800
Aug. 9	26	400	
Oct. 23			400
Dec. 30	29	600	

REQUIRED

a. Assuming Chen uses a periodic inventory system and has 1,000 units on hand at year-end, calculate the amount of ending inventory and cost of goods sold under each of the following pricing methods: first-in, first-out; last-in, first-out; and weighted average.
b. Which inventory pricing method would you choose:
  1. To reflect what is probably the physical flow of goods?
  2. To minimize income tax for the period?
  3. To report the largest amount of income for the period?
  Justify your answers.
c. Assuming Chen uses a perpetual inventory system, prepare a schedule showing the beginning inventory, purchases, cost of goods sold, and the continuous (perpetual) inventory balance for the year under each of the following pricing methods: first-in, first-out; last-in, first-out; and moving average.

INVENTORY PRICING METHODS—PERPETUAL
— OBJ. 3 —

9-29 Fortune Company uses a perpetual inventory system. Transactions for an inventory item during April were as follows:

April 1 Beginning inventory, 60 units @ $325 per unit.
     9 Purchased 20 units @ $345 per unit.
    14 Sold 40 units @ $550 per unit.
    23 Purchased 10 units @ $350 per unit.
    29 Sold 20 units @ $550 per unit.

REQUIRED

Prepare a schedule showing the beginning inventory, purchases, cost of goods sold, and the continuous (perpetual) inventory balance for April. Use the (a) first-in, first-out method; (b) last-in, first-out method; and (c) moving average method.

EFFECTS OF FIFO AND LIFO
— OBJ. 2, 3 —

9-30 Examine the annual data below for Sorkin, Inc., which prices inventory on the last-in, first-out basis and uses the periodic inventory system.

Beginning inventory: 3,000 units @ $5

Purchases		Sales	
Jan. 5	9,000 @ $6	Feb. 8	8,000 @ $ 9
May 19	20,000 @ 7	June 21	19,000 @ 10
Dec. 30	7,000 @ 9	Nov. 28	4,000 @ 12

REQUIRED

a. How much gross profit on sales would Sorkin, Inc., report for the year?
b. By what amount would Sorkin's reported gross profit for the year change if the final merchandise purchase had been postponed for several days?

c. How would Sorkin's reported gross profit differ if the final purchase had been for 14,000 units instead of for 7,000 units?

d. Assuming Sorkin used the first-in, first-out method, calculate the answers to requirements (a), (b), and (c).

LOWER OF COST OR MARKET RULE
— OBJ. 5 —

9-31 Venner Company had the following inventory at December 31, 1993:

		Unit Price	
	Quantity	Cost	Market
Fans			
Model X1	300	$18	$19
Model X2	250	22	24
Model X3	400	29	26
Heaters			
Model B7	500	24	28
Model B8	290	35	32
Model B9	100	40	38

REQUIRED

a. Determine the ending inventory amount by applying the lower of cost or market rule to
   1. Each item of inventory.
   2. Each major category of inventory.
   3. The total inventory.

b. Which of the LCM procedures from requirement (a) results in the lowest net income for 1993? Explain.

GROSS PROFIT METHOD
— OBJ. 6 —

9-32 Cardinal Company, an automobile parts supplier, was robbed of a portion of its inventory on the night of August 16, 1994. The company does not keep perpetual inventory records and must, therefore, estimate the theft loss. To aid in this determination, the accounting staff compiles the following information:

Inventory, August 1, 1994	$414,000
Inventory, August 17, 1994 (Not stolen)	190,000
Purchases, August 1–16, 1994	85,000
Purchases returns, August 1–16, 1994	4,000
Sales, August 1–16, 1994	300,000
Average gross profit margin	38%

REQUIRED

Use the gross profit method to estimate the amount of the inventory theft loss.

RETAIL METHOD
— OBJ. 6 —

9-33 Sales clerks for Dixon Company, a retail concern, took a year-end physical inventory at retail prices and determined that the total retail value of the ending inventory was $220,000. The following information for the year is available:

	Cost	Selling Price
Beginning inventory	$127,000	$190,000
Net purchases	481,000	760,000
Sales		714,000

Management estimates its inventory loss from theft and other causes by comparing its physical ending inventory at retail prices with an estimated ending inventory at retail prices (determined by subtracting sales from goods available for sale at selling prices) and reducing this difference to cost by applying the proper cost ratio.

REQUIRED

a. Compute the estimated cost of the ending inventory using the cost-to-retail percentage from the retail method. This inventory amount will appear in the balance sheet, and the calculation should be based on the physical inventory taken at retail prices.

b. Compute the estimated inventory loss for the year from theft and other causes.

IMPORT ACCOUNTING
— OBJ. 7 —

9-34 On June 18, 1993, Talon, Inc., a U.S. company using the periodic inventory system, purchased merchandise on account from Bourne Company, a French firm. The merchandise cost was 80,000 French francs. Talon paid the amount due (in francs) on July 10, 1993. Talon's fiscal year ends on June 30. Exchange rates for the French franc were the following:

June 18, 1993	$0.178
June 30, 1993	0.165
July 10, 1993	0.157

REQUIRED

a. Prepare the journal entries to account for the Bourne Company transaction on Talon's records for June 18, 1993, June 30, 1993, and July 10, 1993.

b. Assume Talon's accounting year ends December 31 rather than June 30. Prepare the necessary journal entries on Talon's records in 1993 to account for the foreign currency transaction with Bourne Company.

c. Assume Talon's accounting year ends June 30 and the exchange rates for the French franc were as follows:

June 18, 1993	$0.154
June 30, 1993	0.172
July 10, 1993	0.149

Prepare the journal entries to account for the Bourne Company transaction on Talon's records for June 18, 1993, June 30, 1993, and July 10, 1993.

ALTERNATE EXERCISES

ENDING INVENTORY COUNT
— OBJ. 1 —

9-20A The December 31, 1993, inventory of Kachina Company was $126,000. In arriving at this amount, the following items were considered:

1. Excluded from the inventory count were goods costing $10,000 that were owned by Kachina Company but were on consignment to Tolkin Company (Tolkin has physical possession of the goods and will receive a 15% commission upon sale of the goods).

2. Included in the inventory count were goods costing $4,000 that arrived on January 2, 1994. These goods were shipped F.O.B. destination and should have arrived on December 31, 1993. Bad weather caused the local roads to be closed on December 31.

3. Excluded from the inventory count were goods in transit at December 31 to Kachina Company from Adkins, Inc. The goods, costing $2,500, were shipped F.O.B. shipping point and did not arrive until January 6, 1994.

Compute the correct December 31, 1993, inventory for Kachina Company. Kachina has no specific agreement with any party concerning the passage of title to goods bought or sold.

INVENTORY PRICING METHODS—PERIODIC
— OBJ. 2 —

9-21A Toon Company, which uses the periodic inventory system, has the following records for 1993:

	Units	Unit Cost
Beginning inventory	100	$23
Purchases: Jan. 6	650	21
July 15	550	19
Dec. 28	200	18

Ending inventory at December 31 was 350 units. Compute the ending inventory and the cost of goods sold using (a) first-in, first-out; (b) weighted average; and (c) last-in, first-out.

INCOME EFFECTS OF INVENTORY PRICING METHODS
— OBJ. 4 —

9-22A The following is a summary of Archer Company's inventory amounts at the end of each of its first three years of operations, assuming various periodic inventory pricing procedures.

Year-end	First-in, First-out	Last-in, First-out	Weighted Average
1	$ 9,700	$ 9,000	$ 9,200
2	11,400	10,400	11,000
3	9,200	8,500	8,900

Answer each of the following questions, providing supporting computations or other reasoning (disregard income tax effects).

a. For year 1, by how much could reported income change simply by choosing among the three inventory pricing methods?

b. For year 2, which inventory pricing method would result in the *highest* reported income?

c. For year 3, which inventory pricing method would result in the *lowest* reported income?

d. Which inventory pricing method would result in the *highest* reported income for the *three years combined*?

INVENTORY PRICING METHODS—PERPETUAL
— OBJ. 3 —

9-23A The following are June inventory data for Merrit Company, which uses perpetual inventory procedures.

June 1 Beginning inventory, 75 units @ $30 per unit.
     8 Purchased 50 units @ $35 per unit.
    16 Sold 90 units.
    28 Purchased 80 units @ $36 per unit.

Compute the cost of goods sold for June 16 using (a) first-in, first-out; (b) last-in, first-out; and (c) moving average.

LOWER OF COST OR MARKET
— OBJ. 5 —

9-24A The following data refer to Froning Company's ending inventory:

Item Code	Quantity	Unit Cost	Unit Market
LXC	60	$44	$48
KWT	210	38	35
MOR	300	22	20
NES	100	27	32

Determine the ending inventory amount by applying the lower of cost or market rule to (a) each item of inventory and (b) the total inventory.

GROSS PROFIT METHOD
— OBJ. 6 —

9-25A Over the past several years Locust Company's gross profit has averaged 34% of net sales. During the first three months of the current year, net sales are $1,200,000 and net cost of purchases totals $810,000. Inventory at the beginning of the period was $116,000. The company prepares quarterly interim financial statements. Use the gross profit method to determine the estimated cost of the inventory at the end of the current three-month period.

RETAIL METHOD
— OBJ. 6 —

9-26A Ortega Company's inventory at January 1 had a cost of $56,000 and a retail value of $92,000. During the first six months of the current year, Ortega's net merchandise purchases cost $127,000 and had a net retail value of $208,000. Net sales for the six months totaled $240,000. Use the retail method to determine the estimated cost of the inventory at the end of the current six-month period.

IMPORTS AND EXPORTS
— OBJ. 7 —

9-27A a. Storm Company, a U.S. firm, purchased merchandise on account from Downe Company, an Australian supplier, for 80,000 Australian dollars. On the purchase date, the exchange rate was $0.798 per Australian dollar. On the payment date, the exchange rate was $0.823 per Australian dollar. What are the (1) cost of the merchandise purchased, and (2) the foreign exchange gain or loss from the settlement?

b. Banner Company, a U.S. firm, sold merchandise on account to Zurich Industries, a Swiss customer, for 100,000 Swiss francs. On the sale date, the exchange rate was $0.698 per Swiss franc. On the settlement date, the exchange rate was $0.672 per Swiss franc. What are the (1) sales revenue, and (2) the foreign exchange gain or loss from the settlement.

ALTERNATE PROBLEMS

INVENTORY PRICING METHODS—PERIODIC AND PERPETUAL
— OBJ. 2, 3, 4 —

9-28A Gleem Sales, Inc., had a beginning inventory on January 1 of 1,300 units that cost $40 per unit. A summary of purchases and sales during the year follows:

	Unit Cost	Units Purchased	Units Sold
Jan. 3			800
Mar. 8	$44	1,500	
June 13			1,000
Sept. 19	50	400	
Nov. 23	55	600	
Dec. 28			900

REQUIRED

a. Assuming Gleem uses a periodic inventory system and has 1,100 units on hand at year-end, calculate the amount of ending inventory and cost of goods sold under each of the following pricing methods: first-in, first-out; last-in, first-out; and weighted average.

b. Which inventory pricing method would you choose:
1. To reflect what is probably the physical flow of goods?
2. To minimize income tax for the period?
3. To report the largest amount of income for the period?
Justify your answers.

c. Assuming Gleem uses a perpetual inventory system, prepare a schedule showing the beginning inventory, purchases, cost of goods sold, and the continuous (perpetual) inventory balance for the year under each of the following pricing methods: first-in, first-out; last-in, first-out; and moving average.

INVENTORY PRICING METHODS—PERPETUAL
— OBJ. 3 —

9-29A Shiloh Company uses a perpetual inventory system. Transactions for an inventory item during June were as follows:

June   1   Beginning inventory, 30 units @ $40 per unit.
     5   Purchased 20 units @ $50 per unit.
  13   Sold 25 units @ $90 per unit.
  25   Purchased 15 units @ $52 per unit.
  29   Sold 10 units @ $100 per unit.

REQUIRED

Prepare a schedule showing the beginning inventory, purchases, cost of goods sold, and the continuous (perpetual) inventory balance for June. Use the (a) first-in, first-out method; (b) last-in, first-out method; and (c) moving average method.

COMPARISON OF FIFO AND LIFO
— OBJ. 4 —

9-30A Selected operating data follow for Autosound, Inc., a franchised distributor of automobile audio systems:

Beginning inventory	400 units	@ $290
Purchases:	700	@ 320
	300	@ 340
Sales	1,000	@ 600
Operating expenses	$152,000	

Autosound uses the periodic inventory system priced at first-in, first-out. Assume all sales, purchases, operating expenses, and taxes are paid in cash and that a 30% income tax rate is applicable. There are 400 units in the ending inventory.

REQUIRED

a. What is Autosound's net income for the period?

b. What is the net amount of cash generated by the period's activity?

c. Why are the amounts in requirements (a) and (b) different? How would you explain this to a stockholder who expected a cash dividend equal to one-half of the reported net income?

d. What would be your answers to requirements (a) and (b) if the firm used the last-in, first-out method to price its ending inventory?

e. Briefly explain the nature of any phantom profit on inventory in part (a). Also, explain the nature of any tax advantage of the last-in, first-out inventory pricing in requirement (d).

f. Contrast the ending inventory carrying values in requirements (a) and (d). Which figure is more meaningful? Why?

g. Contrast the reported income in requirements (a) and (d). Which figure is more meaningful? Why?

LOWER OF COST OR MARKET RULE
— OBJ. 5 —

9-31A Crane Company had the following inventory at December 31, 1993:

		Unit Price	
	Quantity	Cost	Market
Desks			
Model 9001	70	$190	$200
Model 9002	45	280	268
Model 9003	20	350	360
Cabinets			
Model 7001	120	60	64
Model 7002	80	95	88
Model 7003	50	130	126

REQUIRED

a. Determine the ending inventory amount by applying the lower of cost or market rule to
   1. Each item of inventory.
   2. Each major category of inventory.
   3. The total inventory.

b. Which of the LCM procedures from requirement (a) results in the lowest net income for 1993? Explain.

GROSS PROFIT METHOD
— OBJ. 6 —

9-32A Field Company, a computer supply firm, lost all of its inventory to a flood on March 15, 1993. The company does not keep perpetual inventory records and must, therefore, estimate the flood loss for insurance purposes. To aid in this determination, the accounting staff compiles the following information:

	1991	1992	1993 (to 3/15)
Net sales	$710,000	$800,000	$220,000
Beginning inventory	50,000	40,500	74,500
Purchases	450,000	520,000	111,000
Purchases returns	3,000	4,000	1,000
Purchases discounts	5,000	6,000	2,000
Transportation in	10,000	12,000	4,000
Ending inventory	40,500	74,500	?

REQUIRED

a. Compute the gross profit rates for 1991 and 1992.

b. Using the average of the gross profit rates for 1991 and 1992, use the gross profit method to estimate the amount of the flood loss on March 15, 1993.

RETAIL METHOD
— OBJ. 6 —

9-33A Sales clerks for Morningstar Company, a retail concern, took a year-end physical inventory at retail prices and determined that the total retail value of the ending inventory was $420,000. The following information for the year is available:

	Cost	Selling Price
Beginning inventory	$317,200	$ 450,000
Net purchases	910,400	1,410,000
Sales		1,416,000

Management estimates its inventory loss from theft and other causes by comparing its physical ending inventory at retail prices with an estimated ending inventory at retail prices (determined by subtracting sales from goods available for sale at selling prices) and reducing this difference to cost by applying the proper cost ratio.

REQUIRED

a. Compute the estimated cost of the ending inventory using the cost-to-retail percentage from the retail method. This inventory amount will appear in the balance sheet, and the calculation should be based on the physical inventory taken at retail prices.

b. Compute the estimated inventory loss for the year from theft and other causes.

EXPORT ACCOUNTING — OBJ. 7 —

9-34A On December 20, 1993, Bluemound, Inc., a U.S. firm using the periodic inventory system, sold merchandise on account to Mitsison Company, a Japanese company. The sales price was 8,000,000 yen. Bluemound received the amount due (in yen) on January 18, 1994. Bluemound ends its accounting year on December 31. Exchange rates for the Japanese yen were the following:

December 20, 1993	$0.00724 per yen
December 31, 1993	0.00759
January 18, 1994	0.00792

REQUIRED

a. Prepare the journal entries to account for the Mitsison Company transaction on Bluemound's records for December 20, 1993, December 31, 1993, and January 18, 1994.

b. Assume Bluemound's accounting year ends October 31 rather than December 31. Prepare the necessary journal entries on Bluemound's records in 1993 and 1994 to account for the foreign currency transaction with Mitsison Company.

c. Assume Bluemound's accounting year ends December 31 and the exchange rates for the Japanese yen were as follows:

December 20, 1993	$0.00788 per yen
December 31, 1993	0.00756
January 18, 1994	0.00713

Prepare the journal entries to account for the Mitsison Company transaction on Bluemound's records for December 20, 1993, December 31, 1993, and January 18, 1994.

CASES

Business Decision Case

Salem Company's entire inventory and many of its accounting records were destroyed by fire early in the morning of April 1, 1993. Salem filed an inventory loss claim of $132,000 with Rock Insurance Company. As Rock's representative, you must evaluate the reasonableness of Salem's claim. You and Salem's accountant have gathered the following information from various sources:

1. The January 1, 1993, inventory figure of $75,000 was found on a copy of a personal property tax declaration filed with the local municipality.

2. From a statistical summary filed with a trade association, the sales and cost of goods sold for the preceding three years were as follows:

	1990	1991	1992
Net sales	$780,000	$840,000	$960,000
Cost of goods sold	432,900	457,800	528,000

3. Salem buys an estimated 80% of its merchandise from three wholesale suppliers. According to these three suppliers, Salem's purchases for the first three months of 1993 were as follows:

Supplier	Purchases
Fall Corporation	$56,000
London Company	87,000
Voss, Inc.	37,000

4. Salem's sales average 5% cash and the balance on credit. Adding machine tapes totaling the accounts receivable subsidiary ledger were found and showed $43,000 and $50,000, respectively, for December 31, 1992, and March 31, 1993. An analysis of bank deposit slips indicates that collections from credit customers deposited in the bank in 1993 were $110,000 for January, $106,000 for February, and $119,000 for March.

REQUIRED

Based on the preceding data, use the gross profit method to estimate Salem Company's ending inventory destroyed by fire. Is Salem's loss claim reasonable? Why or why not?

Analytical Application Case

W. W. GRAINGER, INC., headquartered in Skokie, Illinois, is a nationwide distributor of equipment, components, and supplies. FOOD LION, INC., headquartered in Salisbury, North Carolina, operates general food supermarkets. Recent financial data for these two companies are shown below (Year 2 is the more recent year; amounts in thousands):

	Year 2		Year 1	
	Grainger	Food Lion	Grainger	Food Lion
Cost of Goods Sold	$1,259,039	$4,447,177	$1,125,510	$3,772,473
Beginning Inventory	412,365	577,853	329,947	523,081
Ending Inventory	416,651	673,606	412,365	577,853

REQUIRED

a. Compute the inventory turnover and days' sales in inventory for W. W. Grainger, Inc., and Food Lion, Inc., for Years 1 and 2.
b. In evaluating the Year 2 inventory turnover and days' sales in inventory for W. W. Grainger, Inc., is it appropriate to compare these ratios to (1) the Year 1 ratios for Grainger and (2) the Year 2 ratios for Food Lion?
c. Grainger uses the LIFO method of inventory pricing. If FIFO had been used, its inventories (in thousands) would have been as follows: Year 2 ending inventory, $560,716; Year 2 beginning inventory and Year 1 ending inventory, $548,280; and Year 1 beginning inventory, $442,766. Compute Grainger's inventory turnover for Years 1 and 2 under FIFO pricing and comment on the effect that LIFO pricing has on the ratio (compared with FIFO pricing). (*Note:* The change to FIFO will affect both cost of goods sold and average inventory.)

Ethics Case

Reed Kohler is in his last year, before retiring, as controller for Quality Sales Corporation. As a member of top management, Kohler participates in an attractive company bonus plan. The overall size of the bonus is a function of the firm's income before bonus and income taxes (the larger the income, the larger the bonus).

Due to a slowdown in the economy, Quality Sales Corporation has encountered difficulties in managing its cash flows. To improve cash flows (by reducing cash payments for income taxes), the firm's auditors have recommended that the firm change its inventory pricing method from FIFO to LIFO. This change would cause a significant increase in the cost of goods sold for the year. Kohler believes the firm should not switch to LIFO this year because its inventory quantities are too large. He believes the firm should work to reduce its inventory quantities and then switch to LIFO (the switch could be made in a year or two). After expressing this opinion to the firm's treasurer, Kohler is stunned when the treasurer replies: "Reed, I can't believe that after all these years with the firm, you put your personal interests ahead of the firm's interests."

REQUIRED

Explain why Kohler may be viewed as holding a position that favors his personal interests. What can Kohler do to increase his credibility when the possible change to LIFO is discussed at a meeting of the firm's top management next week?

What options
does a firm
have in how
it depreciates
its plant
assets?

All firms have
plant assets,
such as build-
ings, vehicles,
and equipment.
■ Plant assets
may be a large
part of a firm's
total assets—
63% in 1991 for
Vulcan Materials Co., a leading pro-
ducer of construction aggregates and
chemicals, as well as owner of quar-
ries, mining equipment, trucks, and
barges. ■ Plant assets may be depreciated using straight-line, units of
production, sum of the years' digits,
and double-declining balance methods
—all four covered in this chapter.

10 PLANT ASSETS: MEASUREMENT AND DEPRECIATION

CHAPTER OBJECTIVES

1 **PROVIDE** the background to understand the various problems related to the measurement of plant assets (pp. 362–363).

2 **IDENTIFY** the guidelines relating to the initial measurement of plant assets (pp. 363–366).

3 **DISCUSS** the nature of the depreciation process (pp. 366–367).

4 **ILLUSTRATE** four generally accepted methods of computing periodic depreciation (pp. 367–373).

5 **DISCUSS** the distinction between revenue and capital expenditures (pp. 373–376).

6 **ANALYTICAL APPLICATION:** **DEFINE** *return on assets* and **EXPLAIN** its use (p. 376).

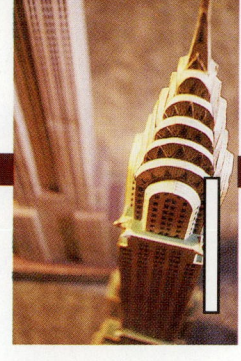

*Little of all we value here
Wakes on the morn of its
hundredth year.*

OLIVER WENDELL HOLMES

n this chapter and the following chapter, we discuss the accounting problems related to the acquisition, use, and disposal of assets whose benefits to a firm extend over many accounting periods. These long-term assets fall in three major balance sheet categories: *plant assets*, *natural resources*, and *intangible assets*. **Plant assets**, or **fixed assets**, refer to a firm's *property*, *plant*, and *equipment*.

The carrying values of these long-term assets are normally based on historical costs. The costs related to the use of these long-term assets must be properly calculated and matched with the revenues they help generate, so that periodic net income is determined correctly. Each period's expired portion of the asset's cost is called *depreciation*, *depletion*, or *amortization*, depending on the type of asset involved. All of these terms have the same meaning in accounting—that is, periodic charging to expense.

Exhibit 10-1 gives several specific examples within each asset category. The exhibit also associates the term for the periodic write-off to expense with the proper asset category. Note that site land—that is, a place on which to operate—usually has an indefinite useful life and therefore does not require any periodic write-off to expense. (Depletion and amortization are discussed more fully in the next chapter.)

OVERVIEW OF PLANT ASSET PROBLEMS

OBJECTIVE ❶ PROVIDE *the background to understand the various problems related to the measurement of plant assets.*

We consider the problems associated with plant assets in the order shown in Exhibit 10-2. This exhibit is a graphic presentation of the typical accounting problems created by plant assets in relation to an asset's life cycle.

Measurement problems associated with plant assets include identifying the types and amounts of expenditures that make up the original recorded cost of the particular asset. During the use period of a limited-life asset, it is important to charge the appropriate amounts against yearly revenue to reflect the asset's consumption. This involves estimating the asset's useful life and its probable salvage value at disposal. Also during the use period, expenditures for simple maintenance (expense) must be properly differentiated from expenditures that increase the capacity or extend the life of the asset (added to asset costs). On disposal, the adjusted accounting cost of the asset must be compared with the net proceeds from disposal in order to determine any related gain or loss. We consider this last problem in the next chapter.

| | EXHIBIT 10—1 | LONG-TERM ASSETS REQUIRING PERIODIC WRITE-OFF |

Asset Category	Examples	Term for Periodic Write-off to Expense
Plant Assets	Buildings, equipment, tools, furniture, fixtures, and vehicles	Depreciation
	Exception: Land for site use is considered to have an indefinite life and is not depreciated.	
Natural Resources	Oil, timber, coal, and other mineral deposits	Depletion
Intangible Assets	Patents, copyrights, leaseholds, franchises, trademarks, and goodwill	Amortization

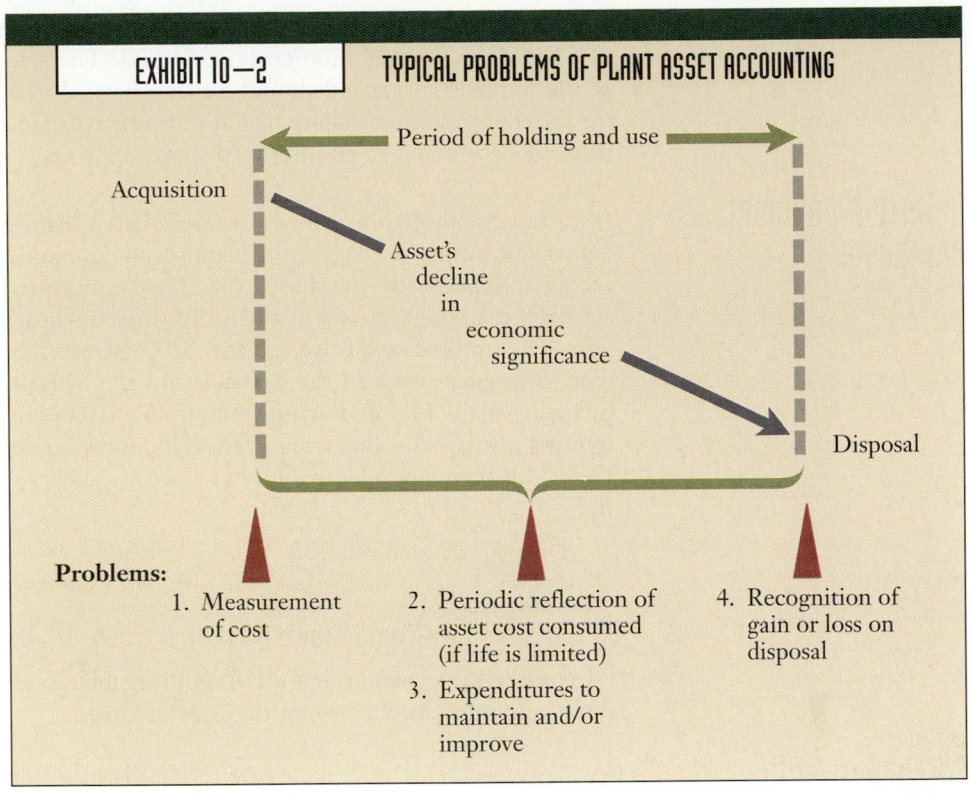

EXHIBIT 10—2   TYPICAL PROBLEMS OF PLANT ASSET ACCOUNTING

Period of holding and use

Acquisition

Asset's
decline
in
economic
significance

Disposal

Problems:
1. Measurement
   of cost

2. Periodic reflection of
   asset cost consumed
   (if life is limited)

3. Expenditures to
   maintain and/or
   improve

4. Recognition of
   gain or loss on
   disposal

ORIGINAL MEASUREMENT OF PLANT ASSETS

OBJECTIVE **2** IDENTIFY *the guidelines relating to the initial measurement of plant assets.*

Plant assets are originally recorded at their cost. These measures are also called *historical costs*, because they provide the basis for accounting for the assets in subsequent periods. Usually we do not attempt to reflect subsequent changes in market values for plant assets. In general, the initial cost of a plant asset is equal to the cash and/or the cash equivalent of that which is given up in order to acquire the asset *and* to prepare it for use. In other words, initial cost includes the asset's (1) implied cash price and (2) cost of preparation for use.

The expenditures to acquire and prepare the asset for use must be reasonable and necessary to be considered part of the asset's cost. Accountants do not capitalize (charge to an asset account) wasteful or inefficient expenditures. Costs of waste and inefficiency are expensed when incurred. For example, suppose equipment is damaged while it is being installed or a firm's receiving dock is damaged while equipment is being unloaded. Expenditures made to repair these damages are not part of the cost of the equipment; they are instead charged to expense.

Cash Purchases

Often an asset's historical cost is simply the amount of cash paid when the asset is acquired and readied for use. Consider, for example, the following expenditures for a certain piece of equipment:

Purchase price factors:		
Gross invoice price	$10,000	
Less: Cash discount (1/10, n/30)	(100)	
Sales tax	500	$10,400
Related expenditures:		
Freight charges	$ 200	
Installation costs	500	
Testing of installed machine	300	1,000
Cost of equipment		$11,400

The total initial equipment cost is $11,400, consisting of a cash purchase price of $10,400 and preparation costs of $1,000. The sales tax is a necessary component of the purchase price and should not be charged to a tax expense account. Similarly, the costs of freight, installation, and testing are expenditures necessary to get the asset to the location and in condition for use.

Deferred Payment Purchases

If an asset's purchase price is not immediately paid in cash, we determine the cash equivalent purchase price at the acquisition date and record that amount in the asset account. Suppose we purchased the above equipment on a financing plan requiring a $1,500 cash down payment and a non-interest-bearing note for $10,000 due in one year. The implied cash price remains $10,400, even though the financing plan is used. The difference between the $10,400 and the $11,500 total disbursement under the financing plan ($1,500 down payment plus $10,000 payment on note) represents the interest cost of the financing plan. The entry to record the purchase of the asset under the financing plan would be:

Equipment	10,400	
Discount on Notes Payable	1,100	
Cash		1,500
Notes Payable		10,000
To record purchase of equipment.		

Of course, the expenditures for freight, installation, and testing are still debited to the Equipment account when they are incurred.

Purchases with Noncash Assets

Sometimes a plant asset may be purchased with a noncash asset, and therefore the implied cash price is not readily apparent. For example, a firm may acquire equipment in exchange for shares of stock that have been held as an investment. Generally accepted accounting principles normally provide that the implied cash price should be the fair value of either the asset given up or the asset received, whichever is more objectively determinable. General-purpose property and equipment (standard office or factory equipment) and widely traded securities usually have more objectively determinable fair values than do highly specialized property or equipment and securities that are seldom traded. In the latter instances, the accountant must exercise professional judgment in determining the appropriate fair value.

A modification to this guideline may occur when a plant asset is exchanged for a similar plant asset used in the same line of business. We consider this modification in the next chapter in our discussion of exchanges of similar plant assets.

Package Purchases

Sometimes several types of assets are purchased concurrently as a package. For example, assume that a company purchased a small freight terminal including land, a building, and some loading equipment for a total price of $190,000. For accounting purposes, the total purchase price should be divided among the three asset forms because (1) they are reported in different accounts, (2) only the building and equipment are subject to depreciation, and (3) the equipment will have an estimated useful life different from that of the building.

The price of package purchases is commonly allocated on the basis of relative market or appraisal values. We assume estimated market values to illustrate this approach.

Asset	Estimated Market Value	Percent of Total	Allocation of Purchase Price	Estimated Useful Life
Land	$ 60,000	30	$ 57,000	Indefinite
Building	120,000	60	114,000	30 years
Equipment	20,000	10	19,000	8 years
Totals	$200,000	100	$190,000	

Actually, the firm may obtain realistic market values from a professional appraiser or from assessed values on related property tax bills.

Capitalization of Interest

Interest cost is part of an asset's initial cost if a period of time is required to get the asset ready for use. The process that adds interest cost to an asset's initial cost is called the **capitalization of interest.** For example, the construction of a factory building takes time to complete. Accordingly, an appropriate portion of the actual interest cost incurred during the construction period is added to the factory building's cost. We compute the amount of interest capitalized by multiplying the periodic interest rate times the period's average accumulated construction expenditures. The average accumulated construction expenditures for a period are usually determined by summing the accumulated expenditures at the beginning of the period and the end of the period, and dividing the sum by 2.

To illustrate, let us assume Miller Company borrowed $500,000 at 12% to finance the construction of a factory building. Interest of $5,000 is paid monthly. During the first month, construction expenditures total $300,000. The interest cost capitalized this first month is $1,500, computed as follows:

Average accumulated construction expenditures:		
Accumulated construction expenditures, beginning of month	$ –0–	
Accumulated construction expenditures, end of month	300,000	
Average accumulated construction expenditures for the month	$300,000 ÷ 2 =	$150,000
Monthly interest rate (1%)		0.01
Interest capitalized for the month		$ 1,500

The entry to record the first month's interest payment is

Factory Building	1,500	
Interest Expense	3,500	
Cash		5,000

To record interest payment, of which $1,500 is capitalized to factory building.

Interest is capitalized until the factory building is completed. Of course, in subsequent months, the average accumulated construction expenditures increase, so larger amounts of interest cost are capitalized. If the average accumulated construction expenditures exceed $500,000, then additional computations based on the company's other borrowings are needed to determine the interest cost associated with the expenditures over $500,000. These computations are covered in intermediate accounting texts.

Related Expenditures

A purchase of land often raises some interesting questions about related expenditures. Suppose a firm retains a local real estate broker at a fee of $2,000 to locate an appropriate site for its new office building. The property eventually chosen has an old residence on it, which will be razed. The terms of the sale include a payment of $40,000 to the seller, with the buyer paying off an existing mortgage of $10,000 and $300 of accrued interest. In addition, the buyer agrees to pay accrued real estate taxes of $800. Other related expenditures include legal fees of $400 and a title insurance premium of $500. A local salvage company will raze the old residence, level the lot, keep all the materials, and pay the firm $200. If we apply the general plant asset measurement rule, we compute the initial cost of the land as follows:

Payment to the seller	$40,000
Commission for finding property	2,000
Payment of mortgage and interest due at time of sale	10,300
Payment of property taxes owed by seller	800
Legal fees	400
Title insurance premium	500
	$54,000
Less: Net recovery from razing	(200)
Cost of land	$53,800

Again, expenditures for the taxes, insurance, legal fees, and interest should be capitalized as part of the land, because they were necessary for its acquisition and preparation for use. Removing the old residence prepares the land for its intended use. The $200 net recovery from razing, therefore, *reduces* the land's cost. A net payment to remove the old building would have *increased* the land's cost.

When a land site is acquired in an undeveloped area, the firm may pay special assessments to the local government for such property improvements as streets, sidewalks, and sewers. These improvements are normally maintained by the local government and, accordingly, are considered relatively permanent improvements by the firm. In these circumstances, the company capitalizes the special assessments as part of the cost of the land.

The firm may make property improvements that have limited lives. Paved parking lots, driveways, private sidewalks, and fences are examples. These expenditures are charged to a separate account, **Land Improvements,** which is depreciated over the estimated lives of the improvements.

THE NATURE OF DEPRECIATION

OBJECTIVE ❸ DISCUSS *the nature of the depreciation process.*

With the exception of site land, the use of plant assets to generate revenue consumes their economic potential. At some point of reduced potential—usually before they are totally worthless—these assets are disposed of and possibly replaced. We can diagram the typical pattern of plant asset utilization (indicated in Exhibit 10-2) as follows:

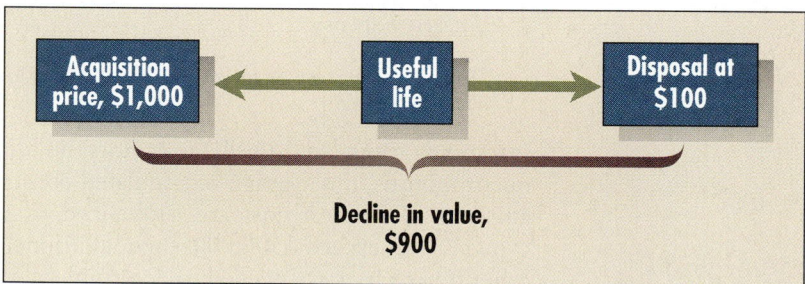

The asset is acquired for $1,000, used for several accounting periods, and then sold for $100. The $900 decline in value is called **depreciation** and, in every sense of the word, is an expense of generating the revenues recognized during the periods that the asset was used. Therefore, if the income figure is to be meaningful, $900 of expense must be allocated to these periods and matched with the revenues. Failure to do so would overstate income for these periods.

Note that in this process we estimate an asset's useful life and salvage value as well as properly determine its acquisition cost. **Useful life** is the expected period of economic usefulness to the current entity—the period from date of acquisition to expected date of disposal. **Salvage value** (or *residual value*) is the expected net recovery (sales proceeds − disposal costs) when the asset is sold or removed from service. When the salvage value is insignificant, it may be ignored in the depreciation process.

Allocation versus Valuation

Although the idea is theoretically appealing, accountants do not specifically base depreciation on the changes in market value or on the measured wear of assets—primarily because a reliable, objective, and practical source for such data rarely exists. Rather, **depreciation accounting** attempts to allocate in a rational and systematic manner the difference between acquisition cost and estimated salvage value over the *estimated* useful life of the asset. Depreciation accounting techniques are convenient expedients for measuring asset expirations and are therefore not precise. Though imprecise, depreciation estimates clearly provide better income determination than would result from completely expensing the asset at either the date of acquisition or the date of disposal.

Several factors are naturally related to the periodic allocation of depreciation. Depreciation can be caused by wear from use, from natural deterioration through interaction of the elements, and from technical obsolescence. Each factor reduces the value of the asset. To some extent maintenance (lubrication, adjustments, parts replacements, and cleaning) may partially arrest or offset wear and deterioration. Quite logically, then, when useful life and salvage values are estimated, a given level of maintenance is assumed. Therefore, the cost of using plant assets tends to be the sum of periodic maintenance expenditures plus some measure of the depreciation that occurs despite the maintenance performed. Maintenance expense normally increases toward the latter stages of most assets' lives.

How to allocate depreciation expense to individual accounting periods is just one facet of the overall problem of matching expenses with revenues. The most defensible reason for choosing one allocation pattern over another is that one pattern may better portray the pattern of services received each period from using the asset. It would be only coincidence if the book value of a particular asset were exactly equal to its market value at any time during its useful life. On the other hand, the general pattern of an asset's book value may be related to its decline in market value. Indeed, the goal is that at the end of an asset's useful life, its book value and market value (that is, salvage value) should be the same.

COMPUTATIONS OF PERIODIC DEPRECIATION

We now illustrate four widely used methods of computing periodic depreciation. For each illustration, we assume that the asset costs $1,000 and has an estimated useful life of five years. The estimated salvage value at the end of the five-year period is $100. Our computations illustrate different ways to *allocate* the amount depreciated among each of the five accounting periods in the asset's life.

Straight Line

OBJECTIVE 4 ILLUSTRATE *four generally accepted methods of computing periodic depreciation.*

The **straight-line method** is probably the simplest depreciation method to use. An equal amount of depreciation expense is allocated to each full period of the asset's useful life. Using straight-line depreciation,

$$\text{Annual Depreciation} = \frac{\text{Original Cost} - \text{Salvage Value}}{\text{Periods of Useful Life}}$$

which in our example is

$$\frac{\$1,000 - \$100}{5 \text{ years}} = \$180 \text{ per year}$$

The basic entry to record each period's depreciation expense is

Depreciation Expense—Equipment	180	
Accumulated Depreciation—Equipment		180
To record depreciation expense for the year.		

Like other expense accounts, Depreciation Expense is deducted from revenue in determining net income and is closed at year-end to the Income Summary account. The offsetting credit is posted to the contra account, Accumulated Depreciation, which is deducted from the related asset account on the balance sheet to compute the asset's book value, or carrying value. In this manner, the original cost of an asset is maintained in the asset account, and the cumulative balance of depreciation taken is carried in the contra account as long as the asset is in service. When an asset is disposed of, the related cost and accumulated depreciation are removed from the accounts.

For our simple illustration, the following table shows account balances and the progression of certain amounts during the asset's five-year life.

Year of Useful Life	Balance of Asset Account	Annual Depreciation Expense	End-of-Period Balance Accumulated Depreciation Account	End-of-Period Balance Asset's Book Value
1	$1,000	$180	$180	$820
2	1,000	180	360	640
3	1,000	180	540	460
4	1,000	180	720	280
5	1,000	180	900	100
		Total $900		

Observe that (1) the asset account always shows the original cost of the asset, (2) each period reflects $180 of depreciation expense, (3) the Accumulated Depreciation account balance is cumulative and shows the portion of the original cost taken as depreciation to date, (4) the asset's book value is the original cost less total accumulated depreciation to date, and (5) the asset's book value at the end of five years equals the estimated salvage value. Thus, the book value decreases to the estimated salvage value as the asset is depreciated during its useful life.

The book value of the asset is shown on the balance sheet by deducting the Accumulated Depreciation account (normally a credit balance) from the asset account (normally a debit balance). At the end of the second year, for example, the asset's balance sheet presentation is as follows:

Equipment (Original cost)	$1,000
Less: Accumulated Depreciation	360
Equipment (Book value)	$ 640

For periods of less than one year, straight-line depreciation amounts are simply proportions of the annual amount. For example, if the asset had been acquired on April 1, depreciation for the period ended December 31 would be $\frac{9}{12} \times \$180 = \$135$. Assets acquired or disposed of during the first half of any month are usually treated as if the acquisition or disposal occurred on the first of the month. When either event occurs during the last half of any month, we assume it occurred on the first of the following month.

Straight-line allocation is best suited to an asset with a relatively uniform periodic usage and a low obsolescence factor. Examples include pipelines, storage tanks, fencing, and surface paving. These types of assets can provide approximately equal utility during all periods of their useful lives.

Units of Production

The **units-of-production method** allocates depreciation in proportion to the asset's use in operations. First, the depreciation per unit of production is computed by dividing the total expected depreciation (in our example, $900) by the asset's projected units-of-production capacity. Therefore,

$$\text{Depreciation per Unit} = \frac{\text{Original Cost} - \text{Salvage Value}}{\text{Estimated Total Units of Production}}$$

Units-of-production capacity may represent miles driven, tons hauled, hours used, or number of cuttings, drillings, or stampings of parts. Assume that our example is a drilling tool that will drill an estimated 45,000 parts during its useful life. The depreciation per unit of production is

$$\frac{\$1,000 - \$100}{45,000 \text{ parts}} = \$0.02 \text{ per part}$$

To find periodic depreciation expense, we multiply the depreciation per unit of production by the number of units produced during the period. Therefore,

Annual Depreciation = Depreciation per Unit × Units of Production for the Year

Assuming the parts drilled over the five years were 8,000, 14,000, 10,000, 4,000, and 9,000, respectively, we calculate each year's depreciation expense as follows:

Year of Useful Life	Depreciation per Unit		Annual Units of Production		Annual Depreciation Expense
1	$0.02	×	8,000	=	$160
2	0.02	×	14,000	=	280
3	0.02	×	10,000	=	200
4	0.02	×	4,000	=	80
5	0.02	×	9,000	=	180
					Total $900

The units-of-production method is particularly appropriate when wear is the major cause of depreciation and the amount of use varies from period to period. Of course, if use is uniformly spread over the asset's life, the same allocation of depreciation would result from either the straight-line or units-of-production method. The units-of-production method may necessitate some extra record keeping to express the periodic use in terms of production capacity. However, this data may already be tabulated as part of a periodic production report.

Sum of the Years' Digits

The **sum-of-the-years'-digits (SYD) method** accelerates depreciation expense so that the amounts recognized in the early periods of an asset's useful life are greater than those recognized in the later periods. This type of depreciation pattern (larger amounts in early periods) identifies an **accelerated depreciation method.** The SYD is found by estimating an asset's useful life in years, assigning consecutive numbers to each year, and totaling these numbers. For n years,

$$SYD = 1 + 2 + 3 + \ldots + n$$

In our example, the SYD for a five-year asset life is $1 + 2 + 3 + 4 + 5 = 15$.

Determining the SYD factor by simple addition can be somewhat laborious for long-lived assets. For these assets, the formula $n(n + 1)/2$, where n = the number of periods in the asset's useful life, can be applied to derive the SYD. In our example,

$$\frac{5(5 + 1)}{2} = \frac{30}{2} = 15$$

The yearly depreciation is then calculated by multiplying the total depreciable amount for the asset's useful life by a fraction whose numerator is the remaining useful life and whose denominator is the SYD. Thus, the formula for yearly depreciation is

$$\text{Annual Depreciation} = (\text{Original Cost} - \text{Salvage Value}) \times \frac{\text{Remaining Useful Life}}{\text{SYD}}$$

The calculations for our example are shown below:

Year of Useful Life	Fraction of Total Depreciation Taken Each Year		Original Cost Less Salvage Value		Annual Depreciation Expense
1	$\frac{5}{15}$	×	$900	=	$300
2	$\frac{4}{15}$	×	900	=	240
3	$\frac{3}{15}$	×	900	=	180
4	$\frac{2}{15}$	×	900	=	120
5	$\frac{1}{15}$	×	900	=	60
SYD 15					Total $900

When the acquisition of an asset does not coincide with the beginning of the fiscal period, the annual depreciation amounts are allocated proportionately to the appropriate fiscal periods. For example, assume we purchased the asset on April 1.

NOT BAD FOR A TEN-YEAR-OLD

Carl Friedrich Gauss ranks among the greatest mathematicians of all time. Certainly, his contributions place him in the company of such mathematical giants as Archimedes and Sir Isaac Newton. Born in Brunswick, Germany, in 1777, Gauss was an infant prodigy. During his 78-year life, he made major contributions to number theory, non-Euclidean geometry, astronomy, and physics. His work in the field of magnetism led to a unit of measure being given his name—the gauss *is the metric unit for measuring electromagnetic induction.*

An episode that occurred when Gauss was ten years old relates to our study of depreciation accounting. One day during arithmetic class, the teacher assigned the students the task of finding the sum of all the numbers 1 through 100. The students did their assignments on slate tablets. As they finished an assignment, they would each place their tablet on a large table. The teacher had barely finished giving this assignment when Gauss placed his tablet on the table, exclaiming "Ligget se!" (There it is). While the other students were still busy writing and computing, the teacher finally took a look at Gauss's slate. There was only one number written on it—5,050, the correct answer!

Gauss got his answer so quickly because he noted a particular numerical relationship: if he paired the first number and the last number (1, 100), the second number and the next to last number (2, 99), the third number and the third from the last number (3, 98), and so on, the sum of each pair was the same, 101. Out of the 100 numbers, there were 50 such pairs. Thus, the sum of all the numbers is 50×101, or 5,050.*

This brilliantly simple solution to the problem of adding up a set of whole numbers explains the formula used in summing up an asset's years in sum-of-the-years'-digits depreciation. If we let n equal the number of years of useful life, then the number of "Gaussian" pairs is $n/2$ and the sum of each pair is $n + 1$. The sum of the numbers, therefore, is $(n/2)(n + 1)$, or, alternatively, $n(n + 1)/2$.

*This episode and other details of Gauss's life may be found in G. Waldo Dunnington, *Carl Friedrich Gauss: Titan of Science* (New York: Exposition Press, 1955).

Depreciation for the period ended December 31 would be $\frac{9}{12} \times \$300 = \$225$. For the next fiscal year, a full year's depreciation would be calculated as $(\frac{3}{12} \times \$300) + (\frac{9}{12} \times \$240) = \$255$.

As an accelerated depreciation method, the SYD approach is most appropriate when the asset renders greater utility during its early life and less in its later life. Accelerated depreciation is suitable for assets with either a high technological obsolescence factor in the early life phase or a high maintenance factor in the late life phase.

Double Declining Balance

Another accelerated depreciation method is the **double declining-balance method,** which derives its name from the fact that a *constant percentage* factor of twice the straight-line rate is applied each year to the *declining balance* of the asset's book value.

The *straight-line rate* is simply the number of years in the asset's useful life divided into 100%. In our example, this would be 100%/5 = 20%. Double the straight-line rate is then 40%. In equation form,

$$\text{Double Declining-balance Rate} = \frac{100\%}{\text{Years of Useful Life}} \times 2$$

To determine the annual double declining-balance depreciation expense, we simply multiply the asset's book value at the beginning of the period by the constant rate (or percentage). Using double declining-balance depreciation, then,

Annual Depreciation = Book Value at Beginning of Year $\times$ Double Declining-balance Rate

Remember that an asset's book value at any time is its original cost less its accumulated depreciation to date. The book value of a depreciable asset *declines* as it is depreciated. The important thing to remember is that the percentage depreciation rate remains constant; the book value—to which the percentage is applied—declines. Salvage value is not considered in the calculations, except that depreciation stops when the asset's book value equals its estimated salvage value.

Applying the general rule for double declining-balance depreciation to our example, we obtain the accelerated depreciation pattern shown in the following table (amounts to nearest dollar).

Year of Useful Life	Original Cost	Beginning Accumulated Depreciation	Beginning Book Value		Twice Straight-line Percentage		Annual Depreciation Expense
1	$1,000	$ 0	$1,000	×	40%	=	$400
2	1,000	400	600	×	40%	=	240
3	1,000	640	360	×	40%	=	144
4	1,000	784	216	×	40%	=	86
5	1,000	870	130				30
						Total	$900

Observe that in the fifth year depreciation expense is only $30, the amount needed to reduce the asset's book value to the estimated salvage value of $100. Assets are not depreciated below their salvage values. If no salvage value has been estimated, the double declining-balance technique automatically provides one. When a fraction (40%, or $\frac{4}{10}$, for example) is applied to an asset's book value, the entire original cost can never be depreciated; some balance, though small, will always remain.

If an asset is purchased during the fiscal period, a pro rata allocation of the first year's depreciation is necessary. If we acquired our asset on April 1, depreciation for the period ended December 31 would be $\frac{9}{12} \times (40\% \times \$1,000) = \$300$. In subsequent periods, the usual procedure is followed; that is, the asset's book value at the beginning of the period is multiplied by the constant rate. The next year, for example, depreciation would be $40\% \times (\$1,000 - \$300) = \$280$.

Because double declining-balance depreciation is also an accelerated depreciation method, it is appropriate in the same situations as the SYD method.

Comparison of Depreciation Methods

The following chart compares the periodic depreciation expense from our example for the straight-line method, the sum-of-the-years'-digits method, and the double declining-balance method. The chart visually displays the accelerated nature of the latter two methods. The units-of-production method is not shown in the chart because there is no general pattern for the annual depreciation. The annual depreciation using the units-of-production method depends on the yearly productive activity of the asset, and this activity will vary from asset to asset.

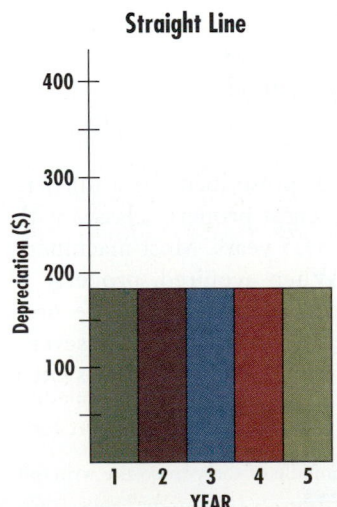

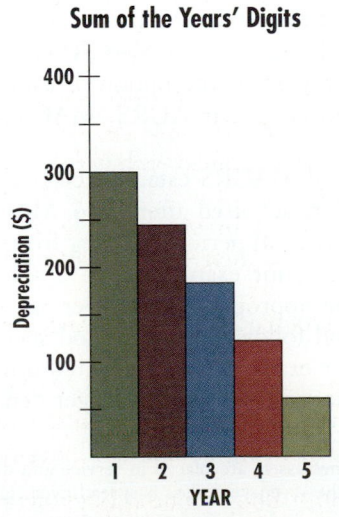

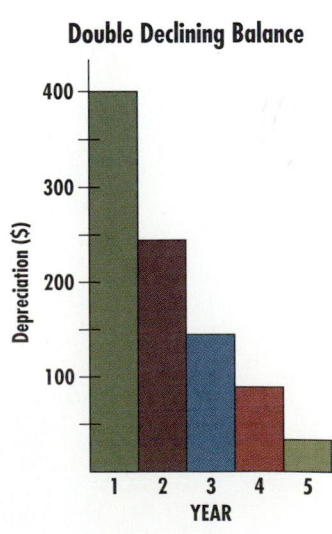

REVISION OF DEPRECIATION

We have stressed that depreciation allocations are based on estimates of both useful lives and salvage values. Circumstances change, however, and original estimates may be too high or too low. Once it is determined that original estimates are wrong, the computation of periodic depreciation expense for the asset's remaining useful life must be revised. We revise a depreciation estimate by allocating the revised undepreciated balance of the asset over the revised remaining useful life. To illustrate this revision procedure, we use the data from our previous examples in which an asset costing $1,000 has a five-year life and an estimated salvage value of $100.

If, based on the original estimates, straight-line depreciation of $180 has been recorded for each of the first three years, the accumulated depreciation would be $3 \times \$180 = \$540$. Now suppose that just before recording the fourth year's depreciation, circumstances indicate that the asset's life will be six years instead of five and that its salvage value at the end of the sixth year will be $40. The revised depreciation expense to be taken during the revised remaining useful life is computed as follows:

Original asset cost	$1,000
Depreciation already recorded (3 years @ $180)	540
Book value at start of fourth year	$ 460
Revised salvage value	40
Revised remaining depreciation	$ 420
Revised remaining useful life	3 years
Revised periodic depreciation expense for fourth, fifth, and sixth years	$420/3 = $140 per year

The revision process does not change depreciation amounts recorded in earlier periods. The earlier computations utilized the best estimates available at the time. A change in an estimate, then, causes depreciation expense to be revised in the year of change and subsequent periods only.

DEPRECIATION FOR TAX PURPOSES

Depreciation expense is deducted by a business on its federal income tax return. The amount on the tax return, however, may differ substantially from the amount reported in the firm's income statement because the calculation of tax depreciation follows income tax regulations. The specific procedures for tax purposes depend on the year the asset was acquired. Assets acquired before 1981 are depreciated over their useful lives, and the acceptable methods include straight line, units of production, sum of the years' digits, and double declining balance. For property acquired from 1981 through 1986, tax depreciation is calculated under a special accelerated method called the **accelerated cost recovery system (ACRS)**. The ACRS procedures are modified (and referred to as **MACRS**) for assets acquired after 1986. Both ACRS and MACRS permit firms the option of using a straight-line method. However, salvage value is ignored under ACRS, MACRS, and the straight-line options to these procedures.

ACRS and MACRS establish classes of property with prescribed write-off periods. For assets acquired after 1986, MACRS establishes eight property classes with prescribed write-off periods ranging from three years to 31.5 years. Most machinery and equipment, for example, is in a seven-year class. When acquired, property is placed in the appropriate class (per tax guidelines) and depreciated over the prescribed period following the method specified for that class. Property in the seven-year class, for example, is depreciated using double declining balance (with a switch to straight line when it gives a larger deduction).[1]

---

[1] MACRS assumes assets are placed in service and disposed of in the middle of the year so the write-off of property in the seven-year class is spread over eight different tax years.

ACRS was introduced into the tax law to encourage companies to invest in plant assets. Because the write-off period under ACRS and MACRS is usually shorter than an asset's useful life, these methods provide larger depreciation deductions during an asset's early years than was previously possible. In a sense, these accelerated deductions provide an interest-free loan to the firm because they allow the firm to pay less tax in the early phase of an asset's life and more in the later phase. During the intervening time, the firm can use the amount of funds equal to the postponed income tax payments.

Change and modification characterize the history of U.S. tax law. Tax depreciation guidelines will likely be modified again in the future. Keep in mind, however, that depreciation changes in the tax law do not affect the depreciation methods a firm may use in preparing its financial statements. Tax depreciation guidelines apply only to the preparation of income tax returns.

REVENUE EXPENDITURES

OBJECTIVE 5 DISCUSS *the distinction between revenue and capital expenditures.*

Revenue expenditures are expenditures relating to plant assets that are expensed when incurred. The following list identifies three common types of revenue expenditures:

1. Expenditures for ordinary maintenance and repairs of existing plant assets.
2. Expenditures to acquire low-cost items that benefit the firm for several periods.
3. Expenditures considered unnecessary or unreasonable in the circumstances.

Maintenance and Repairs

Some level of maintenance and repairs must be assumed when estimating useful lives and salvage values of property, plant, and equipment. For example, a plant asset that is not maintained or repaired will have a shorter useful life than a similar asset that is properly maintained. Periodic upkeep—such as lubrication, cleaning, and replacement of minor parts—is necessary to maintain an asset's expected level and length of usefulness. These periodic upkeep costs are charged to expense as they are incurred.

Low-cost Items

Most businesses purchase items that provide years of service at a relatively small cost, such as paperweights, ashtrays, and wastebaskets. Because of the small dollar amounts involved, establishing these items as assets and depreciating them over their expected useful lives really serves no useful purpose. The effect on the financial statements is not significant. Consequently, expensing these expenditures at the time of purchase is more efficient. The accounting for such low-cost items is thus completed in the period they are purchased. This practice of accounting for small dollar transactions in the most expedient fashion is an example of a basic principle of accounting called *materiality*.

Unnecessary or Unreasonable Costs

As noted earlier, costs of waste and inefficiency related to the acquisition of plant assets are expensed when incurred. Because an asset's initial cost includes only necessary and reasonable expenditures, any unnecessary or unreasonable outlays are expensed. An accountant may need to exercise considerable judgment, however, in determining whether a particular expenditure is necessary and reasonable. Identical expenditures may be treated differently, depending on the circumstances. For example, assume a company pays an overtime premium to have a piece of equipment delivered on a holiday. If it is essential that the equipment be available for use on the next workday, then the overtime premium should be added to the equipment's cost as a necessary and reasonable expenditure. In contrast, if the equipment could just as well be delivered on the next workday, then the overtime premium is an unnecessary and wasteful expenditure that should be expensed.

CAPITAL EXPENDITURES

Capital expenditures increase the book value of long-term assets. To *capitalize* an amount, then, means to increase an asset's book value by that amount. Following are typical capital expenditures related to property, plant, and equipment:

1. Initial acquisitions and additions.
2. Betterments.
3. Extraordinary repairs.

Initial Acquisitions and Additions

Earlier in this chapter, we discussed the guidelines governing the initial measurement of plant assets. Expenditures equal to the asset's implied cash price plus the costs necessary to prepare the asset for use were debited to the asset account. These amounts were capital expenditures.

The same guidelines apply in accounting for additions to existing plant assets. Adding a new wing to a building or expanding the size of an asphalt parking lot are examples of additions. These capital expenditures should also be debited to an asset account. A separate account (and depreciation schedule) should be used for an addition when its estimated useful life differs from the remaining useful life of the existing plant asset.

Betterments

Betterments improve the quality of services rendered by a plant asset but do not necessarily extend its useful life. Examples include adding a power winch to a highway service truck or air conditioning to an automobile. In each instance, the vehicle's services are enhanced, but its useful life is not changed. Expenditures for betterments are debited to the appropriate asset account, and the subsequent periodic depreciation expense is increased to allocate the additional cost over the asset's remaining useful life.

To illustrate, let us assume Tray Service Station purchased a new service truck for $6,500 on January 2, 1993. Its estimated useful life is six years with a salvage value of $500. Using the straight-line method, $1,000 of depreciation expense is recorded in 1993 [($6,500 − $500)/6 = $1,000]. On January 2, 1994, a power winch costing $700 is added to the truck. The truck's useful life does not change, but its estimated salvage value increases to $600. The January 2, 1994, entry to record the new power winch is

Truck	700	
Cash		700

To record cost of power winch added to truck.

Annual depreciation expense of $1,120 for 1994–1998 is computed as follows:

Original truck cost	$6,500
Power winch cost	700
Total cost	$7,200
Depreciation recorded in 1993	1,000
Book value after 1994 betterment	$6,200
Revised salvage value	600
Revised remaining depreciation	$5,600
Remaining useful life	5 years
Revised periodic depreciation expense for 1994–1998	$5,600/5 = $1,120 per year

The December 31, 1994, entry to record depreciation expense is

Depreciation Expense—Truck	1,120	
Accumulated Depreciation—Truck		1,120

To record 1994 depreciation on truck.

Betterments may involve replacing a significant asset component with an improved component. Again, the cost of the new asset component should be added to the asset account and depreciated over the asset's remaining useful life. Further, the cost and accumulated depreciation of the replaced asset component should be removed from the accounts. For example, if a building's gas furnace is replaced by a more efficient model, the cost of the new furnace is added to the Building account, and the cost and applicable depreciation on the old furnace are removed from the accounts. The book value of the old asset component may be difficult to determine if it is not accounted for separately, but a reasonable estimate frequently can be made.

Extraordinary Repairs

Extraordinary repairs are expenditures that extend an asset's expected useful life beyond the original estimate. These capital expenditures are debited to the asset's Accumulated Depreciation account (which increases the asset's book value). We charge Accumulated Depreciation because some of the previous years' depreciation presumably is recovered by the expenditures that extend the asset's useful life. Depreciation entries after an extraordinary repair should lead to the salvage value at the end of the revised (extended) useful life.

For example, assume $12,800 worth of equipment is purchased; it has an estimated useful life of eight years and a salvage value of $800. Annual straight-line depreciation expense is $1,500 [($12,800 − $800)/8]. Six months into the seventh year, the equipment is extensively overhauled at a cost of $1,950. The overhaul extends the equipment's useful life an estimated two years beyond the original eight, with no change in the expected salvage value. The entry to record the overhaul is

Accumulated Depreciation—Equipment	1,950	
Cash		1,950
To record cost of equipment overhaul.		

Depreciation for the seventh year is $1,350, computed as follows:

Depreciation for first six months ($1,500/2)			$ 750
Depreciation for last six months:			
Equipment cost		$12,800	
Depreciation already taken ($6\frac{1}{2}$ years)	$9,750		
Less: Extraordinary repair	1,950	7,800	
Book value after extraordinary repair		$ 5,000	
Salvage value		800	
Remaining depreciation		$ 4,200	
Revised remaining useful life		42 months	
Depreciation for six months: ($4,200/42) × 6			600
Total depreciation expense for seventh year			$1,350

The entry to record depreciation expense at the end of the seventh year is

Depreciation Expense—Equipment	1,350	
Accumulated Depreciation—Equipment		1,350
To record depreciation on equipment.		

Depreciation expense for Years 8, 9, and 10 will be $1,200 each year [($4,200/42) × 12].

In practice, the distinctions among additions, betterments, and extraordinary repairs to plant assets often become blurred. Some expenditures, for example, may improve an asset's quality of services *and* extend its useful life. Accountants must use reasonable judgment to identify (and account for) the primary effect of the transaction.

Preparation of accurate financial statements depends on maintaining the proper distinction between capital expenditures and revenue expenditures. A misclassification of expenditures results in incorrect financial statements for several periods. For example, capitalizing a revenue expenditure overstates the current period's income and understates income in subsequent periods as the amount incorrectly capitalized is depreciated. Similarly, if a capital expenditure is immediately expensed, then the current period's income is understated and income is overstated during the subsequent periods when the incorrectly expensed amount should have been depreciated. Exercising care in analyzing expenditures, of course, will minimize these undesirable effects.

ANALYTICAL APPLICATION

RETURN ON ASSETS

OBJECTIVE 6 DEFINE return on assets *and* EXPLAIN *its use*.

The ability of a firm to use its assets effectively and efficiently in its operations is a sign of a healthy, well-managed company. The rate of return on assets, generally referred to as *return on assets*, is a widely used ratio that focuses on this dimension of a firm's financial profile. In practice, there is some variation in the computation of this ratio. One typical computation of **return on assets** is as follows:

$$\text{Return on Assets} = \frac{\text{Net Income}}{\text{Average Total Assets}}$$

This ratio relates data from two financial statements—the income statement and the balance sheet. The numerator consists of the net income for the year.[2] The denominator in the ratio is the average amount of assets used during the year (sum total assets at the beginning of the year and total assets at the end of the year and divide the sum by 2).

To illustrate the computation of return on assets, we use data from a recent year for THE COCA-COLA COMPANY. The company reported, in thousands, a net income of $1,381,904, total assets at the beginning of the year of $8,282,526, and year-end total assets of $9,278,187. Coca-Cola's return on assets for the year is 15.7%, computed as $1,381,904/[($8,282,526 + $9,278,187)/2].

To evaluate a firm's return on assets, we should consider the trend in the ratio, the return for other firms in the industry, the industry average, and the economic environment. For example, in the year that The Coca-Cola Company generated a 15.7% return on assets, competitor PEPSICO, INC., had a 6.7% return on assets. For that year, The Coca-Cola Company utilized its assets more profitably than did PepsiCo, Inc.

Following are examples of recent returns on assets for several companies in different industries.

NORFOLK SOUTHERN CORPORATION (freight transportation services)	5.4%
THE LESLIE FAY COMPANIES, INC. (women's apparel)	7.0%
HON INDUSTRIES (office furniture)	15.6%
THE STRIDE RITE CORPORATION (footwear)	21.5%

KEY POINTS FOR CHAPTER OBJECTIVES

1 PROVIDE the background to understand the various problems related to the measurement of plant assets (pp. 362–363).

■ The major types of long-term assets requiring periodic write-off are plant assets, natural resources, and intangible assets.

---

[2] An alternate computation adds interest expense to net income in the ratio's numerator. This variation keeps the method of financing the assets from influencing the ratio.

- The label given to the periodic write-off of plant assets, natural resources, and intangible assets varies by asset category, as follows:

  Plant assets: Depreciation

  Natural resources: Depletion

  Intangible assets: Amortization

2 IDENTIFY the guidelines relating to the initial measurement of plant assets (pp. 363–366).

- The initial cost of a plant asset is its implied cash price plus the expenditures necessary to prepare it for use.
- A portion of actual interest cost is included in a plant asset's initial cost if a period of time is required to get the asset ready for use.

3 DISCUSS the nature of the depreciation process (pp. 366–367).

- Depreciation is a cost allocation process; it allocates a plant asset's depreciable cost (acquisition cost less salvage value) in a rational and systematic manner over the asset's estimated useful life.

4 ILLUSTRATE four generally accepted methods of computing periodic depreciation (pp. 367–373).

- The most commonly used depreciation methods are straight line, units of production, sum of the years' digits, and double declining balance.
- Revisions of depreciation are accomplished by recalculating depreciation charges for current and subsequent periods.

5 DISCUSS the distinction between revenue and capital expenditures (pp. 373–376).

- Revenue expenditures, expensed as incurred, include the performance of ordinary repairs and maintenance, the purchase of low-cost items, and the incurrence of unnecessary or unreasonable outlays.
- Capital expenditures, which increase a plant asset's book value, include initial acquisitions, additions, betterments, and extraordinary repairs.

6 ANALYTICAL APPLICATION: DEFINE *return on assets* and EXPLAIN its use (p. 376).

- Return on assets is computed by dividing net income by average total assets.

SELF-TEST QUESTIONS FOR REVIEW

(Answers follow the Solution to Demonstration Problem.)

1. The initial cost of a plant asset is equal to the asset's implied cash price and
   a. The interest paid on any debt incurred to finance the asset's purchase.
   b. The market value of any noncash assets given up to acquire the plant asset.
   c. The reasonable and necessary costs incurred to prepare the asset for use.
   d. The asset's estimated salvage value.

2. Which of the following depreciation methods allocates equal amounts of depreciation to each full period of an asset's useful life?
   a. Units of production.
   b. Straight line.
   c. Double declining balance.
   d. Sum of the years' digits.

3. On January 1, 1993, Rio Company purchased a delivery truck for $10,000. The company estimates the truck will be driven 80,000 miles over its eight-year useful life. The estimated salvage value is $2,000. The truck was driven 12,000 miles in 1993. Which method results in the largest 1993 depreciation expense?
   a. Sum of the years' digits.
   b. Units of production.
   c. Straight line.
   d. Double declining balance.

4. Which of the following statements is false?
   a. A plant asset's useful life is the period from date of acquisition to date of disposal.
   b. When the estimate of a plant asset's useful life is changed, depreciation amounts recorded in earlier periods are revised to reflect the new useful life.
   c. Expenditures for extraordinary repairs are debited to an accumulated depreciation account.
   d. Capitalizing a revenue expenditure in the current period overstates the current period's net income.

5. Which of the following expenditures is expensed when incurred?
   a. The cost of regular monthly maintenance on a firm's copying machines.
   b. The cost of a new table and chairs for a firm's conference room.

    c. Interest paid that relates to the average monthly accumulated construction expenditures on a building under construction.

    d. The cost of razing an unwanted building on newly purchased land.

DEMONSTRATION PROBLEM FOR REVIEW

Segman Company purchased a machine in 1993 for $24,300. The machine has an expected useful life of three years and a salvage value of $900. The company expects to use the machine for 1,400 hours the first year, 2,000 hours the second year, and 1,600 hours the third year.

REQUIRED

a. Assume the machine was purchased on January 2, 1993. Compute each year's depreciation expense for 1993–1995 using each of the following depreciation methods: (1) straight line, (2) units of production (actual usage equals expected usage), (3) sum of the years' digits, and (4) double declining balance.

b. Assume the machine was purchased June 1, 1993. Compute each year's depreciation expense for 1993–1996 using each of the following depreciation methods: (1) straight line, (2) sum of the years' digits, and (3) double declining balance.

SOLUTION TO DEMONSTRATION PROBLEM

a. 1. Straight line:
    1993: ($24,300 − $900)/3 = $7,800
    1994: ($24,300 − $900)/3 = $7,800
    1995: ($24,300 − $900)/3 = $7,800

  2. Units of production:
    Depreciation per hour = ($24,300 − $900)/5,000 hours = $4.68 per hour
    1993: 1,400 hours × $4.68 = $6,552
    1994: 2,000 hours × $4.68 = $9,360
    1995: 1,600 hours × $4.68 = $7,488

  3. Sum of the years' digits:
    SYD = 3 + 2 + 1 = 6
    1993: ($24,300 − $900) × 3/6 = $11,700
    1994: ($24,300 − $900) × 2/6 = $7,800
    1995: ($24,300 − $900) × 1/6 = $3,900

  4. Double declining balance:
    Twice straight-line rate = (100%/3) × 2 = $66\frac{2}{3}$%
    1993: $24,300 × $66\frac{2}{3}$% = $16,200
    1994: ($24,300 − $16,200) × $66\frac{2}{3}$% = $5,400
    1995: ($24,300 − $21,600) × $66\frac{2}{3}$% = $1,800

b. 1. Straight line REFER TO CALCULATIONS IN (a)1.
    1993: $7,800 × $\frac{7}{12}$ = $4,550
    1994: $7,800 (full year's depreciation)
    1995: $7,800 (full year's depreciation)
    1996: $7,800 × $\frac{5}{12}$ = $3,250

  2. Sum of the years' digits REFER TO CALCULATIONS IN (a)3.
    1993: $11,700 × $\frac{7}{12}$ = $6,825
    1994: ($11,700 × $\frac{5}{12}$) + ($7,800 × $\frac{7}{12}$) = $9,425
    1995: ($7,800 × $\frac{5}{12}$) + ($3,900 × $\frac{7}{12}$) = $5,525
    1996: $3,900 × $\frac{5}{12}$ = $1,625

  3. Double declining balance REFER TO CALCULATIONS IN (a)4.
    1993: $16,200 × $\frac{7}{12}$ = $9,450
    1994: ($24,300 − $9,450) × $66\frac{2}{3}$% = $9,900
    1995: ($24,300 − $19,350) × $66\frac{2}{3}$% = $3,300
    1996: $750 [This amount reduces the machine's book value to its salvage value of $900 and is the maximum depreciation expense for 1996. ($24,300 − $22,650) × $66\frac{2}{3}$% = $1,100 gives an amount in excess of the maximum $750 depreciation.]

ANSWERS TO SELF-TEST QUESTIONS

1. c, p. 363   **2.** b, p. 367   **3.** d, p. 370   **4.** b, p. 372   **5.** a, p. 373

GLOSSARY OF KEY TERMS USED IN THIS CHAPTER

accelerated cost recovery system (ACRS, MACRS) A system of accelerated depreciation for tax purposes introduced in 1981 (ACRS) and modified starting in 1987 (MACRS); it prescribes depreciation rates by asset classification for assets acquired after 1980 (p. 372).

accelerated depreciation method Any depreciation method under which the amounts of depreciation expense taken in the early years of an asset's life are larger than the amounts expensed in the later years (p. 369).

betterments Capital expenditures that improve the quality of services rendered by a plant asset but do not necessarily extend its useful life (p. 374).

capital expenditures Expenditures that increase the book value of long-term assets (p. 374).

capitalization of interest A process that adds interest to an asset's initial cost if a period of time is required to prepare the asset for use (p. 365).

depreciation The decline in economic potential of plant assets originating from wear, deterioration, and obsolescence (p. 366).

depreciation accounting The process of allocating the cost of plant assets (less salvage value) to expense in a rational and systematic manner over the time period benefitting from their use (p. 366).

double declining-balance method An accelerated depreciation method that allocates depreciation expense to each year by applying a constant percentage to the declining book value of the asset (p. 370).

extraordinary repairs Expenditures that extend a plant asset's useful life beyond the original estimate (p. 375).

fixed assets An alternate label for plant assets; may also be called *property, plant, and equipment* (p. 362).

Land Improvements Improvements with limited lives made to land sites, such as paved parking lots and driveways (p. 366).

plant assets A firm's property, plant, and equipment (p. 362).

return on assets A financial ratio computed as net income divided by average total assets (p. 376).

revenue expenditures Expenditures related to plant assets that are expensed when incurred (p. 373).

salvage value The expected net recovery when a plant asset is sold or removed from service. Also called *residual value* (p. 366).

straight-line method A depreciation method that allocates equal amounts of depreciation expense to each full period of an asset's useful life (p. 367).

sum-of-the-years'-digits method An accelerated depreciation method that allocates depreciation expense to each year in a fractional proportion, the denominator of which is the sum of the years' digits in the useful life of the asset and the numerator of which is the remaining useful life of the asset at the beginning of the current depreciation period (p. 369).

units-of-production method A depreciation method that allocates depreciation expense to each operating period in proportion to the amount of the asset's expected total production capacity used each period (p. 368).

useful life The period of time an asset is used by an entity in its operating activities, running from date of acquisition to date of disposal (or removal from service) (p. 366).

QUESTIONS

10-1 List the three major types of long-term assets that require a periodic write-off, present examples of each, and indicate for each type the term that denotes the periodic write-off to expense.

10-2 In what way is land different from other plant assets?

10-3 Describe the typical sequence of transactions and related problem areas associated with plant assets.

10-4 In general, what amounts constitute the initial cost of plant assets?

10-5 Wyler Company borrowed $2,600,000 to finance the purchase of a new office building, which was ready for immediate use. May Wyler add a portion of the interest cost on the $2,600,000 to the building's cost? Explain.

10-6 Foss Company bought land with a vacant building for $600,000. Foss will use the building in its operations. Must Foss allocate the purchase price between the land and building? Why or why not? Would your answer be different if Foss intends to raze the building and build a new one? Why or why not?

10-7 Explain why the recognition of depreciation expense is necessary to match revenue and expense properly.

10-8 "Depreciation is a process of periodic reductions in a plant asset's book value to correspond with changes in the asset's market value as it ages." Do you agree? Why or why not?

10-9 How is the use of the contra account Accumulated Depreciation justified when recording depreciation?

10-10 How can we justify the use of accelerated depreciation?

10-11 Briefly describe an operational situation that lends itself naturally to each of the following depreciation methods: (a) straight line, (b) units of production, (c) sum of the years' digits, and (d) double declining balance.

10-12 How should we handle a revision of depreciation charges due to a change in an asset's estimated useful life or salvage value? Which periods—past, present, or future—are affected by the revision?

10-13 Explain the benefit of accelerating depreciation for income tax purposes when the total depreciation taken is no more than if straight-line depreciation were used.

10-14 Identify three types of revenue expenditures. What is the proper accounting for revenue expenditures?

10-15 "We cannot properly estimate an asset's useful life without first considering the level of maintenance employed." Do you agree? Why or why not?

10-16 Lane Company purchased a $25 pencil sharpener with an estimated useful life of 20 years. How should Lane account for this expenditure?

10-17 Identify three types of capital expenditures. What is the proper accounting for capital expenditures?

10-18 What is the difference between an ordinary repair and an extraordinary repair? What is the rationale for charging extraordinary repairs to accumulated depreciation?

10-19 How is *return on assets* computed? What does this ratio show?

EXERCISES

**INITIAL COST OF PLANT
ASSET
— OBJ. 2 —**

10-20 The following data relate to a firm's purchase of a machine used in the manufacture of its product:

Invoice price	$30,000
Applicable sales tax	1,782
Cash discount taken for prompt payment	300
Freight paid	278
Cost of insurance coverage on machine while in transit	100
Installation costs	1,000
Testing and adjusting costs	440
Repair of damages to machine caused by the firm's employees	800
Prepaid maintenance contract for first year of machine's use	264

Compute the initial amount at which the machine should be carried in the firm's accounts.

**ALLOCATION OF PACKAGE
PURCHASE PRICE
— OBJ. 2 —**

10-21 Tamock Company purchased a small established plant from one of its suppliers. The $920,000 purchase price included the land, a building, and factory machinery. Tamock also paid $3,000 in legal fees to negotiate the purchase of the plant. Various property tax bills for the plant showed the following assessed values for the items purchased:

Property	Assessed Value
Land	$119,000
Building	442,000
Machinery	289,000
Total	$850,000

Using the assessed valuations on the property tax bill as a guide, allocate the total purchase price of the plant to the land, building, and machinery accounts in Tamock Company's records.

CAPITALIZATION OF INTEREST
— OBJ. 2 —
$900

10-22 On April 1, 1993, Florida Company borrowed $800,000 at 9% to finance the construction of a new wing on its headquarters office building. The construction will take several months. Interest of $6,000 is paid monthly. Construction begins April 1, 1993, and accumulated construction expenditures are $240,000 at April 30, 1993. Determine how much interest cost should be capitalized for April.

DEPRECIATION METHODS
— OBJ. 4 —

10-23 A delivery truck costing $12,000 is expected to have a $1,200 salvage value at the end of its useful life of four years or 120,000 miles. Assume the truck was purchased on January 2, 1993. Compute the depreciation expense for 1994 using each of the following depreciation methods: (a) straight line, (b) sum of the years' digits, (c) double declining balance, and (d) units of production (assume the truck was driven 34,000 miles in 1994).

DEPRECIATION METHODS
— OBJ. 4 —

10-24 A delivery truck costing $12,000 is expected to have a $1,200 salvage value at the end of its useful life of four years or 120,000 miles. Assume the truck was purchased on April 1, 1993. Compute the depreciation expense for 1994 using each of the following depreciation methods: (a) straight line, (b) sum of the years' digits, (c) double declining balance, and (d) units of production (assume the truck was driven 38,000 miles in 1994).

REVISION OF DEPRECIATION
— OBJ. 4 —

10-25 On January 2, 1990, Mosler, Inc., purchased new equipment for $44,000. The equipment was expected to have a $5,000 salvage value at the end of its estimated six-year useful life. Straight-line depreciation has been recorded. Before adjusting the accounts for 1994, Mosler decided that the useful life of the equipment should be extended by two years and the salvage value decreased to $3,000.
  a. Present a general journal entry to record depreciation expense on the equipment for 1994.
  b. What is the book value of the equipment at the end of 1994 (that is, after recording the depreciation expense for 1994)?

CAPITAL EXPENDITURE AND DEPRECIATION
— OBJ. 4, 5 —

10-26 On January 3, 1987, Trust Company purchased a warehouse for $610,000 with an estimated useful life of 25 years and a salvage value of $60,000. Trust uses straight-line depreciation on the warehouse. On January 1, 1994, Trust spent $45,000 for the installation of a fire detection and sprinkler system in the warehouse. The useful life of the warehouse was unchanged, but its estimated salvage value increased to $69,000.
  a. Prepare the general journal entry to record the cost of the fire detection and sprinkler system.
  b. Compute the 1994 depreciation expense on the warehouse.
  c. Prepare the general journal entry to record the warehouse's 1994 depreciation expense.

REVENUE AND CAPITAL EXPENDITURES
— OBJ. 5 —

10-27 Shively Company built an addition to its chemical plant. Indicate whether each of the following expenditures related to the addition is a revenue expenditure or a capital expenditure.
  a. Shively's initial application for a building permit was denied by the city as not conforming to environmental standards. Shively disagreed with the decision and spent $5,000 in attorney's fees to convince the city to reverse its position and issue the permit.
  b. Due to unanticipated sandy soil conditions, and upon the advice of construction engineers, Shively spent $55,000 to extend the footings for the addition to a greater depth than originally planned.

    c. Shively spent $4,000 to send each of the addition's subcontractors a side of beef as a thank-you gift for completing the project on schedule.

    d. Shively invited the mayor to a ribbon-cutting ceremony to open the plant addition. Shively spent $35 to purchase the ribbon and scissors.

    e. Shively spent $4,800 to have the company logo sandblasted into the concrete above the entrance to the addition.

PROBLEMS

INITIAL COST OF PLANT ASSETS
— OBJ. 2 —

10-28   The items below represent expenditures (or receipts) related to the construction of a new home office for Lowrey Company.

Cost of land site, which included an old apartment building appraised at $70,000	$ 160,000
Legal fees, including fee for title search	2,600
Payment of apartment building mortgage and related interest due at time of sale	8,000
Payment of delinquent property taxes assumed by the purchaser	3,000
Cost of razing the apartment building	12,000
Proceeds from sale of salvaged materials	(2,800)
Grading to establish proper drainage flow on land site	2,100
Architect's fees on new building	200,000
Proceeds from sale of excess dirt (from basement excavation) to owner of adjoining property (dirt was used to fill in a low area on property)	(1,000)
Payment to building contractor	4,000,000
Interest cost incurred during construction (based on average accumulated construction expenditures)	185,000
Payment of medical bills of employee accidentally injured while inspecting building construction	900
Special assessment for paving city sidewalks (paid to city)	16,000
Cost of paving driveway and parking lot	23,000
Cost of installing lights in parking lot	9,700
Premium for insurance on building during construction	5,800
Cost of open house party to celebrate opening of new building	7,000

REQUIRED

From the given data, compute the proper balances for the Land, Building, and Land Improvements accounts of Lowrey Company.

ALLOCATION OF PACKAGE PURCHASE PRICE AND DEPRECIATION METHODS
— OBJ. 2, 4 —

10-29   To expand its business, Small Company paid $645,000 for most of the property, plant, and equipment of a small trucking company that was going out of business. Before agreeing to the price, Small hired a consultant for $5,000 to appraise the assets. The appraised values were as follows:

Land	$ 90,000
Building	360,000
Trucks	120,000
Equipment	30,000
Total	$600,000

Small issued two checks totaling $650,000 to acquire the assets and pay the consultant on July 1, 1993. Small depreciated the assets using the straight-line method on the building, the double declining-balance method on the trucks, and the sum-of-the-years'-digits method on the equipment. Estimated useful lives and salvage values were as follows:

	Useful Life	Salvage Value
Building	20 years	$40,000
Trucks	4 years	15,000
Equipment	7 years	3,500

REQUIRED

a. Compute the amounts allocated to the various types of plant assets acquired on July 1, 1993.

b. Prepare the July 1, 1993, general journal entries to record the purchase of the assets and the payment to the consultant.

c. Prepare the December 31, 1993, general journal entries to record 1993 depreciation expense on the building, trucks, and equipment.

DEPRECIATION METHODS
— OBJ. 4 —

10-30 On January 2, Roth, Inc., purchased a laser cutting machine to be used in the fabrication of a part for one of its key products. The machine cost $72,000, and its estimated useful life was four years or 750,000 cuttings, after which it could be sold for $4,500.

REQUIRED

Compute the depreciation expense for each year of the machine's useful life under each of the following depreciation methods:

a. Straight line.

b. Sum of the years' digits.

c. Double declining balance.

d. Units of production. (Assume annual production in cuttings of 112,000; 238,000; 273,000; and 127,000.)

COMPREHENSIVE PROBLEM
— OBJ. 2, 4, 5 —

10-31 During the first few days of 1993, Coast Company entered into the following transactions:

1. Purchased a parcel of land with a building on it for $800,000 cash. The building, which will be used in operations, has an estimated useful life of 25 years and a salvage value of $40,000. The assessed valuations for property tax purposes show the land at $70,000 and the building at $630,000.

2. Paid $27,600 for the construction of an asphalt parking lot for customers. The parking lot is expected to last 12 years and have no salvage value.

3. Paid $15,000 for the construction of a new entrance to the building.

4. Purchased store equipment, paying the invoice price (including 7% sales tax) of $64,200 in cash. The estimated useful life of the equipment is 8 years, and the salvage value is $6,000.

5. Paid $480 freight on the new store equipment.

6. Paid $1,000 to repair damages to floor caused when the store equipment was accidentally dropped as it was moved into place.

7. Paid $50 for an umbrella holder to place inside front door (customers may place wet umbrellas in the holder). The holder is expected to last 20 years.

REQUIRED

a. Prepare general journal entries to record the above transactions.

b. Prepare the December 31, 1993, general journal entries to record the proper amounts of depreciation expense for the year. Sum-of-the-years'-digits depreciation is used for the equipment, and straight-line depreciation is used for the building and land improvements.

COMPREHENSIVE PROBLEM
— OBJ. 2, 4, 5 —

10-32 Basin Corporation had the following transactions related to its delivery truck:

1993

Jan.   5   Purchased for $12,380 cash a new truck with an estimated useful life of four years and a salvage value of $2,300.

Feb. 20   Installed a new set of side-view mirrors at a cost of $48 cash.

June   9   Paid $185 for an engine tune-up, wheel balancing, and a periodic lubrication.

Aug.   2   Paid a $200 repair bill for the uninsured portion of damages to the truck caused by Basin's own driver.

Dec. 31   Recorded 1993 depreciation on the truck.

1994

May   1   Installed a set of parts bins in the truck at a cost of $960 cash. This expenditure was not expected to increase the salvage value of the truck.

Dec. 31   Recorded 1994 depreciation on the truck.

1995

July 1 Paid $1,810 for a major engine overhaul on the truck. The overhaul should extend the useful life of the truck an additional two years (to December 31, 1998) with a salvage value now estimated at $1,500.

Dec. 31 Recorded 1995 depreciation on the truck.

Basin's depreciation policies include (1) using straight-line depreciation, (2) recording depreciation to the nearest whole month, and (3) expensing all truck expenditures of $500 or less.

REQUIRED

Present general journal entries to record these transactions and adjustments.

REVISION OF DEPRECIATION AND CAPITAL EXPENDITURE
— OBJ. 4, 5 —

10-33 Macon Company uses straight-line depreciation in accounting for its machines. On January 3, 1992, Macon purchased a new machine for $36,000 cash. The machine's estimated useful life was 12 years with a $4,500 salvage value. In 1994, the company decided its original useful life estimate should be reduced by three years. Beginning in 1994, depreciation was based on a seven-year remaining useful life, and no change was made in the salvage value estimate. On January 2, 1995, Macon added an automatic guide and a safety shield to the machine at a cost of $2,400 cash. These improvements did not change the machine's useful life, but they did increase the estimated salvage value to $4,800.

REQUIRED

a. Prepare general journal entries to record (1) the purchase of the machine, (2) 1992 depreciation expense, (3) 1993 depreciation expense, (4) 1994 depreciation expense, (5) the 1995 improvements, and (6) 1995 depreciation expense.

b. Compute the book value of the machine at the end of 1995 (that is, after recording the depreciation expense for 1995).

PLANT ASSET ERRORS AND CORRECTIONS
— OBJ. 2, 4, 5 —

10-34 During 1993, King, Inc., analyzed several transactions relating to its plant assets as described below.

Jan. 2 Paid for robotic equipment purchased and installed today. The invoice price was $180,000 and King was entitled to a 2% cash discount. Entry:

Robotic Equipment	180,000	
Purchases Discounts		3,600
Cash		176,400

Feb. 6 Paid $500 for regular, annual maintenance on the firm's word processors. Entry:

Office Equipment	500	
Cash		500

June 7 Paid $2,900 to clear timber and brush from a land site purchased a few days earlier. King will build a new plant on this land site. Entry:

Land Clearing Expense	2,900	
Cash		2,900

Aug. 1 Paid $42 for a wastebasket purchased today. The wastebasket has an estimated useful life of 30 years. Entry:

Office Equipment	42	
Cash		42

Dec. 30 Paid $15,750 interest on $175,000 borrowed on January 2, 1993, to finance the purchase of the robotic equipment. Entry:

Robotic Equipment	15,750	
Cash		15,750

Dec. 31 Recorded the 1993 straight-line depreciation on the robotic equipment purchased January 2, 1993. The equipment has a 10-year useful life and a $15,000 expected salvage value. The Robotic Equipment account balance before depreciation was $195,750. Entry:

Depreciation Expense—Robotic Equipment 18,075
    Robotic Equipment 18,075

REQUIRED

a. Identify any errors made by King, Inc., in analyzing the above transactions.
b. Prepare journal entries at December 31, 1993, to correct each error noted in requirement (a). The books have not been closed for 1993.

ALTERNATE EXERCISES

INITIAL COST OF PLANT ASSET
— OBJ. 2 —

10-20A Fischer Construction purchased a used front-end loader for $18,000, terms 1/10, n/30, F.O.B. shipping point, freight collect. Fischer paid the freight charges of $210 and sent the seller a check for $17,820 one week after the machine was delivered. The loader required a new battery, which cost Fischer $100. Fischer also spent $140 to have the company name printed on the loader and $225 for one year's insurance coverage on the loader. Fischer hired a new employee to operate it at a wage of $15 per hour; the employee spent one morning (four hours) practicing with the machine and went to work at a construction site that afternoon. Compute the initial amount at which the front-end loader should be carried in the firm's accounts.

ALLOCATION OF PACKAGE PURCHASE PRICE
— OBJ. 2 —

10-21A Andrew Lupino went into business by purchasing a car lubrication station, consisting of land, a building, and equipment. The seller's original asking price was $200,000. Lupino hired an appraiser for $1,000 to appraise the assets. The appraised valuations were land, $36,000; building, $99,000, and equipment, $45,000. After receiving the appraisal, Lupino offered $160,000 for the business. The seller refused this offer. Lupino then offered $170,000 for the business, which the seller accepted. Using the appraisal values as a guide, allocate the total purchase price of the car lubrication station to the land, building, and equipment accounts.

CAPITALIZATION OF INTEREST
— OBJ. 2 —

10-22A On May 1, 1993, Iowa Company borrowed $900,000 at 12% to finance the construction of a new warehouse. Interest of $9,000 is paid monthly. The construction that began during the first week of May will take several months. At May 31, the accumulated construction expenditures were $275,000. At June 30, the accumulated construction expenditures were $535,000. Determine how much interest cost should be capitalized for June.

DEPRECIATION METHODS
— OBJ. 4 —

10-23A A machine costing $72,900 was purchased January 2, 1993. The machine should be obsolete after three years and, therefore, no longer useful to the company. The estimated salvage value is $2,700. Compute the depreciation expense for each year of the machine's useful life using each of the following depreciation methods: (a) straight line, (b) sum of the years' digits, and (c) double declining balance.

DEPRECIATION METHODS
— OBJ. 4 —

10-24A A machine costing $72,900 was purchased May 1, 1993. The machine should be obsolete after three years and, therefore, no longer useful to the company. The estimated salvage value is $2,700. Compute each year's depreciation expense for 1993–1996 using each of the following depreciation methods: (a) straight line, (b) sum of the years' digits, and (c) double declining balance.

REVISION OF DEPRECIATION
— OBJ. 4 —

10-25A Associated Clinic purchased a special machine for use in its laboratory on January 2, 1993. The machine cost $56,000 and was expected to last 10 years. Its salvage value was estimated to be $4,000. By early 1995, it was evident that the machine will be useful for a total of only seven years. The salvage value after seven years was estimated to be $5,000. Associated Clinic uses straight-line depreciation. Compute the proper depreciation expense on the machine for 1995.

Capital Expenditure and Depreciation
— Obj. 4, 5 —

10-26A At the end of last year, the balance sheet of Locust Company shows a building with a cost of $986,000 and an accumulated depreciation of $460,800. The company uses the straight-line method to depreciate the building. When acquired, the building had an estimated 35-year useful life, and its salvage value was $90,000. Early in January of the current year, Locust made major structural repairs to the building costing $284,800. Although the capacity of the building was unchanged, the improvements will extend the useful life of the building to an estimated 48 years, rather than the original 35 years. The salvage value remains $90,000.

a. By the end of last year, how many years had the company depreciated the building?

b. Present the general journal entry to record the cost of the structural repairs.

c. Present the general journal entry to record the building's depreciation expense for the current year.

Revenue and Capital Expenditures
— Obj. 5 —

10-27A Indicate whether each of the following expenditures is a revenue expenditure or a capital expenditure for Blare Company.

a. Paid $200 to replace a truck windshield that was cracked by a stone thrown up by another vehicle while the truck was being used to make a delivery.

b. Paid $8 for a no-smoking sign for the conference room.

c. Paid $900 to add a hard disk to an employee's computer.

d. Paid $12 for a dust cover for a computer printer.

e. Paid $200 to replace a cracked windshield on a used truck that was just purchased for company use. The company bought the truck knowing the windshield was cracked.

f. Paid $80 for a building permit from the city for a storage shed the company is going to have built.

ALTERNATE PROBLEMS

10-28A The items below represent expenditures (or receipts) related to the construction of a new home office for Secrest Investment Company.

Initial Cost of Plant Assets
— Obj. 2 —

Cost of land site, which included an abandoned railroad spur	$ 160,000
Legal fees, including title search, relating to land purchase	4,800
Cost of surveying land to confirm boundaries	1,000
Cost of removing railroad tracks	7,500
Payment of delinquent property taxes assumed by the purchaser	5,000
Proceeds from sale of timber from walnut trees cut down to prepare site for construction	(16,000)
Proceeds from sale of salvaged railroad track	(2,500)
Grading to prepare land site for construction	4,000
Cost of basement excavation (contracted separately)	3,400
Architect's fees on new building	125,000
Payment to building contractor—original contract price	2,800,000
Cost of changes during construction to make building more energy efficient	90,000
Interest cost incurred during construction (based on average accumulated construction expenditures)	112,000
Cost of replacing windows broken by vandals	1,400
Cost of paving driveway and parking lot	19,000
Out-of-court settlement for mud slide onto adjacent property	8,000
Special assessment for paving city sidewalks (paid to city)	20,000
Cost of brick and wrought iron fence installed across front of property	11,500

REQUIRED

From the given data, compute the proper balances for the Land, Building, and Land Improvements accounts of Secrest Investment Company.

ALLOCATION OF PACKAGE PURCHASE PRICE AND DEPRECIATION METHODS — OBJ. 2, 4 —

10-29A In an expansion move, Beam Company paid $1,090,000 for most of the property, plant, and equipment of a small manufacturing firm that was going out of business. Before agreeing to the price, Beam hired a consultant for $10,000 to appraise the assets. The appraised values were as follows:

Land	$ 156,000
Building	456,000
Equipment	564,000
Trucks	24,000
Total	$1,200,000

Beam issued two checks totaling $1,100,000 to acquire the assets and pay the consultant on April 1, 1993. Beam depreciated the assets using the straight-line method on the building, the sum-of-the-years'-digits method on the equipment, and the double declining-balance method on the trucks. Estimated useful lives and salvage values were as follows:

	Useful Life	Salvage Value
Building	15 years	$40,000
Equipment	9 years	52,000
Trucks	5 years	3,000

REQUIRED

a. Compute the amounts allocated to the various types of plant assets acquired on April 1, 1993.
b. Prepare the April 1, 1993, general journal entries to record the purchase of the assets and the payment of the consultant.
c. Prepare the December 31, 1993, general journal entries to record the 1993 depreciation expense on the building, equipment, and trucks.

DEPRECIATION METHODS — OBJ. 4 —

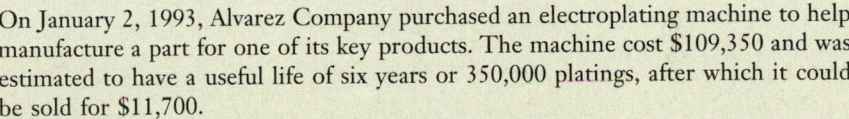

10-30A On January 2, 1993, Alvarez Company purchased an electroplating machine to help manufacture a part for one of its key products. The machine cost $109,350 and was estimated to have a useful life of six years or 350,000 platings, after which it could be sold for $11,700.

REQUIRED

a. Compute each year's depreciation expense for 1993–1998 under each of the following depreciation methods:
   1. Straight line.
   2. Sum of the years' digits.
   3. Double declining balance.
   4. Units of production. (Assume annual production in platings of 70,000, 90,000, 50,000, 55,000, 40,000, and 45,000.)
b. Assume the machine was purchased on September 1, 1993. Compute each year's depreciation expense for 1993–1999 under each of the following depreciation methods:
   1. Straight line.
   2. Sum of the years' digits.
   3. Double declining balance.

COMPREHENSIVE PROBLEM — OBJ. 2, 4, 5 —

10-31A During the first few days of 1994, Chasen Company began business and entered into the following transactions:
   1. Purchased a parcel of land with an old building on it for $200,000 cash. The company plans to tear the building down. The assessed valuations for property tax purposes show the land at $140,000 and the building at $35,000.
   2. Demolished the old building at a cost of $18,000 cash.

3. Erected a prefabricated, modular shell building on the site in three days at a cost of $270,000 cash. The building has an estimated useful life of 18 years and an estimated salvage value of $18,000.
4. Purchased and installed equipment to enable the company to begin operations. The purchase price plus installation costs totaled $86,000 cash. The company expects to replace the equipment after eight years. Its salvage value is estimated to be $6,800.
5. Constructed a chain-link fence around the property border for security purposes. The fence cost $8,500 and is expected to last 20 years and have no salvage value. Chasen has 30 days to pay the bill for the fence.
6. Paid $12 cash to purchase a padlock for the fence gate. The padlock is expected to last 20 years.
7. Paid $3,240 cash to modify switches on the equipment to conform to federal safety standards. The switches do not extend the useful life of the equipment.

REQUIRED

a. Prepare general journal entries to record the above transactions.
b. Prepare the December 31, 1994, general journal entries to record the proper amounts of depreciation expense for the year (take a full year's depreciation). Sum-of-the-years'-digits depreciation is used for the equipment, and straight-line depreciation is used for the building and land improvements.

COMPREHENSIVE PROBLEM
— OBJ. 2, 4, 5 —

10-32A Stellar Delivery Service had the following transactions related to its delivery truck:

1992

Mar. 1 Purchased for $14,250 cash a new delivery truck with an estimated useful life of five years and a $1,400 salvage value.

2 Paid $290 for painting the company name and logo on the truck.

Dec. 31 Recorded 1992 depreciation on the truck.

1993

July 1 Installed air conditioning in the truck at a cost of $904 cash. Although the truck's estimated useful life was not affected, its estimated salvage value was increased by $200.

Sept. 7 Paid $215 for truck tune-up and safety inspection.

Dec. 31 Recorded 1993 depreciation on the truck.

1994

May 2 Paid $1,110 for a major overhaul of the truck. The overhaul should extend the truck's useful life one year (to February 28, 1998), when the revised salvage value should be $1,500.

Sept. 3 Installed a set of front and rear bumper guards at a cost of $65 cash.

Dec. 31 Recorded 1994 depreciation on the truck.

1995

Dec. 31 Recorded 1995 depreciation on the truck.

Stellar's depreciation policies include (1) using straight-line depreciation, (2) recording depreciation to the nearest whole month, and (3) expensing all truck expenditures of $75 or less.

REQUIRED

Present general journal entries to record these transactions and adjustments.

REVISION OF DEPRECIATION
AND CAPITAL EXPENDITURE
— OBJ. 4, 5 —

10-33A Richter Company uses straight-line depreciation in accounting for its machines. On January 2, 1988, Richter purchased a new machine for $61,000 cash. The machine's estimated useful life was seven years with a $5,000 salvage value. In 1993, the company decided its original useful life estimate should be increased by three years. Beginning in 1993, depreciation was based on a 10-year total useful life, and no change was made in the salvage value estimate. On January 3, 1994, Richter added an automatic cut-off switch and a self-sharpening blade mechanism to the machine at a cost of $4,400 cash. These improvements did not change the machine's useful life, but did increase the estimated salvage value to $5,600.

REQUIRED

a. Prepare general journal entries to record (1) the purchase of the machine, (2) 1988 depreciation expense, (3) 1993 depreciation expense, (4) the 1994 improvements, and (5) 1994 depreciation expense.

b. Compute the book value of the machine at the end of 1994 (that is, after recording the depreciation expense for 1994).

PLANT ASSET ERRORS AND CORRECTIONS
— OBJ. 2, 4 —

10-34A On April 1, 1993, Yale Company purchased a new machine. The machine was shipped F.O.B. shipping point, freight collect. The invoice showed the following information:

Machine	$20,000
7% sales tax	1,400
Freight charges	200
Total due	$21,600

Yale immediately paid the invoice and made the following journal entry:

Apr. 1	Machine	20,000	
	Sales Tax Expense	1,400	
	Transportation In	200	
	Cash		21,600

Yale expects the machine to last eight years and have a salvage value of $2,400. Yale uses straight-line depreciation. At year-end, Yale made the following journal entry to record depreciation for 1993 on the machine:

Dec. 31	Depreciation Expense—Machine	2,500	
	Machine		2,500
	($20,000/8 = $2,500)		

REQUIRED

a. Identify any errors made by Yale Company in accounting for the machine in 1993.

b. Prepare journal entries at December 31, 1993, to correct the errors noted in requirement (a). The books have not been closed for 1993.

CASES

Business Decision Case

Lyle Fleming, president of Fleming, Inc., wants you to resolve his dispute with Mia Gooden over the amount of a finder's fee due Gooden. Fleming hired Gooden to locate a new plant site to expand the business. By agreement, Gooden's fee was to be 15% of the "cost of the property (excluding the finder's fee) measured according to generally accepted accounting principles."

Gooden located Site 1 and Site 2 for Fleming to consider. Each site had a selling price of $180,000, and the geographic locations of both sites were equally acceptable to Fleming. Fleming employed an engineering firm to conduct the geological tests necessary to determine the relative quality of the two sites for construction. The tests, which cost $12,000 for each site, showed that Site 1 was superior to Site 2.

The owner of Site 1 initially gave Fleming 30 days—a reasonable period—to decide whether or not to buy the property. However, Fleming procrastinated in contracting the geological tests, and the results were not available by the end of the 30-day period. Fleming requested a two-week extension. The Site 1 owner granted Fleming the additional two weeks but charged him $6,000 for the extension (which Fleming paid). Fleming eventually bought Site 1.

Fleming sent Gooden a fee of $28,800, which was 15% of a cost computed as follows:

Sales price, Site 1	$180,000
Geological tests, Site 1	12,000
Total	$192,000

Gooden believes she is entitled to $31,500, based on a cost computed as follows:

Sales price, Site 1	$180,000
Geological tests, Site 1	12,000
Geological tests, Site 2	12,000
Fee for time extension	6,000
Total	$210,000

REQUIRED

What fee is Gooden entitled to under the agreement? Explain.

Analytical Application Case

SAFETY-KLEEN CORP., headquartered in Elgin, Illinois, provides fluid recovery services to businesses that generate hazardous and semi-hazardous waste fluids. With a primary focus on small-quantity generators of such fluids, the company is the world's largest re-refiner of used lubricating oils. Selected financial data for Safety-Kleen Corp. for three recent years are shown below (amounts in thousands; Year 3 is the most recent year).

	Year 3	Year 2	Year 1
Total assets, beginning of year	$538,002	$398,773	$302,026
Total assets, end of year	718,548	538,002	398,773
Revenues for the year	588,987	478,117	417,174
Net income for the year	55,198	45,987	42,330

REQUIRED

a. Compute the return on assets for Years 1, 2, and 3.
b. In each of the three years, Safety-Kleen's total assets grew by 30–35%. With such a rapid growth in assets, was Safety-Kleen able to maintain its rate of profitability in the utilization of assets throughout the three years? Explain.

Ethics Case

Linda Tristan, assistant controller for Ag-Growth, Inc., a biotechnology firm, has concerns about the accounting analysis for the firm's purchase of a land site and building from Hylite Corporation. The price for this package purchase was $1,500,000 cash. A memorandum from the controller, Greg Fister, stated that the journal entry for this purchase should debit Land for $1,125,000, debit Building for $375,000, and credit Cash for $1,500,000. The building, a used laboratory facility, is to be depreciated over 10 years with a zero salvage value.

The source documents supporting the transaction include two appraisals of the property—one done for Ag-Growth and one done for Hylite Corporation. The appraisal for Ag-Growth valued the land at $800,000 and the building at $400,000. The appraisal for Hylite Corporation (done by a different appraiser) valued the land at $1,200,000 and the building at $600,000. Negotiations between the two firms finally settled on an overall price of $1,500,000 for the land and the building.

Tristan asked Fister how he arrived at the amounts to be recorded for the land and building since each appraisal valued the land at only twice the building's value. "Well," replied Fister, "I used the $1,200,000 land value from Hylite's appraiser and the $400,000 building value from our appraiser. That relationship shows the land to be worth three times the building's value. Using that relationship, I assigned 75% of our actual purchase price of $1,500,000 to the land and 25% of the purchase price to the building."

"But why do it that way?" asked Tristan.

"Because it will improve our profits, before income taxes, by $125,000 over the next decade," replied Fister.

"But it just doesn't seem right," commented Tristan.

REQUIRED

a. How does the accounting analysis by Fister improve profits, before income taxes, by $125,000 over the next decade?

b. Is the goal of improving profits a sufficient rationale to defend the accounting analysis by Fister?

c. Do you agree with Fister's analysis? Briefly explain.

d. What actions are available to Tristan to resolve her concerns with Fister's analysis?

Are natural resources and intangible assets significant long-term assets?

Although reported on balance sheets less frequently than plant assets, natural resources and intangible assets are significant assets for some firms. ■ International Paper Company, for example, reports timberlands as an asset measured in excess of $700 million. ■ The Clorox Company reports "Brands, Trademarks, Patents and Other Intangibles" as 25% of its total assets. ■ A large portion of these intangible assets resulted from Clorox's 1990 purchase of the Pine-Sol cleaner and Combat insecticide brands.

11

PLANT ASSET DISPOSALS, NATURAL RESOURCES, AND INTANGIBLE ASSETS

he preceding chapter dealt with the measurement and depreciation of plant assets. In this chapter, we examine the remaining plant asset problem area—accounting for their disposal. We then consider the accounting issues related to the acquisition and use of natural resources and intangible assets. Although plant assets, natural resources, and intangible assets are separate identifiable categories of long-term assets, the basic accounting procedures related to each category are similar.

DISPOSALS OF PLANT ASSETS

OBJECTIVE ❶ EXPLAIN *and* ILLUSTRATE *the accounting for disposals of plant assets.*

A firm may dispose of a plant asset in a variety of ways. The asset may be sold, retired, exchanged for a dissimilar asset, or traded in as partial payment for a new, similar asset. The asset's usefulness to the firm may also be ended by an unfavorable and unanticipated event—the asset may be stolen or destroyed by a natural disaster.

Depreciation must extend through an asset's total useful life to a firm. Therefore, depreciation must be recorded up to the disposal date, regardless of the manner of the asset's disposal. Should the disposal date not coincide with the end of an accounting period, a journal entry must record depreciation for a partial period (the period from the date depreciation was last recorded to the disposal date). We illustrate this partial period depreciation in two of our subsequent examples.

We use the following basic data to illustrate disposals of plant assets:

Equipment's original cost	$1,000
Estimated salvage value after five years	100
Annual straight-line depreciation	180
(Unless stated otherwise, assume that depreciation to the date of disposal has been recorded.)	

Sale of Plant Assets

Firms normally sell their plant assets once they are no longer efficient or useful. Generally, the asset still has some book value and some sales value in the used market.

Most sales of plant assets involve the following related factors:

1. The sale transaction exchanges a used plant asset for cash. Because the plant asset sold is no longer on hand, the journal entry must remove from both the asset and the accumulated depreciation accounts all amounts related to that asset. These amounts reflect the asset's book value.

2. Because plant assets are most often sold for amounts either greater or less than their book values, gains or losses are produced. Sales proceeds in excess of book values create gains from the sales. Book values in excess of sales proceeds cause losses from the sales.

SOLD FOR MORE THAN BOOK VALUE

Assume the equipment is sold for $230 midway through its fifth year. Depreciation was last recorded at the end of the fourth year. The related entries are

Depreciation Expense—Equipment	90	
Accumulated Depreciation—Equipment		90
To record depreciation expense for six months.		
Cash	230	
Accumulated Depreciation—Equipment	810	
Equipment		1,000
Gain on Sale of Plant Assets		40
To record sale of equipment for $230.		

Note that recording depreciation to the date of sale adds $90 to the Accumulated Depreciation account, which totals (4 × $180) + $90 = $810. To reflect the sale properly, we must remove this entire amount of accumulated depreciation from the books. The gain is the proceeds of $230 minus the asset's book value of $190.

SOLD FOR LESS THAN BOOK VALUE

Assume the equipment is sold for $30 at the end of the fifth year. The correct entry to record this sale is

Cash	30	
Loss on Sale of Plant Assets	70	
Accumulated Depreciation—Equipment	900	
Equipment		1,000
To record sale of equipment for $30.		

The loss equals the book value of $100 minus the sales proceeds of $30. The cash receipt is recorded, and balances from both accounts related to the asset—the asset account and its contra account—are removed from the books.

SOLD FOR BOOK VALUE

Assume the equipment is sold for $280 at the end of the fourth year. The proper entry is

Cash	280	
Accumulated Depreciation—Equipment	720	
Equipment		1,000
To record sale of equipment for $280.		

The equipment's book value at the end of the fourth year is $280 ($1,000 cost − $720 accumulated depreciation). The $280 sales proceeds exactly equal the book value; no gain or loss is involved. Of course, we still remove from the accounts the amounts reflecting the book value of the asset sold.

Destruction or Theft of Plant Assets

A company's plant assets may be destroyed—by fire, flood, earthquake, tornado, or other natural disaster—or they may be stolen. If an uninsured asset is destroyed or stolen, the firm suffers a loss measured by the asset's book value. Assume the equipment in our example is uninsured and after three years is destroyed by fire. Its book value when destroyed is $460 ($1,000 cost − $540 accumulated depreciation). The proper journal entry is

Fire Loss	460	
Accumulated Depreciation—Equipment	540	
Equipment		1,000
To record equipment fire loss.		

Business firms normally insure their property to eliminate, or reduce, the risk of loss by destruction or theft. When an insured asset is destroyed or stolen, a claim is filed with the insurance company. The maximum amount recoverable from the insurance company is the asset's fair market value. Because the accounting records reflect a plant asset's book value—not its fair market value—the accounting analysis of the asset's theft or destruction may show a gain or loss, even when the asset is insured. The gain or loss is the difference between the insurance settlement and the asset's book value. If the insurance settlement equals the insured asset's book value, then no gain or loss is recorded.

To illustrate a gain from an insured asset's destruction, assume the equipment from the preceding example is insured and has a fair market value of $500 when destroyed by fire. The $500 insurance claim exceeds the equipment's book value, so we reflect a $40 gain from the insurance settlement in the following entry:

Receivable from Insurance Company	500	
Accumulated Depreciation—Equipment	540	
Equipment		1,000
Gain on Insurance Settlement		40
To record insurance claim on equipment destroyed by fire.		

Cash is debited and Receivable from Insurance Company is credited when the $500 check settling the claim is received from the insurance company.

Retirement of Plant Assets

When a plant asset that has no sales value in the used market is retired from productive service, we record a loss equal to the asset's book value. Assume the equipment in our example is scrapped at the end of five years. The entry to record this event is

Loss on Retirement of Plant Assets	100	
Accumulated Depreciation—Equipment	900	
Equipment		1,000
To record retirement of equipment.		

Ideally, any plant asset that will be scrapped should have a zero salvage value. Then the asset's book value is zero (accumulated depreciation equals the asset's cost) at the end of its estimated useful life. If the asset is retired on that date, no loss is recorded. The asset's cost and accumulated depreciation, of course, must still be removed from the accounts. To illustrate, let us change our example and assume a zero salvage value for the equipment. Over the equipment's five-year life, we record depreciation totaling $1,000 ($200 per year). The following entry records the equipment's retirement at the end of five years:

Accumulated Depreciation—Equipment	1,000	
Equipment		1,000
To record retirement of equipment.		

Note, however, that the equipment's book value reaches zero only at the end of five years. Should the equipment be retired before that date, a loss equal to the equipment's book value will be recorded.

Exchange of Plant Assets

A plant asset may be traded in for another plant asset. The seller of the new asset establishes a trade-in allowance for the used asset with the balance of the selling price due in cash. The trade-in allowance bears no particular relationship to the used asset's book value. When it is applied against a legitimate cash selling price, the allowance does represent the used asset's fair value. Sometimes, however, the suggested selling price may be higher than the actual cash selling price; in these cases, the trade-in allowance is inflated and does not indicate the used asset's fair value.

With one exception (discussed later), the new plant asset acquired in an exchange of plant assets is recorded at its cash equivalent price (that is, its fair value). Ideally, this amount is determined by using the fair value of the plant asset given up plus any cash paid. However, the fair value of the plant asset given up is not always obvious. Therefore, the new plant asset should be recorded at the fair value of the assets given up or the fair value of the asset received, whichever is more clearly evident.

When plant assets are exchanged, the book value of the asset traded in, of course, is removed from the accounts. We determine any gain or loss on the exchange transaction by comparing the fair value assigned to the new asset with the total of the used asset's book value plus any cash payment. If the new asset's fair value is larger, a gain is recorded. Should the used asset's book value plus cash paid exceed the new asset's fair value, we reflect a loss. No gain or loss is recorded if the two amounts being compared are equal.

GAIN ON EXCHANGE To illustrate an exchange of plant assets resulting in a recorded gain, assume our equipment ($1,000 cost and $100 salvage value) is traded in after two years (accumulated depreciation, $360) on new equipment that has a $1,200 cash price. The old equipment receives a $700 trade-in allowance, so a $500 cash payment is required. The following entry records the exchange:

Equipment (New)	1,200	
Accumulated Depreciation—Equipment	360	
Equipment (Old)		1,000
Cash		500
Gain on Exchange of Plant Assets		60
To record trade of equipment.		

The $60 gain on the transaction is the excess of the new equipment's fair value ($1,200) over the old equipment's book value ($640) plus cash paid ($500).

LOSS ON EXCHANGE Now assume the old equipment exchanged in the preceding example receives a $400 trade-in allowance. With this allowance, an $800 cash payment is required. The journal entry for this exchange of plant assets shows a loss on the exchange, as follows:

Equipment (New)	1,200	
Accumulated Depreciation—Equipment	360	
Loss on Exchange of Plant Assets	240	
Equipment (Old)		1,000
Cash		800
To record trade of equipment.		

The loss on the transaction is the excess of the old equipment's book value ($640) plus cash paid ($800) over the new equipment's fair value ($1,200).

EXCEPTION: NO GAIN RECORDED Accounting guidelines conclude that some exchanges of plant assets should not result in an immediate gain to the company acquiring the new asset. Instead, the new asset is recorded at an amount equal to the sum of the book value of the asset traded in plus any cash paid. *An exchange receiving this treatment is an exchange of similar productive assets where the new asset is used in the same line of business as the old asset and the cash paid is less than 25% of the total fair value exchanged.*[1] A gain in such an exchange is not recognized because the exchange transaction does not complete the earning process for gains. In essence, the firm acquires an asset performing the same function as the asset given up. Further, there is not enough cash involved to warrant recording the new asset at its fair value.

To illustrate, assume the equipment being exchanged in our previous example is similar equipment and that the new equipment will be used in the same line of business as the old equipment. Assume further that the trade-in allowance for the old equipment is $960 (there is a very strong market for this equipment). The $240 required cash payment is 20% of the total fair value exchanged ($240/$1,200 = 20%). The following journal entry records this exchange:

Equipment (New)	880	
Accumulated Depreciation—Equipment	360	
Equipment (Old)		1,000
Cash		240
To record trade of equipment.		

The new equipment is recorded at $880—the sum of the $640 book value of the old equipment and the $240 cash payment. This treatment departs from the general rule that newly acquired plant assets are recorded at their implied cash cost (fair value). The new equipment has a cash price of $1,200, but it is recorded at $880. Essentially, its book value has been reduced by the $320 gain that is not recognized.

Accounting guidelines only require that a gain not be recognized in the situation described. If a loss had been present in the preceding illustration where similar productive assets in the same line of business are exchanged, the loss would be recorded.

---

[1] *Opinions of the Accounting Principles Board, No. 29*, "Accounting for Nonmonetary Transactions" (New York: American Institute of Certified Public Accountants, 1973) and *EITF Abstracts, A Summary of Proceedings of the FASB Emerging Issues Task Force*, Issue No. 86-29, "Nonmonetary Transactions: Magnitude of Boot and the Exceptions to the Use of Fair Value," (Norwalk, CT: Financial Accounting Standards Board, 1991). The Accounting Principles Board, in 1973, concluded that gains should not be recorded when similar productive assets are exchanged. The FASB's Emerging Issues Task Force, at its December 4, 1986, meeting, reached a consensus that a significant amount of cash converts an exchange of similar productive assets that would otherwise be accounted for at recorded amounts into a monetary transaction where both parties should record the exchange at fair value. At the same meeting, consensus was reached that a "same line of business" test be applied to exchanges of similar productive assets. If the new asset is not used in the same line of business as the asset given up, the new asset is recorded at fair value. (*Statement on Auditing Standards No. 69*, "The Meaning of 'Present Fairly in Conformity with Generally Accepted Accounting Principles' in the Independent Auditor's Report," in *Journal of Accountancy*, March 1992, pp. 108–111, confirms that consensus positions of the Emerging Issues Task Force constitute generally accepted accounting principles.)

TRADE-IN AND TAX REGULATIONS

The Internal Revenue Code specifies that any gains or losses on trade-in transactions involving similar assets are not reported in the year of exchange. This treatment differs from the accounting guidelines just discussed. Accounting guidelines recognize all losses and most gains on trade-in transactions involving similiar plant assets (only gains on similar assets used in the same line of business with cash less than 25% of the total fair value exchanged are not recognized).

Under income tax guidelines, the new asset acquired when similar plant assets are exchanged is recorded at the book value of the asset given up plus any cash paid. To illustrate, assume the situation presented earlier showing a loss exchange (new asset's selling price, $1,200; used asset's cost, $1,000; accumulated depreciation, $360; trade-in allowance, $400; and cash payment, $800). The journal entry under income tax guidelines is as follows:

Equipment (New) ($1,200 + $240 loss)	1,440	
Accumulated Depreciation—Equipment	360	
Equipment (Old)		1,000
Cash		800
To record trade of equipment.		

This treatment does not recognize the loss in the year of exchange but increases the depreciation available in future years. While this treatment is not in accord with generally accepted accounting principles, some firms may follow the income tax method when losses and gains are immaterial to avoid keeping a separate record for income tax purposes.

Summary of Plant Asset Disposals

Exhibit 11-1 summarizes our discussion of accounting for plant asset disposals following generally accepted accounting principles. The exhibit shows the different events involving a disposal of plant assets and the various situations leading to the recording of a gain, a loss, or no gain or loss on the disposal. Note that a gain cannot be recorded on the retirement (that is, scrapping) of a plant asset nor on the exchange of similar plant assets in the same line of business with cash paid less than 25% of the total fair value exchanged.

CONTROL OF PLANT ASSETS

OBJECTIVE 2 IDENTIFY *the records used to provide control over plant assets.*

Firms with a large number of plant assets use a system of control accounts and subsidiary ledgers to account for and manage these assets. The general ledger becomes unwieldy if it contains a separate account for each plant asset. Instead, plant assets are divided into functional groups and only the control accounts (asset and accumulated depreciation accounts) for each functional group appear in the general ledger. The plant asset functional groupings vary somewhat from company to company, but typical control accounts include Land Improvements, Buildings, Furniture and Fixtures, Factory Equipment, and Delivery Equipment.

A subsidiary ledger supports each plant asset control account in the general ledger. The subsidiary ledger contains a detailed record for each specific asset in the control group. The subsidiary ledger may be maintained by a manual or a computerized system. Regardless of the record's form, the following basic data are usually incorporated:

Description
Assigned serial number and accounting classification
Date purchased
Assigned physical location
Insurance coverage
Person accountable
Original cost
Major modifications and repairs
Depreciation method and data
Disposition data (date, price, remarks)

EXHIBIT 11—1	PLANT ASSET DISPOSALS			

	Effect on Current Period's Net Income Determination		
Event	**Gain**	**Loss**	**No Gain or Loss**
1. Sale of plant assets			
Sales proceeds > Book value of asset sold	X		
Sales proceeds < Book value of asset sold		X	
Sales proceeds = Book value of asset sold			X
2. Destruction or theft of plant assets			
Insurance settlement > Book value of asset destroyed/stolen	X		
Insurance settlement* < Book value of asset destroyed/stolen		X	
Insurance settlement = Book value of asset destroyed/stolen			X
3. Retirement of plant assets			
Book value of retired asset > 0		X	
Book value of retired asset = 0			X
4. Exchange of plant assets			
a. Exchange of similar plant assets in the same line of business; cash paid is less than 25% of total fair value exchanged			
Fair value of new asset > Book value of old asset + cash payment			X[†]
Fair value of new asset < Book value of old asset + cash payment		X	
Fair value of new asset = Book value of old asset + cash payment			X
b. All other plant asset exchanges			
Fair value of new asset > Book value of old asset + cash payment	X		
Fair value of new asset < Book value of old asset + cash payment		X	
Fair value of new asset = Book value of old asset + cash payment			X

* Insurance settlement is zero for uninsured assets.
† New asset is recorded at amount equal to book value of old asset + cash payment.

Exhibit 11-2 presents the relationship between control accounts for a plant asset functional group (Delivery Equipment) and the related subsidiary ledger. Each purchase and sale of delivery equipment is recorded in the control account and on a separate detailed record in the subsidiary ledger. In this illustration, two delivery vans were purchased in 1993 and they represent the firm's total delivery equipment. Annual depreciation for the individual vans is noted on the subsidiary ledger records and then totaled to get the amount for the general journal entry to record the delivery equipment's annual depreciation. At the end of the accounting period, the control account balances should equal the sum of the balances of the individual assets in the subsidiary ledger (as shown in Exhibit 11-2). The detailed information in the subsidiary ledger is particularly helpful in determining (1) periodic depreciation and (2) a plant asset's book value at time of disposal.

Most firms assign a specific serial number to each plant asset when it is purchased. This is usually done by small decals, stampings, or etchings that are not easily removed or altered. Periodically, the existence and condition of these assets should be verified by a physical count.

NATURAL RESOURCES

Natural resources are assets occurring in a natural state, such as timber, petroleum, natural gas, coal, and other mineral deposits mined by the extractive industries. These resources are also known as **wasting assets.** As with plant assets, natural resources

EXHIBIT 11—2	PLANT ASSET CONTROL ACCOUNTS AND SUBSIDIARY LEDGER

GENERAL LEDGER CONTROL ACCOUNTS

DELIVERY EQUIPMENT   ACCOUNT NO. 164

Date		Description	Post. Ref.	Debit	Credit	Balance
1993						
Jan.	1		J1	9,000		9,000
July	1		J8	10,400		19,400

ACCUMULATED DEPRECIATION—DELIVERY EQUIPMENT   ACCOUNT NO. 165

Date		Description	Post. Ref.	Debit	Credit	Balance
1993						
Dec.	31		J14		2,640	2,640

DELIVERY EQUIPMENT SUBSIDIARY LEDGER

Item Ford Delivery Van, Blue   **Account No.** 164
Purchased From Mann Ford, Madison   **Serial No.** V280
Person Responsible Store 1 Manager   **Insurance** Allgroup, #8750
Service Life 5 years   **Location** Store 1
Depreciation: **Salvage Value** $600
  Method Straight line   **Per Year** $1,680   **Per Month** $140

Date		Descrip.	Asset			Accumulated Depreciation		
			Dr.	Cr.	Balance	Dr.	Cr.	Balance
1993								
Jan.	1		9,000		9,000			
Dec.	31						1,680	1,680

Item Ford Delivery Van, Tan   **Account No.** 164
Purchased From Mann Ford, Madison   **Serial No.** V281
Person Responsible Store 2 Manager   **Insurance** Allgroup, #8750
Service Life 5 years   **Location** Store 2
Depreciation: **Salvage Value** $800
  Method Straight line   **Per Year** $1,920   **Per Month** $160

Date		Descrip.	Asset			Accumulated Depreciation		
			Dr.	Cr.	Balance	Dr.	Cr.	Balance
1993								
July	1		10,400		10,400			
Dec.	31						960	960

OBJECTIVE ③ DISCUSS *the nature of and the accounting for natural resources.*

are initially accounted for at their cost. When known deposits are purchased, the initial measurement is quite simple. When the natural resource is discovered after extensive exploration, however, determining its initial cost is more difficult. Because not all exploration activities are successful, we must determine which activities were necessary to discover the resource. Expenditures for these activities are capitalized as the cost of the resource, and the remaining amounts are expensed. The cost of developing the site so the natural resource may be extracted is another component of initial cost. Expenditures to remove layers of soil and clay, build access roads, and construct mine entrances illustrate these development costs.

Depletion

The term **depletion** refers to the allocation of the cost of natural resources to the units extracted from the ground or, in the case of timberland, the board feet of timber cut. Accounting for the depletion of natural resources is comparable to units-of-production depreciation of plant assets. The average depletion cost per unit of natural resource is computed as follows:

$$\text{Depletion per Unit} = \frac{\text{Cost of Natural Resource} - \text{Residual Value}}{\text{Estimated Total Units of Resource}}$$

The unit measure used depends on the natural resource; the unit may be barrels, tons, board feet, cubic feet, or some other unit appropriate for the resource. Residual value is the expected net recovery (sales proceeds − restoration costs) when the property is eventually sold. Once depletion per unit is computed, periodic depletion is determined as follows:

$$\text{Periodic Depletion} = \text{Depletion per Unit} \times \text{Units Extracted in Current Period}$$

For example, assume that a company acquires for $520,000 a parcel of land whose major commercial value is a soft coal mine that contains an estimated 800,000 tons of extractable coal. Development costs of $100,000 are incurred to prepare the site for mining coal. The property's estimated residual value is $20,000 ($115,000 expected sales value − $95,000 estimated costs to recondition the land). The coal deposit's initial cost is $620,000 ($520,000 acquisition cost + $100,000 development costs). We calculate the depletion per ton of mined coal as follows:

$$\frac{\$620,000 - \$20,000}{800,000 \text{ tons}} = \$0.75 \text{ per ton}$$

If, during the first period, 60,000 tons are extracted, that period's depletion charge would be 60,000 × $0.75 = $45,000. We would make the following entry:

Depletion of Coal Deposit	45,000	
Accumulated Depletion—Coal Deposit		45,000
To record depletion of coal deposit.		

In the balance sheet, Accumulated Depletion is a contra account deducted from the cost of the natural resource as follows:

Coal Deposit (Original cost)	$620,000
Less: Accumulated Depletion	45,000
Coal Deposit (Book value)	$575,000

This treatment is similar to handling accumulated depreciation accounts.

Depreciation of On-site Equipment

The extraction of many natural resources requires the construction of *on-site* equipment, such as drilling and pumping devices, crushing equipment, and conveyor systems. Often in remote places, this equipment may be abandoned when the natural resource is exhausted. If the useful life of these assets expires before the resources are exhausted, ordinary depreciation techniques are appropriate. When the reverse is true—natural resources are exhausted, and the asset is abandoned before the end of its physical life—depreciation should be based on the length of the extraction period. Alternatively, we could use the units-of-production approach based on the estimated total resource to be extracted.

For example, assume coal mining equipment was acquired at a cost of $210,000 in our preceding example. The equipment has an estimated $10,000 salvage value after the coal is mined. If the units-of-production method were used, depreciation per ton for the first year would be

$$\frac{\$210,000 - \$10,000}{800,000 \text{ tons}} = \$0.25 \text{ per ton}$$

The first year's depreciation, when 60,000 tons are mined, is 60,000 × $0.25 = $15,000. The following entry would be made:

Depreciation of Mining Equipment	15,000	
Accumulated Depreciation—Mining Equipment		15,000
To record depreciation of mining equipment.		

Financial Statement Reporting of Depletion Charge

The periodic depletion charge and the depreciation charge on equipment used to extract and process a natural resource are costs incurred to get an inventory of the natural resource. These costs are added to any other extracting and processing costs (and any beginning inventory) to determine the cost of the resource available for sale during the period. The cost of the resource available for sale is allocated in part to the balance sheet as ending inventory (based on units on hand at year-end) and in part to the income statement as the cost of resource sold during the year (based on units sold during the year).

To illustrate using our coal mining example, assume that in the first year, the firm incurred $66,000 of extracting and processing costs in addition to the $45,000 depletion charge and the $15,000 depreciation of mining equipment. The company sold 40,000 of the 60,000 tons of coal that were mined. The following schedule shows the derivation of the ending inventory and cost of coal sold amounts.

Beginning inventory	$ –0–
Depletion of coal deposit	45,000
Depreciation of mining equipment	15,000
Other extracting and processing costs	66,000
Cost of coal available for sale (60,000 tons)	$126,000/60,000 = $2.10 per ton
Less: Ending inventory of coal (20,000 tons × $2.10)	42,000
Cost of coal sold (40,000 tons × $2.10)	$ 84,000

The company will show a $42,000 inventory of coal in its year-end balance sheet. Its income statement will deduct $84,000 from sales revenue as the cost of coal sold during the year.

Revision of Depletion and Depreciation

Estimating accurately the recoverable units of a natural resource is difficult. Imagine trying to estimate the barrels of oil or the ounces of silver located underground. After extracting activities begin, better information may result in revisions of such estimates. When an estimate of recoverable units changes, a revised depletion per unit is computed. The revised depletion per unit becomes effective in the period the estimate of recoverable units changes—depletion amounts computed in prior periods are not changed. The revised depletion per unit is computed as follows:

$$\text{Revised Depletion per Unit} = \frac{\text{Book Value of Natural Resource} - \text{Residual Value}}{\text{Revised Estimate of Remaining Units of Resource}}$$

To illustrate, assume that at the beginning of the second year of our coal mining example, the estimated total amount of recoverable coal is changed to 560,000 tons. Because 60,000 tons have already been mined, an estimated 500,000 tons remain underground. The coal deposit's book value at the start of the second year is $575,000 (Cost − Accumulated Depletion). Therefore, the revised depletion per ton is $1.11, determined as follows:

$$\frac{\$575,000 - \$20,000}{500,000 \text{ tons}} = \$1.11 \text{ per ton}$$

Under the units-of-production method, depreciation per unit must be revised if the estimate of extractable resource units changes. The process is similar to the depletion per unit revision. We compute the revised depreciation per unit by dividing the asset's book value (less any salvage value) by the revised remaining resource units. For example, at the beginning of the second year, the coal mining equipment's book value is $195,000 ($210,000 cost − $15,000 accumulated depreciation). If the coal remaining underground is now estimated at 500,000 tons, then depreciation per ton, beginning in the second year, is $0.37, computed as follows:

$$\frac{\$195,000 - \$10,000}{500,000 \text{ tons}} = \$0.37 \text{ per ton}$$

Depletion for Tax Purposes

The Internal Revenue Code permits a deduction for the depletion of natural resources sold when a firm computes its income tax liability. The depletion deduction may be based on the resource's cost, using the procedures illustrated. Companies mining certain resources, however, may use **percentage depletion** if it gives a larger deduction. Under percentage depletion, the depletion deduction is a specified percentage of the gross revenue from mining activities, with certain limitations. The depletion percentages range from 5% to 22%, depending on the natural resource. Percentage depletion is not limited by the resource's cost and may, over a period of years, result in income tax depletion deductions that exceed total cost. *Percentage depletion is a special income tax feature; it is not permitted under generally accepted accounting principles for financial reporting purposes.*

Supplemental Disclosures of Resource Reserves

Many companies in the extractive industries—especially oil- and gas-producing companies—are holding for future operations large discovered and proven reserve fields. Most often these reserves are carried at historical cost figures that may represent only a small fraction of their current values. In such cases, the financial statements may contain supplemental disclosures about reserve quantities and other data useful in estimating reserve values.[2]

INTANGIBLE ASSETS

OBJECTIVE 4 DISCUSS *the nature of and the accounting for intangible assets.*

In accounting, **intangible assets** include certain resources that benefit an enterprise's operations but lack physical substance. Several intangible assets are exclusive rights or privileges obtained from a governmental unit or by legal contract—such as patents, copyrights, franchises, trademarks, and leaseholds. Other intangible assets (1) arise from the creation of a business enterprise—namely, organization costs—or (2) reflect a firm's ability to generate above-normal earnings—that is, goodwill.

The term *intangible asset* is not used with precision in accounting literature. By convention, only certain assets are included in the intangible category. Some resources that lack physical substance—such as prepaid insurance, receivables, and investments—are not classified as intangible assets. Because intangible assets lack physical characteristics, the related accounting procedures may be more subjective and arbitrary than for tangible assets.

Measurement of Intangible Assets

A firm should record intangible assets acquired from outside entities initially at their cost. Similarly, some intangible assets created internally by a firm are measured at their cost. For example, the costs of forming a business are charged to an Organization Costs account, and the costs to secure a trademark—such as attorney's fees, registration fees, and design costs—are charged to a Trademarks account.

---

[2] Specific disclosure requirements have been established for oil- and gas-producing companies. For details, see *Statement of Financial Accounting Standards No. 69*, "Disclosures about Oil and Gas Producing Activities" (Stamford, CT: Financial Accounting Standards Board, 1982).

Most expenditures related to internally created intangible assets are expensed rather than capitalized. Because these intangibles are not acquired from outside entities, accountants lack an objective measure for the asset account. The accountant responds to uncertainty about an intangible asset's existence, or its proper measure, by expensing the related amounts. This situation is particularly evident in accounting for research and development costs.

RESEARCH AND DEVELOPMENT COSTS

American industry annually spends billions of dollars searching for new knowledge and translating this knowledge into new or significantly improved products or processes. These **research and development costs** are important, but usually a significant uncertainty exists about the future benefits of specific research and development efforts. Only a small portion of research and development projects culminates in a new product or process, and even then commercial success is not certain. The market failure rate is high for new products. Uncertain future benefits of research and development costs influenced the Financial Accounting Standards Board's development of the following accounting guideline: *All research and development costs related to a firm's products and its production processes must be expensed when incurred.*[3]

The preceding guideline does not apply to a firm's selling and administrative activities or to the unique exploration and development efforts of firms in the extractive industries. Also, legal costs of obtaining or defending a patent for a new product or process may be capitalized.

COMPUTER SOFTWARE

The widespread use of computers has spawned an entire industry of companies that produce computer software for sale or lease. The industry's unique product and the rapidly changing computer technology caused the Financial Accounting Standards Board to consider specifically how to account for the costs of developing and producing computer software for sale or lease. The board's conclusions illustrate the application of measurement guidelines relating to research and development costs and intangible assets to a particular industry. It assigns the various development and production costs to three different categories, as follows:[4]

1. **Expensed as research and development costs.** All costs incurred to establish the software's technological feasibility are expensed as research and development costs. This covers all costs of those activities—such as planning, designing, coding, and testing—necessary to establish that the software can be produced to achieve the design specifications.

2. **Capitalized as an intangible asset.** After technological feasibility has been established, the rest of the costs incurred to produce the product masters are capitalized as **computer software production costs,** an intangible asset. Product masters are the completed versions of the software, documentation, and training materials that are then copied to produce the items for sale or lease.

3. **Capitalized as inventory.** The costs incurred to duplicate and physically package the computer software, documentation, and training materials are capitalized in the company's inventory account.

Computer software purchased by a company to use in its selling or administrative activities may be capitalized when it clearly benefits future periods. For example, the purchase cost of a computer software package designed to serve a firm's general management information needs should be capitalized if it will be used several years. Similarly, if a firm develops its own software for internal selling or administrative uses, the development costs may be capitalized when the software will be useful for several

---

[3] *Statement of Financial Accounting Standards No. 2,* "Accounting for Research and Development Costs" (Stamford, CT: Financial Accounting Standards Board, 1974).

[4] *Statement of Financial Accounting Standards No. 86,* "Accounting for the Costs of Computer Software to Be Sold, Leased, or Otherwise Marketed" (Stamford, CT: Financial Accounting Standards Board, 1985).

periods. Many firms, however, follow a policy of expensing immediately all costs of developing software for internal use.

Amortization of Intangibles

The **amortization** of an intangible asset is the periodic write-off to expense of the asset's cost over the term of its expected useful life. Because salvage values are ordinarily not involved, amortization typically entails (1) determining the asset's cost, (2) estimating the period over which it benefits the firm, and (3) allocating the cost in equal amounts to each accounting period involved. *Accounting principles modify this general approach by specifying that the period of amortization for intangibles should not exceed 40 years.*[5] As a result, intangibles are treated as if they have a limited life—even though some, such as trademarks, may legally have indefinite lives. Straight-line amortization must be used for intangible assets unless another method is shown to be more appropriate.[6]

The amortization entry debits the appropriate amortization expense account. The entry's credit normally goes directly to the intangible asset account. An accumulated amortization account could be used for the credit, but generally there is no particular benefit to financial statement users from accumulating amortization in a separate contra asset account. In our examples, we will credit the asset account directly for its periodic amortization.

Intangible assets originally deemed to have specific useful lives should be reviewed periodically to determine if their value or their economic lives have decreased. If so, an immediate write-off or a plan of periodic amortization at an increased rate is appropriate.

Patents

A **patent** is an exclusive privilege, granted to an inventor by the federal government for a period of 17 years. The patent gives the patent holder the right to exclude others from making, using, or selling the invention. Patent laws were originated to encourage inventors by protecting them from imitators who might usurp the invention for commercial gain. Just what a patentable idea is has become quite complex in the modern realm of technical knowledge. Consequently, long periods of patent "searching" and, frequently, successful defense of infringement suits may precede the validation of a patent. Even though patents have a legal life of 17 years, changes in technology or consumer tastes may shorten their economic life. Because of their uncertain value, patents should probably be accounted for conservatively. When patents are purchased some time after having been granted, the buyer enjoys the privilege at most for only the remaining legal life.

To illustrate the accounting for patents, assume that, early in January, a company pays $34,000 legal costs to obtain a patent on a new product. The journal entry is

Patents	34,000	
Cash		34,000
To record legal costs of acquiring patent.		

The company expects the patent to provide benefits for 17 years. The following entry records the first year's straight-line amortization:

Amortization Expense—Patents	2,000	
Patents		2,000
To record patent amortization.		

Because an accumulated amortization account is not used, the asset account balance reflects the asset's book value. The balance sheet presentation at year-end would be

Patents (cost less amortization to date)	$32,000

[5] *Opinions of the Accounting Principles Board, No. 17*, "Accounting for Intangible Assets" (New York: American Institute of Certified Public Accountants, 1970).

[6] Annual amortization of computer software production costs, however, is to be the greater of (1) the straight-line amount or (2) an amount computed using the ratio of the current revenue for the software product to the total current and estimated future revenue for the product.

Copyrights

A **copyright** protects its owner against the unauthorized reproduction of a specific written work or artwork. A copyright lasts for the life of the author plus 50 years. The purchase price of valuable copyrights can be substantial, and proper measurement and amortization are necessary for valid income determination. But even with the related legal fees, the cost of most copyrights is seldom sufficiently material to present accounting problems.

A copyright's legal life exceeds the 40-year maximum amortization period allowed for intangibles. However, copyright costs are generally amortized over periods much shorter than 40 years. Copyright costs should be amortized over the period that the copyrighted work produces revenue—for a proper matching of expenses with revenues—which may be only a few years.

Franchises

Franchises most often involve exclusive rights to operate or sell a specific brand of products in a given geographical area. Franchises may be for definite or indefinite periods. Although many franchises are agreements between two private firms, various governmental units award franchises for public utility operations within their legal jurisdictions. The right to operate a KENTUCKY FRIED CHICKEN restaurant or to sell MIDAS MUFFLERS in a specific area illustrates franchise agreements in the private sector.

Some franchise agreements require a substantial initial payment by the party acquiring the franchise. This amount should be debited to the intangible asset account Franchise and amortized on a straight-line basis over the franchise period or 40 years, whichever is shorter.

Trademarks and Trade Names

Trademarks and **trade names** represent the exclusive and continuing right to use certain terms, names, or symbols, usually to identify a brand or family of products. An original trademark or trade name can be registered with the federal government at nominal cost. A company may spend considerable time and money to determine an appropriate name or symbol for a product. Also, the purchase of well-known, and thus valuable, trademarks or trade names may involve substantial amounts of funds. When the cost of a trademark or trade name is material, the amount is debited to an appropriate intangible asset account—Trademarks, for example—and amortized over the period of expected benefit (not exceeding 40 years).

Organization Costs

Expenditures incurred in launching a business (usually a corporation) are called **organization costs.** These expenditures, which may include attorney's fees, fees paid to the state, and other costs related to preparation for operations, are debited to the intangible asset account Organization Costs. Theoretically, these expenditures benefit the firm throughout its operating life, but all intangibles must be amortized over 40 years or less. Most firms amortize organization costs over a 5- to 10-year period. Income tax guidelines reinforce this practice by permitting the amortization of organization costs for tax purposes over a period of at least five years.

Goodwill

Goodwill is the value derived from a firm's ability to earn more than a normal rate of return on the fair market value of its specific, identifiable net assets. A firm's *net assets* are its assets minus its liabilities. The measurement of goodwill is complex, because it can stem from any factor that can make income rates high relative to investment. Examples of such factors include exceptional customer relations, advantageous location, operating efficiency, superior personnel relations, favorable financial sources, and even monopolistic position. Furthermore, goodwill cannot be severed from a firm and sold separately. Because measuring goodwill is difficult, a firm records it in the accounts only when another firm is purchased and the amount paid to acquire it exceeds the recognized fair market value of the identifiable net assets involved. Determining the amount of goodwill often requires complex negotiations, but the agreed-on amount is almost always based on the anticipated above-normal earnings.

When Cosmair Inc.'s L'Oreal division decided to market green and purple hair dye a couple of years ago, it wanted an equally colorful brand name. What it hoped to do was create a playful, punk image for the product. So, after much brainstorming by professional name consultants and its own marketing executives, the company picked the offbeat name Zazu. ■ The name, alas, wasn't quite unusual enough. In September, a Hinsdale, Ill., hair-styling salon called Zazu Designs won a trademark-infringement suit against L'Oreal and was awarded damages of

$2.1 million as well as rights to the disputed name for its own line of shampoos. Cosmair executives claim that despite an investigation of existing trademarks, they were caught unaware of the shampoos.

PLAYING FOR HIGH STAKES

So it goes these days in the consumer-product name game, which increasingly is turning into a crap shoot. Despite spending hundreds of thousands of dollars to try to come up with original names, marketers say they are running into far more trademark conflicts. The main problem is that the number of available—and appealing—names keeps shrinking. Last year, the U.S. Patent and Trademark Office says, about 47,500 new trademarks were registered—more than triple the number in 1980.

"It's a real challenge to find a clean name without any conflicts," says Mel Owen, a trademark attorney in San Francisco. "The shortage is especially acute for descriptive words that are most effective in selling a product. The safe names are made-up, meaningless words."

Some marketers are managing to sidestep trademark litigation, but it's costing them dearly. Almost routinely these days, they are negotiating six-figure settlements to acquire the rights to previously registered trademarks. "Little-known brand names suddenly become very valuable when companies find out we may be interested in the same names," says John Bissell, senior vice president for special products at Stroh Brewery Co. Stroh had to pay other companies for the rights to brand names for both of its new nonalcoholic beverages—Sundance and High Five—but won't disclose how much.

Revlon, Inc. says it paid a "substantial amount" this year to avoid any trouble over its new Trouble fragrance for women. The company considers the name perfect for its strategy of marketing an image of romantic adventure and fantasy. But it quickly found that Mennen Co. already was selling a Trouble cologne for men in Central America. Revlon felt compelled to buy rights to the name, allowing Mennen to sell its cologne in only some countries. "What good is a successful perfume if we can't go worldwide with it?" says Arne Zimmerman, president of Revlon's classic cosmetics and fragrances group.

In the U.S., the difficulty of coming up with an appealing brand name may ease a bit, thanks to a trademark law passed by Congress last month. The new law allows a company to register its trademark for 10 years, compared with 20 years previously. To renew its registration of the trademark, the company has to prove it is using the name and not just holding it in reserve.

"The pool of available trademarks will be greater since a lot of dead wood will be cleared from the rolls," says Dolores Hanna, trademark attorney for Kraft and chairwoman of a commission that recommended trademark-law changes. "We can't afford to have good trademarks tied up that aren't being used actively."

Aware of the increasing potential for conflict, many companies are taking a cautious approach. They usually search trademark-registration files, brand-name directories, and telephone books to see if they have come up with an original name. Along the way, they often wind up discarding many of their favorite proposals.

Because of the conflicts it found, for instance, Delano Goldman & Young Inc., a New York name-development firm, rejected its top choices—Spirit, Phantom, Invader, Raider, Pacesetter and Westwinds—for two Suzuki motorcycles. Says Chairman Frank Delano: "We would have been walking a legal mine field if we had tried to use any of those names."

OUT OF THE WOODWORK

Even the most thorough searches of trademark registrations and brand-name directories won't turn up every potential conflict. "Name searches are a game of Russian roulette," says Richard Berman, trademark attorney for General Mills Inc. "There isn't mandatory registration of trademarks, so companies can come out of the woodwork after you market your product and claim trademark infringement."

Despite the increasing conflicts over trademarks, there still are those rare occasions when a company hits on a catchy name that nobody else has claimed. The microwave-oven boom, for example, has opened up all sorts of possibilities. General Mills dreamed up the name MicroRave for its microwave cake mixes and hasn't encountered a single conflict.

Accountants expense immediately all costs associated with the internal development or maintenance of goodwill. This means many firms that have created goodwill through their operations do not reflect it in the accounts because it was not purchased.

To illustrate the concept of goodwill, assume that Carley Company is for sale. We know the following information about the company and the industry in which it operates:

Fair market value of Carley Company's identifiable net assets	$2,000,000
Normal rate of return on net assets for industry	× 11%
Normal earnings on $2,000,000 of identifiable net assets	$ 220,000
Average annual earnings for Carley Company (Past four years)	286,000
Above-average earnings for Carley Company	$ 66,000

Carley's $66,000 of superior earnings suggests the presence of an asset—not specifically identifiable—that helps generate these excess earnings. That asset is goodwill—a combination of factors unique to Carley Company that generates the above-average rate of return on its identifiable net assets. The price paid for Carley will exceed $2,000,000 because the goodwill is also being purchased.

How much should be paid for goodwill? Although above-average earnings in the past are evidence of goodwill, the purchaser is interested in future earnings performance. Goodwill estimates are subject to uncertainty about how long the superior earnings may be sustained. A purchaser may use several methods to estimate a goodwill amount. We illustrate the following two methods:

1. Goodwill may be estimated by capitalizing the superior earnings at the normal rate of return. *Capitalizing earnings* here means dividing earnings by the rate of return; this computation for Carley Company is $66,000/0.11 = $600,000. The $600,000 represents the dollar investment that, at an 11% rate of return, will earn $66,000 each year. However, this approach implies that *every* future year will generate the $66,000 excess earnings—a tenuous assumption in a competitive environment. Sometimes excess earnings are capitalized at an above-normal rate of return in recognition of the greater risk of continued superior earnings. The higher the capitalization rate used, the lower the goodwill estimate.

2. Goodwill may be estimated as some multiple of the superior earnings. Carley's purchaser, for example, may pay five times the above-average earnings for goodwill, or 5 × $66,000 = $330,000.

Of course, the seller also estimates goodwill in determining an overall value for the firm. When the buyer and seller agree on the firm's total purchase price, we can establish the portion assignable to goodwill. The difference between the total purchase price and the fair value of the specific, identifiable net assets is the goodwill measure. For example, if Carley Company is purchased for $2,400,000, $2,000,000 is assigned to the identifiable net assets and $400,000 is assigned to goodwill.

Shown as an intangible asset in the financial statements, goodwill must be amortized over 40 years or less.

LEASES

OBJECTIVE 5 IDENTIFY *and* DISTINGUISH *operating and capital leases.*

A firm may rent property for a specified period under a contract called a **lease.** The company acquiring the right to use the property is the **lessee;** the owner of the property is the **lessor.** The rights transferred to the lessee are called a **leasehold.** Examples of leased assets are land, buildings, trucks, factory machinery, office equipment, and automobiles. A lessee's accounting treatment depends on whether a lease is an operating lease or a capital lease.

Operating Lease

The typical rental agreement illustrates an **operating lease:** the lessee pays for the use of an asset for a limited period, and the lessor retains the usual risks and rewards of owning the property. The lessee usually charges each lease payment to rent expense. Sometimes leases extending over long periods require advance payments from the lessee. The lessee debits these payments to a *Leasehold* account, then allocates the amount to rent expense over the period covered by the advance payment. For example, assume Graphic Company makes an $18,000 advance payment for the final year's rent on a 10-year lease of office space. The following entry records the advance payment:

Leasehold	18,000	
Cash		18,000
To record advance lease payment.		

The leasehold amount is an intangible asset. In this illustration, the advance payment relates specifically to Year 10, so the $18,000 is classified as an intangible asset for nine years. In Year 10, the $18,000 will be expensed.

Expenditures made by a lessee to alter or improve leased property are called **leasehold improvements.** For example, a company may construct a building on leased land or make improvements to a leased building. The improvements or alterations become part of the leased property and revert to the lessor at the end of the lease. Under an operating lease, the cost of leasehold improvements is capitalized to a *Leasehold Improvements* account and then amortized over the life of the lease or the life of the improvements, whichever is shorter. The classification of leasehold improvements varies; some businesses classify them as intangible assets, whereas others include them in the property, plant, and equipment section of the balance sheet.

To illustrate, assume Graphic Company improves the office space leased for 10 years by adding new interior walls and built-in bookshelves. The improvements were made at the start of the lease, cost $40,000, and have an estimated life of 40 years. Graphic Company records the expenditures for the improvements as follows:

Leasehold Improvements	40,000	
Cash		40,000
To record office improvements.		

Because Graphic Company benefits from these leasehold improvements only for the 10-year lease period, it should amortize the improvements over 10 years. The following entry is made in each of the 10 years:

Amortization Expense—Leasehold Improvements	4,000	
Leasehold Improvements		4,000
To record amortization of leasehold improvements.		

Capital Lease

A **capital lease** transfers to the lessee substantially all of the benefits and risks related to the ownership of the property. A lease meeting at least one of the following criteria is a capital lease.[7]

1. The lease transfers ownership of the property to the lessee by the end of the lease term.
2. The lease contains a bargain purchase option.
3. The lease term is at least 75% of the estimated economic life of the leased property.
4. The present value of the lease payments[8] is at least 90% of the fair value of the leased property.

The economic effect of a capital lease is similar to that of an installment purchase. The lessee accounts for a capital lease by recording the leased property as an asset and establishing a liability for the lease obligation. The present value of the future lease payments determines the dollar amount of the entry. For example, assume Prescott Company leases equipment under a capital lease for 10 years at

---

[7] *Statement of Financial Accounting Standards No. 13,* "Accounting for Leases" (Stamford, CT: Financial Accounting Standards Board, 1976).

[8] Present values are discussed in Appendix D.

$40,000 per year, and that the proper initial valuation of this lease for accounting purposes is $226,000. Prescott Company records the capital lease as follows:

Leased Equipment	226,000	
Lease Obligation		226,000
To record 10-year capital lease.		

The leased equipment is depreciated over the period it benefits the lessee and appears among the firm's plant assets in the balance sheet. Part of each lease payment made by the lessee is charged to interest expense, and the remainder reduces the lease obligation.

Lessees usually prefer to have their leases classified as operating leases rather than capital leases because this classification avoids showing a lease obligation among the balance sheet liabilities. Having fewer balance sheet liabilities may make it easier to borrow money from lenders. Structuring a lease so that no liability is recorded (that is, having it qualify as an operating lease) is an example of a practice known as **off-balance-sheet financing.**

We have identified the basic differences between operating and capital leases. Accounting for capital leases is quite complex. Similar complexities face lessors because they may treat some leases as sales or financing transactions rather than as typical rental agreements. These areas, which are beyond the scope of this text, are covered in intermediate accounting texts.

BALANCE SHEET PRESENTATION

OBJECTIVE **6** ILLUSTRATE *the balance sheet presentation of plant assets, natural resources, and intangible assets.*

Plant assets, natural resources, and intangible assets usually are presented in the balance sheet below the sections for current assets and investments. Exhibit 11-3 shows how these assets may appear on a balance sheet.

EXHIBIT 11—3	BALANCE SHEET PRESENTATION OF PLANT ASSETS, NATURAL RESOURCES, AND INTANGIBLE ASSETS [IN THOUSANDS OF DOLLARS]

Plant Assets		
Land		$ 800
Buildings	$4,600	
Less: Accumulated Depreciation	1,200	3,400
Fixtures	$ 90	
Less: Accumulated Depreciation	20	70
Equipment	$1,400	
Less: Accumulated Depreciation	300	1,100
Leased Equipment	$ 226	
Less: Accumulated Depreciation	81	145
Total Plant Assets		$5,515
Natural Resources		
Timberland	$ 500	
Less: Accumulated Depletion	200	$ 300
Coal Deposit	$ 900	
Less: Accumulated Depletion	150	750
Total Natural Resources		$1,050
Intangible Assets (Cost less amortization to date)		
Patents		$ 200
Goodwill		500
Organization Costs		100
Total Intangible Assets		$ 800

ANALYTICAL APPLICATION

OBJECTIVE 7 DEFINE *asset turnover and* EXPLAIN *its use.*

ASSET TURNOVER

Firms use assets to generate revenues. The asset turnover ratio measures how effectively a firm generates sales revenue from its investment in assets. The **asset turnover** ratio is computed as follows:

$$\text{Asset Turnover} = \frac{\text{Net Sales}}{\text{Average Total Assets}}$$

This ratio relates data from two financial statements. Net sales in the numerator is taken from the income statement and the average total assets in the denominator is derived from balance sheet information. We calculate the average total assets by summing the beginning of the year total assets and the year-end total assets and dividing the sum by 2.

To illustrate the computation of asset turnover, we use data from a recent year for BETHLEHEM STEEL CORPORATION, a steel manufacturer. The company reported, in millions of dollars, net sales of $5,250.9, total assets at the beginning of the year of $4,448.5, and total assets at year-end of $4,793.3. Bethlehem's asset turnover for the year was 1.14, computed as $5,250.9/[($4,448.5 + $4,793.3)/2]. In the preceding year, Bethlehem's asset turnover was 1.19 (net sales of $5,488.8 million divided by average total assets of $4,611.65 million). The higher the asset turnover is, the more effective the company is in using its assets to generate sales revenue. The decline in Bethlehem's ratio from 1.19 to 1.14 indicates that the company was somewhat less effective in the second year in using its assets to generate sales revenue.

There is considerable variation from industry to industry in the asset turnover ratio. An interpretation of the ratio, therefore, should include a comparison with recent data for the same company, or to a similar company's ratio, or to an industry average. For example, it makes more sense to compare Bethlehem's asset turnover with the asset turnover for INLAND STEEL INDUSTRIES, INC. (whose ratio of 1.40 compares with Bethlehem's 1.14), than it does to compare it with a large retailer like WAL-MART STORES, INC. (whose asset turnover was 3.55 in the year that Bethlehem's was 1.14).

KEY POINTS FOR CHAPTER OBJECTIVES

1 EXPLAIN and ILLUSTRATE the accounting for disposals of plant assets (pp. 394–398).
  - When a firm disposes of a plant asset, depreciation must be recorded on the asset up to the disposal date.
  - Gains and losses on plant asset dispositions are determined by comparing the assets' book values to the proceeds received. Gains are not recognized on exchanges of similar productive assets in the same line of business when cash paid is less than 25% of the total fair value exchanged.

2 IDENTIFY the records used to provide control over plant assets (pp. 398–399, 400).
  - A subsidiary ledger for each plant asset control account contains the detailed information about individual plant assets.

3 DISCUSS the nature of and the accounting for natural resources (pp. 399–403).
  - Natural resources are initially measured at their cost.
  - Depletion is the allocation of a natural resource's cost to the resource units as they are mined, cut, or otherwise extracted from their source.
  - The units-of-production depreciation method may be appropriate for equipment used exclusively in the mining and extracting of natural resources.

4 DISCUSS the nature of and the accounting for intangible assets (pp. 403–408).
  - Intangible assets acquired from outside entities are initially measured at their cost. Some internally created intangible assets are also measured at their cost (such as organization

costs, trademarks, and computer software production costs), but most expenditures related to internally created intangible assets are expensed rather than capitalized.

- Research and development costs related to a firm's products and its production processes are expensed as incurred.
- Amortization is the periodic write-off to expense of an intangible asset's cost over the asset's useful life or 40 years, whichever is shorter.
- Goodwill reflects a firm's ability to generate above-normal earnings. Goodwill may be shown in the accounts only when it has been purchased.

5 IDENTIFY and DISTINGUISH operating leases and capital leases (pp. 408–410).

- Under an operating lease, the lessor retains the usual risks and rewards of owning the property. The lessee records no liability at the start of the lease. Each lease payment made by the lessee is charged to rent expense (unless it is an advance payment, which is initially capitalized).
- A capital lease transfers most of the usual risks and rewards of property ownership to the lessee. At the inception of the lease, the lessee records an asset (a leased asset) and a liability (a lease obligation). The asset is depreciated over its useful life to the lessee, and the liability is reduced as the periodic lease payments are made.

6 ILLUSTRATE the balance sheet presentation of plant assets, natural resources, and intangible assets (p. 410).

- Plant assets, natural resources, and intangible assets usually appear in the balance sheet after current assets and investments.

7 ANALYTICAL APPLICATION: DEFINE *asset turnover* and EXPLAIN its use (p. 411).

- Asset turnover is computed by dividing net sales by average total assets. It measures the effectiveness of assets in generating sales revenues.

SELF-TEST QUESTIONS FOR REVIEW

(Answers follow the Solution to Demonstration Problem.)

1. On the first day of the current year, Blakely Company sold equipment for less than its book value. Which of the following is part of the journal entry to record the sale?
   a. A debit to Equipment.
   b. A credit to Accumulated Depreciation—Equipment.
   c. A credit to Gain on Sale of Plant Assets.
   d. A debit to Loss on Sale of Plant Assets.

2. Which of the following events results in the immediate recognition of a gain?
   a. An uninsured plant asset is destroyed by fire.
   b. Similar plant assets used in the same line of business are exchanged and the fair value of the asset acquired is less than the sum of the book value of the asset given up plus the cash payment.
   c. Dissimilar plant assets are exchanged and the fair value of the asset acquired exceeds the sum of the book value of the asset given up plus the cash payment.
   d. A plant asset is retired before the end of its estimated useful life.

3. Accounting for the periodic depletion of natural resources is similar to which depreciation method?
   a. Straight line.   c. Sum of the years' digits.
   b. Units of production.   d. Double declining balance.

4. Certain costs related to a firm's products and its production processes must be expensed when incurred. These costs are
   a. Research and development costs.
   b. Computer software production costs.
   c. Costs of forming the business (organization costs).
   d. Legal costs to obtain a patent for a new product.

5. The value derived from a firm's ability to earn more than a normal rate of return on its specific, identifiable net assets is called
   a. A franchise.   c. A patent.
   b. Goodwill.   d. Organization costs.

DEMONSTRATION PROBLEM FOR REVIEW

Rochelle Company has an office copier that originally cost $10,250 and that has an $800 expected salvage value at the end of an estimated seven-year useful life. Straight-line depreciation on the machine has been recorded for five years; the last depreciation entry was made at the end of the fifth year. Two months into the sixth year, Rochelle disposes of the copier.

REQUIRED

a. Prepare the journal entry to record depreciation expense to the date of disposal.
b. Prepare journal entries to record the machine's disposal in the following unrelated situations:
   1. Sale of the machine for cash at its book value.
   2. Sale of the machine for $3,000 cash.
   3. Sale of the machine for $5,000 cash.
   4. Exchange of the machine for a new office copier costing $13,000. The trade-in allowance received for the old copier is $4,200. The $8,800 balance is paid in cash. Follow generally accepted accounting principles in recording this transaction.
   5. Destruction of the machine by flood. Unfortunately, Rochelle does not carry flood insurance.

SOLUTION TO DEMONSTRATION PROBLEM

a.

Depreciation Expense—Office Equipment	225	
Accumulated Depreciation—Office Equipment		225
To record depreciation expense for two months.		

Annual depreciation: $\dfrac{\$10,250 - \$800}{7} = \$1,350$

Two months' depreciation: $\$1,350 \times \frac{2}{12} = \$225$

b. 1.

Cash	3,275	
Accumulated Depreciation—Office Equipment	6,975	
Office Equipment		10,250
To record sale of machine for book value.		

Cost		$10,250
Accumulated depreciation:		
5 years × $1,350 = $6,750		
2 months	225	6,975
Book value		$3,275

2.

Cash	3,000	
Loss on Sale of Plant Assets	275	
Accumulated Depreciation—Office Equipment	6,975	
Office Equipment		10,250
To record sale of machine for $3,000.		

3.

Cash	5,000	
Accumulated Depreciation—Office Equipment	6,975	
Office Equipment		10,250
Gain on Sale of Plant Assets		1,725
To record sale of machine for $5,000.		

4.

Office Equipment (New)	13,000	
Accumulated Depreciation—Office Equipment	6,975	
Office Equipment (Old)		10,250
Cash		8,800
Gain on Exchange of Plant Assets		925
To record trade of office copiers.		

5.

Flood Loss	3,275	
Accumulated Depreciation—Office Equipment	6,975	
Office Equipment		10,250
To record flood loss to machine.		

ANSWERS TO SELF-TEST QUESTIONS

1. d, p. 395   2. c, p. 396   3. b, p. 401   4. a, p. 404   5. b, p. 406

GLOSSARY OF KEY TERMS USED IN THIS CHAPTER

amortization The periodic writing off of an account balance to expense; usually refers to the writing off of an intangible asset (p. 405).

asset turnover Net sales divided by average total assets (p. 411).

capital lease A lease that transfers to the lessee substantially all of the benefits and risks related to ownership of the property. The lessee records the leased property as an asset and establishes a liability for the lease obligation (p. 409).

computer software production costs An intangible asset representing the costs incurred (after technological feasibility has been established) to produce computer software masters (p. 404).

copyright An exclusive right that protects an owner against the unauthorized reproduction of a specific written work or artwork (p. 406).

depletion The allocation of the cost of natural resources to the units extracted from the ground or, in the case of timberland, the board feet of timber cut (p. 401).

franchise Generally, an exclusive right to operate or sell a specific brand of products in a given geographical area (p. 406).

goodwill The value that derives from a firm's ability to earn more than a normal rate of return on the fair market value of its specific, identifiable net assets (p. 406).

intangible assets A term applied to a group of long-term assets, including patents, copyrights, franchises, trademarks, and goodwill, that benefit an entity but do not have physical substance (p. 403).

lease A contract between a lessor (owner) and lessee (tenant) for the rental of property (p. 408).

leasehold The rights transferred from the lessor to the lessee by a lease (p. 408).

leasehold improvements Expenditures made by a lessee to alter or improve leased property (p. 409).

lessee The party acquiring the right to the use of property by a lease (p. 408).

lessor The owner of property who transfers the right to use the property to another party by a lease (p. 408).

natural resources Assets occurring in a natural state, such as timber, petroleum, natural gas, coal, and other mineral deposits (p. 399).

off-balance-sheet financing The structuring of a financing arrangement so that no liability shows on the borrower's balance sheet (p. 410).

operating lease A lease by which the lessor retains the usual risks and rewards of owning the property (p. 408).

organization costs Expenditures incurred in launching a business (usually a corporation), including attorney's fees and various fees paid to the state (p. 406).

patent An exclusive privilege granted for 17 years to an inventor that gives the patent holder the right to exclude others from making, using, or selling the invention (p. 405).

percentage depletion A percentage deduction permitted for income tax purposes that is a specified percentage of the gross revenue from mining activities, with certain limitations (p. 403).

research and development costs Expenditures made in the search for new knowledge and in the translation of this knowledge into new or significantly improved products or processes (p. 404).

trademark An exclusive and continuing right to use a certain symbol to identify a brand or family of products (p. 406).

trade name An exclusive and continuing right to use a certain term or name to identify a brand or family of products (p. 406).

wasting assets Another name for natural resources. See *natural resources* (p. 399).

QUESTIONS

11-1 Identify three ways that a firm may dispose of a plant asset.

11-2 What factors determine the gain or loss on the sale of a plant asset?

11-3 Under what condition does a firm show neither a gain nor a loss from (a) the sale of a plant asset and (b) the retirement of a plant asset?

11-4 Policano Company depreciates a piece of equipment $720 per year on a straight-line basis. After the last depreciation entry on December 31, 1992, the equipment's book value is $3,000. On July 31, 1993, the equipment is sold for $3,500 cash. What is the gain (or loss) on the sale of the equipment?

11-5 Courier, Inc., exchanged used office furniture with a $700 book value and $800 cash for office furniture having a cash selling price of $1,900. At what amount should Courier record the office furniture? What is the gain (or loss) on the exchange of assets?

11-6 Assume that a company exchanged a used microcomputer with a $1,900 book value and $800 cash for a new microcomputer having a cash selling price of $3,500. The new microcomputer will be used in the same line of business as the old one. At what amount should the company record the new microcomputer? What is the gain (or loss) on the exchange of assets?

11-7 How is the amount of loss determined when an uninsured plant asset is destroyed by flood?

11-8 Syron Company has a Buildings subsidiary ledger. Identify the general ledger control accounts that are supported by this subsidiary ledger.

11-9 Lahey, Inc., has a Furniture and Fixtures subsidiary ledger. When Lahey purchases furniture, should the purchase be reflected in the general ledger? The subsidiary ledger?

11-10 Define *depletion*. The total depletion charge for a period may not all be expensed in the same period. Explain.

11-11 Folger Company installed a conveyor system that cost $162,000. The system can be used only in the excavation of gravel at a particular site. Folger expects to excavate gravel at the site for nine years. Over how many years should the conveyor be depreciated if its physical life is estimated at (a) 8 years and (b) 12 years?

11-12 Why is computing the depletion of natural resources similar to computing units-of-production depreciation?

11-13 List and briefly explain the nature of six different types of intangible assets.

11-14 How should a firm account for research and development costs related to its products and production processes?

11-15 Which costs of developing and producing computer software for sale or lease are to be capitalized as an intangible asset?

11-16 Abbey Company purchased for $8,500 computer software that is designed to process the firm's payroll, bill customers, and process customer payments. The software should be useful without significant modification for five years. What is the proper accounting for the software's cost?

11-17 What is the maximum amortization period for an intangible asset?

11-18 Briefly describe two methods for estimating the goodwill amount for a firm that is generating above-average earnings.

11-19 What is the difference between an operating lease and a capital lease?

11-20 How is the *asset turnover ratio* computed? What does this ratio show?

EXERCISES

SALE OF PLANT ASSET
— OBJ. 1 —

11-21 Raine Company has a machine that originally cost $89,000. Depreciation has been recorded for five years using the straight-line method, with an $8,000 estimated salvage value at the end of an expected nine-year life. After recording depreciation at the end of the fifth year, Raine sells the machine. Prepare the journal entry to record the machine's sale for
a. $48,000 cash.
b. $44,000 cash.
c. $41,000 cash.

DESTRUCTION OF PLANT
ASSET
— OBJ. 1 —

11-22 A storage building owned by Krueger Company was destroyed by flood exactly eight years after its purchase. The building, purchased for $380,000, had an estimated 20-year useful life and a $40,000 salvage value. Straight-line depreciation was up to date when the building was destroyed. Prepare the journal entry to record the destruction of the building assuming the following:
a. The building was not insured.
b. The building was insured, and Krueger expects a $250,000 insurance settlement.
c. The building was insured, and Krueger expects a $220,000 insurance settlement.

RETIREMENT OF PLANT ASSET
— OBJ. 1 —

11-23 On January 2, 1987, Dome, Inc., purchased a floor maintenance machine costing $3,500. Dome estimates the machine's useful life at seven years with no salvage value. Straight-line depreciation is recorded each year on December 31. Prepare the journal entry to record the machine's disposal in the following situations:
a. The machine is scrapped on December 31, 1993. Assume 1993 depreciation has been recorded.
b. The machine is scrapped on June 30, 1992. Prepare an entry to update depreciation before recording the machine's disposal.

EXCHANGE OF PLANT ASSET
— OBJ. 1 —

11-24 Assume Hawkeye Company trades a used machine for a new machine with a cash price of $28,000. The old machine originally cost $24,000 and has $7,000 of accumulated depreciation. The seller allows $22,000 as a trade-in for the old machine; Hawkeye pays the balance in cash. Following generally accepted accounting principles, prepare the journal entry to record Hawkeye's trade-in transaction assuming the following:
a. The machines are dissimilar plant assets.
b. The machines are similar plant assets used in the same line of business.

EXCHANGE OF PLANT ASSET
— OBJ. 1 —

11-25 Reardon Company exchanges used equipment costing $57,000 (on which $38,000 of depreciation has accumulated) for similar new equipment. The new equipment's cash price, with no trade-in, is $65,000.
a. Following generally accepted accounting principles, prepare the journal entry to record Reardon's trade-in transaction when
  1. The equipment's trade-in allowance is $16,000, and the balance is paid in cash.
  2. The equipment's trade-in allowance is $21,000, and the balance is paid in cash.
b. Following income tax guidelines, prepare the journal entry to record Reardon's trade-in transaction when
  1. The equipment's trade-in allowance is $16,000, and the balance is paid in cash.
  2. The equipment's trade-in allowance is $21,000, and the balance is paid in cash.

COMPUTING DEPLETION AND DEPRECIATION
— OBJ. 3 —

11-26 Cooper Copper Company recently acquired a parcel of land containing an estimated 900,000 tons of commercial grade copper ore. Cooper paid $7,000,000 for the land and acquired extraction equipment at a cost of $954,000. Although the equipment will be worthless when the ore is depleted, Cooper estimates that the land can be sold for $600,000 (after spending $80,000 to recondition the site upon completion of mining operations).
a. Compute the proper depletion charge for a period during which 95,000 tons of ore are extracted and sold.
b. Compute the proper depreciation charge on the extraction equipment, using the units-of-production method, for a period during which 95,000 tons of ore are extracted and sold.

COMPUTING AND RECORDING AMORTIZATION EXPENSE
— OBJ. 4, 5 —

11-27 For each of the following unrelated situations, calculate the annual amortization expense and present a general journal entry to record the expense. Assume contra accounts are not used for accumulated amortization.
a. A two-year-old patent was purchased for $225,000. The patent will probably be commercially exploitable for another nine years.
b. Certain sales counter fixtures, costing $49,500, were constructed and permanently installed in a building leased from another firm. The physical life of the counters was an estimated 20 years. When the counters were installed, the operating lease had 11 years to run and contained no provision for the removal of the fixtures.
c. A trademark is carried at a cost of $132,000, which represents the out-of-court settlement paid to another firm that has agreed to refrain from using or claiming the trademark or one similar to it. The company expects to actively use the trademark as long as the company exists.
d. A patent was acquired on a device designed by a production worker. Although the cost of the patent to date consisted of $32,300 in legal fees for handling the patent application, the patent should be commercially valuable during its entire legal life and is currently worth approximately $340,000.
e. A franchise granting exclusive distribution rights for a new solar water heater within a four-state area for three years was obtained at a cost of $63,000. Satisfactory sales performance over the three years permits renewal of the franchise for another three years (at an additional cost determined at renewal).

**OPERATING LEASE
— OBJ. 5 —**

11-28 On December 20, 1993, Brighton Company signed a three-year lease for office space at a monthly rental of $1,000. The lease starts January 1, 1994. Under the terms of this operating lease, Brighton paid $3,000 on December 20, 1993, as an advance ("good faith") payment of the last three months' rent (Months 34, 35, and 36). On March 1, 1994, with the landlord's permission, Brighton paid $8,500 to install permanent shelving in the office. The shelving is estimated to last 30 years.

a. Prepare the journal entry to record Brighton's $3,000 cash payment on December 20, 1993.

b. Prepare the journal entry to record Brighton's $8,500 cash payment on March 1, 1994.

c. Assume that Brighton makes adjustments once a year. Prepare the appropriate adjusting entry at December 31, 1994, related to the office shelving.

PROBLEMS

**DISPOSALS OF PLANT ASSET
— OBJ. 1 —**

11-29 Citano Company has a used executive charter plane that originally cost $720,000. Straight-line depreciation on the plane has been recorded for six years, with a $60,000 expected salvage value at the end of its estimated eight-year useful life. The last depreciation entry was made at the end of the sixth year. Eight months into the seventh year, Citano disposes of the plane.

REQUIRED

Prepare journal entries to record

577500

a. Depreciation expense to the date of disposal.

b. Sale of the plane for cash at its book value.

c. Sale of the plane for $182,000 cash.

d. Sale of the plane for $160,000 cash.

e. Exchange of the plane for a new aircraft costing $300,000. The trade-in allowance received is $230,000, and the balance is paid in cash. The new plane will be used in the same line of business as the old plane.

f. Destruction of the plane in a fire. Citano expects a $165,000 insurance settlement.

g. Exchange of the plane for a new yacht costing $800,000. The trade-in allowance received is $185,000, and the balance is paid in cash.

**EXCHANGE OF PLANT
ASSETS
— OBJ. 1 —**

11-30 On July 1, 1989, Temple Construction Company purchased a small bulldozer for $24,100. Temple estimates a six-year useful life and a $2,500 salvage value for the bulldozer. On October 1, 1989, the company purchased a flatbed truck for $16,300. Temple estimates the truck's useful life at seven years and its salvage value at $1,600. Temple uses straight-line depreciation for all plant assets and records depreciation on December 31 each year.

On March 31, 1994, Temple traded in the truck for a new truck. The manufacturer's "sticker" price on the new truck was $18,000, but the dealer's cash price was $17,400. After the dealer deducted the allowance for the old truck, Temple paid $11,000 cash for the new truck. Temple estimates the new truck will last five years and have an $1,800 salvage value.

On June 30, 1994, Temple exchanged the bulldozer for a new bulldozer with a cash price of $28,000. Temple's trade-in allowance for the old bulldozer was $7,000, and the company paid $21,000 cash. The new bulldozer's estimated useful life is six years; its estimated salvage value is $1,900.

REQUIRED

Following generally accepted accounting principles, prepare journal entries to record the following events in 1994:

Mar. 31   Update depreciation on the truck.

    31   Exchange of trucks.

June 30   Update depreciation on the bulldozer.

    30   Exchange of bulldozers.

Dec. 31   Depreciation for 1994 on new truck and new bulldozer.

**DEPLETION ACCOUNTING
— OBJ. 3 —**

11-31

Pitt Gravel, Inc., has just purchased a site containing an estimated 2,000,000 tons of high-grade aggregate rock. Pitt makes the following expenditures before starting production:

Purchase price of property	$2,675,000
Legal fees to acquire title and secure proper zoning for operations	8,700
Removal of topsoil and grading for drainage	66,300
Construction of on-site crushing, washing, and loading facilities	600,000

Once the rock deposits are no longer commercially valuable, Pitt estimates the company will spend $50,000 to recondition the land. The land will then sell for an estimated $200,000. Certain parts of the on-site crushing, washing, and loading facilities have an estimated salvage value of $80,000 when operations are terminated.

REQUIRED

a. Prepare the journal entry to record the total depletion charge for the first year, during which 300,000 tons of rock are extracted from the quarry.

b. Prepare the journal entry to record the depreciation of the crushing, washing, and loading facilities for the first year, in which 300,000 tons of rock are extracted. Use the units-of-production depreciation method.

c. Compute the cost of a 30,000-ton inventory of rock at the end of the first year for which all extraction and processing costs except depletion and depreciation of crushing, washing, and loading facilities average $0.80 per ton.

d. At the beginning of the second year, Pitt estimates that only 1,300,000 tons of rock remain in the quarry. Compute the revised (1) depletion per ton of rock and (2) depreciation per ton of rock.

**ACCOUNTING FOR
INTANGIBLE ASSETS
— OBJ. 4, 5 —**

11-32

Berdahl Company owns several retail outlets. In 1993, it expanded operations and entered into the following transactions:

Jan. 2 Signed an eight-year operating lease for additional retail space for an annual rent of $22,200. Paid the first and last years' rent in advance on this date. (*Hint:* Debit the first year's rent to Prepaid Rent.)

3 Paid $15,200 to a contractor for installation of a new oak floor in the leased facility. The oak floor's life is an estimated 50 years with no salvage value.

Mar. 1 Paid $30,000 to obtain an exclusive area franchise for five years to distribute a new line of perfume.

July 1 Paid $42,000 to LogoLab, Inc., for designing a trademark for a new line of gourmet chocolates that Berdahl will distribute nationally. Berdahl will use the trademark for as long as the firm (and the chocolates) remain in business. Berdahl expects to be in business for at least another 50 years.

1 Paid $36,000 for advertisement in a national magazine (June issue) introducing the new line of chocolates and the trademark.

REQUIRED

a. Prepare general journal entries to record these transactions.

b. Prepare the necessary adjusting entries on December 31, 1993, for these transactions. Berdahl makes adjusting entries once a year. Berdahl uses straight-line amortization but does not use contra accounts when amortizing intangible assets.

**ACCOUNTING FOR PLANT
AND INTANGIBLE ASSETS
— OBJ. 1, 4, 5 —**

11-33

Selected 1994 transactions and events for Lund Company are given below:

Jan. 2 Paid $34,000 for a four-year franchise to distribute a product line locally.

Mar. 31 Discovered a computer was stolen from the accountant's office. Lund carries no theft insurance. The computer cost $5,800 when purchased on January 2, 1991, and was being depreciated over six years with a $400 salvage value. Straight-line depreciation was last recorded on December 31, 1993.

Apr. 1 Entered into a nine-year operating lease for additional warehouse space. Paid in advance the rent for the last two months of the nine-year lease, $3,600.

June 30   Discarded office equipment and realized no salvage value. A $600 salvage value, after a six-year useful life, had been estimated when the equipment was acquired for $7,200 on July 1, 1988. Straight-line depreciation was last recorded on December 31, 1993.

Aug. 1   Paid a $5,000 cash bonus to employee for designing and developing a new product.

Sept. 1   Paid a $10,200 legal services fee to obtain a new product patent, which was granted today. Lund estimates the patent will provide effective protection from competitors for 10 years.

Oct. 1   Constructed storage bins at a cost of $30,600 in the warehouse space leased April 1. The physical life of the storage bins is an estimated 15 years. The lease contains no provision for the removal of the bins; the lessor takes control of the bins at the end of the lease.

Nov. 1   Exchanged a used forklift truck for a similar new truck. The used truck cost $9,000 and had accumulated depreciation of $7,500 (through October 31, 1994). The new truck's cash price was $10,000. Lund's trade-in allowance was $1,800, and the company paid $8,200 cash. Lund estimates a 10-year useful life and a $1,000 salvage value for the new truck.

REQUIRED

a. Prepare general journal entries to record these transactions.

b. Prepare the December 31, 1994, general journal entries to record the proper amounts of depreciation and amortization expense for assets acquired during the year. Lund uses straight-line depreciation and amortization but does not use contra accounts when amortizing intangible assets.

PREPARATION OF BALANCE SHEET — **OBJ. 6** —   **11-34**   Dooley Company's December 31, 1993, post-closing trial balance contains the following normal balances:

Cash	$ 6,000
Accounts Payable	12,000
Stone Quarry	270,000
Building	293,000
Long-term Notes Payable	525,000
H. Dooley, Capital	645,000
Accumulated Depreciation—Equipment	120,000
Leasehold	10,000
Accumulated Depletion—Stone Quarry	96,000
Land	44,000
Accounts Receivable	14,000
Timberland	460,000
Accumulated Depreciation—Building	90,000
Wages Payable	4,000
Patent (Net of amortization)	80,000
Accumulated Depletion—Timberland	135,000
Notes Payable (Short term)	90,000
Inventory	140,000
Equipment	400,000

REQUIRED

Prepare a December 31, 1993, classified balance sheet for Dooley Company.

ALTERNATE EXERCISES

SALE OF PLANT ASSET — **OBJ. 1** —

11-21A   Noble Company has equipment that originally cost $48,000. Depreciation has been recorded for six years using the straight-line method, with a $4,000 estimated salvage value at the end of an expected eight-year life. After recording depreciation at the end of the sixth year, Noble sells the equipment. Prepare the journal entry to record the equipment's sale for

a. $17,000 cash.

b. $15,000 cash.

c. $10,000 cash.

**THEFT OF PLANT ASSET
— OBJ. 1 —**

11-22A An automobile owned by Parker Company was stolen exactly two years after its purchase. The automobile, purchased for $24,500, had an estimated six-year useful life and a $3,500 salvage value. Straight-line depreciation was up to date when the automobile was stolen. Prepare the journal entry to record the theft of the automobile, assuming the following:

a. The automobile was not insured against theft.

b. The automobile was insured, and Parker expects a $19,000 insurance settlement.

c. The automobile was insured, and Parker expects a $14,000 insurance settlement.

**RETIREMENT OF PLANT
ASSET
— OBJ. 1 —**

11-23A On January 2, 1988, Farley, Inc., purchased a machine for $5,600. Farley estimates the machine's useful life at eight years with no salvage value. Straight-line depreciation is recorded each year on December 31.

a. Prepare the journal entry to record the retirement (i.e., scrapping) of the machine on December 31, 1995. Assume 1995 depreciation has been recorded.

b. Assume Farley had originally estimated a salvage value of $400 rather than zero. Prepare the journal entry to record the retirement (i.e., scrapping) of the machine on December 31, 1995. Assume 1995 depreciation has been recorded.

**EXCHANGE OF PLANT ASSET
— OBJ. 1 —**

11-24A Assume Zoe Company trades a used machine for a new machine with a cash price of $31,500. The old machine originally cost $30,000 and has $10,000 of accumulated depreciation. The seller allows $24,500 as a trade-in for the old machine; Zoe pays the balance in cash. Following generally accepted accounting principles, prepare the journal entry to record Zoe's trade-in transaction assuming

a. The machines are dissimilar plant assets.

b. The machines are similar plant assets used in the same line of business.

**EXCHANGE OF PLANT ASSET
— OBJ. 1 —**

11-25A Holden Company exchanges used equipment costing $70,000 (on which $49,000 of depreciation has accumulated) for similar new equipment. The new equipment's cash price, with no trade-in, is $84,000.

a. Following generally accepted accounting principles, prepare the journal entry to record Holden's trade-in transaction when

1. The equipment's trade-in allowance is $15,000, and the balance is paid in cash.

2. The equipment's trade-in allowance is $25,000, and the balance is paid in cash.

b. Following income tax guidelines, prepare the journal entry to record Holden's trade-in transaction when

1. The equipment's trade-in allowance is $15,000, and the balance is paid in cash.

2. The equipment's trade-in allowance is $25,000, and the balance is paid in cash.

**COMPUTING DEPLETION
AND DEPRECIATION
— OBJ. 3 —**

11-26A Savage Mining Company purchased Hidden Valley Mine for $10,000,000. The mine contains an estimated 2,500,000 tons of ore. Savage also purchased mining equipment for $400,000 that will be useful only at Hidden Valley Mine. The equipment will be worthless when the ore is depleted. Upon completion of the mining operations, Savage estimates the land can be sold for $500,000 after spending $50,000 to restore the land site.

a. Compute the proper depletion charge for a period during which 250,000 tons of ore are extracted and sold.

b. Compute the proper depreciation charge on the mining equipment, using the units-of-production method, for a period during which 250,000 tons of ore are extracted and sold.

**GOODWILL ESTIMATION
— OBJ. 4 —**

11-27A Serum Company, which is for sale, has identifiable net assets with a fair market value of $4,000,000 and no recorded goodwill. Serum's annual net income in recent years has averaged $574,000 in an industry that considers 10% a normal rate of return on net assets.

a. Compute Serum's above-normal earnings.

b. Estimate Serum's goodwill amount by capitalizing the above-normal earnings at the normal rate of return on net assets.

c. How much will the goodwill estimate from part (b) change if the excess earnings are capitalized at 15%?

**CAPITAL LEASE
— OBJ. 5, 6 —**

11-28A On January 2, 1993, Soper Corporation leased equipment for eight years under a capital lease. The present value of the future lease payments is used to record the lease; this present value amount is $176,000. Soper will use the straight-line method to depreciate the leased equipment to a zero book value over the term of the lease.

a. Prepare the journal entry to record the capital lease on January 2, 1993.

b. Prepare the journal entry to record one year's depreciation on the leased equipment on December 31, 1993.

c. In which section of a classified balance sheet will the leased equipment be presented in the December 31, 1993, balance sheet?

ALTERNATE PROBLEMS

**DISPOSALS OF PLANT ASSET
— OBJ. 1 —**

11-29A Canyon Company has a used delivery truck that originally cost $13,600. Straight-line depreciation on the truck has been recorded for three years, with a $1,000 expected salvage value at the end of its estimated six-year useful life. The last depreciation entry was made at the end of the third year. Four months into the fourth year, Canyon disposes of the truck.

REQUIRED

Prepare journal entries to record

a. Depreciation expense to the date of disposal.

b. Sale of the truck for cash at its book value.

c. Sale of the truck for $7,500 cash.

d. Sale of the truck for $6,000 cash.

e. Exchange of the truck for a new truck costing $12,200. The trade-in allowance received is $9,200, and the balance is paid in cash. The new truck will be used in the same line of business as the old truck.

f. Theft of the truck. Canyon carries no insurance for theft.

g. Exchange of the truck for golf carts costing $16,200 for the company golf course. The trade-in allowance received is $7,200, and the balance is paid in cash.

**EXCHANGE OF PLANT
ASSETS
— OBJ. 1 —**

11-30A On April 1, 1990, Pyle Excavators, Inc., purchased a tractor for $40,500. Pyle estimated a nine-year useful life and a $2,700 salvage value for the tractor. On September 1, 1990, the company paid $30,800 for a new trenching machine. Pyle estimated the machine's useful life at five years and its salvage value at $3,200. Pyle uses straight-line depreciation for all plant assets and records depreciation on December 31 each year.

On June 30, 1995, Pyle traded in the tractor for a new tractor with a cash price of $43,200. The dealer allowed a trade-in value of $17,500 for the old tractor, and Pyle paid the remaining $25,700 in cash. Pyle estimated the new tractor would last seven years and have a $3,300 salvage value.

On August 31, 1995, Pyle exchanged the trenching machine for a new trenching machine with a cash price of $34,400. Pyle's trade-in allowance for the old trenching machine was $4,400, and the company paid $30,000 cash. The new machine's estimated useful life is six years; its estimated salvage value is $3,800.

REQUIRED

Following generally accepted accounting principles, prepare journal entries to record the following events in 1995:

June 30 Update depreciation on the tractor.

30 Exchange of tractors.

Aug. 31 Update depreciation on the trenching machine.

31 Exchange of trenching machines.

Dec. 31 Depreciation for 1995 on new tractor and new trenching machine.

DEPLETION ACCOUNTING
— OBJ. 3 —

11-31A Longview Mining Company has just purchased a site containing an estimated 1,800,000 tons of coal. Longview makes the following expenditures before starting operations:

Cost of land survey	$ 12,000
Purchase price of property	2,075,000
Legal fees to acquire title and secure proper zoning for operations	7,000
Construction of on-site conveyance and loading facilities	360,000

After all the coal has been extracted, Longview expects to spend $75,000 to restore the land site and then sell it for $225,000. Longview also expects to sell certain parts of the conveyance and loading facilities for $36,000.

REQUIRED

a. Prepare the journal entry to record the total depletion charge for the first year, during which 200,000 tons of coal are extracted from the mine.

b. Prepare the journal entry to record the depreciation of the conveyance and loading facilities for the first year, in which 200,000 tons of coal are extracted. Use the units-of-production depreciation method.

c. Compute the cost of a 40,000-ton inventory of coal at the end of the first year for which all extraction and processing costs except depletion and depreciation of conveyance and loading facilities average $1.24 per ton.

d. At the beginning of the second year, Longview estimates that only 1,200,000 tons of coal remain underground. Compute the revised (1) depletion per ton of coal and (2) depreciation per ton of coal.

ACCOUNTING FOR
INTANGIBLE ASSETS
— OBJ. 4, 5 —

11-32A During the first few days of 1993, Lindal Company began business and entered into the following transactions:

1. Paid $10,200 in attorney's fees and other costs related to the organization of the company.

2. Purchased an existing patent on a product for $90,000. The patent's legal protection and useful life cover 12 more years.

3. Entered into a six-year operating lease for additional office space. Paid in advance the rent for the last three months of the six-year lease, $4,200.

4. Paid $9,600 to have recessed lighting installed in the leased office space. The lighting is estimated to last 20 years with no salvage value.

5. Paid $125,000 for a 20-year franchise to distribute a product line in a three-state region.

6. Spent $26,000 on the initial research for a promising new product to complement the patented product.

7. Purchased a computer software package to aid the controller's financial planning and budgeting activities. The software cost $5,200, should be useful without significant modification for four years, and has no salvage value.

REQUIRED

a. Prepare general journal entries to record these transactions.

b. Prepare the December 31, 1993, general journal entries to record the proper amounts of amortization expense for the year. Organization costs are amortized over five years. Lindal uses straight-line amortization but does not use contra accounts when amortizing intangible assets.

ACCOUNTING FOR PLANT AND INTANGIBLE ASSETS
— OBJ. 1, 4, 5 —

11-33A Selected 1994 transactions of Continental Publishers, Inc., are given below:

Jan. 2 Paid $80,000 to purchase copyrights to a series of romantic novels. The copyrights expire in 40 years, although Continental expects sales of the novels to stop after 10 years.

Mar. 1 Discovered a satellite dish antenna has been destroyed by lightning. The loss is covered by insurance and a claim is filed today. The antenna cost $8,620 when installed on July 1, 1992, and was being depreciated over 12 years with a $700 salvage value. Straight-line depreciation was last recorded on December 31, 1993. Continental expects to receive an insurance settlement of $7,600.

Apr. 1 Leased equipment under a nine-year capital lease. The equipment will be returned to the lessor at the end of the lease. The proper initial valuation of this lease is $115,200.

July 1 Paid $150,000 to acquire a patent on a new publishing process. The patent has a remaining legal life of 15 years. Continental estimates the new process will be utilized for 6 years before it becomes obsolete.

Oct. 1 Exchanged old printing equipment for new (similar) printing equipment. The old equipment cost $68,000 and had accumulated depreciation of $51,200 (through September 30, 1994). The new equipment's cash price was $96,000. Continental's trade-in allowance was $16,000 and the company paid $80,000 cash. Continental estimates an eight-year useful life and an $8,000 salvage value for the new equipment.

Nov. 1 Paid $42,000 to obtain a four-year franchise to sell a new series of computerized do-it-yourself manuals.

REQUIRED

a. Prepare general journal entries to record these transactions.
b. Prepare the December 31, 1994, general journal entries to record the proper amounts of depreciation and amortization expense for assets acquired during the year. Continental uses straight-line depreciation and amortization but does not use contra accounts when amortizing intangible assets.

PREPARATION OF BALANCE SHEET
— OBJ. 6 —

11-34A Conlon Corporation's December 31, 1993, post-closing trial balance contains the following normal account balances:

Interest Payable	$ 12,000
Accumulated Depreciation—Equipment	65,000
Inventory	70,000
Organization Costs (Net of amortization)	8,000
Copper Deposit	400,000
Notes Payable (Short term)	40,000
Cash	1,000
Accumulated Depletion—Coal Deposit	63,000
Building	140,000
Accounts Receivable	10,000
Patent (Net of amortization)	25,000
Equipment	133,000
Capital Stock	200,000
Retained Earnings	176,000
Accumulated Depreciation—Building	35,000
Accounts Payable	7,000
Leased Equipment	70,000
Accumulated Depletion—Copper Deposit	160,000
Land	87,000
Long-term Notes Payable	410,000
Coal Deposit	300,000
Accumulated Depreciation—Leased Equipment	11,000
Lease Obligation (Long term)	65,000

REQUIRED

Prepare a December 31, 1993, classified balance sheet for Conlon Corporation.

CASES

Business Decision Case

Tim Lopez wants to buy Bauer Company from Amy Bauer. His first offer was rejected, and he seeks your advice as he prepares another offer. Your discussions with Lopez and an analysis of related data disclose the following:

1. Lopez's first offer of $1,500,000 was equal to the fair market value of Bauer Company's identifiable net assets. Lopez and Bauer agree that this amount represents the fair market value of these net assets.

2. Bauer rejected the first offer because she believes her company has exceptionally good supplier, customer, and employee relationships. These attributes do not appear on the balance sheet, but they are a component of the company's overall value and should be reflected in the purchase price.

3. Lopez recognizes Bauer Company's favorable relationships. However, he is uncertain how long they will last when Bauer leaves the company after the sale.

4. Lopez is willing to incorporate a goodwill amount in his offer and accepts a "capitalization of excess earnings" approach to estimating goodwill. In light of his uncertainty about the long-run continuation of superior earnings, however, the capitalization rate must be twice the average rate of return for the industry.

5. The industry's average rate of return on identifiable net assets is 13%.

6. Over the past several years, Bauer Company's net income has averaged $286,000.

REQUIRED

Estimate a goodwill amount for Bauer Company, and recommend a purchase price that Tim Lopez should offer Amy Bauer.

Analytical Application Case

CAMPBELL SOUP COMPANY produces food products that include, in addition to its soups, such brands as Pepperidge Farm, Swanson, and Le Menu. Selected financial data for Campbell Soup Company for three recent years are shown below (amounts in millions; Year 3 is the most recent year).

	Year 3	Year 2	Year 1
Total assets, beginning of year	$3,932.1	$3,609.6	$3,097.4
Total assets, end of year	4,115.6	3,932.1	3,609.6
Net sales for the year	6,205.8	5,762.1	4,868.9

a. Compute (to two decimal places) the asset turnover for Years 1, 2, and 3.
b. Campbell's total assets grew in each of the three years. Was Campbell able to maintain the effectiveness of its assets in generating sales revenues during this period of asset growth? Comment.

c. In Years 2 and 3, H. J. HEINZ COMPANY, a competitor of Campbell Soup Company, had the following financial data (in millions):

	Year 3	Year 2
Total assets, beginning of year	$4,001.8	$3,605.1
Total assets, end of year	4,487.5	4,001.8
Net sales for the year	6,085.7	5,800.9

Compute (to two decimal places) the asset turnover for H. J. Heinz Company for Years 2 and 3. Compare these figures with the asset turnover ratios for Campbell Soup Company and comment.

Ethics Case

Craig Rehn works in the accounting department of Kensington, Inc. After work one night, he observed the sales manager, a good friend of the controller, loading a company computer into the manager's personal automobile. Upon noticing Rehn, the sales manager explained that he was taking an old company computer home "to play around with" because he had been told it was fully depreciated and had been recently replaced with a newer model. Rehn is aware that the sales manager operates another business from his home.

REQUIRED
What ethical problem does Rehn face in this situation? What possible responses does he have?

What amounts of money will a firm have to pay others during the next year and how will these amounts be recorded and reported?

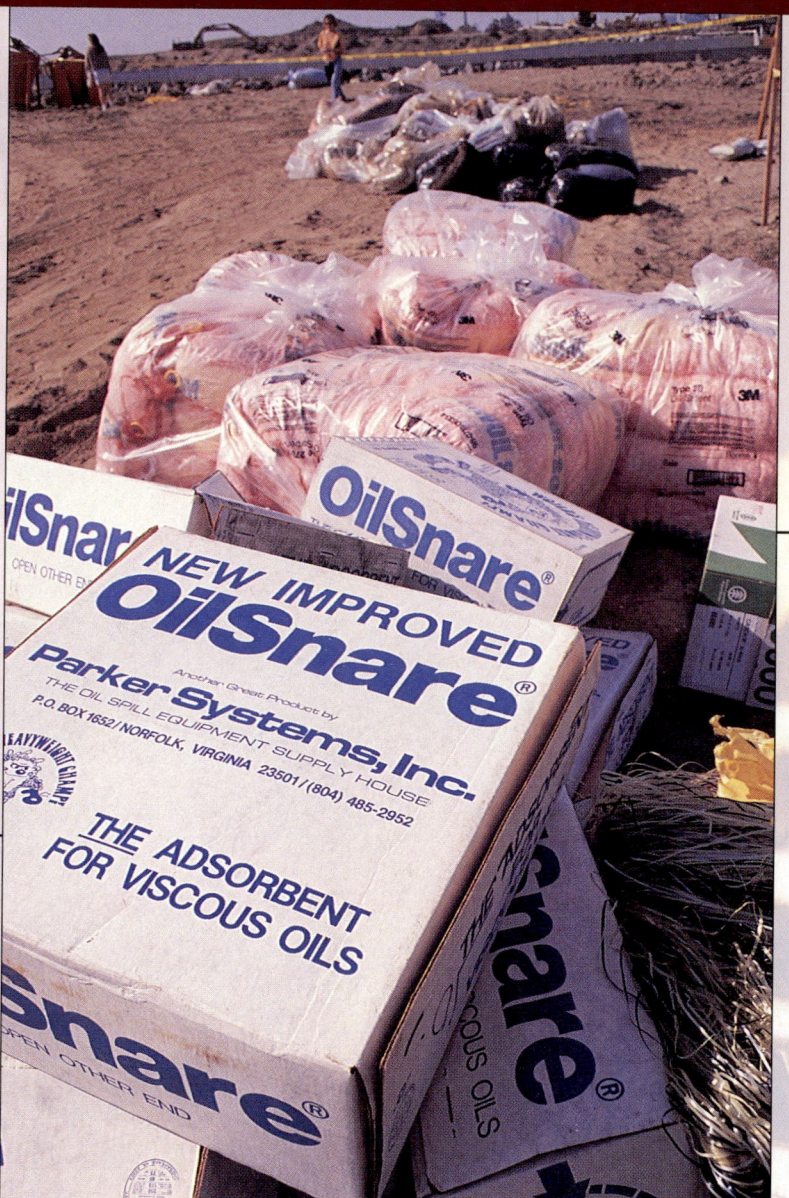

Current liabilities are amounts that a firm owes others during the next year. ■ They are always recorded in the accounting records and reported in the balance sheet. ■ Contingent liabilities are amounts that may or may not require payment of cash during the next year ■ Some contingent liabilities are recorded in the accounting records, others disclosed in financial statement footnotes. ■ Chevron, for example, notes in its annual report a contingent liability for complying with environmental cleanup regulations.

12 CURRENT LIABILITIES AND PAYROLL ACCOUNTING

iabilities, one of the three elements in the accounting equation, generally represent a firm's obligations to nonowners. Total liabilities are divided into two subcategories—current liabilities and long-term liabilities. In this chapter, we focus on current liabilities, and because several liabilities are associated with a firm's payroll, we will examine payroll accounting procedures and requirements in some depth.

THE NATURE OF LIABILITIES

OBJECTIVE ❶ DEFINE *and* **ILLUSTRATE** *the most common types of current and contingent liabilities.*

Liabilities are obligations resulting from past transactions or events that require the firm to pay money, provide goods, or perform services in the future. The existence of a past transaction or event is an important element in the definition of liabilities. For example, a purchase commitment is actually an agreement between a buyer and a seller to enter into a *future* transaction. The performance of the seller that will create the obligation on the part of the buyer is, at this point, a future transaction; hence, a purchase commitment is not a liability. Another example is a company's long-term salary contract with an executive. When the agreement is signed, each party is committed to perform in the future—the executive to render services and the company to pay for those services. The company does not record a liability when the contract is signed, because the executive has not yet rendered any services.

Although they involve definite future cash payments, the foregoing examples are not reported as liabilities because they are related to future transactions. However, significant purchase commitments and executive compensation commitments should be disclosed in notes to the balance sheet.

Items shown as liabilities are often not legally due and payable on the balance sheet date. For example, the accrual of wages expense incurred but not paid during the period results in a credit balance account titled Wages Payable. Accrued wages are not typically due until several days after the balance sheet date. In the case of other accrued expenses—such as property taxes and executive bonuses—payment may not be due until months after the balance sheet date. Bonds payable, although shown as liabilities, may not be actually payable for several decades. These items are all reported as liabilities, however, because they are obligations resulting from past transactions that will be settled as the business continues to operate.

The determination of liabilities is basic to accounting properly for a firm's operations. For example, if a liability is omitted, then either an asset or an expense has been omitted also. If expense is involved, then net income and owners' equity are misstated as well. Thus, the balance sheet or the income statement, or both, may be affected if liabilities are not reported correctly.

Most liabilities are satisfied by the eventual payment of cash. Some may require a firm to furnish goods—for instance, a publisher obligated to provide issues of a magazine to customers who have subscribed in advance. Other liabilities may be obligations to provide services—for example, product warranties and maintenance contracts that accompany a new appliance or automobile.

Definition of Current Liabilities

Current liabilities are all obligations that will require within the coming year or the normal operating cycle, whichever is longer, (1) the use of existing current assets or (2) the creation of other current liabilities. Most current liabilities will be settled by using current assets, but sometimes a current liability is settled by the issuance of another current liability. A past-due account payable, for example, may be settled by issuing a short-term note payable. Note that liabilities are classified as current using the same time frame as is used to classify current assets—the longer of one year or the firm's normal operating cycle.

Measurement of Current Liabilities

Current liabilities are usually measured and shown in the balance sheet at the money amount necessary to satisfy the obligation. When future provision of services or goods is involved, the dollar amount of the liability is only an estimate of the costs to be incurred. Even some current liabilities that will be settled with cash payments are estimates of the dollar amounts of the future cash payments. We will discuss several examples of estimated current liabilities in this chapter.

EXAMPLES OF CURRENT LIABILITIES

In this section, we review the common types of current liabilities. Although not exhaustive, these concepts should enable you to look more deeply into the accounting problems and techniques involved.

Trade Accounts and Notes Payable

In a balance sheet listing of current liabilities, amounts due to short-term creditors on open accounts or notes payable are commonly shown first. Most of the accounting procedures for accounts and notes payable are fairly routine and have been discussed in previous chapters. However, we should carefully account for transactions that occur shortly before and after the end of the accounting period. At the end of the period, recently received inventory items must be reflected as accounts payable, if unpaid, and as purchases of the period. Likewise, items that the company owns and for which a payable has been recorded must be included in inventory whether or not the items have been received. In other words, we need a proper "cut-off" of purchases, payables, and inventory for valid income determination and presentation of financial position.

Dividends Payable

Ordinary dividends are distributions of corporate earnings to stockholders. Because the corporate board of directors determines the timing and amounts of dividends, they do not accrue as does interest expense. Instead, dividends are shown as liabilities only after a formal declaration. Once declared, however, dividends are binding obligations of the corporation. Dividends are current liabilities because they are almost always paid within several weeks of the time they are declared.

Portions of Long-term Debt

The repayment of many long-term obligations involves a series of installments over several years. To report liabilities involving installments properly, we should show the principal amount of the installments due within one year (or the operating cycle, if longer) as a current liability.

Sales and Excise Taxes

Many products and services are subject to sales and excise taxes. The laws governing these taxes usually require the selling firm to collect the tax at the time of sale and to send the collections periodically to the appropriate taxing agency. Assume that a particular product selling for $1,000 is subject to a 6% state sales tax and a 10% federal excise tax. Each tax should be figured on the basic sales price only. We record the above sale as follows:

Accounts Receivable (*or* Cash)	1,160	
Sales		1,000
Sales Tax Payable		60
Excise Tax Payable		100
To record sales and related taxes.		

Recording this transaction as a $1,160 sale is incorrect, because this overstates revenue and may lead to the omission of the liabilities for the taxes collected. The selling firm periodically completes a tax reporting form and sends the period's tax collections with it. The tax liability accounts are then debited and Cash is credited.

Some firms record sales at the gross amount, including taxes collected. Then, to convert the total amount to actual sales, we divide the transaction total of $1,160 by 1.16 to yield $1,000 as the basic sales amount and $160 as the total tax.

Estimated or Accrued Liabilities

Estimated or accrued liabilities are often referred to as *accrued expenses*. Generally they are the credits offsetting a series of debits to various expense accounts that are necessary for matching periodic expenses with revenue. Examples are the accrual of incurred (but unpaid) product warranty expense, various taxes, and vacation pay.

PRODUCT WARRANTIES

Many firms guarantee their products for a period of time after the sale. Proper matching of expenses with revenue requires that the estimated costs of providing these **product warranties** be recognized as an expense in the period of sale rather than in a later period when the warranty costs may actually be paid.

Suppose that a firm sells a product for $300 per unit, which includes a 30-day warranty against defects. Past experience indicates that 3% of the units will prove defective and that the average repair cost is $40 per defective unit. Furthermore, during a particular month, product sales were $240,000, and 13 of the units sold in this month were defective and were repaired during the month. Using this information, we calculate the accrued liability for product warranties at the end of the month as follows:

Number of units sold ($240,000/$300)	800
Rate of defective units	× 0.03
Total units expected to fail	24
Less: Units failed in month of sale	13
Units expected to fail in the remainder of the warranty period	11
Average repair cost per unit	× $ 40
Estimated liability for product warranty provision at end of period	$440

This accrued liability would be recorded at the end of the period of sale as follows:

Product Warranty Expense	440	
Estimated Liability for Product Warranty		440
To record estimated warranty expense.		

When a unit fails in a future period, the repair costs will be recorded by debiting Estimated Liability for Product Warranty and crediting Cash, Supplies, and so forth.

PROPERTY TAXES

Property taxes are a primary source of revenue for city and county governments. The property taxes paid by business firms are, to some extent, the price for the many governmental services from which the firms benefit. Thus, property taxes are considered an operating expense that applies pro rata to each operating period.

Often, firms do not know in advance the amount of tax to be paid. These firms must accrue an estimated amount of property tax expense (and the related liability) each month until they know their actual tax liability.

To illustrate, assume that Morton Company, which ends its accounting year on December 31, is located in a city whose fiscal year runs from July 1 to June 30. City taxes are assessed on October 1 (for the fiscal year started the preceding July 1) and are paid by November 15. The relationship of Morton Company's and the city's accounting years is diagrammed as follows:

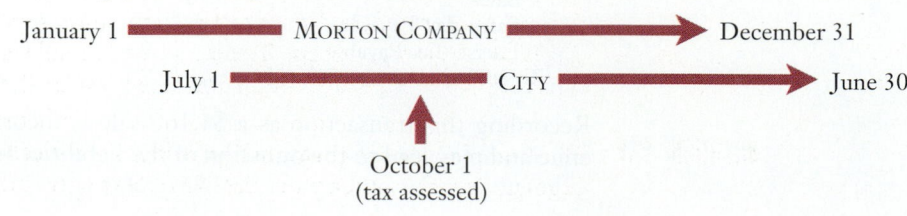

For example, on October 1, 1993, Morton Company knows the amount of its property taxes for the last six months of 1993 and the first six months of 1994. Consequently, property tax expense must be estimated for July, August, and September 1993. Morton Company estimates in July 1993 that its property taxes for the next 12 months will be $18,000. At the end of July, August, and September 1993, the following entry would reflect the estimated monthly property taxes ($18,000/12 = $1,500):

Property Tax Expense	1,500	
Estimated Property Tax Payable		1,500
To record estimated property tax expense for the month.		

On October 1, 1993, Morton Company receives a $19,008 property tax bill from the city. Morton's estimate for July–September is too low by $252 ($19,008/12 = $1,584; $1,584 − $1,500 = $84; $84 × 3 months = $252). The $252 difference may be handled as an increase in the property taxes for October. The entry to record the October taxes would then be the following:

Property Tax Expense ($1,584 + $252)	1,836	
Estimated Property Tax Payable		1,836
To record property tax expense for October.		

The Estimated Property Tax Payable account has a balance of $6,336 after the October entry. The following is the entry on November 15 to record the property tax payment in full:

Estimated Property Tax Payable	6,336	
Prepaid Property Tax	12,672	
Cash		19,008
To record payment of property taxes.		

The balance in the Prepaid Property Tax account is amortized to Property Tax Expense from November 1993 through June 1994 at $1,584 per month.

INCOME TAXES

The federal government, most states, and some municipalities levy income taxes against corporations, individuals, estates, and trusts. Sole proprietorships and partnerships are not taxable entities—their owners include the businesses' income on their personal tax returns. In the United States, income is generally reported annually on one or more income tax forms, and taxpayers compute the amount of tax due. The tax due is determined in accordance with various tax laws, rulings of the taxing agencies, and many applicable court decisions. Because administration of tax laws is quite complex and many honest differences exist in their interpretation, the final tax liability for certain firms may not be settled until several years after a given tax year. Thus, the liability for income taxes is often an estimated obligation for some period of time.

Because corporations are separate taxable entities, they ordinarily incur a legal obligation for income taxes whenever corporate income is earned. Therefore, corporate financial statements are routinely adjusted for income tax liabilities. Assuming income taxes of $1,000, this adjustment is recorded as follows:

Income Tax Expense	1,000	
Income Tax Payable		1,000
To record estimated income tax.		

Income Tax Expense may be included among the operating expenses in the income statement. Alternatively, to highlight the impact of income taxes, some companies derive an intermediate figure in the income statement labeled Income before Income Taxes. All expenses except income taxes are subtracted from revenue to derive this figure. Income taxes are then subtracted last in the income statement.

VACATION PAY

Most employees enjoy vacation privileges—typically, at least two weeks per year with regular pay. Depending on the particular agreement, an employee may earn some fraction of his or her annual vacation each payroll period. Other contracts may require a full year's employment before any vacation is given. In the latter case, the proportion of employees who earn annual vacations depends on the employee turn-over rate.

Generally, an employer accrues **vacation benefit expense** if the employees' vacation benefits relate to service already rendered and they vest over time, as long as payment is probable and can be estimated.[1] Assume that a firm provides an annual two-week vacation for employees who have worked 50 weeks and that with the employee turnover rate, 80% of the staff will receive vacation benefits. These employees earn the two weeks' vacation pay during the 50 weeks worked each year, or at the rate of 4% (2 weeks vacation/50 weeks worked). The proper accrual of vacation benefits expense for a $10,000 payroll would be

$$\$10,000 \times 0.04 \times 0.8 = \$320$$

The appropriate journal entry would be

Vacation Benefits Expense	320	
Estimated Liability for Vacation Benefits		320
To record estimated vacation benefits.		

When the vacation benefits are paid, the amount would be recorded as follows (assume vacation benefit of $150 is paid):

Estimated Liability for Vacation Benefits	150	
Cash		150
To record payment of vacation benefits.		

This treatment reflects the annual vacation expense in the appropriate periods and recognizes throughout the year the accrued liability for vacation benefits.

CONTINGENT LIABILITIES

Even though a past transaction or event has taken place, the existence of some liabilities still depends on the occurrence of a future event. These types of liability are called **contingent liabilities.** Whether or not a contingent liability is currently recorded in the accounts depends on the likelihood of the future event occurring and the measurability of the obligation.

If the future event will *probably occur* and the amount of the liability can be *reasonably estimated*, an estimated liability should be recorded in the accounts.[2] The estimated liability for product warranty discussed earlier in the chapter is an example of this situation. Our analysis assumed that customers were likely to make claims under warranties for goods they had purchased and that a reasonable estimate of the amount of warranty obligation could be made.

Some contingent liabilities are not recorded in the accounts but must be disclosed in a note to the financial statements. Contingent liabilities disclosed in this manner are (1) those for which the likelihood of the future event occurring is probable but no reasonable estimate of the future obligation is determinable or (2) those for which the likelihood of the future event occurring is *reasonably possible* (but not probable), regardless of the ability to measure the future amount. When the future amount is not determinable, the note should state that the amount cannot be estimated.

If the likelihood of the future event occurring is *remote*, the contingent liability is not recorded in the accounts or disclosed in a note to the financial statements,

---

[1] *Statement of Financial Accounting Standards No. 43*, "Accounting for Compensated Absences" (Stamford, CT: Financial Accounting Standards Board, 1980).

[2] *Statement of Financial Accounting Standards No. 5*, "Accounting for Contingencies" (Stamford, CT: Financial Accounting Standards Board, 1975).

MESSY ACCOUNTING

American Cyanamid is involved in legal proceedings over cleaning up pollution at approximately 60 sites. How do we know? Because we searched through the notes tucked away in the back of Cyanamid's latest annual report. The note informs us the $4.6 billion (1990 revenues) biotechnology and chemical company may face "substantial" cleanup costs. ■ Substantial? What does that mean? Ten million dollars, perhaps? Or several hundred million dollars, enough to wipe out an entire year's earnings? The company doesn't say.

We're not picking on Cyanamid. It has plenty of company. Such reticence on the subject of environmental liabilities isn't rare, unfortunately. Most companies offer some kind of boilerplate in their annual report, but they differ widely on how promptly to reveal a problem, or how much to say about it. In most cases, says chemical analyst William Young of Donaldson, Lufkin & Jenrette, "We don't get very much specific disclosure."

Specialty materials company Dexter Corp. (1990 revenues, $907 million), for instance, disclosed in 1989 that it faced possible environmental troubles at its Windsor Locks, Conn. facility. But this was specifically disclosed in the 10-K, not in the annual report, giving the impression that the problem was minor. Since then, Dexter has accrued $9.1 million in pre-tax charges for settlement costs and legal fees. Earnings were down almost 50% from last year, to only $12 million, in part because of these charges. Is there more bad news in the offing? Dexter won't comment.

Houston-based consulting firm Pilko & Associates recently surveyed 200 manufacturing executives representing a broad range of industries. About two-thirds had discovered an environmental problem just within the last year. Half were already involved in some sort of environmental litigation.

Yet the nation's accounting rule-makers have not provided guidelines on when and how to disclose the mess in your backyard. The applicable accounting rule is an old (1975) standard on the broad subject of contingent liabilities. A company must disclose a liability, it decrees, as soon as there is a "reasonable possibility" the liability has been incurred.

"Reasonable possibility," of course, is a bit vague, and practice diverges widely. Late last year a survey of 125 industrial companies by accountants Price Waterhouse found that just over a third disclosed their environmental problems to shareholders as soon as federal or state regulators tapped them on the shoulder. Some others disclosed before such notification.

Accounting guidelines say that as soon as a company considers a liability is "probable" and can reasonably be estimated, it must start accruing charges—that is, deducting amounts from today's earnings to cover the future expense.

But "reasonably estimated" is just as vague as "reasonably possible." Some companies seem to take advantage of this by taking the hits to earnings when it's most convenient. Last year Occidental Petroleum lumped $720 million of environmental charges into a $2.2 billion pretax big bath for "restructuring costs." Others wait for strong earnings to let out the news.

Not all the blame rests with the companies or their accountants. It sometimes takes the bureaucrats at the Environmental Protection Agency as long as 18 to 30 months to come up with estimates for different cleanup alternatives. There's also uncertainty as to whether the company's insurer will cover some or all of costs. And lawsuits with vendors or neighbors have yet to be resolved.

Still, the looming threat is a matter that greatly concerns investors, and they deserve better than they are getting in the way of timely warning. Consider the natural gas transmission company Panhandle Eastern (1990 revenues, $3 billion). In early 1989 Panhandle acquired Texas Eastern, which tentatively expected a contingent liability of $400 million for the cleanup of 89 sites contaminated by polychlorinated biphenyls (PCBs). There was no estimate for other associated costs, like third-party claims.

The day after the merger Panhandle gave security analysts the impression that the $400 million estimate was "not only sufficient but generous." Yet in the second quarter of last year the company revised its estimate to $480 million. With the extras, which Panhandle said could add "more than $250 million," the total cost could come to $730 million.

Of course, you can't entirely blame managements for being coy about these numbers, which can hurt their stock badly. For years, industrial-equipment maker Duriron Co., Inc. said in its annual report it would have to clean its Dayton, Ohio landfill, and the cost "is difficult to project but could be substantial." Many investors shunned the stock, which never broke the $20 range. Last year a study of the site was completed, and the company finally announced it anticipated no "material" expense.

Still, environmental risks are part of the landscape today, and corporate management will have to face the risks. Dennis Beresford, chairman of the Financial Accounting Standards Board, agrees "there will be a call for more standard setting." Beresford warns that the task is a difficult one. Every oil leak, asbestos or landfill situation varies. Nevertheless, he hopes the standard setters will address the issue sometime within the next few years. We'd suggest sooner.

SOURCE: Reed Abelson, "Messy Accounting," *Forbes*, October 14, 1991, pp. 172, 174. Reprinted by permission of *Forbes* magazine. © Forbes, Inc., 1991.

regardless of the ability to measure the future amount. One exception to this guideline, however, is when a company guarantees the credit of others (discussed below). Even remote contingent liabilities associated with credit guarantees must be disclosed in a note to the financial statements.

Additional situations creating contingent liabilities are discussed below. In each of these situations, accountants must assess the likelihood of the future event occurring and the measurability of the future amount because these factors determine the proper accounting treatment.

Lawsuits

In the course of its operations, a firm may prosecute a claim in a court of law by filing a **lawsuit.** At any point, a firm may be the defendant in one or more lawsuits involving potentially sizable settlements. Examples of litigation issues include product liability, patent infringement, unfair labor practices, breach of contract, environmental matters, and tax issues. The resolution of a lawsuit may take several years. During the time a lawsuit is pending, the defendant has a contingent liability for any future settlement or damages.

Environmental Cleanup Costs

Past actions by many companies in disposing of various types of industrial waste, such as acids, solvents, and isotopes, have caused subsequent environmental damage. The magnitude of the problem led to the passage of federal laws and the creation of a federal agency, the Environmental Protection Agency, to ensure that damaged sites are cleaned up. Some estimates of the total cleanup cost run as high as $100 billion. Firms owning sites that require cleanup, or that may require cleanup, face a contingent liability for the cleanup costs. Cleanup costs for a particular site may be very difficult to estimate. The party responsible for bearing the cost—the company or its insurance company—may also be at issue.

Additional Income Tax Assessments

Earlier in this chapter, we explained that many aspects of income tax laws and rulings are subject to a significant degree of interpretation. Consequently, many firms do not know their final income tax liability for a given tax period until the related return has been audited or until the applicable statute of limitations becomes effective. The federal statute of limitations for income taxes is three years. No statute of limitations exists in cases of fraud or failure to file returns. After a firm's income tax return has been audited, the government may determine an **additional income tax assessment.** Proposed assessments for additional taxes often are contested in court for extended periods. During this time, the taxpaying firm is contingently liable for the proposed additional tax.

Credit Guarantees

To accommodate important but less financially secure suppliers or customers, a firm may create a **credit guarantee** by cosigning a note payable. Until the original debtor satisfies the obligation, the cosigning firm is contingently liable for the debt. An event similar to a credit guarantee is the discounting of a note receivable *with recourse.* Until the original maker honors the note, the firm that discounted the note receivable is contingently liable for it. Even when the likelihood of default by the debtor is considered remote, the contingent liability associated with credit guarantees must still be disclosed in a note to the financial statements.

Exhibit 12-1 summarizes the criteria for identifying various types of liabilities and the related financial statement treatment. Observe that all liabilities—noncontingent and contingent—arise from a past transaction or event involving the firm. The unique feature of a contingent liability is that it depends on the occurrence of a future event. When it is probable that the future event will occur and that the future obligation is reasonably estimable, the contingent liability is recorded in the accounts and appears in the firm's balance sheet.

EXHIBIT 12—1	LIABILITIES: CRITERIA AND FINANCIAL STATEMENT TREATMENT

| Criterion | Liability Recorded in Accounts and Reported in Balance Sheet | | Contingent Liability: Disclosed in Footnote to Financial Statements | Contingent Liability: No Disclosure Required |
	Noncontingent	Contingent		
Arises out of past transaction or event	Yes	Yes	Yes	Yes	Yes	Yes
Dependent on occurrence of future event	No	No	Yes	Yes	Yes	Yes
Likelihood of future event occurring	Not applicable	Not applicable	Probable	Probable	Reasonably possible	Remote
Amount of future obligation	Known	Reasonably estimable	Reasonably estimable	Not reasonably estimable	Known, reasonably estimable, or not reasonably estimable	Known, reasonably estimable, or not reasonably estimable
Examples	Notes Payable, Accounts Payable	Income Tax Payable	Estimated Liability for Product Warranty	Lawsuits, environmental cleanup costs, additional income tax assessments, and guarantees of others' credit. Exact classification depends on likelihood of future event occurring and measurability of future amount. Guarantees of others' credit must be disclosed even if likelihood of future event occurring is remote.		

PAYROLL ACCOUNTING

Wages and salaries represent a major element in the cost structure of most businesses. Indeed, the largest single expense incurred by some service businesses may be the compensation paid to employees. As we examine the procedures and requirements associated with accounting for salaries and wages, we see that several different current liabilities are related to a company's payroll expense.

PAYROLL LEGISLATION

Payroll accounting procedures are influenced significantly by legislation enacted by the federal and state governments. These laws levy taxes based on payroll amounts, establish remittance and reporting requirements for employers, and set up certain minimum standards for wages and hours.

Federal Insurance Contributions Act

OBJECTIVE ❷ EXPLAIN *and* ILLUSTRATE *the deductions made in computing net pay and the items included in employers' payroll taxes.*

In the mid-1930s, the federal government enacted a national Social Security program to provide workers with a continuing source of income during retirement. The program has been expanded several times since then, one example being the 1965 enactment of the Medicare program of hospital and medical insurance for persons 65 years of age and older.

Monthly benefit payments under Social Security and hospital insurance protection under Medicare are financed by taxes levied on employees, their employers, and self-employed people. Most employed persons in the United States are currently covered by the Social Security system.

The Federal Insurance Contributions Act **(FICA)** establishes the tax levied on *both* employee and employer. The Social Security (old age, survivors, and disability insurance) tax rate for 1991 was 6.2% each for the employee and the employer; the Medicare (hospital insurance) tax rate for 1991 was 1.45% each for the employee and the employer. These tax rates are subject to change in subsequent years.

The Social Security tax rate and the Medicare tax rate apply to salary and wages paid to an employee during a calendar year. The salary and wage bases for Social Security and Medicare are different. For Social Security, the 1991 salary and wage base was $53,400 for each employee, and the Medicare salary and wage base for 1991 was $125,000 for each employee. These bases are also subject to change in subsequent years.

FICA tax on employees is deducted from each paycheck by the employer. In addition, employers pay an amount equal to the amount deducted from the employees. The maximum amount that could be deducted from the paychecks of one employee during 1991 was $5,123.30 [($53,400 × 6.2%) + ($125,000 × 1.45%)]. The maximum amount that could be paid by the employer per employee during 1991 would also be $5,123.30. As a result, the total maximum combined tax paid per employee in 1991 was $10,246.60.

Federal Unemployment Tax Act

The **Federal Unemployment Tax Act (FUTA)** is also part of the federal Social Security program. The states and the national Social Security Administration work together in a joint unemployment insurance program. FUTA raises funds to help finance the administration of the unemployment compensation programs operated by the states. Generally, funds collected under this act are not paid out as unemployment compensation benefits, but are used to pay administrative costs at the federal and state levels. In times of high unemployment, however, the federal government may appropriate funds from its general revenue to provide extended unemployment benefits.

FUTA generates funds by a payroll tax levied only on the employer. At present, the rate is 6.2% of the first $7,000 of an employee's wages. However, the employer is entitled to a credit against this tax for unemployment taxes paid to the state. The maximum credit allowed is 5.4% of the first $7,000 of each employee's wages. Many states set their basic unemployment tax rates at this maximum credit. In these states, the effective FUTA rate on the employer is generally 0.8% (6.2% − 5.4%). Unless otherwise stated, the rates used in our illustrations and problems are 5.4% for state unemployment tax and 0.8% for the federal unemployment tax.

State Unemployment Compensation Taxes

Benefit payments to compensate individuals for wages lost during unemployment are handled through unemployment compensation programs administered by each state. Generally, a worker who becomes unemployed through no fault of his or her own, is able to work, and is available for work is eligible for unemployment benefits. The duration and amount of benefits typically depend on the worker's length of employment and average wage during a previous base period.

The funds for unemployment benefits are generated in most states by a payroll tax levied exclusively on *employers*. In a few states, the employee must also contribute. Because of the credit allowed against the FUTA tax, states often establish their unemployment tax rate for new employers at 5.4%. However, the rate may vary over time according to an employer's experience rating. Employers with records of stable employment usually pay less than the basic rate, and employers causing high levels of unemployment usually pay more than the basic rate. An employer with a favorable experience rating who pays less than the basic rate is still entitled to the maximum 5.4% credit against the federal unemployment tax. For many years the amount of wages per employee subject to unemployment tax was the same for both state and federal unemployment compensation taxes. Recently, many states have increased the base beyond the $7,000 amount presently established for the federal tax, because of increases in claims.

We should remember that FICA, FUTA, and state unemployment taxes are levied on certain maximum amounts of payroll. Throughout the calendar year, employers must be alert to the fact that a higher amount of each period's wages may no longer be subject to one or more of these taxes.

Federal Income Tax Withholding

Employers are required to withhold federal income taxes from wages and salaries paid to employees. Current withholding of income taxes facilitates the government's collection of the tax and also eliminates the possible burden on the employee of having to pay a tax on income after the income has been used for other purposes.

The amount of income tax withheld from each employee is based on the amount of the employee's wage or salary, the employee's marital status, and the number of withholding allowances to which the employee is entitled. When first employed, each employee reports his or her marital status, Social Security number, and number of withholding allowances to the employer on an **Employee's Withholding Allowance Certificate,** also known as **Form W-4** (see Exhibit 12-2). Employees file new W-4s if withholding allowances or marital status change. Employees are entitled to each of the withholding allowances for which they qualify, including one for the employee, one for his or her spouse, and one for each dependent. An employee may also claim one or more additional allowances based on expected excessive itemized deductions on his or her annual income tax return.

Employers usually use the government's withholding tables to determine the amount of federal income taxes to withhold from each employee. There are separate tables for married and single persons and for a variety of payroll periods. Exhibit 12-3 illustrates a few lines from a recent table.

Alternatively, employers may use the percentage method, which is especially useful when no table pertains to the length of the payroll period in question. Both the tables and the percentage method incorporate a graduated system of withholding. That is, the withholding rates increase as the earnings subject to withholding increase.

EXHIBIT 12—2

Form **W-4**	**Employee's Withholding Allowance Certificate**	OMB No. 1545-0010
Department of the Treasury Internal Revenue Service	▶ For Privacy Act and Paperwork Reduction Act Notice, see reverse.	19**92**

1 Type or print your first name and middle initial	Last name	2 Your social security number
Michael R. Corrigan		374-16-3455

Home address (number and street or rural route)	3 ☐ Single ☒ Married ☐ Married, but withhold at higher Single rate.
145 Canyon Drive	**Note:** If married, but legally separated, or spouse is a nonresident alien, check the Single box.

City or town, state, and ZIP code	4 If your last name differs from that on your social security card,
Madison, WI 53711	check here and call 1-800-772-1213 for more information . ▶ ☐

5	Total number of allowances you are claiming (from line G above or from the Worksheets on back if they apply)	**5**	3
6	Additional amount, if any, you want deducted from each paycheck	**6** $	

7 I claim exemption from withholding and I certify that I meet **ALL** of the following conditions for exemption:
- Last year I had a right to a refund of **ALL** Federal income tax withheld because I had **NO** tax liability; **AND**
- This year I expect a refund of **ALL** Federal income tax withheld because I expect to have **NO** tax liability; **AND**
- This year if my income exceeds $600 and includes nonwage income, another person cannot claim me as a dependent.

If you meet all of the above conditions, enter the year effective and "EXEMPT" here . . ▶ | **7** | 19

8 Are you a full-time student? (**Note:** Full-time students are not automatically exempt.) . . . . | **8** ☐ Yes ☒ No

Under penalties of perjury, I certify that I am entitled to the number of withholding allowances claimed on this certificate or entitled to claim exempt status.

Employee's signature ▶ *Michael Corrigan* Date ▶ November 15 , 19 92

9 Employer's name and address (Employer: Complete 9 and 11 only if sending to the IRS)	10 Office code (optional)	11 Employer identification number

Cat. No. 10220Q

EXHIBIT 12—3	FEDERAL INCOME TAX WITHHOLDING TABLE

WEEKLY Payroll Period—Employee MARRIED

And the wages are—		And the number of withholding allowances claimed is—										
At least	But less than	0	1	2	3	4	5	6	7	8	9	10 or more
		The amount of income tax to be withheld shall be—										
260	270	30	23	17	11	5	0	0	0	0	0	0
270	280	31	25	19	12	6	0	0	0	0	0	0
280	290	33	26	20	14	8	2	0	0	0	0	0
290	300	34	28	22	15	9	3	0	0	0	0	0
300	310	36	29	23	17	11	5	0	0	0	0	0
310	320	37	31	25	18	12	6	0	0	0	0	0
320	330	39	32	26	20	14	8	1	0	0	0	0
330	340	40	34	28	21	15	9	3	0	0	0	0
340	350	42	35	29	23	17	11	4	0	0	0	0
350	360	43	37	31	24	18	12	6	0	0	0	0
360	370	45	38	32	26	20	14	7	1	0	0	0
370	380	46	40	34	27	21	15	9	3	0	0	0
380	390	48	41	35	29	23	17	10	4	0	0	0
390	400	49	43	37	30	24	18	12	6	0	0	0
400	410	51	44	38	32	26	20	13	7	1	0	0
410	420	52	46	40	33	27	21	15	9	2	0	0
420	430	54	47	41	35	29	23	16	10	4	0	0
430	440	55	49	43	36	30	24	18	12	5	0	0
440	450	57	50	44	38	32	26	19	13	7	1	0

State Income Tax Withholding

Most states now have an income tax that is withheld by employers. Payroll procedures for withholding state income taxes are similar to those for withholding federal income taxes.

Taxes related to payroll amounts may be levied on the employee, the employer, or both. Exhibit 12-4 summarizes who pays the various payroll taxes we have just discussed.

Employee versus Independent Contractor

Salaries and wages paid to employees provide the basis for withholding taxes from employees and levying payroll taxes on the employer. Independent contractors are not subject to withholding and are therefore distinguished from employees. In gen-

EXHIBIT 12—4	TAXES RELATED TO PAYROLL AMOUNTS

Tax	Paid By Employer	Paid By Employee
Federal Insurance Contributions Act	X	X
Federal Unemployment Tax Act	X	
State Unemployment Compensation Taxes	X	In a few states
Federal Income Tax Withholding		X
State Income Tax Withholding		X

eral, an *employee* performs services subject to the supervision and control of another party known as the employer. The following variables establish the existence of an employer-employee relationship: (1) the employer has the power to discharge the individual worker, (2) the employer sets the work hours for the individual worker, and (3) the employer furnishes a place to work. An *independent contractor,* on the other hand, may also perform services for a business firm, but that firm does not have the legal right to direct and control the methods used by this person. Independent contractors are in business for themselves; examples are certified public accountants, lawyers, and physicians.

Wages are the earnings of employees who are paid on an hourly or piecework basis. A *salary* is the compensation of employees paid on a monthly or annual basis. Amounts paid to independent contractors are identified as *fees*. For example, the expense account Audit Fees Expense may be charged for the amounts paid to a certified public accountant for audit work, and Legal Fees Expense may be charged for payments to a lawyer for legal work.

Remittance and Reporting Requirements

The legislation levying various taxes on payroll amounts also specifies the procedures for paying these taxes to the government and establishes the reports an employer must file. A sound system of payroll accounting ensures that these payments are made and reports are filed on time.

FICA TAXES AND FEDERAL INCOME TAXES WITHHELD

Employer payment and reporting requirements are the same for both employer's and employees' FICA taxes and federal income taxes withheld, because these taxes are combined for payment and reporting purposes. Generally, payments are deposited in a Federal Reserve bank or authorized commercial bank. The specific payment requirements vary depending on the combined dollar amount of the taxes.

Each quarter, employers file an Employer's Quarterly Federal Tax Return, Form 941, with the Internal Revenue Service. On this form the employer schedules a record of its liability for FICA taxes and withheld income taxes throughout the quarter and reports its deposits of these taxes.

By January 31, an employer must give each employee a **Form W-2,** Wage and Tax Statement, which specifies the employee's total wages paid, the federal income taxes withheld, the wages subject to FICA tax, and the FICA tax withheld for the preceding calendar year (see Exhibit 12-5). The worker attaches one copy of Form W-2 to his or her federal income tax return. The employer sends a copy of each employee's Form W-2 to the Social Security Administration, which, in turn, provides the Internal Revenue Service with the income tax data that it needs from these forms.

FEDERAL UNEMPLOYMENT INSURANCE TAXES

The amount due on federal unemployment insurance taxes must be reviewed quarterly. If undeposited taxes exceed $100 at the end of any of the first three quarters of a year, a deposit must be made in a Federal Reserve bank or authorized commercial bank during the first month after the quarter. If the amount due is $100 or less, no deposit is necessary. By January 31, each employer must file a Form 940, Employer's Annual Federal Unemployment Tax Return, for the preceding year. If the annual tax reported on Form 940, less deposits made, exceeds $100, the entire amount due must be deposited by January 31. If this amount is $100 or less, it may be either deposited or remitted with Form 940.

STATE UNEMPLOYMENT COMPENSATION TAXES

The filing and payment requirements for unemployment compensation taxes vary among the states. Often, however, employers must pay the taxes when they file quarterly reports. Some states require payments more frequently, sometimes monthly, if the taxes owed by an employer exceed a preestablished level.

Fair Labor Standards Act

The **Fair Labor Standards Act** establishes minimum wage, overtime pay, and equal pay standards for employees covered by the act and sets record-keeping requirements for their employers. The act's coverage has been amended several times since its

EXHIBIT 12—5	FORM W-2 WAGE AND TAX STATEMENT 1991

1 Control number 112		OMB No. 1545-0008	This information is being furnished to the Internal Revenue Service. If you are required to file a tax return, a negligence penalty or other sanction may be imposed on you if this income is taxable and you fail to report it.		
2 Employer's name, address, and ZIP code University of Wisconsin System 750 University Avenue Madison, Wisconsin 53706			6 Statutory employee ☐ Deceased ☐ Pension plan ☐ Legal rep. ☐ 942 emp. ☐ Subtotal ☐ Deferred compensation ☐ Void ☐		
			7 Allocated tips	8 Advance EIC payment	
			9 Federal income tax withheld 14,320.50	10 Wages, tips, other compensation 64,300.00	
3 Employer's identification number 39-6006492	4 Employer's state I.D. number 20608		11 Social security tax withheld 3,310.80	12 Social security wages 53,400.00	
5 Employee's social security number 374-16-3455			13 Social security tips	14 Medicare wages and tips 64,300.00	
19 Employee's name, address, and ZIP code Michael R. Corrigan 145 Canyon Drive Madison, Wisconsin 53711			15 Medicare tax withheld 932.35	16 Nonqualified plans	
			17 See Instrs. for Box 17	18 Other	
20 /////////	21 /////////		22 Dependent care benefits	23 Benefits included in Box 10	
24 State income tax 3,752.60	25 State wages, tips, etc. 64,300.00	26 Name of state WI	27 Local income tax	28 Local wages, tips, etc.	29 Name of locality

Department of the Treasury—Internal Revenue Service

passage in 1938. Its provisions now extend, with certain exemptions, to employees directly or indirectly engaged in interstate commerce and to domestic service workers. Executive, administrative, and professional employees are exempt from the act's minimum wage and overtime provisions.

A covered employee must be paid an amount equal to at least $1\frac{1}{2}$ times that employee's regular pay rate for every hour beyond 40 that he or she works in a week. The following are some examples of overtime pay computations under this standard; the examples differ by the basic method of compensating the employee.

1. Heather Green receives $6.10 per hour as her regular rate of pay. Her overtime rate of pay is $9.15 ($6.10 + $3.05) per hour. This week she worked 44 hours. Her gross earnings this week are $280.60, computed as (40 hours × $6.10/hour) + (4 hours × $9.15/hour).

2. Jack Tyler is paid on a piece rate basis. His earnings this week, before any overtime compensation, are $275.20 for 43 hours of work. For overtime pay computations, his regular hourly rate of pay is determined by dividing his weekly earnings on a piece rate basis by the number of hours worked in that week, or $275.20/43 = $6.40. For each hour worked over 40 in the week, Tyler is entitled to an overtime premium of $3.20 ($\frac{1}{2}$ of $6.40). Therefore, his total earnings this week are $275.20 + $9.60 (3 hours × $3.20) = $284.80.

   The act permits an alternative way to compute overtime for piece rate workers, if agreed upon in advance of the work. This method pays $1\frac{1}{2}$ times the piece rate for each piece produced during overtime hours.

Employees may negotiate overtime pay rates in excess of the minimum standard illustrated in the preceding discussion. A union contract, for example, may require double the regular pay rate for hours worked on Sundays and holidays.

Under the Fair Labor Standards Act, employers may not discriminate on the basis of sex in the rates paid to men and women employees performing equal work on jobs demanding equal skill, effort, and responsibility and having similar working conditions. The equal pay provisions also provide that employers must eliminate illegal pay differentials by a means other than reducing employee pay rates. The law does permit wage differentials between men and women when due to a job-related factor other than sex, such as a difference based on a bona fide seniority or merit system.

Employers are required under the law to maintain a detailed record of each employee's wage and hours, including the hour and day the employee's workweek begins, the regular hourly rate of pay, the total overtime pay for any week in which more than 40 hours are worked, the deductions from and additions to wages, and the employee's total wages paid each period. The law does not prescribe any particular form for these records. The payroll records maintained in a typical payroll accounting system contain much of this information, which is also needed to comply with other laws and regulations.

OTHER PAYROLL DEDUCTIONS

In addition to FICA taxes, federal income taxes, and perhaps state and local income taxes, other items may be deducted from an employee's gross earnings in arriving at the net *take-home* pay for the period. Each additional deduction must be authorized by the employee. Following are examples of other payroll deductions:

1. Union dues.
2. Premiums on life, accident, health, or major medical insurance.
3. Installment payment on loan from employees' credit union.
4. Repayment of advance from employer.
5. Purchase of U.S. savings bonds.
6. Contributions to charitable organizations.
7. Payments into a retirement plan.

COMPUTATION OF NET PAY FOR INDIVIDUAL EMPLOYEE

To illustrate the computation of an individual employee's net pay for a payroll period, let us assume that Donald Carter's hourly wage rate is $10. He is married and claims three withholding allowances on Form W-4. He has authorized his employer to deduct $5 per week for group health insurance and $2 per week as a contribution to the United Way charity. During the current week, he works 42 hours. Prior to the current week, his gross earnings for the year are $1,660. FICA tax rates are 6.2% of the first $53,400 earned for Social Security and 1.45% of the first $125,000 earned for Medicare. The amount paid to Donald Carter is computed as follows:

Gross earnings		$430.00
Deductions:		
Federal income tax withheld	$36.00	
FICA taxes withheld	32.90	
Group health insurance	5.00	
United Way contribution	2.00	
Total deductions		75.90
Net earnings		$354.10

An explanation of these amounts follows:

1. *Gross earnings:* Carter's regular hourly rate is $10; his overtime rate is $10 × 1.5, or $15 per hour. Because Carter worked two hours beyond the 40-hour

standard, his gross pay will be ($10 × 40 hours) plus ($15 × 2 hours), or $430.

2. *Federal income tax withheld:* Carter's deduction for federal income tax withheld is determined using the table in Exhibit 12-3. The row for wages of at least $430 but less than $440 and the column for three withholding allowances yields the withholding amount of $36.

3. *FICA taxes withheld:* Carter's earnings for the year exceed neither the Social Security nor the Medicare maximum. Therefore, the amount for Social Security will be $430 × 6.2%, or $26.66, and the Medicare amount will be $430 × 1.45%, or $6.24, for a total of $32.90.

4. *Group health insurance and charitable contribution:* Carter has authorized his employer to make these deductions.

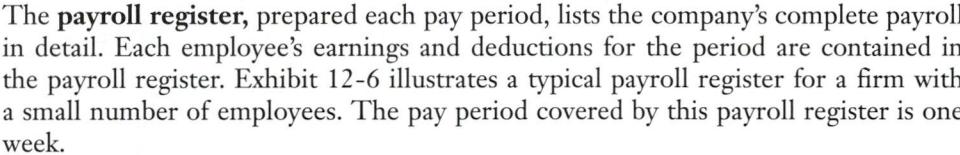

PAYROLL RECORDS

The precise nature of an enterprise's payroll records and procedures depends to a great extent on the size of the work force and the degree to which the record keeping is automated. In some form, however, two records are basic to most payroll systems—the payroll register and individual employee earnings records.

The Payroll Register

OBJECTIVE ❸ DESCRIBE *and* ILLUSTRATE *the records required in payroll accounting.*

The **payroll register,** prepared each pay period, lists the company's complete payroll in detail. Each employee's earnings and deductions for the period are contained in the payroll register. Exhibit 12-6 illustrates a typical payroll register for a firm with a small number of employees. The pay period covered by this payroll register is one week.

In Exhibit 12-6, the column immediately after each employee's name shows the total hours worked by that employee during the week. Data on the hours worked are taken from time cards or similar documents maintained for each employee. In this illustration, overtime pay is computed at $1\frac{1}{2}$ times the regular hourly rate. The employees' gross earnings appear in the final column in the earnings section.

The FICA tax is deducted from each employee's gross earnings. Because the payroll illustrated is early in the calendar year (the week ended February 4, 1993), no employee's earnings have exceeded the maximum amount of wages subject to the FICA tax. As discussed earlier, the federal income tax withheld is based on an employee's earnings, marital status, and number of withholding allowances. In Exhibit 12-6, for example, David Plank's relatively high federal income tax withheld is due to the fact that he is single and claims only one withholding allowance. The deductions for health insurance, contributions to United Way, and purchases of U.S. savings bonds are specifically authorized by each employee affected by the deductions. The health insurance premiums vary with the number of persons covered by the plan.

An employee receives an amount equal to gross earnings less total deductions for the pay period. These net earnings are shown in the payment section of the payroll register, along with the number of the check issued by the company in payment of the wages.

In the last two columns of the payroll register, gross earnings are distributed between the office wages and sales wages categories. This division permits the total salaries and wages for the period to be recorded in the proper expense accounts.

Recording the Payroll and Related Taxes

For some businesses, the payroll register is a special journal; in these cases, the pertinent payroll register information is posted directly to the general ledger. Often, however, the payroll register is the basis for a general journal entry that is then posted

EXHIBIT 12–6   PAYROLL REGISTER FOR THE WEEK ENDED FEBRUARY 4, 1993

Employee	Total Hours	Earnings			Deductions					Payment		Distribution	
		Regular	Overtime	Gross	FICA Tax	Federal Income Tax	Health Insurance	Other (see key)	Total Deductions	Net Earnings	Check No.	Office Wages	Sales Wages
Donald Carter	42	400	30	430	36.00	32.90	5.00	(A) 2.00	75.90	354.10	566	430	
Jane Latt	40	280		280	21.42	20.00	5.00	(B) 4.00	50.42	229.58	567		280
Raul Lopez	44	260	37	297	22.72	22.00	5.00		49.72	247.28	568		297
David Plank	40	360		360	27.54	41.00	2.00	(B) 5.00	75.54	284.46	569		360
Myra Smiken	44	320	48	368	28.15	26.00	5.00		59.15	308.85	570		368
Fred Wells	40	280		280	21.42	20.00	2.00	(A) 1.00	44.42	235.58	571	280	
Beth White	46	320		320	24.48	26.00	5.00		55.48	264.52	572	320	
Totals		2,220	115	2,335	181.73	187.90	29.00	12.00	410.63	1,924.37		1,030	1,305

Key: A—United Way Contribution
B—U.S. Savings Bonds

Handwritten annotations:

7,165

62,700 6

PAYROLL PAYABLE

TOTAL GROSS
EARNINGS

$9000

STAT

TOTAL GROSS
– TOTAL DED.
NET PAY

TOTAL GROSS   62700
EARNINGS

FICA   SS.   6.2%
UNLIMITED MC + 1.45%
7.65%

to the general ledger. The journal entry to record the weekly payroll shown in Exhibit 12-6 follows:

Office Salaries and Wages Expense	1,030.00	
Sales Salaries and Wages Expense	1,305.00	
FICA Tax Payable		181.73
Federal Income Tax Withholding Payable		187.90
Health Insurance Premiums Payable		29.00
United Way Contributions Payable		3.00
U.S. Savings Bond Deductions Payable		9.00
Payroll Payable		1,924.37
To record payroll for week ended February 4, 1993.		

The employer company may, when recording each payroll, also record its payroll tax liabilities. The year-to-date gross earnings for the employees in Exhibit 12-6 have not exceeded the maximum limits for either the FICA or unemployment taxes. The entry to record the employer's taxes for the week's payroll follows:

Payroll Tax Expense	326.50	
FICA Tax Payable (see preceding entry)		181.73
Federal Unemployment Tax Payable (0.8% × $2,335)		18.68
State Unemployment Tax Payable (5.4% × $2,335)		126.09
To record payroll tax expense for week ended February 4, 1993.		

Payment of the Liabilities

The various liabilities established in the entries recording the payroll and the employer's payroll taxes are settled when the employer makes payments to the appropriate parties. The issuance of the employees' payroll checks results in the following entry:

Payroll Payable	1,924.37	
Cash		1,924.37
To pay net payroll for week ended February 4, 1993.		

The FICA taxes, federal income taxes withheld, and federal unemployment insurance taxes are remitted to a depository bank. The state unemployment compensation taxes are remitted to the appropriate state agency, according to the state's requirements. The health insurance premiums are sent to the company providing the coverage, the United Way contributions are paid to that charitable organization, and the deductions for the purchase of U.S. savings bonds are remitted to the financial institution handling the acquisition of the bonds. If any of these liabilities remain unpaid when financial statements are prepared, they are classified as current liabilities in the balance sheet.

Accrual of Employer Payroll Taxes

Employer payroll taxes are based on employees' salaries and wages. A company that accrues salaries and wages with a year-end adjusting entry should also record the related employer payroll taxes as year-end adjustments. Payroll taxes are properly an expense of the period during which the related salaries and wages were earned, although the employer is *legally* obligated for these taxes in the period the salaries and wages are actually paid. This circumstance, coupled with a possibly immaterial amount of payroll taxes, leads some companies to an alternative procedure: they record the total amount of payroll taxes only in the year the payroll is paid.

Individual Employee Earnings Record

Employers maintain an **individual earnings record** for each employee. This record contains much of the information needed for the employer to comply with the various taxation and reporting requirements established by law. Exhibit 12-7 illustrates Donald Carter's individual earnings record for the first five weeks of 1993.

The individual earnings record contains the details on earnings and deductions shown earlier in the payroll register. In addition, the cumulative gross earnings column alerts the employer when an employee's yearly earnings have exceeded the maximum amounts to which the FICA and unemployment taxes apply.

Employers prepare Form W-2—the Wage and Tax Statement sent to every employee each year—from the individual employee earnings records. Although Form

EXHIBIT 12-7

INDIVIDUAL EMPLOYEE EARNINGS RECORD

Employee's Name: Donald Carter
Address: 510 Palm Lane
Archer, Florida 32600
Date of Birth: May 6, 1946
Position: Clerk-Analyst

Social Security No.: 719-23-4866
Male: X
Female: ___
Married: X
Single: ___
Withholding Allowances: 3
Date of Employment: June 1, 1971
Date Employment Ended: ___

Employee No.: 6
Hourly Pay Rate: $10.00

1993 Period Ended	Total Hours	Earnings Regular	Earnings Overtime	Earnings Gross	Deductions FICA Tax	Deductions Federal Income Tax	Deductions Health Insurance	Deductions Other: (A) United Way (B) Savings Bonds	Deductions Total Deductions	Payment Net Earnings	Payment Check No.	Cumulative Gross Earnings
Jan. 7	40	400.00		400.00	30.60	32.00	5.00	(A) 2.00	69.60	330.40	412	400.00
Jan. 14	44	400.00	60.00	460.00	35.19	41.00	5.00	(A) 2.00	83.19	376.81	447	860.00
Jan. 21	40	400.00		400.00	30.60	32.00	5.00	(A) 2.00	69.60	330.40	480	1,260.00
Jan. 28	40	400.00		400.00	30.60	32.00	5.00	(A) 2.00	69.60	330.40	525	1,660.00
Feb. 4	42	400.00	30.00	430.00	32.90	36.00	5.00	(A) 2.00	75.90	354.10	566	2,090.00

Handwritten annotations:

18.64
181.73
280.41

941 PAYMENT
(DR) FICA TAX PAY 260.41
(DR) FED. INC. TAX PAY. 187.90
(CR) CASH

940 PAYMENT
FUTA
DR FUTA PAY 8.00
CR CASH 8.06

W-2 is sent only once and covers an entire year, employers typically provide employees with an earnings statement each pay period, detailing the earnings and deductions for that period. These earnings statements may be a detachable portion of the employee's paycheck or may be enclosed as a separate document with the paycheck.

PAYMENT TO EMPLOYEES

A company with a small number of employees may pay them with checks drawn on the firm's regular bank account. A company with a large number of employees usually establishes a separate bank account to pay the payroll.

Payroll Bank Account

A company with a separate payroll bank account draws a check on its regular bank account each pay period in an amount equal to the total net earnings of the employees. This check is deposited in the payroll bank account. Individual payroll checks are then drawn on this account and delivered to the employees. The issuance of the payroll checks reduces to zero the book balance in the payroll bank account.

One advantage of maintaining a separate payroll bank account is that it divides the work between the preparation and issuance of regular company checks and payroll checks. A related advantage is that it simplifies the monthly reconciliation of the regular bank account. The large number of payroll checks, many of which may be outstanding at month-end, are not run through the regular bank account. The payroll bank account must also be reconciled, but the only reconciling items for this bank account are payroll checks outstanding.

Payment in Cash

Sometimes employees are paid in currency and coin rather than by check. This may happen, for example, if the employees work in a location where it may not be convenient for them to deposit or cash checks. The company prepares and cashes its own checks for the payroll amount. Each employee's pay is delivered to the employee in an envelope. For internal control, and to have evidence of the payment, an employee signs a receipt for the payroll envelope. Often the outside of the envelope contains an itemization of the employee's gross earnings and deductions for the payroll period.

ANALYTICAL APPLICATION

OBJECTIVE ④ DEFINE *the operating cash flow to current liabilities ratio and* EXPLAIN *its use.*

OPERATING CASH FLOW TO CURRENT LIABILITIES RATIO

Two measures previously introduced—the current ratio and the acid test ratio—emphasize the relationship of current assets to current liabilities in an attempt to measure the ability of the firm to liquidate current liabilities when they become due. The **operating cash flow to current liabilities ratio** is another measure of ability to liquidate current liabilities. The ratio is calculated as follows:

$$\text{Operating Cash Flow to Current Liabilities Ratio} = \frac{\text{Net Cash Flow from Operating Activities}}{\text{Average Current Liabilities}}$$

Net cash flow from operating activities is obtained from the statement of cash flows. The net cash flow from operating activities represents the excess amount of cash derived from operations during the year after deducting working capital needs and payments required on current liabilities. The denominator is the average of the beginning and ending current liabilities for the year.

The following amounts (in millions of dollars) were taken from recent financial statements for AMERICAN INFORMATION TECHNOLOGIES CORPORATION (Ameritech), a company headquartered in Chicago that is the parent of five Bell companies serving the Great Lakes region:

Net cash flow from operating activities	$2,885.7
Current liabilities at beginning of the year	3,227.2
Current liabilities at end of the year	4,606.9

The operating cash flow to current liabilities ratio would be calculated as follows:

$$\$2,885.7/[(\$3,227.2 + \$4,606.9)/2] = 0.74$$

Ameritech's operating cash flow to current liabilities ratio for the preceding year was 1.00. The higher this ratio, the stronger is a firm's ability to settle current liabilities as they become due. The decline in Ameritech's ratio from 1.00 to 0.74, however, is not necessarily a sign of financial weakness. A ratio of 0.5 is considered a strong ratio so Ameritech's ratio of 0.74 would be interpreted as quite strong.

KEY POINTS FOR CHAPTER OBJECTIVES

❶ DEFINE and **ILLUSTRATE** the most common types of current and contingent liabilities (pp. 428–435).

- Current liabilities are all obligations that will require within the coming year or the operating cycle, whichever is longer, (1) the use of existing current assets or (2) the creation of other current liabilities.
- Some common examples of current liabilities are trade accounts and notes payable, dividends payable, sales and excise taxes payable, property taxes payable, income taxes payable, and estimated liability for vacation benefits.
- Even though a past transaction or event has taken place, the existence of some liabilities, called *contingent liabilities*, depends on the occurrence of a future event. Whether or not a contingent liability is currently recorded in the accounts depends on the likelihood of the future event occurring and the measurability of the obligation.
  1. If the future event will probably occur and the amount of the liability can be reasonably estimated, then the contingent liability should be recorded in the accounts.
  2. If the likelihood of the future event occurring is probable, but no reasonable estimate of the future obligation is determinable or the likelihood of the future event occurring is reasonably possible (but not probable), regardless of the ability to measure the future amount, then the contingent liability should be disclosed in a note to the financial statements, not recorded in the accounts.
  3. If the likelihood of the future event occurring is remote, the contingent liability is not recorded in the accounts or disclosed in a note to the financial statements. The only exception is a credit guarantee, which must be disclosed in a note to the financial statements.

❷ EXPLAIN and **ILLUSTRATE** the deductions made in computing net pay and the items included in employers' payroll taxes (pp. 435–442).

- Deductions from employees' pay generally required by law are withheld income taxes and FICA taxes. Some deductions may be contractual, such as union dues. Others are voluntary, such as charitable contributions.
- Employers' payroll tax expenses include a matching amount (with employees) of FICA taxes, and state and federal unemployment compensation taxes. Employers may also, by contract, assume other expenses, such as a portion of health premiums.

❸ DESCRIBE and **ILLUSTRATE** the records required in payroll accounting (pp. 442–446).

- Firms with more than a few employees often prepare a payroll register, which itemizes each employee's gross earnings, deductions, and net pay. This can either be posted as a journal or used to support journal entries recording the payroll.
- Most firms maintain an individual earnings record for each employee that contains information necessary for the employer to comply with various taxation and reporting requirements established by law.

❹ ANALYTICAL APPLICATION   DEFINE the *operating cash flow to current liabilities ratio* and **EXPLAIN** its use (pp. 446–447).

- The operating cash flow to current liabilities ratio is calculated by dividing net cash flow from operating activities by the average current liabilities for the year.
- The operating cash flow to current liabilities ratio is a measure of a firm's ability to liquidate its current liabilities.

SELF-TEST QUESTIONS FOR REVIEW

(Answers follow the Solution to Demonstration Problem.)

1. Which of the following is *not* considered to be a contingent liability?
   a. Discounted notes receivable.
   b. Notes payable.
   c. Credit guarantees.
   d. Lawsuit.

2. A firm sold merchandise on account for $1,840, which included a 10% excise tax and a 5% sales tax. The entry to record this sale would include
   a. A debit of $1,600 to Accounts Receivable.
   b. A debit of $2,116 to Accounts Receivable.
   c. A credit of $1,600 to Sales.
   d. A credit of $1,840 to Sales.

3. A firm sells a product for $400 per unit, which includes a 30-day warranty against defects. Experience indicates that 4% of the units will prove defective, requiring an average repair cost of $50 per unit. During the first month of business, product sales were $320,000 and 20 of the units sold were defective and repaired during the month. The accrued liability for product warranties at month-end is
   a. $1,000   b. $600   c. $1,600   d. $2,000

4. Which of the following payroll-related taxes does not represent a deduction from the employees' earnings?
   a. FICA taxes.
   b. Income taxes.
   c. Federal unemployment taxes.
   d. All of the above are deductions from employees' earnings.

5. Janice Sheldon, who is covered by the Fair Labor Standards Act, receives wages of $9 per hour. This week she worked 44 hours. Income tax withheld amounts to $42. Her prior gross earnings for the year were $4,320, and the FICA tax rates are 6.2% of the first $53,400 and 1.45% of the first $125,000. Sheldon's net pay is
   a. $340.33   b. $323.68   c. $307.03   d. $346.18

DEMONSTRATION PROBLEM FOR REVIEW

Archer Corporation had the following payroll data for April 1993:

Office salaries	$ 40,000
Sales salaries	86,000
Federal income taxes withheld	25,600
Health insurance premiums deducted	1,850
United Way contributions deducted	950
Salaries (included above):	
subject to both FICA taxes	126,000
subject to federal unemployment taxes	76,000
subject to state unemployment taxes	88,000

The combined FICA tax rate is 7.65% (6.2% plus 1.45%), the federal unemployment compensation tax rate is 0.8%, and the state unemployment compensation tax rate is 5.4%. The amounts subject to these taxes are given above.

REQUIRED

Present general journal entries to record
a. Accrual of the payroll.
b. Payment of the net payroll.
c. Accrual of employer's payroll taxes.
d. Payment of all liabilities related to the payroll. (Assume that all are settled at the same time.)

SOLUTION TO DEMONSTRATION PROBLEM

a.	Apr. 30	Office Salaries Expense	40,000	
		Sales Salaries Expense	86,000	
		Federal Income Tax Withholding Payable		25,600
		FICA Tax Payable		9,639
		Health Insurance Premiums Payable		1,850
		United Way Contributions Payable		950
		Payroll Payable		87,961

To accrue payroll for April. FICA taxes
(0.0765 × $126,000 = $9,639).

| b. | 30 | Payroll Payable | 87,961 | |
| | | Cash | | 87,961 |

To pay April payroll.

c.	30	Payroll Tax Expense	14,999	
		FICA Tax Payable		9,639
		Federal Unemployment Tax Payable		608
		State Unemployment Tax Payable		4,752

To record employer's payroll taxes (FICA tax = 0.0765
× $126,000 = $9,639; federal unemployment tax =
0.008 × $76,000 = $608; state unemployment tax =
0.054 × $88,000 = $4,752).

d.	30	Federal Income Tax Withholding Payable	25,600	
		FICA Tax Payable	19,278	
		Health Insurance Premiums Payable	1,850	
		United Way Contributions Payable	950	
		Federal Unemployment Tax Payable	608	
		State Unemployment Tax Payable	4,752	
		Cash		53,038

To record payment of payroll-related liabilities.

ANSWERS TO SELF-TEST QUESTIONS

1. b, pp. 432–434   **2.** c, p. 429   **3.** b, p. 430   **4.** c, p. 436   **5.** a, p. 440

GLOSSARY OF KEY TERMS USED IN THIS CHAPTER

additional income tax assessment   An assessment by taxing authorities for an increased income tax payment; if contested by the taxpayer, it will be disclosed as a contingent liability by the company that is assessed the additional tax (p. 434).

contingent liability   A potential obligation, the eventual occurrence of which usually depends on some future event beyond the control of the firm. Contingent liabilities may originate with such things as lawsuits, credit guarantees, and contested income tax assessments (p. 432).

credit guarantee   A guarantee of another company's debt by cosigning a note payable; a guarantor's contingent liability that is usually disclosed in a balance sheet footnote (p. 434).

current liabilities   Obligations that will require within the coming year or operating cycle, whichever is longer, (1) the use of existing current assets or (2) the creation of other current liabilities (p. 428).

Employee's Withholding Allowance Certificate (Form W-4)   A form used by employees to claim income tax withholding allowances (p. 437).

Fair Labor Standards Act   An act establishing minimum wage, overtime pay, and equal pay standards for employees and setting the necessary record-keeping requirements for employers (p. 439).

Federal Unemployment Taxes (FUTA)   A federal tax levied against employers to help finance administration of the various unemployment compensation programs operated by the states (p. 436).

FICA Tax   Federal Insurance Contributions Act tax; under this act, the income of an individual is taxed to support the national Social Security program providing retirement income, medical care, and death benefits. Employers pay a matching amount of tax on their eligible employees (p. 436).

individual earnings records   A detailed record maintained by an employer for each employee that shows gross earnings, overtime premiums, all amounts withheld, payroll tax data, and net earnings paid (p. 444).

lawsuit   A prosecution of a claim in a court of law; may lead to a financial statement footnote disclosure by the defendant as a contingent liability (p. 434).

liabilities   Present obligations resulting from past transactions that require the firm to pay money, provide goods, or perform services in the future (p. 428).

operating cash flow to current liabilities ratio   Net cash flow from operating activities divided by the average current liabilities for the year (p. 446).

payroll register   A detailed list, prepared each pay period, showing each employee's earnings and deductions for the period (p. 442).

product warranties   Guarantees against product defects for a designated period of time after sale (p. 430).

vacation benefit expense   An expense reflecting the cost of employee vacation privileges; this expense is generally accrued over the period in which employees earn vacation (p. 432).

Wage and Tax Statement (Form W-2)   A form an employer must give each employee annually that shows the employee's total gross pay, federal income tax and FICA tax withheld, and the wages subject to FICA tax (p. 444).

QUESTIONS

12-1   For accounting purposes, how are liabilities defined?

12-2   Present a general rule for measuring current liabilities on the balance sheet.

12-3   Define *current liabilities*.

12-4   Describe the difference between accounting for product warranties on (a) failed units repaired in the month of sale and (b) failed units repaired in a subsequent month but that are still covered by the warranty.

12-5   Under what conditions must an employer accrue employees' vacation benefits?

12-6   Define *contingent liabilities*. List three examples of contingent liabilities. When should contingent liabilities be recorded in the accounts?

12-7   On whom is the FICA tax levied? What does the FICA tax finance?

12-8   On whom are the federal and state unemployment insurance taxes levied? What do these taxes finance?

12-9   Why does an employee file a Form W-4, Employee's Withholding Allowance Certificate, with his or her employer?

12-10   What is the difference between an employee and an independent contractor?

12-11   What does Form W-2, Wage and Tax Statement, report? Who receives copies of this form?

12-12   Simon Garcia is employed at $10.20 per hour. Under the Fair Labor Standards Act, how many hours in a week must he work before he is entitled to overtime pay? What is the minimum overtime rate of pay he must receive?

12-13   List at least five examples of deductions from an employee's gross earnings other than FICA taxes and federal income taxes withheld.

12-14   What is a payroll register? How does it differ from an individual employee earnings record?

12-15   If earned but unpaid wages are accrued at year-end, should employer payroll taxes on these wages be accrued at the same time? Explain.

12-16   List two advantages of maintaining a special payroll bank account for the payment of a net payroll.

12-17   Define the *operating cash flow to current liabilities ratio* and explain its use.

EXERCISES

CURRENT LIABILITIES IN BALANCE SHEET
— OBJ. 1 —

12-18   For each of the following situations, indicate the amount shown as a liability on the balance sheet of Kane, Inc., at December 31, 1993.

   a.   Kane has trade accounts payable of $110,000 for merchandise included in the 1993 ending inventory.

   b.   Kane has agreed to purchase a $28,000 drill press in January 1994.

c. During November and December of 1993, Kane sold products to a firm and guaranteed them against product failure for 90 days. Estimated costs of honoring this provision during 1994 are $2,200.

d. On December 15, 1993, Kane declared a $70,000 cash dividend payable on January 15, 1994, to stockholders of record on December 31, 1993.

e. Kane provides a profit-sharing bonus for its executives equal to 5% of the reported before-tax income for the current year. The estimated income (as defined above) for 1993 is $600,000 on June 15, 1993.

EXCISE AND SALES TAX CALCULATIONS — OBJ. 1 —

12-19 Barnes Company has just billed a customer for $974.40, an amount that includes a 10% excise tax and a 6% state sales tax.

a. What amount of revenue is recorded?

b. Present a general journal entry to record the transaction on the books of Barnes Company on June 15, 1993.

PROVIDING FOR VACATION BENEFITS — OBJ. 1 —

12-20 Franklin, Inc.'s current vacation policy for its production workers provides four weeks paid vacation for employees who have worked 48 weeks. An analysis of the company's employee turnover rates indicates that approximately 10% of the employees will forfeit their vacation benefits.

a. Compute the proper provision for estimated vacation benefits for a four-week period in which the total pay earned by the employee group was $104,000.

b. Present a general journal entry to recognize the above on March 20, 1993.

PROVIDING FOR WARRANTY COSTS — OBJ. 1 —

12-21 Milford Company sells a motor that carries a 60-day unconditional warranty against product failure. Based on a reliable statistical analysis, Milford knows that between the sale and lapse of the product warranty, 2% of the units sold will require repair at an average cost of $48 per unit. The following data reflect Milford's recent experience.

	October	November	December	Dec. 31 Total
Units sold	22,000	21,000	25,000	68,000
Known product failures from sales of:				
October	110	180	150	440
November		120	220	340
December			210	210

Calculate and prepare a general journal entry to record properly the estimated liability for product warranties at December 31, 1993. Assume that warranty costs of known failures have already been reflected in the records.

PAYROLL CALCULATIONS FOR AN EMPLOYEE — OBJ. 2 —

12-22 Scott Quinn is an employee subject to the Fair Labor Standards Act. His regular pay rate is $8 per hour, and he is paid overtime at $1\frac{1}{2}$ times his regular pay rate. He worked 43 hours in the current week. His gross earnings prior to the current week are $9,600. He is married and claims four withholding allowances on Form W-4. No deductions other than FICA and federal income taxes are subtracted from his paycheck. Compute the following amounts related to Quinn's current week's wages:

a. Regular earnings.

b. Overtime earnings.

c. FICA taxes (assume 6.2% of first $53,400 plus 1.45% of first $125,000).

d. Federal income tax withheld (use federal income tax withholding table in Exhibit 12-3).

e. Net earnings.

RECORDING PAYROLL TAXES — OBJ. 2 —

12-23 Kaplan Company's August payroll register shows total gross earnings of $200,000. Of this amount, $160,000 is above the maximum amount subject to federal unemployment taxes, and $145,000 is above the maximum amount subject to state unemployment taxes. Kaplan Company has a favorable employment record, so its state unemployment tax rate is 2%. It is subject to an 0.8% federal unemployment tax. The 6.2% FICA rate applies to $170,000 of the gross earnings; the 1.45% rate applies to the entire $200,000. Prepare the general journal entry to record Kaplan Company's payroll tax expense on August 31, 1993.

PAYROLL CALCULATIONS FOR AN EMPLOYEE — OBJ. 2 —

12-24 William Tong is an employee subject to the Fair Labor Standards Act who is paid on a piece rate basis. His earnings for the current week, before any overtime compensation, are $352 for 44 hours of work. For each hour over 40 worked in a week, he receives an overtime premium of one-half his regular hourly pay rate based on the total hours worked in that week. His gross earnings prior to the current week were

$8,875. He is married and claims one withholding allowance on Form W-4. No deductions other than FICA and federal income taxes are subtracted from his paycheck. Compute the following amounts related to Tong's current week's wages:

a. Regular hourly pay rate.

b. Gross earnings.

c. FICA taxes (assume 6.2% of first $53,400 plus 1.45% of first $125,000).

d. Federal income tax withheld (use federal income tax withholding table in Exhibit 12-13).

e. Net earnings.

PROBLEMS

PROPERTY TAX CALCULATIONS — OBJ. 1 —

12-25 Estrella Company prepares monthly financial statements and ends its accounting year on December 31. Its headquarters building is located in the city of Bayfield. City taxes are assessed on September 1 each year, are paid by October 15, and relate to the city's fiscal year that ends the next June 30 (10 months after assessment). For the city tax year July 1, 1992–June 30, 1993, Estrella paid $30,000 in property taxes on its headquarters building.

REQUIRED

a. What amount of property tax expense should be accrued on the financial statements for July 1993, if property taxes for July 1, 1993–June 30, 1994 are an estimated 5% higher than the preceding year?

b. Assume that the 1993–1994 tax bill received on September 1, 1993, was for $33,600 and that the estimate in part (a) was used through August. What is the proper monthly property tax expense for September, 1993, if the deficiencies in the monthly property tax estimates through August are handled as an increase in the property tax expense for September, 1993?

c. How does the payment of the tax bill on October 15, 1993, affect the amount of property tax expense recognized for October?

EXCISE AND SALES TAX CALCULATIONS — OBJ. 1 —

12-26 Fulton Corporation initially records its sales at amounts that exclude any related excise and sales taxes. During June, 1993, Fulton recorded total sales of $210,000. An analysis of June sales indicated the following:

1. Thirty percent of sales were subject to both a 10% excise tax and a 6% sales tax.

2. Fifty percent of sales were subject only to the sales tax.

3. The balance of sales were for labor charges not subject to either excise or sales tax.

REQUIRED

a. Calculate the related liabilities for excise and sales taxes for June 1993.

b. Prepare the necessary journal entry at June 30 to record the monthly payment of excise tax and sales tax to the government.

RECORDING PAYROLL AND PAYROLL TAXES — OBJ. 2 —

12-27 Beamon Corporation had the following payroll for April 1993:

Officers' salaries	$32,000
Sales salaries	67,000
Federal income taxes withheld	19,000
FICA taxes withheld	7,500
Health insurance premiums deducted	1,600
United Way contributions deducted	900
Salaries (included above) subject to federal unemployment taxes	82,000
Salaries (included above) subject to state unemployment taxes	86,000

REQUIRED

Present general journal entries on April 30, 1993, to record

a. Accrual of the monthly payroll.

b. Payment of the net payroll.

c. Accrual of employer's payroll taxes. (Assume that the FICA tax matches the amount withheld, the federal unemployment tax is 0.8%, and the state unemployment tax is 5.4%.)

d. Payment of all liabilities related to this payroll. (Assume all are settled at the same time.)

**RECORDING PAYROLL AND
PAYROLL TAXES
— OBJ. 2 —**

12-28   The following data are taken from Fremont Wholesale Company's May 1993 payroll:

Administrative salaries	$34,000
Sales salaries	47,000
Custodial salaries	7,000
Total payroll	$88,000
Salaries subject to 1.45% FICA tax	$88,000
Salaries subject to 6.2% FICA tax	74,000
Salaries subject to FUTA unemployment taxes	14,000
Salaries subject to state unemployment taxes	20,000
Federal income taxes withheld from all salaries	18,700

Assume that the company is subject to a 2% state unemployment tax (due to a favorable experience rating) and a 0.8% federal unemployment tax.

REQUIRED

Record the following in general journal form on May 31:

a. Accrual of the monthly payroll.
b. Payment of the net payroll.
c. Accrual of the employer's payroll taxes.
d. Payment of the above payroll-related liabilities. (Assume all are settled at the same time.)

**PREPARING PAYROLL
REGISTER AND RECORDING
PAYROLL
— OBJ. 3 —**

12-29   Edgewater Company employs five persons, all of whom are paid an hourly rate. All employees receive overtime pay at $1\frac{1}{2}$ times their regular pay rate. Data relating to the payroll for the week ended March 31, 1993, are given below:

Employee	Hours Worked	Pay Rate	Gross Earnings to End of Prior Week
James Allen	44	$9 per hour	$4,050
Paul Durango	40	$12 per hour	5,500
Ann Poole	42	$8 per hour	3,620
John Scott	40	$9 per hour	4,030
Amy Thorp	40	$8 per hour	3,680

Additional data:

1. Paul Durango's gross earnings are charged to Office Salaries Expense; the gross earnings of the other employees are charged to Sales Salaries Expense.
2. All salaries and wages are subject to FICA tax; the rates are 6.2% of the first $53,400 earned plus 1.45% of the first $125,000 earned.
3. The federal unemployment tax is 0.8% of the first $7,000 of salaries and wages, and the state unemployment tax is 5.4% of the first $10,500 of salaries and wages of each employee.
4. Each employee has a $5 per week deduction for group health insurance.
5. Assume the following federal income tax withheld the last week in March:

Allen	$60
Durango	75
Poole	36
Scott	31
Thorp	24

REQUIRED

a. Prepare the payroll register for the week ended March 31, using the following column headings:

	Earnings			Deductions					
Employee	Regular	Overtime	Gross	FICA Tax	Federal Income Tax	Health Insurance	Total	Net Earnings

b. Prepare the general journal entry on March 31 to record
   1. The week's payroll.
   2. The employer's payroll taxes for the week.

3. The payment of the net payroll.

c. Edgewater Company remits the group health insurance premiums to the Badger Insurance Company monthly. Total premiums withheld in March were $100. Prepare the general journal entry on March 31 to record the monthly remittance of these premiums.

d. The March 31 balances in the FICA Tax Payable and Federal Income Tax Withholding Payable accounts—after posting the entries from part (b)—are $1,245 and $1,090, respectively. Prepare the general journal entry on March 31 to record the monthly remittance of these taxes to an authorized commercial bank.

e. Edgewater Company's total federal unemployment tax for the quarter ended March 31 is $174.20—after posting the entries from requirement (b). Edgewater Company deposits the taxes quarterly in an authorized commercial bank. Prepare the general journal entry on March 31 to record this remittance.

f. The total state unemployment tax for the quarter ended March 31 is $1,169.53— after posting the entries from requirement (b). Prepare the general journal entry on March 31 to record the quarterly remittance of this tax.

ALTERNATE EXERCISES

CURRENT LIABILITIES IN BALANCE SHEET
— OBJ. 1 —

12-18A For each of the following situations, indicate the amount shown as a liability on the balance sheet of Anchor, Inc., at December 31, 1993.

a. Anchor's general ledger shows a credit balance of $125,000 in Long-term Notes Payable; of this amount, a $25,000 installment becomes due on June 30, 1994.

b. Anchor estimates its unpaid income tax liability for 1993 is $34,000; it plans to pay this amount in March 1994.

c. On December 31, 1993, Anchor received a $15,000 invoice for merchandise shipped on December 28. The merchandise has not yet been received. The merchandise was shipped F.O.B. shipping point.

d. During 1993, Anchor collected $10,500 of state sales tax. At year-end, it has not yet remitted $1,400 of these taxes to the state department of revenue.

e. On December 31, 1993, Anchor's bank approved a $5,000, 90-day loan. Anchor plans to sign the note and receive the money on January 2, 1994.

EXCISE AND SALES TAX CALCULATIONS
— OBJ. 1 —

12-19A Allied Company has just billed a customer for $1,102, an amount that includes a 10% excise tax and a 6% state sales tax.

a. What amount of revenue is recorded?

b. Present a general journal entry to record the transaction on the books of Allied Company on November 6, 1993.

PROVIDING FOR VACATION BENEFITS
— OBJ. 1 —

12-20A Dalton, Inc.'s current vacation policy for its production workers provides two weeks paid vacation for employees who have worked 50 weeks. An analysis of the company's employee turnover rates indicates that approximately 15% of the employees will forfeit their vacation benefits.

a. Compute the proper provision for estimated vacation benefits for a four-week period in which the total pay earned by the employee group was $162,000.

b. Present a general journal entry to recognize the above on April 15, 1993.

PROVIDING FOR WARRANTY COSTS
— OBJ. 1 —

12-21A Brigham Company sells an electric timer that carries a 60-day unconditional warranty against product failure. Based on a reliable statistical analysis, Brigham knows that between the sale and lapse of the product warranty, 3% of the units sold will require repair at an average cost of $35 per unit. The following data reflect Brigham's recent experience.

	October	November	December	Dec. 31 Total
Units sold	36,000	30,000	45,000	111,000
Known product failures from sales of:				
October	320	550	210	1,080
November		230	360	590
December			410	410

Calculate and prepare a general journal entry to record properly the estimated liability for product warranties at December 31, 1993. Assume that warranty costs of known failures have already been reflected in the records.

PAYROLL CALCULATIONS FOR AN EMPLOYEE — OBJ. 2 —

12-22A Sheila Butler is an employee subject to the Fair Labor Standards Act. Her regular pay rate is $9 per hour, and she is paid overtime at $1\frac{1}{2}$ times her regular pay rate. She worked 43 hours in the current week. Her gross earnings prior to the current week are $10,540. She is married and claims three withholding allowances on Form W-4. No deductions other than FICA and federal income taxes are subtracted from her paycheck. Compute the following amounts related to Butler's current week's wages:
a. Regular earnings.
b. Overtime earnings.
c. FICA taxes (assume 6.2% of first $53,400 plus 1.45% of first $125,000).
d. Federal income tax withheld (use federal income tax withholding table in Exhibit 12-3).
e. Net earnings.

RECORDING PAYROLL TAXES — OBJ. 2 —

12-23A Taylor Company's September payroll register shows total gross earnings of $196,000. Of this amount, $166,000 is above the maximum amount subject to federal unemployment taxes, and $140,000 is above the maximum amount subject to state unemployment taxes. Taylor Company has a favorable employment record, so its state unemployment tax rate is 1%. It is subject to an 0.8% federal unemployment tax. The 6.2% FICA rate applies to $165,000 of the gross earnings while the 1.45% rate applies to the entire $196,000. Prepare the general journal entry to record Taylor Company's payroll tax expense on September 30, 1993.

PAYROLL CALCULATIONS FOR AN EMPLOYEE — OBJ. 2 —

12-24A Ellen Price is an employee subject to the Fair Labor Standards Act who is paid on a piece rate basis. Her earnings for the current week, before any overtime compensation, are $330 for 44 hours of work. For each hour over 40 worked in a week, she receives an overtime premium of one-half her regular hourly pay rate based on the total hours worked in that week. Her gross earnings prior to the current week were $8,520. She is married and claims two withholding allowances on Form W-4. No deductions other than FICA and federal income taxes are subtracted from her paycheck. Compute the following amounts related to Price's current week's wages:
a. Regular hourly pay rate.
b. Gross earnings.
c. FICA taxes (assume 6.2% of first $53,400 plus 1.45% of first $125,000).
d. Federal income tax withheld (use federal income tax withholding table in Exhibit 12-3).
e. Net earnings.

ALTERNATE PROBLEMS

PROPERTY TAX CALCULATIONS — OBJ. 1 —

12-25A Bryant Company prepares monthly financial statements and ends its accounting year on December 31. The company owns a factory in the city of Ashton, where city taxes are assessed on March 1 each year, are paid by May 1, and relate to the city's fiscal year that ends the next June 30 (four months after assessment). For the city tax year July 1, 1992–June 30, 1993, Bryant paid $48,000 in property taxes on its factory.

REQUIRED

a. What amount of property tax expense should be accrued on the financial statements for July 1993, if property taxes for July 1, 1993–June 30, 1994 are an estimated 6% higher than they were the preceding year?
b. Assume that the 1993–1994 tax bill received on March 1, 1994, was for $52,800 and that the estimate in part (a) was used through February. What is the proper monthly property tax expense for March 1994, if the deficiencies in the monthly property tax estimates through February are handled as an increase in the property tax expense for March 1994?

c. How does the payment of the tax bill on May 1, 1994, affect the amount of property tax expense recognized for May?

EXCISE AND SALES TAX CALCULATIONS — OBJ. 1 —

12-26A Madison Corporation initially records its sales at amounts that exclude any related excise and sales taxes. During May 1993, Madison recorded total sales of $300,000. An analysis of May sales indicated the following:

1. Twenty percent of sales were subject to both a 10% excise tax and a 5% sales tax.

2. Sixty percent of sales were subject only to the sales tax.

3. The balance of sales were for labor charges not subject to either excise or sales tax.

REQUIRED

a. Calculate the related liabilities for excise and sales taxes for May 1993.

b. Prepare the necessary journal entry at May 31 to record the monthly payment of excise tax and sales tax to the government.

RECORDING PAYROLL AND PAYROLL TAXES — OBJ. 2 —

12-27A Manchester, Inc., had the following payroll for March 1993:

Officers' salaries	$39,000
Sales salaries	65,000
Federal income taxes withheld	21,000
FICA taxes withheld	7,900
Health insurance premiums deducted	2,200
Salaries (included above) subject to federal unemployment taxes	74,000
Salaries (included above) subject to state unemployment taxes	82,000

REQUIRED

Present general journal entries on March 31, 1993, to record:

a. Accrual of the monthly payroll.

b. Payment of the net payroll.

c. Accrual of employer's payroll taxes. (Assume that the FICA tax matches the amount withheld, the federal unemployment tax is 0.8%, and the state unemployment tax is 5.4%.)

d. Payment of all liabilities related to this payroll. (Assume all are settled at the same time.)

RECORDING PAYROLL AND PAYROLL TAXES — OBJ. 2 —

12-28A The following data are taken from Jefferson Distribution Company's March 1993 payroll:

Administrative salaries	$29,000
Sales salaries	55,000
Custodial salaries	8,000
Total payroll	$92,000
Salaries subject to FICA tax (6.2% + 1.45%)	$92,000
Salaries subject to FUTA unemployment taxes	68,000
Salaries subject to state unemployment taxes	76,000
Federal income taxes withheld from all salaries	19,100

Assume that the company is subject to a 5.4% state unemployment tax and an 0.8% federal unemployment tax.

REQUIRED

Record the following in general journal form on March 31:

a. Accrual of the monthly payroll.

b. Payment of the net payroll.

c. Accrual of the employer's payroll taxes.

d. Payment of the above payroll-related liabilities. (Assume all are settled at the same time.)

**PREPARING PAYROLL
REGISTER AND RECORDING
PAYROLL
— OBJ. 3 —**

12-29A   Herman Company employs five persons, all of whom are paid an hourly rate. All employees receive overtime pay at $1\frac{1}{2}$ times their regular pay rate. Data relating to the payroll for the week ended March 31, 1993, are given below:

Employee	Hours Worked	Pay Rate	Gross Earnings to End of Prior Week
Janice Carter	43	$10 per hour	$4,650
Dale Farmer	40	$12 per hour	5,610
George Monroe	40	$8 per hour	3,780
James Rider	42	$8 per hour	3,860
Robert Warren	40	$10 per hour	4,430

Additional data:

1. Dale Farmer's gross earnings are charged to Office Salaries Expense; the gross earnings of the other employees are charged to Sales Salaries Expense.
2. All salaries and wages are subject to FICA tax; the rates are 6.2% of the first $53,400 earned plus 1.45% of the first $125,000 earned.
3. The federal unemployment tax is 0.8% of the first $7,000 of salaries and wages, and the state unemployment tax is 5.4% of the first $10,500 of salaries and wages of each employee.
4. Each employee has a $4 per week deduction for group medical insurance.
5. Assume the following federal income tax withheld the last week in March is

Carter	$52
Farmer	60
Monroe	39
Rider	37
Warren	37

REQUIRED

a. Prepare the payroll register for the week ended March 31, using the following column headings:

Employee	Earnings			Deductions				Net Earnings
	Regular	Overtime	Gross	FICA Tax	Federal Income Tax	Medical Insurance	Total	

b. Prepare the general journal entry on March 31 to record
   1. The week's payroll.
   2. The employer's payroll taxes for the week.
   3. The payment of the net payroll.
c. Herman Company remits the group health insurance premiums to the Colonial Insurance Company monthly. Total premiums withheld in March were $100. Prepare the general journal entry on March 31 to record the monthly remittance of these premiums.
d. The March 31 balances in the FICA Tax Payable and Federal Income Tax Withholding Payable accounts—after posting the entries from part (b)—are $1,463.48 and $1,108, respectively. Prepare the general journal entry on March 31 to record the monthly remittance of these taxes to an authorized commercial bank.
e. Herman Company's total federal unemployment tax for the quarter ended March 31 is $158.73—after posting the entries from part (b). Prepare the general journal entry on March 31 to record this remittance.
f. The total state unemployment tax for the quarter ended March 31 is $1,368.90—after posting the entries from part (b). Prepare the general journal entry on March 31 to record the quarterly remittance of this tax.

CASES

Business Decision Case

Statz Enterprises manages office buildings in several Midwestern cities. The firm maintains its own janitorial staff for all buildings managed. The firm manages 10 buildings in Center City, where it maintains a staff of 40 janitorial people, with a total annual payroll of $707,000. All members of the staff earn more than $16,000 per year each. FICA tax rates are 6.2% of the first $53,400 of earnings plus 1.45% of the first $125,000 of earnings per employee. Only one employee's earnings exceeds the $53,400 maximum amount by the amount of $2,000. Statz is subject to a 5.4% state unemployment tax on the first $10,000 wages earned by each employee. Its federal unemployment compensation tax rate is 0.8% of the first $7,000 earned by each employee. The firm's contribution to health insurance cost averages $60 per employee. Annual nonpayroll costs of the Center City operation follow:

Supplies	$25,000
Depreciation on equipment	46,000
Insurance	22,000
Miscellaneous	5,000
	$98,000

The firm has a high employee turnover rate and has not always kept tenants happy with the janitorial service. President Robert Statz has been approached by Maintenance, Inc., a commercial janitorial service chain, which has submitted a bid of $860,000 annually to provide janitorial service for the 10 buildings in Center City. This firm is noted for efficiency and satisfactory service. Statz estimates that hiring an outside firm would save $8,000 annually in bookkeeping costs and costs of contracting with other commercial firms for substitutes for regular help. These costs are not included in the above list of nonpayroll costs.

REQUIRED

Prepare a cost analysis for Statz to help him decide whether to accept the bid of Maintenance, Inc.

Analytical Application Case

PARKER HANNIFIN CORPORATION, headquartered in Cleveland, Ohio, manufactures motion control and fluid system components for a variety of industrial users. The firm's financial statements for three recent years contain the following data (Year 3 is the most recent year; dollar amounts in thousands):

	Year 3	Year 2	Year 1
Current assets at year-end	$1,129,190	$1,103,370	$950,982
Current liabilities at year-end	438,372	472,951	411,268
Current liabilities at beginning of year	472,951	411,268	337,342
Cash provided by operating activities	127,833	132,261	152,254

a. Compute Parker Hannifin's current ratio (current assets/current liabilities) for Years 1, 2, and 3.

b. Compute Parker Hannifin's operating cash flow to current liabilities ratio for Years 1, 2, and 3.

c. Comment on the three-year trend in Parker Hannifin's current ratio and operating cash flow to current liabilities ratio. Do the trends in these two ratios reinforce each other or contradict each other as indicators of Parker Hannifin's ability to pay its current liabilities?

Ethics Case

Sunrise Pools, Inc., is being sued by the Crescent Club for negligence when installing a new pool on Crescent Club's property. Crescent Club alleges that the employees of Sunrise Pools damaged the foundation of the clubhouse and part of the golf course while operating heavy machinery to install the pool.

The lawsuit is for $1.5 million. At the time of the alleged incident Sunrise Pools carried only $600,000 of liability insurance.

While reviewing the draft of Sunrise Pools' annual report, its president deletes all references to this lawsuit. He is concerned that disclosure of this lawsuit in the annual report will be viewed by Crescent Club as admission of Sunrise's wrongdoing, even though he privately admits that Sunrise employees were careless and believes that Sunrise Pools will be found liable for an amount in excess of $1 million. The president sends the amended draft of the annual report to the vice president of finance with a note stating that the lawsuit will not be disclosed in the annual report and also that the lawsuit will not be disclosed to the board of directors.

REQUIRED

Is the president's concern valid? What ethical problems will the vice president of finance face if he follows the president's instructions?

What types of financial information accompany a set of financial statements?

A series of notes and supplementary information, including a section called "management's discussion and analysis," accompany the financial statements in a corporation's annual report to stockholders. ■ This information is usually longer than the statements themselves and helps present a more detailed picture of the firm. ■ For example, note C in AT&T's 1991 annual report focuses on its merger with NCR Corporation, a world leader in computers and transaction processing.

13

ACCOUNTING PRINCIPLES AND FINANCIAL STATEMENT DISCLOSURES

Generally accepted accounting principles (GAAP) are the guidelines by which financial accounting statements are prepared. The phrase *generally accepted accounting principles* encompasses a wide spectrum of accounting guidelines, ranging from basic concepts and standards to detailed methods and procedures. There are principles covering almost every aspect of financial accounting and reporting. We have already discussed many of the methods and procedures within the domain of generally accepted accounting principles, such as inventory pricing methods and depreciation methods. In this chapter, we focus on the fundamental and pervasive principles of accounting, an understanding of which is indispensable to anyone who uses financial accounting data. We also consider the topic of financial statement disclosures.

HISTORICAL DEVELOPMENT

OBJECTIVE ❶ **DISCUSS** *the historical development of accounting principles and the nature of the conceptual framework.*

In contrast to the physical sciences, accounting has no immutable or natural laws, such as the law of gravity. The closest approximation to a law in accounting is probably the use of arithmetic functions and logic. Because no basic natural accounting law exists, accounting principles have developed on the basis of their *usefulness*. Consequently, the growth of accounting is more closely related to experience and practice than to the foundation provided by ultimate law. As such, accounting principles tend to evolve rather than be discovered, to be flexible rather than precise, and to be subject to relative evaluation rather than be ultimate or final.

Conventional accounting comprises a relatively recent body of knowledge. Although the origin of double-entry bookkeeping has been traced back to the fourteenth century, most important accounting developments have occurred in the last century.

The recent rapid development of accounting as an information system is largely explained by the economic history of the last 8 to 10 decades. This period included (1) the development of giant industrial firms, (2) the existence of large stockholders' groups, (3) the pronounced separation of ownership and management of large corporate firms, (4) the rapid growth of industrial and economic activity, and (5) the expansion of government regulation of industry. These factors helped create the large groups of interested parties who require a constant stream of reliable financial information concerning the economic entities they own, manage, or regulate. This information is meaningful only when prepared according to some agreed-on standards and procedures.

Accounting principles—like common law—originate from problem situations such as changes in the law, tax regulations, new business organizational arrangements, or new financing or ownership techniques. In response to the effect such problems have on financial reports, certain accounting techniques or procedures are tried. Through comparative use and analysis, one or more of these techniques are judged most suitable, obtain substantial authoritative support, and are then considered a generally accepted accounting principle. Organizations such as the Financial Accounting Standards Board (FASB), the American Institute of Certified Public Accountants (AICPA), and the Securities and Exchange Commission (SEC) are instrumental in the development of most accounting principles.

The general acceptance of accounting principles is not determined by a formal vote or survey of practicing accountants. An accounting principle must have substantial authoritative support to qualify as generally accepted. References to a particular accounting principle in authoritative accounting literature constitute substantive evidence of its general acceptance.

Pronouncements by the FASB are the most direct evidence of whether or not a specific accounting principle is generally accepted. Organized in 1973, the FASB has issued more than 100 *Statements of Financial Accounting Standards* dealing with generally accepted accounting principles.[1] Before the creation of the FASB, pronouncements by the AICPA—many of which are still in effect—represented the most authoritative indicators of general acceptance.[2]

During the two decades ending in 1959, the Committee on Accounting Procedures of the AICPA issued 51 *Accounting Research Bulletins.* These bulletins dealt with a variety of problems and, although they lacked formal legal status, considerably influenced generally accepted practice. In 1959, the AICPA established the Accounting Principles Board (APB) to issue authoritative opinions on problems related to generally accepted accounting principles. During its existence, the APB issued 31 *Opinions of the Accounting Principles Board.* These opinions increased in importance in 1964 when the AICPA required that any departure from an APB opinion be disclosed in a footnote to the financial statements or in the accompanying auditor's report. When the FASB succeeded the APB in 1973, this requirement was extended to cover FASB pronouncements.

As a federal agency, the SEC's primary focus is to regulate the interstate sale of stocks and bonds. The SEC requires companies under its jurisdiction to submit annual audited financial statements. The SEC has the power to set the accounting principles used by these companies, but, for the most part, the SEC has relied upon the FASB (and earlier, the AICPA) to formulate accounting principles. Because of its interest in full and fair financial reporting, the SEC interacts regularly with the FASB about various accounting problems.

CONCEPTUAL FRAMEWORK

The FASB has developed an overall conceptual framework to guide the formulation of specific accounting principles. The **conceptual framework** is a cohesive set of interrelated objectives and fundamentals for external financial reporting. For business enterprises, the framework consists of (1) financial reporting objectives, (2) financial statement elements, (3) recognition criteria for financial statement items, and (4) qualitative characteristics of accounting information. A recurrent theme throughout the conceptual framework is the importance of providing information that is useful to financial statement readers.

The **financial reporting objectives** focus primarily on information useful to investors and creditors. Financial statements should provide information that is (1) useful in making investment, credit, and similar decisions and (2) helpful in assessing the ability of enterprises to generate future cash flows. Finally, financial statements should (3) contain information about a firm's economic resources, the claims to these resources, and the effects of events that change these resources and claims. This latter information enhances the efforts of investors and creditors to identify financial strengths and weaknesses, predict future performance, or evaluate earlier expectations.

Financial statement elements are the significant components used to put financial statements together. These elements include assets, liabilities, owners' equity, investments by owners, distributions to owners, revenues, expenses, gains, losses,

---

[1] Paralleling the FASB structure, the Governmental Accounting Standards Board (GASB) was organized in 1984 to formulate accounting principles for state and local government financial reporting.

[2] For a hierarchy of sources of generally accepted accounting principles, see *Statement on Auditing Standards No. 69*, "The Meaning of 'Present Fairly in Conformity with Generally Accepted Accounting Principles' in the Independent Auditor's Report," in *Journal of Accountancy*, March 1992, pp. 108–111.

and comprehensive income.[3] The conceptual framework identifies and defines these elements, noting that they reflect the economic resources, claims to resources, and events that are relevant to decisions made by investors and creditors.

The **recognition criteria** specify in broad terms the criteria that must be satisfied before a particular asset, liability, revenue, expense, or the like may be recorded in the accounts. Essentially, the item under consideration must meet the definition of an element and be measurable, and information about the item must achieve the primary qualitative characteristics of accounting information.

The **qualitative characteristics of accounting information** are qualities that contribute to decision usefulness. The two primary qualities are **relevance** and **reliability.** To be relevant, information must contribute to the predictive and evaluative decisions made by investors and creditors. Reliable information contains no bias or material error and faithfully portrays what it intends to represent.

Exhibit 13-1 summarizes the conceptual framework. Various pieces of this conceptual framework were already part of the accounting discipline before their consideration by the FASB. Integrating the pieces into a cohesive framework is important, however. The FASB's intent is to solve individual accounting issues and formulate specific accounting principles within the context of the conceptual framework. Consequently, accounting principles based on this framework should form a consistent and coherent set of guidelines for financial reporting.

BASIC PRINCIPLES

OBJECTIVE ② IDENTIFY *and* **DISCUSS** *the basic principles underlying accounting theory.*

Accounting Entity Concept

In this section, we consider several fundamental principles that underlie the preparation of accounting data. Accountants vary somewhat in the way they refer to these basic guides—terms such as *principle, concept, standard, assumption,* and *convention* have been used to refer to one or more of them. Regardless of the label selected, however, each of these items influences the practice of accounting.

Each entity should be accounted for separately.

The most fundamental concept in accounting is the entity. An **accounting entity** is an economic unit with identifiable boundaries for which accountants accumulate and report financial information. Before accountants can analyze and report activities, they must identify the particular entity (and its boundaries) for which they are accounting. Every financial report specifies the entity in its heading.

Each proprietorship, partnership, and corporation is a separate entity, and separate accounting records should be kept for each unit. In accumulating financial information, we must separate the activities of an accounting entity from the other economic and personal activities of its owners. For example, Matt and Lisa Cook own Good Cook Inn restaurant as partners. The Good Cook Inn partnership is an accounting entity. Matt Cook is also an attorney whose activities constitute a proprietorship. Therefore, he keeps a set of accounting records for his legal activities separate from Good Cook Inn's records of its business activities. Lisa Cook's activities as a realtor also constitute a proprietorship. She keeps a set of accounting records for her realty activities separate from both the records of Good Cook Inn and of Matt Cook, attorney.

An accounting entity may be a unit other than a proprietorship, partnership, or corporation. Data for two or more corporations may be combined to provide financial reports for a larger economic entity. For example, a parent corporation and its

---

[3] *Comprehensive income* includes all changes in owners' equity during a period except investments by or distributions to owners. It is a concept not yet achieved in practice. For example, error corrections related to prior periods are not included in the income statement under current accounting principles.

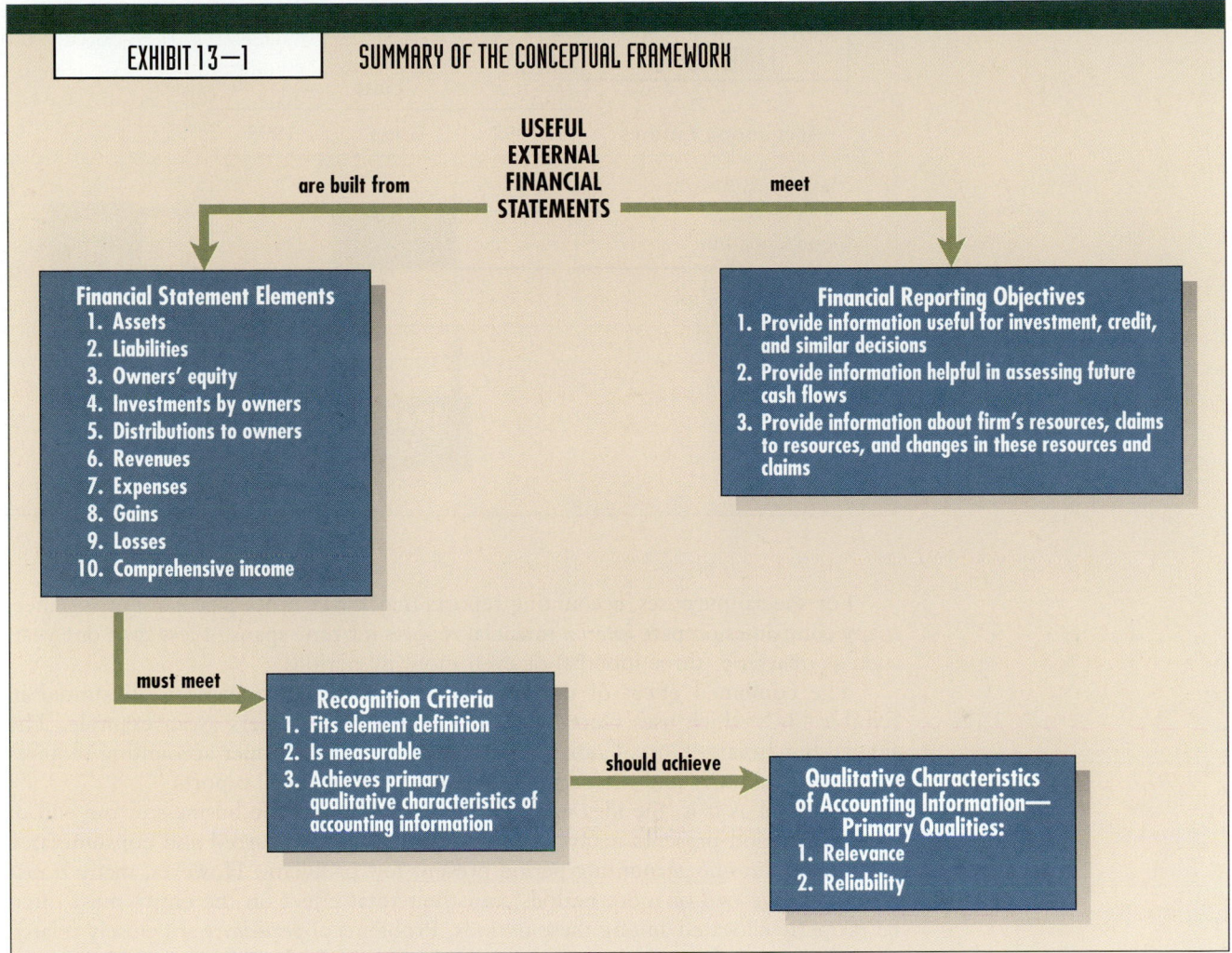

EXHIBIT 13—1   SUMMARY OF THE CONCEPTUAL FRAMEWORK

USEFUL
EXTERNAL
FINANCIAL
STATEMENTS

are built from

meet

Financial Statement Elements
1. Assets
2. Liabilities
3. Owners' equity
4. Investments by owners
5. Distributions to owners
6. Revenues
7. Expenses
8. Gains
9. Losses
10. Comprehensive income

Financial Reporting Objectives
1. Provide information useful for investment, credit, and similar decisions
2. Provide information helpful in assessing future cash flows
3. Provide information about firm's resources, claims to resources, and changes in these resources and claims

must meet

Recognition Criteria
1. Fits element definition
2. Is measurable
3. Achieves primary qualitative characteristics of accounting information

should achieve

Qualitative Characteristics of Accounting Information— Primary Qualities:
1. Relevance
2. Reliability

wholly owned subsidiaries (corporations in their own right) may consolidate their individual financial reports into a set of consolidated statements covering the group of corporations. In contrast, internal reports to corporate management may contain financial data concerning the activities of units as small as a division, a department, a profit center, or a plant. In this type of financial reporting, the entity is the division, the department, the profit center, or the plant.

The entity concept does not negate the legal fact that an all-inclusive legal liability exists in proprietorships and partnerships. In other words, business assets are available to personal creditors, and business creditors may have legal access to both business and personal assets in these noneconomic business organizations.

Accounting Period Concept

Accounting reports relate to specific periods—typically, one year.

The operations of most businesses are virtually continuous except for some changes associated with cyclical time periods, seasons, or dates. Thus, any division of the total life of a business into segments based on annual periods is somewhat artificial. However, the concept of **accounting periods** is useful. Many taxes are assessed on an annual basis, and comprehensive reports to corporation stockholders are made annually. In addition, many other noneconomic factors tend to consider the year a natural division of time.

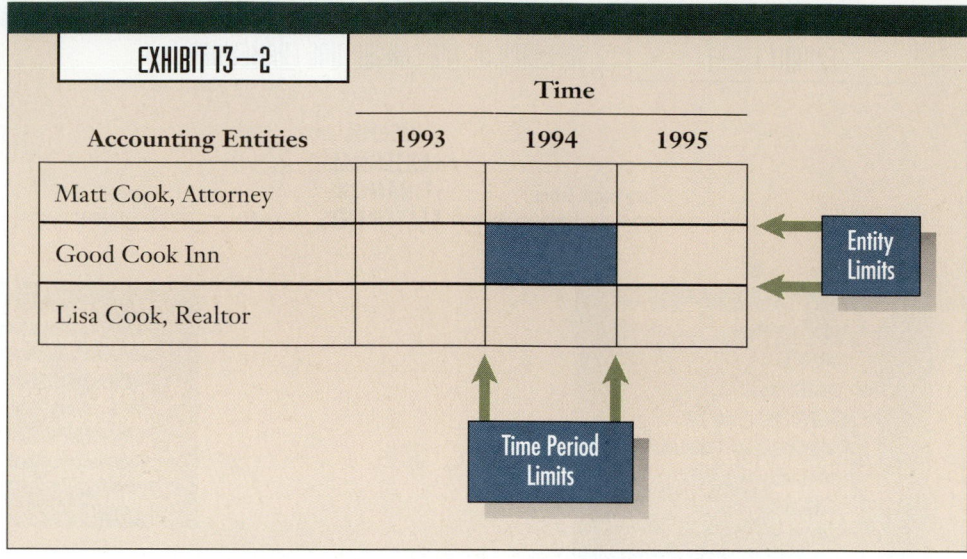

For special purposes, accounting reports may cover other periods. For instance, many companies prepare *interim* financial reports for time spans of less than one year, such as quarterly (three months) or even monthly periods.

The combined effect of the entity and periodicity concepts is illustrated in Exhibit 13-2, which uses Good Cook Inn and its two owners as an example. The shaded box isolates Good Cook Inn's activities for 1994. Proper accounting requires that both the entity and the period be identified in financial reports.

As useful as it is, the idea of artificially "cutting off" the business at the end of a certain period presents many problems. Transactions incurred and consummated entirely within one accounting period present few problems. However, many transactions bridge two or more periods, and their total effect on the entity must often be properly allocated among these periods. Problems of *periodicity* are closely related to the concept of matching expenses with revenue, which is developed later in the chapter.

Going Concern Concept

In the absence of evidence to the contrary, a business entity is assumed to have an indefinite life.

With few exceptions, business organizations have no anticipated termination date. Most firms operate profitably for indefinite periods and are, in fact, **going concerns.** Firms that do not succeed usually have indications of impending termination for some time before operations actually cease.

The going concern assumption has important implications for accounting procedures. It allows firms to defer costs—such as ending inventories, prepaid expenses, and undepreciated asset balances—that will be charged against the revenue of future periods. Furthermore, the going concern concept assumes the use of cost-based accounting measures rather than market-based liquidation values. Firms that expect to continue profitable operations do not ordinarily sell their operating assets; therefore, potential liquidation prices for these assets at the end of an accounting period may not be especially relevant. In this sense, the going concern assumption justifies the use of historical cost as the primary basis for accounting entries.

Measuring Unit Concept

The unit of measure in accounting is the basic unit of money.

Although other descriptive information is often relevant, money is the common **measuring unit** for recording accounting transactions. By expressing all assets and equities in terms of money, the accountant creates a common denominator that permits addition and subtraction of all forms of assets and equities and makes possible the preparation of financial statements. Expressing all statement items in money terms also permits the comparison of (1) various elements in the financial statements of a firm, (2) statements of the same firm from different time periods, and (3) the statements of two or more firms. This principle also assumes that the unit of measure is stable; that is, changes in its general purchasing power are not considered sufficiently important to require adjustments to the basic financial statements.

Cost Principle

Asset measures are based on the prices paid to acquire the assets.

The dollar amounts in account balances represent the accounting measures of the items about which information is collected. Possible sources of these measures are opinions of management, professional appraisals, current market prices, and historical costs. The **cost principle** states that asset measures should be based on historical cost. Most practicing accountants believe that other sources are so subjective that their use should be seriously limited.

We can describe *historical cost* as an item's "historical exchange price." It represents the amount of cash, or its equivalent, paid to acquire an asset. Most accountants agree that no item has a single ultimate value and that for the millions of exchanges that occur daily, the exchange price probably best indicates the value of an item at the time of the transaction. Usually we do not attempt to reflect subsequent changes in market values for assets, so the initial exchange price of an item becomes known as its historical cost.

Historical costs tend to be highly objective because under classical assumptions they are derived in the marketplace by informed, rational, and independent parties. Also, the details of the original transaction can easily be verified by consulting the documents that are customarily executed at the time of exchange (deeds, bills of sale, checks, and mortgages). An overlooked advantage of historical cost measurement is that the data are a natural byproduct of the exchange transaction itself and are therefore available at little additional cost or effort. Relative objectivity may be the primary justification for historical cost–based accounting measures, but their natural availability at negligible cost is also an important factor—especially when the historical cost method is compared with more expensive sources of values such as professional appraisals.

Objectivity Principle

Whenever possible, accounting entries must be based on objectively determined evidence.

The principle of **objectivity** requires bias-free and verifiable accounting data. Users want accounting data that are not subject to the capricious whim of either management or the accountant who prepares or audits the statements. Consequently, whenever possible, accounting determinations are based on actual invoices, documents, bank statements, and physical counts of items involved.

Not all accounting determinations can be totally objective. Periodic depreciation and estimates of the eventual collectibility of credit sales are examples of relatively subjective factors routinely incorporated into accounting reports. Several accountants required to determine independently the depreciation expense for a given period on an item of special-purpose equipment would probably come up with a range of suggested amounts. We might expect the range to be in some proportion to the degree of subjectivity involved.

Variations in accounting measurements, of course, lead to variations in reported income. Thus, the more subjective accounting records are, the greater variety there may be in reported income. Because highly subjective determinations are not readily verifiable, a user of a subjectively derived accounting report does not know where this particular statement falls in the range of reportable income figures. An even greater disadvantage is that the user has no way of knowing the motives of the individual preparing the statements. Was he or she trying to be "fair" or attempting to minimize or maximize reported income? We have no reliable source of answers to this question. For this reason, accountants—particularly independent auditors—look for objective evidence to support the accounting data in financial reports.

Consistency Principle

Unless otherwise disclosed, accounting reports are prepared on a basis consistent with the preceding period.

In many instances, more than one method of applying a generally accepted accounting principle is possible. In other words, two firms that have identical operating situations might each choose a different—but equally acceptable—accounting method and report different amounts for the same types of transactions.

Changes in accounting procedures that lead to different reported values may affect the amount of reported income. Under certain circumstances, a firm could, by design, increase or decrease its reported earnings simply by changing from one generally accepted accounting principle to another that yields different values. This situation justifies the consistency principle. **Consistency** means that the same accounting methods are used from one accounting period to the next. Consistency enhances the utility of financial statements when comparative data for a firm are analyzed.

Sometimes it is appropriate for a firm to change an accounting method. Indeed, progress in improving accounting data almost dictates that some changes will occur. In these cases, financial statement users should know when and to what extent reported earnings result from changes in accounting techniques.

Revenue Recognition Principle
POINT OF SALE

With limited exceptions, revenue is recognized at the point of sale.

At first, a **revenue recognition principle** that states that revenue is normally recognized at the point of sale may seem obvious. However, modern business operations are often so complicated and so extended that practical questions arise concerning the point at which revenue should be recognized. With the exceptions discussed later in this section, generally accepted accounting principles require the recognition of revenue in the accounting period in which the sale occurs.

For services, the sale is deemed to occur when the service is performed. When merchandise is involved, the sale takes place when title to the goods transfers from seller to buyer. In many situations this coincides with the delivery of the merchandise. As a result, accountants usually record revenue when goods are delivered.

To understand the logic of and the exceptions to the principle of recognizing revenue at point of sale, we must consider some underlying factors. Most firms have some sort of cash-to-cash operating cycle, which is diagrammed in Exhibit 13-3. In reality, most firms are engaged in many partially overlapping operating cycles, represented by the following diagram:

Time

For our purposes, it is sufficient to consider the isolated cycle. In Exhibit 13-3, the firm starts with $100 cash and then uses the cash to acquire, handle, store, promote, display, and finally sell the inventory. In a cash sale, inventory is immediately converted to $140 cash. If the sale is made on credit terms, the collection process must be accomplished. The $40 difference between the cash at the cycle's beginning and at its end, reduced by any applicable noncash expenses, is the income generated by the operating cycle.

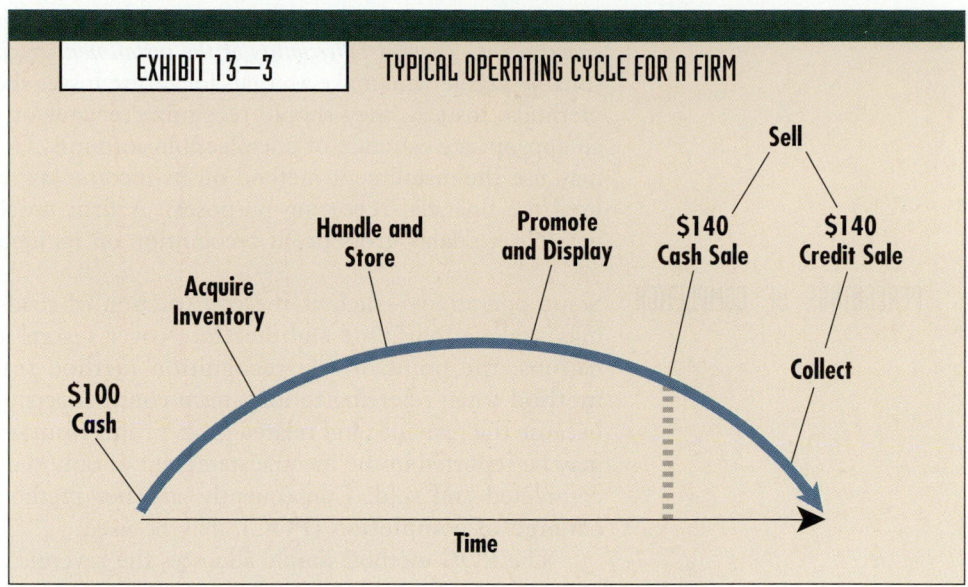

EXHIBIT 13—3 **TYPICAL OPERATING CYCLE FOR A FIRM**

Throughout the cycle, the firm works toward the eventual sale of the goods and collection of the sales price. This cycle is the firm's **earning process,** and it should be substantially complete before revenue is recorded. Also, the revenue should be realized before it is recorded in the accounts. **Realized** means that the goods (or services) are exchanged for cash or claims to cash. It is at the point of sale, then, that the two important conditions for revenue recognition are met—at that time the revenue is both (1) *earned* and (2) *realized.*[4]

COLLECTION BASES
For selected exceptions, revenue recognition occurs at times other than the point of sale. Methods that delay recognition until cash is collected are *collection basis methods.* These methods usually relate to installment credit sales. A conservative method, known as the **cost recovery method,** considers all cash collections a return of cost until all costs are recovered; the remaining collections are considered all gross profit.

Another collection basis method is the **installment method.** The installment method takes its name from the popular sales term for purchases of moderate to large dollar amounts. In effect, the installment method treats each dollar received as part return of cost and part gross profit. The specific proportion of each is determined by the relationship between the cost and the sales price of the merchandise involved. For example, assume that on October 1, 1993, a refrigerator costing $450 is sold for $600, with installment terms consisting of a 20% down payment and the balance due in 24 equal payments of $20 on the last day of each month. Under the installment basis, because the cost was 75% of the selling price ($450/$600), each dollar collected will be considered 75% return of cost and 25% gross profit. The resulting gross profit during the three years would be recognized as follows:

	1993		1994	1995	
	Down Payment	**Three $20 Payments**	**Twelve $20 Payments**	**Nine $20 Payments**	**Totals**
Total received (100%)	$120	$60	$240	$180	$600
Considered return of cost (75%)	90	45	180	135	450
Considered gross profit (25%)	30	15	60	45	150

---

[4] *Statement of Financial Accounting Concepts No. 5,* "Recognition and Measurement in Financial Statements of Business Enterprises" (Stamford, CT: Financial Accounting Standards Board, 1984).

Collection basis methods of revenue recognition are used when firms cannot *reasonably estimate the extent of collectibility of the installment receivables.* Companies that can reasonably predict and make accruals for future losses should not employ collection basis methods. Instead, they should recognize revenue at point of sale and match with it an appropriate estimate of uncollectible accounts. However, in some instances a firm may use the installment method on its income tax return (regardless of the method used for financial reporting purposes). A firm usually considers it desirable, when possible, to delay gross profit recognition on its income tax return.

PERCENTAGE OF COMPLETION

Some operations—such as the construction of roads, dams, and large office buildings—take a long time and therefore cover several accounting periods. In such situations, the point-of-sale recognition method (called the **completed contract method** when referring to long-term contract accounting) does not work very well, because the revenue (and related gross profit) from several years of construction work may be reported in the income statement of only the period in which the project was completed and sold. Consequently, another method of revenue recognition, **percentage of completion (POC),** may be used.

The POC method simply allocates the revenue on a contract among the several accounting periods involved, in proportion to the estimated percentage of the contract completed each period. To use this method, we must have a reasonably accurate and reliable procedure for estimating periodic progress on the contract. Most often, estimates of the percentage of contract completion are tied to the proportion of total costs incurred.

For example, assume that a dam is to be constructed during a two-year period beginning July 1, 1993. The contract price is $3,000,000, and estimated total costs are $2,400,000; thus, estimated gross profit is $600,000. If the total cost incurred in 1993 is $720,000 (that is, 30% of the estimated total), then $900,000 revenue (or 30% of the total revenue) is recognized in 1993. Similarly, if 50% of the total estimated costs ($1,200,000) is incurred in 1994, then 50% of the total revenue ($1,500,000) is recognized in 1994. Incurring the last $480,000 of costs in 1995 (20% of the total) results in 20% of the total revenue ($600,000) being recorded in 1995. Under the POC method then, the revenue is reflected among the three calendar years as follows:

	(Dollars in Thousands)			
	1993	**1994**	**1995**	**Total**
Cost incurred	$720	$1,200	$480	$2,400
Percent of total costs	30%	50%	20%	100%
Revenue recognized	$900	$1,500	$600	$3,000

The periodic gross profit is equal to the revenue recognized less the costs incurred each period.[5] In our example, the gross profit reflected each year is as follows (amounts in thousands):

	1993	**1994**	**1995**	**Total**
Revenue recognized	$900	$1,500	$600	$3,000
Cost incurred	720	1,200	480	2,400
Gross profit	$180	$ 300	$120	$ 600

Clearly, in long-term construction, the POC method of revenue recognition more reasonably reflects reported revenue and gross profit as an indicator of productive effort than the completed contract basis.

---

[5] For simplicity, we assume that the original estimate of total costs is accurate. If estimated total costs change as the project progresses (as usually happens), the periodic percentage of completion is computed as the percentage complete at end of current period − the percentage complete at end of previous period.

Matching Concept

To the extent feasible, all expenses related to given revenue are matched with and deducted from that revenue in the determination of periodic income.

Income determination procedures relate expenses and revenues through the **matching concept.** Matching expenses with revenues occurs in the following ways:

1. Costs that relate to specific revenue are recognized as expenses whenever the related revenue is recognized. For example, cost of goods sold relates to the specific revenue from the sale of goods. Cost of goods sold is recorded, therefore, in the same accounting period as the sales revenue.

2. Costs that relate to the revenue of several accounting periods are expensed in a systematic and rational manner throughout these periods. The impact of some assets benefiting several periods cannot be traced to any specific revenue amounts. Instead, the asset's cost is matched with each period's overall revenue through appropriate depreciation and amortization procedures. The depreciation of office equipment illustrates this category of matching.

3. Costs that relate only to the current period's overall revenue are expensed immediately. Expenditures that benefit only the current accounting period, such as office salaries expense, fit this category.

The proper matching of expenses with revenues is accomplished primarily through the accrual accounting techniques illustrated throughout the text.

Conservatism Concept

Accounting measurements take place in a context of significant uncertainties, and possible errors in measurement of net assets and income should tend toward understatement rather than overstatement.

Accounting determinations are often based on estimates of future events and are therefore subject to a range of optimistic or pessimistic interpretations. In the early 1900s, many abuses were perpetrated on financial statement users who were given overly optimistic measurements of assets and estimates of income. Consequently, the investor was reassured when a company used the "most conservative" accounting procedures. In some instances, banks would write down handsome multistory office buildings, showing them on the balance sheet at a nominal value of $1. The intention was to emphasize the understatement of assets as evidence of conservative accounting and financial strength.

More recently, accountants have recognized that intentional understatement of net assets and income can be as misleading as overly optimistic accounting treatments. For example, stockholders might erroneously decide to sell their stock in a company that grossly understates its income through overly conservative accounting procedures. Also, a conservative treatment in one accounting period may cause the overstatement of reported income for many other periods. For example, the bank that writes its building down to $1 is, in a sense, "overdepreciating" and therefore understating both assets and income for that period. During the building's remaining useful life, the bank's income is overstated because the related building depreciation expense is omitted from the income statements of those periods.

Today, **conservatism** is the accountant's reaction to situations in which significant uncertainties exist about the outcomes of transactions still in progress. In contrast to the intentional understatements of net assets and income, accountants follow conservative accounting procedures when they are unsure of the proper measure to use. For example, if two estimates of future amounts to be received are about equally likely, conservatism requires the less optimistic estimate be used. Thus, possible errors in measuring net assets and income should tend toward understatement rather than overstatement.

Materiality Concept

Accounting transactions so insignificant that they would not affect the actions of financial statement users are recorded as is most expedient.

Sound accounting procedures require effort and cost money. When the amounts involved are too small to affect the overall picture significantly, the application of theoretically correct accounting procedures is hardly worth its cost. For example, accounting theory asserts that assets acquired and used over several accounting periods should first be recorded as assets, with systematic amounts of depreciation expense recognized in each of the periods in which the assets are used (directly or indirectly) to earn revenue. The concept of **materiality,** however, permits a firm to expense the costs of such items as small tools, pencil sharpeners, and waste paper baskets when acquired because they are "immaterial" in amount. Many firms set dollar limits—such as $25 or $100—below which the costs of all items are expensed.

The concept of materiality is relative—an immaterial amount for General Motors Corporation may be material for smaller companies. Also, the nature of the transaction should be considered. A difference of $1,000 in depreciation expense might be immaterial, but the same discrepancy in cash could be material.

The materiality of an item in a financial statement is usually judged in comparison to a related amount. For example, to determine the effect of the inclusion or omission of an income statement item, we express it as a percentage of net income; a current asset item might be expressed as a percentage of total current assets, and so on. Accounting literature is not precise about what quantitative proportions are deemed material. In specific instances, 5–15% of related amounts have been considered material, but this matter is best subject to judgment. Always remember, however, that although a given series of transactions might *each* be considered immaterial in amount, their aggregate effect could be material in certain circumstances.

Full Disclosure Principle

All information necessary for the users' understanding of the financial statements must be disclosed.

Accounting's purpose is to provide useful information to various parties interested in a firm's financial performance and position. Often facts or conditions exist that, although not specifically part of the data in the accounts, have considerable influence on the understanding and interpretation of the financial statements. To inform users properly, a firm should disclose this additional information.

In the following section, we expand on this basic principle of **full disclosure.**

FINANCIAL STATEMENT DISCLOSURES

Disclosures related to financial statements fall into one of three categories: (1) parenthetical disclosures on the face of the financial statements, (2) notes to the financial statements, and (3) supplementary information. Most disclosures amplify or explain information contained in the financial statements. Some disclosures, however, add new kinds of information.

Parenthetical Disclosures

OBJECTIVE ❸ IDENTIFY *and* DESCRIBE *the various types of financial statement disclosures.*

Parenthetical disclosures are placed next to an account title or other descriptive label in the financial statements. Their purpose is to provide succinctly some additional detail about the item. The information disclosed parenthetically could instead be disclosed by a note to the statements. The selection of the particular disclosure technique is at the discretion of individual companies. Because they are presented on the face of the financial statements, parenthetical disclosures probably stand a better chance of being noticed by statement readers than do disclosures in the notes.

Several types of parenthetical disclosures follow, illustrated with examples that relate to topics we have discussed in earlier chapters.

1. A parenthetical disclosure may report contra asset amounts, such as the allowance for uncollectible accounts or accumulated depreciation.

	1995	1994
Accounts Receivable, less allowances for uncollectible accounts (1995—$30,000; 1994—$26,500)	$215,000	$174,000
Plant and Equipment, less accumulated depreciation (1995—$530,000; 1994—$450,000)	997,000	892,000

2. The measurement technique used may be revealed by a parenthetical disclosure.

	1995	1994
Inventories (At last-in, first-out cost)	$620,000	$710,000
Intangibles (Cost less amortization to date)	75,000	80,000

3. An alternate financial measure for the item reported may be disclosed parenthetically.

	1995	1994
Short-term Stock Investments, at market (cost, $250,000 at December 31, 1995, and $600,000 at December 31, 1994)	$210,000	$525,000
Inventories (At last-in, first-out cost; cost using first-in, first-out would have been: 1995—$1,200,000, 1994—$1,000,000)	950,000	800,000

4. A parenthetical disclosure may report an amount that is not otherwise separately reported, such as the amount of interest capitalized during the year.

	1995	1994
Interest Expense (Net of capitalized amounts of $29,000 and $11,000, respectively)	$187,000	$162,000

5. Accounts that have been combined and reported as a single figure in the financial statements may be broken down in a parenthetical disclosure.

	1995	1994
Cash and Cash Equivalents (Including short-term investments of $300,000 and $270,000 at December 31, 1995 and 1994, respectively)	$540,000	$420,000

Notes to Financial Statements

Although much information is gathered, summarized, and reported in financial statements, the statements alone are limited in their ability to convey a complete picture of a firm's financial status. *Notes* are added to financial statements to help fill in the gaps. In fact, accountants have given so much attention to financial statement notes in recent years that today it is not unusual for the notes to take up more space than the statements themselves. Notes may cover a wide variety of topics. Typically, they deal with significant accounting policies, explanations of complex or special transactions, details of reported amounts, commitments, contingencies, segments, quarterly data, and subsequent events.

SIGNIFICANT ACCOUNTING POLICIES

Accounting principles contain several instances for which alternative procedures are acceptable. For example, there are several acceptable depreciation and inventory pricing methods, revenue on long-term construction contracts may be recognized using either the percentage-of-completion or the completed contract method, and revenue from some installment sales may be recognized using collection basis methods. The particular procedures selected obviously affect the financial data presented. Further, unique or complex events may require innovative applications of accounting principles. Knowledge of a firm's specific accounting principles and methods of applying these principles helps users understand the financial statements. Accordingly, these principles and methods are disclosed in a **summary of significant accounting policies.** The summary is either the initial note to the financial statements or immediately precedes the notes. The number of policies listed, of course, will vary from firm to firm, but the policies relating to inventory pricing methods, depreciation methods, and consolidation practices are invariably included.

For example, a recent annual report of FLIGHTSAFETY INTERNATIONAL, INC., contains the following description of its depreciation and amortization policies (FlightSafety offers training to aircraft pilots and crews of ocean-going vessels):

> Depreciation is provided on the straight-line method over estimated useful lives as follows: simulators, training equipment and spare parts, 4 to 20 years; buildings, 25 to 40 years; and furniture, fixtures and equipment, 4 to 10 years. Leasehold improvements, including buildings on leased property, are amortized over the life of the lease or the life of the improvement, whichever is shorter.
>
> Interest cost is capitalized during the construction period of simulators and facilities. These costs are amortized over the life of the related assets. The amount of interest capitalized was $3,425,000 in 1990 ($3,245,000 in 1989 and $1,646,000 in 1988).

EXPLANATIONS OF COMPLEX OR SPECIAL TRANSACTIONS

The complexity of certain transactions means that not all important aspects are likely to be reflected in the accounts. Financial statement notes, therefore, report the additional relevant details about such transactions. Typical examples include notes discussing financial aspects of pension plans, profit-sharing plans, acquisitions of other companies, borrowing agreements, stock option and other incentive plans, and income taxes.

Transactions with related parties are special transactions requiring disclosure in the financial statement notes.[6] *Related-party transactions* include transactions between a firm and its (1) principal owners, (2) members of management, (3) subsidiaries, or (4) affiliates. The transactions may be sales or purchases of property, leases, borrowings or lendings, and the like. These transactions are not arm's length transactions; that is, they are not between independent parties each acting in its own best interests (as is true in most transactions). Because of the relationships between the parties, one party may exert significant influence over the other party and the results may differ from what would occur in an arm's length transaction (for example, the interest rate for funds borrowed may be below the current market rate). A user trying to compare a firm's financial data with that of prior periods or other similar companies will find related-party information useful. It may help identify and explain differences in the data.

 To illustrate, a recent annual report of SKYWEST, INC., contains the following description of related-party transactions (SkyWest provides air services in the western states and is a DELTA CONNECTION air carrier):

> The Company and Delta Air Lines, Inc. (Delta) operate under a joint marketing and code-sharing agreement under which the Company uses the Delta two letter designator code (DL) in displaying its schedules on all flights in the automated airline reservation systems used throughout the industry.
>
> Delta owns 1,035,933 shares or approximately 20% of the outstanding common stock of the Company. The Company leases various terminal facilities from Delta and Delta provides certain services to the Company, including advertising, reservation and ground handling services. Expenses paid to Delta under these agreements were approximately $2,978,000, $2,754,000 and $2,489,000 during the years ended March 31, 1991, 1990 and 1989, respectively.
>
> The Company had net receivables from Delta totaling approximately $2,266,000 and $1,928,000 as of March 31, 1991 and 1990, respectively.

---

[6]*Statement of Financial Accounting Standards No. 57*, "Related Party Disclosures" (Stamford, CT: Financial Accounting Standards Board, 1982).

DETAILS OF REPORTED AMOUNTS

Financial statements often summarize several groups of accounts into a single dollar amount. For example, a balance sheet may show as one asset an amount labeled Property, Plant, and Equipment, or it may list Long-term Debt as a single amount among the liabilities. These aggregated amounts may be sufficient for some financial statement users, but others want more detail about these items. Notes will report this detail, presenting schedules that list the types and amounts of property, plant, and equipment and long-term debt. Other items that may be summarized in the financial statements and detailed in the notes include inventories, other current assets, notes payable, accrued liabilities, owners' equity, and income tax expense.

The notes to DONNELLY CORPORATION's annual report (see Appendix L) contain several examples of financial statement items that are detailed, including inventories (note 2), long-term debt (note 3), preferred and common stock (note 4), and income taxes (note 7).

COMMITMENTS

A firm may have contractual arrangements existing at a balance sheet date in which both parties to the contract still have acts to perform. If performance under these **commitments** will have a significant financial impact on the firm, the existence and nature of the commitments should be disclosed in the financial statement notes. Examples of commitments reported in notes are commitments under operating leases, contracts to purchase materials or equipment, contracts to construct facilities, salary commitments to executives, commitments to retire or redeem stock, and commitments to deliver goods.

A recent annual report of TENNECO, INC., a corporation with diversified business interests, such as natural gas pipelines, farm and construction equipment, automotive parts, and shipbuilding, includes the following example of significant purchase commitments:

> In connection with the financing commitments of certain joint ventures, Tenneco has entered into unconditional purchase obligations for products and services of $285 million ($169 million on a present value basis). Tenneco's annual obligations under these agreements are $27 million for each of the years 1991 and 1992, and $26 million for each of the years 1993, 1994, and 1995. Payments under such obligations, including additional purchases in excess of contractual obligations, were $29 million, $34 million and $36 million for the years 1990, 1989 and 1988, respectively. In addition, in connection with the Great Plains coal gasification project, Tenneco has contracted to purchase 30% of the plant's original design capacity for a remaining period of 19 years.

CONTINGENCIES

We discussed contingent liabilities in an earlier chapter. As noted there, if the future event that would turn a contingency into an obligation is not likely to occur, or if the liability amount cannot be reasonably estimated, the **contingency** is disclosed parenthetically or in a note to the financial statements. Typical contingencies disclosed in notes are lawsuits, possible income tax assessments, credit guarantees, and discounted notes receivable.

THE LESLIE FAY COMPANIES, INC., a firm engaged in the design, manufacture, and sale of apparel, reported the following contingency in a recent annual report:

> The Company is the subject of an ongoing investigation and audit by the United States Customs Service relating to duties on some of the Company's imported products covering the period 1982 through 1987. The Company has made voluntary disclosures and has paid additional duties to the Customs Service, which were charged to cost of goods sold primarily in 1987. During 1990, the Customs Service issued a penalty claim in the amount of $3,145,000, with respect to one of the Company's divisions whose audit had been completed. The Company has responded to this notice, denying any additional liability, and is vigorously defending its position in accordance with Customs Service procedures. Based upon audits of the other divisions completed to date, the Customs Service has advised the Company that an additional $879,000 in duties is owing. The Company is seeking clarification of these

claims but believes that there is little or no liability. While it is not possible to predict the ultimate outcome of the investigation and audit or the contemplated claims, the Company believes that the adjustments, if any, resulting therefrom would not have a material adverse effect on the future financial position of the Company.

SEGMENTS

Many firms diversify their activities and operate in several different industries. The firms' financial statements combine information from all operations into aggregate amounts. This complicates the users' ability to analyze the statements because the interpretation of financial data is influenced by the industry in which a firm operates. Different industries face different types of risk and have different rates of profitability. In making investment and lending decisions, users evaluate risk and required rates of return. Having financial data available by industry segments is helpful to such evaluations.

The FASB recognizes the usefulness of industry data to investors and lenders. Public companies with significant operations in more than one industry must report certain information by industry **segments.** Typically, these disclosures are in the financial statement notes. The major disclosures by industry segment are revenue, operating profit or loss, identifiable assets (the assets used by the segment), capital expenditures, and depreciation.

Other types of segment data may also be disclosed. Business operations in different parts of the world are subject to different risks and opportunities for growth. Thus, public firms with significant operations in foreign countries must report selected financial data by foreign geographic area. The data disclosed are revenue, operating profit or loss (or other profitability measure), and identifiable assets. Also, if a firm has export sales or sales to a single customer that are 10% or more of total revenue, the amount of such sales must be separately disclosed.

An example of the latter type of segment disclosure is SOUTHWESTERN BELL CORPORATION, which reported the following segment information in a recent annual report (Southwestern Bell's primary activity is providing services and products over its local telephone system):

> The Corporation operates predominantly in the telecommunications service industry.
> Approximately 15 percent in 1990, 19 percent in 1989, and 20 percent in 1988 of the Corporation's consolidated revenues were derived from services provided to AT&T. No other customer accounted for more than 10 percent of consolidated revenues.

Note 10 to Donnelly Corporation's financial statements in its 1991 annual report (see Appendix L) illustrates segment disclosures by industry, foreign versus domestic, and major customer.

QUARTERLY DATA

Interim financial reports cover periods shorter than one year. Companies that issue interim reports to investors and others generally do so quarterly. These reports provide users with timely information on a firm's progress and are most useful in predicting what the annual financial results will be. The SEC requires certain companies to disclose selected quarterly financial data in their annual reports to stockholders. Included among the notes, the data reported for each quarter include sales, gross profit, net income, and earnings per share. **Quarterly data** permit users to analyze such things as the seasonal nature of operations, the impact of diversification on quarterly activity, and whether the firm's activities lead or lag general economic trends.

Note 12 to Donnelly Corporation's financial statements (see Appendix L) illustrates a disclosure of quarterly data for a two-year period.

SUBSEQUENT EVENTS

If a company issues a large amount of securities or suffers a casualty loss after the balance sheet date, this information should be reported in a note to the readers, even though the situation arose subsequent to the balance sheet date. Firms are responsible for disclosing any significant events that occur between the balance sheet date and the date the financial statements are issued. This guideline recognizes that it takes several weeks for financial statements to be prepared and audited before they are issued. Events occurring during this period that may have a material effect on the firm's operations are certainly of interest to readers and should be disclosed. Other examples of **subsequent events** requiring disclosure are sales of assets, significant changes in long-term debt, and acquisitions of other companies.

For example, ABBOTT LABORATORIES, whose main business is the development, manufacture, and sale of a broad line of health care products and services, reported the following subsequent event in its 1990 annual report:

> Included in Deferred Charges and Other Assets in the Consolidated Balance Sheet is an investment in common stock which the company sold on February 6, 1991, for an after-tax gain of approximately $125 million.

Supplementary Information

Supplementing the financial statements are several additional disclosures—management's financial discussion and analysis of the statements, selected financial data covering a 5- to 10-year period, and perhaps information on the impact of inflation. These *supplementary* disclosures are either required of certain companies by the SEC or recommended (but not required) by the FASB.

MANAGEMENT'S DISCUSSION AND ANALYSIS

Management may increase the usefulness of financial statements by sharing some of their knowledge about the company's financial condition and operations. This is the purpose of the disclosure devoted to management's discussion and analysis. In this supplement to the financial statements, management identifies and comments on events and trends influencing the firm's liquidity, operating results, and financial resources. Management's closeness to the company not only gives them insights unavailable to outsiders, but also may introduce certain biases into the analysis. Nonetheless, management's comments, interpretations, and explanations should contribute to a better understanding of the financial statements.

COMPARATIVE SELECTED FINANCIAL DATA

The analysis of financial performance is enhanced if a firm's financial data for several years are available. By analyzing trends over time, the analyst learns much more about a company than is possible from only a single year's data. Year-to-year changes may give clues as to future growth or may highlight areas for concern. Corporate annual reports to stockholders present complete financial statements in comparative form, showing the current year and one or two preceding years. Beyond this, however, the financial statements are supplemented by a summary of selected key financial statistics for a 5- or 10-year period. The financial data presented in this historical summary usually include sales, net income, dividends, earnings per share, working capital, and total assets.

INFLATION ACCOUNTING

Inflation has an impact on virtually every aspect of economic affairs, including investment decisions, pricing policies, marketing strategies, and salary and wage negotiations. Persons making economic decisions utilize financial data prepared by accountants. Conventional financial statements, however, contain no explicit adjustments for the impact of inflation on the financial data. In response to this, the FASB encourages companies to disclose supplementary information about the effects of changing prices on the firm's financial data.[7]

The U.S. rate of inflation in the early 1990s has been low, so financial statement users are not demanding information on the impact of changing prices. Because there is a cost to compiling this type of information, few companies are voluntarily making the supplementary disclosures recommended by the FASB. Should the rate of inflation increase to the point where disclosures are required, the current recommended

---

[7] *Statement of Financial Accounting Standards No. 89*, "Financial Reporting and Changing Prices" (Stamford, CT: Financial Accounting Standards Board, 1986).

disclosures will be the likely starting point for the development of the required disclosures. The appendix to this chapter examines the FASB recommended disclosures in more detail.

The preceding catalogue of parenthetical disclosures, notes, and supplementary information demonstrates the breadth and detail of data that accompanies a set of financial statements. To some, the vast and increasing array of financial statement disclosures threatens to turn a wealth of information into an information "overload." Whether there is too much information, of course, depends on the needs and financial sophistication of users. Nonetheless, it should be clear that much may be learned by reading these disclosures.

INTERNATIONAL ACCOUNTING PRINCIPLES

A topic of importance to an increasing number of accountants is the development and implementation of a set of international accounting principles. The term **international accounting principles** refers to a set of accounting guidelines that are acceptable for financial statements that will be presented and utilized in different countries.

Need for International Accounting Principles

Two major reasons for interest in a set of international accounting principles are (1) to improve the operation of international capital markets and (2) to reduce the information-generating costs of multinational companies.

IMPROVE THE OPERATION OF INTERNATIONAL CAPITAL MARKETS

OBJECTIVE 4 DEFINE *and* DISCUSS *international accounting principles.*

Accompanying the movement to a global economy has been the development of an international capital market. A U.S. company in need of funds, for example, may seek financing in one or more foreign countries, or a foreign company may seek financing in the United States. Similarly, a U.S. investor may invest in foreign securities, or a foreign investor may invest in U.S. securities. The movement of capital across borders is sizable. For example, the net capital inflow from foreigners into the United States exceeded $500 billion from 1988 through 1990. In 1991, it was estimated that, worldwide, one of every seven equity trades had a foreign investor on the other side.[8]

At present, there are differences in accounting principles among countries (see pages 480–481). These differences create barriers to, and cause inefficiencies in, the operation of the international capital market. For example, some foreign companies are unwilling to offer their securities in the United States because they do not want to incur the costs of restating their financial data to comply with U.S. accounting principles. Also, in trying to compare corporate performances across borders, U.S. investors and lenders incur extra costs as they adjust their analyses to compensate for the lack of comparability in underlying accounting principles. Lenders may even increase the rate of interest charged to compensate for the uncertainty created by the use of different (and not completely understood) accounting principles. A set of international accounting principles, understood and interpreted consistently throughout the world, would eliminate these types of problems and encourage the flow of capital across borders.

Even the existence of the large amounts of capital currently flowing in the international market does not reduce the need for increased harmonization of accounting principles among countries. Accounting's role in the allocation of resources in capital markets is to provide investors and creditors with relevant and reliable financial information so that informed decisions may be made as to where resources should be

---

[8]Michael Howell, *The Forthcoming 1990s New Issue Boom: Will Smart Money Head to the US?* (Salomon Brothers Inc., March 12, 1991).

allocated. If the underlying accounting data are not comparable across countries (as is currently the case), then it is likely that investors and creditors at present are not making the optimal allocation decisions.

REDUCE THE INFORMATION-GENERATING COSTS OF MULTINATIONAL COMPANIES

A multinational corporation has subsidiary units located outside the firm's home country. To the extent that each country in which a subsidiary is located has different accounting principles, the multinational firm's costs of generating accounting information are increased. For example, a different accounting system must be established for each country in which the firm operates so that local reporting requirements may be met, various personnel must be trained in the similarities and differences in accounting principles used by subsidiary units, and subsidiary financial data must be converted to the home country accounting principles whenever the data from all units are to be merged into one overall set of financial statements. Costs associated with these activities would be eliminated with the implementation of a set of international accounting principles.

Obstacles to International Accounting Principles

Getting a set of international accounting principles identified and accepted by different countries is a difficult task. Among the obstacles are (1) cultural differences among countries, (2) differences among countries as to who establishes accounting principles, and (3) nationalistic tendencies of principle-setting bodies.

CULTURAL DIFFERENCES

Countries differ in economic environment, political structure, and language. These differences contribute to the diversity in accounting principles among countries, and this diversity makes it harder to agree on a common set of principles.

An economic environment with a high rate of inflation, for example, may generate an accounting principle that requires inflation adjustments to the financial statements, but a country with a low inflation rate may not require such adjustments. As an illustration, Mexican accounting principles require inflation adjustments to financial statements, but U.S. principles do not. Similarly, an economy dominated by publicly held corporations may require accounting principles that are not needed in an economy influenced by small, family-owned businesses.

Some political systems place more emphasis on private ownership of property than do other systems, and this may lead to differences in accounting principles. The relationship between tax law and accounting principles also differs among countries. In some countries, financial statements must conform to tax returns, but in other countries, such as the United States, tax returns and financial statements may differ significantly.

Language differences create problems in establishing a uniformly understood set of international accounting principles. Accounting contains many technical terms and not all languages can easily assimilate the fine points of technical definitions. Also, the interpretation of certain concepts, such as the *timeliness* of reporting or the *reliability* of data, may differ among countries.[9]

DIFFERENCES IN NATIONAL PRINCIPLE-SETTING BODIES

The nature of the group with primary responsibility for formulating accounting principles varies from one country to the next. The group may be a committee in the private sector (such as the Financial Accounting Standards Board in the United States and the Accounting Standards Committee in Canada), or it may be a governmental

---

[9]John M. Turner, "International Harmonization: A Professional Goal," *The Journal of Accountancy*, January 1983, pp. 59–60.

NO COMPARISONS

So you want to invest overseas? ■ *That makes sense. After all, foreign stock markets often outperform the U.S. market. Now all you have to do is figure out what you're investing in.* ■ *It won't be easy: Disclosure and accounting rules overseas differ sharply from those in the U.S.—and also differ significantly among the foreign countries.* ■ *Only companies in the United States and Canada, for example, issue reports quarterly on profits and other key financial data. And most companies in Japan and Germany don't consolidate the financial data of majority-owned subsidiaries (see table on page 481).*

Gary Greenberg, a global analyst with Harris Associates, says that in other nations the lack of a strong enforcement body like the Securities and Exchange Commission permits overseas companies to be more foot-loose and fancy-free with disclosures. And insider trading is often greeted with a wink by government regulators. In Holland, Spain and France, where stock exchanges are relatively small, government regulation and oversight of company disclosures are "very relaxed," Mr. Greenberg says.

As a result, many experts advise individuals to avoid investing in foreign markets on their own. And, in fact, some countries such as Brazil, India, South Korea and Taiwan make it difficult, if not impossible, for individuals to invest in companies within their borders. "Overseas mutual funds are better because professional fund managers can lead you through the foreign stock-market jungle with all its perils and pitfalls," says Martin Skala, senior editor of Standard & Poor's *Outlook* publication on U.S. and world investment.

But even the most sophisticated funds can be fooled. For example, the Acorn Fund in Chicago, which invests in small start-up companies overseas, recently saw its investment of $575,000 in the stock of Lafe Holdings Ltd., an electronics manu-facturer in Hong Kong, decline by 54% after the company's chairman sold all his stock but didn't disclose it.

"Such undisclosed insider dealings are much more common overseas, and you've really got to keep your eye on management," says Ralph Wanger, the Acorn Fund's president.

Differences in accounting rules make for a wide divergence of financial results in various countries.

To illustrate how tough it is to compare such profits, three accounting professors at Rider College in Lawrenceville, N.J., set up a computer model of an imaginary company's financial reports in four nations. Starting with the same gross operating profit of $1.5 million, the company had net profit of $34,600 in the United States, $260,600 in the United Kingdom, $240,600 in Australia and $10,402 in Germany—all because of varying accounting rules in each country.

Although many companies have world-wide operations, their financial results in different countries aren't comparable, the professors say. They term this a "serious problem" for "accountants who may be called upon to analyze a foreign company's financial statements."

The results of companies in Japan, Germany, Switzerland and Spain are among the most difficult to compare with those of their U.S. counterparts, says Kenneth Oberman, manager of the Oppenheimer Global Fund. In Japan and Germany, he says, many corporations don't consolidate results of their majority-owned subsidiaries; in Switzerland and Spain, some concerns set up hidden reserves, which result in lower reported profits.

"When I invest in a Swiss company," says Mr. Oberman, "I usually add a fudge factor of 25% to its financial results, and sometimes I find I should have added 40%."

Investing in Korean companies can also be tricky. Some Korean companies create "special gains and losses" that sometimes don't relate to company successes or failures, says Robert Kim, a portfolio manager for the Korea Fund, managed by Scudder Stevens & Clark. "If a Korean company wants to pay less taxes or quiet worker demands for higher wages, it can do this with depreciation schedules much more easily than in the United States," Mr. Kim says.

Because financial reports can lose something in translation, some managers of overseas funds hire country nationals to analyze stocks. Five years ago the Merrill Lynch Pacific Fund hired Etsuko Nakajima, a Japanese financial analyst. "She has been very helpful in spelling out language nuances," says Stephen Silverman, the Pacific Fund portfolio manager.

In researching a Japanese investment company, the fund found that the Japanese-language version of the company's policy of refunds to clients was less generous than the U.S. translation had indicated. "This made the stock more attractive to us," Mr. Silverman adds.

SOURCE: Lee Berton, "No Comparisons," *The Wall Street Journal*, September 22, 1989, p. R30. Reprinted with permission of *The Wall Street Journal*. © 1989 Dow Jones & Co., Inc. All rights reserved worldwide.

Let the Investor Beware
Accounting rules vary world-wide.

All Company Financial Reports Include	AUSTRALIA	AUSTRIA	BRITAIN	CANADA	FRANCE	GERMANY	HONG KONG	JAPAN	NETHERLANDS	SINGAPORE	SPAIN	SWITZERLAND	UNITED STATES
Quarterly data*				●									●
Accruals for deferred taxes	●		●	●	●		●		●	●			●
Consolidation of parent and majority owned subsidiaries†	●		●	●	●		●		●	●	●	●	●
Discretionary or hidden reserves		●			●	●					●	●	
Immediate deduction of research and development costs‡	●		●	●	●	●		●	●			●	●

* In Austria, companies issue only annual data. Other countries besides the United States and Canada issue semiannual data. In the Netherlands, companies issue quarterly or semiannual data.

† In Austria, Japan, and Germany, the minority of companies fully consolidate.

‡ In Austria, Hong Kong, Singapore, and Spain, the accounting treatment for R&D costs—whether they are immediately deducted or capitalized and deducted over later years—isn't disclosed in financial reports.

SOURCE: Center for International Financial Analysis and Research, Princeton, N.J.

body (in Germany, for example, Parliament sets accounting standards through the Ministry of Finance), or it may be a combined effort of a private-sector committee and a governmental body.[10] The group's membership may consist of accountants only, or it may be a mix of accountants and nonaccountants. A governmental body containing nonaccountants is likely to have a different perspective about appropriate accounting principles than is a private-sector committee composed of accountants only. The variety among countries in the nature and composition of principle-setting bodies, then, contributes to the problem of achieving agreement on international accounting principles.

NATIONALISTIC TENDENCIES OF PRINCIPLE-SETTING BODIES

To achieve a set of international accounting principles that is acceptable to all countries, each country's principle-setting body will probably have to compromise its views somewhat. These compromises may be difficult to achieve. For example, although the FASB supports the development of international accounting principles, situations may arise in which it believes its current accounting principles are best and should not be "watered down" to meet a proposed international standard. Further, the appropriate role for a nation's principle-setting body once international principles are in place is still open to question. A strong national principle-setting group, for example, may not want its role to be only that of advocate for its country's interests at the international level. Concerns about compromise and future roles create a tendency in principle-setting bodies to resist, or slow down, the movement toward international harmonization of accounting principles. For substantial progress toward international harmonization to occur, however, nationalistic attitudes would have to be modified.

---

[10] S. E. C. Purvis, Helen Gernon, and Michael A. Diamond, "The IASC and Its Comparability Project: Prerequisites for Success," *Accounting Horizons*, June 1991, p. 25.

International Accounting Standards Committee

Although several organizations are working to increase international harmonization in accounting, the organization that has taken the lead in formulating international accounting principles is the *International Accounting Standards Committee (IASC)*. Organized in 1973 and headquartered in London, the IASC's 1991 membership consisted of 106 professional accounting organizations from 79 countries. The IASC has no authoritative status in any country, nor does it have any enforcement powers. Instead, the IASC depends on its members to persuade the principle setters in their home countries that financial statements should comply with the international accounting standards it formulates.

During its existence, the IASC has issued more than 30 international accounting standards. The IASC is governed by a 14-member board, and standards must be approved by at least 75% of the board members. Through the late 1980s, most of the standards identified a range of acceptable practice—usually two acceptable alternatives were established—rather than specifying a single accounting principle for each situation considered. For the most part, the practices allowed by these standards were compatible with generally accepted accounting principles (GAAP) in the United States.

Beginning in 1988 and continuing to the present, the IASC has worked to eliminate a large number of the alternatives allowed in its existing standards. Some of the revised standards may well conflict with GAAP. At this writing, for example, the IASC has proposed that the completed contract method be eliminated as an acceptable accounting procedure and that goodwill should be amortized over a maximum 5-year period unless a longer life can be justified (in which case the maximum write-off period would be 20 years).[11]

The *International Organization of Securities Commissions (IOSCO)* supports the IASC's efforts to eliminate alternatives in its standards. IOSCO comprises securities regulators from all over the world (the U.S. member is the Securities and Exchange Commission). Should the IASC develop a set of principles acceptable to securities regulators, then an intermediate approach to accounting internationalism may be possible. Under this approach, the securities regulators would adopt the principles as a set of international standards. Foreign companies wishing to issue securities in a particular country would then be required to reconcile their financial statements to the international standards (and not the local country's standards).[12] As a result, the international flow of capital would be improved without requiring national principle setters to compromise their standards for domestic companies. The 1990s should reveal whether this intermediate approach will be successful.

ANALYTICAL APPLICATION

OPERATING CASH FLOW TO CAPITAL EXPENDITURES RATIO

OBJECTIVE 5 DEFINE *the* **operating cash flow to capital expenditures ratio** *and* EXPLAIN *its use.*

To remain competitive, an entity must be able to replace, and expand when appropriate, its property, plant, and equipment. A ratio that helps assess a firm's ability to do this is the **operating cash flow to capital expenditures ratio,** which is computed as follows:

$$\text{Operating Cash Flow to Capital Expenditures Ratio} = \frac{\text{Net Cash Flow from Operating Activities}}{\text{Annual Capital Expenditures}}$$

---

[11] *Exposure Draft 32*, "Comparability of Financial Statements: Proposed Amendments to International Accounting Standards 2, 5, 8, 9, 11, 16, 17, 18, 19, 21, 22, 23 and 25 (London: International Accounting Standards Committee, 1989).

[12] Philip R. Lochner, Jr., "The Role of U.S. Standard Setters in International Harmonization of Accounting Standards," *The Journal of Accountancy*, September 1991, p. 108.

The numerator in this ratio comes from the first section of the statement of cash flows—the section reporting the net cash flow from operating activities. Information for the denominator may be found in one or more places in the financial statements and related disclosures. Data on capital expenditures are part of the required industry segment disclosures in the notes to the financial statements. Capital expenditures may also be shown in the investing activities section of the statement of cash flows. Also, capital expenditures often appear in the comparative selected financial data presented as supplementary information to the financial statements. Finally, management's discussion and analysis of the statements may identify the annual capital expenditures.

A ratio in excess of 1.0 means that the firm's current operating activities are providing cash in excess of the amount needed to provide the desired level of plant capacity and would normally be considered a sign of financial strength. This ratio may also be viewed as an indicator of long-term solvency—a ratio exceeding 1.0 means that there is an operating cash flow in excess of capital needs that may be used to repay outstanding long-term debt.

The interpretation of this ratio for a firm is influenced by its trend in recent years, the ratio size being achieved by other firms in the same industry, and the stage of the firm's life cycle. A firm in the early stages of its life cycle—when periods of rapid expansion may occur—may be expected to experience a lower ratio than a firm in the mature stage of its life cycle—when maintenance of plant capacity may be more likely than expansion of capacity.

To illustrate the ratio's computation, ABBOTT LABORATORIES (a manufacturer of pharmaceutical and other health care products) reported capital expenditures in a recent year of $629,500,000. In the same year, Abbott's net cash flow from operating activities was $1,200,884,000. Abbott's operating cash flow to capital expenditures ratio for that year was $1,200,884,000/$629,500,000 = 1.91. Following are recent operating cash flow to capital expenditures ratios for several companies:

GRUMMAN CORPORATION (aerospace)	5.10
THE QUAKER OATS COMPANY (consumer grocery products)	2.21
FEDERAL MOGUL CORPORATION (precision parts)	1.53
NORFOLK SOUTHERN CORPORATION (freight transportation services)	1.43
FIGGIE INTERNATIONAL INC. (diversified products and services)	0.69

KEY POINTS FOR CHAPTER OBJECTIVES

❶ DISCUSS the historical development of accounting principles and the nature of the conceptual framework (pp. 462–464).
- The FASB, the AICPA, and the SEC have been instrumental in the development of generally accepted accounting principles.
- The conceptual framework is a cohesive set of interrelated objectives and fundamentals for external financial reporting.

❷ IDENTIFY the basic principles underlying accounting theory (pp. 464–472).
- Each of the following is an important basic accounting principle:

accounting entity	consistency
accounting period	revenue recognition
going concern	matching
measuring unit	conservatism
cost	materiality
objectivity	full disclosure

- Revenue is usually recognized at point of sale because it is then both earned and realized.
- The installment method of revenue recognition treats each dollar received as part return of cost and part gross profit.
- The percentage-of-completion method recognizes revenue in proportion to the amount of the total contract completed in the period.

❸ IDENTIFY and **DESCRIBE** the various types of financial statement disclosures (pp. 472–478).
- Financial statement disclosures provide additional information about financial performance and position and appear as parenthetical disclosures, notes, or supplementary information.

④ **DEFINE** and **DISCUSS** international accounting principles (pp. 478–482).

■ International accounting principles would (1) improve the operation of international capital markets and (2) reduce the information-generating costs of multinational companies.

■ Obstacles to the acceptance of international accounting principles include (1) cultural differences, (2) differences in who establishes accounting principles, and (3) nationalistic tendencies of principle-setting bodies.

⑤ **ANALYTICAL APPLICATION:** **DEFINE** the *operating cash flow to capital expenditures ratio* and **EXPLAIN** its use (pp. 482–483).

■ The operating cash flow to capital expenditures ratio is computed by dividing a firm's net cash flow from operating activities by its annual capital expenditures.

■ The ratio helps assess a firm's (1) ability to maintain its plant capacity and (2) long-run solvency.

SELF-TEST QUESTIONS FOR REVIEW

(Answers follow the Solution to Demonstration Problem.)

1. Which of the following is not included in the overall conceptual framework for business enterprises?
   a. Financial reporting objectives.
   b. Financial statement elements.
   c. Inflation accounting disclosures.
   d. Qualitative characteristics of accounting information.

2. Plant assets are depreciated over their useful lives. Which basic principle of accounting does this procedure reflect?
   a. Full disclosure.
   b. Matching.
   c. Consistency.
   d. Objectivity.

3. On August 1, 1994, Perry Company sold a computer costing $3,500 for $5,000. The customer paid 25% down with the balance due in 30 equal monthly payments of $125 starting September 1, 1994. Using the installment method, how much gross profit is recognized in 1994?
   a. $525   b. $1,500   c. $150   d. $1,225

4. During 1994, Switzer Company made interest-free loans totaling $2,500,000 to certain of its officers. The money is used to finance construction of a special facility that will then be leased to Switzer. Switzer discloses this situation in a note to its 1994 financial statements. This note is an example of a
   a. Contingency disclosure.
   b. Significant accounting policy disclosure.
   c. Related party disclosure.
   d. Subsequent event disclosure.

5. Which organization has provided the leadership in developing a set of international accounting principles?
   a. Financial Accounting Standards Board.
   b. Securities and Exchange Commission.
   c. International Organization of Securities Commissions.
   d. International Accounting Standards Committee.

DEMONSTRATION PROBLEM FOR REVIEW

On November 1, 1993, Dent Company sold a sofa for $900 on terms of 20% down on the purchase date, and 18 equal monthly payments of $40 beginning December 1, 1993. The sofa cost $540. Compute the amount of gross profit shown in each calendar year involved using the following revenue recognition methods:
a. Point-of-sale method.
b. Installment method.
c. Cost recovery method.

SOLUTION TO DEMONSTRATION PROBLEM

a. Under the point-of-sale method, all of the revenue and gross profit would be recognized in November 1993, as follows:

Sales	$900
Cost of goods sold	540
Gross profit	$360

b. Under the installment method, the gross profit percentage is $360/$900 = 40%. Cash collected is treated as 60% cost recovery and 40% gross profit.

	1993	1994	1995
Cash collected			
1993: Down payment ($180) + one $40			
monthly payment	$220		
1994: Twelve $40 monthly payments		$480	
1995: Five $40 monthly payments			$200
Considered return of cost (60%)	132	288	120
Considered gross profit (40%)	88	192	80

c. Under the cost recovery method, no gross profit is recorded until the cost of the item sold ($540) has been collected in cash; all cash collected after the cost has been recovered is gross profit.

	1993	1994	1995
Cash collected	$220	$480	$200
Considered return of cost (first $540)	220	320	0
Considered gross profit (last $360)	0	160	200

ANSWERS TO SELF-TEST QUESTIONS

1. c, p. 463   2. b, p. 471   3. a, p. 469   4. c, p. 474   5. d, p. 482

APPENDIX C

The Financial Accounting Standards Board has developed supplemental disclosure guidelines that firms may use to show the effects of changing prices on their financial data.[1] The recommended supplementary data combine two types of adjustments for changing prices. One, **constant dollar accounting,** adjusts financial data for changes in the general purchasing power of the dollar. The other, **current cost accounting,** reflects the impact of specific price changes on a firm by incorporating current value measurements into the data. We now examine the nature of these adjustments.

CONSTANT DOLLAR ACCOUNTING

The general purchasing power of the dollar is a measure of its ability to buy goods and services. *Price-level changes* are changes in the prevailing exchange ratio between money and goods or services. Whenever a rise in the general level of prices for goods and services occurs, the general purchasing power of the dollar declines; this is **inflation.** In contrast, **deflation** is an increase in the dollar's general purchasing power as the general level of prices declines. Our discussion is in the context of inflation, the prevailing price-level movement of the last several decades.

Price indexes measure price-level changes. A **price index** represents a series of measurements, stated as percentages, indicating the relationship between (1) the weighted average price of a sample of goods and services at various points in time and (2) the weighted average price of a similar sample of goods and services at a common, or base, date.

For example, assume that we wish to construct a price index for a single commodity that was priced at $1.60 in December 1992, $2 in December 1993, and $2.50 in December 1994. If we select December 1993 as our base date, our price index expresses the price of this commodity in December of 1992, 1993, and 1994 as a percentage of its price in December 1993. The 1992 price is 80% ($1.60/$2) of the 1993 price, and the 1994 price is 125% ($2.50/$2) of the 1993 price. The percentage relationship on the base date is, of course, always 100%. The price index for each date is as follows (the percent sign is understood and usually not shown with index numbers):

December 1992	80
December 1993	100
December 1994	125

Prominent examples of price indexes are the Consumer Price Index for All Urban Consumers and the Gross National Product Implicit Price Deflator. The FASB recommends the use of the Consumer Price Index for any general purchasing power adjustments. The monthly calculation of the Consumer Price Index is one advantage it has over the GNP Implicit Price Deflator, which is calculated quarterly.

With index numbers, amounts stated in terms of dollars of general purchasing power at a particular time may be restated in terms of dollars of different purchasing power at another time. We simply multiply the amount to be restated by the following *conversion factor:*

$$\frac{\text{Index You Are Converting TO}}{\text{Index You Are Converting FROM}}$$

---

[1] *Statement of Financial Accounting Standards No. 89,* "Financial Reporting and Changing Prices" (Stamford, CT: Financial Accounting Standards Board, 1986).

For example, suppose we acquired a parcel of land for $5,000 in December 1993, when the general price index was 100. Suppose also that the general price indexes for various times were as follows:[2]

December 1992	80
December 1993	100
December 1994	125
Average for 1994	110

We restate the cost of the land in terms of the December 1994 dollar by multiplying the $5,000 by the conversion factor 125/100 (December 1994 index/December 1993 index). The resulting measure is $6,250, the cost of the land stated in dollars of December 1994 general purchasing power. The cost of the land in terms of the 1994 average dollar is $5,000 × 110/100 = $5,500. Each of the amounts $5,000, $6,250, and $5,500 represents the cost of the land, but the cost is expressed in a different unit of measure in each case.

Current market values may also be expressed in different units of general purchasing power. Assume at December 31, 1994, the current market value of the land is $7,500. This amount exceeds the land's historical cost adjusted for changes in the dollar's general purchasing power to December 31, 1994 ($6,250), indicating that the specific price of this land has increased more than prices in general. The land's current market value is a financial measure taken at December 31, 1994, so it is stated in terms of the dollar's general purchasing power at that date (price index of 125). As with any dollar amount, we may restate this measure to other units of general purchasing power by using the proper conversion factor. For example, the land's December 31, 1994, current market value restated to the 1994 average purchasing power of the dollar is $7,500 × 110/125 = $6,600.

Generally accepted accounting principles use the dollar as a measuring unit and assume that it is stable (that is, that no significant general price-level changes occur); therefore, all dollars are considered economically equal. Some single-year levels of inflation have strained the stable-dollar assumption, and certainly, some multiyear periods have invalidated it. A benefit of adjusting for changes in the general purchasing power of the dollar is that better comparisons of financial data through time are achieved.

To illustrate, assume that the average price-level indexes and Company A's sales revenue for 1992–1994 are as shown:

	Average Price-level Index	Unadjusted Sales
1992	75	$1,500,000
1993	88	1,650,000
1994	110	1,900,000

Events that occur fairly evenly throughout the year, such as sales, are assumed to be initially stated in dollars of the average purchasing power for the year. The 1992 unadjusted sales, then, are stated in dollars of 1992 average purchasing power; 1993 sales are measured in dollars of 1993 average purchasing power; and 1994 sales are stated in dollars of 1994 average purchasing power.

The unadjusted sales figures indicate a healthy increase in sales. However, if we convert the dollars stated in the average price-level for 1992, 1993, and 1994 to a common unit of general purchasing power—a dollar with the 1994 average purchasing power—we discover the following sales levels:

---

[2] The assumed price indexes used in this appendix are selected for ease of calculation and illustrative clarity. They do not represent actual price indexes for the dates used.

	Average Price-level Index	Unadjusted Sales	Conversion Factor	Restated Sales
1992	75	$1,500,000	110/75	$2,200,000
1993	88	1,650,000	110/88	2,062,500
1994	110	1,900,000	110/110	1,900,000

Adjusting the data to a common dollar indicates a decrease in sales activity rather than an increase. During periods of significant inflation, other comparative data, such as net income and dividends, may be similarly affected. Putting comparative data in the same unit of general purchasing power, then, may help users to better analyze and interpret the data.

A new item computed from constant dollar adjustments is the **purchasing power gain or loss on net monetary items.** Net monetary items are monetary assets less monetary liabilities. Monetary assets include cash and other assets—such as receivables—that represent the right to receive a fixed number of dollars in the future, regardless of price-level changes. Monetary liabilities are obligations to disburse a fixed number of dollars in the future, regardless of price-level changes. Most liabilities are monetary. By their nature, monetary items in a balance sheet are stated in dollars of current purchasing power at the balance sheet date.

Holding monetary items during a period of rising prices creates purchasing power gains and losses on these items. For example, suppose you hold $1,000 cash during a period when the general price level increases from 100 to 125. At the end of the period, your $1,000 will buy fewer goods and services than it would at the beginning of the period. This decrease in your ability to buy goods and services as a result of inflation is a *purchasing power loss on cash*. The amount of the loss, stated in end-of-year general purchasing power, is $250, calculated by multiplying the percentage increase in prices, 25%, by the $1,000 cash you held.

Assume that you also had a note payable of $800 outstanding during the time the general price index increased from 100 to 125. As a result of inflation, you owe dollars whose general purchasing power at the end of the period is less than it was at the beginning of the period. The decrease in the general purchasing power of the dollars with which you will settle the liability represents a *purchasing power gain on the note payable*. The amount of the gain, stated in end-of-year general purchasing power, is $200 (25% × $800).

Combining the $250 purchasing power loss on cash and the $200 purchasing power gain on the note payable gives a $50 purchasing power loss on *net* monetary items, stated in year-end general purchasing power. Purchasing power gains and losses have no counterpart in conventional financial statements. They are computed only by making constant dollar adjustments. The net purchasing power gain or loss is one indicator of how well management handled monetary items during a period of inflation or deflation and may, therefore, be useful to financial statement readers.

CURRENT COST ACCOUNTING

Current cost accounting is a system for incorporating current values into the financial data. The current cost of an asset is the estimated cost to acquire a similar asset at current prices. Under a system of current cost accounting, net income is determined by subtracting from revenue the current cost of assets used in the earning process. Assets at year-end are measured at their current cost. Changes in the current cost of an asset are reflected in the period in which the change in value occurs.

A simple example illustrates the basic concepts of current cost accounting. Assume that Densmore, Inc., started business on January 1, 1994, with the following assets:

Cash	$10,000
Inventory (7,500 units @ $10)	75,000
Land	15,000

During 1994, Densmore, Inc., sold 5,000 inventory units at $16 each and incurred cash operating expenses of $18,000. Densmore's 1994 historical cost income statement follows:

Historical Cost

Sales (5,000 units @ $16)	$80,000
Cost of Goods Sold (5,000 units @ $10)	$50,000
Operating Expenses	18,000
Total Expenses	$68,000
Net Income	$12,000

Now assume that before any inventory was sold in 1994, its current cost increased to $11 per unit and remained there until year-end. Densmore's 1994 income statement using current cost procedures follows:

Current Cost

Sales	$80,000
Cost of Goods Sold (5,000 units @ $11)	$55,000
Operating Expenses	18,000
Total Expenses	$73,000
Net Income	$ 7,000

The $7,000 current cost net income shows earnings after first providing for the replacement of assets used in operations. Expenses are measured at their current costs when incurred. Current cost net income, therefore, indicates the profitability of operations at the company's current level of operating costs. It also represents the maximum dividend the company could pay and still maintain its present level of operations.

Changes in the specific prices of assets held during the year are identified using current cost procedures. To continue our Densmore, Inc., illustration, assume that the replacement cost of land increased to $19,000 by year-end. Current cost procedures will show a 1994 increase of $11,500 in the current cost of inventory and land held during the year, computed as follows:

Inventory: Increase from $10 to $11 on 7,500 units	$ 7,500
Land: Increase from $15,000 to $19,000	4,000
Increase in current cost during 1994	$11,500

Note that the current cost increase includes $5,000 that relates to the inventory units sold during 1994. The increase in their replacement cost occurred before they were sold, so the increase does belong as part of the value change that occurred while Densmore held the assets.

One issue in current cost accounting is whether the changes in the current costs of assets held should be included as part of net income or handled separately. The disclosures encouraged by the FASB use the latter treatment.

FASB DISCLOSURES

From December 25, 1979, through December 2, 1986, the FASB required large, publicly held companies to disclose supplementary inflation information. During this time, the FASB experimented with, and evaluated, various constant dollar and current cost disclosures. By the end of 1986, the inflation rate was low enough that the disclosures were made voluntary. Most of the disclosures encouraged by the FASB are current cost amounts stated in a constant unit of general purchasing power. It believes that this combination encompasses the best aspects of both constant dollar and current cost accounting. Constant dollar adjustments stabilize the purchasing power of the unit of measure and reveal the purchasing power gain or loss on net monetary items, while current cost calculations show the impact of specific price changes during the period.

The disclosures encouraged by the FASB consist of a five-year schedule of selected data (all stated in the same unit of general purchasing power) and a few additional current year disclosures. Included in the five-year schedule are such items as net sales, net income[3] computed using current cost accounting, the purchasing power gain or loss on net monetary items, and the increase or decrease in the current cost of inventory and plant assets. Included among the additional current year disclosures are the year-end current costs of inventory and plant assets.

Because there is a cost to compile constant dollar and current cost data, few companies are voluntarily making these supplementary disclosures. Should the future rate of inflation increase to the point where disclosures are again required, the current recommended disclosures will be the likely starting point for the development of the required disclosures.

GLOSSARY OF KEY TERMS USED IN THIS CHAPTER AND APPENDIX

accounting entity An economic unit that has identifiable boundaries and that is the focus for the accumulation and reporting of financial information (p. 464).

accounting period The time period, typically one year, to which accounting reports are related (p. 465).

commitments A contractual arrangement by which both parties to the contract still have acts to perform (p. 475).

completed contract method A point-of-sale (that is, completion of the contract) revenue recognition method for long-term contracts (p. 470).

conceptual framework A cohesive set of interrelated objectives and fundamentals for external financial reporting developed by the FASB (p. 463).

conservatism An accounting principle stating that judgmental determinations should tend toward understatement rather than overstatement of net assets and income (p. 471).

consistency An accounting principle stating that, unless otherwise disclosed, accounting reports should be prepared on a basis consistent with the preceding period (p. 468).

constant dollar accounting An accounting process that adjusts financial data for changes in the general purchasing power of the dollar (p. 486).

contingency A possible future event; significant contingent liabilities must be disclosed in the notes to the financial statements (p. 475).

cost principle An accounting principle stating that asset measures are based on the prices paid to acquire the assets (p. 467).

cost recovery method A revenue recognition method for installment transactions that treats all cash collections as a return of cost until all costs are recovered; the remaining cash collections are considered all gross profit (p. 469).

current cost accounting A system of accounting that reflects assets and expenses at their current replacement amounts (p. 486).

deflation A decrease in the general level of prices for goods and services (p. 486).

earning process The entire productive effort put forth by an entity to generate and collect revenue. Normally, this process should be substantially complete before revenue is recorded (p. 469).

financial reporting objectives A component of the conceptual framework that specifies that financial statements should provide information (1) useful for investment and credit decisions, (2) helpful in assessing an entity's ability to generate future cash flows, and (3) about

---

[3] If a company reports extraordinary items or discontinued operations, then income from continuing operations rather than net income is reported on a current cost basis. We discuss extraordinary items, discontinued operations, and income from continuing operations in the chapter Corporations: Dividends, Retained Earnings, and Earnings Disclosures.

an entity's resources, claims to those resources, and the effects of events causing changes in these items (p. 463).

financial statement elements A part of the conceptual framework that identifies the significant components—such as assets, liabilities, owners' equity, revenues, and expenses—used to put financial statements together (p. 463).

full disclosure An accounting principle stipulating the disclosure of all facts necessary to make financial statements useful to readers (p. 472).

generally accepted accounting principles (GAAP) A group of standards or guides to action in preparing financial accounting reports (p. 462).

going concern concept An accounting principle that assumes that, in the absence of evidence to the contrary, a business entity will have an indefinite life (p. 466).

inflation An increase in the general level of prices for goods and services (p. 486).

installment method A method of revenue recognition for installment transactions that treats each cash collection as part return of cost and part gross profit (p. 469).

international accounting principles A set of accounting guidelines that is acceptable for financial statements that will be presented and used in different countries (p. 478).

matching concept An accounting guideline that states that income is determined by relating expenses, to the extent feasible, with revenues that have been recorded (p. 471).

materiality An accounting guideline that states that transactions so insignificant that they would not affect a user's actions may be recorded in the most expedient manner (p. 472).

measuring unit concept An accounting guideline noting that the accounting unit of measure is the basic unit of money (p. 466).

objectivity An accounting principle requiring that, whenever possible, accounting entries be based on objectively determined evidence (p. 467).

operating cash flow to capital expenditures ratio A financial ratio calculated by dividing a firm's net cash flow from operating activities by its annual capital expenditures (p. 482).

percentage-of-completion (POC) method A revenue recognition method that allocates revenue on a long-term contract among the accounting periods involved in proportion to the estimated percentage of the contract completed each period (p. 470).

price index A series of measurements, stated as percentages, indicating the relationship between the weighted average price of a sample of goods and services at various points of time and the weighted average price of a similar sample of goods and services at a common, or base, date (p. 486).

purchasing power gain or loss on net monetary items The gain or loss in general purchasing power that results from holding monetary assets or owing monetary liabilities during periods of inflation or deflation (p. 488).

qualitative characteristics of accounting information The characteristics of accounting information that contribute to decision usefulness. The primary qualities are *relevance* and *reliability* (p. 464).

quarterly data Selected quarterly financial information that is reported in annual reports to stockholders (p. 476).

realized A criterion for revenue recognition that states that goods or services must be exchanged for cash or claims to cash before revenue may be recorded (p. 469).

recognition criteria The criteria that must be met before a financial statement element may be recorded in the accounts. Essentially, the item must meet the definition for an element and must be measurable, and the resultant information about the item must be relevant and reliable (p. 464).

relevance A qualitative characteristic of accounting information; relevant information contributes to the predictive and evaluative decisions made by financial statement users (p. 464).

reliability A qualitative characteristic of accounting information; reliable information contains no bias or error and faithfully portrays what it intends to represent (p. 464).

revenue recognition principle An accounting principle requiring that, with few exceptions, revenue be recognized at the point of sale (p. 468).

segments Subdivisions of a firm for which supplemental financial information is disclosed (p. 476).

subsequent events Events occurring shortly after a fiscal year-end that will be reported as supplemental information to the financial statements of the year just ended (p. 477).

summary of significant accounting policies A financial statement disclosure, usually the initial note to the statements, that identifies the major accounting policies and procedures used by the firm (p. 474).

QUESTIONS

13-1 How would you determine whether a particular accounting procedure is a generally accepted accounting principle?

13-2 Discuss the origin of accounting principles.

13-3 Why has the FASB developed a conceptual framework?

13-4 Identify two primary qualities of accounting information that contribute to decision usefulness.

13-5 In one sentence, describe each of the following accounting principles:

accounting entity	consistency
accounting period	revenue recognition
going concern	matching
measuring unit	conservatism
cost	materiality
objectivity	full disclosure

13-6 Why is the accounting entity the most fundamental accounting concept?

13-7 Why do accounting principles emphasize historical cost as a basis for measuring assets?

13-8 How do accountants justify using the point of sale for revenue recognition?

13-9 Explain the procedures and justification for using the following methods of revenue recognition: (a) the installment method and (b) the percentage-of-completion method.

13-10 Identify the three categories of financial statement disclosures.

13-11 NORFOLK SOUTHERN CORPORATION owns a major freight railroad, NORFOLK SOUTHERN RAILWAY COMPANY and a motor carrier, NORTH AMERICAN VAN LINES, INC. Where in Norfolk Southern's financial report should you look to determine when it recognizes revenue on freight shipments?

13-12 GANNETT CO., INC., publisher of *USA Today*, operates principally in three industries: newspaper publishing, broadcasting, and outdoor advertising. What financial information about these industry activities should be available in Gannett's financial report? Where and why is this information disclosed?

13-13 SOTHEBY'S HOLDINGS, INC., is a leading fine art auctioneer. Its 1990 annual report shows loans to officers and directors of $2,404,000 among the assets in the balance sheet. Where in Sotheby's financial report should you look to find out more information about these loans?

13-14 LANDS' END, INC., sells apparel as well as bed and bath products by direct mail. For the fiscal year ended January 31, 1991, Lands' End reported net sales of $603,975,000. Where in Lands' End's financial report should you look to find whether its pattern of sales is seasonal or not?

13-15 What authoritative status do principles formulated by the International Accounting Standards Committee have?

13-16 Where in a company's financial report should you look to find the annual amount of capital expenditures?

13-17 For a recent year, OUTBOARD MARINE CORPORATION'S operating cash flow to capital expenditures ratio was 0.70. Explain how this ratio was calculated and indicate how large the ratio should be before it would be considered a sign of financial strength.

EXERCISES

CONCEPTUAL FRAMEWORK
— OBJ. 1 —

13-18 The Financial Accounting Standards Board worked several years to develop a conceptual framework.
a. What is the basic purpose of a conceptual framework?
b. Identify the financial reporting objectives that are specified in the conceptual framework.

BASIC PRINCIPLES
— OBJ. 2 —

13-19 Indicate the basic principle or principles of accounting that underlie each of the following independent situations:

a. Dr. Kline is a practicing pediatrician. Over the years, she has accumulated a personal investment portfolio of securities, virtually all of which have been purchased from her earnings as a pediatrician. The investment portfolio is not reflected in the accounting records of her medical practice.

b. A company purchases a desk tape dispenser for use by the office secretary. The tape dispenser cost $10 and has an estimated useful life of 25 years. The purchase is debited to the Office Supplies Expense account.

c. A company sells a product that has a two-year warranty covering parts and labor. In the same period that sales are recorded, an estimate of future warranty costs is debited to the Product Warranty Expense account.

d. A company pays $80,000 for a patent that has an estimated useful life of 10 years and no salvage value. The amount, debited to the Patent account, is amortized over a 10-year period.

REVENUE RECOGNITION
— OBJ. 2 —

13-20   For each of the following independent situations, determine how much revenue should be reported in the current period and how much should be deferred to a future period. If a collection basis method applies, determine the appropriate gross profit amounts under the installment method.

a. Purchased merchandise for $56,000 that will be sold early in the next period for $84,000.

b. Began work on a long-term construction contract with a price of $750,000. Expected costs total $500,000, of which $160,000 were incurred this period. The percentage of completion method is used.

c. Sold undeveloped real estate lots for $120,000 on installment terms. Of the $120,000, 30% was collected during this period. No reasonable estimate of the collectibility of the remaining balances is possible. The cost of the property sold is $78,000.

REVENUE RECOGNITION
— OBJ. 2 —

13-21   On October 1, 1993, London Appliance Company sold a combination refrigerator–freezer for $700 on terms of $100 down on the purchase date, and 15 equal monthly payments of $40 beginning November 1, 1993. The appliance cost $490. Compute the amount of gross profit shown in each calendar year involved using the following revenue recognition methods:

a. The cost recovery method.

b. The installment method.

c. The point-of-sale method.

FINANCIAL STATEMENT
NOTES
— OBJ. 3 —

13-22   Notes to financial statements present information on significant accounting policies, complex or special transactions, details of reported amounts, commitments, contingencies, segments, quarterly data, and subsequent events. Indicate which type of note disclosure is illustrated by each of the following notes.

a. The company has agreed to purchase seven EMB-120 aircraft and related spare parts. The aggregate cost of these aircraft is approximately $35,500,000, subject to a cost escalation provision. The aircraft are scheduled to be delivered over the next two fiscal years.

b. The company has deferred certain costs related to major accounting and information systems enhancements that are anticipated to benefit future years. Upon completion, the related cost is amortized over a period not exceeding five years.

c. The company has guaranteed loans and leases of independent distributors approximating $26,800,000 as of December 31 of the current year.

d. An officer of the company is also a director of a major raw material supplier of the company. The amount of raw material purchases from this supplier approximated $365,000 in the current year.

INTERNATIONAL
ACCOUNTING PRINCIPLES
— OBJ.4 —

13-23   The acceptance by nations of a set of international accounting principles will provide certain benefits.

a. What group has taken the lead in developing a set of international accounting principles?

b. Identify and briefly discuss two major benefits that would result from the adoption by nations of a set of international accounting principles.

CONSTANT DOLLAR
ACCOUNTING
— APPENDIX C —

13-24   In 1991, Conif Company purchased a parcel of land for $150,000 when the general price-level index was 120. By the end of 1995, the land's current market value was $188,000. Assume that general price-level indexes for 1992–1995 are as follows:

December 1992	132
December 1993	150
December 1994	156
December 1995	180
Average for 1995	171

a. Restate the land's cost in terms of the dollar's general purchasing power at (1) December 1992, (2) December 1993, (3) December 1994, (4) December 1995, and (5) for the year 1995 (average for 1995).

b. Restate the land's December 1995 market value in terms of the dollar's average purchasing power for 1995.

**CURRENT COST
ACCOUNTING
— APPENDIX C —**

13-25 On January 2, 1994, Locket Company started business and bought 9,000 inventory items at $60 each. On January 3, the unit purchase price increased to $64 and remained there until year-end. During 1994, Locket sold 6,800 of these items (and made no more purchases). If Locket followed current cost accounting procedures, what would be the amount of (a) the 1994 cost of goods sold expense, and (b) the increase in the current cost of inventory during 1994?

PROBLEMS

**BASIC PRINCIPLES
— OBJ. 2 —**

13-26 The following are certain unrelated accounting situations and the accounting treatment, in general journal form, that has been followed in each firm's records.

1. Martin Company mounts a $500,000, year-long advertising campaign on a new national cable television network. The firm's annual accounting period is the calendar year. The television network required full payment in December at the beginning of the campaign. Accounting treatment is

Advertising Expense	500,000	
Cash		500,000

2. Because of a local bankruptcy, machinery worth $160,000 was acquired at a "bargain" purchase price of $130,000. Accounting treatment is

Machinery	130,000	
Cash		130,000

3. Tim Vagly, a consultant operating a sole proprietorship, withdrew $10,000 from the business and purchased securities as a gift to his wife. Accounting treatment is

Investments	10,000	
Cash		10,000

4. The Solid State Bank, by action of the board of directors, wrote down the book value of its home office building to the nominal amount of $100. The objective was to bolster its customers' confidence in the bank's financial strength by obviously understating bank assets. Accounting treatment is

Retained Earnings	1,999,900	
Buildings		1,999,900

5. Frandor, Inc., ends its fiscal year on June 30. Financial statements for the year just ended are prepared on July 10. During the July 4 holiday weekend, a fire destroyed most of the inventories of the company. Because the company may have violated local fire regulations, the loss may not be covered by insurance. This possible loss is reflected in the financial statements for the year just ended. Accounting treatment is

Fire Loss	292,000	
Merchandise Inventory		292,000

6. Sioux Company received a firm offer of $85,000 for a parcel of land it owns that cost $63,000 two years ago. The offer was refused, but the indicated gain was recorded in the accounts. Accounting treatment is

Land	22,000	
Income from Increase in Value of Land		22,000

7. In December 1993, Ames Company adopted a policy of paying its salespersons a 6% commission on sales made, payable in the month following the sale. Sales during December 1993 were $250,000. Accounting treatment at December 31, 1993, is

Sales Commissions Expense	15,000	
Sales Commissions Payable		15,000

REQUIRED

a. In each of the given situations, indicate which basic generally accepted accounting principles apply and whether they have been used appropriately.
b. If you decide the accounting treatment is not generally accepted, discuss the effect of the departure on the balance sheet and the income statement.

**INSTALLMENT METHOD
— OBJ. 2 —**

13-27   During December 1993, Gator Realty Company sold several residential lots on an installment basis. The sales totaled $400,000. Terms were 30% down on the date of purchase, and 20 equal monthly payments beginning January 2, 1994. The cost of property sold on the installment basis was $232,000. Gator Realty Company elects the installment method to report the gross profit from these sales on its income tax return. On its books, the company recognizes the revenue and related cost of property sold when the sale is made.

REQUIRED

a. Comment on why Gator Realty Company would elect the installment method to report the gross profit on its income tax return.
b. Assuming all installment payments are collected as scheduled, calculate how much gross profit from these December installment sales Gator Realty Company will report on its income tax return for (1) 1993, (2) 1994, and (3) 1995.
c. Assuming all installment payments are collected as scheduled, calculate how much gross profit from these December installment sales Gator Realty Company will report on its books for (1) 1993, (2) 1994, and (3) 1995.

**PERCENTAGE-OF-
COMPLETION ACCOUNTING
— OBJ. 2 —**

13-28   On December 1, 1993, Fulcom, Inc., signed a contract to build a communications satellite. Completion and sale of the satellite were scheduled for November 1995. The total contract price for the satellite was $38,000,000, and total estimated cost was $30,000,000. The contract specified the following cash payments by the buyer:

$9,500,000 on signing the contract.
$13,300,000 when the satellite is considered one-half completed.
$14,060,000 when the satellite is completed.
$1,140,000 90 days after completion.

The degree of completion is considered equal to the proportion of estimated total cost incurred by the builder. Fulcom accounts for operations on a calendar-year basis. Costs for the satellite were incurred and paid as follows:

December 1993	$ 5,100,000
1994	16,800,000
1995	8,100,000

The satellite was finished and the sale was consummated November 8, 1995.

REQUIRED

a. Calculate the gross profit (or loss) that would be reported each year if a cash basis of accounting (cash receipts less cash disbursements) were used.
b. Calculate the gross profit that would be reported each year on an accrual basis of accounting using (1) the completed contract (point-of-sale) method of revenue recognition and (2) the percentage-of-completion method of revenue recognition.
c. Comment on the relative usefulness of these approaches to periodic income determination.

**FINANCIAL STATEMENT
NOTES: QUARTERLY DATA
— OBJ. 3 —**

13-29   Actual recent quarterly data are presented below for Company A and Company B. One of these companies is GIBSON GREETINGS, INC., which manufactures and sells greeting cards. The other company is HON INDUSTRIES INC., which manufactures and sells office furniture. Both companies are on a calendar-year basis.

	First Quarter	Second Quarter	Third Quarter	Fourth Quarter	Year
Company A					
Net sales	$173,803	$158,156	$162,529	$169,408	$663,896
Gross profit	53,404	47,344	50,600	54,026	205,374
Net income	11,517	8,190	10,804	12,667	43,178
Company B					
Net sales	$ 80,466	$ 79,049	$145,161	$206,535	$511,211
Gross profit	50,593	46,575	69,456	90,405	257,029
Net income	6,225	1,957	12,723	18,895	39,800

(Amounts in Thousands)

REQUIRED

a. Compute the percent of annual net sales generated each quarter by Company A. Round to the nearest percent.

b. Compute the percent of annual net sales generated each quarter by Company B. Round to the nearest percent.

c. Which company has the most seasonal business? Briefly explain.

d. Which company is Gibson Greetings, Inc.? Hon Industries Inc.? Briefly explain.

e. Which company's interim quarterly data are probably most useful for predicting annual results? Briefly explain.

CONSTANT DOLLAR ACCOUNTING — APPENDIX C —

13-30 The following are the 1993 year-end asset accounts of Gale Company under historical cost accounting and the general price-level index that reflects the purchasing power of the dollar used to measure each asset.

	Balance	Price-level Index
Cash	$ 20,000	150
Notes Receivable	50,000	150
Supplies	30,000	125
Building (Net of accumulated depreciation)	600,000	60
Equipment (Net of accumulated depreciation)	300,000	80
Total assets	$1,000,000	

The average general price-level index for 1993 is 135, and the year-end index is 150.

REQUIRED

a. Restate each asset balance to a constant unit of general purchasing power—the 1993 *year-end* purchasing power of the dollar—and compute the total assets.

b. Restate each asset balance to a constant unit of general purchasing power—the 1993 *average* purchasing power of the dollar—and compute the total assets.

c. Prepare a schedule showing the percent of total assets each asset represents using (1) historical cost measures, (2) constant dollar (end-of-year dollar) measures, and (3) constant dollar (average-for-the-year dollar) measures. Round answers to the nearest percent.

d. Based on your answers to (c), does changing the unit of measure from one constant dollar to another constant dollar alter the relationships among assets?

CURRENT COST ACCOUNTING — APPENDIX C —

13-31 Malek Corporation began operations on January 2, 1994, with the following assets:

Cash	$ 40,000
Inventory (15,000 units @ $28)	400,000
Land	115,000

During 1994, Malek sold 10,000 inventory units at $50 each and incurred cash operating expenses of $130,000. Malek's historical cost income statement for 1994 was as follows:

Sales		$500,000
Cost of Goods Sold	$280,000	
Operating Expenses	130,000	
Total Expenses		410,000
Net Income		$ 90,000

Malek did not purchase any inventory units after January 2, 1994. Before any inventory was sold, its current cost increased to $32 per unit and remained there until year-end. The current cost of the land at December 31, 1994, was $126,000.

REQUIRED

a. Prepare a schedule showing Malek's 1994 net income using current cost accounting procedures.

b. Prepare a schedule showing the year-end current cost of inventory and land, and a schedule showing the year-end historical cost of inventory and land.

c. Prepare a schedule showing the increase in the current cost of inventory and land that occurred during 1994.

d. How much of the increase computed in (c) relates to inventory units sold during 1994 and how much relates to assets on hand at year-end?

ALTERNATE EXERCISES

CONCEPTUAL FRAMEWORK
— OBJ. 1 —

13-18A The Financial Accounting Standards Board worked several years to develop a conceptual framework.

a. Identify the financial statement elements that are specified in the conceptual framework.

b. Before a financial statement element may be recorded in the accounts, certain recognition criteria must be met. What are these recognition criteria?

BASIC PRINCIPLES
— OBJ. 2 —

13-19A Indicate the basic principle or principles of accounting that underlie each of the following independent situations:

a. GRUMMAN CORPORATION reports in its 1990 annual report that "sales under fixed-price production contracts are recorded at the time of delivery."

b. The annual financial report of FREDERICK'S OF HOLLYWOOD, INC. and subsidiaries includes the financial data of its operating subsidiaries: FREDERICK'S OF HOLLYWOOD RETAIL STORES, PRIVATE MOMENTS RETAIL STORES, and FREDERICK'S OF HOLLYWOOD MAIL ORDER. All significant intercompany transactions are eliminated when the data are combined.

c. A company purchased a parcel of land several years ago for $60,000. The land's estimated current market value is $75,000. The Land account balance is not increased but remains at $60,000.

d. A company has a calendar-year accounting period. On January 8, 1993, a tornado destroyed its largest warehouse, causing a $760,000 loss. This information is reported in a footnote to the 1992 financial statements.

REVENUE RECOGNITION
— OBJ. 2 —

13-20A For each of the following independent situations, determine how much revenue should be reported in the current period and how much should be deferred to a future period. If a collection basis method applies, determine the appropriate gross profit amounts under the installment method.

a. Took a special order for merchandise from a customer and, in turn, placed an order with our supplier to have the special merchandise delivered to the customer during the next period. The merchandise costs $7,200 and sells for $10,400.

b. Began work on a long-term construction contract with a price of $1,900,000. Expected costs total $1,200,000, of which $300,000 were incurred this period. The contract will be finished near the end of the next accounting period. The completed contract method is used.

c. Sold a deluxe hot tub for $2,500 on October 1, 1993. Terms were $300 down and $200 installments for 11 months, beginning November 1, 1993. The hot tub cost $1,600 and we are able to estimate that the customer will make the installment payments on schedule.

REVENUE RECOGNITION
— OBJ. 2 —

13-21A On September 1, 1994, Mainstreet Appliance Company sold a television set for $900 on terms of 20% down on the purchase date and 24 equal monthly payments beginning October 1, 1994. The television set cost $540. Compute the amount of gross profit to be shown in 1994, 1995, and 1996 using the following revenue recognition methods:

a. Installment method.

b. Point-of-sale method.

FINANCIAL STATEMENT
NOTES
— OBJ. 3 —

13-22A Notes to financial statements present information on significant accounting policies, complex or special transactions, details of reported amounts, commitments, contingencies, segments, quarterly data, and subsequent events. Indicate which type of note disclosure is illustrated by each of the following notes.

a. Sales by the Farm and Equipment segment to independent dealers are recorded at the time of shipment to those dealers. Sales through company-owned retail stores are recorded at the time of sale to retail customers.

b. Members of the board of directors, the advisory board, and employees are not charged the vendor's commission on property sold at auction for their benefit. (From the notes of an auctioneer company.)

c. Sales to an airline company accounted for approximately 43% of the company's net sales in the current year.

d. The company's product liability insurance coverage with respect to insured events occurring after January 1 of the current year is substantially less than the amount of that insurance available in the recent past. The company is now predominantly self-insured in this area. The reduction in insurance coverage reflects trends in the liability insurance field generally and is not unique to the company.

INTERNATIONAL
ACCOUNTING PRINCIPLES
— OBJ. 4 —

13-23A Although there are benefits to the acceptance by nations of a set of international accounting principles, several obstacles would have to be overcome before such acceptance could occur.

a. Identify and briefly discuss three obstacles to the acceptance by nations of a set of international accounting principles.

b. What role might the International Organization of Securities Commissions play in implementing a set of international accounting principles?

CONSTANT DOLLAR
ACCOUNTING
— APPENDIX C —

13-24A Lucsiak Corporation has reported sales revenue for the past three years as follows:

1992	$5,500,000
1993	6,600,000
1994	7,800,000

Assume that the average general price-level indexes for these three years are as follows: 1992, 120; 1993, 150; and 1994, 180. The price-level index at the end of 1994 is 198. Prepare a schedule of sales revenue for 1992–1994 stated in the general purchasing power of the dollar (a) at the end of 1994 and (b) for the year 1994 (average for 1994).

PURCHASING POWER GAIN
OR LOSS ON MONETARY
ITEMS
— APPENDIX C —

13-25A Listed below are the year-end monetary assets and liabilities of Breen Company and the general price-level index on the date each account balance was established.

	Balance	Price-level Index
Cash	$20,000	256
Accounts Receivable	60,000	250
Notes Receivable	36,000	300
Accounts Payable	61,500	246
Notes Payable	21,000	240

The year-end price index is 320. Assume the balance of each monetary item has not changed since it was established.

a. Compute the purchasing power gain or loss on each monetary item, stated in terms of the year-end purchasing power of the dollar.

b. What is the purchasing power gain or loss on net monetary items?

ALTERNATE PROBLEMS

BASIC PRINCIPLES
— OBJ. 2 —

13-26A The following are several unrelated accounting practices:

1. A recession has caused slow business and low profits for Balke Company. Consequently, the firm takes no depreciation on its plant assets this year.

2. Gail Derry, a consultant operating a sole proprietorship, used her business car for a personal, month-long vacation. A full year's depreciation on the car is charged to the firm's depreciation expense account.

3. Vine Company purchased a new $18 snow shovel that is expected to last six years. The shovel is used to clear the firm's front steps during the winter months. The shovel's cost is debited to the Snow Shovel asset account and will be depreciated over six years.

4. Filene Corporation has been named as the defendant in a $40,000,000 pollution lawsuit. Because the lawsuit will take several years to resolve and the outcome is uncertain, Filene's management decides not to mention the lawsuit in the current year financial statements.

5. Drummond Corporation's portfolio of short-term stock investments has an aggregate market value below cost. Management believes that stock prices will rise soon and, therefore, does not write down the portfolio at year-end to its lower market value amount.

6. The management of Newell Corporation, a U.S. company, prepares and issues its financial statements in constant units of purchasing power rather than the U.S. dollar unadjusted for the effect of inflation.

REQUIRED

a. For each of the given practices, indicate which basic generally accepted accounting principles apply and whether they have been used appropriately.

b. For each inappropriate accounting practice, indicate the proper accounting procedure.

**INSTALLMENT METHOD
— OBJ. 2 —**

13-27A   Kroon Company sells residential building lots and makes all sales on an installment basis. Selected financial data for its first three years of operations are shown below.

	1992	1993	1994
Sales	$300,000	$500,000	$600,000
Cost of property sold	195,000	310,000	360,000
Gross profit	$105,000	$190,000	$240,000
Cash collections from 1992 sales	$140,000	$120,000	$ 40,000
Cash collections from 1993 sales		200,000	170,000
Cash collections from 1994 sales			250,000

Kroon Company elects the installment method to report the gross profit from its installment sales on its income tax return. On its books, the company recognizes the revenue and related cost of property sold when the sale is made.

REQUIRED

a. What is the gross profit percentage on sales for 1992, 1993, and 1994?

b. How much gross profit will Kroon report on its income tax returns in 1992, 1993, and 1994?

c. For the three-year period 1992–1994, how much less gross profit will Kroon have reported on its income tax returns compared with the gross profit recorded on its books?

**PERCENTAGE-OF-
COMPLETION ACCOUNTING
— OBJ. 2 —**

13-28A   On November 1, 1993, Seaworthy, Inc., signed a contract to build a large seagoing oil tanker. Completion and sale of the ship were scheduled for October 1995. The total contract price for the ship was $18,000,000 and the total estimated cost was $14,000,000. The contract specified the following cash payments by the buyer:

$1,800,000 on signing the contract.
$9,000,000 when the ship is considered one-half completed.
$6,000,000 when the ship is completed.
$1,200,000 90 days after completion.

The degree of completion is considered equal to the proportion of estimated total cost incurred by the builder. The company accounts for operations on a calendar-year basis. Costs for the ship were incurred and paid as follows:

November and December, 1993	$2,100,000
1994	8,400,000
1995	3,500,000

The ship was finished and the sale was consummated October 20, 1995.

REQUIRED

a. Calculate the gross profit (or loss) that would be reported each year if a cash basis of accounting (cash receipts less cash disbursements) were used.

b. Calculate the gross profit that would be reported each year on an accrual basis of accounting using (1) the completed contract (point-of-sale) method of revenue recognition and (2) the percentage-of-completion method of revenue recognition.

c. Comment on the relative usefulness of these approaches to periodic income determination.

FINANCIAL STATEMENT NOTES: QUARTERLY DATA — OBJ. 3 —

13-29A Actual recent quarterly data are presented below for Company C and Company D. One of these companies is 50-OFF STORES, INC., a regional chain of off-price retail stores selling apparel, toys, housewares, and related items. The company's fiscal year ends on the Friday nearest to January 31. The other company is DIEBOLD, INCORPORATED. Diebold manufacturers and sells financial self-service transaction systems (automated teller machines) and other financial equipment. Diebold is on a calendar-year basis.

	(Amounts in Thousands)				
	First Quarter	Second Quarter	Third Quarter	Fourth Quarter	Year
Company C:					
Net sales	$113,218	$119,365	$115,212	$128,259	$476,054
Gross profit	34,681	32,876	30,936	43,949	142,442
Company D:					
Net sales	$ 15,505	$ 15,223	$ 18,606	$ 28,789	$ 78,123
Gross profit	5,044	4,756	6,156	9,451	25,407

REQUIRED

a. Compute the percentage of annual net sales generated each quarter by Company C. Round to the nearest percent.

b. Compute the percentage of annual net sales generated each quarter by Company D. Round to the nearest percent.

c. Which company has the most seasonal business? Briefly explain.

d. Which company is 50-OFF Stores, Inc.? Diebold, Incorporated? Briefly explain.

CONSTANT DOLLAR ACCOUNTING — APPENDIX C —

13-30A Appearing below are Lamb Company's sales for three years under historical cost accounting and the average general price-level index for each year.

	Sales	Average Price-level Index
1993	$3,600,000	120
1994	4,500,000	144
1995	6,500,000	160

The 1995 year-end general price-level index is 180.

REQUIRED

a. Restate each year's sales amount to a constant unit of general purchasing power—the 1995 *year-end* purchasing power of the dollar.

b. Restate each year's sales amount to a constant unit of general purchasing power—the 1995 *average* purchasing power of the dollar.

c. Prepare a schedule showing the percentage of sales increase from 1993 to 1994, and from 1994 to 1995 using (1) historical cost measures, (2) constant dollar (end-of-year dollar) measures, and (3) constant dollar (average-for-the-year dollar) measures. Round to the nearest percent.

d. Based on your answers to (c), does changing the unit of measure from one constant dollar to another constant dollar change the year-to-year relationships between sales amounts?

CURRENT COST ACCOUNTING — APPENDIX C —

13-31A Siegel Corporation began operations on January 2, 1993, with the following assets:

Cash	$20,000
Inventory (6,000 units @ $15)	90,000
Land	80,000

During 1993, Siegel sold 3,500 inventory units at $25 each and incurred cash operating expenses of $15,000. Siegel's historical cost income statement for 1993 was as follows:

Sales		$87,500
Cost of Goods Sold	$52,500	
Operating Expenses	15,000	
Total Expenses		67,500
Net Income		$20,000

Before any inventory was sold, its current cost increased to $17 per unit. After the last sale in 1993, Siegel's supplier announced a year-end price increase to $18 per unit. The current cost of the land at December 31, 1993, was $88,000.

REQUIRED

a. Prepare a schedule showing Siegel's 1993 net income using current cost accounting procedures.
b. Prepare a schedule showing the year-end current cost of inventory and land, and a schedule showing the year-end historical cost of inventory and land.
c. Prepare a schedule showing the increase in the current cost of inventory and land that occurred during 1993.
d. How much of the increase computed in (c) relates to inventory units sold during 1993 and how much relates to assets on hand at year-end?

CASES

Business Decision Case

Topcopter, Inc., started operations on January 1, 1994. Its primary assets are two helicopters, which are used in the following ways:

1. For carrying passengers between a major air terminal and a downtown heliport. As a new business promotion, the company sold 900 booklets of one-way tickets. Each booklet contained 10 tickets and was priced at $200. During 1994, purchasers of the booklets used 6,000 tickets.

2. For passenger charter flights. A local corporation charters a helicopter to transport executives to and from an island conference facility. A deposit of 25% of the charter fee is required when a charter flight is booked. On December 31, 1994, the company had deposits of $3,400 for scheduled charter flights. The company received a total of $32,000 for charter flights flown during 1994.

3. For construction material and equipment transportation. Building contractors rent a helicopter for $160 per hour for moving material and equipment to and from construction sites. Contractors used the helicopters a total of 150 hours during 1994. Of this total, 15 hours occurred in December, for which the company has not yet received payment.

4. For "Save a Life" efforts during holidays. The state rents a helicopter for $120 per hour on holiday weekends to carry a medical team to accident locations. The state used the helicopters a total of 230 hours in 1994. The company has not yet collected for 30 hours of use in December.

Topcopter's accountant has prepared the following schedule of revenue for 1994:

One-way ticket booklets (900 @ $200)	$180,000
Charter flights made	32,000
Deposits on charter flights scheduled	3,400
Contractors (135 hours @ $160)	21,600
"Save a Life" program (200 hours @ $120)	24,000
Total revenue	$261,000

The president of Topcopter, Inc., has asked you to evaluate whether the accountant has correctly determined the 1994 revenue in accordance with generally accepted accounting principles.

REQUIRED

Has the accountant correctly determined the 1994 revenue? If not, prepare a revised 1994 revenue schedule. Give reasons for any changes you make from the accountant's schedule.

Analytical Application Case

The GAP, INC., is headquartered in San Francisco and THE LESLIE FAY COMPANIES, INC., is headquartered in New York City. Both firms are specialty retailers dealing in various apparel lines. Following are selected financial data for these two firms over a recent three-year period (amounts in thousands; Year 3 is the most recent year):

	Year 3	Year 2	Year 1
The Gap, Inc.			
Net income	$144,522	$ 97,628	$ 74,231
Net cash flow from operating activities	256,892	118,093	152,079
Annual capital expenditures	193,734	88,398	64,448
The Leslie Fay Companies, Inc.			
Net income	$ 29,078	$ 25,762	$ 22,251
Net cash flow (outflow) from operating activities	(12,341)	2,483	7,692
Annual capital expenditures	7,062	5,601	4,001

REQUIRED

a. Compute the operating cash flow to capital expenditures ratio for The Gap, Inc., for Years 1 through 3. Comment on the trend.

b. Compute the operating cash flow to capital expenditures ratio for The Leslie Fay Companies, Inc., for Years 1 through 3. Comment on the trend.

c. Based only on the operating cash flow to capital expenditures ratio, which of these two companies is better able to provide for its plant capacity needs out of operating cash flows? Which company is a better long-run solvency risk?

Ethics Case

Frank Limad, president of Restoration, Inc., is concerned about entering into a large contract with a supplier. The contract has been arranged by Sheri Cosgrove, controller of Restoration, Inc. Among its various activities, Restoration, Inc., refurbishes cruise line ships. A major refurbishing contract may take from 18 to 24 months to complete. A memorandum dated September 1, 1993, from Cosgrove explained the contract as follows:

> As you know, Frank, we have a contract to refurbish the cruise ship *Viking Moon* for $4,000,000. We estimate the total costs will be $2,500,000. We plan to begin actual work on the project in January 1994 and finish in the fall of 1995. I have arranged to buy all of the materials for this project in November 1993 from a major supplier of ours; these materials include the deck planking and all fixtures and furnishings. The total materials will cost us $1,000,000. We will send payment (a $1,000,000 check) in November 1993. The supplier has agreed not to ship any materials until we are ready for them. With this arrangement, we will be able to book 1993 revenues from this project of $1,600,000 and a gross profit of $600,000.

On September 5, 1993, Limad sent Cosgrove the following note:

> With regard to the *Viking Moon* project—how can we earn revenues by making purchases? Why are we doing this?

On September 8, 1993, Cosgrove replied as follows:

> I use percentage-of-completion accounting for our long-term refurbishing contracts. The portion of revenue earned each year is based on the costs incurred on the project. The $1,000,000 materials cost represents 40% of the estimated total cost of the project, so we may record $1,600,000 of revenue (40% of $4,000,000 contract price) in 1993. The $600,000 gross profit is the $1,600,000 revenue less the $1,000,000 materials cost.
>
> The $600,000 gross profit that we will book will cause 1993's net income to show a nice increase over 1992. We both own Restoration common stock that we acquired

under a plan that restricted our ability to sell the stock. Early in 1994 is the first time we may sell it, and we want the market price to be as high as possible, don't we? I know I need an immediate improvement in my personal cash flow.

Limad must decide whether to sign the contract. Usually, the company does not pay for its materials so far in advance of the material's use.

REQUIRED

a. Does the percentage-of-completion accounting proposed by Cosgrove seem appropriate?

b. What are the ethical implications of Cosgrove's proposal? Should Limad sign the contract?

How does a partnership operate, how is it accounted for, and what type of businesses typically establish themselves as partnerships?

A partnership is a voluntary association of two or more individuals to operate a business. ■ *Very few well-known businesses are organized as partnerships.* ■ *The six largest public accounting firms are partnerships—Arthur Andersen & Co., Coopers & Lybrand, Deloitte & Touche, Ernst & Young, KPMG Peat Marwick, and Price Waterhouse & Co.* ■ *Limited partnerships are often the means raising the capital needed to build major real estate projects such as office buildings, hotels, and shopping centers.*

14

PARTNERSHIP ACCOUNTING

he essence of the partnership form of business organization is captured by the proverb, "Two heads are better than one." A **partnership** is a voluntary association of two or more persons for the purpose of conducting a business for profit. The Uniform Partnership Act governs the formation and operation of partnerships in many states. A partnership is easily formed—the parties need only agree to it. The ease of formation makes the partnership an attractive form of organization for a business that requires more capital than a single proprietor can provide or for persons who want to combine specialized talents. Professional people, such as physicians, attorneys, and public accountants, as well as individuals in many small business concerns, often operate as partnerships.

Partnership agreements may be oral, but sound business practice demands a written agreement to avoid misunderstandings. A written partnership agreement constitutes the **articles of copartnership.** The articles of copartnership should detail the important provisions of the partnership arrangement, including the name and location of the partnership, the nature and duration of the business, the duties of partners, the capital contribution of each partner, the understanding for sharing profits and losses, permitted withdrawal of assets, the method of accounting, the procedure for withdrawals of partners, and the procedure for dissolving the business.

CHARACTERISTICS OF A PARTNERSHIP

Mutual Agency

OBJECTIVE ❶ DESCRIBE *the partnership form of organization and the formation of a partnership.*

Unlimited Liability

Limited Life

Although a partnership is an accounting entity, it is not a legal entity separate from its owners. Several characteristics—in addition to ease of formation—relate to this aspect of partnerships.

Mutual agency means that every partner is an agent for the firm, with the authority to bind the partnership to contracts. This authority applies to all acts of a partner engaging in the usual activities of the firm. Although the partners may limit the authority of one or more partners to act on customary matters, a partner acting contrary to a restriction may still contractually bind the partnership if the other party to the contract is unaware of the limitation. The partnership would not be bound, however, if the other party knew of the restriction.

Most partnerships are **general partnerships,** in which each partner is individually liable for the firm's obligations, regardless of the amount of personal investment. Thus, creditors of a general partnership unable to pay its debts may obtain payment from the personal assets of individual partners. Also, each general partner is an agent of the firm and can bind the partnership to contracts.

In contrast, a **limited partnership** has two classes of partners, general partners and limited partners. There must be at least one general partner to assume unlimited liability for the firm's obligations. Normally, the limited partners are investors who participate in the profits or losses of the firm, but their liability for losses is limited to the amount of their investment. Limited partners do not participate actively in the management of the firm. For a number of years, limited partnerships provided significant tax advantages for investors, but these advantages have been curtailed substantially by recent tax legislation.

Because a partnership is a voluntary association of persons, many events may cause its dissolution. These events include the expiration of the agreed-on partnership term; the accomplishment of the business objective; the admission of a new partner;

the withdrawal, death, or bankruptcy of an existing partner; and the issuance of a court decree because of a partner's incapacity or misconduct. Even though a change in membership dissolves a partnership, business continuity is often unaffected. A new partnership may continue the operations of the former partnership without interruption.

Co-ownership of Property

Assets contributed by partners become partnership property jointly owned by all partners. Individual partners no longer separately own the specific resources invested in the firm. Unless an agreement to the contrary exists, each partner has an equal right to the firm's property for partnership purposes.

Nontaxable Entity

Although a partnership must file an information return for federal income tax purposes, the organization itself is not a taxable entity. The information return shows the distributive shares of the partnership's net income that the partners include on their individual tax returns. The individual members must pay income taxes on their respective shares of partnership earnings whether or not these amounts have been withdrawn from the firm.

ADVANTAGES AND DISADVANTAGES OF A PARTNERSHIP

In contrast with a corporation, a partnership is easier and less expensive to organize and is subject to less government regulation and fewer reporting requirements. Certain corporate actions require the approval of stockholders or directors; partners have fewer constraints on their actions. Businesses of modest size or of planned short duration may find these features advantageous. The same may be true for new businesses hesitant to incur the cost of incorporation until their ventures prove successful.

Disadvantages of the partnership form of organization are mutual agency, unlimited liability, and limited life. The first two in particular underscore the importance of selecting partners with great care and are no doubt partially responsible for the rule that no person may be admitted to a partnership without the consent of all existing partners. A corporation, which offers limited liability to investors, is better able than a partnership to raise large amounts of capital.

The impact of taxes varies from one circumstance to the next. A partnership is a nontaxable entity; a corporation is a taxable entity. Partners' earnings are taxable whether distributed to the partners or not; corporate income is taxable a second time, but only when distributed as dividends. The tax rate on individuals in high tax brackets has often exceeded the corporate tax rate. Determination of the most advantageous form of organization for tax purposes requires careful analysis of existing tax laws and the tax status of the persons going into business.

CAPITAL, DRAWING, AND LOAN ACCOUNTS

Accounting for partnerships is similar in most respects to accounting for sole proprietorships. Each partner has a capital account and a drawing account that serve the same functions as the related accounts for a sole proprietor. A partner's capital account is credited for his or her investments, and each individual drawing account is debited to reflect assets withdrawn from the partnership. At the end of each accounting period, the balances in the drawing accounts are closed to the related capital accounts.

Occasionally, a partner may advance amounts to the partnership beyond the intended permanent investment. These advances should be credited to the partner's loan account and classified among the liabilities, separate from liabilities to outsiders. Similarly, if a partner withdraws money with the intention of repaying it, the debit should go to the partner's advance (or loan receivable) account and be classified separately among the partnership's receivables.

The formation of partnerships, the division of profits and losses, the admission and retirement of partners, and the liquidation of partnerships represent areas of particular interest in accounting for these entities. We focus on these issues in the remainder of the chapter.

FORMATION OF A PARTNERSHIP

A partnership's books are opened with an entry reflecting the net contribution of each partner to the firm. Asset accounts are debited for assets invested in the partnership, liability accounts are credited for any liabilities assumed by the partnership, and separate capital accounts are credited for the amount of each partner's net investment (Assets − Liabilities).

Assume that Earl Ames, a sole proprietor, and John Baker form a partnership. Ames invests $8,000 cash, office equipment with a current fair value of $25,000, and office supplies worth $2,000. The partnership agrees to assume the $5,000 balance on a note issued by Ames when he acquired the equipment. Baker invests $10,000 cash. The following opening entries on the books of the partnership record the investments of Ames and Baker:

Cash	8,000	
Office Equipment	25,000	
Office Supplies	2,000	
Notes Payable		5,000
E. Ames, Capital		30,000
To record Ames' investment in the partnership of Ames and Baker.		
Cash	10,000	
J. Baker, Capital		10,000
To record Baker's investment in the partnership of Ames and Baker.		

Assets invested in the partnership should be recorded at their current fair values. These assets (less any liabilities assumed by the partnership) determine the opening capital balances for each partner. If the assets are not recorded initially at their fair values, inequities develop among the partners in terms of their respective capital balances.

For example, assume the office equipment invested by Ames was recorded incorrectly at $22,000 (its book value from his proprietorship records). If the partnership immediately sold the equipment for its current fair value of $25,000, the resulting $3,000 gain, on closing, would increase the capital balances of both Ames and Baker. This is not equitable. The $3,000 "gain" was not added to the asset by the operations of the partnership. Baker should not be credited with any part of this amount. A similar inequity develops if the equipment is used in operations rather than sold. Owing to a lower total depreciation over the life of the equipment, income would be $3,000 higher over the same period. To avoid such inequities, the partnership records the office equipment initially at $25,000. The values assigned to assets invested in a partnership are important and should be agreeable to all partners.

DIVISION OF PARTNERSHIP PROFITS AND LOSSES

OBJECTIVE ② ILLUSTRATE *various methods for the division of profits and losses.*

In the absence of a profit and loss sharing agreement, partnership profits and losses are divided equally. Partners who do not wish to share profits equally must specify, preferably in a formal written agreement, the manner in which profit and loss distributions are made. Such arrangements may specify a fixed ratio (such as $\frac{2}{3}$ to $\frac{1}{3}$, 60% to 40%, or 5:3) or a sharing formula of some kind based on the relative financial participation of the partners, the services performed by the partners, or both. Any arrangement can be made, and losses may be shared differently from profits. If an agreement specifies the manner of sharing profits but is silent on the sharing of losses, losses will be divided in the same manner as profits. In the following sections, we discuss several common arrangements.

Capital Ratios

When the services performed or skills provided by the various partners are considered equal, profits and losses may be divided according to the partners' relative investments in the firm. Assume that the Ames and Baker partnership had a profit of $18,000 for 1993 and that the partners' capital balances before any profit distribution at year-end were as follows:

E. AMES, CAPITAL			J. BAKER, CAPITAL		
	1993			1993	
	Jan. 1	30,000		Jan. 1	10,000
				July 1	10,000

The $18,000 profit might be divided according to the beginning capital investment ratio or the average capital investment ratio for the year.

BEGINNING CAPITAL RATIO

At the beginning of 1993, the total capital investment in the firm was $40,000— $30,000 for Ames and $10,000 for Baker. If they shared according to the ratio of *beginning* capital balances, the profit distribution would be 3:1, or $13,500 for Ames and $4,500 for Baker, computed as follows:

	Beginning Capital	Percent of Total	Division of Profit
Ames	$30,000	75	$13,500
Baker	10,000	25	4,500
	$40,000	100	$18,000

The following entry would be made to distribute the balance in the Income Summary account:

Income Summary	18,000	
E. Ames, Capital		13,500
J. Baker, Capital		4,500
To close the Income Summary account.		

AVERAGE CAPITAL RATIO

Because partners' investments may change during the year, the partners may decide that using *average* capital balances rather than beginning capital balances provides a more equitable division of profits. Under this scheme, investment balances are *weighted* by multiplying the amount of the investment by the portion of the year that these funds were invested. Because Baker invested an additional $10,000 on July 1, his average capital would be based on a $10,000 investment for the first six months and a $20,000 investment for the last six months. The computation might be as follows:

		Dollars × Months	Average Investment
Ames			
$30,000 × 12 months =		$360,000 ÷ 12 =	$30,000
Baker			
$10,000 × 6 months =	$ 60,000		
$20,000 × 6 months =	120,000	$180,000 ÷ 12 =	15,000
			$45,000

Profit Distribution

$$\text{Ames: } \frac{\$30,000}{\$45,000} \times \$18,000 = \$12,000$$

$$\text{Baker: } \frac{\$15,000}{\$45,000} \times \$18,000 = \underline{6,000}$$

$$\$18,000$$

The entry to close the Income Summary account would credit E. Ames, Capital with $12,000 and J. Baker, Capital with $6,000.

Salary and Interest Allowances

A sharing agreement may provide for variations in the personal services contributed by partners and in their relative investments. **Salary allowances** provide for differences in personal services; **allowances for interest** on capital balances provide for differences in the financial participation of partners.

The terms *salary allowances* and *allowances for interest* describe only the process of dividing net income among partners. These terms should not be confused with any salary expense and interest expense appearing in the firm's records or with any cash withdrawals the partners make. For example, the partnership agreement may provide that partners may make withdrawals equal to their salary allowances. These withdrawals would be debited to each partner's drawing account, which is eventually closed to his or her capital account. The cash withdrawals in no way affect the division of net income among partners—the division of net income is governed by the sharing agreement.

SALARY ALLOWANCE

Suppose Ames and Baker render different degrees of personal services and therefore specify a salary allowance in their sharing agreement—$6,000 for Ames and $4,000 for Baker. The remainder of net income is divided equally. The division of the $18,000 net income is as follows:

	Ames	Baker	Total
Earnings to be divided			$18,000
Salary allowances:			
Ames	$ 6,000		
Baker		$4,000	10,000
Remainder			$ 8,000
Remainder ($8,000) divided equally	4,000	4,000	
Partner's shares	$10,000	$8,000	

The $18,000 balance in the Income Summary account would be closed by crediting E. Ames, Capital for $10,000 and J. Baker, Capital for $8,000.

SALARY AND INTEREST ALLOWANCES

Next, assume that Ames and Baker wish to acknowledge the differences in their financial involvement as well as in their personal services. They have the following sharing agreement: salaries of $6,000 to Ames and $4,000 to Baker; 8% interest on *average* capital balances; and the remainder divided equally. We computed average investments for Ames and Baker earlier at $30,000 and $15,000, respectively. The $18,000 net income would therefore be divided as follows:

	Ames	Baker	Total
Earnings to be divided			$18,000
Salary allowances:			
Ames	$ 6,000		
Baker		$4,000	10,000
			$ 8,000
Allowance for interest on average capital:			
Ames ($30,000 × 0.08)	2,400		
Baker ($15,000 × 0.08)		1,200	3,600
Remainder			$ 4,400
Remainder ($4,400) divided equally	2,200	2,200	
Partners' shares	$10,600	$7,400	

The entry closing the $18,000 net income in the Income Summary account would credit E. Ames, Capital for $10,600 and J. Baker, Capital for $7,400.

If Ames and Baker had withdrawn cash equal to their salary allowances, their drawing accounts at the end of the year would contain debit balances of $6,000 and $4,000, respectively. The entry to close the drawing accounts would be

E. Ames, Capital	6,000	
J. Baker, Capital	4,000	
E. Ames, Drawing		6,000
J. Baker, Drawing		4,000
To close the partners' drawing accounts.		

ALLOWANCES EXCEED EARNINGS

Unless a special provision is included in the sharing agreement, the same allocation procedures apply in the event of a loss or of earnings insufficient to cover allowances for salary and interest. For example, assume that net income for the year was only $8,000. After salary and interest allowances are allocated, a *sharing agreement loss* of $5,600 would be divided equally between the partners to fulfill their agreement. The following are the computations:

	Ames	Baker	Total
Earnings to be divided			$ 8,000
Salary allowances	$6,000	$4,000	
Interest allowances	2,400	1,200	
Total salary and interest	$8,400	$5,200	13,600
Remainder (sharing agreement loss)			($ 5,600)
Remainder divided equally	(2,800)	(2,800)	
Partners' shares	$5,600	$2,400	

The entry closing the $8,000 net income in the Income Summary account would credit E. Ames, Capital with $5,600 and J. Baker, Capital with $2,400.

PARTNERSHIP FINANCIAL STATEMENTS

A few unique features of partnership financial statements arise because a partnership consists of co-owners. The partnership income statement may show, at the bottom, how the net income is divided among the partners. A capital account for each partner appears in the owners' equity section of the balance sheet. The statement of partners' (or owners') capital portrays the changes in the capital balances of each partner, as shown in Exhibit 14-1.

ADMISSION OF A PARTNER

New partners may be admitted to a partnership either by purchasing an interest from current members or by investing in the firm. When a person buys an interest from one or more of the current partners, the assets of the firm are not affected. Payment

---

EXHIBIT 14—1

AMES AND BAKER
STATEMENT OF PARTNERS' CAPITAL
FOR THE YEAR ENDED DECEMBER 31, 1993

	Ames	Baker	Total
Capital Balances, January 1, 1993	$30,000	$10,000	$40,000
Add: Additional Contributions during 1993		10,000	10,000
Net Income for 1993	10,600	7,400	18,000
Totals	$40,600	$27,400	$68,000
Less: Withdrawals during 1993	6,000	4,000	10,000
Capital Balances, December 31, 1993	$34,600	$23,400	$58,000

OBJECTIVE ❸ PRESENT *the methods for admitting a new partner.*

is made personally to the member or members from whom the interest is obtained, resulting in merely a transfer among capital accounts. When an investment is made in the firm, however, total assets increase by the amount contributed.

Economic circumstances usually dictate a new partner's mode of entry. A firm with sufficient capital may seek the skills and services of a particular new partner. Or current partners may wish to liquidate part of their interests and scale down their individual investments. In these situations, the firm may sell an interest in the current partnership. On the other hand, if additional capital is needed, adding a partner who will contribute assets may be a proper solution.

For the benefit of the existing partners, the net assets of the current partnership should reflect their current fair values when a new partner is admitted. This may require a revaluation of certain assets. The resultant gain or loss would be apportioned to the current partners in their profit and loss sharing ratio. If the net assets do not reflect their fair values, the new partner may share in gains and losses that developed before admission to the firm. In the following examples of new partner admissions, we assume that the recorded book values of the current partnership's assets do not require restatement.

Purchase of an Interest

Suppose that Ames and Baker have capital balances of $30,000 and $10,000, respectively, and that Ames sells one-half of his interest to Kelsey Carter. For Carter to become a partner, both Ames and Baker must consent to the sale. The entry to record Carter's admission would be

E. Ames, Capital	15,000	
K. Carter, Capital		15,000
To record admission of Carter.		

The actual cash amount paid to Ames is entirely a personal matter between the two persons and is not relevant in recording Carter's admission. Whether an interest is purchased from one partner or several, a transfer of capital is made only for the amounts of the interests purchased without regard to the payment made. Suppose that Carter purchased a one-fourth interest in the firm by obtaining one-fourth of each partner's current share. One-fourth interest would amount to $10,000 (one-fourth of $40,000 present capital). The entry for Carter's admission would be

E. Ames, Capital	7,500	
J. Baker, Capital	2,500	
K. Carter, Capital		10,000
To record admission of Carter.		

Admission by Investment

Clearly, if an incoming partner contributes assets to the firm, total capital increases. If the current partners' capital balances are realistically stated, the new partner simply contributes assets equal to the desired proportionate interest in the total capital of the new firm. In our example, present capital is $40,000—$30,000 for Ames and $10,000 for Baker. Carter wants to contribute enough cash to obtain one-third interest in the new firm. The current partners' capital of $40,000 represents two-thirds of the new firm's capital; therefore, Carter should contribute $20,000. The entry for admission would be

Cash	20,000	
K. Carter, Capital		20,000
To record admission of Carter.		

BONUS TO CURRENT PARTNERS

If a partnership interest is especially attractive because of a superior earnings record or the promise of exceptional future earnings, the current partners may require the new partner to pay an additional amount as a **bonus** for admission. Suppose that Ames and Baker required a $35,000 payment for a one-third interest in the new firm.

The total capital of the new firm would then be $75,000, of which a one-third interest would be $25,000, as follows:

E. Ames, capital	$30,000
J. Baker, capital	10,000
Present capital	$40,000
Contribution of Carter	35,000
Capital of new firm	$75,000
One-third interest	$25,000

The $10,000 difference between Carter's payment of $35,000 and her interest of $25,000 is a bonus to the former partners, to be divided according to their profit and loss sharing ratio. If the agreement provides for equal sharing, the entry to admit Carter is

Cash	35,000	
E. Ames, Capital		5,000
J. Baker, Capital		5,000
K. Carter, Capital		25,000
To record admission of Carter.		

BONUS TO NEW PARTNER A firm eager to add a partner who has ready cash or unique skills, management potential, or other desirable characteristics may award the new partner a larger interest than would be warranted by his or her contribution. Because the capital of the new partner will be greater than his or her asset contribution, the current partners must make up the difference (bonus to new partner) by reducing their capital balances. Assume that Carter receives a one-third interest by contributing only $14,000 to the new firm. The capital of the new firm increases to $54,000 ($40,000 + $14,000), of which a one-third interest is $18,000, as shown below:

E. Ames, capital	$30,000
J. Baker, capital	10,000
Present capital	$40,000
Contribution of Carter	14,000
Capital of new firm	$54,000
One-third interest	$18,000

The $4,000 difference between Carter's $14,000 contribution and her $18,000 interest is a bonus to Carter. Ames and Baker reduce their capital balances accordingly, with amounts based on the profit and loss sharing ratio. With equal sharing, the entry to admit Carter as a partner in the firm is

Cash	14,000	
E. Ames, Capital	2,000	
J. Baker, Capital	2,000	
K. Carter, Capital		18,000
To record admission of Carter.		

RETIREMENT OF A PARTNER

A retiring partner may (1) sell his or her interest to an outsider, (2) sell that interest to one or more of the remaining partners, or (3) receive payment for the interest from partnership funds.

Sale of Partnership Interest

The procedure for recording the sale of a retiring partner's interest to an outsider is similar to that illustrated earlier for the purchase of an interest. Suppose that retiring partner Baker, with the firm's approval, sells his $10,000 interest to Stan Dodge.

OBJECTIVE 4 DESCRIBE *the alternatives when a partner retires.*

Regardless of the personally determined amount of Dodge's actual payment to Baker, the entry to record Dodge's admission and Baker's departure is

J. Baker, Capital	10,000	
S. Dodge, Capital		10,000
To record Dodge's purchase of Baker's interest.		

This transaction is a personal one between Baker and his partners. If Baker sells his interest to remaining partners Ames and Carter, Baker's interest is merely transferred to their capital accounts, regardless of the actual amount of the payments. If Baker sells equal portions of his interest to the remaining partners, the entry is

J. Baker, Capital	10,000	
E. Ames, Capital		5,000
K. Carter, Capital		5,000
To record sale of Baker's interest to Ames and Carter.		

Payment from Partnership Funds

A partner's retirement may be an occasion for reviewing partners' capital balances. Because of such factors as appreciation of assets or an exceptional partnership performance record, the capital balances may not provide a realistic basis for determining the value of partnership interests. In such situations, the partners may recognize any amount by which the current fair value of the retiring partner's partnership interest exceeds his or her capital balance by paying a bonus to the retiring partner.

SETTLEMENT EXCEEDS CAPITAL BALANCE

If the retiring partner receives funds from the partnership for his or her interest, any difference between the amount of this interest and the sum paid affects the capital balances of the remaining partners. For example, assume that the capital balances of Ames, Baker, and Carter are $35,000, $15,000, and $25,000, respectively, when Baker retires and that the firm pays $20,000 for Baker's interest. Baker's $5,000 bonus is divided by the other partners according to their profit and loss sharing ratio (assumed here to be equal). The entry would be

E. Ames, Capital	2,500	
K. Carter, Capital	2,500	
J. Baker, Capital	15,000	
Cash		20,000
To record Baker's withdrawal from the partnership.		

When the fair value of a retiring partner's interest exceeds his or her related capital balance, the remaining partners might revalue total partnership assets upward proportionately, distribute the increase to all partners in their profit and loss sharing ratio, and then pay the retiring partner an amount equal to his or her new capital balance. Such an approach, however, obviously departs from the principle of historical cost. Although the increased value of the partnership interest is properly considered in settling with the retiring partner, revaluing total partnership assets above their historical cost is not acceptable.

CAPITAL BALANCE EXCEEDS SETTLEMENT

In certain circumstances, a retiring partner may accept a settlement less than his or her capital balance. Examples include a history of poor partnership earnings or recognition of operating disadvantages resulting from the partner's retirement. In such cases, the excess of the retiring partner's capital balance over the settlement constitutes a bonus to the remaining partners. Assume that Baker, who has a capital balance of $15,000, accepts $11,000 rather than $20,000 for his interest. The $4,000 bonus is allocated to the remaining partners in their profit and loss sharing ratio (assumed here to be equal). The entry to record this bonus is

J. Baker, Capital	15,000	
E. Ames, Capital		2,000
K. Carter, Capital		2,000
Cash		11,000
To record Baker's withdrawal from the partnership.		

LIQUIDATION OF A PARTNERSHIP

OBJECTIVE 5   EXPLAIN *how partnerships are liquidated.*

The situations that arise during partnership liquidations can be quite complex. Because liquidations are treated comprehensively in advanced accounting texts, we will provide only a basic approach to them here. When a business partnership is discontinued, the assets are sold, the liabilities are paid, and the remaining cash is distributed to the partners. The conversion of the partnership assets into cash (by selling the assets) is called **realization.** Essentially, gains and losses realized in selling assets are carried to the partners' capital accounts (in the established profit and loss sharing ratio), and each partner eventually receives the balance remaining in his or her capital account.

Let us suppose that Ames, Baker, and Carter share profits and losses in the ratio of 40%, 40%, and 20%, respectively, and that before liquidation the partnership's balance sheet can be summarized as follows (assume that for the final operating period, the partnership books have been adjusted and closed and the profit or loss allocated to each partner):

Cash	$ 15,000	Liabilities	$ 40,000
Other Assets (Net)	100,000	E. Ames, Capital	35,000
		J. Baker, Capital	15,000
		K. Carter, Capital	25,000
	$115,000		$115,000

Capital Balances Exceed Losses

If Other Assets in the balance sheet in our example are sold for $80,000, the firm sustains a $20,000 loss. Because the partners share the loss, their capital balances are ultimately reduced by the following amounts: Ames, $8,000; Baker, $8,000; and Carter, $4,000. The appropriate entries might be as follows:

Cash	80,000	
Loss on Realization of Assets	20,000	
Other Assets (Net)		100,000
To record loss on sale of other assets.		
E. Ames, Capital	8,000	
J. Baker, Capital	8,000	
K. Carter, Capital	4,000	
Loss on Realization of Assets		20,000
To distribute loss on sale of other assets.		

After these entries have been recorded, the firm's balance sheet accounts would be as follows:

Cash	$95,000	Liabilities	$40,000
		E. Ames, Capital	27,000
		J. Baker, Capital	7,000
		K. Carter, Capital	21,000
	$95,000		$95,000

Finally, the entries to pay the liabilities and distribute the remaining cash to the partners would be

Liabilities	40,000	
Cash		40,000
To record payment of liabilities.		
E. Ames, Capital	27,000	
J. Baker, Capital	7,000	
K. Carter, Capital	21,000	
Cash		55,000
To record cash distribution to partners.		

Observe that upon liquidation *only gains and losses* are shared in the profit and loss sharing ratio—not the residual cash. Residual cash is distributed to partners *in the amounts of their capital balances* after all gains and losses have been shared.

HOW TO ACHIEVE A PRODUCTIVE PARTNERSHIP

Deborah Heller and Linda Cunningham of Heller, Hunt, and Cunningham of Brookline, Massachusetts, report three key dimensions to successful partnerships: ■ *Professional competence of all partners.* ■ *Respect for personality differences.* ■ *Clear agreements about the business relationship.* ■ *There are nine critical factors that must be clarified in business partnerships:*

1. Each partner's degree of autonomy.
2. The firm's business goals.
3. Compensation amounts and process.
4. Decision-making methods.
5. Division of overhead.
6. Procedure for entrance and exit of partners.
7. Division of firm equity.
8. Firm management issues.
9. Type of partnership.

Each firm will make different decisions about these critical factors. There is no correct way to deal with any one of them.

More important than what is decided is how the decision is made. It is critical that each partner perceives he or she has been

■ Included in decision making.
■ Influential (that is, listened to, understood and taken seriously) in affecting the outcome.
■ Given a chance to use his or her resources and skills in arriving at the decision.

If these critical process factors are attended to, partners will feel committed to implementing the decisions made. If not, problems will eventually emerge.

CLARIFYING THE BUSINESS RELATIONSHIP

The key reason for clarifying business relationships among partners is to minimize conflict and create trust. Conflicts in troubled business partnerships almost always result from disruptions of expectations. Often these expectations have never been discussed explicitly. Usually, one or more partners either have mistakenly believed there was an agreement about an aspect of the business or have not taken the time to clarify their agreements. Dialogues about key aspects of the business relationship can help turn the implicit into the explicit. Trust is a direct result of making clear agreements and keeping them over time.

NINE BUSINESS RELATIONSHIP FACTORS

Autonomy. This is what a partner can decide alone, without consulting other partners. Limits on autonomy must be clear in areas such as budgets, work schedules, new client acceptance, hiring staff, assuming debt and taking vacations.

Business goals. At the outset, agreements must be reached about

Losses Exceed Partner's Capital

When liquidation losses occur, a partner's share of losses may exceed his or her capital balance. That partner will be expected to contribute cash to the partnership to offset the capital account debit balance. For example, suppose that in our illustration, the $100,000 of Other Assets are sold for only $60,000. The resulting $40,000 loss on realization of assets is recorded and then distributed in the 40%:40%:20% sharing ratio, reducing partners' capital accounts as follows: Ames, $16,000; Baker, $16,000; and Carter, $8,000. Entries to record and distribute the loss and to pay the liabilities are as follows:

Cash	60,000	
Loss on Realization of Assets	40,000	
Other Assets (Net)		100,000
To record loss on sale of other assets.		

what kinds of services are to be offered to what kinds of clients. Eventually, decisions must be made about whether to expand the business and how (such as those on cost leadership, differentiation and focus).

Compensation. Perhaps more important than the amount of each partner's compensation are the criteria and method for making compensation decisions. Will hours billed, dollars collected, clients originated or some other factor be used in determining how much each partner takes home? How will the decision be made? How will the amount relate to profits? When will it be disbursed?

Decision making. Probably most basic among these nine factors is a clear agreement about the decision-making process itself. Three aspects must be considered:

1. Which decisions must involve all partners (hiring, firing, spending, business strategy)?
2. What decision-making method will be used (for example, one person–one vote, consensus, or executive committee recommendation)?
3. Will votes be equal or weighted in some way?

Division of overhead. This determines which expenses (office space, equipment, insurance, licenses, staff salaries, and parking) will be shared by partners and which are each one's individual responsibility.

Entrance and exit of partners. Discussions about changing the partnership's composition often are avoided. In admitting new partners, decisions must be reached about admission criteria, the type of partnership to be offered and whether there will be a financial buy-in. For partners leaving the partnership, decisions must be made about disbursement of assets and how to handle the partner's capital investment. In addition, grounds and policies must be set for expulsion from the partnership and for handling a partner's death or disability.

Equity. This includes agreements about how both tangible (equipment, furnishings, accounts receivable, clients) and intangible assets (goodwill associated with the firm's name) will be divided if the partnership should be dissolved.

Firm management. Partners must reach clear agreements about who is responsible for the tasks required to stay in business. This means determining who will market the firm, pay the bills and taxes, keep the books and serve as lead contact with the outside world. If there is a managing partner, a first among equals, the limits of his or her authority must be determined and a decision made about how he or she will be compensated.

Type of partnership. Clarifying whether the partners are going to be equal or not is fundamental to a clear business relationship. If not, there must be criteria for assigning weights to ownership units, such as investment of capital, book of clients or professional activities and reputation, for example.

A PARTNERSHIP'S WORK IS NEVER DONE

The work of making a partnership an effective one is never done. Agreements must be revisited as the partnership's market and structure evolve. However, the benefits of continuing this work include satisfaction in accomplishment, personal growth and companionship on the journey.

SOURCE: *Journal of Accountancy*, May 1992, pp. 113–118. Reprinted with permission from the Journal of Accountancy. Copyright © 1992 by American Institute of Certified Public Accountants, Inc. Opinions of the authors are their own and do not necessarily reflect the policies of the AICPA.

E. Ames, Capital	16,000	
J. Baker, Capital	16,000	
K. Carter, Capital	8,000	
Loss on Realization of Assets		40,000
To distribute loss on sale of other assets.		
Liabilities	40,000	
Cash		40,000
To record payment of liabilities.		

After recording and distributing the loss on the sale of other assets and payment of the liabilities, the following account balances remain:

Cash	$35,000	E. Ames, Capital	$19,000
		J. Baker, Capital (Debit)	(1,000)
		K. Carter, Capital	17,000
	$35,000		$35,000

Note that Baker's $16,000 share of the loss on realization of the other assets absorbs his $15,000 capital balance and leaves a $1,000 capital deficit (debit balance) in his capital account.

If Baker pays the firm $1,000 to make up his deficit, the resulting $36,000 cash balance is the amount distributed to Ames ($19,000) and Carter ($17,000). If Baker cannot make the contribution, the $1,000 is treated as a loss distributed to Ames and Carter in their profit and loss sharing ratio. Because the ratio of their respective shares is 40:20, Ames sustains 40/60, or two-thirds, of the $1,000 loss and Carter, 20/60, or one-third. The entry to redistribute Baker's debit balance would be

E. Ames, Capital	667	
K. Carter, Capital	333	
J. Baker, Capital		1,000

To record distribution of Baker's capital deficit to Ames and Carter.

The $35,000 cash is then paid to Ames and Carter in the amounts of their final capital balances.

E. Ames, Capital	18,333	
K. Carter, Capital	16,667	
Cash		35,000

To record cash distribution to partners.

Sometimes a partner with a capital account deficit may be uncertain about making up the deficit. At the same time, the other partners may want to distribute whatever cash is available after creditors have been paid. In our illustration, if Ames and Carter had doubts about receiving $1,000 from Baker, cash might be distributed as shown in the last entry—$18,333 to Ames and $16,667 to Carter. This would leave sufficient amounts in their capital accounts—$667 for Ames and $333 for Carter—to absorb a $1,000 loss in the sharing ratio if Baker defaults on payment. If he does contribute the amount needed, the other partners will be paid the balances of their capital accounts.

Statement of Partnership Liquidation

Liquidation of a partnership can continue over an extended period. To provide interested parties with a comprehensive report of the initial assets and liabilities, the sale of noncash assets, the payment of liabilities, and the final distribution of cash to the partners, the partnership may prepare a **statement of partnership liquidation.** Using data from our illustration, Exhibit 14-2 presents a statement of liquidation for the Ames, Baker, and Carter partnership. We assume that other assets are sold for $60,000 and that Baker does not cover his $1,000 capital deficit.

Observe the following about the statement of partnership liquidation:

1. The statement is dated to reflect the period during which the liquidation took place.
2. The initial numbers on the statement reflect the partnership balance sheet at the beginning of the liquidation.
3. Each line that reflects a step in the liquidation (sale of other assets, allocation of loss, payment of liabilities, allocation of partner's capital deficit, and final cash distribution) matches related journal entries in the illustration.
4. The statement shows how each step affects the liquidation and is therefore an excellent vehicle for analysis.

EXHIBIT 14—2

AMES, BAKER, AND CARTER (PARTNERSHIP)
STATEMENT OF PARTNERSHIP LIQUIDATION
FROM JANUARY 1 TO MARCH 31, 1993

	Cash	Other Assets	Liabilities	E. Ames, Capital (40%)	J. Baker, Capital (40%)	S. Carter, Capital (20%)	Realization Gain (Loss)
Beginning Balances	$15,000	$100,000	$40,000	$35,000	$15,000	$25,000	
Sale of Other Assets	60,000	(100,000)					($40,000)
	$75,000	$ –0–	$40,000	$35,000	$15,000	$25,000	($40,000)
Allocation of Loss to Partners				(16,000)	(16,000)	(8,000)	40,000
	$75,000		$40,000	$19,000	$ (1,000)	$17,000	$ –0–
Payment of Liabilities	(40,000)		(40,000)				
	$35,000		$ –0–	$19,000	$ (1,000)	$17,000	
Allocation of Baker's Capital Deficit				(667)	1,000	(333)	
	$35,000			$18,333	$ –0–	$16,667	
Final Distribution of Cash	(35,000)			(18,333)		(16,667)	
	$ –0–			$ –0–		$ –0–	

ANALYTICAL APPLICATION

OBJECTIVE 6 DEFINE common-size income statement *and* EXPLAIN *its usefulness*.

COMMON-SIZE INCOME STATEMENT

The relative importance of various items in financial statements for a single year can be highlighted by showing them as percentages of an important total. Such percentages are especially useful in presenting income statement data. The important total used in income statements as the base for calculating the percentages is *total revenues* (or net sales for a merchandising firm). That is, all items in the income statement are presented as a percentage of total revenues. The presentation of income statement percentages is referred to as a **common-size income statement.**

The income statement (in thousands of dollars and percentages) for a recent year for ALLIANCE CAPITAL MANAGEMENT L.P. is presented below. Headquartered in New York City, Alliance Capital Management L.P. is a limited partnership that provides investment services to sponsored cash management accounts and mutual funds and distributes shares in the mutual funds.

Revenues		
Investment advisory and service fees	$161,718	87.1%
Commission income	7,985	4.3
Shareholder servicing and administration fees	11,905	6.4
Interest, dividend, and other income	4,097	2.2
Total revenues	$185,705	100.0%

Expenses

Employee compensation and benefits	$ 76,543	41.2%
General and administrative	28,744	15.5
Interest	3,847	2.1
Advertising	3,341	1.8
Other promotion and servicing	31,092	16.7
Amortization of intangible assets	6,872	3.7
Total expenses	$150,439	81.0%
Income before income taxes	$ 35,266	19.0%
Income taxes	1,351	0.7
Net income	$ 33,915	18.3%

The common-size income statement reveals that more than 87% of the firm's revenues come from its investment advisory and service fees. It also shows, for example, that employee compensation and benefits expense consumes 41.2% of total revenues. The relatively large net income percentage (18.3%) reflects the fact that the partnership is not subject to federal or state income taxes (the income tax shown in the income statement is a New York City unincorporated business tax).

Percentages from a common-size income statement have a number of uses. Management can compare the actual percentages to budgeted percentages to assist in determining where the company did better and worse than planned. In addition, investors and creditors can compare the percentages to industry averages to determine how the company is doing compared to other companies in the same industry. A comparison may also be made to previous years' common-size income statements to identify any significant changes that have occurred.

KEY POINTS FOR CHAPTER OBJECTIVES

❶ DESCRIBE the partnership form of organization and the formation of a partnership (pp. 506–508).
- A partnership is a voluntary association of persons who agree to become joint owners of a business. Each general partner is an agent for the partnership, has unlimited liability for partnership debts, and co-owns firm property with all partners. A partnership is a nontaxable entity and may be dissolved by any membership change or by court decree.
- Partnership assets should be recorded initially at their current fair values, which precludes future inequities in partners' capital balances resulting from the use of these assets.

❷ ILLUSTRATE various methods for the division of profits and losses (pp. 508–511).
- Partnership profits and losses are divided among partners according to their sharing agreement. If no sharing agreement exists, profits and losses are divided equally.
- Besides using ratios and percentages in allocating profits and losses, agreements may include salary allowances and interest on capital investments. In certain cases, some partners may receive an increase in capital and others may suffer a decrease when profits and losses are allocated.

❸ PRESENT the methods for admitting a new partner (pp. 511–513).
- When all or part of a partner's interest is purchased by another party, there is merely a transfer of capital from the selling partner to the other party. Total capital remains unchanged.
- When an incoming partner contributes assets to the firm, he or she may be credited with the amount of the investment if there is no bonus arrangement. If the incoming partner is credited with less than the investment, the bonus is accorded current partners in their profit and loss sharing ratio. If the incoming partner is credited with more than the investment, current partners absorb the bonus in their profit and loss sharing ratio.

❹ DESCRIBE the alternatives when a partner retires (pp. 513–514).
- When a retiring partner sells his or her interest to a new partner or current partners, there is merely a transfer of recorded capital, regardless of the amount paid.
- When payment is made from partnership funds, however, a bonus may be involved. If the settlement exceeds the retiring partner's capital balance, the bonus is absorbed by the remaining partners in their profit and loss sharing ratio. If the capital balance exceeds the settlement, the bonus is accorded the remaining partners in their profit and loss sharing ratio.

5 EXPLAIN how partnerships are liquidated (pp. 515–519).
- ■ The following steps are followed in a typical partnership liquidation: (1) noncash assets are sold and any gain or loss on sale is distributed to the partners' capital accounts, (2) liabilities are paid, and (3) partners are paid the amounts in their capital accounts.
- ■ If step 1 above results in a deficit for any partner(s) who is unable to make up the deficit, such deficit should be distributed to partners having credit balances in their capital accounts according to their profit and loss sharing ratio before any cash distributions are made to partners.

6 ANALYTICAL APPLICATION: DEFINE *common-size income statement* and EXPLAIN its usefulness (pp. 519–520).
- ■ A common-size income statement presents data as percentages of a key figure.
- ■ The base amount for a common-size income statement is total revenues (or net sales).

SELF-TEST QUESTIONS FOR REVIEW

(Answers follow the Solution to Demonstration Problem.)

1. Partners A and B have beginning investments of $40,000 and $60,000, respectively. Profit and loss sharing is as follows: interest at 20% on beginning capital balances, salaries to A and B of $10,000 and $5,000, respectively, and the remainder shared in the ratio 2:3. How much of $30,000 net income would be distributed to A?
   a. $18,000   b. $16,000   c. $15,500   d. $14,000

2. Partners Hill and Draper have capital balances of $50,000 and $30,000, respectively, and share profits and losses equally. Brown purchases one-half of Hill's interest for $28,000. The entry for Brown's admission is

   a. | Hill, Capital | 28,000 | |
      | Brown, Capital | | 28,000 |

   b. | Cash | 28,000 | |
      | Brown, Capital | | 28,000 |

   c. | Hill, Capital | 25,000 | |
      | Brown, Capital | | 25,000 |

   d. | Hill, Capital | 26,500 | |
      | Draper, Capital | 1,500 | |
      | Brown, Capital | | 28,000 |

3. Bauer and Carr have capital balances of $80,000 and $70,000, respectively, and share profits and losses equally. Drumm invests an amount to give him exactly a one-third interest in the firm. No bonuses are to be awarded to any partners.
   a. Drumm should invest $75,000 and be credited with $75,000.
   b. Drumm should invest $50,000 and be credited with $50,000.
   c. Drumm should invest $50,000 and be credited with $75,000.
   d. Drumm should invest $75,000 and be credited with $50,000.

4. Partners Doyle, Katz, and Gibbs have capital balances of $50,000, $60,000, and $70,000, respectively, and share profits and losses in the ratio 3:2:1. Doyle retires and is paid $56,000 with partnership funds. The entry to record Doyle's retirement will include a
   a. Debit to Doyle, Capital for $56,000.
   b. Debit to Katz, Capital for $3,000.
   c. Credit to Katz, Capital for $4,000.
   d. Debit to Gibbs, Capital for $2,000.

5. Partners Hughes, Judd, and Sanchez share profits and losses in the ratio 3:5:2. Just before liquidation, the partnership has the following balance sheet:

Cash	$ 20,000	Hughes, Capital	$ 60,000
Other Assets	140,000	Judd, Capital	20,000
		Sanchez, Capital	80,000
	$160,000		$160,000

Other Assets are sold for $80,000. Assuming that none of the partners can make up any resulting capital deficit, the final cash distribution to partner Sanchez is

a. $68,000   **b.** $64,000   **c.** $20,000   **d.** $72,000

DEMONSTRATION PROBLEM FOR REVIEW

J. Porter and M. Kantor have been partners for several years, operating Fast Moves, a moving business. The business has had its ups and downs but overall has been quite successful. In recognition of Porter's administrative responsibilities, the profit and loss sharing agreement allows her a salary of $5,000, with the remainder shared equally.

On January 1, 1993, Porter and Kantor had capital balances of $14,000 and $9,000, respectively. During 1993, Porter withdrew $4,000 cash from the partnership, and 1993 net income was $11,000. On December 31, 1993, the partnership had the following assets and liabilities: Cash, $4,000; Other Assets, $29,000; and Accounts Payable, $3,000.

Porter and Kantor liquidate the partnership on January 1, 1994. On that date, other assets are sold for $35,000, creditors are paid, and the partners receive the remaining cash.

REQUIRED

a. Prepare a schedule showing how the $11,000 net income for 1993 should be divided between Porter and Kantor.
b. Prepare a statement of partners' capital for 1993.
c. Prepare a balance sheet at December 31, 1993.
d. Give the January 1, 1994, journal entries to record the sale of other assets and recognition of any related gain or loss, the distribution of any gain or loss to partners' capital accounts, the payment of liabilities, and the distribution of cash to the partners.

SOLUTION TO DEMONSTRATION PROBLEM

a.

	Porter	Kantor	Total
Earnings to be divided			$11,000
Salary allowance	$5,000		5,000
Remainder			$ 6,000
Remainder divided equally	3,000	$3,000	
Partners' shares	$8,000	$3,000	

b.

FAST MOVES
STATEMENT OF PARTNERS' CAPITAL
FOR THE YEAR 1993

	Porter	Kantor	Total
Capital Balances, January 1, 1993	$14,000	$ 9,000	$23,000
Add: Net Income for 1993	8,000	3,000	11,000
Totals	$22,000	$12,000	$34,000
Less: Withdrawals	4,000		4,000
Capital Balances, December 31, 1993	$18,000	$12,000	$30,000

c.

FAST MOVES
BALANCE SHEET
DECEMBER 31, 1993

Assets		Liabilities	
Cash	$ 4,000	Accounts Payable	$ 3,000
Other Assets	29,000		
		Owners' Equity	
		J. Porter, Capital	$18,000
		M. Kantor, Capital	12,000
			30,000
Total Assets	$33,000	Total Liabilities and Owners' Equity	$33,000

d.   1994

Jan. 1	Cash	35,000	
	Other Assets		29,000
	Gain on Realization of Assets		6,000
	To record sale of other assets.		
1	Gain on Realization of Assets	6,000	
	J. Porter, Capital		3,000
	M. Kantor, Capital		3,000
	To distribute gain on sale of other assets.		
1	Accounts Payable	3,000	
	Cash		3,000
	To record payment of liabilities.		
1	J. Porter, Capital	21,000	
	M. Kantor, Capital	15,000	
	Cash		36,000
	To record cash distribution to partners.		

ANSWERS TO SELF-TEST QUESTIONS   **1.** b, p. 510   **2.** c, p. 512   **3.** a, p. 513   **4.** d, p. 514   **5.** b, pp. 515–518

GLOSSARY OF KEY TERMS USED IN THIS CHAPTER

allowance for interest   A provision in a partnership profit and loss sharing agreement that allows credit for the relative investments of partners (p. 510).

articles of copartnership   The formal written agreement among partners setting forth important aspects of the partnership, such as name, nature, duration, and location of the business, capital contributions, duties, and profit and loss ratios (p. 506).

bonus   In the context of partnership admissions, a bonus is the difference between the amount invested by a new partner and the amount credited to the new partner's capital account (p. 512).

common-size income statement   A form of the income statement that displays each item as a percentage of total revenues (or net sales) (p. 519).

general partnership   A partnership in which each partner is individually liable for the firm's obligations regardless of the amount of personal investment (p. 506).

limited partnership   A partnership in which one class of partner limits its liability for losses to the amount of the limited partners' investment; there must be at least one general partner in a limited partnership (p. 506).

partnership   A voluntary association of two or more persons for the purpose of conducting a business for profit (p. 506).

realization   The conversion of an entity's assets into cash (p. 515).

salary allowance   A provision in a partnership profit and loss sharing agreement that allows credit for the partners' personal services to the partnership (p. 510).

statement of partnership liquidation   A comprehensive report on the liquidation of a partnership that includes the initial assets and liabilities, the sale of noncash assets, the payment of liabilities, and the final distribution of cash to the partners (p. 518).

QUESTIONS

14-1   What is meant by *mutual agency*? By *unlimited liability*?

14-2   A corporation is said to have continuity of existence, whereas a partnership is characterized by a limited life. Name several events that may cause the dissolution of a partnership.

14-3   Porter understands that a partnership is a nontaxable entity and believes that if she does not withdraw any assets from the firm this year, she will not have any taxable income from her partnership activities. Is she correct? Why or why not?

14-4   Carlin invests in his partnership a machine that originally cost him $25,000. At the time of the investment, his personal records carry it at a book value of $13,000. Its current market value is $19,000. At what amount should the partnership record the machine? Why?

14-5 What factors should persons going into partnership consider in deciding how to share profits and losses?

14-6 If a partnership agreement is silent on the sharing of profits and losses, how will they be divided? What if the agreement indicates the method of sharing profits, but states nothing about the sharing of losses?

14-7 What are salary allowances? What is the difference between a salary allowance and a salary expense?

14-8 In what ways do the financial statements of a partnership differ from those of a sole proprietorship? What is the purpose of a statement of partners' capital?

14-9 Distinguish between the admission of a partner by the purchase of an interest and by an investment in the firm.

14-10 What circumstances might cause (a) current partners to receive a bonus when admitting a new partner and (b) an incoming partner to receive a bonus?

14-11 Boyd and Houk, who share profits and losses equally, admit Lowe as a new partner. Lowe contributes $100,000 for a one-fourth interest in the new firm. The entry to admit Lowe shows a $20,000 bonus each to Boyd and Houk. What is the apparent total capital of the new partnership?

14-12 When a partner retires, are the assets and capital of the partnership reduced? Explain.

14-13 When a partnership liquidates, how do accountants handle the gains and losses realized in selling the assets?

14-14 In a partnership liquidation, the residual cash is distributed to partners in the amounts of their capital balances just prior to the distribution. Why is this the proper distribution procedure?

14-15 Assume that during liquidation a debit balance arises in a partner's capital account and the partner is unable to contribute any more assets to the partnership. How does the partnership dispose of the debit balance in the capital account?

14-16 How is a statement of partnership liquidation dated and what accounting information does this statement contain?

14-17 Describe a common-size income statement and explain how it might be used.

EXERCISES

**PARTNERSHIP FORMATION
— OBJ. 1 —**

14-18 R. Diaz and S. Kaman form a partnership on May 1, 1993. Diaz contributes $80,000 cash, and Kaman contributes the following items from a separate business:

Marketable securities—cost of $14,000; current fair value of $18,000
Equipment—cost of $60,000; accumulated depreciation of $24,000, current fair value of $30,000
Land—cost of $45,000; current fair value of $58,000
Note payable (secured by equipment)—$21,000 assumed by partnership

Prepare the opening general journal entries of the partnership to record the investments of Diaz and Kaman.

**PROFIT AND LOSS SHARING
— OBJ. 2 —**

14-19 T. Roberts and J. Witmer are partners whose profit and loss sharing agreement gives salary allowances of $25,000 to Roberts and $15,000 to Witmer, with the remainder divided equally.
a. Net income for 1993 is $58,000. Prepare the general journal entry to distribute the income to Roberts and Witmer at December 31, 1993.
b. Assume a $20,000 net loss for 1993. Prepare the general journal entry to distribute the loss to Roberts and Witmer at December 31, 1993.

**STATEMENT OF PARTNERS'
CAPITAL
— OBJ. 3 —**

14-20 Use the following data to prepare a 1993 statement of partners' capital for W. Stevens and S. Jessen, who share profits and losses in the ratio of 60% to Stevens and 40% to Jessen.

W. Stevens, Capital, January 1, 1993	$95,000
S. Jessen, Capital, January 1, 1993	50,000
W. Stevens, Drawing	20,000
S. Jessen, Drawing	26,000
Additional investments by Stevens	5,000
Net income for 1993	50,000

ADMISSION OF A PARTNER
— OBJ. 3 —

14-21 C. Peters and M. Schmidt are partners with capital balances of $90,000 and $60,000, respectively. They share profits and losses in the ratio of 60% to Peters and 40% to Schmidt. J. Walsh receives a one-fourth interest in the firm by investing $70,000 cash on May 4, 1993.

a. Prepare the general journal entry to record Walsh's admission assuming a bonus is allowed Peters and Schmidt.

b. Briefly explain circumstances that might cause existing partners to receive a bonus when admitting a new partner.

RETIREMENT OF A PARTNER
— OBJ. 4 —

14-22 D. Charles, R. Gibson, and M. Kramer are partners sharing profits and losses in the ratio 5:3:2, respectively. Their capital balances are Charles, $80,000; Gibson, $120,000; and Kramer, $120,000. Charles retires from the firm on June 30, 1993, and is paid $100,000 from partnership funds.

a. Prepare the general journal entry to record Charles' retirement, assuming that Gibson and Kramer absorb the bonus paid Charles.

b. Briefly explain circumstances that might cause a retiring partner to receive a bonus.

PARTNERSHIP LIQUIDATION
— OBJ. 5 —

14-23 In the liquidation of the ABC Partnership, noncash assets were sold for $60,000, and the related gain or loss on realization resulted in debits to the capital accounts of partners A, B, and C for $16,000, $12,000, and $12,000, respectively.

a. Were the noncash assets sold at a gain or a loss? How do you know? How much was the gain or the loss?

b. What is the partners' apparent profit and loss sharing ratio?

c. What was the apparent book value of the noncash assets sold?

PARTNERSHIP LIQUIDATION
— OBJ. 5 —

14-24 Just before liquidation, the balance sheet of the partnership of A. Rosen and W. Travis, who share profits and losses equally, appeared as follows:

Cash	$ 72,000	Liabilities	$ 20,000
Other Assets	128,000	A. Rosen, Capital	120,000
		W. Travis, Capital	60,000
	$200,000		$200,000

a. If other assets are sold for $120,000, what amounts will Rosen and Travis receive as the final cash distribution?

b. If other assets are sold for $140,000, what amounts will Rosen and Travis receive as the final cash distribution?

c. If Rosen receives $102,000 and Travis receives $42,000 as the final (and only) cash distribution, what amount was received from the sale of the other assets?

PARTNERSHIP LIQUIDATION
— OBJ. 5 —

14-25 Davis, Frye, Hahn, and Gordon are liquidating their partnership. All assets have been converted to cash, and all liabilities have been paid. At this point, the capital accounts show the following: Davis, $11,000 credit balance; Frye, $16,000 credit balance; Hahn, $9,000 debit balance; and Gordon, $14,000 credit balance. Profits and losses are shared equally.

a. How much cash is available to distribute to partners?

b. If there is doubt concerning Hahn's ability to make up the $9,000 deficit, how should the available cash be distributed?

PROBLEMS

PROFIT AND LOSS SHARING
— OBJ. 2 —

14-26 H. Gordon and L. Madden form a partnership on January 1, 1993, and invest $140,000 and $100,000, respectively. During 1993, the partnership earned a $48,000 net income.

REQUIRED

a. Prepare the entry to close the Income Summary account and distribute the $48,000 net income under each of the following independent assumptions:

1. The partnership agreement is silent on the sharing of profits and losses.

2. Profits and losses are shared in the ratio of beginning capital investments.

3. Profits and losses are shared by allowing 10% interest on beginning capital investments, with the remainder divided equally.

b. Assume that the partnership had a $24,000 loss during 1993. Prepare the entry to close the Income Summary account and distribute the $24,000 loss under each of the foregoing assumptions.

PROFIT AND LOSS SHARING
— OBJ. 2 —

14-27 The capital accounts and the Income Summary account as of December 31, 1993, of the Dole, Fine, and Thomas partnership appear below. None of the partners withdrew capital during 1993.

G. DOLE, CAPITAL			J. FINE, CAPITAL		
	1993			1993	
	Jan. 1	48,000		Jan. 1	64,000
	July 1	64,000		Oct. 1	64,000

M. THOMAS, CAPITAL			INCOME SUMMARY		
	1993			1993	
	Jan. 1	160,000		Dec. 31	120,000

REQUIRED

a. Prepare the entry to distribute the $120,000 net income if Dole, Fine, and Thomas share profits and losses:
  1. Equally.
  2. In the ratio 5:3:2, respectively.
  3. In the ratio of *average* capital balances for the year.
  4. Under an agreement allowing $40,000 salary to Thomas, 10% interest on *beginning* investments, with the remainder shared equally.

b. Assume that net income was $42,000 rather than $120,000. Prepare the entry to distribute the $42,000 earnings if the agreement allows $40,000 salary to Thomas, 10% interest on beginning investments, with the remainder shared equally.

ADMISSION OF A PARTNER
— OBJ. 3 —

14-28 J. Brady and T. Dalton are partners with capital balances of $80,000 and $64,000, respectively. Profits and losses are shared equally.

REQUIRED

Give the entries to record the admission of a new partner, S. Felton, under each of the following separate circumstances:

a. Felton purchases one-half of Dalton's interest, paying Dalton $36,000 personally.

b. Felton invests sufficient funds to receive exactly one-fourth interest in the new partnership. (No bonuses are recorded.)

c. Felton invests $46,000 for a one-fifth interest, with any bonus distributed to the capital accounts of Brady and Dalton.

d. Felton invests $32,000 for a one-fourth interest, with any bonus credited to Felton's capital account.

e. In requirements (c) and (d) above, what do the terms of admission imply regarding the relative negotiating positions of the new partner and the old partners?

RETIREMENT OF A PARTNER
— OBJ. 4 —

14-29 C. Bower, F. Green, and N. Klein are partners with capital balances of $140,000, $80,000, and $100,000, respectively. Profits and losses are shared equally. Klein retires from the firm.

REQUIRED

Record the entries for Klein's retirement in each of the following separate circumstances:

a. Klein's interest is sold to R. Winston, a new partner, for $116,000.

b. Bower and Green each acquire one-half of Klein's interest for $56,000 apiece.

c. Klein receives $116,000 of partnership funds for his interest. The remaining partners absorb the bonus paid Klein.

d. The partners agree that Klein's abrupt retirement presents operating disadvantages and therefore Klein should receive only $92,000 for his interest. Payment is from partnership funds, with any bonuses going to Bower and Green.

SHARING OF LOSS,
ADMISSION AND
WITHDRAWAL OF PARTNERS
— OBJ. 2, 3, 4 —

14-30 W. Fletcher and S. Marshall formed a partnership on January 1, 1991, with capital investments of $62,000 and $124,000, respectively. The profit and loss sharing agreement allowed Fletcher a salary of $16,000, with the remainder divided equally. During the year, Marshall made withdrawals of $10,000; no other investments or withdrawals were made in 1991. The partnership incurred a net loss of $20,000 in 1991.

On January 1, 1992, J. Kiley was admitted to the partnership. Kiley purchased one-third of Marshall's interest, paying $30,000 directly to Marshall. Fletcher, Marshall, and Kiley agreed to share profits and losses in the ratio 3:5:2, respectively. No provision was made for salaries. The partnership earned a net income of $120,000 in 1992.

On January 1, 1993, Marshall withdrew from the partnership. Marshall received $130,000 of partnership funds for her interest. Fletcher and Kiley absorbed the bonus paid Marshall.

REQUIRED

a. Prepare the December 31, 1991, entry to close the Income Summary account and distribute the $20,000 loss for 1991.
b. Compute the capital balances of Fletcher and Marshall at December 31, 1991.
c. Prepare the entry to record the admission of Kiley on January 1, 1992.
d. Prepare the December 31, 1992, entry to close the Income Summary account and distribute the $120,000 income for 1992.
e. Compute the December 31, 1992, capital balances of Fletcher, Marshall, and Kiley.
f. Prepare the January 1, 1993, entry to record Marshall's withdrawal.

STATEMENT OF PARTNERS' CAPITAL
— OBJ. 2 —

14-31 Litton and Meyer formed a partnership in 1991, agreeing to share profits and losses equally. On December 31, 1991, their capital balances were: Litton, $160,000; Meyer, $96,000.

On January 1, 1992, Nelson was admitted to a one-fourth interest in the firm by investing $96,000 cash. Nelson's admission was recorded by according bonuses to Litton and Meyer. The profit and loss sharing agreement of the new partnership allowed salaries of $32,000 to Litton and $40,000 to Nelson, with the remainder divided in the ratio 3:3:2 among Litton, Meyer, and Nelson, respectively.

Net income for 1992 was $168,000. Litton and Meyer withdrew cash during the year equal to their salary allowances. Immediately after the net income had been closed to the partners' capital accounts, Nelson retired from the firm. Nelson received $140,000 of partnership funds for his interest, and the remaining partners absorbed the bonus paid to him.

REQUIRED

Prepare a statement of partners' capital for 1992.

PARTNERSHIP LIQUIDATION
— OBJ. 5 —

14-32 R. Frain, S. Hawk, and T. Lund are partners who share profits and losses in the ratio of 5:3:2, respectively. Just before the partnership's liquidation, its balance sheet accounts appear as follows:

Cash	$100,000	Accounts Payable	$120,000
Other Assets	300,000	R. Frain, Capital	60,000
		S. Hawk, Capital	120,000
		T. Lund, Capital	100,000
	$400,000		$400,000

REQUIRED

a. Assuming that other assets are sold for $240,000, prepare the entries to record the sale of the other assets and distribute the related loss, pay liabilities, and distribute the remaining cash to the partners on February 15, 1993.
b. Assuming that other assets are sold for $160,000, prepare the entries to record the sale of the other assets and distribute the related loss, pay liabilities, apportion any partner's deficit among the other partners (assuming any such deficit is not made up by the partner involved), and distribute the remaining cash to the appropriate partners on February 15, 1993.
c. Assuming that liquidation procedures occurred between January 1 and February 15, 1993, prepare a statement of partnership liquidation using the data in requirement (b).

SHARING OF LOSS AND PARTNERSHIP LIQUIDATION
— OBJ. 5 —

14-33 G. Abner, H. Boyd, J. Case, and K. Dunn are partners whose profit and loss sharing agreement provides for annual interest at 20% on partners' beginning capital balances, annual salaries of $24,000 and $8,000 to Abner and Case, respectively, with the remainder divided in the ratio of 4:3:2:1, respectively.

Due to a history of modest earnings, they liquidate their partnership at December 31, 1992. Just prior to completing the closing of the partnership books for 1992, the trial balance is summarized as follows:

Cash	$148,000	Liabilities	$120,000
Other Assets (Net)	220,000	G. Abner, Capital	60,000
G. Abner, Drawing	24,000	H. Boyd, Capital	140,000
J. Case, Drawing	8,000	J. Case, Capital	40,000
Income Summary (loss)	60,000	K. Dunn, Capital	100,000
	$460,000		$460,000

REQUIRED

a. Assuming that none of the partners made any capital contributions during the year, prepare journal entries to complete the closing of the books at December 31, 1992. During the year, Abner and Case withdrew amounts equal to their salary allowances.

b. Starting with the partnership post-closing trial balance at December 31, 1992, prepare a statement of partnership liquidation assuming that
   1. Other assets were sold for $140,000 cash.
   2. All liabilities were paid in cash.
   3. Any partner experiencing a capital deficit would be unable to make up the deficit to the partnership.
   4. The final distribution of cash to partners was made on February 20, 1993.

ALTERNATE EXERCISES

PARTNERSHIP FORMATION
— OBJ. 1 —

14-18A J. Lopez and W. Garcia form a partnership on July 1, 1993. Lopez contributes $75,000 cash and Garcia contributes the following items from a separate business:

Marketable securities—cost of $15,000; current fair value of $12,000
Equipment—cost of $50,000; accumulated depreciation of $20,000, current fair value of $25,000
Land—cost of $50,000; current fair value of $62,000
Note payable (secured by equipment)—$11,000 assumed by partnership

Prepare the opening general journal entries of the partnership to record the investments of Lopez and Garcia.

PROFIT AND LOSS SHARING
— OBJ. 2 —

14-19A T. Ecker and M. Ward are partners whose profit and loss sharing agreement gives salary allowances of $30,000 to Ecker and $18,000 to Ward, with the remainder divided equally.
   a. Net income for 1993 is $72,000. Prepare the general journal entry to distribute the income to Ecker and Ward on December 31, 1993.
   b. Assume a $12,000 net loss for 1993. Prepare the general journal entry to distribute the loss to Ecker and Ward on December 31, 1993.

STATEMENT OF PARTNERS'
CAPITAL
— OBJ. 3 —

14-20A Use the following data to prepare a 1993 statement of partners' capital for H. Gomez and C. Bard, who share profits and losses in the ratio of 60% to Gomez and 40% to Bard.

H. Gomez, Capital, January 1, 1993	$90,000
C. Bard, Capital, January 1, 1993	56,000
H. Gomez, Drawing	21,000
C. Bard, Drawing	18,000
Additional investments by Gomez	8,000
Net income for 1993	40,000

ADMISSION OF A PARTNER
— OBJ. 3 —

14-21A B. Falk and T. Hardy are partners with capital balances of $100,000 and $70,000; respectively. They share profits and losses in the ratio of 60% to Falk and 40% to Hardy. J. Jerold receives a one-fourth interest in the firm by investing $90,000 cash on June 15, 1993.
   a. Prepare the general journal entry to record Jerold's admission assuming a bonus is allowed Falk and Hardy.
   b. Briefly explain circumstances that might cause existing partners to receive a bonus when admitting a new partner.

RETIREMENT OF A PARTNER — OBJ. 4 —

14-22A F. Lane, D. Potter, and L. Neuman are partners sharing profits and losses in the ratio 5:3:2, respectively. Their capital balances are Lane, $60,000; Potter, $90,000; and Neuman, $90,000. Lane retires from the firm on June 30, 1993, and is paid $75,000 from partnership funds.
   a. Prepare the general journal entry to record Lane's retirement, assuming that Potter and Neuman absorb the bonus paid Lane.
   b. Briefly explain circumstances that might cause a retiring partner to receive a bonus.

PARTNERSHIP LIQUIDATION — OBJ. 5 —

14-23A In the liquidation of the HJK Partnership, noncash assets were sold for $75,000, and the related gain or loss on realization resulted in credits to the capital accounts of partners H, J, and K for $15,000, $9,000, and $6,000, respectively.
   a. Were the noncash assets sold at a gain or a loss? How do you know? How much was the gain or the loss?
   b. What is the partners' apparent profit and loss sharing ratio?
   c. What was the apparent book value of the noncash assets sold?

PARTNERSHIP LIQUIDATION — OBJ. 5 —

14-24A Just before liquidation, the balance sheet of the partnership of T. Harris and C. Moyer, who share profits and losses equally, appeared as follows:

Cash	$ 54,000	Liabilities	$ 15,000
Other Assets	96,000	T. Harris, Capital	90,000
		C. Moyer, Capital	45,000
	$150,000		$150,000

   a. If other assets are sold for $90,000, what amounts will Harris and Moyer receive as the final cash distribution?
   b. If other assets are sold for $105,000, what amounts will Harris and Moyer receive as the final cash distribution?
   c. If Harris receives $76,500 and Moyer receives $31,500 as the final (and only) cash distribution, what amount was received from the sale of the other assets?

PARTNERSHIP LIQUIDATION — OBJ. 5 —

14-25A Case, Earl, Kason, and Perl are liquidating their partnership. All assets have been converted to cash, and all liabilities have been paid. At this point, the capital accounts show the following: Case, $10,000 credit balance; Earl, $19,000 credit balance; Kason, $12,000 debit balance; and Perl, $16,000 credit balance. Profits and losses are shared equally.
   a. How much cash is available to distribute to partners?
   b. If there is doubt concerning Kason's ability to make up the $12,000 deficit, how should the available cash be distributed?

ALTERNATE PROBLEMS

PROFIT AND LOSS SHARING — OBJ. 2 —

14-26A S. Ritter and N. Varney form a partnership on February 1, 1993, and invest $120,000 and $60,000, respectively. During 1993, the partnership earned $42,000 net income.

REQUIRED

   a. Prepare the entry to close the Income Summary account and distribute the $42,000 net income under each of the following independent assumptions:
      1. The partnership agreement is silent on the sharing of profits and losses.
      2. Profits and losses are shared in the ratio of beginning capital investments.
      3. Profits and losses are shared by allowing 10% interest on beginning capital investments with the remainder divided equally.
   b. Assume the partnership had a $24,000 loss in 1993. Prepare the entry to close the Income Summary account and distribute the $24,000 loss under each of the foregoing assumptions.

PROFIT AND LOSS SHARING — OBJ. 2 —

14-27A The capital accounts and the Income Summary account as of December 31, 1993, of the Baker, Kane, and Quinn partnership appear below. None of the partners withdrew capital during 1993.

R. BAKER, CAPITAL		
	1993	
	Jan. 1	120,000
	Sept. 1	120,000

B. KANE, CAPITAL		
	1993	
	Jan. 1	60,000
	July 1	40,000

J. QUINN, CAPITAL		
	1993	
	Jan. 1	48,000

INCOME SUMMARY		
	1993	
	Dec. 31	72,000

REQUIRED

a. Prepare the entry to distribute the $72,000 net income if Baker, Kane, and Quinn share profits and losses:

1. Equally.
2. In the ratio 3:2:1, respectively.
3. In the ratio of *average* capital balances for the year.
4. Under an agreement allowing $36,000 salary to Baker, 10% interest on *beginning* investments, with the remainder shared equally.

b. Assume that net income was $48,000 rather than $72,000. Prepare the entry to distribute the $48,000 earnings if the agreement allows $36,000 salary to Baker, 10% interest on beginning investments, with the remainder shared equally.

ADMISSION OF A PARTNER
— OBJ. 3 —

14-28A A. Curtis and P. James are partners with capital balances of $120,000 and $72,000, respectively. Profits and losses are shared equally.

REQUIRED

Prepare the entries to record the admission of a new partner, D. Pierce, under each of the following separate circumstances:

a. Pierce purchases one-half of James' interest, paying James $44,000 personally.
b. Pierce invests sufficient funds to receive exactly one-fourth interest in the new partnership. (No bonuses are recorded.)
c. Pierce invests $68,000 for a one-fifth interest, with any bonus distributed to the capital accounts of Curtis and James.
d. Pierce invests $56,000 for a one-fourth interest, with any bonus credited to Pierce's capital account.
e. In requirements (c) and (d) above, what do the terms of admission imply regarding the relative negotiating positions of the new partner and the old partners?

RETIREMENT OF A PARTNER
— OBJ. 4 —

14-29A G. Anderson, K. Carroll, and Q. Warren are partners with capital balances of $120,000, $100,000, and $80,000, respectively. Profits and losses are shared equally. Warren retires from the firm.

REQUIRED

Record the entries for Warren's retirement in each of the following separate circumstances:

a. Warren's interest is sold to V. Hines, a new partner, for $90,000.
b. One-half of Warren's interest is sold to each of the remaining partners for $44,000 apiece.
c. Warren receives $92,000 of partnership funds for his interest. The remaining partners absorb the bonus paid to Warren.
d. The partners agree that Warren's abrupt retirement presents operating disadvantages and therefore Warren should receive only $72,000 for his interest. Payment is from partnership funds, with any bonuses going to Anderson and Carroll.

SHARING OF LOSS,
ADMISSION AND
WITHDRAWAL OF PARTNERS
— OBJ. 2, 3, 4 —

14-30A H. Allen and R. Kohl formed a partnership on January 1, 1991, with capital investments of $82,000 and $130,000, respectively. The profit and loss sharing agreement allowed Allen a salary of $20,000 with the remainder divided equally. During the year, Kohl made withdrawals of $18,000; no other investments or withdrawals were made in 1991. The partnership incurred a net loss of $24,000 in 1991.

On January 1, 1992, M. Richards was admitted to the partnership. Richards purchased one-third of Kohl's interest, paying $36,000 directly to Kohl. Allen, Kohl, and Richards agreed to share profits and losses in the ratio 5:3:2, respectively. No provision was made for salaries. The partnership earned a net income of $100,000 in 1992.

On January 1, 1993, Kohl withdrew from the partnership. Kohl received $104,000 of partnership funds for his interest. Allen and Richards absorbed the bonus paid Kohl.

REQUIRED

a. Prepare the December 31, 1991, entry to close the Income Summary account and distribute the $24,000 loss for 1991.
b. Compute the capital balances of Allen and Kohl at December 31, 1991.
c. Prepare the entry to record the admission of Richards on January 1, 1992.
d. Prepare the December 31, 1992, entry to close the Income Summary account and distribute the $100,000 income for 1992.
e. Compute the December 31, 1992, capital balances of Allen, Kohl, and Richards.
f. Prepare the January 1, 1993, entry to record Kohl's withdrawal.

STATEMENT OF PARTNERS' CAPITAL — OBJ. 2 —

14-31A Arnold and Brown formed a partnership in 1991, agreeing to share profits and losses equally. On December 31, 1991, their capital balances were Arnold, $140,000; Brown, $108,000.

On January 1, 1992, Carter was admitted to a one-fourth interest in the firm by investing $112,000 cash. Carter's admission was recorded by according bonuses to Arnold and Brown. The profit and loss sharing agreement of the new partnership allowed salaries of $28,000 to Arnold and $32,000 to Carter, with the remainder divided in the ratio 4:3:3 among Arnold, Brown, and Carter, respectively.

Net income for 1992 was $144,000. Arnold and Carter withdrew cash during the year equal to their salary allowances. Immediately after net income had been closed to the partners' capital accounts, Carter retired from the firm. Carter received $118,000 for his interest, and the remaining partners absorbed the bonus paid Carter.

REQUIRED

Prepare a statement of partners' capital for 1992.

PARTNERSHIP LIQUIDATION — OBJ. 5 —

14-32A H. Cody, T. Lyon, and J. Parker are partners who share profits and losses in the ratio of 5:3:2, respectively. Just before the partnership's liquidation, its balance sheet appears as follows:

Cash	$ 60,000	Accounts Payable	$ 40,000
Other Assets (Net)	160,000	H. Cody, Capital	32,000
		T. Lyon, Capital	60,000
		J. Parker, Capital	88,000
	$220,000		$220,000

REQUIRED

a. Assuming that other assets are sold for $130,000, prepare the entries to record the sale of the other assets and distribute the related loss, pay liabilities, and distribute the remaining cash to the partners on February 8, 1993.
b. Assuming that other assets are sold for $88,000, prepare the entries to record the sale of the other assets and distribute the related loss, apportion any partner's deficit among the other partners (assuming any such deficit is not made up by the partner involved), and distribute the remaining cash to the appropriate partners on February 8, 1993.
c. Assuming that liquidation procedures occurred between January 1 and February 8, 1993, prepare a statement of partnership liquidation using the data in requirement (b).

SHARING OF LOSS AND PARTNERSHIP LIQUIDATION — OBJ. 5 —

14-33A C. Beard, F. Dale, K. Gregg, and N. Ritt are partners whose profit and loss sharing agreement provides for annual interest at 20% on partners' beginning capital balances, annual salaries of $10,000 and $20,000 to Beard and Dale, respectively, with the remainder divided in the ratio of 5:3:1:1, respectively.

Due to a history of modest earnings, they liquidate their partnership on December 31, 1992. Just prior to completing the closing of the partnership books for 1992, the trial balance is summarized as follows:

Cash	$ 54,000	Liabilities	$ 34,000
Other Assets (Net)	160,000	C. Beard, Capital	50,000
Beard, Drawing	20,000	F. Dale, Capital	40,000
Dale, Drawing	30,000	K. Gregg, Capital	100,000
Income Summary (loss)	20,000	N. Ritt, Capital	60,000
	$284,000		$284,000

REQUIRED

a. Assuming that none of the partners made any capital contributions during the year, prepare journal entries to complete the closing of the books at December 31, 1992.

b. Starting with the partnership post-closing trial balance at December 31, 1992, prepare a statement of partnership liquidation assuming that
  1. Other assets were sold for $120,000 cash.
  2. All liabilities were paid in cash.
  3. Any partner experiencing a capital deficit would be unable to make up the deficit to the partnership.
  4. The final distribution of cash to partners was made on January 31, 1993.

CASES

Business Decision Case

Bill Campbell and John Miller were in business for several years, sharing profits and losses equally. Because of Miller's poor health, they liquidated the partnership. Campbell managed the liquidation because Miller was in the hospital. Just before liquidation, the partnership balance sheet contained the following information:

Cash	$ 160,000	Liabilities	$ 100,000
Other Assets	440,000	Campbell, Capital	200,000
		Miller, Capital	300,000
	$600,000		$600,000

Campbell (1) sold the other assets at the best prices obtainable, (2) paid off all the creditors, and (3) divided the remaining cash between Miller and himself equally, according to their profit and loss sharing ratio.

Miller received a note from Campbell that read "Good news—sold other assets for $500,000. Have $280,000 check waiting for you. Get well soon." Because he will not be released from the hospital for several days, Miller asks you to review Campbell's liquidation and cash distribution procedures.

REQUIRED

Do you approve of Campbell's liquidation and cash distribution procedures? Explain. If you believe Campbell erred, what amount of final cash settlement should Miller receive?

Analytical Application Case

CHAPARRAL STEEL COMPANY, located in Midlothian, Texas, manufactures a variety of steel products. Shown below are income statements for two recent years (dollar amounts in thousands; Year 2 is the more recent year):

	Year 2	Year 1
Net Sales	$404,155	$451,490
Costs and Expenses:		
Cost of Sales	$323,967	$324,719
Selling, General, and Administrative Expenses	16,566	23,774
Depreciation Expense	19,865	17,671
Amortization Expense	252	251
Interest Expense	12,556	15,050
Other Income	(5,701)	(4,650)
Total Costs and Expenses	$367,505	$376,815
Income before Income Taxes	$ 36,650	$ 74,675
Income Taxes	12,604	25,569
Net Income	$ 24,046	$ 49,106

REQUIRED

a. Prepare common-size income statements for Years 1 and 2 for Chaparral Steel Company.

b. Compare the common-size income statements prepared in (a) and comment.

Ethics Case

Gary Cunningham and Dennis Stanton are partners in Good Times Recording Studios. Gary manages the New York City office while Dennis manages the Los Angeles office.

Gary borrows $50,000 from a bank in the partnership name, using partnership assets as collateral without discussing it with Dennis. Although Gary is going to use the money for personal reasons, he intends to pay it back promptly and instructs Helen Terry, the accountant, not to bother telling Dennis about the loan.

REQUIRED

What ethical considerations does Helen face? What are her alternatives?

How does a corporation account for the interests of its owners?

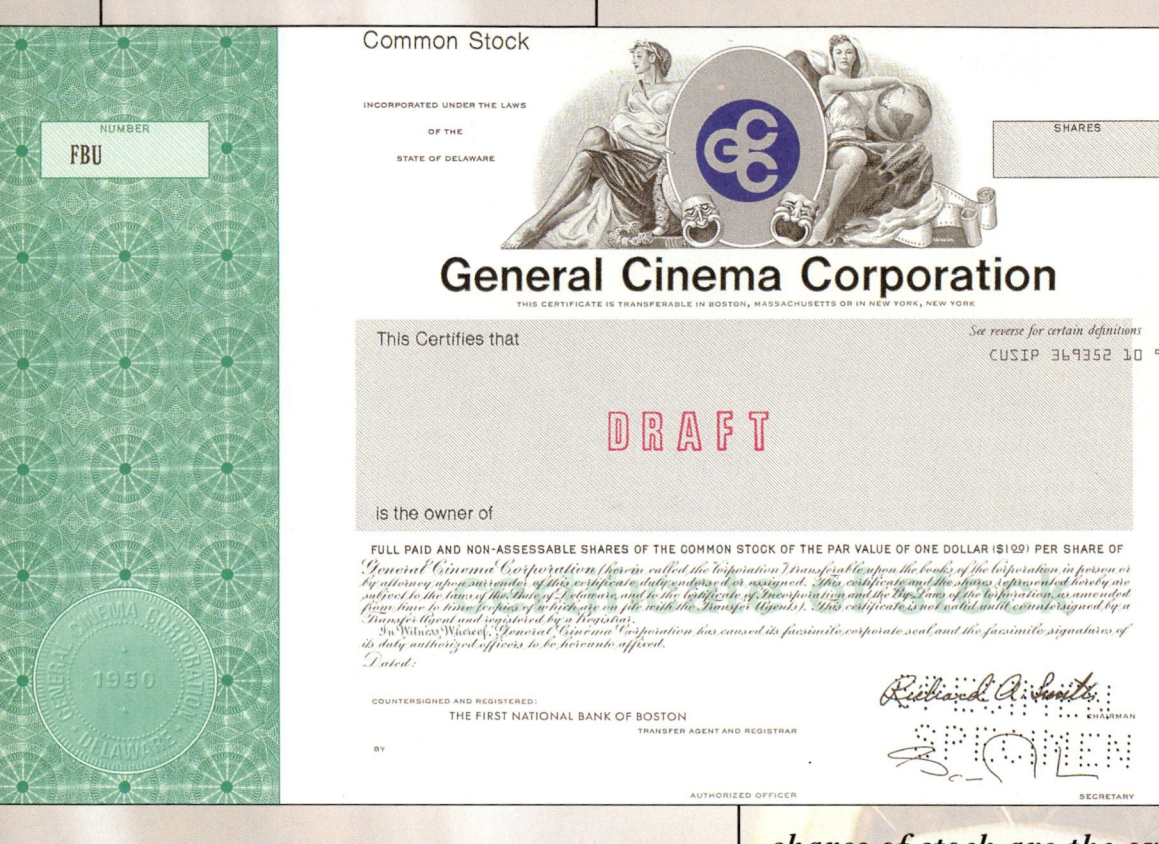

Common Stock

INCORPORATED UNDER THE LAWS
OF THE
STATE OF DELAWARE

NUMBER
FBU

SHARES

General Cinema Corporation

THIS CERTIFICATE IS TRANSFERABLE IN BOSTON, MASSACHUSETTS OR IN NEW YORK, NEW YORK

This Certifies that

See reverse for certain definitions
CUSIP 369352 10 9

DRAFT

is the owner of

FULL PAID AND NON-ASSESSABLE SHARES OF THE COMMON STOCK OF THE PAR VALUE OF ONE DOLLAR ($1.00) PER SHARE OF

General Cinema Corporation (herein called the Corporation) transferable upon the books of the Corporation in person or by attorney upon surrender of this certificate duly endorsed or assigned. This certificate and the shares represented hereby are subject to the laws of the State of Delaware and to the Certificate of Incorporation and the By-Laws of the Corporation, as amended from time to time (copies of which are on file with the Transfer Agent). This certificate is not valid until countersigned by a Transfer Agent and registered by a Registrar.

In Witness Whereof, General Cinema Corporation has caused its facsimile corporate seal and the facsimile signatures of its duly authorized officers to be hereunto affixed.

Dated:

COUNTERSIGNED AND REGISTERED:
THE FIRST NATIONAL BANK OF BOSTON
TRANSFER AGENT AND REGISTRAR

BY

CHAIRMAN

SPECIMEN

SECRETARY

AUTHORIZED OFFICER

The owners of a publicly held corporation are called stockholders or shareholders, because shares of stock are the ownership units for a corporation. ■ Stockholders may be individuals or large pension funds or mutual funds, holding from a few to millions of shares. ■ Thus a large number of shares can be held by relatively few stockholders. ■ Historically, corporations issued stock certificates as evidence of shares acquired by the owner, but entries on computerized records are making ornate certificates obsolete.

15

CORPORATIONS: ORGANIZATION AND CAPITAL STOCK

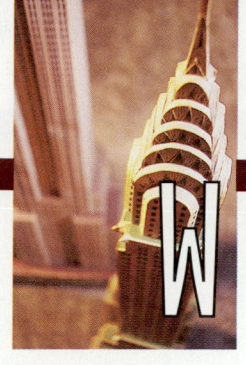

ithout a doubt, the modern corporation dominates the national and international economic landscape. In the United States, corporations generate well over three-fourths of the combined business receipts of corporations, partnerships, and proprietorships, even though fewer than one of every five businesses is organized as a corporation. The corporate form of organization is used for a variety of business efforts—from the large, multinational corporation with more than a million owners operating in countries all over the world to the small, family-owned business in a single community. In this chapter, we emphasize the organization of the corporation and the accounting procedures for its capital stock transactions.

NATURE AND FORMATION OF A CORPORATION

OBJECTIVE ① DEFINE *and* **DISCUSS** *the corporate form of organization.*

A **corporation** is a legal entity—an artificial legal "person"—created on the approval of the appropriate governmental authority. The right to conduct business as a corporation is a privilege granted by the state in which the corporation is formed. All states have laws specifying the requirements for creating a corporation. In some instances, such as the formation of a national bank, the federal government must approve the creation of a corporation.

To form a corporation, the incorporators (often at least three are required) must apply for a charter. The incorporators prepare and file the **articles of incorporation,** which delineate the basic structure of the corporation, including the purposes for which it is formed, the amount of capital stock to be authorized, and the number of shares into which the stock is to be divided. If the incorporators meet the requirements of the law, the government issues a charter or certificate of incorporation. After the charter has been granted, the incorporators (or, in some states, the subscribers to the corporation's capital stock) hold an organizational meeting to elect the first board of directors and adopt the corporation's bylaws.

Because assets are essential to corporate operations, the corporation issues *certificates of capital stock* to obtain the necessary funds. As owners of the corporation, *stockholders*, or *shareholders*, are entitled to a voice in the control and management of the company. Stockholders with voting stock may vote on specific issues at the annual meeting and participate in the election of the board of directors. The board of directors establishes the overall policies of the corporation and declares dividends. Normally, the board selects such corporate officers as a president, one or more vice-presidents, a controller, a treasurer, and a secretary. The officers implement the policies of the board of directors and actively manage the day-to-day affairs of the corporation. The other employees of the corporation execute the operating plans and policies developed by management. Exhibit 15-1 depicts the organizational structure of a corporation.

ADVANTAGES OF THE CORPORATE FORM

A corporation has several organizational advantages compared with a sole proprietorship or partnership. These advantages are discussed in the following sections.

Separate Legal Entity

A business with a corporate charter is empowered to conduct business affairs apart from its owners. The corporation, as a legal entity, may acquire assets, incur debt, enter into contracts, sue, and be sued—all in its own name. The owners, or stockholders, of the corporation receive stock certificates as evidence of their ownership

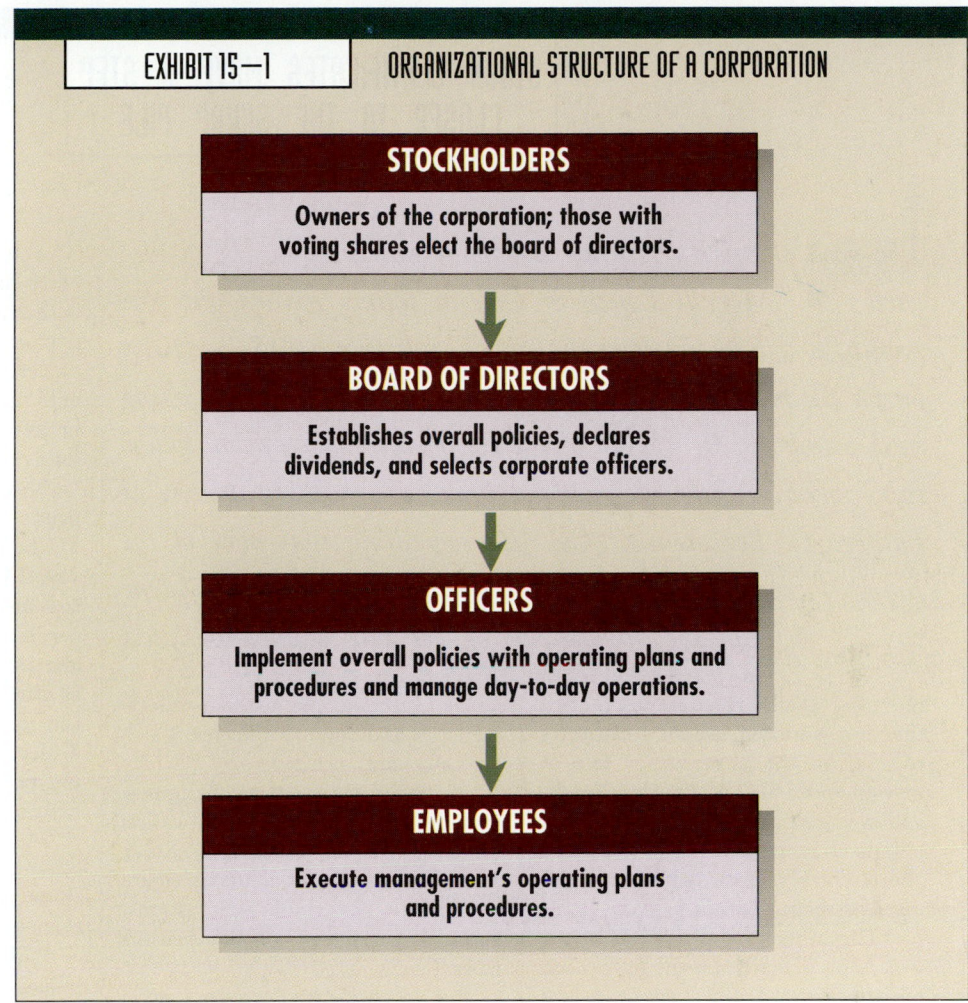

EXHIBIT 15—1   ORGANIZATIONAL STRUCTURE OF A CORPORATION

STOCKHOLDERS

Owners of the corporation; those with voting shares elect the board of directors.

BOARD OF DIRECTORS

Establishes overall policies, declares dividends, and selects corporate officers.

OFFICERS

Implement overall policies with operating plans and procedures and manage day-to-day operations.

EMPLOYEES

Execute management's operating plans and procedures.

interests; the stockholders, however, are separate and distinct from the corporation. This characteristic contrasts with proprietorships and partnerships, which are accounting entities but not legal entities apart from their owners.

Limited Liability

The liability of shareholders with respect to company affairs is usually limited to their investment in the corporation. In contrast, owners of proprietorships and partnerships can be held responsible separately and collectively for unsatisfied obligations of the business. Because of the limited liability of corporate shareholders, state laws restrict distributions to shareholders. Most of these laws have fairly elaborate provisions that define the various forms of owners' equity and describe distribution conditions. To protect creditors, the state controls the distribution of contributed capital. Distributions of retained earnings (undistributed profits) are not legal unless the board of directors formally declares a dividend. Because of the legal delineation of owner capital available for distribution, corporations must maintain careful distinctions in the accounts to identify the different elements of stockholders' equity.

Transferability of Ownership

Shares in a corporation may be routinely transferred without affecting the company's operations. The corporation merely notes such transfers of ownership in the stockholder records (ledger). Although a corporation must have stockholder records to notify shareholders of meetings and to pay dividends, the price at which shares transfer between owners is not recognized in the corporation's accounts.

STOCK CERTIFICATES MOVE A STEP CLOSER TO THE SCRAP PILE

The good ol' stock certificate is rapidly marching to the grave-yard. ■ Merrill Lynch & Co., in letters mailed out this month, is telling investors that it will institute a $15-a-security fee for the privilege of holding a stock or bond certificate, starting in September. ■ "Most of the rest of the industry will follow suit," predicts Guy Moszkowski, brokerage-industry analyst at Sanford C. Bernstein & Co. "It's something that most of the firms have wanted to do away with for quite some time." ■ But the introduction of fees will be only the latest move by Wall Street to discourage the time-honored use of certificates to confirm the purchase or sale of investments. Stocks, mutual funds, and even certificates of deposit are all being converted to computerized "book-entry" form, whether small investors like it or not.

"The other capital markets of the world, particularly Japan, have been moving toward the certificate-less society," says Frank G. Zarb, chairman of Primerica Corp.'s Smith Barney, Harris Upham & Co. securities unit. Smith Barney doesn't rule out following Merrill's lead.

Until certificates have entirely departed, a growing number of investors will have to weigh the costs and-benefits of holding certificates vs. opting for book entry (in which investors' holdings are confirmed only on account statements).

For example, investors can face problems if they try to transfer accounts from a brokerage firm without having a stock certificate in hand.

And some people just like collecting stock and bond certificates, which typically are printed on specially made paper with ornate designs—including a security identification number. On all New York Stock Exchange certificates, a human figure with plainly discernible features must appear with at least a three-quarters frontal view.

But stock-market investors don't actually have to take possession of the certificate. They can request computerized book entry through the issuer, in which case the company issuing the shares keeps track of the investor's holding. Or they can take book entry through their brokerage firm, in which case their stock is held by the firm in a so-called street name account.

The major advantage for holding stock in a street name through a brokerage firm is that the certificates can't be lost or stolen, and time isn't wasted sending the certificate to the broker before selling.

A big disadvantage of the book-entry-only system, certificate fans say, is that it delays dividend and interest payments. Such payments go directly to certificate holders, but for book-entry shares, they pass through the brokerage firm—which pockets the funds for at least a brief time.

Northern Bank Note Co., which prints certificates, says 85% of the 115 bank trust officers it recently surveyed favor certificates. Among the reasons, the company says, are that certificates provide collateral for loans and makes it easier to give securities as gifts. Book-entry-only transactions can make the sale of securities more difficult because an investor can't simply take his stock to any brokerage firm to sell, the company added.

Merrill says that only 2.1% of its clients actually request certificates these days, despite the outcry over the issue by many investors.

The American Association of Individual Investors, a non-profit group of 110,000 investors, says 71% of its members favored "certificate-less" trading in stocks and other investments in an October 1990 survey. But James Cloonan, the group's president, says it's "essential" that investors have the option to keep their own certificates because it would make some investors feel more "secure."

SOURCE: William Power and Michael Siconolfi, "Stock Certificates Move a Step Closer to the Scrap Pile," *The Wall Street Journal*, July 10, 1991, p. C1. Reprinted by permission of *The Wall Street Journal*. © 1991 Dow Jones & Co., Inc. All rights reserved worldwide.

Continuity of Existence

Because routine transfers of ownership do not affect a corporation's affairs, the corporation is said to have continuity of existence. In this respect, a corporation is completely different from a partnership. In a partnership, any change in ownership technically results in discontinuance of the old partnership and formation of a new one.

(Many large professional service partnerships, however, follow procedures that provide for continuity with changes in ownership.)

Absence of Mutual Agency

The absence of mutual agency for a corporation means that a stockholder, acting as an owner, cannot enter into a contract for the corporation and bind the corporation to the contract. Mutual agency is present in a partnership, however, meaning that every partner is an agent for the firm with the authority to bind the partnership to contracts.

Capital-raising Capability

The limited liability of stockholders and the ease with which shares of stock may be transferred from one investor to another are attractive features to potential stockholders. These characteristics enhance the ability of the corporation to raise large amounts of capital by issuing shares of stock. Because both large and small investors may acquire ownership interests in a corporation, a wide spectrum of potential investors exists. Corporations with thousands of stockholders are not uncommon. The ability to accumulate and use tremendous amounts of capital makes the corporation the dominant form of business organization in the U.S. economy.

DISADVANTAGES OF THE CORPORATE FORM

Organization Costs

There are disadvantages to organizing as a corporation rather than as a proprietorship or partnership. We identify three disadvantages below.

Creating a corporation is more costly than organizing a proprietorship or partnership. The expenditures incurred to organize a corporation are charged to Organization Costs, an intangible asset account. These costs include attorney's fees, fees paid to the state, and costs of promoting the enterprise. Organization costs typically are amortized over a period of 5 to 10 years.

Taxation

As legal entities, corporations are subject to federal income taxes on their earnings, whether distributed or not. In addition, shareholders must pay income taxes on earnings received as dividends. In many small corporations in which the shareholders themselves manage the business affairs, large salaries may reduce earnings to a point where the double taxation feature is not onerous. However, the firm may have to justify the reasonableness of such salaries to the Internal Revenue Service. Under certain circumstances, a corporation with 35 or fewer shareholders may elect partnership treatment for tax purposes. Although partnerships must submit "information" tax returns, an income tax is not imposed on their earnings. Instead, the partners report their respective shares of partnership earnings on their individual income tax returns.

Usually, corporations are subject to state income taxes in the states in which they are incorporated or are doing business. They may also be subject to real estate, personal property, and franchise taxes.

Regulation and Supervision

Corporations are subject to greater degrees of regulation and supervision than are proprietorships and partnerships. Each state has the right to regulate the corporations it charters. State laws limit the powers a corporation may exercise, identify reports that must be filed, and define the rights and liabilities of stockholders. If stock is issued to the public, the corporation must comply with the laws governing the sale of corporate securities. Furthermore, corporations whose stock is listed and traded on organized security exchanges—such as the New York Stock Exchange—are subject to the various reporting and disclosure requirements of these exchanges.

OWNERS' EQUITY AND ORGANIZATIONAL FORMS

Differences arise between accounting for the owners' equity of a corporation and for that of a sole proprietorship or partnership. In a sole proprietorship, only a single owner's capital account is needed to reflect increases from capital contributions and net earnings as well as decreases from withdrawals and net losses. In practice, many sole proprietors keep a separate drawing account to record withdrawals of cash and other business assets. This separate record is kept only for convenience, however; no subdivision of the owner's capital account is required either by law or by accounting principles.

A similar situation exists in most partnerships, which customarily maintain capital and drawing accounts for each partner. A partnership is simply an association of two or more persons who agree to become joint owners of a business. Because more than one individual is involved in the business, a written agreement should govern the financial participation and business responsibilities of the partners. However, no legal or accounting requirement demands that a distinction be maintained between contributed capital and undistributed earnings.

A corporation, on the other hand, is subject to certain legal restrictions imposed by the government approving its creation. These restrictions focus on the distinction between contributed capital and retained earnings and make accounting for the owners' equity somewhat more complex for corporations than for other types of business organizations. Note that much of the accounting for corporate owners' equity is actually a polyglot of legal prescription and accounting convention. The detailed reporting of stockholders' equity transactions, however, provides analytical information that is often useful and, in many instances, required by law.

In a proprietorship or partnership, the individual owners' capital accounts indicate their relative interests in the business. The stockholders' equity section of a corporate balance sheet does not present individual stockholder accounts. A shareholder, however, can easily compute his or her interest in the corporation by calculating the proportion of the total shares outstanding that his or her shares represent. For example, if only one class of stock is outstanding and it totals 1,000 shares, an individual owning 200 shares has a 20% interest in the corporation's total stockholders' equity, which includes all contributed capital and retained earnings. The dollar amount of this interest, however, is a book amount, rarely coinciding with the market value. A stockholder who liquidates his or her investment would sell it at a price negotiated with a buyer or, if the stock is traded on a stock exchange, at the exchange's quoted market price.

PAR AND NO-PAR VALUE STOCK

OBJECTIVE ② EXPLAIN *the difference between par and no-par value stock.*

The corporate charter may specify a face value, or **par value,** for each share of a stock of any class. In the early days of corporate stock issuances, par value represented the market value of the stock when it was issued. In this century, however, par values have typically been set at amounts well below the stock's market value at date of issue. Par value today, therefore, has no economic significance.

Par value may have legal implications.[1] In some states, par value may represent the minimum amount that must be paid in per share of stock. If stock is issued at a *discount* (that is, at less than par value), the stockholder may have a liability for the discount should creditor claims remain unsatisfied after the company's liquidation. Issuing stock at a discount has been a rare event in this century, though, because boards of directors have generally established par values below market values at time

---

[1]For a more complete discussion of the legal implications of par value stock, see Philip McGough, "The Legal Signification of the Par Value of Common Stock: What Accounting Educators Should Know," *Issues in Accounting Education*, Fall 1988, pp. 330–50.

of issue. Following are some examples of corporations whose most basic class of stock (common stock) has a par value below $1.

Corporation	Common Stock Par Value per Share
THE CHARLES SCHWAB CORPORATION	$0.01
LANDS' END, INC.	0.01
PEPSICO., INC.	$0.01\frac{2}{3}$
PFIZER INC.	0.10
THE STRIDE RITE CORPORATION	0.50
GEORGIA-PACIFIC CORPORATION	0.80

Par value may also be used in some states to define a corporation's legal capital. *Legal capital* is the minimum amount of contributed capital that must remain in the corporation as a margin of protection for creditors. A distribution of assets to stockholders would not be allowed if it reduced stockholders' equity below the amount of legal capital. Given the role that par value may play in defining legal capital, accountants carefully segregate and record the par value of stock transactions in an appropriate capital stock account.

Most states permit the issuance of stock without a par value—that is, **no-par stock.** The company's board of directors usually sets a **stated value** for the no-par stock. In such cases, the stated value will determine the corporation's legal capital. Again, the stated value figure is usually set well below market value at time of issue, but in contrast to par value, the stated value is not printed on the stock certificate. For accounting purposes, stated value amounts are treated in a manner similar to par value amounts. In the absence of a stated value, the entire proceeds from the issuance of no-par stock will likely establish the corporation's legal capital.

TYPES OF STOCK

OBJECTIVE ③ IDENTIFY *and* **DISCUSS** *the types of stock and their basic rights.*

The amounts and kinds of stock that a corporation may issue are enumerated in the company's charter. Providing for several classes of stock permits the company to raise capital from different types of investors. The charter also specifies the corporation's **authorized stock**—the maximum number of shares of each class of stock that may be issued. A corporation that wishes to issue more shares than its authorized number must first amend its charter. Shares that have been sold and issued to stockholders constitute the **issued stock** of the corporation. Some of this stock may be repurchased by the corporation. Shares actually held by stockholders are called **outstanding stock,** whereas those reacquired by the corporation (and not retired) are *treasury stock.* We discuss treasury stock later in the chapter.

Common Stock

When only one class of stock is issued, it is called **common stock.** Common shareholders compose the basic ownership class. They have rights to vote, to share in earnings, to participate in additional issues of stock, and—in the case of liquidation—to share in assets after prior claims on the corporation have been settled. We now consider each of these rights.

As the owners of a corporation, the common shareholders elect the board of directors and vote on other matters requiring the approval of owners. Common shareholders are entitled to one vote for each share of stock they own. Owners who do not attend the annual stockholders' meetings may vote by proxy (this may be the case for most stockholders in large corporations).

A common stockholder has the right to a proportionate share of the corporation's earnings that are distributed as dividends. All earnings belong to the corporation, however, until the board of directors formally declares a dividend.

Each shareholder of a corporation has a **preemptive right** to maintain his or her proportionate interest in the corporation. If the company issues additional shares of stock, current owners of that type of stock receive the first opportunity to acquire, on a pro rata basis, the new shares. In certain situations, management may request shareholders to waive their preemptive rights. For example, the corporation may wish to issue additional stock to acquire another company. Further, stockholders of firms incorporated in some states do not receive preemptive rights.

A liquidating corporation converts its assets to a form suitable for distribution, usually cash, which it then distributes to parties having claims on the corporate assets. Any assets remaining after all claims have been satisfied belong to the residual ownership interest in the corporation—the common stockholders. These owners are entitled to the final distribution of the balance of the assets.

A company may occasionally use *classified* common stock; that is, it may issue more than one class of common stock. Two classes of common stock issued are identified as Class A and Class B. The two classes usually differ in either their respective dividend rights or their respective voting powers. Usually, classified common stock is issued when the organizers of the corporation wish to acquire funds from the public while retaining voting control. To illustrate, let us assume 10,000 shares of Class A stock are issued to the public at $40 per share, and 20,000 shares of Class B stock are issued to the organizers at $5 per share. If each shareholder receives one vote per share of stock, the Class B stockholders have twice as many votes as the Class A stockholders. Yet the total investment of Class B stockholders is significantly less than that of the Class A stockholders. To offset the difference in the voting power per dollar of investment, the Class A stockholders may have better dividend rights, such as being entitled to dividends in early years, whereas the Class B stockholders may not receive dividends until a certain level of earning power is reached.

Preferred Stock

Preferred stock is a class of stock with various characteristics that distinguish it from common stock. Preferred stock has one or more preferences over common stock, usually with reference to (1) dividends and (2) assets when the corporation liquidates. To determine the features of a particular issue, we must examine the stock contract. The majority of preferred issues, however, have certain typical features, which we discuss below.

DIVIDEND PREFERENCE

When the board of directors declares a distribution of earnings, preferred stockholders are entitled to a certain annual amount of dividends before common stockholders receive any distribution. The amount is usually specified in the preferred stock contract as a percentage of the par value of the stock or in dollars per share if the stock does not have a par value. Thus, if the preferred stock has a $100 par value and a 6% dividend rate, the preferred shareholders receive $6 per share in dividends. However, the amount is owed to the stockholders only if declared.

Preferred dividends are usually **cumulative**—that is, regular dividends to preferred stockholders omitted in past years must be paid in addition to the current year's dividend before any distribution is made to common shareholders. If a preferred stock is noncumulative, omitted dividends do not carry forward. Because investors normally consider the noncumulative feature unattractive, noncumulative preferred stock is rarely issued.

To illustrate the difference between cumulative and noncumulative preferred stock, assume that a company ending its second year of operations has outstanding 1,000 shares of $100 par value, 6% preferred stock and 10,000 shares of $20 par value common stock. The company declared no dividends last year. This year a total dividend of $27,000 is declared. The distribution of the $27,000 to the two stockholder classes depends on whether the preferred stock is cumulative or noncumulative. If it is cumulative, preferred shareholders receive $12 per share before common shareholders receive anything.

	Preferred	Common	Total
Outstanding stock (total par value)	$100,000	$200,000	$300,000
Preferred stock is cumulative			
Preferred dividends in arrears (6%)	$ 6,000		$ 6,000
Regular preferred dividend (6%)	6,000		6,000
Remainder to common		$15,000	15,000
Total distribution	$12,000	$15,000	$27,000
Preferred stock is noncumulative			
Regular preferred dividend (6%)	$6,000		$ 6,000
Remainder to common		$21,000	21,000
Total distribution	$6,000	$21,000	$27,000

Dividends in arrears (that is, omitted in past years) on cumulative preferred stock are not an accounting liability and do not appear in the liability section of the balance sheet. They do not become an obligation of the corporation until the board of directors formally declares such dividends. Any arrearages are typically disclosed to investors in a footnote to the balance sheet.

Ordinarily, preferred stockholders receive a fixed amount and do not participate further in distributions made by the corporation. Occasionally, however, the stock contract may make the preferred a **participating** stock. A participating preferred stock shares dividend distributions with common stock beyond the regular preferred dividend rate. To illustrate the participating feature, let us assume that our previous company has outstanding 1,000 shares of $100 par value, 6% *fully participating* cumulative preferred stock and 10,000 shares of $20 par value common stock. Assume also that the company declares total dividends of $27,000 and that no preferred dividends are in arrears. The distribution would be made as follows:

	Preferred	Common	Total
Outstanding stock (total par value)	$100,000	$200,000	$300,000
Preferred dividends in arrears	$ –0–		$ –0–
Regular dividend (6%) and matching rate to common (6%)	6,000	$12,000	18,000
Remainder of $9,000 ($27,000 − $18,000) divided to give each class the same rate: $9,000/$300,000 = 3%	3,000	6,000	9,000
Total distribution	$9,000	$18,000	$27,000
Rate of distribution (based on total par value)	9%	9%	

Note that, after the preferred stock is accorded its regular 6% dividend, a like rate of 6% ($12,000) is allocated to the common stock. The remaining $9,000 is then apportioned so both classes of stock receive the same *rate* of distribution. This rate is determined by dividing the remainder to be distributed by the total par value of both classes of stock ($300,000). It is important to note that the preferred stock does not participate until the common stock is accorded an amount corresponding to the regular preferred dividend rate. Also, a preferred stock's dividend preference applies only to its regular dividend rate; it does not apply to the participation feature.

Any arrearage on cumulative preferred stock must first be awarded to the preferred shareholders. Therefore, had there been one year's arrearage on the fully participating stock in the foregoing example, $12,000 ($6,000 dividends in arrears and $6,000 current dividends) would have been allocated to the preferred stock and then the normal 6%, or $12,000, to the common stock. Of the remaining $3,000, $1,000 would be assigned to the preferred stock and $2,000 to the common stock.

Preferred stock may also be *partially* participating. For example, suppose that the preferred shares participate to 8%. They would then be entitled only to an additional 2% over their regular 6% dividend, and any remaining amount would be accorded to the common shares. The Demonstration Problem at the end of the chapter illustrates a dividend distribution to a partially participating preferred stock.

If either the common stock or the preferred stock is no-par value stock, preferred stock participation is determined on some basis other than total par values. For example, the participation may be achieved by allocating dividends of equal dollar amounts per share to each class of stock.

ASSET DISTRIBUTION PREFERENCE

Preferred stockholders normally have a preference over common stockholders as to the receipt of assets when a corporation liquidates. As the corporation goes out of business, the claims of creditors are settled first. Then preferred stockholders have the right to receive assets equal to the par value of their stock or a larger stated liquidation value per share before any assets are distributed to common stockholders. The preferred stockholders' preference to assets in liquidation also includes any dividends in arrears.

OTHER FEATURES

Although preferred shareholders do not ordinarily have the right to vote in the election of directors, this right can be accorded by contract. Some state laws require that all stock issued by a corporation be given voting rights. Sometimes, a preferred stock contract confers full or partial voting rights under certain conditions—for example, when dividends have not been paid for a specified period.

Preferred stock contracts may contain features that cause the stock to resemble the common stock equity at one end of a spectrum or a debt obligation at the other end. The stock may, for example, be *convertible* into common stock at some specified rate. With this feature, the market price of the preferred often moves with that of the common. When the price of the common stock rises, the value of the conversion feature is enhanced. Preferred stock may also be convertible into long-term debt securities (bonds).

Preferred stock may be *callable*, which means the corporation can redeem the stock after a length of time and at a price specified in the contract. The call feature makes the stock similar to a bond, which frequently is callable or has a limited life. Most preferred stocks are callable, with the call or redemption price set slightly above the original issuance price.

To be successful in selling its preferred stock, a corporation often must cater to current market vogues. Features are added or omitted, depending on market conditions and the desires of the investor group the corporation wishes to attract. Management must balance market requirements with its own goals. Sometimes management must compromise and issue securities that it hopes to change over time, perhaps through conversion or refinancing, to arrive at the desired financial plan.

Preferred stocks appeal to investors who want a steady rate of return that is normally somewhat higher than that on bonds. These investors often believe that preferred stock entails less risk than common stock, although the common will pay off more if the company does well.

From both the legal and the accounting standpoint, preferred stock is part of stockholders' equity. Dividends are distributions of earnings and, unlike interest on bonds, are not shown as expenses on the income statement. Also, because of the legal classification of preferred stock as stockholders' equity, the company cannot deduct dividends as expenses for income tax purposes, whereas interest on debt can be deducted as an expense.

STOCK ISSUANCES FOR CASH

In issuing its stock, a corporation may use the services of an investment banker, a specialist in marketing securities to investors. The investment banker may *underwrite* a stock issue; that is, the banker buys the stock from the corporation and resells it to investors. The corporation does not risk being unable to sell its stock. The under-

OBJECTIVE **4** **DESCRIBE** *the accounting for issuances of stock for cash, by subscription, and for noncash assets.*

writer bears this risk in return for the profits generated by selling the stock to investors at a price higher than that paid the corporation. An investment banker who is unwilling to underwrite a stock issue may handle it on a *best efforts* basis. In this case, the investment banker agrees to sell as many shares as possible at a set price, but the corporation bears the risk of unsold stock.

When capital stock is issued, the appropriate capital stock account is always credited with the par value of the shares, or if the stock is no-par, with its stated value, if any. The asset received for the stock (usually cash) is debited, and any difference is placed in an appropriately named account.

To illustrate the journal entries to record various stock issuances for cash, let us assume that in its first year of operations a corporation issued three different types of stock, as follows:

1. Issued 1,000 shares of $100 par value, 9% preferred stock at $107 cash per share.

Cash	107,000	
9% Preferred Stock		100,000
Paid-in Capital in Excess of Par Value		7,000

In this transaction, the preferred stock is issued at a *premium* (that is, at more than par value). The par value of the preferred stock issued is credited to the 9% Preferred Stock account and the $7,000 premium is credited to Paid-in Capital in Excess of Par Value. If there is more than one class of par value stock, the account title may indicate the class of stock to which the premium relates, in this case Paid-in Capital in Excess of Par Value—9% Preferred Stock. An alternative account title for the $7,000 premium is Premium on Preferred Stock. The account title used in the journal entry, however, is more typical.

2. Issued 1,000 shares of $100 par value, 6% preferred stock at $98 cash per share.

Cash	98,000	
Excess of Par Value over Amount Paid In	2,000	
6% Preferred Stock		100,000

This preferred stock is issued at a discount. Again, a capital stock account (in this case, 6% Preferred Stock) is credited for the par value of the shares issued. The account Excess of Par Value over Amount Paid In (or, alternatively, Discount on Preferred Stock) is debited for the $2,000 discount.

3. Issued 5,000 shares of no-par common stock, stated value $20, at $30 cash per share.

Cash	150,000	
Common Stock		100,000
Paid-in Capital in Excess of Stated Value		50,000

When no-par stock has a stated value, as in entry 3, the stated value of the total shares issued is credited to the proper capital stock account, and any additional amount received is credited to an account called Paid-in Capital in Excess of Stated Value. If no stated value for no-par stock exists, the entire proceeds should be credited to the appropriate capital stock account. In entry 3, if the common stock had no stated value, the entire $150,000 amount would have been credited to the Common Stock account.

These three stock issuances are reflected in Exhibit 15-2, which presents the stockholders' equity section in the company's year-end balance sheet. (Retained earnings are assumed to be $25,000.) The stockholders' equity section is divided into two major categories: **1** paid-in capital and **2** retained earnings. **Paid-in capital** is the amount of capital contributed to the corporation by various transactions, such as by

EXHIBIT 15—2	STOCKHOLDERS' EQUITY SECTION: VARIOUS STOCK ISSUANCES

Paid-in Capital:

9% Preferred Stock, $100 Par Value, 1,000 shares authorized, issued, and outstanding	$100,000	
Paid-in Capital in Excess of Par Value	7,000	$107,000
6% Preferred Stock, $100 Par Value, 1,000 shares authorized, issued, and outstanding	$100,000	
1 Excess of Par Value over Amount Paid In	(2,000)	98,000
No-par Common Stock, Stated Value $20, 10,000 shares authorized; 5,000 shares issued and outstanding	$100,000	
Paid-in Capital in Excess of Stated Value	50,000	150,000
Total Paid-in Capital		$355,000
2 Retained Earnings		25,000
Total Stockholders' Equity		$380,000

issuance of preferred stock and common stock. The capital contributed by owners through the issuance of stock is broken down between the legal capital (par or stated value of the stock) and amounts received in excess of the legal capital (or, in rare instances, the discount below legal capital). Later in this chapter we discuss other events (treasury stock transactions and donations) that may increase a corporation's paid-in capital. *Retained earnings* represent the cumulative net earnings and losses of the company that have not been distributed to owners as dividends.

In Exhibit 15-2, we assume that all authorized amounts of both classes of preferred stock and half of the 10,000 shares of common stock authorized have been issued. Note that both the premium on the 9% preferred stock and the excess received over stated value of the no-par common stock are added to the par and stated values, respectively. On the other hand, the $2,000 discount on the 6% preferred stock is deducted from par value to show the amount received for this class. All the accounts in the illustration have credit balances in the general ledger, except Excess of Par Value over Amount Paid In on the 6% preferred stock, which has a $2,000 debit balance.

STOCK SUBSCRIPTIONS

Sometimes a corporation may sell stock directly to investors on a subscription basis. The subscription contract often provides for installment payments and shares are not issued until full payment is received. When subscriptions to commmon shares are obtained, the corporation debits the amount to an account titled Stock Subscriptions Receivable—Common, credits a paid-in capital account called *Common Stock Subscribed* for the par or stated value of the shares subscribed, and, if the subscription price exceeds the stock's par or stated value, credits the usual paid-in capital account for such excess amounts. Some accountants classify Stock Subscriptions Receivable—Common as an asset; others classify it as a contra stockholders' equity account so that the equity increase will only equal the amount of cash received. (We will use the asset classification.) The Common Stock Subscribed account signifies that the shares have not yet been fully paid for or issued. This account is classified on the balance sheet immediately after the regular Common Stock account. When the stock is issued after receipt of all payments, the journal entry debits Common Stock Subscribed and credits Common Stock.

To illustrate the journal entries for stock subscription transactions, let us assume that 5,000 shares of $10 par value common stock were sold on subscription for $12 a share, paid in installments of $4 and $8. The entries would be as follows:

To record receipt of subscriptions

Stock Subscriptions Receivable—Common	60,000	
Common Stock Subscribed		50,000
Paid-in Capital in Excess of Par Value		10,000
Received subscriptions for 5,000 shares at $12 per share.		

To record collection of first installment

Cash	20,000	
Stock Subscriptions Receivable—Common		20,000
Collected first installment of $4 per share.		

To record collection of final installment and issuance of shares

Cash	40,000	
Stock Subscriptions Receivable—Common		40,000
Collected final installment of $8 per share.		
Common Stock Subscribed	50,000	
Common Stock		50,000
Issued 5,000 common shares on receipt of final installment payment.		

STOCK ISSUANCES FOR ASSETS OTHER THAN CASH

When stock is issued for property other than cash or for services, the accountant must carefully determine the amount recorded. We should not assume that the par or stated value of the shares issued automatically sets a value for the property or services received. In the early years of U.S. corporations, such an assumption frequently resulted in the recording and reporting of excessive asset valuations.

Property or services acquired should be recorded at their current fair value or at the fair value of the stock issued, whichever is more clearly determinable. If the stock is actively traded on a securities exchange, the market price of the stock issued may indicate an appropriate value. For example, if the current market price is $14 per share and 5,000 shares are issued for a parcel of land, this land may be valued, in the absence of other price indicators, at $70,000. An effort should be made, however, to determine a fair value for the property. Certainly, all aspects of the transaction should be carefully scrutinized to ascertain that the number of shares issued was objectively determined. If no market value for the stock is available, we would seek an independently determined value for the property or services received.

Let us suppose the stock issued for the land is $10 par value common stock and its market value is the best indicator of the property's fair value. The entry to record the transaction would be the following:

Land	70,000	
Common Stock		50,000
Paid-in Capital in Excess of Par Value		20,000
To record issuance of 5,000 shares of common stock for land valued at $70,000.		

STOCK SPLITS

OBJECTIVE 5 DEFINE *and* DISCUSS *stock splits.*

Occasionally, a corporation reduces the par or stated value of its common stock and issues additional shares to its stockholders. This type of transaction, called a **stock split,** does not change the balances of the stockholders' equity accounts—only a memorandum entry is made in the records to show the altered par or stated value of the stock. For example, if a company that has outstanding 10,000 shares of $10 par value common stock announced a 2-for-1 stock split, it would simply reduce the par value of its stock to $5 per share. After the stock split, each shareholder would have twice the number of shares held before the split.

The major reason for a stock split is to reduce the market price of the stock. Some companies like their stock to sell within a certain price range. They may believe that higher prices narrow the breadth of their market, because investors often prefer to buy 100-share lots (purchases of fewer shares are odd-lot purchases and may be subject to higher brokers' fees). Many small investors cannot afford to purchase high-priced stocks in 100-share lots.

When shares are selling below the desired price, a *reverse split* can be accomplished by increasing the par value of the shares and reducing the number outstanding. Such transactions are encountered less frequently than stock splits.

TREASURY STOCK

OBJECTIVE 6 EXPLAIN *the accounting for treasury stock and donated capital.*

When a corporation reacquires its own outstanding shares for a purpose other than retiring them, the reacquired shares are called **treasury stock.** Treasury stock may be purchased for a variety of reasons, which include reissuing them to officers and employees in profit-sharing schemes or stock-option plans. Whatever the purpose, the corporation is reducing owner capital for a period of time. Consequently, treasury stock is not regarded as an asset. The shares do not carry voting privileges or pre-emptive rights, are not paid dividends, and do not receive assets on the corporation's liquidation.

Because treasury stock is stock that has been issued before, it differs in one significant way from unissued stock. If the treasury stock was fully paid for when first issued (that is, it was initially issued for an amount equal to or more than its par value), then it may be reissued at less than par value without any discount liability attaching to it. As we mentioned earlier, some states may attach a liability to shares initially issued at a discount, whereas other states do not even permit such issuances.

Purchase of Treasury Stock

Accountants commonly record treasury stock at cost, debiting the Treasury Stock account. The aggregate cost is deducted from total stockholders' equity in the balance sheet. Suppose a corporation had outstanding 20,000 shares of $10 par value common stock and then repurchased 1,000 shares at $12 per share. The entry for the repurchase would be as follows:

Treasury Stock—Common	12,000	
Cash		12,000
To record purchase of 1,000 shares of treasury stock at $12 per share.		

If a balance sheet is prepared after this transaction, the stockholders' equity section would appear as follows (amounts for paid-in capital in excess of par value and retained earnings are assumed):

Stockholders' Equity

Paid-in Capital:	
Common Stock, $10 Par Value, authorized and issued 20,000 shares; 1,000 shares in treasury, 19,000 shares outstanding	$200,000
Paid-in Capital in Excess of Par Value	20,000
Total Paid-in Capital	$220,000
Retained Earnings	40,000
	$260,000
Less: Treasury Stock (1,000 shares) at Cost	12,000
Total Stockholders' Equity	$248,000

Note that the $200,000 par value of all *issued* stock is shown, although 1,000 shares are no longer outstanding. The total cost of the 1,000 shares, however, is later deducted from total stockholders' equity.

In the above owners' equity situation, the corporation apparently has $40,000 retained earnings unfettered by any legal restrictions; the entire amount might be distributed as dividends if the corporation's cash position permits. In many states, however, the corporation must restrict (reduce) the retained earnings available for declaration of dividends by the cost of any treasury stock held. Then, in our illustration, only $28,000 in retained earnings would be available for dividends. The statutory restriction exists because a corporation that reduces its paid-in capital by repurchasing shares must protect creditors by "buffering" the reduced capital with its retained earnings in an amount equal to the resources expended.

Reissue of Treasury Stock for More than Cost

The corporation may accept any price for the reissue of treasury stock. Treasury stock transactions are not part of a firm's normal operating activities, and any additional capital obtained from reissuing such shares at more than cost is not regarded as earnings and is not added to retained earnings. The corporation should regard any additional amounts paid by subsequent purchasers as paid-in capital. Therefore, increases in capital from the reissue of purchased treasury shares are credited to a paid-in capital account such as Paid-in Capital from Treasury Stock.

Let us assume that 500 shares of the treasury stock are resold by the corporation at $13 per share. The entry to record the reissue would be as follows:

Cash	6,500	
Treasury Stock—Common		6,000
Paid-in Capital from Treasury Stock		500
To record sale of 500 shares of treasury stock at $13 per share.		

Observe that Treasury Stock—Common is credited at the cost price of $12 per share, a basis consistent with the original debit to the account. The excess over cost is credited to Paid-in Capital from Treasury Stock.

Reissue of Treasury Stock for Less than Cost

When treasury stock is reissued for an amount less than the treasury stock's cost, the difference first reduces any previously recorded paid-in capital from treasury stock for that class of stock. If there is not enough paid-in capital from treasury stock, the remaining amount is debited to Retained Earnings. To illustrate, assume that the remaining 500 treasury shares from our previous example are reissued for $9 per share. The journal entry would be as follows:

Cash	4,500	
Paid-in Capital from Treasury Stock	500	
Retained Earnings	1,000	
Treasury Stock—Common		6,000
To record sale of 500 shares of treasury stock at $9 per share.		

DONATED CAPITAL

Occasionaliy, a corporation may acquire treasury stock when a shareholder donates shares to the corporation. Perhaps the donor received the shares in exchange for a patent on a product and now wishes the corporation to raise additional capital to promote and market the product. As noted, because treasury shares represent stock that has been issued once, they can be reissued at any price. Thus, the corporation may find it easier to market these shares than to sell unissued shares, especially if investors have shown little interest in the venture and the unissued shares could be sold only at a discount.

The reacquisition of treasury shares by donation, whatever the reason, is usually not recorded—except for a memorandum entry—at the time of reacquisition. When such shares are subsequently sold, the amount received is credited to **Donated Capital,** a form of paid-in capital. To illustrate, suppose a stockholder donates 500 shares of common stock to a corporation, which then resells the shares at $25 per share. The entries for these transactions would be as follows:

To record receipt of donated treasury shares

(Memorandum) Received 500 shares of donated common stock.

To record sale of donated treasury shares

Cash	12,500	
Donated Capital		12,500
To record sale of 500 donated shares at $25 per share.		

The Donated Capital account may also be credited for the fair market value of any property donated to the corporation, assuming that a value can be determined objectively. For example, communities wanting to attract industry have donated land sites to corporations. If fair values can be established by appraisal or by study of prices for similar local property, the amount may be recorded.

Assume that a city donates a plant site to a corporation. An independent appraiser values the land at $26,000, which is accepted by the board of directors as an appropriate valuation. The entry to record the donation would be as follows:

Land	26,000	
Donated Capital		26,000
To record receipt of donated land valued at $26,000.		

Exhibit 15-3 illustrates the presentation of donated capital in stockholders' equity, along with examples of other paid-in capital items that we have discussed in this chapter.

BOOK VALUE PER SHARE

OBJECTIVE 7 DEFINE *and* DISCUSS *the terms book value, market value, and liquidation value per share of stock.*

Book value per share is often calculated for a class of stock, particularly common stock. **Book value per share,** which is the dollar amount of net assets represented by one share of stock, is computed by dividing the amount of stockholders' equity associated with a class of stock by the number of outstanding shares in that class. The computation uses stockholders' equity, because a corporation's net assets (assets − liabilities) equals its stockholders' equity. The measure is based on amounts recorded in the books and presented in the balance sheet—hence, the term *book* value per share.

For example, assume the following stockholders' equity section of a balance sheet:

Stockholders' Equity

Paid-in Capital:	
Common Stock, $50 Par Value, 5,000 shares authorized, issued, and outstanding	$250,000
Paid-in Capital in Excess of Par Value	100,000
Total Paid-in Capital	$350,000
Retained Earnings	80,000
Total Stockholders' Equity	$430,000

Because this corporation has only one class of stock, the book value per share is the total stockholders' equity divided by the shares outstanding—that is, $430,000/5,000 = $86. Note that the divisor is shares outstanding; it does not include shares of unissued common stock or treasury stock.

To compute book values per share when more than one class of stock is outstanding, we must determine the portion of stockholders' equity attributable to each class of stock. Preferred stocks are assigned the amounts their owners would receive

EXHIBIT 15—3	STOCKHOLDERS' EQUITY SECTION: VARIOUS PAID-IN CAPITAL ITEMS

Paid-in Capital:

6% Preferred Stock, $100 Par Value, 2,000 shares authorized, issued, and outstanding	$200,000	
Paid-in Capital in Excess of Par Value—Preferred Stock	30,000	$230,000
Common Stock, $1 Par Value, 250,000 shares authorized; 150,000 shares issued, 5,000 shares subscribed; and 3,000 shares in the treasury	$150,000	
Common Stock Subscribed, 5,000 shares	5,000	
Paid-in Capital in Excess of Par Value—Common Stock	455,000	610,000
Paid-in Capital from Treasury Stock		4,000
Donated Capital		26,000
Total Paid-in Capital		$870,000
Retained Earnings		115,000
		$985,000
Less: Treasury Stock (3,000 common shares) at Cost		15,000
Total Stockholders' Equity		$970,000

if the corporation liquidated—that is, the liquidation preference of preferred stock plus any dividend arrearages on cumulative stock. The common shares receive the remainder of the stockholders' equity. For example, assume the following stockholders' equity section:

Stockholders' Equity

Paid-in Capital:

9% Preferred Stock, $100 Par Value, 1,000 shares authorized, issued, and outstanding	$100,000
Paid-in Capital in Excess of Par Value—Preferred Stock	5,000
No-par Common Stock, Stated Value $40, 3,000 shares authorized, issued, and outstanding	120,000
Paid-in Capital in Excess of Stated Value—Common Stock	6,000
Total Paid-in Capital	$231,000
Retained Earnings	73,000
Total Stockholders' Equity	$304,000

Assume that the stated liquidation preference is $103 per share for the preferred stock, with no dividends in arrears. The book value per share for the preferred stock, therefore, is also $103. The computation for the book value per share of common stock follows:

Total stockholders' equity	$304,000
Less: Equity applicable to preferred stock (1,000 × $103)	103,000
Equity allocated to common stock	$201,000
Shares of common stock outstanding	3,000
Book value per share of common stock ($201,000/3,000)	$67

The book value per share of common stock may be used in many ways. Management may include the book value per share—and any changes in it for the year—in the annual report to stockholders. Two corporations negotiating a merger through an exchange of stock may find their respective book values per share to be one of several factors influencing the final exchange ratio. Or an individual may acquire an option to buy stock in the future, with the purchase price related to the future book value of the stock. Also, book values are used by many investors in selecting stocks to buy. Such investors concentrate on buying stocks that are selling below or close to their book value because they believe this is the best way to identify undervalued stocks.

MARKET VALUE AND LIQUIDATION VALUE

The book value of common stock is different from its market value and its liquidation value. The **market value per share** is the current price at which the stock may be bought or sold. This price reflects such things as the earnings potential of the company, dividends, book values, capital structure, and general economic conditions. Because book value is only one of several variables influencing market price (and usually not the most significant one at that), market values and book values rarely coincide.

The **liquidation value per share** of common stock is the amount that would be received if the corporation liquidated. The amounts recorded in the books do not portray liquidation proceeds, so no correlation exists between liquidation values and book values of common stocks. Liquidation values may not be easy to determine, but corporate managements must be alert to the relationship between the market value and the approximate liquidation value of their common stock. A corporation whose liquidation value exceeds its market value may be the object of a "raid." A raider acquires control of a corporation (by buying stock at market values) and then liquidates the business (at liquidation values), keeping the difference as a gain.

ANALYTICAL APPLICATION

RETURN ON COMMON STOCKHOLDERS' EQUITY

OBJECTIVE 8 DEFINE return on common stockholders' equity *and* EXPLAIN *its use.*

A financial ratio of particular interest to common stockholders is the return on common stockholders' equity. This ratio measures the profitability of the common stockholders' equity in the corporation. The **return on common stockholders' equity** is computed as follows:

$$\text{Return on Common Stockholders' Equity} = \frac{\text{Net Income} - \text{Preferred Dividends}}{\text{Average Common Stockholders' Equity}}$$

By subtracting the preferred dividend requirements from net income, the numerator represents the net income available to the common stockholders. The denominator averages the common stockholders' equity for the year (sum the beginning and ending common stockholders' equity and divide the sum by 2). If a corporation has preferred stock outstanding, the common stockholders' equity is computed by subtracting the preferred stockholders' equity (the same equity as is used to compute the preferred stock's book value per share) from total stockholders' equity.

To illustrate the computation of return on common stockholders' equity, we will use financial data from a recent annual report of BALL CORPORATION, headquartered in Muncie, Indiana. Ball manufactures a variety of packaging, industrial, and consumer products (glass home canning jars, for example) and provides aerospace systems services to the federal government. The financial data are as follows (in millions of dollars):

Net income	$ 50.2
Preferred dividends	5.8
Preferred stockholders' equity, beginning of year	1.3
Preferred stockholders' equity, end of year	53.6
Common stockholders' equity, beginning of year	383.0
Common stockholders' equity, end of year	403.9

Ball Corporation's return on common stockholders' equity for the year is 11.3%, computed as follows: ($50.2 − $5.8)/[($383.0 + $403.9)/2]. Ball Corporation's return on common stockholders' equity for the preceding year was 8.2%, therefore, the 11.3% return represents a nice improvement over the preceding year. On the other hand, one of the corporate financial objectives specified by Ball is to achieve a minimum return on common stockholders' equity of 15%. An 11.3% return falls below the specified financial objective.

KEY POINTS FOR CHAPTER OBJECTIVES

1 DEFINE and DISCUSS the corporate form of organization (pp. 536–540).
- A corporation is a separate legal entity chartered by the state in which it is formed or, in some cases, by the federal government.
- The liability of corporate shareholders is usually limited to their ownership investment, whereas claims against partners and sole proprietors may extend to their personal resources.
- Unlike proprietorships and partnerships, corporations must report paid-in capital separately from the accumulated balance of retained earnings. Distributions to shareholders are limited by the amount of retained earnings and other capital as specified by state law.

2 EXPLAIN the difference between par and no-par value stock (pp. 540–541).
- Par value is the face value printed on a stock certificate. It has no economic significance but may have legal significance.
- No-par stock has no face value printed on the stock certificate, although generally the board of directors sets a stated value for the stock.

3 IDENTIFY and DISCUSS the types of stock and their basic rights (pp. 541–544).
- Common stock represents a corporation's basic ownership class of stock.
- Preferred stocks may differ from common stock in any of several characteristics. Typically, preferred stocks have some type of dividend preference and a prior claim to assets in liquidation.

4 DESCRIBE the accounting for issuances of stock for cash, by subscription, and for noncash assets (pp. 544–547).
- When capital stock is issued, the appropriate capital stock account is credited with the par or stated value of the shares issued; the asset received for the stock is debited; and any difference is placed in an appropriately named account.

5 DEFINE and DISCUSS stock splits (pp. 547–548).
- Stock splits change the par or stated value of stock and affect the number of shares outstanding. Only a memorandum notation records stock splits.

6 EXPLAIN the accounting for treasury stock and donated capital (pp. 548–550).
- Treasury stock represents reacquired shares of the firm's own stock. It is commonly recorded at cost and deducted from total stockholders' equity in the balance sheet.
- Donated capital results from gifts to the corporation that, if feasible, should be recorded at fair market value.

7 DEFINE and DISCUSS the terms book value, market value, and liquidation value per share of stock (pp. 550–552).
- The book value per share of common stock indicates the net assets, based on recorded amounts, associated with a share of common stock. Common stock book values are different from market values or liquidation values.

8 ANALYTICAL APPLICATION: DEFINE *return on common stockholders' equity* and EXPLAIN its use (pp. 552–553).
- Return on common stockholders' equity is computed as (Net Income − Preferred Dividends)/Average Common Stockholders' Equity. It indicates the profitability of the common stockholders' equity.

SELF-TEST QUESTIONS FOR REVIEW

(Answers follow the Solution to Demonstration Problem.)

1. The liability of stockholders for corporation actions is usually
   a. Unlimited.
   b. Limited to the par or stated value of the stock they hold.
   c. Limited to the amount of their investment in the corporation.
   d. Limited to the amount of the corporation's retained earnings.

2. Which type of stock may have dividends in arrears?
   a. Cumulative preferred stock.
   b. Common stock.
   c. Noncumulative preferred stock.
   d. Treasury stock.

3. Wyler Company issues 20,000 shares of $10 par value common stock in exchange for a building with a current fair value of $1,000,000. In recording this transaction, what amount should be credited to Paid-in Capital in Excess of Par Value?
   a. $1,000,000
   b. $200,000
   c. $800,000
   d. $980,000

4. Which of the following accounts has a normal debit balance?
   a. Common Stock Subscribed.
   b. Paid-in Capital in Excess of Stated Value.
   c. Donated Capital.
   d. Treasury Stock.

5. Caffey Corporation has a total stockholders' equity of $1,860,000. Caffey has 20,000 shares of $25 par value, 6% preferred stock issued and outstanding, and 60,000 shares of $10 par value common stock issued and outstanding. The preferred stock has a liquidation preference of $27 per share and no dividends in arrears. What is the book value per share of common stock?
   a. $31.00
   b. $22.00
   c. $22.67
   d. $10.00

DEMONSTRATION PROBLEM FOR REVIEW

Goodwin Corporation has outstanding 6,000 shares of $50 par value, 5% preferred stock and 30,000 shares of $30 par value common stock. This year the company declares and pays a total cash dividend of $90,000.

REQUIRED

For each of the following independent cases, calculate the total dividends paid to each class of stock.
a. The preferred stock is noncumulative and nonparticipating.
b. The preferred stock is cumulative and nonparticipating; dividends are in arrears one year.
c. The preferred stock is cumulative and participating to 7%; there is no dividend arrearage.
d. The preferred stock is cumulative and fully participating; there is no dividend arrearage.
e. The preferred stock is cumulative and fully participating; dividends are in arrears three years.

SOLUTION TO DEMONSTRATION PROBLEM

	Preferred	Common	Total
Outstanding stock (total par value)	$300,000	$900,000	$1,200,000
a. Regular preferred dividend (5%)	$15,000		$15,000
Remainder to common		$75,000	75,000
Total distribution	$15,000	$75,000	$90,000
b. Dividend in arrears one year (5%)	$15,000		$15,000
Regular preferred dividend (5%)	15,000		15,000
Remainder to common		$60,000	60,000
Total distribution	$30,000	$60,000	$90,000
c. Regular preferred dividend (5%) and matching rate to common (5%)	$15,000	$45,000	$60,000
Preferred participation dividend (2%) and matching rate to common (2%)	6,000	18,000	24,000
Remainder to common		6,000	6,000
Total distribution	$21,000	$69,000	$90,000
d. Regular preferred dividend (5%) and matching rate to common (5%)	$15,000	$45,000	$60,000
Remainder of $30,000 divided to give each class the same rate: $30,000/$1,200,000 = 2.5%	7,500	22,500	30,000
Total distribution	$22,500	$67,500	$90,000

e. Dividends in arrears three years [3 × 5% = 15%]	$45,000	$45,000
Regular preferred dividend (5%)	15,000	15,000
Remainder to common (not enough to achieve a 5% rate)	$30,000	30,000
Total distribution	$60,000 $30,000	$90,000

ANSWERS TO SELF-TEST QUESTIONS

1. c, p. 537 **2.** a, p. 542 **3.** c, p. 547 **4.** d, p. 548 **5.** b, p. 550

GLOSSARY OF KEY TERMS USED IN THIS CHAPTER

articles of incorporation A document prepared by persons organizing a corporation in the United States that sets forth the structure and purpose of the corporation and specifics regarding the stock to be issued (p. 536).

authorized stock The maximum number of shares in a class of stock that a corporation may issue (p. 541).

book value per share The dollar amount of net assets represented by one share of stock; computed by dividing the amount of stockholders' equity associated with a class of stock by the outstanding shares of that class of stock (p. 550).

common stock The basic ownership class of corporate capital stock, carrying the rights to vote, share in earnings, participate in future stock issues, and share in any liquidation proceeds after prior claims have been settled (p. 541).

corporation A legal entity created by the granting of a charter from an appropriate governmental authority and owned by stockholders who have limited liability for corporate debt (p. 536).

cumulative (preferred stock) A feature associated with preferred stock whereby any dividends in arrears must be paid before dividends may be paid on common stock (p. 542).

donated capital The amount received by a corporation from the donation of assets or the donation of the corporation's own stock (p. 550).

issued stock Shares of stock that have been sold and issued to stockholders; issued stock may be either outstanding or in the treasury (p. 541).

liquidation value per share The amount that would be received by a holder of a share of stock if the corporation liquidated (p. 552).

market value per share The current price at which shares of stock may be bought or sold (p. 552).

no-par stock Stock that does not have a par value (p. 541).

outstanding stock Shares of stock that are currently owned by stockholders (p. 541).

paid in capital The amount of capital contributed to a corporation by various transactions; the primary source of paid-in capital is from the issuance of shares of stock (p. 545).

participating (preferred stock) A feature associated with preferred stock that permits stockholders to share in dividend distributions with common stockholders beyond the preferred stock's regular dividend rate (p. 543).

par value (stock) An amount specified in the corporate charter for each share of stock and imprinted on the face of each stock certificate. Often determines the legal capital of the corporation (p. 540).

preemptive right The right of a stockholder to maintain his or her proportionate interest in a corporation by having the right to purchase an appropriate share of any new stock issue (p. 541).

preferred stock A class of corporate capital stock typically receiving priority over common stock in dividend payments and distribution of assets should the corporation be liquidated (p. 542).

return on common stockholders' equity A financial ratio computed as (net income − preferred dividends) divided by average common stockholders' equity (p. 552).

stated value A nominal amount that may be assigned to each share of no-par stock and accounted for much as if it were a par value (p. 541).

stock split Additional shares of its own stock issued by a corporation to its current stockholders in proportion to their current ownership interests without changing the balances in the related stockholders' equity accounts. A formal stock split increases the number of shares outstanding and reduces proportionately the stock's per-share par value (p. 547).

treasury stock Shares of outstanding stock that have been reacquired by the issuing corporation for purposes other than retiring the stock. Treasury stock is recorded at cost and deducted from stockholders' equity in the balance sheet (p. 548).

QUESTIONS

15-1 Explain the meaning of each of the following terms and, when appropriate, how they interrelate: *corporation, articles of incorporation, corporate charter, board of directors, corporate officers,* and *organization costs.*

15-2 What is meant by the limited liability of a shareholder? Does this characteristic enhance or reduce a corporation's ability to raise capital?

15-3 Contrast the federal income taxation of corporations with that of sole proprietorships and partnerships. Which of the three types of organizations must file a federal income tax return?

15-4 Define *par value stock.* What is the significance of a stock's par value?

15-5 What is the preemptive right of a shareholder?

15-6 What are the basic differences between preferred stock and common stock? What are the typical features of preferred stock?

15-7 What features make preferred stock similar to debt? Similar to common stock?

15-8 What is meant by dividend arrearage on preferred stock? If dividends are two years in arrears on $400,000 of 8% preferred stock and dividends are declared this year, what amount of total dividends must preferred shareholders receive before any distributions can be made to common shareholders?

15-9 What is fully participating preferred stock? Partially participating preferred stock?

15-10 Distinguish between authorized stock and issued stock. Why might the number of shares issued be greater than the number of shares outstanding?

15-11 Distinguish between premium and discount on stock. Where do such amounts appear in the balance sheet?

15-12 A company acquired machines with a fair market value of $80,000 in exchange for 14,000 shares of $5 par value common stock. How should this transaction be recorded in the accounts?

15-13 Define *stock split.* What is the major reason for a stock split?

15-14 Define *treasury stock.* Why might a corporation acquire treasury stock? How is treasury stock shown in the balance sheet?

15-15 If a corporation purchases 600 shares of its own common stock at $10 per share and resells it at $14 per share, where would the $2,400 increase in capital appear in the financial statements? Why is no gain reported?

15-16 A corporation has total stockholders' equity of $4,550,000 and one class of $20 par value common stock. The corporation has 200,000 shares authorized; 150,000 shares issued; 130,000 shares outstanding; and 20,000 shares as treasury stock. What is the book value per share?

15-17 Define and contrast the terms *book value, market value,* and *liquidation value per share* of common stock.

15-18 Assume that a corporation has preferred stock outstanding. How is the return on common stockholders' equity computed?

EXERCISES

**DIVIDEND DISTRIBUTION
— OBJ. 3 —**

15-19 Lakeside Company has outstanding 10,000 shares of $40 par value, 7% cumulative preferred stock and 50,000 shares of $10 par value common stock. The company declared cash dividends amounting to $135,000.
  a. If no arrearage on the preferred stock exists, how much in total dividends, and in dividends per share, is paid to each class of stock?
  b. If one year's dividend arrearage on the preferred stock exists, how much in total dividends, and in dividends per share, is paid to each class of stock?
  c. Assume that no arrearage on the preferred stock exists but that the stock is fully participating. How much in total dividends, and in dividends per share, is paid to each class of stock?

**STOCK ISSUANCES
FOR CASH
— OBJ. 4 —**

15-20 On June 1, 1993, Finlay, Inc., issued 6,000 shares of $50 par value preferred stock at $58 per share and 9,000 shares of no-par common stock at $16 per share. The common stock has no stated value. All issuances were for cash.
   a. Prepare the general journal entries to record the stock issuances.
   b. Prepare the entry for the issuance of the common stock, assuming it had a stated value of $10 per share.
   c. Prepare the entry for the issuance of the common stock, assuming it had a par value of $1 per share.

**STOCK SUBSCRIPTIONS
— OBJ. 4 —**

15-21 On May 1, 1993, Peters Company received subscriptions for 8,000 shares of $10 par value common stock at $30 per share, with the following payment schedule from each subscriber: 50% on May 30, 30% on June 15, and 20% on July 1. All payments were received on schedule, and the shares were issued on July 1, 1993. Prepare the general journal entries made during 1993 on May 1, May 30, June 15, and July 1.

**STOCK SPLIT
— OBJ. 5 —**

15-22 On March 1 of the current year, Sentry Corporation has 250,000 shares of $20 par value common stock that are issued and outstanding. The general ledger shows the following account balances relating to the common stock:

Common Stock	$5,000,000
Paid-in Capital in Excess of Par Value	2,250,000

On March 2, Sentry Corporation splits its stock 2 for 1 and reduces the par value to $10 per share.
   a. How many shares of common stock are issued and outstanding immediately after the stock split?
   b. What is the balance in the Common Stock account immediately after the stock split?
   c. What is the balance in the Paid-in Capital in Excess of Par Value account immediately after the stock split?
   d. Is a general journal entry required to record the stock split? If yes, prepare the entry.

**TREASURY STOCK
— OBJ. 6 —**

15-23 Coastal Corporation issued 20,000 shares of $10 par value common stock at $19 per share and 5,000 shares of $50 par value, 8% preferred stock at $70 per share. Later, the company purchased 4,000 shares of its own common stock at $22 per share.
   a. Prepare the general journal entries to record the stock issuances and the purchase of the common shares.
   b. Assume that Coastal resold 3,000 shares of the treasury stock at $25 per share. Prepare the general journal entry to record the resale of this treasury stock.
   c. Assume that Coastal resold the remaining 1,000 shares of treasury stock at $18 per share. Prepare the general journal entry to record the resale of this treasury stock.

**DONATED CAPITAL
— OBJ. 6 —**

15-24 Dexter, Inc., has 15,000 shares of $5 par value common stock outstanding. Prepare the general journal entries (if required) to record the following 1993 transactions:

   Aug. 12   The community in which Dexter, Inc., is building a new plant donated the land site to the company. The appraised value of the land is $82,000.
   Oct.   7   Shareholders donated 1,000 shares of Dexter stock to the corporation.
        22   The company sold the donated shares for $26 cash per share.

**BOOK VALUE PER SHARE
— OBJ. 7 —**

15-25 The stockholders' equity section of Caravan Company's balance sheet appears as follows:

Paid-in Capital:		
8% Cumulative Preferred Stock, $50 Par Value,		
10,000 shares authorized, issued, and outstanding	$500,000	
Paid-in Capital in Excess of Par Value—		
Preferred Stock	120,000	$ 620,000
No-par Common Stock, $5 Stated Value, 80,000		
shares authorized, issued, and outstanding	$400,000	
Paid-in Capital in Excess of Stated Value—		
Common Stock	480,000	880,000
Paid-in Capital from Treasury Stock		30,000
Total Paid-in Capital		$1,530,000
Retained Earnings		280,000
Total Stockholders' Equity		$1,810,000

The preferred stock has a liquidation preference of $53 per share, and no dividends are in arrears. Compute the book value per share of the common stock.

PROBLEMS

DIVIDEND DISTRIBUTION
— **OBJ. 3** —

15-26 Rydon Corporation has outstanding 30,000 shares of $100 par value, 7%, cumulative preferred stock and 100,000 shares of $10 par value common stock. The company has declared cash dividends of $760,000.

REQUIRED

a. Calculate the total dividends and the dividends per share paid to each class of stock. There are no dividend arrearages.

b. Assuming that one year's dividend arrearage exists on the preferred stock, calculate the total dividends and the dividends per share paid to each class of stock.

c. Assuming that the 7% preferred stock is participating only to 10% (and no dividend arrearages exist), calculate the total dividends and the dividends per share paid to each class of stock.

d. Assuming that the 7% preferred stock is fully participating (and no dividend arrearages exist), calculate the total dividends and the dividends per share paid to each class of stock.

STOCKHOLDERS' EQUITY:
TRANSACTIONS AND
BALANCE SHEET
PRESENTATION
— **OBJ. 4, 6** —

15-27 Tunic Corporation was organized on April 1, 1993, with an authorization of 25,000 shares of 6%, $50 par value preferred stock and 100,000 shares of $5 par value common stock. During April, the following transactions affecting stockholders' equity occurred:

Apr. 1 Issued 60,000 shares of common stock at $15 cash per share.

3 Issued 700 shares of common stock to attorneys and promoters in exchange for their services in organizing the corporation. The services were valued at $10,500.

8 Issued 2,000 shares of common stock in exchange for equipment with a fair market value of $32,000.

17 Received land valued at $65,000 as a donation from the city to attract Tunic to its present location. The land will allow Tunic to have adequate parking for its operations.

20 Issued 5,000 shares of preferred stock for cash at $66 per share.

30 Closed the $47,000 net income for April from the Income Summary account to Retained Earnings.

REQUIRED

a. Prepare general journal entries to record the foregoing transactions.

b. Prepare the stockholders' equity section of the balance sheet at April 30, 1993.

STOCKHOLDERS' EQUITY:
TRANSACTIONS, BALANCE
SHEET PRESENTATION, AND
BOOK VALUE PER SHARE
— **OBJ. 4, 6, 7** —

15-28 The stockholders' equity of Windham Corporation at January 1, 1993, appears below:

8% Preferred Stock, $25 Par Value, 15,000 shares authorized;	
5,800 shares issued and outstanding	$145,000
Paid-in Capital in Excess of Par Value—Preferred Stock	87,000
Common Stock, $10 Par Value, 200,000 shares authorized;	
40,000 shares issued and outstanding	400,000
Paid-in Capital in Excess of Par Value—Common Stock	240,000
Retained Earnings	270,000

During 1993, the following transactions occurred:

Jan. 10 Issued 16,000 shares of common stock for $18 cash per share.

23 Purchased 6,000 shares of common stock for the treasury at $20 per share.

Mar. 2 Shareholders donated 4,000 shares of common stock to the corporation.

14 Sold one-half of the treasury shares acquired January 23 for $21 per share.

14 Sold the donated shares at $21 per share.

July 15 Issued 3,200 shares of preferred stock to acquire special equipment with a fair market value of $144,000.

Sept. 15 Received subscriptions to 18,000 shares of common stock at $25 per share.

Oct. 15 Received cash payment from each subscriber for 40% of the common stock subscription price.

Nov. 15 Received the balance due on the September 15 stock subscriptions in cash and issued the stock certificates.

Dec. 31 Closed the net income of $52,200 from the Income Summary account to Retained Earnings.

REQUIRED

a. Set up T accounts for the stockholders' equity accounts at the beginning of the year and enter January 1 balances.

b. Prepare general journal entries to record the foregoing transactions and post to T accounts (set up any additional T accounts needed). Determine the ending balances for the stockholders' equity accounts.

c. Prepare the December 31, 1993, stockholders' equity section of the balance sheet.

d. Assume the preferred stock has a liquidation preference of $27 per share. No dividends are in arrears. Compute the book value per share of common stock at December 31, 1993.

STOCKHOLDERS' EQUITY: TRANSACTIONS AND BALANCE SHEET PRESENTATION — OBJ. 4, 5, 6 —

15–29 The stockholders' equity of Summit Corporation at January 1, 1993, is shown below:

7% Preferred Stock, $100 Par Value, 20,000 shares authorized; 6,000 shares issued and outstanding	$ 600,000
Paid-in Capital in Excess of Par Value—Preferred Stock	24,000
Common Stock, $15 Par Value, 100,000 shares authorized; 60,000 shares issued and outstanding	900,000
Paid-in Capital in Excess of Par Value—Common Stock	360,000
Retained Earnings	328,000
Total Stockholders' Equity	$2,212,000

The following transactions, among others, occurred during the year:

Jan. 12 Announced a 3-for-1 common stock split, reducing the par value of the common stock to $5 per share. The authorization was increased to 300,000 shares.

20 Received subscriptions for the sale of 20,000 shares of common stock at $8 per share.

29 Received one-half of the January 20 subscription price in cash from each subscriber.

Feb. 9 Received the remainder of payment for the shares subscribed on January 20 in cash and issued the stock certificates.

Apr. 14 Received a plant site valued at $110,000 as a gift from the city.

June 1 Acquired equipment with a fair market value of $66,000 in exchange for 600 shares of preferred stock.

Sept. 1 Reacquired 3,000 shares of common stock for cash at $10 per share.

Oct. 12 Resold 500 treasury shares at $11 per share.

Dec. 21 Received subscriptions for the sale of 10,000 shares of common stock at $9 per share.

Dec. 28 Resold 800 of the remaining treasury shares at $9 per share.

31 Closed the Income Summary account. with net earnings of $88,000, to Retained Earnings.

REQUIRED

a. Set up T accounts for the stockholders' equity accounts at the beginning of the year and enter January 1 balances.

b. Prepare general journal entries for the given transactions and post them to the T accounts (set up any additional T accounts needed). Determine the ending balances for the stockholders' equity accounts.

c. Prepare the stockholders' equity section of the balance sheet at December 31, 1993.

STOCKHOLDERS' EQUITY:
INFORMATION AND ENTRIES
FROM COMPARATIVE DATA
— OBJ. 4, 6 —

15-30 Comparative stockholders' equity sections from two successive years' balance sheets of Smiley, Inc., are as follows:

	Dec. 31, 1994	Dec. 31, 1993
Paid-in Capital:		
8% Preferred Stock, $50 Par Value, authorized 15,000 shares; issued and outstanding, 1993: 8,000 shares; 1994: 10,000 shares	$ 500,000	$ 400,000
Paid-in Capital in Excess of Par Value— Preferred Stock	226,000	176,000
Common Stock, No-par Value, $20 Stated Value, authorized 60,000 shares; outstanding, 1993: 25,000 shares (6,000 shares in treasury); 1994: 35,000 shares.	700,000	620,000
Common Stock Subscribed, 1993: 1,000 shares		20,000
Paid-in Capital in Excess of Stated Value— Common Stock	300,000	255,000
Paid-in Capital from Treasury Stock	12,000	
Donated Capital	90,000	
Retained Earnings	292,000	229,000
		$1,700,000
Less: Treasury Stock (6,000 shares common) at Cost		180,000
Total Stockholders' Equity	$2,120,000	$1,520,000

No dividends were declared or paid during 1994. The company received a donated parcel of land from the city in 1994.

REQUIRED

Prepare the general journal entries for the transactions affecting stockholders' equity that evidently occurred during 1994. Assume that cash was received for stock transactions involving the receipt of an asset.

BOOK VALUE PER SHARE
— OBJ. 7 —

15-31 Sanders Corporation has the following stockholders' equity section in its balance sheet:

Paid-in Capital:		
7% Preferred Stock, $100 Par Value, 9,000 shares authorized, issued, and outstanding	$900,000	
Paid-in Capital in Excess of Par Value— Preferred Stock	108,000	
Common Stock, $5 Par Value, 200,000 shares authorized; 100,000 shares issued and outstanding	500,000	
Paid-in Capital in Excess of Par Value— Common Stock	650,000	
Paid-in Capital from Treasury Stock	32,000	$2,190,000
Retained Earnings		357,000
Total Stockholders' Equity		$2,547,000

REQUIRED

For each of the following independent cases, compute the book value per share for the preferred stock and the common stock.

a. The preferred stock is noncumulative, nonparticipating, and has a liquidation preference of $103 per share.

b. The preferred stock is cumulative, nonparticipating, and has a liquidation preference per share equal to par value plus dividends in arrears. No dividends are in arrears.

c. The preferred stock is cumulative, nonparticipating, and has a liquidation preference of $102 per share plus dividends in arrears. Dividends are three years in arrears.

ALTERNATE EXERCISES

DIVIDEND DISTRIBUTION
— OBJ. 3 —

15-19A Bower Corporation has outstanding 10,000 shares of $50 par value, 8% preferred stock and 40,000 shares of $5 par value common stock. During its first three years in business, the firm declared no dividends in the first year, $200,000 of dividends in the second year, and $40,000 of dividends in the third year.
a. If the preferred stock is cumulative, determine the total amount of dividends paid to each class of stock in each of the three years.
b. If the preferred stock is noncumulative, determine the total amount of dividends paid to each class of stock in each of the three years.

CASH AND NONCASH STOCK ISSUANCES
— OBJ. 4 —

15-20A Chavoy Corporation was organized in 1993. The company's charter authorizes 100,000 shares of $10 par value common stock. On August 1, 1993, the attorney who helped organize the corporation accepted 500 shares of Chavoy common stock as settlement for the services provided (the services were valued at $7,000). On August 15, 1993, Chavoy issued 4,000 common shares for $60,000 cash. On October 15, 1993, Chavoy issued 3,000 common shares to acquire a vacant land site appraised at $54,000. Prepare the general journal entries to record the stock issuances on August 1, August 15, and October 15.

STOCK SUBSCRIPTIONS
— OBJ. 4 —

15-21A On July 1, 1993, Monitor Corporation received subscriptions for 5,000 shares of $5 par value common stock at $18 per share, with the following payment schedule from each subscriber: 40% on August 1, 35% on August 15, and 25% on September 1. All payments were received on schedule and the shares were issued on September 1, 1993. Prepare the journal entries to record the 1993 transactions on July 1, August 1, August 15, and September 1.

STOCK SPLIT
— OBJ. 5 —

15-22A On September 1, 1993, Oxford Company has 150,000 shares of $15 par value common stock that are issued and outstanding. The general ledger shows the following account balances relating to the common stock:

Common Stock	$2,250,000
Paid-in Capital in Excess of Par Value	1,050,000

On September 2, Oxford splits its stock 3 for 2 and reduces the par value to $10 per share.
a. How many shares of common stock are issued and outstanding immediately after the stock split?
b. What is the balance in the Common Stock account immediately after the stock split?
c. What is the likely reason that Oxford Company split its stock?

STOCK ISSUANCE AND TREASURY STOCK
— OBJ. 4, 6 —

15-23A Diva, Inc., recorded certain capital stock transactions shown in the following respective journal entries: (1) issuance of common stock for $22 cash per share, (2) subsequent repurchase of some shares at $25 per share, and (3) reissuance of some of the reacquired shares.

1. Cash		418,000	
Common Stock			95,000
Paid-in Capital in Excess of Par Value			323,000
2. Treasury Stock		52,500	
Cash			52,500
3. Cash		31,900	
Treasury Stock			27,500
Paid-in Capital from Treasury Stock			4,400

a. How many shares were originally issued?
b. What was the par value of the shares issued?
c. How many shares of treasury stock were reacquired?
d. How many shares of treasury stock were reissued?
e. At what price per share was the treasury stock reissued?

DONATED CAPITAL
— OBJ. 6 —

15-24A Flavin Company has 40,000 shares of $20 par value common stock outstanding and holds 5,000 donated shares of common stock in the treasury (when donated to the company, the treasury stock had a market value of $150,000). Prepare the general journal entries to record the following 1993 transactions:

June 15 The company exchanged 3,000 shares of the donated treasury stock for a land site valued at $105,000.

Aug. 10 The company received a small parcel of land valued at $25,000 as a donation from the city. This land adjoins the land acquired on June 15 and will permit the company to proceed with the construction of a new building.

Oct. 20 The company exchanged 2,000 shares of the donated treasury stock for specialized equipment valued at $50,000.

BOOK VALUE PER SHARE
— OBJ. 7 —

15-25A The stockholders' equity section of Avalon Corporation's balance sheet appears as follows:

Paid-in Capital:		
Common Stock, $10 par value, 300,000 shares authorized; 200,000 shares issued; 10,000 shares in the treasury	$2,000,000	
Paid-in Capital in Excess of Par Value	2,800,000	$4,800,000
Paid-in Capital from Treasury Stock		90,000
Donated Capital		100,000
Total Paid-in Capital		$4,990,000
Retained Earnings		659,000
		$5,649,000
Less: Treasury Stock (10,000 shares) at Cost		310,000
Total Stockholders' Equity		$5,339,000

Compute the book value per share of the common stock.

ALTERNATE PROBLEMS

DIVIDEND DISTRIBUTION
— OBJ. 3 —

15-26A Gardner Corporation has outstanding 9,000 shares of $50 par value, 6%, cumulative preferred stock and 60,000 shares of $15 par value common stock. The company has declared cash dividends of $189,000.

REQUIRED

a. Calculate the total dividends and the dividends per share paid to each class of stock. There are no dividend arrearages.

b. Assuming that two years' dividend arrearages exist on the preferred stock, calculate the total dividends and the dividends per share paid to each class of stock.

c. Assuming that the 6% preferred stock is participating only to 10% (and no dividend arrearages exist), calculate the total dividends and the dividends per share paid to each class of stock.

d. Assuming that the 6% preferred stock is fully participating (and no dividend arrearages exist), calculate the total dividends and the dividends per share paid to each class of stock.

STOCKHOLDERS' EQUITY:
TRANSACTIONS AND
BALANCE SHEET
PRESENTATION
— OBJ. 4, 6 —

15-27A Beaker Corporation was organized on July 1, 1993, with an authorization of 40,000 shares of $4 no-par value preferred stock ($4 is the annual dividend) and 80,000 shares of $20 par value common stock. During July, the following transactions affecting stockholders' equity occurred:

July 1 Issued 28,000 shares of common stock at $30 cash per share.

5 The local municipality donated a vacant building to the corporation as an inducement to operate the business in the community. The fair market value of the building was $600,000.

12 Issued 2,500 shares of common stock in exchange for equipment with a fair market value of $80,000.

15 Issued 5,000 shares of preferred stock for cash at $58 per share.

16 Received subscriptions for 5,000 shares of common stock at $34 per share.

July 31 Received a 25% cash payment on the common stock subscriptions from each subscriber. The balance of the subscription price is due on August 31.

     31 Closed the $54,000 net income for July from the Income Summary account to Retained Earnings.

REQUIRED

a. Prepare general journal entries to record the foregoing transactions.

b. Prepare the stockholders' equity section of the balance sheet at July 31, 1993.

STOCKHOLDERS' EQUITY: TRANSACTIONS, BALANCE SHEET PRESENTATION, AND BOOK VALUE PER SHARE — OBJ. 4, 6, 7 —

15-28A The stockholders' equity of Scott Corporation at January 1, 1993, appears below:

Common Stock, $5 Par Value, 350,000 shares authorized; 50,000 shares issued and outstanding	$250,000
Paid-in Capital in Excess of Par Value	650,000
Retained Earnings	346,000

During 1993, the following transactions occurred:

Jan.   5 Issued 9,000 shares of common stock for $22 cash per share.

     18 Purchased 4,000 shares of common stock for the treasury at $23 cash per share.

Mar. 10 Shareholders donated 3,000 shares to the corporation.

     12 Sold one-fourth of the treasury shares acquired January 18 for $26 per share.

     12 Sold the donated shares at $26 per share.

July 17 Sold 800 shares of the remaining treasury stock for $21 per share.

Sept. 20 Received subscriptions to 6,000 shares of common stock at $27 per share.

Oct. 20 Received cash payment for one-third of the common stock subscription price from each subscriber.

Nov. 25 Received the balance due on the September 20 stock subscription in cash, and issued the stock certificates.

Dec. 31 Closed the net income of $60,800 from the Income Summary account to Retained Earnings.

REQUIRED

a. Set up T accounts for the stockholders' equity accounts at the beginning of the year and enter January 1 balances.

b. Prepare general journal entries to record the foregoing transactions and post to T accounts (set up any additional T accounts needed). Determine the ending balances for the stockholders' equity accounts.

c. Prepare the December 31, 1993, stockholders' equity section of the balance sheet.

d. Compute the book value per share of common stock at December 31, 1993.

STOCKHOLDERS' EQUITY: TRANSACTIONS AND BALANCE SHEET PRESENTATION — OBJ. 4, 5, 6 —

15-29A The following is the stockholders' equity of Clipper Corporation at January 1, 1993:

8% Preferred Stock, $50 Par Value, 8,000 shares authorized; 6,000 shares issued and outstanding	$ 300,000
Paid-in Capital in Excess of Par Value—Preferred Stock	57,000
Common Stock, $20 Par Value, 50,000 shares authorized; 35,000 shares issued and outstanding	700,000
Paid-in Capital in Excess of Par Value—Common Stock	385,000
Retained Earnings	239,000
Total Stockholders' Equity	$1,681,000

The following transactions, among others, occurred during the year:

Jan. 15 Issued 1,000 shares of preferred stock for $60 cash per share.

     20 Received subscriptions for the sale of 8,000 shares of common stock at $33 per share.

     30 Received one-third of the January 20 subscription price in cash from each subscriber.

Feb.   9 Received the remainder of payment for the shares subscribed on January 20 in cash and issued the stock certificates.

Mar. 10 Received a vacant school building valued at $550,000 as a gift from the city. The company plans to remodel the building for additional office space.

May 18   Announced a 2-for-1 common stock split, reducing the par value of the common stock to $10 per share. The authorization was increased to 100,000 shares.

June 1   Acquired equipment with a fair market value of $72,000 in exchange for 4,000 shares of common stock.

Sept. 1   Purchased 2,500 shares of common stock for the treasury at $20 cash per share.

Oct. 12   Resold 900 treasury shares at $21 per share.

Dec. 22   Received subscriptions for the sale of 5,000 shares of common stock at $18 per share.

28   Resold 1,100 of the remaining treasury shares at $18 per share.

31   Closed the Income Summary account, with net earnings of $55,000, to Retained Earnings.

REQUIRED

a. Set up T accounts for the stockholders' equity accounts at the beginning of the year and enter January 1 balances.

b. Prepare general journal entries for the given transactions and post them to the T accounts (set up any additional T accounts needed). Determine the ending balances for the stockholders' equity accounts.

c. Prepare the stockholders' equity section of the balance sheet at December 31, 1993.

STOCKHOLDERS' EQUITY: TRANSACTION DESCRIPTIONS FROM ACCOUNT DATA — OBJ. 4, 6 —

15-30A   The following T accounts contain keyed entries representing seven transactions involving the stockholders' equity of Riverview, Inc.

CASH			
(1)	69,600	(4)	7,000
(2)	45,000		
(6)	3,200		

STOCK SUBSCRIPTIONS RECEIVABLE—COMMON	
(7)	54,000

LAND	
(3)	62,000
(5)	85,000

PREFERRED STOCK, $50 PAR	
(1)	60,000

PAID-IN CAPITAL IN EXCESS OF PAR VALUE—PREFERRED STOCK	
(1)	9,600

COMMON STOCK, $10 PAR	
(2)	45,000
(3)	50,000

COMMON STOCK SUBSCRIBED	
(7)	30,000

PAID-IN CAPITAL IN EXCESS OF PAR VALUE—COMMON STOCK	
(3)	12,000
(7)	24,000

TREASURY STOCK			
(4)	(500 shares of common) 7,000	(6)	2,800

PAID-IN CAPITAL FROM TREASURY STOCK	
(6)	400

DONATED CAPITAL	
(5)	85,000

REQUIRED

Using this information, give detailed descriptions, including number of shares and price per share when applicable, for each of the seven transactions.

BOOK VALUE PER SHARE — OBJ. 7 —

15-31A Yambert, Inc., has the following stockholders' equity section in its balance sheet:

Paid-in Capital:		
8% Preferred Stock, $75 Par Value, 10,000 shares authorized, issued, and outstanding	$750,000	
Paid-in Capital in Excess of Par Value— Preferred Stock	150,000	
Common Stock, $1 Par Value, 800,000 shares authorized; 200,000 shares issued and outstanding	200,000	
Paid-in Capital in Excess of Par Value— Common Stock	950,000	
Donated Capital	180,000	$2,230,000
Retained Earnings		420,000
Total Stockholders' Equity		$2,650,000

REQUIRED

For each of the following independent cases, compute the book value per share for the preferred stock and the common stock.

a. The preferred stock is noncumulative, nonparticipating, and has a liquidation preference of $77 per share.

b. The preferred stock is cumulative, nonparticipating, and has a liquidation preference per share equal to par value plus dividends in arrears. No dividends are in arrears.

c. The preferred stock is cumulative, nonparticipating, and has a liquidation preference of $76 per share plus dividends in arrears. Dividends are two years in arrears.

CASES

Business Decision Case

Brett Barr has operated Barr's Hardware very successfully as a sole proprietorship. He believes that the continued growth and success of his business depends on increasing its scale of operations, which requires additional working capital. He also wishes to relocate his store from its rented quarters to a new retail shopping area. After exploring several opportunities that would result in large personal debts, Barr incorporates his business, taking in as stockholders Dr. Alec Frost, who invests cash, and Elise Moore, a real estate developer who owns land and a suitable vacant building in the desired shopping area.

As an initial step, Barr and his attorney secure a corporate charter for Hardware City, Inc., authorizing it to issue 60,000 shares of $10 par value common stock. On June 1, 1993, the date of incorporation, the post-closing trial balance of Barr's Hardware is as follows:

	Debit	Credit
Cash	$ 3,800	
Accounts Receivable	11,200	
Allowance for Uncollectible Accounts		$ 100
Merchandise Inventory	180,000	
Store Equipment	72,000	
Accumulated Depreciation—Store Equipment		37,000
Accounts Payable		8,600
Note Payable (due two years hence)		25,000
B. Barr, Capital		196,300
	$267,000	$267,000

Other details of the agreement follow:

1. After a detailed review of the accounts of Barr's Hardware, the new stockholders agree that:
   a. The allowance for uncollectible accounts should increase by $250.
   b. Because of damaged and obsolete goods, the merchandise inventory should be written down by $20,000.

c. The store equipment will be recorded in the corporate accounts at its fair market value of $40,000 with no accumulated depreciation.

d. The new corporation assumes at face value the recorded liabilities of the proprietorship.

2. Barr has agreed to accept shares in the new corporation at par value in exchange for his adjusted equity in the assets of the proprietorship. He will purchase for cash at par value any additional shares necessary to bring his total holdings to the next even 100 shares.

3. The total value of Moore's building and land is agreed to be $177,000, of which $27,000 is associated with the land. Moore has agreed to accept stock at $12 per share for her land and building.

4. In an effort to stimulate local business, the Business Development Commission of the local city government has deeded to the corporation, for a token fee of $500, a small strip of land that will provide better delivery access to the rear of Moore's building. The fair value of the parcel is $5,000.

5. Frost has agreed to purchase for cash 6,000 shares at $12 per share. He will subscribe to an additional 1,000 shares at $14 per share, paying the subscription price in two equal installments, 90 and 180 days later.

6. Legal and accounting costs of $9,500 associated with acquiring the corporate charter and issuing the stock are paid from corporate funds. (Treat these as the asset, Organization Costs.)

REQUIRED

a. As Barr's accountant, you must prepare a balance sheet for the new corporation reflecting the shares issued, the stock subscription received, the parcel of land received from the city, and payment of legal and accounting costs. *Hint:* You may wish to prepare a worksheet with the following headings:

Accounts	Barr's Hardware Trial Balance		Adjustments and Organizational Transactions		Hardware City, Inc. Trial Balance	
	Dr.	Cr.	Dr.	Cr.	Dr.	Cr.

Properly combining and extending the amounts in the first two pairs of columns provide amounts for the trial balance of Hardware City, Inc. When recording Barr's Hardware trial balance, leave extra lines for the several transactions that will affect the Cash and B. Barr, Capital accounts. Also leave extra lines when entering the Common Stock and Paid-in Capital in Excess of Par Value accounts on the worksheet. For purposes of review, you may wish to key your adjustments and transactions to the letters and numbers used in the problem data.

b. In contrast to what they contributed to the corporation, what specifically do Barr, Frost, and Moore "own" after the incorporation?

c. From Barr's viewpoint, what are the advantages and disadvantages of incorporating the hardware store?

Analytical Application Case

GRUMMAN CORPORATION, headquartered in Bethpage, New York; MCDONNELL DOUGLAS CORPORATION, headquartered in St. Louis; and NORTHROP CORPORATION, headquartered in Los Angeles, are three firms in the aerospace industry in the United States. During a recent year, the average return on common stockholders' equity for the aerospace industry was 11.8%. In the same year, the relevant financial data for Grumman, McDonnell Douglas, and Northrop were as follows (in millions):

	Grumman	McDonnell Douglas	Northrop
Preferred stockholders' equity, beginning	$ 37.6	$ –0–	$ –0–
Preferred stockholders' equity, ending	32.4	–0–	–0–
Preferred dividends	3.8	–0–	–0–
Common stockholders' equity, beginning	817.7	3,287.0	875.1
Common stockholders' equity, ending	867.5	3,514.0	1,032.6
Net income	85.6	306.0	210.4

REQUIRED

a. Compute Grumman Corporation's return on common stockholders' equity.
b. Evaluate Grumman Corporation's return on common stockholders' equity by comparing it with the following:
   1. The average for the aerospace industry.
   2. The return earned by McDonnell Douglas Corporation.
   3. The return earned by Northrop Corporation.
   4. The return earned by Grumman Corporation in the previous year (in the previous year, Grumman's net income was $67.3 million, preferred dividend requirements were $4.5 million, and average common stockholders' equity was $799.9 million).

Ethics Case

Colin Agee, chairperson of the board of directors and chief executive officer of Image, Inc., is pondering a recommendation to make to the firm's board of directors in response to actions taken by Sam Mecon. Mecon recently informed Agee and other board members that he (Mecon) had purchased 15% of the voting stock of Image at $11 per share and is considering an attempt to take control of the company. His effort to take control would include offering $15 per share to stockholders to induce them to sell shares to him. Mecon also indicated he would abandon his takeover plans if the company would buy back his stock at a price 50% over its current market price of $12 per share.

Agee views the proposed takeover by Mecon as a hostile maneuver. Mecon has a reputation of identifying companies that are undervalued (that is, their underlying net assets are worth more than the price of the outstanding stock), buying enough stock to take control of such a company, replacing top management, and, on occasion, breaking up the company (that is, selling off the various divisions to the highest bidder). The process has proven profitable to Mecon and his financial backers. Stockholders of the companies taken over also benefited because Mecon paid them attractive prices to buy their stock.

Agee recognizes that Image is currently undervalued by the stock market but believes that eventually the company will significantly improve its financial performance to the long-run benefit of its stockholders.

REQUIRED

What are the ethical issues that Agee should consider in arriving at a recommendation to make to the board of directors regarding Mecon's offer to be "bought out" of his takeover plans?

How are events outside a firm's ordinary operating activities reported in the income statement?

In 1990, Phillips Petroleum Co. recorded a $101 million gain from the settlement of litigation related to the 1979 expropriate of its interest in offshore Iranian oilfields. ■ *How such items are reported is important because the income statement not only reflects past performance but helps predict future performance.* ■ *Thus accountants use separate sections of the income statement to report discontinued operations, extraordinary items (such as Phillips' gain), and changes in accounting principles.*

16

CORPORATIONS: DIVIDENDS, RETAINED EARNINGS, AND EARNINGS DISCLOSURE

All things have their place, knew we how to place them.

GEORGE HERBERT

he two major components of stockholders' equity are paid-in capital and retained earnings. The preceding chapter focused on events affecting paid-in capital; in this chapter we emphasize retained earnings and its components.

Retained earnings represents the stockholders' equity arising from the corporation's retention of assets generated from profit-directed activities. At the end of an accounting period, the Retained Earnings account is credited with the corporation's net income (when the Income Summary account is closed to it) or debited with a net loss. A debit balance in the Retained Earnings account resulting from accumulated losses is called a **deficit.** The board of directors may decide, based on the income performance of the corporation, to declare a dividend. The dividend declaration reduces retained earnings.

Profits (or net income) cause retained earnings to increase. Profits play a significant role in the organization and functioning of economic activity in the United States. A corporation's profitability is vitally important both to its owners and to potential investors. For this reason, data reported in the income statement are usually considered the most important financial information presented by corporations. Because of the importance of income data, accountants have developed several guidelines for their disclosure. After discussing the accounting for dividends and retained earnings, we will discuss the guidelines for reporting income data.

DIVIDENDS

OBJECTIVE ❶ IDENTIFY *and* DISTINGUISH *between cash dividends and stock dividends.*

Dividends are distributions of assets or stock from a corporation to its stockholders. A corporation can distribute dividends to shareholders only after its board of directors has formally declared a distribution. Dividends are usually paid in cash but may also be property or additional shares of stock in the firm. Legally, declared dividends are an obligation of the firm, and an entry to record the dividend obligation is made on the *declaration date.* Cash and property dividends payable are carried as liabilities, and stock dividends to be issued are shown in the stockholders' equity section of the balance sheet. At the declaration, a *record date* and *payment date* are established. For example, on April 25 (declaration date), the board of directors might declare a dividend payable June 1 (payment date) to those who own stock on May 15 (record date). Stockholders owning stock on the record date receive the dividend even if they dispose of their shares before the payment date. Therefore, shares sold between the record date and payment date are sold *ex-dividend* (without right to the dividend).

Most dividend declarations reduce retained earnings; under certain conditions, however, state laws may permit distributions from paid-in capital. Shareholders should be informed of the source of such dividends, because, in a sense, they are a return of capital rather than a distribution of earnings.

Cash Dividends

The majority of dividends distributed by corporations are paid in cash. Although companies may pay such dividends annually, many large firms pay quarterly dividends. The QUAKER OATS COMPANY and PEPSICO, INC., for example, usually pay quarterly dividends. Some companies occasionally pay an extra dividend at year-end. Usually this is done when the company wishes to increase the total annual distribution without departing from a standard quarterly amount that was established by custom or announced in advance.

In declaring cash dividends, a company must have both an appropriate amount of retained earnings and the necessary amount of cash. Uninformed investors often believe that a large Retained Earnings balance automatically permits generous dividend distributions. A company, however, may successfully accumulate earnings and at the same time not be sufficiently liquid to pay large dividends. Many companies, especially new firms in growth industries, finance their expansion from assets generated through earnings and pay out small cash dividends or none at all.

Cash dividends are based on the number of shares of stock outstanding. When a company's directors declare a cash dividend, an entry is made debiting Cash Dividends and crediting Dividends Payable. Assume, for example, that a company has outstanding 1,000 shares of $100 par value, 6% preferred stock and 6,000 shares of $10 par value common stock. If the company declares the regular $6 dividend on the preferred stock and a $2 dividend on the common stock, the dividend payment totals $18,000. The following entry is made at the declaration date:

Cash Dividends	18,000	
Dividends Payable—Preferred Stock		6,000
Dividends Payable—Common Stock		12,000
To record declaration of $6 dividend on preferred stock and $2 dividend on common stock.		

The Cash Dividends account is a temporary account that is closed to Retained Earnings at year-end.[1] Dividends Payable—Preferred Stock and Dividends Payable—Common Stock are reported as current liabilities on the balance sheet. On the dividend payment date, the following entry is made:

Dividends Payable—Preferred Stock	6,000	
Dividends Payable—Common Stock	12,000	
Cash		18,000
To record payment of dividends on preferred and common stocks.		

Stock Dividends

Companies frequently distribute shares of their own stock as dividends to shareholders in lieu of, or in addition to, cash dividends. A company may issue **stock dividends** when it does not wish to deplete its working capital by paying a cash dividend. Young and growing companies often issue stock dividends, because cash is usually needed to acquire new facilities and to expand. The use of stock dividends is by no means confined to such companies, however.

The accounting for a stock dividend results in a transfer of a portion of retained earnings to the paid-in capital accounts. Thus, distribution of a stock dividend signals management's desire to "plow back" earnings into the company. Although stock dividends may take a number of forms, usually common shares are distributed to common shareholders. We limit our discussion to this type of distribution.

SMALL STOCK DIVIDENDS

Small stock dividends are dividends in which the additional shares issued are fewer than 20–25% of the number previously outstanding. These stock dividends are *recorded at the market value* of the shares involved, causing retained earnings to decrease and paid-in capital to increase by this amount. In some respects, the issuance of new shares in the form of a dividend can be viewed as a transaction that avoids the test of the marketplace. If the shareholders receive cash and immediately purchase additional shares of the firm's stock, the purchases are made at market value. Thus, the number of shares issued in exchange for a given amount of retained earnings should be related to the market value of the shares.

To illustrate the entries reflecting a declaration of a small stock dividend, we assume that the stockholders' equity of a company is as follows before declaration of a 10% stock dividend:

Common Stock, $5 Par Value, 20,000 shares issued and outstanding	$100,000
Paid-in Capital in Excess of Par Value	20,000
Total Paid-in Capital	$120,000
Retained Earnings	65,000
Total Stockholders' Equity	$185,000

---

[1] Some companies, especially those paying dividends annually, debit Retained Earnings directly on the dividend declaration date.

THE LURE OF DIVIDEND REINVESTMENT PLANS

Dividend reinvestment programs represent a truly "win-win" situation for shareholders and corporations. On the one hand, they offer a low-cost—often no-cost—way for stockholders to accumulate shares. For the sponsoring corporations, they provide a way to raise equity capital inexpensively. ■ These programs— about 900 corporations and closed-end funds now offer them— usually permit current shareholders to purchase additional shares directly, without using brokers. The purchases are made with dividends that the company reinvests for them. In many programs,

additional shares can be bought by paying cash.

Among the many attractions for investors:

■ Most companies charge no commission for purchasing the stock, and those that do charge only a nominal fee.

■ Over 100 firms have dividend reinvestment plans that permit participants to buy stock at discounts to prevailing market prices. These discounts usually range from 3% to 10%.

■ Most plans permit investors to send optional cash payments directly to the company to purchase additional shares. The minimum purchase, in many cases, is tiny. Sometimes, it's even possible to purchase shares (or, more likely, a fraction of one) for as little as $10. . . .

When it comes time to sell, many companies will let you unload your shares through the plan. Usually, you pay a fee, but one lower than a broker would charge. (A few plans even allow

you to redeem shares at no charge.)
. . .

There are some downsides, of course. . . . Perhaps the biggest negative is the fact that investors have little control over the price at which shares are bought and sold. The stock is bought only on certain dates, usually once a month or quarter. Therefore, there may be quite a lag between when you make a buy decision and when the transaction is executed. Thus, the plans are best suited for a long-term investment strategy.

For companies, the benefits of dividend reinvestment plans include:

■ Improving shareholder relationships. The low investment requirements build goodwill with shareholders, goodwill that can pay off nicely. For example, Procter & Gamble has one of the more interesting dividend reinvestment plans. P&G investors can make optional cash payments of just $2 at a time. In addition, P&G is one of a handful of companies that allows investors to make first-time purchases of stock directly. In P&G's case, this

---

With 20,000 shares outstanding, declaration of a 10% stock dividend requires the issuance of an additional 2,000 shares. Let us assume that the market price per share is $11. The total market value of the shares to be distributed is $22,000, resulting in the following entry:

Stock Dividends	22,000	
Stock Dividend Distributable		10,000
Paid-in Capital in Excess of Par Value		12,000
To record declaration of 10% stock dividend on common shares.		

The amount of the credit to Stock Dividend Distributable is the par value of the shares to be distributed. If a balance sheet is prepared between the declaration date and the distribution date of a stock dividend, the Stock Dividend Distributable account is shown in stockholders' equity immediately after the Common Stock account. When the stock is distributed, the following entry is made:

Stock Dividend Distributable	10,000	
Common Stock		10,000
To record issuance of stock dividend on common shares.		

The Stock Dividends account is a temporary account that is closed to Retained Earnings at year-end, as appears on the following page:

initial investment can be as low as the cost of just one share. Such minimal investment requirements have made the P&G plan quite popular with investors, a fact not lost on P&G. . . .

McDonald's also has one of the more successful plans, which it actively promotes and which includes roughly 48% of its shareholders. This builds brand awareness and reinforces customer relationships. In other words, it helps sell a lot of Big Macs.

- Stabilizing the shareholder base. Corporations generally like wide ownership of their shares. If a relatively small amount of stock is held by a relatively large number of individuals, a corporate raider or unfriendly suitor would have trouble accumulating shares for a proxy battle or hostile takeover. Also, as a group, individual investors are more loyal than institutional holders and generally invest for the long term. They're unlikely to be actively trading the issue and increasing its volatility.

Linked is another benefit: Wide ownership and continuous purchases through a reinvestment plan provide market support for the share price.

- Holding down costs. Dividend reinvestment plans reduce the number of dividend checks and stock certificates that must be prepared and mailed. These savings offset some of the cost of operating a reinvestment program.

- Raising equity capital. Companies make purchases for participants in two ways—by acting as an agent for the shareholders to buy stock on the open market, or by issuing new shares from the treasury. In the former case, no new equity capital is generated. But in the latter, the corporation receives the funds in return for the issued shares. This is no different than raising money by having an investment banker make a public offering of new shares. In most reinvestment plans, companies give themselves the flexibility to purchase shares in either way. . . .

But if dividend reinvestment programs are so great, why don't all corporations provide them, especially those facing high costs for equity capital? A Conference Board study sheds some light. One obvious reason: Some corporations' dividend policies (or lack of a dividend) preclude them from offering a plan. Other reasons include the costs of operating a program and low expected participation levels, based on the profiles of the company's typical shareholders.

Another reason cited in the Conference Board study was fear of damaging relationships with shareholders, especially if clerical or record-keeping errors were made. And some corporations simply view a reinvestment plan as being more of a hassle than it's worth, while others fret that repeated issuance of new shares will hurt the stock price. . . .

SOURCE: Charles Carlson, "A Lot for (Almost) Nothing; The Lure of Dividend Reinvestment Plans," *Barrons*, February 17, 1992, p. 17. Reprinted by permission of *Barrons*, © 1992 Dow Jones & Company, Inc. All Rights Reserved Worldwide.

Retained Earnings	22,000	
Stock Dividends		22,000
To close the Stock Dividends account.		

After the stock is distributed and the Stock Dividends account is closed, a comparison of the stockholders' equity and outstanding shares before and after the stock dividend appears below. Note that retained earnings decreased $22,000 and paid-in capital increased $22,000, but total stockholders' equity did not change.

	Before Stock Dividend	After Stock Dividend
Common Stock, $5 par value	$100,000	$110,000
Paid-in Capital in Excess of Par Value	20,000	32,000
Total Paid-in Capital	$120,000	$142,000
Retained Earnings	65,000	43,000
Total Stockholders' Equity	$185,000	$185,000
Common shares issued and outstanding	20,000	22,000

The relative position of a common shareholder is not altered by the receipt of a common stock dividend. If a 10% stock dividend is distributed, all shareholders increase their proportionate holdings by 10%, and the total stock outstanding is increased in the same proportion. No income is realized by the shareholders. If the stock dividend distributed is not large in relation to the outstanding shares, little or no change may occur in the market value of the stock. If the market value does not decrease and the company continues the same cash dividends per share, shareholders have benefited by the distribution.

LARGE STOCK DIVIDENDS

When the number of shares issued as a stock dividend is large enough to reduce materially the per-share market value, the shareholders may not perceive the same benefits as they do for small stock dividends. Accordingly, the accounting analysis is different for large stock dividends (those over 20–25%). The journal entry to record the declaration of a large stock dividend debits Stock Dividends and credits Stock Dividend Distributable for *the minimum increase in paid-in capital required by law for the issuance of new shares.* Usually this amount is the par or stated value of the stock. Once the stock is issued, the increase in paid-in capital is reflected in the Common Stock account.[2]

RETAINED EARNINGS STATEMENT

OBJECTIVE **2** ILLUSTRATE *a retained earnings statement and a statement of stock-holders' equity.*

A **retained earnings statement** presents an analysis of the Retained Earnings account for the accounting period. The statement begins with the retained earnings balance at the beginning of the period, shows the items that caused retained earnings to change during the period, and ends with the period-end retained earnings balance. An example of a retained earnings statement is shown in Exhibit 16-1.

STATEMENT OF STOCKHOLDERS' EQUITY

Rather than reporting a retained earnings statement, corporations often integrate information about retained earnings into a more comprehensive statement called a **statement of stockholders' equity.** This statement presents an analysis of all components of stockholders' equity for the accounting period. The statement begins with the beginning balances of the various stockholders' equity components, reports the items causing changes in these components, and ends with the period-end balances.

Exhibit 16-2 presents a statement of stockholders' equity for Geyser Corporation. This statement reveals all of the events affecting Geyser's stockholders' equity during 1993. These events are the issuance of common stock, the issuance of treasury stock, the earning of net income, the declaration of cash dividends, and the acquisition of treasury stock. Note that the information in the Retained Earnings column contains the same information as a retained earnings statement.

PRIOR PERIOD ADJUSTMENTS

Essentially, **prior period adjustments** correct errors made in financial statements of prior periods.[3] Errors may result from mathematical mistakes, oversights, incorrect applications of accounting principles, or improper analyses of existing facts when the financial statements are prepared.

---

[2] A large stock dividend is similar in many respects to a stock split (discussed in the preceding chapter). A stock's par or stated value per share is not changed by a stock dividend, however, whereas a stock split reduces the par or stated value in proportion to the increase in shares of stock. This difference leads to a difference in analysis—only a memorandum entry is made for a stock split, whereas a large stock dividend requires a journal entry to transfer the legal capital of shares to be issued from retained earnings to paid-in capital.

[3] *Statement of Financial Accounting Standards No. 16,* "Prior Period Adjustments" (Stamford, CT: Financial Accounting Standards Board, 1977).

EXHIBIT 16—1

GEYSER CORPORATION
RETAINED EARNINGS STATEMENT
FOR THE YEAR ENDED DECEMBER 31, 1993

Retained Earnings, January 1, 1993	$48,000
Add: Net Income	32,000
	$80,000
Less: Cash Dividends Declared	19,000
Retained Earnings, December 31, 1993	$61,000

OBJECTIVE ③ DISCUSS *the accounting for prior period adjustments, changes in accounting estimates, and the process of restricting retained earnings.*

Prior period adjustments are not included in the current year's income statement. Instead, corrections of material errors of past periods are charged or credited directly to Retained Earnings and are reported as adjustments to the beginning balance of Retained Earnings in the current year's retained earnings statement or statement of stockholders' equity. The prior period adjustment should be shown net of any related income tax effects.

For example, assume that Geyser Corporation discovered in 1994 that it charged $10,000 of equipment installation costs on December 31, 1993, to Repairs Expense rather than capitalizing it to the Equipment account. Assuming a 40% income tax rate, 1993 net income was understated by $6,000 (Repairs Expense was overstated $10,000 and Income Tax Expense was understated $4,000.) Because of this error, the company owes another $4,000 of income taxes for 1993. The journal entry in 1994 to correct for the 1993 error is as follows:

Equipment	10,000	
Retained Earnings		6,000
Income Tax Payable		4,000
To correct for error in recording 1993 equipment installation costs.		

The company reports the $6,000 prior period adjustment in the 1994 retained earnings statement, as follows:

Retained Earnings, January 1, 1994	$61,000
Add: Correction of Prior Period Equipment Error (net of $4,000 income taxes)	6,000
Adjusted Balance, January 1, 1994	$67,000

EXHIBIT 16—2

GEYSER CORPORATION
STATEMENT OF STOCKHOLDERS' EQUITY
FOR THE YEAR ENDED DECEMBER 31, 1993

	Common Stock	Paid-in Capital in Excess of Par Value	Paid-in Capital from Treasury Stock	Retained Earnings	Treasury Stock	Total
Balance, January 1, 1993	$200,000	$120,000	$18,000	$48,000	($14,000)	$372,000
6,000 Common Shares Issued	30,000	24,000				54,000
500 Treasury Shares Issued			2,000		3,500	5,500
Net Income				32,000		32,000
Cash Dividends Declared				(19,000)		(19,000)
200 Treasury Shares Acquired					(2,000)	(2,000)
Balance, December 31, 1993	$230,000	$144,000	$20,000	$61,000	($12,500)	$442,500

CHANGES IN ACCOUNTING ESTIMATES

Estimates play an integral part in accounting. In preparing periodic financial statements, we estimate the effects of transactions continuing in the future. For example, we must estimate uncollectible accounts, useful lives of plant and intangible assets, salvage values of plant assets, and product warranty costs. As a normal consequence of such estimates, new information, changed conditions, or more experience may require the revision of previous estimates.

It is important to distinguish a change in accounting estimate from a prior period adjustment because the accounting treatment differs between the two items. The effect of a **change in accounting estimate** should be reflected in the income statements of *current and future periods* to the extent appropriate in each case. The estimated amounts reported in prior period financial statements are not changed. Presumably, the previous estimates were the best possible, given the information then available.

The total impact of some changes in estimates is included in the current year's income statement. A revision of an estimated liability recorded in prior periods is one example. Assume that unanticipated cost increases have caused a company to underestimate its liability for product warranty carried into the current year by $900. The estimated liability is revised as follows:

Product Warranty Expense	900	
Estimated Liability for Product Warranty		900
To record change in estimated warranty liability.		

An estimate revision may affect both the period of change and future periods. If so, the effect of the revision should be accounted for over the current and future periods. The revision of depreciation discussed earlier, in the chapter on depreciation methods, illustrates this type of change.

RESTRICTIONS ON RETAINED EARNINGS

Portions of retained earnings are often *restricted* (or *appropriated*), so that these amounts are not available for the declaration of dividends. To the extent that dividends are not declared and paid, assets are kept within the corporation. **Retained earnings restrictions** may be voluntary, contractual, or statutory.

Voluntary restrictions are restrictions placed on retained earnings by the board of directors for particular corporate objectives. The board of directors may want to have corporate funds available, for example, to enlarge a plant or to settle a pending lawsuit. By restricting retained earnings, assets needed for these purposes will not be distributed as dividends.

Note, however, that restricting retained earnings for a particular objective restricts only dividend amounts. The restriction does not ensure that specific funds will be available for the stated objective. A company may have a large retained earnings balance without having an ample amount of liquid assets. It is management's responsibility to see that the right kind of assets are available when needed.

Contractual restrictions result from certain types of contracts entered into by a corporation. When a company issues long-term debt, for example, the debt agreement may limit the amount of dividends the company may pay until the debt is settled. This restriction helps protect the availability of the company's working capital for debt payment purposes.

Statutory restrictions are retained earnings restrictions imposed by law. In the previous chapter, we mentioned a statutory restriction in connection with treasury stock purchases—many states require that retained earnings be restricted in an amount equal to the cost of treasury stock purchased by the corporation. This restriction prevents a corporation from distributing assets to stockholders through a combination of dividends and treasury stock purchases that exceeds the retained earnings balance. This restriction, therefore, protects creditors by limiting the assets that may be distributed to owners.

Retained earnings restrictions are usually disclosed in a note to the financial statements. The following note from an annual report of DONNELLY CORPORATION illustrates the disclosure of a contractual restriction on retained earnings (Donnelly Corporation manufactures automotive mirrors, automotive window systems, and solid-state glass coatings for electronics products):

> The various borrowings subject the Company to certain restrictions relating to, among other things, minimum net worth, payment of dividends and maintenance of certain financial ratios. Retained earnings available for dividends at June 30, 1991, are $4,201,000.

CONTENT AND FORMAT OF THE INCOME STATEMENT

OBJECTIVE 4 IDENTIFY *and* DISCUSS *the content and format of the income statement.*

Accountants believe that the income statement is more useful when certain types of transactions and events are reported in separate sections. For this reason, information about extraordinary items, discontinued operations, and effects of changes in accounting principles are disclosed separately in an income statement. Segregating these categories of information from the results of ordinary, continuing operations should make it easier for financial statement users to estimate the future earnings performance of the company.

The creation of several sections in the income statement, however, complicates the reporting of income tax expense. Items affecting the overall amount of income tax expense may appear in more than one section. If this is the case, accountants allocate the income tax expense among those sections of the statement in which the items affecting the tax expense appear.

The income statement's usefulness is also enhanced if it contains information on earnings per share. Accordingly, earnings per share are reported in the income statement immediately after the net income amount.

We now examine these areas in more detail.

TAX ALLOCATION WITHIN A PERIOD

The process of allocating a period's total income tax expense to different sections of an income statement is known as **tax allocation within a period.** This process is necessary when items affecting the income tax amount appear in different income statement sections.

To illustrate, assume that a company will be preparing an income statement with two sections, one section reporting income from ordinary, continuing operations ($100,000 before income taxes) and a second section reporting an extraordinary gain of $20,000 (extraordinary items will be discussed presently). Using a 40% income tax rate, the total income tax expense for the period is $48,000 (40% × $120,000). The $48,000 will be allocated to the two sections of the income statement as shown in the following schedule.

Income Statement Section	Taxable Amount in Section	Income Tax Allocated to Section
Ordinary, continuing operations	$100,000	$40,000
Extraordinary items	20,000	8,000

Now assume that the company had a $30,000 extraordinary loss rather than a $20,000 extraordinary gain. Combining the $30,000 loss with the $100,000 income before income taxes from ordinary, continuing operations gives a total of $70,000 subject to income tax. With a 40% income tax rate, total income tax expense for the period is $28,000 (40% × $70,000). Because the $30,000 extraordinary loss caused a reduction in income taxes, the total tax expense of $28,000 allocated to the two income statement sections consists of a tax expense of $40,000 and a tax reduction of $12,000, as shown in the following schedule.

Income Statement Section	Taxable Amount or (Loss) in Section	Income Tax or (Tax Reduction) Allocated to Section
Ordinary, continuing operations	$100,000	$40,000
Extraordinary items	(30,000)	(12,000)

When tax allocation within a period is used, the income tax amount reported in an income statement section relates only to the revenues, expenses, gains, or losses included in that section. Thus, the income statement section presents a normal relationship between income taxes and the items in that section affecting the tax calculation. Later chapter exhibits will illustrate the income statement presentation of tax allocation within a period.

SECTIONS OF THE INCOME STATEMENT

Ordinary, Continuing Operations

The first section (and many times the only section) of an income statement presents information on the period's *ordinary, continuing operations*. Either one of two basic formats may be used to report this information: a multiple-step format and a single-step format. Both the multiple-step and single-step formats are acceptable.

MULTIPLE-STEP FORMAT

A **multiple-step income statement** derives one or more intermediate amounts before the final amount for ordinary, continuing income is reported. Examples of intermediate amounts that may be derived are Gross Profit on Sales and Income before Taxes. The following is a brief illustration of a multiple-step income statement:

Sales		$260,000
Cost of Goods Sold		150,000
Gross Profit on Sales		$110,000
Selling Expenses	$32,000	
Administrative Expenses	43,000	75,000
Income before Taxes		$ 35,000
Income Tax Expense		14,000
Net Income		$ 21,000

SINGLE-STEP FORMAT

A **single-step income statement** derives the ordinary, continuing income of the business in one step—by subtracting total expenses from total revenues. A brief single-step income statement is illustrated below:

Sales		$260,000
Expenses:		
Cost of Goods Sold	$150,000	
Selling Expenses	32,000	
Administrative Expenses	43,000	
Income Tax Expense	14,000	
Total Expenses		239,000
Net Income		$ 21,000

Discontinued Operations

When a company sells, abandons, or otherwise disposes of a segment of its operations, a **discontinued operations** section of the income statement reports information about the discontinued segment. The discontinued operations section presents two categories of information:

1. The income or loss from the segment's operations for the portion of the year before its discontinuance.
2. The gain or loss from the disposal of the segment.

EXHIBIT 16—3	INCOME STATEMENT SHOWING DISCONTINUED OPERATIONS

PACIFIC CORPORATION
INCOME STATEMENT
FOR THE YEAR ENDED DECEMBER 31, 1993

Sales		$700,000
Cost of Goods Sold		360,000
Gross Profit on Sales		$340,000
Selling Expenses	$75,000	
Administrative Expenses	45,000	120,000
Income from Continuing Operations before Taxes		$220,000
Income Tax Expense		88,000
Income from Continuing Operations		$132,000
Discontinued Operations:		
Loss from Operations of Discontinued Division Y (Net of $16,000 reduction of income taxes)	$24,000	
Loss on Disposal of Division Y (Net of $40,000 reduction of income taxes)	60,000	84,000
Net Income		$ 48,000
Earnings per Common Share:		
Income from Continuing Operations		$3.30
Discontinued Operations		(2.10)
Net Income		$1.20

The section is placed immediately after information about ordinary, continuing operations.

A *segment* of a business is a unit—such as a department or a division—whose activities constitute a separate major line of business or serve a particular class of customer. The assets and operating results of the segment must be clearly distinguishable from the rest of the company. For example, a furniture manufacturing division of a diversified manufacturing company is a segment of the business.

To illustrate the reporting of discontinued operations, we assume that on July 1, 1993, Pacific Corporation sold its Division Y. From January 1 through June 30, Division Y had operated at a loss, net of taxes, of $24,000 ($40,000 operating loss less a $16,000 reduction in income taxes caused by the operating loss). The loss, net of taxes, from the sale of the division was $60,000 ($100,000 loss on the sale less a $40,000 reduction in income taxes caused by the loss). Exhibit 16-3 illustrates the income statement for Pacific Corporation, including the information about Division Y in the discontinued operations section. Note that when there is a discontinued operations section, the difference between the ordinary revenues and expenses is labeled Income from Continuing Operations.

Extraordinary Items

Extraordinary items are transactions and events that are both *unusual in nature* and *occur infrequently*.[4] An item that is unusual in nature is highly abnormal and significantly different from the firm's ordinary and typical activities. To determine a firm's ordinary and typical activities, we must consider such things as the types of operations, lines of business, operating policies, and the environment in which the firm operates. The operating environment includes the characteristics of the industry, the geographic location of the firm's facilities, and the type of government regulations

---

[4]*Opinions of the Accounting Principles Board, No. 30*, "Reporting the Results of Operations—Reporting the Effects of Disposal of a Segment of a Business, and Extraordinary, Unusual and Infrequently Occurring Events and Transactions" (New York: American Institute of Certified Public Accountants, 1973).

imposed. A transaction or event is considered to occur infrequently if the firm does not expect it to recur in the foreseeable future.

The fact that the two criteria—unusual nature and infrequent occurrence—must *both* be present considerably restricts the events and transactions that qualify as extraordinary items. For example, suppose a tobacco grower suffers crop loss from a flood, which normally happens every few years in this area. The history of floods creates a reasonable expectation that another flood will occur in the foreseeable future. The loss, therefore, does not meet the criteria for an extraordinary item. Now consider a different tobacco grower who suffers flood damage to his crop for the first time from a broken dam. The dam is repaired and is not expected to fail in the foreseeable future. The flood loss in this circumstance is an extraordinary item.

Other events that may generate extraordinary losses are earthquakes, expropriation of property, and prohibitions under newly enacted laws (such as a government ban on a product currently marketed). An extraordinary gain may result from a nonrecurring sale of an asset never used in operations. Assume that a manufacturing company acquired land several years ago for future use but then changed its plans and held the land for appreciation. If this is the only undeveloped land the company owns and it will not speculate in land in the foreseeable future, any gain from the sale of the land is considered extraordinary.

One exception to the criteria defining extraordinary items relates to gains and losses incurred when a company extinguishes its own debt. These gains and losses are aggregated and, if material, are classified as extraordinary items.[5] An example of a debt extinguishment loss is presented in the next chapter.

Exhibit 16-4 is an income statement for a corporation with an extraordinary item. During 1993, Atlantic Corporation, a manufacturing concern, sold a block of common stock of Z Company, a publicly traded company, at a gain of $80,000. The shares of stock were the only security investment the company had ever owned, and it does not plan to acquire other stocks in the foreseeable future. For Atlantic Corporation, this gain is unusual, infrequent, and properly considered an extraordinary item. The gain is reported net of $32,000 of income taxes on the gain, as shown in Exhibit 16-4 **1**.

UNUSUAL OR NONRECURRING ITEMS Events and transactions that are unusual *or* nonrecurring, but not both, are not extraordinary items. *Accounting Principles Board Opinion No. 30* notes several examples of gains and losses that are not extraordinary either because they are typical or because they may recur as a result of continuing business activities. Examples of such items are gains and losses from (1) the write-down or write-off of receivables, inventories, and intangible assets; (2) the exchange or translation of foreign currencies; (3) the sale or abandonment of property, plant, or equipment used in the business; (4) the effects of a strike; and (5) the adjustments of long-term contract accruals. An unusual or infrequently occurring item of a material amount should be reported as a separate component of income from ordinary, continuing operations.

Assume that during 1993 Atlantic Corporation incurred a $45,000 loss because of a labor strike at one of its plants. The strike was not part of the company's ordinary activities, but Atlantic Corporation has a history of labor difficulties. Therefore, even though the strike loss was unusual, it was not infrequent because it will likely happen again in the foreseeable future. Because it did not qualify as an extraordinary item, the before-tax amount of the strike loss was reported as a separate item among the ordinary expenses, as shown in Exhibit 16-4 **2**.

---

[5]Unless the gains or losses result from extinguishments of debt made to satisfy sinking-fund requirements that must be met within one year. See *Statement of Financial Accounting Standards No. 64*, "Extinguishments of Debt Made to Satisfy Sinking-fund Requirements" (Stamford, CT: Financial Accounting Standards Board, 1982).

EXHIBIT 16—4 | **INCOME STATEMENT SHOWING EXTRAORDINARY ITEM, UNUSUAL OR NONRECURRING ITEM, AND CHANGE IN ACCOUNTING PRINCIPLE**

ATLANTIC CORPORATION
INCOME STATEMENT
FOR THE YEAR ENDED DECEMBER 31, 1993

Sales		$1,900,000
Expenses:		
Cost of Goods Sold	$1,100,000	
Selling Expenses	195,000	
Administrative Expenses	160,000	
2 Loss from Plant Strike	45,000	
Income Tax Expense	160,000	
Total Expenses		1,660,000
Income before Extraordinary Item and Cumulative Effect of a Change in Accounting Principle		$ 240,000
1 Extraordinary Item:		
Gain from Sale of Z Company Stock (Net of $32,000 income taxes)		48,000
3 Cumulative Effect on Prior Years of Changing to a Different Depreciation Method (Net of $8,000 income taxes)		12,000
Net Income		$ 300,000
Earnings per Common Share:		
Income before Extraordinary Item and Cumulative Effect of a Change in Accounting Principle		$2.00
Extraordinary Gain		.40
Cumulative Effect on Prior Years of Changing to a Different Depreciation Method		.10
Net Income		$2.50

Changes in Accounting Principles

Occasionally a company may implement a **change in accounting principle**—that is, switch from one generally accepted method to another.[6] Examples include a change in inventory pricing method—such as from FIFO to weighted average—or a change in depreciation method—such as from double declining balance to straight line. Because the comparability of financial data through time is enhanced by the consistent use of accounting principles, a company should change principles only when it can demonstrate that the new principle is preferable.

Almost all changes in accounting principles introduce a new item into the income statement—the **cumulative effect of a change in principle.** This item represents the total difference in the cumulative income for all prior years had the new principle been used in those years. It is equal to the difference between (1) the retained earnings at the beginning of the year and (2) the retained earnings amount at the beginning of the year had the new principle been used in all years in which the previous principle was followed for the items in question. The cumulative effect is disclosed immediately before the net income figure.

To illustrate the reporting of the cumulative effect of a change in principle, we assume that Atlantic Corporation in Exhibit 16-4 changed its method of depreciating

---

[6] The phrase *generally accepted accounting principles* covers a wide spectrum of accounting guidelines, ranging from basic standards to specific methods. In accounting principle changes, the focus is on changes in specific methods.

plant equipment in 1993, switching from an accelerated method to the straight-line method. Cumulative income before income taxes for years prior to 1993 would have been $20,000 greater if the straight-line method had been used to depreciate the plant equipment in those years. If we assume an income tax rate of 40%, the $12,000 after-tax amount of the effect of the change in principle would be reported on Atlantic Corporation's income statement as shown in Exhibit 16-4 **3**.

In addition to reporting the cumulative effect, the company should, in a note to the financial statements, justify the change and disclose the effect of the change on the current year's income exclusive of the cumulative adjustment. The effect of the change on earnings per share should also be reported.

Annual financial reports often include financial statements for prior periods for comparative purposes. These prior period statements are not revised to reflect the new principle adopted this period. For each period reported, however, the net income and the related earnings per share are recomputed as if the new principle had been in effect in that period.[7] Each period's income statement will disclose these recomputed amounts.

The above disclosure requirements accommodate two conflicting positions on the appropriate method of disclosing a change in accounting principle. One position stresses the possible dilution of public confidence in financial statements if previously reported statements are revised to reflect a new principle—hence, the inclusion of a cumulative effect on prior years' income in the current year's income statement with no revision of prior period statements. The other position emphasizes the importance of consistency in the use of accounting principles for comparative analysis of data—hence, the disclosure of selected, significant pieces of information, recomputed using the new principle, for all periods presented in the financial statements.

EARNINGS PER SHARE

OBJECTIVE 5   IDENTIFY and ILLUSTRATE the computation and disclosure of earnings per share.

A financial statistic of great interest to corporation shareholders and potential investors is the **earnings per share (EPS)** of common stock. Consequently, earnings per share data are widely disseminated, reaching interested persons through such channels as annual stockholder reports, financial newspapers, and financial statistical services. Because this financial information is so important, accounting guidelines require the disclosure of earnings per share data on the income statement.

Earnings per share is computed by dividing the earnings available to common stockholders by the weighted average number of common shares outstanding during the year. The earnings available to common stockholders is the net income less any preferred stock dividend. Thus, the earnings per share computation is as follows:

$$\text{Earnings per Share} = \frac{\text{Net Income} - \text{Preferred Dividends}}{\text{Weighted Average Common Shares Outstanding}}$$

Simple Capital Structure

In determining the presentation of earnings per share data, accountants distinguish between corporations with simple capital structures and those with complex capital structures. An entity with a **simple capital structure** has no securities outstanding (or agreements to issue securities) that have the potential to dilute (reduce) earnings per share. For example, corporations whose capital structures consist only of common stock or common stock and preferred stock that cannot be converted into common stock have simple capital structures.

A corporation with a simple capital structure computes and presents one earnings per share number. The computation utilizes actual data only (as we shall see shortly, complex capital structure computations incorporate assumed data). To illustrate the calculation for a firm with a simple capital structure, suppose that Owens Corporation had a 1993 net income of $39,000. On January 1, 1993, 10,000 shares of common

---

[7] If an extraordinary item is reported, the income before extraordinary item and the related per-share amount must also be recomputed using the new principle.

stock were outstanding. An additional 6,000 common shares were issued on July 1, 1993. The company has no preferred stock.

Because Owens Corporation has no preferred stock, the numerator for the earnings per share calculation will be the $39,000 net income. The computation of average shares outstanding weights the common shares by the length of time they were outstanding. The 1993 weighted average common shares outstanding for Owens Corporation is 13,000, computed as follows:

Shares		Months Outstanding		Share Months
10,000	$\times$	6	=	60,000
16,000	$\times$	6	=	96,000
		12		156,000

$$\text{Weighted Average Common Shares Outstanding} = \frac{156,000}{12} = 13,000$$

Owen Corporation's 1993 earnings per share, then, is computed as follows:

$$\text{Earnings per Share} = \frac{\$39,000 - \$0}{13,000} = \$3.00$$

Complex Capital Structure

An entity with a **complex capital structure** contains one or more securities that have the potential to dilute earnings per share. For example, preferred stock convertible into common stock (convertible preferred stock) or debt convertible into common stock (convertible debt) are potentially dilutive securities because, if converted, these securities cause common shares outstanding to increase without providing the corporation with any additional assets to use to generate additional earnings.

A corporation with a complex capital structure presents two earnings per share amounts—a primary earnings per share and a fully diluted earnings per share. The computation of **primary earnings per share** includes the actual common stock plus any common stock equivalents. A common stock equivalent is a potentially dilutive security that is likely to be converted into common stock (accounting guidelines contain criteria for determining when a potentially dilutive security is a common stock equivalent). The calculation of **fully diluted earnings per share** is based on the assumption that all dilutive securities are converted into common stock (whether or not such conversion is likely). The difference between the two per-share amounts shows the maximum possible dilution in earnings per share from any outstanding dilutive securities that are not common stock equivalents.

To illustrate the computation of primary and fully diluted earnings per share, let us suppose that Bodeen Company had a net income of $90,000 for 1993. All year the company had 40,000 shares of common stock and 5,000 shares of convertible preferred stock outstanding. The annual dividend on the convertible preferred stock is 80 cents per share, and each share is convertible into two shares of common stock. The convertible preferred stock is a potentially dilutive security; we assume it is not a common stock equivalent.

Because Bodeen Company has no common stock equivalents, its calculation of primary earnings per share is the same as if it had a simple capital structure. Bodeen's preferred stock dividend is $4,000 (5,000 $\times$ $0.80) and its weighted average number of actual common shares outstanding is 40,000 (40,000 shares outstanding all year). Thus, primary earnings per share is computed as follows:

$$\text{Primary Earnings per Share} = \frac{\$90,000 - \$4,000}{40,000} = \$2.15$$

The calculation of Bodeen's fully diluted earnings per share incorporates the *assumption* that the preferred stock is converted into common stock at the beginning of 1993. Under this assumption, there would be no 1993 preferred stock dividend. Also, under this assumption the weighted average common shares outstanding would be 50,000 (40,000 actual common shares outstanding all year + 10,000 assumed common shares outstanding all year from the conversion of 5,000 shares of preferred stock). Thus, fully diluted earnings per share is computed as follows:

$$\text{Fully Diluted Earnings per Share} = \frac{\$90,000 - \$0}{50,000} = \$1.80$$

The variety of potentially dilutive securities and of events that affect outstanding common stock can make the computations of earnings per share quite complex. The analysis required for such computations is covered in advanced courses.

Additional Per-Share Disclosures

The form in which earnings per share are disclosed should correspond to the income statement content. Thus, if a firm reports discontinued operations, earnings per share should be disclosed for income from continuing operations as well as for net income. Companies may also disclose the per-share effect of discontinued operations, although this disclosure is optional. Exhibit 16-3 illustrates an earnings per share presentation with discontinued operations.

Similarly, if a firm reports extraordinary gains or losses, earnings per share should be reported for income before extraordinary items. At the company's option, the per-share effect of each extraordinary item may also be shown. If a firm reports the cumulative effect of a change in an accounting principle, accounting standards require the disclosure of the per-share amount of the cumulative effect. Exhibit 16-4 illustrates the earnings per share presentation for an income statement that contains both an extraordinary item and a change in an accounting principle.

SUMMARY OF THE INCOME STATEMENT

Reporting the income of a corporation with the variety of items discussed in this chapter can be complex. Exhibit 16-5 summarizes these items and indicates their placement on the income statement, the order in which they are normally reported, and whether each is reported before or net of its income tax effect. Each of these items on the statement is keyed with the number of its related explanation.

Note that changes in accounting estimates and unusual *or* nonrecurring items are reported without any related income tax amounts because they are included in the computation of income from continuing operations. Income tax expense in this section relates to all preceding items of revenue and expense. All items below income from continuing operations are reported at amounts net of their income tax effects. The income statement in Exhibit 16-5 is a single-step income statement. Income from continuing operations is computed in one step, subtracting total expenses from sales. A single-step statement may include sections other than income from continuing operations.

Note also that when the income statement contains special sections, the number of per-share disclosures increases. In Exhibit 16-5, the required earnings per share disclosures are per-share amounts for income from continuing operations, income before extraordinary items and cumulative effect of a change in accounting principle, cumulative effect of change in accounting principle, and net income.

ANALYTICAL APPLICATION

OBJECTIVE 6 DEFINE price-earnings ratio *and* EXPLAIN *its use.*

PRICE-EARNINGS RATIO

A financial ratio used by investors is the price-earnings ratio. The **price-earnings ratio** is computed by dividing the market price of a firm's stock by its earnings per share. Thus,

| EXHIBIT 16—5 | SUMMARY OF INCOME STATEMENT FORMAT |

ABC CORPORATION
INCOME STATEMENT
FOR THE YEAR ENDED DECEMBER 31, 1993

EXPLANATIONS

1 Changes in Accounting Estimates

Before-tax amounts are reported as part of related ordinary expenses.

2 Unusual or Nonrecurring Items

Before-tax amounts are separate items listed among the ordinary expenses.

3 Income Tax Expense

The initial allocation of income taxes applies to the net of all preceding revenue and expense items. All items appearing below income from continuing operations are reported net of income taxes.

4 Discontinued Operations

Involves reporting separately for the discontinued segment:
(a) Gain or loss from operations net of income taxes.
(b) Gain or loss on disposal net of income taxes.

5 Extraordinary Items

Reported net of income taxes.

6 Cumulative Effect of Change in Accounting Principle

Reported net of income taxes as the last item before net income on the income statement.

7 Earnings per Share

Items in bold type are required disclosures; others are optional. Complex capital structures require reporting of primary and fully diluted earnings per share amounts.

Sales			$XXX
Expenses:			
1 Ordinary Expenses (including effects of changes in accounting estimates)		$XX	
2 Unusual or Nonrecurring Items		XX	
3 Income Tax Expense		XX	
Total Expenses			XXX
Income from Continuing Operations			$XXX
4 Discontinued Operations:			
Gain or Loss from Operations (net of income taxes)		$XX	
Gain or Loss on Disposal (net of income taxes)		XX	XX
Income before Extraordinary Items and Cumulative Effect of a Change in Accounting Principle			$XXX
5 Extraordinary Items (net of income taxes)			XX
6 Cumulative Effect on Prior Years of Change in Accounting Principle (net of income taxes)			XX
Net Income			$XXX
7 Earnings per Common Share:			
Income from Continuing Operations			**$X**
Discontinued Operations			X
Income before Extraordinary Items and Cumulative Effect of a Change in Accounting Principle			**$X**
Extraordinary Item			X
Cumulative Effect of Change in Accounting Principle			**X**
Net Income			**$X**

$$\text{Price-Earnings Ratio} = \frac{\text{Market Price per Common Share}}{\text{Earnings per Share}}$$

The current market price of the firm's common stock and the earnings per share for the most recent four quarters of operations are typically used in calculating this ratio. For firms with complex capital structures, primary earnings per share is used. Also, if a firm's income statement includes data from discontinued operations or extraordinary items, the per-share amount before these items is generally used as the denominator in the ratio. The price-earnings ratio, abbreviated P/E, is reported with the stock listings in *The Wall Street Journal*.

To illustrate, we previously computed a 1993 primary earnings per share of $2.15 for Bodeen Corporation. If Bodeen's common stock had a market price per share of $39 at December 31, 1993, Bodeen's price-earnings ratio at the end of 1993 is $39/$2.15 = 18.1. With this price-earnings ratio, Bodeen's common stock would be characterized as selling at 18.1 times earnings, or as having an earnings multiple of 18.1, at the end of 1993.

After analyzing a firm, an investor may have determined what he or she believes is an appropriate earnings multiple for the firm. The investor will then compare it with the actual price-earnings ratio to evaluate whether the firm's stock is overpriced or underpriced.

A high price-earnings ratio for a firm usually indicates that investors expect higher than average earnings growth for the company. Firms in high growth industries, therefore, will generally have higher price-earnings ratios than will firms in stable, mature industries. The ratio will also vary within an industry, thus giving an indication of the relative attractiveness of firms to investors. For example, near the end of 1991, three firms in the computer hardware industry had the following price-earnings ratios: AMERICAN POWER CONVERSION, 47; APPLE COMPUTER, 22; and IBM, 16. The average price-earnings ratio near the end of 1991 for the stocks composing Standard & Poor's 500-stock index was 22.7.

KEY POINTS FOR CHAPTER OBJECTIVES

❶ IDENTIFY and DISTINGUISH between cash dividends and stock dividends (pp. 570–574).
- Cash dividends reduce retained earnings and are a current liability when declared.
- Stock dividends are accounted for by a transfer of retained earnings to the appropriate stock and paid-in capital accounts at the market value of the shares for small stock dividends and at the legal minimum for large stock dividends.

❷ ILLUSTRATE a retained earnings statement and a statement of stockholders' equity (pp. 574, 575).
- A retained earnings statement presents the events causing retained earnings to change during an accounting period.
- A statement of stockholders' equity presents the events causing each component of stockholders' equity (including retained earnings) to change during an accounting period.

❸ DISCUSS the accounting for prior period adjustments, changes in accounting estimates, and the process of restricting retained earnings (pp. 574–577).
- Prior period adjustments are corrections of material errors made in previous periods. They are charged or credited directly to Retained Earnings.
- The effects of changes in accounting estimates are spread over the appropriate current and future periods.
- Restrictions placed on retained earnings reduce the amount of retained earnings available for dividends.

❹ IDENTIFY and DISCUSS the income statement content and format (pp. 577–582).
- Tax allocation within a period improves the reporting of income taxes by disclosing both the tax effect and the item causing that effect in the same location in the income statement.
- The ordinary, continuing income may be reported in a single-step format or in a multiple-step format.
- Gains and losses from discontinued operations are reported in a special income statement section immediately following income from continuing operations.
- Extraordinary items are both unusual *and* nonrecurring; they are reported in a separate section of the income statement. Unusual *or* nonrecurring items are not reported in a separate section, but they may be separately identified in the first section of the income statement reporting data on ordinary and continuing operations.
- The cumulative effects of most changes in accounting principles are disclosed in the income statement in a special section immediately preceding net income.

❺ DISCUSS and ILLUSTRATE the computation and disclosure of earnings per share (pp. 582–584, 585).
- Corporations with complex capital structures present data on both primary and fully diluted earnings per share. A single presentation of earnings per share is appropriate for a corporation with a simple capital structure.
- Per-share amounts in addition to net income per share are reported when there are special sections in the income statement.

❻ ANALYTICAL APPLICATION: DEFINE *price-earnings ratio* and **EXPLAIN** its use (pp. 584–586).
- The price-earnings ratio is computed by dividing the current market price per share of common stock by the earnings per share.

SELF-TEST QUESTIONS FOR REVIEW

(Answers follow the Solution to Demonstration Problem.)

1. Which of the following events decreases a corporation's stockholders' equity?
   a. A payment of a previously declared cash dividend.
   b. A declaration of a 6% stock dividend.
   c. A $100,000 retained earnings restriction.
   d. A declaration of a $1 cash dividend per share of preferred stock.

2. In 1993, Corliss, Inc., discovered that an arithmetic error had been made in 1992, causing 1992's depreciation expense to be overstated. Corliss corrected the error in 1993 with a journal entry that included a credit to Retained Earnings. This situation illustrates a
   a. Prior period adjustment.
   b. Change in an accounting estimate.
   c. Change in an accounting principle.
   d. Restriction on retained earnings.

3. Assume that an income statement contains each of the four sections listed below. Which will be the last section in the income statement?
   a. Extraordinary item.
   b. Cumulative effect of a change in accounting principle.
   c. Income from continuing operations.
   d. Discontinued operations.

4. Which of the following items will appear in either a single-step or a multiple-step income statement for a merchandising firm?
   a. Restriction of retained earnings.
   b. Gross profit on sales.
   c. Income before extraordinary item.
   d. Prior period adjustment.

5. A corporation will make a dual presentation of earnings per share (primary and fully diluted earnings per share) when it
   a. Has two classes of stock outstanding (preferred and common stock).
   b. Uses a multiple-step income statement format.
   c. Has a capital structure that contains at least one potentially dilutive security (a complex capital structure).
   d. Has restrictions on the amount of earnings that may be paid out as dividends.

DEMONSTRATION PROBLEM FOR REVIEW

Information related to the income and retained earnings of Alpha, Inc., for 1993 is listed below. For simplicity, amounts are limited to three digits. Using these data, prepare a single-step income statement and a retained earnings statement for Alpha, Inc., for 1993. Assume that all changes in income are subject to a 40% income tax rate. Disregard earnings per share disclosures.

Additional uncollectible accounts expense due to revised estimate of percentage of anticipated uncollectible accounts (considered a selling expense)	$ 20
Cost of goods sold	420
Cash dividends declared	70
Overstatement of 1992 ending inventory (caused by error)	10
Gain on condemnation of property (considered unusual and infrequent)	40
Gain on disposal of discontinued Beta Division	80

Increase in prior years' reported income before income taxes due to change in depreciation method	$ 20
Loss from labor strike (considered unusual but recurring)	40
Loss from operations of discontinued Beta Division	50
Other operating expenses	230
Retained earnings balance at end of 1992	454
Sales	980
Selling and administrative expenses (before revised estimate of uncollectible accounts)	170

SOLUTION TO DEMONSTRATION PROBLEM   (Selected computations appear as notes to the financial statements.)

ALPHA, INC.
INCOME STATEMENT
FOR THE YEAR ENDED DECEMBER 31, 1993

Sales		$980
Expenses:		
Cost of Goods Sold	$420	
Other Operating Expenses	230	
Selling and Administrative Expenses (Note A)	190	
Loss from Labor Strike	40	
Income Tax Expense (Note B)	40	
Total Expenses		920
Income from Continuing Operations		$ 60
Discontinued Operations:		
Loss from Operations of Discontinued Beta Division (Net of $20 reduction of income taxes) (Note C)	($ 30)	
Gain on Disposal of Discontinued Beta Division (Net of $32 income taxes) (Note D)	48	18
Income before Extraordinary Item and Cumulative Effect of a Change in Accounting Principle		$ 78
Extraordinary Item:		
Gain on Condemnation of Property (Net of $16 income taxes) (Note E)		24
Cumulative Effect on Prior Years of Changing to a Different Depreciation Method (Net of $8 income taxes) (Note F)		12
Net Income		$114

ALPHA, INC.
RETAINED EARNINGS STATEMENT
FOR THE YEAR ENDED DECEMBER 31, 1993

Retained Earnings, January 1, 1993	$454
Less: Correction of Prior Period Inventory Error (Net of $4 reduction of income taxes) (Note G)	6
Adjusted Balance, January 1, 1993	$448
Add: Net Income	114
	$562
Less: Cash Dividends Declared	70
Retained Earnings, December 31, 1993	$492

Notes to financial statements:
  (A) $170 + $20 = $190
  (B) 40% [$980 − ($420 + $230 + $190 + $40)] = $40
  (C) $50 − [0.4($50)] = $30
  (D) $80 − [0.4($80)] = $48
  (E) $40 − [0.4($40)] = $24
  (F) $20 − [0.4($20)] = $12
  (G) $10 − [0.4($10)] = $6

ANSWERS TO SELF-TEST QUESTIONS

1. d, p. 571   **2.** a, p. 574   **3.** b, p. 581   **4.** c, p. 580   **5.** c, p. 583

GLOSSARY OF KEY TERMS USED IN THIS CHAPTER

change in accounting estimate A revision of an estimate used in an accounting analysis, such as the revision of the useful life of a plant asset (p. 576).

change in accounting principle A switch from one generally accepted accounting method to another generally accepted method, such as changing depreciation methods (p. 581).

complex capital structure A corporate capital structure containing one or more potentially dilutive securities. Complex capital structures normally require a dual presentation of earnings per share (p. 583).

cumulative effect of a change in principle An item appearing in a separate section of the income statement resulting from a change in accounting principle. It represents the total difference in the cumulative net income for all prior years affected by the change, assuming that the new principle had been used in those years (p. 581).

deficit A negative (debit) balance in a corporation's Retained Earnings account (p. 570).

discontinued operations Operating segments of a company that have been sold, abandoned, or disposed of during the accounting period. Related operating income (or loss) and related gains and losses on disposal are reported separately on the income statement (p. 578).

dividends Distributions of assets (usually cash) or stock from a corporation to its stockholders (p. 570).

earnings per share A financial ratio computed as net income less preferred stock dividends divided by the weighted average common shares outstanding for the period (p. 582).

extraordinary items Transactions and events that are unusual in nature and occur infrequently. Gains and losses on such items are shown separately, net of tax effects, on the income statement (p. 579).

fully diluted earnings per share An earnings per share presentation for corporations with complex capital structures that assumes all dilutive securities are converted into common stock (p. 583).

multiple-step income statement An income statement in which one or more intermediate amounts, such as gross profit on sales, are derived before the ordinary, continuing income is reported (p. 578).

price-earnings ratio A financial ratio computed as the current market price per common share divided by the earnings per share (p. 584).

primary earnings per share An earnings per share presentation that considers the actual common stock outstanding plus any dilutive common stock equivalents; generally, a required presentation for corporations with complex capital structures (p. 583).

prior period adjustment A correction of an error made in the financial statements of a prior accounting period (p. 574).

retained earnings The amount of stockholders' equity resulting from a corporation's retention of assets generated from operating activities (p. 570).

retained earnings restrictions Voluntary, contractual, or statutory restrictions placed on the availability of retained earnings for dividend declarations (p. 576).

retained earnings statement A financial statement showing the changes that occurred in retained earnings during the accounting period (p. 574).

simple capital structure A corporate capital structure that does not contain any securities with the potential to dilute earnings per share (p. 582).

single-step income statement An income statement in which the ordinary, continuing income is derived in one step by subtracting total expenses from total revenues (p. 578).

statement of stockholders' equity A financial statement that presents the changes that occurred in all components of stockholders' equity during the accounting period (p. 574).

stock dividends Additional shares of its own stock issued by a corporation to its current stockholders in proportion to their ownership interests (p. 571).

tax allocation within a period The apportionment of total income tax expense among the various sections of an income statement (p. 577).

QUESTIONS

16-1 What is a stock dividend? How does a common stock dividend paid to common shareholders affect their respective ownership interests?

16-2 Distinguish between the accounting for a small stock dividend and the accounting for a large stock dividend.

16-3 What information is presented in a retained earnings statement? a statement of stockholders' equity?

16-4 Niro Company discovered this year that a significant portion of its inventory was overlooked during its inventory count at the end of last year. How should the correction of this error be disclosed in the financial statements?

16-5 Distinguish between an error and a change in accounting estimate. How is reporting corrections of errors different from reporting changes in accounting estimates?

16-6 What is a restriction of retained earnings? Why and by whom are such restrictions made?

16-7 Where do the following accounts (and their balances) appear in the balance sheet?
   a. Dividends Payable—Common Stock
   b. Stock Dividend Distributable

16-8 What is meant by *tax allocation within a period*? What is the purpose of this type of tax allocation?

16-9 What is the difference between a single-step income statement and a multiple-step income statement?

16-10 Which one of the following amounts would appear only in a multiple-step income statement?

Income from continuing operations.
Income before extraordinary item.
Gross profit on sales.
Net income.

16-11 What is a business *segment*? Why are gains and losses from a discontinued segment reported in a separate section of the income statement?

16-12 Define *extraordinary items*. How are extraordinary items shown in the income statement?

16-13 A manufacturing plant of Park Corporation was destroyed by an earthquake, which is rare in the region where the plant was located. Where should this loss be classified in the income statement?

16-14 A Florida citrus grower incurs substantial frost damage to crops. Frost damage typically is experienced every few years. How should the loss on the crops be shown in the income statement?

16-15 This year, Bradley Company switched from the FIFO method of inventory pricing to the weighted average method. Cumulative income before income taxes for previous years would have been $70,000 lower if the weighted average method had been used.
   a. Assuming a 40% income tax rate, how should the effect of this inventory pricing change be shown in the income statement?
   b. If a comparative income statement is presented in the annual report, should Bradley revise last year's income statement using the weighted average method?

16-16 Distinguish between corporations with simple capital structures and those with complex capital structures. What does the type of capital structure imply regarding the presentation of earnings per share data?

16-17 In 1993, Milford Company earned a net income of $250,800. The company, which has a simple capital structure, started the year with 36,000 shares of common stock outstanding and issued an additional 6,000 shares on September 1. (There is no preferred stock.) What is Milford Company's 1993 earnings per share?

16-18 What assumption underlies the computation of fully diluted earnings per share? What does the difference between the amounts of primary earnings per share and fully diluted earnings per share reveal?

16-19 For 1993, Cray Company's primary earnings per share was $3.25 and its fully diluted earnings per share was $3.07. At December 31, 1993, Cray's common stock had a market price of $55.25 per share. What is Cray's price-earnings ratio at December 31, 1993?

EXERCISES

CASH DIVIDENDS — OBJ. 1 —

16-20 Sanders Corporation has outstanding 5,000 shares of $50 par value, 6% preferred stock, and 20,000 shares of $1 par value common stock. The company has $225,000 of retained earnings. At year-end, the company declares the regular $3 per share cash dividend on the preferred stock and a $2.10 per share cash dividend on the common stock. Three weeks later, the company pays the dividends.
   a. Prepare the journal entry for the declaration of the cash dividends.
   b. Prepare the journal entry for the payment of the cash dividends.

STOCK DIVIDENDS — OBJ. 1 —

16-21 Witt Corporation has outstanding 50,000 shares of $5 par value common stock. At year-end, the company declares a 4% stock dividend. The market price of the stock on the declaration date is $35 per share. Four weeks later, the company issues the shares of stock to shareholders.

a. Prepare the journal entry for the declaration of the stock dividend.

b. Prepare the journal entry for the issuance of the stock dividend.

c. Assume that the company declared a 40% stock dividend rather than a 4% stock dividend. Prepare the journal entries for (1) the declaration of the stock dividend and (2) the issuance of the stock dividend.

RETAINED EARNINGS STATEMENT — OBJ. 2 —

16-22 Use the following data to prepare a retained earnings statement for Shepler Corporation for 1993. Assume a 40% income tax rate.

Total retained earnings originally reported at December 31, 1992	$190,000
Cash dividends declared in 1993	40,000
Understatement of 1992 ending inventory discovered late in 1993 (Caused by arithmetic errors)	15,000
Net income for 1993	105,000
Stock dividends declared in 1993	22,000

PRIOR PERIOD ADJUSTMENT — OBJ. 3 —

16-23 Late in 1994, Lowe Corporation receives a notice from the Internal Revenue Service that Lowe had made an arithmetic error on its 1993 income tax return (the multiplication of the income tax rate times taxable income was wrong). As a result, Lowe owes another $5,500 of income taxes for 1993.

a. Prepare the 1994 journal entry to record the additional income taxes owed for 1993.

b. Where will Lowe Corporation report this event in its 1994 financial statements?

INCOME STATEMENT SECTIONS — OBJ. 4 —

16-24 During the current year, Dale Corporation incurred an extraordinary tornado loss of $200,000 and sold a segment of its business at a gain of $175,000. Until it was sold, the segment had a current period operating loss of $80,000. Also, the company discovered that an error caused last year's ending inventory to be understated by $25,000 (a material amount). The company had $600,000 income from continuing operations for the current year. Prepare the lower part of the income statement, beginning with the $600,000 income from continuing operations. Follow tax allocation procedures, assuming that all changes in income are subject to a 40% income tax rate. Disregard earnings per share disclosures.

ACCOUNTING CHANGES AND PRIOR PERIOD ADJUSTMENT — OBJ. 3, 4 —

16-25 For each of the following current year events for Prince, Inc., (1) identify the type of accounting change or other category of event involved, (2) indicate where each would be reported on the current year's income or retained earnings statement, and (3) illustrate how each would be disclosed including the relevant dollar amounts. Assume that the income tax rate for all years is 40%.

a. The company changed from the sum-of-the-years'-digits to the straight-line method of depreciating its equipment. Cumulative income before income taxes for prior years would have been $60,000 higher under the straight-line method.

b. The company discovered that, because of a new employee's oversight, depreciation of $20,000 on an addition to the plant had been omitted last year. The amount is material.

c. A patent acquired at a cost of $150,000 five years ago (including the current year) has been amortized under the straight-line method using an estimated useful life of 15 years. In reviewing accounts for the year-end adjustments, the company revised its estimate of the total useful life to 9 years.

EARNINGS PER SHARE — OBJ. 5 —

16-26 Lucky Corporation began the year with a simple capital structure consisting of 100,000 shares of common stock outstanding. On April 1, 5,000 additional shares were issued, and another 15,000 shares were issued on August 1. The company had a net income for the year of $308,000.

a. Compute the earnings per share of common stock.

b. Assume that the company also had 11,000 shares of 6%, $50 par value cumulative preferred stock outstanding throughout the year. Compute the earnings per share of common stock.

EARNINGS PER SHARE — OBJ. 5 —

16-27 During 1993, Dogwood Corporation had 80,000 shares of $10 par value common stock and 10,000 shares of 5%, $100 par value convertible preferred stock outstanding. The preferred stock is not a common stock equivalent. Each share of preferred stock may be converted into two shares of common stock. Dogwood Corporation's 1993 net income was $490,000.

a. Compute the primary earnings per share for 1993.
b. Compute the fully diluted earnings per share for 1993.

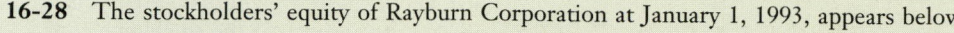

PROBLEMS

Retained Earnings: Transactions and Statement
— Obj. 1, 2 —

16-28 The stockholders' equity of Rayburn Corporation at January 1, 1993, appears below.

Common Stock, $5 Par Value, 200,000 shares authorized; 80,000 shares issued and outstanding	$400,000
Paid-in Capital in Excess of Par Value	539,000
Retained Earnings	285,000

During 1993, the following transactions occurred:

June 7   Declared a 10% stock dividend; market value of the common stock was $12 per share.

28   Issued the stock dividend declared on June 7.

Dec. 5   Declared a cash dividend of $1 per share.

26   Paid the cash dividend declared on December 5.

31   Closed the net income of $238,000 from the Income Summary account to Retained Earnings

31   Closed the dividend accounts to Retained Earnings.

REQUIRED

a. Prepare general journal entries to record the foregoing transactions.
b. Prepare a retained earnings statement for 1993.

Retained Earnings: Transactions and Statement
— Obj. 1, 2, 3 —

16-29 The stockholders' equity of Cyclone Corporation at January 1, 1993, follows.

6% Preferred Stock, $25 Par Value, 20,000 shares authorized; 10,000 shares issued and outstanding	$ 250,000
Common Stock, $5 Par Value, 300,000 shares authorized; 60,000 shares issued and outstanding	300,000
Paid-in Capital in Excess of Par Value—Common Stock	540,000
Retained Earnings	460,000
Total Stockholders' Equity	$1,550,000

The following transactions, among others, occurred during 1993:

Feb. 10   Discovered that the accountant overlooked a 1991 adjusting entry for $8,000 of goodwill amortization. Goodwill amortization was not deductible for tax purposes, so this error has no income tax effect.

June 18   Declared a 50% stock dividend on all outstanding shares of common stock. The market value of the stock was $15 per share.

July 1   Issued the stock dividend declared on June 18.

Dec. 20   Declared the annual cash dividend on the preferred stock and a cash dividend of $1.25 per share of common stock, payable on January 20 to stockholders of record on December 28.

31   Closed the Income Summary account, with net earnings of $392,000, to Retained Earnings.

31   Closed the dividend accounts to Retained Earnings.

REQUIRED

a. Prepare journal entries to record the foregoing transactions.
b. Prepare a retained earnings statement for 1993.

Stockholders' Equity: Transactions and Statement
— Obj. 1, 2 —

16-30 The stockholders' equity section of Day Corporation at December 31, 1992, follows:

Common Stock, $10 Par Value, 100,000 shares authorized, 25,000 shares issued, 4,000 shares are in the treasury	$250,000
Paid-in Capital in Excess of Par Value	325,000
Paid-in Capital from Treasury Stock	12,000
Retained Earnings (See Note)	198,000
	$785,000
Less: Treasury Stock (4,000 shares) at Cost	100,000
Total Stockholders' Equity	$685,000

Note: The availability of retained earnings for cash dividends is restricted by $100,000 due to the purchase of treasury stock.

The following transactions affecting stockholders' equity occurred during 1993:

Jan.   8   Issued 10,000 shares of previously unissued common stock for $26 cash per share.

Mar. 12   Sold all of the treasury shares for $27 cash per share.

June 30   Declared a 6% stock dividend on all outstanding shares of common stock. The market value of the stock was $30 per share.

July 10   Issued the stock dividend declared on June 30.

Oct.   7   Acquired 1,100 shares of common stock for the treasury at $28 cash per share.

Dec. 18   Declared a cash dividend of 80 cents per outstanding common share, payable on January 9 to stockholders of record on December 31.

       31   Closed the Income Summary account, with net income of $183,000, to Retained Earnings.

       31   Closed the dividend accounts to Retained Earnings.

REQUIRED

a. Prepare journal entries to record the foregoing transactions.

b. Prepare a statement of stockholders' equity for 1993.

INCOME STATEMENT FORMAT — OBJ. 4 —

16-31   The following information from Belvidere Company's 1993 operations is available:

Administrative expenses	$ 80,000
Cost of goods sold	580,000
Sales	965,000
Flood loss (considered unusual and infrequent)	30,000
Selling expenses	106,000
Interest expense	9,000
Loss from operations of discontinued segment	75,000
Gain on disposal of discontinued segment	40,000
Income taxes:	
Amount applicable to ordinary operations	76,000
Reduction applicable to flood loss	12,000
Reduction applicable to loss from operations of discontinued segment	30,000
Amount applicable to gain on disposal of discontinued segment	16,000

REQUIRED

a. Prepare a multiple-step income statement for 1993. (Disregard earnings per share amounts.)

b. Prepare a single-step income statement for 1993. (Disregard earnings per share amounts.)

EARNINGS PER SHARE — OBJ. 5 —

16-32   Leland Corporation began 1993 with 60,000 shares of common stock and 8,000 shares of convertible preferred stock outstanding. On March 1 an additional 5,000 shares of common stock were issued. On August 1, another 8,000 shares of common stock were issued. On November 1, 3,000 shares of common stock were reacquired for the treasury. The preferred stock has a $1.50 per-share dividend rate, and each share may be converted into one share of common stock. The preferred stock is not a common stock equivalent. Leland Corporation's 1993 net income is $213,000.

REQUIRED

a. Compute primary earnings per share for 1993.

b. Compute fully diluted earnings per share for 1993.

c. If the preferred stock were not convertible, Leland Corporation would have a simple capital structure. What would be its earnings per share for 1993?

EARNINGS PER SHARE AND MULTIPLE-STEP INCOME STATEMENT — OBJ. 4, 5 —

16-33   Bowden Corporation discloses earnings per share amounts for extraordinary items. The following summarized data relate to the company's 1993 operations:

Sales	$990,000
Cost of goods sold	600,000
Selling expenses	77,000
Administrative expenses	95,000

Loss from earthquake damages (considered unusual and infrequent)	$55,000
Loss on sale of equipment	8,000
Income tax expense (not allocated)	62,000

Shares of common stock:	
Outstanding at January 1, 1993	27,000 shares
Additional issued at May 1, 1993	4,000 shares
Additional issued at November 1, 1993	2,000 shares

REQUIRED

Prepare a multiple-step income statement for Bowden Corporation for 1993. Assume a 40% income tax rate. Allocate income tax expense within the income statement. Include earnings per share disclosures for 1993 at the bottom of the income statement. Bowden Corporation has no preferred stock.

ALTERNATE EXERCISES

CASH AND STOCK DIVIDENDS
— OBJ. 1 —

16-20A Mandrich Corporation has outstanding 20,000 shares of $10 par value common stock. The company has $306,000 of retained earnings. At year-end, the company declares a cash dividend of $1.70 per share and a 5% stock dividend. The market price of the stock at the declaration date is $20 per share. Four weeks later, the company pays the dividends.
a. Prepare the journal entry for the declaration of the cash dividend.
b. Prepare the journal entry for the declaration of the stock dividend.
c. Prepare the journal entry for the payment of the cash dividend.
d. Prepare the journal entry for the payment of the stock dividend.

LARGE STOCK DIVIDEND AND STOCK SPLIT
— OBJ. 1 —

16-21A Key Corporation has 25,000 shares of $20 par value common stock outstanding and retained earnings of $620,000. The company declares a 100% stock dividend. The market price at the declaration date is $26 per share.
a. Prepare the general journal entries for (1) the declaration of the dividend and (2) the issuance of the dividend.
b. Assume that the company splits its stock two shares for one share and reduces the par value from $20 to $10 rather than declaring a 100% stock dividend. How does the accounting for the stock split differ from the accounting for the 100% stock dividend?

RETAINED EARNINGS STATEMENT
— OBJ. 2 —

16-22A Use the following data to prepare a retained earnings statement for Schauer Corporation for 1993. Assume a 40% income tax rate.

Total retained earnings originally reported at December 31, 1992	$224,000
Stock dividends declared in 1993	30,000
Cash dividends declared in 1993	14,000
Understatement of 1992 depreciation expense discovered late in 1993 (Caused by arithmetic errors)	5,000
Net income for 1993	86,000

PRIOR PERIOD ADJUSTMENT
— OBJ. 3 —

16-23A Early in 1994, Wall Corporation discovered that its accountant had made an error in determining the firm's interest income for 1993. Due to an arithmetic error, the adjusting entry at the end of 1993 to record interest earned on investments in municipal obligations was understated by $15,000. The interest will be received in December 1994. The interest is exempt from income taxes, so there is no income tax effect.
a. Prepare the 1994 journal entry to correct the 1993 mistake in recording interest income.
b. Assume that Wall reported an ending retained earnings balance of $186,000 in its 1993 retained earnings statement. Prepare the first part of the 1994 retained earnings statement to show the correction of the 1994 beginning retained earnings balance.

INCOME STATEMENT SECTIONS
— OBJ. 4 —

16-24A During the current year, Newtech Corporation sold a segment of its business at a loss of $120,000. Until it was sold, the segment had a current period operating loss of $100,000. Also, the company had an extraordinary gain of $60,000 during the year as the result of an expropriation settlement received from a foreign government.

The company also changed depreciation methods during the year. Depreciation expense in prior years would have been smaller by $90,000 had the new principle been used in those years. The company has $900,000 income from continuing operations for the current year. Prepare the lower part of the income statement, beginning with the $900,000 income from continuing operations. Follow tax allocation procedures, assuming that all changes in income are subject to a 40% income tax rate. Disregard earnings per share disclosures.

ACCOUNTING CHANGES AND PRIOR PERIOD ADJUSTMENT — OBJ. 3, 4 —

16-25A For each of the following current year events for Lordkin, Inc., (1) identify the type of accounting change or other category of event involved, (2) indicate where each would be reported on the current year's income or retained earnings statement, and (3) illustrate how each would be disclosed including the relevant dollar amounts. Assume that the income tax rate for all years is 40%.

a. The company changed from FIFO to the weighted average method of inventory pricing. Cumulative income before income taxes for prior years would have been $75,000 lower under the weighted average method.

b. The company discovered that depreciation on certain assets had been recorded twice last year. The amount of excess depreciation recorded because of the mistake was $30,000.

c. The company recorded $300,000 of goodwill 11 years ago (including the current year) and has been amortizing it using the straight-line method over a 20-year period. Upon review, the company now believes the maximum amortization period of 40 years should be used.

EARNINGS PER SHARE — OBJ. 5 —

16-26A Ewing Corporation began the year with a simple capital structure consisting of 34,000 shares of common stock outstanding. On May 1, 10,000 additional shares were issued, and another 4,000 shares were issued on September 1. The company had a net income for the year of $231,000.

a. Compute the earnings per share of common stock.

b. Assume that the company also had 5,000 shares of 7%, $30 par value cumulative preferred stock outstanding throughout the year. Compute the earnings per share of common stock.

EARNINGS PER SHARE — OBJ. 5 —

16-27A During 1993, Boxer Corporation had 25,000 shares of $10 par value common stock and 5,000 shares of 6%, $50 par value convertible preferred stock outstanding. The preferred stock is not a common stock equivalent. Each share of preferred stock may be converted into three shares of common stock. Boxer Corporation's 1993 net income was $180,000.

a. Compute the primary earnings per share for 1993.

b. Compute the fully diluted earnings per share for 1993.

ALTERNATE PROBLEMS

16-28A The stockholders' equity of Striker Corporation at January 1, 1993, appears below.

RETAINED EARNINGS: TRANSACTIONS AND STATEMENT — OBJ. 1, 2 —

Common Stock, $10 Par Value, 100,000 shares authorized; 50,000 shares issued and outstanding	$500,000
Paid-in Capital in Excess of Par Value	350,000
Retained Earnings	270,000

During 1993, the following transactions occurred:

May 12 Declared a 7% stock dividend; market value of the common stock was $20 per share.

June 6 Issued the stock dividend declared on May 12.

Dec. 5 Declared a cash dividend of 90 cents per share.

30 Paid the cash dividend declared on December 5.

31 Closed the net income of $169,000 from the Income Summary account to Retained Earnings

31 Closed the dividend accounts to Retained Earnings.

REQUIRED

a. Prepare general journal entries to record the foregoing transactions.

b. Prepare a retained earnings statement for 1993.

Retained Earnings:
Transactions and
Statement
— Obj. 1, 2, 3 —

16-29A The stockholders' equity of Elson Corporation at January 1, 1993, is shown below.

5% Preferred Stock, $100 Par Value, 10,000 shares authorized; 5,000 shares issued and outstanding	$ 500,000
Paid-in Capital in Excess of Par Value—Preferred Stock	40,000
Common Stock, $5 Par Value, 200,000 shares authorized; 60,000 shares issued and outstanding	300,000
Paid-in Capital in Excess of Par Value—Common Stock	520,000
Retained Earnings	516,000
Total Stockholders' Equity	$1,876,000

The following transactions, among others, occurred during 1993:

Feb. 12 Elson Corporation carries life insurance on its key officers (with the corporation as beneficiary), and in 1992 it paid insurance premiums of $12,600 covering the three-year period 1992–1994. Today the company discovered that none of the $12,600 had been charged to Insurance Expense in 1992 (it all remained in Prepaid Insurance). These premiums are not deductible for tax purposes, so this error has no tax effect.

Apr. 1 Declared a 100% stock dividend on all outstanding shares of common stock. The market value of the stock was $15 per share.

15 Issued the stock dividend declared on April 1.

Dec. 7 Declared a 3% stock dividend on all outstanding shares of common stock. The market value of the stock was $13 per share.

17 Issued the stock dividend declared on December 7.

20 Declared the annual cash dividend on the preferred stock and a cash dividend of 75 cents per common share, payable on January 15 to stockholders of record on December 31.

31 Closed the Income Summary account, with net earnings of $274,000, to Retained Earnings.

31 Closed the dividend accounts to Retained Earnings.

REQUIRED

a. Prepare journal entries to record the foregoing transactions.
b. Prepare a retained earnings statement for 1993.

Income Statement and
Dividend Relationships
— Obj. 4, 5 —

16-30A Tricon Company presented the following earnings per share data:

Earnings per Share of Common Stock:	
Income before Extraordinary Item	$4.20
Extraordinary Gain (net of tax)	1.05
Net Income	$5.25

The company, which has a simple capital structure, began the year with 47,000 shares of $10 par value common stock and 7,500 shares of 5%, $40 par value preferred stock outstanding. On September 1, an additional 9,000 shares of common stock were issued. Cash dividends were distributed to both preferred and common stockholders.

REQUIRED

a. What is the annual preferred stock dividend requirement?
b. What was the net income for the current year for Tricon Company?
c. What was the amount of the extraordinary gain, net of the tax effect? What was the amount of the gain before the tax effect, assuming a 40% tax rate on the gain?
d. If the tax rate on ordinary income is 40%, what amount of income tax expense was reported in the income before extraordinary item section of the income statement?

Single-step Income
Statement and Retained
Earnings Statement
— Obj. 2, 4 —

16-31A The information listed below is related to Saglin Corporation's 1993 income and retained earnings.

Administrative expenses	$ 68,000
Stock dividends declared	43,000
Cash dividends declared	24,000
Cost of goods sold	508,000
Understatement of 1992 depreciation expense (caused by an error)	15,000

Increase in prior years' income before income taxes due to change in inventory pricing method (from weighted average to FIFO)	$ 75,000
Loss from uninsured portion of brushfire damages (considered unusual but recurring)	25,000
Loss from expropriation of property by foreign government (considered unusual and infrequent)	50,000
Retained earnings (balance at December 31, 1992)	361,000
Sales	848,000
Selling expenses	47,000
Income taxes:	
Amount applicable to ordinary operations	80,000
Reduction applicable to loss from expropriation of property	20,000
Amount applicable to increase in prior years' income before income taxes due to change in inventory pricing method	30,000
Reduction applicable to 1992 depreciation expense error	6,000

REQUIRED

a. Prepare a single-step income statement for Saglin Corporation for 1993. (Disregard earnings per share amounts.)

b. Prepare a retained earnings statement for Saglin Corporation for 1993.

EARNINGS PER SHARE
— OBJ. 5 —

16-32A Island Corporation began the year 1993 with 36,000 shares of common stock and 3,500 shares of convertible preferred stock outstanding. On May 1, an additional 12,000 shares of common stock were issued. On July 1, 6,000 shares of common stock were reacquired for the treasury. On September 1, the 6,000 treasury shares of common stock were reissued. The preferred stock has a $4 per-share dividend rate, and each share may be converted into two shares of common stock. The preferred stock is not a common stock equivalent. Island Corporation's 1993 net income is $143,000.

REQUIRED

a. Compute primary earnings per share for 1993.

b. Compute fully diluted earnings per share for 1993.

c. If the preferred stock were not convertible, Island Corporation would have a simple capital structure. What would be its earnings per share for 1993?

EARNINGS PER SHARE AND
MULTIPLE-STEP INCOME
STATEMENT
— OBJ. 4, 5 —

16-33A  Garner Corporation discloses earnings per share amounts for extraordinary items. The following summarized data are related to the company's 1993 operations:

Sales	$1,480,000
Cost of goods sold	860,000
Selling expenses	120,000
Administrative expenses	95,000
Gain from expropriation of property by foreign government (negotiated settlement; considered unusual and infrequent)	125,000
Loss from plant strike	65,000
Shares of common stock:	
Outstanding at January 1, 1993	46,000 shares
Additional issued at April 1, 1993	17,000 shares
Additional issued at August 1, 1993	3,000 shares

REQUIRED

Prepare a multiple-step income statement for Garner Corporation for 1993. Assume a 40% income tax rate. Include earnings per share disclosures for 1993 at the bottom of the income statement. Garner Corporation has no preferred stock.

CASES

Business Decision Case

The stockholders' equity section of Pillar Corporation's comparative balance sheet at the end of 1993 and 1994 is presented below. It is part of the financial data just reviewed at a stockholders' meeting.

	December 31, 1994	December 31, 1993
Common Stock, $10 Par Value, 600,000 shares authorized; issued at December 31, 1994, 220,000 shares; 1993, 200,000 shares	$2,200,000	$2,000,000
Paid-in Capital in Excess of Par Value	3,660,000	3,300,000
Retained Earnings (See Note)	2,480,000	2,460,000
Total Stockholders' Equity	$8,340,000	$7,760,000

Note: The availability of retained earnings for cash dividends is restricted by $1,500,000 due to a planned plant expansion.

The following items were also disclosed at the stockholders' meeting: net income for 1994 was $910,000; a 10% stock dividend was issued December 14, 1994; when the stock dividend was declared, the market value was $28 per share; the market value per share at December 31, 1994, was $26; management plans to borrow $350,000 to help finance a new plant addition, which is expected to cost a total of $1,750,000; and the customary $1.65 per share cash dividend had been revised to $1.50 when declared and issued the last week of December, 1994.

As part of its investor relations program, during the stockholders' meeting management asked stockholders to write any questions they might have concerning the firm's operations or finances. As assistant controller, you are given the stockholders' questions.

REQUIRED

Prepare brief but reasonably complete answers to the following questions:

a. What did Pillar do with the cash proceeds from the stock dividend issued in December?
b. What was my book value per share at the end of 1993 and 1994?
c. I owned 6,000 shares of Pillar in 1993 and have not sold any shares. How much more or less of the corporation do I own at December 31, 1994, and what happened to the market value of my interest in the company?
d. I heard someone say that stock dividends don't give me anything I didn't already have. Why did you issue one? Are you trying to fool us?
e. Instead of a stock dividend, why didn't you declare a cash dividend and let us buy the new shares that were issued?
f. Why are you cutting back on the dividends I receive?
g. If you have $1,500,000 put aside in retained earnings for the new plant addition, which will cost $1,750,000, why are you borrowing $350,000 instead of just the $250,000 needed?

Analytical Application Case

THE HOME DEPOT, INC., and TIFFANY & CO. are both specialty retailers. The Home Depot, headquartered in Atlanta, sells home improvement materials and supplies; Tiffany, headquartered in New York City, specializes in fine jewelry, china, crystal, and silver. As is typical of retailers, each company ends its fiscal year a few weeks after the December holiday season. The Home Depot's fiscal year ends on the Sunday nearest January 31 and Tiffany's fiscal year ends on January 31. Neither company has any outstanding preferred stock. For a recent fiscal year, the two companies reported the following financial data.

	Home Depot	Tiffany
Net income	$163,428,000	$36,661,000
Weighted average common shares outstanding	120,835,000	15,694,000

REQUIRED

a. For the fiscal year presented, compute The Home Depot's earnings per share.
b. For the fiscal year presented, compute Tiffany's earnings per share.
c. A few months after these financial results were issued, the stock of both companies was trading on the New York Stock Exchange at approximately the same price, The Home Depot at $50.88 and Tiffany & Co. at $51.63. Using these market prices, compute the price-earnings ratio for The Home Depot and Tiffany & Co.
d. At the time of the above price-earnings ratio, which of the two companies was apparently favored more by investors?

Ethics Case

Melanie Samson, vice president and general counsel, chairs the Executive Compensation Committee for Sunlight Corporation. Four and one-half years ago, the compensation committee designed a performance bonus plan for top management that was approved by the board of directors. The plan provides an attractive bonus for top management if the firm's earnings per share grows each year over a five-year period. The plan is now in its fifth year; for the past four years, earnings per share has grown each year. Last year, earnings per share was $1.95 (net income was $3,900,000 and the weighted average common shares outstanding was 2,000,000). Sunlight Corporation has no preferred stock and has had 2,000,000 common shares outstanding for several years. Samson has recently seen an estimate that Sunlight's net income this year will decrease about 5% from last year because of a slight recession in the economy.

Samson is disturbed by an item on the agenda for the board of directors meeting on June 20 and an accompanying note from John Kirk. Kirk is vice president and chief financial officer for Sunlight. Kirk is proposing to the board that Sunlight buy back 300,000 shares of its own common stock on July 1. Kirk's explanation is that the firm's stock is undervalued now and that Sunlight has excess cash on hand. When the stock subsequently recovers in value, Kirk notes, Sunlight will reissue the shares and generate a nice increase in contributed capital.

Kirk's note to Samson merely states, "Look forward to your support of my proposal at the board meeting."

REQUIRED

Why is Samson disturbed by Kirk's proposal and note? What possible ethical problem does Samson face when Kirk's proposal is up for a vote at the board meeting?

*L*ong-term *borrowed funds may come from a single source, such as an insurance company, or from numerous creditors by the firm's issuance of bonds.* ■ *Bond-holders receive bond certificates as evidence of the debt they purchased, and these certificates represent a contract to repay the debt with interest.* ■ *In its 1991 financial statement notes, Southwestern Bell, a communications corporation, reported $5,675,400,000 in total long-term debt, including debenture bonds like the one pictured here.*

17

LONG-TERM LIABILITIES

ome of the most frequently encountered or significant long-term liabilities of business firms are bonds payable, mortgage notes payable, employee pension liability, deferred tax liability, and capital lease liabilities. We discuss the accounting treatment of the first four of these long-term liabilities in this chapter; accounting for capital leases, a direct method of financing plant and equipment, was discussed in an earlier chapter.

BONDS PAYABLE

OBJECTIVE ① IDENTIFY *the reasons for issuing bonds and* **DESCRIBE** *various types of bonds.*

At various times in the course of business operations, particularly during phases of expansion, firms must secure additional long-term funds. When they choose long-term borrowing, it is often accomplished by issuing bonds. A **bond** is a long-term debt instrument that promises to pay interest periodically as well as a principal amount at maturity. The interest is usually paid semiannually. The principal amount is referred to as the bond's *face value* (because it is printed on the face of the bond certificate) or *par value*.

Bonds are used most often when a borrower receives funds from a large number of lenders contributing various amounts. In contrast, a note payable is used when all of the funds are borrowed from one lender. Consequently, bonds are usually drawn up to be negotiable. Because many parties are involved, the borrower should select a *trustee*—often a large bank—to represent the group of bondholders. As a third party to the transaction, the trustee may take security title to any pledged property and is likely to initiate any action necessitated by failure to meet the terms of the bond agreement. The trustee may also maintain a record of current bond owners and may act as a disbursing agent for the interest and principal payments.

Advantages and Disadvantages of Issuing Bonds

The advantages of obtaining long-term funds by issuing bonds rather than common stock include the following:

1. **No dilution of ownership interest.** Bondholders are creditors, not owners, of a corporation. Issuing bonds rather than common stock, therefore, maintains outstanding shares at their current level.

2. **Tax deductibility of bond interest expense.** Interest expense is currently deductible as an expense on a corporation's income tax return. Dividend payments to stockholders are not tax deductible. With combined federal and state income tax rates approaching 40% for many corporations, the tax deductibility of bond interest expense is an attractive aspect of financing through bonds.

3. **Return on stockholders' equity may increase.** The term **trading on the equity** or **leveraging** identifies the use of borrowed funds, particularly long-term debt, in the capital structure of a firm. Trading *profitably* on the equity means that the borrowed funds generate a higher rate of return than the interest rate paid for the use of the funds. The excess accrues to the benefit of the common shareholders because it magnifies, or increases, their earnings. Corporations that show a return on common stockholders' equity higher than their return on assets are trading profitably on the equity.

Exhibit 17-1 illustrates the profitable use of trading on the equity by comparing two different ways to finance a $2,000,000 expansion of Whitt Corporation—issuing common stock or issuing 10% bonds payable. Before the financing, the corporation

EXHIBIT 17–1
TRADING ON THE EQUITY: FINANCING ALTERNATIVES FOR WHITT CORPORATION $2,000,000 EXPANSION

	Financed by	
	Issuing Common Stock	Issuing Bonds
Capital structure before financing		
10% Bonds payable	—	—
Common stockholders' equity	$3,000,000	$3,000,000
Capital structure after financing		
10% Bonds payable	—	$2,000,000
Common stockholders' equity	$5,000,000	3,000,000
Total equity (= Total assets)	$5,000,000	$5,000,000
Annual results with financing		
Income before interest expense and income taxes	$1,100,000	$1,100,000
Bond interest expense	—	200,000
Income before income taxes	$1,100,000	$ 900,000
Income tax expense (40% rate)	440,000	360,000
Net income	$ 660,000	$ 540,000
Return on common stockholders' equity*:		
$660,000/$5,000,000 =	13.2%	
$540,000/$3,000,000 =		18.0%

*(Net Income – Preferred Dividends)/Average Common Stockholders' Equity. Whitt has no preferred stock and distributes cash dividends equal to net income; therefore, ending common stockholders' equity equals the beginning common stockholders' equity.
Average Common Stockholders' Equity = ($5,000,000 + $5,000,000)/2 = $5,000,000, and
($3,000,000 + $3,000,000)/2 = $3,000,000

has $3,000,000 of common stockholders' equity and no debt. Whitt earns a return of 22% (before interest expense and income taxes) on assets it puts to use and distributes cash dividends equal to its net income. Assuming a 40% income tax rate, Exhibit 17-1 shows that Whitt's return on common stockholders' equity is 13.2% when the financing is done with common stock. When the financing is done with the 10% bonds, the return on common stockholders' equity jumps to 18.0%. By borrowing funds and putting them to work earning a return greater than their cost, Whitt increases its return on common stockholders' equity.

Not all aspects of issuing bonds are necessarily desirable for the borrowing company. Among the disadvantages of issuing bonds are the following:

1. **Bond interest expense is a contractual obligation.** In contrast with dividends on common stock, bond interest represents a fixed periodic expenditure that the firm is contractually obligated to make. Fixed interest charges can be a financial burden when operations do not develop as favorably as expected.

2. **Funds borrowed have specific repayment date.** Because bonds normally have a definite maturity date, the borrower has a specific obligation to repay the face value of the bonds at maturity. This obligation, too, can be a significant burden when a company's financial performance does not reach expected levels. Funds received from issuing common stock, on the other hand, have no specific repayment date; instead, they usually represent a permanent increase in a firm's paid-in capital.

3. **Borrowing agreement may restrict company actions.** The legal document setting forth the terms of a bond issue is called a *bond indenture*. Among the provisions in the bond indenture may be restrictions on dividend payments, restrictions on additional financing, specification of a minimum cash balance, and specification of minimum financial ratios that must be maintained. These provisions are intended to provide protection for the bondholders, but they do limit management's flexibility to act.

Types of Bonds

Bond agreements may be formulated to capitalize on certain lending situations, appeal to special investor groups, or provide special repayment patterns. We now list several types of bonds and discuss their characteristics.

Secured bonds pledge some specific property as security for meeting the terms of the bond agreement. The specific title of the bonds may indicate the type of property pledged—for example, real estate mortgage bonds (land or buildings), chattel mortgage bonds (machinery or equipment), and collateral trust bonds (negotiable securities). If property is subject to two or more mortgages, the relative priority of each mortgage is denoted by its identification as a "first," "second," or even "third" mortgage.

Bonds that have no specific property pledged as security for their repayment are **debenture bonds.** Holders of such bonds rely on the borrower's general credit reputation. Because the lender's risk is usually greater than with secured bonds, the sale of unsecured bonds may require offering a higher interest rate.

The maturity dates of **serial bonds** are staggered over a series of years. For example, a serial bond issue of $15 million may provide for $1 million of the bonds to mature each year for 15 years. An advantage of serial bonds is that lenders can choose bonds with maturity dates that correspond with their desired length of investment.

The issuing corporation (or its trustee) maintains a record of the owners of **registered bonds.** At appropriate times, interest payments are mailed to the registered owners. Interest on **coupon bonds** is paid in a different manner. A coupon for interest payable to the bearer is attached to the bond for each interest period. Whenever interest is due, the bondholder detaches a coupon and deposits it with his or her bank for collection.

Callable bonds allow the borrower to *call in* (retire) the bonds and pay them off after a stated date. Usually, an extra amount or premium must be paid to the holders of the called bonds. Callable bonds offer borrowers an additional flexibility that may be significant if funds become available at interest rates substantially lower than those being paid on the bonds. To some degree, borrowers can in effect "call" any of their bonds by buying them in the open market.

Convertible bonds grant the holder the right to convert them to capital stock at some specific exchange ratio. This provision gives an investor the security of being a creditor during a certain stage of a firm's life, with the option of becoming a stockholder if the firm becomes sufficiently profitable.

Bond Prices

OBJECTIVE ❷ DISCUSS *the relationship of bond prices to interest rates and* ILLUSTRATE *accounting for bond issuance, interest, and straight-line amortization.*

Most bonds are sold in units of $1,000 face (maturity) value, and the market price is expressed as a percentage of face value. For example, a $1,000 face value bond quoted at 98 sells for $980, and a bond quoted at 103 sells for $1,030. Generally, bond prices fluctuate in response to changes in market interest rates, which are determined by government monetary policies (managing the demand and supply of money) and economic expectations. They are also affected by the outlook for the issuing firm. Market prices are quoted in the financial news at the nearest $\frac{1}{8}$% of the true market price.

A bond specifies a pattern of future cash flows—a series of interest payments and a single payment at maturity equal to the face value. The amount of the periodic interest payment is determined by the **nominal** or **contract rate** stated on the bond certificate. Interest rates are stated as annual rates, so the nominal rate needs to be converted to fit the interest period when interest is paid more than once a year. For

BEWARE REDEMPTION

Many bondholders who have been savoring returns from high-yielding instruments purchased over the past 10 years are in for a rude awakening. Those bonds may not be around much longer: Issuers are taking advantage of ways to retire the debt early. ■ The threat of early redemption, or calls, is something overlooked by most individual investors, who generally focus on yields and credit quality. But a call provision is one of the most important aspects of any bond. It's nice to get an attractive yield, but that doesn't matter much if the yield lasts only 5 or 10 years, rather than the anticipated 20 or 30.

There are billions of dollars of long-term municipal and corporate bonds issued in the high-rate environment of the early to mid-1980s that are being called as companies, cities, and states sell new debt at lower rates and use the funds to pay off existing bondholders. People holding 9% or 10% municipal bonds or 11% or 12% corporate bonds are having their investments called, forcing them to put the cash back to work at current rates of 7% or 8%. The danger of calls on newly issued bonds may not seem great; rates today are way below their peaks of the 1980s. But if they fall a percentage point or two, new bonds would be vulnerable, too.

So it's imperative to determine whether any bonds purchased over the past decade have call provisions, and, when buying new bonds, to ask about the call feature.

In theory, when bonds are sold, brokers should state on confirmation slips whether bonds are callable. But in practice, the "confirms" often fail to include all the call features, observes James Lynch, a money manager and editor of the Santa Fe, N.M.-based Lynch Municipal Bond Advisory. And because many investors are easily seduced by high-yielding bonds, they don't bother to ask whether the instrument can be called.

"Whenever you see an unusually high yield, you have to wonder," says Daniel Scotto, head of fixed-income research at Donaldson, Lufkin & Jenrette. If a broker offers a bond with a yield that seems too high, he adds, the investor should ask whether other bonds of the same issuer carry a similar rate. It may turn out that the true yield on the bond is lower because it can be called.

A callable bond offers a bad trade-off: If rates rise, the issuer does nothing, and the investor is stuck holding a bond that declines in value and pays a below-market rate. And if rates fall, the issuer pays the bond off early and the investor must reinvest funds at a lower rate. Telephone companies, for example, still benefit from the 4% and 5% debt they sold in the 1960s, but very few have much 15% debt from the 1980s outstanding.

Institutions have wised up during the past few years and are demanding more non-callable bonds, but individuals have been slower to learn. Lynch contends that "individuals should get paid when they're buying a callable bond," meaning that they should get higher yields than they would receive on non-callable bonds. Hugh Lamle, executive vice president at M.D. Sass Investors Services, a New York money-management firm, observes that it's important to evaluate a bond on a "yield-to-worst-case scenario" basis.

Most bond calls are made at a price of par (100 cents on the dollar) or slightly higher. So, if a bond is purchased above par, the buyer should find out if it's callable, because the true yield measured to the call date can be much lower than the yield to maturity.

SOURCE: Andrew Bary, "Beware Redemption," *Barrons*, July 15, 1991, p. 15. Reprinted by permission of Barron's, © 1991 Dow Jones & Company, Inc. All rights reserved worldwide.

example, bond interest is usually paid semiannually, with the payments six months apart. Thus, the amount of interest paid semiannually is calculated by multiplying one-half the nominal rate of interest times the bond's face value.

A bond's market price is determined by discounting the bond's future cash flows to the present using the current **market rate** of interest for the bond as the discount rate—a process known as *computing the bond's present value*. The market rate is the rate of return investors expect on their investment. Present value factors are available in tables to help simplify the calculations (also, certain calculators are programmed to compute present values). When issued, a bond's price may be equal to, less than, or more than its face value. Bonds sell at *face value* when the market rate of interest equals the nominal rate. Bonds sell at a *discount* (less than face value) when the market interest rate exceeds the nominal rate, and bonds sell at a *premium* (more than face value) when the market interest rate is less than the nominal rate.

Since bonds are usually printed and sold at different times, the two interest rates often differ. Also, a firm may desire a nominal rate expressed in even percentages or in easily recognized fractions of a percent (that is, 10% or $9\frac{1}{2}$%), whereas the market rate for a particular bond issue may be expressed in a more complex fraction or decimal amount.

Exhibit 17-2 shows the calculation of a bond's price using different market rates of interest. (See the appendix to this chapter for a discussion of the calculation of a bond's present value.) The bond is a $1,000, 10%, four-year bond with interest payable semiannually; the periodic interest payment is $50 ($1,000 × 0.10 × $\frac{1}{2}$). As shown in the exhibit, the bond will

1. Sell at a *discount* ($938 bond price) when the market rate (12%) exceeds the nominal rate (10%).
2. Sell at *face value* ($1,000 bond price) when the market rate (10%) equals the nominal rate (10%).
3. Sell at a *premium* ($1,068 bond price) when the market rate (8%) is less than the nominal rate (10%).

Recording Bond Issues

Firms often authorize more bonds than they actually anticipate issuing at one time. Authorization of bonds usually includes (1) formal action by the board of directors, (2) application to and approval of some government agency, (3) retention of a trustee, and (4) all the attendant negotiations and legalities. For secured bonds, the total value of the bonds authorized is typically some fraction of the value of the property pledged. The difference between the dollar amount of the bonds issued and the value of the pledged property represents a margin of safety to bondholders.

Because individual bond issues may have widely varying characteristics, separate accounts with reasonably descriptive titles should be used for each bond issue. When the bonds are authorized, an account is opened in the general ledger, and a memo-

---

EXHIBIT 17—2	CALCULATION OF BOND PRICE AT DIFFERENT INTEREST RATES

Bond being priced is a $1,000, 10%, four-year bond with interest payable semiannually. There are eight semiannual interest payments of $50 ($1,000 × 10% × $\frac{1}{2}$).

	Priced to Yield Investor an Interest Rate, Compounded Semiannually, of		
	12%	10%	8%
Present value of $1,000 due at maturity:			
$1,000 × 0.627 present value factor* =	$627		
$1,000 × 0.677 present value factor =		$ 677	
$1,000 × 0.731 present value factor =			$ 731
Present value of eight $50 interest payments (rounded to nearest dollar):			
$50 × 6.210 present value factor* =	311		
$50 × 6.463 present value factor =		323	
$50 × 6.733 present value factor =			337
Bond price	$938	$1,000	$1,068
Bond priced at	Discount	Face value	Premium

*See the appendix to this chapter for a discussion of present value factors and present value tables.

randum entry may be made in the account stating the total amount of bonds authorized.

BONDS ISSUED AT FACE VALUE

To provide a simple illustration, we will use a short bond life. Assume that on December 31, Reid, Inc., issues at face value ten $10,000, 10% bonds that mature in four years with interest paid on June 30 and December 31. The following entry records the bond issue:

Dec. 31	Cash	100,000	
	Bonds Payable		100,000
	To record issuance of bonds.		

Interest of $5,000 ($100,000 $\times$ 0.10 $\times \frac{6}{12}$) will be paid on each of the eight payment dates (four years, semiannual payments). For example, the entry on June 30, the first interest payment date, is

June 30	Bond Interest Expense	5,000	
	Cash		5,000
	To record payment of semiannual interest on bonds payable.		

When the bonds mature, Reid, Inc., records their retirement in the following manner:

(final year)

Dec. 31	Bonds Payable	100,000	
	Cash		100,000
	To record retirement of bonds.		

BONDS ISSUED AT A DISCOUNT

If the nominal rate of interest on the bonds issued is less than the current market rate of interest for the type and quality of the bonds, they can be sold only at a price less than their face value. In such cases, investors "discount" the bonds to earn the amount of interest reflected in the current money market. For example, assume that Reid, Inc.'s $100,000 issue of 10%, four-year bonds are sold on December 31 at 98— 98% of their face value—because the applicable market rate exceeds the 10% nominal rate. The following entry records the issue of these bonds:

Dec. 31	Cash	98,000	
	Discount on Bonds Payable	2,000	
	Bonds Payable		100,000
	To record issuance of bonds at 98.		

The $2,000 discount is not an immediate loss or expense to Reid, Inc. Rather, it represents an adjustment of interest expense over the life of the bonds. We illustrate this by comparing the funds that Reid, Inc., receives with the funds it must pay to the bondholders. Regardless of their selling price, the bonds are an agreement to pay $140,000 to the bondholders ($100,000 principal plus eight semiannual interest payments of $5,000 each).

Total funds paid to bondholders	$140,000
Total funds received from bond sale	98,000
Difference equals total interest paid	$ 42,000
Average expense per year ($42,000/4)	$ 10,500

Although Reid, Inc., makes only two $5,000 interest payments—a total of $10,000— each year, its full annual interest expense on the bonds exceeds that amount. To reflect the larger periodic interest expense, the bond discount is *amortized*. Amortization of bond discount means that periodically an amount is transferred from Discount on Bonds Payable to Bond Interest Expense.

Basically, there are two methods of amortization—the straight-line method and the effective interest method. Under the *straight-line method*, equal amounts are transferred from bond discount to interest expense for equal periods of time. For Reid,

Inc., this amount is $250 every six months ($2,000 total bond discount ÷ 8 semi-annual interest periods). The more complex *effective interest method* reflects a constant rate of interest over the life of the bonds. The effective interest method is discussed later in this chapter.

Assuming the straight-line method of amortization, the journal entries each year to record interest expense for Reid, Inc., are as follows. (We assume that the bond sale is already recorded as illustrated above and that the bonds were issued on the day they are dated.)

June 30	Bond Interest Expense		5,250	
	Discount on Bonds Payable			250
	Cash			5,000
	To record semiannual interest payment and amortization of bond discount.			
Dec. 31	Bond Interest Expense		5,250	
	Discount on Bonds Payable			250
	Cash			5,000
	To record semiannual interest payment and amortization of bond discount.			

These entries result in two debits to the Bond Interest Expense account each year, a total of $10,500 annual interest expense. Amortizing the bond discount over the four-year life of the bonds at $250 every six months leaves a zero balance in the Discount on Bonds Payable account at the maturity date of the bonds. The retirement of the bonds is then recorded by debiting Bonds Payable and crediting Cash for $100,000, the amount of their face value.

BONDS ISSUED AT A PREMIUM

If the market rate of interest had been below the 10% offered by Reid, Inc.'s bonds, investors would have been willing to pay a premium for them. Like a bond discount, a bond premium is considered an adjustment of interest expense over the life of the bonds. We just saw that bond discount increases interest expense; now we see that bond premium reduces interest expense. The following entries illustrate the sale of Reid, Inc., bonds at 104 (104% of face value), the payments of interest, the amortization of bond premium, and the retirement of the bonds at maturity:

Dec. 31	Cash		104,000	
	Bonds Payable			100,000
	Premium on Bonds Payable			4,000
	To record sale of bonds at a premium.			
June 30	Bond Interest Expense		4,500	
	Premium on Bonds Payable		500	
	Cash			5,000
	To record semiannual interest payment and amortization of bond premium.			
Dec. 31	Bond Interest Expense		4,500	
	Premium on Bonds Payable		500	
	Cash			5,000
	To record semiannual interest payment and amortization of bond premium.			
(final year)				
Dec. 31	Bonds Payable		100,000	
	Cash			100,000
	To retire bonds at maturity.			

The eight semiannual $500 debit entries to the Premium on Bonds Payable account leave it with a zero balance when the bonds mature. We can verify the $9,000 total annual interest expense reflected by the above entries as follows:

Total funds paid to bondholders	$140,000
Total funds received from bondholders	104,000
Difference equals total interest paid	$ 36,000
Average interest expense per year ($36,000/4)	$ 9,000

YEAR-END OR INTERIM ADJUSTMENTS

When a periodic interest payment date does not correspond with the fiscal year-end, adjustment of the general ledger accounts should include an entry reflecting the amount of interest expense incurred but not paid and a pro rata amortization of bond discount or bond premium for the portion of the year involved. Similar adjustments are appropriate when interim financial statements are prepared and the interim date does not correspond with an interest payment date.

Assume the bonds issued by Reid, Inc., at 104 were dated and issued April 30 and had interest payment dates on October 31 and April 30. At December 31 of each year, the following entry would be made:

Dec. 31	Bond Interest Expense	1,500	
	Premium on Bonds Payable	167	
	Bond Interest Payable		1,667

To accrue interest expense and amortize bond premium for two months [($4,000/48) × 2 = $167 (rounded); $100,000 × 0.10 × $\frac{2}{12}$ = $1,667 (rounded)].

If the bonds were issued at a discount rather than at a premium, the adjusting entry would amortize the bond discount for two months. The Bond Interest Payable account is classified as a current liability in the balance sheet.

On the next interest payment date, April 30, the following entry would be made (assuming Reid, Inc., does not make reversing entries):

Apr. 30	Bond Interest Payable	1,667	
	Bond Interest Expense	3,000	
	Premium on Bonds Payable	333	
	Cash		5,000

To record semiannual interest payment and amortization of bond premium for four months [($4,000/48) × 4 = $333 (rounded)].

ISSUANCE BETWEEN INTEREST DATES

Not all bonds are sold on the exact day on which their interest begins to accumulate (the date on the bond certificates). For example, issuance may be delayed in anticipation of a more favorable bond market. Investors who buy bonds after the interest begins to accrue are expected to "buy" the accrued interest. Such bonds are said to be sold at some price "plus accrued interest." To illustrate, let us assume that Reid, Inc., sold its $100,000, 10%, four-year bonds at 104 on February 28 instead of on December 31, the date on the bond certificates. The following entry would be made:

Feb. 28	Cash	105,667	
	Bonds Payable		100,000
	Premium on Bonds Payable		4,000
	Bond Interest Payable		1,667

To record bond issuance at 104 plus two months' accrued interest.

The interest accrued on the bonds on February 28 is $1,667 ($100,000 × 0.10 × $\frac{2}{12}$, rounded). On the first interest payment date, June 30, Reid, Inc., would make the following entry:

June 30	Bond Interest Payable	1,667	
	Bond Interest Expense	2,985	
	Premium on Bonds Payable	348	
	Cash		5,000

To record semiannual interest payment and amortization of bond premium for four months.

In this situation, the $4,000 bond premium would be amortized over the period the bonds are outstanding, or 46 months. Therefore, on June 30, the amount of the premium to be amortized is $348 [($4,000/46) × 4 months, rounded]. Thus, bond interest expense for the four months ended June 30 is $2,985 (four months' interest paid of $3,333 less the $348 premium amortization).

A similar treatment would be used if the bonds had been sold at a discount. In other words, the amortization period for premium or discount extends from the date of sale to the maturity date of the bonds.

Bonds Payable on the Balance Sheet

OBJECTIVE ❸ ILLUSTRATE *the classification of bonds on the balance sheet and* **DISCUSS** *effective interest amortization.*

In this section, we use the data relating to Reid, Inc., bonds with interest payment dates of June 30 and December 31 and straight-line amortization. The schedule in Exhibit 17-3 shows that regardless of whether bond premium or bond discount is involved, the book value of bonds progresses toward and equals their face value at the time of maturity.

Assume that Reid, Inc., issued first and second mortgage bonds on December 31, 1992, corresponding to the premium and discount examples above. At the end of 1994, the firm's trial balance would include the following accounts:

	Debit	Credit
Discount on Bonds Payable, Second Mortgage Series	$1,000	
Bonds Payable, 10%, 1996, First Mortgage Series		$100,000
Bonds Payable, 10%, 1996, Second Mortgage Series		100,000
Premium on Bonds Payable, First Mortgage Series		2,000

The Premium on Bonds Payable and Discount on Bonds Payable accounts are classified properly as an addition to and as a deduction from, respectively, the face value of the bonds in the balance sheet, as follows:

Long-term Liabilities

Bonds Payable, 10%, 1996, First Mortgage Series	$100,000	
Add: Premium on Bonds Payable	2,000	$102,000
Bonds Payable, 10%, 1996, Second Mortgage Series	$100,000	
Less: Discount on Bonds Payable	1,000	99,000

Bonds payable maturing within the next year should be classified as a current liability. An exception to this guideline arises when a *bond sinking fund*, a noncurrent asset, is used to retire the bonds. (Bond sinking funds are discussed shortly.) In that case, because a current asset is not utilized to retire the bonds, the bonds payable may be classified as long-term liabilities.

Effective Interest Method of Amortization

Many business firms use the straight-line method of amortizing bond discount and premium because of its simplicity. This method recognizes equal amounts of interest expense each year. However, because the *book value* (*carrying value*) of the bonds

---

EXHIBIT 17–3	SCHEDULE OF BOOK VALUE OF BONDS

	REID, INC., $100,000 OF FOUR-YEAR BONDS SOLD AT 104 (PREMIUM) (STRAIGHT-LINE AMORTIZATION)			REID, INC., $100,000 OF FOUR-YEAR BONDS SOLD AT 98 (DISCOUNT) (STRAIGHT-LINE AMORTIZATION)		
	Balances			**Balances**		
At Year-end	Bonds Payable (Credit)	Premium on Bonds Payable (Credit)	Book Value	Bonds Payable (Credit)	Discount on Bonds Payable (Debit)	Book Value
At issue	$100,000	$4,000	$104,000	$100,000	$2,000	$ 98,000
1993	100,000	3,000	103,000	100,000	1,500	98,500
1994	100,000	2,000	102,000	100,000	1,000	99,000
1995	100,000	1,000	101,000	100,000	500	99,500
1996	100,000	–0–	100,000	100,000	–0–	100,000

changes each year (see Exhibit 17-3), the interest, expressed as a percentage of the book value, changes over the life of the bonds. Theoretically, this percentage should be constant; otherwise, the firm's borrowing rate appears to change each year. The **effective interest method** of amortization corrects this deficiency. With this method, a constant percentage of the book value of the bonds is recognized as interest expense each year, resulting in unequal recorded amounts of interest expense. Accounting guidelines recommend the use of the effective interest method whenever the two methods yield materially different results.

To obtain a period's interest expense under the effective interest method, we multiply the bonds' book value at the beginning of each period by the effective interest rate. The **effective rate** is the market rate of interest used to price the bonds when they were issued. The difference between this amount and the amount of interest paid (Nominal Interest Rate × Face Value of Bonds) is the amount of discount or premium amortized. When using the effective interest method of amortization, accountants often prepare an amortization schedule similar to the one in Exhibit 17-4, explained in the following example.

BONDS ISSUED AT A DISCOUNT

Assume that on March 31, 1993, a firm issues four-year bonds of $100,000 face value with an 8% annual interest rate and interest dates of September 30 and March 31. Also assume that the bonds are dated March 31, 1993, so that there is no accrued interest at the time of sale, and that the maturity date is four years from the date of sale. The selling price is $93,552, which provides an effective interest rate of 10% (for computations, see the appendix to this chapter). Exhibit 17-4 gives an amortization schedule for the life of the bonds, with amounts rounded to the nearest dollar.

The schedule shows six-month interest periods; therefore, the interest rates shown in columns A and B are one-half the annual rates. Column A lists the constant amounts of interest paid each six months, that is, the nominal interest rate times face value (4% × $100,000). The amounts in column B are obtained by multiplying the book value at the beginning of each period (column E) by the 5% effective interest rate. For example, the $4,678 interest expense for the first period is 5% of $93,552;

EXHIBIT 17—4	BONDS SOLD AT A DISCOUNT: PERIODIC INTEREST EXPENSE, EFFECTIVE INTEREST AMORTIZATION, AND BOOK VALUE OF BONDS

$100,000 of 8%, four-year bonds with interest payable semiannually issued at $93,552 to yield 10%.

Year	Interest Period	A Interest Paid (4% of face value)	B Interest Expense (5% of bond book value)	C Periodic Amortization (B – A)	D Balance of Unamortized Discount (D – C)	E Book Value of Bonds, End of Period ($100,000 – D)
(at issue)					$6,448	$ 93,552
1	1	$4,000	$4,678	$678	5,770	94,230
	2	4,000	4,712	712	5,058	94,942
2	3	4,000	4,747	747	4,311	95,689
	4	4,000	4,784	784	3,527	96,473
3	5	4,000	4,824	824	2,703	97,297
	6	4,000	4,865	865	1,838	98,162
4	7	4,000	4,908	908	930	99,070
	8	4,000	4,930*	930	–0–	100,000

*Adjusted for cumulative rounding error of $24.

for the second period, it is 5% of $94,230, or $4,712, and so on. Note that the amount changes each period. For discounted bonds, the amount increases each period because the book value increases over the life of the bonds until it reaches face value at the maturity date. The amount of discount amortization for each period, given in column C, is the difference between the corresponding amounts in columns A and B. Column D lists the amount of unamortized discount at the end of each period.

The amounts recorded for the issuance of the bonds and each interest payment can be read directly from the amortization schedule. The following entry records the issuance:

Mar. 31	Cash		93,552	
	Discount on Bonds Payable		6,448	
	Bonds Payable			100,000
	To record issuance of bonds.			

The following entry records interest expense and discount amortization on September 30, 1993:

Sept. 30	Bond Interest Expense		4,678	
	Discount on Bonds Payable			678
	Cash			4,000
	To record semiannual interest expense and discount amortization.			

BONDS ISSUED AT A PREMIUM

Suppose that the bonds in our illustration carried an 8% nominal interest rate but that the effective interest rate was 6%. These bonds would be issued at $106,980 (for computations, see the appendix to this chapter). The amortization schedule for the bond issue is given in Exhibit 17-5. The nominal interest rate of 4% in column A and the effective interest rate of 3% in column B are one-half the annual rates for the bonds, because the calculations are for six-month periods. The issuance of the bonds is recorded as follows:

Mar. 31	Cash		106,980	
	Bonds Payable			100,000
	Premium on Bonds Payable			6,980
	To record issuance of bonds.			

The entry to record interest expense and premium amortization on September 30, 1993, is the following:

Sept. 30	Bond Interest Expense		3,209	
	Premium on Bonds Payable		791	
	Cash			4,000
	To record semiannual interest expense and premium amortization.			

YEAR-END ADJUSTING ENTRIES

We record interest and amortization of the discount or premium on the bonds in our two examples on March 31 and September 30. Therefore, at December 31, adjustments are needed to accrue interest and amortize the discount or premium for three months.

The amounts can be computed from those shown for the second interest period in the amortization schedules. For our earlier example (bonds issued at a discount), one-half of the amount shown for the second interest period in Exhibit 17-4, column A, [($4,000/2) = $2,000] is the interest payable. In the same fashion, from column B, [($4,712/2) = $2,356] is the interest expense, and from column C, [($712/2) = $356] is the discount amortization. The year-end adjusting entry follows:

Dec. 31	Bond Interest Expense		2,356	
	Discount on Bonds Payable			356
	Bond Interest Payable			2,000
	To accrue interest for three months and amortize one-half of the discount for the interest period.			

		EXHIBIT 17—5		**BONDS SOLD AT A PREMIUM: PERIODIC INTEREST EXPENSE, EFFECTIVE INTEREST AMORTIZATION, AND BOOK VALUE OF BONDS**		

$100,000 of 8%, four-year bonds with interest payable semiannually issued at $106,980 to yield 6%.

Year	Interest Period	**A** Interest Paid (4% of face value)	**B** Interest Expense (3% of bond book value)	**C** Periodic Amorti-zation (A – B)	**D** Balance of Unamor-tized Premium (D – C)	**E** Book Value of Bonds, End of Period ($100,000 + D)
(at issue)					$6,980	$106,980
1	1	$4,000	$3,209	$791	6,189	106,189
	2	4,000	3,186	814	5,375	105,375
2	3	4,000	3,161	839	4,536	104,536
	4	4,000	3,136	864	3,672	103,672
3	5	4,000	3,110	890	2,782	102,782
	6	4,000	3,083	917	1,865	101,865
4	7	4,000	3,056	944	921	100,921
	8	4,000	3,079*	921	–0–	100,000

*Adjusted for cumulative rounding error of $51.

When interest is paid at the next interest payment date, the remaining amounts of bond interest expense and discount amortization for the six-month period are recognized. Assuming that Reid, Inc., does not use reversing entries, the entry to record the interest payment on March 31, 1994, would be as follows:

Mar. 31	Bond Interest Payable	2,000	
	Bond Interest Expense	2,356	
	Discount on Bonds Payable		356
	Cash		4,000
	To record semiannual interest payment and discount amortization for three months.		

For our second example (bonds issued at a premium), we follow the same procedure, using the second interest period in Exhibit 17-5. Again we use one-half of the amounts shown to derive the amounts for our year-end adjusting entry:

Dec. 31	Bond Interest Expense	1,593	
	Premium on Bonds Payable	407	
	Bond Interest Payable		2,000
	To accrue interest for three months and amortize one-half of the premium for the interest period.		

Here, too, the remaining amounts of bond interest expense and premium amortization for the six-month period are recognized at the next interest payment date. Assuming that Reid, Inc., does not use reversing entries, the entry on March 31, 1994, to record the interest payment would be the following:

Mar. 31	Bond Interest Payable	2,000	
	Bond Interest Expense	1,593	
	Premium on Bonds Payable	407	
	Cash		4,000
	To record semiannual interest payment and premium amortization for three months.		

Retirement of Bonds before Maturity

OBJECTIVE ④ ILLUSTRATE *the retirement and conversion of bonds and the use of sinking funds.*

Bonds are usually retired at their maturity dates with an entry debiting Bonds Payable and crediting Cash for the amount of the face value of the bonds. However, bonds may be retired before maturity—for example, to take advantage of more attractive financing terms.

In accounting for the retirement of bonds before maturity, the following analysis should be used:

1. Remove the book value of the bonds being retired from the accounts (that is, remove the Bonds Payable amount and any related bond premium or discount).
2. Record the cash paid to retire the bonds.
3. Recognize any difference between the bonds' book value and the cash paid as a gain or loss on bond retirement.

To illustrate, assume that the bonds issued for $106,980 in our previous example were called for retirement at 105 at the end of the third year, just after paying the semiannual interest on March 31, Year 3. According to Exhibit 17-5, the bonds' book value at the end of Year 3 is $101,865. The following entry properly reflects the bond retirement:

Mar. 31	Bonds Payable	100,000	
	Premium on Bonds Payable	1,865	
	Loss on Bond Retirement	3,135	
	Cash		105,000
	To retire bonds at 105 and record loss on retirement.		

Accounting guidelines require that a gain or loss on bond retirement, if material, be classified as an extraordinary item on the income statement.

Conversion of Bonds

Few convertible bonds are redeemed for cash, since at some point these bonds are usually converted into common stock. Because, as noted earlier, the conversion feature is attractive to potential investors, a company may issue convertible bonds at a lower interest rate than it would pay without the conversion feature.

A company may also issue convertible bonds to reduce the dilutive effect that a common stock issue would have on earnings per share. This occurs because the conversion price is higher than the current market price of the stock when the convertible bonds are issued. For example, suppose a company that needs $100,000 of funds could issue additional common stock at $20 per share. The company needs to issue 5,000 shares to obtain $100,000. Alternatively, the firm may issue $100,000 of convertible bonds and establish a conversion price of $25 per share. When the bonds are converted into stock (and the company expects this to happen), the number of common shares issued will be 4,000 ($100,000/$25). The fewer number of common shares associated with the convertible bonds produces higher earnings per share than if common stock had been issued initially.

Convertible bonds usually include a call feature. When the market value of the stock to be received on conversion is significantly higher than the call price on the bond, a company may force conversion by calling in the bonds. Of course, one of the risks of issuing convertible bonds is that the market price of the stock may not increase in the future. Bondholders may then decide it is not to their advantage to convert the bonds, and the company cannot force conversion by exercising the call feature.

The entry to record a bond conversion transfers the book value of the bonds to the common stock accounts. For example, assume that the bonds issued for $93,552 in our previous example were convertible into 4,000 shares of $20 par value common stock. All the bonds were converted into stock at the end of the second year, just after paying the semiannual interest on March 31, Year 2. Exhibit 17-4 shows the book value of the bonds at the end of Year 2 to be $96,473. The entry on the following page records the conversion:

Mar. 31	Bonds Payable		100,000	
	Discount on Bonds Payable			3,527
	Common Stock			80,000
	Paid-in Capital in Excess of Par Value			16,473
	To record conversion of bonds into 4,000 shares of $20 par value common stock.			

BOND SINKING FUNDS

As additional security to bondholders, some bond agreements require the borrower to make periodic cash deposits to a **bond sinking fund,** which is used to retire the bonds. The fund is often controlled by a trustee—usually a bank or a trust company. The trustee invests the cash deposited periodically in the sinking fund in income-producing securities. The objective is to accumulate investments and investment income sufficient to retire the bonds at their maturity.

We now illustrate typical transactions for a simple bond sinking fund managed by a trustee. Assume that Reid, Inc., establishes such a fund to retire its $100,000 bond issue, which matures in four years. Reid, Inc., makes equal annual deposits to the sinking fund at the end of each of the four years.

Periodic Deposit of Cash to the Fund

The amount of the equal periodic contributions is determined by compound interest tables and assumes an average annual rate of net investment income.[1] If the trustee estimates that the sinking-fund securities will earn 8% annually, Reid, Inc.'s annual cash payment to the trustee should be $22,192. Earning 8% annually, the fund will grow to $100,000 after four years, as follows:

Year	Annual Cash Deposit	8% Annual Interest	Fund Balance at Year-end
1	$22,192	—	$ 22,192
2	22,192	$1,775	46,159
3	22,192	3,693	72,044
4	22,192	5,764	100,000

The entry to record the annual cash deposit is

Bond Sinking Fund	22,192	
Cash		22,192

Income Reported on Sinking-fund Securities

Reid, Inc., records on its books the trustee's periodic reports on the earnings of the sinking-fund securities. For example, if the fund earned $1,775 during the second year, Reid, Inc., makes the following journal entry:

Bond Sinking Fund	1,775	
Bond Sinking Fund Income		1,775

Retirement of Bonds

Usually, the trustee sells the sinking-fund securities and pays the bondholders with the proceeds. Reid, Inc., then records the retirement of the bonds as follows:

Bonds Payable	100,000	
Bond Sinking Fund		100,000

Any deficit in the sinking fund needed to retire the bonds requires an additional cash payment from Reid, Inc. Any surplus is transferred to the Cash account in closing out the sinking fund.

The Bond Sinking Fund is classified in the balance sheet as an investment. Bond Sinking Fund Income is reported under Other Income and Expenses in the income statement.

---

[1] An example showing how such periodic contributions are determined is given in the appendix to this chapter.

MORTGAGE NOTES PAYABLE

OBJECTIVE 5 DESCRIBE *and* ILLUSTRATE *accounting for mortgage notes payable.*

A firm may borrow long-term funds by issuing a **mortgage note,** which is actually two related agreements. The note is an agreement to repay the money borrowed with interest; the mortgage is a legal agreement pledging certain property of the borrower as security for repayment of the note.

Mortgage notes are usually repaid in equal periodic installments. The agreement may require installment payments to be made monthly, quarterly, or semiannually. Each payment contains an interest amount and a repayment of principal. Because the installment payments are equal, each installment payment contains different amounts of interest and principal repayment. These component amounts change with each installment because the interest is computed on the unpaid principal, and the unpaid principal is reduced with each payment.

To illustrate, assume that on December 31, 1992, Reid, Inc., borrows $100,000 on a 12%, 10-year mortgage note payable. The note is to be repaid with equal quarterly installments of $4,326 (for computation see the appendix to this chapter). Thus, there will be 40 quarterly payments and the quarterly interest rate is 3%. Exhibit 17-6 shows the first eight quarterly payments and their division between interest expense and principal repayment. The journal entry to record the first quarterly payment follows:

1993
Mar. 31   Interest Expense   3,000
   Mortgage Note Payable   1,326
    Cash   4,326
  To record quarterly mortgage payment.

PENSION PLANS AND OTHER POSTRETIREMENT BENEFITS

Pension Plans

OBJECTIVE 6 DESCRIBE *the basic ideas of accounting for postretirement benefits.*

Many companies have established plans to pay benefits to their employees after they retire. The cost of these **pension plans** may be paid entirely by the employer. Sometimes, the employees pay part of the cost through deductions from their salaries and wages. The employer and employee contributions are usually paid into a pension fund that is managed by another company. Retirement benefits are paid from the assets in the pension fund.

The employer's pension plan cost must be expensed during the years the employees work for the company. For some plans, this accounting analysis is fairly simple; for other plans, it is not. In a *defined contribution plan*, for example, the employer's responsibility is to contribute a certain defined amount to the pension fund each year (a percentage of employee salaries, perhaps). The assets available in the pension fund, then, determine the size of the retirement benefits. The employer's pension accounting analysis is straightforward—when the required contribution is made, Pension Expense is debited and Cash is credited.

The analysis becomes more complex in *defined benefit plans*. These plans specify the retirement benefits to be received in the future; typically, the retirement benefits are a function of the number of years an employee works for the company and the salary or wage level at or near retirement. One complexity under such plans is the determination of the periodic pension expense and contribution amounts. These amounts are influenced by such factors as employee turnover, employee life expectancies, future salary and wage levels, and pension fund investment performance. Actuaries make the required pension estimates.

When a defined benefit plan is first adopted, the company usually gives employees credit for their years of employment prior to the plan's adoption. The cost of providing the retirement benefits earned by this earlier service is called **prior service cost.** Prior service cost may be quite sizable, and the company may take many years to fund it. A similar situation may develop when a company amends a plan to increase

EXHIBIT 17—6	PARTIAL MORTGAGE PAYMENT SCHEDULE

$100,000 mortgage note payable with quarterly payments of $4,326 and quarterly interest rate of 3%.

Payment Date	A Cash Payment	B Interest Expense (3% × D)*	C Principal Repaid (A − B)	D Book Value of Note (Unpaid Principal)
1992				
December 31 (issue date)				$100,000
1993				
March 31	$4,326	$3,000	$1,326	98,674
June 30	4,326	2,960	1,366	97,308
September 30	4,326	2,919	1,407	95,901
December 31	4,326	2,877	1,449	94,452
1994				
March 31	4,326	2,834	1,492	92,960
June 30	4,326	2,789	1,537	91,423
September 30	4,326	2,743	1,583	89,840
December 31	4,326	2,695	1,631	88,209

*3% × unpaid principal after previous payment, rounded to the nearest dollar.

benefit levels. Another complexity in a defined benefit plan, then, is that the accumulated pension retirement benefits may exceed the assets in the pension fund. In such cases, the FASB requires companies to record a liability equal to the excess amount.[2]

Other Postretirement Benefits

In addition to pensions, employers may provide retired employees with other benefits, such as health care and legal services. Until recently, companies followed a "pay-as-you-go" system of accounting for these benefits; that is, no expense was recorded until a benefit payment was made. Since 1993, however, accounting guidelines have required companies to expense the cost of providing these benefits during the years the employees work for the company.[3] The benefits are not paid until after the employees retire, so a long-term liability for these benefits will also be recorded. These long-term liabilities may be quite large, particularly when health care benefits are involved.

DEFERRED INCOME TAXES

Corporations pay income taxes based on the amount of taxable income they report on their income tax returns. Most of the revenues and expenses used to compute taxable income are exactly the same as the firm reports in its income statement. There are several areas, however, in which the tax law either requires or permits a firm to report revenues and expenses in a different pattern on the tax return than on the income statement.

[2] *Statement of Financial Accounting Standards No. 87*, "Employers' Accounting for Pensions" (Stamford, CT: Financial Accounting Standards Board, 1985).

[3] *Statement of Financial Accounting Standards No. 106*, "Employers' Accounting for Postretirement Benefits Other Than Pensions" (Norwalk, CT: Financial Accounting Standards Board, 1990).

Deferred Tax Liabilities

OBJECTIVE 7 DESCRIBE and ILLUSTRATE *deferred income taxes and present a comprehensive balance sheet.*

Following are two examples of differences between when a transaction affects taxable income and when it affects the income statement:

1. A company purchases a plant asset in the current year that it is allowed to expense immediately on its income tax return. In its current year financial statements, the company establishes an asset that will be depreciated over its useful life. On the current year tax return, the company immediately expenses the entire payment.

2. A company purchases a plant asset in the current year and depreciates it in its financial statements using the straight-line method with no expected salvage value. On the tax return, the company depreciates the asset using the *modified accelerated cost recovery system (MACRS)*. The first year's MACRS depreciation exceeds the straight-line amount.

Both transactions create a situation in which, at the end of the current year, the book value of the related plant asset exceeds the asset's tax basis (that is, the remaining amount that can be expensed on future tax returns). The difference is only temporary, however, because eventually both the asset's book value and its tax basis will be zero (as the expensing of the asset is completed in the financial statements and on the tax return). Further, in the future year(s) when the temporary difference (excess of book value over tax basis) is expensed in the financial statements, the company will owe income taxes on that amount (because there will not be any corresponding expense in that year's tax return). These future income taxes payable represent a deferred tax consequence, therefore, from a situation in which an asset's book value temporarily exceeds its tax basis.

Accounting standards require that a **deferred tax liability** be recorded for the deferred tax consequences of temporary differences.[4] In other words, an accounting liability must be recognized when a temporary difference between an asset's book value and its tax basis will result in future taxable amounts. The deferred tax liability is an appropriate liability to report in the balance sheet—it represents an estimate of future income taxes payable resulting from an already existing temporarydifference. The deferred tax liability is computed by applying the proper income tax rate to the future taxable amount.

To illustrate, assume that on January 2, 1993, Lenscape, Inc., purchases equipment for $10,000 and debits the expenditure to the Equipment account. The equipment is expected to last two years with no salvage value and will be depreciated in 1993 and 1994 using the straight-line method. Lenscape deducts the full $10,000 as an expense on its 1993 income tax return. Lenscape owns no other plant assets. This is the only difference between Lenscape's financial statements and tax returns. The income tax rate is 40% for 1993 and 1994.

Assume Lenscape's income before depreciation expense and income taxes is $50,000 in 1993 and $70,000 in 1994. Lenscape's pretax financial income and taxable income for 1993 and 1994 will then be as follows:

	1993		1994	
	Financial Income	**Taxable Income**	**Financial Income**	**Taxable Income**
Income before depreciation expense and income taxes	$50,000	$50,000	$70,000	$70,000
Depreciation expense	5,000	10,000	5,000	–0–
Pretax financial income	$45,000		$65,000	
Taxable income		$40,000		$70,000

---

[4] *Statement of Financial Accounting Standards No. 109,* "Accounting for Income Taxes" (Norwalk, CT: Financial Accounting Standards Board, 1992).

The book value and tax basis of the equipment at December 31, 1993, and December 31, 1994, are as follows:

| | December 31, 1993 | | December 31, 1994 | |
	Book Value	Tax Basis	Book Value	Tax Basis
Equipment	$5,000	–0–	–0–	–0–

The following observations may be drawn from Lenscape's handling of the equipment expenditure:

1. Deducting the equipment on 1993's tax return causes a $5,000 difference between the book value and tax basis of the equipment at December 31, 1993.

2. The $5,000 difference at December 31, 1993, between the equipment's book value and its tax basis is temporary. It is eliminated in 1994.

3. The elimination of the $5,000 temporary difference in 1994 causes taxable income that year to be $5,000 greater than pretax financial income. Lenscape, therefore, will pay an income tax on the $5,000 in 1994 of $2,000 (0.40 × $5,000). This is the liability that must be recognized at December 31, 1993, as a deferred tax liability.

The journal entry to record income taxes at December 31, 1993, is

1993
Dec. 31	Income Tax Expense	18,000	
	Income Tax Payable		16,000
	Deferred Tax Liability		2,000
	To record 1993 income taxes.		

The entry to Deferred Tax Liability is the amount necessary to establish the proper year-end account balance. At December 31, 1993, there should be a deferred tax liability of $2,000 (0.40 × $5,000). Lenscape has no previous balance in the Deferred Tax Liability account, so the credit entry is for the full $2,000. The entry to Income Tax Payable reflects the income taxes currently due to the government—it is computed by multiplying the 1993 taxable income by the 1993 tax rate ($40,000 × 0.40 = $16,000). The debit to Income Tax Expense is the balancing amount in the journal entry; in this case, it is determined by combining the income tax payable and deferred tax liability amounts.

The journal entry to record income taxes at December 31, 1994 is

1994
Dec. 31	Income Tax Expense	26,000	
	Deferred Tax Liability	2,000	
	Income Tax Payable		28,000
	To record 1994 income taxes.		

The $2,000 debit to Deferred Tax Liability brings this account balance to zero. This is the correct balance at December 31, 1994, because the temporary difference is eliminated in 1994. The $28,000 credit to Income Tax Payable correctly records the 1994 income tax owed to the government ($70,000 × 0.40 = $28,000). The balancing debit to Income Tax Expense is determined by netting the income tax payable and deferred tax liability amounts.

Income Tax Rate

The proper income tax rate to use in determining a deferred tax liability is the tax rate scheduled to be in effect when the future taxable amount occurs. If a new tax rate has been enacted into law for the future year, then that tax rate is used. To illustrate using the Lenscape, Inc., example, assume that the tax rates enacted into law are 40% for 1993 and 35% for 1994. The journal entries to record income taxes for 1993 and 1994 would then be as appears on the following page:

1993
Dec. 31 Income Tax Expense   17,750
      Income Tax Payable   16,000
      Deferred Tax Liability   1,750
  To record 1993 income taxes
  [Deferred tax liability: $5,000 × 0.35 = $1,750; Income
  tax payable: $40,000 × 0.40 = $16,000; Income tax
  expense: $1,750 + $16,000 = $17,750].

1994
Dec. 31 Income Tax Expense   22,750
     Deferred Tax Liability   1,750
      Income Tax Payable   24,500
  To record 1994 income taxes
  [Deferred tax liability: to eliminate account balance;
  Income tax payable: $70,000 × 0.35 = $24,500; Income
  tax expense: $24,500 − $1,750 = $22,750.

If tax rates change after a deferred tax liability has been recorded, a journal entry will be necessary to revise the account balance to its proper amount (with an offsetting debit or credit to Income Tax Expense).

Balance Sheet Presentation

Deferred income tax accounts are classified on a firm's balance sheet as current or noncurrent based on the classification of the related asset or liability. For example, Lenscape's deferred tax liability at December 31, 1993, would be classified as a noncurrent liability because the related asset, Equipment, is classified as a noncurrent asset.

    The amounts reported as deferred tax liabilities may be quite large, often millions of dollars (or more) for major corporations. As one example, PHILLIPS PETROLEUM COMPANY reported deferred tax liabilities of $1,283,000,000 in its December 31, 1990, balance sheet.

Other Temporary Differences

Differences in the accounting for revenues may also create temporary differences that will result in deferred tax liabilities. An example of one such situation is a company that recognizes revenue from installment sales at point of sale in its financial statements and uses the installment method in its income tax return.[5]

    Some temporary differences cause an asset's book value to be *less* than its tax basis. For example, a firm may use the allowance method in its financial statements to account for uncollectible accounts expense and use the direct write-off method for tax purposes. Also, some temporary differences may create a liability with a book value larger than its tax basis. For example, a company may receive an advance payment for future services to be performed (crediting a liability account for the advance payment) but include the payment in taxable income in the year it is received. These temporary differences create deferred tax assets (future reductions or refunds of income taxes). The guidelines for measuring deferred tax assets, however, are more complex than those that apply to deferred tax liabilities and are beyond the scope of this textbook.

CORPORATION BALANCE SHEET

Exhibit 17-7 is a comprehensive illustration of a corporation's balance sheet that contains many of the items discussed in this and the preceding chapters.

---

[5] At this writing, the tax law permits the installment method to be used for installment sales of residential lots, timeshare units, and property used in the trade or business of farming.

EXHIBIT 17—7	CORPORATION BALANCE SHEET

SUPERIOR CORPORATION
BALANCE SHEET
DECEMBER 31, 1993

Assets

Current Assets

Cash			$ 20,000
Short-term Investments (At lower of cost or market)			10,000
Accounts Receivable		$65,000	
Less: Allowance for Uncollectible Accounts		5,000	60,000
Inventories (At lower of cost or market)			120,000
Prepaid Expenses			10,000
Total Current Assets				$220,000

Investments

Bond Sinking Fund	50,000

Plant Assets

Land	$ 30,000	
Buildings (Less accumulated depreciation of $50,000)	380,000	
Machinery and Equipment (Less accumulated depreciation of $30,000)	140,000	
Total Plant Assets		550,000

Intangible Assets (Cost less amortization to date)

Goodwill	$ 28,000	
Patents	12,000	
Total Intangible Assets		40,000
Total Assets		$860,000

Liabilities

Current Liabilities

Accounts Payable	$ 45,000	
Income Tax Payable	18,000	
Dividends Payable	15,000	
Accrued Payables	2,000	
Total Current Liabilities		$ 80,000

Long-term Liabilities

First Mortgage, 9% Bonds Payable (Due 1998)	$100,000	
Premium on First Mortgage Bonds	6,000	
	$106,000	
Deferred Tax Liability	30,000	
Total Long-term Liabilities		136,000
Total Liabilities		$216,000

Stockholders' Equity

Paid-in Capital

Common Stock, $10 Par Value, 40,000 shares authorized and issued; 500 shares in treasury	$400,000	
Paid-in Capital in Excess of Par Value	80,000	
Total Paid-in Capital		$480,000
Retained Earnings		170,000
		$650,000
Less: Treasury Stock (500 shares) at Cost		6,000
Total Stockholders' Equity		$644,000
Total Liabilities and Stockholders' Equity		$860,000

ANALYTICAL APPLICATION

TIMES INTEREST EARNED RATIO

OBJECTIVE 8 DEFINE times interest earned ratio *and* EXPLAIN *its use.*

A financial ratio of particular interest to present and potential long-term creditors is the times interest earned ratio (also known as the *interest coverage ratio*). The **times interest earned ratio** is computed as follows:

$$\text{Times Interest Earned Ratio} = \frac{\text{Income before Interest Expense and Income Taxes}}{\text{Interest Expense}}$$

The principal on long-term debt such as bonds payable is not due until maturity, which may be many years into the future. Interest payments, however, are due each year. Thus, creditors look at the times interest earned ratio to help assess the ability of a firm to meet its annual interest commitments. The ratio shows the number of times the fixed interest charges were earned during the year. Many financial analysts consider that the times interest earned ratio should be at least in the range of 3.0–4.0 for the extension of long-term credit to be considered a safe investment. The trend of the ratio in recent years and the nature of the industry (volatile or stable, for example) may also influence the interpretation of this ratio.

Both the numerator and denominator in the times interest earned ratio come from the income statement. The numerator uses income before interest expense and income taxes, because that is the amount available to cover the interest charges. The denominator is the firm's total interest expense for the period. To illustrate, Reid, Inc., in this chapter's first example, issued $100,000 of 10% bonds at face value. The annual interest expense was $10,000. If this were Reid's only interest expense and Reid's income before interest expense and income taxes the first year were $35,000, Reid's times interest earned ratio that year would be $35,000/$10,000 = 3.5.

The times interest earned ratio may differ considerably among firms. Following are examples of recent times interest earned ratios for several companies in different industries.

THE QUAKER OATS COMPANY (grocery products)	5.0
CSX CORPORATION (transportation)	2.8
SOUTHWESTERN BELL CORPORATION (communications)	3.6
LANDS' END, INC. (direct mail merchandising)	25.5
BAXTER INTERNATIONAL INC. (health care)	1.4

KEY POINTS FOR CHAPTER OBJECTIVES

1 IDENTIFY the reasons for issuing bonds and DESCRIBE various types of bonds (pp. 602–604).

- The advantages of issuing bonds rather than common stock include (1) no dilution of ownership interest, (2) tax deductibility of interest expense, and (3) return on stockholders' equity may increase.

- Trading on the equity means that borrowed funds are used in the expectation that they will generate a rate of return higher than the interest rate.

- The disadvantages of issuing bonds include the following: (1) interest is a contractual obligation, (2) the funds borrowed have a specific repayment date, and (3) the borrowing agreement may restrict company actions.

- Bonds permit borrowing from a large number of investors, who are usually represented by a trustee. Bonds may be secured or unsecured (debenture bonds). Bonds may all come due at the same time or may have staggered maturities (serial bonds). For registered bonds, the issuer keeps records of owners and mails them interest payments. Owners of coupon bonds detach the interest coupons when due and deposit them in a bank. Bonds may be callable after a certain date, and some bonds are convertible into the firm's stock at a specified exchange ratio.

❷ **DISCUSS** the relationship of bond prices to interest rates and **ILLUSTRATE** accounting for bond issuance, interest, and amortization (pp. 604–610).
- Bond prices are expressed as a percentage of face value.
- The nominal rate of interest, stated on the bond certificate, dictates the amount of interest paid each period. The effective, or market, rate of interest is the rate investors expect to receive on their investment.
- When the market interest rate exceeds the nominal rate on bonds, they are sold at a discount; when the nominal rate exceeds the market rate, the bonds are sold at a premium. Discounts and premiums are recorded when the bonds are issued.
- Discounts and premiums are amortized each interest date under the straight-line method by adding a pro rata share to interest expense for discounts, or deducting a pro rata share for premiums.

❸ **ILLUSTRATE** the classification of bonds on the balance sheet and **DISCUSS** effective interest amortization (pp. 610–614).
- Bonds payable are shown in the long-term liabilities section of the balance sheet, with unamortized premium added or unamortized discount deducted.
- In certain cases the effective interest method is used instead of the straight-line method. The effective interest method results in a constant rate of interest on the bond book value throughout the life of the bonds.

❹ **ILLUSTRATE** the retirement and conversion of bonds and the use of sinking funds (pp. 614–615).
- The entry for retirement of bonds removes both the bonds payable and any related bond premium or bond discount from the accounts at the date of retirement and recognizes any gain or loss on retirement.
- The entry for bond conversion into common stock removes both the appropriate portion of the bonds payable and any related bond premium or bond discount from the accounts at the date of conversion. The par value of common stock issued is recorded, together with the appropriate amount of paid-in capital in excess of par value.
- Some bond agreements require the borrower to make periodic payments to a sinking fund controlled by a trustee, who invests the amounts. The invested amounts plus accumulated income are used to retire the bonds at maturity.

❺ **DESCRIBE** and **ILLUSTRATE** accounting for mortgage notes payable (pp. 616, 617).
- Mortgages involve an agreement, evidenced by a note, to repay the principal amount borrowed with interest on certain dates, and an agreement to pledge certain property as security for repayment of the note.
- Mortgage notes are usually repaid in equal periodic installments, with each payment containing different amounts of interest and principal.

❻ **DESCRIBE** the basic ideas of accounting for postretirement benefits (pp. 616–617).
- In a defined contribution pension plan, the employer contributes a defined amount to the pension fund each year, debiting Pension Expense and crediting Cash. The fund assets determine the size of benefits.
- Defined benefit pension plans specify retirement benefits to be received in the future. They are often a function of years worked and the salary or wage level at retirement. Pension expense and contributions are influenced by such variables as employee turnover, life expectancies, and future salary and wage levels, and actuaries are needed to make estimates.
- Other postretirement benefits, such as health care and legal services, must be accounted for by expensing the cost of providing these benefits during the years of employee service.

❼ **DESCRIBE** and **ILLUSTRATE** deferred income taxes and present a comprehensive balance sheet (pp. 617–621).
- When a difference in tax accounting and financial reporting results in the related asset having a book value in excess of its tax basis, a deferred tax liability results.
- The deferred tax liability is phased out as the difference in book value and tax basis disappears.

❽ **ANALYTICAL APPLICATION:** **DEFINE** *times interest earned ratio* and **EXPLAIN** its use (p. 622).
- The times interest earned ratio is computed as income before interest expense and income taxes divided by interest expense. It measures the ability of a firm to meet its annual interest commitments.

SELF-TEST QUESTIONS FOR REVIEW

(Answers follow the Solution to Demonstration Problem.)

1. On May 1, 1993, a firm issued $400,000 of 12-year, 9% bonds payable at $96\frac{1}{2}$ plus accrued interest. The bonds are dated January 1, 1993, and interest is payable on January 1 and July 1 of each year. The amount the firm receives on May 1 is
   a. $386,000   **b.** $422,000   **c.** $392,000   **d.** $398,000

2. The amount of discount on the bonds in question 1 to be amortized (straight line) on July 1, 1993, is
   a. $200   **b.** $194.44   **c.** $600   **d.** $583.33

3. A firm issued $250,000 of 10-year, 12% bonds payable on January 1, 1993, for $281,180, yielding an effective rate of 10%. Interest is payable on January 1 and July 1 each year. The firm records amortization on each interest date. Bond interest expense for the first six months of 1993, using effective interest amortization, is
   a. $15,000   **b.** $16,870.80   **c.** $14,059   **d.** $14,331

4. In financial statement presentations, the Discount on Bonds Payable account is
   a. Added to Bond Interest Expense.
   b. Deducted from Bonds Payable.
   c. Added to Bonds Payable.
   d. Deducted from Bond Interest Expense.

5. A firm started operations in 1993. In 1993, it expensed $6,000 on its income tax return that it will not deduct in its financial statements until 1994. The firm's pretax financial income in 1993 was $100,000. The income tax rate for 1993 is 35%; the enacted tax rate for 1994 is 40%. In its December 31, 1993 balance sheet, the company should show a deferred tax liability of
   a. $35,000   **b.** $2,100   **c.** $40,000   **d.** $2,400

DEMONSTRATION PROBLEM FOR REVIEW

The following are selected transactions of Tyler, Inc., for 1993, 1994, and 1995. The firm closes its books on December 31.

1993
Dec. 31   Issued $500,000 of 12%, 10-year convertible bonds for $562,360, yielding an effective rate of 10%. Interest is payable June 30 and December 31. The holder of each $1,000 bond may convert it into 90 shares of $10 par value Tyler, Inc., common stock.

1994
June 30   Paid semiannual interest and recorded semiannual premium amortization on bonds.
Dec. 31   Paid semiannual interest and recorded semiannual premium amortization on bonds.

1995
Jan. 1   Converted $250,000 of convertible bonds to common stock.

REQUIRED

a. Record these transactions in general journal form. Use straight-line amortization.
b. Record the 1994 transactions using effective interest amortization. Round amounts to nearest dollar.

SOLUTION TO DEMONSTRATION PROBLEM

a.   **1993**
Dec. 31   Cash 562,360
              Bonds Payable 500,000
              Premium on Bonds Payable 62,360
          Issued $500,000 of 12%, 10-year convertible bonds for $562,360.

1994

June 30	Bond Interest Expense		26,882	
	Premium on Bonds Payable		3,118	
	Cash			30,000

To record semiannual interest payment and premium amortization [$\$500,000 \times 0.12 \times \frac{6}{12} = \$30,000$; $\$62,360/20$ periods $= \$3,118$].

Dec. 31	Bond Interest Expense		26,882	
	Premium on Bonds Payable		3,118	
	Cash			30,000

To record semiannual interest payment and premium amortization.

1995

Jan. 1	Bonds Payable		250,000	
	Premium on Bonds Payable		28,062	
	Common Stock			225,000
	Paid-in Capital in Excess of Par Value			53,062

Conversion of $250,000 convertible bonds into 22,500 shares of $10 par value common stock.
Book value of bonds converted:

Face amount	$250,000
Add: Premium (50% of total premium)	28,062
Book Value	$278,062

b. **1994**

June 30	Bond Interest Expense		28,118	
	Premium on Bonds Payable		1,882	
	Cash			30,000

To record semiannual interest payment and premium amortization [$\$562,360 \times 0.05 = \$28,118$].

Dec. 31	Bond Interest Expense		28,024	
	Premium on Bonds Payable		1,976	
	Cash			30,000

To record semiannual interest payment and premium amortization [$(\$562,360 - \$1,882) \times 0.05 = \$28,024$, rounded].

ANSWERS TO SELF-TEST QUESTIONS

1. d, p. 609　　**2.** a, p. 609　　**3.** c, p. 611　　**4.** b, p. 610　　**5.** d, p. 619

In this appendix, we explain the concept of present value and the techniques of bond valuation, expand on the subject of effective interest amortization, and introduce the concept of future value.

PRESENT VALUES

Concept of Present Value

Would you rather receive a dollar now or a dollar one year from now? Most persons would answer, "a dollar now." Intuition tells us that a dollar received now is more valuable than the same amount received sometime in the future. Sound reasons exist for choosing the earlier dollar, the most obvious of which concerns risk. Because the future is always uncertain, some event may prevent us from receiving the dollar at the later date. To avoid this risk, we choose the earlier date.

A second reason for choosing the earlier date is that the dollar received now could be invested; one year from now, we could have not only the dollar but also the interest income for the period. Using these risk and interest factors, we can generalize that (1) the right to receive an amount of money now—its **present value**—is normally worth more than the right to receive the same amount later—its future value; (2) the longer we must wait to receive an amount, the less attractive the receipt is; and (3) the difference between the present value of an amount and its future value is a function of interest (Principal × Interest Rate × Time). The more risk associated with any situation, the higher the appropriate interest rate.

We support these generalizations with an illustration. What amount could we accept now that would be as valuable as receiving $100 one year from now if the appropriate interest rate is 10%? We recognize intuitively that with a 10% interest rate, we should accept less than $100, or approximately $91. We base this estimate on the realization that the $100 received in the future must equal the present value (100%) plus 10% interest on the present value. Thus, in our example, the $100 future receipt must be 1.10 times the present value. Dividing ($100/1.10), we obtain a present value of $90.90. In other words, under the given conditions, we would do as well to accept $90.90 now as to wait one year and receive $100. To confirm the equality of a $90.90 receipt now to a $100 receipt one year later, we calculate the future value of $90.90 at 10% for one year as follows:

$$\$90.90 \times 1.10 \times 1 \text{ year} = \$100 \text{ (rounded)}$$

Thus, we compute the present value of a future receipt by discounting (deducting an interest factor) the future receipt back to the present at an appropriate interest rate. We present this schematically below:

Present value $90.90	⟵	Discounted for one year at 10%	⟵	Future value $100

If either the time period or the interest rate were increased, the resulting present value would decrease. If more than one time period is involved, compound interest computations are appropriate.

Use of Present Value Tables

Because present value tables, such as Table I (on page 632) are widely available, we need not present here the various formulas for interest computations. Table I can be used to compute the present value amounts in the illustrations and problem materials that follow. Simply stated, present value tables provide a multiplier for many combinations of time periods and interest rates that, when applied to the dollar amount of a future cash flow, determines its present value.

Present value tables are used as follows. First, determine the number of interest compounding periods involved (three years compounded annually is 3 periods, three years compounded semiannually is 6 periods, three years compounded quarterly is

12 periods, and so on). The extreme left-hand column indicates the number of periods covered in the table.

Next, determine the interest rate per compounding period. Note that interest rates are usually quoted on a *per year* basis. Therefore, only in the case of annual compoundings is the quoted interest rate the interest rate per compounding period. In other cases, the rate per compounding period is the annual rate divided by the number of compounding periods in a year. For example, an interest rate of 10% per year would be 10% for one compounding period if compounded annually, 5% for two compounding periods if compounded semiannually, and $2\frac{1}{2}$% for four compounding periods if compounded quarterly.

Locate the factor that is to the right of the appropriate number of compounding periods and beneath the appropriate interest rate per compounding period. Multiply this factor by the number of dollars involved.

Note the logical progressions among multipliers in Table I. All values are less than 1.0 because the present value is always smaller than the $1 future amount if the interest rate is greater than zero. Also, as the interest rate increases (moving from left to right in the table) or the number of periods increases (moving from top to bottom), the multipliers become smaller.

EXAMPLE 1 Compute the present value of $100 one year hence, at 10% interest compounded annually.

> Number of periods (one year, annually) = 1
> Rate per period (10%/1) = 10%
> Multiplier = 0.909
> Present value = $100.00 × 0.909 = $90.90
> (Note that this agrees with our earlier illustration.)

EXAMPLE 2 Compute the present value of $116.99 two years hence, at 8% compounded semiannually.

> Number of periods (two years, semiannually) = 4
> Rate per period (8%/2) = 4%
> Multiplier = 0.855
> Present value = $116.99 × 0.855 = $100 (rounded)

Annuity Form of Cash Flow

Using present value tables like Table I, we can compute the present value of any single future cash flow or series of future cash flows. One frequent pattern of cash flows, however, is subject to a more convenient treatment. This pattern, known as an **annuity,** can be described as *equal amounts equally spaced over a period*.

For example, $100 is to be received at the end of each of the next three years as an annuity. When annuity cash flows occur at the end of each period, the annuity is called an *ordinary annuity*. As shown below, the present value of this ordinary annuity can be computed from Table I by computing the present value of each of the three individual receipts and summing them (assuming 5% annual interest).

Future Receipts (ordinary annuity)				PV Multiplier (Table I)		Present Value
Yr. 1	Yr. 2	Yr. 3				
$100			×	0.952	=	$ 95.20
	$100		×	0.907	=	90.70
		$100	×	0.864	=	$ 86.40
				Total present value		$272.30

Table II (on page 633) provides a single multiplier for computing the present value of a series of future cash flows in the ordinary annuity form. Referring to Table II in the three periods hence row and the 5% column, we see that the multiplier is 2.723. When applied to the $100 annuity amount, the multiplier gives a present value of $272.30. As shown above, the same present value is derived from the several multipliers of Table I. For annuities of 5, 10, or 20 years, considerable computations are avoided by using annuity tables.

Bond Valuations

We have explained previously that (1) a bond agreement specifies a pattern of future cash flows—usually a series of interest payments and a single payment at maturity equal to the face value—and (2) bonds are sold at premiums or discounts to adjust their effective interest rates to the prevailing market rate when they are issued.

Because of the role played by interest, the selling price (or valuation) of a bond that is necessary to yield a specific rate can be determined as follows:

1. Use Table I to compute the present value of the future principal repayment at the desired (or effective) rate of interest.

2. Use Table II to compute the present value of the future series of interest payments at the desired (or effective) rate of interest.

3. Add the present values obtained in steps 1 and 2.

We illustrate in Exhibit D-1 the pricing of a $100,000 issue of 8%, four-year bonds paying interest semiannually and sold on the date of issue to yield 8%.

We use the 4% column in both Tables I and II, because the interest rate is 8% compounded semiannually (8%/2 = 4% per compounding period), and we use the eight periods hence row because there are eight semiannual periods in four years. The multiplier from Table I is applied to the $100,000 because the principal repayment is a single sum. Because the eight semiannual interest payments are in the annuity form, we use the multiplier from Table II to compute their present value. Note that the computation in Exhibit D-1 confirms the observation that the price of 8% bonds sold to yield 8% should be face (or par) value.

Installment Payment Computation

When a creditor lends money that is repaid in equal periodic installments, such as a mortgage note payable, the creditor needs to determine the amount of the installment payment. This is done by dividing the amount loaned (a present value amount) by the present value factor for an annuity at the desired rate of interest.

For example, a creditor lends $100,000 on a 10-year mortgage note to be repaid in equal quarterly payments. The creditor wants to earn a return of 12% annually. Because there are four payments each year, the present value factor selected is for 40 periods at 3%. From Table II, this factor is 23.115. The quarterly payment, then, is determined as follows:

Present Value	÷	Factor	=	Periodic Payment
$100,000	÷	23.115	=	$4,326 (rounded)

EXHIBIT D—1	CALCULATION OF BOND PRICE USING PRESENT VALUE TABLES

$100,000 of 8%, four-year bonds with interest payable semiannually priced to yield 8%.

Future Cash Flows	Multiplier (Table I)	Multiplier (Table II)	Present Values
Principal repayment, $100,000 (a single amount received eight semiannual periods hence)	0.731		$ 73,100
Interest payments, $4,000 at end of each of eight semiannual interest periods		6.733	26,900 (rounded)
Total present value (or issue price) of bonds			$100,000

EFFECTIVE INTEREST AMORTIZATION

Most bonds sell at more or less than their face value, and therefore accounting for them involves amortizing bond premium or bond discount. For the remainder of this illustration, we show (1) how the $100,000, 8% bond issue used earlier would be valued if it were sold to yield either 6% or 10% compounded semiannually and (2) how the bond discount and premium amounts would be determined under the *effective interest method* of amortization.

We calculate the amount of discount and premium in the illustration as follows:

Future Cash Flows	Bonds Sold at Discount (to yield 10%)		Bonds Sold at Premium (to yield 6%)	
	Present Value Multiplier	Present Value	Present Value Multiplier	Present Value
Principal repayment of $100,000 (eight semiannual periods hence, factors from Table I)	0.677	$67,700	0.789	$ 78,900
Interest payments of $4,000 each (a series of eight in ordinary annuity form, factors from Table II)	6.463	25,852	7.020	28,080
Selling price of bond issues		$93,552		$106,980
Amount of bond discount or premium		$ 6,448		$ 6,980

According to these results, an investor wishing to earn 10%, compounded semiannually, must discount the bonds by $6,448 (that is, pay only $93,552 for them). An investor paying a $6,980 premium for the bonds would earn 6%, compounded semiannually, on the investment.

The book value of bonds consists of their face value plus any unamortized premium or less any unamortized discount. Thus, at issuance, the book value of the bonds is equal to their selling price. To calculate the periodic amount of amortization using the effective interest method use the following steps:

1. Determine the period's interest expense by multiplying the bonds' book value at the beginning of the period by the effective interest rate.

2. Determine the period's amortization by comparing the period's interest expense (step 1 above) to the amount of interest actually paid. If the interest expense is more than the amount of interest paid, the difference is discount amortization; if the expense is less than the interest paid, the difference is premium amortization.

Face value of bonds	$100,000
Less: Discount	6,448
Book value of bonds at beginning of period	$ 93,552
Multiply by the interest rate per interest period (10%/2 = 5%)	$\times$ 0.05
Interest expense for first period (rounded)	$ 4,678
Actual interest paid ($100,000 $\times$ 0.08 $\times \frac{6}{12}$)	4,000
First period's discount amortization	$ 678

Exhibits D-2 and D-3 summarize the calculations, related account balances, and the general progressions involved in the other periods of our illustration. These

EXHIBIT D—2	BONDS SOLD AT A DISCOUNT: PERIODIC INTEREST EXPENSE, EFFECTIVE INTEREST AMORTIZATION, AND BOOK VALUE OF BONDS

$100,000 of 8%, four-year bonds with interest payable semiannually issued at $93,552 to yield 10%.

Year	Interest Period	A Interest Paid (4% of face value)	B Interest Expense (5% of bond book value)	C Periodic Amortization (B – A)	D Balance of Unamortized Discount (D – C)	E Book Value of Bonds, End of Period ($100,000 – D)
(at issue)					$6,448	$ 93,552
1	1	$4,000	$4,678	$678	5,770	94,230
	2	4,000	4,712	712	5,058	94,942
2	3	4,000	4,747	747	4,311	95,689
	4	4,000	4,784	784	3,527	96,473
3	5	4,000	4,824	824	2,703	97,297
	6	4,000	4,865	865	1,838	98,162
4	7	4,000	4,908	908	930	99,070
	8	4,000	4,930*	930	–0–	100,000

*Adjusted for cumulative rounding error of $24.

amortization schedules also appear in the accompanying chapter and are explained there. We repeat them here for your convenience.

The effective interest method of amortization is often justified as being more precise than the straight-line method. This contention probably rests on the fact that, by incorporating a changing amount of total interest expense, the effective interest method results in a uniform interest rate throughout the life of the bonds. This

EXHIBIT D—3	BONDS SOLD AT A PREMIUM: PERIODIC INTEREST EXPENSE, EFFECTIVE INTEREST AMORTIZATION, AND BOOK VALUE OF BONDS

$100,000 of 8%, four-year bonds with interest payable semiannually issued at $106,980 to yield 6%.

Year	Interest Period	A Interest Paid (4% of face value)	B Interest Expense (3% of bond book value)	C Periodic Amortization (A – B)	D Balance of Unamortized Premium (D – C)	E Book Value of Bonds, End of Period ($100,000 + D)
(at issue)					$6,980	$106,980
1	1	$4,000	$3,209	$791	6,189	106,189
	2	4,000	3,186	814	5,375	105,375
2	3	4,000	3,161	839	4,536	104,536
	4	4,000	3,136	864	3,672	103,672
3	5	4,000	3,110	890	2,782	102,782
	6	4,000	3,083	917	1,865	101,865
4	7	4,000	3,056	944	921	100,921
	8	4,000	3,079*	921	–0–	100,000

*Adjusted for cumulative rounding error of $51.

increased precision is offset by the added complexity and the fact that the difference between the two methods is often considered immaterial.

FUTURE VALUES

Future Value of a Single Amount

The **future value** of a single sum is the amount a specified investment will be worth at a future date if invested at a given rate of compound interest. Suppose we decide to invest $6,000 in a savings account that pays 6% annual interest, and that we intend to leave the principal and interest in the account for five years. We assume that interest is credited to the account at the end of each year. The balance in the account at the end of five years is determined using Table III (on page 634), which furnishes the future value of a dollar after a given number of time periods, as follows:

$$\textbf{Principal} \times \textbf{Factor} = \textbf{Future Value}$$
$$\$6,000 \times 1.338 = \$8,028$$

The factor 1.338 is in the row for five periods and the column for 6%.

Suppose the interest is credited to the account semiannually, rather than annually. In this situation, there are 10 compounding periods, and we use a 3% rate (one-half the annual rate). The future value calculation is as follows:

$$\textbf{Principal} \times \textbf{Factor} = \textbf{Future Value}$$
$$\$6,000 \times 1.344 = \$8,064$$

Future Value of an Annuity

If, instead of investing a single amount at the beginning of a series of periods, we invest a specified amount each period, we are investing in the annuity form. Suppose we decide to invest $2,000 at the end of each year for five years at an 8% annual rate of return. To determine the accumulated amount of principal and interest, we refer to Table IV (on page 635), which furnishes the future value of a dollar invested at the end of each period. The factor 5.867 is in the row for five periods and the column for 8%, and the calculation is as follows:

$$\textbf{Periodic Payment} \times \textbf{Factor} = \textbf{Future Value}$$
$$\$2,000 \times 5.867 = \$11,734$$

If we decide to invest $1,000 at the end of each six months for five years at an 8% annual rate of return, we would use the factor for 10 periods at 4%, as follows:

$$\textbf{Periodic Payment} \times \textbf{Factor} = \textbf{Future Value}$$
$$\$1,000 \times 12.01 = \$12,010$$

When the future value is some desired amount and the periodic payment is to be calculated, you need only to *divide* the future value by the factor to determine the periodic payment.

For example, a corporation issued $100,000 of 10-year bonds payable and agreed to contribute the necessary amounts to a sinking fund at the end of each year in order to retire the bonds in 10 years. It is expected that the sinking fund will earn a 12% annual rate of return over the period. The factor for 10 periods at 12%, taken from Table IV, is 17.55. The annual contribution to the sinking fund is as follows:

$$\textbf{Future Value} \div \textbf{Factor} = \textbf{Periodic Payment}$$
$$\$100,000 \div 17.55 = \$5,698 \text{ (rounded)}$$

PRESENT VALUE TABLES

TABLE I	PRESENT VALUE OF $1

Periods Hence	Rate per Compounding Period									
	2%	3%	4%	5%	6%	8%	10%	12%	15%	20%
1	0.980	0.971	0.962	0.952	0.943	0.926	0.909	0.893	0.870	0.833
2	0.961	0.943	0.925	0.907	0.890	0.857	0.826	0.797	0.756	0.694
3	0.942	0.915	0.889	0.864	0.840	0.794	0.751	0.712	0.658	0.579
4	0.924	0.889	0.855	0.823	0.792	0.735	0.683	0.636	0.572	0.482
5	0.906	0.863	0.822	0.784	0.747	0.681	0.621	0.567	0.497	0.402
6	0.888	0.838	0.790	0.746	0.705	0.630	0.564	0.507	0.432	0.335
7	0.871	0.813	0.760	0.711	0.665	0.583	0.513	0.452	0.376	0.279
8	0.854	0.789	0.731	0.677	0.627	0.540	0.467	0.404	0.327	0.233
9	0.837	0.766	0.703	0.645	0.592	0.500	0.424	0.361	0.284	0.194
10	0.821	0.744	0.676	0.614	0.558	0.463	0.386	0.322	0.247	0.162
11	0.804	0.722	0.650	0.585	0.527	0.429	0.350	0.287	0.215	0.135
12	0.789	0.701	0.625	0.557	0.497	0.397	0.319	0.257	0.187	0.112
13	0.773	0.681	0.601	0.530	0.469	0.368	0.290	0.229	0.163	0.093
14	0.758	0.661	0.577	0.505	0.442	0.340	0.263	0.205	0.141	0.078
15	0.743	0.642	0.555	0.481	0.417	0.315	0.239	0.183	0.123	0.065
16	0.728	0.623	0.534	0.458	0.394	0.292	0.218	0.163	0.107	0.054
17	0.714	0.605	0.513	0.436	0.371	0.270	0.198	0.146	0.093	0.045
18	0.700	0.587	0.494	0.416	0.350	0.250	0.180	0.130	0.081	0.038
19	0.686	0.570	0.475	0.396	0.331	0.232	0.164	0.116	0.070	0.031
20	0.673	0.554	0.456	0.377	0.312	0.215	0.149	0.104	0.061	0.026
30	0.552	0.412	0.308	0.231	0.174	0.099	0.057	0.033	0.015	0.004
40	0.453	0.307	0.208	0.142	0.097	0.046	0.022	0.011	0.004	0.001
50	0.372	0.228	0.141	0.087	0.054	0.021	0.009	0.003	0.001	—

TABLE II	PRESENT VALUE OF AN ORDINARY ANNUITY OF $1 PER PERIOD

Periods Hence	Rate per Compounding Period									
	2%	**3%**	**4%**	**5%**	**6%**	**8%**	**10%**	**12%**	**15%**	**20%**
1	0.980	0.971	0.962	0.952	0.943	0.926	0.909	0.893	0.870	0.833
2	1.942	1.914	1.886	1.859	1.833	1.783	1.736	1.690	1.626	1.528
3	2.884	2.829	2.775	2.723	2.673	2.577	2.487	2.402	2.283	2.106
4	3.808	3.717	3.630	3.546	3.465	3.312	3.170	3.037	2.855	2.589
5	4.714	4.580	4.452	4.330	4.212	3.993	3.791	3.605	3.352	2.991
6	5.601	5.417	5.242	5.076	4.917	4.623	4.355	4.111	3.784	3.326
7	6.472	6.230	6.002	5.786	5.582	5.206	4.868	4.564	4.160	3.605
8	7.326	7.020	6.733	6.463	6.210	5.747	5.335	4.968	4.487	3.837
9	8.162	7.786	7.435	7.108	6.802	6.247	5.760	5.328	4.772	4.031
10	8.983	8.530	8.111	7.722	7.360	6.710	6.145	5.650	5.019	4.192
11	9.787	9.253	8.761	8.306	7.887	7.139	6.495	5.988	5.234	4.327
12	10.575	9.954	9.385	8.863	8.384	7.536	6.814	6.194	5.421	4.439
13	11.348	10.635	9.986	9.394	8.853	7.904	7.103	6.424	5.583	4.533
14	12.106	11.296	10.563	9.899	9.295	8.244	7.367	6.628	5.724	4.611
15	12.849	11.938	11.118	10.380	9.712	8.560	7.606	6.811	5.847	4.675
16	13.578	12.561	11.652	10.838	10.106	8.851	7.824	6.974	5.954	4.730
17	14.292	13.166	12.166	11.274	10.477	9.122	8.022	7.120	6.047	4.775
18	14.992	13.754	12.659	11.690	10.828	9.372	8.201	7.250	6.128	4.812
19	15.679	14.324	13.134	12.085	11.158	9.604	8.365	7.366	6.198	4.844
20	16.351	14.878	13.590	12.462	11.470	9.818	8.514	7.469	6.259	4.870
30	22.397	19.600	17.292	15.373	13.765	11.258	9.427	8.055	6.566	4.979
40	27.356	23.115	19.793	17.159	15.046	11.925	9.779	8.244	6.642	4.997
50	31.424	25.730	21.482	18.256	15.762	12.234	9.915	8.304	6.661	4.999

FUTURE VALUE TABLES

TABLE III		FUTURE VALUE OF $1								

Periods Hence	Rate per Compounding Period									
	2%	3%	4%	5%	6%	8%	10%	12%	15%	20%
1	1.020	1.030	1.040	1.050	1.060	1.080	1.100	1.120	1.150	1.200
2	1.040	1.061	1.082	1.103	1.124	1.166	1.210	1.254	1.323	1.440
3	1.061	1.093	1.125	1.158	1.191	1.260	1.331	1.405	1.521	1.728
4	1.082	1.126	1.170	1.216	1.262	1.360	1.464	1.574	1.749	2.074
5	1.104	1.159	1.217	1.276	1.338	1.469	1.611	1.762	2.011	2.488
6	1.126	1.194	1.265	1.340	1.419	1.587	1.772	1.974	2.313	2.986
7	1.149	1.230	1.316	1.407	1.504	1.714	1.949	2.211	2.660	3.583
8	1.172	1.267	1.369	1.477	1.594	1.851	2.144	2.476	3.059	4.300
9	1.195	1.305	1.423	1.551	1.689	1.999	2.358	2.773	3.518	5.160
10	1.219	1.344	1.480	1.629	1.791	2.159	2.594	3.106	4.046	6.192
11	1.243	1.384	1.539	1.710	1.898	2.332	2.853	3.479	4.652	7.430
12	1.268	1.426	1.601	1.796	2.012	2.518	3.138	3.896	5.350	8.916
13	1.294	1.469	1.665	1.886	2.133	2.720	3.452	4.363	6.153	10.699
14	1.319	1.513	1.732	1.980	2.261	2.937	3.798	4.887	7.076	12.839
15	1.346	1.558	1.801	2.079	2.397	3.172	4.177	5.474	8.137	15.407
16	1.373	1.605	1.873	2.183	2.540	3.426	4.595	6.130	9.358	18.488
17	1.400	1.653	1.948	2.292	2.693	3.700	5.054	6.866	10.761	22.186
18	1.428	1.702	2.026	2.407	2.854	3.996	5.560	7.690	12.375	26.623
19	1.457	1.754	2.107	2.527	3.026	4.316	6.116	8.613	14.232	31.948
20	1.486	1.806	2.191	2.653	3.207	4.661	6.728	9.646	16.367	38.338
30	1.811	2.427	3.243	4.322	5.743	10.06	17.45	29.96	66.212	237.376
40	2.208	3.262	4.801	7.040	10.29	21.72	45.26	93.05	267.864	1,469.772
50	2.692	4.384	7.107	11.47	18.42	46.90	117.4	289.0	1,083.657	9,100.438

TABLE IV		FUTURE VALUE OF AN ORDINARY ANNUITY OF $1 PER PERIOD								
Periods Hence	Rate per Compounding Period									
	2%	**3%**	**4%**	**5%**	**6%**	**8%**	**10%**	**12%**	**15%**	**20%**
1	1.000	1.000	1.000	1.000	1.000	1.000	1.000	1.000	1.000	1.000
2	2.020	2.030	2.040	2.050	2.060	2.080	2.100	2.120	2.150	2.200
3	3.060	3.091	3.122	3.153	3.184	3.246	3.310	3.374	3.473	3.640
4	4.122	4.184	4.246	4.310	4.375	4.506	4.641	4.779	4.993	5.368
5	5.204	5.309	5.416	5.526	5.637	5.867	6.105	6.353	6.742	7.442
6	6.308	6.468	6.633	6.802	6.975	7.336	7.716	8.115	8.754	9.930
7	7.434	7.662	7.898	8.142	8.394	8.923	9.487	10.09	11.07	12.92
8	8.583	8.892	9.214	9.549	9.897	10.64	11.44	12.30	13.73	16.50
9	9.755	10.16	10.58	11.03	11.49	12.49	13.58	14.78	16.79	20.80
10	10.95	11.46	12.01	12.58	13.18	14.49	15.94	17.55	20.30	25.96
11	12.17	12.81	13.49	14.21	14.97	16.65	18.53	20.65	24.35	32.15
12	13.41	14.19	15.03	15.92	16.87	18.98	21.38	24.13	29.00	39.58
13	14.68	15.62	16.63	17.71	18.88	21.50	24.52	28.03	34.35	48.50
14	15.97	17.09	18.29	19.60	21.02	24.21	27.98	32.39	40.50	59.20
15	17.29	18.60	20.02	21.58	23.28	27.15	31.77	37.28	47.58	72.04
16	18.64	20.16	21.82	23.66	25.67	30.32	35.95	42.75	55.72	87.44
17	20.01	21.76	23.70	25.84	28.21	33.75	40.54	48.88	65.08	105.9
18	21.41	23.41	25.65	28.13	30.91	37.45	45.60	55.75	75.84	128.1
19	22.84	25.12	27.67	30.54	33.76	41.45	51.16	63.44	88.21	154.7
20	24.30	26.87	29.78	33.07	36.79	45.76	57.28	72.05	102.4	186.7
30	40.57	47.58	56.08	66.44	79.06	113.3	164.5	241.3	434.7	1,181.2
40	60.40	75.40	95.03	120.8	154.8	259.1	442.6	767.1	1,779	7,343
50	84.58	112.8	152.7	209.3	290.3	573.8	1,164	2,400	7,218	45,497

GLOSSARY OF KEY TERMS USED IN THIS CHAPTER AND THE APPENDIX

annuity   A pattern of cash flows in which equal amounts are spaced equally over a number of periods (p. 627).

bond   A long-term debt instrument that promises to pay interest periodically and a principal amount at maturity, usually issued by the borrower to a group of lenders. Bonds may incorporate a wide variety of provisions relating to security for the debt involved, methods of paying the periodic interest, and maturity and retirement provisions (p. 602).

bond sinking fund   A fund accumulated through required periodic contributions (and investment income thereon) to be used for the retirement of a specific bond issue (p. 615).

callable bonds   Bonds that allow the borrower to retire (call in) the bonds after a stated date (p. 604).

contract rate   The rate of interest stated on a bond certificate (p. 604).

convertible bond   A bond incorporating the holder's right to convert the bond to capital stock under prescribed terms (p. 604).

coupon bond   A bond with coupons for interest payable to bearer attached to the bond for each interest period. Whenever interest is due, the bondholder detaches a coupon and deposits it with his or her bank for collection (p. 604).

debenture bond   A bond that has no specific property pledged as security for the repayment of funds borrowed (p. 604).

deferred tax liability   A liability representing the estimated future income taxes payable resulting from an existing temporary difference between an asset's book value and its tax basis (p. 618).

effective interest method   A method of amortizing bond premium or discount that results in a constant rate of interest each period and varying amounts of premium or discount amortized each period (p. 611).

effective rate   The current rate of interest in the market for a bond or other debt instrument. When issued, a bond is priced to yield the market rate of interest at the date of issuance (p. 611).

future value   The amount a specified investment (or series of investments) will be worth at a future date if invested at a given rate of compound interest (p. 632).

leveraging   The use of borrowed funds in the capital structure of a firm. The expectation is that the funds will earn a return greater than the rate of interest on the borrowed funds (p. 602).

market rate   The current rate of interest in the market for a bond or other debt instrument (p. 605).

mortgage note   A note combined with a mortgage; the mortgage is a legal agreement pledging certain property of the borrower as security for repayment of the note (p. 616).

nominal rate   The rate of interest stated on a bond certificate (p. 604).

pension plan   A plan to pay benefits to employees after they retire from the company. The plan may be a defined contribution plan or a defined benefit plan (p. 616).

present value   The current worth of amounts to be paid (or received) in the future; computed by discounting the future payments (or receipts) at a specified interest rate (p. 626).

prior service cost   The cost of providing retirement benefits earned by employees prior to the adoption or amendment of a pension plan (p. 616).

registered bond   A bond for which the issuer (or the trustee) maintains a record of owners and, at the appropriate times, mails out interest payments (p. 604).

secured bond   A bond that pledges specific property as security for meeting the terms of the bond agreement (p. 604).

serial bond   A bond issue that staggers the bond maturity dates over a series of years (p. 604).

times interest earned ratio   Income before interest expense and income taxes divided by interest expense. Sometimes called *interest coverage ratio* (p. 622).

trading on the equity   The use of borrowed funds in the capital structure of a firm. The expectation is that the funds will earn a return higher than the rate of interest on the borrowed funds (p. 602).

QUESTIONS

17-1   Define the following terms: (a) mortgage notes, (b) bonds payable, (c) trustee, (d) secured bonds, (e) serial bond, (f) callable bonds, (g) convertible bonds, (h) face value, (i) nominal rate, (j) bond discount, (k) bond premium, and (l) amortization of bond premium or discount.

17-2 Identify the advantages and disadvantages of issuing bonds rather than common stock.

17-3 Explain how issuing bonds at a premium or discount "adjusts the nominal rate to the applicable market rate of interest."

17-4 A $2,000,000 issue of 10-year, 9% bonds was sold at 97 plus accrued interest three months after the bonds were dated. What net amount of cash is received?

17-5 Regardless of whether premium or discount is involved, what generalization can be made about the change in the book value of bonds payable during the period in which they are outstanding?

17-6 How should premium and discount on bonds payable be presented in the balance sheet?

17-7 On April 30, 1993, one year before maturity, Eastern Company retired $100,000 of 9% bonds payable at 101. The book value of the bonds on April 30 was $98,800. Bond interest was last paid on April 30, 1993. What is the gain or loss on the retirement of the bonds?

17-8 Give reasons why a convertible bond may be attractive to both an investor and the issuing company. Why do corporations typically include a call feature in a convertible bond?

17-9 What is the purpose of a bond sinking fund? Where is the bond sinking fund classified in the balance sheet?

17-10 Under what conditions should the effective interest method be used to amortize discount or premium on bonds payable?

17-11 If the effective interest amortization method is used for bonds payable, how does the periodic interest expense change over the life of the bonds when they are issued (a) at a discount and (b) at a premium?

17-12 Sax Company borrowed money by issuing a 20-year mortgage note payable. The note will be repaid in equal monthly installments. The interest expense component of each payment decreases with each payment. Why?

17-13 In employee pension plans, what does the term *prior service cost* mean?

17-14 What accounting analysis is required when the accumulated retirement benefits under a firm's pension plan exceed the assets in the pension fund?

17-15 Give three examples of temporary differences that will result in the recognition of deferred tax liabilities.

17-16 During 1994, its first year of operations, Hunter, Inc., recorded $10,000 of sales revenue in its financial statements that will not be reported as revenue on its income tax return until 1995. The tax rate is 40% for 1994 and 1995. What amount of deferred tax liability related to this temporary difference should appear in Hunter's December 31, 1994, balance sheet?

17-17 A firm records an outlay as an asset in 1993 but deducts the outlay as an expense on its 1993 income tax return. In 1994 the entire amount will be expensed for financial reporting. In 1993, tax rates enacted into law were 35% for 1993 and 40% for 1994. Which rate is used in determining the deferred tax liability at December 31, 1993? Explain.

17-18 When are deferred tax liabilities classified as current liabilities? as long-term liabilities?

17-19 What does the times interest earned ratio show and how is it used?

EXERCISES

**BONDS PAYABLE ENTRIES;
STRAIGHT-LINE
AMORTIZATION
— OBJ. 2 —**

17-20 On May 1, 1993, Rajor Company issued $300,000 of 10-year, 10% bonds at 103. Interest is payable semiannually on November 1 and May 1. Prepare journal entries to reflect (a) the issuance of the bonds, (b) the semiannual interest payment and premium amortization (straight-line method) on November 1, 1993, and (c) the retirement of the bonds (after the final interest payment) on May 1, 2003.

**BONDS PAYABLE ENTRIES;
STRAIGHT-LINE
AMORTIZATION
— OBJ. 2 —**

17-21 On March 1, 1993, Tolson Company issued $400,000 of 10-year, 9% bonds at 97. Interest is payable semiannually on September 1 and March 1. Prepare journal entries to reflect (a) the issuance of the bonds, (b) the semiannual interest payment and discount amortization (straight-line method) on September 1, 1993, and (c) the retirement of the bonds (after the final interest payment) on March 1, 2003.

FINANCIAL STATEMENT PRESENTATION OF BOND ACCOUNTS
— OBJ. 3, 7 —

17-22 Indicate the proper financial statement classification for each of the following accounts:

> Gain on Bond Retirement (material amount)
> Discount on Bonds Payable
> Mortgage Notes Payable
> Bonds Payable
> Bond Sinking Fund
> Bond Interest Payable
> Premium on Bonds Payable

BONDS PAYABLE ENTRIES; EFFECTIVE INTEREST AMORTIZATION
— OBJ. 3 —

17-23 On December 31, 1993, Daggett Company issued $500,000 of 10-year, 9% bonds payable for $468,895, yielding an effective interest rate of 10%. Interest is payable semiannually on June 30 and December 31. Prepare journal entries to reflect (a) the issuance of the bonds, (b) the semiannual interest payment and discount amortization (effective interest method) on June 30, 1994, and (c) the semiannual interest payment and discount amortization on December 31, 1994. Round amounts to the nearest dollar.

BONDS PAYABLE ENTRIES; EFFECTIVE INTEREST AMORTIZATION
— OBJ. 3 —

17-24 On December 31, 1993, Coffey Company issued $200,000 of 15-year, 10% bonds payable for $234,520, yielding an effective interest rate of 8%. Interest is payable semiannually on June 30 and December 31. Prepare journal entries to reflect (a) the issuance of the bonds, (b) the semiannual interest payment and premium amortization (effective interest method) on June 30, 1994, and (c) the semiannual interest payment and premium amortization on December 31, 1994. Round amounts to the nearest dollar.

EARLY RETIREMENT OF BONDS
— OBJ. 4 —

17-25 Elston Corporation issued $400,000 of 11%, 20-year bonds at 102 on January 1, 1993. Interest is payable semiannually on July 1 and January 1. Elston uses the straight-line method to amortize bond premiums. On January 1, 1998, Elston retired the bonds at 103 (after making the interest payment on that date). Prepare the journal entry to record the bond retirement on January 1, 1998.

MORTGAGE NOTES PAYABLE
— OBJ. 5 —

17-26 On December 31, 1993, Thomas, Inc., borrowed $600,000 on a 12%, 15-year mortgage note payable. The note is to be repaid in equal semiannual installments of $43,589 (payable on June 30 and December 31). Prepare journal entries to reflect (a) the issuance of the mortgage note payable, (b) the payment of the first installment on June 30, 1994, and (c) the payment of the second installment on December 31, 1994. Round amounts to the nearest dollar.

DEFERRED INCOME TAXES
— OBJ. 7 —

17-27 Fisk, Inc., purchased $200,000 of special manufacturing tools on January 1, 1993. The tools are being depreciated on a straight-line basis over five years with no expected salvage value. MACRS depreciation is being used on the firm's tax returns. At December 31, 1994, the tools' book value is $120,000 and their tax basis is $44,000 (this is Fisk's only temporary difference). Over the next three years, straight-line depreciation will exceed MACRS depreciation by $10,000 in 1995, $26,000 in 1996, and $40,000 in 1997. The income tax rate in effect for all years is 40%.
a. What amount of deferred tax liability should appear in Fisk's December 31, 1994, balance sheet?
b. What amount of deferred tax liability should appear in Fisk's December 31, 1995, balance sheet?
c. What amount of deferred tax liability should appear in Fisk's December 31, 1996, balance sheet?
d. Where should the deferred tax liability accounts be classified in Fisk's 1994, 1995, and 1996 year-end balance sheets?

DETERMINING BOND PRICE
— APPENDIX D —

17-28 Lunar, Inc., plans to issue $800,000 of 10% bonds that will pay interest semiannually and mature in five years. Assume that the effective interest rate is 12% per year compounded semiannually. Compute the selling price of the bonds. Use Tables I and II (on pages 632, 633).

PROBLEMS

**BONDS PAYABLE ENTRIES;
STRAIGHT-LINE
AMORTIZATION
— OBJ. 2, 4 —**

17-29 On December 31, 1993, Knighton, Inc., sold at 96 a $600,000 issue of 7% bonds that mature in 10 years. Bond interest is payable on June 30 and December 31. The firm uses the straight-line method of amortization.

REQUIRED

a. Show all entries pertaining to the bonds for 1993 and 1994.

b. Prepare the entry necessary to record properly the retirement of one-half the bonds at 98 on June 30, 1997 (immediately after the interest payment on that date).

**BONDS PAYABLE ENTRIES;
STRAIGHT-LINE
AMORTIZATION
— OBJ. 2, 4 —**

17-30 Askew, Inc., which closes its books on December 31, is authorized to issue $900,000 of 9%, 15-year bonds dated May 1, 1993, with interest payments on November 1 and May 1.

REQUIRED

Prepare general journal entries to record the following events, assuming the bonds were (a) sold at 97 on May 1, 1993; and (b) sold at $103\frac{1}{2}$ plus accrued interest on October 1, 1993.

1. The bond issuance.

2. Payment of the first semiannual period's interest and amortization on that date of any related bond premium or discount (straight-line).

3. Accrual of bond interest expense and any related bond premium or discount amortization at December 31, 1993.

4. Payment of the semiannual interest and amortization of any related bond premium or discount (straight line) on May 1, 1994. (The firm does not make reversing entries.)

5. Retirement of $300,000 of the bonds at 101 on May 1, 1998 (immediately after the interest payment on that date).

**EFFECTIVE INTEREST
AMORTIZATION
— OBJ. 3 —**

17-31 On December 31, 1993, Caper, Inc., issued $600,000 of 8%, 10-year bonds for $525,288, yielding an effective interest rate of 10%. Semiannual interest is payable on June 30 and December 31 each year. The firm uses the effective interest method to amortize the discount.

REQUIRED

a. Prepare an amortization schedule showing the necessary information for the first two interest periods. Round amounts to the nearest dollar.

b. Prepare the journal entry for the bond issuance on December 31, 1993.

c. Prepare the entry to record the bond interest payment and discount amortization at June 30, 1994.

d. Prepare the entry to record the bond interest payment and discount amortization at December 31, 1994.

**EFFECTIVE INTEREST
AMORTIZATION
— OBJ. 3 —**

17-32 On March 31, 1993, Eagle, Inc., issued $400,000 of 9%, 20-year bonds for $439,474, yielding an effective interest rate of 8%. Semiannual interest is payable on September 30 and March 31 each year. The firm uses the effective interest method to amortize the premium.

REQUIRED

a. Prepare an amortization schedule showing the necessary information for the first two interest periods. Round amounts to the nearest dollar.

b. Prepare the journal entry for the bond issuance on March 31, 1993.

c. Prepare the entry to record the bond interest payment and premium amortization at September 30, 1993.

d. Prepare the adjusting entry to record interest expense and premium amortization at December 31, 1993, the close of the firm's accounting year.

e. Prepare the entry to record the bond interest payment and premium amortization at March 31, 1994. (The firm does not make reversing entries.)

**SINKING-FUND ENTRIES
— OBJ. 4 —**

17-33 Linden, Inc., issued $750,000 of bonds and is required by its bond agreement to maintain a bond sinking fund managed by a trustee. The following transactions relate to the fund at various times in its life.

1. Linden remits a periodic cash deposit of $51,760 to the fund.
2. The trustee reports sinking fund earnings of $8,613 during the period.
3. The trustee reports the sale of sinking-fund securities and the retirement of the $750,000 of outstanding bonds. Just before this report, the Bond Sinking Fund account for Linden, Inc., showed a balance of $750,000. The trustee also reports the sale of the securities generated an unexpected gain of $8,250, and a check for this amount accompanies the trustee's report (credit to Bond Sinking Fund Income).

REQUIRED

Prepare general journal entries for these sinking-fund transactions.

CONVERTIBLE BONDS PAYABLE; STRAIGHT-LINE AMORTIZATION
— **OBJ. 2, 4** —

17-34 The following transactions of Sphere Corporation for 1993 and 1994 relate to the firm's convertible bonds. The company closes its books on December 31.

1993

May 31 Issued $500,000 of 9%, 10-year convertible bonds, dated May 31, 1993, at 97. Interest is payable semiannually on November 30 and May 31. The holder of each $1,000 bond may convert it into 180 shares of $5 par value Sphere Corporation common stock.

Nov. 30 Paid semiannual interest and recorded semiannual discount amortization (straight line) on convertible bonds.

Dec. 31 Recorded accrued interest payable and discount amortization (straight line) on convertible bonds. (Sphere Corporation does not use reversing entries.)

1994

May 31 Paid semiannual interest and recorded discount amortization (straight line) on all convertible bonds.

May 31 Converted $100,000 of convertible bonds to common stock.

REQUIRED

Record these transactions in general journal form.

MORTGAGE NOTES PAYABLE
— **OBJ. 5, APPENDIX D** —

17-35 On December 31, 1994, Finley Corporation borrowed $250,000 on a 10%, 10-year mortgage note payable. The note is to be repaid with equal semiannual installments, beginning June 30, 1995.

REQUIRED

a. Compute the amount of the semiannual installment payment. Use Table II (on page 633) and round amount to the nearest dollar.
b. Prepare the journal entry to record Finley's borrowing of funds on December 31, 1994.
c. Prepare the journal entry to record Finley's installment payment on June 30, 1995.
d. Prepare the journal entry to record Finley's installment payment on December 31, 1995. (Round amounts to the nearest dollar.)

DEFERRED INCOME TAXES
— **OBJ. 7** —

17-36 Early in January 1994, Wade, Inc., purchased equipment costing $8,000 and debited the amount to the Equipment account. The equipment had a two-year useful life and was depreciated $4,000 in each of the years 1994 and 1995. Wade deducted the entire $8,000 as an expense on its 1994 income tax return. Wade had no other plant assets and the accounting for this equipment represented the only difference between Wade's financial statements and income tax returns. Wade's income before depreciation expense and income taxes was $184,000 in 1994 and $244,000 in 1995. Tax rates enacted into law at December 31, 1994, were 40% for both 1994 and 1995.

REQUIRED

a. What amount of deferred tax liability should be reported in Wade's year-end balance sheets for 1994 and 1995?
b. Prepare journal entries to record income taxes at December 31, 1994, and December 31, 1995.
c. Assume the tax rates enacted into law at December 31, 1994, are 35% for 1994 and 40% for 1995. Prepare journal entries to record income taxes at December 31, 1994, and December 31, 1995.

COMPUTING VARIOUS
PRESENT VALUES
— APPENDIX D —

17-37 Compute the present value of each of the following (use Tables I and II, pages 632, 633):

 a. $70,000 10 years hence if the annual interest rate is
  1. 8% compounded annually.
  2. 8% compounded semiannually.
  3. 8% compounded quarterly.
 b. $800 received at the end of each year for the next eight years if money is worth 10% per year compounded annually.
 c. $500 received at the end of each six months for the next 15 years if the interest rate is 8% per year compounded semiannually.
 d. $300,000 inheritance 10 years hence if money is worth 10% per year compounded annually.
 e. $2,000 received each half-year for the next 10 years plus a single sum of $75,000 at the end of 10 years if the interest rate is 12% per year compounded semiannually.

ALTERNATE EXERCISES

BONDS PAYABLE ENTRIES;
STRAIGHT-LINE
AMORTIZATION
— OBJ. 2 —

17-20A On June 1, 1993, Kerry Company issued $900,000 of 20-year, 12% bonds at 104. Interest is payable semiannually on December 1 and June 1. Prepare journal entries to reflect (a) the issuance of the bonds, (b) the semiannual interest payment and premium amortization (straight-line method) on December 1, 1993, and (c) the retirement of the bonds (after the final interest payment) on June 1, 2003.

BONDS PAYABLE ENTRIES;
STRAIGHT-LINE
AMORTIZATION
— OBJ. 2 —

17-21A On January 1, 1993, Crane Company issued $300,000 of 15-year, 8% bonds at 96. Interest is payable semiannually on July 1 and January 1. Prepare journal entries to reflect (a) the issuance of the bonds, (b) the semiannual interest payment and discount amortization (straight-line method) on July 1, 1993, and (c) the retirement of the bonds (after the final interest payment) on January 1, 2003.

BONDS PAYABLE ON
BALANCE SHEET
— OBJ. 3, 7 —

17-22A The adjusted trial balance for the Lancer Corporation at the end of the current year contains the following accounts:

Bond Interest Payable	$ 15,000
9% Bonds Payable	500,000
10% Bonds Payable	800,000
Discount on 9% Bonds Payable	9,000
Premium on 10% Bonds Payable	5,000
Bond Sinking Fund	250,000

Prepare the long-term liabilities section of the balance sheet. Indicate the proper balance sheet classification for accounts listed above that do not belong in the long-term liabilities section.

BONDS PAYABLE ENTRIES;
EFFECTIVE INTEREST
AMORTIZATION
— OBJ. 3 —

17-23A On December 31, 1993, Blair Company issued $400,000 of 20-year, 11% bonds payable for $369,812, yielding an effective interest rate of 12%. Interest is payable semiannually on June 30 and December 31. Prepare journal entries to reflect (a) the issuance of the bonds, (b) the semiannual interest payment and discount amortization (effective interest method) on June 30, 1994, and (c) the semiannual interest payment and discount amortization on December 31, 1994. Round amounts to the nearest dollar.

BONDS PAYABLE ENTRIES;
EFFECTIVE INTEREST
AMORTIZATION
— OBJ. 3 —

17-24A On December 31, 1993, Kay Company issued $200,000 of five-year, 13% bonds payable for $223,186, yielding an effective interest rate of 10%. Interest is payable semiannually on June 30 and December 31. Prepare journal entries to reflect (a) the issuance of the bonds, (b) the semiannual interest payment and premium amortization (effective interest method) on June 30, 1994, and (c) the semiannual interest payment and premium amortization on December 31, 1994. Round amounts to the nearest dollar.

CONVERSION OF BONDS
— OBJ. 4 —

17-25A Barton Corporation issued $500,000 of 9%, 10-year convertible bonds at 96 on January 1, 1993. Interest is payable semiannually on July 1 and January 1. After five years, each $1,000 bond may be converted into 40 shares of $20 par value common stock. Barton uses the straight-line method to amortize bond discounts. On January 1, 1999, all bonds are converted into common stock (after making the interest payment on that date). Prepare the journal entry to record the bond conversion on January 1, 1999.

MORTGAGE NOTES PAYABLE
— OBJ. 5 —

17-26A On December 31, 1993, Beam Inc., borrowed $250,000 on an 8%, 10-year mortgage note payable. The note is to be repaid in equal quarterly installments of $9,139 (beginning March 31, 1994). Prepare journal entries to reflect (a) the issuance of the mortgage note payable, (b) the payment of the first installment on March 31, 1994, and (c) the payment of the second installment on June 30, 1994. Round amounts to the nearest dollar.

DEFERRED INCOME TAXES
— OBJ. 7 —

17-27A Miner Corporation paid $9,000 on December 31, 1993 for equipment with a three-year useful life (1994-1996) and debited the payment to Equipment. The equipment will be depreciated $3,000 per year in 1994, 1995, and 1996. Miner took the $9,000 payment as an expense on its 1993 income tax return. This amount is Miner's only temporary difference between its books and its tax return. Miner's income tax rate is 40%.

a. What amount of deferred tax liability should appear in Miner's December 31, 1993, balance sheet?

b. Where should the deferred tax liability be classified in the balance sheet at December 31, 1993?

c. What amount of deferred tax liability should appear in Miner's December 31, 1994, balance sheet?

DETERMINING BOND PRICE
— APPENDIX D —

17-28A Tide, Inc., plans to issue $600,000 of 10% bonds that will pay interest semiannually and mature in 10 years. Assume that the effective interest is 8% per year compounded semiannually. Compute the selling price of the bonds. Use Tables I and II (on pages 632, 633).

ALTERNATE PROBLEMS

BONDS PAYABLE ENTRIES; STRAIGHT-LINE AMORTIZATION
— OBJ. 2, 4 —

17-29A On December 31, 1993, Bolden, Inc., sold at 102 a $500,000 issue of 10% bonds that mature in 20 years. Bond interest is payable on June 30 and December 31. The firm uses the straight-line method of amortization.

REQUIRED

a. Show all entries pertaining to the bonds for 1993 and 1994.

b. Present the entries necessary to record properly the retirement of $200,000 of the bonds at 101 on December 31, 1999 (immediately after the interest payment on that date).

BONDS PAYABLE ENTRIES; STRAIGHT-LINE AMORTIZATION
— OBJ. 2, 4 —

17-30A Cheney, Inc., which closes its books on December 31, is authorized to issue $800,000 of 9%, 20-year bonds dated March 1, 1993, with interest payments on September 1 and March 1.

REQUIRED

Prepare general journal entries to record the following events, assuming the bonds were (a) sold for $785,000 on March 1, 1993; and (b) sold for $851,920 plus accrued interest on July 1, 1993.

1. The bond issuance.

2. Payment of the semiannual interest and amortization of any related bond premium or discount (straight line) on September 1, 1993.

3. Accrual of bond interest expense and any related bond premium or discount amortization at December 31, 1993. Cheney does not use reversing entries.

4. Payment of the semiannual interest and amortization of any related bond premium or discount (straight line) on March 1, 1994.

5. Retirement of $200,000 of the bonds at 101 on March 1, 2003 (immediately after the interest payment on that date).

EFFECTIVE INTEREST AMORTIZATION
— OBJ. 3 —

17-31A On December 31, 1993, Echo, Inc., issued $700,000 of 11%, 10-year bonds for $659,995, yielding an effective interest rate of 12%. Semiannual interest is payable on June 30 and December 31 each year. The firm uses the effective interest method to amortize the discount.

REQUIRED

a. Prepare an amortization schedule showing the necessary information for the first two interest periods. Round amounts to the nearest dollar.
b. Prepare the journal entry for the bond issuance on December 31, 1993.
c. Prepare the entry to record bond interest expense and discount amortization at June 30, 1994.
d. Prepare the entry to record bond interest expense and discount amortization at December 31, 1994.

EFFECTIVE INTEREST AMORTIZATION
— OBJ. 3 —

17-32A On April 30, 1993, Raines, Inc., issued $300,000 of 10%, 15-year bonds for $351,780, yielding an effective interest rate of 8%. Semiannual interest is payable on October 31 and April 30 each year. The firm uses the effective interest method to amortize the discount.

REQUIRED

a. Prepare an amortization schedule showing the necessary information for the first two interest periods. Round amounts to the nearest dollar.
b. Prepare the journal entry for the bond issuance on April 30, 1993.
c. Prepare the entry to record the bond interest payment and premium amortization at October 31, 1993.
d. Prepare the adjusting entry to record bond interest expense and premium amortization at December 31, 1993, the close of the firm's accounting year.
e. Prepare the entry to record bond interest expense and premium amortization at April 30, 1994. (The firm does not make reversing entries.)

SINKING-FUND ENTRIES
— OBJ. 4 —

17-33A Leisure, Inc., issued $450,000 of bonds and is required by its bond agreement to maintain a bond sinking fund managed by a trustee. The following transactions relate to the fund at various times in its life.

1. Leisure remits a periodic cash deposit of $16,575 to the fund.
2. The trustee reports sinking fund earnings of $4,305 during the period.
3. The trustee reports the sale of sinking-fund securities and the retirement of the $450,000 of outstanding bonds. Just before this report, the Bond Sinking Fund account for Leisure, Inc., showed a balance of $450,000. The trustee also reports that the sale of the securities generated an unexpected gain of $6,450, and a check for this amount accompanies the trustee's report (credit to Bond Sinking Fund Income).

REQUIRED

Prepare general journal entries for these sinking-fund transactions.

CONVERTIBLE BONDS PAYABLE; STRAIGHT-LINE AMORTIZATION
— OBJ. 2, 4 —

17-34A The following transactions of Nylan, Inc., for 1993 and 1994 relate to the firm's convertible bonds. The company closes its books on December 31.

1993

Jan. 31   Issued $1,200,000 of 13%, 20-year convertible bonds, dated January 31, 1993, at 105. Interest is payable semiannually on July 31 and January 31. The holder of each $1,000 bond may convert it into 48 shares of $20 par value Nylan, Inc., common stock.

July 31   Paid semiannual interest and recorded premium amortization (straight line) on convertible bonds.

Dec. 31   Recorded accrued interest payable and premium amortization (straight line) on convertible bonds. (Nylan, Inc., does not use reversing entries.)

1994

Jan. 31   Paid semiannual interest and recorded premium amortization (straight line) on all convertible bonds.

Jan. 31   Converted $300,000 of convertible bonds to common stock.

REQUIRED

Record these transactions in general journal form.

MORTGAGE NOTES
PAYABLE
— OBJ. 5, APPENDIX D —

17-35A On December 31, 1994, Comray Corporation borrowed $500,000 on an 8%, five-year mortgage note payable. The note is to be repaid with equal quarterly installments, beginning March 31, 1995.

REQUIRED

a. Compute the amount of the quarterly installment payment. Use Table II (on page 633) and round amount to the nearest dollar.

b. Prepare the journal entry to record the borrowing of funds by Comray Corporation on December 31, 1994.

c. Prepare the journal entry to record the installment payment by Comray Corporation on March 31, 1995.

d. Prepare the journal entry to record the installment payment by Comray Corporation on June 30, 1995. (Round amounts to the nearest dollar.)

DEFERRED INCOME TAXES
— OBJ. 7 —

17-36A Viking Company paid $10,000 on December 31, 1993 for special equipment with a two-year useful life and debited the payment to Equipment. The equipment was depreciated $5,000 per year in 1994 and 1995. Viking owned no other plant assets. Viking deducted the entire $10,000 as an expense on its 1993 income tax return. This represented the only difference between Viking's financial statements and income tax returns. Viking's income before depreciation expense and income taxes was $300,000 in 1993, $380,000 in 1994, and $410,000 in 1995. Tax rates enacted into law at December 31, 1993 were 35% for 1993, 35% for 1994, and 40% for 1995.

REQUIRED

a. What is the book value of equipment at December 31, 1993; December 31, 1994; and December 31, 1995?

b. What is the tax basis of equipment at December 31, 1993; December 31, 1994; and December 31, 1995?

c. What amount of deferred tax liability should be reported in the year-end balance sheets for 1993, 1994, and 1995?

d. Prepare journal entries to record income taxes at December 31, 1993; December 31, 1994; and December 31, 1995.

DETERMINING BOND
SINKING-FUND
CONTRIBUTION AND
VARIOUS FUTURE VALUES
— APPENDIX D —

17-37A Compute the amounts specified below (use Tables III and IV, pages 634, 635).

a. A firm issued $500,000 of 10-year bonds payable. The bond agreement requires annual year-end contributions to a sinking fund in order to accumulate $500,000 to retire the bonds at maturity. Calculate the amount of the annual contribution if an 8% rate of return is expected.

b. Calculate the future value of a single amount of $6,000 invested for 15 years at 10% compounded annually.

c. Calculate the future value of a single amount of $6,000 invested for 15 years at 10% compounded semiannually.

d. Calculate the future value of an annuity of $10,000 invested at the end of each year for eight years at an annual rate of 8%.

e. Calculate the future value of an annuity of $5,000 invested at the end of each six months for eight years at an annual rate of 8%.

CASES

Business Decision Case

Kingston Corporation has total assets of $4,500,000 and has been earning an average of $700,000 before income tax the past several years. The firm is planning to expand plant facilities to manufacture a new product and needs an additional $1,500,000 in funds, on which it expects to earn 18% before income tax. The income tax rate is expected to be 40% for the next several years. The firm has no long-term debt outstanding and presently has 80,000 shares of common stock outstanding. The firm is considering three alternatives:

1. Obtain the $1,500,000 by issuing 20,000 shares of common stock at $75 per share.

2. Obtain the $1,500,000 by issuing $750,000 of 10%, 20-year bonds at face value and 10,000 shares of common stock at $75 per share.

3. Obtain the $1,500,000 by issuing $1,500,000 of 10%, 20-year bonds at face value.

REQUIRED

As a stockholder of Kingston Corporation, which alternative would you prefer, if your main concern is enhancing the firm's earnings per share?

Analytical Application Case

DIEBOLD, INCORPORATED, headquartered in Canton, Ohio, manufactures financial self-service transaction systems (such as automated teller systems) and security products. IMO INDUSTRIES INC., headquartered in Lawrenceville, New Jersey, manufactures analytical and optical instruments, electronic and mechanical controls, and engineered power products. Three years of selected financial information for these two companies are presented below (Year 3 is the most recent year; amounts in thousands).

	Year 3	Year 2	Year 1
Diebold			
Interest expense	$ 793	$ 530	$ 586
Income before income taxes	37,478	53,863	43,870
Imo			
Interest expense	57,510	43,078	29,442
Income before income taxes	42,077	57,138	46,304

REQUIRED

a. Compute the times interest earned ratio for Diebold, Incorporated for Years 1 through 3 and comment on the trend.
b. Compute the times interest earned ratio for Imo Industries, Inc., for Years 1 through 3 and comment on the trend.
c. Assume that you were going to acquire $100,000 of 10-year bonds issued by one of these two companies. Based on the ratios computed in requirements (a) and (b), to which company would you prefer to lend your money?

Ethics Case

Sexton Corporation is in the third quarter of the current year and projections are that net income will be down about $500,000 from the previous year. Sexton's return on assets is also projected to decline from its usual 15% to approximately 13%. If earnings do decline, this year will be the second consecutive year of decline. Sexton's president is quite concerned about these projections (and his job) and has called a meeting of the firm's officers for next week to consider ways to "turn things around and fast."

Shane Smith, treasurer of Sexton Corporation, has received a memorandum from his assistant, Ann Hathaway. Smith had asked Hathaway if she had any suggestions as to how Sexton might improve its earnings performance for the current year. Hathaway's memo reads as follows:

> As you know, we have $2,000,000 of 8%, 20-year bonds payable outstanding. We issued these bonds 10 years ago at face value. When they mature, we would probably replace them with other bonds. The economy right now is in a phase of high inflation, and interest rates for bonds have soared to about 16%. My proposal is to replace these bonds right now. More specifically, I propose:
>
> 1. Immediately issue $2,000,000 of 20-year, 16% bonds payable. These bonds will be issued at face value.
> 2. Use the proceeds from the new bonds to buy back and retire our outstanding 8% bonds. Because of the current high rates of interest, these bonds are trading in the market at $1,200,000.
> 3. The benefits to Sexton are that (a) the retirement of the old bonds will generate an $800,000 gain for the income statement and (b) there will be an extra $800,000 of cash available for other uses.

Smith is intrigued by the possibility of generating an $800,000 gain for the income statement. However, he is not sure this proposal is in the best long-run interests of the firm and its stockholders.

REQUIRED

a. How is the $800,000 gain calculated from the retirement of the old bonds? Where would this gain be reported in Sexton's income statement?
b. Why might this proposal not be in the best long-run interests of the firm and its stockholders?
c. What possible ethical conflict is present in this proposal?

How are a corporation's financial statements affected when it owns more than 50% of the stock of another corporation?

Corporations with a majority ownership of other companies must prepare financial statements that consolidate the data of the subsidiary companies. ■ The consolidated financial statements of American Brands, Inc., for example, contain financial results based on its ownership of a diverse group of subsidiaries: The American Tobacco Co., MasterBrand Industries, Inc. (makers of Master locks and Moen faucets), The Franklin Life Insurance Co., Jim Beam Brands Co., Acushnet Co., and Golden Belt Manufacturing Co.

18

LONG-TERM INVESTMENTS AND CONSOLIDATED FINANCIAL STATEMENTS

he stocks and bonds issued by corporations may be acquired by a variety of investors, including individuals, partnerships, corporations, mutual funds, pension funds, foundations, and trusts. Our focus in this chapter will be on long-term investments in these securities made by corporations. Long-term bond investments and long-term stock investments representing less than a majority ownership are presented on the balance sheet in a noncurrent asset category called *Investments*. The Investments category is usually placed just after a firm's presentation of current assets.

Most business combinations today are achieved by stock acquisitions. Practically all of the corporations listed on the organized stock exchanges own all or a majority of the voting stock of other companies. Accounting for such business combinations is discussed later in this chapter.

LONG-TERM BOND INVESTMENTS

Purchase of Bonds

OBJECTIVE ❶ DESCRIBE *and* **ILLUSTRATE** *accounting for long-term bond investments.*

Bonds may be purchased when they are originally issued, or they may be purchased on the open market—corporate bonds trade on organized securities exchanges and on the over-the-counter market. Bond investments are recorded by the purchaser at cost, including any brokerage commission. If a firm makes numerous long-term bond investments, a control account, Long-term Bond Investments, is established in the general ledger and a subsidiary ledger is maintained to show the detail for each bond investment.

To illustrate, assume that a firm purchases $100,000 face value of Natco Company 8% bonds at 98 on a semiannual interest date (January 1) 10 years prior to maturity. The brokerage commission is $200. The following entry records the purchase:

Jan. 1	Long-term Bond Investment—Natco Company	98,200	
	Cash		98,200
	To record purchase of $100,000 of bonds at 98 plus $200 commission.		

Note that although the bonds are purchased at a discount of $1,800, no separate account is used for the discount. In contrast to the accounting for bonds payable, the cost of a bond investment is usually recorded in a single account, whether the bond is purchased at par, a discount, or a premium.

Amortization of Discount and Premium

Because bonds acquired as a long-term investment may be held for extended periods, any related discount or premium is usually amortized to interest income. The *straight-line method* of amortization is commonly used; however, as with bonds payable accounting, the *effective interest method* should be used when the two methods yield materially different results. In our example, we use the straight-line method.

The $1,800 discount on the investment in Natco bonds will be amortized $90 for each of the 20 remaining semiannual interest periods ($1,800/20 = $90). Because no separate account is used for the bond discount, the amortization amount is debited directly to the bond investment account. The Natco bonds pay $4,000 interest semiannually ($100,000 × 0.08 × $\frac{1}{2}$). On July 1, the first interest date since acquiring the bonds, the entry on the following page records the receipt of interest and the discount amortization:

BOND INVESTMENTS AND THEIR RATINGS

*I*nvestments in bonds generally provide less risk than stock investments. Bond prices do not fluctuate as much as stock prices, and they always have some value as long as the issuing firm can pay interest. On the other hand, stock prices can plummet drastically when a firm has a sustained period of losses and pays no dividends. Also, when a firm goes bankrupt, bondholders' claims to assets have priority over those of stockholders. ■ *The quality of bonds varies a great deal. Investors who want to know the relative quality of a particular bond issue can consult a bond rating service. Companies providing*

bond ratings include Standard and Poor's, Moody's, Fitch, and Duff and Phelps. For example, Standard and Poor's rates bonds as AAA, AA, A, BBB, BB, and so on, down to D, which means "defaulted." The diagram shows the relationship between the ratings and the degree of risk, using Standard and Poor's bond ratings system as an example.

At one time, top-quality (AAA) bonds were referred to as "gilt edge" investments, but one rarely hears that term anymore. *The Wall Street Journal* defines "junk bonds" as bonds with a BB rating or lower.* These are bonds

of dubious quality, some of which have been featured in "leveraged buy-out" takeovers (a popular tactic during the 1980s). The cautious investor usually buys bonds rated A or higher.

Generally, bonds with poor ratings offer higher interest rates than highly rated bonds. However, bond interest rates are affected by other factors, such as the type of bond, the general level of interest rates, the state of the stock market, and the length of time to maturity.

The Wall Street Journal, 1990/91 Educational Edition, p. 12.

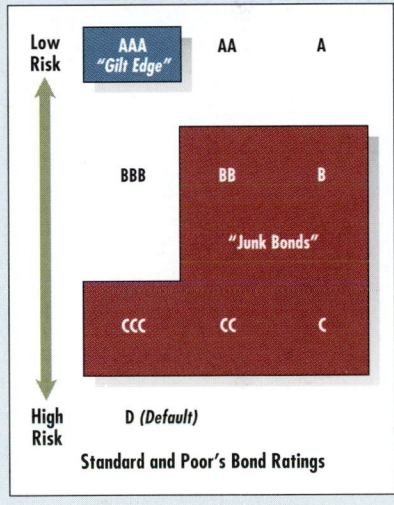

Standard and Poor's Bond Ratings

July 1	Cash	4,000	
	Long-term Bond Investment—Natco Company	90	
	Bond Interest Income		4,090
	To record receipt of semiannual interest and discount amortization.		

The discount amortization each six months causes the carrying value of the bond investment to increase to its $100,000 face value at the maturity date. It also causes the periodic interest income to be larger than the cash received as interest.

When the purchase price of a bond exceeds its maturity value, the bond is still recorded at cost and the related premium amortization entry is credited directly to the bond investment account. Thus, the carrying value of bonds acquired at a premium progresses downward toward maturity value. Also, the amount of interest income reported is less (by the amount of premium amortized) than the cash received as interest income each period.

Sale of Bonds

Bonds may be sold before they reach maturity. Assume that on January 1, five years after they were purchased, the Natco Company bonds were sold at 99½ less a $150 commission. Discount amortization over the 10 semiannual interest periods during which the bonds were held would have raised their carrying value to $99,100 [$98,200 + (10 × $90) = $99,100]. As we do for the sale of any asset, we figure the gain or loss by comparing the book value of the asset to the net proceeds from the sale. This sale results in a gain and is recorded as follows:

Jan. 1	Cash	99,350	
	Long-term Bond Investment—Natco Company		99,100
	Gain on Sale of Investments		250
	To record sale of bond investment at 99½ less a commission of $150.		

LONG-TERM STOCK INVESTMENTS

OBJECTIVE ❷ DESCRIBE *the various kinds of long-term stock investments and the accounting for them.*

Noncontrolling and Noninfluential Interest

Although all long-term investments in stock are first entered in the accounts at cost, the subsequent accounting procedures differ according to the circumstances. Basically, the accounting treatment used depends on whether the ownership interest acquired is a controlling interest—that is, an interest that permits the investor company to exercise significant influence over the company whose stock is held—or an interest that is neither controlling nor influential.

Long-term investments of less than 20% of a corporation's voting stock are considered small enough to preclude the investor company from significantly influencing the policies of the company whose stock is acquired. Such investments are initially recorded at cost, and, depending on company policy, cash dividends are recorded as income either when declared or received. These procedures are known as the **cost method** of accounting for investments. On the balance sheet, however, these investments are carried at the lower of cost or market value of the portfolio, determined at the balance sheet date. Thus, like temporary stock investments, their carrying value may increase or decrease from period to period (but never above cost). Unlike temporary stock investments, however, any unrealized losses or recoveries of unrealized losses are not shown in the income statement; instead, the net unrealized loss on the portfolio of long-term stock investments is reported separately as a contra stockholders' equity account in the balance sheet.

The journal entries for noncontrolling and noninfluential investments are similar to those for temporary stock investments. To illustrate, suppose that 100 shares of Hytex, Inc., common stock are acquired on October 1 at a cost of $6,600, including commissions and taxes. The investment is recorded as follows:

Oct. 1	Long-term Stock Investment—Hytex, Inc.	6,600	
	Cash		6,600
	To record purchase of 100 shares of Hytex, Inc., common stock for $6,600.		

DIVIDENDS

As in the case of temporary investments, cash dividends received are credited to the Dividend Income account, whereas a memorandum entry records any stock dividends received, since they do not constitute income. The entry for the stock dividend reveals the new average cost of the stock held. Assume that on December 10, Hytex, Inc., paid a cash dividend of $2 per share and a stock dividend of 10%. The following entries record the cash and stock dividends:

Dec. 10	Cash	200	
	Dividend Income		200
	To record receipt of $200 dividend on Hytex, Inc., stock.		

Dec. 10 (Memorandum) Received 10 shares of Hytex, Inc., common stock as stock dividend. Average cost per share of 110 shares held is now $60 ($6,600/110).

LOWER OF COST OR MARKET FOR PORTFOLIO

All of a company's noncontrolling and noninfluential investments in long-term stocks constitute a portfolio. At the end of the accounting period, they are reported on the balance sheet at the lower of the aggregate cost or market value of the portfolio. Should the aggregate market value drop below total cost, an unrealized loss is recorded and a contra asset account (to offset long-term stock investments) is credited. To illustrate, assume that a company has the following portfolio of long-term stock investments at the end of its first year of operations:

Stock	Cost	Market Value
Hytex, Inc., Common	$ 6,600	$ 4,800
Intersouth, Inc., Common	20,000	21,500
Wade Corporation Common	15,400	12,000
Total	$42,000	$38,300

Because the total market value ($38,300) is less than total cost ($42,000), the company makes the following journal entry:

Dec. 31	Unrealized Loss on Long-term Stock Investments	3,700	
	Allowance to Reduce Long-term Stock Investments to Market		3,700
	To record unrealized loss on portfolio of long-term stock investments.		

The Unrealized Loss on Long-term Stock Investments is reported separately as a contra stockholders' equity account in the balance sheet (thereby reducing total stockholders' equity). On the balance sheet, the Allowance to Reduce Long-term Stock Investments to Market is deducted from the cost of long-term stock investments, or the investment is shown in the following condensed form:

Long-term Stock Investments, at market (Cost $42,000)	$38,300

If the portfolio's market value exceeds its total cost, the investments are reported at cost and no allowance is created.

SALE OF LONG-TERM INVESTMENTS

When a long-term stock investment is sold, a gain or loss is recorded equal to the difference between the sale proceeds and the stock's original cost (or the original cost adjusted for the effect of a stock dividend). For example, if all 110 shares of Hytex, Inc., stock discussed above were sold on March 1 of the next year for $4,800, the following entry would be made:

Mar. 1	Cash	4,800	
	Loss on Sale of Investments	1,800	
	Long-term Stock Investment—Hytex, Inc.		6,600
	To record sale of stock for $4,800.		

RECOVERY OF UNREALIZED LOSS

The difference between the total cost and market value of a stock portfolio will likely change from one year-end to the next because of changes in market values or in the portfolio's composition. Thus, the contra asset account increases or decreases each year-end to reflect the net unrealized portfolio loss at that time. If the net unrealized loss at year-end is smaller than it was the year before, the adjusting entry records a decrease in the unrealized loss. Assume that the company whose investments we have been analyzing has the following portfolio of long-term stock investments at the end of its second year of operations:

Stock	Cost	Market Value
Intersouth, Inc., Common	$20,000	$22,100
Wade Corporation Common	15,400	12,800
Total	$35,400	$34,900

The net unrealized loss is now $500 ($35,400 − $34,900); at the end of the preceding year, it had been $3,700. The following entry would adjust the allowance account:

Dec. 31	Allowance to Reduce Long-term Stock Investments to Market	3,200	
	Unrealized Loss on Long-term Stock Investments		3,200
	To record decrease in net unrealized loss on long-term stock investments.		

On the year-end balance sheet, the contra amount to stockholders' equity is only $500, and the long-term investments would be shown at market value ($35,400 cost − $500 allowance).

Influential but Noncontrolling Interest

A corporation that owns 20% or more of another corporation's voting stock may exert a significant influence on the operating or financial decisions of that company. However, if 50% or less of the total voting stock is owned, the investment will not usually represent a controlling interest. Investments in the 20–50% ownership range may therefore be considered influential but noncontrolling interests. The **equity method** of accounting is appropriate for investments in this category.

When stock is purchased, it is initially recorded at cost under the equity method (just as it would be under the cost method). Assume, for example, that on January 1, 1993, Warner Company purchased 1,500 shares of Rave, Inc., common stock for $18,000. These shares represent 30% of Rave's voting stock. The following entry records the purchase.

Jan. 1	Long-term Stock Investment—Rave, Inc.	18,000	
	Cash		18,000
	To record purchase of 1,500 common shares of Rave, Inc.		

Under the equity method, the investor company records as income or loss each period its proportionate share of the income or loss reported for that period by the company whose stock is held. For example, if Rave, Inc., reports a 1993 net income of $20,000, Warner Company makes the following entry:

Dec. 31	Long-term Stock Investment—Rave, Inc.	6,000	
	Income from Investment in Rave, Inc., Stock		6,000
	To record as income 30% of Rave, Inc.'s 1993 net income of $20,000.		

As this entry shows, when the investor company records its share of the other corporation's income, the investment amount also increases. When cash dividends are received, however, the investor company reports no income. The receipt of a dividend is treated as a reduction of the stock investment account. To illustrate, assume that Rave, Inc., declared and paid a 1993 dividend of $7,000 and that Warner Company received its share of the dividend ($2,100) on December 31. Warner Company records the dividend in the following entry:

Dec. 31	Cash	2,100	
	Long-term Stock Investment—Rave, Inc.		2,100
	To record receipt of $2,100 dividend from Rave, Inc.		

Controlling Interest

A company holding more than 50% of another corporation's stock owns a controlling interest. In some cases—such as by agreement with other stockholders—control may exist with a lesser percentage of stock ownership. The financial data of controlled corporations are usually *consolidated* with the data of the investor company in **consolidated financial statements.** Either the cost or equity method may be used for investments in these controlled corporations; in either case, the application of consolidation procedures yields the same result.

PARENT-SUBSIDIARY RELATIONSHIP

OBJECTIVE ❸ **DEFINE** *parent-subsidiary relationships and* **ILLUSTRATE** *how their balance sheet data are consolidated.*

A corporation that controls the policies and operations of other corporations through ownership of the latters' stock commonly presents financial statements of the combined group in published reports. Such consolidated statements present the financial position and operating results of affiliated companies as a single economic unit. The company holding all or a majority of the stock of the others is the **parent company,** and the wholly owned or majority-held companies are **subsidiaries.** It is important to observe that the individual companies of a group are *legal entities*, each with separate financial statements. When the financial data of these legal entities are combined, the resulting statements represent the group as an *economic entity*, as shown in Exhibit 18-1.

Consolidated financial statements present both the total resources controlled by a parent company and the aggregate results of the group's operations that are difficult to perceive when viewing only the separate reports of the individual companies. Consolidated statements are particularly valuable to the managers and stockholders of the parent company. In addition, creditors, government agencies, and the general public are informed of the magnitude and scope of an economic enterprise through consolidated statements.

Virtually all companies prepare consolidated statements when they hold more than 50% of the subsidiary's stock. With this degree of control, the parent can usually direct the policies and activities of the subsidiary. For many years, the accounts of majority-held and wholly owned subsidiaries engaged in activities completely unrelated to those of the parent and other affiliates were routinely excluded from consolidated financial statements. Thus, a retailer such as SEARS, ROEBUCK and COMPANY excluded its insurance subsidiary, and automobile manufacturers such as FORD and GENERAL MOTORS excluded their wholly owned finance companies. It was believed that the economic operations and accounts of such firms were not compatible in financial statements with merchandising and manufacturing operations. The huge growth in conglomerate firms—firms with subsidiaries in several different industries—complicated this viewpoint, however, because most of these firms consolidated their diverse subsidiaries. For this reason, and because past practice permitted omission of significant amounts of assets, liabilities, revenues, and expenses,

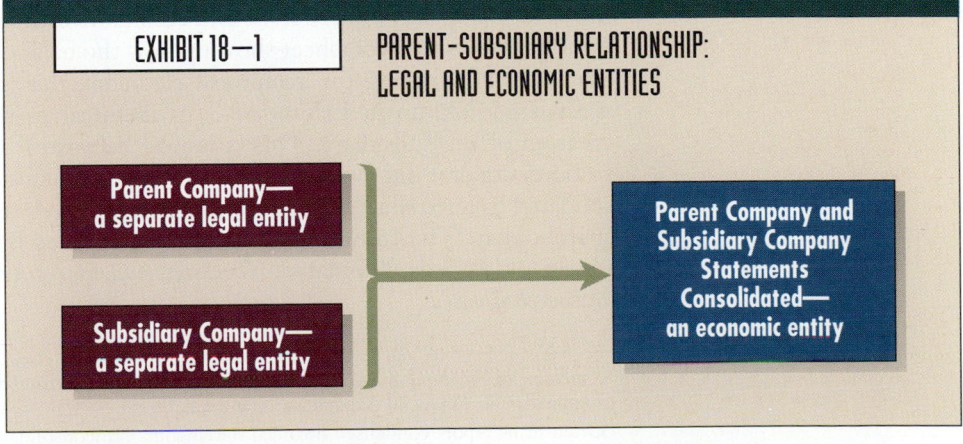

| EXHIBIT 18—1 | PARENT-SUBSIDIARY RELATIONSHIP: LEGAL AND ECONOMIC ENTITIES |

Parent Company—a separate legal entity

Subsidiary Company—a separate legal entity

Parent Company and Subsidiary Company Statements Consolidated—an economic entity

the exclusion of nonhomogenous subsidiaries is no longer permitted.[1] At present, the major exceptions to the rule are subsidiaries in bankruptcy and foreign subsidiaries with severe exchange restrictions.

Whenever a majority-held or wholly owned subsidiary's accounts are excluded from the consolidated financial statements, the parent company's investment is shown in the consolidated balance sheet as Investment in Unconsolidated Subsidiary.[2] Because the viability of excluded subsidiaries is often in doubt, they should be carried at cost.

ACQUISITION OF SUBSIDIARIES

A corporation may obtain a subsidiary either by establishing a new firm and holding more than 50% of its voting stock or by acquiring more than 50% of the voting stock of an existing firm. Both methods have been extensively used. When an existing firm is acquired, however, the method of acquisition may play an important role in the manner of accounting for the subsidiary.

One common method of acquiring an existing firm is to give up cash, other assets, notes, or debt securities. Generally, this is a *purchase* of a subsidiary, and the **purchase method** of reporting is used in consolidated financial statements. We discuss this method of acquisition first. Another method, called *pooling of interests*, involves exchanging stock of the acquiring company for substantially all of the shares of another firm. We discuss the accounting and reporting for pooling of interests later in the chapter.

WHOLLY OWNED SUBSIDIARIES: CONSOLIDATION AT ACQUISITION DATE

Creating a Subsidiary Company

Let us assume that, on January 1, 1993, P Company established a new, wholly owned subsidiary, S Company, to market P Company's products. P Company acquired all of S Company's common stock for $100,000 cash. To record this transaction, P Company debits Investment in S Company and credits Cash for $100,000. In its records, S Company debits Cash and credits Common Stock for $100,000. Condensed balance sheets before and after the creation of the subsidiary are given in Exhibit 18-2.

Notice that the only change in P Company's balance sheet is a shift of $100,000 from Cash and Other Assets to Investment in S Company. The latter represents the 100% ownership of S Company common stock, giving P Company control over the resources of S Company ($100,000 cash). Thus, the $100,000 shown in Investment in S Company on P Company's balance sheet and the $100,000 shown in Common Stock on the subsidiary's balance sheet are called *reciprocal* items. If we *consolidate* the accounts on the balance sheets of the two companies at January 1, the reciprocal items must be eliminated; otherwise, assets and stockholders' equity would be double counted. The eliminating entry made in a consolidated worksheet debits Common Stock (S Company) for $100,000 and credits Investment in S Company for $100,000. Exhibit 18-3 is the worksheet showing how the balance sheets are consolidated. Note that after eliminating the reciprocal elements, the consolidated balance sheet (the right-hand column in Exhibit 18-3) is identical to that of P Company before the creation of the subsidiary. This is logical because P Company commands no more resources than it did formerly. Also, observe that the stockholders' equity on the consolidated balance sheet is the equity of P Company's stockholders—that is, the *outside* shareholders. The stockholders' equity represented by P Company's ownership of S Company stock is eliminated. *The intercompany equity existing on the balance sheets is always eliminated.*

---

[1] *Statement of Financial Accounting Standards No. 94*, "Consolidation of All Majority-owned Subsidiaries" (Stamford, CT: Financial Accounting Standards Board, 1987).

[2] Often firms report condensed financial statements of unconsolidated subsidiaries in notes to the consolidated financial statements.

EXHIBIT 18—2	CONDENSED BALANCE SHEETS BEFORE AND AFTER CREATION OF A WHOLLY OWNED SUBSIDIARY

Before Creating S Company	**After Creating S Company**	
P COMPANY BALANCE SHEET JANUARY 1, 1993	**P COMPANY BALANCE SHEET JANUARY 1, 1993**	**S COMPANY BALANCE SHEET JANUARY 1, 1993**
Cash and Other Assets $750,000	Cash and Other Assets $650,000	Cash $100,000
	Investment in S Company 100,000	
Total Assets $750,000	Total Assets $750,000	$100,000
Liabilities $200,000	Liabilities $200,000	Liabilities $ —
Common Stock 400,000	Common Stock 400,000	Common Stock 100,000
Retained Earnings 150,000	Retained Earnings 150,000	Retained Earnings —
Total Liabilities and Stockholders' Equity $750,000	Total Liabilities and Stockholders' Equity $750,000	Total Liabilities and Stk. Equity $100,000

Reciprocal Items

Acquisition of an Existing Firm

The general concept of consolidating affiliated companies is always the same, whether a subsidiary is created or an existing firm is acquired. Intercompany items—such as intercompany stockholders' equity—are eliminated so that the consolidated statements show only the interests of outsiders.

Suppose that P Company, instead of creating a new firm, purchased 100% of the common stock of an existing firm, Z Company, on January 1, 1993, for $100,000. Z Company's total stockholders' equity of $100,000 is composed of $80,000 of common stock and $20,000 of retained earnings. The entry on P Company's books to record the acquisition debits Investment in Z Company for $100,000 and credits Cash for $100,000. Z Company makes no entry because payment is made directly to the shareholders of Z Company.

Also assume that on January 1, 1993, P Company loaned Z Company $25,000 cash in exchange for a six-month promissory note. P Company's entry debits Notes

EXHIBIT 18—3	CONSOLIDATED BALANCE SHEET WORKSHEET FOR PARENT AND WHOLLY OWNED SUBSIDIARY: CONSOLIDATION AT ACQUISITION DATE

P AND S COMPANIES
CONSOLIDATED BALANCE SHEET WORKSHEET
JANUARY 1, 1993

	P Company	S Company	Eliminations Debit	Eliminations Credit	Consolidated Balance Sheet
Cash and Other Assets	650,000	100,000			750,000
Investment in S Company	100,000	—		100,000	—
	750,000	100,000			750,000
Liabilities	200,000	—			200,000
Common Stock					
P Company	400,000				400,000
S Company		100,000	100,000		—
Retained Earnings					
P Company	150,000				150,000
	750,000	100,000	100,000	100,000	750,000

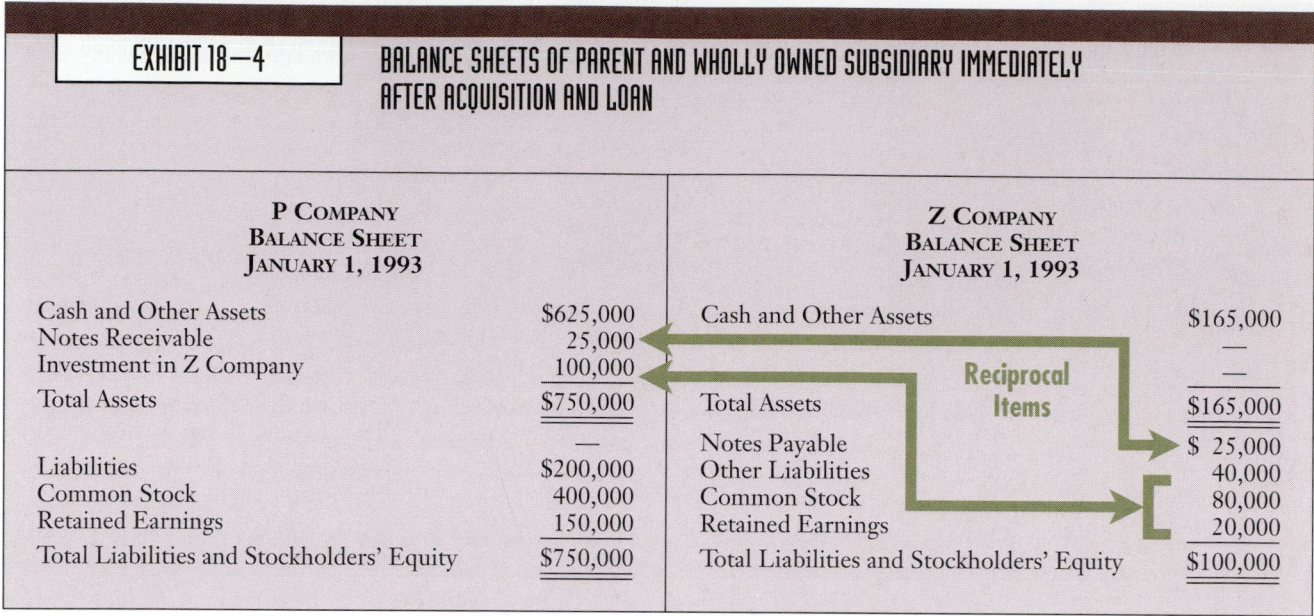

	EXHIBIT 18—4		BALANCE SHEETS OF PARENT AND WHOLLY OWNED SUBSIDIARY IMMEDIATELY AFTER ACQUISITION AND LOAN	

P Company
Balance Sheet
January 1, 1993

Cash and Other Assets	$625,000
Notes Receivable	25,000
Investment in Z Company	100,000
Total Assets	$750,000
	—
Liabilities	$200,000
Common Stock	400,000
Retained Earnings	150,000
Total Liabilities and Stockholders' Equity	$750,000

Z Company
Balance Sheet
January 1, 1993

Cash and Other Assets	$165,000
Notes Receivable	—
Investment in Z Company	—
Total Assets	$165,000
Notes Payable	$ 25,000
Other Liabilities	40,000
Common Stock	80,000
Retained Earnings	20,000
Total Liabilities and Stockholders' Equity	$100,000

Reciprocal Items

Receivable for $25,000 and credits Cash for $25,000; Z Company debits Cash for $25,000 and credits Notes Payable for $25,000.

The balance sheets of the two companies *immediately after the acquisition and loan* are shown in Exhibit 18-4. There are two examples of reciprocal items in these balance sheets: (1) the intercompany $25,000 of Notes Receivable for P Company and Notes Payable for Z Company and (2) the $100,000 Investment in Z Company on P Company's balance sheet and the Common Stock and Retained Earnings ($80,000 + $20,000) on Z Company's balance sheet.

When consolidating the accounts of the two firms, both of the reciprocal situations must be eliminated. Exhibit 18-5 shows the worksheet used to prepare the consolidated balance sheet as of January 1, 1993. A consolidated balance sheet should show receivables and payables only with *outsiders;* otherwise, both total receivables and payables of the consolidated entity are overstated. Therefore, the reciprocal receivable and payable of $25,000 must be eliminated in preparing the consolidated balance sheet. To accomplish this, elimination entry (1) on the worksheet in Exhibit 18-5 debits Notes Payable for $25,000 and credits Notes Receivable for $25,000.

To avoid double counting assets and stockholders' equity, we must eliminate the reciprocal investment and stockholders' equity accounts. Elimination entry (2) on the worksheet in Exhibit 18-5 does this by debiting Common Stock (Z Company) for $80,000, debiting Retained Earnings (Z Company) for $20,000, and crediting Investment in Z Company for $100,000.

WHOLLY OWNED SUBSIDIARIES: CONSOLIDATION AFTER ACQUISITION DATE

In accounting periods following a parent-subsidiary affiliation, the parent company may account for its investment in the subsidiary by either the cost or the equity method. In all of our examples and problems, we use the equity method, because it is easier to understand.[3] Recall that under this method, the parent periodically reflects in its own records its share (100% in our example) of the subsidiary's earnings by debiting the Investment in Subsidiary account and crediting Income from Investment in Subsidiary. The latter item eventually increases the parent company's retained earnings. (If the subsidiary has a loss, the entry would be a debit to Loss from Invest-

---

[3] As we mentioned earlier in this chapter, both methods yield the same results when appropriate procedures are used. Consolidation procedures for both methods are taught in advanced accounting courses.

EXHIBIT 18—5	CONSOLIDATED BALANCE SHEET WORKSHEET FOR PARENT AND WHOLLY OWNED SUBSIDIARY: CONSOLIDATION AT ACQUISITION DATE

P AND Z COMPANIES
CONSOLIDATED BALANCE SHEET WORKSHEET
JANUARY 1, 1993

	P Company	Z Company	Eliminations Debit	Eliminations Credit	Consolidated Balance Sheet
Cash and Other Assets	625,000	165,000			790,000
Notes Receivable	25,000	—		(1) 25,000	—
Investment in Z Company	100,000	—		(2)100,000	—
	750,000	165,000			790,000
Notes Payable	—	25,000	(1) 25,000		—
Liabilities	200,000	40,000			240,000
Common Stock					
P Company	400,000				400,000
Z Company		80,000	(2) 80,000		—
Retained Earnings					
P Company	150,000				150,000
Z Company		20,000	(2) 20,000		—
	750,000	165,000	125,000	125,000	790,000

ment in Subsidiary and a credit to Investment in Subsidiary, the debit eventually reducing the parent's retained earnings.) Whenever the subsidiary pays dividends, the parent company debits Cash and credits the Investment in Subsidiary account for the amount received.

To illustrate, let us return to the example (Exhibit 18-2) in which P Company created a subsidiary by purchasing 100% of S Company's stock for $100,000 cash. We assume that during the year following acquisition, P Company earned $40,000 *before* adding its earnings from S Company and paid no dividends. We also assume that S Company earned $20,000, paying $10,000 in dividends.

To record its share of S Company's earnings and to record the dividends received, P Company makes the following entries *in its own records:*

Investment in S Company	20,000	
Income from Investment in S Company (Retained Earnings)		20,000
To record 100% of S Company's earnings for the current year.		
Cash	10,000	
Investment in S Company		10,000
To record dividends received from S Company.		

The balance sheets of P Company and S Company at December 31, 1993, are given in Exhibit 18-6.

Let us review the changes that have occurred in these two balance sheets since the date of acquisition. P Company's Cash and Other Assets has increased $50,000. This increase consists of P Company's own net income of $40,000 plus $10,000 in dividends received from S Company. (For simplicity, we assume that all of P Company's net income increases Cash and Other Assets, with liabilities remaining unchanged.) The Investment in S Company has increased $10,000 ($20,000 S Company earnings less $10,000 dividends received). P Company's Retained Earnings has increased $60,000 ($40,000 of its own net income plus $20,000 S Company net income).

For S Company, Cash and Other Assets has increased $15,000, along with a $5,000 increase in liabilities. Thus, net assets have increased $10,000. The corresponding $10,000 increase in Retained Earnings resulted from $20,000 net income

EXHIBIT 18—6	BALANCE SHEETS OF PARENT AND WHOLLY OWNED SUBSIDIARY ONE YEAR AFTER ACQUISITION

P COMPANY BALANCE SHEET DECEMBER 31, 1993		S COMPANY BALANCE SHEET DECEMBER 31, 1993	
Cash and Other Assets	$700,000	Cash and Other Assets	$115,000
Investment in S Company	110,000		—
Total Assets	$810,000	Total Assets	$115,000
Liabilities	$200,000	Liabilities	$ 5,000
Common Stock	400,000	Common Stock	100,000
Retained Earnings	210,000	Retained Earnings	10,000
Total Liabilities and Stockholders' Equity	$810,000	Total Liabilities and Stockholders' Equity	$115,000

less $10,000 dividends declared and paid. Exhibit 18-7 shows a worksheet from which to prepare a consolidated balance sheet at December 31, 1993.

When consolidated statements are prepared after the acquisition date, the worksheet entries eliminate the intercompany equity existing *at the date of the consolidated statements*. P Company's 100% interest in S Company includes all of the subsidiary's common stock and retained earnings. Therefore, the eliminating entry on the worksheet debits Common Stock (S Company) for $100,000, debits Retained Earnings (S Company) for $10,000, and credits Investment in S Company for $110,000.

A formal consolidated balance sheet is given in Exhibit 18-8. Note that the Cash and Other Assets accounts of both firms have been combined, as have been the liabilities. The intercompany equity—100% of S Company stockholders' equity—has been eliminated; therefore, the stockholders' equity is that of the parent company.

EXHIBIT 18—7	CONSOLIDATED BALANCE SHEET WORKSHEET FOR PARENT AND WHOLLY OWNED SUBSIDIARY: CONSOLIDATION ONE YEAR AFTER ACQUISITION

P AND S COMPANIES
CONSOLIDATED BALANCE SHEET WORKSHEET
DECEMBER 31, 1993

	P Company	S Company	Eliminations Debit	Eliminations Credit	Consolidated Balance Sheet
Cash and Other Assets	700,000	115,000			815,000
Investment in S Company	110,000	—		110,000	—
	810,000	115,000			815,000
Liabilities	200,000	5,000			205,000
Common Stock					
P Company	400,000				400,000
S Company		100,000	100,000		—
Retained Earnings					
P Company	210,000				210,000
S Company		10,000	10,000		—
	810,000	115,000	110,000	110,000	815,000

EXHIBIT 18—8	CONSOLIDATED BALANCE SHEET OF PARENT AND WHOLLY OWNED SUBSIDIARY ONE YEAR AFTER ACQUISITION

P AND S COMPANIES
CONSOLIDATED BALANCE SHEET
DECEMBER 31, 1993

Cash and Other Assets	$815,000	Liabilities	$205,000
		Common Stock	400,000
		Retained Earnings	210,000
Total Assets	$815,000	Total Liabilities and Stockholders' Equity	$815,000

MAJORITY-HELD SUBSIDIARIES: CONSOLIDATION AT ACQUISITION DATE

When a firm owns more than a 50% but less than a 100% interest in another firm, the parent company's interest is a *majority interest*. The interest of the other (outside) stockholders of the subsidiary company is called the **minority interest.** In preparing a consolidated balance sheet for a parent company and a majority-held subsidiary, the assets and liabilities of the affiliated companies are combined in the usual way to show their total resources and liabilities. The parent company's equity in the subsidiary at the date of the consolidated statements is eliminated as before, but in this case, the equity represents less than 100% of the subsidiary's common stock and retained earnings. The amount of the subsidiary's common stock and retained earnings not eliminated, which represents the minority interest in the subsidiary, will appear on the consolidated balance sheet.

For example, assume that P Company purchased 80% of Q Company's voting stock on January 1, 1993, for $160,000. After the acquisition, the separate balance sheets of the two firms appeared as shown in Exhibit 18-9.

Note that Q Company's stockholders' equity is $200,000 ($150,000 Common Stock and $50,000 Retained Earnings). The equity acquired by P Company is therefore $160,000 (80% of $200,000), which is the amount P Company paid for its interest. This intercompany equity at the date of the consolidated statements is eliminated. The remaining 20% minority interest, however, must be shown in the consolidated balance sheet. In other words, the minority, or outside, shareholders have a $40,000

EXHIBIT 18—9	BALANCE SHEETS OF PARENT AND MAJORITY-HELD SUBSIDIARY IMMEDIATELY AFTER ACQUISITION

P AND Q COMPANIES
BALANCE SHEETS
JANUARY 1, 1993

	P Company	Q Company
Cash and Other Assets	$590,000	$220,000
Investment in Q Company	160,000	—
Total Assets	$750,000	$220,000
Liabilities	$200,000	$ 20,000
Common Stock	400,000	150,000
Retained Earnings	150,000	50,000
Total Liabilities and Stockholders' Equity	$750,000	$220,000

interest in the stockholders' equity of Q Company (20% of $200,000). The worksheet entry to eliminate the intercompany equity and to reflect the minority interest debits Common Stock (Q Company) for $150,000, debits Retained Earnings (Q Company) for $50,000, credits Investment in Q Company for $160,000, and credits Minority Interest for $40,000. The worksheet from which to prepare the consolidated balance sheet is given in Exhibit 18-10.

A formal consolidated balance sheet for the two companies, prepared from the right-hand column of the worksheet, is given in Exhibit 18-11. Note that the total consolidated stockholders' equity of $590,000 consists of the parent company's common stock and retained earnings (totaling $550,000) and the $40,000 minority interest. Thus, the interests of outside shareholders (the parent firm's shareholders and the subsidiary's minority shareholders) are portrayed in the consolidated balance sheet. Sometimes, in formal consolidated balance sheets, the minority interest

---

EXHIBIT 18—10	CONSOLIDATED BALANCE SHEET WORKSHEET FOR PARENT AND MAJORITY-HELD SUBSIDIARY: CONSOLIDATION AT ACQUISITION DATE

P AND Q COMPANIES
CONSOLIDATED BALANCE SHEET WORKSHEET
JANUARY 1, 1993

	P Company	Q Company	Eliminations Debit	Eliminations Credit	Consolidated Balance Sheet
Cash and Other Assets	590,000	220,000			810,000
Investment in Q Company	160,000	—		160,000	—
	750,000	220,000			810,000
Liabilities	200,000	20,000			220,000
Minority Interest				40,000	40,000
Common Stock					
P Company	400,000				400,000
Q Company		150,000	150,000		—
Retained Earnings					
P Company	150,000				150,000
Q Company		50,000	50,000		—
	750,000	220,000	200,000	200,000	810,000

EXHIBIT 18—11	CONSOLIDATED BALANCE SHEET OF PARENT AND MAJORITY-HELD SUBSIDIARY AT ACQUISITION DATE

P AND Q COMPANIES
CONSOLIDATED BALANCE SHEET
JANUARY 1, 1993

Cash and Other Assets	$810,000	Liabilities		$220,000
		Stockholders' Equity:		
		Minority Interest	$ 40,000	
		Common Stock	400,000	
		Retained Earnings	150,000	590,000
Total Assets	$810,000	Total Liabilities and Stockholders' Equity		$810,000

amount is shown between the liabilities and the stockholders' equity. Most financial analysts, however, consider the minority interest part of stockholders' equity, and it is probably a better practice to classify it with the stockholders' equity.

MAJORITY-HELD SUBSIDIARIES: CONSOLIDATION AFTER ACQUISITION DATE

Assume that the separate balance sheets of P Company and Q Company (of our previous example) one year after the acquisition date are as shown in the first two columns of Exhibit 18-12. During the year following acquisition, Q Company earned $25,000 net income and paid $5,000 in dividends. Therefore, its Retained Earnings increased by $20,000, to $70,000. Since P Company would reflect 80% of the increase in its Investment in Q Company under the equity method, the balance of this account at year-end would be $176,000 ($160,000 + $16,000). As shown in Exhibit 18-12, this amount would be eliminated in preparing a consolidated balance sheet. Likewise, the Common Stock and Retained Earnings of Q Company would be eliminated, and 20% of the $220,000 total stockholders' equity of Q Company, $44,000, would be established as minority interest. Note that the $4,000 increase in this amount consists of 20% of the increase in Q Company's retained earnings since acquisition. The formal consolidated balance sheet taken from the last column of the worksheet is shown in Exhibit 18-13.

DIFFERENCES BETWEEN ACQUISITION COST AND BOOK VALUE

So far in our examples, we have assumed that the amount paid by the parent company to acquire a particular interest in a subsidiary exactly equals the book value of the interest acquired. In the real world this rarely happens. In fact, the parent firm almost always pays more for its interest than the book values shown on the subsidiary's balance sheet. This occurs for one of two reasons, or a combination of them. First, the recorded values of the subsidiary's assets are often understated in terms of current

EXHIBIT 18—12	CONSOLIDATED BALANCE SHEET WORKSHEET FOR PARENT AND MAJORITY-HELD SUBSIDIARY: CONSOLIDATION ONE YEAR AFTER ACQUISITION

P AND Q COMPANIES
CONSOLIDATED BALANCE SHEET WORKSHEET
DECEMBER 31, 1993

	P Company	Q Company	Eliminations Debit	Eliminations Credit	Consolidated Balance Sheet
Cash and Other Assets	624,000	250,000			874,000
Investment in Q Company	176,000	—		176,000	—
	800,000	250,000			874,000
Liabilities	210,000	30,000			240,000
Minority Interest				44,000	44,000
Common Stock					
P Company	400,000				400,000
Q Company		150,000	150,000		—
Retained Earnings					
P Company	190,000				190,000
Q Company		70,000	70,000		—
	800,000	250,000	220,000	220,000	874,000

EXHIBIT 18—13	CONSOLIDATED BALANCE SHEET FOR PARENT AND MAJORITY-HELD SUBSIDIARY ONE YEAR AFTER ACQUISITION

P AND Q COMPANIES
CONSOLIDATED BALANCE SHEET
DECEMBER 31, 1993

Cash and Other Assets	$874,000	Liabilities		$240,000
		Stockholders' Equity:		
		Minority Interest	$ 44,000	
		Common Stock	400,000	
		Retained Earnings	190,000	634,000
Total Assets	$874,000	Total Liabilities and Stockholders' Equity		$874,000

OBJECTIVE ④ DISCUSS *the treatment of acquisitions when cost exceeds the book value acquired in a subsidiary.*

fair market values, a common situation given the impact of inflation. Second, the parent firm may be willing to pay an additional amount for an unrecorded asset of the subsidiary—**goodwill**—if the subsidiary's earning power or its potential earning power is higher than normal for similar firms.

Suppose that P Company acquires a 100% interest in Y Company's voting stock for $125,000 when Y Company has the balance sheet shown in Exhibit 18-14. Note that P Company is paying $125,000 for a 100% interest in a firm with a net book value of $100,000. Negotiations for the purchase, however, reveal that Y Company's plant and equipment are undervalued by $15,000 and that its potential for future superior earnings is valued at an additional $10,000.

In preparing a consolidated balance sheet, we make a worksheet entry that eliminates the intercompany equity and reflects the additional asset values established by the acquisition. The entry includes the following debits: Common Stock (Y Company), $80,000; Retained Earnings (Y Company), $20,000; Plant and Equipment, $15,000; and Goodwill from Consolidation, $10,000. A credit of $125,000 would be made to Investment in Y Company. Thus, the intercompany equity in the recorded book values of the subsidiary is eliminated, and an additional amount of assets, $25,000, is reflected in the consolidated balance sheet. The goodwill from

---

EXHIBIT 18—14	BALANCE SHEETS OF PARENT AND WHOLLY OWNED SUBSIDIARY AT ACQUISITION DATE: ACQUISITION COST EXCEEDS SUBSIDIARY'S BOOK VALUE

P COMPANY **BALANCE SHEET** **JANUARY 1, 1993**		**Y COMPANY** **BALANCE SHEET** **JANUARY 1, 1993**	
Cash and Other Assets	$XXX,XXX	Current Assets	$ 40,000
Investment in Y Company	125,000	Plant and Equipment	60,000
Total Assets	$XXX,XXX	Total Assets	$100,000
Liabilities	$XXX,XXX	Liabilities	$ —
Common Stock	XXX,XXX	Common Stock	80,000
Retained Earnings	XXX,XXX	Retained Earnings	20,000
Total Liabilities and Stockholders' Equity	$XXX,XXX	Total Liabilities and Stockholders' Equity	$100,000

consolidation[4] appears as an intangible asset on the consolidated balance sheet. In the consolidated statements of subsequent years, the amount paid in excess of the equity acquired in the subsidiary is amortized over the life of the assets to which the amount has been assigned. In the case of goodwill, the period cannot exceed 40 years.

The Demonstration Problem at the end of this chapter illustrates a consolidation that has both a minority interest and goodwill from consolidation.

On occasion, we encounter a situation in which the parent company pays less than the equity acquired for a particular interest in a subsidiary company. If this situation occurs, accounting guidelines attribute the difference to an overvaluation of the subsidiary's noncurrent assets (other than long-term investments in marketable securities). The eliminating entry on the worksheet credits such assets.

CONSOLIDATED INCOME STATEMENT

OBJECTIVE 5 EXPLAIN *and* ILLUSTRATE *the consolidation of parent and subsidiary income statements.*

So far we have dealt only with consolidated balance sheets. Now we look at the problem of consolidating the income statements of affiliated firms. If we wish to show the scope of operations of affiliated companies as an entity, combining the revenue, cost of goods sold, and expenses of the several companies is logical. In preparing a consolidated income statement, however, we should present only the results of transactions with firms and individuals *outside* the entity. Any intercompany transactions—such as intercompany sales and purchases—should be eliminated. Likewise, revenue and expense amounts representing services rendered by one firm to an affiliated firm should be eliminated. Otherwise, the consolidated income statement would distort the extent of the group's operations.

For example, if a single company has two divisions—one manufacturing products and another marketing them—transfers of products from the manufacturing division to the marketing division are not regarded as sales transactions. Only sales by the marketing division are reflected in the firm's income statement. The same situation exists when two separate firms make up one consolidated entity.

To illustrate the procedures for preparing a consolidated income statement, we use Exhibit 18-15, the separate income statements of P Company and its 75%-held

EXHIBIT 18—15	INCOME STATEMENTS OF PARENT AND MAJORITY-HELD SUBSIDIARY PRIOR TO CONSOLIDATION

P COMPANY INCOME STATEMENT FOR THE YEAR ENDED DECEMBER 31, 1993		Z COMPANY INCOME STATEMENT FOR THE YEAR ENDED DECEMBER 31, 1993	
Sales	$500,000	Sales (Including $30,000 sold to P Company)	$200,000
Cost of Goods Sold (Including $30,000 of purchases from Z Company)	300,000	Cost of Goods Sold	140,000
Gross Profit	$200,000	Gross Profit	$ 60,000
Operating Expenses (Including income taxes)	160,000	Operating Expenses (Including income taxes)	40,000
Net Income	$ 40,000	Net Income	$ 20,000

---

[4]Often this is called *Excess of Cost over Book Value of Investment in Subsidiary*. Many accountants and financial analysts, however, prefer to call it *Goodwill from Consolidation*.

subsidiary, Z Company. For simplicity, we assume that P Company has not yet reflected its 75% share of Z Company's net income in its own income statement.[5]

We have indicated in the income statements that $30,000 of Z Company's sales were to P Company. Assume that P Company, in turn, sold all of this merchandise to outsiders. In preparing a consolidated income statement, we must eliminate $30,000 from the sales reported by Z Company and from the purchases (in cost of goods sold) reported by P Company. The worksheet from which to prepare a consolidated income statement for the two firms is given in Exhibit 18-16.

In Exhibit 18-16, the $30,000 in Z Company's sales and the reciprocal amount in P Company's cost of goods sold have been eliminated so that only sales to outsiders are reflected in the consolidated income statement. Notice that this elimination does not affect consolidated net income, because the same amount is excluded from both sales and cost of goods sold. It does, however, avoid distorting the sales volume and costs of the group. Of the $60,000 aggregate net income of the two firms, the $5,000 minority interest (25% of Z Company's net income) is deducted, so the consolidated net income of the affiliated firms is $55,000. Thus, the $55,000 consolidated net income consists of $40,000 (the parent's net income from its own operations) plus $15,000 (the parent's 75% interest in the $20,000 subsidiary net income). The consolidated net income statement, shown in Exhibit 18-17, is prepared directly from the last column of the worksheet.

Other Intercompany Accounts and Consolidated Statements

Because affiliated companies often engage in a variety of intercompany transactions, treating the resulting amounts in consolidated statements can be fairly complex. For example, a complication relating to goods sold between affiliates is that all of the goods may not, in turn, have been sold to outside parties by the end of the period. Other intercompany transactions may include intercompany bond and preferred stock holdings or plant and equipment transfers.

In addition to a consolidated balance sheet and income statement, other consolidated financial statements include a consolidated statement of cash flows, a consolidated statement of retained earnings, and a consolidated statement of stockholders' equity. The preparation of these consolidated statements, as well as the accounting for the intercompany transactions noted above, is beyond the scope of our introductory discussion.

EXHIBIT 18—16	CONSOLIDATED INCOME STATEMENT WORKSHEET FOR PARENT AND MAJORITY-HELD SUBSIDIARY

P AND Z COMPANIES
CONSOLIDATED INCOME STATEMENT WORKSHEET
FOR THE YEAR ENDED DECEMBER 31, 1993

	P Company	Z Company	Eliminations Debit	Eliminations Credit	Consolidated Income Statement
Sales	500,000	200,000	30,000		670,000
Cost of Goods Sold	300,000	140,000		30,000	410,000
Gross Profit	200,000	60,000			260,000
Expenses (Including income taxes)	160,000	40,000			200,000
Net Income	40,000	20,000			60,000
Minority Interest in Net Income of Z Company (25% of $20,000)					(5,000)
Consolidated Net Income					55,000

---

[5] If P Company had already included its share of Z Company's earnings in its own income statement, this amount would have to be eliminated to avoid double counting when the revenues and expenses of the two firms are consolidated.

EXHIBIT 18—17	CONSOLIDATED INCOME STATEMENT FOR PARENT AND MAJORITY-HELD SUBSIDIARY

P AND Z COMPANIES
CONSOLIDATED INCOME STATEMENT
FOR THE YEAR ENDED DECEMBER 31, 1993

Sales	$670,000
Cost of Goods Sold	410,000
Gross Profit	$260,000
Expenses (Including income taxes)	200,000
Net Income before Minority Interest	$ 60,000
Less: Minority Interest in Net Income of Z Company	5,000
Consolidated Net Income	$ 55,000

CONSOLIDATED STATEMENTS: POOLING METHOD

OBJECTIVE 6 PROVIDE *an overview of accounting for acquisitions under the pooling of interests method.*

In all of the foregoing examples, we assumed that an acquiring company *purchased* a controlling interest in the shares of another firm by issuing cash, other assets, or debt. Thus, a purchase and sale transaction occurred, and we used the *purchase method* to prepare consolidated statements.

On the other hand, if the acquiring company obtains substantially all (90% or more) of a subsidiary company's shares by *issuing its own shares* (and by meeting certain other criteria),[6] a **pooling of interests** has occurred. In a pooling of interests, stockholders of the subsidiary company become stockholders of the parent company. Basically, two sets of interests "unite" rather than have a purchase and sale transaction take place.

If a combination is a pooling of interests, the parent's investment and the consolidated financial statements are prepared according to the **pooling method** of accounting. In a consolidated balance sheet prepared under the pooling method, the *book values* of the affiliated companies are combined. Of course, the market values of each firm's stock play an important part in determining the number of shares exchanged for the subsidiary's shares. However, once the negotiations are completed, the market values of the shares play no role in recording the parent's investment or in preparing consolidated financial statements.

Because the consolidated statements under the pooling method reflect the book values of the subsidiary's assets, we do not revalue these assets, nor does any goodwill (excess of cost over equity acquired) emerge from the consolidation. On the other hand, under the purchase method, the subsidiary's assets are revalued (almost invariably upward during periods of rising prices), and goodwill often appears in the consolidated balance sheet. Also, the increase in tangible assets and any goodwill are amortized over future periods. Consequently, future yearly consolidated earnings are less under the purchase method than under the pooling method.

Another facet of the pooling method is that the subsidiary's and the parent's net incomes for the entire period of the acquisition year can be combined regardless of the date of acquisition. For example, suppose a parent company earned $500,000 net income in the year that it used the pooling method to acquire a 100% interest in a subsidiary that earned $400,000. The acquisition occurred October 1, and the sub-

---

[6]The criteria for determining whether a pooling has occurred are set forth in *Opinions of the Accounting Principles Board, No. 16*, "Business Combinations" (New York: American Institute of Certified Public Accountants, 1970), p. 297.

sidiary's earnings for the last quarter were $100,000. The pooling method combines the subsidiary's entire $400,000 with the parent's earnings, for a total consolidated net income of $900,000. With the purchase method, only the last quarter's earnings of the subsidiary ($100,000) are combined with the parent's $500,000 earnings, for a net income of $600,000.

We summarize the pooling method as follows:

1. With the pooling method, total consolidated assets do not increase, because book values of each firm are combined. With the purchase method, asset revaluation and goodwill (excess of cost over equity acquired) often increase total consolidated assets.

2. Without amortization of revaluation increases or goodwill, the pooling method results in higher future earnings than the purchase method.

3. When pooling is used, parent company and subsidiary earnings for the entire year are combined in the year of acquisition. With the purchase method, only the subsidiary's earnings after the acquisition date are included with parent company earnings.

At one time, companies had wide latitude in selecting between the purchase method and the pooling method in accounting for a business combination. The pooling method was often selected because this method enabled companies to show an immediate (often synthetic) improvement in their earnings *purely as a result of the combination* rather than through improved operations. Current guidelines, however, are more restrictive and identify specific criteria that combining firms must meet to use the pooling method.

USEFULNESS OF CONSOLIDATED STATEMENTS

Consolidated statements present an integrated report of an economic unit comprising a number of business enterprises related through stock ownership. In fact, no other way can depict, fairly concisely, the extent of resources and scope of operations of many companies subject to common control.

The statements do have certain limitations, however. The status or performance of weak constituents in a group can be "masked" through consolidation with successful units. Rates of return, ratios, and trend percentages calculated from consolidated statements may sometimes prove deceptive because they are really composite calculations. Shareholders and creditors of controlled companies who are interested in their legal rights and prerogatives should examine the separate financial statements of the relevant constituent companies.

Supplemental disclosures do improve the quality of consolidated statements, particularly those of *conglomerates*—entities with diversified lines of business. Both the Financial Accounting Standards Board and the Securities and Exchange Commission have stipulated that certain firms disclose information regarding revenues, income from operations, and identifiable assets for various business segments.

ANALYTICAL APPLICATION

OBJECTIVE 7 DEFINE dividend yield *and* EXPLAIN *its use.*

DIVIDEND YIELD

Stock investors differ in their expectations regarding their investments—some investors are primarily interested in appreciation in the market price of the stock, and other investors focus on receiving current income in the form of dividends. Dividend yield is a ratio that is helpful to the latter group of investors. **Dividend yield** measures the current rate of return in dividends from an investment in the stock. It is computed by dividing the latest annual dividends per share by the current market price of the stock. Therefore,

$$\text{Dividend Yield} = \frac{\text{Annual Dividends per Share}}{\text{Market Price per Share}}$$

For example, during the fiscal year ending May 31, 1991, WORTHINGTON INDUSTRIES, a manufacturer of metal and plastic products headquartered in Columbus, Ohio, declared cash dividends per common share of $0.61. At May 31, 1991, Worthington's common stock had a per-share market price of $24.38. At May 31, 1991, then, Worthington's dividend yield was $0.61/$24.38 = 2.5%.

Dividend yields are included in the stock tables published in *The Wall Street Journal* and *Barrons*, so it is easy for investors to compare current dividend yields from investments in different stocks. Listed below are dividend yields for several common stocks from early in 1992.

THE COCA-COLA COMPANY	1.3%
HEWLETT PACKARD COMPANY	0.8%
IBM CORPORATION	5.0%
PEPSICO, INC.	1.4%
TEXACO, INC.	5.2%
WAL-MART STORES, INC.	0.3%
WESTINGHOUSE ELECTRIC CORPORATION	7.5%

HEY POINTS FOR CHAPTER OBJECTIVES

① **DESCRIBE** and **ILLUSTRATE** accounting for long-term bond investments (pp. 648–650).

- Long-term bond investments are recorded at cost, including brokerage commissions.
- Discounts or premiums are amortized each interest date by deducting a pro rata share of premiums from interest income or adding a pro rata share for discounts. The investment account is debited for amortized discounts or credited for amortized premiums.
- When sold, the book value of bond investments is removed as of the sale date, and any gain or loss is recorded.

② **DESCRIBE** the various kinds of long-term stock investments and the accounting for them (pp. 650–653).

- Long-term stock investments are of three types:
  1. Noncontrolling and noninfluential interest—that is, interest amounting to less than 20% of the investee's voting stock. Such investments are recorded at cost, and the portfolio is valued at the lower of total cost or market at each year-end. Unrealized losses are shown contra to stockholders' equity.
  2. Influential but noncontrolling interest—that is, interest amounting to 20–50% of the investee's voting stock. Such investments are initially recorded at cost, then adjusted periodically according to the equity method. The firm's share of the investee's earnings is added to and the dividends are deducted from the investment's carrying value.
  3. Controlling interest—that is, interest amounting to more than 50% of the investee's voting stock. The investment may be carried on either the cost or equity basis; the application of consolidation procedures results in the same consolidated statements under either method.

③ **DEFINE** parent-subsidiary relationships and **ILLUSTRATE** how their balance sheet data are consolidated (pp. 653–661).

- With few exceptions, all wholly owned or majority-held subsidiaries are consolidated with the parent firm.
- A parent company that carries its investment in a subsidiary under the equity method—as illustrated in this chapter—uses the following accounting procedures:
  1. The parent periodically debits Investment in Subsidiary and credits Income from Subsidiary for its share of subsidiary earnings. Dividends received from the subsidiary are debited to Cash and credited to Investment in Subsidiary.
  2. The parent eliminates its equity in the subsidiary existing when the consolidated balance sheet is prepared.
  3. If a subsidiary is majority held, the portion of the subsidiary's stockholders' equity not eliminated in procedure 2 above is presented as minority interest.
  4. Any amounts owing between the parent and subsidiaries are eliminated in preparing consolidated statements.

④ **DISCUSS** the treatment of acquisitions when cost exceeds the book value acquired in a subsidiary (pp. 661–663).

■ In a purchase combination, the acquiring company initially records its investment at cost. In preparing consolidated statements, any amount in excess of the book value acquired in the subsidiary is allocated among specific assets when possible. Any unallocated amount is goodwill, which must be amortized over a period of years.

⑤ **EXPLAIN** and **ILLUSTRATE** the consolidation of parent and subsidiary income statements (pp. 663–665).

■ A consolidated income statement presents only the results of transactions with firms and individuals outside the entity. Any intercompany transactions, such as intercompany sales and purchases, are eliminated from sales and cost of goods sold.

■ After revenues, cost of goods sold, and expenses are combined and a combined net income is determined, any minority interest in the subsidiary's earnings is deducted to determine consolidated net income.

⑥ **PROVIDE** an overview of accounting for acquisitions under the pooling of interests method (pp. 665–666).

■ When an acquiring firm obtains 90% or more of another firm's shares by issuing its own shares, the transaction may be treated as a pooling of interests.

■ In a pooling combination, the parent firm records its investment in accordance with the book value of the acquired firm's net assets. Cost (as measured by the market value of shares exchanged) is ignored. The acquired firm's retained earnings at acquisition date are added to those of the acquiring firm in preparing consolidated statements. Earnings of both firms are likewise combined for the period when the acquisition occurred.

⑦ **ANALYTICAL APPLICATION:** **DEFINE** *dividend yield* and **EXPLAIN** its use (pp. 666–667).

■ Dividend yield is computed by dividing a stock's annual dividends per share by its current market price. For investors, the ratio identifies the annual rate of return in dividends from an investment in the stock.

SELF-TEST QUESTIONS FOR REVIEW

(Answers follow the Solution to Demonstration Problem.)

1. A firm purchased $20,000 of 10-year, 9% bonds as an investment at 96 on January 1, 1992, 10 years before maturity. The firm records interest and straight-line amortization on interest dates (July 1 and January 1). On January 1, 1995, the firm sold the bonds at 98. The gain or loss to be recorded on the date of sale is
   a. $160 loss   b. $160 gain   c. $240 loss   d. $240 gain

2. A firm purchased noncontrolling and noninfluential long-term stock investments that cost $65,000. At the close of the year, the portfolio had a market value of $60,000. The entry to adjust the carrying value of the investments at the end of the year includes a
   a. Credit of $5,000 to Unrealized Loss on Long-term Stock Investments.
   b. Debit of $5,000 to Long-term Stock Investments.
   c. Credit of $5,000 to Allowance to Reduce Long-term Stock Investments to Market.
   d. Debit of $60,000 to Long-term Stock Investments.

3. Artway Company purchased 30% of the voting stock of Barton Company for $60,000 on January 1 of the current year. During the year, Barton Company earned $50,000 net income and paid $15,000 in dividends. At the end of the year, Artway Company's account, Investment in Barton Company, should have a balance of
   a. $110,000   b. $70,500   c. $95,000   d. $60,000

4. X Company purchased an 80% interest in Y Company for $225,000 at the beginning of the current year. At that time, X Company had $500,000 common stock and $150,000 retained earnings, and Y Company had $200,000 common stock and $60,000 retained earnings. On the consolidated balance sheet prepared at the time of the acquisition, consolidated retained earnings should be
   a. $150,000   b. $210,000   c. $198,000   d. $48,000

5. Brown Company, which owns 70% of Greene Company's voting stock, sold merchandise during the year to Greene Company for $60,000. The merchandise had cost Brown Company $40,000. Greene Company sold all of the merchandise to outsiders during the year. The eliminating entry to prepare a consolidated income statement for the year should reduce the sales amount and the cost of goods sold amount by
   a. $60,000   b. $40,000   c. $20,000   d. $28,000

DEMONSTRATION PROBLEM FOR REVIEW

On January 1, 1994, Montana Company purchased 75% of the common stock of Utah Company for $200,000, after which the separate balance sheets of the two firms were as follows:

MONTANA AND UTAH COMPANIES
BALANCE SHEETS
JANUARY 1, 1994

Assets	Montana	Utah
Accounts Receivable	$ 30,000	$ 25,000
Investment in Utah	200,000	—
Other Assets	270,000	275,000
Total Assets	$500,000	$300,000

Liabilities and Stockholders' Equity		
Accounts Payable	$ 50,000	$ 60,000
Common Stock	350,000	200,000
Retained Earnings	100,000	40,000
Total Liabilities and Stockholders' Equity	$500,000	$300,000

On January 1, 1994, Utah Company owed $7,000 to Montana Company on account for purchases made during 1993. The amount paid by Montana in excess of the equity acquired in Utah is attributable to goodwill.

REQUIRED

Prepare a consolidated balance sheet worksheet at January 1, 1994.

SOLUTION TO DEMONSTRATION PROBLEM

MONTANA AND UTAH COMPANIES
CONSOLIDATED BALANCE SHEET WORKSHEET
JANUARY 1, 1994

	Montana	Utah	Eliminations Debit	Eliminations Credit	Consolidated Balance Sheet
Accounts Receivable	30,000	25,000		(1) 7,000	48,000
Investment in Utah	200,000	—		(2) 200,000	—
Other Assets	270,000	275,000			545,000
Goodwill from Consolidation			(2) 20,000		20,000
	500,000	300,000			613,000
Accounts Payable	50,000	60,000	(1) 7,000		103,000
Minority Interest				(2) 60,000	60,000
Common Stock					
Montana Company	350,000				350,000
Utah Company		200,000	(2) 200,000		—
Retained Earnings					
Montana Company	100,000				100,000
Utah Company		40,000	(2) 40,000		—
	500,000	300,000	267,000	267,000	613,000

Montana Company's January 1, 1994, acquisition of 75% of Utah Company's common stock resulted in goodwill of $20,000 ($200,000 acquisition price − 75% of $240,000 stockholders' equity acquired). At January 1, 1994, the minority interest is $60,000—25% of the $240,000 total stockholders' equity of Utah Company. Elimination entry (1) eliminates the intercompany receivable and payable. Elimination entry (2) eliminates the intercompany equity and establishes the goodwill from consolidation and minority interest.

ANSWERS TO SELF-TEST QUESTIONS

1. b, p. 650   2. c, p. 651   3. b, p. 652   4. a, p. 659   5. a, p. 664

Many business firms expand by opening new outlets, or *branches*, at different locations. The development of suburban shopping centers has provided the impetus for branch marketing of goods and services by many firms, especially retail stores and banks. Both wholesale and retail merchandising companies have expanded their marketing territories through widespread branch operations.

Typically, the various branches offer the same goods or services and follow fairly standardized operations. A manager appointed for each branch normally is responsible for that outlet's profitability. From a managerial viewpoint, each branch is an accounting entity, even though branches are usually segments of a single legal entity—a corporation, partnership, or sole proprietorship. The principal outlet, from which the firm's activities are normally directed, is often referred to as the **home office.**

Generally, merchandising policies, advertising, and promotion are directed or heavily influenced by the home office. Although branches may be given some latitude in acquiring merchandise, often the major portion of goods is purchased centrally.

The accounting system for branch operations should furnish management with complete and timely information to measure branch profitability. The size and complexity of branch operations, geographic location, and degree of autonomy, among other things, may influence the type of accounting system adopted. Most **branch accounting systems,** however, are variations of two basic schemes—centralized accounting by the home office and decentralized accounting by the branch.

CENTRALIZED BRANCH RECORDS

Under a **centralized accounting system,** the home office maintains most of the records needed to account for branch operations. Thus, separate asset, liability, revenue, and expense records for each branch are maintained at the home office. Typically, cash is transferred to the branch to establish a working fund for small disbursements. This fund is ordinarily kept on an imprest basis (like a petty cash fund) and is replenished regularly by the home office on the basis of expense vouchers or summaries submitted by the branch. A branch that collects any amounts in its operations must often deposit such amounts in a home office bank account and transmit deposit slips and lists of the remittances to the home office for recording. The branch also transmits other documents such as copies of sales invoices and credit memos to the home office for recording. The data needed to record branch transactions may be transmitted by a telecommunication or similar device, with the documents forwarded periodically. In some cases, the documents may be filed at the branch, with periodic audits by either home office auditors or independent accountants.

DECENTRALIZED BRANCH RECORDS

Under a **decentralized accounting system,** each branch ordinarily maintains a comprehensive set of accounting records for its operations and forwards periodic financial statements to the home office. Normally, the forms of the records and statements are standardized for all branches, so that they may be conveniently analyzed by the home office and integrated into the financial reports of the whole organization. Emphasis is often placed on the operating, or income statement, accounts. Also, the branch may keep accounts for current assets—such as cash, accounts receivable, and inventory—but the home office may retain the accounts for equipment, fixtures, and accumulated depreciation.

In place of owners' equity accounts, the branch has an account called *Home Office*, which represents amounts of advances or assets received from the home office plus accumulated branch earnings not transferred to the home office. A reciprocal account called *Branch Office* is maintained in the ledger of the home office. When both accounts are posted and up to date, the dollar balances should be identical.

From the branch's viewpoint, the Home Office account may be regarded as either a capital account or a liability. Likewise, the Branch Office balance on the books of the home office may be viewed either as an investment or as a receivable. The classification of these accounts is not especially important; the branch is only an accounting segment, and when its accounts are combined with those of the home office, the balances of these two accounts offset each other and do not appear in the combined financial statements.

ILLUSTRATION OF DECENTRALIZED ACCOUNTING

Assume that on May 1, 1994, Foto-Art Company, retailer of photographic equipment, opened its Western Branch in another city, leasing the store facilities and fixtures. The home office transferred $20,000 cash and $40,000 in merchandise to the branch to begin operations. The following entries record the transfer establishing the branch:

Home Office Records			Western Branch Records		
Western Branch	60,000		Cash	20,000	
Cash		20,000	Shipments from Home Office	40,000	
Shipments to Western Branch		40,000	Home Office		60,000

This entry established the investment in the branch (or receivable from the branch) for the amount of cash and merchandise advanced to the new outlet. The $60,000 amount shown in Western Branch's reciprocal account equals the amount of capital received from the home office.

Generally, merchandise shipped from the home office to the branch should be differentiated from branch acquisitions purchased from outsiders. Therefore, a Shipments to Branch account is credited on the home office records, and a Shipments from Home Office account is debited on the branch records whenever the home office transfers merchandise to the branch. Under a periodic inventory system, the Shipments to Branch account can be considered a contra account to the Purchases account on the home office records. On the branch records, the Shipments from Home Office debit balance can be considered a purchases amount. When the branch closes its books, it closes the Shipments from Home Office account to the Income Summary account. Likewise, the home office closes the Shipments to Branch balance to its own Income Summary account.

The following transactions, including the asset transfer establishing the branch, are shown in summary form:

Summary of May Transactions	Home Office Records			Western Branch Records		
1. Home office opened Western Branch, transferring $20,000 cash and $40,000 merchandise.	Western Branch	60,000		Cash	20,000	
	Cash		20,000	Shipments from		
	Shipments to			Home Office	40,000	
	Western Branch		40,000	Home Office		60,000
2. Purchased $15,000 merchandise from outsiders.				Purchases	15,000	
				Accounts Payable		15,000
3. Sold merchandise on account for $30,000.				Accounts Receivable	30,000	
				Sales		30,000
4. Incurred $5,000 selling expenses and $3,000 general expenses; of the total, $2,000 was on account.				Selling Expenses	5,000	
				General Expenses	3,000	
				Cash		6,000
				Accounts Payable		2,000
5. Collected $24,000 on account from customers.				Cash	24,000	
				Accounts Receivable		24,000
6. Paid $12,000 to creditors on account.				Accounts Payable	12,000	
				Cash		12,000

Summary of May Transactions	Home Office Records		Western Branch Records	
7. Sent $10,000 cash to home office.	Cash	10,000	Home Office	10,000
	Western Branch	10,000	Cash	10,000
8. Attributed $1,000 home office general expenses to Western Branch.	Western Branch	1,000	General Expenses	1,000
	General Expenses	1,000	Home Office	1,000

After the foregoing entries have been posted to Western Branch's ledger, the trial balance for the branch would appear as shown in Exhibit E-1.

Western Branch next records any necessary end-of-period adjustments in the usual fashion. For the sake of simplicity, we assume that none are needed.

BRANCH FINANCIAL STATEMENTS

After the branch has recorded any necessary adjusting entries, financial statements can be prepared. Exhibits E-2 and E-3 show the May income statement and the May 31 balance sheet for Western Branch. Note in the balance sheet that the net income for the period increases the balance of the Home Office account. The branch's net income is closed to the Home Office account at the end of the accounting period, as shown later in the closing entries.

COMBINED FINANCIAL STATEMENTS

At the end of the accounting period, the various branches submit their financial statements (or alternatively, adjusted trial balances) to the home office, which combines the data into a single set of statements for the whole enterprise. The worksheets in Exhibit E-4 (on page 674) provide a convenient vehicle for compiling and integrating the data for the company. In the illustration, the data for home office operations are assumed. Note that the reciprocal amounts of $40,000 representing shipments from the home office to the branch are eliminated and the accounts do not appear in the combined income statement. Likewise, the home office and branch office accounts, with $54,000 balances, are eliminated when the combined balance sheet is prepared.

EXHIBIT E—1

Foto-Art Company
Western Branch
Trial Balance
May 31, 1994

	Debit	Credit
Cash	$16,000	
Accounts Receivable	6,000	
Home Office		$51,000
Accounts Payable		5,000
Sales		30,000
Purchases	15,000	
Shipments from Home Office	40,000	
Selling Expenses	5,000	
General Expenses	4,000	
	$86,000	$86,000

EXHIBIT E—2

FOTO-ART COMPANY
WESTERN BRANCH
INCOME STATEMENT
FOR THE MONTH OF MAY, 1994

Sales			$30,000
Cost of Goods Sold:			
Beginning Inventory		—	
Purchases		$15,000	
Shipment from Home Office		40,000	
Goods Available for Sale		$55,000	
Less: Ending Inventory		37,000	
Cost of Goods Sold			18,000
Gross Profit on Sales			$12,000
Operating Expenses:			
Selling Expenses		$ 5,000	
General Expenses		4,000	
Total Operating Expenses			9,000
Net Income			$ 3,000

CLOSING ENTRIES

After financial statements are prepared, the following closing entries are recorded by the branch:

May 31	Inventory		37,000	
	Sales		30,000	
	Income Summary			67,000
	To record the ending inventory and to close income statement account with credit balance.			
31	Income Summary		64,000	
	Purchases			15,000
	Shipments from Home Office			40,000
	Selling Expenses			5,000
	General Expenses			4,000
	To close income statement accounts with debit balances.			
31	Income Summary		3,000	
	Home Office			3,000
	To close the Income Summary account to the Home Office account.			

EXHIBIT E—3

FOTO-ART COMPANY
WESTERN BRANCH
BALANCE SHEET
MAY 31, 1994

Assets		Liabilities and Home Office Equity	
Cash	$16,000	Accounts Payable	$ 5,000
Accounts Receivable	6,000	Home Office	54,000
Inventory	37,000	Total Liabilities and	
Total Assets	$59,000	Home Office Equity	$59,000

| EXHIBIT E—4 |

FOTO-ART COMPANY
HOME OFFICE AND WESTERN BRANCH
INCOME STATEMENT WORKSHEET
FOR THE MONTH OF MAY, 1994

	Home Office	Western Branch	Eliminations Debit	Eliminations Credit	Combined Income Statement
Sales	65,000	30,000			95,000
Cost of Goods Sold:					
Inventory, May 1	38,000	—			38,000
Purchases	70,000	15,000			85,000
Shipments to Branch	(40,000)		40,000		
Shipments from Home Office		40,000		40,000	
Goods Available for Sale	68,000	55,000			123,000
Less: Inventory, May 31	28,000	37,000			65,000
Cost of Goods Sold	40,000	18,000			58,000
Gross Profit on Sales	25,000	12,000			37,000
Operating Expenses:					
Selling Expenses	9,000	5,000			14,000
General Expenses	7,000	4,000			11,000
Total Operating Expenses	16,000	9,000			25,000
Net Income	9,000	3,000	40,000	40,000	12,000

FOTO-ART COMPANY
HOME OFFICE AND WESTERN BRANCH
BALANCE SHEET WORKSHEET
MAY 31, 1994

Assets	Home Office	Western Branch	Eliminations Debit	Eliminations Credit	Combined Balance Sheet
Cash	20,000	16,000			36,000
Accounts Receivable	36,000	6,000			42,000
Inventory	28,000	37,000			65,000
Western Branch	54,000			54,000	
Plant Assets, Net of Accumulated Depreciation	80,000				80,000
Total Assets	218,000	59,000			223,000

Liabilities and Stockholders' Equity	Home Office	Western Branch	Eliminations Debit	Eliminations Credit	Combined Balance Sheet
Accounts Payable	18,000	5,000			23,000
Accrued Liabilities	2,000				2,000
Home Office		54,000	54,000		
Common Stock	150,000				150,000
Retained Earnings	48,000				48,000
Total Liabilities and Stockholders' Equity	218,000	59,000	54,000	54,000	223,000

On May 31, the home office reflects the branch net income by making a corollary entry to the last entry shown on the preceding page:

May 31	Western Branch	3,000	
	Net Income—Western Branch		3,000
	To reflect net income of Western Branch.		

In closing its records, the home office closes the Net Income—Western Branch account to its Income Summary account.

As world trade has grown, so have the number and size of multinational corporations. A **multinational corporation** conducts operations in more than one country by locating branches, divisions, or subsidiaries outside its home country. EXXON CORPORATION, for example, has divisions and affiliated companies operating in the United States and more than 80 other countries. Exhibit F-1 lists the 10 largest U.S. multinational corporations in 1991.

U.S. multinational corporations frequently use foreign subsidiary companies to conduct their foreign activities. If the foreign subsidiary is more than 50% owned, its financial statements are usually consolidated with the U.S. parent's statements. Of course, when the subsidiary's accounting records are kept in the foreign currency, its financial statements must be converted to U.S. dollars before consolidation can occur.

CONVERSION PROCEDURES

Two different procedures may be used to convert foreign financial statements to U.S. dollars:

1. *Translation* procedures.
2. *Remeasurement* procedures.

The **functional currency** of a foreign subsidiary determines which of these two procedures is used. It is defined by the Financial Accounting Standards Board:

> An entity's functional currency is the currency of the primary economic environment in which the entity operates; normally, that is the currency of the environment in which an entity primarily generates and expends cash.[1]

Depending on the circumstances, the functional currency may be either the foreign currency or the U.S. dollar. For example, a German subsidiary manufactures and sells its own products. Its expenses as well as cash generated by its operations are primarily in German marks and have little impact on its parent's cash flows. This subsidiary's operations are well integrated with the German economy. Thus, its functional currency is the foreign currency (mark). In contrast, consider a German subsidiary that is a sales outlet for its U.S. parent's goods. The subsidiary takes orders,

	EXHIBIT F—1	TEN LARGEST U.S. MULTINATIONALS IN 1991	
Rank	Company	Foreign Revenue (millions)	Foreign Assets (millions)
1	Exxon	$78,073	$51,118
2	IBM	40,358	50,210
3	General Motors	39,083	43,125
4	Mobil	38,778	23,858
5	Ford Motor	34,477	55,053
6	Texaco	24,754	8,497
7	Chevron	17,180	11,566
8	E. I. du Pont de Nemours	17,086	14,386
9	Citicorp	16,848	95,027
10	Philip Morris Cos.	13,152	12,114

Adapted from "The 100 Largest U.S. Multinationals," *Forbes*, July 20, 1992, p. 298. Reprinted by permission.

---

[1] *Statement of Financial Accounting Standards No. 52*, "Foreign Currency Translation" (Stamford, CT: Financial Accounting Standards Board, 1981), p. 3.

bills and collects the invoice price, warehouses the goods to facilitate delivery, and remits its net cash flows primarily to the parent. This subsidiary is essentially an agent for the parent company. Its functional currency would be the U.S. dollar.

The functional currency is also the U.S. dollar for foreign subsidiaries that operate in highly inflationary economies (economies whose cumulative inflation over a three-year period is approximately 100% or more). The U.S. dollar is deemed the functional currency, because it is the more stable currency; the foreign currency is too unstable. Argentina and Brazil are recent examples of countries whose three-year cumulative inflation exceeds 100%.

Once the functional currency is determined, the specific conversion procedures are selected as follows:

1. *Foreign currency is functional currency:* Use translation procedures.
2. *U.S. dollar is functional currency:* Use remeasurement procedures.

To illustrate these two procedures for converting foreign financial statements to U.S. dollars, we assume that Wyso Company was organized in Germany on January 1, 1993, as a wholly owned subsidiary of Minor Corporation, a U.S. company. Wyso's opening balance sheet, in German marks (M), consisted of the following assets and stockholders' equity:

Assets		Stockholders' Equity	
Cash	M 40,000	Common Stock	M800,000
Inventory	160,000		
Plant Assets	600,000		
		Total Liabilities and	
Total Assets	M800,000	Stockholders' Equity	M800,000

After one year of operation, Wyso's 1993 income statement and December 31, 1993, balance sheet, in marks, are as follows:

Wyso Company
Income Statement
For the Year Ended December 31, 1993

Sales		M750,000
Cost of Goods Sold	M500,000	
Depreciation Expense	30,000	
Other Expenses	70,000	
Total Expenses		600,000
Net Income		M150,000

Wyso Company
Balance Sheet
December 31, 1993

Assets		Liabilities		
Cash	M 60,000	Accounts Payable		M 30,000
Accounts Receivable (Net)	140,000			
Inventory	210,000	**Stockholders' Equity**		
Plant Assets (Net)	570,000	Common Stock	M800,000	
		Retained Earnings	150,000	950,000
		Total Liabilities and		
Total Assets	M980,000	Stockholders' Equity		M980,000

Assume that exchange rates for the mark are as follows:

January 1, 1993	$0.64
Average for 1993	0.60
December 31, 1993	0.56

Translation Procedures

Assume that Wyso Company's operations are fully integrated with Germany's economy. Thus, its functional currency is the mark and translation procedures are used. **Translation procedures** convert foreign financial statements to U.S. dollars as follows:

1. All asset and liability accounts are converted using the exchange rate at the balance sheet date (current rate).

2. Capital stock accounts are converted using the exchange rate on the date the stock was issued (historical rate).

3. All revenue and expense accounts are converted using the exchange rate at the date these items were recognized. If revenues and expenses are generated in a relatively uniform pattern during the year, an average exchange rate for the year may be used (average rate).

The purpose of these translation procedures is to retain, in the converted data, the financial results and relationships among assets and liabilities that were created by the subsidiary's operation in its foreign environment.

Exhibit F-2 shows these translation procedures applied to Wyso Company's financial statements. Note the $70,000 **translation adjustment** in the exhibit, shown as a reduction of stockholders' equity in U.S. dollars. Translation procedures create a translation adjustment. The translation adjustment balances the balance sheet and occurs because the same exchange rate is not used to convert all accounts. The $70,000 may be calculated as follows:

Common Stock $\times$ (Historical Rate − Current Rate)	
M800,000 $\times$ ($0.64 − $0.56) =	$64,000
Net Income $\times$ (Average Rate − Current Rate)	
M150,000 $\times$ ($0.60 − $0.56) =	6,000
Translation adjustment	$70,000

EXHIBIT F—2	TRANSLATION OF WYSO COMPANY FINANCIAL STATEMENTS, DECEMBER 31, 1993 GERMAN MARK = FUNCTIONAL CURRENCY

	German Marks	Exchange Rate	U.S. Dollars
Balance Sheet			
Cash	M 60,000	$0.56	$ 33,600
Accounts Receivable (Net)	140,000	0.56	78,400
Inventory	210,000	0.56	117,600
Plant Assets (Net)	570,000	0.56	319,200
Total	M980,000		$548,800
Accounts Payable	M 30,000	0.56	$ 16,800
Common Stock	800,000	0.64	512,000
Retained Earnings	150,000	See Net Income	90,000
Translation Adjustment			(70,000)
Total	M980,000		$548,800
Income Statement			
Sales	M750,000	0.60	$450,000
Cost of Goods Sold	M500,000	0.60	$300,000
Depreciation Expense	30,000	0.60	18,000
Other Expenses	70,000	0.60	42,000
Total Expenses	M600,000		$360,000
Net Income	M150,000		$ 90,000

The translation adjustment is reported as a separate component of stockholders' equity. Depending on the direction of exchange rate changes, it may reduce (as in our illustration) or increase stockholders' equity.

Remeasurement Procedures

Now assume that Wyso Company's operations are essentially a direct extension of Minor Corporation's (the parent) activities. In this circumstance, Wyso's functional currency is the U.S. dollar and remeasurement procedures are used. **Remeasurement procedures** convert foreign financial statements to U.S. dollars as follows:

1. Monetary asset and liability accounts (basically all cash, receivables, and payables) are converted using the exchange rate at the balance sheet date (current rate).

2. All other balance sheet accounts are converted using the exchange rate in effect when the item was initially recorded on the books (historical rate).

3. Revenue and expense accounts are converted using the exchange rate related to the transaction. Generally, the average exchange rate for the period is used. However, expenses that relate to assets converted at historical rates are converted at the appropriate historical rate. Depreciation expense and cost of goods sold are in this latter category.

The objective of these remeasurement procedures is to produce the same U.S. dollar financial statements as if the foreign entity's accounting records had been initially maintained in the U.S. dollar.

Exhibit F-3 shows these remeasurement procedures applied to Wyso Company's financial statements. Schedule A at the bottom of the exhibit details the remeasure-

EXHIBIT F—3	REMEASUREMENT OF WYSO COMPANY FINANCIAL STATEMENTS, DECEMBER 31, 1993 U.S. DOLLAR = FUNCTIONAL CURRENCY		
	German Marks	**Exchange Rate**	**U.S. Dollars**
Balance Sheet			
Cash	M 60,000	$0.56	$ 33,600
Accounts Receivable (Net)	140,000	0.56	78,400
Inventory	210,000	0.58	121,800
Plant Assets (Net)	570,000	0.64	364,800
Total	M980,000		$598,600
Accounts Payable	M 30,000	0.56	$ 16,800
Common Stock	800,000	0.64	512,000
Retained Earnings	150,000	See Net Income	69,800
Total	M980,000		$598,600
Income Statement			
Sales	M750,000	0.60	$450,000
Cost of Goods Sold	M500,000	See Schedule A	$310,600
Depreciation Expense	30,000	0.64	19,200
Other Expenses	70,000	0.60	42,000
Foreign Exchange Loss			8,400
Total Expenses	M600,000		$380,200
Net Income	M150,000		$ 69,800
Schedule A			
Inventory (Beginning)	M160,000	0.64	$102,400
Purchases	550,000	0.60	330,000
	M710,000		$432,400
Inventory (Ending)	210,000	0.58	121,800
Cost of Goods Sold	M500,000		$310,600

ment of cost of goods sold (using a periodic inventory system), which requires converting the beginning inventory, purchases, and ending inventory at historical exchange rates. The average rate for the year ($0.60) applies to the purchases of M550,000, and a rate of $0.58 applies to the ending inventory (the average exchange rate during the latter part of the year when the ending inventory was acquired). Also, note the $8,400 foreign exchange loss among the income statement expenses in U.S. dollars.[2] Remeasurement procedures produce foreign gains or losses—the effects on assets and liabilities of exchange rate changes. These foreign exchange gains and losses are included in net income.

Generally Accepted Accounting Principles

At present, there are no international accounting principles that are broadly accepted and enforced. Accounting principles vary among countries because legal, economic, and regulatory systems differ, just as social values and traditions do. Foreign company financial statements, therefore, may vary in some respects from U.S. generally accepted accounting principles. If they do, the statements must be changed to conform to U.S. generally accepted accounting principles *before* the conversion to U.S. dollars may occur.

GLOSSARY OF KEY TERMS USED IN THIS CHAPTER AND APPENDIXES

branch accounting system   The procedures for maintaining the financial records of various outlets of a single firm and coordinating the data with home office records (p. 670).

centralized accounting system   In the context of accounting for branches, a system whereby the home office maintains most of the records needed to account for branch operations (p. 670).

consolidated financial statements   Financial statements prepared with intercompany (reciprocal) accounts eliminated to portray the financial position and results of operations of two or more affiliated companies as a single economic entity (p. 653).

cost method   A method of accounting by a parent company for investments in subsidiary companies in which the parent company maintains the investment in subsidiary account at its initial cost (p. 650).

decentralized accounting system   In the context of accounting for branches, a system whereby each branch maintains a comprehensive set of accounting records for its operations and forwards periodic financial statements to the home office (p. 670).

dividend yield   Annual dividends per share divided by the market price per share (p. 666).

equity method   A method of accounting by a parent company for investments in subsidiary companies by which the parent's share of subsidiary income or loss is periodically recorded in the parent company accounts (p. 652).

functional currency   The currency of the primary economic environment in which a foreign entity operates (p. 675).

goodwill   The value that derives from a firm's ability to earn more than a normal rate of return on the fair market value of its specific, identifiable net assets. Goodwill is recognized only when it is acquired through purchase of another entity (p. 662).

home office   For a firm with several branches, the principal outlet from which the firm's activities are directed (p. 670).

minority interest   The portion of capital stock in a subsidiary corporation that is not owned by the controlling (parent) company (p. 659).

multinational corporation   A corporation that conducts operations in more than one country by locating branches, divisions, or subsidiaries outside its home country (p. 675).

parent company   A company holding all or a majority of the voting stock of another company, which is called a *subsidiary* (p. 653).

pooling method   The method used to prepare consolidated financial statements for a business combination treated as a pooling of interests. Under this method, the book values of the affiliated companies are combined in the consolidated balance sheet and annual earnings are combined in the income statement in the year of acquisition (p. 665).

---

[2] The $8,400 foreign exchange loss is the amount needed to obtain a $69,800 net income. When transferred to retained earnings, the $69,800 balances the balance sheet.

pooling of interests Uniting the ownership interests of two or more companies through the exchange of 90% or more of the firms' voting stock (p. 665).

purchase method The method used to prepare consolidated financial statements for a business combination treated as a purchase transaction. Under this method, the net assets of the acquired company appear at fair market value in the consolidated balance sheet and goodwill from consolidation appear if the purchase price exceeds the fair market value of the specific net assets acquired (p. 654).

remeasurement procedures A process of converting foreign currency financial statements to U.S. dollars that essentially produces the same U.S. dollar financial statements as if the foreign entity's records had been initially maintained in U.S. dollars (p. 678).

subsidiaries Corporations that have at least a majority of their voting stock owned by another company, called the *parent company* (p. 653).

translation adjustment A component of stockholders' equity (either an increase or a decrease) resulting from the use of translation procedures to convert foreign currency financial statements. The adjustment arises because the same exchange rate is not used to convert all accounts (p. 677).

translation procedures A process of converting foreign currency financial statements to U.S. dollars that retains, in the converted data, the financial results and relationships among assets and liabilities that were created by the entity's operations in its foreign environment (p. 677).

QUESTIONS

18-1 Caldwell Company invested in bonds at a premium on a long-term basis. Should the bond premium be amortized? Where should the bond investment be classified in the balance sheet?

18-2 What is a noncontrolling and noninfluential long-term stock investment?

18-3 How are noncontrolling and noninfluential long-term stock investments reported in the balance sheet? Where are unrealized losses on the portfolio of such investments reported?

18-4 Describe the accounting procedures used when a stock investment represents 20–50% of the voting stock.

18-5 Describe the accounting procedures used when a stock investment represents more than 50% of the voting stock.

18-6 What is the purpose of consolidated financial statements?

18-7 In a recent annual report, MASCO CORPORATION's consolidated financial statements showed an amount under Equity Investments that included a 50% interest in MASCO CAPITAL CORPORATION. Explain why the accounts of Masco Capital Corporation were not consolidated with the accounts of Masco Corporation and its other subsidiaries. On what accounting basis is the investment in this unconsolidated subsidiary carried?

18-8 What is the difference between a purchase acquisition and a pooling of interests?

18-9 P Company purchases all of the common stock of S Company for $800,000 when S Company has $500,000 of common stock and $300,000 of retained earnings. If a consolidated balance sheet is prepared immediately after the acquisition, what amounts are eliminated in preparing it?

18-10 P Company purchases 75% of S Company's common stock for $600,000 when S Company has $500,000 of common stock and $300,000 of retained earnings. If a consolidated balance sheet is prepared immediately after the acquisition, what amounts are eliminated in preparing this statement? What amount of minority interest appears in the consolidated balance sheet?

18-11 Explain the entries made in a parent company's records under the equity method of accounting to (a) reflect its share of the subsidiary's net income for the period and (b) record the receipt of dividends from the subsidiary.

18-12 On January 1 of the current year, P Company purchased 40% of the common stock of S Company for $580,000. During the year, S Company had $90,000 of net income and paid $50,000 in cash dividends. At year-end, what amount appears in P Company's balance sheet as Investment in S Company under the equity method?

18-13 Madd Company purchased an interest in West Company for $550,000 when West Company had $400,000 of common stock and $125,000 of retained earnings.
   a. If Madd Company had acquired a 100% interest in West Company, what amount of Goodwill from Consolidation would appear on the consolidated balance sheet? (Assume that West's assets are fairly valued.)
   b. If Madd had acquired only an 80% interest in West Company, what amount of Goodwill from Consolidation would appear?

18-14 Nelson Company purchased a 90% interest in Wells Company on January 1 of the current year. Nelson Company had $450,000 net income for the current year before reflecting its share of Wells Company's net income. If Wells Company had net income of $120,000 for the year, what is the consolidated net income for the year?

18-15 Kern Company, which owns 75% of Snell Company, sold merchandise during the year to Snell Company for $80,000. The merchandise cost Kern Company $60,000. If Snell Company in turn sold all of the merchandise to outsiders for $105,000, what eliminating entry related to these transactions does Kern make in preparing a consolidated income statement for the year?

18-16 P Company acquired 100% of S Company on September 1 of the current year. Explain why the consolidated earnings of the two firms for the current year might be higher if the transaction is treated as a pooling of interests rather than as a purchase.

18-17 What are the inherent limitations of consolidated financial statements?

18-18 How is a corporation's *dividend yield* computed?

EXERCISES

BOND INVESTMENT ENTRIES
— OBJ. 1 —

18-19 As a long-term investment, $16,000 face value of 10-year, 10% bonds were purchased at 103 on the first day of their first semiannual interest period. Prepare journal entries to record (a) their purchase for cash, (b) the receipt of the first semiannual interest payment and the first semiannual amortization of bond premium (straight line), and (c) the sale of the bonds at 101 two years after they were purchased.

ENTRIES FOR STOCK INVESTMENT: COST METHOD
— OBJ. 2 —

18-20 As a long-term investment, 6,000 shares of World Company common stock were acquired on March 10, 1993, at a total cost of $210,000. The investment represented 15% of the company's voting stock. On December 28, 1993, World Company declared a cash dividend of $1.10 per share, which was received on January 15, 1994. Dividend income is recorded when received. Prepare the necessary journal entries to reflect (a) the purchase of the stock and (b) the receipt of the cash dividend.

ENTRIES FOR STOCK INVESTMENT: EQUITY METHOD
— OBJ. 2 —

18-21 As a long-term investment, 7,000 shares of Sioux Company common stock were acquired on March 20, 1993, at a total cost of $140,000. The investment represented 35% of the company's voting stock. On December 28, 1993, Sioux Company declared a cash dividend of $1.25 per share, which was received on January 18, 1994. Sioux Company's 1993 net income was $80,000. Using the equity method, prepare the journal entries to reflect (a) the purchase of the stock, (b) the proportionate share of Sioux Company's 1993 net income (dated December 31, 1993), and (c) the receipt of the cash dividend.

CALCULATING UNREALIZED LOSS IN INVESTMENT PORTFOLIO
— OBJ. 2 —

18-22 During its first year of operations, Barley, Inc., purchased the following noncontrolling and noninfluential long-term stock investments:

   3,000 shares of A Company stock at $25 per share
   5,000 shares of B Company stock at $40 per share

At year-end, the market value of A Company stock was $21 per share, and the market value of B Company stock was $42 per share. What was the unrealized loss at year-end, and where does it appear in Barley's financial statements?

ELIMINATING ENTRY AND STOCKHOLDERS' EQUITY IN CONSOLIDATION
— OBJ. 3 —

18-23 On January 1 of the current year, Halen Company purchased all of the common shares of Jolson Company for $480,000 cash. On this date, the stockholders' equity of Halen Company consisted of $600,000 in common stock and $110,000 in retained earnings. Jolson Company had $400,000 in common stock and $80,000 in retained earnings.
   a. Give the worksheet eliminating entry to prepare a consolidated balance sheet on the acquisition date.
   b. What amount of total stockholders' equity appears on the consolidated balance sheet?

STOCKHOLDERS' EQUITY IN CONSOLIDATED BALANCE SHEET
— OBJ. 3 —

18-24   Baylor Company purchased 70% of the common stock of Reed Company for $350,000 in cash and notes when the stockholders' equity of Reed Company consisted of $400,000 in common stock and $100,000 in retained earnings. On the acquisition date, the stockholders' equity of Baylor Company consisted of $600,000 in common stock and $240,000 in retained earnings. Prepare the stockholders' equity section in the consolidated balance sheet as of the acquisition date.

ELIMINATING ENTRY INCLUDING ASSET REVALUATION AND GOODWILL
— OBJ. 4 —

18-25   On January 1 of the current year, Pyramid Company purchased all of the common shares of Pound Company for $400,000 cash and notes. Balance sheets of the two firms immediately after the acquisition were as follows:

	Pyramid	Pound
Current Assets	$1,600,000	$120,000
Investment in Pound Company	400,000	—
Plant and Equipment (Net)	3,000,000	320,000
Total Assets	$5,000,000	$440,000
Liabilities	$ 700,000	$ 90,000
Common Stock	3,500,000	300,000
Retained Earnings	800,000	50,000
Total Liabilities and Stockholders' Equity	$5,000,000	$440,000

During the negotiations for the purchase, Pound's plant and equipment were appraised at $350,000. Furthermore, Pyramid concluded that an additional $20,000 demanded by Pound's shareholders was warranted because Pound's earning power was somewhat better than the industry average. Prepare the worksheet eliminating entry needed to prepare a consolidated balance sheet on the acquisition date.

ELIMINATING ENTRY FOR INTERCOMPANY SALES
— OBJ. 5 —

18-26   Pate Company has an 80% interest in Benson Company. During the current year, Benson Company sold merchandise costing $22,000 to Pate Company for $40,000. Assuming that Pate Company sold all of the merchandise to outsiders for $58,000, what worksheet eliminating entry should be made in preparing a consolidated income statement for the period?

ENTRIES TO HOME OFFICE ACCOUNT BY BRANCH
— APPENDIX E —

18-27   Westwood Branch had a beginning balance of $66,000 in its Home Office account. During the current month, Westwood received $88,000 in merchandise shipments from the home office. At month-end, the branch's share of home office general expenses was $6,300. After closing its records, Westwood Branch determined its net income as $25,800. The branch then sent $22,000 cash to the home office.
a. Prepare the branch's journal entry made on receiving the $88,000 in merchandise from the home office.
b. What amount would be in the Home Office account after all entries had been posted for the current month?

TRANSLATION PROCEDURES
— APPENDIX F —

18-28   Assume that translation procedures are being used to convert the financial statements of a foreign subsidiary to U.S. dollars. Indicate which exchange rate—current, historical, or average for the year—should be used to convert each of the following categories of accounts:
a. Assets.
b. Liabilities.
c. Capital stock.
d. Revenues generated uniformly throughout the year.
e. Expenses incurred uniformly throughout the year.

PROBLEMS

BOND INVESTMENT ENTRIES
— OBJ. 1 —

18-29   The following transactions relate to bonds acquired by Bloom Corporation as long-term investments:

1993
June 30   Purchased $100,000 face value of Dynamo, Inc., 20-year, 9% bonds dated June 30, 1993, for $107,600. Interest is paid December 31 and June 30.

Dec. 31 Received semiannual interest payment from Dynamo, Inc., and amortized bond premium (straight-line method).

31 Purchased $200,000 face value of Link, Inc., 10-year, 7% bonds dated December 31, 1993, for $197,000. Interest is paid June 30 and December 31.

1994

June 30 Received semiannual interest payment from Dynamo, Inc., and amortized bond premium.

30 Received semiannual interest payment from Link, Inc., and amortized bond discount (straight-line method).

1995

June 30 Sold Dynamo, Inc., bonds at 103 less a sales commission of $500. (Assume that all receipts of interest and premium amortization through June 30, 1995, are already recorded.)

Dec. 31 Sold Link, Inc., bonds at 99 less a sales commission of $300. (Assume that all receipts of interest and discount amortization through December 31, 1995, are already recorded.)

REQUIRED

Prepare the journal entries to record these transactions.

ENTRIES FOR NONINFLUENTIAL AND NONCONTROLLING STOCK INVESTMENTS — OBJ. 2 —

18-30 The following selected transactions and information are for Steen Corporation for 1993 and 1994.

1993

July 1 Purchased, as a long-term investment, 1,000 shares of Polk, Inc., common stock at a total cost of $56,200. This interest is noninfluential and noncontrolling.

Oct. 1 Purchased, as a long-term investment, 3,000 shares of Wynn, Inc., common stock at a total cost of $72,000, and 2,000 shares of Maple, Inc., common stock at a total cost of $64,800. Both investments are noninfluential and noncontrolling interests.

Nov. 9 Received a cash dividend of 75 cents per share on the Wynn, Inc., stock.

Dec. 31 The Polk, Inc., shares have a market value of $53 per share; the Wynn, Inc., shares have a market value of $21 per share; and the Maple, Inc., shares have a market value of $35 per share. (An entry should be made to adjust the carrying value of the portfolio to the lower of cost or market.)

1994

Feb. 1 Sold the Wynn, Inc., stock for $20 per share less a $100 commission fee.

Dec. 31 The market value of the long-term stock investment portfolio is as follows: Polk, Inc., $54 per share; Maple, Inc., $33 per share. (An entry should be made to adjust the carrying value of the investments and the unrealized loss account.)

REQUIRED

Prepare the journal entries to record these transactions and adjustments.

CONTRASTING ENTRIES FOR STOCK INVESTMENTS: COST AND EQUITY METHODS — OBJ. 2 —

18-31 On January 2, 1993, Trubek Corporation purchased, as a long-term investment, 10,000 shares of Forge Company common stock for $28 per share, including commissions and taxes. On December 31, 1993, Forge Company announced a net income of $66,000 for the year and a dividend of $1.35 per share, payable January 20, 1994, to stockholders of record on January 10, 1994. Trubek Corporation received its dividend on January 23, 1994.

REQUIRED

a. Assume that the stock acquired by Trubek Corporation represents 15% of Forge Company's voting stock. Prepare all journal entries appropriate for this investment, beginning with the purchase on January 2, 1993, and ending with the receipt of the dividend on January 23, 1994. (Trubek Corporation recognizes dividend income when received.)

b. Assume that the stock acquired by Trubek Corporation represents 25% of Forge Company's voting stock. Prepare all journal entries appropriate for this investment, beginning with the purchase on January 2, 1993, and ending with the receipt of the dividend on January 23, 1994.

DETERMINING ELIMINATIONS AND CONSOLIDATED DATA ON DATE OF ACQUISITION (WHOLLY OWNED SUBSIDIARY)
— OBJ. 3, 4 —

18-32   Elder Company purchased all of Hart Company's common stock for cash on January 1, 1994, after which the separate balance sheets of the two corporations appeared as follows:

ELDER AND HART COMPANIES
BALANCE SHEETS
JANUARY 1, 1994

	Elder	Hart
Investment in Hart Company	$ 750,000	—
Other Assets	2,350,000	$800,000
Total Assets	$3,100,000	$800,000
Liabilities	$ 900,000	$130,000
Common Stock	1,600,000	500,000
Retained Earnings	600,000	170,000
Total Liabilities and Stockholders' Equity	$3,100,000	$800,000

During the negotiations for the purchase, Elder Company determined that the appraised value of Hart Company's Other Assets amounted to $845,000.

REQUIRED

a. Prepare the worksheet entry to eliminate the intercompany equity and to reflect the appraised value of Hart Company's assets.

b. What amount of total assets should appear on a January 1 consolidated balance sheet?

c. What amount of total stockholders' equity should appear on a January 1 consolidated balance sheet?

DETERMINING INTERCOMPANY DATA ONE YEAR AFTER ACQUISITION (WHOLLY OWNED SUBSIDIARY)
— OBJ. 2, 3 —

18-33   On January 1, 1993, Texas Company purchased all of the common stock of Austin Company for $520,000 cash. The stockholders' equity of Austin consisted of $400,000 in common stock and $120,000 in retained earnings. On December 31, 1993, the separate balance sheets of the two firms were as follows:

TEXAS AND AUSTIN COMPANIES
BALANCE SHEETS
DECEMBER 31, 1993

	Texas	Austin
Cash	$ 30,000	$ 50,000
Accounts Receivable	40,000	80,000
Investment in Austin Company (At equity)	580,000	—
Other Assets	340,000	510,000
Total Assets	$990,000	$640,000
Accounts Payable	$ 70,000	$ 60,000
Common Stock	700,000	400,000
Retained Earnings	220,000	180,000
Total Liabilities and Stockholders' Equity	$990,000	$640,000

During the year, Austin Company had net income of $75,000. At December 31, Austin owed Texas $25,000 on account for merchandise.

REQUIRED

a. What amount of dividends did Austin Company declare and pay during the year?

b. Prepare Texas Company's journal entries for 1993 that affect the Investment in Austin Company account.

c. What amount of total assets would appear in a December 31, 1993, consolidated balance sheet?

PREPARING CONSOLIDATED BALANCE SHEET WORKSHEET ON ACQUISITION DATE (MINORITY INTEREST)
— **OBJ. 3, 4** —

18-34 On January 1, 1994, Katt Company purchased 85% of the common stock of Harbor Company for $490,000 cash, after which the separate balance sheets of the two firms were as follows:

KATT AND HARBOR COMPANIES
BALANCE SHEETS
JANUARY 1, 1994

	Katt	Harbor
Investment in Harbor Company	$ 490,000	—
Other Assets	1,210,000	$600,000
Total Assets	$1,700,000	$600,000
Liabilities	$ 310,000	$100,000
Common Stock	1,000,000	380,000
Retained Earnings	390,000	120,000
Total Liabilities and Stockholders' Equity	$1,700,000	$600,000

REQUIRED

Prepare a consolidated balance sheet worksheet at January 1, 1994. Assume that any amount paid by Katt Company in excess of the equity acquired in Harbor Company's net assets is attributable to goodwill.

PREPARING CONSOLIDATED INCOME STATEMENT WORKSHEET
— **OBJ. 5** —

18-35 Oxford Company owns 70% of the common stock of Cherokee Company. The income statements of the two companies for 1994 are shown below. In its income statement, Oxford Company has not recorded its share of Cherokee Company's net income.

OXFORD AND CHEROKEE COMPANIES
INCOME STATEMENTS
FOR THE YEAR ENDED DECEMBER 31, 1994

	Oxford	Cherokee
Sales	$640,000	$270,000
Cost of Goods Sold	410,000	160,000
Gross Profit	$230,000	$110,000
Expenses (Including income taxes)	130,000	65,000
Net Income	$100,000	$ 45,000

During the year, Oxford Company sold Cherokee Company merchandise for $35,000, which had cost Oxford $22,000. Cherokee Company sold all of this merchandise to outsiders for $55,000.

REQUIRED

Prepare a consolidated income statement worksheet for 1994.

ANALYZING DATA FROM STATEMENTS CONSOLIDATED ONE YEAR AFTER ACQUISITION
— **OBJ. 3, 6** —

18-36 On January 1, 1993, Ross Company acquired an interest in Lance Company for $310,000 cash. The following information is available about the two companies at December 31, 1993:

Assets	Ross	Lance	Consolidated
Cash	$ 40,000	$ 20,000	$ 60,000
Accounts Receivable	60,000	50,000	100,000
Inventory	80,000	70,000	150,000
Investment in Lance (At equity)	340,000	—	
Other Assets	420,000	260,000	680,000
Total Assets	$940,000	$400,000	$990,000

Liabilities and Stockholders' Equity			
Accounts Payable	$ 70,000	$ 50,000	$110,000
Notes Payable	140,000	10,000	150,000
Common Stock	550,000	250,000	550,000
Retained Earnings	180,000	90,000	180,000
Total Liabilities and Stockholders' Equity	$940,000	$400,000	$990,000

REQUIRED

a. Is the acquisition of Lance Company by Ross Company a purchase or a pooling of interests? Explain.

b. What ownership percentage of Lance Company did Ross Company acquire?

c. What were Lance Company's 1993 earnings? (Lance declared and paid no dividends in 1993.)

d. How much of Lance Company's retained earnings is included in the consolidated retained earnings?

e. What were the amounts of intercompany receivables and payables at December 31?

ENTRIES ON BRANCH AND HOME OFFICE RECORDS — APPENDIX E —

18-37 Robbins, Inc., which operates a large music store in Chicago, arranged in May 1994 to open a branch in Rockford, Illinois. Record keeping for the branch is decentralized and a periodic inventory system is used. A summary of the branch's transactions for May follows:

May 1 The Chicago store transferred $40,000 cash and $100,000 in merchandise to the Rockford branch.

3 Purchased $30,000 in merchandise on account from various dealers.

10 Paid $25,000 on accounts payable.

15 Sales to date: cash, $15,000; on account $28,000.

18 Collected $16,500 on account from customers.

20 Selling expenses for the branch were $12,000 and general expenses were $5,200; of the total, $3,200 was on account and the remainder paid in cash.

25 Sent $25,000 cash to the Chicago store.

30 Sales during the last half of the month: cash, $17,000; on account, $31,000.

REQUIRED

a. Journalize the May transactions on the books of the Rockford branch.

b. Make the necessary closing entries on the Rockford branch records, assuming that the May 31 inventory is $95,000.

c. Journalize the May transactions requiring entries on the books of the Chicago home office, including the entry to record the branch's net income.

d. State the May 31 Home Office account balance in the Rockford branch's ledger.

CONVERSION OF FOREIGN CURRENCY FINANCIAL STATEMENTS: TRANSLATION PROCEDURES — APPENDIX F —

18-38 Zurich Company was organized in Switzerland on January 1, 1994, as a wholly owned subsidiary of Starr, Inc., a U.S. company. Zurich's opening balance sheet, in Swiss francs (SF), consisted of the following assets and stockholders' equity:

Assets		Stockholders' Equity	
Cash	SF 20,000	Common Stock	SF600,000
Inventory	130,000		
Plant Assets	450,000		
		Total Liabilities and	
Total Assets	SF600,000	Stockholders' Equity	SF600,000

Zurich's 1994 income statement and December 31, 1994, balance sheet, in Swiss francs, follow:

ZURICH COMPANY
INCOME STATEMENT
FOR THE YEAR ENDED DECEMBER 31, 1994

Sales		SF800,000
Cost of Goods Sold	SF500,000	
Depreciation Expense	50,000	
Other Expenses	60,000	
Total Expenses		610,000
Net Income		SF190,000

ZURICH COMPANY
BALANCE SHEET
DECEMBER 31, 1994

Assets		**Liabilities**		
Cash	SF 90,000	Accounts Payable		SF 30,000
Accounts Receivable (Net)	150,000			
Inventory	180,000	**Stockholders' Equity**		
Plant Assets (Net)	400,000	Common Stock	SF600,000	
		Retained Earnings	190,000	790,000
		Total Liabilities and		
Total Assets	SF820,000	Stockholders' Equity		SF820,000

Assume the following exchange rates for the Swiss franc:

January 1, 1994	$0.74
Average for 1994	0.71
December 31, 1994	0.68

REQUIRED

Assume that the functional currency for Zurich Company is the Swiss franc. Use translation procedures to convert Zurich's 1994 income statement and December 31, 1994, balance sheet to U.S. dollars. Follow the format of Exhibit F-2.

ALTERNATE EXERCISES

BOND INVESTMENT ENTRIES
— OBJ. 1 —

18-19A As a long-term investment, $60,000 face value of 15-year, 8% bonds were purchased at 95 on the first day of their semiannual interest period. Prepare journal entries to record (a) their purchase for cash, (b) the receipt of the first semiannual interest payment and the first semiannual amortization of bond discount (straight line), and (c) the sale of the bonds at 98 two years after they were purchased.

ENTRIES FOR STOCK INVESTMENT: COST METHOD
— OBJ. 2 —

18-20A As a long-term investment, 5,000 shares of Bolden Company common stock were acquired on February 8, 1994, at a total cost of $110,000. The investment represented 10% of the company's voting stock. On December 18, 1994, Bolden Company declared a cash dividend of 60 cents per share, which was received on January 9, 1995. Dividend income is recorded when received. Prepare the necessary journal entries to reflect (a) the purchase of the stock and (b) the receipt of the cash dividend.

ENTRIES FOR STOCK INVESTMENT: EQUITY METHOD
— OBJ. 2 —

18-21A As a long-term investment, 20,000 shares of Scanner Company common stock were purchased on January 15, 1994, at a total cost of $660,000. The investment represented 40% of the company's voting stock. On December 20, 1994, Scanner Company declared a cash dividend of $1 per share, which was received on January 11, 1995. Scanner Company's 1994 net income was $150,000. Using the equity method, prepare the journal entries to reflect (a) the purchase of the stock, (b) the proportionate share of Scanner Company's 1994 net income (dated December 31, 1994), and (c) the receipt of the cash dividend.

ADJUSTING ENTRIES FOR LONG-TERM STOCK INVESTMENT PORTFOLIO
— OBJ. 2 —

18-22A At the end of its first year of operations, Grant Corporation's portfolio of noncontrolling and noninfluential long-term stock investments had a total cost of $135,000 and a total market value of $124,000. At the end of its second year, the same portfolio had a total cost of $135,000 and a total market value of $132,000. Prepare the adjusting entry related to this investment portfolio that should be made (a) at the end of the first year and (b) at the end of the second year.

ELIMINATING ENTRIES FOR CONSOLIDATED BALANCE SHEET
— OBJ. 3 —

18-23A On January 1, 1994, Pratt Corporation purchased all of the common stock of Steere Company for $740,000. On this same date, Steere Company borrowed $60,000 from Pratt Corporation and signed a promissory note agreeing to repay the money plus interest in six months. Steere Company's stockholders' equity on January 1, 1994, consisted of $600,000 of common stock and $140,000 of retained earnings. Prepare the worksheet eliminating entries needed to prepare a consolidated balance sheet on January 1, 1994.

ELIMINATING ENTRIES FOR CONSOLIDATED BALANCE SHEET
— OBJ. 3 —

18-24A On July 1, 1994, Travis Company purchased 80% of the common stock of Kiley Company for $520,000 cash when the stockholders' equity of Kiley Company consisted of $575,000 in common stock and $75,000 in retained earnings. Also on July 1, 1994, Travis Company purchased $80,000 of supplies on account from Kiley Company ($80,000 was also Kiley's cost). Prepare the worksheet eliminating entries needed to prepare a consolidated balance sheet on July 1, 1994.

CALCULATING AMOUNTS ON CONSOLIDATED STATEMENTS
— OBJ. 3, 4 —

18-25A On January 1, 1994, Gem Company purchased for $450,000 cash an 85% stock interest in Alpine, Inc., which then had common stock of $420,000 and retained earnings of $80,000. On December 31, 1994, after Gem had taken its share of Alpine's earnings, the balance sheets of the two companies were as follows:

	Gem	Alpine
Investment in Alpine, Inc. (At equity)	$501,000	—
Other Assets	414,000	$620,000
Total Assets	$915,000	$620,000
Liabilities	$ 50,000	$ 60,000
Common Stock	700,000	420,000
Retained Earnings	165,000	140,000
Total Liabilities and Stockholders' Equity	$915,000	$620,000

Alpine, Inc., did not declare or pay dividends during the year.

a. Assuming that Alpine, Inc., assets are properly stated, what amount of goodwill from consolidation would be reported on a consolidated balance sheet at January 1, 1994?

b. What was the net income of Alpine, Inc., for 1994?

c. The consolidated balance sheet prepared December 31, 1994, would show

1. What amount of common stock?
2. What amount of retained earnings?
3. What amount of minority interest?

ELIMINATING ENTRY FOR INTERCOMPANY SALES
— OBJ. 5 —

18-26A Skinner Company has a 90% interest in Flint Company. During the current year, Skinner Company sold merchandise costing $45,000 to Flint Company for $75,000. Assuming that Flint Company sold all of the merchandise to outsiders for $95,000, what worksheet eliminating entry should be made in preparing a consolidated income statement for the period?

RECONCILING BRANCH ACCOUNT WITH HOME OFFICE ACCOUNT
— APPENDIX E —

18-27A The reciprocal accounts of the home office and branch operations of Orion Specialty Stores as they appear near the end of the accounting year follow:

BRANCH ACCOUNT (HOME OFFICE RECORDS)

Date		Description	Post. Ref.	Debit	Credit	Balance
Nov.	30	Balance				58,700
Dec.	5	Merchandise shipped		18,900		77,600
	28	Equipment sent		3,500		81,100

HOME OFFICE (BRANCH RECORDS)

Date		Description	Post. Ref.	Debit	Credit	Balance
Nov.	30	Balance				58,700
Dec.	5	Merchandise received			19,800	78,500
	31	Net income			9,500	88,000
	31	Cash remitted		8,100		79,100

a. Review these accounts in terms of any needed updating and the appropriateness of their ending balances. If you discover any apparent bookkeeping errors, assume that the home office records are correct. Prepare any needed journal entries to update and correct the accounts.

b. Prepare a brief analysis of what you consider to be the correct year-end balances for these accounts.

c. What eliminating entry would be appropriate on a worksheet used to prepare combined balance sheets for the home office and the branch?

REMEASUREMENT PROCEDURES — APPENDIX F —

18-28A Assume that remeasurement procedures are being used to convert the financial statements of a foreign subsidiary to U.S. dollars. Indicate which exchange rate—current, historical, or average for the year—should be used to convert each of the following categories of accounts.

a. Monetary assets and liabilities.

b. Assets and liabilities that are not monetary.

c. Capital stock.

d. Revenues generated uniformly throughout the year.

e. Expenses incurred uniformly throughout the year (other than depreciation expense and cost of goods sold).

f. Depreciation expense and cost of goods sold.

ALTERNATE PROBLEMS

BOND AND STOCK INVESTMENT ENTRIES — OBJ. 1, 2 —

18-29A The following transactions relate to bonds and stocks acquired by Kopler Company as long-term investments:

1993

Mar. 1 Purchased 4,000 common shares of Fister, Inc., for $68,000. These shares represent 5% of Fister's voting stock.

June 30 Purchased $200,000 face value of Nectar, Inc., 15-year, 11% bonds dated June 30, 1993, for $204,800. Interest is paid December 31 and June 30.

Dec. 20 Received cash dividend of 50 cents per share on Fister, Inc., stock investment. (Kopler recognizes dividend income when received.)

31 Received semiannual interest payment from Nectar, Inc., and amortized bond premium (straight-line method).

31 Made adjusting entry to reflect that year-end market value of Fister, Inc., stock owned is $64,000. (The investment in Fister, Inc., stock is Kopler's only long-term stock investment accounted for by the cost method.)

1994

May 5 Purchased 15,000 common shares of Billboard Company for $135,000. These shares represent 25% of Billboard's voting stock.

June 30 Received semiannual interest payment from Nectar, Inc., and amortized bond premium.

30 Sold Nectar, Inc., bonds at 104 less a sales commission of $400.

Dec. 31 Sold Fister, Inc., stock for net proceeds of $67,000.

31 Made adjusting entry to eliminate unrealized loss associated with stock investment in Fister, Inc.

31 Made adjusting entry to Billboard Company stock investment to reflect appropriate portion of Billboard Company's 1994 net income of $200,000.

1995

Jan. 10 Received cash dividend of $1.20 per share on Billboard Company stock investment.

REQUIRED

Prepare the journal entries to record these transactions and adjustments.

ENTRIES FOR NONINFLUENTIAL AND NONCONTROLLING STOCK INVESTMENTS — OBJ. 2 —

18-30A The following selected transactions and information are for Monroe Corporation for 1993 and 1994.

1993

Aug. 1 Purchased, as a long-term investment, 4,500 shares of Feller, Inc., common stock at a total cost of $90,000. This interest is noninfluential and noncontrolling.

Nov. 3 Purchased, as a long-term investment, 6,000 shares of Hahn, Inc., common stock at a total cost of $258,000, and 3,000 shares of Alvin, Inc., common stock at a total cost of $48,000. Both investments are noninfluential and noncontrolling interests.

21 Received a cash dividend of $1.50 per share on the Hahn, Inc., stock.

Dec. 31   The Feller, Inc., shares have a market value of $17 per share; the Hahn, Inc., shares have a market value of $41 per share; and the Alvin, Inc., shares have a market value of $18 per share. (An entry should be made to adjust the carrying value of the portfolio to the lower of cost or market.)

1994

Jan. 15   Sold the Hahn, Inc., stock for $40 per share less a $150 commission fee.

Dec. 31   The market value of the long-term stock investment portfolio is as follows: Feller, Inc., $19 per share; Alvin, Inc., $15 per share. (An entry should be made to adjust the carrying value of the investments and the unrealized loss account.)

REQUIRED

Prepare the journal entries to record these transactions and adjustments.

CONTRASTING ENTRIES FOR STOCK INVESTMENTS: COST AND EQUITY METHODS
— OBJ. 2 —

18-31A   On January 2, 1993, Clemens, Inc., purchased, as a long-term investment, 10,000 shares of Baer, Inc., common stock for $45 per share, including commissions and taxes. On December 31, 1993, Baer, Inc., announced a net income of $140,000 for the year and a dividend of 80 cents per share, payable January 15, 1994, to stockholders of record on January 5, 1994. Clemens, Inc., received its dividend on January 18, 1994.

REQUIRED

a. Assume that the stock acquired by Clemens, Inc., represents 10% of Baer, Inc.'s voting stock. Prepare all journal entries appropriate for this investment, beginning with the purchase on January 2, 1993, and ending with the receipt of the dividend on January 18, 1994. (Clemens, Inc., recognizes dividend income when received.)

b. Assume that the stock acquired by Clemens, Inc., represents 40% of Baer, Inc.'s voting stock. Prepare all journal entries appropriate for this investment, beginning with the purchase on January 2, 1993, and ending with the receipt of the dividend on January 18, 1994.

DETERMINING ELIMINATIONS AND CONSOLIDATED DATA ON DATE OF ACQUISITION (MAJORITY-HELD SUBSIDIARY)
— OBJ. 3, 4 —

18-32A   Skokie Company purchased 70% of Lavin Company's voting stock on January 1, 1994, after which the separate balance sheets of the two companies appeared as follows:

SKOKIE AND LAVIN COMPANIES
BALANCE SHEETS
JANUARY 1, 1994

	Skokie	Lavin
Investment in Lavin Company	$ 600,000	—
Other Assets	1,200,000	$870,000
Total Assets	$1,800,000	$870,000
Liabilities	$ 300,000	$120,000
Common Stock	1,000,000	575,000
Retained Earnings	500,000	175,000
Total Liabilities and Stockholders' Equity	$1,800,000	$870,000

In purchasing Lavin Company's shares, Skokie Company attributed the excess of the amount paid over the equity acquired in Lavin entirely to that company's superior earning potential.

REQUIRED

a. Prepare the worksheet entry to eliminate the intercompany equity and to reflect the goodwill.

b. What amount of total assets should appear on a January 1 consolidated balance sheet?

c. What amount of total stockholders' equity should appear on a January 1 consolidated balance sheet?

DETERMINING INTERCOMPANY DATA ONE YEAR AFTER ACQUISITION (WHOLLY OWNED SUBSIDIARY) — OBJ. 3 —

18-33A On January 1, 1994, Joliet Company purchased all of the common stock of Graf Company for $300,000 cash. The stockholders' equity of Graf Company consisted of $250,000 of common stock and $50,000 of retained earnings. On December 31, 1994, the separate balance sheets of the two firms were as follows:

JOLIET AND GRAF COMPANIES
BALANCE SHEETS
DECEMBER 31, 1994

	Joliet	Graf
Cash	$ 30,000	$ 20,000
Accounts Receivable	65,000	70,000
Investment in Graf Company (At equity)	325,000	—
Other Assets	680,000	295,000
Total Assets	$1,100,000	$385,000
Accounts Payable	$ 120,000	$ 60,000
Common Stock	800,000	250,000
Retained Earnings	180,000	75,000
Total Liabilities and Stockholders' Equity	$1,100,000	$385,000

During the year, Graf Company had net income of $40,000. At December 31, 1994, Graf owed Joliet $17,000 on account for merchandise.

REQUIRED

a. What amount of dividends did Graf Company declare and pay during the year?

b. Prepare Joliet Company's journal entries for 1994 that affect the Investment in Graf Company account.

c. What amount of total assets would appear in a December 31, 1994, consolidated balance sheet?

PREPARING CONSOLIDATED BALANCE SHEET WORKSHEET ON DATE OF ACQUISITION (MINORITY INTEREST) — OBJ. 3, 4 —

18-34A On January 1, 1994, Weaver, Inc. purchased 75% of the voting stock of Ogden, Inc., for $530,000, after which the separate balance sheets of the two companies were as follows:

WEAVER, INC., AND OGDEN, INC.
BALANCE SHEETS
JANUARY 1, 1994

	Weaver	Ogden
Accounts Receivable	$ 90,000	$ 40,000
Investment in Ogden, Inc.	530,000	—
Other Assets	995,000	760,000
Total Assets	$1,615,000	$800,000
Accounts Payable	$ 240,000	$140,000
Common Stock	900,000	600,000
Retained Earnings	475,000	60,000
Total Liabilities and Stockholders' Equity	$1,615,000	$800,000

At January 1, 1994, Ogden, Inc., owed $10,000 to Weaver, Inc., on account for purchases made during 1993.

REQUIRED

Prepare a consolidated balance sheet worksheet at January 1, 1994. Assume that any amount paid by Weaver in excess of the equity acquired in Ogden is attributable to a $20,000 undervaluation of Ogden's Other Assets and the existence of goodwill (for the remainder).

PREPARING CONSOLIDATED INCOME STATEMENT WORKSHEET — OBJ. 5 —

18-35A Kline Company purchased a 60% interest in Voight Company on January 1, 1993. The income statements for the two companies for 1993 are given below. Kline Company has not recorded its share of Voight Company's net income.

KLINE AND VOIGHT COMPANIES
INCOME STATEMENTS
FOR THE YEAR ENDED DECEMBER 31, 1993

	Kline	Voight
Sales	$490,000	$270,000
Cost of Goods Sold	310,000	160,000
Gross Profit	$180,000	$110,000
Operating Expenses (Including income taxes)	135,000	80,000
Net Income	$ 45,000	$ 30,000

Voight Company did not pay any dividends in 1993. During the year, Kline sold merchandise costing $29,000 to Voight for $47,000, all of which Voight sold to outsiders for $65,000.

REQUIRED

Prepare a consolidated income statement worksheet for 1993.

ANALYZING DATA FROM STATEMENTS CONSOLIDATED AT ACQUISITION DATE — OBJ. 3, 6 —

18-36A   On January 2, 1994, Prime Company acquired an interest in Spock Company by issuing to Spock Company stockholders 10,000 shares of Prime Company $15 par value common stock in exchange for all Spock Company common shares. On January 2, 1994, Prime Company shares had a market value of $28 per share. The separate balance sheets of the two firms on January 1, 1994, and a consolidated balance sheet on January 2, 1994, are shown below.

	January 1, 1994 Before Investment		January 2, 1994 Consolidated
	Prime	Spock	
Total Assets	$580,000	$270,000	$850,000
Liabilities	$ 50,000	$ 40,000	$ 90,000
Common Stock	400,000	150,000	550,000
Retained Earnings	130,000	80,000	210,000
Total Liabilities and Stockholders' Equity	$580,000	$270,000	$850,000

REQUIRED

a. Is the acquisition of Spock Company by Prime Company treated as a purchase or a pooling of interests? Explain.

b. What ownership percentage of Spock Company did Prime Company acquire? Explain.

c. If Prime Company issued 10,000 shares of its own stock worth $28 per share, why doesn't goodwill from consolidation appear on the consolidated balance sheet?

ENTRIES ON BRANCH AND HOME OFFICE RECORDS — APPENDIX E —

18-37A   Emery, Inc., operates a store selling men's shoes, hosiery, and other men's furnishings in Houston. The firm opened a branch in Austin on June 1, 1994. Recordkeeping for the branch is decentralized, and a periodic inventory system is used. A summary of the branch's June transactions follows:

June 1   Received $50,000 cash and $80,000 merchandise from the home office in Houston.

   12   Purchased $25,000 of merchandise on account from various dealers.

   15   Sales to date: cash, $24,000; on account $22,000.

   19   Collected $20,000 on account from customers.

   21   Paid $19,000 on accounts payable.

   25   Selling expenses for the branch were $18,200 and general expenses were $6,300; of the total, $8,500 was on account and the remainder paid in cash.

   26   The home office informed the Austin branch that $3,000 home office general expense was allocated to the branch.

   30   Sales during the last half of the month: cash, $27,000; on account, $17,000.

REQUIRED

a. Journalize the June transactions on the Austin branch's books.

b. Make the necessary closing entries on the Austin branch's records, assuming that the June 30 inventory is $60,000.

c. Journalize the June transactions requiring entries on the home office's books, including the entry to record the branch's net income.

d. Determine the June 30 balance in the Home Office account in the Austin branch's ledger.

CONVERSION OF FOREIGN CURRENCY FINANCIAL STATEMENTS: REMEASUREMENT PROCEDURES
— APPENDIX F —

18-38A Refer to the data given for Zurich Company in Problem 18-38. In addition, the historical exchange rate applicable to the ending inventory is $0.69 and the historical exchange rate applicable to the 1994 purchases of SF550,000 is $0.71.

REQUIRED

Assume that the functional currency for Zurich Company is the U.S. dollar. Use remeasurement procedures to convert Zurich's 1994 income statement and December 31, 1994, balance sheet to U.S. dollars. There is a 1994 foreign exchange loss of $6,900 from the remeasurement procedures. Follow the format of Exhibit F-3.

CASES

Business Decision Case

Redding, Inc., manufactures heating and cooling systems. It has a 75% interest in Guardian Company, which manufactures thermostats, switches, and other controls for heating and cooling products. It also has a 100% interest in Redding Finance Company, created by the parent company to finance sales of its products to contractors and other consumers. The parent company's only other investment is a 15% interest in the common stock of Dawson, Inc., which produces certain circuits used by Redding, Inc. A condensed consolidated balance sheet of the entity for the current year follows:

REDDING, INC., AND SUBSIDIARIES
CONSOLIDATED BALANCE SHEET
DECEMBER 31, 1993

Assets

Current Assets	$19,300,000
Investment in Stock of Dawson, Inc. (15%) at Cost	2,600,000
Other Assets	71,400,000
Excess of Cost over Equity Acquired in Net Assets of Guardian Company	1,700,000
Total Assets	$95,000,000

Liabilities and Stockholders' Equity

Current Liabilities		$10,300,000
Long-term Liabilities		14,200,000
Stockholders' Equity:		
Minority Interest	$ 3,800,000	
Common Stock	50,000,000	
Retained Earnings	16,700,000	70,500,000
Total Liabilities and Stockholders' Equity		$95,000,000

This balance sheet, along with other financial statements, was furnished to shareholders before their annual meeting, and all shareholders were invited to submit questions to be answered at the meeting. As chief financial officer of Redding, Inc., you have been appointed to respond to the questions at the meeting.

REQUIRED

Answer the following stockholder questions:

a. What is meant by *consolidated* financial statements?

b. Why is the investment in Dawson, Inc., shown on the consolidated balance sheet, but the investments in Guardian Company and Redding Finance Company are omitted?

c. Explain the meaning of the asset Excess of Cost over Equity Acquired in Net Assets of Guardian Company.

d. What is meant by *minority interest* and to what company is this account related?

Analytical Application Case

Following is a listing of the 1990 annual dividends per share of common stock for several major corporations:

SOUTHWESTERN BELL CORPORATION (communications)	$2.76
TRANSAMERICA CORPORATION (insurance and financial services)	1.94
GEORGIA-PACIFIC CORPORATION (pulp, paper, and building products)	1.60
BALL CORPORATION (packaging products)	1.14
NORTHERN TRUST CORPORATION (multibank holding company)	0.78

At December 31, 1990, the market price per share of common stock for these corporations was as follows:

Southwestern Bell Corporation	$56.00
Transamerica Corporation	32.63
Georgia-Pacific Corporation	37.25
Ball Corporation	26.88
Northern Trust Corporation	29.50

REQUIRED

a. Compute the dividend yield at December 31, 1990, for each of the corporations listed above.

b. At the end of 1990, which corporation had the most attractive dividend yield? the least attractive dividend yield?

Ethics Case

A few days ago, Lisa Goren, controller of Farley Corporation, received a note from a recently terminated assistant treasurer. The note read as follows:

> As I leave this company, I think you should know about the way Bill Clayton is manipulating the classification of stock investments for financial statement purposes. To show you what I mean, here is how he has classified Farley's short-term and long-term stock investments at year-end for the last two years:

	This Year		Last Year	
	Cost	**Market**	**Cost**	**Market**
Short-term Stock Investments				
Wysot, Inc.	$ 10,000	$ 22,000	—	—
Bailey Company	15,000	26,000	—	—
Other stocks	90,000	70,000	$ 65,000	$ 75,000
Total	$115,000	$118,000	$ 65,000	$ 75,000
Long-term Stock Investments				
Wysot, Inc.	—	—	$ 10,000	$ 18,000
Bailey Company	—	—	15,000	23,000
Other stocks	$165,000	$168,000	165,000	173,000
Total	$165,000	$168,000	$190,000	$214,000

> There is no way the Wysot and Bailey stocks should be classified as short-term investments. These companies are long-term suppliers of Farley Corporation, and Farley holds these investments to demonstrate good faith to these suppliers. Bill Clayton is manipulating these stock classifications so that he and Farley Corporation will look good.

Lisa asked Bill Clayton (Farley Corporation's treasurer) about the current year-end classification of the Wysot and Bailey stocks. Bill's reply was: "The classification of an investment as short term or long term depends on management's intent. We might sell the Wysot and Bailey investments next year, although it is not likely. If we do sell these two stocks, their classification is consistent with generally accepted accounting principles. If we don't sell them, we'll just tell the outside auditors we changed our minds. Generally accepted accounting principles can't legislate management intent, nor can our outside auditors read our minds. Besides, why shouldn't we take advantage of the flexibility in GAAP to avoid showing a loss on our short-term stock investments this year?"

REQUIRED

a. How does the reclassification of the Wysot and Bailey stocks keep Farley Corporation from recording a loss on its short-term stock investments in the current year?

b. Is it ethical for Bill Clayton to reclassify the Wysot and Bailey stocks?

What information must a company report about its cash flows?

For financial reporting purposes, cash flows for a period must be divided into three types of activities: operating activities, investing activities, and financing activities. ■ The statement of cash flows provides useful perspectives to data presented in the other financial statements. ■ In 1990, for example, railroad owner Norfolk Southern Corporation reported net income of $556.1 million, but its statement of cash flows showed a cash increase of $994.7 million from operating activities.

19 STATEMENT OF CASH FLOWS

he **statement of cash flows** is a basic financial statement that summarizes information about the flow of cash into and out of a company. The statement of cash flows complements the balance sheet and the income statement. The balance sheet reports the company's financial position at a point in time (the end of each period) whereas the statement of cash flows explains the change in one component of financial position—cash—from one balance sheet date to the next. The income statement reveals the results of the company's operating activities for the period, and these operating activities are a major contributor to the change in cash reported in the statement of cash flows.

CASH AND CASH EQUIVALENTS

OBJECTIVE 1 PROVIDE *a basis for understanding a statement of cash flows.*

Even though it is called a statement of cash flows, the statement actually encompasses a somewhat broader concept than just cash. More precisely, the statement is to explain the change in a firm's cash and cash equivalents. **Cash equivalents** are short-term, highly liquid investments that firms acquire with temporarily idle cash to earn interest on these excess funds. To qualify as a cash equivalent, an investment must (1) be easily convertible into a known cash amount and (2) be close enough to maturity so that its market value is not sensitive to interest rate changes (generally, investments with initial maturities of three months or less).[1] Typical examples of cash equivalents are Treasury bills, commercial paper (short-term notes issued by corporations), and money market funds.

Some firms may invest in these types of securities primarily in the hope of benefiting from favorable price changes and, thus, do not view them as the equivalent of cash. For these firms, the investments should be classified as short-term investments, not as cash equivalents. Because firms may differ in how they view these short-term, highly liquid investments, the Financial Accounting Standards Board requires a firm to set, and disclose, a policy for deciding which qualifying investments are treated as cash equivalents.

When preparing a statement of cash flows, the cash and cash equivalents are added together and treated as a single sum. This is done because the purchase and sale of investments in cash equivalents are considered to be part of a firm's overall management of cash rather than a source or use of cash. As statement users evaluate and project cash flows, for example, it may matter very little to them whether the cash is on hand, deposited in a bank account, or invested in cash equivalents. Transfers back and forth between a firm's Cash account and its investments in cash equivalents, therefore, are not treated as cash inflows and cash outflows in its statement of cash flows.

The period-end cash and cash equivalents reported in a statement of cash flows must agree with the amount of cash and cash equivalents reported in the firm's balance sheet. Items treated as cash equivalents, therefore, are distinct from assets classified in the balance sheet as short-term investments or marketable securities. Purchases and sales of these latter items *do* create cash outflows and cash inflows that are reported in the statement of cash flows.

When discussing the statement of cash flows, accountants generally use the word *cash* rather than the term *cash and cash equivalents*. We will follow the same practice in this chapter.

---

[1] *Statement of Financial Accounting Standards No. 95*, "Statement of Cash Flows" (Stamford, CT: Financial Accounting Standards Board, 1987), par. 8.

CLASSIFICATIONS IN THE STATEMENT OF CASH FLOWS

A statement of cash flows classifies cash receipts and payments into three major categories: operating activities, investing activities, and financing activities. Grouping cash flows into these categories identifies the effects on cash of each of the major activities of a firm. The combined effects on cash of all three categories explain the net change in cash for the period. The period's net change in cash is then reconciled with the beginning and ending amounts of cash. Exhibit 19-1 illustrates the basic format for a statement of cash flows.

Operating Activities

A company's income statement reflects the transactions and events that constitute its operating activities. Generally, the cash effects of these transactions and events are what determine the net cash flow from operating activities. The usual focus of a firm's operating activities is on selling goods or rendering services. Cash flows from **operating activities** are defined broadly enough, however, to encompass any cash receipts or payments that are not classified as investing or financing activities. For example, cash received as lawsuit settlements and cash payments to charity are treated as cash flows from operating activities. The following are examples of cash inflows and outflows relating to operating activities.

Operating Activities

Cash Inflows	Cash Outflows
1. Receipts from customers for sales made or services rendered.	1. Payments to suppliers.
2. Receipts of interest and dividends.	2. Payments to employees.
3. Other receipts that are not related to investing or financing activities, such as lawsuit settlements and refunds received from suppliers.	3. Payments of interest to creditors.
	4. Payments of taxes to government.
	5. Other payments that are not related to investing or financing activities, such as contributions to charity.

Investing Activities

A firm's transactions involving (1) the acquisition and disposal of plant assets and intangible assets, (2) the purchase and sale of stocks, bonds, and other securities (that are not cash equivalents), and (3) the lending and subsequent collection of money

---

EXHIBIT 19–1	FORMAT FOR THE STATEMENT OF CASH FLOWS

SAMPLE COMPANY
STATEMENT OF CASH FLOWS
FOR THE YEAR ENDED DECEMBER 31, 1993

Cash Flows from Operating Activities		
(DETAILS OF NET CASH FLOW FROM OPERATING ACTIVITIES)	$XXX	
Net Cash Provided (Used) by Operating Activities		$XXX
Cash Flows from Investing Activities		
(DETAILS OF INDIVIDUAL INVESTING CASH INFLOWS AND OUTFLOWS)	$XXX	
Net Cash Provided (Used) by Investing Activities		XXX
Cash Flows from Financing Activities		
(DETAILS OF INDIVIDUAL FINANCING CASH INFLOWS AND OUTFLOWS)	$XXX	
Net Cash Provided (Used) by Financing Activities		XXX
Net Increase (Decrease) in Cash		$XXX
Cash at Beginning of Year		XXX
Cash at End of Year		$XXX

constitute the basic components of its **investing activities.**[2] The related cash receipts and payments appear in the investing activities section of the statement of cash flows. Examples of these cash flows follow.

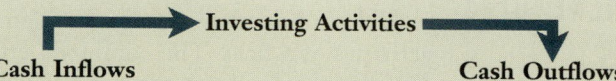

Investing Activities

Cash Inflows	**Cash Outflows**
1. Receipts from sales of plant assets and intangible assets.	1. Payments to purchase plant assets and intangible assets.
2. Receipts from sales of investments in stocks, bonds, and other securities (other than cash equivalents).	2. Payments to purchase stocks, bonds, and other securities (other than cash equivalents).
3. Receipts from repayments of loans by borrowers.	3. Payments made to lend money to borrowers.

Financing Activities

A firm engages in **financing activities** when it obtains resources from owners, returns resources to owners, borrows resources from creditors, and repays amounts borrowed. Cash flows related to these events are reported in the financing activities section of the statement of cash flows. Examples of these cash flows are listed below.

Financing Activities

Cash Inflows	**Cash Outflows**
1. Receipts from issuing common stock and preferred stock.	1. Payments to reacquire treasury stock.
2. Receipts from issuing bonds payable, mortgage notes payable, and other notes payable.	2. Payments of dividends.
	3. Payments to settle outstanding bonds payable, mortgage notes payable, and other notes payable.

Observe that paying cash to settle such obligations as accounts payable, wages payable, interest payable, and income tax payable are operating activities, not financing activities.

The classification of cash flows into three categories of activities helps financial statement users interpret cash flow data. To illustrate, assume that companies D, E, and F are similar companies operating in the same industry. Each company showed a $100,000 cash increase during the current year. Information from their current year statements of cash flows is summarized below.

	D	E	F
Net Cash Provided by Operating Activities	$100,000	$ –0–	$ –0–
Cash Flows from Investing Activities:			
Sale of Plant Assets	–0–	100,000	–0–
Cash Flows from Financing Activities:			
Issuance of Notes Payable	–0–	–0–	100,000
Net Increase in Cash	$100,000	$100,000	$100,000

Although each company's cash increase was the same, the source of the increase varied by company. This variation affects the analysis of the cash flow data, particularly for potential short-term creditors who must evaluate the likelihood of obtaining repayment in the future for any funds loaned to the company. Based only on these cash flow data, a potential creditor would feel more comfortable lending money to D than to either E or F. D's cash increase came from its operating activities, whereas both E and F could only break even on their cash flows from operations. E's cash increase came from the sale of plant assets, a source that is not likely to recur reg-

---

[2] There are exceptions to the classification of these events as investing activities. For example, the purchase and sale of mortgage loans by a mortgage banker and the purchase and sale of securities in the trading account of a broker and dealer in securities represent operating activities for these businesses.

ularly. F's cash increase came entirely from borrowed funds. F faces additional cash burdens in the future when the interest and principal payments on the note payable become due.

NONCASH INVESTING AND FINANCING ACTIVITIES

A secondary objective of cash flow reporting is to present summary information about a firm's investing and financing activities. Of course, many of these activities affect cash and are therefore already included in the investing and financing sections of the statement of cash flows. Some significant investing and financing events, however, do not affect current cash flows. Examples of **noncash investing and financing activities** are the issuance of stocks or bonds in exchange for plant assets or intangible assets, the exchange of long-term assets for other long-term assets, and the conversion of long-term debt into common stock. Information about these events must be reported as a supplement to the statement of cash flows.

Noncash investing and financing transactions generally do affect future cash flows, however. Issuing bonds payable to acquire equipment, for example, requires future cash payments for interest and principal on the bonds. On the other hand, converting bonds payable into common stock eliminates future cash payments related to the bonds. Knowledge of these types of events, therefore, should be helpful to users of cash flow data who wish to assess a firm's future cash flows.

The information on noncash investing and financing transactions is disclosed in a schedule that is separate from the statement of cash flows. The separate schedule may be placed immediately below the statement of cash flows or it may be placed among the notes to the financial statements.

USEFULNESS OF THE STATEMENT OF CASH FLOWS

The Financial Accounting Standards Board believes that one objective of financial reporting is to help external users assess the amount, timing, and uncertainty of future cash flows to the enterprise.[3] These assessments, in turn, help users evaluate their own prospective cash receipts from their investments in, or loans to, the firm. Although statements of cash flows report past cash flows, these statements should be useful for assessing the future cash flows of firms.

A statement of cash flows shows the periodic cash effects of a firm's operating, investing, and financing activities. Distinguishing among these different categories of cash flows helps users compare, evaluate, and predict cash flows. With cash flow information, creditors and investors are better able to assess a firm's ability to settle its liabilities and pay its dividends. A firm's need for outside financing may also be better evaluated. Over time, the statement of cash flows permits users to observe and analyze management's investing and financing policies.

A statement of cash flows also provides information useful in evaluating a firm's financial flexibility. *Financial flexibility* is a firm's ability to generate sufficient amounts of cash to respond to unanticipated needs and opportunities. Information about past cash flows, particularly cash flows from operations, helps in assessing financial flexibility. An evaluation of a firm's ability to survive an unexpected drop in demand, for example, may include a review of its past cash flows from operations. The larger these cash flows, the greater will be the firm's ability to withstand adverse changes in economic conditions. Other financial statements, particularly the balance sheet and its notes, also contain information useful for judging financial flexibility.

---

[3] *Statement of Financial Accounting Concepts No. 1,* "Objectives of Financial Reporting by Business Enterprises" (Stamford, CT: Financial Accounting Standards Board, 1978), p. 18. The FASB also believes information should be reported about earnings. It notes that earnings measured by accrual accounting are a better indicator of periodic financial performance than information about current cash receipts and payments.

Some investors and creditors find the statement of cash flows useful in evaluating the "quality" of a firm's income. As we know, determining income under accrual accounting procedures requires many accruals, deferrals, allocations, and valuations. These adjustment and measurement procedures introduce more subjectivity into income determination than some financial statement users prefer. These users will relate a more objective performance measure—cash flow from operations—to net income. To these users, the higher this ratio is, the higher is the quality of the income.

NET CASH FLOW FROM OPERATING ACTIVITIES

The first section of a statement of cash flows presents a firm's net cash flow from operating activities. There are two alternative formats for reporting the net cash flow from operating activities: the direct method and the indirect method. The *direct method* shows individual amounts of cash inflows and cash outflows from major operating activities, with the net difference between the inflows and outflows being the net cash flow from operating activities. The *indirect method* (or *reconciliation method*) starts with net income and applies a series of adjustments to net income to convert it to a cash-basis income number, which is the net cash flow from operating activities. The indirect method does not show individual amounts of operating cash inflows and outflows.

The Financial Accounting Standards Board encourages companies to use the direct method but permits use of the indirect method. We will first discuss the preparation of the statement of cash flows using the direct method to present the net cash flow from operating activities. We will then discuss the preparation of the statement of cash flows using the indirect method to present the net cash flow from operating activities.

PREPARING THE STATEMENT OF CASH FLOWS UNDER THE DIRECT METHOD

OBJECTIVE 2 DISCUSS *the preparation of a statement of cash flows using the direct method.*

To prepare a statement of cash flows, we need a firm's income statement, comparative balance sheets, and some additional data taken from the accounting records. Exhibit 19-2 presents this information for Bennett Company. We will use these data to prepare Bennett's 1994 statement of cash flows using the direct method.

Bennett's statement of cash flows will explain the $25,000 increase in cash that occurred during 1994 (from $10,000 to $35,000) by classifying the firm's cash flows into operating, investing, and financing categories. To get the information to construct the statement, therefore, we do the following:

1. *Use the direct method to determine the individual cash flows from operating activities.* In doing this, we will utilize changes that occurred during 1994 in various current asset and current liability accounts.

2. *Determine cash flows from investing activities.* We will do this by analyzing changes in the noncash asset accounts not used in the direct method.

3. *Determine cash flows from financing activities.* We will do this by analyzing changes in the liability and stockholders' equity accounts not used in the direct method.

Net Cash Flow from Operating Activities under the Direct Method

CONVERT REVENUES AND EXPENSES TO CASH FLOWS

The **direct method** presents the net cash flow from operating activities by showing the major categories of operating cash receipts and payments. The operating cash receipts and payments are usually determined by converting the accrual-basis revenues and expenses to corresponding cash amounts. It is efficient to do it this way, because the accrual-basis revenues and expenses are readily available in the income statement. We will now explain and illustrate the process of converting Bennett Company's 1994 revenues and expenses to corresponding cash flows from operating activities.

EXHIBIT 19–2	FINANCIAL DATA OF BENNETT COMPANY

BENNETT COMPANY
INCOME STATEMENT
FOR THE YEAR ENDED DECEMBER 31, 1994

Sales		$250,000
Cost of Goods Sold	$140,000	
Wages Expense	52,000	
Insurance Expense	5,000	
Depreciation Expense	10,000	
Income Tax Expense	11,000	
Total Expenses		218,000
Net Income		$ 32,000

BENNETT COMPANY
BALANCE SHEETS

	Dec. 31, 1994	Dec. 31, 1993
Assets		
Cash	$ 35,000	$ 10,000
Accounts Receivable	39,000	34,000
Inventory	54,000	60,000
Prepaid Insurance	17,000	4,000
Long-term Investments	5,000	—
Plant Assets	250,000	200,000
Accumulated Depreciation	(50,000)	(40,000)
Total Assets	$350,000	$268,000
Liabilities and Stockholders' Equity		
Accounts Payable	$ 10,000	$ 19,000
Income Tax Payable	5,000	3,000
Common Stock	260,000	190,000
Retained Earnings	75,000	56,000
Total Liabilities and Stockholders' Equity	$350,000	$268,000

Additional Data for 1994

1. Purchased long-term stock investments and equipment for cash.
2. All accounts payable relate to merchandise purchases.
3. Issued common stock at par for cash.
4. Declared and paid cash dividends of $13,000.

CONVERT SALES TO CASH RECEIVED FROM CUSTOMERS During 1994, accounts receivable increased $5,000. This increase means that during 1994, cash collections on account (which decrease accounts receivable) were less than credit sales (which increase accounts receivable). We compute cash received from customers, then, as follows:[4]

Sales	$250,000
+ Beginning accounts receivable	34,000
− Ending accounts receivable	(39,000)
= Cash received from customers	$245,000

CONVERT COST OF GOODS SOLD TO CASH PAID FOR MERCHANDISE PURCHASED The conversion of cost of goods sold to cash paid for merchandise purchased is a two-step process. First, cost of goods sold is adjusted for the change in inventory to determine the amount of purchases during the year. Then the purchases amount is adjusted for the change in accounts payable to derive the cash paid for merchandise purchased.

Inventory decreased from $60,000 to $54,000 during 1994. This $6,000 decrease indicates that the cost of goods sold exceeded the cost of goods purchased during the year. The year's purchases amount is computed as follows:

Cost of goods sold	$140,000
+ Ending inventory	54,000
− Beginning inventory	(60,000)
= Purchases	$134,000

---

[4]This computation assumes that no accounts were written off as uncollectible during the period. The impact on the computation of an allowance account and uncollectible accounts expense is beyond the scope of this discussion.

A LOOK AT THE FASB'S DECISION-MAKING PROCESS

How does the FASB weigh the often competing interests of different segments of its constituency? Chairman Dennis Beresford used the Board's recently published statement on cash flows to explain . . . some of the inner workings of the FASB. ■ *The Board and staff spent nine months on the project, and received 450 comment letters, Beresford explained. On eight occasions, the Board met to discuss cash flow reporting issues, and three times it held meetings with knowledgeable outsiders on the more controversial issues. One meeting was on the direct/indirect method.*

By the time the process had concluded, two Board members had changed the position on the direct/indirect issue that they had taken in the exposure draft. The swing vote in the final four-to-three tally depended on, he said, "a tradeoff between requiring the direct method or changing the status of other issues that that Board member considered more important."

The majority of comment letters came from bank lending officers, said Beresford, as a result of an effort by Robert Morris Associates to encourage comments. "Many of those letters made eloquent arguments in favor of requiring the use of the direct method of reporting operating cash flows." Preparers, on the other hand, had little incentive to argue against this issue, he added, because the exposure draft allowed either the direct or the indirect method.

As part of the process, Beresford said, a researcher was engaged to determine whether the cost to provide the direct method information would be excessive. "The limited study showed," he said, "that most companies could not obtain amounts of gross operating cash receipts and payments directly from their accounting system. But it also showed that information about those major classes might be determined indirectly by adjusting revenue and expense amounts for the change during the period in related asset and liability accounts."

The direct method was not required in the final statement, Beresford said, "but the users' preference for separately reporting noncash items was adopted. Furthermore, the final statement strongly encourages the use of the direct method for reporting cash flows from operating activities."

And while most preparers agreed with the final decision on the direct/indirect method, Beresford said, "I'm sure that preparers weren't happy with several other parts of the standard, such as including the reporting currency equivalent of foreign currency cash flows, and requiring that all banks and other financial institutions prepare a cash flow statement."

SOURCE: From "Technically Speaking." Reprinted with permission from *Financial Executive* (January/February 1989), copyright © 1989 by Financial Executives Institute, 10 Madison Ave., P.O. Box 1938, Morristown, NJ 07962-1938. (201) 898–4600.

During 1994, accounts payable decreased $9,000. This decrease reflects the fact that cash payments for merchandise purchased on account (which decrease accounts payable) exceeded purchases on account (which increase accounts payable). The cash paid for merchandise purchased, therefore, is computed as follows:

	Purchases	$134,000
+	Beginning accounts payable	19,000
−	Ending accounts payable	(10,000)
=	Cash paid for merchandise purchased	$143,000

CONVERT WAGES EXPENSE TO CASH PAID TO EMPLOYEES

No adjustment to wages expense is needed. The absence of any beginning or ending accrued liability for wages payable means that wages expense and cash paid to employees as wages are the same amount: $52,000.

CONVERT INSURANCE EXPENSE TO CASH PAID FOR INSURANCE

Prepaid insurance increased $13,000 during 1994. The $13,000 increase reflects the excess of cash paid for insurance during 1994 (which increases prepaid insurance) over the year's insurance expense (which decreases prepaid insurance). Starting with insurance expense, then, the cash paid for insurance is computed as follows:

Insurance expense	$ 5,000
+ Ending prepaid insurance	17,000
− Beginning prepaid insurance	(4,000)
= Cash paid for insurance	$18,000

ELIMINATE DEPRECIATION EXPENSE AND OTHER NONCASH OPERATING EXPENSES

Depreciation expense is a noncash expense. Because it does not represent a cash payment, depreciation expense is completely eliminated as we convert accrual expense amounts to the corresponding amounts of cash payments. If Bennett Company had any amortization expense or depletion expense, it also would be eliminated for the same reason. The amortization of an intangible asset and the depletion of a natural resource are entirely noncash expenses.

CONVERT INCOME TAX EXPENSE TO CASH PAID FOR INCOME TAXES

The increase in income tax payable from $3,000 at December 31, 1993, to $5,000 at December 31, 1994, means that 1994's income tax expense (which increases income tax payable) was $2,000 more than 1994's tax payments (which decrease income tax payable). If we start with income tax expense, then we calculate cash paid for income taxes in the following manner:

Income tax expense	$11,000
+ Beginning income tax payable	3,000
− Ending income tax payable	(5,000)
= Cash paid for income taxes	$ 9,000

OMIT GAINS AND LOSSES RELATED TO INVESTING AND FINANCING ACTIVITIES

The income statement may contain gains and losses related to investing and financing activities. Examples include gains and losses from the sale of plant assets and gains and losses from the retirement of bonds payable before maturity. Because these gains and losses are not related to operating activities, we ignore them as we convert income statement items to various cash flows from operating activities. These gains and losses are considered when cash flows from investing and financing activities are determined.

Bennett Company has no 1994 gains and losses related to investing and financing activities. The worksheet illustration later in the chapter and the demonstration problems at the end of the chapter contain examples of such gains or losses.

We have now applied the proper adjustments to convert each accrual basis revenue and expense to the corresponding operating cash flow. We will use these individual cash flows to prepare the operating activities section of the statement of cash flows. This section will appear as follows:

Cash Received from Customers		$245,000
Cash Paid for Merchandise Purchased	$143,000	
Cash Paid to Employees	52,000	
Cash Paid for Insurance	18,000	
Cash Paid for Income Taxes	9,000	222,000
Net Cash Provided by Operating Activities		$ 23,000

Exhibit 19-3 summarizes the procedures for converting individual income statement items to corresponding cash flows from operating activities. To be more efficient, only the changes in the balance sheet accounts during the period (increases or decreases) are used rather than both the beginning and ending account balances.

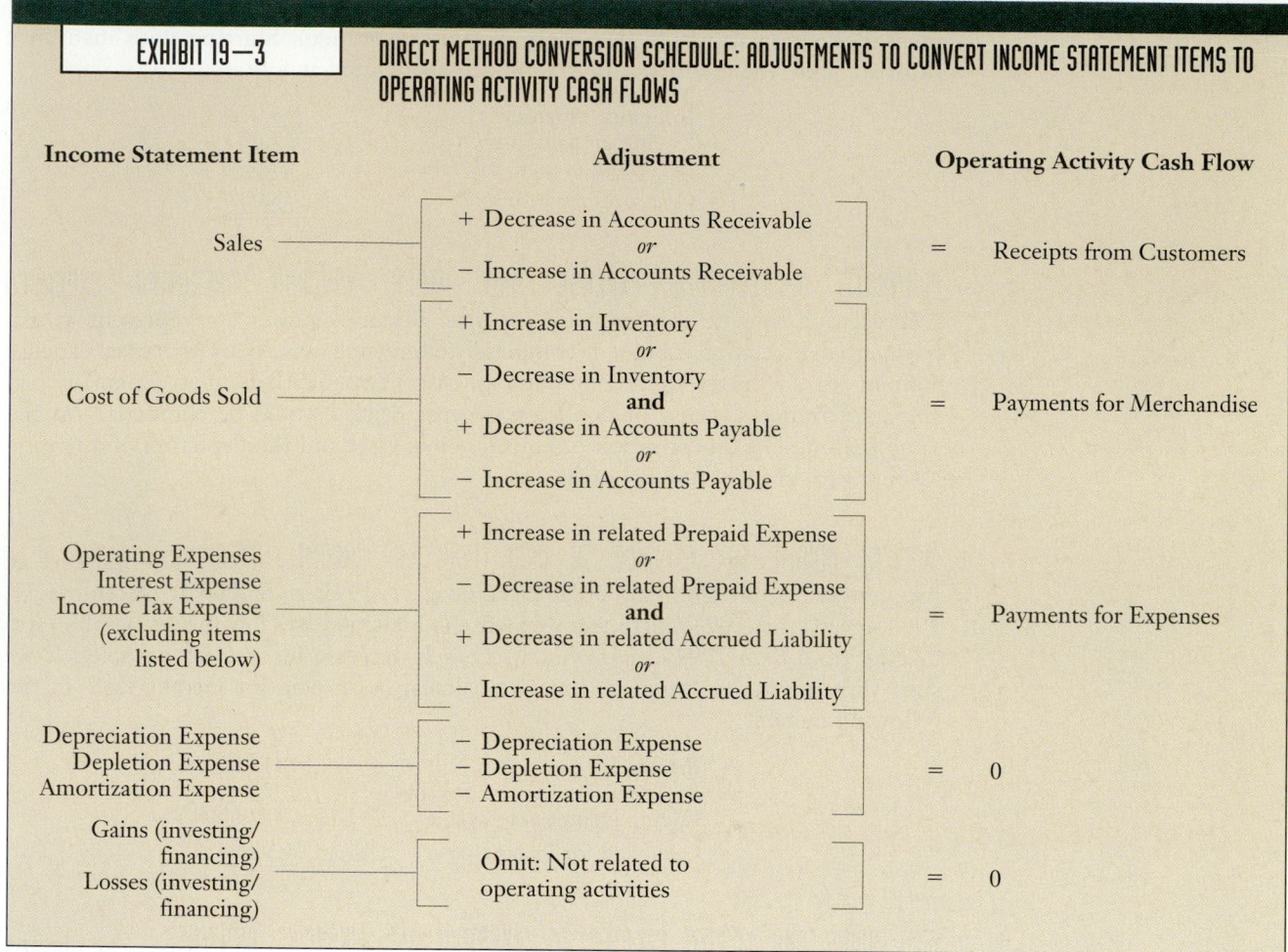

EXHIBIT 19—3 — DIRECT METHOD CONVERSION SCHEDULE: ADJUSTMENTS TO CONVERT INCOME STATEMENT ITEMS TO OPERATING ACTIVITY CASH FLOWS

Income Statement Item	Adjustment	Operating Activity Cash Flow
Sales	+ Decrease in Accounts Receivable *or* − Increase in Accounts Receivable	= Receipts from Customers
Cost of Goods Sold	+ Increase in Inventory *or* − Decrease in Inventory **and** + Decrease in Accounts Payable *or* − Increase in Accounts Payable	= Payments for Merchandise
Operating Expenses Interest Expense Income Tax Expense (excluding items listed below)	+ Increase in related Prepaid Expense *or* − Decrease in related Prepaid Expense **and** + Decrease in related Accrued Liability *or* − Increase in related Accrued Liability	= Payments for Expenses
Depreciation Expense Depletion Expense Amortization Expense	− Depreciation Expense − Depletion Expense − Amortization Expense	= 0
Gains (investing/ financing) Losses (investing/ financing)	Omit: Not related to operating activities	= 0

Cash Flows from Investing Activities

ANALYZE CHANGES IN REMAINING NONCASH ASSET ACCOUNTS

Investing activities cause changes in asset accounts. Usually the accounts affected other than cash are noncurrent asset accounts such as plant assets and long-term investments, although short-term investment accounts may also be affected. To determine the cash flows from investing activities, we analyze the changes in all noncash asset accounts not used in computing the net cash flow from operating activities. Our objective is to identify any investing cash flows related to these changes. Related contra asset accounts should also be analyzed.

ANALYZE CHANGE IN LONG-TERM INVESTMENTS Bennett's comparative balance sheets show that long-term investments increased $5,000 during 1994. The increase means that investments must have been purchased, and the additional data indicate that cash was spent to purchase long-term stock investments. Purchasing stock is an investing activity. Thus, a $5,000 purchase of stock investments will be shown as a cash outflow from investing activities in the statement of cash flows.

ANALYZE CHANGE IN PLANT ASSETS Bennett's plant assets increased $50,000 during 1994. Plant assets increase as the result of purchases, and the additional data for Bennett Company indicate that equipment was purchased for cash in 1994. Purchasing equipment is an investing activity. Thus, a $50,000 purchase of equipment will be shown as a cash outflow from investing activities in the statement of cash flows.

ANALYZE CHANGE IN ACCUMULATED DEPRECIATION Bennett's accumulated depreciation increased $10,000 during 1994. Accumulated depreciation increases when depreciation expense is recorded. Bennett's 1994 depreciation expense was $10,000, so the total change in accumulated depreciation is the result of the recording of depreciation expense. As previously discussed, there is no cash flow related to the recording of depreciation expense.

Cash Flows from Financing Activities

ANALYZE CHANGES IN REMAINING LIABILITY AND STOCKHOLDERS' EQUITY ACCOUNTS

Financing activities cause changes in liability and stockholders' equity accounts. Usually the accounts affected are noncurrent accounts such as bonds payable and common stock, although a current liability such as short-term notes payable may also be affected. To determine the cash flows from financing activities, we analyze the changes in all liability and stockholders' equity accounts that were not used in computing the net cash flow from operating activities. Our objective is to identify any financing cash flows related to these changes.

ANALYZE CHANGE IN COMMON STOCK Bennett's common stock increased $70,000 during 1994. Common stock increases when shares of stock are issued and the additional data show that shares were issued for cash during 1994. Issuing common stock is a financing activity. A $70,000 issuance of common stock, therefore, will appear as a cash inflow from financing activities in the statement of cash flows.

ANALYZE CHANGE IN RETAINED EARNINGS Retained earnings grew from $56,000 to $75,000 during 1994—a $19,000 increase. This increase is the net result of Bennett's $32,000 of net income (which increased retained earnings) and a $13,000 cash dividend (which decreased retained earnings). Because every item in Bennett's income statement was considered in computing the net cash provided by operating activities, only the cash dividend remains to be considered at this point. Paying a cash dividend is a financing activity. Thus, a $13,000 cash dividend will show as a cash outflow from financing activities in the statement of cash flows.

We have now completed the analysis of all of Bennett's noncash balance sheet accounts and can prepare the 1994 statement of cash flows. Exhibit 19-4 shows this statement.

If there are cash inflows and outflows from similar types of investing and financing activities, the inflows and outflows are reported separately (rather than reporting only the net difference). For example, proceeds from the sale of plant assets are reported separately from outlays made to acquire plant assets. Similarly, funds borrowed are reported separately from debt repayments, and proceeds from issuing stock are reported separately from outlays to acquire treasury stock.

SEPARATE DISCLOSURES UNDER THE DIRECT METHOD

When the direct method is used in the statement of cash flows, three separate disclosures are required: (1) a reconciliation of net income to the net cash flow from operating activities, (2) a schedule or description of all noncash investing and financing transactions, and (3) the firm's policy for determining which highly liquid, short-term investments are treated as cash equivalents.

The required reconciliation is the indirect method of computing the net cash flow from operating activities. *Thus, when the direct method is used in the statement of cash flows, the indirect method is a required separate disclosure.* We discuss and illustrate the indirect method later in this chapter.

EXHIBIT 19—4	STATEMENT OF CASH FLOWS UNDER THE DIRECT METHOD

BENNETT COMPANY
STATEMENT OF CASH FLOWS
FOR THE YEAR ENDED DECEMBER 31, 1994

Cash Flows from Operating Activities		
Cash Received from Customers		$245,000
Cash Paid for Merchandise Purchased	$143,000	
Cash Paid to Employees	52,000	
Cash Paid for Insurance	18,000	
Cash Paid for Income Taxes	9,000	222,000
Net Cash Provided by Operating Activities		$ 23,000
Cash Flows from Investing Activities		
Purchase of Stock Investments	($ 5,000)	
Purchase of Equipment	(50,000)	
Net Cash Used by Investing Activities		(55,000)
Cash Flows from Financing Activities		
Issuance of Common Stock	$ 70,000	
Payment of Dividends	(13,000)	
Net Cash Provided by Financing Activities		57,000
Net Increase in Cash		$ 25,000
Cash at Beginning of Year		10,000
Cash at End of Year		$ 35,000

WORKSHEET FOR PREPARING THE STATEMENT OF CASH FLOWS UNDER THE DIRECT METHOD

OBJECTIVE ③ ILLUSTRATE *a worksheet approach to preparing a statement of cash flows using the direct method.*

A worksheet may be helpful in constructing a statement of cash flows. A worksheet is designed to analyze the changes in all the noncash balance sheet accounts and identify, by type of activity, the cash inflows and outflows for the period. We review all noncash balance sheet accounts for two reasons:

1. Because of the basic accounting equation (Assets = Liabilities + Owners' Equity), the net change in cash during a period must equal the net change in all other balance sheet accounts. By analyzing the changes in all noncash balance sheet accounts, we will be able to identify all events affecting cash flows.

2. A required disclosure accompanying the statement of cash flows is a presentation of all noncash investing and financing activities. An analysis of the changes in all noncash balance sheet accounts will permit us to identify these events also.

To illustrate the use of a worksheet, we use the financial data of Superior Corporation shown in Exhibit 19-5. As the comparative balance sheets show, Superior's cash increased $12,000 during 1994. This is the change that will be explained by the 1994 statement of cash flows.

Exhibit 19-6 (on page 710) shows the worksheet for Superior Corporation under the direct method. Note that the worksheet has a description column and four amount columns. Each of the two headings, Changes in Noncash Accounts and Analyzing Entries, has a Debit and a Credit column.

Changes in Noncash Balance Sheet Accounts

The content of the worksheet focuses on the company's noncash balance sheet accounts.

1 First, a list of all noncash balance sheet accounts is entered in the Description column. Then the debit or credit change in each account balance for the

EXHIBIT 19—5	FINANCIAL DATA OF SUPERIOR CORPORATION

SUPERIOR CORPORATION
INCOME STATEMENT
FOR THE YEAR ENDED DECEMBER 31, 1994

Sales		$360,000
Cost of Goods Sold	$200,000	
Wages and Other Operating Expenses	78,000	
Depreciation Expense	13,000	
Interest Expense	10,000	
Income Tax Expense	12,000	
Gain on Sale of Equipment	(16,000)	
Loss on Bond Retirement*	9,000	306,000
Net Income		$ 54,000

Additional Data for 1994

1. Sold equipment having a book value of $4,000 ($10,000 cost – $6,000 accumulated depreciation) for $20,000 cash.
2. Purchased new equipment for $65,000 cash.
3. Retired $80,000 of bonds payable for $89,000 cash.
4. Acquired equipment worth $30,000 by issuing 3,000 shares of common stock.
5. Issued additional common stock at par for $120,000 cash.
6. Declared and paid cash dividends of $11,000.

SUPERIOR CORPORATION
BALANCE SHEETS

Assets	Dec. 31, 1994	Dec. 31, 1993	Increase (Decrease)
Current Assets			
Cash	$ 25,000	$ 13,000	$ 12,000
Accounts Receivable (Net)	55,000	60,000	(5,000)
Inventory	94,000	80,000	14,000
Prepaid Expenses	13,000	10,000	3,000
Total Current Assets	$187,000	$163,000	$ 24,000
Plant Assets			
Building and Equipment	$418,000	$333,000	$ 85,000
Accumulated Depreciation	(75,000)	(68,000)	7,000
Total Plant Assets	$343,000	$265,000	$ 78,000
Total Assets	$530,000	$428,000	$102,000
Liabilities and Stockholders' Equity			
Current Liabilities			
Accounts Payable	$ 32,000	$ 42,000	($ 10,000)
Interest Payable	1,000	3,000	(2,000)
Income Tax Payable	2,000	1,000	1,000
Total Current Liabilities	$ 35,000	$ 46,000	($ 11,000)
Long-term Debt			
Bonds Payable	$ 40,000	$120,000	($ 80,000)
Stockholders' Equity			
Common Stock ($10 par value)	$350,000	$200,000	$150,000
Retained Earnings	105,000	62,000	43,000
Total Stockholders' Equity	$455,000	$262,000	$193,000
Total Liabilities and Stockholders' Equity	$530,000	$428,000	$102,000

* If material, this loss is extraordinary. Separate disclosure of cash flows relating to extraordinary items is not required. For simplicity, a separate extraordinary section is not used here.

period is entered in the appropriate column under the Changes in Noncash Accounts heading. If an account increased, the amount of the increase is shown in the column representing the side of the account where increases are recorded. If an account decreased, the amount of the decrease is shown in the column representing the side of the account where decreases are recorded.

2 After the changes for all noncash balance sheet accounts are entered, the two columns are totaled. The difference between the column totals equals the change in cash for the year. The cash change is entered on the worksheet—an increase in the Debit column, a decrease in the Credit column—and the two columns are totaled and double ruled to show their equality. Exhibit 19-6 shows the $12,000 cash increase for Superior Corporation in the Debit column.

3 At this point, the label "cash flows from operating activities" is written in the Description column. Beneath this, labels for the appropriate categories of operating cash flows are entered, leaving several lines for each category. A firm using the direct method must, at a minimum, disclose the following categories of operating cash receipts and payments:

- Cash received from customers.
- Cash received as dividends and interest.
- Cash received from other operating activities, if any.
- Cash paid to employees and other suppliers of goods and services, including suppliers of insurance, advertising, and the like.

EXHIBIT 19—6

SUPERIOR CORPORATION
WORKSHEET FOR STATEMENT OF CASH FLOWS (DIRECT METHOD)
FOR THE YEAR ENDED DECEMBER 31, 1994

Description	Changes in Noncash Accounts Debit	Credit	Analyzing Entries Debit	Credit
1			**4**	
Accounts Receivable		5,000		(2) 5,000
Inventory	14,000		(3) 14,000	
Prepaid Expenses	3,000		(3) 3,000	
Building and Equipment	85,000		(9) 65,000	(7) 10,000
			(10)* 30,000	
Accumulated Depreciation		7,000	(7) 6,000	(4) 13,000
Accounts Payable	10,000		(3) 10,000	
Interest Payable	2,000		(5) 2,000	
Income Tax Payable		1,000		(6) 1,000
Bonds Payable	80,000		(8) 80,000	
Common Stock		150,000		(10)* 30,000
				(11) 120,000
Retained Earnings		43,000	(8) 9,000	(1) 47,000
			(12) 11,000	(7) 16,000
2				
	194,000	206,000		
Increase in Cash	12,000			
	206,000	206,000		
3				
Cash Flows from Operating Activities				
Cash Received from Customers				
Sales			(1) 360,000	
Add: Accounts Receivable Decrease			(2) 5,000	
Cash Paid to Employees and Suppliers				
Employee and Supplier Expenses				(1) 291,000
Add: Combined changes in Inventory, Prepaid Expenses, and Accounts Payable				(3) 27,000
Less: Depreciation			(4) 13,000	
Cash Paid for Interest				
Interest Expense				(1) 10,000
Add: Interest Payable Decrease				(5) 2,000
Cash Paid for Income Taxes				
Income Tax Expense				(1) 12,000
Less: Income Tax Payable Increase			(6) 1,000	
Cash Flows from Investing Activities				
Sale of Equipment			(7) 20,000	
Purchase of Equipment				(9) 65,000
Cash Flows from Financing Activities				
Retirement of Bonds Payable				(8) 89,000
Issuance of Common Stock			(11) 120,000	
Payment of Dividends				(12) 11,000
			749,000	749,000
5				

- Cash paid for interest.
- Cash paid for income taxes.
- Cash paid for other operating activities, if any.[5]

---

[5] *Statement of Financial Accounting Standards No. 95*, "Statement of Cash Flows" (Stamford, CT: Financial Accounting Standards Board, 1987), par. 27.

We will use these categories when preparing the worksheet. Because accrual-basis revenues and expenses are the starting points for calculating the various operating cash flows under the direct method, we review the income statement to establish which of the minimum categories required by the FASB are present. At this point, we ignore any gains or losses that relate to investing or financing activities.

Superior has the following categories of operating cash receipts and payments:

■ *Cash received from customers*—this amount will be computed by starting with the sales revenue of $360,000.

■ *Cash paid to employees and suppliers*—this amount will be computed by starting with the $291,000 combined expenses of cost of goods sold, wages and other operating expenses, and depreciation expense (we label these combined expenses "employee and supplier expenses"). Generally, we combine all expenses other than interest expense and income tax expense to obtain the starting point for this category of operating cash outflow. *Note that noncash operating expenses such as depreciation, amortization, and depletion are included in this starting point; they will subsequently be eliminated.*

■ *Cash paid for interest*—this amount will be computed by starting with the $10,000 of interest expense.

■ *Cash paid for income taxes*—this amount will be computed by starting with the $12,000 of income tax expense.

Labels and spacing for these four categories of operating cash flows are entered on the worksheet. Next, the label "cash flows from investing activities" is written in the Description column. Several lines are skipped and the label "cash flows from financing activities" is entered in the column. The worksheet is now ready for the analyzing entries.

Analyzing Entries under the Direct Method

Analyzing entries **4** summarize, and explain, the changes that occurred in the non-cash accounts during the period. If the change affected cash flows, we enter the appropriate amount on the worksheet in the proper cash flow category. When all changes in noncash accounts have been explained, our analysis is complete.

Essentially, the analysis consists of two sets of analyzing entries. The initial set determines the various operating cash flows. The second set completes the analysis and identifies any investing or financing cash flows.

ANALYZING ENTRIES FOR OPERATING CASH FLOWS

1. The first analyzing entry places on the worksheet the revenue and expense amounts that are the starting points for calculating operating cash flows and also shows their net effect on retained earnings (because net income has been closed to Retained Earnings). Revenue amounts—the starting points for calculating cash inflows—are recorded in the Debit column; expense amounts—the starting points for calculating cash outflows—are recorded in the Credit column. The entry debits Sales for $360,000 under *cash received from customers*, credits Employee and Supplier Expenses for $291,000 under *cash paid to employees and suppliers*, credits Interest Expense for $10,000 under *cash paid for interest*, credits Income Tax Expense for $12,000 under *cash paid for income taxes*, and credits Retained Earnings for $47,000.

The remaining entries in this set reflect the adjustments needed to convert revenues and expenses to cash amounts. As discussed earlier, changes in accounts receivable, inventory, prepaid expenses, accounts payable, and accrued liabilities affect these conversions. Changes in these accounts are *added* to revenues or expenses if the change means that the cash flow exceeds the accrual amount; the changes are *deducted* if the change means that the cash flow is smaller than the accrual amount. We also must eliminate any noncash operating expenses such as depreciation, amortization, and depletion from accrual expenses; we accomplish this by deducting the noncash expense from the accrual expense amount. (These adjustments are summarized in Exhibit 19-3 on page 706.)

2. The $5,000 decrease in accounts receivable must be added to sales to obtain the cash received from customers. To accomplish this, entry 2 debits Accounts Receivable Decrease as an addition under *cash received from customers* and credits Accounts Receivable for $5,000.

3. Entry 3 reflects the impact of changes in inventory, prepaid expenses, and accounts payable in converting the combined expenses of $291,000 to a cash amount. Changes in all three accounts cause the related cash outflows to be larger than the accrual amounts. The entry debits Inventory for $14,000, debits Prepaid Expenses for $3,000, debits Accounts Payable for $10,000, and credits Combined Changes in Inventory, Prepaid Expenses, and Accounts Payable as an addition under *cash paid to employees and suppliers* for the combined effect of $27,000.

4. Entry 4 eliminates depreciation expense by debiting Depreciation as a deduction under *cash paid to employees and suppliers* and crediting Accumulated Depreciation for $13,000.

5. Entry 5 adjusts interest expense for the change in interest payable to derive the cash outflow for interest payments. The $2,000 decrease in interest payable is debited to Interest Payable and credited to Interest Payable Decrease as an addition under *cash paid for interest*.

6. Entry 6 adjusts income tax expense for the change in income tax payable to derive the cash outflow for income tax payments. The $1,000 increase in income tax payable is debited to Income Tax Payable Increase as a deduction under *cash paid for income taxes* and credited to Income Tax Payable.

ANALYZING ENTRIES TO COMPLETE THE ANALYSIS

The second set of analyzing entries explains the changes in the noncash balance sheet accounts that were not analyzed in determining the operating cash flows. This set of entries derives any cash flows from investing or financing activities and also identifies the noncash investing and financing transactions. We begin this set of entries by reconstructing on the worksheet the investing or financing transactions whose related gains or losses appear in the income statement. Superior Corporation has a $16,000 gain related to an investing transaction and a $9,000 loss related to a financing transaction.

7. Entry 7 reconstructs the entry for the sale of equipment at a gain. The transaction generated a cash inflow of $20,000, which is debited to Sale of Equipment under *cash flows from investing activities*. The $6,000 accumulated depreciation is debited to Accumulated Depreciation, the equipment's $10,000 cost is credited to Building and Equipment, and the $16,000 gain is credited to Retained Earnings (to reflect the impact of the gain on retained earnings).

8. Entry 8 reconstructs the entry for the retirement of bonds payable at a loss. The transaction caused a cash outflow of $89,000. The entry debits Bonds Payable for $80,000, debits Retained Earnings for $9,000 (to reflect the impact of the loss on retained earnings), and credits the $89,000 cash payment to Retirement of Bonds Payable under *cash flows from financing activities*.

At this point, we review each noncash balance sheet account whose change has not been fully explained by our previous analyzing entries and reconstruct the entries, in summary form, to explain these remaining changes. Any effects of these transactions on cash are entered in the worksheet's lower portion as either a cash inflow or a cash outflow. Cash inflows are entered as debits and cash outflows as credits. Not every analyzing entry will necessarily affect cash. An analyzing entry that does not affect cash, however, may reflect a noncash investing and financing transaction that must be separately disclosed. Analyzing entries 9–12 explain the remaining changes in the noncash balance sheet accounts.

9. The cash purchase of equipment for $65,000 was an investing transaction. Entry 9 debits $65,000 to Building and Equipment and credits $65,000 to Purchase of Equipment under *cash flows from investing activities*.

10. Entry 10 reconstructs the entry for the acquisition of equipment in exchange for common stock. The entry debits Building and Equipment and credits Common Stock for $30,000. This event is a noncash investing and financing transaction that must be disclosed in a supplementary schedule. We highlight the analyzing entry with an asterisk (*) to identify it as an event requiring special disclosure treatment.

11. The issuance of common stock for cash was a financing event that caused a $120,000 cash inflow. Entry 11 debits this $120,000 event to Issuance of Common Stock under *cash flows from financing activities* and credits Common Stock for $120,000.

12. The dividend of $11,000 declared and paid in 1994 was a financing event that reduced cash. Entry 12 reconstructs the effect of the dividend by debiting $11,000 to Retained Earnings and crediting the $11,000 outflow to Payment of Dividends under *cash flows from financing activities*.

For each noncash account, the debit or credit balance of the analyzing entries now equals the change shown in the first two columns. Our analysis is complete, and ▉5 we total and double rule the last two columns to complete the worksheet. *The analyzing entries help us compile information for a statement of cash flows; they are not recorded in the accounts.*

The worksheet classifies cash flows in the proper categories for the statement of cash flows. For each category of cash flow related to operating activities, the debit and credit entries are combined into a single amount. For Superior Corporation, Cash Received from Customers is $360,000 + $5,000 = $365,000; Cash Paid to Employees and Suppliers is $291,000 + $27,000 − $13,000 = $305,000; Cash Paid for Interest is $10,000 + $2,000 = $12,000; and Cash Paid for Income Taxes is $12,000 − $1,000 = $11,000.

Exhibit 19-7 shows the statement of cash flows for Superior Corporation, along with the required separate disclosures. The reconciliation of net income to net cash flow from operating activities is discussed later in the chapter (it is the indirect method). As shown by the asterisks on the worksheet, Superior Corporation has one noncash investing and financing transaction, and it is separately disclosed. The firm has no short-term investments, so separate disclosure of a policy for determining cash equivalents is not needed.

PREPARING THE STATEMENT OF CASH FLOWS UNDER THE INDIRECT METHOD

OBJECTIVE ④ DISCUSS *the preparation of a statement of cash flows using the indirect method.*

To prepare a statement of cash flows, we need a firm's income statement, comparative balance sheets, and some additional data taken from the accounting records. Exhibit 19-8 presents this information for Bennett Company. We will use these data to prepare Bennett's 1994 statement of cash flows using the indirect method.

Bennett's statement of cash flows will explain the $25,000 increase in cash that occurred during 1994 (from $10,000 to $35,000) by classifying the firm's cash flows into operating, investing, and financing categories. To get the information to construct the statement, therefore, we do the following:

1. *Use the indirect method to determine the net cash flow from operating activities.* In doing this, we will apply a series of adjustments to the firm's net income. The adjustments include changes in various current asset and current liability accounts.

2. *Determine cash flows from investing activities.* We will do this by analyzing changes in the noncash asset accounts not used in the indirect method.

3. *Determine cash flows from financing activities.* We will do this by analyzing changes in the liability and stockholders' equity accounts not used in the indirect method.

EXHIBIT 19—7	STATEMENT OF CASH FLOWS UNDER THE DIRECT METHOD WITH SUPPLEMENTARY DISCLOSURES

SUPERIOR CORPORATION
STATEMENT OF CASH FLOWS
FOR THE YEAR ENDED DECEMBER 31, 1994

Cash Flows from Operating Activities

Cash Received from Customers		$365,000
Cash Paid to Employees and Suppliers	$305,000	
Cash Paid for Interest	12,000	
Cash Paid for Income Taxes	11,000	328,000
Net Cash Provided by Operating Activities		$ 37,000

Cash Flows from Investing Activities

Sale of Equipment	$ 20,000	
Purchase of Equipment	(65,000)	
Net Cash Used by Investing Activities		(45,000)

Cash Flows from Financing Activities

Issuance of Common Stock	$120,000	
Retirement of Bonds Payable	(89,000)	
Payment of Dividends	(11,000)	
Net Cash Provided by Financing Activities		20,000
Net Increase in Cash		$ 12,000
Cash at Beginning of Year		13,000
Cash at End of Year		$ 25,000

Reconciliation of Net Income to Net Cash Flow from Operating Activities

Net Income	$54,000
Add (Deduct) Items to Convert Net Income to Cash Basis:	
Depreciation	13,000
Gain on Sale of Equipment	(16,000)
Loss on Bond Retirement	9,000
Accounts Receivable Decrease	5,000
Inventory Increase	(14,000)
Prepaid Expenses Increase	(3,000)
Accounts Payable Decrease	(10,000)
Interest Payable Decrease	(2,000)
Income Tax Payable Increase	1,000
Net Cash Provided by Operating Activities	$37,000

Schedule of Noncash Investing and Financing Activities

Issuance of Common Stock to Acquire Equipment	$30,000

Net Cash Flow from Operating Activities under the Indirect Method

The **indirect method** presents the net cash flow from operating activities by applying a series of adjustments to net income to convert it to a cash-basis amount. We will now explain and illustrate the adjustments to convert Bennett Company's 1994 net income to a corresponding net cash flow from operating activities.

CONVERT NET INCOME TO CASH BASIS AMOUNT

DEPRECIATION, AMORTIZATION, AND DEPLETION EXPENSES Depreciation, amortization, and depletion expenses are expenses that represent write-offs of previously recorded assets and are, therefore, totally noncash expenses. One type of adjustment to net income under the indirect method is to add noncash expenses. Thus, any depreciation, amortization, or depletion expenses are added to net income. Bennett Company had $10,000 of depreciation expense in 1994, so this amount is added to Bennett's net income.

EXHIBIT 19—8	FINANCIAL DATA OF BENNETT COMPANY

BENNETT COMPANY
INCOME STATEMENT
FOR THE YEAR ENDED DECEMBER 31, 1994

Sales		$250,000
Cost of Goods Sold	$140,000	
Wages Expense	52,000	
Insurance Expense	5,000	
Depreciation Expense	10,000	
Income Tax Expense	11,000	
Total Expenses		218,000
Net Income		$ 32,000

Additional Data for 1994

1. Purchased long-term stock investments and equipment for cash.
2. All accounts payable relate to merchandise purchases.
3. Issued common stock at par for cash.
4. Declared and paid cash dividends of $13,000.

BENNETT COMPANY
BALANCE SHEETS

	Dec. 31, 1994	Dec. 31, 1993
Assets		
Cash	$ 35,000	$ 10,000
Accounts Receivable	39,000	34,000
Inventory	54,000	60,000
Prepaid Insurance	17,000	4,000
Long-term Investments	5,000	—
Plant Assets	250,000	200,000
Accumulated Depreciation	(50,000)	(40,000)
Total Assets	$350,000	$268,000
Liabilities and Stockholders' Equity		
Accounts Payable	$ 10,000	$ 19,000
Income Tax Payable	5,000	3,000
Common Stock	260,000	190,000
Retained Earnings	75,000	56,000
Total Liabilities and Stockholders' Equity	$350,000	$268,000

GAINS AND LOSSES RELATED TO INVESTING AND FINANCING ACTIVITIES The income statement may contain gains and losses related to investing and financing activities. Examples include gains and losses from the sale of investments and plant assets and gains and losses from the retirement of bonds payable before maturity. Because these gains and losses are not related to operating activities, we eliminate their impact on net income as we convert net income to a net cash flow from operating activities. To eliminate their impact on net income, gains are subtracted and losses are added to net income.

Bennett Company had no 1994 gains and losses related to investing and financing activities. The worksheet illustration later in the chapter and the demonstration problems at the end of the chapter contain examples of such gains or losses.

ACCOUNTS RECEIVABLE CHANGE A decrease in accounts receivable during a year means that cash collections on account exceeded sales on account; an increase in accounts receivable means that sales on account exceeded cash collections. An accounts receivable decrease is added to net income, and an accounts receivable increase is subtracted from net income as we convert net income to a cash basis amount. Bennett's accounts receivable increased $5,000 during 1994, so this increase is subtracted from net income under the indirect method.

INVENTORY CHANGE A decrease in inventory during a period means that the cost of merchandise purchased was less than the cost of goods sold. An inventory decrease, therefore, is added to net income under the indirect method because the cost of purchases is more closely related to cash outflows than the cost of goods sold. (Any variation between the cost of purchases and the cash paid for purchases is handled with a later adjustment for the change in accounts payable.) An inventory increase means that purchases exceeded the cost of goods sold; the adjustment in this case is to subtract the inventory increase from net income. Bennett's inventory decreased $6,000 during 1994, so this decrease is added to net income.

PREPAID EXPENSES CHANGE   The indirect method adds a decrease in prepaid expenses to net income because a decrease means that the cash prepayment during the year was less than the related expense amount. Similarly, an increase in prepaid expenses is subtracted from net income because an increase means that the cash prepayment during the year was more than the related expense amount. Bennett's prepaid insurance increased $13,000 during 1994, so this increase is deducted from net income.

ACCOUNTS PAYABLE CHANGE   A decrease in accounts payable during a year means that cash payments for purchases were more than the cost of purchases. An accounts payable decrease, therefore, is subtracted from net income under the indirect method. In contrast, an increase in accounts payable means that cash payments for purchases were less than the cost of purchases during the period, so an accounts payable increase is added to net income. Bennett's 1994 decrease of $9,000 in accounts payable will be subtracted from its net income.

ACCRUED LIABILITIES CHANGE   Changes in accrued liabilities are interpreted the same way as changes in accounts payable. A decrease means that cash payments exceeded the related expense amount; an increase means that cash payments were less than the related expense amount. Decreases are subtracted from net income; increases are added to net income. Bennett has one accrued liability, Income Tax Payable, and it increased by $2,000 during 1994. The $2,000 increase will be added to net income.

We have now identified the proper adjustments to convert Bennett's net income to its net cash flow from operating activities. The operating activities section of the statement of cash flows will appear as follows under the indirect method:

Net Income	$32,000
Add (Deduct) Items to Convert Net Income to Cash Basis:	
Depreciation	10,000
Accounts Receivable Increase	(5,000)
Inventory Decrease	6,000
Prepaid Insurance Increase	(13,000)
Accounts Payable Decrease	(9,000)
Income Tax Payable Increase	2,000
Net Cash Provided by Operating Activities	$23,000

If there is a net loss for the period, the indirect method begins with the net loss. It is possible, of course, for the net amount of add-backs to exceed the loss so that there is a positive net cash flow from operating activities even when there is an accrual-basis net loss.

Exhibit 19-9 summarizes the adjustments to convert net income to a corresponding net cash flow from operating activities. Note that all current asset changes are handled the same way (add decreases and subtract increases) and all current liability changes are handled the same way (add increases and subtract decreases).

Cash Flows from Investing Activities

ANALYZE CHANGES IN REMAINING NONCASH ASSET ACCOUNTS

Investing activities cause changes in asset accounts. Usually the accounts affected other than cash are noncurrent asset accounts such as plant assets and long-term investments, although short-term investment accounts may also be affected. To determine the cash flows from investing activities, we analyze the changes in all noncash asset accounts not used in computing the net cash flow from operating activities. Our objective is to identify any investing cash flows related to these changes. Related contra asset accounts should also be analyzed.

ANALYZE CHANGE IN LONG-TERM INVESTMENTS   Bennett's comparative balance sheets show that long-term investments increased $5,000 during 1994. The increase means

> **EXHIBIT 19—9**   INDIRECT METHOD CONVERSION SCHEDULE:
> ADJUSTMENTS TO CONVERT NET INCOME TO NET CASH
> FLOW FROM OPERATING ACTIVITIES
>
> | **Add to Net Income** | **Deduct from Net Income** |
> |---|---|
> | Depreciation Expense | |
> | Amortization Expense | |
> | Depletion Expense | |
> | Losses (investing/financing) | Gains (investing/financing) |
> | Decrease in Accounts Receivable | Increase in Accounts Receivable |
> | Decrease in Inventory | Increase in Inventory |
> | Decrease in Prepaid Expenses | Increase in Prepaid Expenses |
> | Increase in Accounts Payable | Decrease in Accounts Payable |
> | Increase in Accrued Liabilities | Decrease in Accrued Liabilities |

that investments must have been purchased, and the additional data indicates that cash was spent to purchase long-term stock investments. Purchasing stock is an investing activity. Thus, a $5,000 purchase of stock investments will be shown as a cash outflow from investing activities in the statement of cash flows.

ANALYZE CHANGE IN PLANT ASSETS   Bennett's plant assets increased $50,000 during 1994. Plant assets increase as the result of purchases, and the additional data for Bennett Company indicate that equipment was purchased for cash in 1994. Purchasing equipment is an investing activity. Thus, a $50,000 purchase of equipment will be shown as a cash outflow from investing activities in the statement of cash flows.

ANALYZE CHANGE IN ACCUMULATED DEPRECIATION   Bennett's accumulated depreciation increased $10,000 during 1994. Accumulated depreciation increases when depreciation expense is recorded. Bennett's 1994 depreciation expense was $10,000, so the total change in accumulated depreciation is the result of the recording of depreciation expense. As previously discussed, there is no cash flow related to the recording of depreciation expense.

Cash Flows from Financing Activities

ANALYZE CHANGES IN REMAINING LIABILITY AND STOCKHOLDERS' EQUITY ACCOUNTS

Financing activities cause changes in liability and stockholders' equity accounts. Usually the accounts affected are noncurrent accounts such as bonds payable and common stock, although a current liability such as short-term notes payable may also be affected. To determine the cash flows from financing activities, we analyze the changes in all liability and stockholders' equity accounts that were not used in computing the net cash flow from operating activities. Our objective is to identify any financing cash flows related to these changes.

ANALYZE CHANGE IN COMMON STOCK   Bennett's common stock increased $70,000 during 1994. Common stock increases when shares of stock are issued, and the additional data show that shares were issued for cash during 1994. Issuing common stock is a financing activity. A $70,000 issuance of common stock, therefore, will appear as a cash inflow from financing activities in the statement of cash flows.

ANALYZE CHANGE IN RETAINED EARNINGS   Retained earnings grew from $56,000 to $75,000 during 1994—a $19,000 increase. This increase is the net result of Bennett's

$32,000 of net income (which increased retained earnings) and a $13,000 cash dividend (which decreased retained earnings). Because every item in Bennett's income statement was considered in computing the net cash provided by operating activities, only the cash dividend remains to be considered at this point. Paying a cash dividend is a financing activity. Thus, a $13,000 cash dividend will show as a cash outflow from financing activities in the statement of cash flows.

We have now completed the analysis of all of Bennett's noncash balance sheet accounts and can prepare the 1994 statement of cash flows. Exhibit 19-10 shows this statement.

If there are cash inflows and outflows from similar types of investing and financing activities, the inflows and outflows are reported separately (rather than reporting only the net difference). For example, proceeds from the sale of plant assets are reported separately from outlays made to acquire plant assets. Similarly, funds borrowed are reported separately from debt repayments, and proceeds from issuing stock are reported separately from outlays to acquire treasury stock.

SEPARATE DISCLOSURES UNDER THE INDIRECT METHOD

When the indirect method is used in the statement of cash flows, three separate disclosures are required: (1) two specific operating cash outflows—cash paid for interest and cash paid for income taxes, (2) a schedule or description of all noncash investing and financing transactions, and (3) the firm's policy for determining which highly liquid, short-term investments are treated as cash equivalents.

EXHIBIT 19—10	STATEMENT OF CASH FLOWS UNDER THE INDIRECT METHOD

BENNETT COMPANY
STATEMENT OF CASH FLOWS
FOR THE YEAR ENDED DECEMBER 31, 1994

Net Cash Flow from Operating Activities		
Net Income	$ 32,000	
Add (Deduct) Items to Convert Net Income to Cash Basis:		
Depreciation	10,000	
Accounts Receivable Increase	(5,000)	
Inventory Decrease	6,000	
Prepaid Insurance Increase	(13,000)	
Accounts Payable Decrease	(9,000)	
Income Tax Payable Increase	2,000	
Net Cash Provided by Operating Activities		$ 23,000
Cash Flows from Investing Activities		
Purchase of Stock Investments	($ 5,000)	
Purchase of Equipment	(50,000)	
Net Cash Used by Investing Activities		(55,000)
Cash Flows from Financing Activities		
Issuance of Common Stock	$ 70,000	
Payment of Dividends	(13,000)	
Net Cash Provided by Financing Activities		57,000
Net Increase in Cash		$ 25,000
Cash at Beginning of Year		10,000
Cash at End of Year		$ 35,000

WORKSHEET FOR PREPARING THE STATEMENT OF CASH FLOWS UNDER THE INDIRECT METHOD

OBJECTIVE **⑤** ILLUSTRATE *a worksheet approach to preparing a statement of cash flows using the indirect method.*

A worksheet may be helpful in constructing a statement of cash flows. A cash flow worksheet is designed to analyze the changes in all the noncash balance sheet accounts and identify the period's cash flows by type of activity. We review all noncash balance sheet accounts for two reasons:

1. Because of the basic accounting equation (Assets = Liabilities + Owners' Equity), the net change in cash during a period must equal the net change in all other balance sheet accounts. By analyzing the changes in all noncash balance sheet accounts, we will be able to identify all events affecting cash flows.

2. A required disclosure accompanying the statement of cash flows is a presentation of all noncash investing and financing activities. A review of all noncash balance sheet accounts will permit us to identify these events also.

To illustrate the use of a worksheet, we use the financial data of Superior Corporation shown in Exhibit 19-11. As the comparative balance sheets show, Superior's cash increased $12,000 during 1994. This is the change that will be explained by the 1994 statement of cash flows.

Exhibit 19-12 shows the worksheet for Superior Corporation under the indirect method. Note that the worksheet has a Description column and four amount columns. Each of the two headings, Changes in Noncash Accounts and Analyzing Entries, has a Debit and a Credit column.

EXHIBIT 19—11	**FINANCIAL DATA OF SUPERIOR CORPORATION**

SUPERIOR CORPORATION
INCOME STATEMENT
FOR THE YEAR ENDED DECEMBER 31, 1994

Sales		$360,000
Cost of Goods Sold	$200,000	
Wages and Other Operating Expenses	78,000	
Depreciation Expense	13,000	
Interest Expense	10,000	
Income Tax Expense	12,000	
Gain on Sale of Equipment	(16,000)	
Loss on Bond Retirement*	9,000	306,000
Net Income		$ 54,000

Additional Data for 1994

1. Sold equipment having a book value of $4,000 ($10,000 cost – $6,000 accumulated depreciation) for $20,000 cash.
2. Purchased new equipment for $65,000 cash.
3. Retired $80,000 of bonds payable for $89,000 cash.
4. Acquired equipment worth $30,000 by issuing 3,000 shares of common stock.
5. Issued additional common stock at par for $120,000 cash.
6. Declared and paid cash dividends of $11,000.

SUPERIOR CORPORATION
BALANCE SHEETS

Assets	Dec. 31, 1994	Dec. 31, 1993	Increase (Decrease)
Current Assets			
Cash	$ 25,000	$ 13,000	$ 12,000
Accounts Receivable (Net)	55,000	60,000	(5,000)
Inventory	94,000	80,000	14,000
Prepaid Expenses	13,000	10,000	3,000
Total Current Assets	$187,000	$163,000	$ 24,000
Plant Assets			
Building and Equipment	$418,000	$333,000	$ 85,000
Accumulated Depreciation	(75,000)	(68,000)	7,000
Total Plant Assets	$343,000	$265,000	$ 78,000
Total Assets	$530,000	$428,000	$102,000
Liabilities and Stockholders' Equity			
Current Liabilities			
Accounts Payable	$ 32,000	$ 42,000	($ 10,000)
Interest Payable	1,000	3,000	(2,000)
Income Tax Payable	2,000	1,000	1,000
Total Current Liabilities	$ 35,000	$ 46,000	($ 11,000)
Long-term Debt			
Bonds Payable	$ 40,000	$120,000	($ 80,000)
Stockholders' Equity			
Common Stock ($10 par value)	$350,000	$200,000	$150,000
Retained Earnings	105,000	62,000	43,000
Total Stockholders' Equity	$455,000	$262,000	$193,000
Total Liabilities and Stockholders' Equity	$530,000	$428,000	$102,000

* If material, this loss is extraordinary. Separate disclosure of cash flows relating to extraordinary items is not required. For simplicity, a separate extraordinary section is not used here.

EXHIBIT 19—12

SUPERIOR CORPORATION
WORKSHEET FOR STATEMENT OF CASH FLOWS (INDIRECT METHOD)
FOR THE YEAR ENDED DECEMBER 31, 1994

Description	Changes in Noncash Accounts		Analyzing Entries	
	Debit	Credit	Debit	Credit
1 Accounts Receivable		5,000	**4**	(5) 5,000
Inventory	14,000		(6) 14,000	
Prepaid Expenses	3,000		(7) 3,000	
Building and Equipment	85,000		(11) 65,000	(3) 10,000
			(12)* 30,000	
Accumulated Depreciation		7,000	(3) 6,000	(2) 13,000
Accounts Payable	10,000		(8) 10,000	
Interest Payable	2,000		(9) 2,000	
Income Tax Payable		1,000		(10) 1,000
Bonds Payable	80,000		(4) 80,000	
Common Stock		150,000		(12)* 30,000
				(13) 120,000
Retained Earnings		43,000	(14) 11,000	(1) 54,000
2				
	194,000	206,000		
Increase in Cash	12,000			
	206,000	206,000		

3

Net Cash Flow from Operating Activities

Net Income			(1) 54,000	
Add: Depreciation			(2) 13,000	
Less: Gain on Sale of Equipment				(3) 16,000
Add: Loss on Bond Retirement			(4) 9,000	
Add: Accounts Receivable Decrease			(5) 5,000	
Less: Inventory Increase				(6) 14,000
Less: Prepaid Expenses Increase				(7) 3,000
Less: Accounts Payable Decrease				(8) 10,000
Less: Interest Payable Decrease				(9) 2,000
Add: Income Tax Payable Increase			(10) 1,000	

Cash Flows from Investing Activities

Sale of Equipment			(3) 20,000	
Purchase of Equipment				(11) 65,000

Cash Flows from Financing Activities

Retirement of Bonds Payable				(4) 89,000
Issuance of Common Stock			(13) 120,000	
Payment of Dividends				(14) 11,000
			443,000	443,000

5

Changes in Noncash Balance Sheet Accounts

The content of the worksheet focuses on the company's noncash balance sheet accounts.

1 First, a list of all noncash balance sheet accounts is entered in the Description column. Then the debit or credit change in each account balance for the period is entered in the appropriate column under the Changes in Noncash Accounts heading. If an account increased, the amount of the increase is shown in the column representing the side of the account where increases are recorded. If an account decreased, the amount of the decrease is shown in the column representing the side of the account where decreases are recorded.

2 After the changes for all noncash balance sheet accounts are entered, the two columns are totaled. The difference between the column totals equals the change in cash for the year. The cash change is entered on the worksheet— an increase in the Debit column, a decrease in the Credit column—and the two columns are totaled and double ruled to show their equality. Exhibit 19-12 shows the $12,000 cash increase for Superior Corporation in the Debit column.

3 At this point, the label "net cash flow from operating activities" is written in the Description column. Several lines are skipped to allow for the determination of the net cash flow from operating activities. Next, the label "cash flows from investing activities" is written in the Description column. Several lines are skipped and the label "cash flows from financing activities" is entered in the column. The worksheet is now ready for the analyzing entries.

Analyzing Entries under the Indirect Method

Analyzing entries **4** summarize, and explain, the changes that occurred in the noncash accounts during the period. If the change affected cash flows, we enter the appropriate amount on the worksheet in the proper cash flow category. When all changes in noncash accounts have been explained, our analysis is complete.

The analysis consists of two sets of analyzing entries. The initial set determines the net cash flow from operating activities using the indirect method. The second set completes the analysis and identifies any investing or financing cash flows.

ANALYZING ENTRIES TO COMPUTE NET CASH FLOW FROM OPERATING ACTIVITIES

1. The first analyzing entry establishes the starting point for computing the net cash flow from operating activities: accrual-basis net income or net loss. If there is net income, it is recorded in the Debit column; a net loss would be recorded in the Credit column. On the worksheet, Superior Corporation's $54,000 net income is debited to Net Income under *net cash flow from operating activities* and credited to Retained Earnings.

The remaining entries in this set reflect the adjustments needed to convert net income to a cash amount. These adjustments are summarized in Exhibit 19-9 on page 717. When these adjustments reflect gains and losses related to investing or financing activities, the analyzing entry will present the entire transaction. As a result, some investing and financing cash flows may be identified in this set of analyzing entries.

2. Entry 2 adds depreciation expense to net income (thus eliminating its effect on net income). The entry debits $13,000 to Depreciation as an addition under *net cash flow from operating activities* and credits $13,000 to Accumulated Depreciation.

3. Entry 3 eliminates the effect of the gain on sale of equipment from net income (and, therefore, from the net operating cash flow). The equipment sale was an investing event resulting in a $20,000 cash inflow. The entry debits $20,000 to Sale of Equipment under *cash flows from investing activities*, debits the equipment's $6,000 of accumulated depreciation to Accumulated Depreciation, credits the equipment's $10,000 cost to Building and Equipment, and credits the $16,000 gain to Gain on Sale of Equipment as a deduction under *net cash flow from operating activities* (to eliminate the effect of the gain on net income).

4. Entry 4 eliminates the effect of the loss on bond retirement from net income (and, therefore, from the net operating cash flow). The bond retirement was a financing event resulting in an $89,000 cash outflow. The entry debits Bonds Payable for $80,000, debits Loss on Bond Retirement for $9,000 as an addition under *net cash flow from operating activities* (to eliminate the effect of the loss on net income), and credits Retirement of Bonds Payable for $89,000 under *cash flows from financing activities*.

5. Entry 5 adds the decrease in accounts receivable to net income. The entry debits Accounts Receivable Decrease as an addition under *net cash flow from operating activities* and credits Accounts Receivable for $5,000.

6. Entry 6 subtracts the inventory increase from net income by debiting Inventory and crediting Inventory Increase as a deduction under *net cash flow from operating activities* for $14,000.

7. Entry 7 subtracts the increase in prepaid expenses from net income by debiting Prepaid Expenses and crediting Prepaid Expenses Increase as a deduction under *net cash flow from operating activities* for $3,000.

8. Entry 8 subtracts the decrease in accounts payable from net income with a debit of $10,000 to Accounts Payable and a credit of $10,000 to Accounts Payable Decrease as a deduction under *net cash flow from operating activities*.

9. Entry 9 subtracts the decrease in interest payable from net income with a $2,000 debit to Interest Payable and a $2,000 credit to Interest Payable Decrease as a deduction under *net cash flow from operating activities*.

10. Entry 10 adds the increase in income tax payable to net income by debiting Income Tax Payable Increase as an addition under *net cash flow from operating activities* and crediting Income Tax Payable for $1,000.

ANALYZING ENTRIES TO COMPLETE THE ANALYSIS

At this point, we review each noncash balance sheet account whose change has not been fully explained by our previous analyzing entries and reconstruct the entries, in summary form, to explain these remaining changes. Any effects of these transactions on cash are entered in the worksheet's lower portion as either a cash inflow (entered as a debit) or a cash outflow (entered as a credit). Not every analyzing entry necessarily affects cash. An analyzing entry that does not affect cash, however, may reflect a noncash investing and financing transaction that must be separately disclosed. Analyzing entries 11–14 explain the remaining changes in the noncash balance sheet accounts.

11. The $65,000 cash purchase of equipment was an investing transaction. Entry 11 debits $65,000 to Building and Equipment and credits $65,000 to Purchase of Equipment under *cash flows from investing activities*.

12. Entry 12 reconstructs the entry for the acquisition of equipment in exchange for common stock. The entry debits Building and Equipment and credits Common Stock for $30,000. This event is a noncash investing and financing transaction that must be disclosed in a supplementary schedule. We highlight the analyzing entry with an asterisk (*) to identify it as an event requiring special disclosure treatment.

13. The issuance of common stock for cash was a financing activity that caused a $120,000 cash inflow. Entry 13 analyzes this event with a $120,000 debit to Issuance of Common Stock under *cash flows from financing activities* and a $120,000 credit to Common Stock.

14. The dividend of $11,000 declared and paid in 1994 was a financing event that reduced cash. Entry 14 reconstructs the effect of the dividend by debiting $11,000 to Retained Earnings and crediting the $11,000 outflow to Payment of Dividends under *cash flows from financing activities*.

For each noncash account, the debit or credit balance of the analyzing entries now equals the change shown in the first two columns. Our analysis is complete, and **5** we total and double rule the last two columns to complete the worksheet. The analyzing entries help us compile information for a statement of cash flows; they are not recorded in the accounts.

Exhibit 19-13 shows the statement of cash flows for Superior Corporation, along with the required separate disclosures. As shown by the asterisks on the worksheet, Superior Corporation has one noncash investing and financing transaction, and it is separately disclosed. The firm has no short-term investments, so separate disclosure of a policy for determining cash equivalents is not needed.

| EXHIBIT 19—13 | STATEMENT OF CASH FLOWS UNDER THE INDIRECT METHOD WITH SUPPLEMENTARY DISCLOSURES |

SUPERIOR CORPORATION
STATEMENT OF CASH FLOWS
FOR THE YEAR ENDED DECEMBER 31, 1994

Net Cash Flow from Operating Activities

Net Income	$ 54,000	
Add (Deduct) Items to Convert Net Income to Cash Basis:		
Depreciation	13,000	
Gain on Sale of Equipment	(16,000)	
Loss on Bond Retirement	9,000	
Accounts Receivable Decrease	5,000	
Inventory Increase	(14,000)	
Prepaid Expenses Increase	(3,000)	
Accounts Payable Decrease	(10,000)	
Interest Payable Decrease	(2,000)	
Income Tax Payable Increase	1,000	
Net Cash Provided by Operating Activities		$37,000
Cash Flows from Investing Activities		
Sale of Equipment	$ 20,000	
Purchase of Equipment	(65,000)	
Net Cash Used by Investing Activities		(45,000)
Cash Flows from Financing Activities		
Issuance of Common Stock	$120,000	
Retirement of Bonds Payable	(89,000)	
Payment of Dividends	(11,000)	
Net Cash Provided by Financing Activities		20,000
Net Increase in Cash		$12,000
Cash at Beginning of Year		13,000
Cash at End of Year		$25,000
Supplemental Cash Flow Disclosures		
Cash Paid for Interest		$12,000
Cash Paid for Income Taxes		11,000
Schedule of Noncash Investing and Financing Activities		
Issuance of Common Stock to Acquire Equipment		$30,000

The separate disclosure of cash paid for interest is computed by adjusting interest expense for the change during the year in interest payable. Superior Corporation's 1994 cash paid for interest is $12,000 ($10,000 + $2,000). Cash paid for income taxes is computed by adjusting income tax expense for the change during the year in income tax payable. Superior Corporation's 1994 cash paid for income taxes is $11,000 ($12,000 − $1,000).

ANALYTICAL APPLICATION

DIVIDEND PAYOUT RATIO

OBJECTIVE 6 **DEFINE divi-dend payout ratio *and ex-plain its use.***

Some investors in common stocks are interested primarily in possible future growth of the stock's market price, whereas other investors focus on the amount of annual dividends that may be received. Investors in the latter group are interested in a corporation's dividend payout ratio. The **dividend payout ratio** is the percentage of earnings available to common stockholders that is paid out as dividends. The ratio is computed as follows:

$$\text{Dividend Payout Ratio} = \frac{\text{Annual Dividends per Share}}{\text{Earnings per Share}}$$

Dividend payout ratios vary considerably among corporations. Companies that are considered "growth" companies often have low payout ratios because they use the assets generated by earnings to help finance their expansion. In contrast, utilities often distribute a high percentage of their earnings as dividends. Utilities generally do much of their financing with long-term debt and, thus, have less need to utilize assets generated by earnings to finance their activities.

Some corporations try to maintain a reasonably constant dividend payout ratio, so their payout ratios do not vary much from one year to the next. Other corporations try to keep the per-share dividend amount either constant or increasing each year at a constant rate. If net income fluctuates quite a bit from year to year, these latter corporations will show dividend payout ratios that are quite variable through time.

Following are the dividend payout ratios of several corporations for a recent year.

ATMOS ENERGY CORPORATION (natural gas service)	78.9%
ENRON CORP. (natural gas and liquid fuels transmission and marketing)	70.5%
TRANSAMERICA CORPORATION (financial services)	59.0%
GANNET CO., INC. (newspaper publishing)	51.3%
GEORGIA-PACIFIC CORPORATION (pulp, paper, and building products)	37.4%
H. B. FULLER COMPANY (specialty chemical products)	25.9%

KEY POINTS FOR CHAPTER OBJECTIVES

❶ PROVIDE a basis for understanding a statement of cash flows (pp. 698–702).
■ A statement of cash flows explains the net increase or decrease in cash and cash equivalents during the period.
■ A statement of cash flows separates cash flows into operating, investing, and financing categories.
■ A secondary objective of cash flow reporting is to provide information about a firm's investing and financing activities. A required supplemental disclosure reports noncash investing and financing activities.
■ A statement of cash flows should help users compare, evaluate, and predict a firm's cash flows and also help evaluate its financial flexibility.

❷ DISCUSS the preparation of a statement of cash flows using the direct method (pp. 702–708).
■ The direct method shows the major categories of operating cash receipts and payments.
■ The FASB encourages use of the direct method but permits use of either the direct or the indirect method.
■ A firm using the direct method must separately disclose the reconciliation of net income to net cash flow from operating activities.

❸ ILLUSTRATE a worksheet approach to preparing a statement of cash flows using the direct method (pp. 708–713, 714).
■ The worksheet contains entries analyzing the changes in all noncash balance sheet accounts to determine their effects, if any, on cash flows. The analyzing entries that determine operating cash flows convert operating revenues and expenses to the related cash amounts.
■ The worksheet also identifies noncash investing and financing transactions.

❹ DISCUSS the preparation of a statement of cash flows using the indirect method (pp. 713–718).
■ The indirect method reconciles net income to net cash flow from operating activities.
■ A firm using the indirect method must separately disclose the cash paid for interest and the cash paid for income taxes.

❺ ILLUSTRATE a worksheet approach to preparing a statement of cash flows using the indirect method (pp. 719–723).
■ The worksheet contains entries analyzing the changes in all noncash balance sheet accounts to determine their effects, if any, on cash flows. The analyzing entries that relate to cash

flow from operating activities reconcile net income to net cash flow from operating activities.
- The worksheet also identifies noncash investing and financing transactions.

6 ANALYTICAL APPLICATION: DEFINE *dividend payout ratio* and EXPLAIN its use (pp. 723–724).
- The dividend payout ratio is computed by dividing the annual dividends per share by the earnings per share.

SELF-TEST QUESTIONS FOR REVIEW

(Answers follow Solution to Demonstration Problem 2).

1. Which of the following is not disclosed in a statement of cash flows?
   a. A transfer of cash to a cash equivalent investment.
   b. The amount of cash on hand at year-end.
   c. Cash outflows from investing activities during the period.
   d. Cash inflows from financing activities during the period.

2. Which of the following events will appear in the cash flows from financing activities section of the statement of cash flows?
   a. Cash purchase of equipment.
   b. Cash purchase of bonds issued by another company.
   c. Cash received as repayment for funds loaned.
   d. Cash purchase of treasury stock.

3. Which of the following methods will disclose the cash received from customers in the statement of cash flows?
   a. Indirect method.
   b. Reconciliation method.
   c. Direct method.
   d. Both direct and indirect methods.

4. Tyler Company has a net income of $49,000 and the following related items:

Depreciation expense	$ 5,000
Accounts receivable increase	2,000
Inventory decrease	10,000
Accounts payable decrease	4,000

   Using the indirect method, what is Tyler's net cash flow from operations?
   a. $42,000   b. $46,000   c. $58,000   d. $38,000

5. A worksheet for a statement of cash flows analyzes the changes in
   a. Each of the firm's bank accounts.
   b. All of the firm's noncash balance sheet accounts.
   c. The firm's working capital accounts only.
   d. The firm's noncurrent balance sheet accounts only.

DEMONSTRATION PROBLEM 1 FOR REVIEW: THE DIRECT METHOD

Terry Company's 1994 income statement and comparative balance sheets at December 31, 1994 and 1993, are as follows:

TERRY COMPANY
INCOME STATEMENT
FOR THE YEAR ENDED DECEMBER 31, 1994

Sales		$385,000
Dividend Income		5,000
		$390,000
Cost of Goods Sold	$233,000	
Wages Expense	82,000	
Advertising Expense	10,000	
Depreciation Expense	11,000	
Income Tax Expense	17,000	
Loss on Sale of Investments	2,000	355,000
Net Income		$ 35,000

TERRY COMPANY
BALANCE SHEETS

Assets	Dec. 31, 1994	Dec. 31, 1993
Cash	$ 8,000	$ 12,000
Accounts Receivable	22,000	28,000
Inventory	94,000	66,000
Prepaid Advertising	12,000	9,000
Long-term Investments	30,000	41,000
Plant Assets	178,000	130,000
Accumulated Depreciation	(72,000)	(61,000)
Total Assets	$272,000	$225,000

Liabilities and Stockholders' Equity		
Accounts Payable	$ 27,000	$ 14,000
Wages Payable	6,000	2,500
Income Tax Payable	3,000	4,500
Common Stock	139,000	125,000
Retained Earnings	97,000	79,000
Total Liabilities and Stockholders' Equity	$272,000	$225,000

Cash dividends of $17,000 were declared and paid during 1994. Plant assets were purchased for cash, and, later in the year, additional common stock was issued for cash. Investments costing $11,000 were sold for cash at a $2,000 loss.

REQUIRED

a. Compute the change in cash that occurred during 1994.

b. Prepare a 1994 statement of cash flows using the direct method.

SOLUTION TO DEMONSTRATION PROBLEM 1

a. $8,000 ending balance − $12,000 beginning balance = $4,000 decrease in cash

b. 1. Use the direct method to determine the individual cash flows from operating activities.

- $385,000 Sales + $6,000 Accounts Receivable decrease = $391,000 Cash Received from Customers
- $5,000 Dividend Income = $5,000 Cash Received as Dividends
- $233,000 Cost of Goods Sold + $28,000 Inventory increase − $13,000 Accounts Payable increase = $248,000 Cash Paid for Merchandise Purchased
- $82,000 Wages Expense − $3,500 Wages Payable increase = $78,500 Cash Paid to Employees
- $10,000 Advertising Expense + $3,000 Prepaid Advertising increase = $13,000 Cash Paid for Advertising
- $17,000 Income Tax Expense + $1,500 Income Tax Payable decrease = $18,500 Cash Paid for Income Taxes

2. Analyze changes in remaining noncash asset (and contra asset) accounts to determine cash flows from investing activities.

- Long-term Investments: $11,000 decrease resulted from sale of investments for cash at a $2,000 loss. Cash received from sale of investments = $9,000 ($11,000 cost − $2,000 loss).
- Plant Assets: $48,000 increase resulted from purchase of plant assets for cash. Cash paid to purchase plant assets = $48,000.
- Accumulated Depreciation: $11,000 increase resulted from the recording of 1994 depreciation. No cash flow effect.

3. Analyze changes in remaining liability and stockholders' equity accounts to determine cash flows from financing activities.

- Common Stock: $14,000 increase resulted from the issuance of stock for cash. Cash received from issuance of common stock = $14,000.
- Retained Earnings: $18,000 increase resulted from net income of $35,000 and dividend declaration of $17,000. Cash paid as dividends = $17,000.

The statement of cash flows is as follows:

TERRY COMPANY
STATEMENT OF CASH FLOWS
FOR THE YEAR ENDED DECEMBER 31, 1994

Cash Flows from Operating Activities		
Cash Received from Customers	$391,000	
Cash Received as Dividends	5,000	$396,000
Cash Paid for Merchandise Purchased	$248,000	
Cash Paid to Employees	78,500	
Cash Paid for Advertising	13,000	
Cash Paid for Income Taxes	18,500	358,000
Net Cash Provided by Operating Activities		$ 38,000
Cash Flows from Investing Activities		
Sale of Investments	$ 9,000	
Purchase of Plant Assets	(48,000)	
Net Cash Used by Investing Activities		(39,000)
Cash Flows from Financing Activities		
Issuance of Common Stock	$ 14,000	
Payment of Dividends	(17,000)	
Net Cash Used by Financing Activities		(3,000)
Net Decrease in Cash		($ 4,000)
Cash at Beginning of Year		12,000
Cash at End of Year		$ 8,000

DEMONSTRATION PROBLEM 2 FOR REVIEW: THE INDIRECT METHOD

SOLUTION TO DEMONSTRATION PROBLEM 2

Refer to the data for Terry Company presented in Demonstration Problem 1.

REQUIRED

a. Compute the change in cash that occurred during 1994.
b. Prepare a 1994 statement of cash flows using the indirect method.

a. $8,000 ending balance − $12,000 beginning balance = $4,000 decrease in cash
b. 1. Use the indirect method to determine the net cash flow from operating activities.
   - The adjustments to convert Terry Company's net income of $35,000 to a net cash provided by operating activities of $38,000 are shown in the following statement of cash flows.
   2. Analyze changes in remaining noncash asset (and contra asset) accounts to determine cash flows from investing activities.
   - Long-term Investments: $11,000 decrease resulted from sale of investments for cash at a $2,000 loss. Cash received from sale of investments = $9,000 ($11,000 cost − $2,000 loss).
   - Plant Assets: $48,000 increase resulted from purchase of plant assets for cash. Cash paid to purchase plant assets = $48,000.
   - Accumulated Depreciation: $11,000 increase resulted from the recording of 1994 depreciation. No cash flow effect.
   3. Analyze changes in remaining liability and stockholders' equity accounts to determine cash flows from financing activities.
   - Common Stock: $14,000 increase resulted from the issuance of stock for cash. Cash received from issuance of common stock = $14,000.
   - Retained Earnings: $18,000 increase resulted from net income of $35,000 and dividend declaration of $17,000. Cash paid as dividends = $17,000.

The statement of cash flows appears on the following page:

TERRY COMPANY
STATEMENT OF CASH FLOWS
FOR THE YEAR ENDED DECEMBER 31, 1994

Net Cash Flow from Operating Activities

Net Income	$35,000	
Add (Deduct) Items to Convert Net Income to Cash Basis:		
Depreciation	11,000	
Loss on Sale of Investments	2,000	
Accounts Receivable Decrease	6,000	
Inventory Increase	(28,000)	
Prepaid Advertising Increase	(3,000)	
Accounts Payable Increase	13,000	
Wages Payable Increase	3,500	
Income Tax Payable Decrease	(1,500)	
Net Cash Provided by Operating Activities		$38,000
Cash Flows from Investing Activities		
Sale of Investments	$ 9,000	
Purchase of Plant Assets	(48,000)	
Net Cash Used by Investing Activities		(39,000)
Cash Flows from Financing Activities		
Issuance of Common Stock	$14,000	
Payment of Dividends	(17,000)	
Net Cash Used by Financing Activities		(3,000)
Net Decrease in Cash		($ 4,000)
Cash at Beginning of Year		12,000
Cash at End of Year		$ 8,000

ANSWERS TO SELF-TEST QUESTIONS

1. a, p. 698   **2.** d, p. 700   **3.** c, p. 709   **4.** c, p. 717   **5.** b, p. 708, 719

Some accountants prefer to use a T-account approach to accumulate the information needed for a statement of cash flows. Although the basic analysis is similar to the worksheet approach discussed in the chapter, the T-account method may be faster to set up and complete when the situation is not too complicated. In this appendix, we explain the T-account approach for a statement of cash flows prepared using the indirect method.

FIVE STEPS IN THE T-ACCOUNT APPROACH UNDER THE INDIRECT METHOD

Preparing a statement of cash flows under the indirect method and the related separate disclosures using a T-account approach involves five steps:

1. Set up a large T account for Cash showing the net change in cash that occurred during the year.
2. Set up T accounts for all other balance sheet accounts showing the net change in each account that occurred during the year.
3. Record entries in the T accounts to account for and explain the net change that occurred in each account.
4. Prepare the statement of cash flows using information from the Cash T account.
5. Determine the information for the required separate disclosures.

ILLUSTRATION OF T-ACCOUNT APPROACH

We will illustrate the T-account approach for the indirect method using the data for Superior Corporation presented in the chapter (on page 719).

STEP 1 Set up a large T account labeled Cash and enter the period's net change in cash in the account—a cash increase is entered on the debit side and a cash decrease is entered on the credit side. Superior Corporation's cash increased $12,000 during 1994, so $12,000 is entered on the debit side and identified as "Net Change." Place a single rule beneath this entry to separate it from the analyzing entries that will be reflected in the account.

Divide the T account into the following six categories, leaving space for entries in each category:

Debit Side	Credit Side
Operating Activities—Increases	Operating Activities—Decreases
Investing Activities—Increases	Investing Activities—Decreases
Financing Activities—Increases	Financing Activities—Decreases

STEP 2 Set up T accounts for each remaining balance sheet account and enter the period's net change on the appropriate side of each account. During 1994, Superior Corporation's accounts receivable decreased $5,000, so $5,000 is entered on the credit side of the Accounts Receivable T account; inventory increased $14,000, so $14,000 is entered on the debit side of the Inventory T account, and so on. Place a single rule beneath the net change entered in each account.

Exhibit G-1 shows the T accounts for Superior Corporation after all the net changes have been entered and ruled. The net change for each account is the *target number* for that account. Our objective is to analyze all changes in the noncash balance sheet accounts to determine the events affecting cash flows. Entries recorded in each account will eventually equal that account's target number. Our analysis is complete when the target numbers in all T accounts are equaled by the entries in the T accounts.

EXHIBIT G—1	

CASH

Net Change	12,000	
Operating Activities—Increases		Operating Activities—Decreases
Investing Activities—Increases		Investing Activities—Decreases
Financing Activities—Increases		Financing Activities—Decreases

ACCOUNTS RECEIVABLE

	Net Change	5,000

INVENTORY

Net Change	14,000	

PREPAID EXPENSES

Net Change	3,000	

BUILDING AND EQUIPMENT

Net Change	85,000	

ACCUMULATED DEPRECIATION

	Net Change	7,000

ACCOUNTS PAYABLE

Net Change	10,000	

INTEREST PAYABLE

Net Change	2,000	

INCOME TAX PAYABLE

	Net Change	1,000

BONDS PAYABLE

Net Change	80,000	

COMMON STOCK

	Net Change	150,000

RETAINED EARNINGS

	Net Change	43,000

STEP 3 Record entries in the T accounts to account for and explain the net changes in the accounts. These entries are placed directly into the T accounts; for ease of study, we also present them in a general journal format. Entries to the Cash T account need a descriptive label because this account provides the data for the statement of cash flows.

The T-account entries are divided into two sets. The *first set* of entries determines the net cash flow from operating activities using the indirect method. The indirect method begins with net income (or net loss) and applies a series of adjustments to convert the net income (or net loss) to a cash amount. (These adjustments are summarized in Exhibit 19-9 on page 717.) When these adjustments deal with gains and losses related to investing and financing activities, the T-account entry will present the entire transaction. The *second set* of entries explains the remaining changes in the T accounts.

Entries 1–10 compose the first set of entries and determine the net cash flow from operating activities for Superior Corporation. (You should trace each entry into the completed T-account analysis shown in Exhibit G-2 on page 732.)

T-Account Entries Only

1. Cash—Operating Activities (Net Income)   54,000
      Retained Earnings   54,000

This entry establishes net income as the starting point for computing the net cash flow from operating activities and shows the increase in retained earnings caused by the period's net income.

2. Cash—Operating Activities (Depreciation)   13,000
      Accumulated Depreciation   13,000

The period's depreciation expense is added to net income in computing the net cash flow from operating activities. Depreciation expense also increased accumulated depreciation.

3. Cash—Investing Activities (Sale of Equipment)   20,000
   Accumulated Depreciation   6,000
      Building and Equipment   10,000
      Cash—Operating Activities (Gain on Sale of Equipment)   16,000

This entry reflects the sale of equipment and its impact on cash flows. The sale provided cash from investing activities of $20,000. The $16,000 gain on sale of equipment is deducted from net income in determining the net cash flow from operating activities.

4. Bonds Payable   80,000
      Cash—Operating Activities (Loss on Bond Retirement)   9,000
         Cash—Financing Activities (Retirement of Bonds Payable)   89,000

The retirement of bonds payable is a financing activity that used $89,000 of cash. The $9,000 loss on bond retirement is added to net income in computing the net cash flow from operating activities.

5. Cash—Operating Activities (Accounts Receivable Decrease)   5,000
      Accounts Receivable   5,000

A decrease in accounts receivable is added to net income in computing the net cash flow from operating activities.

6. Inventory   14,000
      Cash—Operating Activities (Inventory Increase)   14,000

An increase in inventory is deducted from net income in computing the net cash flow from operating activities.

EXHIBIT 6—2

CASH

Net Change	12,000		

Operating Activities—Increases		Operating Activities—Decreases	
(1) Net Income	54,000	(3) Gain on Sale of Equipment	16,000
(2) Depreciation	13,000	(6) Inventory Increase	14,000
(4) Loss on Bond Retirement	9,000	(7) Prepaid Expenses Increase	3,000
(5) Accounts Receivable Decrease	5,000	(8) Accounts Payable Decrease	10,000
(10) Income Tax Payable Increase	1,000	(9) Interest Payable Decrease	2,000
Investing Activities—Increases		Investing Activities—Decreases	
(3) Sale of Equipment	20,000	(11) Purchase of Equipment	65,000
Financing Activities—Increases		Financing Activities—Decreases	
(13) Issuance of Common Stock	120,000	(4) Retirement of Bonds Payable	89,000
	222,000	(14) Payment of Dividends	11,000
			210,000

ACCOUNTS RECEIVABLE

		Net Change	5,000
		(5)	5,000

INVENTORY

Net Change	14,000		
(6)	14,000		

PREPAID EXPENSES

Net Change	3,000		
(7)	3,000		

BUILDING AND EQUIPMENT

Net Change	85,000		
(11)	65,000	(3)	10,000
(12)*	30,000		

ACCUMULATED DEPRECIATION

		Net Change	7,000
(3)	6,000	(2)	13,000

ACCOUNTS PAYABLE

Net Change	10,000		
(8)	10,000		

INTEREST PAYABLE

Net Change	2,000		
(9)	2,000		

INCOME TAX PAYABLE

		Net Change	1,000
		(10)	1,000

BONDS PAYABLE

Net Change	80,000		
(4)	80,000		

COMMON STOCK

		Net Change	150,000
		(12)*	30,000
		(13)	120,000

RETAINED EARNINGS

		Net Change	43,000
(14)	11,000	(1)	54,000

7. Prepaid Expenses   3,000

     Cash—Operating Activities (Prepaid Expenses Increase)   3,000

An increase in prepaid expenses is deducted from net income in computing the net cash flow from operating activities.

8. Accounts Payable   10,000

     Cash—Operating Activities (Accounts Payable Decrease)   10,000

A decrease in accounts payable is deducted from net income in computing the net cash flow from operating activities.

9. Interest Payable   2,000

     Cash—Operating Activities (Interest Payable Decrease)   2,000

A decrease in interest payable is deducted from net income in computing the net cash flow from operating activities.

10. Cash—Operating Activities (Income Tax Payable Increase)   1,000

     Income Tax Payable   1,000

An increase in income tax payable is added to net income in computing the net cash flow from operating activities.

At this point, all of the T-account entries affecting the net cash flow from operating activities have been recorded. Any noncash T account whose target amount is not equaled by the entries to date is identified. For Superior Corporation, these accounts are Building and Equipment, Common Stock, and Retained Earnings. The transactions affecting these accounts are reviewed and T-account entries are then prepared to explain these remaining changes. Entries 11–14 are the second set of T-account entries for Superior Corporation; they explain the remaining changes in the T accounts.

11. Building and Equipment   65,000

     Cash—Investing Activities (Purchase of Equipment)   65,000

The purchase of equipment for $65,000 increased the Building and Equipment account and used cash for an investing activity.

12. Building and Equipment   30,000

     Common Stock   30,000

This entry reconstructs the entry for the acquisition of equipment in exchange for common stock. This event is a noncash investing and financing transaction that must be disclosed in a supplementary schedule. We highlight the T-account entry with an asterisk (*) to identify it as an event requiring special disclosure treatment.

13. Cash—Financing Activities (Issuance of Common Stock)   120,000

     Common Stock   120,000

The issuance of common stock was a financing activity that provided $120,000 of cash.

14. Retained Earnings   11,000

     Cash—Financing Activities (Payment of Dividends)   11,000

The $11,000 dividend declared and paid in 1994 reduced retained earnings and used cash for a financing activity.

After these 14 entries, the T-account entries equal the target amounts for all of the noncash balance sheet accounts. The entries in the Cash T account should also equal the target amount; we total the debit entries and credit entries to confirm this. The totals show the following:

Cash debit entries	$222,000
Cash credit entries	210,000
Cash target amount—debit	$ 12,000

Exhibit G-2 shows the T accounts with all of the entries recorded in the accounts. We are now ready to prepare the statement of cash flows.

STEP 4 Prepare the statement of cash flows from the information in the Cash T account. This T account provides the adjustments necessary to reconcile net income to the net cash flow from operating activities. It also provides the various cash inflows and outflows from the investing activities and the financing activities. The sum of the operating, investing, and financing cash flows will equal the period's change in cash. In the statement of cash flows, the change in cash is reconciled with the beginning and ending cash balances. The statement of cash flows for Superior Corporation, using the indirect method, is shown in Exhibit 19-13 (on page 723).

STEP 5 Determine the information for the required separate disclosures. Cash paid for interest is computed by adjusting interest expense for the change during the year in interest payable. Superior Corporation's 1994 cash paid for interest is $12,000 ($10,000 + $2,000). Cash paid for income taxes is computed by adjusting income tax expense for the change during the year in income tax payable. Superior Corporation's 1994 cash paid for income taxes is $11,000 ($12,000 − $1,000). Exhibit 19-13 shows these amounts as supplemental disclosures to the statement of cash flows.

The noncash investing and financing transactions are identified in the T accounts (the entries containing an asterisk identify these events). Exhibit 19-13 shows the supplemental disclosure of Superior Corporation's one noncash investing and financing transaction: the $30,000 issuance of common stock to acquire equipment.

Superior Corporation has no short-term investments, so a separate disclosure to indicate which highly liquid, short-term investments are treated as cash equivalents is not needed.

GLOSSARY OF KEY TERMS USED IN THIS CHAPTER AND APPENDIX

cash equivalents Short-term, highly liquid investments that firms acquire with temporarily idle cash to earn interest on these excess funds. To qualify as a cash equivalent, an investment must be easily convertible into a known amount of cash and be close enough to maturity so that its market value is not sensitive to interest rate changes (p. 698).

direct method A presentation of net cash flow from operating activities in a statement of cash flows that shows the major categories of operating cash receipts and payments (p. 702).

dividend payout ratio A financial ratio showing the percentage of earnings available to common stockholders that is paid out as dividends; computed as annual dividends per share divided by earnings per share (p. 724).

financing activities A section in the statement of cash flows that reports cash flows associated with obtaining resources from owners and creditors, returning resources to owners, and repaying amounts borrowed (p. 700).

indirect method A presentation of net cash flow from operating activities in a statement of cash flows that begins with net income and applies a series of adjustments to convert the net income to a cash basis amount. Also known as the *reconciliation method* (p. 714).

investing activities A section in the statement of cash flows that reports cash flows involving (1) the purchase and sale of plant and intangible assets, (2) the purchase and sale of stocks, bonds, and other securities, and (3) the lending and subsequent collection of money (p. 700).

noncash investing and financing activities Investing activities and financing activities that do not affect current cash flows; information about these events must be reported as a supplement to the statement of cash flows (p. 701).

operating activities   A section in the statement of cash flows that reports cash flows from all activities that are not classified as investing or financing activities. Generally, the activities reported in the income statement constitute a company's operating activities (p. 699).

statement of cash flows   A financial statement showing a firm's cash inflows and cash outflows for a specific period, classified into operating, investing, and financing categories (p. 698).

QUESTIONS

19-1 Define *cash equivalents*. Give three examples of cash equivalents.

19-2 Why are cash equivalents included with cash in a statement of cash flows?

19-3 Identify the three major types of activities classified on a statement of cash flows and give an example of a cash inflow and a cash outflow in each classification.

19-4 Identify in which of the three activity categories of a statement of cash flows each of the following items would appear, and indicate for each item whether it represents a cash inflow or a cash outflow:
a. Cash purchase of equipment.
b. Cash collections on loans.
c. Cash dividends paid.
d. Cash dividends received.
e. Cash proceeds from issuing stock.
f. Cash receipts from customers.
g. Cash interest paid.
h. Cash interest received.

19-5 Traverse Company acquired a $2,000,000 building by issuing $2,000,000 worth of bonds payable. In terms of cash flow reporting, what type of transaction is this? What special disclosure requirements apply to a transaction of this type?

19-6 Why are noncash investing and financing transactions disclosed as supplemental information to a statement of cash flows?

19-7 Why is a statement of cash flows a useful financial statement?

19-8 Distinguish between the direct method and the indirect method of presenting net cash flow from operating activities.

19-9 A firm is converting its accrual basis revenues and expenses to corresponding cash amounts using the direct method. Sales on the income statement are $725,000. Beginning and ending accounts receivable on the balance sheet are $53,000 and $44,000, respectively. What is the amount of cash received from customers?

19-10 A firm reports $280,000 cost of goods sold in its income statement. Beginning and ending inventories are $62,000 and $57,000, respectively, and beginning and ending accounts payable (for merchandise purchased) are $21,000 and $18,000, respectively. What is the amount of cash paid for merchandise purchased?

19-11 A firm reports $77,000 wages expense in its income statement. If beginning and ending wages payable are $1,900 and $1,300, respectively, what is the amount of cash paid to employees?

19-12 A firm reports $38,000 advertising expense in its income statement. If beginning and ending prepaid advertising are $5,000 and $7,500, respectively, what is the amount of cash paid for advertising?

19-13 Rusk Company sold equipment for $4,200 cash that had cost $26,000 and had $21,000 of accumulated depreciation. Describe how this event is handled in a statement of cash flows using the direct method.

19-14 What separate disclosures are required for a company that reports a statement of cash flows using the direct method?

19-15 A firm uses the indirect method of presenting net cash flow from operating activities. Calculate this net cash flow using the following information:

Net income	$55,000
Accounts receivable decrease	10,000
Inventory increase	8,000
Accounts payable decrease	4,500
Income tax payable increase	2,000
Depreciation expense	7,500

19-16　In determining net cash flow from operating activities using the indirect method, why must we add depreciation back to net income? Give an example of another item that is added back to net income under the indirect method.

19-17　Vista Company sold for $43,000 cash long-term investments originally costing $28,000. The company recorded a gain on the sale of $15,000. Describe how this event is handled in a statement of cash flows using the indirect method.

19-18　What separate disclosures are required for a company that reports a statement of cash flows using the indirect method?

19-19　If a business had a net loss for the year, under what circumstances would the statement of cash flows show a positive net cash flow from operating activities?

19-20　What is the purpose of the analyzing entries on a worksheet for a statement of cash flows?

19-21　Bleaker Company declares and pays its annual dividend near the end of its fiscal year. For the current year, Bleaker's dividend payout ratio was 30%, its earnings per common share was $5.50, and it had 20,000 shares of common stock outstanding all year. What total amount of dividends did Bleaker declare and pay in the current year?

EXERCISES

CLASSIFICATION OF CASH FLOWS
— OBJ. 1 —

19-22　For each of the items below, indicate whether the cash flow relates to an operating activity, an investing activity, or a financing activity.
   a. Cash receipts from customers for services rendered.
   b. Sale of long-term investments for cash.
   c. Acquisition of plant assets for cash.
   d. Payment of income taxes.
   e. Bonds payable issued for cash.
   f. Payment of cash dividends declared in previous year.
   g. Purchase of short-term investments (not cash equivalents) for cash.

CLASSIFICATION OF CASH FLOWS
— OBJ. 1 —

19-23　For each of the items below, indicate whether it is (1) a cash flow from an operating activity, (2) a cash flow from an investing activity, (3) a cash flow from a financing activity, (4) a noncash investing and financing activity, or (5) none of the above.
   a. Paid cash to retire bonds payable at a loss.
   b. Received cash as settlement of a lawsuit.
   c. Acquired a patent in exchange for common stock.
   d. Received advance payments from customers on orders for custom-made goods.
   e. Gave large cash contribution to local university.
   f. Invested cash in 60-day commercial paper (a cash equivalent).

OPERATING CASH FLOWS (DIRECT METHOD)
— OBJ. 2 —

19-24　Calculate the cash flow asked for in each of the following cases.
   a. Cash paid for advertising:

Advertising expense	$43,000
Prepaid advertising, January 1	14,000
Prepaid advertising, December 31	17,000

   b. Cash paid for income taxes:

Income tax expense	$26,000
Income tax payable, January 1	6,800
Income tax payable, December 31	4,500

   c. Cash paid for merchandise purchased:

Cost of goods sold	$160,000
Inventory, January 1	32,000
Inventory, December 31	29,000
Accounts payable, January 1	8,000
Accounts payable, December 31	12,000

OPERATING CASH FLOWS (DIRECT METHOD)
— OBJ. 2 —

19-25　Lincoln Company, a sole proprietorship that owns no plant assets, had the following income statement for the current year:

Sales		$720,000
Cost of Goods Sold	$460,000	
Wages Expense	100,000	
Rent Expense	40,000	
Insurance Expense	18,000	618,000
Net Income		$102,000

Additional information about the company follows:

	End of Year	Beginning of Year
Accounts Receivable	$41,000	$38,000
Inventory	75,000	86,000
Prepaid Insurance	8,000	6,000
Accounts Payable	29,000	23,000
Wages Payable	7,000	11,000

Use the preceding information to calculate the net cash flow from operating activities using the direct method. Show a related cash flow for each revenue and expense.

STATEMENT OF CASH FLOWS (DIRECT METHOD)
— OBJ. 2 —

19-26 Use the following information about the 1994 cash flows of Mason Corporation to prepare a statement of cash flows using the direct method.

Cash balance, end of 1994	$ 18,000
Cash paid to employees and suppliers	186,000
Cash received from sale of land	22,000
Cash paid to acquire treasury stock	7,000
Cash balance, beginning of 1994	23,000
Cash received as interest	9,000
Cash paid as income taxes	15,000
Cash paid to purchase equipment	78,000
Cash received from customers	225,000
Cash received from issuing bonds payable	35,000
Cash paid as dividends	10,000

NET CASH FLOW FROM OPERATING ACTIVITIES (INDIRECT METHOD)
— OBJ. 4 —

19-27 Refer to the information in Exercise 19-25. Calculate the net cash flow from operating activities using the indirect method.

STATEMENT OF CASH FLOWS (INDIRECT METHOD)
— OBJ. 4 —

19-28 Use the following information about Lund Corporation for 1994 to prepare a statement of cash flows using the indirect method.

Accounts payable increase	$ 8,000
Accounts receivable increase	3,000
Accrued liabilities decrease	2,000
Amortization expense	5,000
Cash balance, beginning of 1994	27,000
Cash balance, end of 1994	21,000
Cash paid as dividends	20,000
Cash paid to purchase land	88,000
Cash paid to retire bonds payable at par	50,000
Cash received from issuance of common stock	25,000
Cash received from sale of equipment	14,000
Depreciation expense	32,000
Gain on sale of equipment	2,000
Inventory decrease	10,000
Net income	66,000
Prepaid expenses increase	1,000

INVESTING AND FINANCING CASH FLOWS
— OBJ. 2, 4 —

19-29 During 1994, Paxon Corporation's Long-term Investments account increased $20,000, the net result of purchasing stocks costing $90,000 and selling stocks costing $70,000 at a $5,000 loss. Also, the Bonds Payable account decreased $50,000, the net result of issuing $100,000 of bonds at 105 and retiring bonds with a face value (and book value) of $150,000 at a $10,000 gain. What items and amounts will appear in the (a) cash flows from investing activities and the (b) cash flows from financing activities sections of a 1994 statement of cash flows?

PROBLEMS

STATEMENT OF CASH
FLOWS (DIRECT METHOD)
— OBJ. 2 —

19-30   Wolff Company's 1994 income statement and comparative balance sheets at December 31 of 1994 and 1993 are shown below.

WOLFF COMPANY
INCOME STATEMENT
FOR THE YEAR ENDED DECEMBER 31, 1994

Sales		$615,000
Cost of Goods Sold	$420,000	
Wages Expense	95,000	
Insurance Expense	9,000	
Depreciation Expense	15,000	
Interest Expense	10,000	
Income Tax Expense	20,000	569,000
Net Income		$ 46,000

WOLFF COMPANY
BALANCE SHEETS

Assets	Dec. 31, 1994	Dec. 31, 1993
Cash	$ 10,000	$ 3,000
Accounts Receivable	42,000	30,000
Inventory	90,000	57,000
Prepaid Insurance	3,000	8,000
Plant Assets	245,000	180,000
Accumulated Depreciation	(62,000)	(47,000)
Total Assets	$328,000	$231,000

Liabilities and Stockholders' Equity		
Accounts Payable	$ 12,000	$ 18,000
Wages Payable	7,000	4,000
Income Tax Payable	4,000	6,000
Bonds Payable	135,000	60,000
Common Stock	100,000	100,000
Retained Earnings	70,000	43,000
Total Liabilities and Stockholders' Equity	$328,000	$231,000

Cash dividends of $19,000 were declared and paid during 1994. Plant assets were purchased for cash and bonds payable were issued for cash. Bond interest is paid semiannually on June 30 and December 31. Accounts payable relate to merchandise purchases.

REQUIRED

a. Compute the change in cash that occurred during 1994.
b. Prepare a 1994 statement of cash flows using the direct method.

STATEMENT OF CASH
FLOWS (DIRECT METHOD)
— OBJ. 2 —

19-31   Arctic Company's 1994 income statement and comparative balance sheets at December 31 of 1994 and 1993 are shown below.

ARCTIC COMPANY
INCOME STATEMENT
FOR THE YEAR ENDED DECEMBER 31, 1994

Sales		$520,000
Cost of Goods Sold	$382,000	
Wages Expense	136,000	
Advertising Expense	23,000	
Depreciation Expense	16,000	
Interest Expense	13,000	
Gain on Sale of Land	(18,000)	552,000
Net Loss		($ 32,000)

ARCTIC COMPANY
BALANCE SHEETS

Assets	Dec. 31, 1994	Dec. 31, 1993
Cash	$ 42,000	$ 20,000
Accounts Receivable	30,000	36,000
Inventory	77,000	81,000
Prepaid Advertising	7,000	9,000
Plant Assets	258,000	150,000
Accumulated Depreciation	(56,000)	(40,000)
Total Assets	$358,000	$256,000

Liabilities and Stockholders' Equity		
Accounts Payable	$ 12,000	$ 22,000
Interest Payable	4,000	—
Bonds Payable	160,000	—
Common Stock	175,000	175,000
Retained Earnings	27,000	59,000
Treasury Stock	(20,000)	—
Total Liabilities and Stockholders' Equity	$358,000	$256,000

During 1994, Arctic sold land for $50,000 that had originally cost $32,000. Arctic also purchased equipment for cash, reacquired treasury stock for cash, and issued bonds payable for cash. Accounts payable relate to merchandise purchases.

REQUIRED

a. Compute the change in cash that occurred during 1994.

b. Prepare a 1994 statement of cash flows using the direct method.

STATEMENT OF CASH FLOWS (DIRECT METHOD) WITH WORKSHEET — OBJ. 2, 3 —

19-32 Dairy Company's 1994 income statement and comparative balance sheets at December 31 of 1994 and 1993 are presented below.

DAIRY COMPANY
INCOME STATEMENT
FOR THE YEAR ENDED DECEMBER 31, 1994

Sales		$876,000
Cost of Goods Sold	$555,000	
Wages and Other Operating Expenses	119,000	
Depreciation Expense	27,000	
Goodwill Amortization Expense	9,000	
Interest Expense	13,000	
Income Tax Expense	45,000	
Loss on Bond Retirement	6,000	774,000
Net Income		$102,000

DAIRY COMPANY
BALANCE SHEETS

Assets	Dec. 31, 1994	Dec. 31, 1993
Cash	$ 34,000	$ 23,000
Accounts Receivable	66,000	60,000
Inventory	129,000	137,000
Prepaid Expenses	15,000	12,000
Plant Assets	450,000	420,000
Accumulated Depreciation	(108,000)	(105,000)
Goodwill	54,000	63,000
Total Assets	$640,000	$610,000

Liabilities and Stockholders' Equity

Accounts Payable	$ 40,000	$ 33,000
Interest Payable	5,000	9,000
Income Tax Payable	7,000	10,000
Bonds Payable	75,000	150,000
Common Stock	315,000	285,000
Retained Earnings	198,000	123,000
Total Liabilities and Stockholders' Equity	$640,000	$610,000

During the year, the company sold for $21,000 old equipment that had cost $45,000 and had $24,000 accumulated depreciation. New equipment worth $75,000 was acquired in exchange for $75,000 of bonds payable. Bonds payable of $150,000 were retired for cash at a loss. A $27,000 cash dividend was declared and paid in 1994. All stock issuances were for cash.

REQUIRED

a. Prepare a worksheet for a statement of cash flows using the direct method.

b. Prepare a 1994 statement of cash flows using the direct method.

c. Prepare separate schedules showing (1) a reconciliation of net income to net cash flow from operating activities (see Exhibit 19-9, page 717) and (2) noncash investing and financing transactions.

STATEMENT OF CASH FLOWS (DIRECT METHOD) WITH WORKSHEET — OBJ. 2, 3 —

19-33 Rainbow Company's income statement for 1994 and comparative balance sheets at December 31 of 1994 and 1993 are shown below.

RAINBOW COMPANY
INCOME STATEMENT
FOR THE YEAR ENDED DECEMBER 31, 1994

Sales		$600,000
Dividend Income		12,000
		$612,000
Cost of Goods Sold	$352,000	
Wages and Other Operating Expenses	104,000	
Depreciation Expense	31,000	
Patent Amortization Expense	6,000	
Interest Expense	10,000	
Income Tax Expense	35,000	
Loss on Sale of Equipment	4,000	
Gain on Sale of Investments	(8,000)	534,000
Net Income		$ 78,000

RAINBOW COMPANY
BALANCE SHEETS

Assets	Dec. 31, 1994	Dec. 31, 1993
Cash and Cash Equivalents	$ 15,000	$ 20,000
Accounts Receivable	32,000	24,000
Inventory	82,000	62,000
Prepaid Expenses	8,000	5,000
Long-term Investments	24,000	64,000
Land	153,000	80,000
Buildings	355,000	280,000
Accumulated Depreciation—Buildings	(73,000)	(60,000)
Equipment	143,000	180,000
Accumulated Depreciation—Equipment	(33,000)	(37,000)
Patents	40,000	26,000
Total Assets	$746,000	$644,000

Liabilities and Stockholders' Equity

Accounts Payable	$ 20,000	$ 13,000
Interest Payable	5,000	4,000
Income Tax Payable	6,000	8,000
Bonds Payable	120,000	100,000
Preferred Stock ($100 par value)	80,000	60,000
Common Stock ($5 par value)	328,000	316,000
Paid-in Capital in Excess of Par Value—Common	105,000	99,000
Retained Earnings	82,000	44,000
Total Liabilities and Stockholders' Equity	$746,000	$644,000

During the year, the following transactions occurred:
1. Purchased land for cash.
2. Sold long-term investments costing $40,000 for $48,000 cash.
3. Capitalized an expenditure of $75,000 made to improve the building.
4. Sold equipment for $11,000 cash that originally cost $37,000 and had $22,000 accumulated depreciation.
5. Issued bonds payable at face value for cash.
6. Acquired a patent with a fair value of $20,000 by issuing 200 shares of preferred stock at par value.
7. Declared and paid a $40,000 cash dividend.
8. Issued 2,400 shares of common stock for cash at $7.50 per share.
9. Recorded depreciation of $13,000 on buildings and $18,000 on equipment.

REQUIRED

a. Prepare a worksheet for a statement of cash flows using the direct method.
b. Prepare a 1994 statement of cash flows using the direct method.
c. Prepare separate schedules showing (1) a reconciliation of net income to net cash flow from operating activities (see Exhibit 19-9, page 717) and (2) noncash investing and financing transactions.

STATEMENT OF CASH FLOWS (INDIRECT METHOD) — OBJ. 4 —

19-34 Refer to the data given for Wolff Company in Problem 19-30.

REQUIRED

a. Compute the change in cash that occurred during 1994.
b. Prepare a 1994 statement of cash flows using the indirect method.

STATEMENT OF CASH FLOWS (INDIRECT METHOD) — OBJ. 4 —

19-35 Refer to the data given for Arctic Company in Problem 19-31.

REQUIRED

a. Compute the change in cash that occurred during 1994.
b. Prepare a 1994 statement of cash flows using the indirect method.

STATEMENT OF CASH FLOWS (INDIRECT METHOD) WITH WORKSHEET — OBJ. 4, 5 —

19-36 Refer to the data given for Dairy Company in Problem 19-32.

REQUIRED

a. Prepare a worksheet for a statement of cash flows using the indirect method.
b. Prepare a 1994 statement of cash flows using the indirect method.
c. Prepare separate schedules showing (1) cash paid for interest and for income taxes and (2) noncash investing and financing transactions.

STATEMENT OF CASH FLOWS (INDIRECT METHOD) WITH WORKSHEET — OBJ. 4, 5 —

19-37 Refer to the data given for Rainbow Company in Problem 19-33.

REQUIRED

a. Prepare a worksheet for a statement of cash flows using the indirect method.
b. Prepare a 1994 statement of cash flows using the indirect method.
c. Prepare a separate schedules showing (1) cash paid for interest and for income taxes and (2) noncash investing and financing transactions.

STATEMENT OF CASH FLOWS (INDIRECT METHOD) USING T-ACCOUNT APPROACH — APPENDIX G —

19-38 Refer to the data given for Wolff Company in Problem 19-30.

REQUIRED

a. Use the T-account approach to compile data for a statement of cash flows using the indirect method.
b. Prepare a 1994 statement of cash flows using the indirect method.

STATEMENT OF CASH
FLOWS (INDIRECT
METHOD) USING
T-ACCOUNT APPROACH
— APPENDIX G —

19-39 Refer to the data given for Arctic Company in Probem 19-31.

REQUIRED

a. Use the T-account approach to compile data for a statement of cash flows using the indirect method.

b. Prepare a 1994 statement of cash flows using the indirect method.

STATEMENT OF CASH
FLOWS (INDIRECT
METHOD) USING
T-ACCOUNT APPROACH
— APPENDIX G —

19-40 Refer to the data given for Dairy Company in Problem 19-32.

REQUIRED

a. Use the T-account approach to compile data for a statement of cash flows using the indirect method.

b. Prepare a 1994 statement of cash flows using the indirect method.

c. Prepare separate schedules showing (1) cash paid for interest and for income taxes and (2) noncash investing and financing transactions.

STATEMENT OF CASH
FLOWS (INDIRECT
METHOD) USING
T-ACCOUNT APPROACH
— APPENDIX G —

19-41 Refer to the data given for Rainbow Company in Problem 19-33.

REQUIRED

a. Use the T-account approach to compile data for a statement of cash flows using the indirect method.

b. Prepare a 1994 statement of cash flows using the indirect method.

c. Prepare separate schedules showing (1) cash paid for interest and for income taxes and (2) noncash investing and financing transactions.

ALTERNATE EXERCISES

CLASSIFICATION OF CASH
FLOWS
— OBJ. 1 —

19-22A For each of the items below, indicate whether the cash flow relates to an operating activity, an investing activity, or a financing activity.

a. Cash loaned to borrowers.

b. Cash paid as interest on bonds payable.

c. Cash received from issuance of preferred stock.

d. Cash paid as state income taxes.

e. Cash received as dividends on stock investments.

f. Cash paid to acquire treasury stock.

g. Cash paid to acquire franchise to distribute a product line.

CLASSIFICATION OF CASH
FLOWS
— OBJ. 1 —

19-23A For each of the items below, indicate whether it is (1) a cash flow from an operating activity, (2) a cash flow from an investing activity, (3) a cash flow from a financing activity, (4) a noncash investing and financing activity, or (5) none of the above.

a. Received cash as interest earned on bond investment.

b. Received cash as refund from supplier.

c. Borrowed cash from bank on six-month note payable.

d. Exchanged, at a gain, stock held as an investment for a parcel of land.

e. Invested cash in a money market fund (cash may be easily withdrawn from the fund).

f. Loaned cash to help finance the start of a new biotechnology firm.

OPERATING CASH FLOWS
(DIRECT METHOD)
— OBJ. 2 —

19-24A Calculate the cash flow asked for in each of the following cases.

a. Cash paid for rent:

Rent expense	$50,000
Prepaid rent, January 1	12,000
Prepaid rent, December 31	9,000

b. Cash received as interest:

Interest income	$15,000
Interest receivable, January 1	2,000
Interest receivable, December 31	2,600

c. Cash paid for merchandise purchased:

Cost of goods sold	$95,000
Inventory, January 1	11,000
Inventory, December 31	15,000
Accounts payable, January 1	10,000
Accounts payable, December 31	8,000

**OPERATING CASH FLOWS
(DIRECT METHOD)
— OBJ. 2 —**

19-25A Howell Company's current year income statement contains the following data:

Sales	$940,000
Cost of Goods Sold	630,000
Gross Profit	$310,000

Howell's comparative balance sheets show the following data (accounts payable relate to merchandise purchases):

	End of Year	Beginning of Year
Accounts Receivable	$ 59,000	$50,000
Inventory	120,000	98,000
Prepaid Expenses	5,000	9,000
Accounts Payable	36,000	41,000

Compute Howell's current-year cash received from customers and cash paid for merchandise purchased.

**STATEMENT OF CASH
FLOWS (DIRECT METHOD)
— OBJ. 2 —**

19-26A Use the following information about the 1994 cash flows of Gilbert Corporation to prepare a statement of cash flows using the direct method.

Cash balance, end of 1994	$ 25,000
Cash paid to employees and suppliers	126,000
Cash received from sale of equipment	81,000
Cash paid to retire bonds payable	60,000
Cash balance, beginning of 1994	16,000
Cash paid as interest	6,000
Cash paid as income taxes	20,000
Cash paid to purchase patent	55,000
Cash received from customers	180,000
Cash received from issuing common stock	30,000
Cash paid as dividends	15,000

**NET CASH FLOW FROM
OPERATING ACTIVITIES
(INDIRECT METHOD)
— OBJ. 4 —**

19-27A The following information was obtained from Galena Company's comparative balance sheets.

	Dec. 31, 1994	Dec. 31, 1993
Cash	$ 17,000	$ 8,000
Accounts Receivable	38,000	31,000
Inventory	48,000	43,000
Prepaid Rent	6,000	8,000
Long-term Investments	18,000	30,000
Plant Assets	130,000	92,000
Accumulated Depreciation	(34,000)	(28,000)
Accounts Payable	21,000	17,000
Income Tax Payable	3,000	5,000
Common Stock	105,000	80,000
Retained Earnings	94,000	82,000

Assume that Galena Company's 1994 income statement showed depreciation expense of $6,000, a gain on sale of investments of $8,000, and a net income of $40,000. Calculate the net cash flow from operating activities using the indirect method.

**NET CASH FLOW FROM
OPERATING ACTIVITIES
(INDIRECT METHOD)
— OBJ. 4 —**

19-28A Cairo Company had a $14,000 net loss from operations for 1994. Depreciation expense for 1994 was $6,500 and a 1994 dividend of $5,000 was declared and paid. Balances of the current asset and current liability accounts at the beginning and end of 1994 are as follows:

	End	Beginning
Cash	$ 3,500	$ 7,000
Accounts Receivable	12,000	19,000
Inventory	38,000	40,000
Prepaid Expenses	4,500	7,000
Accounts Payable	9,000	6,000
Accrued Liabilities	2,000	5,500

Did Cairo Company's 1994 operating activities provide or use cash? Use the indirect method to determine your answer.

INVESTING AND FINANCING CASH FLOWS — OBJ. 2, 4 —

19-29A Refer to the information in Exercise 19-27A. During 1994, Galena Company purchased plant assets for cash, sold investments for cash, and issued common stock for cash. The firm also declared and paid cash dividends in 1994. What items and amounts will appear in (a) the cash flows from investing activities and (b) the cash flows from financing activities sections of a 1994 statement of cash flows?

ALTERNATE PROBLEMS

STATEMENT OF CASH FLOWS (DIRECT METHOD) — OBJ. 2 —

19-30A Rural Company's 1994 income statement and comparative balance sheets at December 31 of 1994 and 1993 are shown below.

RURAL COMPANY
INCOME STATEMENT
FOR THE YEAR ENDED DECEMBER 31, 1994

Sales		$525,000
Cost of Goods Sold	$313,000	
Wages Expense	90,000	
Depreciation Expense	16,000	
Rent Expense	24,000	
Income Tax Expense	25,000	468,000
Net Income		$ 57,000

RURAL COMPANY
BALANCE SHEETS

Assets	Dec. 31, 1994	Dec. 31, 1993
Cash	$ 17,000	$ 31,000
Accounts Receivable	43,000	50,000
Inventory	114,000	92,000
Prepaid Rent	12,000	10,000
Plant Assets	350,000	250,000
Accumulated Depreciation	(105,000)	(89,000)
Total Assets	$431,000	$344,000

Liabilities and Stockholders' Equity		
Accounts Payable	$ 24,000	$ 14,000
Wages Payable	10,000	6,000
Income Tax Payable	4,000	7,000
Common Stock	245,000	210,000
Paid-in Capital in Excess of Par Value	60,000	48,000
Retained Earnings	88,000	59,000
Total Liabilities and Stockholders' Equity	$431,000	$344,000

Cash dividends of $28,000 were declared and paid during 1994. Plant assets were purchased for cash and additional common stock was issued for cash. Accounts payable relate to merchandise purchases.

REQUIRED

a. Compute the change in cash that occurred during 1994.

b. Prepare a 1994 statement of cash flows using the direct method.

STATEMENT OF CASH FLOWS (DIRECT METHOD) — OBJ. 2 —

19-31A Sweet Company's 1994 income statement and comparative balance sheets at December 31 of 1994 and 1993 are presented on the following page.

SWEET COMPANY
INCOME STATEMENT
FOR THE YEAR ENDED DECEMBER 31, 1994

Sales		$728,000
Cost of Goods Sold	$390,000	
Wages Expense	156,000	
Depreciation Expense	46,000	
Insurance Expense	10,000	
Interest Expense	9,000	
Income Tax Expense	44,000	
Gain on Sale of Equipment	(12,000)	643,000
Net Income		$ 85,000

SWEET COMPANY
BALANCE SHEETS

Assets	Dec. 31, 1994	Dec. 31, 1993
Cash	$ 18,000	$ 24,000
Accounts Receivable	52,000	33,000
Inventory	136,000	97,000
Prepaid Insurance	7,000	9,000
Plant Assets	683,000	593,000
Accumulated Depreciation	(146,000)	(135,000)
Total Assets	$750,000	$621,000

Liabilities and Stockholders' Equity		
Accounts Payable	$ 29,000	$ 21,000
Interest Payable	4,000	—
Income Tax Payable	9,000	12,000
Bonds Payable	105,000	60,000
Common Stock	500,000	450,000
Retained Earnings	143,000	78,000
Treasury Stock	(40,000)	—
Total Liabilities and Stockholders' Equity	$750,000	$621,000

During the year, Sweet Company sold equipment for $21,000 cash that originally cost $44,000 and had $35,000 accumulated depreciation. New equipment was purchased for cash. Bonds payable and common stock were issued for cash. Cash dividends of $20,000 were declared and paid. At the end of the year, shares of treasury stock were purchased for cash. Accounts payable relate to merchandise purchases.

REQUIRED

a. Compute the change in cash that occurred during 1994.
b. Prepare a 1994 statement of cash flows using the direct method.

STATEMENT OF CASH FLOWS (DIRECT METHOD) WITH WORKSHEET — OBJ. 2, 3 —

19-32A Huber Company's 1994 income statement and comparative balance sheets at December 31 of 1994 and 1993 are presented below.

HUBER COMPANY
INCOME STATEMENT
FOR THE YEAR ENDED DECEMBER 31, 1994

Sales		$900,000
Cost of Goods Sold	$600,000	
Wages and Other Operating Expenses	191,000	
Depreciation Expense	30,000	
Patent Amortization Expense	7,000	
Interest Expense	20,000	
Income Tax Expense	28,000	
Gain on Exchange of Land for Patent	(40,000)	836,000
Net Income		$ 64,000

HUBER COMPANY
BALANCE SHEETS

Assets	Dec. 31, 1994	Dec. 31, 1993
Cash	$ 38,000	$ 18,000
Accounts Receivable	71,000	55,000
Inventory	95,000	71,000
Land	130,000	180,000
Building and Equipment	490,000	400,000
Accumulated Depreciation	(132,000)	(110,000)
Patent	83,000	—
Total Assets	$775,000	$614,000

Liabilities and Stockholders' Equity

	Dec. 31, 1994	Dec. 31, 1993
Accounts Payable	$ 40,000	$ 29,000
Interest Payable	14,000	6,000
Income Tax Payable	8,000	13,000
Bonds Payable	200,000	80,000
Common Stock	400,000	400,000
Retained Earnings	113,000	86,000
Total Liabilities and Stockholders' Equity	$775,000	$614,000

During 1994, $37,000 of cash dividends were declared and paid. A patent valued at $90,000 was obtained in exchange for land. Equipment that originally cost $20,000 and had $8,000 accumulated depreciation was sold for $12,000 cash. Bonds payable were sold for cash and cash was used to pay for structural improvements to the building.

REQUIRED

a. Prepare a worksheet for a statement of cash flows using the direct method.
b. Prepare a 1994 statement of cash flows using the direct method.
c. Prepare separate schedules showing (1) a reconciliation of net income to net cash flow from operating activities (see Exhibit 19-9, page 717) and (2) noncash investing and financing transactions.

STATEMENT OF CASH FLOWS (DIRECT METHOD) WITH WORKSHEET — OBJ. 2, 3 —

19-33A Towne Company's income statement for 1994 and comparative balance sheets at December 31 of 1994 and 1993 are presented below.

TOWNE COMPANY
INCOME STATEMENT
FOR THE YEAR ENDED DECEMBER 31, 1994

Service Fees Earned		$250,000
Dividend and Interest Income		26,000
		$276,000
Wages and Other Operating Expenses	$234,000	
Depreciation Expense	43,000	
Franchise Amortization Expense	9,000	
Loss on Sale of Equipment	10,000	
Gain on Sale of Investments	(14,000)	282,000
Net Loss		($ 6,000)

TOWNE COMPANY
BALANCE SHEETS

Assets	Dec. 31, 1994	Dec. 31, 1993
Cash	$ 36,000	$ 30,000
Accounts Receivable	11,000	15,000
Interest Receivable	4,000	3,000
Prepaid Expenses	10,000	7,000
Long-term Investments	155,000	225,000

Assets (continued)	Dec. 31, 1994	Dec. 31, 1993
Plant Assets	$428,000	$420,000
Accumulated Depreciation	(149,000)	(118,000)
Franchise	75,000	18,000
Total Assets	$570,000	$600,000

Liabilities and Stockholders' Equity

Accrued Liabilities	$ 10,000	$ 13,000
Notes Payable	—	25,000
Common Stock ($10 par value)	550,000	500,000
Retained Earnings	46,000	62,000
Treasury Stock	(36,000)	—
Total Liabilities and Stockholders' Equity	$570,000	$600,000

During the year, the following transactions occurred:

1. Sold equipment for $20,000 cash that originally cost $42,000 and had $12,000 accumulated depreciation.
2. Sold long-term investments that had cost $70,000 for cash.
3. Paid cash to extend the company's exclusive franchise for another three years.
4. Paid off a note payable at the bank on January 1.
5. Declared and paid a $10,000 dividend.
6. Purchased treasury stock for cash.
7. Acquired land valued at $50,000 by issuing 5,000 shares of common stock.

REQUIRED

a. Prepare a worksheet for a statement of cash flows using the direct method.
b. Prepare a 1994 statement of cash flows using the direct method.
c. Prepare separate schedules showing (1) a reconciliation of net loss to net cash flow from operating activities (see Exhibit 19-9, page 717) and (2) noncash investing and financing transactions.

STATEMENT OF CASH FLOWS (INDIRECT METHOD) — OBJ. 4 —

19-34A Refer to the data given for Rural Company in Problem 19-30A.

REQUIRED

a. Compute the change in cash that occurred during 1994.
b. Prepare a 1994 statement of cash flows using the indirect method.

STATEMENT OF CASH FLOWS (INDIRECT METHOD) — OBJ. 4 —

19-35A Refer to the data given for Sweet Company in Problem 19-31A.

REQUIRED

a. Compute the change in cash that occurred during 1994.
b. Prepare a 1994 statement of cash flows using the indirect method.

STATEMENT OF CASH FLOWS (INDIRECT METHOD) WITH WORKSHEET — OBJ. 4, 5 —

19-36A Refer to the data given for Huber Company in Problem 19-32A.

REQUIRED

a. Prepare a worksheet for a statement of cash flows using the indirect method.
b. Prepare a 1994 statement of cash flows using the indirect method.
c. Prepare separate schedules showing (1) cash paid for interest and for income taxes and (2) noncash investing and financing transactions.

STATEMENT OF CASH FLOWS (INDIRECT METHOD) WITH WORKSHEET — OBJ. 4, 5 —

19-37A Refer to the data given for Towne Company in Problem 19-33A.

REQUIRED

a. Prepare a worksheet for a statement of cash flows using the indirect method.
b. Prepare a 1994 statement of cash flows using the indirect method.
c. Prepare a supplemental disclosure showing noncash investing and financing transactions.

STATEMENT OF CASH FLOWS (INDIRECT METHOD) USING T-ACCOUNT APPROACH — APPENDIX G —

19-38A Refer to the data given for Rural Company in Problem 19-30A.

REQUIRED

a. Use the T-account approach to compile data for a statement of cash flows using the indirect method.
b. Prepare a 1994 statement of cash flows using the indirect method.

STATEMENT OF CASH
FLOWS (INDIRECT
METHOD) USING
T-ACCOUNT APPROACH
— APPENDIX G —

19-39A Refer to the data given for Sweet Company in Problem 19-31A.

REQUIRED

a. Use the T-account approach to compile data for a statement of cash flows using the indirect method.

b. Prepare a 1994 statement of cash flows using the indirect method.

STATEMENT OF CASH
FLOWS (INDIRECT
METHOD) USING
T-ACCOUNT APPROACH
— APPENDIX G —

19-40A Refer to the data given for Towne Company in Problem 19-33A.

REQUIRED

a. Use the T-account approach to compile data for a statement of cash flows using the indirect method.

b. Prepare a 1994 statement of cash flows using the indirect method.

c. Prepare a supplemental disclosure showing noncash investing and financing transactions.

STATEMENT OF CASH
FLOWS (INDIRECT
METHOD) USING
T-ACCOUNT APPROACH
— APPENDIX G —

19-41A Refer to the data given for Huber Company in Problem 19-32A.

REQUIRED

a. Use the T-account approach to compile data for a statement of cash flows using the indirect method.

b. Prepare a 1994 statement of cash flows using the indirect method.

c. Prepare separate schedules showing (1) cash paid for interest and for income taxes and (2) noncash investing and financing transactions.

CASES

Business Decision Case

Recently hired as assistant controller for Finite, Inc., you are sitting next to the controller as she responds to questions at the annual stockholders' meeting. The firm's financial statements contain a statement of cash flows prepared using the indirect method. A stockholder raises his hand.

Stockholder: "I notice depreciation expense is shown as an addition in the calculation of the net cash flow from operating activities."

Controller: "That's correct."

Stockholder: "What depreciation method do you use?"

Controller: "We use the straight-line method for all plant assets."

Stockholder: "Well, why don't you switch to an accelerated depreciation method, such as double declining balance, increase the annual depreciation amount, and thus increase the net cash flow from operating activities?"

The controller pauses, turns to you, and replies: "My assistant will answer your question."

REQUIRED

Prepare an answer to the stockholder's question.

Analytical Application Case

Listed below are selected financial data for four corporations: BROWN-FORMAN CORPORATION (consumer products), GRUMMAN CORPORATION (aerospace), OSMONICS, INC. (filtration products), and ZERO CORPORATION (enclosures and cases). These data cover five years (Year 5 is the most recent year; net income in thousands).

	Year 5	Year 4	Year 3	Year 2	Year 1
Brown-Forman Corporation					
Net income	$145,233	$92,505	$144,497	$103,399	$89,584
Earnings per common share	$5.21	$3.29	$5.15	$3.25	$2.78
Dividend per common share	$2.16	$1.88	$1.52	$1.24	$0.90
Grumman Corporation					
Net income	$85,572	$67,264	$86,465	$35,650	$78,690
Earnings per common share	$2.48	$1.91	$2.50	$0.94	$2.32
Dividend per common share	$1.00	$1.00	$1.00	$1.00	$1.00
Osmonics, Inc.					
Net income	$3,714	$4,047	$2,990	$1,151	$836
Earnings per common share	$0.90	$0.77	$0.57	$0.22	$0.17
Dividend per common share	$–0–	$–0–	$–0–	$–0–	$–0–

	Year 5	Year 4	Year 3	Year 2	Year 1
Zero Corporation					
Net income	$14,592*	$16,114	$16,063	$13,290	$11,602
Earnings per common share	$0.92*	$1.02	$1.02	$0.85	$0.74
Dividend per common share	$0.40	$0.39	$0.34	$0.29	$0.25

*Excluding provision for plant relocation.

REQUIRED

a. Compute the dividend payout ratio for each company for each of the five years.
b. Companies may differ in their dividend policy; that is, they may differ in whether they emphasize a constant dividend amount per share, a steady growth in dividend amount per share, a target or constant dividend payout ratio, or some other criterion. Based on the data available, identify what appears to be each of the above firm's dividend policy over the five-year period.

Ethics Case

Due to an economic recession, Anton Corporation faces severe cash flow problems. Management forecasts that payments to some suppliers will have to be delayed for several months. Jay Newton, controller, has asked his staff for suggestions on selecting the suppliers for which payments will be delayed.

"That's a fairly easy decision," observes Tim Haslem. "Some suppliers charge interest if our payment is late, but others do not. We should pay those suppliers that charge interest and delay payments to the ones that do not charge interest. If we do this, the savings in interest charges will be quite substantial."

"I disagree," states Tara Wirth. "That position is too 'bottom line' oriented. It's not fair to delay payments only to suppliers who don't charge interest for late payments. Most suppliers in that category are ones we have dealt with for years; selecting these suppliers would be taking advantage of the excellent relationships we have developed over the years. The fair thing to do is to make pro rata payments to each supplier."

"Well, making pro rata payments to each supplier means that *all* our suppliers will be upset because no one receives full payment," comments Sue Myling. "I believe it is most important to maintain good relations with our long-term suppliers; we should pay them currently and delay payments to our newer suppliers. The interest costs we end up paying these newer suppliers is the price we must pay to keep our long-term relationships solid."

REQUIRED

Which suppliers should Jay Newton select for delayed payments? Discuss.

What financial statement relationships are of interest to financial statement users?

"**S**tride Rite has now sustained a compounded annual growth rate in earnings per share of 51% since 1984. And our return on equity has climbed steadily to 31.6% in 1990 – one of the highest rates of return among New York Stock Exchange companies..."

Knowing the importance of financial statement relationships, firms may include certain ratios in their annual reports. ■ With more than $1.7 billion of liabilities in 1990, for example, Gannett Co., Inc., reported its 1990 times interest earned ratio (a healthy 9.6) as well. ■ In the same year, The Stride Rite Corporation noted on the cover of its annual report: "And our return on equity has climbed steadily to 31.6% in 1990—one of the highest rates of return among New York Stock Exchange companies...."

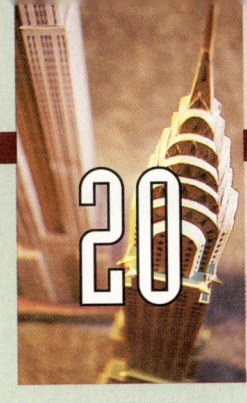

20

ANALYSIS AND INTERPRETATION OF FINANCIAL STATEMENTS

CHAPTER OBJECTIVES

1 **IDENTIFY** sources of financial information for analysts and **DESCRIBE** horizontal analysis of financial statements (pp. 752–757).

2 **DESCRIBE** vertical analysis of financial statements (pp. 757–758).

3 **DEFINE** and **DISCUSS** financial ratios for analyzing profitability (pp. 759–761).

4 **DEFINE** and **DISCUSS** financial ratios for analyzing short-term liquidity (pp. 761–765).

5 **DEFINE** and **DISCUSS** financial ratios for analyzing long-term solvency (pp. 765–768).

6 **DEFINE** and **DISCUSS** financial ratios for analysis by common stock investors (pp. 768–769).

7 **DISCUSS** the limitations of financial analysis (pp. 769–770).

Many individuals and groups, including managers, owners, prospective investors, creditors, labor unions, governmental agencies, and the public, are interested in the data appearing in a firm's financial statements. These parties are usually interested in the profitability and financial strength of the firm in question, although such factors as size, growth, and the firm's efforts to meet its social responsibilities may also be of interest. Managers, owners, and prospective investors may ask the following questions: How do profits this year compare with those of previous years? How do profits compare with those of other firms in the same industry? Creditors may ask: Will our debt be repaid on time? Will the interest payments be met? Unions may ask: How can we show that the firm can support a particular wage increase? Regulatory agencies may ask: What rate of return should the firm be permitted? Is the firm enjoying windfall profits? These kinds of questions can be answered by interpreting the data in financial reports.

Various techniques are used to analyze and interpret financial statement data. In the following pages, we concentrate on some widely used methods of evaluation. In many cases, management may profitably use these techniques to plan and control its own operations, but in this discussion, our viewpoint is primarily that of an outsider.

SOURCES OF INFORMATION

OBJECTIVE ❶ IDENTIFY *sources of financial information for analysts and* DESCRIBE *horizontal analysis of financial statements.*

Except for closely held companies, business firms publish financial statements at least annually, and most large companies also issue them quarterly. Normally, annual statements are attested to by certified public accountants, and the careful analyst reads the accountants' opinion to determine the reliability of the given data. Companies listed on stock exchanges submit annual statements to the Securities and Exchange Commission (SEC). These statements, which are available to any interested party, are generally more useful than annual reports because they furnish a greater amount of detail. Even more detail can be found in *prospectuses* submitted to the SEC by certain companies issuing large amounts of new securities.

For data not provided by the financial statements, a trained analyst has a number of sources: personal interviews with company management, contacts with research organizations, trade association data, and subscriptions to financial services that periodically publish analytical data for many firms. The analyst also can obtain useful information from financial newspapers, such as *The Wall Street Journal* and *Barron's*, and from magazines devoted to financial and economic reporting, such as *Business Week* and *Forbes*. The analyst may want to compare the performance of a particular firm with that of the industry. Data on industry norms, average ratios, and other relationships are available from such agencies as Dun & Bradstreet and Robert Morris Associates. Both Dun & Bradstreet and Robert Morris Associates compile industry statistics for a variety of manufacturers, wholesalers, and retailers. In addition, some brokerage firms compile various industry norms and average ratios from their own computer data bases.

ANALYTICAL TECHNIQUES

Absolute dollar amounts of profits, sales, assets, and other key data are not meaningful when studied individually. For example, knowing that a company's annual earnings are $1 million is of little value unless these earnings can be related to other data. A $1 million profit might represent excellent performance for a company with less than $10 million in invested capital. On the other hand, such earnings would be meager for a firm that has several hundred million dollars in invested capital. Thus, the most significant information derived in analysis concerns the relationships between two or more variables, such as earnings to assets, earnings to sales, and earnings to stockholders' investment. To describe these relationships clearly and to make comparisons easy, the analyst states these relationships in terms of ratios and percentages.

For example, we might express the relationship of $15,000 in earnings to $150,000 in sales as a 10% ($15,000/$150,000) rate of earnings on sales. To describe the relationship between sales of $150,000 and inventory of $20,000, we might use a ratio or a percentage; ($150,000/$20,000) may be expressed as 7.5, 7.5:1, or 750%.

Changes in selected items compared in successive financial statements are often expressed as percentages. For example, if a firm's earnings increased from $40,000 last year to $48,000 this year, the $8,000 increase related to last year (the base year) is expressed as a 20% increase ($8,000/$40,000). To express a dollar increase or decrease as a percentage, however, the analyst must make the base-year amount a positive figure. If, for example, a firm had a net loss of $4,000 in one year and earnings of $20,000 in the next, the $24,000 increase cannot be expressed as a percentage. Similarly, if a firm showed no marketable securities in last year's balance sheet but showed $15,000 of such securities in this year's statement, the $15,000 increase cannot be expressed as a percentage.

When evaluating a firm's financial statements for two or more years, analysts often use **horizontal analysis.** This type of analysis is useful in detecting improvement or deterioration in a firm's performance and in spotting trends. The term **vertical analysis** describes the study of a single year's financial statements.

Horizontal Analysis

COMPARATIVE FINANCIAL STATEMENTS

The form of horizontal analysis encountered most often is **comparative financial statements** for two or more years, showing dollar and/or percentage changes for important items and classification totals. Dollar increases and decreases are divided by the earliest year's data to obtain percentage changes. The 1992 and 1993 financial statements of Alliance Company, an electronic components and accessories manufacturer, are shown in Exhibits 20-1, 20-2, and 20-3. We use the data in these statements throughout this chapter to illustrate various analytical techniques.

When examining financial statements, the analyst focuses immediate attention on significant items only. Although percentage changes are helpful in identifying items to focus on, sometimes they may be misleading. An unusually large percentage change may occur primarily because the dollar amount of the base year is small. This is illustrated by the percentage increase exceeding 1,787% for net cash provided by financing activities (Exhibit 20-3). Large percentage changes also frequently occur in items whose dollar amounts may not be significant compared with other items on the statements. For example, although a large percentage change in Alliance Company's balance sheet occurred in Prepaid Expenses (Exhibit 20-1), the analyst would scarcely notice this item in an initial examination of changes. Instead, attention would be directed first to changes in totals—current assets, total assets, current liabilities, and so on. Next, changes in significant individual items, such as receivables and inventory, would be examined. These changes may be related to certain changes in income statement items or cash flows to determine whether they are favorable.

For example, Alliance Company's total assets increased 17.4% (Exhibit 20-1), and sales increased 29.7% (Exhibit 20-2). A fairly large percentage increase in sales was supported by a much smaller rate of increase in assets. Furthermore, the 19.0% increase in inventory was also considerably less than the increase in sales. These results reflect favorably on the firm's performance. In addition, the 29.7% increase in sales was accompanied by an increase in accounts receivable of only 14.6%; on the surface, the company's sales growth was not associated with a relaxation in credit policy.

EXHIBIT 20—1				
ALLIANCE COMPANY **COMPARATIVE BALANCE SHEETS** **(THOUSANDS OF DOLLARS)**				
	Dec. 31, 1993	Dec. 31, 1992	Increase (Decrease)	Percent Change
Assets				
Current Assets:				
Cash and Cash Equivalents	$ 5,500	$ 4,200	$ 1,300	31.0%
Marketable Securities	2,500	2,400	100	4.2
Accounts Receivable (Net)	59,600	52,000	7,600	14.6
Inventory [Lower of cost (first-in, first-out) or market]	75,000	63,000	12,000	19.0
Prepaid Expenses	900	600	300	50.0
Total Current Assets	$143,500	$122,200	$21,300	17.4
Investments	1,800	1,600	200	12.5
Property, Plant, and Equipment (Net of accumulated depreciation)	47,000	40,000	7,000	17.5
Total Assets	$192,300	$163,800	$28,500	17.4
Liabilities				
Current Liabilities:				
Notes Payable	$ 3,500	$ 3,000	$ 500	16.7
Accounts Payable	25,100	24,100	1,000	4.1
Accrued Liabilities	30,000	27,300	2,700	9.9
Total Current Liabilities	$ 58,600	$ 54,400	$ 4,200	7.7
Long-term Liabilities:				
12% Debenture Bonds Payable	25,000	20,000	5,000	25.0
Total Liabilities	$ 83,600	$ 74,400	$ 9,200	12.4
Stockholders' Equity				
10% Preferred Stock, $100 Par Value	$ 8,000	$ 8,000	$ —	—
Common Stock, $5 Par Value	20,000	14,000	6,000	42.9
Paid-in Capital in Excess of Par Value—Common Stock	6,600	5,500	1,100	36.4
Retained Earnings	74,100	61,900	12,200	19.7
Total Stockholders' Equity	$108,700	$ 89,400	$19,300	21.6
Total Liabilities and Stockholders' Equity	$192,300	$163,800	$28,500	17.4

We see on the income statement that the 38.9% gross profit increase outstripped the rate of increase in sales, indicating a higher mark-up rate in 1993. Net income, however, increased only 21.8%; therefore, expenses must have grown disproportionately. Indeed, selling and administrative expenses increased 44.7% and 52.3%, respectively. Further, the net cash provided by operating activities decreased 28.5% (Exhibit 20-3). This is not a favorable sign; combined with the 7.7% increase in current liabilities, it may signal a problem developing in the firm's ability to pay off its current obligations as they become due.

From this limited analysis of comparative financial statements, an analyst may conclude that operating performance for 1993 was generally favorable when compared with that for 1992. Further analysis using some of the techniques summarized later in the chapter, however, may cause the analyst to modify that opinion. The foregoing analysis has revealed two reservations: selling and administrative expenses increased at a fairly high rate and net cash provided by operating activities decreased even though net income increased.

EXHIBIT 20—2

ALLIANCE COMPANY
COMPARATIVE INCOME STATEMENTS
(THOUSANDS OF DOLLARS)

	Year Ended Dec. 31, 1993	Year Ended Dec. 31, 1992	Increase (Decrease)	Percent Change
Net Sales	$415,000	$320,000	$95,000	29.7%
Cost of Goods Sold	290,000	230,000	60,000	26.1
Gross Profit on Sales	$125,000	$ 90,000	$35,000	38.9
Operating Expenses:				
Selling Expenses	$ 39,500	$ 27,300	$12,200	44.7
Administrative Expenses	49,640	32,600	17,040	52.3
Total Operating Expenses	$ 89,140	$ 59,900	$29,240	48.8
Income before Interest Expense and Income Taxes	$ 35,860	$ 30,100	$ 5,760	19.1
Interest Expense	3,000	2,400	600	25.0
Income before Income Taxes	$ 32,860	$ 27,700	$ 5,160	18.6
Income Tax Expense	14,100	12,300	1,800	14.6
Net Income	$ 18,760	$ 15,400	$ 3,360	21.8
Earnings per Share	$5.28	$5.21		
Dividends per Share	1.44	0.85		

ALLIANCE COMPANY
COMPARATIVE RETAINED EARNINGS STATEMENTS
(THOUSANDS OF DOLLARS)

	Year Ended Dec. 31, 1993	Year Ended Dec. 31, 1992	Increase (Decrease)	Percent Change
Retained Earnings, January 1	$61,900	$49,680	$12,220	24.6%
Net Income	18,760	15,400	3,360	21.8
Total	$80,660	$65,080	$15,580	23.9
Dividends:				
On Preferred Stock	$ 800	$ 800	$ —	—
On Common Stock	5,760	2,380	3,380	142.0
Total	$ 6,560	$ 3,180	$ 3,380	106.3
Retained Earnings, December 31	$74,100	$61,900	$12,200	19.7

TREND ANALYSIS To observe percentage changes over time in selected data, analysts compute **trend percentages.** Most companies provide summaries of data for the past 5 or 10 years in their annual reports. With such information, the analyst may examine changes over a period longer than two years. For example, suppose you were interested in sales and earnings trends for Alliance Company for the past five years. The following are the dollar data for the years 1989–1993):

ALLIANCE COMPANY
ANNUAL PERFORMANCE (MILLIONS OF DOLLARS)

	1989	1990	1991	1992	1993
Sales	$202.0	$215.0	$243.0	$320.0	$415.0
Net income	10.9	11.7	13.5	15.4	18.8

The above data suggest a fairly healthy growth pattern for this company, but we can determine the pattern of change from year to year more precisely by calculating trend percentages. To do this, we select a *base year* and then divide the data for each of the other years by the base-year data. The resultant figures are actually indexes of the

EXHIBIT 20—3

ALLIANCE COMPANY
COMPARATIVE STATEMENTS OF CASH FLOWS
(THOUSANDS OF DOLLARS)

	Year Ended		Increase (Decrease)	Percent Change
	Dec. 31, 1993	Dec. 31, 1992		
Net Cash Flow from Operating Activities				
Net Income	$18,760	$15,400		
Add (Deduct) Items to Convert Net Income to Cash Basis:				
Depreciation	3,000	2,800		
Accounts Receivable Increase	(7,600)	(4,000)		
Inventory Increase	(12,000)	(8,400)		
Prepaid Expenses Increase	(300)	—		
Accounts Payable Increase	1,000	200		
Accrued Liabilites Increase	2,700	1,780		
Net Cash Provided by Operating Activities	$ 5,560	$ 7,780	($2,220)	(28.5)%
Cash Flows from Investing Activities				
Purchase of Marketable Securities	($ 100)	($ 400)	(300)	(75.0)
Purchase of Long-term Investments	(200)	—	200	—
Purchase of Property, Plant, and Equipment	(10,000)	(7,300)	2,700	37.0
Net Cash Used by Investing Activities	($10,300)	($ 7,700)	2,600	33.8
Cash Flows from Financing Activities				
Borrowing on Notes Payable	$ 500	$ 500	—	—
Issuance of Bonds Payable	5,000	3,000	2,000	66.7
Issuance of Common Stock	7,100	—	7,100	—
Payment of Dividends	(6,560)	(3,180)	3,380	106.3
Net Cash Provided by Financing Activities	$ 6,040	$ 320	5,720	1,787.5
Net Increase in Cash and Cash Equivalents	$ 1,300	$ 400		
Cash and Cash Equivalents at Beginning of Year	4,200	3,800		
Cash and Cash Equivalents at End of Year	$ 5,500	$ 4,200		

changes occurring throughout the period. If we choose 1989 as the base year, all data for 1990 through 1993 will be related to 1989, which is represented as 100%.

To create the following table, we divided each year's sales—from 1990 through 1993—by $202, the 1989 sales in millions of dollars. Similarly, the net incomes for 1990 through 1993 were divided by $10.9, the 1989 net income in millions of dollars.

ALLIANCE COMPANY
ANNUAL PERFORMANCE (PERCENTAGE OF BASE YEAR)

	1989	1990	1991	1992	1993
Sales	100	106	120	158	205
Net income	100	107	124	141	172

The trend percentages reveal that the growth in earnings outstripped the growth in sales for 1990 and 1991, then fell below the sales growth in the last two years. We saw in our analysis of comparative statements that a disproportionate increase in selling and administrative expenses emerged in 1993. We might therefore analyze the 1992 data to determine whether net income was affected for the same reason or whether the reduced growth was caused by other factors.

We must exercise care in interpreting trend percentages. Remember that all index percentages are related to the *base year*. Therefore, the change between the 1990 sales index (106%) and the 1991 sales index (120%) represents a 14% increase in terms of *base year* dollars. To express the increase as a percentage of 1990 dollars, we divide the 14% increase by the 106% 1990 sales index to obtain an increase of 13%. We must also be careful to select a *representative* base year. For example, consider the following sales and earnings data during the identical period for a competing company, Century Company:

CENTURY COMPANY
ANNUAL PERFORMANCE

	1989	1990	1991	1992	1993
Sales (millions of dollars)	$192.3	$204.4	$225.0	$299.0	$414.6
Percentage of base year	100	106	117	155	216
Net income (millions of dollars)	$ 1.9	$ 3.0	$ 4.0	$ 6.5	$ 10.0
Percentage of base year	100	158	210	342	526

Note that Century Company's sales growth pattern is similar to Alliance Company's. When judged from trend percentages, however, the net income growth is more than three times that of Alliance Company. Using an unrepresentative base year for Century Company—when earnings were depressed—makes the earnings trend misleading. In 1989, Century Company earned less than 1% of sales ($1.9/$192.3). But in the later years of the period, a more normal relationship between earnings and sales prevailed, and earnings were roughly $2-2\frac{1}{2}\%$ of sales. The earnings/sales relationship for Alliance Company was relatively normal in 1989.

Other data that the analyst may relate to sales and earnings over a period of years include total assets, plant investment, and expenditures for research and development.

Vertical Analysis

OBJECTIVE **2** DESCRIBE *vertical analysis of financial statements.*

The relative importance of various items in financial statements for a single year can be highlighted by showing them as percentages of a key figure. A financial statement that presents the various items as percentages of a key figure is called a **common-size financial statement.** Net sales (or net revenues) is the key figure used in a common-size income statement; total assets is the typical key figure used in a common-size balance sheet.

A financial statement may present both the dollar amounts and common-size percentages. For example, Exhibit 20-4 presents Alliance Company's 1993 income

---

EXHIBIT 20—4

ALLIANCE COMPANY
INCOME STATEMENT WITH COMMON-SIZE PERCENTAGES
FOR THE YEAR ENDED DECEMBER 31, 1993
(THOUSANDS OF DOLLARS)

Net Sales	$415,000	100.0%
Cost of Goods Sold	290,000	69.9
Gross Profit on Sales	$125,000	30.1%
Operating Expenses:		
Selling Expenses	$ 39,500	9.5%
Administrative Expenses	49,640	12.0
Total Operating Expenses	$ 89,140	21.5%
Income before Interest and Taxes	$ 35,860	8.6%
Interest Expense	3,000	0.7
Income before Income Taxes	$ 32,860	7.9%
Income Tax Expense	14,100	3.4
Net Income	$ 18,760	4.5%

statement in dollars and common-size percentages. The common-size percentages show each item in the income statement as a percentage of net sales.

Alliance Company's common-size income statements for 1992 and 1993 are compared with Century Company's in Exhibit 20-5. We see in Exhibit 20-5 that Century Company has a smaller gross profit percentage than does Alliance Company. The disparity might be due either to lower sales prices or higher production costs for Century Company. Selling and administrative expenses as a percentage of sales are fairly comparable, except that, combined, they are a higher percentage of the sales dollar for Alliance Company than for Century Company in 1993. Interest expense as a percentage of sales in 1993 is somewhat higher for Century Company than for Alliance Company. If we consider Century Company's low rate of net income to net sales (2.2% in 1993), the interest percentage is significant. Yet Alliance Company's higher rate of return on sales (about double that of Century Company) is due mainly to its better gross profit margin.

We may also use common-size percentages to analyze balance sheet data, although less successfully than with income statement data. For example, if for a period of several years we state current assets and long-term assets as a percentage of total assets, we can determine whether a company is becoming more or less liquid. The best use of common-size percentages with balance sheet data is probably with the sources of capital (equities). The proportions of the total capital supplied by short-term creditors, long-term creditors, preferred stockholders, and common stockholders of Alliance Company are shown below for 1993:

	Amount (Millions of Dollars)	Common-size Percentage
Current debt	$ 58.6	30.5%
Long-term debt	25.0	13.0
Preferred stock equity	8.0	4.1
Common stock equity	100.7	52.4
	$192.3	100.0%

EXHIBIT 20–5

ALLIANCE AND CENTURY COMPANIES
COMMON-SIZE COMPARATIVE INCOME STATEMENTS
(PERCENTAGE OF NET SALES)

	Alliance Company		Century Company	
	Year Ended Dec. 31, 1993	Year Ended Dec. 31, 1992	Year Ended Dec. 31, 1993	Year Ended Dec. 31, 1992
Net Sales	100.0%	100.0%	100.0%	100.0%
Cost of Goods Sold	69.9	71.9	73.8	74.9
Gross Profit on Sales	30.1%	28.1%	26.2%	25.1%
Operating Expenses:				
Selling Expenses	9.5%	8.5%	8.6%	8.2%
Administrative Expenses	12.0	10.2	12.3	11.4
Total Operating Expenses	21.5%	18.7%	20.9%	19.6%
Income before Interest and Taxes	8.6%	9.4%	5.3%	5.5%
Interest Expense	0.7	0.8	1.0	0.8
Income before Income Taxes	7.9%	8.6%	4.3%	4.7%
Income Tax Expense	3.4	3.8	2.1	2.3
Net Income	4.5%	4.8%	2.2%	2.4%

ANALYSIS OF PROFITABILITY

OBJECTIVE ③ DEFINE *and* DISCUSS *financial ratios for analyzing profitability.*

We have introduced a number of financial ratios in the preceding chapters. At this point, we will classify the ratios by their overall objective and review their computations by calculating them for a single company. Alliance Company's financial statements provide the data for the calculations (all dollar amounts are in thousands). Also, representative industry averages will be presented when available.[1]

Several ratios assist in evaluating how efficiently and effectively a firm operates in its quest for profits; in other words, these ratios analyze various aspects of a firm's profitability. These ratios are (1) gross profit percentage, (2) return on sales, (3) asset turnover, (4) return on assets, and (5) return on common stockholders' equity.

Gross Profit Percentage

The **gross profit percentage** is a closely watched ratio for retailers and manufacturers. The ratio is computed as follows:

$$\text{Gross Profit Percentage} = \frac{\text{Gross Profit on Sales}}{\text{Net Sales}}$$

This ratio reflects the net impact on profitability of changes in a firm's pricing structure, sales mix, and merchandise costs. Both managers and analysts monitor movements in the gross profit percentage.

Alliance's common-size income statements (Exhibit 20-5) reveal that its gross profit percentage improved from 28.1% in 1992 to 30.1% in 1993. These percentages are derived using the following amounts:

	1993	1992
Gross profit	$125,000	$ 90,000
Net sales	415,000	320,000
Gross profit percentage	30.1%	28.1%
Industry average	33.1%	

Although Alliance's ratio improved, the 1993 ratio falls below the industry average.

Return on Sales

Another important measure of operating performance is **return on sales.** An overall test of operating efficiency, this ratio reveals the percentage of each dollar of net sales generated as profit. Return on sales is computed as follows:

$$\text{Return on Sales} = \frac{\text{Net Income}}{\text{Net Sales}}$$

When common-size income statements are available, return on sales equals the net income percentage. Alliance's common-size income statements (Exhibit 20-5) reveal that its return on sales decreased from 4.8% in 1992 to 4.5% in 1993. These percentages are computed using the following amounts:

	1993	1992
Net income	$ 18,760	$ 15,400
Net sales	415,000	320,000
Return on sales	4.5%	4.8%
Industry average	3.9%	

The decline in return on sales is unfavorable, particularly in light of the gross profit percentage increase from 1992 to 1993. This is further evidence that Alliance's selling and administrative expenses increased at a relatively high rate during 1993. Even at that, however, Alliance's 1993 return on sales exceeds the industry average.

---

[1] Although assumed, the industry averages are based on data for manufacturers of electronic components and accessories compiled in 1990 by Robert Morris Associates and Dun & Bradstreet and in 1991 by Standard & Poor's Compustat Services (for *Business Week*).

Return on sales and gross profit percentages should be used only when analyzing similar companies in the same industry or when comparing different periods for the same company (as above). These ratios vary widely by industry. Retail jewelers, for example, have much larger gross profit percentages (industry average around 45%) and returns on sales (industry average around 6%) than retail grocers (industry averages are about 16% for gross profit percentage and about 2% for return on sales). Averages for these industries would also be expected to vary significantly in the next ratio we consider, asset turnover.

Asset Turnover

Asset turnover measures how efficiently a firm utilizes its assets to generate sales revenue. The ratio is computed as follows:

$$\text{Asset Turnover} = \frac{\text{Net Sales}}{\text{Average Total Assets}}$$

The following calculations are for Alliance Company (total assets were $146,100 at the end of 1991):

		1993	1992
Net sales		$415,000	$320,000
Total assets:			
Beginning of year	(a)	163,800	146,100
End of year	(b)	192,300	163,800
Average [(a + b)/2]		178,050	154,950
Asset turnover		2.33	2.07
Industry average		2.0	

Alliance's asset turnover increased from 1992 to 1993, indicating that assets were used more efficiently in 1993 to generate sales revenue. The 1993 ratio also exceeds the industry average.

Some industries that are characterized by low gross profit percentages and returns on sales manage relatively high asset turnovers. Retail grocers, for example, typically turn over assets four to five times per year. In contrast, retail jewelers average one to two asset turnovers per year.

Return on Assets

The rate of return on total assets, generally called **return on assets,** is an overall measure of a firm's profitability and efficiency. It shows the rate of profit earned per dollar of assets under a firm's control. Return on assets is calculated as follows:[2]

$$\text{Return on Assets} = \frac{\text{Net Income}}{\text{Average Total Assets}}$$

Alliance Company's return on assets is calculated as follows:

	1993	1992
Net income	$ 18,760	$ 15,400
Average total assets	178,050	154,950
(see asset turnover calculation)		
Return on assets	10.5%	9.9%
Industry average	8.1%	

Alliance Company improved its return on assets to 10.5% in 1993, a return that is nicely above the industry average.

The return on assets summarizes, in one ratio, the impact of two component ratios: return on sales and asset turnover. Return on assets is the product of these latter ratios, as follows:

---

[2]An alternative computation adds interest expense to net income in the ratio's numerator. This variation keeps the method of financing the assets from influencing the ratio.

Ratio title:	Return on Sales	×	Asset Turnover	=	Return on Assets
Ratio computation:	$\dfrac{\text{Net Income}}{\text{Net Sales}}$	×	$\dfrac{\text{Net Sales}}{\text{Average Total Assets}}$	=	$\dfrac{\text{Net Income}}{\text{Average Total Assets}}$
Alliance Company:	4.5%	×	2.33	=	10.5%

Return on Common Stockholders' Equity

The **return on common stockholders' equity** measures the ultimate profitability of the ownership interest held by common stockholders. The ratio shows the percentage of profit earned on each dollar of common stockholders' equity. The return is earned on the stockholders' equity invested throughout the year, so the ratio uses the average common stockholders' equity, as follows:

$$\frac{\text{Return on Common}}{\text{Stockholders' Equity}} = \frac{\text{Net Income} - \text{Preferred Dividends}}{\text{Average Common Stockholders' Equity}}$$

The return on common stockholders' equity for Alliance Company is calculated below (common stockholders' equity was $69,180 at the end of 1991):

		1993	1992
Net income		$ 18,760	$15,400
Less: Preferred dividends		800	800
Common stock earnings		$ 17,960	$14,600
Common stockholders' equity:			
Beginning of year	(a)	$ 81,400	$69,180
End of year	(b)	101,700	81,400
Average [(a + b)/2]		91,550	75,290
Return on common stockholders' equity		19.6%	19.4%
Industry average		16.0%	

Alliance Company's return on common stockholders' equity improved slightly from 1992 to 1993; it also exceeds the industry average for 1993.

ANALYSIS OF SHORT-TERM LIQUIDITY

OBJECTIVE ④ DEFINE *and* **DISCUSS** *financial ratios for analyzing short-term liquidity.*

A firm's *working capital* is the difference between its current assets and current liabilities. Adequate working capital enables a firm to meet its current obligations on time and take advantage of available discounts. Shortages of working capital can sometimes force a company into disadvantageous borrowing at inopportune times and unfavorable interest rates. Many long-term debt contracts contain provisions that require the borrowing firm to maintain an adequate working capital position.

The adequacy of a firm's working capital is best judged by examining various financial relationships in addition to calculating the working capital amount. For example, compare the following working capital positions of Alliance Company and Dover Company:

	(Thousands of Dollars)	
	Alliance	**Dover**
Current assets	$143,500	$988,700
Current liabilities	58,600	903,800
Working capital	$ 84,900	$ 84,900

Both firms have the same amount of working capital, yet their working capital positions are not equal. Alliance's working capital exceeds its current liabilities whereas Dover's working capital is less than 10% of its current liabilities.

Analysis of a firm's short-term liquidity utilizes several financial ratios that relate to various aspects of working capital. These ratios are (1) current ratio, (2) quick ratio, (3) operating cash flow to current liabilities ratio, (4) accounts receivable turnover and average collection period, and (5) inventory turnover and days' sales in inventory.

Current Ratio

The **current ratio** is simply the current assets divided by the current liabilities.

$$\text{Current Ratio} = \frac{\text{Current Assets}}{\text{Current Liabilities}}$$

This ratio is a widely used measure of a firm's ability to meet its current obligations on time and to have funds readily available for current operations. The following calculations show that Alliance Company improved its current ratio to 2.45 (or 2.45:1) in 1993.

	1993	1992
Current assets	$143,500	$122,200
Current liabilities	58,600	54,400
Current ratio	2.45	2.25
Industry average	2.1	

Evaluating the adequacy of a firm's current ratio may involve comparing it with the recent past (Alliance's current ratio went up in 1993) or with an industry average (Alliance's ratio exceeds the industry average). What is considered an appropriate current ratio will vary by industry. A service firm with little inventory, such as a car wash service, would be expected to have a smaller current ratio than would a firm carrying a large inventory, such as a hardware retailer. At the end of a recent year, for example, the median current ratio for the car wash industry was 0.9; the median current ratio for the retail hardware industry was 2.4. The composition of current assets, therefore, influences the evaluation of short-term liquidity. The quick ratio, which we discuss next, considers the composition of current assets.

Quick Ratio

The **quick ratio** (or *acid-test ratio*) shows the relationship between a firm's liquid, or *quick*, assets and its current liabilities. Quick assets are cash and cash equivalents, short-term investments, and current receivables. Compared with the current ratio, the main item omitted is inventory. Prepaid items are also omitted, but they are usually not material in amount. The quick ratio may give a better picture than the current ratio of a company's ability to meet current debts and to take advantage of discounts offered by creditors. The quick ratio and the current ratio together indicate the influence of the inventory figure in the company's working capital position. For example, a company might have an acceptable current ratio, but if its quick ratio falls much below 1.0, the analyst might be uneasy about the size of the inventory and analyze the inventory position more carefully. The 1.0 rule of thumb for the quick ratio is an arbitrary standard used only to alert the analyst to the need for further scrutiny.

The quick ratio is computed as follows:

$$\text{Quick Ratio} = \frac{\text{Cash and Cash Equivalents} + \text{Short-term Investments} + \text{Current Receivables}}{\text{Current Liabilities}}$$

We calculate the quick ratio for Alliance Company as follows:

	1993	1992
Cash and cash equivalents, marketable securities, and receivables	$67,600	$58,600
Current liabilities	58,600	54,400
Quick ratio	1.15	1.08
Industry average	1.2	

Alliance's quick ratio improved from 1992 to 1993, and its 1993 quick ratio of 1.15 is consistent with the industry average of 1.2.

Operating Cash Flow to Current Liabilities Ratio

Ultimately, cash is needed to settle current liabilities. Another ratio dealing with the ability to pay current liabilities as they become due focuses on the firm's cash flow from operations. The **operating cash flow to current liabilities ratio** is calculated as follows:

$$\text{Operating Cash Flow to Current Liabilities Ratio} = \frac{\text{Net Cash Flow from Operating Activities}}{\text{Average Current Liabilities}}$$

Working capital components are constantly changing as a firm engages in its operating activities—inventory is bought and sold, services are rendered, receivables are collected, employees work, suppliers provide various goods and services, and payments are made to employees and suppliers. This ratio relates the net cash available as a result of these activities for a year to the average current liabilities outstanding during the period. The higher the ratio, the stronger the firm's ability to settle current liabilities as they become due.

Alliance Company's operating cash flow to current liabilities ratio is computed as follows (current liabilities at the end of 1991 were $51,920; no industry average is available):

		1993	1992
Net cash flow from operating activities		$ 5,560	$ 7,780
Current liabilities:			
Beginning of year	(a)	54,400	51,920
End of year	(b)	58,600	54,400
Average [(a + b)/2]		56,500	53,160
Operating cash flow to current liabilities ratio		0.10	0.15

Alliance's ratio worsened from 1992 to 1993, a result of both a decline in cash provided by operating activities and an increase in average current liabilities.

Accounts Receivable Turnover

The speed with which account receivable are collected is of interest in evaluating short-term liquidity. **Accounts receivable turnover** indicates how many times a year a firm collects its average receivables and, thus, measures how fast a firm converts its accounts receivable into cash. Accounts receivable turnover is computed as follows:

$$\text{Accounts Receivable Turnover} = \frac{\text{Net Sales}}{\text{Average Accounts Receivable}}$$

The accounts receivable turnover for Alliance Company is computed below (accounts receivable at the end of 1991 were $48,000):

		1993	1992
Net sales		$415,000	$320,000
Average accounts receivable (net):			
Beginning of year	(a)	52,000	48,000
End of year	(b)	59,600	52,000
Average [(a + b)/2]		55,800	50,000
Accounts receivable turnover		7.44	6.40
Industry average		7.0	

The higher the accounts receivable turnover is, the faster accounts receivable are being converted into cash. Alliance's turnover increased from 6.40 in 1992 to 7.44 in 1993, which is an improvement in the ratio. Alliance's 1993 accounts receivable turnover is also above the industry average of 7.0 for the year.

Average Collection Period

A variation (or extension) of accounts receivable turnover is the **average collection period.** The average collection period, sometimes called *days' sales outstanding,* shows how many days it takes on average to collect an account receivable. It is computed as follows:

$$\text{Average Collection Period} = \frac{365}{\text{Accounts Receivable Turnover}}$$

Alliance Company's average collection period is calculated as follows:

	1993	1992
Average collection period:		
1993: 365/7.44; 1992: 365/6.40	49.1 days	57.0 days
Industry average	52.1 days	

Alliance reduced its average collection period by almost eight days during 1993, so that it is three days less than the industry average. This may have resulted from such actions as a tightening of credit standards or a shortening of the credit period. Or it may reflect that customers have improved their cash flows and are thus able to pay more promptly. Knowledge of Alliance's credit terms would permit us to evaluate its average collection period further. If, for example, Alliance's credit terms are net 30 days, then an average collection period of 49.1 days indicates that it has a problem with slow-paying customers. On the other hand, if the terms are that payment is due within 45 days, then the 1993 average collection period shows no particular problem with the speed of collection.

Inventory Turnover

An analyst concerned about a company's inventory position may compute the company's **inventory turnover.** This figure indicates whether the inventory amount is disproportionate to the amount of sales. Excessive inventories not only tie up company funds and increase storage costs but may also lead to subsequent losses if the goods become outdated or unsaleable. The computation of inventory turnover is as follows:

$$\text{Inventory Turnover} = \frac{\text{Cost of Goods Sold}}{\text{Average Inventory}}$$

Using this measure for Alliance Company gives the following results (inventory at the end of 1991 was $54,600):

		1993	1992
Cost of goods sold		$290,000	$230,000
Inventory:			
Beginning of year	(a)	63,000	54,600
End of year	(b)	75,000	63,000
Average [(a + b)/2]		69,000	58,800
Inventory turnover		4.20	3.91
Industry average		4.6	

Alliance improved its inventory turnover from 1992 to 1993. Its 1993 inventory turnover of 4.20, however, is below the industry average of 4.6.

We use cost of goods sold in the calculation because the inventory measure in the denominator is a *cost* figure; we should therefore use a cost figure in the numerator. However, some financial information services use net sales instead of cost of goods sold to calculate inventory turnover. Analysts who compare a firm's inventory turnover with industry averages should be alert to how the industry average for inventory turnover is computed.

Usually, the average inventory is obtained by adding the year's beginning and ending inventories and dividing by 2. Since inventories taken at the beginning and end of the year are likely to be lower than the typical inventory, an unrealistically high turnover ratio may result. We should use a 12-month average if monthly inventory figures are available. Furthermore, we should be careful in calculating inventory turnover ratios for companies that use last-in, first-out inventory measurement methods, because the inventory amounts may deviate substantially from current costs.

A low inventory turnover can result from an overextended inventory position or from inadequate sales volume. For this reason, appraisal of inventory turnover should be accompanied by scrutiny of the quick ratio and analysis of trends in both inventory and sales.

Days' Sales in Inventory

Days' sales in inventory is derived from a firm's inventory turnover. It shows how many days it takes a firm to sell its average inventory and is computed as follows:

$$\text{Days' Sales in Inventory} = \frac{365}{\text{Inventory Turnover}}$$

Days' sales in inventory for Alliance Company is calculated below:

	1993	1992
Days' sales in inventory 1993: 365/4.20; 1992: 365/3.91	86.9 days	93.4 days
Industry average	79.3 days	

Alliance decreased the time it takes to sell its average inventory from 93.4 days in 1992 to 86.9 days in 1993. Even with this improvement, however, Alliance's length of time exceeds the industry average by more than seven days.

By combining days' sales in inventory with the average collection period, we can estimate the average time period running from the acquisition of inventory to the eventual collection of cash. In 1993, for example, it took Alliance 136.0 days (86.9 days' sales in inventory + 49.1 days for the average collection period) to sell its average inventory and collect the related cash from its customers. Although this time period exceeds the industry average of 131.4 days by more than four days, it is more than two weeks shorter than Alliance's 1992 time period of 150.4 days (93.4 days + 57.0 days). Alliance has improved its performance in this area, but there apparently is still room for more improvement.

ANALYSIS OF LONG-TERM SOLVENCY

OBJECTIVE 5 DEFINE *and* DISCUSS *financial ratios for analyzing long-term solvency.*

Debt-to-Equity Ratio

The preceding set of ratios examined a firm's short-term liquidity. Another set of ratios analyzes long-term solvency. Ratios in the latter group are (1) debt-to-equity ratio, (2) operating cash flow to total liabilities ratio, (3) times interest earned ratio, and (4) operating cash flow to capital expenditures ratio.

The **debt-to-equity ratio** looks at the financial structure of a firm by relating total liabilities to total owners' equity, as follows:

$$\text{Debt-to-Equity Ratio} = \frac{\text{Total Liabilities}}{\text{Total Owners' Equity}}$$

We use year-end balances for the elements in this ratio rather than averages because we are interested in the capital structure at a particular point in time. The total owners' equity for a corporation is its total stockholders' equity.

The debt-to-equity ratio gives potential creditors an indication of the margin of protection available to them (creditors' claims to assets have priority over owners' claims). The lower the ratio, the better the protection being provided to creditors. A firm with a low ratio usually has more flexibility in seeking borrowed funds than does a firm with a high ratio.

Alliance Company's debt to equity ratio is computed as follows:

	1993	1992
Total liabilities (year-end)	$ 83,600	$74,400
Total stockholders' equity (year-end)	108,700	89,400
Debt-to-equity ratio	0.77	0.83
Industry average	0.98	

Alliance's debt-to-equity ratio dropped from 0.83 in 1992 to 0.77 in 1993; the 1993 ratio is also below the industry average. Both the trend in the ratio and its relationship to the industry average would be interpreted as positive aspects of the firm's long-term financial strength.

Operating Cash Flow to Total Liabilities Ratio

Another measure of long-term solvency is the **operating cash flow to total liabilities ratio.** This ratio indicates the extent to which operating activities provide cash that is available to service a firm's liabilities. A firm's operating activities are constantly creating and settling its current liabilities; any positive net cash flow from operations is available to settle long-term liabilities or utilize for other purposes. The ratio is computed as follows:

$$\text{Operating Cash Flow to Total Liabilities Ratio} = \frac{\text{Net Cash Flow from Operating Activities}}{\text{Average Total Liabilities}}$$

The operating cash flow to total liabilities ratio for Alliance Company is calculated as follows (total liabilities at the end of 1991 were $68,920; no industry average is available):

		1993	1992
Net cash flow from operating activities		$ 5,560	$ 7,780
Total liabilities:			
Beginning of year	(a)	74,400	68,920
End of year	(b)	83,600	74,400
Average [(a + b)/2]		79,000	71,660
Operating cash flow to total liabilities ratio		0.07	0.11

The higher this ratio is, the more positive is the indication of long-term financial strength. The drop in Alliance's ratio from 0.11 in 1992 to 0.07 in 1993 would be considered an unfavorable change.

Times Interest Earned Ratio

To evaluate further the size of a company's debt, an analyst may observe the relationship of interest charges to earnings. For example, an extremely high debt-to-equity ratio for a company may indicate heavy borrowing. However, if its earnings are sufficient, even in poor years, to meet the interest charges on the debt several times over, the analyst may regard the situation quite favorably.

Analysts, particularly long-term creditors, almost always calculate the **times interest earned ratio.** This ratio is determined by dividing the income before interest expense and income taxes by the annual interest expense:

$$\text{Times Interest Earned Ratio} = \frac{\text{Income before Interest Expense and Income Taxes}}{\text{Interest Expense}}$$

The computations for Alliance Company are as follows:

	1993	1992
Income before interest expense and income taxes	$35,860	$30,100
Interest expense	3,000	2,400
Times interest earned ratio	11.95	12.54
Industry average	3.2	

Alliance Company's income available to meet interest charges each year was approximately 12 times the amount of its interest expense. The 1993 ratio is well above the industry average. Alliance Company has an exceptionally good margin of safety. Generally speaking, a company that earns its interest several times before taxes in its poor years is regarded as a satisfactory risk by long-term creditors.

Operating Cash Flow to Capital Expenditures Ratio

The ability of a firm's operations to provide sufficient cash to replace, and expand when appropriate, its property, plant, and equipment is shown by the **operating cash flow to capital expenditures ratio.** To the extent that acquisitions of plant assets can be financed out of cash provided by operating activities, a firm does not have to use other financing sources, such as long-term debt. The ratio is calculated as follows:

$$\text{Operating Cash Flow to Capital Expenditures Ratio} = \frac{\text{Net Cash Flow from Operating Activities}}{\text{Annual Capital Expenditures}}$$

A ratio of 1.0 means that the firm's current operating activities are providing sufficient cash to provide the desired level of plant capacity. A ratio in excess of 1.0 means that there is net cash available from operations in excess of plant asset needs that may be used for other purposes, such as retiring long-term debt.

FOCUS FOR INVESTORS

Baruch Lev, *an accounting professor at the University of California at Berkeley, has tested several gauges that analysts typically use, to see which of them is best in measuring a company's earnings potential, and in predicting its stock performance, too.* ■ *The most important items on financial statements, he says, are trends in inventory, accounts receivable, and order backlogs. "These are the strongest indicators, and are much more closely related to stock returns than reported earnings," he says.*

TRACKING INVENTORIES

In particular, investors should look at how companies' inventories of finished goods track their sales. If inventories are rising faster than sales, "It's a bad signal, because it shows the company is having difficulty selling its product, and suggests a hit to future earnings as a result of management's efforts to get rid of those inventories," he says.

For similar reasons, he says, it pays to watch accounts receivable, or IOUs from customers that have received goods but not yet paid for them. If these are rising faster than sales, not only can this signal trouble with sales but may show vulnerability to customer defaults.

Mr. Lev also advises comparing the percentage change in a company's order backlog to the percentage change in its sales. This "turns out to be a *very* important indicator for future stock returns," he says. If the order backlog is growing faster than sales, this is a good sign for investors, but if it is lagging, this spells trouble.

Companies aren't required to report their order backlogs, however. If a particular company doesn't do this, Mr. Lev says, check the trend in its gross operating margins compared with its sales trend. If margin growth lags behind sales growth, this can mean future earnings are on shaky footing; if margin growth is outpacing sales growth, this can be a sign of strength. . . .

Aside from balance sheet data, accounting signals can tell a lot about the integrity of a company's earnings, Mr. Lev says. For example, last-in, first-out accounting produces much more reliable earnings figures than first-in, first-out methods, because LIFO more accurately captures the real cost of sales, he says. And when auditors qualify a company's results, or don't give an opinion, he says this is "obviously a strong negative."

In general, lax accounting policies mean a company's reported earnings aren't as good as they look. For example, companies that use 40-year depreciation schedules, or that suddenly shift to a longer depreciation schedule from a shorter one, are probably overstating earnings.

'STRONG BALANCE SHEET'

High debt is another red flag, particularly in these days of scarce credit and economic uncertainty, professional investors say. "You really want a strong balance sheet, just in case after doing all this work, your assessment is wrong," Boniface Zaino, managing director at Trust Co. of the West, says.

If long-term debt as a percentage of a company's equity is high, relative to other companies in the same industry or the market as a whole, this means the company doesn't have much of a buffer against lean times. "Until we're past the eye of the economic storm, you really don't want any part of leverage," Richard Bernstein, senior quantitative analyst at Merrill Lynch & Co., says.

By contrast, a large cash position is a big plus, not only for safety but also because it indicates the company is in a position to take advantage of competitors' problems. . . .

The operating cash flow to capital expenditures ratio for Alliance Company is computed below (no industry average is available):

	1993	1992
Net cash flow from operating activities	$ 5,560	$7,780
Annual capital expenditures (see Exhibit 20-3)	10,000	7,300
Operating cash flow to capital expenditures ratio	0.56	1.07

Alliance's ratio decreased from 1.07 in 1992 to 0.56 in 1993. Not only did the net cash provided by operations decrease in 1993, but capital expenditures increased. The increase in capital expenditures, however, may reflect the decision to do some financing with common stock in 1993, a source that was not used in 1992 (see Exhibit 20-3).

ANALYSIS FOR COMMON STOCK INVESTORS

OBJECTIVE ⑥ DEFINE *and* DISCUSS *financial ratios for analysis by common stock investors.*

Present and potential common stockholders share an interest with other parties in analyzing the profitability, short-term liquidity, and long-term solvency of a corporation. There are other financial ratios, however, that are primarily of interest to common stockholders. These ratios are (1) earnings per share, (2) price-earnings ratio, (3) dividend yield, and (4) dividend payout ratio.

Earnings per Share

Because stock market prices are quoted on a per-share basis, the reporting of **earnings per share** of common stock is useful to investors. Our discussion of earnings per share in an earlier chapter noted that the computation for corporations with simple capital structures is as follows:

$$\text{Earnings per Share} = \frac{\text{Net Income} - \text{Preferred Dividends}}{\text{Weighted Average Common Shares Outstanding}}$$

Earnings per share must be reported on the income statement, so the analyst does not have to compute this ratio. Alliance Company's income statements show the following earnings per share (Exhibit 20-2; no industry average is available):

	1993	1992
Earnings per share	$5.28	$5.21

Even though Alliance Company's net income increased almost 22% in 1993, earnings per share increased only slightly because a large number of additional common shares were issued during the year.

Price-Earnings Ratio

The **price-earnings ratio** is the result of dividing the market price of a share of common stock by the earnings per share.

$$\text{Price-Earnings Ratio} = \frac{\text{Market Price per Share}}{\text{Earnings per Share}}$$

For many analysts and investors, this ratio is an important tool in assessing stock values. For example, after evaluating the strong and weak points of several companies in an industry, the analyst may compare price-earnings ratios to determine the "best buy."

When determining the price-earnings ratio, we customarily use the latest market price and the earnings per share for the last four quarters of a company's operations. Alliance Company's price-earnings ratios at the end of 1992 and 1993 are computed as follows (year-end market prices follow):

	1993	1992
Market price per share (at year-end)	$55.50	$53.75
Earnings per share	5.28	5.21
Price-earnings ratio	10.5	10.3
Industry average	12	

The market price of a share of Alliance's common stock was slightly more than 10 times the amount that share earned in both 1992 and 1993. Alliance's price-earnings ratio at the end of 1993 is a little below the industry average.

Dividend Yield

Investors' expectations vary a great deal with personal economic circumstances and with the overall economic outlook. Some investors are more interested in the price appreciation of a stock investment than in present income in the form of dividends.

When shares are disposed of in the future, the capital gains provision of the income tax laws may tax any gains at a rate that is lower than the rate applied to other income. Other investors are more concerned with dividends than with price appreciation. Such investors desire a high **dividend yield** on their investments. Dividend yield is calculated by dividing the current annual dividends per share by the current price of the stock:

$$\text{Dividend Yield} = \frac{\text{Annual Dividends per Share}}{\text{Market Price per Share}}$$

Alliance Company's dividend yields are computed as follows (dividends per share are disclosed in Exhibit 20-2; no industry average is available):

	1993	1992
Annual dividends per share	$ 1.44	$ 0.85
Market price per share (at year-end)	55.50	53.75
Dividend yield	2.6%	1.6%

Even though Alliance's dividend yield was higher at the end of 1993 than it was at the end of 1992, the dividend yields for both years would be considered low.

Dividend Payout Ratio

Investors who emphasize the yield on their investments may also be interested in a firm's **dividend payout ratio,** which is the percentage of the common stock earnings paid out in dividends. The payout ratio indicates whether a firm has a conservative or a liberal dividend policy and may also indicate whether the firm is conserving funds for internal financing of growth. We calculate the dividend payout ratio as follows:

$$\text{Dividend Payout Ratio} = \frac{\text{Annual Dividends per Share}}{\text{Earnings per Share}}$$

Alliance Company's dividend payout ratios are calculated as follows (no industry average is available):

	1993	1992
Annual dividends per share	$1.44	$0.85
Earnings per share	5.28	5.21
Dividend payout ratio	27.3%	16.3%

Alliance increased its dividend payout ratio in 1993 compared with 1992. The payout ratios in both years, however, would be considered relatively low.

Payout ratios for typical, seasoned industrial corporations vary between 40% and 60%. Many corporations, however, need funds for internal financing of growth and pay out little or nothing in dividends. At the other extreme, some companies—principally utility companies—may pay out as much as 70% or 80% of their earnings. Utilities have less need to retain funds for growth because the bulk of their financing is through long-term debt.

LIMITATIONS OF FINANCIAL ANALYSIS

OBJECTIVE 7 DISCUSS *the limitations of financial analysis.*

The ratios, percentages, and other relationships we have described in this chapter are merely the result of analytical techniques. They may only isolate areas requiring further investigation. Moreover, we must interpret them with due consideration to general economic conditions, conditions of the industry in which the companies operate, and the positions of individual companies within the industry.

We should also be aware of the inherent limitations of financial statement data. Problems of comparability are frequently encountered. Companies otherwise similar may use different accounting methods, which can cause problems in comparing certain key relationships. For instance, inventory turnover is different for a company using LIFO inventory costing than for one using FIFO. Inflation may distort certain computations, especially those resulting from horizontal analysis. For example, trend percentages calculated from data unadjusted for inflation may be deceptive.

We must be careful even when comparing companies in a particular industry. Such factors as size, diversity of product, and mode of operations can make the firms completely dissimilar. Some firms, particularly conglomerates, are difficult to classify by industry. If segment information—particularly product-line data—is available, the analyst may compare the statistics for several industries. Often, trade associations prepare industry statistics that are stratified by size of firm or type of product, making analysis easier.

KEY POINTS FOR CHAPTER OBJECTIVES

1 IDENTIFY sources of financial information for analysts and DESCRIBE horizontal analysis of financial statements (pp. 752–757).
- Data sources include published financial statements, filings with the SEC, and statistics available from financial services.
- A common form of horizontal analysis is inspecting dollar and percentage changes in comparative financial statements for two or more years.
- Analyzing trend percentages of key figures, such as net sales, net income, and total assets for a number of years, related to a base year, is often useful.

2 DESCRIBE vertical analysis of financial statements (pp. 757–758).
- Vertical analysis deals with the relationships of financial statement data for a single year.
- Common-size statements express items on a financial statement as a percentage of a key item, such as expressing income statement items as a percentage of net sales.

3 DEFINE and DISCUSS financial ratios for analyzing profitability (pp. 759–761).
- Ratios for analyzing profitability are gross profit percentage, return on sales, asset turnover, return on assets, and return on common stockholders' equity.

4 DEFINE and DISCUSS financial ratios for analyzing short-term liquidity (pp. 761–765).
- Ratios for analyzing short-term liquidity are current ratio, quick ratio, operating cash flow to current liabilities ratio, accounts receivable turnover, average collection period, inventory turnover, and days' sales in inventory.

5 DEFINE and DISCUSS financial ratios for analyzing long-term solvency (pp. 765–768).
- Ratios for analyzing long-term solvency are debt-to-equity ratio, operating cash flow to total liabilities ratio, times interest earned ratio, and operating cash flow to capital expenditures ratio.

6 DEFINE and DISCUSS financial ratios for analysis by common stock investors (pp. 768–769).
- Ratios of particular interest to common stock investors are earnings per share, price-earnings ratio, dividend yield, and dividend payout ratio.

7 DISCUSS the limitations of financial analysis (pp. 769–770).
- When analyzing statements, one must be aware of the firm's accounting methods, the effects of inflation, and the difficulty of identifying a firm's industry classification.

SUMMARY OF FINANCIAL STATEMENT RATIOS

Analysis of Profitability

$$\text{Gross Profit Percentage} = \frac{\text{Gross Profit on Sales}}{\text{Net Sales}}$$

$$\text{Return on Sales} = \frac{\text{Net Income}}{\text{Net Sales}}$$

$$\text{Asset Turnover} = \frac{\text{Net Sales}}{\text{Average Total Assets}}$$

$$\text{Return on Assets} = \frac{\text{Net Income}}{\text{Average Total Assets}}$$

$$\text{Return on Common Stockholders' Equity} = \frac{\text{Net Income} - \text{Preferred Dividends}}{\text{Average Common Stockholders' Equity}}$$

Analysis of Short-term Liquidity

$$\text{Current Ratio} = \frac{\text{Current Assets}}{\text{Current Liabilities}}$$

$$\text{Quick Ratio} = \frac{\text{Cash and Cash Equivalents} + \text{Short-term Investments} + \text{Current Receivables}}{\text{Current Liabilities}}$$

$$\frac{\text{Operating Cash Flow to}}{\text{Current Liabilities Ratio}} = \frac{\text{Net Cash Flow from Operating Activities}}{\text{Average Current Liabilities}}$$

$$\text{Accounts Receivable Turnover} = \frac{\text{Net Sales}}{\text{Average Accounts Receivable}}$$

$$\text{Average Collection Period} = \frac{365}{\text{Accounts Receivable Turnover}}$$

$$\text{Inventory Turnover} = \frac{\text{Cost of Goods Sold}}{\text{Average Inventory}}$$

$$\text{Days' Sales in Inventory} = \frac{365}{\text{Inventory Turnover}}$$

Analysis of Long-term Solvency

$$\text{Debt-to-Equity Ratio} = \frac{\text{Total Liabilities}}{\text{Total Owners' Equity}}$$

$$\frac{\text{Operating Cash Flow to}}{\text{Total Liabilities Ratio}} = \frac{\text{Net Cash Flow from Operating Activities}}{\text{Average Total Liabilities}}$$

$$\text{Times Interest Earned Ratio} = \frac{\text{Income before Interest Expense and Income Taxes}}{\text{Interest Expense}}$$

$$\frac{\text{Operating Cash Flow to}}{\text{Capital Expenditures Ratio}} = \frac{\text{Net Cash Flow from Operating Activities}}{\text{Annual Capital Expenditures}}$$

Analysis for Common Stock Investors

$$\text{Earnings per Share} = \frac{\text{Net Income} - \text{Preferred Dividends}}{\text{Weighted Average Common Shares Outstanding}}$$

$$\text{Price-Earnings Ratio} = \frac{\text{Market Price per Share}}{\text{Earnings per Share}}$$

$$\text{Dividend Yield} = \frac{\text{Annual Dividends per Share}}{\text{Market Price per Share}}$$

$$\text{Dividend Payout Ratio} = \frac{\text{Annual Dividends per Share}}{\text{Earnings per Share}}$$

SELF-TEST QUESTIONS FOR REVIEW

(Answers follow the Solution to Demonstration Problem.)

All of the self-test questions are based on the following data:

THERMO COMPANY
BALANCE SHEET
DECEMBER 31, 1993

Cash	$ 40,000	Current Liabilities	$ 80,000
Accounts Receivable (Net)	80,000	10% Bonds Payable	120,000
Inventory	130,000	Common Stock	200,000
Plant and Equipment (Net)	250,000	Retained Earnings	100,000
		Total Liabilities and	
Total Assets	$500,000	Stockholders' Equity	$500,000

Net sales for 1993 were $800,000, gross profit was $320,000, and net income was $36,000. The income tax rate was 40%. A year ago accounts receivable (net) were $76,000, inventory was $110,000, and common stockholders' equity was $260,000. The bonds payable were outstanding all year and 1993 interest expense was $12,000.

1. The current ratio of Thermo Company at 12/31/93, calculated from the above data, was 3.13, and the working capital was $170,000. If the firm paid $20,000 of its current liabilities, immediately after this transaction,
   a. Both the current ratio and the working capital would decrease.
   b. Both the current ratio and the working capital would increase.
   c. The current ratio would increase, but the working capital would remain the same.
   d. The current ratio would increase, but the working capital would decrease.

2. The firm's inventory turnover for the year was
   a. 6.67   b. 4   c. 6   d. 3.69

3. The firm's return on common stockholders' equity was
   a. 25.7%   b. 12.9%   c. 17.1%   d. 21.4%

4. The firm's average collection period for receivables was
   a. 36.5 days   b. 37.4 days   c. 35.6 days   d. 18.3 days

5. The firm's times interest earned ratio for the year was
   a. 4   b. 3   c. 5   d. 6

DEMONSTRATION PROBLEM FOR REVIEW

Knox Instruments, Inc., is a manufacturer of various medical and dental instruments. Financial statement data for the firm follow.

1993	(Thousands of Dollars, except per Share Amount)
Net Sales	$200,000
Cost of Goods Sold	98,000
Net Income	10,750
Dividends	4,200
Net Cash Provided by Operating Activities	7,800
Earnings per Share	2.71

KNOX INSTRUMENTS, INC.
BALANCE SHEETS
(THOUSANDS OF DOLLARS)

Assets	Dec. 31, 1993	Dec. 31, 1992
Cash	$ 3,000	$ 2,900
Accounts Receivable (Net)	28,000	28,800
Inventory	64,000	44,000
Total Current Assets	$ 95,000	$ 75,700
Plant Assets	76,000	67,300
Total Assets	$171,000	$143,000

Liabilities and Stockholders' Equity		
Current Liabilities	$ 45,200	$ 39,750
10% Bonds Payable	20,000	14,000
Total Liabilities	$ 65,200	$ 53,750
Common Stock, $10 Par Value	$ 40,000	$ 30,000
Retained Earnings	65,800	59,250
Total Stockholders' Equity	$105,800	$ 89,250
Total Liabilities and Stockholders' Equity	$171,000	$143,000

REQUIRED

a. Using the given data, calculate items 1 through 9 for 1993. Compare the performance of Knox Instruments, Inc., with the following industry averages and comment on its operations.

	Median Ratios for the Industry
1. Current ratio	2.7
2. Quick ratio	1.6
3. Average collection period	73 days
4. Inventory turnover	2.3
5. Operating cash flow to current liabilities ratio	NA
6. Debt-to-equity ratio	0.50
7. Return on assets	4.9%
8. Return on common stockholders' equity	10.2%
9. Return on sales	4.1%

b. Calculate the dividends paid per share of common stock. (Use average number of shares outstanding during the year.) What was the dividend payout ratio?

c. If the 1993 year-end price per share of common stock is $25, what is (1) the price-earnings ratio? (2) the dividend yield?

SOLUTION TO DEMONSTRATION PROBLEM

a. 1.
$$\text{Current ratio} = \frac{\$95,000}{\$45,200} = 2.10$$

2.
$$\text{Quick ratio} = \frac{\$31,000}{\$45,200} = 0.69$$

3. Average collection period:

$$\text{Accounts receivable turnover} = \frac{\$200,000}{(\$28,800 + \$28,000)/2} = 7.04$$

$$\text{Average collection period} = \frac{365}{7.04} = 51.8 \text{ days}$$

4.
$$\text{Inventory turnover} = \frac{\$98,000}{(\$44,000 + \$64,000)/2} = 1.81$$

5.
$$\text{Operating cash flow to current liabilities ratio} = \frac{\$7,800}{(\$39,750 + \$45,200)/2} = 0.18$$

6.
$$\text{Debt-to-equity ratio} = \frac{\$65,200}{\$105,800} = 0.62$$

7.
$$\text{Return on assets} = \frac{\$10,750}{(\$143,000 + \$171,000)/2} = 6.8\%$$

8.
$$\text{Return on common stockholders' equity} = \frac{\$10,750}{(\$89,250 + \$105,800)/2} = 11.0\%$$

9.
$$\text{Return on sales} = \frac{\$10,750}{\$200,000} = 5.4\%$$

Although the firm's current ratio, 2.10, is below the industry median, it is still acceptable. However, the quick ratio, 0.69, is far below the industry median. This indicates that the inventory (which is omitted from this calculation) is excessive; this is borne out by the firm's inventory turnover of 1.81 times, which compares with the industry median of 2.3 times. The firm's average collection period of 51.8 days is significantly better than the industry median of 73 days. No industry median is available for the operating cash flow to current liabilities ratio. The debt-to-equity ratio of 0.62 indicates that the firm has proportionately more debt in its capital structure than the median industry firm, which has a debt-to-equity ratio of 0.50. The firm's operations appear efficient, because its return on assets, return on stockholders' equity, and return on sales all exceed the industry medians.

b. Average number of shares outstanding = (4,000,000 + 3,000,000)/2 = 3,500,000 shares.
$4,200,000 dividends/3,500,000 shares = $1.20 dividends per share.
Dividend payout ratio = $4,200,000 dividends/$10,750,000 net income = 39.1%.

c. Earnings per share = $10,750,000/3,500,000 shares = $3.07.
Price-earnings ratio = $25/$3.07 = 8.1.
Dividend yield = $1.20/$25 = 4.8%.

ANSWERS TO SELF-TEST QUESTIONS   1. c, p. 762   2. b, p. 764   3. b, p. 761   4. c, p. 763   5. d, p. 766

GLOSSARY OF KEY TERMS USED IN THIS CHAPTER

accounts receivable turnover   Annual net sales divided by average accounts receivable (net) (p. 763).

asset turnover   Net income divided by average total assets (p. 760).

average collection period   365 days divided by accounts receivable turnover (p. 763).

common-size financial statement   A financial statement in which each item is presented as a percentage of a key figure (p. 757).

comparative financial statements   A form of horizontal analysis involving comparison of two or more periods' financial statements showing dollar and percentage changes (p. 753).

current ratio   A firm's current assets divided by its current liabilities (p. 762).

days' sales in inventory   365 days divided by inventory turnover (p. 764).

debt-to-equity ratio   A firm's total liabilities divided by its total owners' equity (p. 765).

dividend payout ratio   Annual dividends per share divided by the earnings per share (p. 769).

dividend yield   Annual dividends per share divided by the market price per share (p. 769).

earnings per share   Net income less preferred stock dividends divided by the weighted average common shares outstanding for the period (p. 768).

gross profit percentage   Gross profit on sales divided by net sales (p. 759).

horizontal analysis   Analysis of a firm's financial statements that covers two or more years (p. 753).

inventory turnover   Cost of goods sold divided by average inventory (p. 764).

operating cash flow to capital expenditures ratio   A firm's net cash flow from operating activities divided by its annual capital expenditures (p. 766).

operating cash flow to current liabilities ratio   A firm's net cash flow from operating activities divided by its average current liabilities (p. 762).

operating cash flow to total liabilities ratio   A firm's net cash flow from operating activities divided by its average total liabilities (p. 765).

price-earnings ratio   Current market price per common share divided by earnings per share (p. 768).

quick ratio   Quick assets (that is, cash and cash equivalents, short-term investments, and current receivables) divided by current liabilities (p. 762).

return on assets   Net income divided by average total assets (p. 760).

return on common stockholders' equity   Net income less preferred stock dividends divided by average common stockholders' equity (p. 761).

return on sales   Net income divided by net sales (p. 759).

times interest earned ratio   Income before interest expense and income taxes divided by interest expense (p. 766).

trend percentages   A comparison of the same financial item over two or more years stated as a percentage of a base-year amount (p. 755).

vertical analysis   Analysis of a firm's financial statements that focuses on the statements of a single year (p. 753).

QUESTIONS

20-1   Distinguish between horizontal analysis and vertical analysis of financial statements.

20-2   "Analysts should focus attention on each item showing a large percentage change from one year to the next." Is this statement correct? Comment.

20-3   What are trend percentages and how are they calculated? What pitfalls must an analyst avoid when preparing trend percentages?

20-4   The following data are taken from the income statements of Maste Company. Using 1990 as the base year, calculate trend percentages.

	1990	1991	1992	1993
Sales	$500,000	$560,000	$625,000	$700,000
Net income	25,000	29,000	31,500	36,000

20-5   What are common-size financial statements and how are they used?

20-6   What item is the key figure (that is, 100%) in a common-size income statement? a common-size balance sheet?

20-7 During the past year, Lite Company had net income of $4 million, and Scanlon Company had net income of $7 million. Both companies manufacture electrical components for the building trade. What additional information would you need to compare the profitability of the two companies? Discuss your answer.

20-8 Under what circumstances can return on sales be used to appraise the profitability of a company? Can this ratio be used to compare the profitability of companies from different industries? Explain.

20-9 What is the relationship between asset turnover, return on assets, and return on sales?

20-10 For 1994, Blare Company had a return on sales of 5.5% and an asset turnover of 2.60. What is Blare's 1994 return on assets?

20-11 What does the return on common stockholders' equity measure?

20-12 How does the quick ratio differ from the current ratio?

20-13 For each of the following ratios, indicate whether a high ratio or low ratio would be considered, in general, a positive sign:
  a. Current ratio.
  b. Quick ratio.
  c. Operating cash flow to current liabilities ratio.
  d. Accounts receivable turnover.
  e. Average collection period.
  f. Inventory turnover.
  g. Days' sales in inventory.

20-14 Discuss the significance of the debt-to-equity ratio and explain how it is computed.

20-15 Why do we determine the times interest earned ratio and how is it calculated?

20-16 What does the operating cash flow to capital expenditures ratio measure?

20-17 Clair, Inc., earned $5.50 per share of common stock in the current year and paid dividends of $2.53 per share. The most recent market price of the common stock is $63.25 per share. Calculate (a) the price-earnings ratio, (b) the dividend yield, and (c) the dividend payout ratio.

20-18 Identify two inherent limitations of financial statement data.

EXERCISES

COMPARATIVE INCOME STATEMENTS
— OBJ. 1 —

20-19 Consider the following income statement data from Ross Company for 1993 and 1994.

	1994	1993
Sales	$875,000	$750,000
Cost of Goods Sold	560,000	465,000
Selling Expenses	175,000	165,000
Administrative Expenses	100,000	90,000
Income Tax Expense	13,000	9,000

  a. Prepare a comparative income statement, showing increases and decreases in dollars and in percentages.
  b. Comment briefly on the changes between the two years.

COMMON-SIZE INCOME STATEMENTS
— OBJ. 2 —

20-20 Refer to the income statement data given in Exercise 20-19.
  a. Prepare common-size income statements for each year.
  b. Compare the common-size income statements and comment briefly.

RATIOS ANALYZING PROFITABILITY
— OBJ. 3 —

20-21 The following information is available for Buhler Company:

Annual data	1993	1992
Net sales	$8,500,000	$8,000,000
Gross profit on sales	2,932,500	2,720,000
Net income	535,500	472,000

Year-end data	Dec. 31, 1993	Dec. 31, 1992
Total assets	$6,400,000	$5,800,000
Common stockholders' equity	3,700,000	3,300,000

Calculate the following ratios for 1993:
a. Gross profit percentage.
b. Return on sales.
c. Asset turnover.
d. Return on assets.
e. Return on common stockholders' equity (Buhler Company has no preferred stock outstanding).

WORKING CAPITAL AND SHORT-TERM LIQUIDITY RATIOS
— OBJ. 4 —

20-22   Bell Company has a current ratio of 3.34 (3.34:1) on December 31, 1993. On that date its current assets are as follows:

Cash	$ 30,000
Short-term investments	56,000
Accounts receivable (net)	192,000
Inventory	228,200
Prepaid expenses	11,500
	$517,700

Bell Company's current liabilities at December 31, 1992, were $125,000 and during 1993 its operating activities provided a net cash flow of $56,000.
a. What are the firm's current liabilities on December 31, 1993?
b. What is the firm's working capital on December 31, 1993?
c. What is the quick ratio on December 31, 1993?
d. What is the 1993 operating cash flow to current liabilities ratio?

RECEIVABLE AND INVENTORY RATIOS
— OBJ. 4 —

20-23   Bell Company, whose current assets at December 31, 1993, are shown in Exercise 20-22, had 1993 net sales of $940,000 and cost of goods sold of $531,100. At January 1, 1993, accounts receivable (net) were $176,000 and inventory was $220,800.
a. What is the 1993 accounts receivable turnover?
b. What is the 1993 average collection period?
c. What is the 1993 inventory turnover?
d. What is the 1993 days' sales in inventory?

RATIOS ANALYZING LONG-TERM SOLVENCY
— OBJ. 5 —

20-24   The following information is available for Antler Company:

Annual data	1993	1992
Interest expense	$ 75,000	$ 62,000
Income tax expense	183,500	145,000
Net income	448,500	375,000
Capital expenditures	332,000	420,000
Net cash provided by operating activities	415,000	390,000

Year-end data	Dec. 31, 1993	Dec. 31, 1992
Total liabilities	$1,800,000	$1,400,000
Total owners' equity	3,000,000	2,600,000

Calculate the following:
a. 1993 year-end debt-to-equity ratio.
b. 1993 operating cash flow to total liabilities ratio.
c. 1993 times interest earned ratio.
d. 1993 operating cash flow to capital expenditures ratio.

RATIOS FOR COMMON STOCK INVESTORS
— OBJ. 6 —

20-25   Kluster Corporation has only common stock issued and outstanding. The firm reported earnings per share of $4.80 for 1994. During 1994, Kluster paid dividends of $1.44 per share. On December 31, 1994, the current market price of the stock was $18 per share. Calculate the following:
a. 1994 year-end price-earnings ratio.
b. 1994 dividend yield.
c. 1994 dividend payout ratio.

PROBLEMS

TREND PERCENTAGES
— OBJ. 1 —

20-26 Net sales, net income, and total asset figures for Vibrant Controls, Inc., for five consecutive years are given below (Vibrant manufactures pollution controls):

	Annual Amounts (Thousands of Dollars)				
	1990	**1991**	**1992**	**1993**	**1994**
Net sales	$81,500	$88,350	$97,200	$103,600	$108,400
Net income	3,600	3,950	4,350	4,875	6,500
Total assets	42,500	44,200	48,960	52,225	54,600

REQUIRED

a. Calculate trend percentages, using 1990 as the base year.
b. Calculate the return on sales for each year. (Rates above 2.6% are considered good for manufacturers of pollution controls; rates above 6.6% are considered very good.)
c. Comment on the results of your analysis.

CHANGES IN VARIOUS
RATIOS
— OBJ. 1, 3, 4, 5 —

20-27 Selected information follows for Brimmer Company, taken from the 1993 and 1994 financial statements:

	1994	**1993**
Net sales	$920,000	$840,000
Cost of goods sold	580,000	542,000
Interest expense	20,000	20,000
Income tax expense	27,000	24,000
Net income	60,000	52,000
Net cash flow from operating activities	68,000	55,000
Capital expenditures	40,000	45,000
Accounts receivable (net), December 31	126,000	110,000
Inventory, December 31	195,000	160,000
Common stockholders' equity, December 31	440,000	400,000
Total assets, December 31	750,000	650,000

REQUIRED

a. Calculate the following ratios for 1994. The 1993 results are given for comparative purposes.

		1993
1.	Gross profit percentage	35.5%
2.	Return on assets	8.3%
3.	Return on sales	6.2%
4.	Return on common stockholders' equity (no preferred stock was outstanding)	13.9%
5.	Accounts receivable turnover	8.00
6.	Average collection period	45.6 days
7.	Inventory turnover	3.61
8.	Times interest earned ratio	4.80
9.	Operating cash flow to capital expenditures ratio	1.22

b. Comment on the changes between the two years.

RATIOS FROM
COMPARATIVE AND
COMMON-SIZE DATA
— OBJ. 1, 2, 3, 4, 5 —

20-28 Consider the following financial statements for Waverly Company for 1993 and 1994.

During 1994, management obtained additional bond financing to enlarge its production facilities. The company faced higher production costs during the year for such things as fuel, materials, and freight. Because of temporary government price controls, a planned price increase on products was delayed several months.

As a holder of both common and preferred stock, you analyze the financial statements for 1993 and 1994.

WAVERLY COMPANY
BALANCE SHEETS
(THOUSANDS OF DOLLARS)

	Dec. 31, 1994	Dec. 31, 1993
Assets		
Cash and Cash Equivalents	$ 19,000	$ 13,000
Accounts Receivable (Net)	57,000	42,000
Inventory	110,000	100,000
Prepaid Expenses	21,000	12,000
Plant and Other Assets (Net)	474,000	408,000
Total Assets	$681,000	$575,000
Liabilities and Stockholders' Equity		
Current Liabilities	$ 88,000	$ 84,000
10% Bonds Payable	225,000	150,000
9% Preferred Stock, $50 Par Value	75,000	75,000
Common Stock, $10 Par Value	200,000	200,000
Retained Earnings	93,000	66,000
Total Liabilities and Stockholders' Equity	$681,000	$575,000

WAVERLY COMPANY
INCOME STATEMENTS
(THOUSANDS OF DOLLARS)

	1994	1993
Sales	$810,000	$675,000
Cost of Goods Sold	526,500	425,250
Gross Profit on Sales	$283,500	$249,750
Selling and Administrative Expenses	173,400	150,100
Income before Interest Expense and Income Taxes	$110,100	$ 99,650
Interest Expense	22,500	15,000
Income before Income Taxes	$ 87,600	$ 84,650
Income Tax Expense	23,250	22,450
Net Income	$ 64,350	$ 62,200
Other financial data (thousands of dollars):		
Net cash provided by operating activities	$ 66,200	$ 63,500
Preferred dividends	6,750	6,750

REQUIRED

a. Calculate the following for each year: current ratio, quick ratio, operating cash flow to current liabilities ratio (current liabilities were $78,000,000 at December 31, 1992), inventory turnover (inventory was $86,000,000 at December 31, 1992), debt-to-equity ratio, times interest earned ratio, return on assets (total assets were $493,000,000 at December 31, 1992), and return on common stockholders' equity (common stockholders' equity was $249,000,000 at December 31, 1992).

b. Calculate common-size percentages for each year's income statement.
c. Comment on the results of your analysis.

CONSTRUCTING
STATEMENTS FROM RATIO
DATA
— OBJ. 3, 4 —

20-29   The following are the 1993 financial statements for Omicron Company, with almost all dollar amounts missing.

OMICRON COMPANY
BALANCE SHEET
DECEMBER 31, 1993

Cash	$?	Current Liabilities	$?
Accounts Receivable (Net)	?	8% Bonds Payable	?
Inventory	?	Common Stock	?
Equipment (Net)	?	Retained Earnings	650,000
		Total Liabilities and	
Total Assets	$3,500,000	Stockholders' Equity	$3,500,000

OMICRON COMPANY
INCOME STATEMENT
FOR THE YEAR ENDED DECEMBER 31, 1993

Net Sales	$?
Cost of Goods Sold	?
Gross Profit	?
Selling and Administrative Expenses	?
Income before Interest Expense and Income Taxes	?
Interest Expense	40,000
Income before Income Taxes	?
Income Tax Expense (35%)	?
Net Income	$260,000

The following information is available about Omicron Company's 1993 financial statements:

1. Quick ratio, 0.90.
2. Inventory turnover (inventory at January 1, 1993 was $790,000), 4 times.
3. Return on sales, 5.2%.
4. Accounts receivable turnover [accounts receivable (net) at January 1, 1993 were $590,000], 8 times.
5. Gross profit percentage, 32%.
6. Return on common stockholders' equity (common stockholders' equity at January 1, 1993 was $1,850,000), 13%.
7. The interest expense relates to the bonds payable that were outstanding all year.

REQUIRED

Compute the missing amounts, and complete the financial statements of Omicron Company. *Hint:* Complete the income statement first.

RATIOS COMPARED WITH
INDUSTRY AVERAGES
— OBJ. 3, 4, 5 —

20-30 Because you own common stock of Phantom Corporation, a paper manufacturer, you are analyzing the firm's performance for the most recent year. The following data are taken from the firm's latest annual report.

	Dec. 31, This Year	Dec. 31, Last Year
Quick Assets	$ 500,000	$ 460,000
Inventory and Prepaid Expenses	310,000	260,000
Other Assets	3,990,000	3,480,000
Total Assets	$4,800,000	$4,200,000
Current Liabilities	$ 520,000	$ 450,000
10% Bonds Payable	1,200,000	1,200,000
8% Preferred Stock, $100 Par Value	400,000	400,000
Common Stock, $10 Par Value	2,250,000	1,800,000
Retained Earnings	430,000	350,000
Total Liabilities and Stockholders' Equity	$4,800,000	$4,200,000

For this year, net sales amount to $9,400,000, net income is $479,000, and preferred dividends declared and paid are $32,000.

REQUIRED

a. Calculate the following for this year:
   1. Return on sales.
   2. Return on assets.
   3. Return on common stockholders' equity.
   4. Quick ratio.
   5. Current ratio.
   6. Debt-to-equity ratio.
b. Trade association statistics and information provided by credit agencies reveal the following data on industry norms:

	Median	Upper Quartile
Return on sales	4.9%	8.6%
Return on assets	6.5%	11.2%
Return on common stockholders' equity	10.6%	17.3%
Quick ratio	1.0	1.8
Current ratio	1.8	3.0
Debt-to-equity ratio	1.08	0.66

Compare Phantom Corporation's performance with industry performance.

**RATIOS COMPARED WITH
INDUSTRY AVERAGES
— OBJ. 3, 4, 5, 6 —**

20-31 Packard Plastics, Inc., manufactures various plastic and synthetic products. Financial statement data for the firm are as follows:

	1994 (Thousands of Dollars, except Earnings per Share)
Net Sales	$520,000
Cost of Goods Sold	358,000
Net Income	34,500
Dividends	9,500
Earnings per Share	2.76

**PACKARD PLASTICS, INC.
BALANCE SHEETS
(THOUSANDS OF DOLLARS)**

	Dec. 31, 1994	Dec. 31, 1993
Assets		
Cash	$ 6,500	$ 5,400
Accounts Receivable (Net)	50,300	45,500
Inventory	120,000	110,000
Total Current Assets	$176,800	$160,900
Plant Assets (Net)	172,000	155,000
Other Assets	4,200	3,100
Total Assets	$353,000	$319,000
Liabilities and Stockholders' Equity		
Notes Payable—Banks	$ 25,000	$ 20,000
Accounts Payable	22,100	18,400
Accrued Liabilities	20,600	20,300
Total Current Liabilities	$ 67,700	$ 58,700
10% Bonds Payable	100,000	100,000
Total Liabilities	$167,700	$158,700
Common Stock, $10 Par Value (12,500,000 shares)	$125,000	$125,000
Retained Earnings	60,300	35,300
Total Stockholders' Equity	$185,300	$160,300
Total Liabilities and Stockholders' Equity	$353,000	$319,000

REQUIRED

a. Using the given data, calculate items 1 through 8 below for 1994. Compare the performance of Packard Plastics, Inc., with the following industry averages and comment on its operations.

	Median Ratios for Manufacturers of Plastic and Synthetic Products
1. Quick ratio.	1.2
2. Current ratio.	1.9
3. Accounts receivable turnover	7.9
4. Inventory turnover	7.8
5. Debt-to-equity ratio	0.95
6. Gross profit percentage	32.7%
7. Return on sales	3.5%
8. Return on assets	6.3%

b. Calculate the dividends paid per share of common stock. What was the dividend payout ratio?

c. If the most recent price per share of common stock is $34.50, what is the price-earnings ratio? The dividend yield?

ALTERNATE EXERCISES

COMPARATIVE BALANCE SHEET
— OBJ. 1 —

20-19A Consider the following balance sheet data for LANDS' END, INC., a direct mail merchant, at January 31, 1991 and 1990 (amounts in thousands):

	Jan. 31, 1991	Jan. 31, 1990
Cash and Cash Equivalents	$ 27,264	$ 8,254
Inventory	73,863	85,709
Other Current Assets	6,697	5,751
Current Assets	$107,824	$ 99,714
Property, Plant, and Equipment (Net)	77,576	67,218
Total Assets	$185,400	$166,932
Current Liabilities	$ 60,774	$ 43,915
Long-term Liabilities	7,800	8,413
Total Liabilities	68,574	52,328
Common Stock	$ 201	$ 201
Paid-in and Donated Capital	31,136	30,781
Retained Earnings	98,381	87,516
Treasury Stock	(12,892)	(3,894)
Total Stockholders' Equity	$116,826	$114,604
Total Liabilities and Stockholders' Equity	$185,400	$166,932

a. Prepare a comparative balance sheet, showing increases and decreases in dollars and percentages.
b. Comment briefly on the changes between the two years.

COMMON-SIZE BALANCE SHEETS
— OBJ. 2 —

20-20A Refer to the balance sheet data given in Exercise 20-19A.

a. Prepare common-size balance sheets for each year (use total assets as the base amount for computing percentages).
b. Compare the common-size balance sheets and comment briefly.

RATIOS ANALYZING PROFITABILITY
— OBJ. 3 —

20-21A The following information is available for Crest Company:

Annual Data	1994	1993
Net sales	$5,400,000	$5,000,000
Cost of goods sold	3,391,200	3,100,000
Net income	221,400	212,500

Year-end Data	Dec. 31, 1994	Dec. 31, 1993
Total assets	$2,650,000	$2,350,000
Common stockholders' equity	1,900,000	1,800,000

Calculate the following ratios for 1994:
a. Gross profit percentage.
b. Return on sales.
c. Asset turnover.
d. Return on assets.
e. Return on common stockholders' equity (Crest Company declared and paid preferred dividends of $15,000 in 1994).

WORKING CAPITAL AND SHORT-TERM LIQUIDITY RATIOS
— OBJ. 4 —

20-22A Favor Company has a current ratio of 1.95 (1.95:1) on December 31, 1993. On that date its current assets are as follows:

Cash and cash equivalents	$ 18,000
Short-term investments	67,000
Accounts receivable (net)	125,000
Inventory	193,500
Prepaid expenses	9,900
	$413,400

Favor Company's current liabilities at December 31, 1992, were $190,000 and during 1993 its operating activities provided a net cash flow of $30,150.
a. What are the firm's current liabilities on December 31, 1993?
b. What is the firm's working capital on December 31, 1993?
c. What is the quick ratio on December 31, 1993?
d. What is the 1993 operating cash flow to current liabilities ratio?

RECEIVABLE AND INVENTORY RATIOS — OBJ. 4 —

20-23A Favor Company, whose current assets at December 31, 1993, are shown in Exercise 20-22A, had 1993 net sales of $566,100 and cost of goods sold of $374,600. At January 1, 1993, accounts receivable (net) were $126,600 and inventory was $188,700.
a. What is the 1993 accounts receivable turnover?
b. What is the 1993 average collection period?
c. What is the 1993 inventory turnover?
d. What is the 1993 days' sales in inventory?

RATIOS ANALYZING LONG-TERM SOLVENCY — OBJ. 5 —

20-24A The following information is available for Percy Company:

Annual data	1993	1992
Interest expense	$ 176,000	$ 160,000
Income tax expense	112,800	105,000
Net income	263,200	245,000
Capital expenditures	390,000	250,000
Net cash provided by operating activities	204,000	198,000

Year-end data	Dec. 31, 1993	Dec. 31, 1992
Total liabilities	$3,200,000	$2,900,000
Total owners' equity	2,000,000	1,900,000

Calculate the following:
a. 1993 year-end debt-to-equity ratio.
b. 1993 operating cash flow to total liabilities ratio.
c. 1993 times interest earned ratio.
d. 1993 operating cash flow to capital expenditures ratio.

RATIOS FOR COMMON STOCK INVESTORS — OBJ. 6 —

20-25A Henshue Corporation has only common stock issued and outstanding. The firm reported earnings per share of $1.39 for 1994. During 1994, Henshue paid dividends of $0.50 per share. On December 31, 1994, the current market price of the stock was $33.50 per share. Calculate the following:
a. 1994 year-end price-earnings ratio.
b. 1994 dividend yield.
c. 1994 dividend payout ratio.

ALTERNATE PROBLEMS

TREND PERCENTAGES — OBJ. 1 —

20-26A Sales of automotive products for FORD MOTOR COMPANY and GENERAL MOTORS CORPORATION for the five years 1986–1990 are given below:

	Sales of Automotive Products (Millions of Dollars)				
	1986	1987	1988	1989	1990
Ford Motor Company	$62,868	$71,797	$82,193	$82,879	$81,844
General Motors Corporation	90,863	89,891	97,777	99,106	97,312

Net sales for PEPSICO., Inc., and net operating revenues (comparable to net sales) for THE COCA-COLA COMPANY for the five years 1986–1990 are given on the following page:

Net Sales/Net Operating Revenues (Millions of Dollars)

	1986	1987	1988	1989	1990
PepsiCo, Inc.	$9,017	$11,018	$12,533	$15,242	$17,803
The Coca-Cola Company	6,977	7,658	8,065	8,622	10,236

REQUIRED

a. Calculate trend percentages for all four companies, using 1986 as the base year.
b. Comment on the trend percentages of Ford Motor Company and General Motors Corporation.

c. Comment on the trend percentages of PepsiCo, Inc. and The Coca-Cola Company.

CHANGES IN VARIOUS RATIOS
— OBJ. 1, 3, 4, 5 —

20-27A Selected information follows for Cycle Company, taken from the 1993 and 1994 financial statements:

	1994	1993
Net sales	$580,000	$520,000
Cost of goods sold	352,000	310,000
Interest expense	15,000	14,000
Income tax expense	5,400	5,100
Net income	21,500	20,300
Net cash flow from operating activities	30,600	26,500
Capital expenditures	50,000	25,000
Accounts receivable (net), December 31	132,000	118,000
Inventory, December 31	198,000	160,000
Common stockholders' equity, December 31	175,000	159,000
Total assets, December 31	370,000	340,000

REQUIRED

a. Calculate the following ratios for 1994. The 1993 results are given for comparative purposes.

	1993
1. Gross profit percentage	40.4%
2. Return on assets.	6.3%
3. Return on sales.	3.9%
4. Return on common stockholders' equity (no preferred stock was outstanding).	14.0%
5. Accounts receivable turnover	4.77
6. Average collection period.	76.5 days
7. Inventory turnover.	2.07
8. Times interest earned ratio.	2.81
9. Operating cash flow to capital expenditures ratio	1.06

b. Comment on the changes between the two years.

RATIOS FROM COMPARATIVE AND COMMON-SIZE DATA
— OBJ. 1, 2, 3, 4, 5 —

20-28A Consider the following financial statements for Vega Company for 1993 and 1994.
During 1994, management obtained additional bond financing to enlarge its production facilities. The plant addition produced a new high-margin product, which is supposed to improve the average rate of gross profit and return on sales.
As a potential investor, you analyze the financial statements for 1993 and 1994.

VEGA COMPANY
BALANCE SHEETS
(THOUSANDS OF DOLLARS)

Assets	Dec. 31, 1994	Dec. 31, 1993
Cash	$ 17,000	$ 14,000
Accounts Receivable (Net)	23,000	11,000
Inventory	70,000	48,000
Prepaid Expenses	1,000	2,000
Plant and Other Assets (Net)	309,000	285,000
Total Assets	$420,000	$360,000

Liabilities and Stockholders' Equity

Current Liabilities	$ 50,700	$ 30,000
9% Bonds Payable	125,000	100,000
8% Preferred Stock, $50 Par Value	40,000	40,000
Common Stock, $10 Par Value	150,000	150,000
Retained Earnings	54,300	40,000
Total Liabilities and Stockholders' Equity	$420,000	$360,000

VEGA COMPANY
INCOME STATEMENTS
(THOUSANDS OF DOLLARS)

	1994	1993
Sales	$560,000	$465,000
Cost of Goods Sold	368,000	316,000
Gross Profit on Sales	$192,000	$149,000
Selling and Administrative Expenses	154,000	116,000
Income before Interest Expense and Income Taxes	$ 38,000	$ 33,000
Interest Expense	11,000	9,000
Income before Income Taxes	$ 27,000	$ 24,000
Income Tax Expense	9,500	8,400
Net Income	$ 17,500	$ 15,600
Other financial data (thousands of dollars):		
Net cash provided by operating activities	$ 20,000	$ 17,000
Preferred dividends	3,200	3,200

REQUIRED

a. Calculate the following for each year: current ratio, quick ratio, operating cash flow to current liabilities ratio (current liabilities were $28 million at December 31, 1992), inventory turnover (inventory was $45 million at December 31, 1992), debt-to-equity ratio, times interest earned ratio, return on assets (total assets were $315 million at December 31, 1992), and return on common stockholders' equity (common stockholders' equity was $177.6 million at December 31, 1992).

b. Calculate common-size percentages for each year's income statement.

c. Comment on the results of your analysis.

CONSTRUCTING STATEMENTS FROM RATIO DATA
— OBJ. 3, 4 —

20-29A The following are the 1993 financial statements for Timber Company, with almost all dollar amounts missing.

TIMBER COMPANY
BALANCE SHEET
DECEMBER 31, 1993

Cash	$?	Current Liabilities	$?
Accounts Receivable (Net)	?	10% Bonds Payable	120,000
Inventory	?	Common Stock	?
Equipment (Net)	?	Retained Earnings	40,000
		Total Liabilities and	
Total Assets	$480,000	Stockholders' Equity	$480,000

TIMBER COMPANY
INCOME STATEMENT
FOR THE YEAR ENDED DECEMBER 31, 1993

Net Sales	$?
Cost of Goods Sold	?
Gross Profit on Sales	?
Selling and Administrative Expenses	?
Income before Interest Expense and Income Taxes	?
Interest Expense	?
Income before Income Taxes	?
Income Tax Expense (35%)	?
Net Income	$ 58,500

The following information is available about Timber Company's 1993 financial statements:

1. Quick ratio, 1.65.

2. Current ratio, 3.15.

3. Return on sales, 7.5%.

4. Return on common stockholders' equity (common stockholders' equity at January 1, 1993 was $285,000), 20%.

5. Gross profit percentage, 30%.

6. Accounts receivable turnover [accounts receivable (net) at January 1, 1993 were $81,000], 10 times.

7. The interest expense relates to the bonds payable that were outstanding all year.

REQUIRED

Compute the missing amounts, and complete the financial statements of Timber Company.

RATIOS COMPARED WITH INDUSTRY AVERAGES — OBJ. 3, 4, 5 —

20-30A You are analyzing the performance of Lumite Corporation, a manufacturer of personal care products, for the most recent year. The following data are taken from the firm's latest annual report.

	Dec. 31, This Year	Dec. 31, Last Year
Quick Assets	$ 320,000	$ 280,000
Inventory and Prepaid Expenses	1,050,000	900,000
Other Assets	4,630,000	4,120,000
Total Assets	$6,000,000	$5,300,000
Current Liabilities	$ 600,000	$ 430,000
10% Bonds Payable	1,400,000	1,400,000
7% Preferred Stock	1,000,000	1,000,000
Common Stock, $5 Par Value	2,100,000	2,000,000
Retained Earnings	900,000	470,000
Total Liabilities and Stockholders' Equity	$6,000,000	$5,300,000

For this year, net sales amount to $9,600,000, net income is $750,000, and preferred dividends declared and paid are $70,000.

REQUIRED

a. Calculate the following for this year:

1. Return on sales.

2. Return on assets.

3. Return on common stockholders' equity.

4. Quick ratio.

5. Current ratio.

6. Debt-to-equity ratio.

b. Trade association statistics and information provided by credit agencies reveal the following data on industry norms:

	Median	Upper Quartile
Return on sales	3.7%	10.6%
Return on assets	5.8%	14.2%
Return on common stockholders' equity	18.5%	34.2%
Quick ratio	1.0	1.8
Current ratio	2.2	3.7
Debt-to-equity ratio	1.07	0.37

Compare Lumite Corporation's performance with industry performance.

RATIOS COMPARED WITH INDUSTRY AVERAGES
— OBJ. 3, 4, 5, 6 —

20-31A Avery Instruments, Inc., is a manufacturer of various measuring and controlling instruments. Financial statement data for the firm are as follows:

	1994 (Thousands of Dollars, except Earnings per Share)
Net Sales	$140,000
Cost of Goods Sold	83,000
Net Income	5,500
Dividends	1,100
Earnings per Share	2.50

AVERY INSTRUMENTS, INC.
BALANCE SHEETS
(THOUSANDS OF DOLLARS)

	Dec. 31, 1994	Dec. 31, 1993
Assets		
Cash	$ 12,200	$12,000
Accounts Receivable (Net)	30,500	27,400
Inventory	26,300	29,100
Total Current Assets	$ 69,000	$68,500
Plant Assets (Net)	22,600	21,300
Other Assets	10,400	9,200
Total Assets	$102,000	$99,000
Liabilities and Stockholders' Equity		
Notes Payable—Banks	$ 4,000	$ 4,000
Accounts Payable	15,000	13,300
Accrued Liabilities	11,000	14,100
Total Current Liabilities	$ 30,000	$31,400
9% Bonds Payable	25,000	25,000
Total Liabilities	$ 55,000	$56,400
Common Stock, $15 Par Value (2,200,000 shares)	$ 33,000	$33,000
Retained Earnings	14,000	9,600
Total Stockholders' Equity	$ 47,000	$42,600
Total Liabilities and Stockholders' Equity	$102,000	$99,000

REQUIRED

a. Using the given data, calculate items 1 through 8 below for 1994. Compare the performance of Avery Instruments, Inc., with the following industry averages and comment on its operations.

	Median Ratios for Manufacturers of Measuring and Controlling Instruments
1. Quick ratio	1.3
2. Current ratio	2.4
3. Accounts receivable turnover	5.9
4. Inventory turnover	3.5
5. Debt-to-equity ratio	0.73
6. Gross profit percentage	42.8%
7. Return on sales	4.5%
8. Return on assets	7.6%

b. Calculate the dividends paid per share of common stock. What was the dividend payout ratio?

c. If the most recent price per share of common stock is $47.50, what is the price-earnings ratio? The dividend yield?

CASES

Business Decision Case

Crescent Paints, Inc., a paint manufacturer, has been in business five years. The company has had modest profits and has experienced few operating difficulties until this year (1994), when president Alice Becknell discusses her company's working capital problems with you, a loan officer at Granite Bank. Becknell explains that expanding her firm has created difficulties in meeting obligations when they come due and in taking advantage of cash discounts offered by manufacturers for timely payment. She would like to borrow $50,000 from Granite Bank. At your request, Becknell submits the following financial data for the past two years:

	1993	1992
Net sales	$1,600,000	$1,400,000
Cost of goods sold	1,056,000	935,000
Net income	33,600	26,900
Dividends	15,600	12,000
December 31, 1991 data:		
Total assets		$ 900,000
Accounts receivable (net)		164,000
Inventory		280,000

CRESCENT PAINTS, INC.
BALANCE SHEETS

	Dec. 31, 1993	Dec. 31, 1992
Assets		
Cash	$ 25,000	$ 40,000
Accounts Receivable (Net)	276,000	200,000
Inventory	420,000	340,000
Prepaid Expenses	9,000	5,000
Total Current Assets	$ 730,000	$585,000
Plant Assets (Net)	380,000	355,000
Total Assets	$1,110,000	$940,000
Liabilities and Stockholders' Equity		
Notes Payable—Banks	$ 80,000	$ 30,000
Accounts Payable	195,000	152,000
Accrued Liabilities	77,000	68,000
Total Current Liabilities	$ 352,000	$250,000
10% Mortgage Payable	150,000	200,000
Total Liabilities	$ 502,000	$450,000
Common Stock	$ 530,000	$430,000
Retained Earnings	78,000	60,000
Total Stockholders' Equity	$ 608,000	$490,000
Total Liabilities and Stockholders' Equity	$1,110,000	$940,000

You calculate the following items for both years from the given data and compare them with the median ratios for paint manufacturers provided by a commercial credit firm:

	Median Ratios for Paint Manufacturers
1. Current ratio	2.5
2. Quick ratio	1.3
3. Accounts receivable turnover	8.1
4. Average collection period	44.9 days
5. Inventory turnover	4.9
6. Debt-to-equity ratio	0.78
7. Return on assets	4.8%
8. Return on sales	2.4%

REQUIRED

Based on your analysis, decide whether and under what circumstances you would grant Becknell's request for a loan. Explain the reasons for your decision.

Analytical Application Case

Refer to the actual financial statements of DONNELLY CORPORATION for fiscal years 1990 and 1991 presented in Appendix L at the end of the textbook. Donnelly Corporation is headquartered in Holland, Michigan. Approximately 85–90% of its business is the manufacture of automotive vision systems (such as interior and exterior rearview mirrors) and automotive modular window systems; other operations focus on the manufacture of solid-state glass coatings for products used in the computer and electronics industries.

REQUIRED

a. For both fiscal years (1990 and 1991), compute (or identify) the following financial ratios:

1. Gross profit percentage.
2. Return on sales.
3. Asset turnover.
4. Return on assets.
5. Return on common stockholders' equity. (Use common stockholders' equity in schedule of selected financial data.)
6. Current ratio.
7. Quick ratio.
8. Operating cash flow to current liabilities ratio.
9. Accounts receivable turnover (June 30, 1989, accounts receivable = $28,986,000).
10. Average collection period.
11. Inventory turnover (June 30, 1989, inventory = $16,207,000).
12. Days' sales in inventory.
13. Debt-to-equity ratio.
14. Operating cash flow to total liabilities ratio (June 30, 1989, total liabilities = $65,343,000).
15. Times interest earned ratio.
16. Operating cash flow to capital expenditures ratio.
17. Earnings per share.
18. Price-earnings ratio. (Use the high stock price in the fourth quarter each year.)
19. Dividend yield.
20. Dividend payout ratio.

b. Comment briefly on the changes from fiscal 1990 to fiscal 1991 in the ratios computed above.

Ethics Case

Chris Nelson, new assistant controller for Grand Company, is preparing for the firm's year-end closing procedures. On December 30, 1993, a memorandum from the controller directed Nelson to make a journal entry debiting Cash and crediting Long-term Advances to Officers for $1,000,000. Not finding the $1,000,000 in the cash deposit prepared for the bank that day, Nelson went to the controller for a further explanation. In response, the controller took from her desk drawer a check for $1,000,000 payable to Grand Company from Jason Grand, chief executive officer of the firm. Attached to the check was a note from Jason Grand saying that if this check were not needed to return it to him next week.

"This check is paying off a $1,000,000 advance the firm made to Jason Grand six years ago," stated the controller. "Mr. Grand has done this every year since the advance; each time we have returned the check to him in January of the following year. We plan to do so again this time. In fact, when Mr. Grand retires in four years, I expect the board of directors will forgive this advance. However, if the firm really needed the cash, we would deposit the check."

"Then why go through this charade each year?" inquired Nelson.

"It dresses up our year-end balance sheet," replied the controller. "Certain financial statement ratios are improved significantly. Further, the notes to the financial statements don't have to reveal a related-party loan. Lots of firms engage in year-end transactions designed to dress up their financial statements."

REQUIRED

a. What financial statement ratios are improved by making the journal entry contained in the controller's memorandum?

b. Is the year-end handling of Jason Grand's advance an ethical practice? Discuss.

How does a manufacturing firm determine the cost of the products that it produces?

Manufacturers accumulate a variety of costs to determine the cost of their products. ■ These include the costs of materials, labor, and operating and maintaining the factory. ■ The product costs are accumulated and accounted for in manufacturing inventory accounts. ■ Factory automation has changed the product cost structure for many manufacturers. ■ Companies like General Motors have built modern new facilities such as its Saturn plant shown here to incorporate modern production technology.

21

ACCOUNTING FOR MANUFACTURING OPERATIONS

CHAPTER OBJECTIVES

1 **IDENTIFY** key objectives of a manufacturing accounting system and **DEFINE** *product costs* and *period costs* (p. 792).

2 **DESCRIBE** the three manufacturing inventories—materials, work in process, and finished goods—and **DISCUSS** the categories of manufacturing cost and how these costs flow among the inventories and cost of goods sold (pp. 793–794).

3 **DEFINE** *total manufacturing costs, cost of goods manufactured,* and *cost of goods sold,* and **ILLUSTRATE** the schedule of cost of goods manufactured and sold and the income statement (pp. 794–796).

4 **ILLUSTRATE** the journal entries to record product cost flows using the perpetual inventory system (pp. 797–798).

5 **PRESENT** the year-end accounting procedures for a manufacturing firm, including the preparation of a worksheet, adjusting entries, financial statements, closing entries, and schedule of cost of goods manufactured and sold (pp. 799–804).

6 **DISCUSS** just-in-time (JIT) inventory systems and factory automation (pp. 804–806).

We are made to create, from
the poet to the potter.

After BENJAMIN DISRAELI

anufacturing firms are companies that take materials (such as sheets of steel and coils of wire) and components (such as electric motors and microprocessors) and turn them into finished products. The manufacturer utilizes human labor, utilities (such as electricity, natural gas, and water), and factory assets (such as buildings, machinery, and computers) to convert the materials and components into products.

In previous chapters, our discussion of accounting systems and procedures related primarily to merchandising and service firms. Even though the accounting principles and techniques described earlier also apply to manufacturing firms, accounting for manufacturing operations is usually more complex because more activities are involved in producing a product than in purchasing and selling merchandise or providing a service.

KEY OBJECTIVES OF A MANUFACTURING ACCOUNTING SYSTEM

Product Costing

OBJECTIVE ❶ IDENTIFY *key objectives of a manufacturing accounting system and* DEFINE *product costs and* **period costs.**

Manufacturing operations vary widely in complexity. However, all manufacturing accounting systems have two common primary objectives: product costing and cost control. **Product costing** involves accumulating and allocating the costs of all inputs in the manufacturing process to individual products. The manufacturer must know its product costs in order to measure inventory values and the profitability of its products. Using product costing information, management can determine which products to continue producing and which products to drop. This chapter emphasizes product costing.

Product costs are all costs necessary to bring a manufactured product to completion, regardless of the period in which completed. All costs of material and components, human labor, utilities, and use of factory assets are included in product costs. When accounting for merchandising and service companies, items such as salaries and wages, utilities, and depreciation are immediately expensed. In manufacturing accounting, however, all such costs incurred in the factory are product costs, which are initially taken into inventory accounts.

Period costs are expenditures charged (debited) to expense in the period incurred. The benefits associated with such costs are considered to expire in that period rather than relate to whatever product may have been produced in that period. Traditionally, selling expenses and nonfactory administrative expenses are considered period costs. Some departments in a manufacturing firm, such as personnel, may benefit both factory and nonfactory activities. The costs of such departments, therefore, are partly product cost and partly period cost.

Based on the above concepts, the income statement of a manufacturing firm would include the following:

Sales		$6,000,000
Cost of Goods Sold (*Product cost of units sold*)		2,800,000
Gross Profit on Sales		$3,200,000
Operating Expenses (*Period costs*):		
Selling Expenses	$1,200,000	
Nonfactory Administrative Expenses	700,000	1,900,000
Income from Operations		$1,300,000

Cost Control

The second primary objective of manufacturing accounting systems is cost control. Cost control is vital to all companies, especially manufacturing firms. **Cost control** involves the accumulation of information to measure management performance and evaluate operational efficiency. Subsequent chapters present cost control approaches and techniques that are used by manufacturing companies.

MANUFACTURING INVENTORIES AND COST CATEGORIES

Manufacturing Inventories

OBJECTIVE ❷ DESCRIBE *the three manufacturing inventories—materials, work in process, and finished goods—and* DISCUSS *the categories of manufacturing cost and how they flow among the inventories and cost of goods sold.*

At any point in time, manufacturing operations typically have units of product at various stages of completion. Three inventories are usually maintained on a perpetual basis to reflect these stages—materials, work in process, and finished goods.

1. The **materials inventory** includes factory materials and components that have been purchased but not yet placed into production. Some of the items in the materials inventory, such as sheets of steel or microprocessors, were finished products to the supplying company but are materials and components to the purchasing company. All items in the Materials Inventory account are recorded at their net delivered cost.

2. The **work in process inventory** includes units of product that have been placed in production but have not yet been completed. All the costs of material and components, human labor, utilities, and use of factory assets are included in the work in process inventory. All items in the Work in Process Inventory account are recorded at cost.

3. The **finished goods inventory** includes all units of product that have been completed but have not been sold. All items in the Finished Goods Inventory account were recorded at cost in the Work in Process Inventory account and transferred to the Finished Goods Inventory account.

Merchandising firms have one primary inventory, merchandise inventory. Manufacturing firms have three primary inventories: materials, work in process, and finished goods. These inventories are reported in the current assets section of the balance sheet as follows:

Merchandising Firm		Manufacturing Firm	
Current Assets		**Current Assets**	
Cash	$10,000	Cash	$10,000
Short-term Investments	20,000	Short-term Investments	20,000
Receivables	45,000	Receivables	45,000
Merchandise Inventory	80,000	Inventories:	
Prepaid Expenses	15,000	Materials	35,000
Total Current Assets	$170,000	Work in Process	55,000
		Finished Goods	25,000
		Factory Supplies	5,000
		Prepaid Expenses	15,000
		Total Current Assets	$210,000

Many manufacturing firms also maintain an inventory of factory supplies for the manufacturing operation. *Factory supplies* are consumable items, such as cleaning supplies and machinery lubricants, used in the factory but not incorporated into the product. The inventory of factory supplies is usually maintained on a periodic basis, so the cost of factory supplies used during a period is determined at period-end after the supplies on hand are counted.

Manufacturing Cost Categories

Manufacturing costs are usually accounted for in the following categories:

1. **Direct material** includes all of the important materials and components that physically make up the product (such as sheets of steel and electric motors). Incidental material items, such as glue and fasteners, are considered **indirect material** and are included in factory overhead. Both direct material items and indirect material items are included in the materials inventory. Therefore, all items in the materials inventory will be used as either direct material or indirect material.

2. **Direct labor** includes the salary and wage costs of factory employees who work directly on the product (such as machine operators, assemblers, and painters). The salary and wage cost of factory employees who do not work directly on the product (such as supervisors, inspectors, and material handlers) is considered **indirect labor,** which is included in factory overhead. The total

amount of factory labor (direct and indirect) is identified on a manufacturing firm's factory payroll.

3. **Factory overhead,** also called *manufacturing overhead, factory burden,* or *indirect manufacturing costs,* consists of all manufacturing costs not included in direct material and direct labor. Factory overhead includes indirect material, indirect labor, factory supplies used, factory payroll tax and fringe benefit costs, factory utilities, and factory building and machinery costs (such as depreciation, insurance, property taxes, and repairs and maintenance). Factory overhead specifically *excludes* selling and nonfactory administrative expenses since these expenses are not incurred in the manufacturing process.

COMBINED COSTS The manufacturing cost categories are frequently combined when analyzing manufacturing costs. The sum of direct material and direct labor for a particular product is known as **prime cost.** Prime cost is made up of the elements of product cost that are easily and directly traceable to individual products. **Conversion cost** is the sum of direct labor and factory overhead. Conversion cost represents the elements of product cost necessary to convert the materials and components to the final finished products.

PRODUCT COST FLOWS

OBJECTIVE ❸ DEFINE total manufacturing costs, cost of goods manufactured, and cost of goods sold, and ILLUSTRATE the schedule of cost of goods manufactured and sold and the income statement.

Exhibit 21-1 illustrates the flow of product costs through a manufacturing firm. Materials and components in the materials inventory flow to the work in process inventory (as direct material) and to factory overhead (as indirect material). The factory payroll is distributed between the work in process inventory (as direct labor) and factory overhead (as indirect labor). Factory overhead is the third major element that flows into the work in process inventory. Factory overhead is applied to the work in process inventory using procedures we describe in the next chapter. As a result of these flows, total manufacturing costs are accumulated in the work in process inventory.

All costs that are accumulated in the work in process inventory eventually flow to the finished goods inventory and finally to cost of goods sold. The product cost that flows from the work in process inventory to the finished goods inventory during

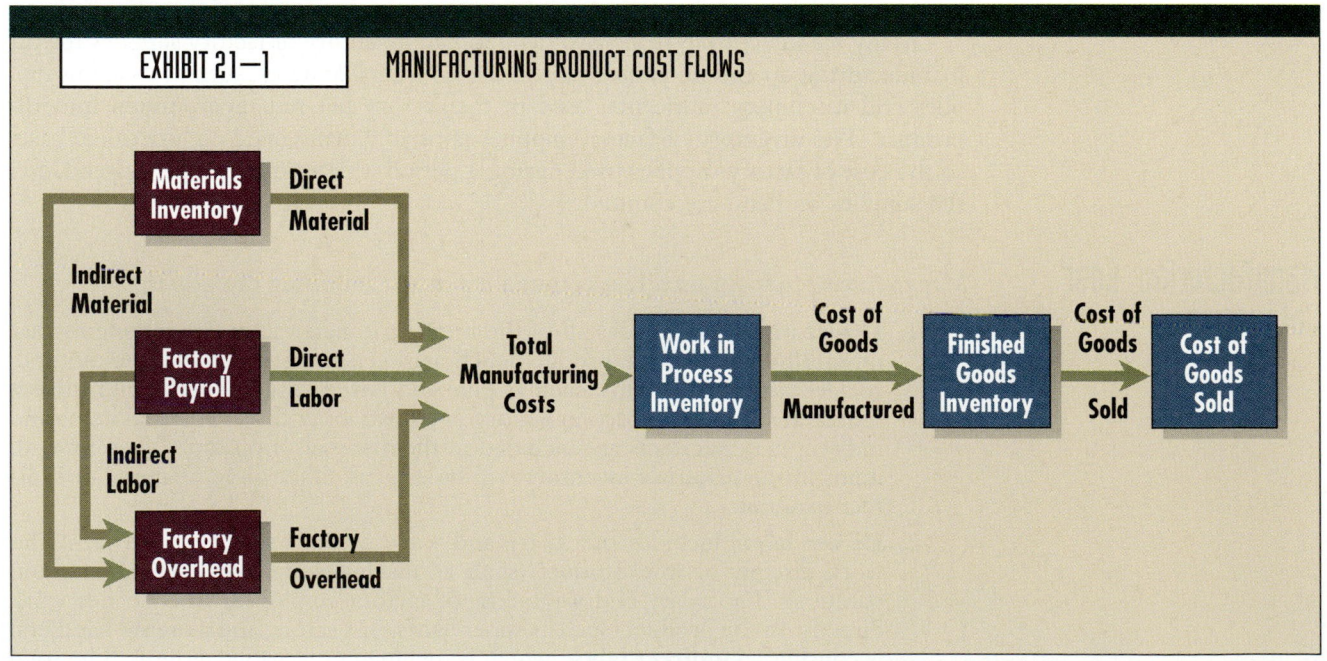

EXHIBIT 21—1   MANUFACTURING PRODUCT COST FLOWS

an accounting period is known as **cost of goods manufactured;** the product cost that flows from the finished goods inventory to the cost of goods sold account is known as **cost of goods sold.**

SCHEDULE OF COST OF GOODS MANUFACTURED AND SOLD

The schedule of cost of goods manufactured and sold presents information about an entity's flow of product costs for an accounting period. Exhibit 21-2 shows the schedule of cost of goods manufactured and sold for 1993 for Columbus Manufacturing Corporation. The schedule has three sections. The first section **1** summarizes the **total manufacturing costs** for the year: the total direct material, direct labor, and factory overhead incurred in the manufacturing process during the year. In the presentation of direct material used during the year, the net delivered cost of materials purchased is added to the beginning materials inventory to determine the cost of material available during the year. The cost of material not used (ending materials

EXHIBIT 21—2

COLUMBUS MANUFACTURING CORPORATION
SCHEDULE OF COST OF GOODS MANUFACTURED AND SOLD
FOR THE YEAR ENDED DECEMBER 31, 1993

Direct Material:		
Beginning Materials Inventory	$ 12,000	
Net Delivered Cost of Materials Purchased	144,000	
Cost of Material Available	$156,000	
Less: Ending Materials Inventory	7,000	
Total Material Used	$149,000	
Less: Indirect Material Used	3,000	
Direct Material Used		$146,000
Direct Labor		102,000
Factory Overhead:		
Indirect Material	$ 3,000	
Indirect Labor	28,000	
Factory Supplies Used	10,000	
Factory Utilities	31,000	
Factory Insurance	8,000	
Factory Property Taxes	12,000	
Depreciation—Factory Building	40,000	
Depreciation—Factory Machinery	15,000	
Other Factory Overhead	13,000	
Total Factory Overhead		160,000
Total Manufacturing Costs for the Year		$408,000
Add: Beginning Work in Process Inventory		18,000
Total Cost of Work in Process during the Year		$426,000
Less: Ending Work in Process Inventory		16,000
Cost of Goods Manufactured		$410,000
Add: Beginning Finished Goods Inventory		25,000
Cost of Goods Available for Sale		$435,000
Less: Ending Finished Goods Inventory		35,000
Cost of Goods Sold		$400,000

inventory) is then subtracted to identify the cost of all material used during the year. This total represents both direct material used and indirect material used. We subtract indirect material used to determine the direct material used. Direct labor is presented on a single line. The detail of factory overhead is shown by summing all of the individual components of factory overhead.

The second section **2** of the schedule of cost of goods manufactured and sold determines the *cost of goods manufactured*—the cost of goods completed during the year and transferred to finished goods. In this section, total manufacturing costs for the year is added to the amount representing the work in process at the beginning of the year to determine the total cost of work in process during the year. The cost of uncompleted units (ending work in process inventory) is then subtracted to determine the cost associated with the completed units (cost of goods manufactured).

The third section **3** of the schedule of cost of goods manufactured and sold presents information related to *cost of goods sold.* The cost of the beginning finished goods inventory is added to cost of goods manufactured to report the cost of goods available for sale during the year. The cost of unsold units (ending finished goods inventory) is then subtracted to identify the cost associated with the units that were sold during the year (cost of goods sold).

The schedule of cost of goods manufactured and sold presents useful information about product costs in support of the income statement. It is not, however, a required financial statement.

INCOME STATEMENT FOR A MANUFACTURING FIRM

The income statement for 1993 for Columbus Manufacturing Corporation is presented in Exhibit 21-3. The format is virtually the same as the income statement for a merchandising firm that uses the perpetual inventory system. Because Columbus Manufacturing Corporation uses the perpetual inventory system for its finished goods inventory, the cost of goods sold amount is available in a general ledger account. The schedule of cost of goods manufactured and sold (see Exhibit 21-2) supports the cost of goods sold amount in the income statement and provides additional information about the flow of product costs.

EXHIBIT 21–3

COLUMBUS MANUFACTURING CORPORATION
INCOME STATEMENT
FOR THE YEAR ENDED DECEMBER 31, 1993

Sales		$700,000
Cost of Goods Sold		**400,000**
Gross Profit on Sales		$300,000
Operating Expenses:		
Selling Expenses	$ 90,000	
Nonfactory Administrative Expenses	130,000	220,000
Income from Operations		$ 80,000
Other Income and Expense:		
Interest Expense		5,000
Income before Income Tax		$ 75,000
Income Tax Expense		20,000
Net Income		$ 55,000

ILLUSTRATION OF PRODUCT COST ACCUMULATION

OBJECTIVE ④ ILLUSTRATE *the journal entries to record product cost flows using the perpetual inventory system.*

The following illustration for Davis Manufacturing Corporation presents summary transaction and adjustment entries for 1993 related to the accounts used to accumulate product costs. Each entry is keyed to Exhibit 21-4, which diagrams these cost flows. Assume that Davis Manufacturing Corporation had the following manufacturing inventory account balances at January 1, 1993:

Materials Inventory	$ 9,000
Work in Process Inventory	20,000
Finished Goods Inventory	16,000

The following entries summarize many transactions that would have occurred during the year (the perpetual inventory system is used):

1 Acquisition of Materials

Materials Inventory	116,000	
Accounts Payable		116,000

To record the delivered cost of materials purchased.

2 Use of Direct Material and Indirect Material

Work in Process Inventory	107,000	
Factory Overhead	3,000	
Materials Inventory		110,000

To record the transfer of direct material ($107,000) to the work in process inventory and the transfer of indirect material ($3,000) to factory overhead.

3 Incurrence of Factory Payroll

Factory Payroll	120,000	
Factory Payroll Payable		120,000

To record the factory payroll.

4 Use of Direct Labor and Indirect Labor

Work in Process Inventory	87,000	
Factory Overhead	33,000	
Factory Payroll		120,000

To record the distribution of the factory payroll as direct labor ($87,000) to the work in process inventory and as indirect labor ($33,000) to factory overhead.

5 Incurrence of Factory Overhead Costs during Year

Factory Overhead	85,000	
Accounts Payable or Cash		85,000

To record various factory costs incurred during the year as factory overhead.

6 Recognition of Certain Factory Overhead Costs with Year-end Adjustments

Factory Overhead	10,000	
Factory Supplies		4,000
Accumulated Depreciation—Factory Machinery		6,000

To record cost of factory supplies used and depreciation on factory machinery.

7 Application of Factory Overhead

Work in Process Inventory	131,000	
Factory Overhead		131,000

To record the application of factory overhead to the work in process inventory. (The procedures for determining this application will be described in a subsequent chapter.)

8 Recognition of Cost of Goods Manufactured

Finished Goods Inventory	327,000	
Work in Process Inventory		327,000

To record the transfer of the cost associated with goods completed from the work in process inventory to the finished goods inventory.

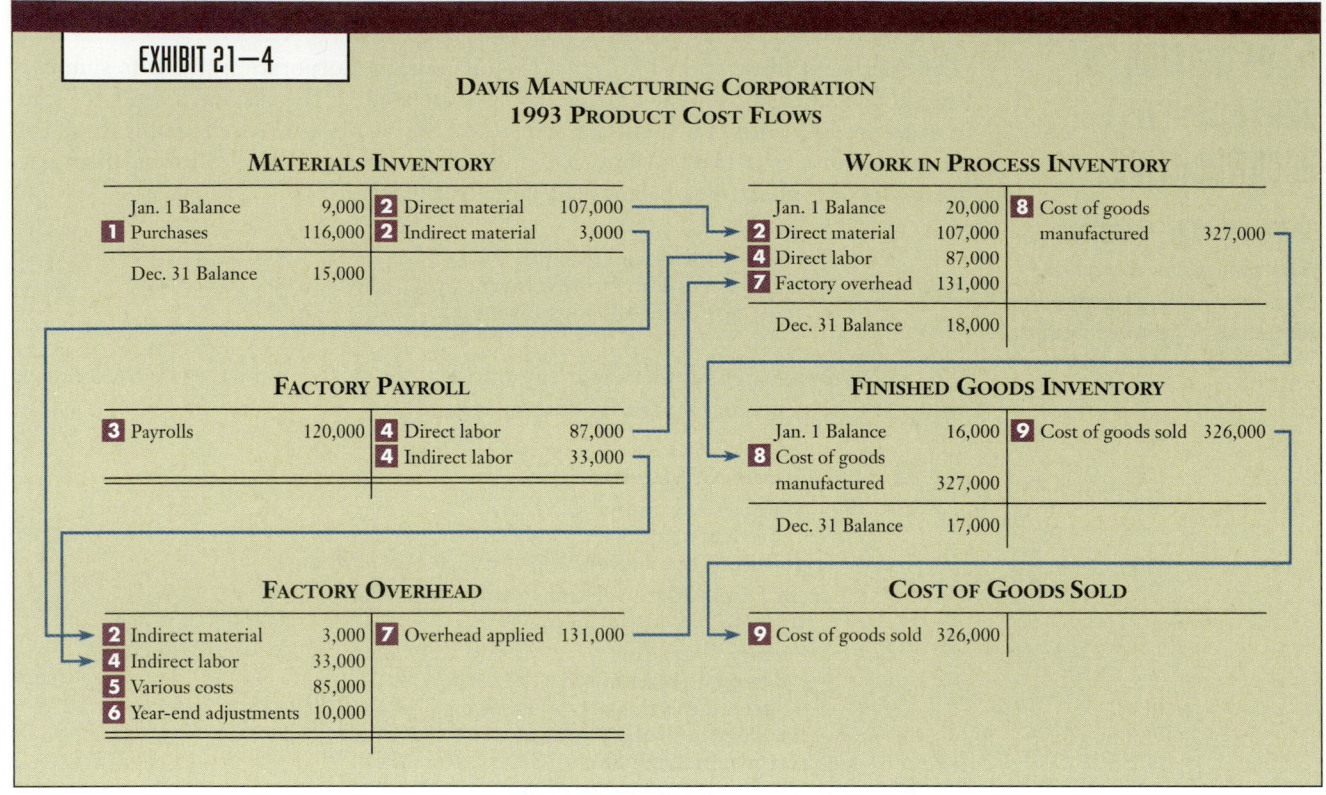

EXHIBIT 21-4

DAVIS MANUFACTURING CORPORATION
1993 PRODUCT COST FLOWS

9   **Recognition of Cost of Goods Sold**

Cost of Goods Sold	326,000	
Finished Goods Inventory		326,000

To record the transfer of the cost associated with goods
sold to customers from the finished goods inventory to
cost of goods sold.

At the same time entry **9** is recorded, another entry would record the sale—debit
Cash or Accounts Receivable and credit Sales for the selling price of the goods.

Cost Flows

Exhibit 21-4 presents T accounts to which the above summary entries have been
posted. The arrows in Exhibit 21-4 indicate the flows of product cost. Direct material
flows from Materials Inventory to Work in Process Inventory, whereas indirect material flows from Materials Inventory to Factory Overhead. Direct labor flows from
Factory Payroll to Work in Process Inventory, whereas indirect labor flows from Factory Payroll to Factory Overhead. Actual factory overhead comes from several
sources, and factory overhead applied flows to Work in Process Inventory. Cost of
goods manufactured (the product cost of goods completed during the accounting
period) flows from Work in Process Inventory to Finished Goods Inventory. The
cost of goods sold flows from Finished Goods Inventory to the Cost of Goods Sold
account.

YEAR-END ACCOUNTING PROCEDURES FOR A MANUFACTURING FIRM

Most of the year-end accounting procedures for manufacturing firms are similar to
those presented for merchandising firms. The following illustration of these procedures for Davis Manufacturing Corporation includes the preparation and use of a
worksheet to adjust the general ledger accounts, the preparation of financial statements from worksheet data, and the closing of the temporary accounts. The illustration highlights the unique aspects of manufacturing accounting.

Worksheet for a Manufacturing Firm

OBJECTIVE 5 PRESENT *the year-end accounting procedures for a manufacturing firm, including the preparation of a worksheet, adjusting entries, financial statements, closing entries, and schedule of cost of goods manufactured and sold.*

As previously discussed, a **worksheet** makes adjusting the general ledger accounts and preparing financial statements easier in the following ways:

1. It places in one location the debit and credit balances of all general ledger accounts.
2. It makes apparent the effects of any adjustment.
3. It groups all adjusted balances involved in preparing each financial statement.

The following basic steps in preparing the worksheet are similar for all firms:

1. Copy the unadjusted trial balance from the general ledger to the first set of amount columns.
2. Formulate appropriate adjustments in the second set of amount columns, with dollars of debits equal to dollars of credits.
3. Combine unadjusted account balances from the first set of columns with the adjustments from the second set of columns to determine the adjusted trial balance, which is placed in the third set of amount columns.
4. Extend amounts in the adjusted trial balance columns to either the income statement set of columns or the balance sheet set of columns.
5. Balance each set of financial statement columns in turn to check the mathematical accuracy of the worksheet.

Exhibit 21-5 presents the worksheet for Davis Manufacturing Corporation for the year ended December 31, 1993. The unadjusted trial balance reflects the summary journal entries recorded earlier in this chapter *except* for the summary adjusting entry (entry **6**).

Davis' three primary inventories had the following balances at the beginning and end of 1993:

	January 1, 1993	December 31, 1993
Materials	$ 9,000	$15,000
Work in process	20,000	18,000
Finished goods	16,000	17,000

Since Davis Manufacturing Corporation uses the perpetual inventory system, the December 31, 1993, balances will appear in the trial balance columns of the worksheet.

Adjusting Entries

Adjusting entry data for Davis Manufacturing Corporation at December 31, 1993, are as follows:

1. Uncollectible accounts expense is estimated to be $9,000.
2. Factory supplies on hand at December 31, 1993, are $13,000.
3. Office supplies on hand at December 31, 1993, are $2,000.
4. Depreciation on factory machinery for 1993 is $6,000.
5. Estimated income tax expense for 1993 is $11,000.

Following are the entries to record these adjustments, with each adjustment keyed to the number of the data item listed above.

1. Uncollectible Accounts Expense	9,000	
Allowance for Uncollectible Accounts		9,000
To estimate uncollectible accounts expense.		
2. Factory Overhead	4,000	
Factory Supplies		4,000
To record the amount of factory supplies used during the year.		
3. Office Supplies Expense	3,000	
Office Supplies		3,000
To record the amount of office supplies used during the year.		

EXHIBIT 21–5

Davis Manufacturing Corporation
Worksheet (Perpetual Inventory System)
For the Year Ended December 31, 1993

Description	Trial Balance Debit	Trial Balance Credit	Adjustments Debit	Adjustments Credit	Adjusted Trial Balance Debit	Adjusted Trial Balance Credit	Income Statement Debit	Income Statement Credit	Balance Sheet Debit	Balance Sheet Credit
Cash	13,500				13,500				13,500	
Accounts Receivable	45,000				45,000				45,000	
Allowance for Uncollectible Accounts		1,000		(1) 9,000		10,000				10,000
Materials Inventory	15,000				15,000				15,000	
Work in Process Inventory	18,000				18,000				18,000	
Finished Goods Inventory	17,000				17,000				17,000	
Factory Supplies	17,000			(2) 4,000	13,000				13,000	
Office Supplies	5,000			(3) 3,000	2,000				2,000	
Factory Machinery	90,000				90,000				90,000	
Accumulated Depreciation		20,000		(4) 6,000		26,000				26,000
Accounts Payable		7,000				7,000				7,000
Long-term Notes Payable—10%		40,000				40,000				40,000
Common Stock—$10 Par Value		50,000				50,000				50,000
Retained Earnings		24,000				24,000				24,000
Cash Dividends	5,500				5,500				5,500	
Sales		470,000				470,000		470,000		
Factory Overhead		10,000	(2) 4,000 (4) 6,000							
Cost of Goods Sold	326,000				326,000		326,000			
Office Rent Expense	6,500				6,500		6,500			
Sales Rent Expense	21,000				21,000		21,000			
Office Salaries Expense	13,000				13,000		13,000			
Sales Salaries Expense	18,000				18,000		18,000			
Advertising Expense	7,500				7,500		7,500			
Interest Expense	4,000				4,000		4,000			
	622,000	622,000								
Uncollectible Accounts Expense			(1) 9,000		9,000		9,000			
Office Supplies Expense			(3) 3,000		3,000		3,000			
Income Tax Expense			(5) 11,000		11,000		11,000			
Income Tax Payable				(5) 11,000		11,000				11,000
			33,000	33,000	638,000	638,000	419,000	470,000	219,000	168,000
Net Income							51,000			51,000
							470,000	470,000	219,000	219,000

4. Factory Overhead 6,000
 Accumulated Depreciation 6,000
 To record depreciation on factory machinery.

5. Income Tax Expense 11,000
 Income Tax Payable 11,000
 To record estimated income taxes for 1993.

The preceding adjusting journal entries are listed in the second set of columns of the worksheet in Exhibit 21-5. The total of the debits ($33,000) equals the total of the credits ($33,000) in the adjustments columns of the worksheet.

Unadjusted account balances from the first set of columns are combined with the adjustments from the second set of columns to determine the adjusted trial balance. These combined amounts are placed in the third set of amount columns. The adjusted trial balance is then extended to either the income statement columns or the balance sheet columns. The data in these columns are used to prepare the income statement, retained earnings statement, and balance sheet.

Financial Statements

Exhibit 21-6 presents the income statement for Davis Manufacturing Corporation. This statement may be prepared directly from the worksheet income statement columns shown in Exhibit 21-5.

Exhibit 21-7 shows the retained earnings statement for Davis Manufacturing Corporation. Davis Manufacturing Corporation declared cash dividends of $5,500 during 1993.

Exhibit 21-8 presents the December 31, 1993, balance sheet for Davis Manufacturing Corporation. Note the presentation of the multiple inventory accounts among the current assets.

Schedule of Cost of Goods Manufactured and Sold

When a manufacturing firm uses the perpetual inventory system for Materials Inventory, Work in Process Inventory, and Finished Goods Inventory, cost of goods sold can be determined directly by reference to the Cost of Goods Sold account in the general ledger. Total manufacturing costs and cost of goods manufactured, however, are not directly available in a general ledger account or from the worksheet. The schedule of cost of goods manufactured and sold can, however, be created from the data from subsidiary records.

EXHIBIT 21-6

DAVIS MANUFACTURING CORPORATION
INCOME STATEMENT
FOR THE YEAR ENDED DECEMBER 31, 1993

Sales			$470,000
Cost of Goods Sold			326,000
Gross Profit on Sales			$144,000
Operating Expenses:			
Selling Expenses:			
Sales Rent Expense	$21,000		
Sales Salaries Expense	18,000		
Advertising Expense	7,500	$46,500	
Nonfactory Administrative Expenses:			
Office Rent Expense	$ 6,500		
Office Salaries Expense	13,000		
Uncollectible Accounts Expense	9,000		
Office Supplies Expense	3,000	31,500	
			78,000
Income from Operations			$ 66,000
Other Income and Expense:			
Interest Expense			4,000
Income before Income Tax			$ 62,000
Income Tax Expense			11,000
Net Income			$ 51,000
Earnings per Share of Common Stock (5,000 shares outstanding)			$10.20

EXHIBIT 21—7

DAVIS MANUFACTURING CORPORATION
RETAINED EARNINGS STATEMENT
FOR THE YEAR ENDED DECEMBER 31, 1993

Retained Earnings, January 1, 1993	$24,000
Add: Net Income for 1993	51,000
	$75,000
Less: Dividends Declared	5,500
Retained Earnings, December 31, 1993	$69,500

EXHIBIT 21—8

DAVIS MANUFACTURING CORPORATION
BALANCE SHEET
DECEMBER 31, 1993

Assets

Current Assets

Cash		$ 13,500
Accounts Receivable	$45,000	
Less: Allowance for Uncollectible Accounts	10,000	35,000
Inventories:		
Materials	$15,000	
Work in Process	18,000	
Finished Goods	17,000	50,000
Factory Supplies		13,000
Office Supplies		2,000
Total Current Assets		$113,500

Plant Assets

Factory Machinery	$90,000	
Less: Accumulated Depreciation	26,000	64,000
Total Assets		$177,500

Liabilities

Current Liabilities

Accounts Payable		$ 7,000
Income Tax Payable		11,000
Total Current Liabilities		$ 18,000

Long-term Liabilities

Notes Payable (10%, due 5 years hence)		40,000
Total Liabilities		$ 58,000

Stockholders' Equity

Common Stock, $10 Par Value, 5,000 Shares		
Authorized, Issued, and Outstanding	$50,000	
Retained Earnings	69,500	119,500
Total Liabilities and Stockholders' Equity		$177,500

Subsidiary records for Davis Manufacturing Corporation for 1993 contain the following data:

1. Net delivered cost of materials purchased was $116,000.
2. Direct labor totaled $87,000.
3. Factory overhead consists of the following:

Indirect material	$ 3,000
Indirect labor	33,000
Depreciation on factory machinery	6,000
Factory supplies used	4,000
Factory utilities	23,000
Factory insurance	5,000
Factory repairs	12,000
Factory rent	45,000
	$131,000

These data are combined with the worksheet data and the data related to beginning and ending inventory balances to create the schedule of cost of goods manufactured and sold. Exhibit 21-9 presents the schedule of cost of goods manufactured and sold for Davis Manufacturing Corporation for the year ended December 31, 1993.

EXHIBIT 21-9

DAVIS MANUFACTURING CORPORATION
SCHEDULE OF COST OF GOODS MANUFACTURED AND SOLD
FOR THE YEAR ENDED DECEMBER 31, 1993

Direct Material:		
Beginning Materials Inventory	$ 9,000	
Net Delivered Cost of Materials Purchased	116,000	
Cost of Material Available	$125,000	
Less: Ending Materials Inventory	15,000	
Total Material Used	$110,000	
Less: Indirect Material Used	3,000	
Direct Material Used		$107,000
Direct Labor		87,000
Factory Overhead:		
Indirect Material	$ 3,000	
Indirect Labor	33,000	
Depreciation—Factory Machinery	6,000	
Factory Supplies Used	4,000	
Factory Utilities	23,000	
Factory Insurance	5,000	
Factory Repairs	12,000	
Factory Rent	45,000	
Total Factory Overhead		131,000
Total Manufacturing Costs for the Year		$325,000
Add: Beginning Work in Process Inventory		20,000
Total Cost of Work in Process during the Year		$345,000
Less: Ending Work in Process Inventory		18,000
Cost of Goods Manufactured		$327,000
Add: Beginning Finished Goods Inventory		16,000
Cost of Goods Available for Sale		$343,000
Less: Ending Finished Goods Inventory		17,000
Cost of Goods Sold		$326,000

Closing Entries

Four closing entries are needed for Davis Manufacturing Corporation at December 31, 1993. These closing entries may be taken directly from the worksheet shown in Exhibit 21-5.

1.	Sales	470,000	
	Income Summary		470,000
	To close the revenue account.		
2.	Income Summary	419,000	
	Cost of Goods Sold		326,000
	Office Rent Expense		6,500
	Sales Rent Expense		21,000
	Office Salaries Expense		13,000
	Sales Salaries Expense		18,000
	Advertising Expense		7,500
	Interest Expense		4,000
	Uncollectible Accounts Expense		9,000
	Office Supplies Expense		3,000
	Income Tax Expense		11,000
	To close the expense accounts.		
3.	Income Summary	51,000	
	Retained Earnings		51,000
	To close the Income Summary account.		
4.	Retained Earnings	5,500	
	Cash Dividends		5,500
	To close the Cash Dividend account.		

MAJOR TRENDS IN MANUFACTURING

Two major trends in manufacturing have been affecting manufacturing product costs and manufacturing inventories: just-in-time inventory systems and automation of the manufacturing process. These two trends have tended to increase manufacturing efficiency and thereby reduce product cost.

Just-in-time Inventory Systems

OBJECTIVE ⑥ DISCUSS *just-in-time (JIT) inventory systems and factory automation.*

Manufacturing firms typically maintain inventories (materials, work in process, and finished goods) as buffers against unforeseen delays. For example, a manufacturer would keep a supply of various materials on hand to protect against a supplier's being late in the delivery of materials needed to produce a particular product. This approach is sometimes referred to as maintaining *just-in-case inventories* (just-in-case the supplier does not deliver when scheduled). Just-in-case inventories create carrying costs for the manufacturer, including casualty insurance, building usage costs, and the cost of capital on the investment in the inventory. Higher levels of inventory create higher levels of carrying costs.

Just-in-time (JIT) inventory systems seek to eliminate the just-in-case inventory balances. A company operating under a complete just-in-time philosophy would have *no* inventories at the end of each day of operations, that is, zero balances of materials, work in process, and finished goods. Materials would be ordered so that only the materials needed for production each day would be received each morning. Production would be scheduled so that all products started during the day would be completed by the end of the day (resulting in no work in process inventory) and shipped to customers by the end of the day (resulting in no finished goods inventory). *Just-in-time* means that materials are received just in time to be placed into production and that products are completed just in time to be shipped to customers.

Most manufacturing companies have been unable to reach the ideal zero balance level of all three manufacturing inventories. To guard against delayed shipments due to inclement weather or other problems, manufacturers may order materials so they arrive one or two days before they are actually needed. Even with this approach, the true just-in-case quantities are still minimized. In addition, manufacturers may be subject to seasonal demand for their product, so that they may be required to build

JUST-IN-TIME INVENTORY AND THE BUSINESS CYCLE

Inventory swings always have played a major role in business cycle fluctuations in both theory and practice. Business cycle theories assign inventories a central part.* And inventory swings historically have accounted for a disproportionate share of the fluctuations in output: Liquidation accentuates recessions, whereas reaccumulation bolsters the ensuing recovery. **However, the cyclical dynamics of inventories are changing in a way that dampens the business cycle, both down and up.** *The spread of just-in-time (JIT) production and inventory management techniques*

has shaved the peaks and valleys off of the business cycle. Such techniques dampened the 1990–91 recession.

Over the past six years or so, this innovation has reduced permanently companies' desired *level* of inventories by shortening the pipeline—or lead time—between demand and production. As a result, fluctuations in demand now translate more quickly into production adjustments, but the adjustments are smaller than in the past. JIT limits the excessive accumulation of inventories in the early stages of recession and reduces the need to restock. Smaller production adjustments—evident in smaller inventory swings—dampen the amplitude of both recessions and recoveries.

JIT is an approach to production and distribution aimed at reducing costs and improving quality. Reducing inventories is only a byproduct of this approach. However, JIT targets inventories for cost reduction, because they are viewed as wasteful.

Holding inventory ties up capital. Storage, depreciation, and other incidental costs add as much as 10% to the total cost of holding stocks.†

Traditionally, firms have realized benefits as well as costs by holding inventories. The benefits include having enough materials on hand to meet demand fluctuations, smoothing the production process, producing or purchasing the most efficient lot size, reducing the risks of "stocking-out," and minimizing transportation costs. Traditional inventory management techniques trade off those benefits against the cost.

Two factors spurred JIT's adoption: (1) high real inventory carrying costs and (2) the availability of new, lower-cost technological solutions to improve productivity and efficiency.

JIT sees the "benefits" of holding inventories as inefficient cover-ups that fail to solve the real problem, which is how to make production more efficient. It realizes these goals by other means. Small but frequent

deliveries ensure material supplies. Production processes are smoothed by designing assembly with fewer steps, thereby eliminating cleaning, inspection, and rework by improving quality and using scanners and computers to eliminate paperwork. Lot sizes are trimmed by reducing setup times. Stockout risks are reduced by producing to meet customer orders, made possible by computerized order systems and air delivery companies such as Federal Express.

JIT is used at all stages of the production and distribution process. First used in the automotive industry, it soon spread to other manufacturers. Black and Decker, Hewlett-Packard, Xerox, and General Electric have become JIT zealots. Wholesalers and retailers also use the system successfully. However, JIT has proved to be particularly valuable in reducing materials and work in process inventories in the machinery and automotive industries.

---

* See, for example, Lloyd A. Metzler, "The Nature and Stability of Inventory Cycles," *The Review of Economic Statistics*, August 1941.

† See Alan S. Blinder and Louis Maccini, "The Resurgence of Inventory Research: What Have We Learned?" *Journal of Economic Perspectives*, Winter 1991.

SOURCE: Richard B. Berner, "The New Inventory Cycle: Dampening the Recovery," *United States Fixed-Income Research: Economic Issues* [a report], July 12, 1991. Reprinted with permission of Salomon Brothers Inc. All rights reserved.

---

finished goods inventory during low demand periods of the year so they can meet customer demand during high demand periods of the year.

CONCEPTS TO IMPLEMENT JUST-IN-TIME SYSTEMS

Four important concepts are necessary for the successful operation of a just-in-time inventory system. First, a manufacturer typically relies on a limited number of materials suppliers. Each supplier is required to sign a contract of at least one year with the manufacturer. The contract usually specifies price, delivery terms and schedule, and performance conditions necessary for renewal of the contract. Material quality and delivery performance are monitored and rated for each supplier. Suppliers with poor ratings are replaced.

Second, suppliers must be willing and able to make frequent, often daily, deliveries of materials in relatively small quantities. The manufacturer's purchasing department must work closely with the supplier to facilitate the deliveries.

Third, the manufacturer must develop a system of **total quality control** to continually monitor materials and work in process for defective units. All defective units must be eliminated from the process as quickly as possible and the cause of the defects must be corrected.

Fourth, the physical arrangement of the factory operations area is usually different when the just-in-time inventory system is used. Traditionally, machines in the factory operations area are grouped by type of machine—all shearing equipment is in one location with all welding equipment in another location. With just-in-time inventory systems, machines are organized in multiple **manufacturing cells.** Each cell, or group of machines, contains one or more of various types of machines needed to manufacture the product. As a result, welding equipment may be found in 20 different locations in the factory rather than in one place. This new structure in the factory usually results in better scheduling of material flows, a necessity when the just-in-time inventory approach is being used.

Factory Automation

Factory automation is a widely recognized trend in modern manufacturing facilities. Factory automation exists in many forms. **Stand-alone automation** incorporates a robot or computer-controlled machine into an existing manufacturing process to perform a single function, such as welding. Stand-alone automation is usually undertaken to reduce both labor costs and material costs.

Flexible-manufacturing-system automation involves multiple cells of two or more automated machines. All of the machines in each cell are controlled by a computer. The machines in each cell are interconnected to allow an automated flow of product through the manufacturing cell. This type of automated system produces the product from start to finish. The functions performed within the cell can be changed quickly by changing the program in the computer that controls the process.

When deciding whether to automate all or part of a manufacturing process, a manufacturer must compare the costs associated with the automation with the benefits to be derived from the automation. The costs include the cost of the automated equipment, the costs of eliminating direct labor workers, and the costs of reorganizing the manufacturing operation. The benefits include lower direct labor costs, better product quality, and fewer defective units. In general, automation should reduce direct labor costs and increase factory overhead costs. However, the increase in factory overhead should be less than the decrease in direct labor costs.

KEY POINTS FOR CHAPTER OBJECTIVES

❶ **IDENTIFY** key objectives of a manufacturing accounting system and **DEFINE** *product costs* and *period costs* (p. 792).
- The two primary objectives of all manufacturing accounting systems are *product costing* and *cost control.*
- *Product costs* are all costs necessary to bring a manufactured product to completion. Factory costs are considered product costs.
- *Period costs* are expenditures charged to expense in the period incurred. Selling expenses and nonfactory administrative expenses are considered period costs.

❷ **DESCRIBE** the three manufacturing inventories—materials, work in process, and finished goods—and **DISCUSS** the categories of manufacturing cost and how they flow among the inventories and cost of goods sold (pp. 793–794).
- *Materials inventory* includes all factory materials and components that have been purchased but not yet placed into production.

- *Work in process inventory* includes all units of product that have been placed into production but not yet completed.
- *Finished goods inventory* includes all units of product that have been completed but not yet sold.
- *Total product costs* consist of direct material, direct labor, and factory overhead (which includes indirect material and indirect labor).
- *Prime cost* is direct material plus direct labor. *Conversion cost* is direct labor plus factory overhead.
- Product cost flows from the Materials Inventory account to the Work in Process Inventory account to the Finished Goods Inventory account and finally to the Cost of Goods Sold account.

③ DEFINE *total manufacturing costs*, *cost of goods manufactured*, and *cost of goods sold*, and **ILLUSTRATE** the schedule of cost of goods manufactured and sold and the income statement (pp. 794–796).
- *Total manufacturing costs* is the sum of direct material, direct labor, and factory overhead incurred during the accounting period.
- *Cost of goods manufactured* (cost of product transferred to finished goods inventory during the accounting period) is total manufacturing costs plus beginning work in process inventory minus ending work in process inventory.
- *Cost of goods sold* is cost of goods manufactured plus beginning finished goods inventory minus ending finished goods inventory.
- The schedule of cost of goods manufactured and sold has subtotals that reveal total manufacturing costs, cost of goods manufactured, and cost of goods sold.

④ ILLUSTRATE the journal entries to record product cost flows using the perpetual inventory system (pp. 797–798).
- Direct material, direct labor, and factory overhead costs are accumulated in the Work in Process Inventory account.
- When manufacturing is completed, product costs are transferred from the Work in Process Inventory account to the Finished Goods Inventory account.
- When goods are sold, product costs are transferred from the Finished Goods Inventory account to Cost of Goods Sold.

⑤ PRESENT the year-end accounting procedures for a manufacturing firm, including the preparation of a worksheet, adjusting entries, financial statements, closing entries, and schedule of cost of goods manufactured and sold (pp. 799–804).
- The manufacturing worksheet has five pairs of amount columns: Trial Balance, Adjustments, Adjusted Trial Balance, Income Statement, and Balance Sheet.
- Revenues, expenses, and Cost of Goods Sold are closed to the Income Summary account.
- The schedule of cost of goods manufactured and sold is prepared using data from the worksheet and subsidiary records.

⑥ DISCUSS just-in-time (JIT) inventory systems and factory automation (pp. 804–806).
- Traditional manufacturing inventories are used as buffers against unforeseen delays.
- Just-in-time inventory systems (rather than just-in-case inventory systems) minimize the amount of each inventory that is on hand.
- Just-in-time inventory systems rely on four basic concepts: (1) a limited number of materials suppliers, (2) suppliers who are willing and able to make frequent deliveries in small quantities, (3) total quality control of the materials and products, and (4) the arrangement of the factory operations area in manufacturing cells.
- Stand-alone automation of a factory incorporates a robot or computer-controlled machine into an existing manufacturing process. Flexible-manufacturing-system automation of a factory operation involves the use of multiple cells of two or more automated machines. Each cell produces a product from start to finish.

SELF-TEST QUESTIONS FOR REVIEW

(Answers follow the Solution to Demonstration Problem.)

1. Which of the following is never an element of product cost?
   a. Insurance.
   b. Utilities.
   c. Advertising.
   d. Supplies.

2. Which of the following is not an element of factory overhead?
   a. Factory office salaries.
   b. Plant manager's salary.
   c. Product inspector's salary.
   d. Company president's salary.

3. The sum of direct materials, direct labor, and factory overhead plus beginning work in process inventory minus ending work in process inventory computes
   a. Total manufacturing costs.
   c. Cost of goods sold.
   b. Cost of goods manufactured.
   d. Total cost of work in process.

4. The journal entry to record the distribution of the factory payroll requires
   a. A debit to Work in Process Inventory for direct labor.
   b. A debit to Work in Process Inventory for indirect labor.
   c. A Debit to Factory Overhead for direct labor.
   d. A credit to Factory Overhead for direct labor.

5. A manufacturer incurred $20,000 of direct material, $10,000 of direct labor, and $15,000 of factory overhead during 1993. Beginning work in process inventory was $8,000. If cost of goods manufactured was $47,000, what was the amount of the ending work in process inventory?
   a. $55,000.
   c. $10,000.
   b. $6,000.
   d. $53,000.

DEMONSTRATION PROBLEM FOR REVIEW

At December 31, 1993, the end of its fiscal year, Perez Manufacturing Corporation collected the following data for 1993:

Materials inventory, January 1	$ 80,000
Materials inventory, December 31	60,000
Work in process inventory, January 1	100,000
Work in process inventory, December 31	140,000
Finished goods inventory, January 1	120,000
Finished goods inventory, December 31	110,000
Net delivered cost of materials purchased	180,000
Direct labor	280,000
Indirect material	15,000
Indirect labor	75,000
Factory supplies used	16,000
Factory depreciation	30,000
Factory repairs and maintenance	22,000
Selling expenses	64,000
Nonfactory administrative expenses	58,000

REQUIRED

Prepare a schedule of cost of goods manufactured and sold for Perez Manufacturing Corporation for the year ended December 31, 1993, assuming that there were no other factory overhead items than those listed above.

SOLUTION TO DEMONSTRATION PROBLEM

PEREZ MANUFACTURING CORPORATION
SCHEDULE OF COST OF GOODS MANUFACTURED AND SOLD
FOR THE YEAR ENDED DECEMBER 31, 1993

Direct Material:		
Beginning Materials Inventory	$ 80,000	
Net Delivered Cost of Materials Purchased	180,000	
Cost of Material Available	$260,000	
Less: Ending Materials Inventory	60,000	
Total Material Used	$200,000	
Less: Indirect Material Used	15,000	
Direct Material Used		$185,000
Direct Labor		280,000
Factory Overhead:		
Indirect Material	$ 15,000	
Indirect Labor	75,000	
Factory Supplies Used	16,000	
Factory Depreciation	30,000	
Factory Repairs and Maintenance	22,000	
Total Factory Overhead		158,000
Total Manufacturing Costs for the Year		$623,000

Add: Beginning Work in Process Inventory	100,000
Total Cost of Work in Process during the Year	$723,000
Less: Ending Work in Process Inventory	140,000
Cost of Goods Manufactured	$583,000
Add: Beginning Finished Goods Inventory	120,000
Cost of Goods Available for Sale	$703,000
Less: Ending Finished Goods Inventory	110,000
Cost of Goods Sold	$593,000

ANSWERS TO SELF-TEST QUESTIONS   **1.** c, p. 792   **2.** d, p. 794   **3.** b, p. 795   **4.** a, p. 797   **5.** b, p. 796

GLOSSARY OF KEY TERMS USED IN THIS CHAPTER

conversion cost   The sum of direct labor cost plus factory overhead cost in a manufacturing operation (p. 794).

cost control   Accumulation of information to measure management performance and evaluate operational efficiency (p. 792).

cost of goods manufactured   The cost of goods completed during the accounting period and transferred to finished goods. It is calculated by adding the beginning balance of Work in Process Inventory to total manufacturing costs for the year and subtracting the ending balance of Work in Process Inventory (p. 795).

cost of goods sold   The cost of inventory sold to customers during the accounting period. It is calculated by adding the beginning balance of Finished Goods Inventory to cost of goods manufactured and subtracting the ending balance of Finished Goods Inventory (p. 795).

direct labor   Refers to the wage cost of factory workers applying their skills directly to the manufacture of products. The wage cost of factory workers indirectly supporting the manufacturing process is accounted for as indirect labor, part of factory overhead (p. 793).

direct material   Refers to the cost of all important materials and components that physically make up the product (p. 793).

factory overhead   All manufacturing costs not considered direct material or direct labor, including indirect material, indirect labor, and factory depreciation, taxes, and insurance (p. 794).

finished goods inventory   Units of product for which production has been completed (p. 793).

flexible-manufacturing-system automation   An arrangement of two or more automated machines used in a manufacturing environment in which all the machines are interconnected and controlled by a computer (p. 806).

indirect labor   The salary and wage cost of factory employees who do not work directly on the product (such as supervisors, inspectors, and material handlers) (p. 793).

indirect material   Incidental material items, such as glue and fasteners, that are included in factory overhead rather than direct material (p. 793).

just-in-time (JIT) inventory systems   A system in which manufacturing inventories are maintained on a full just-in-time basis; that is, all inventories are replenished exactly when the item is needed; material is received just in time to be placed into production and goods are finished just in time to ship them to customers (p. 804).

manufacturing cells   A grouping of dissimilar machines used in manufacturing to facilitate just-in-time manufacturing (p. 806).

materials inventory   All factory materials acquired but not yet placed into production (p. 793).

period costs   Costs associated with the period in which they are incurred, rather than with the product (p. 792).

prime cost   The sum of direct material plus direct labor in a manufacturing operation (p. 794).

product costing   Accumulating and allocating the costs of all inputs in the manufacturing process to individual products (p. 792).

product costs   All costs necessary to bring a manufactured product to completion (p. 792).

stand-alone automation   Incorporating a robot or computer-controlled machine into an existing manufacturing process to perform a single function (p. 806).

total manufacturing cost   The total direct material, direct labor, and factory overhead incurred in the manufacturing process during the year (p. 795).

total quality control   A system for continually monitoring materials and work in process for defective units (p. 806).

work in process inventory   All units of product that are in the process of being manufactured (p. 793).

worksheet   An informal accounting document used to facilitate the preparation of financial statements (p. 799).

QUESTIONS

21-1   How are product costs accounted for differently from period costs? Give examples of each.

21-2   What is the basic format of the income statement of a manufacturing firm?

21-3   Name the three inventory accounts maintained by manufacturing firms and briefly describe the nature of each.

21-4   Name and briefly describe the three major categories used to account for manufacturing costs.

21-5   Define *prime cost* and *conversion cost*.

21-6   List six examples of factory overhead costs.

21-7   In what way is total manufacturing cost different from cost of goods manufactured?

21-8   If cost of work in process during the year is $480,000 and ending work in process inventory is $50,000, what is the amount of cost of goods manufactured?

21-9   If beginning and ending finished goods inventories are $55,000 and $45,000, respectively, and the cost of goods sold is $420,000, what is the cost of goods manufactured?

21-10   What journal entry would be made to record the transfer of $12,000 of direct material and $2,500 of indirect material from the material inventory?

21-11   What journal entry would be made to record the distribution of a factory payroll consisting of $11,000 of direct labor and $4,000 of indirect labor?

21-12   What journal entry would be made to record the payment of $1,500 cash for factory utilities?

21-13   What journal entry would be required to record the transfer of completed products costing $15,000?

21-14   Contrast just-in-case inventories and just-in-time inventories.

21-15   Describe a manufacturing cell and contrast a cell to the equipment arrangement in a traditional manufacturing operation.

21-16   Describe and contrast stand-alone automation and flexible-manufacturing-system automation.

EXERCISES

SCHEDULE OF COST OF GOODS MANUFACTURED AND SOLD
— OBJ. 3 —

21-17   At December 31, 1993, the end of its fiscal year, Lederman Manufacturing Corporation collected the following data for 1993:

Materials inventory, January 1	$ 25,000
Materials inventory, December 31	15,000
Work in process inventory, January 1	30,000
Work in process inventory, December 31	41,000
Finished goods inventory, January 1	51,000
Finished goods inventory, December 31	36,000
Net delivered cost of materials purchased	125,000
Direct labor	148,000
Indirect material	12,000
Indirect labor	37,000
Factory supplies used	10,000
Factory depreciation	65,000
Factory repairs and maintenance	21,000
Selling expenses (total)	62,000
Nonfactory administrative expenses (total)	58,000

Prepare a schedule of cost of goods manufactured and sold for Lederman Manufacturing Corporation for the year ended December 31, 1993, assuming that there were no other factory overhead items than those listed above.

INCOME STATEMENT
— OBJ. 3 —

21-18   Lederman Manufacturing Corporation (see Exercise 21-17) sold 15,000 units of product for $40 each during 1993. During the year, 5,000 shares of common stock were outstanding. Prepare an income statement for the year (ignore income taxes).

COST OF GOODS MANUFACTURED AND COST OF GOODS SOLD
— OBJ. 3 —

21-19   For each of the following unrelated columns of data for the year, compute the cost of goods manufactured and the cost of goods sold.

	A	B	C
Selling expenses	$ 500	$ 800	$ 600
Factory insurance	260	245	140
Ending finished goods inventory	810	750	515
Nonfactory administrative expenses	250	450	350
Direct labor	2,560	2,760	2,120
Beginning materials inventory	520	670	350
Beginning work in process inventory	1,120	840	1,070
Indirect material used	390	420	230
Factory utilities	240	275	150
Factory depreciation	730	760	380
Ending work in process inventory	1,360	790	950
Ending materials inventory	440	710	410
Indirect labor	425	280	160
Beginning finished goods inventory	850	725	480
Factory repairs and maintenance	215	230	175
Net delivered cost of materials purchased	3,140	4,410	2,870
Factory supplies used	330	310	210

PRIME COST AND CONVERSION COST
— OBJ. 3 —

21-20   Piper Manufacturing Company incurred the following during 1993:

Direct material	$25,000
Direct labor	30,000
Factory overhead	45,000
Selling expenses	40,000
Nonfactory administrative expenses	35,000

Calculate prime cost and conversion cost for Piper Manufacturing Company during 1993.

ENTRIES FOR PRODUCT COST FLOW
— OBJ. 4 —

21-21   The following transactions occurred during January 1993 for Richards Manufacturing Company:

Jan.   5   Acquired $3,000 of material on account that will be used to produce product for resale.

11   Requisitioned $2,500 of material for use as direct material in the factory.

16   Completed the manufacturing of products with a total product cost of $11,000 and transferred them to the warehouse.

Record these transactions in general journal form. Assume that Richard Manufacturing Company uses the perpetual inventory system.

ENTRIES FOR PRODUCT COST FLOW
— OBJ. 4 —

21-22   Record the following transactions that occurred during March 1993 for Harris Manufacturing Company, which uses the perpetual inventory system:

Mar. 12   Transferred $10,000 of completed goods from the factory to the warehouse.

15   Requisitioned $6,000 of material for use in the factory as direct material and $1,000 for indirect material.

18   Sold goods costing $8,000 for $12,000 on account.

JUST-IN-TIME MATERIAL INVENTORY
— OBJ. 6 —

21-23   Imperial Manufacturing Company operates its factory 200 days each year. Its typical annual output has a total product cost of $400,000 ($180,000 direct material, $110,000 direct labor, $20,000 indirect material, $15,000 indirect labor, and $75,000 other factory overhead). Imperial keeps an average of $11,000 of materials inventory on hand. Imperial wants to convert to a just-in-time inventory system that would store only the material needed for the next day's production. How much could Imperial reduce its material inventory if it adopted the new system?

PROBLEMS

SCHEDULE OF COST OF GOODS MANUFACTURED AND SOLD
— OBJ. 3 —

21-24 The following amounts are available for 1993 for Bourne Manufacturing Company:

Administrative salaries (nonfactory)	$ 70,000
Administrative rent (nonfactory)	35,000
Advertising and promotion expense	41,000
Depreciation—administrative	22,000
Depreciation—factory	30,000
Depreciation—selling	17,000
Direct labor	175,000
Factory rent	18,000
Factory supplies used	12,000
Finished goods inventory (January 1)	57,000
Finished goods inventory (December 31)	52,000
Indirect material used	14,000
Indirect labor	19,000
Materials inventory (January 1)	13,000
Materials inventory (December 31)	20,000
Net delivered cost of materials purchased	138,000
Other factory overhead	26,000
Sales	845,000
Sales salaries expense	72,000
Work in process inventory (January 1)	18,000
Work in process inventory (December 31)	31,000

REQUIRED

Using the above data, prepare a schedule of cost of goods manufactured and sold.

COST OF GOODS MANUFACTURED AND SOLD
— OBJ. 3 —

21-25 The following data relate to three independent production periods of Riverside Manufacturing Company. Missing data are indicated by question marks.

	A	B	C
Materials:			
Beginning inventory	$ 52	$164	$110
Purchases	?	700	500
Ending inventory	74	100	?
Total material used	330	?	440
Direct labor	580	960	800
Factory overhead:			
Indirect material	96	?	120
Indirect labor	160	150	350
Other	?	200	340
Total factory overhead	520	480	?
Work in process inventories:			
Beginning	?	90	260
Ending	70	?	100
Finished goods inventories:			
Beginning	?	400	80
Ending	335	120	330
Cost of goods manufactured	1,384	?	?
Cost of goods sold	1,339	2,324	?

REQUIRED

Using the above data, determine the missing amounts. (You should set up a schedule of cost of goods manufactured and sold, fill in the known data, and calculate the missing amounts.)

JOURNAL ENTRIES
— OBJ. 4 —

21-26   Taylor Manufacturing Company uses the perpetual inventory system to record transactions related to its manufacturing inventories. The following transactions occurred
during March 1993:

Mar. 6   Prepared and recorded the factory payroll of $12,000.

 6   Recorded the distribution of the payroll: $10,000 of direct labor and $2,000
of indirect labor.

 8   Received $14,000 of materials and components that had been ordered on
account.

10   Completed product costing $22,000 and transferred it to the warehouse.

11   Requisitioned $5,000 of material for use in the factory; $4,000 was used as
direct material and the remainder was used as indirect material.

12   Sold on account product costing $3,000 for $4,500.

15   Applied $6,000 of factory overhead cost to the product currently being
worked on.

21   Paid $500 cash for a special material component that was shipped via over-
night delivery.

27   Sold product costing $2,900 for $5,000 cash.

REQUIRED
Prepare general journal entries to record these transactions.

JOURNAL ENTRIES
— OBJ. 4 —

21-27   Paulson Manufacturing Company uses the perpetual inventory system to account for
its manufacturing inventories. The following are Paulson's transactions during July
1993:

July 5   Received material costing $2,000 from a supplier. The material was pur-
chased on account.

 9   Requisitioned $6,000 of material for use in the factory, consisting of $5,000
of direct material and $1,000 of indirect material.

11   Recorded the incurrence of the $15,000 factory payroll.

11   Distributed the factory payroll: $13,500 of direct labor and $1,500 of indirect labor.

17   Incurred various overhead costs totaling $14,000. (Credit Accounts Payable.)

20   Applied $20,000 of factory overhead to the products being manufactured.

23   Completed product costing $16,000 and moved it to the warehouse.

26   Sold goods with a product cost of $3,000 on account for $5,000.

REQUIRED
a. Set up a T account for the following four accounts and post the July 1, 1993,
balance listed after the account title: Materials Inventory, $7,000; Work in Process
Inventory, $25,000; Finished Goods Inventory, $10,000; and Cost of Goods Sold,
$30,000.
b. Record the transactions listed above in general journal form, post relevant portions
to the four T accounts, and balance the four accounts.

TOTAL MANUFACTURING
COST, INCOME
STATEMENT, UNIT COST,
AND SELLING PRICE
— OBJ. 3 —

21-28   Two inventors, recently organized as Innovation, Inc., consult you regarding a planned
new product. They have estimates of the costs of materials, labor, overhead, and other
expenses for 1993 but need to know how much to charge for each unit to earn a profit
in 1993 equal to 15% of their estimated total long-term investment of $400,000
(ignore income taxes).

Their plans indicate that each unit of the new product requires the following:

> **Direct Material**
> 4 lbs. of a material costing $5/lb.
> **Direct Labor**
> 2 hrs. of a metal former's time at $11/hr.
> 0.6 hr. of an assembler's time at $8/hr.

Major items of production overhead would be annual rent of $46,460 for a factory building, $28,660 rent for machinery, and $21,700 of indirect material. Other production overhead is estimated to be $233,280. Selling expenses are an estimated 30% of total sales, and nonfactory administrative expenses are 20% of total sales.

The consensus at Innovation is that during 1993 10,000 units of product should be produced for selling and another 2,000 units should be produced for the next year's beginning inventory. Also, an extra 3,000 pounds of material will be purchased as beginning inventory for the next year. Because of the nature of the manufacturing process, all units started must be completed, so work in process inventories are negligible.

REQUIRED

a. Incorporate the above data into a schedule of estimated total manufacturing costs and compute the unit production cost for 1993.

b. Prepare an estimated income statement that would provide the target amount of profit for 1993.

c. What unit sales price should Innovation charge for the new product?

WORKSHEET, FINANCIAL STATEMENTS, AND SCHEDULE OF COST OF GOODS MANUFACTURED AND SOLD — OBJ. 5 —

21-29 The trial balance for Newton Manufacturing Corporation at the end of 1993 follows:

	Debit	Credit
Cash	$ 40,000	
Accounts Receivable	248,000	
Allowance for Uncollectible Accounts		$ 5,600
Materials Inventory	136,000	
Work in Process Inventory	80,000	
Finished Goods Inventory	64,000	
Land	140,000	
Factory Buildings	800,000	
Accumulated Depreciation—Factory Buildings		184,000
Factory Equipment	700,000	
Accumulated Depreciation—Factory Equipment		68,000
Accounts Payable		168,400
Long-term Notes Payable—8%		224,000
Common Stock, $40 Par Value (All outstanding)		1,120,000
Retained Earnings		228,000
Sales		1,680,000
Factory Overhead		72,000
Cost of Goods Sold	1,194,800	
Selling Expenses	203,200	
Nonfactory Administrative Expenses	144,000	
	$3,750,000	$3,750,000

The following information is available (adjusting entries have not been recorded):

1. Annual amounts of depreciation are factory buildings, $44,000 and factory equipment, $28,000.

2. Uncollectible accounts expense, $\frac{1}{2}$% of sales. (Debit this expense to Selling Expenses.)

3. Estimated income taxes, $26,000.

4. January 1 inventories were materials, $164,000; work in process, $72,000; and finished goods, $92,000.

5. Additional data needed for schedule of cost of goods manufactured and sold:

Net delivered cost of materials purchased	$380,000
Direct labor	512,400
Indirect material	47,000
Indirect labor	126,800
Factory utilities	21,600
Factory repairs and maintenance	16,000
Factory property taxes	18,000

REQUIRED

a. Prepare a manufacturing worksheet for 1993.

b. Prepare an income statement.

c. Prepare a balance sheet.

d. Prepare a schedule of cost of goods manufactured and sold.

WORKSHEET, INCOME
STATEMENT, AND
SCHEDULE OF COST OF
GOODS MANUFACTURED
AND SOLD
— OBJ. 5 —

21-30 The trial balance of Hyde Company at December 31, 1993, is given below, together with the worksheet adjustments. Hyde Company uses perpetual inventory procedures.

	Trial Balance		Adjustments	
	Debit	**Credit**	**Debit**	**Credit**
Cash	28,000			
Materials Inventory	52,000			
Work in Process Inventory	30,000			
Finished Goods Inventory	42,000			
Prepaid Insurance	2,800			(1) 1,400
Factory Machinery	240,000			
Accumulated Depreciation—				
Factory Machinery		50,000		(2) 17,000
Patents	40,800			(3) 3,200
Accounts Payable		66,200		
Common Stock, $17 Par				
Value		170,000		
Retained Earnings		25,400		
Sales		620,000		
Factory Overhead		17,000	(2) 17,000	
Cost of Goods Sold	414,000			
Sales Salaries Expense	52,000			
Advertising Expense	13,600			
Nonfactory			(1) 1,400	
Administrative Expenses	33,400		(3) 3,200	
	948,600	948,600		
Income Tax Expense			(4) 20,000	
Income Tax Payable				(4) 20,000
			41,600	41,600

Additional information:

1. January 1,1993, inventories were materials, $36,000; work in process, $27,800; and finished goods, $42,000.

2. Net delivered cost of materials purchased was $142,800.

3. Direct labor was $180,800.

4. Factory overhead included the following:

Indirect labor	$61,000
Factory utilities	8,200
Repairs and maintenance	4,400
Factory buildings rent	18,000
Indirect material	15,000

REQUIRED

a. Complete the manufacturing worksheet.

b. Prepare an income statement.

c. Prepare a schedule of cost of goods manufactured and sold.

JUST-IN-TIME INVENTORIES
— OBJ. 6 —

21-31 Glendale Manufacturing Company plans to produce 120,000 units of its only product during 1994. At December 31, 1993, Glendale, which uses perpetual inventory procedures, had the following inventories:

Materials inventory	$20,000
Work in process inventory	15,000
Finished goods inventory	40,000

Glendale plans to operate its factory 240 days during 1994, running one 8-hour shift each day. The level of production will be the same each day. All items in the materials inventory will be used as direct material. Each unit of product requires the following:

Direct Material

2 lbs. of a material costing $3 per lb.

Direct Labor

$\frac{1}{2}$ hr. of labor at $10 per hr.

Factory Overhead

Equals 1.6 times the direct labor cost

Glendale has decided to work toward just-in-time inventories for material, work in process, and finished goods. The planned inventory levels at the end of each day, beginning July 1, 1994, are the following:

Materials

2 days' production

Work in Process

0.5 day's production

Finished Goods

3 days' production

REQUIRED

a. Determine the planned inventory dollar amounts for the three manufacturing inventories.
b. Calculate the planned reduction in inventory dollar amount between December 31, 1993, and July 1, 1994.

ALTERNATE EXERCISES

SCHEDULE OF COST OF GOODS MANUFACTURED AND SOLD
— OBJ. 3 —

21-17A At December 31, 1993, the end of its fiscal year, Kelly Metal Products Corporation collected the following data for 1993:

Materials inventory, January 1	$ 32,000
Materials inventory, December 31	22,000
Work in process inventory, January 1	34,000
Work in process inventory, December 31	45,000
Finished goods inventory, January 1	21,000
Finished goods inventory, December 31	18,000
Net delivered cost of materials purchased	210,000
Direct labor	135,000
Indirect material	13,000
Indirect labor	25,000
Factory supplies used	12,000
Factory depreciation	78,000
Factory repairs and maintenance	28,000
Selling expenses (total)	63,000
Nonfactory administrative expenses (total)	57,000

REQUIRED

Prepare a schedule of cost of goods manufactured and sold for Kelly Metal Products Corporation for the year ended December 31, 1993, assuming that there were no other factory overhead items than those listed above.

INCOME STATEMENT
— OBJ. 3 —

21-18A Kelly Metal Products Corporation (see Exercise 21-17A) sold 20,000 units of product for $35 each during 1993. During the year, 10,000 shares of common stock were outstanding. Prepare an income statement for the year (ignore income taxes).

COST OF GOODS MANUFACTURED AND COST OF GOODS SOLD
— OBJ. 3 —

21-19A For each of the following unrelated columns of data for the year, compute the cost of goods manufactured and the cost of goods sold.

	A	B	C
Selling expenses	$ 600	$ 700	$ 900
Factory insurance	180	270	300
Ending finished goods inventory	620	660	930
Nonfactory administrative expenses	300	400	800
Direct labor	2,130	2,850	3,160
Beginning materials inventory	425	575	850
Beginning work in process inventory	840	920	1,290
Indirect material used	270	325	520
Factory utilities	350	360	500
Factory depreciation	820	740	965
Ending work in process inventory	790	985	1,425
Ending materials inventory	385	610	820
Indirect labor	225	410	365
Beginning finished goods inventory	565	680	950
Factory repairs and maintenance	330	250	415
Net delivered cost of materials purchased	2,780	3,620	8,170
Factory supplies used	210	230	260

PRIME COST AND CONVERSION COST
— OBJ. 3 —

21-20A Benton Manufacturing Company incurred the following during 1993:

Direct material	$42,000
Direct labor	47,000
Factory overhead	63,000
Selling expenses	56,000
Nonfactory administrative expenses	51,000

Calculate prime cost and conversion cost for Benton Manufacturing Company during 1993.

ENTRIES FOR PRODUCT COST FLOW
— OBJ. 4 —

21-21A The following transactions occurred during February 1993 for Thompson Manufacturing Company:

Feb. 10 Acquired $5,000 of material on account that will be used to produce product for resale.

11 Requisitioned $4,000 of material for use as direct material in the factory.

16 Completed the manufacturing of products with a total product cost of $24,000 and transferred them to the warehouse.

Record these transactions in general journal form. Assume that Thompson Manufacturing Company uses the perpetual inventory system.

ENTRIES FOR PRODUCT COST FLOW
— OBJ. 4 —

21-22A Record the following transactions that occurred during April 1993 for Boyd Manufacturing Corporation, which uses the perpetual inventory system:

Apr. 21 Transferred $16,000 of completed goods from the factory to the warehouse.

25 Requisitioned $9,000 of material for use in the factory as direct material and $2,000 for indirect material.

28 Sold goods costing $6,000 for $10,000 on account.

· JUST-IN-TIME MATERIAL INVENTORY
— OBJ. 6 —

21-23A Grand Manufacturing Company operates its factory 200 days each year. Its typical annual output has a total product cost of $600,000 ($270,000 direct material, $165,000 direct labor, $30,000 indirect material, $22,500 indirect labor, and $112,500 other factory overhead). Grand keeps an average of $15,000 of materials inventory on hand. Grand wants to convert to a just-in-time inventory system that would store only the material needed for the next day's production. How much could Grand reduce its material inventory if it adopted the new system?

ALTERNATE PROBLEMS

SCHEDULE OF COST OF GOODS MANUFACTURED AND SOLD
— OBJ. 3 —

21-24A The following amounts are available for 1993 for Bishop Manufacturing Company:

Administrative salaries (nonfactory)	$ 85,000
Administrative rent (nonfactory)	47,000
Advertising and promotion expense	93,000
Depreciation—administrative	77,000
Depreciation—factory	95,000
Depreciation—selling	36,000
Direct labor	325,000
Factory rent	68,000
Factory supplies used	23,000
Finished goods inventory (January 1)	61,000
Finished goods inventory (December 31)	63,000
Indirect material used	27,000
Indirect labor	44,000
Materials inventory (January 1)	22,000
Materials inventory (December 31)	30,000
Net delivered cost of materials purchased	210,000
Other factory overhead	55,000
Sales	938,000
Sales salaries expense	71,000
Work in process inventory (January 1)	33,000
Work in process inventory (December 31)	29,000

REQUIRED

Using the above data, prepare a schedule of cost of goods manufactured and sold.

COST OF GOODS MANUFACTURED AND SOLD
— OBJ. 3 —

21-25A The following data relate to three independent production periods of Randolph Manufacturing Company. Missing data are indicated by question marks.

	A	B	C
Materials:			
Beginning inventory	$ 78	$ 410	$ 220
Purchases	?	1,750	1,000
Ending inventory	111	250	?
Total material used	495	?	880
Direct labor	870	2,400	1,600
Factory overhead:			
Indirect material	144	?	110
Indirect labor	240	375	700
Other	?	500	680
Total factory overhead	780	1,000	?
Work in process inventories:			
Beginning	?	225	520
Ending	105	?	200
Finished goods inventories:			
Beginning	?	1,000	160
Ending	495	300	660
Cost of goods manufactured	2,076	?	?
Cost of goods sold	2,016	5,275	?

REQUIRED

Using the above data, determine the missing amounts. (You should set up a schedule of cost of goods manufactured and sold, fill in the known data, and calculate the missing amounts.)

JOURNAL ENTRIES
— OBJ. 4 —

21-26A Travis Manufacturing Company uses the perpetual inventory system to record transactions related to its manufacturing inventories. The following transactions occurred during August 1993:

Aug. 5   Received $9,000 of materials and components that had been ordered on account.

     7   Prepared and recorded the factory payroll, which totaled $8,000.

     7   Recorded the distribution of the payroll: $6,500 of direct labor and $1,500 of indirect labor.

Aug. 11 Sold on account product costing $3,500 for $5,200.

16 Completed product costing $16,000 and transferred it to the warehouse.

20 Requisitioned $7,000 of material for use in the factory; $5,900 was used as direct material and the remainder was used as indirect material.

25 Applied $10,000 of factory overhead cost to the product currently being worked on.

29 Paid $400 cash for a special material component that was shipped via overnight delivery.

31 Sold product costing $1,000 for $1,700 cash.

REQUIRED

Prepare general journal entries to record these transactions.

JOURNAL ENTRIES — OBJ. 4 —

21-27A Porter Manufacturing Company uses the perpetual inventory system to account for its manufacturing inventories. The following are Porter's transactions during September 1993:

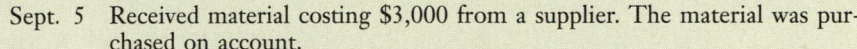

Sept. 5 Received material costing $3,000 from a supplier. The material was purchased on account.

9 Requisitioned $7,000 of material for use in the factory, consisting of $5,600 of direct material and $1,400 of indirect material.

11 Recorded the incurrence of the $16,000 factory payroll.

11 Distributed the factory payroll: $14,000 of direct labor and $2,000 of indirect labor.

17 Incurred various overhead costs totaling $15,000. (Credit Accounts Payable.)

20 Applied $21,000 of factory overhead to the products being manufactured.

23 Completed product costing $17,000 and moved it to the warehouse.

26 Sold goods with a product cost of $4,000 on account for $6,000.

REQUIRED

a. Set up a T account for the following four accounts and post the September 1, 1993, balance listed after the account title: Materials Inventory, $8,000; Work in Process Inventory, $26,000; Finished Goods Inventory, $11,000; and Cost of Goods Sold, $32,000.

b. Record the transactions listed above in general journal form, post relevant portions to the four T accounts, and balance the four accounts.

TOTAL MANUFACTURING COSTS, INCOME STATEMENT, UNIT COST, AND SELLING PRICE — OBJ. 3 —

21-28A You are consulted by Investors, Inc., a group of investors planning a new product. They have estimates of the costs of materials, labor, overhead, and other expenses for 1993 but need to know how much to charge for each unit to earn a profit in 1993 equal to 10% of their estimated investment of $500,000 (ignore income taxes).

Their plans indicate that each unit of the new product requires the following:

Direct Material

4 lbs. of a material costing $6/lb.

Direct Labor

3 hrs. of a die cutter's time at $9/hr.
2 hrs. of an assembler's time at $8 hr.

Major items of production overhead would be annual rent of $40,000 on the factory building and $25,000 on machinery as well as indirect material of $21,000. Other production overhead is an estimated 60% of total direct labor costs. Selling expenses are an estimated 20% of total sales, and nonfactory administrative expenses are 10% of total sales.

The consensus at Investors is that during 1993 4,000 units of product should be produced for selling and another 1,000 units should be produced for the next year's beginning inventory. Also, an extra 6,000 pounds of material will be purchased as beginning inventory for the next year. Because of the nature of the manufacturing process, all units started must be completed, so work in process inventories are negligible.

REQUIRED

a. Incorporate the above data into a schedule of estimated total manufacturing costs and compute the unit production cost for 1993.
b. Prepare an estimated income statement that would provide the target amount of profit for 1993.
c. What unit sales price should Investors charge for the new product?

WORKSHEET, FINANCIAL STATEMENTS, AND SCHEDULE OF COST OF GOODS MANUFACTURED AND SOLD
— OBJ. 5 —

21-29A The trial balance for the Niagara Boatbuilders Corporation at the end of 1993 follows:

	Debit	Credit
Cash	$ 40,000	
Accounts Receivable	151,200	
Allowance for Uncollectible Accounts		$ 7,200
Materials Inventory	50,000	
Work in Process Inventory	44,000	
Finished Goods Inventory	54,000	
Land	104,000	
Factory Buildings	550,000	
Accumulated Depreciation—Factory Buildings		148,000
Factory Machinery	740,000	
Accumulated Depreciation—Factory Machinery		108,000
Accounts Payable		128,400
Long-term Notes Payable—9%		216,000
Common Stock, $100 Par Value (All outstanding)		360,000
Retained Earnings		510,000
Sales		1,476,000
Factory Overhead		58,000
Cost of Goods Sold	988,800	
Selling Expenses	175,600	
Nonfactory Administrative Expenses	114,000	
	$3,011,600	$3,011,600

The following information is available (adjusting entries have not been recorded):
1. Annual amounts of depreciation are factory buildings, $32,000 and factory machinery, $26,000.
2. Uncollectible accounts expense, 1% of sales. (Debit this expense to Selling Expenses.)
3. Estimated income taxes, $38,840.
4. January 1 inventories were materials, $64,000; work in process, $32,000; and finished goods, $80,000.
5. Additional data needed for schedule of cost of goods manufactured and sold:

Net delivered cost of materials purchased	$416,000
Direct labor	302,000
Indirect material	37,000
Indirect labor	111,000
Factory utilities	31,800
Factory repairs and maintenance	18,000
Factory property taxes	24,000

REQUIRED

a. Prepare a manufacturing worksheet for 1993.
b. Prepare an income statement.
c. Prepare a balance sheet.
d. Prepare a schedule of cost of goods manufactured and sold.

**WORKSHEET, INCOME
STATEMENT, AND
SCHEDULE OF COST OF
GOODS MANUFACTURED
AND SOLD
— OBJ. 5 —**

21-30A The trial balance of Hunter Company at December 31, 1993, is given below, together with the worksheet adjustments. Hunter Company uses perpetual inventory.

	Trial Balance		Adjustments	
	Debit	**Credit**	**Debit**	**Credit**
Cash	34,000			
Materials Inventory	78,000			
Work in Process Inventory	34,000			
Finished Goods Inventory	66,000			
Prepaid Insurance	10,000			(1) 5,000
Factory Machinery	570,000			
Accumulated Depreciation—				
Factory Machinery		48,000		(2) 22,400
Copyright	98,000			(3) 6,000
Accounts Payable		154,000		
Common Stock, $20 Par				
Value		224,000		
Retained Earnings		156,000		
Sales		1,900,000		
Factory Overhead		22,400	(2) 22,400	
Cost of Goods Sold	1,294,400			
Sales Salaries Expense	134,000			
Advertising Expense	62,000			
Nonfactory Administrative			(3) 6,000	
Expenses	124,000		(1) 5,000	
	2,504,400	2,504,400		
Income Tax Expense			(4) 52,840	
Income Tax Payable				(4) 52,840
			86,240	86,240

Additional information:
1. January 1, 1993, inventories were materials, $68,000; work in process, $50,000; and finished goods, $84,000.
2. Net delivered cost of materials purchased was $504,000.
3. Direct labor was $490,000.
4. Factory overhead included the following:

Indirect labor	$186,000
Factory utilities	26,000
Repairs and maintenance	12,000
Factory building rent	30,000
Indirect material	42,000

REQUIRED

a. Complete the manufacturing worksheet.
b. Prepare an income statement.
c. Prepare a schedule of cost of goods manufactured and sold.

**JUST-IN-TIME INVENTORIES
— OBJ. 6 —**

21-31A Grafton Manufacturing Company plans to produce 200,000 units of its only product during 1994. At December 31, 1993, Grafton had the following inventories (Grafton uses perpetual inventory procedures):

Materials inventory	$ 14,000
Work in process inventory	35,000
Finished goods inventory	100,000

Grafton plans to operate its factory 250 days during 1994, running one 8-hour shift each day. The level of production will be the same each day. All items in the materials inventory will be used as direct material. Each unit of product requires the following:

Direct Material

3 lbs. of material costing $2 per lb.

Direct Labor

1 hr. of labor at $12 per hr.

Factory Overhead

Equal to 1.5 times the direct labor cost

Grafton has decided to work toward just-in-time inventories for material, work in process, and finished goods. The planned inventory levels at the end of each day, beginning August 1, 1994, are as follows:

Materials

2 days' production

Work in Process

1 day's production

Finished Goods

3 days' production

REQUIRED

a. Determine the planned inventory dollar amounts for the three manufacturing inventories.

b. Calculate the planned reduction in inventory dollar amounts between December 31, 1993, and August 1, 1994.

CASES

Business Decision Case

James Alvarez, an engineer, needs some accounting advice. In their spare time during the past year, Alvarez and his college-aged son, Robert, have manufactured a small weed-trimming sickle in a rented building near their home. Robert, who has had one accounting course in college, keeps the books.

Alvarez is pleased about the results of their first year's operations. He asks you to look over the following income report prepared by Robert before they leave on a well-deserved vacation to Hawaii, after which they plan to expand their business significantly.

Sales (34,000 units at $10 each)		$340,000
Costs of producing 35,000 units:		
Materials:		
Precast blades at $1.50 each	$ 57,000	
Preturned handles at $1 each	40,000	
Labor costs of hired assemblers	26,600	
Labor costs of hired painters	33,000	
Rent on building	14,900	
Rent on machinery	7,100	
Utilities for production	8,000	
Other production costs	11,900	
Advertising expense	26,200	
Sales commissions	35,700	
Delivery of products to customers	14,350	
Total costs	$274,750	
Less: Ending inventory of 1,000 units at average production costs of $7.85 (or $274,750/35,000 units)	7,850	
Cost of goods sold		266,900
Net income		$ 73,100

After you examine the income report, Alvarez responds to your questions and assures you that (1) no theft or spoilage of materials has occurred, (2) no partially completed units are involved, and (3) he and his son have averaged 30 hours each per week in the business for 50 weeks. Ignore income taxes in this situation.

REQUIRED

a. Identify any apparent discrepancy in the income report in the cost of materials used.

b. Recalculate the cost of goods manufactured, the average cost per unit produced, and the net income for the year.

c. What factors should Alvarez consider regarding the profitability of his venture before deciding to expand it significantly?

Ethics Case

Great Cakes is a large bakery known for its quality "boxed cake" products. Its motto is "We Use Only the Best Ingredients."

Ralph Sands, the purchasing supervisor, is responsible for ordering the ingredients for all the bakery products. He is being considered for a promotion based on his proven ability to purchase ingredients at the best price available.

The cost of all the ingredients has risen substantially over the past few months. Sands decides to purchase 25% of the ingredients at a lower quality than Great Cakes normally uses because the cost is significantly less. Without relying on the company's test kitchens, he believes this substitution will not be noticed by the customers and the lower cost will counterbalance the increased costs of the other ingredients.

Sands explains this decision to his friend, Lynn Pall, the company's accountant, one day at lunch. He also tells her that he does not intend to inform management of the inclusion of the lower-quality ingredients in the bakery's products.

REQUIRED

What ethical considerations arise from Ralph Sands' decisions? What problems face Lynn Pall because of his actions?

How does a manufacturing firm account for product cost when production is characterized by a series of different products or jobs?

Many manufacturing firms make their products in batches or produce special orders for customers. ■ These manufacturers use job order costing procedures to accumulate and account for product cost. ■ At Ford Motor Co., car or truck models with optional equipment packages are made for inventory and to fill orders. ■ A complicating factor in job order costing is applying factory overhead to products. ■ Firms from computer maker Hewlett-Packard to tractor manufacturer John Deere do so using activity-based costing.

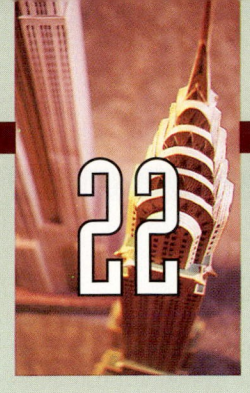

22

COST ACCOUNTING SYSTEMS: JOB ORDER COSTING

irtually all manufacturing firms have a cost accounting system consisting of forms, procedures, and records used to develop and report timely information about product costs. Any orderly method of developing product or service cost information constitutes a cost accounting system. Typically, some amount of cost is accumulated and related to some unit of activity or accomplishment. Examples include accumulating the cost of cutting and forming materials, assembling parts, and painting the final product that results in a completed unit of product such as a lawnmower, a computer, or a custom-designed executive jet aircraft. Although a cost accounting system could be maintained independently of a firm's formal accounting system, most comprehensive cost accounting systems are integrated into the formal accounting system.

Cost accounting systems are usually illustrated for manufacturing situations involving product costs per unit. Note, however, that reliable cost-per-unit-of-accomplishment information is vital to managerial decision making in all types of entities, including service firms and governmental operations. For example, a hospital may need to know the cost per patient of providing a specific surgical procedure; an insurance company may want to know the cost of providing health care insurance to a particular group; and a city may need to know the cost per ton of trash removal. Many of the cost accounting concepts and techniques that we discuss in this and subsequent chapters, therefore, apply to nonmanufacturing as well as manufacturing entities.

TWO BASIC TYPES OF COST ACCOUNTING SYSTEMS

OBJECTIVE ❶ INTRODUCE *and* DISCUSS *the two basic types of cost accounting systems— job order costing systems and process costing systems—and* DISCUSS *the need for timely product costing.*

Two basic types of cost accounting systems are used by manufacturing firms: job order costing systems and process costing systems. Both systems are designed to develop timely information about product costs, manufacturing inventories, and cost per unit.

A **job order costing system** is used for production that is characterized by a series of different products or jobs undertaken either to fill specific orders from customers or to produce a general stock of products from which future customer orders are filled. In a job order costing system, the costs of direct material, direct labor, and factory overhead are accumulated separately for each job or product. Job order costing is used by construction companies (cost of each construction project), printing companies (cost of each printing job), manufacturers of consumer products (cost per unit of each product manufactured), and hospitals (cost per patient).

A **process costing system** lends itself to the production of a large volume of products manufactured in a continual flow operation, such as the distillation of fuels or manufacture of paint or wire. Essentially, the materials and operations are involved repetitively during each manufacturing period. Direct material, direct labor, and factory overhead are accumulated by production department or process. Assembly line operations of entities such as breweries or flour mills and mass production operations such as power plants and chemical companies would use process costing.

Both job order and process costing systems allocate manufacturing costs to determine unit costs. In a job order system, costs are identified with specific jobs or products, but a process costing system identifies costs with production processes and averages them over all products made during the period. The type of cost accounting system used by a particular company depends on the nature of the company's manufacturing operation. One company may, in fact, use job order costing to account for one part of its manufacturing operation and use process costing to account for another part of its manufacturing operation.

Timely Product Costing

A cost accounting system—either job order costing or process costing—must provide for the timely determination of product costs. Product costs are needed to arrive at inventory amounts for work in process inventory and finished goods inventory. These amounts are needed in the preparation of financial statements. To determine income properly, a method to identify costs with products sold and products that remain on hand, either finished or unfinished, must be established.

Management uses engineering studies and cost analyses to establish budgets. Actual product costs are compared to budgets so that problems can be identified and remedial action taken when necessary. Management also uses product costs as one of the components in setting product prices.

To identify costs with a product or group of products, a manufacturer must trace factory costs—direct material, direct labor, and factory overhead—to products. To account for material used, a company may keep track of the costs of material requisitioned for production by job, product, or department. Labor costs can similarly be accounted for by timekeeping methods or by identifying the product or job with the payroll costs of personnel in the factory production departments. A manufacturing firm cannot, however, directly determine the amount of factory overhead that should be identified with different products or group of products. Consequently, manufacturing firms typically assign factory overhead costs to products by using predetermined overhead rates.

PREDETERMINED FACTORY OVERHEAD RATES

OBJECTIVE ❷ DISCUSS *the need for a predetermined overhead rate,* DEMONSTRATE *its calculation, and* PRESENT *a comparison of annual and monthly rates.*

Predetermined factory overhead rates are so named because (1) they are predetermined (calculated prior to the beginning of each fiscal year), (2) they deal with factory overhead (all manufacturing costs other than direct material and direct labor), and (3) they are usually stated in terms of a rate (such as "$20 per direct labor hour"). Before the beginning of each year, management normally prepares budgets. Included in the total budget is a production budget, which estimates utilization of the factory's productive capacity in terms of a common measure of activity. Traditionally, the common measure of activity is direct labor hours, direct labor costs, or machine hours. Also included in the total budget is an estimate of factory overhead costs for the year.

The **predetermined overhead rate** is computed by dividing the estimated total factory overhead cost for the year by the estimated utilization of the factory productive capacity for the year. Calculations of predetermined rates are typically based on one-year production periods.

Assume that the most appropriate measure of activity for applying overhead in a given situation is direct labor hours. If the estimated number of direct labor hours for 1993 is 100,000 and the estimated total factory overhead cost for 1993 is $150,000, the overhead rate for 1993 may be calculated as follows:

$$\begin{aligned}
\text{1993 Predetermined Overhead Rate} &= \frac{\text{Estimated Factory Overhead for 1993}}{\text{Estimated Direct Labor Hours for 1993}} \\[2mm]
&= \frac{\$150,000}{100,000 \text{ hours}} \\[2mm]
&= \$1.50/\text{direct labor hour}
\end{aligned}$$

If, during March 1993, a particular product requires 50 direct labor hours of production time, $75 of factory overhead (50 × $1.50) is charged to this product.

Before selecting the basis for applying overhead to products, a firm should analyze carefully the relationship between overhead incurred and various alternative measures of activity. Direct labor hours or direct labor costs would be used as the measure of activity in a factory that has labor-intensive manufacturing. However, in a factory in which automation has replaced many of the production workers, machine hours may be a more appropriate measure.

Using a predetermined overhead rate, management can estimate the overhead costs of any job at any stage of production, computing "costs to date" both for control purposes and for inventory costing. This method also eliminates wide fluctuations in unit costs that might result if actual recorded overhead costs were assigned to products during short interim periods when production departed markedly from average levels.

Annual versus Monthly Rates

Assume, for example, that normal production is 100,000 direct labor hours per year and that production fluctuates seasonally throughout the year. Suppose also that a large share of actual factory overhead cost is spread fairly evenly over the year. (Such costs as depreciation, maintenance, utilities, and supervisory costs remain fairly constant from month to month.) Exhibit 22-1 illustrates the possible differences between assigned overhead costs based on actual monthly overhead rates and those based on an annual overhead rate. The predetermined annual rate in this example is $1.50 per direct labor hour ($150,000/100,000 direct labor hours). The actual monthly rates vary from $3.10 in February to $1.10 in July, with only the months of April, September, and October even approaching the annual average of $1.50 per direct labor hour. Using actual monthly rates and assuming that a particular unit of product requires 3 direct labor hours, a unit produced in July when production activity was highest would be assigned overhead costs of $3.30 (3 × $1.10). In contrast, a unit produced in February when production activity was lowest would be assigned overhead costs of $9.30 (3 × $3.10). The $6 difference is hardly defensible, especially when the two units of product may be virtually indistinguishable physically. Clearly, basing product costs on allocations of actual monthly overhead amounts is unrealistic. The use of a predetermined overhead rate employing a yearly average produces more meaningful unit cost figures.

JOB ORDER COSTING SYSTEMS

Job order costing systems are designed to accumulate product costs—direct material, direct labor, and factory overhead—by job and in total. Exhibits 22-2 through 22-6 are examples of the forms and records used in a manual job order costing system.

EXHIBIT 22–1	COMPARISON OF ACTUAL MONTHLY AND PREDETERMINED ANNUAL OVERHEAD RATES			
	Factory Overhead Costs Incurred Each Month*	Direct Labor Hours Worked Each Month	Actual Monthly Overhead Rates	Predetermined Annual Overhead Rate
January	$ 9,900	4,000	$2.48	$1.50
February	9,300	3,000	3.10	1.50
March	10,500	5,000	2.10	1.50
April	12,300	8,000	1.54	1.50
May	14,100	11,000	1.28	1.50
June	14,700	12,000	1.23	1.50
July	16,500	15,000	1.10	1.50
August	15,300	13,000	1.18	1.50
September	13,500	10,000	1.35	1.50
October	12,300	8,000	1.54	1.50
November	11,100	6,000	1.85	1.50
December	10,500	5,000	2.10	1.50
Annual Amounts	$150,000	100,000		

*Assumed to be $7,500 each month plus 60 cents per direct labor hour.

EXHIBIT 22—2   MATERIALS LEDGER CARD

Materials Ledger Card

Stock No. _32_
Description _1/8" Steel Wire_   Reorder Quantity _4,000 ft._
Supplier _Steel Supply Corp._   Minimum Quantity _1,000 ft._

Date	Received				Issued				Balance		
	Rec'g. Report No.	Units	Price	Total Price	Mat'l. Req'n. No.	Units	Price	Total Price	Units	Price	Total Price
1993											
8/1	320	4,000	0.20	800.00					4,000	0.20	800.00
8/5					567	700	0.20	140.00	3,300	0.20	660.00
8/9	332	4,000	0.21	840.00					3,300	0.20	660.00
									4,000	0.21	840.00

OBJECTIVE ③ DESCRIBE *a job order costing system and* PRESENT *examples of forms and records used in job order costing.*

Each of the three manufacturing inventory accounts—Materials Inventory, Work in Process Inventory, and Finished Goods Inventory—has a subsidiary ledger in which unit costs are accounted for. There is a **materials ledger card** (Exhibit 22-2) for each type of direct material or indirect material used. These cards make up the subsidiary ledger for the Materials Inventory account; the cards show quantities received, issued, and on hand, unit costs, and total amounts. **Materials requisition forms** (Exhibit

EXHIBIT 22—3   MATERIALS REQUISITION FORM

Materials Requisition

Date ___8/5/93___   Job. No. ___372___   Requisition No. ___567___

Item	Quantity		Unit Price	Amount
	Authorized	Issued		
Stock No. 32 (1/8" wire)	700 ft.	700 ft.	0.20	$140
Total				$140

Authorized by: ___G. E. K.___   Issued by: ___G. A. P.___   Received by: ___F. W. E.___

EXHIBIT 22—4 | **TIME TICKET**

Time Ticket

Employee Name Robert Smith   Employee No. 42
Skill Specification Machine Operator   Payroll Period Ending 8/16/93

Time Started	Time Stopped	Total Time	Hourly Labor Rate	Department	Job No.	Total Cost
8:00	12:00	4.0	$8.00	B	372	$32.00
1:00	2:00	1.0	8.00	B	372	8.00
Total		5.0				$40.00

Approved by: _R. L. T._

EXHIBIT 22—5 | **JOB COST SHEET**

Job Cost Sheet

Customer Gordon Sales Company   Job No. 372
Product Bracket-H3   Date Promised 9/1/93
Quantity 200   Dates: Started 8/1/93 Completed 8/20/93

Direct Material		Direct Labor			Cost Summary	
Mat'l. Req'n. No.	Amount	Payroll Summary Dated	Dept.	Amount		
567	140.00	8/2	A	70.00	**Direct Material**	700.00
573	180.00	8/9	A	240.00	**Direct Labor**	600.00
591	200.00	8/16	B	190.00	**Factory Overhead (applied at):**	
603	180.00	8/23	B	100.00	150% of direct labor cost	900.00
					Total Cost	2,200.00
Totals	700.00			600.00	**Units Finished** 200 **Unit Cost**	11.00

EXHIBIT 22—6	FINISHED GOODS LEDGER CARD

Finished Goods Ledger Card

Stock No. __H3__
Item __Bracket-H3__   Minimum Quantity __50__

Manufactured			Sales			Balance			
Job No.	Quantity	Total Cost	Invoice No.	Quantity	Total Cost	Date	Quantity	Unit Cost	Total Cost
372	200	2,200.00				8/20	200	11.00	2,200.00
			123	100	1,100.00	8/25	100	11.00	1,100.00

22-3) authorize the issuance of direct material for various jobs or of indirect material. **Time tickets** (Exhibit 22-4) document the amount of time spent on each job and the individual employee labor cost incurred as direct labor for individual jobs or as a part of factory overhead.

Job cost sheets (Exhibit 22-5) make up the subsidiary ledger for the Work in Process Inventory account. For each job in process, the sheet indicates the cost of direct material, direct labor, and applied overhead identified with the job. When a job is completed, the total cost is divided by the number of units in the lot to obtain a unit cost. The job's cost sheet is then removed from the work in process subsidiary ledger and an entry is made on a **finished goods ledger card** (Exhibit 22-6). These cards make up the subsidiary ledger for finished goods inventory. The cards in this last ledger identify the stock number and name of the product and show quantities, unit costs, and total costs of the various lots of product awaiting sale.

Another subsidiary ledger is maintained for factory overhead. Because factory overhead consists of many different costs, the Factory Overhead account in the general ledger is a control account. The *factory overhead ledger* is the subsidiary ledger containing the individual amounts for each component of factory overhead.

ILLUSTRATION OF JOB ORDER COSTING

We now turn to a comprehensive illustration of job order costing, which shows how to use these forms. In this illustration, we make the following three assumptions:

1. Bradley Company uses materials A and B to produce job 1 and job 2.
2. Bradley also uses material C, which is classified as indirect material.
3. Bradley uses a predetermined overhead rate based on annual direct labor hours to assign factory overhead to jobs.

Accounting for Materials

Assume that Bradley Company had no beginning inventory balances for Materials Inventory, Work in Process Inventory, and Finished Goods Inventory. Bradley buys the materials it needs to manufacture its product. Thus, the first transaction to record is the *purchase* of materials. Bradley Company purchased on account $2,500 of

OBJECTIVE ④ PRESENT *an illustration of job order costing that details the journal entries, general ledger postings, and subsidiary dual postings used and the flows of product costs.*

material A, $1,500 of material B, and $500 of material C. Following is the entry to record this purchase when the material is received.

1 Materials Inventory	4,500	
Accounts Payable		4,500

To record the purchase of materials—A, $2,500; B, $1,500; and C, $500.

GENERAL LEDGER POSTING   An accounting clerk would post this entry in the general ledger, debiting the Materials Inventory account $4,500 and crediting the Accounts Payable account $4,500.

SUBSIDIARY LEDGER POSTING   A materials clerk would post the detail of the materials purchases on the materials ledger cards (the materials inventory subsidiary ledger). He or she would post $2,500 in the Received column on the material A card, $1,500 in the Received column on the material B card, and $500 in the Received column on the material C card.

The next transaction is the *requisition* of the following materials from the materials inventory: $1,000 of material A, $500 of material B, and $200 of material C. This material is used as follows: $900 direct material (materials A and B) on job 1, $600 direct material (materials A and B) on job 2, and $200 indirect material (material C). The entry to record the requisitioning and use of this material is as follows:

2 Work in Process Inventory	1,500	
Factory Overhead	200	
Materials Inventory		1,700

To record the requisitioning of material—A, $1,000; B, $500; and C, $200—and the use of the material—Job 1, $900; Job 2, $600; and indirect material, $200.

GENERAL LEDGER POSTING   An accounting clerk would post this entry in the general ledger, debiting the Work in Process Inventory account $1,500, debiting the Factory Overhead account $200, and crediting the Materials Inventory account $1,700.

SUBSIDIARY LEDGER POSTING   A materials clerk would post the detail of the materials requisitions on the materials ledger cards. $1,000 would be posted in the Issued column of the card for material A, $500 would be posted in the Issued column of the card for material B, and $200 would be posted in the Issued column of the card for material C.

A cost accounting clerk would post the job cost sheets (the work in process inventory subsidiary ledger) and the factory overhead ledger. A $900 amount would be posted in the Direct Material column of the job cost sheet for job 1, a $600 amount would be posted in the Direct Material column of the job cost sheet for job 2, and $200 would be posted in the Debit column of the Indirect Material account in the factory overhead ledger.

The effect of the various postings of these transactions is shown in Exhibit 22-7. The general ledger is shown on the left side of the exhibit, and the subsidiary ledgers are shown on the right side. The postings of the materials transactions are highlighted in bold type.

Accounting for Labor

Manufacturing firms typically use **clock cards** to collect the total amount of time that each employee worked during a particular pay period. Clock cards collect only total time worked; time tickets collect hours worked on particular jobs. Clock cards are used to prepare the factory payroll. Assume that the total factory payroll for Bradley Company was $3,400. The journal entry to record the factory payroll is as follows:

3 Factory Payroll	3,400	
Factory Payroll Payable		3,400

To record the factory payroll.

An accounting clerk would post this entry in the general ledger.

| EXHIBIT 22—7 | ENTRIES FOR PURCHASE AND REQUISITION OF MATERIALS |

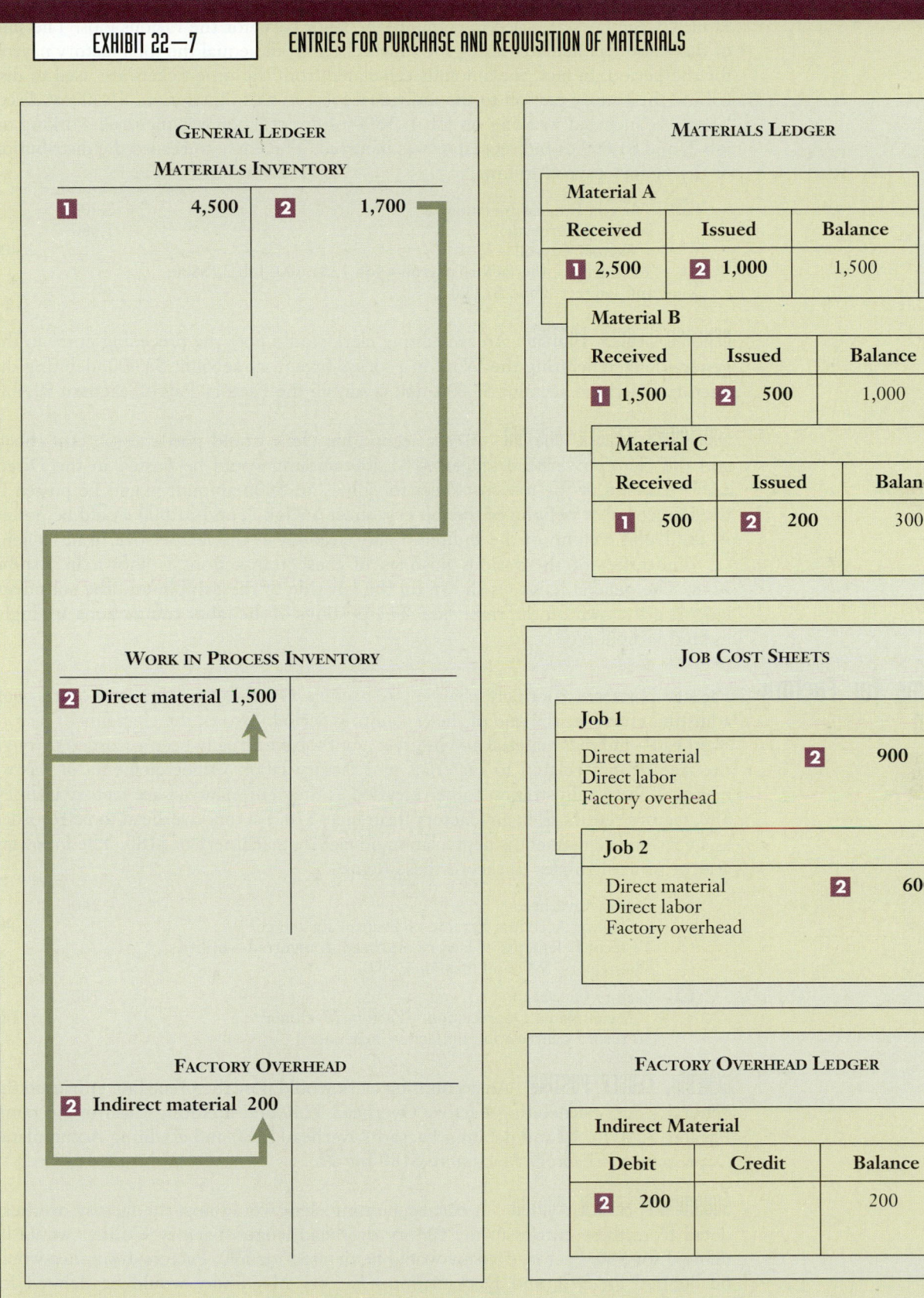

Manufacturing firms use time tickets to identify labor costs with specific jobs. Hourly wage rates are used to compute the labor costs for the various jobs. The sum of the amounts calculated using the time tickets should equal the total factory payroll for the period. In fact, the amounts calculated from the time tickets are used to distribute the factory payroll to the individual jobs. In this illustration, $1,600 of direct labor was incurred working on job 1, $800 of direct labor was incurred working on job 2, and $1,000 of indirect labor was incurred. The entry to record the distribution of the factory payroll follows:

4	Work in Process Inventory	2,400	
	Factory Overhead	1,000	
	Factory Payroll		3,400
	To distribute the factory payroll—Job 1, $1,600; Job 2, $800; and indirect labor, $1,000.		

GENERAL LEDGER POSTING An accounting clerk would post the preceding entry in the general ledger, debiting the Work in Process Inventory account $2,400, debiting the Factory Overhead account $1,000, and crediting the Factory Payroll account $3,400.

SUBSIDIARY LEDGER POSTING A cost accounting clerk would post the job cost sheets and the factory overhead ledger. A $1,600 amount would be posted in the Direct Labor column of the job cost sheet for job 1, an $800 amount would be posted in the Direct Labor column of the job cost sheet for job 2, and $1,000 would be posted in the Debit column of the Indirect Labor account in the factory overhead ledger.

The effect of the various postings of these transactions is shown in Exhibit 22-8. The general ledger is shown on the left side of the exhibit, and the subsidiary ledgers are shown on the right side. The postings of the labor transactions are highlighted in bold type.

Accounting for Factory Overhead

Factory costs are routinely charged to Factory Overhead as incurred or through adjusting entries at the end of the accounting period. Two of the elements of factory overhead—indirect material and indirect labor—have already been recorded through the transactions related to materials and factory labor. Other elements of factory overhead in this illustration to be recorded as they are incurred are factory utilities, $80; factory repairs, $90; and factory insurance, $70. Factory overhead to be recorded as a year-end adjustment is depreciation on factory machinery of $180. The following are the journal entries to record these items:

5	Factory Overhead	240	
	Cash or Accounts Payable or Prepaid Insurance		240
	To record elements of factory overhead as incurred—utilities, $80; repairs, $90; and insurance, $70.		
6	Factory Overhead	180	
	Accumulated Depreciation—Factory Machinery		180
	To record depreciation on factory machinery.		

GENERAL LEDGER POSTING An accounting clerk would post the preceding entries to the general ledger by debiting Factory Overhead $240 and crediting Cash or Accounts Payable $240 for **5** and debiting Factory Overhead $180 and crediting Accumulated Depreciation—Factory Machinery $180 for **6**.

SUBSIDIARY LEDGER POSTING A cost accounting clerk would post the factory overhead detail from these entries to the factory overhead ledger. Factory Utilities would be debited for $80, Factory Repairs would be debited for $90, Factory Insurance would be debited for $70, and Depreciation—Factory Machinery would be debited for $180.

As explained earlier, actual factory overhead costs are not assigned directly to individual jobs. Instead, through the use of a predetermined overhead rate, the Work

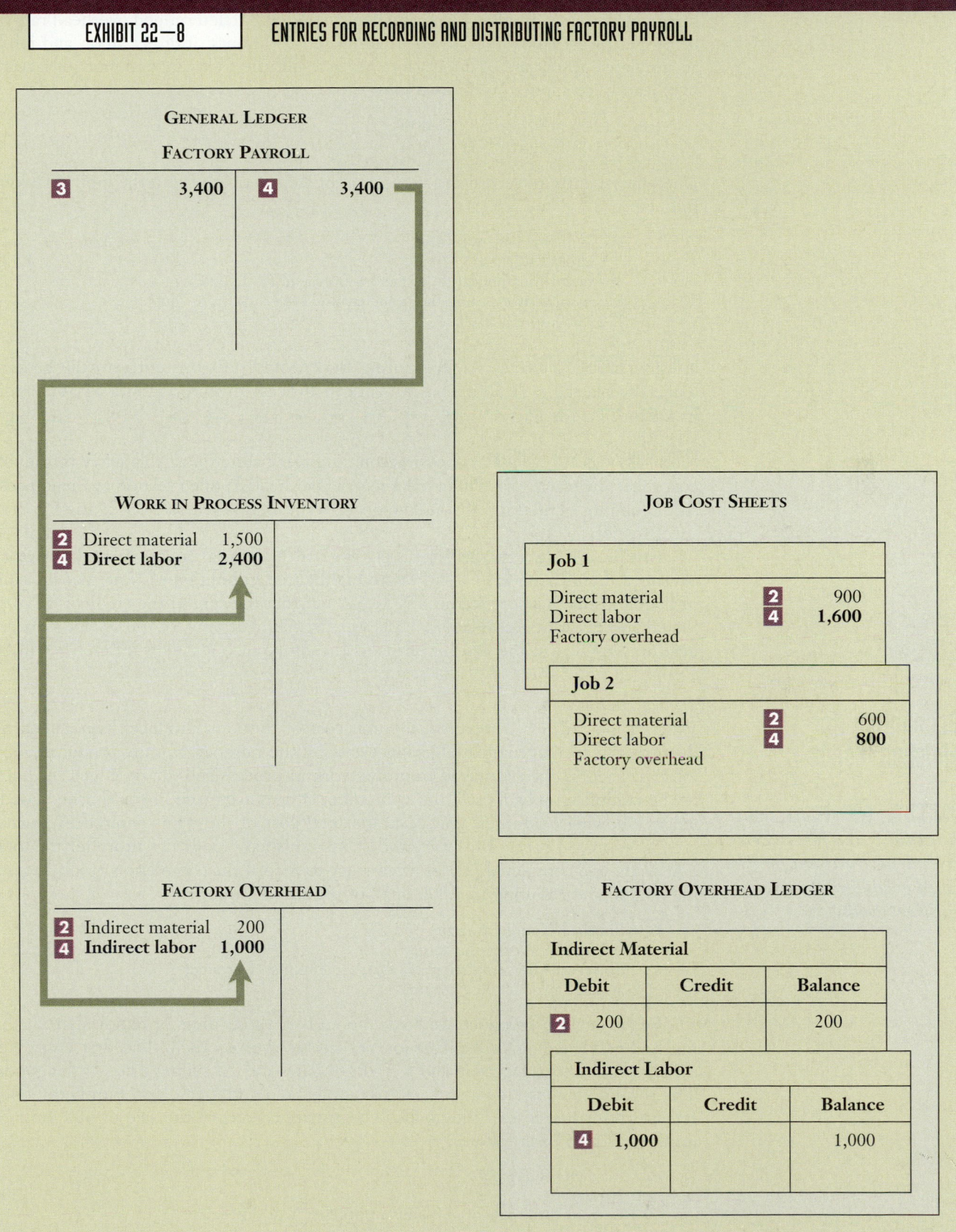

EXHIBIT 22—8   ENTRIES FOR RECORDING AND DISTRIBUTING FACTORY PAYROLL

in Process Inventory account is charged with factory overhead applied. During the budgeting process, Bradley Company determined its predetermined overhead rate to be $5 per direct labor hour. Job 1 accumulated 200 hours of direct labor, and job 2 accumulated 100 hours of direct labor. As a result, the following amounts of factory overhead were applied to the two jobs:

Job 1 (200 hours × $5) $1,000
Job 2 (100 hours × $5)   500

The journal entry to record the application of factory overhead to the individual jobs follows:

7 Work in Process Inventory 1,500
    Factory Overhead 1,500
    To record the application of factory overhead to the work in
    process inventory using the predetermined overhead rate—job
    1, $1,000; job 2, $500.

GENERAL LEDGER POSTING An accounting clerk would post this entry to the general ledger by placing a $1,500 debit in Work in Process Inventory and a $1,500 credit in Factory Overhead.

SUBSIDIARY LEDGER POSTING A cost accounting clerk would post this entry to the job cost sheets by placing $1,000 in the Factory Overhead Applied section of the job cost sheet for job 1 and $500 in the Factory Overhead Applied section of the job cost sheet for job 2.

Exhibit 22-9 reflects the various postings of the journal entries related to factory overhead. Items from **5**, **6**, and **7** are highlighted in bold type. Note that the sum of the debits in Factory Overhead is $1,620 but that the sum of the credits is $1,500. Stated another way, actual factory costs were $1,620, but only $1,500 of factory overhead was applied to the Work in Process Inventory account. This difference will be accounted for at the end of the year.

Accounting for Finished Goods

OBJECTIVE 5 DISCUSS *the procedures and journal entries used to account for finished goods and the sale of finished goods.*

When a job order is completed, the unit cost of the item produced is obtained by dividing the total accumulated product cost by the number of units produced. The job cost sheet is then removed from the work in process subsidiary ledger and filed in the completed jobs file. At the same time, entries are made in the finished goods ledger, showing quantities, unit cost, and total cost of the items entered. A journal credits Work in Process Inventory and debits Finished Goods Inventory for the total cost of the job completed. The journal entry to record the completion of job 1, costing $3,500 and resulting in 1,000 units of product Y, follows:

8 Finished Goods Inventory 3,500
    Work in Process Inventory 3,500
    To record the completion of job 1, 1,000 units of product Y,
    at $3.50 product cost per unit.

When units of product are sold, the cost of those units is removed from the finished goods ledger cards. Two journal entries are recorded. The first entry is a debit to Accounts Receivable and a credit to Sales for the selling price of the goods. The second entry is a debit to Cost of Goods Sold and a credit to Finished Goods Inventory for the cost of the goods. The entries to record the sale of 400 units of product Y at $6 each follow:

9 Accounts Receivable 2,400
    Sales 2,400
    To record the sale of 400 units of product Y at $6 each.

10 Cost of Goods Sold 1,400
    Finished Goods Inventory 1,400
    To record the cost of 400 units of product Y sold
    (400 × $3.50).

EXHIBIT 22—9	ENTRIES FOR RECORDING AND APPLYING FACTORY OVERHEAD

GENERAL LEDGER

WORK IN PROCESS INVENTORY

2	Direct material	1,500
4	Direct labor	2,400
7	**Factory overhead**	**1,500**

FACTORY OVERHEAD

2	Indirect material	200	**7**	Applied	1,500
4	Indirect labor	1,000			
5	**Various**	**240**			
6	**Depreciation**	**180**			

JOB COST SHEETS

Job 1

Direct material	**2**	900
Direct labor	**4**	1,600
Factory overhead	**7**	**1,000**

Job 2

Direct material	**2**	600
Direct labor	**4**	800
Factory overhead	**7**	**500**

FACTORY OVERHEAD LEDGER

Indirect Material

Debit	Credit	Balance
2 200		200

Indirect Labor

Debit	Credit	Balance
4 1,000		1,000

Factories Utilities

Debit	Credit	Balance
5 80		80

Factory Repairs

Debit	Credit	Balance
5 90		90

Factory Insurance

Debit	Credit	Balance
5 70		70

Depreciation—Factory Machinery

Debit	Credit	Balance
6 180		180

Disposition of Under- and Overapplied Overhead

It would be unusual in any month for the amount of applied overhead to equal the actual overhead cost. There are several reasons for this. First, estimates of the total annual overhead cost and the activity in direct labor hours were used to calculate the overhead rate. Second, production activity normally fluctuates from month to month. Third, the actual pattern of incurring overhead cost may also vary from month to month. Therefore, we can expect either debit or credit balances monthly in the Factory Overhead account. A debit balance in the account is called **underapplied** (or underabsorbed) **overhead**. A credit balance would be **overapplied** (or overabsorbed) **overhead.**

At year-end, a journal entry is made to dispose of the underapplied or overapplied amount of factory overhead. If the amount of underapplied or overapplied overhead is insignificant, an entry is made to transfer the amount to the Cost of Goods Sold account. An overapplied amount is transferred by debiting Factory Overhead and crediting Cost of Goods Sold. An underapplied amount is transferred by debiting Cost of Goods Sold and crediting Factory Overhead.

When the underapplied or overapplied amount is significant, it should be allocated to all of the jobs that were worked on during the year. This is accomplished by a journal entry that transfers the amount to Work in Process Inventory, Finished Goods Inventory, and Cost of Goods Sold. An overapplied amount is transferred by debiting Factory Overhead and crediting Work in Process Inventory, Finished Goods Inventory, and Cost of Goods Sold. An underapplied amount is transferred by debiting Work in Process Inventory, Finished Goods Inventory, and Cost of Goods Sold and crediting Factory Overhead. The amount transferred is distributed among Work in Process Inventory, Finished Goods Inventory, and Cost of Goods Sold based on the amount of applied overhead that is in each of the three accounts at the end of the year.

In our illustration, actual factory overhead totaled $1,620, whereas applied overhead totaled $1,500. Therefore, overhead was underapplied by $120. Assume that this amount is significant. At year-end, the amounts of applied overhead included in the balances of Work in Process Inventory, Finished Goods Inventory, and Cost of Goods Sold are as follows:

Work in Process Inventory

Total applied	$1,500	
Less: Amount applied to job 1, which was transferred to Finished Goods Inventory	1,000	
Applied overhead in year-end Work in Process Inventory		$ 500

Finished Goods Inventory

Amount applied to job 1, which was transferred from Work in Process Inventory (1,000 units)	$1,000	
Less: Applied overhead associated with 400 units transferred to Costs of Goods Sold	400	
Applied overhead in year-end Finished Goods Inventory		600

Cost of Goods Sold

Applied overhead associated with 400 units sold during the year		400
Total overhead applied		$1,500

The amount of underapplied overhead to be transferred to each of the three accounts is determined by using the ratio of applied overhead in the year-end balance to the total amount applied:

Work in Process Inventory
$120 \times (\$500/\$1,500) = \$ 40$
Finished Goods Inventory
$120 \times (\$600/\$1,500) = 48$
Cost of Goods Sold
$120 \times (\$400/\$1,500) = 32$
Total $120

The journal entry to record the transfer of the underapplied overhead follows:

11	Work in Process Inventory	40	
	Finished Goods Inventory	48	
	Cost of Goods Sold	32	
	Factory Overhead		120

To record the transfer of underapplied overhead to the jobs that were worked on during the year: $40 to job 2 (job cost sheets), $48 to unsold product Y (finished goods ledger), and $32 to product Y sold (Cost of Goods Sold account).

After this entry is posted to the general ledger, the balance in the Factory Overhead account will be zero. Balances of the accounts in the factory overhead ledger have served their purpose of providing detailed information on actual factory overhead for the year. At year-end, the individual accounts in the factory overhead ledger are double ruled to separate current year information from next year's data. The compilation of next year's data will start from zero in each of these accounts.

After entries **8** through **11** are posted, the relevant accounts and subsidiary ledgers would appear as in Exhibit 22-10. Note three points: (1) a parallel exists between the physical flow of goods and the related accounting entries, (2) the job cost sheets contain a detailed analysis of the balance showing in the Work in Process Inventory account in the general ledger, and (3) the sale of finished goods inventory involves entries of both the selling price and the cost amount.

When perpetual inventory procedures are used in cost accounting systems, the ending balances in the Materials Inventory, Work in Process Inventory, and Finished Goods Inventory accounts reflect all the transactions of the accounting period that increase and decrease inventories. These ending balances are adjusted only if a discrepancy is discovered when the year-end physical counts of inventory are taken.

TRADITIONAL OVERHEAD RATES AND ACTIVITY-BASED COSTING

Manufacturing companies that use traditional overhead rates typically use either a plantwide overhead rate or departmental overhead rates. A **plantwide overhead rate** is determined by dividing estimated total factory overhead for the year by estimated utilization of the total factory productive capacity for the year. The discussions and illustration in this chapter have incorporated a plantwide overhead rate. When a plantwide overhead rate is adopted, the cost accounting system uses a single predetermined rate for applying overhead to work done in all the producing departments, such as shearing, bending, drilling, welding, assembling, and painting.

Departmental Overhead Rates

OBJECTIVE 6 CONTRAST *plantwide overhead rates to departmental overhead rates and DISCUSS activity-based costing.*

Some manufacturing companies have adopted a cost accounting system that uses **departmental overhead rates.** When departmental overhead rates are used, a separate overhead rate is predetermined for each producing department in the factory by dividing the estimated overhead associated with each department by the estimated utilization of the capacity of that department.

A manufacturer would use departmental overhead rates for two primary reasons. First, the ratio of factory overhead cost to the capacity measure in one department may be significantly different than the ratio in another department. For instance, in department 1, the overhead rate might be $5 per direct labor hour, whereas the overhead rate in department 2 might be $9 per direct labor hour. Second, the capacity measure in one department may be different than the capacity measure in another department. For example, if department 1 is highly automated, then machine hours would be an appropriate measure of capacity for department 1. However, if department 2 is direct labor intensive, then direct labor hours would be an appropriate measure of capacity for department 2.

When departmental overhead rates are used, the manufacturer accumulates the appropriate measure of capacity for each department for each job so that the appropriate overhead rates can be applied. Assume that a particular manufacturer has three

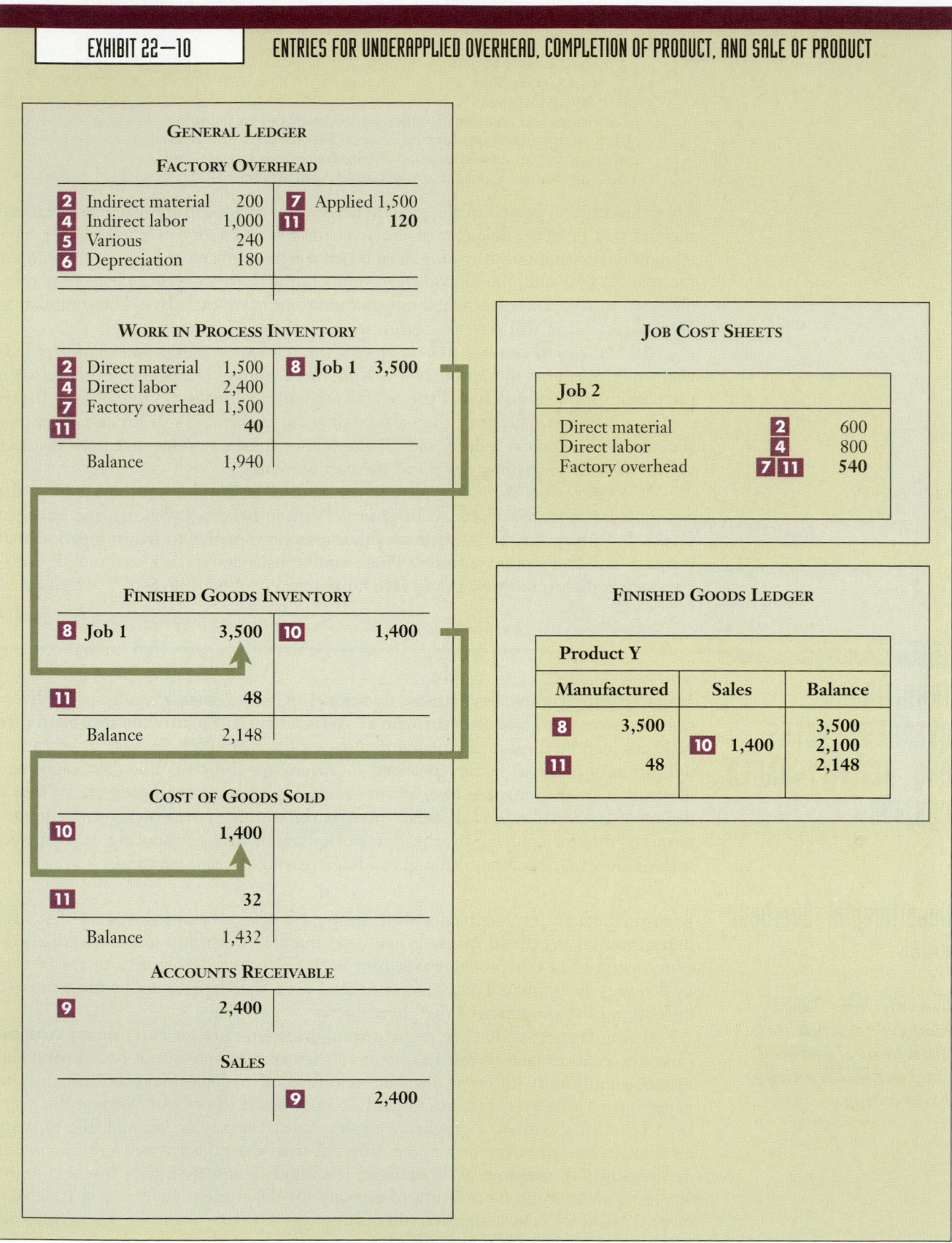

EXHIBIT 22—10 ENTRIES FOR UNDERAPPLIED OVERHEAD, COMPLETION OF PRODUCT, AND SALE OF PRODUCT

GENERAL LEDGER

FACTORY OVERHEAD

2 Indirect material	200	7 Applied 1,500
4 Indirect labor	1,000	11 120
5 Various	240	
6 Depreciation	180	

WORK IN PROCESS INVENTORY

2 Direct material	1,500	8 Job 1 3,500
4 Direct labor	2,400	
7 Factory overhead	1,500	
11	40	
Balance	1,940	

FINISHED GOODS INVENTORY

8 Job 1	3,500	10 1,400
11	48	
Balance	2,148	

COST OF GOODS SOLD

10	1,400	
11	32	
Balance	1,432	

ACCOUNTS RECEIVABLE

| 9 | 2,400 | |

SALES

| | | 9 2,400 |

JOB COST SHEETS

Job 2

Direct material	2	600
Direct labor	4	800
Factory overhead	7 11	540

FINISHED GOODS LEDGER

Product Y

Manufactured		Sales		Balance
8	3,500			3,500
		10	1,400	2,100
11	48			2,148

producing departments: machining, painting, and assembling. The capacity measure for machining and painting is machine hours, whereas the capacity measure for assembly is direct labor hours. For job 368, the factory accumulated 30 machine hours of machining, 20 machine hours of painting, and 40 direct labor hours of assembling. Machining has a predetermined overhead rate of $4 per machine hour, painting has a predetermined overhead rate of $3 per machine hour, and assembling has a predetermined overhead rate of $2 per direct labor hour. Factory overhead would be applied to job 368 as follows:

Machining (30 machine hours × $4)	$120
Painting (20 machine hours × $3)	60
Assembling (40 direct labor hours × $2)	80
Total factory overhead applied to job 368	$260

Departmental overhead rates usually provide a more equitable application of factory overhead to individual jobs than do plantwide rates. However, when there are significant variations in volume or complexity among the individual jobs, neither plantwide nor departmental overhead rates may provide an equitable application of factory overhead among the individual jobs. Instead, activity-based costing may then be appropriate.

Activity-based Costing

A number of manufacturing firms use activity-based costing rather than departmental overhead rates to apply factory overhead to individual jobs. Rather than viewing the factory as one operation (plantwide rate) or as a series of departments (departmental rates), **activity-based costing** views the factory as a group of activities. Factory overhead costs are associated with each activity and a predetermined overhead rate is established for each activity.

Activity-based costing arises from the principle that the products that a company manufactures do not generate costs; rather, the manufacturing activities that are performed in planning, procuring, and producing products generate costs. Product costs are calculated by determining how each product or job is supported by the manufacturing activities being performed. Activities create cost and products consume activities.

A manufacturing activity is often referred to as a **cost driver**—that is, the manufacturing activity causes factory costs to be incurred. As manufacturing companies have automated their production facilities, the number of cost drivers in the manufacturing operation has increased. For example, a welding robot would have a number of cost drivers associated with it, including programming, setup, and machine operation.

Listed below are examples of manufacturing activities that would be considered cost drivers. Listed next to each activity is the basis that might be used to apply its costs to jobs or products.

Manufacturing Activity	**Basis for Application**
Purchasing	Number of purchase orders
Quality control	Number of inspections
Material handling	Number of times moved
Machine setup	Number of setups
Production engineering	Number of change orders
Machine operation	Number of machine hours
Production scheduling	Number of production orders

It is important to note that an individual product or job may not use all activities (just as an individual product may not flow through all departments). As a result, activity-based costing applies very different amounts of factory overhead to the various jobs and products as they flow through the factory. Complex products or jobs that require a large number of activities accumulate a large amount of applied factory overhead.

TRADITIONAL VERSUS COST-DRIVER APPROACHES

The following illustrates the allocation of cleanup costs in a printing company under both the traditional and cost-driver approaches. These cleanup costs include labor, supervision, cleaning supplies, etc., of a large printing press designed for relatively long, high-volume production runs. The press has seven printing units, each used to print a particular color. (A job requiring four colors uses four printing units, while a job requiring two colors uses only two.)

TRADITIONAL APPROACH

Traditionally, the accumulation and allocation of these costs were based on machine hours. Assume the estimated total annual operating cost of the press is $4,550,000; this includes cleanup costs of $325,000. Estimated annual production run time of the press is 6,500 machine hours. We compute a cost application rate of $700 per machine hour ($4,550,000/6,500 = $700). Therefore, a seven-color printing job that runs for 10 hours is assigned a cost of $7,000 (10 × $700). Cleanup costs constitute $50 of the $700 application rate—$325,000/6,500 = $50.

This allocation method does not consider differences between jobs that actually affect cost. Thus, the cost assigned to cleanup for both a one-color and a seven-color job, each of which takes 10 printing hours, would be $500. Although it is suitable for external financial reporting purposes, the traditional approach falls short of providing accurate costs for individual products.

COST-DRIVER APPROACH

The cost-driver approach examines the printing operation to find what causes cleanup costs. In searching for the causes of the $325,000 budgeted cleanup cost, we note that only printing units actually used in the printing process require cleanup. It becomes apparent the use of additional colors causes additional cleanup costs and, therefore, the cause of cleanup costs—the cost driver—is the number of colors used. From this information, we develop an application rate for cleanup costs based on the number of colors to be used. Estimating 1,250 colors will be used annually, the rate is $260 per color ($325,000/1,250 = $260). Based on the cost-driver approach, the cleanup cost allocated to the seven-color order would be $1,820 (7 × $260) or $1,320 more than the cost assigned using the traditional method. In the traditional approach, a product requiring multiple colors and having the same printing run time will have the same overhead cost per job as one requiring only two colors. This results in cost from the more complex product being shifted to the simpler product and obscuring the true profitability of both.

SOURCE: Frank Collins and Michael L. Werner, "Improving Performance with Cost Drivers," *Journal of Accountancy*, June 1990, pp. 131–34. Reprinted by permission of the Journal of Accountancy, copyright © 1990 by American Institute of Certified Public Accountants, Inc. Opinions of the authors are their own and do not necessarily reflect the policies of the AICPA.

KEY POINTS FOR CHAPTER OBJECTIVES

❶ INTRODUCE and **DISCUSS** the two basic types of cost accounting systems—job order costing systems and process costing systems—and **DISCUSS** the need for timely product costing (pp. 826–827).

- A *job order costing system* is used when production is characterized by a series of different products or jobs undertaken either to fill specific orders from customers or to produce a general stock from which future orders will be filled.
- A *process costing system* lends itself to the production of a large volume of products manufactured in a continual flow operation.
- A cost accounting system must trace, on a timely basis, direct material, direct labor, and factory overhead to products or jobs.

❷ DISCUSS the need for a predetermined overhead rate, **DEMONSTRATE** its calculation, and **PRESENT** a comparison of annual and monthly rates (pp. 827–828).

- The *predetermined overhead rate* is calculated by dividing the estimated total factory overhead cost for the year by the estimated utilization of the factory productive capacity during the upcoming year.

- The overhead rate should be calculated on an annual basis. Monthly overhead rates fluctuate significantly from month to month.

3 DESCRIBE a job order costing system and PRESENT examples of forms and records used in job order costing (pp. 828–831).

- The control accounts and subsidiary ledgers used are Materials Inventory (subsidiary is materials ledger), Work in Process Inventory (subsidiary consists of job cost sheets), and Finished Goods Inventory (subsidiary is finished goods ledger).
- *Materials requisitions* authorize issuances from the materials inventory.
- *Time tickets* document the labor time by job.
- The *job cost sheet* summarizes the product costs—direct material, direct labor, and factory overhead applied—for one job; the predetermined overhead rate is used to apply factory overhead.

4 PRESENT an illustration of job order costing that details the journal entries, general ledger postings, and subsidiary dual postings used and the flows of product costs (pp. 831–836).

- When material is requisitioned from the materials inventory, Work in Process Inventory is debited for the cost of direct material and Factory Overhead is debited for the cost of indirect material.
- When the factory payroll is distributed, Work in Process Inventory is debited for the cost of direct labor and Factory Overhead is debited for the cost of indirect labor.
- Actual factory overhead costs are recorded by debiting Factory Overhead.
- Factory overhead is applied to jobs by debiting Work in Process Inventory and crediting Factory Overhead.

5 DISCUSS the procedures and journal entries used to account for finished goods and the sale of finished goods (pp. 836–839).

- The cost of finished goods is recorded by debiting Finished Goods Inventory and crediting Work in Process Inventory.
- The sale of finished goods is recorded by debiting Cost of Goods Sold and crediting Finished Goods Inventory for the cost of the goods sold *and* by debiting Accounts Receivable and crediting Sales for the selling price.

6 CONTRAST plantwide overhead rates to departmental overhead rates and DISCUSS activity-based costing (pp. 839–842).

- When departmental overhead rates are used, a separate rate is calculated for each producing department in the factory.
- When activity-based costing is used, an overhead rate is developed for each manufacturing activity related to planning, procuring, and producing products.
- A manufacturing activity is often referred to as a *cost driver*, since it causes factory overhead costs to be generated.

SELF-TEST QUESTIONS FOR REVIEW

(Answers follow the Solution to Demonstration Problem.)

1. Predetermined overhead rates should be
   a. Higher than actual overhead rates.
   b. Lower than actual overhead rates.
   c. Based on monthly budgets.
   d. Based on annual budgets.

2. Which account is debited to record the issuance of material to production for incorporation into the product?
   a. Direct Material.
   b. Materials Inventory.
   c. Work in Process Inventory.
   d. Factory Supplies.

3. Which of the following is usually not found on a job cost sheet?
   a. Factory overhead applied.
   b. Finished units currently on hand.
   c. Direct material.
   d. Unit cost.

4. When should the balance of the Factory Overhead account be zero?
   a. At the end of each month.
   b. After year-end closing.
   c. Never.
   d. Each time a job is completed.

5. Which of the following has job cost sheets as its subsidiary ledger?
   a. Work in Process Inventory.
   b. Cost of Goods Sold.
   c. Materials Inventory.
   d. Finished Goods Inventory.

DEMONSTRATION PROBLEM FOR REVIEW

The annual budget for Diamond Corporation for 1993 included the following costs and expenses:

Direct material	$ 30,000
Direct labor ($8 per hour)	120,000
Sales commissions	28,000
Factory supervision	16,000
Indirect labor	27,000
Factory depreciation	25,000
Factory taxes	7,000
Factory insurance	6,000
Factory utilities	9,000

REQUIRED

a. Compute the plantwide predetermined factory overhead rate for 1993 using direct labor hours as the activity measure.

b. Determine the amount of factory overhead that would be applied to jobs during March 1993 when 1,100 direct labor hours were actually incurred.

SOLUTION TO DEMONSTRATION PROBLEM

a. Budgeted factory overhead:

Factory supervision	$16,000
Indirect labor	27,000
Factory depreciation	25,000
Factory taxes	7,000
Factory insurance	6,000
Factory utilities	9,000
Budgeted factory overhead	$90,000

Budgeted direct labor hours:

$$\frac{\$120,000}{\$8/hour} = 15,000 \text{ budgeted direct labor hours}$$

Predetermined overhead rate:

$$\frac{\text{Budgeted Factory Overhead}}{\text{Budgeted Direct Labor Hours}} = \frac{\$90,000}{15,000} = \$6 \text{ per direct labor hour}$$

b. 1,100 hours × $6 = $6,600 applied factory overhead

ANSWERS TO SELF-TEST QUESTIONS

1. d, p. 827   **2.** c, p. 832   **3.** b, p. 830   **4.** b, p. 838   **5.** a, p. 831

GLOSSARY OF KEY TERMS USED IN THIS CHAPTER

activity-based costing   A technique for determining product cost in a manufacturing operation by which the factory is viewed as a group of activities. Factory overhead costs are associated with each activity and a predetermined overhead rate is established for each activity (p. 841).

clock card   A document used to collect total time worked by an employee (p. 832).

cost driver   A manufacturing activity that causes factory costs to be incurred (p. 841).

departmental overhead rates   The separate, predetermined overhead rates that are calculated for each producing department in a manufacturing operation (p. 839).

finished goods ledger card   A record of the amounts acquired, sold, and on hand, and the related costs of a specific finished product. In aggregate, finished goods ledger cards are the subsidiary ledger for the Finished Goods Inventory account maintained on a perpetual basis (p. 831).

job cost sheet   A record of the specific manufacturing costs applied to a given job. When fully recorded, job cost sheets are a subsidiary ledger to the Work in Process Inventory account (p. 831).

job order costing system A method of cost accounting by which manufacturing costs are assigned to specific jobs or batches of specialized products (p. 826).

materials ledger card A subsidiary record maintained for each type of material (direct or indirect) that shows quantity received, issued, and on hand; unit costs; and total amounts (p. 829).

materials requisition form A form used to authorize the issuance of direct material for various jobs or indirect material (p. 829).

overapplied overhead The excess of overhead applied to production over the amount of overhead incurred (p. 838).

plantwide overhead rate A single predetermined factory overhead rate, determined on an annual basis, that incorporates all of the manufacturing operations. The rate is calculated by dividing estimated total factory overhead for the year by estimated utilization of the total factory productive capacity for the year (p. 839).

predetermined overhead rate An estimated overhead rate determined in advance for a one-year period for applying factory overhead cost to production. The rate is calculated by dividing estimated factory overhead costs by estimated factory utilization of factory productive capacity for the year (p. 827).

process costing system A method of assigning costs to relatively homogeneous products in an often continual, high-volume manufacturing operation (p. 826).

time ticket A record for each employee used in job order costing to accumulate data on hours worked, jobs worked on, and the labor cost assigned to jobs (p. 831).

underapplied overhead The excess of actual overhead cost incurred over the amount applied to production (p. 838).

QUESTIONS

22-1 Briefly describe a cost accounting system.

22-2 What types of entities, other than manufacturers, use cost accounting systems?

22-3 Contrast a job order costing system and a process costing system.

22-4 Give three examples of types of companies that would use job order costing.

22-5 Why are predetermined factory overhead rates so named?

22-6 How is a predetermined factory overhead rate determined?

22-7 Briefly justify the use of an annual predetermined factory overhead rate as opposed to actual monthly factory overhead.

22-8 Wesley Manufacturing Company uses a predetermined plantwide factory overhead rate of $25 per direct labor hour. During April, job 541 had $3,000 of direct material assigned to it; 60 hours of direct labor at $10 per hour were incurred on it. What is the total product cost accumulated on job 541 during April?

22-9 Parker Manufacturing, Inc., employs an overhead rate of 140% of direct labor cost. The job 783 cost sheet shows that $5,000 in direct material has been used and that $8,000 in direct labor has been incurred. If 1,000 units of product have been produced on job 783, what is the unit cost of the product?

22-10 Briefly explain the sequential flow of product costs through a cost accounting system.

22-11 What type of records would be used or maintained for the following manufacturing activities?
a. Determining the amount of a specific material on hand.
b. Issuing direct material for production.
c. Assigning the direct labor costs for a particular worker.
d. Accumulating the cost of a particular product or batch of products.
e. Determining the amounts and cost of completed products on hand.

22-12 Explain the general format and give examples of the data that would appear on (a) a materials ledger card, (b) a job cost sheet, and (c) a finished goods ledger card.

22-13 Why can we say that the sale of a manufactured product is recorded at two different amounts?

22-14 Slaton Company records both actual overhead and applied overhead in one account, Factory Overhead. On January 31, the account has a credit balance. Has overhead been underapplied or overapplied during January?

22-15 Lyle Manufacturing Company applies factory overhead at the rate of 150% of direct labor cost. During October 1993, Lyle incurred $82,000 of direct labor costs and $120,000 of factory overhead costs. What is the amount of over- or underapplied factory overhead for October 1993?

22-16 Briefly describe activity-based costing.

EXERCISES

CALCULATE AND USE OVERHEAD RATE
— OBJ. 2 —

22-17 Selected data for the fabrication department of Austin Manufacturing, Inc., follow:

Estimated factory overhead cost for the year	$270,000
Estimated direct labor cost for the year (@ $9/hr.)	180,000
Actual factory overhead cost for January	16,000
Actual direct labor cost for January (1,200 hours)	11,000

Assuming that direct labor *cost* is the basis for applying factory overhead,
a. Calculate the predetermined overhead rate.
b. Prepare a journal entry that applies factory overhead for January.
c. By what amount is factory overhead over- or underapplied in January?

CALCULATE AND USE OVERHEAD RATE
— OBJ. 2 —

22-18 Using the data in Exercise 22-17, but assuming that the basis for applying factory overhead is direct labor *hours*, complete requirements (a) through (c).

CALCULATE AND USE OVERHEAD RATE
— OBJ. 2 —

22-19 During the coming accounting year, Baker Manufacturing, Inc., anticipates the following costs, expenses, and operating data:

Direct material (16,000 lb.)	$ 80,000
Direct labor (@ $10/hr.)	140,000
Indirect material	12,000
Indirect labor	22,000
Sales commissions	34,000
Factory administration	16,000
Nonfactory administrative expenses	20,000
Other factory overhead*	48,000

*Provides for operating 35,000 machine hours.

a. Calculate the predetermined overhead rate for the coming year for each of the following application bases: (1) direct labor hours, (2) direct labor costs, and (3) machine hours.
b. For each item in requirement a, determine the proper application of factory overhead to job 63, to which 16 direct labor hours, $150 of direct labor cost, and 40 machine hours have been charged.

APPLIED VS. ACTUAL OVERHEAD
— OBJ. 4 —

22-20 Davis Manufacturing Corporation applies factory overhead on the basis of 150% of direct labor cost. An analysis of the related accounts and job cost sheets indicates that during the year total factory overhead incurred was $315,000 and that at year-end Work in Process Inventory, Finished Goods Inventory, and Cost of Goods Sold included $40,000, $20,000, and $140,000, respectively, of direct labor incurred during the current year.
a. Determine the underapplied overhead at year-end (assume it is significant).
b. Prepare a journal entry to record the disposition of the underapplied overhead.

FLOW OF PRODUCT COSTS THROUGH ACCOUNTS
— OBJ. 4 —

22-21 Assuming a routine manufacturing activity, present journal entries (account titles only) for each of the following transactions:
a. Purchased material on account.
b. Recorded factory payroll earned but not paid.
c. Requisitioned both direct material and indirect material.
d. Assigned direct and indirect labor costs.
e. Recorded factory depreciation and accrued factory property tax.
f. Applied factory overhead to production.
g. Completed work on products.
h. Sold finished goods on account.

JOB COST RECORDS
— OBJ. 3 —

22-22 For each of the manufacturing transactions or activities indicated in Exercise 22-21, briefly identify the detailed forms, records, or documents (if any) that would probably underlie each journal entry.

**PERPETUAL INVENTORIES
— OBJ. 4, 5 —**

22-23 The following summary data are from the job cost sheets of Hampton Company:

	Dates			Total Costs Assigned at April 30	Total Production Costs Added in May
Job	Started	Finished	Shipped		
1	4/10	4/20	5/9	$7,300	
2	4/18	4/30	5/20	5,400	
3	4/24	5/10	5/25	2,900	$5,700
4	4/28	5/20	6/3	3,600	4,800
5	5/15	6/10	6/20		2,600
6	5/22	6/18	6/28		3,800

Using the above data, compute (a) the finished goods inventory at May 1 and May 31, (b) the work in process inventory at May 1 and May 31, and (c) the cost of goods sold for May. Hampton began operations with job 1.

**FINISHED GOODS AND COST
OF GOODS SOLD
— OBJ. 5 —**

22-24 Before the completed production for June is recorded, the Work in Process Inventory account for James Company appears as follows:

WORK IN PROCESS INVENTORY

Balance, June 1	16,000
Direct material	45,000
Direct labor	32,000
Factory overhead applied	34,000

Assume that completed production for June includes jobs 107, 108, and 109 with total costs of $28,000, $59,000, and $25,000, respectively.

a. Determine the cost of unfinished jobs at June 30 and prepare a journal entry to record completed production.

b. Using general journal entries, record the sale of job 107 for $40,000 on account.

**JOB COST SHEET
— OBJ. 4 —**

22-25 Riverwood Manufacturing Company has the following account in its cost records:

WORK IN PROCESS INVENTORY

Direct material	50,000	To finished goods	84,000
Direct labor	20,000		
Factory overhead	28,000		

Riverwood applies overhead to production at a predetermined rate based on direct labor costs. Assume that Riverwood uses a job order costing system and that job 110, the only job in process at the end of the period, has been charged with direct material of $6,800. Complete the following cost sheet for job 110.

Cost Sheet—Job 110 (in process)

Direct material	_____
Direct labor	_____
Factory overhead	_____
Total cost	_____

**ACTIVITY-BASED COSTING
— OBJ. 6 —**

22-26 Pioneer Manufacturing Company uses activity-based costing to determine product cost. An analysis of its factory has identified 28 unique manufacturing activities, which have been numbered 1 through 28. Robots are used to manufacture product A; no direct labor is required. A batch of 100 units of product A uses $1,400 of direct material, 60 units of activity 3, 5 units of activity 15, 10 units of activity 21, and 100 units of activity 27. The cost accounting system has predetermined overhead costs per activity, including the following:

Activity	Cost per Unit of the Activity
3	$ 2
15	50
21	13
27	4

What is the unit product cost for product A?

PROBLEMS

Note: In all problems and alternate problems, assume perpetual inventory procedures, a single Factory Overhead account, first-in, first-out costing of inventories, and that the Materials Inventory account is the control account for both direct material and indirect material.

DETERMINE AND USE OVERHEAD RATE
— OBJ. 2, 4 —

22-27 Cortez Manufacturing, Inc., expects the following costs and expenses during the coming year:

Direct material	$ 85,000
Direct labor (@ $9/hr.)	162,000
Sales commissions	37,000
Indirect material	14,000
Indirect labor	41,600
Factory depreciation	43,000
Factory taxes	10,200
Factory insurance	9,400
Factory supplies used	8,600
Factory utilities	17,200

REQUIRED

a. Compute a predetermined factory overhead rate applied on the basis of direct labor hours.
b. Prepare a general journal entry to apply factory overhead during an interim period when 1,500 direct labor hours were worked.
c. What amount of overhead would be assigned to job 466, to which $180 in direct labor had been charged?

DETERMINE AND USE OVERHEAD RATE
— OBJ. 2, 4 —

22-28 The following selected ledger accounts of Cameron Company are for February (the second month of its accounting year):

MATERIALS INVENTORY

Feb. 1 balance	31,500	February credits	113,000
February debits	104,000		

FACTORY OVERHEAD

February debits	137,200	Feb. 1 balance	11,600
		February credits	136,350

WORK IN PROCESS INVENTORY

Feb. 1 balance	22,400	February credits	345,000
February debits:			
Direct material	95,000		
Direct labor	151,500		
Factory overhead	136,350		

FACTORY PAYROLL PAYABLE

February debits	193,500	Feb. 1 balance	45,000
		February credits	177,000

FINISHED GOODS INVENTORY

Feb. 1 balance	76,500	February credits	383,700
February debits	345,000		

REQUIRED

a. Determine the amount of indirect material requisitioned for production during February.
b. How much indirect labor cost was apparently incurred during February?
c. Calculate the factory overhead rate based on direct labor cost.
d. Was factory overhead for February under- or overapplied, and by what amount?

e. Was factory overhead for the first two months of the year under- or overapplied, and by what amount?

f. What is the cost of production completed in February?

g. What is the cost of goods sold in February?

JOB COST JOURNAL ENTRIES — OBJ. 4 —

22-29 Holiday Manufacturing had the following inventories at December 31, 1992, the end of its fiscal year:

Materials inventory	19,000
Work in process inventory	20,000
Finished goods inventory	13,000

During January 1993, the following transactions occurred:

1. Purchased materials on account, $126,000.
2. Incurred factory payroll, $61,000.
3. Requisitioned direct material of $110,000 and indirect material of $20,000.
4. Assigned total factory payroll, of which $11,000 was considered indirect labor.
5. Incurred other factory overhead, $32,800. (Credit Accounts Payable.)
6. Applied factory overhead on the basis of 110% of direct labor costs.
7. Determined completed production, $206,000.
8. Determined cost of goods sold, $203,000.

REQUIRED

a. Prepare general journal entries to record these transactions.

b. If the above transactions covered a full year's operations, prepare a journal entry to dispose of the overhead account balance. Assume that the balance is significant. Also assume that the following accounts contained the indicated amounts of factory overhead applied during 1993:

Work in process inventory	$ 6,000
Finished goods inventory	4,000
Cost of goods sold	45,000

JOB COST JOURNAL ENTRIES — OBJ. 4, 5 —

22-30 Prior to the beginning of 1993, Lowe Company estimated that it would incur $176,000 of factory overhead cost during 1993, using 16,000 direct labor hours to produce the desired volume of goods. On January 1, 1993, beginning balances of Materials Inventory, Work in Process Inventory, and Finished Goods Inventory were $28,000, $–0–, and $43,000, respectively.

REQUIRED

Prepare general journal entries to record the following for 1993:

a. Purchased materials on account, $39,000.

b. Of the total dollar value of materials used, $31,000 represented direct material and $11,000 indirect material.

c. Determined total factory labor, $135,000 (15,000 hrs. at $9/hr.).

d. Of the factory labor, 80% was direct and 20% indirect.

e. Applied factory overhead based on direct labor hours to work in process.

f. Determined actual factory overhead other than those items already recorded, $92,000. (Credit Accounts Payable.)

g. Ending inventories of work in process and finished goods were $32,000 and $57,000, respectively. (Make separate entries.)

h. Transferred the balance in Factory Overhead to Cost of Goods Sold.

JOB COST JOURNAL ENTRIES AND T ACCOUNTS — OBJ. 4, 5 —

22-31 Following are certain operating data for Durango Manufacturing Company for January 1993:

	Materials Inventory	Work in Process Inventory	Finished Goods Inventory
Beginning inventory	$57,000	$24,000	$75,000
Ending inventory	33,000	40,500	48,000

Total sales were $1,800,000, on which the company earned a 40% gross profit. Durango uses a predetermined factory overhead rate of 120% of direct labor costs. Factory overhead applied was $360,000. Exclusive of indirect material used, total factory overhead incurred was $243,000; it was overapplied by $22,500.

REQUIRED

Compute the following items. (Set up T accounts for Materials Inventory, Work in Process Inventory, Finished Goods Inventory, and Factory Overhead; fill in the known amounts; and then use the normal relationships among the various accounts to compute the unknown amounts.)

a. Cost of goods sold.
b. Cost of goods manufactured.
c. Direct labor incurred.

d. Direct material used.
e. Indirect material used.
f. Total materials purchased.

JOB COST JOURNAL ENTRIES AND T ACCOUNTS — OBJ. 4, 5 —

22-32 Summarized data for the first month's operations of Dobson Welding Foundry during 1993 are presented below. A job order costing system is used.

1. Materials purchased on account, $58,000.
2. Amounts of materials requisitioned and foundry labor used:

Job	Materials	Foundry Labor
1	$ 4,400	$2,600
2	7,000	5,000
3	3,200	2,400
4	12,000	4,600
5	4,800	2,800
6	1,400	1,200
Indirect material	6,200	
Indirect labor		3,400

3. Foundry overhead is applied at the rate of 200% of direct labor costs.
4. Miscellaneous foundry overhead incurred:

Prepaid foundry insurance written off	$1,480
Property taxes on foundry building accrued	2,360
Foundry utilities payable accrued	5,280
Depreciation on foundry equipment	7,440
Other costs incurred on account	10,320

5. Ending work in process consisted of jobs 4 and 6.
6. Jobs 1 and 3 and one-half of job 2 were sold on account for $20,000, $17,400, and $14,400, respectively.

REQUIRED

a. Open general ledger T accounts for Materials Inventory, Foundry Payroll, Foundry Overhead, Work in Process Inventory, Finished Goods Inventory, and Cost of Goods Sold. Also set up subsidiary T accounts as job cost sheets for each job.
b. Prepare general journal entries to record the summarized transactions for the month, and post appropriate entries to any accounts listed in requirement (a). Key each entry parenthetically to the related number in the problem data.
c. Determine the balances of any accounts necessary and prepare schedules of jobs in ending work in process and jobs in ending finished goods to confirm that they agree with the related control accounts.

COMPLEX JOB COST JOURNAL ENTRIES AND ANALYSIS — OBJ. 4, 5 —

22-33 During June 1993, its first month of operations, Weston Manufacturing Company completed the transactions listed below. Weston uses a job order costing system. Materials requisitions and the factory payroll summary are analyzed on the 15th and the last day of each month, and charges for direct material and direct labor are entered directly on specific job cost sheets. Factory overhead at the rate of 140% of direct labor costs is recorded on individual job cost sheets when a job is completed and at month-end for any job then in process. At month-end, entries to the general ledger accounts summarize materials requisitions, distribution of factory payroll costs, and the application of factory overhead for the month. All other entries to general ledger accounts are made as they occur.

1. Purchased materials on account, $130,000.
2. Paid miscellaneous factory overhead costs, $32,600.
3. Paid the semimonthly factory payroll, $99,000.
4. An analysis of materials requisitions and the factory payroll summary for June 1–15 indicates the following cost distribution:

Job	Materials	Factory Labor
1	$21,600	$36,800
2	10,400	16,000
3	4,400	10,800
Indirect material	7,600	
Indirect labor		35,400
	$44,000	$99,000

5. Jobs 1 and 2 were completed on June 15 and transferred to finished goods inventory on the next day. (Enter the appropriate factory overhead amounts on the job cost sheets, mark them completed, and make a general journal entry transferring the appropriate amount of cost to the Finished Goods Inventory account.)
6. Paid miscellaneous factory overhead costs, $23,400.
7. Sold job 1 on account, $185,600 (recognized its cost of sales in the general journal).
8. Paid the semimonthly factory payroll, $96,200.
9. An analysis of materials requisitions and factory payroll summary for June 16–30 indicates the following cost distribution:

Job	Materials	Factory Labor
3	$22,800	$16,800
4	18,000	32,400
5	7,800	13,000
6	3,000	4,600
Indirect material	6,800	
Indirect labor		29,400
	$58,400	$96,200

10. Jobs 3 and 4 were completed on June 30 and transferred to finished goods inventory on the same day. (See transaction 5.)
11. Sold job 3 on account, $155,600 (recognized its cost of sales in the general journal).
12. Recorded the following additional factory overhead:

Depreciation on factory building	$26,000
Depreciation on factory equipment	15,200
Expiration of prepaid factory insurance	4,200
Accrual of factory property taxes payable	7,000
	$52,400

13. Recorded monthly general journal entry for the costs of all materials used.
14. Recorded monthly general journal entry for the distribution of factory payroll costs.
15. Recorded factory overhead on the job cost sheets for jobs in ending work in process and in the general journal for all factory overhead applied during the month.

REQUIRED

a. Set up the following general ledger T accounts: Materials Inventory, Factory Payroll, Factory Overhead, Work in Process Inventory, Finished Goods Inventory, Cost of Goods Sold, and Sales.
b. Set up subsidiary ledger T accounts for each of jobs 1–6 as job cost sheets.
c. Noting the accounting procedures described in the first paragraph of the problem, do the following:
 1. Record general journal entries for all transactions. Note that general journal entries are *not* required in transactions 4 and 9. Post only those portions of these entries affecting the general ledger accounts set up in requirement (a).
 2. Enter the applicable amounts directly on the appropriate job cost sheets for transactions 4, 5, 9, 10, and 15. Note parenthetically the nature of each amount entered.
d. Present a brief analysis showing that the general ledger accounts for Work in

Process Inventory and for Finished Goods Inventory agree with the related job cost sheets.

e. Explain in one sentence each what the balance of each general ledger account established in requirement (a) represents.

PLANTWIDE, DEPARTMENTAL, AND ACTIVITY-BASED COSTING — OBJ. 6 —

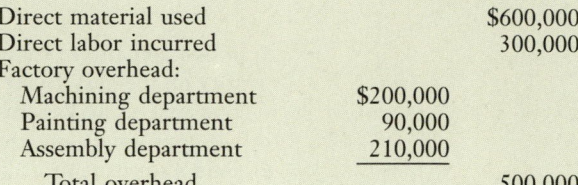

22-34 Thunderbird Manufacturing, Inc., produces five products that require very similar assembly processes. The budget for 1993 for Thunderbird Manufacturing includes the following items:

Direct material used		$600,000
Direct labor incurred		300,000
Factory overhead:		
Machining department	$200,000	
Painting department	90,000	
Assembly department	210,000	
Total overhead		500,000

The best measure of capacity utilization in the machining department is considered to be machine hours, whereas the best measure of capacity utilization in the painting department and the assembly department as well as the factory as a whole is considered to be direct labor hours. Budgeted hours for 1993 follow:

	Direct Labor Hours	Machine Hours
Machining	4,000	10,000
Painting	6,000	3,000
Assembly	15,000	0
Total	25,000	13,000

The engineering and accounting departments of Thunderbird Manufacturing conducted a study of the factory that categorized all of the planned factory operations for 1993 and the related overhead costs into the following activities (budgeted amounts are for 1993):

Activity	Budgeted Overhead	Budgeted Activity for 1993	
Purchasing	$ 50,000	2,000	purchase orders
Metal shearing	75,000	30,000	shearings
Metal bending	40,000	10,000	bends
Welding	60,000	20,000	welds
Painting	80,000	100,000	sq. ft. painted
Assembly	160,000	2,000	units
Packaging	35,000	2,000	units
Total	$500,000		

REQUIRED

a. Calculate a predetermined plantwide overhead rate for 1993.
b. Calculate predetermined departmental overhead rates for 1993.
c. Calculate predetermined overhead rates for 1993 for each factory activity.
d. Job 352 was started and finished during 1993. The following were accumulated for job 352:

Direct material used		$15,000
Direct labor incurred:		

	Hours	Dollars
Machining	100	$1,250
Painting	150	1,900
Assembly	300	3,800
Total	550	$6,950

Machine hours used: machining, 200; painting, 55

Factory activities utilized were as follows:

Purchasing	45 purchase orders
Metal shearing	620 shearings

Metal bending	260 bends
Welding	50 welds
Painting	2,400 sq. ft. painted
Assembly	50 units
Packaging	50 units

Calculate the product cost of job 352 under three different assumptions:
1. The use of a plantwide overhead rate.
2. The use of departmental overhead rates.
3. The use of activity-based costing.

ALTERNATE EXERCISES

CALCULATE AND USE OVERHEAD RATE — OBJ. 2 —

22-17A   Selected data for the welding department of Kingman Manufacturing, Inc., follow:

Estimated factory overhead cost for the year	$405,000
Estimated direct labor cost for the year (@ $9/hr.)	324,000
Actual factory overhead cost for May	26,000
Actual direct labor cost for May (2,400 hrs.)	22,000

Assuming that direct labor cost is the basis for applying factory overhead,
a. Calculate the predetermined overhead rate.
b. Prepare a journal entry that applies factory overhead for May.
c. By what amount is factory overhead over- or underapplied in May?

CALCULATE AND USE OVERHEAD RATE — OBJ. 2 —

22-18A   Using the data in Exercise 22-17A, but assuming that the basis for applying factory overhead is direct labor *hours*, complete requirements (a) through (c).

CALCULATE AND USE OVERHEAD RATE — OBJ. 2 —

22-19A   During the coming accounting year, Ester Manufacturing, Inc., anticipates the following costs, expenses, and operating data:

Direct material (15,000 lb.)	$45,000
Direct labor (@ $12/hr.)	96,000
Indirect material	7,000
Indirect labor	12,000
Sales commissions	18,000
Factory administration	13,000
Nonfactory administrative expenses	14,000
Other factory overhead*	28,000

*Provides for operating 30,000 machine hours.

a. Calculate the predetermined overhead rate for the coming year for each of the following application bases: (1) direct labor hours, (2) direct labor costs, and (3) machine hours.
b. For each item in requirement (a), determine the proper application of factory overhead to job 128, to which 9 direct labor hours, $100 of direct labor cost, and 32 machine hours have been charged.

APPLIED VS. ACTUAL OVERHEAD — OBJ. 4 —

22-20A   Sloan Manufacturing Corporation applies factory overhead on the basis of 120% of direct labor cost. An analysis of the related accounts and job cost sheets indicates that during the year total factory overhead incurred was $210,000 and that at year-end Work in Process Inventory, Finished Goods Inventory, and Cost of Goods Sold included $30,000, $20,000, and $150,000, respectively, of direct labor incurred during the current year.
a. Determine the overapplied overhead at year-end (assume it is significant).
b. Prepare a journal entry to record the disposition of the overapplied overhead.

FLOW OF PRODUCT COSTS THROUGH ACCOUNTS — OBJ. 4 —

22-21A   The following T accounts present a cost flow in which all or part of typical manufacturing transactions are indicated by parenthetical letters on the debit or credit side of each account.

MATERIALS INVENTORY		FACTORY PAYROLL		FACTORY OVERHEAD	
(a)	(c)	(b)	(d)	(c)	(f)
				(d)	
				(e)	

WORK IN PROCESS INVENTORY		FINISHED GOODS INVENTORY		COST OF GOODS SOLD
(c) (d) (f)	(g)	(g)	(h)	(h)

For each parenthetical letter, present a general journal entry with explanation indicating the apparent transaction or procedure that has occurred (disregard amounts).

JOB COST RECORDS — OBJ. 3 —

22-22A For each of the manufacturing transactions or activities indicated by the parenthetical letters in Exercise 22-21A, briefly identify the detailed forms, records, or documents (if any) that would probably underlie each journal entry.

PERPETUAL INVENTORIES — OBJ. 4, 5 —

22-23A The following summary data are from the job cost sheets of Castle Company:

	Dates			Total Costs Assigned at September 30	Total Production Costs Added in October
Job	Started	Finished	Shipped		
1	9/11	9/19	10/10	$9,000	
2	9/17	9/29	10/22	6,600	
3	9/25	10/11	10/27	3,500	$7,100
4	9/27	10/19	11/4	4,400	5,700
5	10/14	11/10	11/18		3,200
6	10/23	11/17	11/29		4,900

Using the above data, compute (a) the finished goods inventory at October 1 and October 31, (b) the work in process inventory at October 1 and October 31, and (c) the cost of goods sold for October. Castle began operations with job 1.

FINISHED GOODS AND COST OF GOODS SOLD — OBJ. 5 —

22-24A Before the completed production for August is recorded, the Work in Process Inventory account for Bayfield Company appears as follows:

WORK IN PROCESS INVENTORY

Balance, August 1	13,000
Direct material	39,000
Direct labor	16,000
Factory overhead	20,000

Assume that completed production for August includes jobs 317, 318, and 319 with total costs of $31,000, $18,000, and $22,000, respectively.

a. Determine the cost of unfinished jobs at August 31 and prepare a journal entry to record completed production.

b. Using general journal entries, record the sale of job 317 for $45,000 on account.

JOB COST SHEET — OBJ. 4 —

22-25A Everglade Manufacturing Company has the following account in its cost records:

WORK IN PROCESS INVENTORY

Direct material	60,000	To finished goods	147,600
Direct labor	48,000		
Factory overhead	57,600		

Everglade applies overhead to production at a predetermined rate based on direct labor costs. Assume that Everglade uses a job order costing system and that job 505, the only job in process at the end of the period, has been charged with direct material of $4,800. Complete the following cost sheet for job 505.

Cost Sheet—Job 505 (in process)

Direct material	_____
Direct labor	_____
Factory overhead	_____
Total cost	_____

ACTIVITY-BASED COSTING
— OBJ. 6 —

22-26A Cascade Manufacturing Company uses activity-based costing to determine product cost. An analysis of its factory has identified 31 unique manufacturing activities, which have been numbered 1 through 31. Robots are used to manufacture product X; no direct labor is required. A batch of 200 units of product X uses $2,260 of direct material, 20 units of activity 5, 50 units of activity 12, 4 units of activity 18, and 200 units of activity 25. The cost accounting system has predetermined overhead costs per activity, including the following:

Activity	Cost per Unit of the Activity
5	$ 12
12	10
18	200
25	5

What is the unit product cost for product X?

ALTERNATE PROBLEMS

DETERMINE AND USE
OVERHEAD RATE
— OBJ. 2, 4 —

22-27A Oxford Manufacturing, Inc., expects the following costs and expenses during the coming year:

Direct material	$355,000
Direct labor (@ $8/hr.)	336,000
Sales commissions	72,000
Factory supervision	74,400
Indirect labor	138,000
Factory depreciation	85,600
Indirect material	31,000
Factory taxes	19,500
Factory insurance	16,200
Factory utilities	13,300

REQUIRED

a. Compute a predetermined factory overhead rate applied on the basis of direct labor hours.
b. Prepare a general journal entry to apply factory overhead during an interim period when 3,500 direct labor hours were worked.
c. What amount of overhead would be assigned to job 325, to which $304 in direct labor had been charged?

DETERMINE AND USE
OVERHEAD RATE
— OBJ. 2, 4 —

22-28A The following selected ledger accounts of the Lakewood Manufacturing Company are for May (the fifth month of its accounting year):

MATERIALS INVENTORY

May 1 balance	40,000	May credits	150,000
May debits	125,000		

FACTORY OVERHEAD

May debits	160,000	May 1 balance	14,000
		May credits	144,000

WORK IN PROCESS INVENTORY

May 1 balance	28,000	May credits	440,000
May debits:			
Direct material	129,000		
Direct labor	180,000		
Factory overhead	144,000		

FACTORY PAYROLL PAYABLE

May debits	228,000	May 1 balance	50,000
		May credits	196,000

FINISHED GOODS INVENTORY

May 1 balance	102,000	May credits	510,000
May debits	440,000		

REQUIRED

a. Determine the amount of indirect material requisitioned for production during May.
b. How much indirect labor cost was apparently incurred during May?
c. Calculate the factory overhead rate based on direct labor cost.
d. Was factory overhead for May under- or overapplied, and by what amount?
e. Was factory overhead for the first five months of the year under- or overapplied, and by what amount?
f. What is the cost of production completed in May?
g. What is the cost of goods sold in May?

JOB COST JOURNAL
ENTRIES
— OBJ. 4 —

22-29A Dillon Manufacturing had the following inventories at December 31, 1992, the end of its fiscal year:

Materials inventory	$15,000
Work in process inventory	17,000
Finished goods inventory	30,000

During January 1993, the following transactions occurred:
1. Purchased materials on account, $125,000.
2. Incurred factory payroll, $105,000.
3. Requisitioned total materials of $130,000, of which $8,000 was considered indirect material.
4. Assigned total factory payroll, of which $15,000 was considered indirect labor.
5. Incurred other factory overhead, $57,000. (Credit Accounts Payable.)
6. Applied factory overhead on the basis of 80% of direct labor costs.
7. Determined ending work in process, $14,000.
8. Determined ending finished goods, $26,000.

REQUIRED

a. Prepare general journal entries to record these transactions.
b. If the above transactions covered a full year's operations, prepare a journal entry to dispose of the overhead account balance. Assume that the balance is significant. Also assume that the following accounts contained the indicated amounts of factory overhead applied during 1993:

Work in process inventory	$ 3,000
Finished goods inventory	6,000
Cost of goods sold	71,000

JOB COST JOURNAL
ENTRIES
— OBJ. 4, 5 —

22-30A Prior to the beginning of 1993, Stapleton Company estimated that it would incur $153,000 of factory overhead cost during 1993, using 17,000 direct labor hours to produce the desired volume of goods. On January 1, 1993, beginning balances of Materials Inventory, Work in Process Inventory, and Finished Goods Inventory were $48,000, $-0-, and $87,000, respectively.

REQUIRED

Prepare general journal entries to record the following for 1993:
a. Purchased materials on account, $316,000.
b. Of the total dollar value of materials used, $284,000 represented direct material and $35,000 indirect material.
c. Determined total factory labor, $189,000 (18,000 hrs. @ $10.50/hr.).
d. Of the factory labor, 15,800 were direct labor hours.
e. Applied factory overhead based on direct labor hours to work in process.
f. Determined actual factory overhead other than those items already recorded, $83,000. (Credit Accounts Payable.)
g. Ending inventories of work in process and finished goods were $57,000 and $71,800, respectively. (Make separate entries.)
h. Transferred the balance in Factory Overhead to Cost of Goods Sold.

**JOB COST JOURNAL
ENTRIES AND T ACCOUNTS
— OBJ. 4, 5 —**

22-31A   Following are certain operating data for Redwood Manufacturing Company for January 1993:

	Materials Inventory	Work in Process Inventory	Finished Goods Inventory
Beginning inventory	$40,000	$50,000	$80,000
Ending inventory	70,000	60,000	56,000

Total sales were $2,000,000, on which the company earned a 40% gross profit. Redwood uses a predetermined factory overhead rate of 110% of direct labor costs. Factory overhead applied was $396,000. Exclusive of indirect material used, total factory overhead incurred was $300,000; it was underapplied by $24,000.

REQUIRED

Compute the following items. (Set up T accounts for Materials Inventory, Work in Process Inventory, Finished Goods Inventory, and Factory Overhead; fill in the known amounts; and then use the normal relationships among the various accounts to compute the unknown amounts.)

a. Cost of goods sold.
b. Cost of goods manufactured.
c. Direct labor incurred.
d. Direct material used.
e. Indirect material used.
f. Total materials purchased.

**JOB COST JOURNAL
ENTRIES AND T ACCOUNTS
— OBJ. 4, 5 —**

22-32A   Summarized data for the first month's operations of Slater Foundry during 1993 are presented below. A job order costing system is used.

1. Materials purchased on account, $88,000.
2. Amounts of materials requisitioned and foundry labor used:

Job	Materials	Foundry Labor
1	$ 4,600	$ 3,600
2	5,200	6,000
3	3,800	8,800
4	13,400	12,000
5	6,400	7,200
6	4,000	2,000
Indirect material	11,000	
Indirect labor		18,000

3. Foundry overhead is applied at the rate of 150% of direct labor costs.
4. Miscellaneous foundry overhead incurred:

Prepaid foundry insurance written off	$ 1,880
Property taxes on foundry building accrued	3,760
Foundry utilities payable accrued	4,400
Depreciation on foundry equipment	8,400
Other costs incurred on account	14,640

5. Ending work in process consisted of jobs 4 and 6.
6. Jobs 1 and 3 and one-half of job 2 were sold on account for $25,200, $31,600, and $18,920, respectively.

REQUIRED

a. Open general ledger T accounts for Materials Inventory, Foundry Payroll, Foundry Overhead, Work in Process Inventory, Finished Goods Inventory, and Cost of Goods Sold. Also set up subsidiary T accounts as job cost sheets for each job.
b. Prepare general journal entries to record the summarized transactions for the month, and post appropriate entries to any accounts listed in requirement (a). Key each entry parenthetically to the related number in the problem data.
c. Determine the balances of any accounts necessary and prepare schedules of jobs in ending work in process and jobs in ending finished goods to confirm that they agree with the related control accounts.

**COMPLEX JOB COST
JOURNAL ENTRIES AND
ANALYSIS
— OBJ. 4, 5—**

22-33A   During June 1993, its first month of operations, Logan Manufacturing Company completed the transactions listed below. Logan uses a job order costing system. Materials requisitions and the factory payroll summary are analyzed on the 15th and the last day of each month, and charges for direct material and direct labor are entered directly on specific job cost sheets. Factory overhead at the rate of 160% of direct labor costs is recorded on individual job cost sheets when a job is completed and at month-end for any job then in process. At month-end, entries to the general ledger accounts summarize materials requisitions, distribution of factory payroll costs, and the application of factory overhead for the month. All other entries to general ledger accounts are made as they occur.

1. Purchased materials on account, $210,000.
2. Paid miscellaneous factory overhead costs, $52,000.
3. Paid the semimonthly factory payroll, $160,000.
4. An analysis of materials requisitions and the factory payroll summary for June 1–15 indicates the following cost distribution:

Job	Materials	Factory Labor
1	$34,000	$ 60,000
2	16,000	26,000
3	8,000	18,000
Indirect material	14,000	
Indirect labor		56,000
	$72,000	$160,000

5. Jobs 1 and 2 were completed on June 15 and transferred to finished goods inventory on the next day. (Enter the appropriate factory overhead amounts on the job cost sheets, mark them completed, and make a general journal entry transferring the appropriate amount of cost to the Finished Goods Inventory account.)
6. Paid miscellaneous factory overhead costs, $38,000.
7. Sold job 1 on account, $300,000 (recognized its cost of sales in the general journal).
8. Paid the semimonthly factory payroll, $156,000.
9. An analysis of materials requisitions and factory payroll summary for June 16–30 indicates the following cost distribution:

Job	Materials	Factory Labor
3	$36,000	$ 28,000
4	30,000	54,000
5	12,000	20,000
6	6,000	8,000
Indirect material	10,000	
Indirect labor		46,000
	$94,000	$156,000

10. Jobs 3 and 4 were completed on June 30 and transferred to finished goods inventory on the same day. (See transaction 5.)
11. Sold job 3 on account, $250,000 (recognized its cost of sales in the general journal).
12. Recorded the following additional factory overhead:

Depreciation on factory building	$42,000
Depreciation on factory equipment	24,000
Expiration of prepaid factory insurance	7,000
Accrual of factory property taxes payable	13,000
	$86,000

13. Recorded monthly general journal entry for the costs of all materials used.
14. Recorded monthly general journal entry for the distribution of factory payroll costs.
15. Recorded factory overhead on the job cost sheets for jobs in ending work in process and in the general journal for all factory overhead applied during the month.

REQUIRED

a. Set up the following general ledger T accounts: Materials Inventory, Factory Payroll, Factory Overhead, Work in Process Inventory, Finished Goods Inventory, Cost of Goods Sold, and Sales.

b. Set up subsidiary ledger T accounts for each of jobs 1–6 as job cost sheets.

c. Noting the accounting procedures described in the first paragraph of the problem, do the following:

    1. Record general journal entries for all transactions. Note that general journal entries are *not* required in transactions 4 and 9. Post only those portions of these entries affecting the general ledger accounts set up in requirement (a).

    2. Enter the applicable amounts directly on the appropriate job cost sheets for transactions 4, 5, 9, 10, and 15. Note parenthetically the nature of each amount entered.

d. Present a brief analysis showing that the general ledger accounts for Work in Process Inventory and for Finished Goods Inventory agree with the related job cost sheets.

e. Explain in one sentence each what the balance of each general ledger account established in requirement (a) represents.

PLANTWIDE, DEPARTMENTAL, AND ACTIVITY-BASED COSTING — OBJ. 6 —

22-34A Bicknell Manufacturing, Inc., produces six products that require very similar assembly processes. The budget for 1993 for Bicknell Manufacturing includes the following items:

Direct material used		$840,000
Direct labor incurred		420,000
Factory overhead:		
Machining department	$280,000	
Painting department	126,000	
Assembly department	336,000	
Total overhead		742,000

The best measure of capacity utilization in the machining department is considered to be machine hours, whereas the best measure of capacity utilization in the painting department and the assembly department as well as the factory as a whole is considered to be direct labor hours. Budgeted hours for 1993 follow:

	Direct Labor Hours	Machine Hours
Machining	5,600	14,000
Painting	8,400	4,000
Assembly	21,000	0
Total	35,000	18,000

The engineering and accounting departments of Bicknell Manufacturing conducted a study of the factory that categorized all of the planned factory operations for 1993 and the related overhead costs into the following activities (budgeted amounts are for 1993):

Activity	Budgeted Overhead	Budgeted Activity for 1993	
Purchasing	$ 56,000	2,000	purchase orders
Metal shearing	105,000	30,000	shearings
Metal bending	56,000	10,000	bends
Welding	84,000	21,000	welds
Painting	117,000	130,000	sq. ft. painted
Assembly	276,000	3,000	units
Packaging	48,000	3,000	units
Total	$742,000		

REQUIRED

a. Calculate a predetermined plantwide overhead rate for 1993.

b. Calculate predetermined departmental overhead rates for 1993.

c. Calculate predetermined overhead rates for 1993 for each factory activity.

d. Job 217 was started and finished during 1993. The following were accumulated for job 217:

Direct material used $20,000
Direct labor incurred:

	Hours	**Dollars**
Machining	140	$1,700
Painting	200	2,500
Assembly	430	5,200
Total	770	$9,400

Machine hours used: machining, 270; painting, 80

Factory activities utilized were as follows:

Purchasing	42 purchase orders
Metal shearing	630 shearings
Metal bending	250 bends
Welding	50 welds
Painting	3,200 sq. ft. painted
Assembly	75 units
Packaging	75 units

Calculate the product cost of job 217 under three different assumptions:
1. The use of a plantwide overhead rate.
2. The use of departmental overhead rates.
3. The use of activity-based costing.

CASES

Business Decision Case

Elizabeth Flanigan and Associates is an engineering and design firm that specializes in developing plans for recycling plants for municipalities. The firm uses a job costing system to accumulate the cost associated with each design project. Flanigan employs three levels of employee: senior engineers, associate engineers, and clerical staff. The salary cost of the senior engineers and the associate engineers is assigned to each project as direct labor. The salary cost of the clerical staff is included in overhead, along with the cost of engineering supplies, automobile travel, and equipment depreciation. The cost of airline travel, motels, building permits, and fees from other consultants is charged to each project as direct material. Overhead is applied to projects using a predetermined overhead rate based on total engineering hours. The rate for 1993 is $5 per hour.

The six different salary levels for 1993 for the employees of Elizabeth Flanigan and Associates are listed below. The hourly rate is determined by dividing the yearly salary by 2,000 hours per year.

Senior engineer
     Level 1: $44,000 per year ($22 per hour)
     Level 2: $36,000 per year ($18 per hour)

Associate engineer
     Level 3: $30,000 per year ($15 per hour)
     Level 4: $24,000 per year ($12 per hour)

Clerical staff
     Level 5: $16,000 per year ($8 per hour)
     Level 6: $12,000 per year ($6 per hour)

The billings that are sent to the municipalities for engineering services utilize cost-plus billing. Typically, the total costs accumulated for a project (direct material, direct labor, and overhead) are multiplied by 140% to determine the amount of the billing. The difference between the billed amount and the accumulated cost is the "plus" in cost plus.

During March 1993, Flanigan accumulated the following information related to job 295 for Johnson Creek City:

Senior engineer hours
Level 1	52
Level 2	84

Associate engineer hours	
Level 3	106
Level 4	44
Clerical hours	
Level 5	20
Level 6	66
Building permits	$1,500
Airline travel and motel	$ 865

REQUIRED

a. What amount should be billed to Johnson Creek City for March 1993?

b. How much profit was earned on job 295 during March 1993?

Ethics Case

Metal Creations, Inc., is a custom manufacturer that uses a job order costing system. Currently, Metal Creations has 35% excess capacity in its factory. Charlie Rollins, the president, has instituted a campaign to obtain new customers. Rollins has offered the salespeople a bonus equal to 25% of the gross profit on work for new customers. The average gross profit rate has been 30% of the contract price.

Steve Starling, the sales manager for Metal Creations, wants to submit a proposal to a new customer that undercuts the usual pricing structure by 30%. As a result, this job would have no gross profit using the regular job order costing system. Instead, Starling suggests that the overhead rate applied to this job should be only 40% of the normal overhead rate, resulting in a gross profit of 28%. Starling suggests that the controller should handle this contract herself, and that no one else in the organization should know about it, especially the other salespeople, because the creative approach to overhead application might create problems.

REQUIRED

Does taking an order at a significantly reduced price create an ethical problem? Does altering the accounting for a particular order create an ethical problem? Does asking the controller to handle the contract and keep the accounting confidential create an ethical problem?

How does a manufacturing firm account for product cost when large volumes of product are manufactured in a continual flow operation?

Manufacturing firms that produce large volumes of a product in a continual flow operation typically use process costing to accumulate and account for product cost. ■ *The refining operations of companies such as Exxon, whose refinery is shown here, and Shell Oil represent this type of manufacturing.* ■ *The FIFO method of process costing is presented in the chapter and the weighted average method is presented in an appendix.*

23

COST ACCOUNTING SYSTEMS: PROCESS COSTING

CHAPTER OBJECTIVES

❶ COMPARE and CONTRAST job order costing and process costing (p. 864).

❷ DESCRIBE the basic concepts of process costing (pp. 864–865).

❸ EXPLAIN techniques for determining unit costs when process costing is used (pp. 866–868).

❹ ILLUSTRATE the journal entries used with process costing (pp. 868–870).

❺ DESCRIBE the calculation of equivalent units and costs per equivalent unit using the FIFO method in a multiple department process costing system (pp. 870–871, 873).

❻ EXPLAIN the procedures used to prepare the production cost report using the FIFO method in a process costing system (pp. 871–872, 874).

❼ IDENTIFY the journal entries to transfer product cost from work in process inventory accounts to Finished Goods Inventory to Cost of Goods Sold (pp. 872, 875–876).

❽ DESCRIBE the procedures for cost allocation for service departments (pp. 876–878).

❾ IDENTIFY joint product costs and byproduct costs and describe techniques to account for them (pp. 878–880).

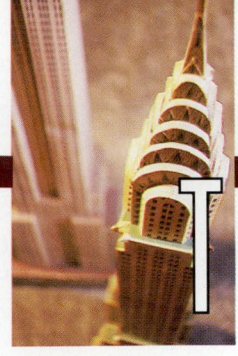

For which of you, desiring to build a tower, does not first sit down and count the cost . . . ?

LUKE 14:28

OBJECTIVE ❶ COMPARE *and* **CONTRAST** *job order costing and process costing.*

he early sections of this chapter explain and illustrate the concepts and procedures typical of a process costing system that involves more than one processing department. The concluding sections of the chapter deal with accounting for the costs of service departments, joint products, and byproducts.

In previous chapters, we introduced and discussed the concepts used in job order costing. Exhibit 23-1 presents the typical flow of product cost in a job order costing system. Direct material and direct labor are accumulated, by job or product, in the work in process inventory. Overhead cost is applied to the work in process inventory using an annual predetermined overhead rate.

Actual overhead costs, including indirect material and indirect labor, are accumulated in the Factory Overhead account as debits, and the applied overhead is recorded in the same account as a credit. Perpetual inventory techniques are used to move product cost from the Work in Process Inventory to Finished Goods Inventory and finally to Cost of Goods Sold.

Job order costing is adopted whenever production is characterized by a series of different products or jobs undertaken either to fill specific orders from customers or to produce a stock of products from which future orders can be filled. **Process costing,** however, is used when large volumes of product are manufactured in a continual flow operation, such as the production of fuels, chemicals, small appliances, building materials, and electricity. With process costing, product costs are accumulated by department, not by job or product.

CHARACTERISTICS OF PROCESS COSTING

OBJECTIVE ❷ DESCRIBE *the basic concepts of process costing.*

Exhibit 23-2 presents the typical flow of product cost in a process costing system. The following characteristics of process costing are evident in Exhibit 23-1 and Exhibit 23-2:

1. There is a separate work in process inventory account for each manufacturing department when process costing is used, whereas there is only one work in process inventory account when job order costing is used. In Exhibit 23-2, there are two work in process inventory accounts since there are two manufacturing departments.

2. Direct material, direct labor, and factory overhead costs can be added to the work in process inventory account in each department. Exhibit 23-2 shows all three elements of product cost being added to both work in process inventory accounts.

3. Perpetual inventory techniques are not used to flow product costs from one work in process inventory account to another when process costing is used. Nor are perpetual inventory techniques used to flow product cost to the Finished Goods Inventory account (or to Cost of Goods Sold) during the accounting period when process costing is used. The accounting techniques introduced in this chapter will provide a means of transferring product cost at the end of the accounting period.

Manufacturing Departments

Typically, multiple manufacturing departments are identified when process costing is used. Products will flow through these departments at different stages of the manufacturing process. For example, a consumer product might be processed through three departments, machining, painting, and assembling. In any particular manufacturing plant, some products may go through many departments, and other products

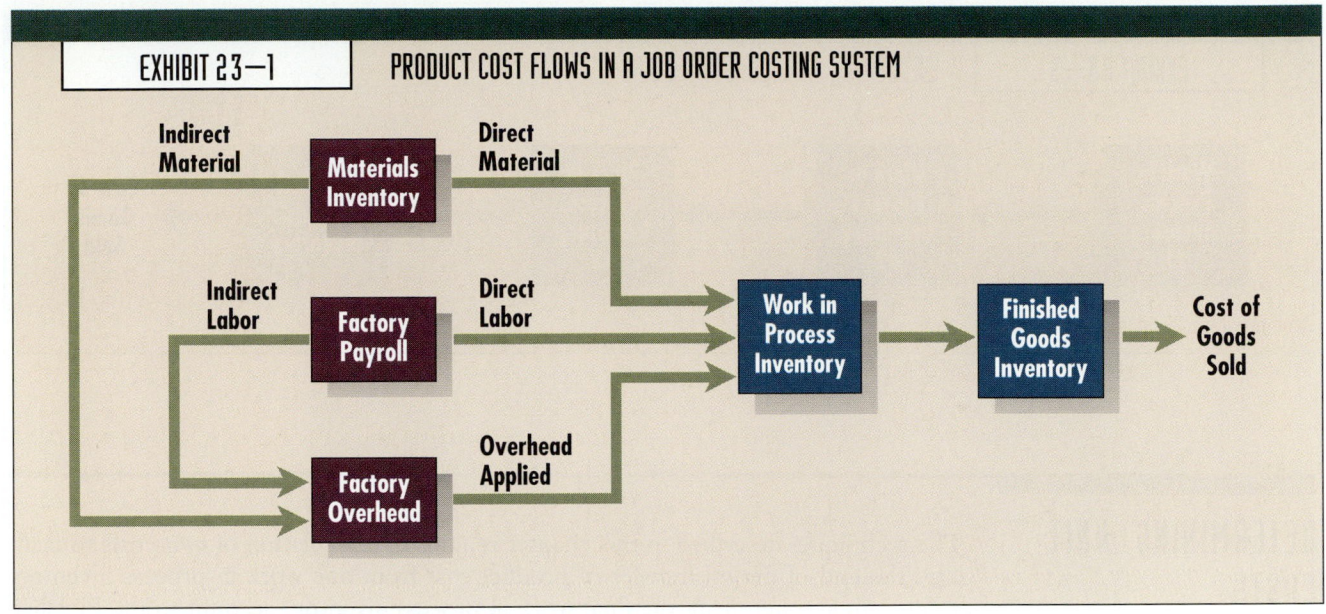

EXHIBIT 23—1   PRODUCT COST FLOWS IN A JOB ORDER COSTING SYSTEM

may go through only a few departments, depending on the nature of the work to be done. Regardless, the work in any department must be performed uniformly on all units and the output of the department must be uniform in nature.

Basic Processing Patterns

There are two basic patterns for arranging the departments in a process costing situation: sequential and parallel. Exhibit 23-3 presents a *sequential* product processing pattern. With sequential processing, there is a single path through the manufacturing process. Exhibit 23-4 presents a simple example of *parallel* product processing. Numerous variations of parallel processing are possible. The process costing techniques described in this chapter can be used regardless of which pattern a particular manufacturing process follows.

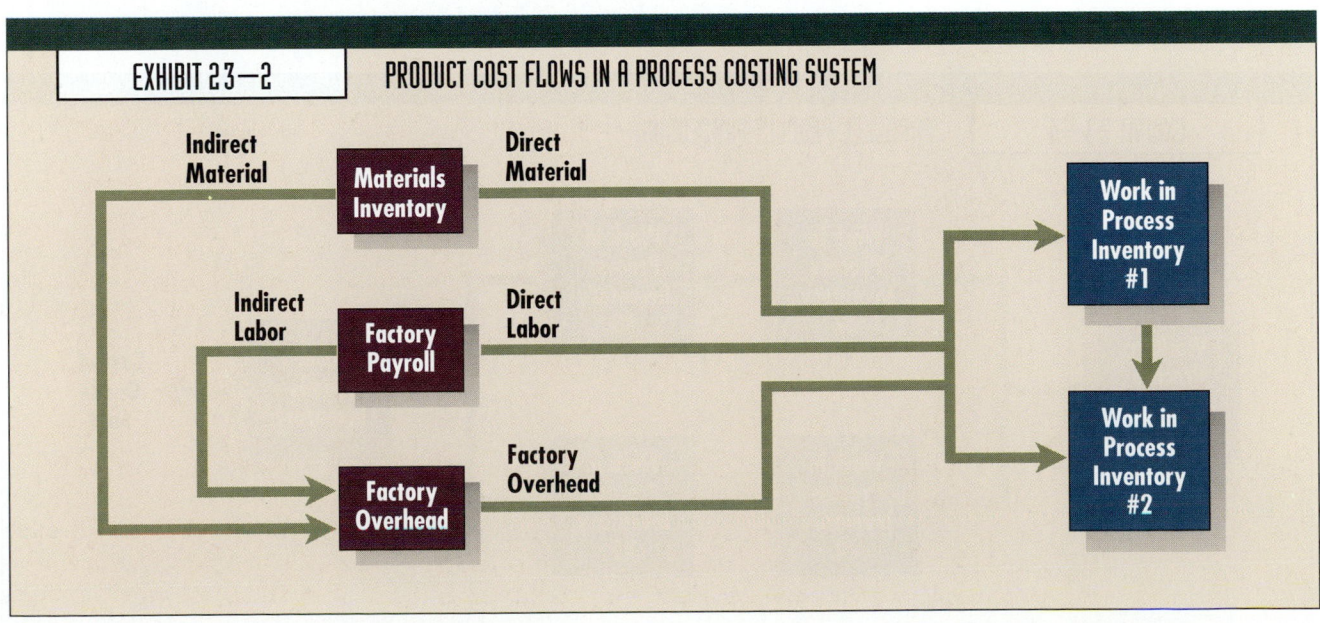

EXHIBIT 23—2   PRODUCT COST FLOWS IN A PROCESS COSTING SYSTEM

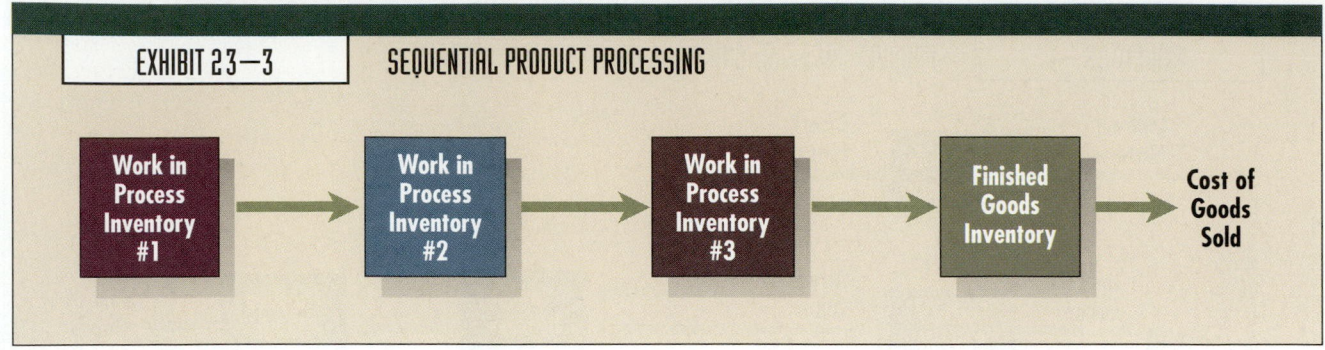

EXHIBIT 23—3   SEQUENTIAL PRODUCT PROCESSING

DETERMINING UNIT COSTS

OBJECTIVE 3   EXPLAIN *techniques for determining unit costs when process costing is used.*

The techniques described in this chapter require the calculation of *unit* costs to facilitate the end-of-period transfer of product cost from one work in process inventory account to another, from the final work in process inventory account to the Finished Goods Inventory account, and from the Finished Goods Inventory account to Cost of Goods Sold. With process costing, unit costs are usually calculated on a monthly basis. These unit costs can be compared to unit costs of prior accounting periods to determine when additional cost control measures are necessary.

Equivalent Units

Assume that Department 1 of Bower Company uses process costing and that it had the following results for January:

Direct material added	$1,400
Direct labor incurred	2,000
Factory overhead cost	800
Total costs	$4,200

Units in process at January 1 (20% complete)	200 units
Units started and finished during January	500 units
Units in process at January 31 (40% complete)	100 units

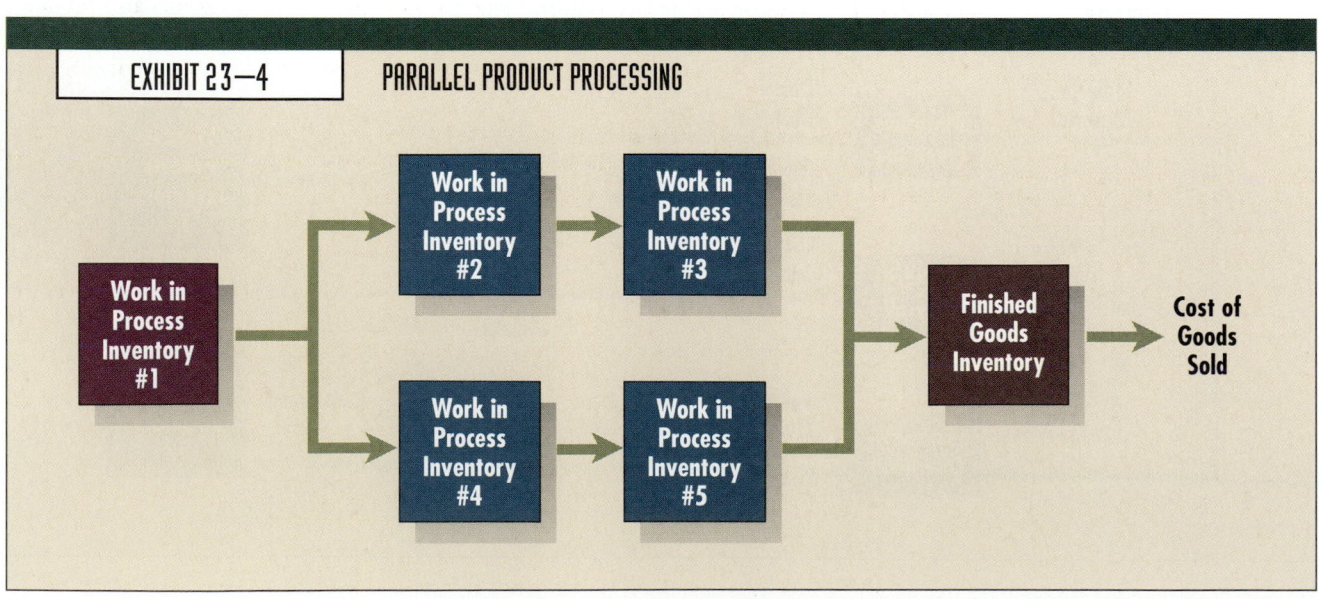

EXHIBIT 23—4   PARALLEL PRODUCT PROCESSING

To properly determine unit costs, we need to calculate the amount of work completed during the month of January, which, in turn, will require the calculation of the number of equivalent units of completed work during the month. **Equivalent units** are the smaller number of full measures of work accomplished that is the equivalent of a larger number of partially accomplished units of work. Using the data for Department 1 of Bower Company, we can calculate the number of equivalent units for January as follows:

	Units Involved		Proportion Completed This Month		Equivalent Units
Beginning inventory	200	$\times$	80%	=	160
Started and finished during January	500	$\times$	100%	=	500
Ending inventory	100	$\times$	40%	=	40
	800				700

The units in the beginning inventory are assumed to be completed during January. Therefore, the percentage complete went from 20% at the beginning of the month to 100% by the end of the month. Therefore, 80% of the work was accomplished during the month. If we assume that material, labor, and overhead are added gradually throughout processing, the unit cost for Department 1 for January would be as follows:

$$\frac{\text{Total Costs for January}}{\text{Equivalent Units Processed}} = \frac{\$4,200}{700 \text{ gallons}} = \$6 \text{ per gallon}$$

In process cost systems, unit cost calculations may be complicated by the fact that materials are added at a different rate or at a different time than are labor and overhead, which are usually grouped together and called **conversion costs.** For example, materials may be added at the beginning of the process, but conversion costs (direct labor plus factory overhead) are added evenly throughout the process. In this case, the number of equivalent units used to calculate the unit cost of materials is different from the number of equivalent units used to compute the unit cost of conversion.

Exhibit 23-5 graphically presents the revised computation of equivalent units when all materials are added initially and conversion costs are incurred evenly throughout the process. Because all materials for beginning work in process were added during the previous period (when these units were started), this batch has no equivalent units for materials in this period. However, any unit of product started this period has all materials added this period, so the 500 units started and finished and the 100 units only started (ending work in process) are assigned full equivalent units for material. For conversion costs, (1) the 200 units in beginning work in process represent only 160 (80% $\times$ 200) equivalent units because only the final 80% of processing occurred this period; (2) each of the 500 units of product started and finished this period equals one equivalent unit because all conversion was accomplished this period; and (3) the 100 units in ending work in process equal only 40 (40% $\times$ 100) equivalent units because only 40% of their processing was accomplished this period. Under these assumptions, the number of equivalent units completed for the period is not the same for material as for conversion costs. Consequently, the computation of cost per equivalent unit requires separate calculations for the two cost components, which are then totaled. In our illustration, these are the following:

$$\frac{\text{Material Cost}}{\text{Equivalent Units}} = \frac{\$1,400}{600} = \$2.333 \text{ for material}$$

$$\frac{\text{Conversion Costs}}{\text{Equivalent Units}} = \frac{\$2,000 + \$800}{700} = 4.000 \text{ for conversion}$$

Total cost for a unit processed this period $\underline{\$6.333}$

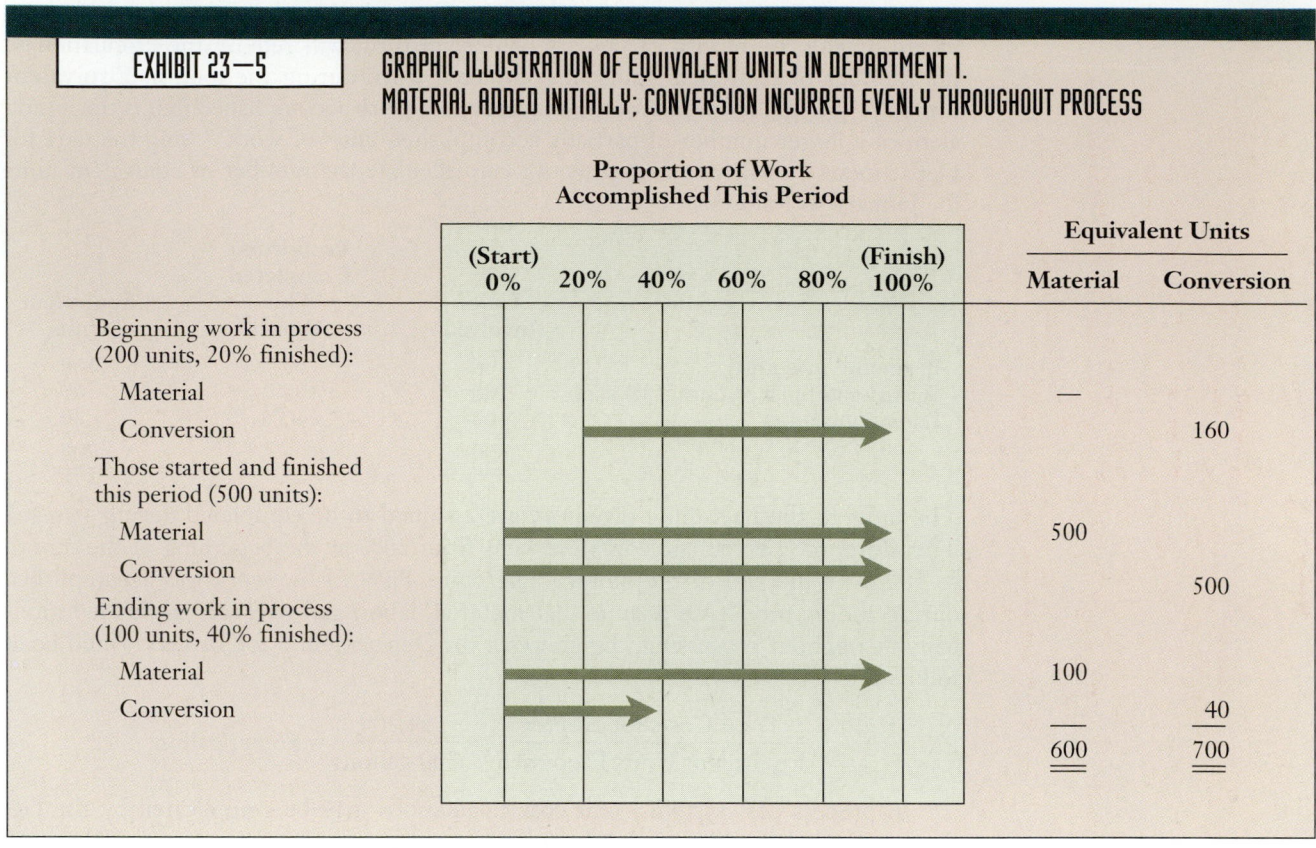

| EXHIBIT 23—5 | GRAPHIC ILLUSTRATION OF EQUIVALENT UNITS IN DEPARTMENT 1. MATERIAL ADDED INITIALLY; CONVERSION INCURRED EVENLY THROUGHOUT PROCESS |

Note again that equivalent unit costs for a specific period are derived by dividing the total costs for the period by the related amount of work accomplished during that period.

COST FLOWS ILLUSTRATED

OBJECTIVE 4   ILLUSTRATE *the journal entries used with process costing.*

For an example of the operation of a process costing system, assume that Northbrook Chemical Company produces an industrial cleaner called Kleeno, which Northbrook markets in one-gallon bottles. The production of Kleeno involves two sequential processing departments: the Mixing Department (where the product is formulated) and the Bottling Department (where the product is bottled, subjected to heat treating, and inspected).

In the Mixing Department, various materials are added at the beginning of the process, and conversion costs are incurred evenly throughout the process. In the Bottling Department, additional materials are added at the beginning of the processing in this department, and conversion costs occur evenly throughout the process. Northbrook uses a predetermined overhead rate to assign overhead cost, which is included in the conversion cost.

On June 1, the Mixing Department had 10,000 gallons in work in process that was 25% complete with respect to conversion cost. This inventory had a cost of $106,500 assigned to it at that date. Also on June 1, the Bottling Department had 8,000 gallons in work in process that was 30% complete with respect to conversion cost. This inventory had a cost of $184,880 assigned to it at that date.

Material

During June, Northbrook purchased $950,000 of material on account. The following is a summary journal entry for the June purchases:

Materials Inventory	950,000	
Accounts Payable		950,000
To record June material purchases.		

The direct material requisitioned during June for each processing department and the indirect material for general factory use are shown in the following summary entry:

Work in Process—Mixing Department	704,000	
Work in Process—Bottling Department	240,000	
Factory Overhead	42,000	
Materials Inventory		966,000
To record direct and indirect material used during June.		

Labor

During June, Northbrook accrued $587,200 of factory payroll. A summary journal entry to record this payroll would be as follows:

Factory Payroll	587,200	
Factory Payroll Payable		587,200
To record the factory payroll for June.		

The factory payroll for June was made up of $298,400 of direct labor for the Mixing Department and $186,500 of direct labor for the Bottling Department. Indirect labor costs amounted to $102,300. The following summary entry distributes these costs:

Work in Process—Mixing Department	298,400	
Work in Process—Bottling Department	186,500	
Factory Overhead	102,300	
Factory Payroll		587,200
To distribute the June factory payroll.		

Factory Overhead

At this point, we have recorded $42,000 of indirect material and $102,300 of indirect labor in the Factory Overhead account. Assume that other overhead costs (such as maintenance, depreciation, and utilities) total $467,500. To record these amounts, we normally would credit various accounts such as Accumulated Depreciation, Accounts Payable, and Prepaid Expenses. For simplicity in this example, we will credit these other accounts in the following summary entry:

Factory Overhead	467,500	
[Other accounts]		467,500
To record various factory overhead costs.		

Northbrook applies overhead to work in process using predetermined overhead rates. The following entry records the amount of applied factory overhead for the two processing departments:

Work in Process—Mixing Department	486,800	
Work in Process—Bottling Department	123,900	
Factory Overhead		610,700
To apply factory overhead to work in process inventories.		

Actual costs charged to the Factory Overhead account total $611,800 ($42,000 + $102,300 + $467,500). The previous entry assigned only $610,700 to the inventory accounts, resulting in $1,100 of underapplied overhead. Recall that underapplied or overapplied factory overhead is disposed of at year-end. If the amount is significant, it should be allocated to the work in process inventories, Finished Goods Inventory, and Cost of Goods Sold based on the amount of factory overhead previously applied. If the amount is insignificant, it should be assigned to Cost of Goods Sold.

As a result of the journal entries recorded during the month, the two work in process accounts contain the following balances as of the end of the month:

	Mixing Department	Bottling Department
Beginning balance	$ 106,500	$184,880
Direct material	704,000	240,000
Direct labor	298,400	186,500
Factory overhead	486,800	123,900
	$1,595,700	$735,280

At the end of the month, additional journal entries are needed to transfer product costs from the Mixing Department to the Bottling Department, from the Bottling Department to finished goods, and from finished goods to cost of goods sold.

FIFO METHOD FOR PROCESS COSTING

OBJECTIVE 5 *DESCRIBE the calculation of equivalent units and costs per equivalent unit using the FIFO method in a multiple department process costing system.*

We have explained how material and conversion costs are debited to work in process accounts for each processing department during the month. At the end of each month, we must calculate the cost of goods transferred out and the cost of goods remaining uncompleted for each department. Calculations can be performed using either the first-in, first-out (FIFO) accounting method or the weighted average accounting method. We illustrate the FIFO method in this chapter and the weighted average method in Appendix H.

Exhibit 23-6 shows the June 1993 **production report** for the two processing departments. Note the following key observations regarding the production report:

1. All unit figures are in whole gallons rather than in equivalent units.
2. In the Mixing Department, the beginning work in process units (10,000) plus units started (80,000) constitute the total number of units to be accounted for (90,000). The 90,000 units are accounted for as units transferred out (75,000) plus units in ending work in process (15,000) of the Mixing Department.
3. For the Bottling Department, the beginning work in process units (8,000) plus units transferred in from the Mixing Department (75,000) constitute the total number of units to be accounted for (83,000). The 83,000 units are accounted for as units transferred out to finished goods (78,000) plus units in ending work in process (5,000) of the Bottling Department.
4. The number of units transferred out of the Mixing Department (75,000) is equal to the number of units transferred into the Bottling Department (75,000).

We now examine how costs are allocated to the various units, beginning with the Mixing Department.

Mixing Department

Remember that in the Mixing Department, materials are added at the start of the mixing process, but conversion costs are incurred evenly throughout the process. Therefore, we must calculate equivalent units and cost per equivalent unit separately for material and conversion costs. Exhibit 23-7 presents these calculations in a **cost**

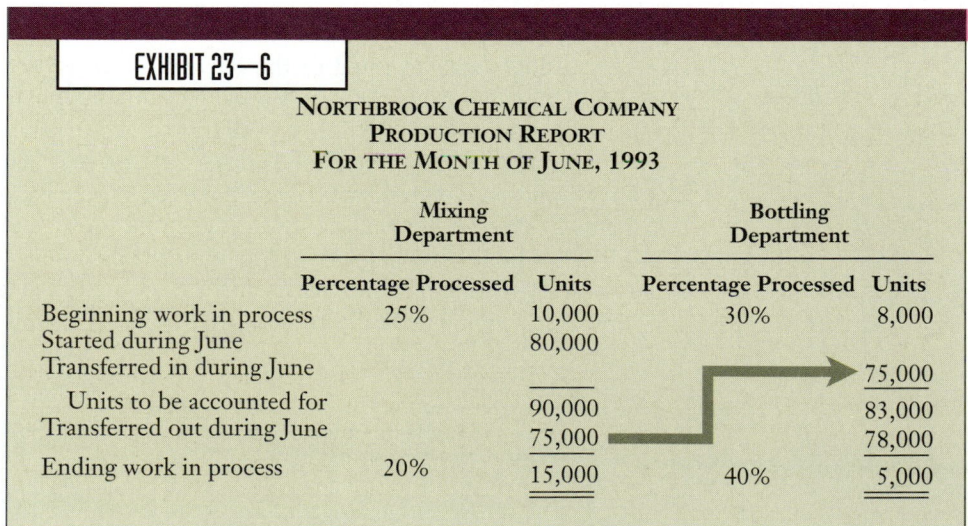

EXHIBIT 23—6

NORTHBROOK CHEMICAL COMPANY
PRODUCTION REPORT
FOR THE MONTH OF JUNE, 1993

	Mixing Department		Bottling Department	
	Percentage Processed	Units	Percentage Processed	Units
Beginning work in process	25%	10,000	30%	8,000
Started during June		80,000		
Transferred in during June				75,000
Units to be accounted for		90,000		83,000
Transferred out during June		75,000		78,000
Ending work in process	20%	15,000	40%	5,000

| EXHIBIT 23—7 | NORTHBROOK CHEMICAL COMPANY MIXING DEPARTMENT COST PER EQUIVALENT UNIT REPORT FOR THE MONTH OF JUNE, 1993 | | | |

FIFO Method	Units Involved	Conversion Completed This Month	Material (added initially)	Conversion (added throughout)
Current equivalent units:				
Transferred out:				
Beginning work in process (25%)	10,000	75%	–0–	7,500
Started and finished this month	65,000	100%	65,000	65,000
Units transferred out this month	75,000			
Ending work in process (20%)	15,000	20%	15,000	3,000
Units accounted for	90,000			
Current equivalent units			80,000	75,500
Current costs:				
Direct material			$704,000	
Direct labor				$298,400
Factory overhead				486,800
Current costs			$704,000	$785,200
Current cost per current equivalent unit			$8.80	$10.40

per equivalent unit report. It is important to note that, with the FIFO method, only current month equivalent units and current month costs are included in the cost per equivalent unit calculations.

In allocating costs to various units of product, three batches of Kleeno are considered: (1) units finished from the June 1 inventory, (2) units started and finished in June, and (3) units started but not finished in June. The composition of costs for the three batches of product handled by the Mixing Department is explained below and in the **production cost report** in Exhibit 23-8:

OBJECTIVE **6** EXPLAIN *the procedures used to prepare the production cost report using the FIFO method in a process costing system.*

1. **Beginning inventory** The 10,000 gallons in the beginning inventory had all the material and 25% of the required conversion work added in May, for a $106,500 total cost in that month. The remaining 75% of the conversion work was completed in June. We multiply the conversion cost of a full unit ($10.40) by the equivalent units (7,500 gallons) to obtain the $78,000 cost to finish this batch.

2. **Started and finished in June** During June, all required material and conversion work were applied to the 65,000 gallons started and finished. The material added this month at $8.80 per gallon and the conversion work completed at $10.40 per unit are applied to each of the 65,000 units. The total cost of the 75,000 gallons in the two batches transferred to the Bottling Department amounts to $1,432,500, and the average cost of the two batches is $19.10 per gallon ($1,432,500/75,000).

3. **Ending inventory** The 15,000 units started but not finished in June contain all required material but only 20% of the needed conversion work. Therefore, we multiply the per-unit material cost of $8.80 by 15,000 gallons to obtain the $132,000 material cost. We then multiply the $10.40 conversion cost by the 3,000 equivalent units of conversion work performed to obtain the $31,200 conversion cost.

EXHIBIT 23—8		

NORTHBROOK CHEMICAL COMPANY
MIXING DEPARTMENT
PRODUCTION COST REPORT
FOR THE MONTH OF JUNE, 1993

FIFO Method	Total Cost	Unit Cost
Costs to be accounted for:		
Prior month costs	$ 106,500	
Direct material	704,000	
Direct labor	298,400	
Factory overhead	486,800	
Total costs to be accounted for	$1,595,700	
Costs accounted for:		
Transferred out:		
Beginning work in process:		
Prior month	$ 106,500	
Material (0 × $8.80)	–0–	
Conversion (7,500 × $10.40)	78,000	
Started and finished:		
Material (65,000 × $8.80)	572,000	
Conversion (65,000 × $10.40)	676,000	
Total costs transferred out	$1,432,500	$19.10
Ending work in process:		
Material (15,000 × $8.80)	$ 132,000	
Conversion (3,000 × $10.40)	31,200	
Ending work in process	$ 163,200	
Total costs accounted for	$1,595,700	

Notice that the production cost report fully accounts for both the 90,000 units of product involved and the total costs of $1,595,700 charged to the Mixing Department.

OBJECTIVE 7 IDENTIFY *the journal entries to transfer product cost from work in process inventory accounts to Finished Goods Inventory to Cost of Goods Sold.*

The following journal entry transfers the cost of the work completed in the Mixing Department during June to the Bottling Department:

Work in Process—Bottling Department	1,432,500	
Work in Process—Mixing Department		1,432,500
To transfer cost of completed work from Mixing to Bottling.		

The work in process inventory account for the Mixing Department would now appear as follows:

WORK IN PROCESS—MIXING DEPARTMENT

June 1 (beginning balance)	106,500	Transferred to Bottling	
Direct material	704,000	Department	1,432,500
Direct labor	298,400		
Factory overhead	486,800		
June 30 (ending balance)	163,200		

All costs charged to this account have now been accounted for as either transferred out or as ending work in process inventory.

Bottling Department

OBJECTIVE 5   DESCRIBE *the calculation of equivalent units and costs per equivalent unit using the FIFO method in a multiple department process costing system.*

In the Bottling Department, materials are added at the start of the process, and conversion costs are incurred evenly throughout the process. The units handled during June include 8,000 units from the beginning work in process inventory of the Bottling Department and the 75,000 units transferred in from the Mixing Department. The 8,000 units in the beginning inventory had $184,880 of product cost assigned to them in the prior month. The 75,000 units had $1,432,500 assigned to them in the Mixing Department prior to being transferred to the Bottling Department.

Again, we must convert the work performed into equivalent units and obtain costs per equivalent unit. Exhibit 23-9 presents the cost per equivalent unit report for the Bottling Department, and Exhibit 23-10 presents the production cost report for the Bottling Department.

The cost per equivalent unit report for the Bottling Department differs from the same report for the Mixing Department in that transferred-in costs must be accounted for in the Bottling Department. As a result, there is a Transferred In column added to the cost per equivalent unit report for the Bottling Department. As Exhibit 23-9 demonstrates, three cost per equivalent unit amounts are calculated: transferred in, material, and conversion.

The percentages of conversion completed this month in Exhibit 23-9 are calculated exactly as before. Since the beginning work in process inventory in the Bottling Department was 30% complete, and since we assume these units were finished during June, then the percentage of conversion work completed during June was 70% (100% − 30%).

It should be noted that the transferred-in cost per equivalent unit in Exhibit 23-9 is the same as the transferred-out unit cost in Exhibit 23-8. When the FIFO method is used, this relationship is always true, since the Transferred-in column in the cost per equivalent unit report contains units and costs transferred in during the current month only.

EXHIBIT 23—9

NORTHBROOK CHEMICAL COMPANY
BOTTLING DEPARTMENT
COST PER EQUIVALENT UNIT REPORT
FOR THE MONTH OF JUNE, 1993

FIFO Method	Units Involved	Conversion Completed This Month	Transferred in	Material (added initially)	Conversion (added throughout)
Current equivalent units:					
Transferred out:					
Beginning work in process (30%)	8,000	70%	–0–	–0–	5,600
Transferrred in and finished	70,000	100%	70,000	70,000	70,000
Units transferred out this month	78,000				
Ending work in process (40%)	5,000	40%	5,000	5,000	2,000
Units accounted for	83,000				
Current equivalent units			75,000	75,000	77,600
Current costs:					
Costs transferred in from Mixing Department			$1,432,500		
Direct material				$240,000	
Direct labor					$186,500
Factory overhead					123,900
Current costs			$1,432,500	$240,000	$310,400
Current cost per current equivalent unit			$19.10	$3.20	$4.00

EXHIBIT 23—10

NORTHBROOK CHEMICAL COMPANY
BOTTLING DEPARTMENT
PRODUCTION COST REPORT
FOR THE MONTH OF JUNE, 1993

FIFO Method	Total Cost	Unit Cost
Costs to be accounted for:		
Prior month costs	$ 184,880	
Transferred in this month	1,432,500	
Direct material	240,000	
Direct labor	186,500	
Factory overhead	123,900	
Total costs to be accounted for	$2,167,780	
Costs accounted for:		
Transferred out:		
Beginning work in process:		
Prior month	$ 184,880	
Material (0 × $3.20)	–0–	
Conversion (5,600 × $4.00)	22,400	
Transferred in and finished:		
Transferred in (70,000 × $19.10)	1,337,000	
Material (70,000 × $3.20)	224,000	
Conversion (70,000 × $4.00)	280,000	
Total costs transferred out	$2,048,280	$26.26
Ending work in process:		
Transferred in (5,000 × $19.10)	$ 95,500	
Material (5,000 × $3.20)	16,000	
Conversion (2,000 × $4.00)	8,000	
Ending work in process	$ 119,500	
Total costs accounted for	$2,167,780	

OBJECTIVE 6 EXPLAIN *the procedures used to prepare the production cost report using the FIFO method in a process costing system.*

Three groups of cost are to be accounted for on the production cost report in Exhibit 23-10: (1) prior month costs (beginning work in process for the Bottling Department), (2) costs transferred in this month (transferred into the Bottling Department from the Mixing Department), and (3) direct material, direct labor, and factory overhead (current month costs incurred in the Bottling Department). All of these costs are accounted for either as transferred out (to finished goods) or ending work in process (for the Bottling Department).

All prior month costs ($184,880) are included with the beginning work in process in the transferred-out section. Because materials are added only at the start of the bottling process, no material cost for June is added to the beginning work in process. Since 5,600 equivalent units of conversion work were added during June, $22,400 of conversion cost is added (5,600 × $4). These conversion costs completed the 8,000 units in the beginning work in process inventory.

The transferred in and finished section and the ending work in process section are handled the same way the started and finished section and the ending work in process section were handled for the Mixing Department. As a result of the calculations of Exhibit 23-10, $2,048,280 representing 78,000 units was transferred from the Bottling Department work in process inventory to the finished goods inventory with a unit cost of $26.26.

WHAT IS PRODUCTIVITY?

Productivity can mean different things to different people. In our view, productivity, in its simplest terms, means maximizing the return on investment of manufacturing resources, whether those resources are facilities, equipment, or people. ■ Improving productivity is not merely making more products per hour or shift but making more usable units of production at the same cost. For many manufacturers, the key to achieving greater productivity is increasing the efficiency and effectiveness of their manufacturing process by eliminating labor and materials waste. How can this

be accomplished? By simplifying product and component design, streamlining process flow, reducing production runs, and managing for quality.

As more and more American manufacturers today realize, unless they are concurrently improving quality, cost, and speed of delivery, they are not truly enhancing productivity.

In our view, despite their investment in technology, manufacturers for whom productivity is a problem have not made adequate investment in their work force. We find this to be a common situation among many growing manufacturers. After committing to a major investment in capital goods, they overlook training, incentive compensation, flexible benefits, and other programs that have a positive impact on the "people" side of their productivity equation.

SOURCE: *Grant Thornton Survey of American Manufacturers* (New York: Grant Thornton, 1990), pp. 23–25. Reprinted with permission from The Grant Thornton Survey of American Manufacturers, 1990.

OBJECTIVE ⑦ IDENTIFY *the journal entries to transfer product cost from work in process inventory accounts to Finished Goods Inventory to Cost of Goods Sold.*

The following journal entry transfers the cost of finished work in the Bottling Department during June:

Finished Goods Inventory	2,048,280	
Work in Process—Bottling Department		2,048,280

To transfer cost of finished work from the Bottling Department to finished goods inventory.

The work in process inventory account for the Bottling Department would now appear as follows:

WORK IN PROCESS—BOTTLING DEPARTMENT

June 1 (beginning balance)	184,880	Transferred to finished goods	2,048,280
Transferred in from Mixing Department	1,432,500		
Direct material	240,000		
Direct labor	186,500		
Factory overhead	123,900		
June 30 (ending balance)	119,500		

All costs accumulated to this point have now been accounted for.

Finished Goods and Cost of Goods Sold

In the cost flows for a process costing system, the journal entries to record sales are similar to those made in a job order system. We assume that, during June, Northbrook sold goods costing $1,800,000 for $2,400,000. In summary form, the following journal entries reflect the sales:

Accounts Receivable	2,400,000	
Sales		2,400,000
To record June sales.		
Cost of Goods Sold	1,800,000	
Finished Goods Inventory		1,800,000
To record cost of goods sold in June.		

An Overview of Process Costing

As you review the Northbrook Chemical Company example, note these basic patterns and relationships in process costing:

1. Product costs are accumulated in three pools: direct material, direct labor, and factory overhead; the latter two are grouped together and called *conversion costs.*
2. Physical units to be accounted for include any beginning work in process and any units started (or transferred in). Physical units are accounted for by transferring them out or retaining them as ending work in process.
3. All cost factors, including any beginning inventory costs, are combined as work in process and must be accounted for.
4. Two primary methods—FIFO and weighted average—are used to assign costs.

ACCOUNTING FOR SERVICE DEPARTMENTS

OBJECTIVE 8 DESCRIBE *the procedures for cost allocation for service departments.*

Service Departments as Cost Centers

Most factories are so large and so complex that a high degree of organizational specialization naturally exists in their operations. Production usually involves a series of specialized departments, such as cutting, preshaping, grinding, subassembly, final assembly, painting, and packaging. In addition to these production departments, a typical factory also has highly specialized **service departments,** which may be involved with purchasing, materials handling, personnel, warehousing, inspection, maintenance, and even food service (cafeterias). Whereas production departments work directly on products, service departments provide production departments with support services that contribute indirectly to the completion of products.

Service departments are often viewed by management as cost centers. That is, the costs of each service department are accumulated separately so management can identify the total cost of such services. Also, unit costs for each service—such as maintenance cost per square foot of floor space—can be derived for comparison with other operating periods and/or other sources of the service such as outside contractors. A well-designed accounting system accounts for service departments as cost centers.

Service Department Costs as Product Costs

Although service departments do not perform actual work on specific products, they do provide essential services to the production departments. Thus, service department costs are appropriately considered among the related production department costs and are included in final product costs. This section explains how service costs are accumulated and assigned to individual products.

By their nature, service departments do not use direct material or direct labor. Their costs are part of factory overhead. However, these departments do not work directly on a product, so overhead rates, in the strict sense, are not computed for them. Instead, service department costs are usually allocated to various production departments according to the approximate benefits received by each production department. In other words, service department costs become part of product costs by being allocated among several production departments, using the most appropriate allocation base for each, and becoming part of each production department's overhead to be applied to work in process.

The T-account diagram (with typical titles and amounts) in Exhibit 23-11 illustrates how service department costs (1) are accumulated on a cost center basis, (2) are allocated to one or more production departments, and (3) become part of the product costs when factory overhead is applied to work in process for each produc-

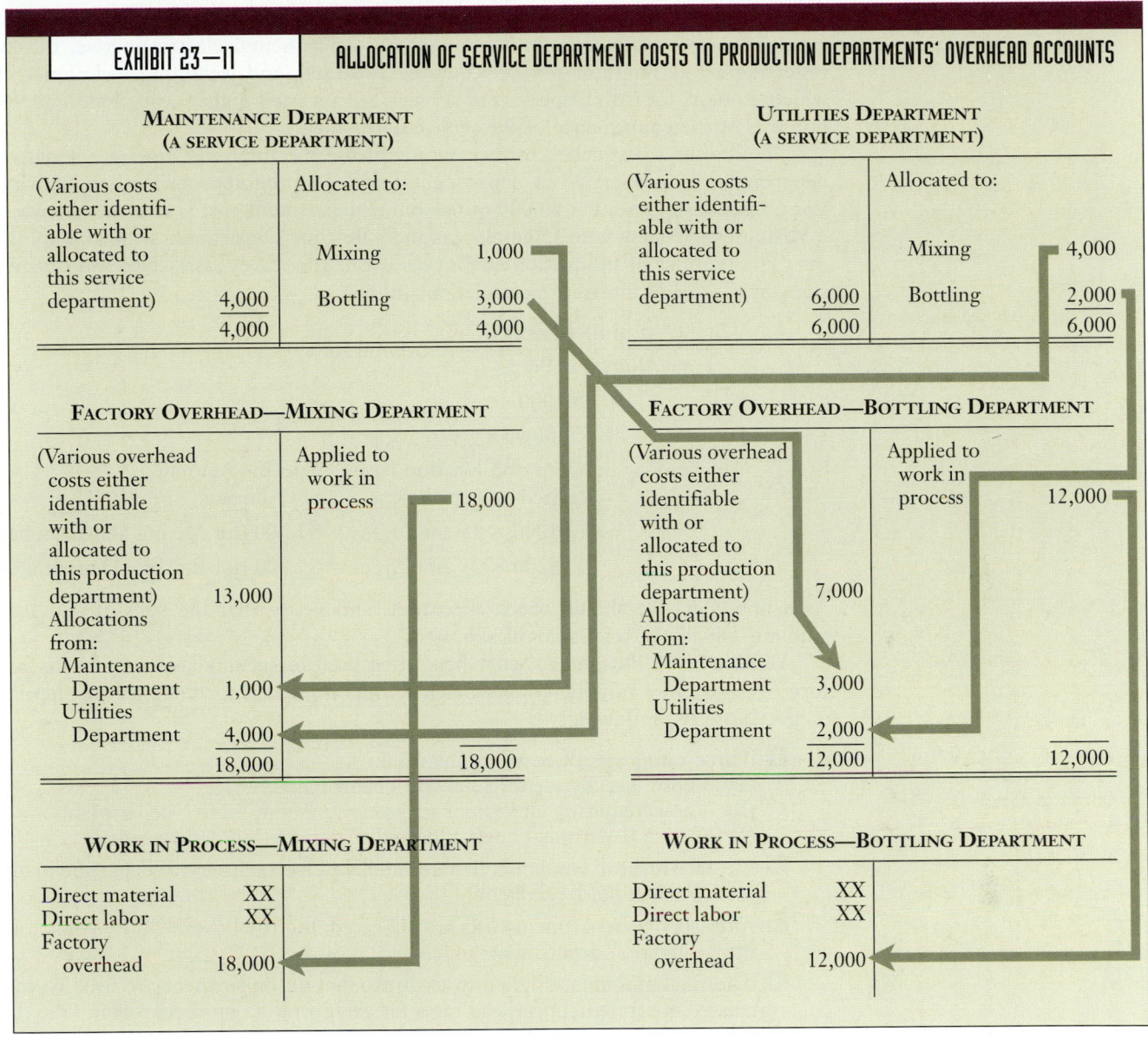

EXHIBIT 23—11 ALLOCATION OF SERVICE DEPARTMENT COSTS TO PRODUCTION DEPARTMENTS' OVERHEAD ACCOUNTS

tion department. To simplify this illustration, we assume that these amounts result in no over- or underapplied overhead.

Note that $4,000 is accumulated as the total cost for the Maintenance Department; then $1,000 and $3,000 are allocated to the Mixing and Bottling Departments, respectively. The allocated service department costs are in turn included in the totals of $18,000 and $12,000 of overhead costs applied from the respective production departments. Similar observations can be made for the Utilities Department.

Method of Cost Allocation

Costs are allocated among various departments on a basis that reflects the proportion of the service or activity that benefits each department. Some examples of allocated costs and their possible allocation bases follow:

Service Cost	Possible Allocation Basis
Personnel salaries	Number of employees in each department
Building depreciation	Square feet of floor space used
Utilities	Machine hours used
Building maintenance	Square feet of floor space used
Machine maintenance	Machine hours used
Heat and light	Cubic feet of building space used

The concern for cost control may justify the use of elaborate devices and schemes to measure service benefits. Some examples are departmental electric meters, tickets reflecting actual hours of service requested and used, and weighting techniques in which requests for rush or peak hour services are assigned higher costs than requests honored at the convenience of the service department.

To allocate a particular cost, we simply divide the total cost among a series of departments in proportion to departmental shares of the appropriate base activity. For example, suppose that $8,000 of personnel department cost is allocated between a Mixing Department with 15 employees and a Bottling Department with 25 employees. The number of production employees is the allocation basis. The two distinct steps involved and illustrative calculations follow:

1. $\dfrac{\text{Total Cost to Be Allocated}}{\text{Total Allocation Base}} = \text{Allocation Rate}$

$$\dfrac{\$8,000}{40 \text{ employees}} = \$200 \text{ per employee}$$

2. $\dfrac{\text{Allocation}}{\text{Rate}} \times \dfrac{\text{Amount of Allocation Basis}}{\text{Related to Department}} = \dfrac{\text{Specific Amount}}{\text{Allocated}}$

$$\$200 \times 15 \text{ employees} = \$3,000 \text{ (for Mixing Department)}$$
$$\$200 \times 25 \text{ employees} = \$5,000 \text{ (for Bottling Department)}$$

As a final step, we should check allocations and verify that the sum of allocated amounts equals the total amount allocated.

Exhibit 23-12 illustrates a worksheet often used to accumulate and allocate factory overhead in a multidepartment factory operation that includes service departments. Note the following:

1 Three categories of costs are involved:
  (a) Those directly identifiable with departments.
  (b) Those requiring allocations to production and service departments.
  (c) Service department costs allocated to production departments.

2 A total overhead amount is first accumulated for each service department and each production department.

3 After service department costs are allocated, the total overhead is assigned to the production departments only.

4 The final amounts assigned to each production department are used to calculate departmental overhead rates for each production department. (See the footnotes to Exhibit 23-12.)

The amounts, proportions, and variety of costs shown in Exhibit 23-12 have been chosen for simplicity of presentation to stress the basic concepts.

We might ask why service department costs are not allocated to other service departments. More sophisticated allocation techniques may involve allocations of some service department costs to other service departments and even mutual assignment of all of one or more service department costs to all other service departments. In many instances, these refinements do not result in materially different allocations; such detailed discussions are beyond our present objectives.

JOINT PRODUCTS

OBJECTIVE **9** IDENTIFY *joint product costs and byproduct costs and* DESCRIBE *techniques to account for them.*

Often, the processing of direct material results in two or more products of significant commercial value. Such products derived from a common input are **joint products,** and the related cost of the direct material is a **joint product cost.** An obvious example of a direct material whose processing results in joint products is crude oil, from which a variety of fuels, solvents, lubricants, and residual petrochemical pitches are derived. Cattle, from which the meat packer obtains many cuts and grades of meat, hides, and other products, are another example.

| **EXHIBIT 23—12** | **OVERHEAD DISTRIBUTION WORKSHEET FOR THE YEAR ENDED DECEMBER 31, 1993** |

	Totals	Service Departments		Production Departments		Allocation Basis
		Building Maintenance	Machine Repairs	Mixing	Bottling	
1 **Directly identifiable with departments**						
Indirect labor	85,000	8,000	20,000	38,500	18,500	Factory payroll analysis
Factory supplies used	24,000	3,000	2,000	9,000	10,000	Requisition forms
1 **Allocated to production and service departments**						
Building depreciation	6,000	600	1,200	3,000	1,200	Square feet of floor space
Personal property taxes	4,000	400	800	1,500	1,300	Assessed value of equipment used
2 Total overhead cost to be allocated	119,000	12,000	24,000	52,000	31,000	
1 **Allocation of service departments**						
Building maintenance (assumed as $\frac{2}{3}$ for mixing and $\frac{1}{3}$ for bottling)		(12,000)		8,000	4,000	Square feet of factory area used
Machinery repairs (assumed as $\frac{1}{6}$ for mixing and $\frac{5}{6}$ for bottling)			(24,000)	4,000	20,000	Machine hours
3 Totals	119,000	–0–	–0–	64,000*	55,000†	

4 *Assuming a factory overhead allocation basis of 20,000 machine hours, the overhead rate for the Mixing Department is $3.20 per machine hour ($64,000/20,000 machine hours).

†Assuming a factory overhead allocation basis of $110,000 direct labor, the overhead rate for the Bottling Department is 50 cents per direct labor dollar ($55,000/$110,000 direct labor).

It is impossible to allocate a joint product cost among joint products in such a way that management can decide whether to continue production or what price to charge for a joint product. To decide to produce one joint product is to decide to produce all related joint products, even if some are discarded. Therefore, to make informed decisions about joint products, management must compare the total revenue generated by all joint products with their total production costs.

The primary reason for allocating a joint product cost among two or more products is to assign cost to the ending inventories of joint products when determining periodic income. The most popular method of allocating joint product costs for inventory costing purposes is the **relative sales value method.** Like the cost allocations explained earlier, this approach uses arithmetic proportions. The total joint product cost is allocated to the various joint products in the proportions of their individual sales values to the total sales value of all joint products at the *split-off point*—that is, where physical separation takes place. For example, assume that 50,000 55-gallon barrels of crude oil costing $1,200,000 are processed into 800,000 gallons of fuel selling for 75 cents per gallon; 400,000 gallons of lubricants selling for $2 per gallon; and 1,000,000 gallons of petrochemical residues selling for 20 cents per gallon. The following calculations illustrate the joint product cost allocation using the relative sales value approach:

Joint Products	Quantity Produced (gallons)		Unit Sales Value		Product Sales Value	Proportion of Total Sales Value
Fuel	800,000	×	$0.75	=	$ 600,000	6/16
Lubricants	400,000	×	2.00	=	800,000	8/16
Residues	1,000,000	×	0.20	=	200,000	2/16
Total sales value					$1,600,000	16/16

Allocations of joint product costs would be undertaken as follows:

	Proportion of Materials Cost	Allocated Cost		Quantity Produced		Cost per Unit
Fuel	6/16 × $1,200,000	$ 450,000	÷	800,000	=	$0.5625 per gallon
Lubricants	8/16 × $1,200,000	600,000	÷	400,000	=	$1.50 per gallon
Residues	2/16 × $1,200,000	150,000	÷	1,000,000	=	$0.15 per gallon
		$1,200,000				

Note that the relative sales value approach results in assigned unit costs that are the same percentage of the selling price for each product. In our illustration, the cost per unit equals 75% of the sales value per unit.

BYPRODUCTS

Byproducts have relatively little sales value compared with the other products derived from a particular process. Byproducts are considered incidental to the manufacture of the more important products. For example, the sawdust and shavings generated in a lumber planing mill or in a furniture factory's cutting department are byproducts.

We may account for byproducts by assigning them a cost equal to their sales value less any disposal costs. This net amount is charged to an inventory account for the byproduct and credited to the work in process account that was charged with the original materials. For example, consider a furniture factory in which walnut boards are processed through a cutting and shaping department. In processing $40,000 worth of lumber, 800 bushels of sawdust and shavings are generated, which, after treatment costing $80, can be sold for $1 per bushel. The following accounts illustrate the amounts and entries involved:

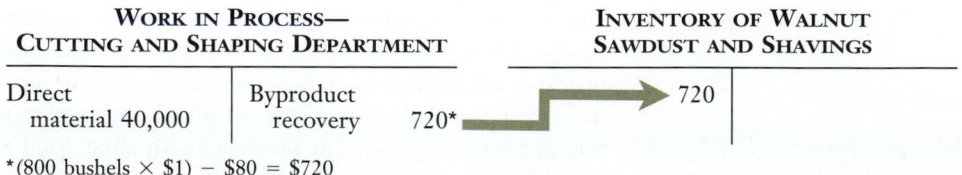

WORK IN PROCESS— CUTTING AND SHAPING DEPARTMENT		**INVENTORY OF WALNUT SAWDUST AND SHAVINGS**
Direct material 40,000	Byproduct recovery 720*	720

*(800 bushels × $1) − $80 = $720

This procedure reduces the costs of the main products by the net amount recovered from byproducts.

KEY POINTS FOR CHAPTER OBJECTIVES

① COMPARE and CONTRAST job order costing and process costing (p. 864).
- Job order costing is used when production consists of a variety of different products or customer orders. Process costing is used when production consists of a large volume of the same product produced in a continual flow.

② DESCRIBE the basic concepts of process costing (pp. 864–865).
- There is a separate work in process account for each department with process costing, whereas there is only one work in process account with job order costing.
- Perpetual inventory techniques flow product cost from work in process to finished goods to cost of goods sold during the accounting period when job order costing is used; end-of-period entries are required to flow product cost from work in process to finished goods to cost of goods sold when process costing is used.
- Products flow through multiple departments that are arranged in either a sequential pattern or a parallel pattern.

③ EXPLAIN techniques for determining unit costs when process costing is used (pp. 866–868).
- When work in process inventories exist at the beginning and the end of the accounting period, the measurement of work accomplished requires that partially finished units be converted to equivalent units for accounting purposes.
- When materials are added at a different rate than conversion work is accomplished, equivalent units must be computed separately for material and conversion.

④ ILLUSTRATE the journal entries used with process costing (pp. 868–870).
- Product cost flows and the related journal entries during the accounting period are similar for process costing and job order costing except for the transfer of product cost to finished goods and cost of goods sold.

⑤ DESCRIBE the calculation of equivalent units and costs per equivalent unit using the FIFO method in a multiple department process costing system (pp. 870–871, 873).
- In assigning manufacturing costs, one must consider three batches of product: units from beginning work in process, units started and finished this period, and units remaining in the ending work in process.
- Under the FIFO method, costs per equivalent unit are calculated by dividing current costs by current equivalent units; prior period costs and equivalent units are excluded from these calculations but are included in the total costs to be accounted for.

⑥ EXPLAIN the procedures used to prepare the production cost report using the FIFO method in a process costing system (pp. 871–872, 874).
- The total cost accounted for in any particular department includes costs associated with units transferred in from prior departments.
- Costs associated with the prior accounting period are included as part of the cost of the units transferred out.

⑦ IDENTIFY the journal entries to transfer product cost from work in process inventory accounts to Finished Goods Inventory to Cost of Goods Sold (pp. 872, 875–876).

⑧ DESCRIBE the procedures for cost allocation for service departments (pp. 876–878).
- Service department costs are overhead costs that are allocated to production departments and eventually assigned to products as part of the production department's overhead.
- Each different service cost may be allocated using a different allocation basis.

⑨ IDENTIFY joint product costs and byproduct costs and DESCRIBE techniques to account for them (pp. 878–880).
- Joint products are products of significant value originating from a common direct material or process. Joint product costs are allocated among joint products primarily for inventory costing purposes.
- Byproducts have relatively insignificant sales values and are assigned costs equal to their net recoverable value, which is removed from the related work in process account and charged to an appropriate inventory account.

SELF-TEST QUESTIONS FOR REVIEW

(Answers follow the Solution to Demonstration Problem 2.)

1. Which of the following costs will not be part of product cost when using a process costing system?

      a. Prior department cost.   **c.** Byproduct cost.
      b. Conversion cost.   **d.** Material cost.

  2. For which of the following will there be multiple accounts in the general ledger when using process costing?
      a. Finished goods.   **c.** Materials.
      b. Work in process.   **d.** Factory payroll.

  3. Which of the following will be excluded from the calculation of equivalent units when FIFO is used?
      a. Prior department units transferred in.
      b. Ending inventory units.
      c. Beginning inventory units.
      d. Units sold.

  4. Which of the following is not one of the categories of cost involved in the allocation of service department costs?
      a. Service department costs allocated to production departments.
      b. Costs directly identifiable with departments.
      c. Costs requiring allocation to departments.
      d. Selling department costs.

  5. What basis should be used to allocate joint product costs to the individual products?
      a. Quantity Sold × Unit Sales Price.
      b. Quantity Produced × Unit Sales Price.
      c. Quantity Sold × Unit Cost.
      d. Quantity Produced × Unit Cost.

DEMONSTRATION PROBLEM 1 FOR REVIEW

Arlington Manufacturing, Inc., produces a liquid polish in two sequential processes organized as the Mixing Department and the Bottling Department. Direct material is added initially in the Mixing Department and evenly throughout the Bottling Department. All conversion cost in both departments is added evenly throughout the process. The following are cost data for May 1993:

	Mixing Department	Bottling Department
Beginning work in process inventory	$ 42,360	$126,100
Operating costs for May:		
Direct material	360,000	242,900
Direct labor	211,200	109,200
Factory overhead	316,800	203,100
	$930,360	$681,300

Beginning work in process consisted of 20,000 gallons (30% complete) in the Mixing Department and 25,000 gallons (20% complete) in the Bottling Department. During May, 180,000 gallons were started in the Mixing Department. Ending work in process consisted of 30,000 gallons (40% complete) in the Mixing Department and 22,000 gallons (25% complete) in the Bottling Department. Assume that Arlington uses the FIFO method for process costing.

REQUIRED

a. Prepare a production report for May for the two departments.
b. For the Mixing Department
   1. Prepare a cost per equivalent unit report for May.
   2. Prepare a production cost report for May.
   3. Prepare journal entries to record the transfer of completed units.
c. For the Bottling Department
   1. Prepare a cost per equivalent unit report for May.
   2. Prepare a production cost report for May.
   3. Prepare journal entries to record the transfer of completed units.

SOLUTION TO DEMONSTRATION PROBLEM 1

a.

ARLINGTON MANUFACTURING, INC.
PRODUCTION REPORT
FOR THE MONTH OF MAY, 1993

	Mixing Department		Bottling Department	
	Percentage Processed	Units	Percentage Processed	Units
Beginning work in process	30%	20,000	20%	25,000
Started during May		180,000		
Transferred in during May				170,000
Units to be accounted for		200,000		195,000
Transferred out during May		170,000		173,000
Ending work in process	40%	30,000	25%	22,000

b. 1.

ARLINGTON MANUFACTURING, INC.
MIXING DEPARTMENT
COST PER EQUIVALENT UNIT REPORT
FOR THE MONTH OF MAY, 1993

FIFO Method	Units Involved	Conversion Completed This Month	Material (added initially)	Conversion (added throughout)
Current equivalent units:				
Transferred out:				
Beginning work in process (30%)	20,000	70%	–0–	14,000
Started and finished this month	150,000	100%	150,000	150,000
Units transferred out this month	170,000			
Ending work in process (40%)	30,000	40%	30,000	12,000
Units accounted for	200,000			
Current equivalent units			180,000	176,000
Current costs:				
Direct material			$360,000	
Direct labor				$211,200
Factory overhead				316,800
Current costs			$360,000	$528,000
Current cost per current equivalent unit			$2	$3

b. 2.

ARLINGTON MANUFACTURING, INC.
MIXING DEPARTMENT
PRODUCTION COST REPORT
FOR THE MONTH OF MAY, 1993

FIFO Method	Total Cost	Unit Cost
Costs to be accounted for:		
Prior month costs	$ 42,360	
Direct material	360,000	
Direct labor	211,200	
Factory overhead	316,800	
Total costs to be accounted for	$930,360	
Costs accounted for:		
Transferred out:		
Beginning work in process:		
Prior month	$ 42,360	
Material (0 × $2)	–0–	
Conversion (14,000 × $3)	42,000	

Started and finished:		
Material (150,000 × $2)	300,000	
Conversion (150,000 × $3)	450,000	
Total costs transferred out	$834,360	$4.908
Ending work in process:		
Material (30,000 × $2)	$ 60,000	
Conversion (12,000 × $3)	36,000	
Ending work in process	$ 96,000	
Total costs accounted for	$930,360	

b. 3. Work in Process—Bottling Department 834,360
Work in Process—Mixing Department 834,360
To record completion of 170,000 units at a cost of $4.908 per unit
and their transfer to the Bottling Department.

c. 1.
ARLINGTON MANUFACTURING, INC.
BOTTLING DEPARTMENT
COST PER EQUIVALENT UNIT REPORT
FOR THE MONTH OF MAY, 1993

FIFO Method:	Units Involved	Conversion Completed This Month	Transferred In	Material (added throughout)	Conversion (added throughout)
Current equivalent units:					
Transferred out:					
Beginning work in process (20%)	25,000	80%	–0–	20,000	20,000
Transferred in and finished	148,000	100%	148,000	148,000	148,000
Units transferred out this month	173,000				
Ending work in process (25%)	22,000	25%	22,000	5,500	5,500
Units accounted for	195,000				
Current equivalent units			170,000	173,500	173,500
Current costs:					
Costs transferred in from Mixing Department			$834,360		
Direct material				$242,900	
Direct labor					$109,200
Factory overhead					203,100
Current costs			$834,360	$242,900	$312,300
Current cost per current equivalent unit			$4.908	$1.40	$1.80

c. 2.
ARLINGTON MANUFACTURING, INC.
BOTTLING DEPARTMENT
PRODUCTION COST REPORT
FOR THE MONTH OF MAY, 1993

FIFO Method	Total Cost	Unit Cost
Costs to be accounted for:		
Prior month costs	$ 126,100	
Transferred in this month	834,360	
Direct material	242,900	
Direct labor	109,200	
Factory overhead	203,100	
Total costs to be accounted for	$1,515,660	
Costs accounted for:		
Transferred out:		
Beginning work in process:		
Prior month	$ 126,100	
Material (20,000 × $1.40)	28,000	
Conversion (20,000 × $1.80)	36,000	

Transferred in and finished:

Transferred in (148,000 × $4.908)	726,384	
Material (148,000 × $1.40)	207,200	
Conversion (148,000 × $1.80)	266,400	
Total costs transferred out	$1,390,084	$8.035

Ending work in process:

Transferred in (22,000 × $4.908)	$ 107,976
Material (5,500 × $1.40)	7,700
Conversion (5,500 × $1.80)	9,900
Ending work in process	$ 125,576
Total costs accounted for	$1,515,660

c. 3.

Finished Goods Inventory	1,390,084	
Work in Process—Bottling Department		1,390,084

To record completion of 173,000 units at a cost of $8.035 per unit and their transfer to finished goods inventory.

This chapter illustrates the concept of equivalent units, the cost flows and journal entries in process costing, and the FIFO method of assigning product cost to the goods transferred out of processing departments as well as the ending work in process accounts of the processing departments. This appendix illustrates the use of the weighted average method to assign product cost to the goods transferred out and to the ending work in process inventories.

In this appendix, we will continue the Northbrook Chemical Company example introduced in the chapter. Recall that, as a result of the journal entries recorded during the month, the work in process accounts at the end of June contained the following balances:

	Mixing Department	Bottling Department
Beginning balance	$ 106,500	$184,880
Direct material	704,000	240,000
Direct labor	298,400	186,500
Factory overhead	486,800	123,900
	$1,595,700	$735,280

Exhibit H–1 shows the June production report for the two processing departments. Note the following key observations about the production report:

1. All unit figures are in whole gallons rather than in equivalent units.

2. In the Mixing Department, the beginning work in process (10,000) plus units started (80,000) constitute the total number of units to be accounted for (90,000). The 90,000 units are accounted for as units transferred out (75,000) plus units in ending work in process (15,000) of the Mixing Department.

3. For the Bottling Department, the beginning work in process (8,000) plus units transferred in from the Mixing Department (75,000) constitute the total number of units to be accounted for (83,000). The 83,000 units are accounted for as units transferred out to finished goods (78,000) plus units in ending work in process (5,000) of the Bottling Department.

4. The number of units transferred out of the Mixing Department (75,000) is equal to the number of units transferred into the Bottling Department (75,000).

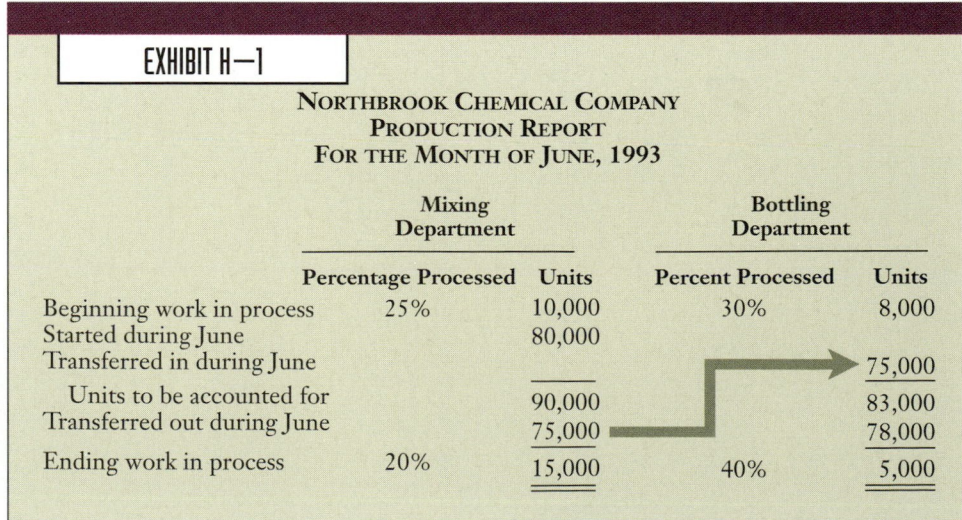

EXHIBIT H–1

NORTHBROOK CHEMICAL COMPANY
PRODUCTION REPORT
FOR THE MONTH OF JUNE, 1993

	Mixing Department		Bottling Department	
	Percentage Processed	Units	Percent Processed	Units
Beginning work in process	25%	10,000	30%	8,000
Started during June		80,000		
Transferred in during June				75,000
Units to be accounted for		90,000		83,000
Transferred out during June		75,000		78,000
Ending work in process	20%	15,000	40%	5,000

We now examine how costs are allocated to the various units, beginning with the Mixing Department.

Mixing Department

In the Mixing Department, materials are added at the start of the mixing process, but conversion costs are incurred evenly throughout the process. Therefore, we must calculate equivalent units and cost per equivalent unit separately for material and conversion costs. Exhibit H-2 presents these calculations in a cost per equivalent unit report. It is important to note that, with the weighted average method, total equivalent units and total costs are included in the cost per equivalent unit calculations. *Total* means that both prior month and current month amounts are included.

In allocating costs to various units of product, three batches of Kleeno are considered: (1) units finished from the June 1 inventory, (2) units started and finished in June, and (3) units started but not finished in June. The composition of costs for the three batches of product handled by the Mixing Department is explained below and in the production cost report in Exhibit H-3.

1. **Beginning inventory** The 10,000 gallons in the beginning inventory had all the material ($84,400 cost) and 25% of the required conversion work ($22,100 cost) added in May, for a $106,500 total cost in that month. The remaining 75% of the conversion work was completed in June. All of the costs, both current month and prior month, were included in the costs per equivalent unit. Therefore, we multiply the equivalent units of material (10,000) by the cost per equivalent unit for material ($8.76) and the equivalent units of conversion (10,000) by the cost per equivalent unit for conversion ($10.35) to obtain the cost assigned to the units in the beginning work in process—$87,600 for material and $103,500 for conversion.

EXHIBIT H-2

NORTHBROOK CHEMICAL COMPANY
MIXING DEPARTMENT
COST PER EQUIVALENT UNIT REPORT
FOR THE MONTH OF JUNE, 1993

Weighted Average Method	Units Involved	Total Conversion Completed	Material (added initially)	Conversion (added throughout)
Total equivalent units:				
Transferred out:				
Beginning work in process (25%)	10,000	100%	10,000	10,000
Started and finished this month	65,000	100%	65,000	65,000
Units transferred out this month	75,000			
Ending work in process (20%)	15,000	20%	15,000	3,000
Units accounted for	90,000			
Total equivalent units			90,000	78,000
Total costs:				
Prior month			$ 84,400	$ 22,100
Direct material			704,000	
Direct labor				298,400
Factory overhead				486,800
Total costs			$788,400	$807,300
Total cost per total equivalent unit			$8.76	$10.35

EXHIBIT H—3

Northbrook Chemical Company
Mixing Department
Production Cost Report
For the Month of June, 1993

Weighted Average Method	Total Cost	Unit Cost
Costs to be accounted for:		
Prior month costs	$ 106,500	
Direct material	704,000	
Direct labor	298,400	
Factory overhead	486,800	
Total costs to be accounted for	$1,595,700	
Costs accounted for:		
Transferred out:		
Beginning work in process:		
Material (10,000 × $8.76)	$ 87,600	
Conversion (10,000 × $10.35)	103,500	
Started and finished:		
Material (65,000 × $8.76)	569,400	
Conversion (65,000 × $10.35)	672,750	
Total costs transferred out	$1,433,250	$19.11
Ending work in process:		
Material (15,000 × $8.76)	$ 131,400	
Conversion (3,000 × $10.35)	31,050	
Ending work in process	$ 162,450	
Total costs accounted for	$1,595,700	

2. **Started and finished in June**   During June, all required material and conversion work were applied to the 65,000 gallons started and finished. The material added this month at $8.76 per gallon and the conversion work completed at $10.35 are applied to each of the 65,000 gallons. The total cost of the 75,000 gallons in the two batches transferred to the Bottling Department amounts to $1,433,250, and the average cost of the two batches is $19.11 per gallon ($1,433,250/75,000).

3. **Ending inventory**   The 15,000 units started but not finished in June contain all required material but only 20% of the needed conversion work. Therefore, we multiply the per-unit material cost of $8.76 by 15,000 gallons to obtain the $131,400 material cost. We then multiply the $10.35 conversion cost by the 3,000 equivalent units of conversion to obtain the $31,050 conversion cost.

Notice that the production cost report fully accounts for both the 90,000 units of product involved and the total costs of $1,595,700 charged to the Mixing Department.

The following entry transfers the cost of the work completed in the Mixing Department during June to the Bottling Department:

Work In Process—Bottling Department	1,433,250	
Work In Process—Mixing Department		1,433,250

To transfer cost of completed work from Mixing to Bottling.

The work in process inventory account for the Mixing Department would now appear as follows:

WORK IN PROCESS—MIXING DEPARTMENT

June 1 (beginning balance)	106,500	Transferred to Bottling	
Direct material	704,000	Department	1,433,250
Direct labor	298,400		
Factory overhead	486,800		
June 30 (ending balance)	162,450		

Note that all costs charged to this account have been accounted for either as transferred out or as ending work in process inventory.

Bottling Department

In the Bottling Department, materials are added at the start of the process, and conversion costs are incurred evenly throughout the process. The units handled during June include 8,000 units from the beginning work in process inventory of the Bottling Department and the 75,000 units transferred in from the Mixing Department. The 8,000 units in the beginning inventory had $184,880 of product cost assigned to them in the prior month. The 75,000 units had $1,433,250 assigned to them in the Mixing Department prior to being transferred to the Bottling Department.

Again, we must convert the work performed into equivalent units and obtain costs per equivalent unit. Exhibit H-4 presents the cost per equivalent unit report for the Bottling Department, and Exhibit H-5 presents the production cost report for the Bottling Department.

The cost per equivalent unit report for the Bottling Department differs from the same report for the Mixing Department in that transferred-in costs must be accounted for in the Bottling Department. As a result, there is a Transferred in column added to the cost per equivalent unit report for the Bottling Department. As Exhibit H-4 demonstrates, three cost per equivalent unit amounts are calculated: transferred in, material, and conversion.

EXHIBIT H—4

NORTHBROOK CHEMICAL COMPANY
BOTTLING DEPARTMENT
COST PER EQUIVALENT UNIT REPORT
FOR THE MONTH OF JUNE, 1993

Weighted Average Method	Units Involved	Total Conversion Completed	Transferred In	Material (added initially)	Conversion (added throughout)
Total equivalent units:					
Transferred out:					
Beginning work in process (30%)	8,000	100%	8,000	8,000	8,000
Transferred in and finished	70,000	100%	70,000	70,000	70,000
Units transferred out this month	78,000				
Ending work in process (40%)	5,000	40%	5,000	5,000	2,000
Units accounted for	83,000				
Total equivalent units			83,000	83,000	80,000
Total costs:					
Prior month (detail from prior month)			$ 154,540	$ 23,940	$ 6,400
Costs transferred in from Mixing Department			1,433,250		
Direct material				240,000	
Direct labor					186,500
Factory overhead					123,900
Total costs			$1,587,790	$263,940	$316,800
Total cost per total equivalent unit			$19.13	$3.18	$3.96

EXHIBIT H—5

NORTHBROOK CHEMICAL COMPANY
BOTTLING DEPARTMENT
PRODUCTION COST REPORT
FOR THE MONTH OF JUNE, 1993

Weighted Average Method	Total Cost	Unit Cost
Costs to be accounted for:		
Prior month costs	$ 184,880	
Transferred in from Mixing Department	1,433,250	
Direct material	240,000	
Direct labor	186,500	
Factory overhead	123,900	
Total costs to be accounted for	$2,168,530	
Costs accounted for:		
Transferred out:		
Beginning work in process:		
Transferred in (8,000 × $19.13)	$ 153,040	
Material (8,000 × $3.18)	25,440	
Conversion (8,000 × $3.96)	31,680	
Transferred in and finished:		
Transferred in (70,000 × $19.13)	1,339,100	
Material (70,000 × $3.18)	222,600	
Conversion (70,000 × $3.96)	277,200	
Total costs transferred out	$2,049,060	$26.27
Ending work in process:		
Transferred in (5,000 × $19.13)	$ 95,650	
Material (5,000 × $3.18)	15,900	
Conversion (2,000 × $3.96)	7,920	
Ending work in process	$ 119,470	
Total costs accounted for	$2,168,530	

The percentages of conversion completed this month in Exhibit H-4 are calculated exactly as before. Since the beginning work in process inventory in the Bottling Department was 30% finished, and since we assume that these units were finished during June, then the percentage of conversion work finished during June was 70% (100% − 30%).

It should be noted that the transferred-in cost per equivalent unit in Exhibit H-4 is not the same as the transferred-out unit cost in Exhibit H-3. When the weighted average method is used, the two amounts usually are not the same, since the calculation for the Bottling Department's transferred-in cost per equivalent unit includes both the cost transferred in during the current month and the cost transferred in during the prior month.

Three groups of cost are to be accounted for on the production cost report in Exhibit H-5: (1) prior month costs (beginning work in process for the Bottling Department); (2) costs transferred in this month (transferred into the Bottling Department from the Mixing Department); and (3) direct material, direct labor, and factory overhead (current month costs incurred in the Bottling Department). All of these costs are accounted for as either transferred out (to finished goods) or as ending work in process (for the Bottling Department).

All prior month costs ($184,880) are included in the costs per equivalent unit. Therefore, cost is assigned to the units in the beginning work in process by multiplying the 8,000 total equivalent units by the cost per equivalent unit for transferred in ($19.13), material ($3.18), and conversion cost ($3.96). The resulting costs are $153,040, $25,440, and $31,680, respectively.

The transferred in and finished section and the ending work in process section are handled the same way the started and finished section and the ending work in process section were handled in the Mixing Department for the weighted average method. As a result of the calculations of Exhibit H-5, $2,049,060 representing 78,000 units were transferred from the Bottling Department work in process inventory to the finished goods inventory with a unit cost of $26.27.

The following entry transfers the cost of completed work in the Bottling Department during June:

Finished Goods Inventory	2,049,060	
Work In Process—Bottling Department		2,049,060
To transfer cost of completed work from the Bottling Department		
to finished goods inventory.		

The work in process inventory account for the Bottling Department would now appear as follows:

WORK IN PROCESS—BOTTLING DEPARTMENT

June 1 (beginning balance)	184,880	Transferred to	
Transferred in from		finished goods	2,049,060
Mixing Department	1,433,250		
Direct material	240,000		
Direct labor	186,500		
Factory overhead	123,900		
June 30 (ending balance)	119,470		

Again, note that all costs accumulated to this point have been accounted for.

Finished Goods and Cost of Goods Sold

In the cost flows for a process costing system, the journal entries to record sales are similar to those made in a job order costing system. We assume that, during June, Northbrook sold goods costing $1,800,000 for $2,400,000. In summary form, the following entries reflect the sales:

Accounts Receivable	2,400,000	
Sales		2,400,000
To record June sales.		
Cost of Goods Sold	1,800,000	
Finished Goods Inventory		1,800,000
To record cost of goods sold during June.		

DEMONSTRATION PROBLEM 2 FOR REVIEW

Using the data for Arlington Manufacturing, Inc., that is presented in Demonstration Problem 1, assume that Arlington uses the weighted average method for process costing. The beginning work in process inventories include the following costs:

	Mixing Department	Bottling Department
Material cost	$28,000	$3,430
Conversion cost	14,360	5,430

REQUIRED

a. Prepare a production report for May for the two departments.
b. For the Mixing Department
  1. Prepare a cost per equivalent unit report for May.
  2. Prepare a production cost report for May.

3. Prepare a journal entry to record the transfer of completed units.

c. For the Bottling Department

1. Prepare a cost per equivalent unit report for May.

2. Prepare a production cost report for May.

3. Prepare a journal entry to record the transfer of completed units.

SOLUTION TO DEMONSTRATION   **a.**
PROBLEM 2

ARLINGTON MANUFACTURING, INC.
PRODUCTION REPORT
FOR THE MONTH OF MAY, 1993

	Mixing Department		Bottling Department	
	Percentage Processed	**Units**	**Percentage Processed**	**Units**
Beginning work in process	30	20,000	20	25,000
Started during May		180,000		
Transferred in during May				170,000
Units to be accounted for		200,000		195,000
Transferred out during May		170,000		173,000
Ending work in process	40	30,000	25	22,000

b. 1.

ARLINGTON MANUFACTURING, INC.
MIXING DEPARTMENT
COST PER EQUIVALENT UNIT REPORT REPORT
FOR THE MONTH OF MAY, 1993

Weighted Average Method	**Units Involved**	**Total Conversion Completed**	**Material (added initially)**	**Conversion (added throughout)**
Total equivalent units:				
Transferred out:				
Beginning work in process (30%)	20,000	100%	20,000	20,000
Started and finished this month	150,000	100%	150,000	150,000
Units transferred out this month	170,000			
Ending work in process (40%)	30,000	40%	30,000	12,000
Units accounted for	200,000			
Total equivalent units			200,000	182,000
Total costs:				
Prior month			$ 28,000	$ 14,360
Direct material			360,000	
Direct labor				211,200
Factory overhead				316,800
Total costs			$388,000	$542,360
Total cost per total equivalent unit			$1.94	$2.98

b. 2.

ARLINGTON MANUFACTURING, INC.
MIXING DEPARTMENT
PRODUCTION COST REPORT
FOR THE MONTH OF MAY, 1993

Weighted Average Method	**Total Cost**	**Unit Cost**
Costs to be accounted for:		
Prior month costs	$ 42,360	
Direct material	360,000	
Direct labor	211,200	
Factory overhead	316,800	
Total costs to be accounted for	$930,360	

Costs accounted for:
  Transferred out:
    Beginning work in process:

Material (20,000 × $1.94)	$ 38,800	
Conversion (20,000 × $2.98)	59,600	

    Started and finished:

Material (150,000 × $1.94)	291,000	
Conversion (150,000 × $2.98)	447,000	
Total costs transferred out	$836,400	$4.92

  Ending work in process:

Material (30,000 × $1.94)	$ 58,200
Conversion (12,000 × $2.98)	35,760
Ending work in process	$ 93,960
Total costs accounted for	$930,360

b. 3.

Work in Process—Bottling Department	836,400	
Work in Process—Mixing Department		836,400

To record completion of 170,000 units at a cost of $4.92 per unit and their transfer to the Bottling Department.

c. 1.

ARLINGTON MANUFACTURING, INC.
BOTTLING DEPARTMENT
COST PER EQUIVALENT UNIT REPORT
FOR THE MONTH OF MAY, 1993

Weighted Average Method:	Units Involved	Total Conversion Completed	Transferred In	Material (added throughout)	Conversion (added throughout)
Total equivalent units:					
Transferred out:					
Beginning work in process (20%)	25,000	100%	25,000	25,000	25,000
Transferred in and finished	148,000	100%	148,000	148,000	148,000
Units transferred out this month	173,000				
Ending work in process (25%)	22,000	25%	22,000	5,500	5,500
Units accounted for	195,000				
Total equivalent units			195,000	178,500	178,500
Total costs:					
Prior month			$117,240	$ 3,430	$ 5,430
Costs transferred in from Mixing Department			834,360		
Direct material				242,900	
Direct labor					109,200
Factory overhead					203,100
Total costs			$951,600	$246,330	$317,730
Total cost per total equivalent unit			$4.88	$1.38	$1.78

c. 2.

ARLINGTON MANUFACTURING, INC.
BOTTLING DEPARTMENT
PRODUCTION COST REPORT
FOR THE MONTH OF MAY, 1993

Weighted Average Method	Total Cost	Unit Cost
Costs to be accounted for:		
Prior month costs	$ 126,100	
Transferred in from department 1	834,360	
Direct material	242,900	
Direct labor	109,200	
Factory overhead	203,100	
Total costs to be accounted for	$1,515,660	

Costs accounted for:
Transferred out:
Beginning work in process:

Transferred in (25,000 × $4.88)	$ 122,000	
Material (25,000 × $1.38)	34,500	
Conversion (25,000 × $1.78)	44,500	

Transferred in and finished:

Transferred in (148,000 × $4.88)	722,240	
Material (148,000 × $1.38)	204,240	
Conversion (148,000 × $1.78)	263,440	
Total costs transferred out	$1,390,920	$8.04

Ending work in process:

Transferred in (22,000 × $4.88)	$ 107,360	
Material (5,500 × $1.38)	7,590	
Conversion (5,500 × $1.78)	9,790	
Ending work in process	$ 124,740	
Total costs accounted for	$1,515,660	

c. 3. Finished Goods Inventory	1,390,920	
Work in Process—Bottling Department		1,390,920

To record completion of 173,000 units at a cost of $8.04 per unit
and their transfer to finished goods inventory.

ANSWERS TO SELF-TEST QUESTIONS

1. c, p. 873   **2.** b, p. 864   **3.** d, p. 873   **4.** d, p. 877   **5.** b, p. 880

GLOSSARY OF KEY TERMS USED IN THIS CHAPTER

byproducts Those products having relatively little sales value compared with other products derived from a process. An example would be the wood shavings generated in the shaping department of a furniture factory (p. 880).

conversion costs The direct labor and factory overhead costs in a manufacturing process (p. 867).

cost per equivalent unit report A report for a manufacturing department that identifies the period's production in equivalent units, the materials and conversion costs, and the cost per equivalent unit of production (p. 871).

equivalent units The smaller number of full measures of work accomplished that is the equivalent of a larger number of partially accomplished work units. For example, 1,000 units 60% processed is equivalent to 600 units fully processed (p. 867).

joint product cost The product cost associated with joint products that is derived from the common inputs (p. 878).

joint products Two or more products having significant value and derived from common inputs such as materials (p. 878).

process costing A method of assigning costs to relatively homogeneous products in an often continual, high-volume manufacturing process (p. 864).

production cost report A report that allocates a department's total production costs for a period to units transferred out and to units in ending work in process (p. 871).

production report A report (usually for a department) showing the beginning inventory of units, units started, units finished and transferred out, and ending inventory of units (p. 870).

relative sales value method A method of allocating joint product costs among two or more products. The joint cost is allocated to the products in the proportions of their individual sales values to the total sales value of all the joint products at the split-off point (p. 880).

service departments Departments or cost centers that provide special support activities to various production departments. Examples include purchasing, personnel, and maintenance (p. 876).

QUESTIONS

23-1 What are the important differences between job order and process costing systems? Give as examples two industries that might use each system.

23-2 How are all manufacturing costs for a series of processing departments accumulated as finished goods inventory?

23-3 Why do unit cost computations in a manufacturing process require equivalent unit computations?

23-4 Why do we say that process cost accounting is basically an averaging computation?

23-5 What is meant by the term *equivalent unit*?

23-6 Why must we sometimes compute equivalent units separately for materials and for conversion costs?

23-7 Describe the three batches of products that are typically involved in a period's production under the FIFO accounting method. In what special situation are there only two batches?

23-8 What is meant by the expression that in each department's work in process account all charges must be accounted for either as being transferred out or as ending work in process inventory?

23-9 Contrast service departments with production departments. Give three examples of a service department.

23-10 Why might service departments be treated as cost centers?

23-11 Explain what each of the following statements means:
a. Service departments do not work directly on products.
b. Service department costs are factory overhead costs.
c. Overhead rates are not used for service departments.
d. In spite of part (c), service department costs become part of product costs.

23-12 How do we choose a basis for allocating a cost to several departments?

23-13 How is an allocation rate calculated? How is the specific amount allocated to a department calculated?

23-14 Briefly describe the general format, data, and calculations that would appear on an overhead distribution worksheet for a company with a number of production and service departments.

23-15 Define *joint product*, and give as examples two industries that have joint products because of the nature of the materials used.

23-16 If allocated joint product costs are irrelevant for management decisions, how do we justify allocating joint costs among joint products?

23-17 Define *byproduct*, and briefly describe an accepted procedure in accounting for byproducts.

EXERCISES

PRODUCTION REPORT AND EQUIVALENT UNITS — OBJ. 5, 6 —

23-18 Ferris Corporation makes a powdered rug shampoo in two sequential departments, Compounding and Drying. Materials are added initially in the Compounding Department and evenly throughout the Drying Department. Conversion costs are added evenly throughout each process. The FIFO method is used for process costing. In the Compounding Department, beginning work in process was 4,000 pounds (70% processed), 37,000 pounds were started in process, 36,000 pounds transferred out, and ending work in process was 60% processed. In the Drying Department, beginning work in process was 2,000 pounds (25% processed), 32,000 pounds were transferred out, and the ending work in process was 40% processed. Prepare a production report for March 1993, and calculate equivalent units for each department.

COST FLOWS THROUGH JOURNAL ENTRIES — OBJ. 4, 7 —

23-19 The Mixing Department performs the last of a series of processes in which a fluid chemical is concentrated. Records indicate that the Mixing Department has been charged with $180,000 of transferred-in costs from the Compounding Department and $64,000 of direct labor costs. The factory overhead rate is 150% of direct labor costs. Beginning work in process was $44,000, and ending work in process totaled $34,000. One-half of this period's completed product is sold on account at a price equal to 160% of its cost. Prepare journal entries to record (1) various costs charged to the Mixing Department this period, (2) transfer of this period's completed product, and (3) sale of one-half of this period's production.

EQUIVALENT UNITS
CALCULATIONS
— OBJ. 5 —

23-20 The following are selected operating data for the Blending Department for August. Painting and packaging operations are carried out subsequently in other departments.

Beginning inventory	3,000 units, 70% complete
Started and completed	60,000 units
Ending inventory	5,000 units, 40% complete

Calculate the equivalent units accomplished using the FIFO method, assuming that
a. All material is added and conversion accomplished evenly throughout the process.
b. The material is added initially and conversion costs are incurred evenly throughout.

EQUIVALENT UNITS AND
PRODUCT COST
ASSIGNMENT
— OBJ. 5, 6 —

23-21 In its first month's operation, Department 1 incurred charges for direct material (10,000 units) of $120,000, direct labor of $33,000, and factory overhead of $58,000. At month-end, 8,800 units had been finished and transferred out; those remaining were finished with respect to material but only 25% finished with respect to conversion. Assuming that the FIFO method is used and that materials are added initially and conversion occurs evenly, compute the following:
a. The equivalent units for material and conversion.
b. The cost per equivalent unit for material and conversion.
c. The total cost assigned to the units transferred out.
d. The total cost assigned to the ending inventory. Demonstrate that your solutions to requirements (c) and (d) account for the total cost involved.

EQUIVALENT UNITS AND
COSTS ANALYSES
— OBJ. 5, 6 —

23-22 Following is the work in process account (and certain annotations) for the first of four departments in which Crocker Company makes its only product.

WORK IN PROCESS—DEPARTMENT 1

Beginning balance (2,000 units, 70% complete)	25,100	Transferred to Department 2: (20,000 units)	_____	(a)
Direct material (21,000 units)	157,500			
Direct labor	145,200			
Factory overhead	48,300			
Ending balance [_____ (b) units, 25% complete]	_____ (c)			

Assuming that the FIFO method is used and that materials are added initially and conversion costs are incurred evenly throughout, compute the amounts necessary to fill in the three blanks.

EQUIVALENT UNITS AND
PRODUCT COST
ASSIGNMENT
— OBJ. 5, 6 —

23-23 Following are the June charges (and certain annotations) appearing in the work in process account for Sutter Company's final processing department:

Beginning inventory (700 units, 40% complete)	$10,780
Transferred in from preceding department (5,000 units)	50,000
Direct labor	59,600
Factory overhead applied	22,800

The FIFO method is used. Conversion costs are incurred evenly throughout and ending work in process totals 900 units, 70% complete. Compute the following:
a. Equivalent units for transferred in and conversion.
b. Cost per equivalent unit for transferred in and conversion.
c. Total cost assigned to the units transferred out.

SERVICE DEPARTMENT
COST ALLOCATION
— OBJ. 8 —

23-24 Presented below are certain operating data for the four departments of Tally Manufacturing Company.

	Service		Production	
	1	2	1	2
Total overhead costs either identifiable with or allocated to each department	$60,000	$72,000	$90,000	$98,000
Square feet of factory floor space			40,000	80,000
Number of factory workers			50	10
Planned direct labor hours for the year			20,000	30,000

Allocate to the two production departments the costs of service departments 1 and 2 using factory floor space and number of workers, respectively, as bases. What is the apparent overhead rate for each production department if planned direct labor hours is the overhead application base?

JOINT PRODUCT COST ALLOCATION
— OBJ. 9 —

23-25 Windsor Manufacturing, Inc., produces joint products A, B, and C from a common material, a batch of which costs $2,400,000. At the point at which each product is separated, the following quantities and unit sales prices are available:

Product	Quantity (pounds)	Selling Price per Pound
A	72,000	$15.00
B	60,000	36.00
C	240,000	1.50

Using the relative sales value method, calculate the amount of joint product cost assigned to a pound of each product.

PROBLEMS

CALCULATE UNITS STARTED AND EQUIVALENT UNITS
— OBJ. 5 —

23-26 Easton Corporation manufactures quality placemats in three consecutive processing departments: Cutting, Printing, and Packaging. The following information is taken from unit product reports for July, 1993:

	Units in Beginning Inventory	Percentage Complete	Units Started in July	Units in Ending Inventory	Percentage Complete
Cutting Department	6,000	70	60,000	7,000	40
Printing Department	10,000	40	?	11,000	60
Packaging Department	9,000	30	?	6,000	20

Materials are added at the start of the process in the Cutting Department and evenly throughout processing in the Packaging Department. No material is used in the Printing Department. Conversion costs are incurred evenly in all processing departments. The FIFO method is used to compute equivalent units and cost inventories.

REQUIRED

a. Calculate the number of units started or transferred in during July in the Printing and Packaging Departments.
b. Calculate the equivalent units relating to transferred-in, material, and conversion costs in each department.

CALCULATE EQUIVALENT UNITS AND COSTS; JOURNAL ENTRIES
— OBJ. 5, 7 —

23-27 Stevens, Inc., produces a film developer in two sequential processes designated Phase I and Phase II. Stevens shut down during June, 1993, when all employees took their annual vacations. As a result, there were no work in process inventories on July 1. Production resumed on July 1. The following operating data apply to July:

	Phase I	Phase II
Units started in process	220,000	
Units transferred in from Phase I		190,000
Ending work in process:		
Units	30,000	30,000
Percent complete	40%	30%
Costs charged to departments:		
Direct material	$444,400	$253,500
Direct labor	136,500	135,800
Factory overhead	146,300	168,400

Assume all manufacturing costs are incurred evenly throughout each process, that 80% of July's production was sold on account at a price equal to 150% of its cost, and that the FIFO method was used.

REQUIRED

a. Briefly explain the July 31 status of the units started in process during July.
b. For each department, prepare a cost per equivalent unit report for July.

c. Prepare journal entries to record the completion and transfer of products from each department and the sale of 80% of July's production.

CALCULATE UNITS, COSTS, AND TRANSFERRED COSTS — OBJ. 5, 6 —

23-28 Godfrey Manufacturing, Inc., operates a plant that produces its own regionally marketed Spicy Steak Sauce. The sauce is produced in two processes, blending and bottling. In the Blending Department, all materials are added at the start of the process, and labor and overhead are incurred evenly throughout the process. Godfrey uses the FIFO method. The Work in Process—Blending Department account for January 1993 with some items missing follows:

WORK IN PROCESS—BLENDING DEPARTMENT

January 1 inventory (5,000 gallons, 60% processed)	17,900	Transferred to Bottling Department (60,000 gallons)	_____
January charges:			
Direct material (61,000 gallons)	152,500		
Direct labor	73,600		
Factory overhead	48,800		
January 31 inventory (_____ gallons, 70% processed) _____			

REQUIRED

Calculate the following amounts for the Blending Department:
a. Number of units in the January 31 inventory.
b. Equivalent units for material cost and conversion cost.
c. January cost per equivalent unit for conversion.
d. Cost of the units transferred to the Bottling Department.
e. Cost of the incomplete units in the January 31 inventory.

CALCULATE UNITS, COSTS, AND TRANSFERRED COSTS — OBJ. 5, 6 —

23-29 Arrow Company processes a food seasoning powder through its Compounding Department and Packaging Department. In the Packaging Department, costs of direct material, direct labor, and factory overhead are incurred evenly throughout the process. Arrow uses the FIFO method. Costs in the Packaging Department for August 1993 follow:

Inventory, August 1 (2,000 units, 40% complete)	$ 5,080
Transferred in from Compounding Department (31,000 units)	93,000
Direct material	15,050
Direct labor	28,560
Factory overhead	34,650
	$176,340

At August 31, 3,000 units were in process, 30% finished.

REQUIRED

Calculate the following for the Packaging Department:
a. Equivalent units during August.
b. Costs per equivalent unit.
c. Total cost of units transferred to finished goods inventory.
d. Inventory cost at August 31.

JOURNAL ENTRIES WITH SUPPORTING CALCULATIONS — OBJ. 4, 7 —

23-30 Patterson Laboratories, Inc., produces one of its products in two successive departments. All materials are added at the beginning of the process in Department 1; no materials are used in Department 2. Conversion costs are incurred evenly in both departments. Patterson uses the FIFO method for process costing. January 1, 1993, inventory account balances are as follows:

Materials Inventory	$30,000
Work in Process—Department 1 (3,000 units, 30% complete)	15,200
Work in Process—Department 2 (4,000 units, 40% complete)	48,100
Finished Goods Inventory (2,000 units @ $16)	32,000

During January, the following transactions occurred:
1. Purchased material on account, $90,000.

2. Placed $84,000 of material into process in Department 1. This represented 24,000 units.
3. Distributed total payroll costs: $108,000 of direct labor to Department 1, $62,700 of direct labor to Department 2, and $51,000 of indirect labor to Factory Overhead.
4. Incurred other actual factory overhead costs, $81,000. (Credit Other Accounts.)
5. Applied overhead to the two processing departments: $88,000 to Department 1 and $43,900 to Department 2.
6. Transferred 25,000 completed units from Department 1 to Department 2. The 2,000 units remaining in Department 1 were 20% completed with respect to conversion costs.
7. Transferred 26,000 completed units from Department 2 to finished goods inventory. The 3,000 units remaining in Department 2 were 75% completed with respect to conversion costs.
8. Sold 20,000 units on account at $27 per unit. Patterson uses FIFO inventory costing procedures for the finished goods inventory.

REQUIRED
a. Record the January transactions in general journal form.
b. Determine the balances remaining in the Materials Inventory account, in each work in process account, and in the Finished Goods Inventory account.

**PRODUCTION COST
REPORT
— OBJ. 5, 6 —**

23-31 Reston Manufacturing Corporation produces a cosmetic product in three consecutive processes. The costs of Department 2 for May 1993 were as follows:

Cost of beginning inventory		$ 26,390
Cost from Department 1		580,000
Costs added in Department 2:		
Direct material	$80,400	
Direct labor	81,550	
Factory overhead	55,130	217,080

Department 2 handled the following units during May:

Units in process, May 1	2,000
Units transferred in from Department 1	40,000
Units transferred to Department 3	39,000
Units in process, May 31	3,000

On average, the May 1 units were 30% complete; the May 31 units were 60% complete. Both material and conversion costs occur evenly throughout the process in Department 2. Reston uses the FIFO method for process costing.

REQUIRED
Prepare the production cost report for Department 2 for May.

**OVERHEAD DISTRIBUTION
WORKSHEET
— OBJ. 8 —**

23-32 The following are selected operating data for the production and service departments of Bluestone Company for 1993.

	Departments			
	Service		Production	
	1	2	1	2
Overhead costs (identified by department)				
Indirect material	$48,400	$ 82,200	$254,400	$ 516,000
Indirect labor	$97,200	$144,000	$325,840	$1,439,000
Square feet of building floor space used	4,800	7,200	12,000	24,000
Assessed value of equipment used	$21,000	$ 63,000	$126,000	$ 210,000
Cubic yards of factory space used			88,000	132,000
Machine hours			51,200	204,800
Direct labor			$200,000	$ 400,000

Building depreciation of $96,000 is allocated on the basis of square feet of floor space. Personal property taxes of $36,000 are allocated on the basis of assessed values of equipment used. Costs for service departments 1 and 2 are allocated to production departments on the basis of cubic yards of factory space and machine hours, respectively.

REQUIRED

a. Prepare a 1993 overhead distribution worksheet for Bluestone Company similar to the one prepared for Exhibit 23-12.
b. Compute the factory overhead rates for production departments 1 and 2 using machine hours and direct labor costs, respectively, for allocation bases.

ALLOCATING JOINT PRODUCT COSTS — OBJ. 9 —

23-33 McGregor Company produces joint products R and S and byproduct T from a common material and manufacturing process involving sequential processing departments for blending and distilling. After distilling, the three products are separable and considered finished goods.

Because of the nature of the operation, no beginning or ending work in process inventories exist. During March 1993, charges to Work in Process—Distilling Department were as follows:

Transferred in from Blending Department	$152,200
Direct labor	36,300
Factory overhead	58,700
	$247,200

REQUIRED

Assume that the following quantities and sales prices are available when the products are separable:

Product	Quantity (pounds)	Unit Price
R	20,000	$ 6
S	30,000	12
T	5,000	2*

*Special freight charges of $800 are incurred in selling byproduct T for this price.

a. Allocate the joint product costs to each joint product on the basis of relative sales value.
b. Prepare March 31 journal entries to record the product completed in and transferred from the Distilling Department to Finished Goods Inventory during March.

STARTED AND EQUIVALENT UNITS — APPENDIX H —

23-34 Using the data in Problem 23-26, assume that Easton Corporation uses the weighted average method for process costing.

REQUIRED

a. Calculate the number of units started or transferred in during July in the Printing and Packaging departments.
b. Calculate the equivalent units relating to transferred-in, material, and conversion costs in each department.

PRODUCTION COST REPORT — APPENDIX H —

23-35 Morrow Manufacturing Company uses the weighted average method for process costing. Morrow produces processed food products that pass through three sequential departments. The costs for Department 2 for September 1993 were as follows:

Cost of beginning inventory:		
Transferred in from Department 1	$30,000	
Material	850	
Conversion	1,480	$ 32,330
Cost from Department 1 during September		730,000
Costs added in Department 2 during September:		
Direct material	$71,750	
Direct labor	72,370	
Factory overhead	51,990	196,110

Department 2 handled the following units during September:

Units in process, September 1	2,000
Units transferred in from Department 1	48,000
Units transferred out to Department 3	46,000
Units in process, September 30	4,000

On average, the September 1 units were 30% complete, and the September 30 units were 60% complete. Both material and conversion costs occur evenly throughout the process in Department 2.

REQUIRED

Prepare the production cost report for September for Department 2.

ALTERNATE EXERCISES

PRODUCTION REPORT AND EQUIVALENT UNITS
— OBJ. 5, 6 —

23-18A Terrace Corporation makes an industrial cleaner in two sequential departments, Compounding and Drying. All material is added initially in the Compounding Department. Conversion costs are added evenly throughout each process. The FIFO method is used for process costing. In the Compounding Department, beginning work in process was 2,000 pounds (60% processed), 34,000 pounds were started, 32,000 pounds transferred out, and ending work in process was 70% processed. In the Drying Department, beginning work in process was 4,000 pounds (25% processed), 30,000 pounds were transferred out, and the ending work in process was 30% processed. Prepare a production report for August 1993, and calculate equivalent units for each department.

COST FLOWS THROUGH JOURNAL ENTRIES
— OBJ. 4, 7 —

23-19A The Mixing Department performs the last of a series of processes in which a fluid chemical is concentrated. Records indicate that the Mixing Department has been charged with $140,000 of transferred-in costs from the Compounding Department and $50,000 of direct labor costs. The factory overhead rate is 170% of direct labor costs. Beginning work in process was $30,000, and ending work in process totaled $36,000. One-half of this period's completed product is sold on account at a price equal to 150% of its cost. Prepare journal entries to record (1) various costs charged to the Mixing Department this period, (2) transfer of this period's completed product, and (3) sale of one-half of this period's production.

EQUIVALENT UNITS CALCULATIONS
— OBJ. 5 —

23-20A The following are selected operating data for the Blending Department for April. Tinting and packaging operations are carried out subsequently in other departments.

Beginning inventory	4,000 units, 60% complete
Started and completed	70,000 units
Ending inventory	6,000 units, 30% complete

Calculate the equivalent units accomplished using the FIFO method, assuming that

a. All material is added and conversion accomplished evenly throughout the process.

b. The material is added initially and conversion costs are incurred evenly throughout.

EQUIVALENT UNITS AND PRODUCT COST ASSIGNMENT
— OBJ. 5, 6 —

23-21A In its first month's operation, Department 1 incurred charges for direct material (9,000 units) of $72,000, direct labor of $38,700, and factory overhead of $13,500. At month-end, 8,500 units had been finished and transferred out; those remaining were finished with respect to material but only 40% finished with respect to conversion. Assuming that the FIFO method is used and that materials are added initially and conversion occurs evenly, compute the following:

a. The equivalent units for material and conversion.

b. The cost per equivalent unit for material and conversion.

c. The total cost assigned to the units transferred out.

d. The total cost assigned to the ending inventory. Prove that your solutions to requirements (c) and (d) account for the total cost involved.

EQUIVALENT UNITS AND COSTS ANALYSES
— OBJ. 5, 6 —

23-22A Following is the work in process account (and certain annotations) for the first of four departments in which Olympus Company makes its only product.

WORK IN PROCESS—DEPARTMENT 1

Beginning balance (3,000 units, 40% complete)	18,200	Transferred to Department 2: (23,000 units)	_____ (a)
Direct material (24,000 units)	96,000		
Direct labor	77,300		
Factory overhead	36,700		
Ending balance [_____ (b) units, 25% complete]	_____ (c)		

Assuming that the FIFO method is used and that materials are added initially and that conversion costs are incurred evenly throughout, compute the amounts necessary to fill in the three blanks.

EQUIVALENT UNITS AND PRODUCT COST ASSIGNMENT
— OBJ. 5, 6 —

23-23A Following are the September charges (and certain annotations) appearing in the work in process account for Empire Company's final processing department:

Beginning inventory (1,500 units, 70% complete)	$31,950
Transferred in from preceding department (6,000 units)	72,000
Direct labor	32,500
Factory overhead applied	52,200

The FIFO method is used. Conversion costs are incurred evenly throughout and ending work in process totals 1,000 units, 60% complete. Compute the following:
a. Equivalent units for transferred in and conversion.
b. Cost per equivalent unit for transferred in and conversion.
c. Total cost assigned to the units transferred out.

SERVICE DEPARTMENT COST ALLOCATION
— OBJ. 8 —

23-24A Presented below are certain operating data for the four departments of Modern Manufacturing Company.

	Service		Production	
	1	2	1	2
Total overhead costs either identifiable with or allocated to each department	$45,000	$60,000	$55,000	$116,000
Square feet of factory floor space			90,000	45,000
Number of factory workers			20	60
Planned direct labor hours for the year			25,000	32,000

Allocate to the two production departments the costs of service departments 1 and 2 using factory floor space and number of workers, respectively, as bases. What is the apparent overhead rate for each production department if planned direct labor hours is the overhead application base?

JOINT PRODUCT COST ALLOCATION
— OBJ. 9 —

23-25A Rullo Manufacturing, Inc., produces joint products A, B, and C from a common material, a batch of which costs $500,000. At the point at which each product is separated, the following quantities and unit sales prices are available:

Product	Quantity (pounds)	Selling Price per Pound
A	20,000	$10
B	25,000	20
C	10,000	30

Using the relative sales value method, calculate the amount of joint product cost assigned to a pound of each product.

ALTERNATE PROBLEMS

23-26A Dornbeck Corporation manufactures decorated planters in three consecutive processing departments: Construction, Painting, and Packaging. The following information is taken from unit product reports for September 1993:

CALCULATE UNITS STARTED AND EQUIVALENT UNITS — OBJ. 5 —	Units in Beginning Inventory	Percentage Complete	Units Started in September	Units in Ending Inventory	Percentage Complete
Construction Department	8,000	40	75,000	9,000	30
Painting Department	15,000	60	?	13,000	70
Packaging Department	12,000	20	?	11,000	40

Materials are added at the start of the process in the Construction Department and evenly throughout processing in the Packaging Department. No material is used in the Painting Department. Conversion costs are incurred evenly in all processing departments. The FIFO method is used to compute equivalent units and cost inventories.

REQUIRED

a. Calculate the number of units started or transferred in during September in the Painting and Packaging Departments.
b. Calculate the equivalent units relating to transferred in, material, and conversion costs in each department.

CALCULATE EQUIVALENT UNITS AND COSTS; JOURNAL ENTRIES — OBJ. 5, 7 —

23-27A Davidson, Inc., produces a shoe polish in two sequential processes designated Phase I and Phase II. Davidson shut down during August 1993, when all employees took their annual vacations. As a result, there were no work in process inventories on September 1. Production resumed on September 1. The following operating data apply to September:

	Phase I	Phase II
Units started in process	130,000	
Units transferred in from Phase I		110,000
Units in ending work in process (on the average, 40% processed)	20,000	10,000
Costs charged to departments:		
Direct material	$141,600	$187,200
Direct labor	206,900	147,100
Factory overhead	123,500	185,700

Assume that all manufacturing costs are incurred evenly throughout each process, that three-fourths of September production was sold on account at a price equal to 140% of its cost, and that the FIFO method was used.

REQUIRED

a. Briefly explain the September 30 status of the units started in process during September.
b. For each department, prepare a cost per equivalent unit report for September.
c. Prepare journal entries to record the finishing and transfer of products from each department and the sale of three-fourths of September's production.

CALCULATE UNITS, COSTS, AND TRANSFERRED COSTS — OBJ. 5, 6 —

23-28A Kipling Manufacturing, Inc., operates a plant that produces its own regionally marketed Super Salad Dressing. The dressing is produced in two processes, blending and bottling. In the Blending Department, all materials are added at the start of the process, and labor and overhead are incurred evenly throughout the process. Kipling uses the FIFO method. The Work in Process—Blending Department account for January 1993 follows:

WORK IN PROCESS—BLENDING DEPARTMENT

January 1 inventory (4,000 gallons, 75% finished)	40,000	Transferred to Bottling Department (70,000 gallons)	———
January charges:			
Direct material (71,000 gallons)	568,000		
Direct labor	164,000		
Factory overhead	186,000		
January 31 inventory (——— gallons, 60% processed)	———		

REQUIRED

Calculate the following amounts for the Blending Department:

a. Number of units in the January 31 inventory.
b. Equivalent units for material cost and conversion cost.
c. January cost per equivalent unit for conversion.
d. Cost of the units transferred to the Bottling Department.
e. Cost of the incomplete units in the January 31 inventory.

CALCULATE UNITS, COSTS,
AND TRANSFERRED COSTS
— OBJ. 5, 6 —

23-29A Bradford Company processes a scouring powder through its Compounding Department and Packaging Department. In the Packaging Department, costs of direct material, direct labor, and factory overhead are incurred evenly throughout the process. Bradford uses the FIFO method. Costs charged to the Packaging Department in October 1993 follow:

Inventory, October 1 (5,000 units, 25% complete)	$ 4,250
Transferred in from Compounding Department	
(82,000 units)	164,000
Direct material	81,550
Direct labor	31,770
Factory overhead	33,470
	$315,040

At October 31, 7,000 units were in process, 40% completed.

REQUIRED

Calculate the following for the Packaging Department:

a. Equivalent units during October.
b. Costs per equivalent unit.
c. Total cost of units transferred to finished goods inventory.
d. Inventory cost at October 31.

JOURNAL ENTRIES WITH
SUPPORTING
CALCULATIONS
— OBJ. 4, 7 —

23-30A Parker Laboratories, Inc., produces one of its products in two successive departments. All materials are added at the beginning of the process in Department 1; no materials are used in Department 2. Conversion costs are incurred evenly in both departments. August 1, 1993, inventory account balances are as follows:

Materials Inventory	$15,000
Work in Process—Department 1 (6,000 units, 25% finished)	30,250
Work in Process—Department 2 (4,000 units, 35% finished)	41,000
Finished Goods Inventory (4,000 units @ $12.50)	50,000

During August, the following transactions occurred:

1. Purchased material on account, $58,000.
2. Placed 16,000 units of material at $4 per unit into process in Department 1.
3. Distributed total payroll costs: $83,770 of direct labor to Department 1, $42,300 of direct labor to Department 2, and $19,100 of indirect labor to Factory Overhead.
4. Incurred other actual factory overhead costs, $21,200. (Credit Other Accounts.)
5. Applied overhead to the two processing departments: Department 1, $21,280, Department 2, $17,900.
6. Transferred 20,000 completed units from Department 1 to Department 2. The 2,000 units remaining in Department 1 were 30% completed with respect to conversion costs.
7. Transferred 15,000 completed units from Department 2 to Finished Goods Inventory. The 9,000 units remaining in Department 2 were 40% completed with respect to conversion costs.
8. Sold 13,000 units on account at $24 per unit. Parker uses FIFO inventory costing for finished goods inventory.

REQUIRED

a. Record the August transactions in general journal form.
b. Determine the balances remaining in the Materials Inventory account, in each work in process account, and in the Finished Goods Inventory account.

**PRODUCTION COST
REPORT
— OBJ. 5, 6 —**

23-31A Gomez Manufacturing Corporation produces a dandruff shampoo in three consecutive processes. The costs of Department 2 for June 1993 were as follows:

Cost of beginning inventory		$ 18,240
Cost from Department 1		540,000
Costs added in Department 2:		
Direct material	$59,670	
Direct labor	96,300	
Factory overhead	41,400	197,370

Department 2 handled the following units during June:

Units in process, June 1	2,000
Units transferred in from Department 1	45,000
Units transferred to Department 3	46,000
Units in process, June 30	1,000

On average, the June 1 units were 40% complete; the June 30 units were 70% complete. Both material and conversion costs occur evenly throughout the process in Department 2. Gomez uses the FIFO method for process costing.

REQUIRED

Prepare the production cost report for Department 2 for June.

**OVERHEAD DISTRIBUTION
WORKSHEET
— OBJ. 8 —**

23-32A The following are selected operating data for the production and service departments of Danville Company for 1993.

	Departments			
	Service		Production	
	1	2	1	2
Overhead costs (identified by department)				
Factory supplies used	$12,800	$21,440	$67,840	$137,600
Indirect labor	$25,920	$38,400	$86,400	$384,000
Square feet of building floor space used	7,200	10,800	18,000	36,000
Assessed value of equipment used	$28,000	$84,000	$168,000	$280,000
Cubic yards of factory space used			132,000	198,000
Machine hours			51,200	204,800
Direct labor ($10 per hour)			$250,000	$500,000

Building depreciation of $51,200 is allocated on the basis of square feet of floor space. Personal property taxes of $19,200 are allocated on the basis of assessed values of equipment used. Costs for service departments 1 and 2 are allocated to production departments on the basis of cubic yards of factory space and machine hours, respectively.

REQUIRED

a. Prepare a 1993 overhead distribution worksheet for Danville Company similar to the one prepared for Exhibit 23-12.

b. Compute the factory overhead rates for production departments 1 and 2 using machine hours and direct labor hours, respectively, for allocation bases.

**ALLOCATING JOINT
PRODUCT COSTS
— OBJ. 9 —**

23-33A Carlton Company produces joint products F and G and byproduct H from a common material and manufacturing process involving two sequential processing departments. After the second process, the three products are separable and considered finished goods.

Because of the nature of the operation, no beginning or ending work in process inventories exist. During June 1993, charges to Work in Process—Department 2 were as follows:

Transferred in from Department 1	$ 66,500
Direct labor	17,100
Factory overhead	26,800
	$110,400

REQUIRED

Assume that the following quantities and sales prices are available when the products are separable:

Product	Quantity (pounds)	Unit Price
F	15,000	$ 8.00
G	12,000	15.00
H	5,000	1.00*

*Special freight charges of $600 are incurred in selling product H for this price.

a. Allocate the joint product costs to each joint product on the basis of relative sales value.

b. Prepare June 30 journal entries to record the product completed in and transferred from Department 2 to finished goods inventory during June.

CALCULATE UNITS, COSTS, AND TRANSFERRED COSTS — APPENDIX H —

23-34A Using the data in Problem 23-28, assume that Godfrey Manufacturing, Inc., uses the weighted average method for process costing. The beginning work in process cost includes $9,332 of material and $8,568 of conversion cost.

REQUIRED

Calculate the following amounts for the Blending Department:

a. Number of units in the January 31 inventory.

b. Equivalent units for material and conversion cost.

c. January cost per equivalent unit of conversion.

d. Cost of the units transferred to the Bottling Department.

e. Cost of the incomplete units in the Jaunary 31 inventory.

PRODUCTION REPORT, COST PER EQUIVALENT UNIT REPORT, AND PRODUCTION COST REPORT — APPENDIX H —

23-35A Summers Manufacturing Corporation produces chemical products using a continual process. The weighted average method is used for process costing. All manufacturing is accomplished in one department. Material is added initially; conversion costs are incurred evenly throughout the process.

The work in process inventory at the beginning of February 1993 consisted of 10,000 units that were 20% complete. The work in process at the end of February consisted of 15,000 units that were 40% complete. During February 195,000 units were transferred to finished goods.

The beginning inventory contained $90,000 of material cost and $30,000 of conversion cost. Product costs incurred during February consisted of $2,010,000 of material and $3,186,000 of conversion.

REQUIRED

Prepare the production report, cost per equivalent unit report, and production cost report for Summers Manufacturing Corporation for the month of February.

CASES

Business Decision Case

Hall Manufacturing Corporation makes a new high-tech adhesive in a single process that blends and bottles the product, which currently sells for $20 per gallon. Market demand for the product seems good, but management is not satisfied with the product's seemingly low profit margin and has sought your advice.

Because of its concern, management has allocated a $60,000 fund for a program of product promotion or cost reduction, or both. Members of the firm's controller's office and marketing staff have identified the following three possible plans:

1. Plan A: Devote all funds to product promotion, which allows all costs and the sales volume to remain the same, but permits a $3.50 per gallon sales price increase.

2. Plan B: Spend $32,000 on product promotion and $28,000 on cost reduction techniques, which maintains sales volume, permits a price increase of $2 per gallon, and reduces conversion costs by 10% per gallon.

3. Plan C: Devote all funds to cost reduction efforts. Sales volume and price do not change. For each gallon produced, however, direct material cost decreases 10%, and conversion cost decreases 20%.

The controller's office also provides you with the following operating data for a typical period (all materials are added initially; conversion costs occur evenly throughout the process; the FIFO method is used for process costing):

Beginning work in process (2,500 gallons, 60% processed)	$ 32,250
Units started in process (34,000 gallons)	
Ending work in process (3,500 gallons, 60% processed)	
Costs charged to the department:	
Direct material	275,400
Direct labor	186,390
Factory overhead	156,330
	$650,370

Using the data from this representative production period, analyze the apparent relative benefits derived from each plan and make a recommendation supported by relevant calculations. Assume that sales for each period will equal units completed in that period.

Ethics Case

Sweet Fragrances Company uses process costing to account for the manufacture of its perfume. The factory consists of three departments: blending, bottling, and packaging.

The production manager of the bottling department, Janine Post, has recommended that her department not be charged for new labels that are more elaborate and expensive than those used in previous years. The new labels were designed as a tie-in for the marketing and advertising campaigns. Post recommends that the costs of the labels be charged to advertising expense. This would result in slightly lower product costs charged to the bottling department than last year.

The company has instituted a bonus plan for all managers based on keeping costs within a range of previous years' costs.

Sam Block, the accounting manager, reviews all recommendations by all managers before they are presented to top management.

REQUIRED

What ethical considerations may arise from Janine Post's recommendation? What alternative recommendations might be made?

What factors should a business consider when planning its future operations so it will break even or generate a profit?

When an entrepreneur considers starting a business, he or she estimates the demand for the planned product or service and calculates the level of sales required for the business to make money or at least break even. ■ When management of PepsiCo, Inc., is considering a new location for a Taco Bell, Pizza Hut, or KFC (Kentucky Fried Chicken) restaurant, it is very interested in the level of sales of their fast-food products necessary to achieve a desired level of profitability.

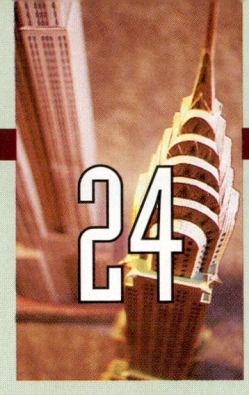

24

COST-VOLUME-PROFIT RELATIONSHIPS

anagement must study a number of factors when planning the future course for an organization. One of the most important factors is the relationship of sales (revenue), costs (expenses), and profit (net income). Cost-volume-profit analysis is used to study this relationship.

Cost-volume-profit analysis is appropriately used by for-profit organizations as well as not-for-profit organizations. The latter type of organization uses the analysis with a target profit of zero. All of the relationships studied in the analysis are equally valid for both types of organizations.

COST BEHAVIOR ANALYSIS

OBJECTIVE ① DEVELOP *an understanding of how specific types of costs change in response to volume changes.*

Cost behavior analysis is the study of the ways in which specific costs respond to changes in the volume of business activity. Each specific cost incurred by an organization may be affected differently by changes in the volume of business activity. Some costs will increase proportionately as volume increases, some costs will change disproportionately, and some costs will remain the same. Other factors besides volume can also cause changes in specific costs; an increase in the assessment rate, for example, can raise property tax expense, whereas a decrease in electricity rates can lower utility expense. These types of changes, however, are not typically caused by fluctuation in the volume of business activity.

Selecting the Activity Basis

For meaningful managerial analysis, costs must be related to some measure of volume of business activity. In a manufacturing operation, such measures include units of product, direct labor hours, machine hours, and percentage of capacity. The cost analyst must consider the use of the analysis when selecting the most relevant and useful activity basis to which costs can be related. For example, if management uses the analysis for control purposes and for establishing responsibility for costs, the analyst selects measures that are meaningful to those responsible for incurring costs. We may use several bases, depending on the objectives of the analysis.

Cost-Volume Graphs

One of the most useful analytic tools for relating cost changes to volume changes is the *cost-volume graph*. Exhibits 24-1 and 24-2 are examples of cost-volume graphs. In these two exhibits, costs (in thousands of dollars) are measured on the vertical axis, and volume (in thousands of units) is measured on the horizontal axis. Point A in Exhibit 24-1 shows that at a volume level of 30,000 units the associated cost is $20,000. Similarly, point B in Exhibit 24-1 represents a cost of $30,000 for a volume level of 50,000 units.

Cost-volume graphs are particularly valuable when available cost-volume data are plotted on the same graph and other cost-volume relationships are estimated by fitting a line to the known points. In Exhibit 24-2, for example, we use three known data points (an increased number of known data points should be used to develop a reliable graph). The known data points, represented by solid points, are as follows:

Volume (units)	Cost (dollars)
10,000	10,000
20,000	15,000
40,000	25,000

By connecting the known data points with a straight line, we may impute the costs associated with other levels of volume. For example, the open points indicate that for volumes of 5,000, 35,000, and 50,000 units, the related costs would be $7,500,

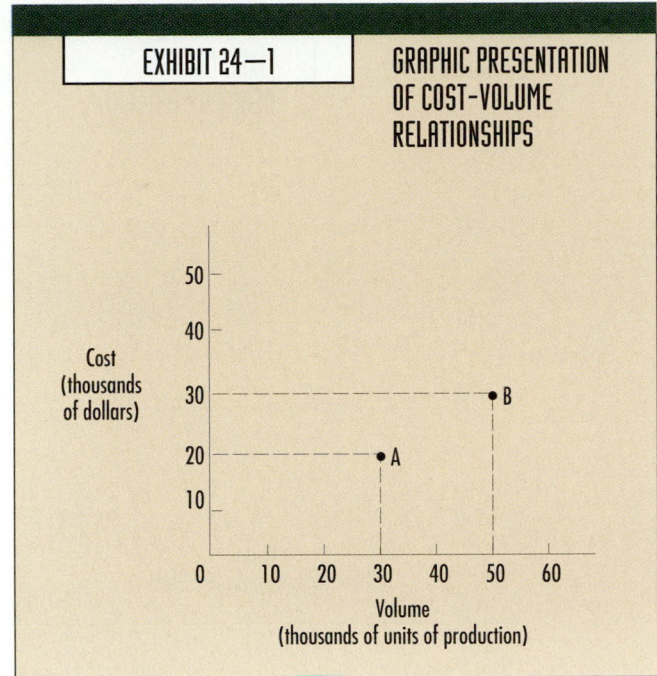

EXHIBIT 24—1 GRAPHIC PRESENTATION OF COST-VOLUME RELATIONSHIPS

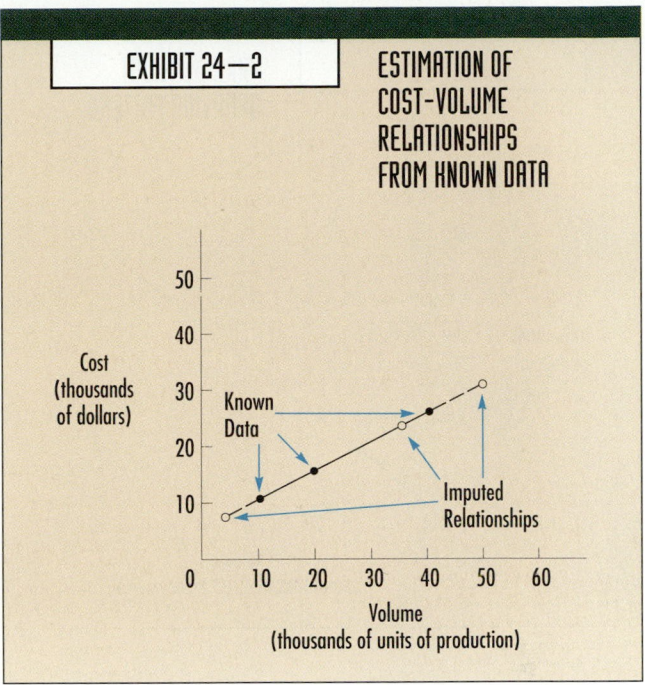

EXHIBIT 24—2 ESTIMATION OF COST-VOLUME RELATIONSHIPS FROM KNOWN DATA

$22,500, and $30,000, respectively. Some important limitations to the validity of this type of imputed cost-volume relationship are discussed later in the chapter.

Classifications of Cost Behavior Patterns

For purposes of analyzing their behavior patterns, costs are usually classified as *variable*, *fixed*, or *semivariable*. However, the classification of costs into these distinct groups is seldom a simple matter.

Despite the difficulties of classification, the study of approximate cost behavior patterns can aid in planning and analyzing operations. Let us examine the ways in which cost-volume graphs vary among the three cost classifications.

Variable costs change proportionately with changes in the volume of activity. Direct material cost and direct labor cost, for example, are variable costs.

Exhibit 24-3 is a typical variable cost graph. As illustrated here, a purely variable cost pattern always passes through the origin, because zero cost is associated with zero volume. Also, because variable costs respond in direct proportion to changes in volume, a variable cost line always slopes upward to the right. The steepness of the slope depends on the amount of cost associated with each unit of volume; the greater the unit cost, the steeper the slope. In Exhibit 24-3, volume is measured in direct labor hours, and the total variable dollar cost is twice as great at 40,000 hours as at 20,000 hours, as expected.

Fixed costs do not change when the volume of activity changes. Examples are depreciation on buildings and property taxes.

Since fixed costs do not respond to changes in volume, they are represented by horizontal lines on a cost-volume graph. In Exhibit 24-4, fixed costs are $80,000 regardless of the volume level considered.

Semivariable costs—sometimes called *mixed costs*—can be described analytically as having both fixed and variable components. A semivariable cost changes linearly with changes in activity, but is some positive amount at zero activity, as shown in Exhibit 24-5. Changes in total semivariable cost are therefore not proportional to changes in operating volume.

As an example of a semivariable cost, consider a firm's utility expense. Even if the firm shuts down production for one period, it typically must pay a minimum

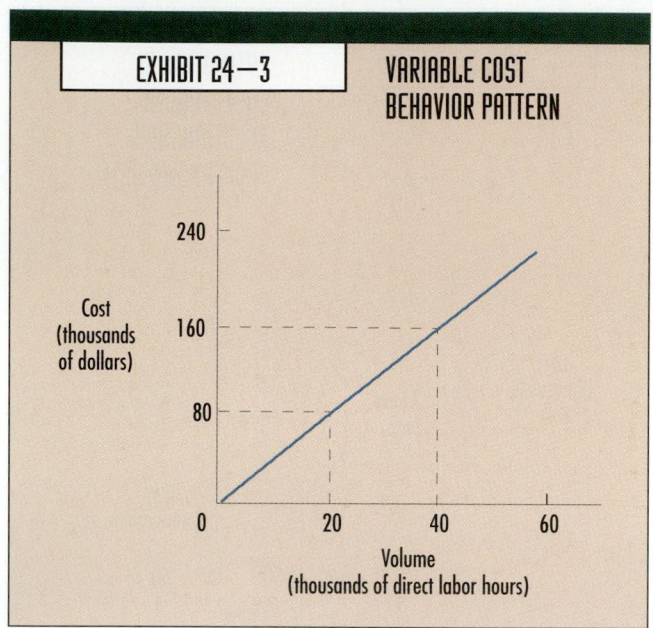

EXHIBIT 24—3   VARIABLE COST BEHAVIOR PATTERN

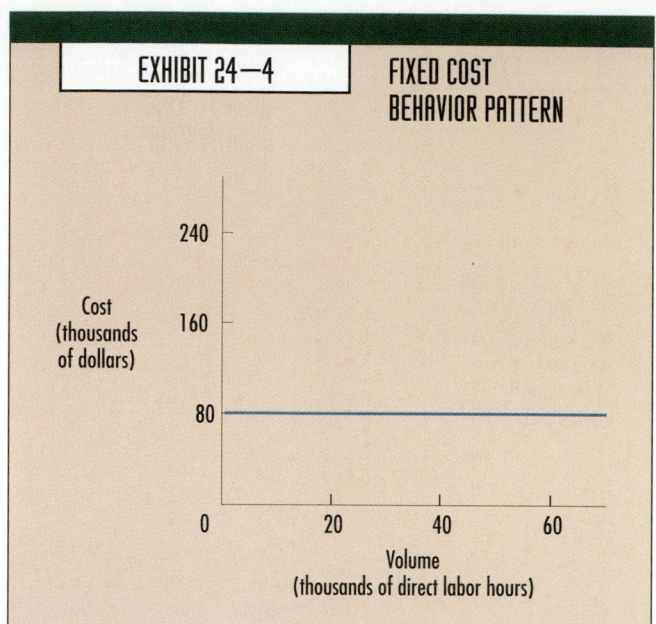

EXHIBIT 24—4   FIXED COST BEHAVIOR PATTERN

amount for utilities. When production resumes, the costs of heat, light, and power increase as production increases.

For purposes of cost analysis, a semivariable cost is divided into its fixed and variable components. We accomplish this by any one of several approaches that vary in their degree of sophistication. One simple method entails plotting on a graph the cost experienced at several levels of volume. If cost behavior in actual situations were perfectly correlated, the observations (points) would form a straight line. More realistically, however, we expect only a discernible pattern as shown in Exhibit 24-6.

The line in Exhibit 24-6 has been subjectively determined to approximate the pattern of data points. Extending this line to the vertical axis indicates a $1,000 fixed portion. We subtract this $1,000 fixed cost from the total $4,000 cost at 60,000 direct labor hours to find a total variable portion of $3,000. Therefore, the rate of variation

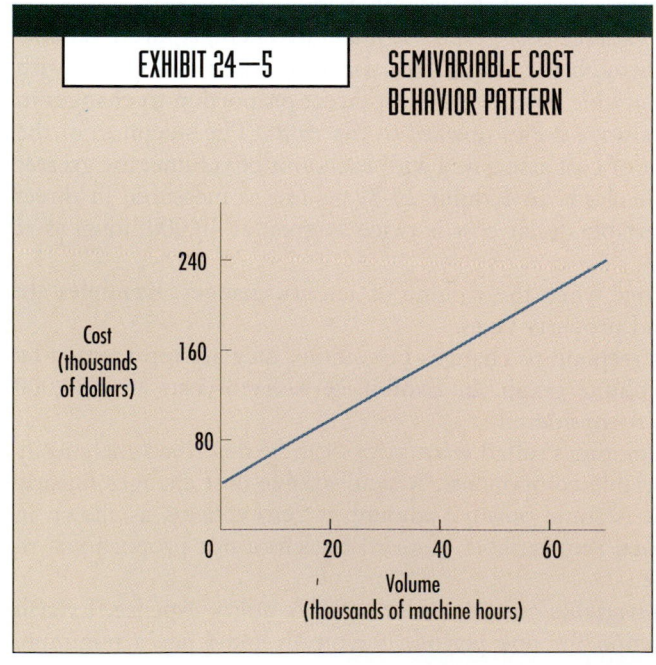

EXHIBIT 24—5   SEMIVARIABLE COST BEHAVIOR PATTERN

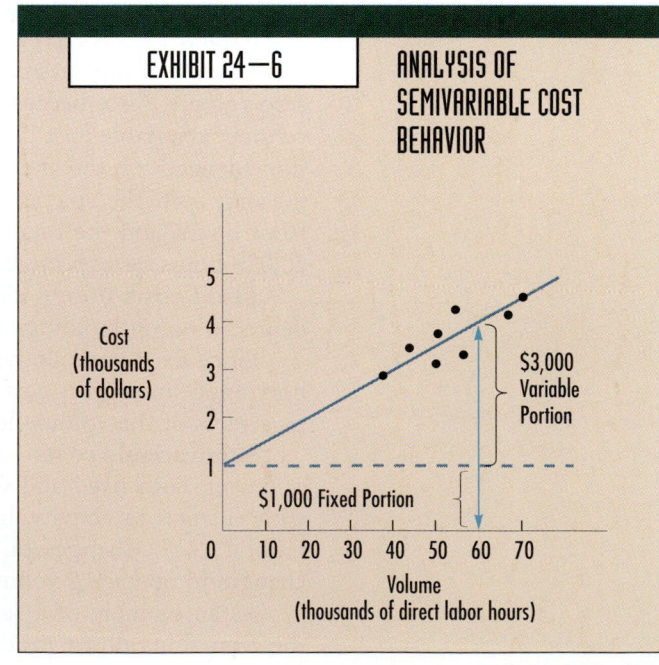

EXHIBIT 24—6   ANALYSIS OF SEMIVARIABLE COST BEHAVIOR

is $3,000/60,000, or 5 cents, per direct labor hour. Hence, we could describe this semivariable cost as $1,000 plus 5 cents per direct labor hour.

We can obtain a better approximation by fitting the line to the cost observation pattern (data points) by the method of least squares. That technique, which is beyond the scope of this text, is illustrated in most introductory statistics texts.

High-Low Method

When too few cost observations are available to plot a graph, or when the analyst wishes to avoid fitting lines to data, the **high-low method** can be used to approximate the position and slope of the cost line. This relatively simple method compares costs at the highest and lowest levels of activity for which representative cost data are available. The variable cost per activity unit (here, per direct labor hour) is determined by dividing the difference in costs at these two levels by the difference in activity. The fixed element of cost is then isolated by multiplying the variable cost per unit by either the top or bottom level of activity and then subtracting the resulting product from the total cost at the selected activity level.

For example, assume that the lowest and highest levels of activity are 40,000 and 60,000 direct labor hours, respectively, and that the following are the total costs for these two levels:

	Level of Activity	Total Cost
High	60,000 direct labor hours	$4,200
Low	40,000 direct labor hours	3,000
Difference	20,000 (increase)	$1,200 (increase)

Because an increase of 20,000 direct labor hours causes a $1,200 increase in total cost (and only the variable portion of the cost could increase), the variable portion of the total semivariable cost must be $1,200/20,000 direct labor hours, or 6 cents per direct labor hour. Subtracting the total variable portion from the total semivariable cost at the high and low activity levels gives us the fixed portion of total cost as follows:

	Volume Levels	
	Low	**High**
Total semivariable cost	$3,000	$4,200
Less variable portions:		
$0.06 × 40,000 direct labor hours	2,400	
$0.06 × 60,000 direct labor nours		3,600
Fixed portion of total cost	$ 600	$ 600

The high-low analysis tells us that any volume level has $600 of fixed cost plus a variable portion of 6 cents per direct labor hour, which can be formulated as follows:

$$\text{Total Cost} = \$600 + (\$0.06 \times \text{Direct Labor Hours})$$

In other words, we can now easily compute the total cost for varying levels of direct labor hours. If either the high or low value used in this method is not representative of the actual cost behavior, the resulting cost formula is inexact.

Relevant Range

OBJECTIVE 2 DEFINE *the concept of* **relevant range.**

The foregoing illustrations of cost behavior are oversimplified because they portray linear cost behavior over the entire range of possible activity. Actually, plotting costs against volume may not always produce a single straight line. For example, certain costs may increase abruptly at intervals in a "step" pattern; others may exhibit a curvilinear pattern when plotted over a wide range of activity. Examples of these cost patterns are shown graphically in Exhibit 24-7.

Clearly, an assumption of linear costs over the entire scale on either axis in these two cases causes some degree of error. The significance of this error is often minimized by the fact that many of the firm's decisions involve relatively small changes in volume around some **relevant range** of activity. The actual cost pattern at

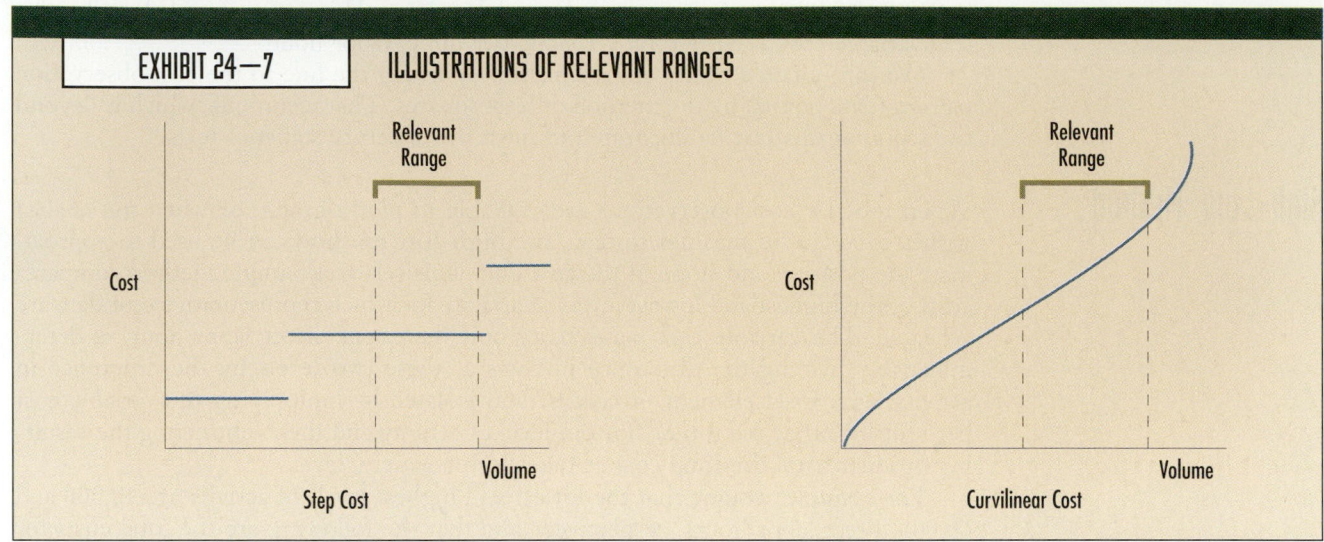

EXHIBIT 24—7   ILLUSTRATIONS OF RELEVANT RANGES

extremely low or high volume levels is not relevant to the firm's decisions. The cost pattern need be only reasonably linear within this relevant range of activity.

Total versus Per-unit Costs

OBJECTIVE ③ OUTLINE *the approach to developing cost formulas.*

The cost-volume relationships for fixed cost, variable cost, and semivariable cost typically remain the same for only one range of activity and for only one time period (frequently one year). Fixed, variable, and semivariable costs are assumed to react only to changes in volume within the relevant range during the given time period. The cost relationships, however, may change when moving to a different range of activity or a different time period. For example, a higher level of activity (above the current relevant range) could require a higher level of supervisory personnel, which would result in a higher level of fixed salary expense. Similarly, next year could have a higher fixed property tax expense due to a higher property tax assessment rate.

It is important for many forms of managerial analysis that managers fully understand the behavior patterns of total fixed and variable costs and per-unit fixed and variable costs. Exhibit 24-8 presents an example of total and per-unit cost behavior for a relevant range of 200 to 1,000 units.

An analysis of Exhibit 24-8 reveals the following:

1. Total variable cost increases proportionately with increases in volume, whereas per-unit variable cost remains constant.

2. Total fixed cost remains constant with increases in volume, whereas per-unit fixed cost decreases proportionately.

EXHIBIT 24—8   ANALYSIS OF TOTAL AND PER-UNIT COSTS

Activity Level	Variable Cost ($1.00 per unit)		Fixed Cost ($600 per month)		Total Cost ($600 + $1.00 per unit)	
Units	Total	Per-unit	Total	Per-unit	Total	Per-unit
200	$ 200	$1.00	$600	$3.00	$ 800	$4.00
600	600	1.00	600	1.00	1,200	2.00
1,000	1,000	1.00	600	0.60	1,600	1.60

3. Total variable plus fixed cost increases with increases in volume (but not proportionately), whereas per-unit variable plus fixed cost decreases (but not proportionately).

These patterns hold true for all feasible relevant ranges and are summarized in Exhibit 24-9.

Total fixed cost and per-unit variable cost are *stable* cost expressions, because they remain constant as volume is changed. Per-unit fixed cost and total variable cost are *unstable* cost expressions because they are valid at only one volume level. In the following section, we show how the stable forms of cost expression—*total* fixed cost and *per-unit* variable cost—are incorporated in a general formula for total cost that is valid over a wide range of operating volumes.

Planning Total Costs

The budget for a business firm, which is treated in detail in a later chapter, is a financial plan that reflects anticipated or planned amounts of such items as revenue, costs, cash balances, and net income. Underlying most aspects of budgeting is some assumed number of units or dollars of sales, as well as an analysis of the total cost incurred for that level of operation.

As stated previously, all costs are variable, semivariable, or fixed. For most cost analyses, semivariable costs are separated into their two components, fixed and variable, with the variable component added to the variable costs and the fixed component added to the fixed costs. The following formula and example use this approach.

For an example, we assume that total fixed cost is $10,000, semivariable cost has a fixed portion of $5,000 and a variable portion of $2 per unit, and that variable costs are $4 per unit. The formulation for planning or budgeting a total cost, using the stable forms of cost expression, follows:

$$\text{Total Cost} = \text{Total Fixed Cost} + \left(\begin{array}{c} \text{Variable} \\ \text{Cost} \\ \text{per Unit} \end{array} \times \begin{array}{c} \text{Number of} \\ \text{Units} \end{array} \right)$$

In our example:

$$\text{Total cost} = \$15,000 + (\$6 \times \text{Units})$$

Therefore, at zero units total cost is $15,000, or the total of all fixed costs. At 5,000 units total cost is $45,000, or [$15,000 + ($6 × 5,000)]. At 10,000 units, total cost is $75,000, or [$15,000 + ($6 × 10,000)]. Notice that when the number of units doubles from 5,000 to 10,000, total cost increases, but less than proportionately.

By using this formula, a firm can forecast costs at different levels of activity. In Exhibit 24-10, each type of cost behavior pattern is considered in the formula. The

EXHIBIT 24—9	PATTERNS OF TOTAL AND PER-UNIT COSTS AS VOLUME INCREASES	
Cost Category	**Total Cost**	**Per-unit Cost**
Variable	Increases proportionately	Remains constant
Fixed	Remains constant	Decreases proportionately
Variable Plus Fixed	Increases, but not proportionately	Decreases, but not proportionately

EXHIBIT 24—10		COST FACTORS IN A FORMULA FOR TOTAL COST AT 10,000 UNITS				
Type of Cost	**Total Cost**	=	**Total Fixed Cost**	+ (**Variable Cost per Unit**	×	**Number of Units**)
Direct material (variable)	$20,000	=		($2.00	×	10,000 units)
Direct labor (variable)	25,000	=		(2.50	×	10,000 units)
Factory overhead:						
Factory supplies (variable)	10,000	=		(1.00	×	10,000 units)
Property taxes (fixed)	4,000	=	$ 4,000			
Maintenance (semivariable)	7,000	=	5,000	+ (0.20	×	10,000 units)
Selling and administrative expense						
(semivariable)	9,000	=	6,000	+ (0.30	×	10,000 units)
Total cost	$75,000	=	$15,000	+ ($6.00	×	10,000 units)

dollar amounts have been chosen for ease of manipulation, and the 10,000-unit activity level is incorporated for illustrative purposes.

We see in Exhibit 24-10 that by combining the various cost factors into the aggregate formula, we determine expected costs not only at the 10,000-unit level but also at other levels simply by inserting the appropriate volume figure in the final formula. For example, total planned cost at 8,000 units is [$15,000 + ($6 × 8,000) = $63,000]; at 12,000 units, it is [$15,000 + ($6 × 12,000) = $87,000].

A word of caution is appropriate here. Because the cost formula relies so heavily on cost analysis, all the limitations of the latter (assumed linearity, relevant ranges, and so on) apply. Also, analyzing many costs into fixed and variable components is often quite complex and inexact. All of these limitations to some degree affect the potential contribution of managerial accounting. In many cases, the analytical approach presented here is the best available.

COST-VOLUME-PROFIT ANALYSIS

For purposes of illustration, we use the following data for Johnson Company throughout the next several sections.

JOHNSON COMPANY
CONDENSED INCOME STATEMENT

Sales (10,000 units @ $20)		$200,000
Costs:		
Variable Cost (10,000 units @ $12)	$120,000	
Fixed Cost	60,000	
Total Cost		180,000
Net Income		$ 20,000

This information assumes that any semivariable costs have been divided into their fixed and variable components and combined with the fixed and variable cost elements. We now examine some of the uses of this information.

Break-even Analysis

OBJECTIVE ④ PRESENT *a discussion of and a formula for calculating the break-even point.*

Management frequently wants to know the level of revenue or number of units of sales at which there is no net income or loss. The level at which total revenue equals total cost or expense is the **break-even point.** Typically, it is expressed in dollars or in units of sales. Let us calculate Johnson Company's break-even point, using the above condensed income statement data.

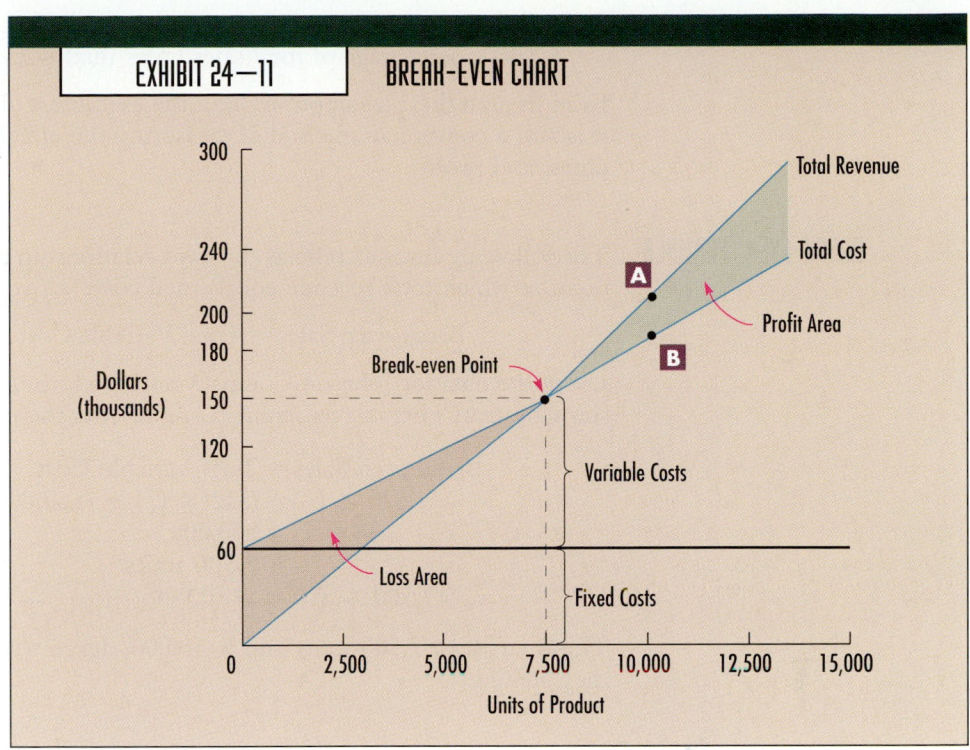

EXHIBIT 24—11   BREAK-EVEN CHART

THE BREAK-EVEN CHART

To prepare a break-even chart, we use the same basic graph employed earlier to explain and portray cost behavior patterns. In Exhibit 24-11 the vertical axis measures both total revenue and total cost. As before, volume is measured along the horizontal axis. For Johnson Company, the activity basis is units of product. Total revenue and total cost are measured in thousands of dollars along the vertical axis.

With zero revenue for zero sales, the graph of total revenue always passes through the origin, which is one point on the line. In general, then, we draw the total revenue line by connecting the origin with any other point that represents total revenue for some volume amount. For Johnson Company, total revenue for 10,000 units is $200,000—**A** in Exhibit 24-11. To construct the total revenue line, we simply draw a straight line from the origin to **A** and extend it beyond **A**.

We now construct the total cost line in the same manner. With fixed costs of $60,000, the total cost line must intersect the vertical axis at $60,000. For Johnson Company, we are given total cost of $180,000 for 10,000 units. From this we can plot **B** and draw the total cost line for Johnson Company as shown in Exhibit 24-11.

Extending the dashed lines as indicated from the point of intersection of the two graphed lines to the two axes, we find Johnson Company's break-even point (where total revenue equals total cost) to be 7,500 units of production, or $150,000 of total sales revenue. Note that all points lying below the break-even point indicate a loss, and points above the break-even level represent profit. The profit and loss areas are shaded on our graph. The amount of profit or loss at any volume level is determined by measuring the vertical distance between the total cost and total revenue lines. A profit is indicated when the total revenue line is above the total cost line, and a loss is indicated when the reverse is true.

THE BASIC ASSUMPTIONS OF BREAK-EVEN ANALYSIS

In our construction of a break-even chart, we assumed linear relationships over a wide range of activity. This approach implies the following:

1. Total fixed cost and variable cost per unit are constant over the entire range of analysis.
2. Selling price per unit remains the same regardless of the volume of sales.

3. When more than one product is involved and sales volume varies, each product's percentage of total sales (sales mix) does not change.

Even though these assumptions limit the usefulness of break-even analysis somewhat, it is still a convenient method of measuring the effect of changes in sales, costs, volumes, and profits.

BREAK-EVEN FORMULA

The following formula reflects the basic relationship that the break-even point is that point at which total revenue equals total cost:

$$\text{Break-even Sales} = \text{Total Variable Cost} + \text{Total Fixed Cost}$$

Using the data for Johnson Company and the formula above, we can calculate Johnson Company's break-even point (U represents the number of units):

$$\text{Break-even Sales} = \text{Total Variable Cost} + \text{Total Fixed Cost}$$
$$(\$20 \times U) = (\$12 \times U) + (\$60,000)$$
$$\$8 \times U = \$60,000$$
$$U = \textbf{7,500 units}$$
$$7,500 \times \$20 = \textbf{\$150,000}$$

These answers, 7,500 units and \$150,000, agree with the graphic solutions, which they should.

CONTRIBUTION MARGIN

OBJECTIVE 5 DEFINE **contribution margin *and* contribution margin ratio.**

Since variable costs change proportionately with changes in revenue, each time additional revenue is generated, additional variable cost is also generated. The difference between the revenue generated and the variable cost generated is called **contribution margin.** This can be demonstrated in the following restructured income statement for Johnson Company:

JOHNSON COMPANY
CONDENSED INCOME STATEMENT

	Total	Per Unit
Sales (10,000 units)	$200,000	$20
Less: Variable Cost	120,000	12
Contribution Margin	$ 80,000	$ 8
Less: Fixed Cost	60,000	
Net Income	$ 20,000	

At 10,000 units, the total contribution margin is \$80,000. For each additional unit sold beyond 10,000 units, \$8 of additional contribution margin is generated (\$20 of sales revenue less \$12 of variable cost).

CONTRIBUTION MARGIN RATIO

A related concept that is used in break-even analysis is **contribution margin ratio,** which is the ratio of contribution margin to sales. The formula to calculate contribution margin ratio can use either *total* amounts:

$$\text{Contribution Margin Ratio} = \frac{\text{Contribution Margin}}{\text{Sales}}$$

or *per-unit* amounts:

$$\text{Contribution Margin Ratio} = \frac{\text{Unit Contribution Margin}}{\text{Unit Sales Price}}$$

Using the data for Johnson Company,

$$\text{Contribution margin ratio} = \frac{\$80,000}{\$200,000} = 0.4$$

or

$$\text{Contribution margin ratio} = \frac{\$8}{\$20} = 0.4$$

ALTERNATE BREAK-EVEN FORMULAS

OBJECTIVE 6 PRESENT *alternate break-even formulas and examples of their application.*

Two alternate break-even formulas can be used to calculate the break-even point either in *units:*

$$\text{Break-even Units} = \frac{\text{Total Fixed Cost}}{\text{Unit Contribution Margin}}$$

or in *dollars of sales:*

$$\frac{\text{Break-even Sales}}{\text{(in dollars)}} = \frac{\text{Total Fixed Cost}}{\text{Contribution Margin Ratio}}$$

Using the data for Johnson Company, we can calculate the break-even point using these two formulas.

Using the first formula,

$$\text{Break-even units} = \frac{\$60,000}{\$8} = 7,500 \text{ units}$$

Using the second formula,

$$\text{Break-even sales} = \frac{\$60,000}{0.4} = \$150,000$$

The results of either formula can be translated to the results of the other formula as follows:

$$7,500 \text{ units} \times \$20 \text{ per unit} = \$150,000$$
$$\$150,000/\$20 \text{ per unit} = 7,500 \text{ units}$$

The results from using any of the break-even formulas can be verified by placing the results in income statement format and determining that net income does equal zero.

Planning Net Income

OBJECTIVE 7 DISCUSS *approaches to planning net income using cost-volume-profit analyses.*

Business firms use a more generalized form of break-even analysis when they are analyzing cost-volume-profit relationships. Rather than make the calculations for break-even analysis, they use formulas that include a *desired profit*. These formulas are similar to the break-even formulas:

$$\text{Desired Sales} = \text{Total Variable Cost} + \text{Total Fixed Cost} + \frac{\text{Desired Net Income}}{\text{before Income Tax}}$$

$$\text{Desired Units} = \frac{\text{Total Fixed Cost} + \text{Desired Net Income before Income Tax}}{\text{Unit Contribution Margin}}$$

$$\text{Desired Sales} = \frac{\text{Total Fixed Cost} + \text{Desired Net Income before Income Tax}}{\text{Contribution Margin Ratio}}$$

Assume that Johnson Company wants to attain a net income before income tax of $24,000. Using the formulas above, we make the following calculations:

Using the first formula,

$$\text{Desired sales} = \text{Total variable cost} + \$60,000 + \$24,000$$
$$(\$20 \times U) = (\$12 \times U) + \$84,000$$
$$\$8 \times U = \$84,000$$
$$U = 10,500 \text{ units}$$

Using the second formula,

$$\text{Desired units} = \frac{\$60,000 + \$24,000}{\$8}$$
$$= 10,500 \text{ units}$$

Using the third formula,

$$\text{Desired sales} = \frac{\$60,000 + \$24,000}{0.4}$$

$$= \$210,000$$

Again, the results can be translated using the unit sales price:

$$10,500 \text{ units} \times \$20 \text{ per unit} = \$210,000$$

$$\$210,000/\$20 \text{ per unit} = 10,500 \text{ units}$$

Effect of Income Taxes

A company's management might want to develop plans using net income (after tax) rather than net income before income taxes. In this case, net income must be converted to net income before income tax so the formulas presented above can be used:

$$\text{Net Income before Income Tax} = \frac{\text{Net Income}}{1 - \text{Income Tax Rate}}$$

Assume that Johnson Company's management wants to attain a net income of $16,800 when the income tax rate is 30%. Net income before income tax can be calculated as follows:

$$\text{Net income before income tax} = \frac{\$16,800}{1 - 0.3} = \frac{\$16,800}{0.7} = \$24,000$$

A brief income statement verifies the calculations made in the preceding sections:

Sales (10,500 units × $20)	$210,000
Less: Variable Cost (10,500 units × $12)	126,000
Contribution Margin	$ 84,000
Less: Fixed Cost	60,000
Net Income before Income Tax	$ 24,000
Income Tax ($24,000 × 0.30)	7,200
Net Income	$ 16,800

Margin of Safety

Margin of safety is the amount by which the actual sales level of a company exceeds the break-even sales level. If sales decrease by more than the margin of safety, then the company will incur an operating loss. The formula for calculating margin of safety follows:

$$\text{Margin of Safety} = \text{Actual Sales} - \text{Break-even Sales}$$

Using Cost-Volume-Profit Relationships

Cost-volume-profit relationships can be used in a number of ways during planning and budgeting sessions to test possible courses of action. The following three independent situations reveal ways that Johnson Company might use cost-volume-profit relationships.

SITUATION 1 Assume that Johnson Company's managers are considering reducing the price of its product per unit from $20 to $18. *How would this change affect the break-even point in units?*

$$\text{Break-even Units} = \frac{\text{Total Fixed Cost}}{\text{Unit Contribution Margin}}$$

$$= \frac{\$60,000}{\$18 - \$12}$$

$$= 10,000 \text{ units}$$

The $2 price decrease would cause the break-even point to increase from 7,500 units (previously calculated) to 10,000 units.

COST-VOLUME-PROFIT ANALYSIS FOR RESTAURANTS

*M*ost retailing industries have developed relationships between product cost and retail price that need to be maintained in order to be profitable. Each segment of each industry has its own ideal relationship. For example, a men's clothing store would typically have a lower ratio of retail price to product cost than would a retail furrier, whereas a downhill ski shop would typically have a higher ratio than a department store would have. ■ Many restaurants strive to have the price of their meals set at 2.5 times the cost of the food used in the meal. Portion control is a key element in applying this ratio. For each food item or ingredient to be included in one portion or meal, a standard quantity (weight or volume) is established. This standard recipe can be used to determine the food cost of a meal. For example, 8 ounces of ingredient A costing 35 cents per ounce plus 2 ounces of ingredient B costing 25 cents per ounce would yield a food cost of $3.30 per portion and a target price of $8.25.

Retail establishments also have variable staffing levels. The number of employees on duty will vary, depending on the time of day. For example, a restaurant might have two cooks and five waiters working from 11:00 a.m. to 2:00 p.m., one cook and two waiters working from 2:00 p.m. to 5:00 p.m., and two cooks and five waiters working from 5:00 p.m. to 9:00 p.m. The number and type of employees to have on duty has to be predetermined. Therefore, the cost of these employees is fixed. They are typically paid the same amount regardless of how many meals are served. Customer tips (which are not an expense of the restaurant) would vary, depending in part on the number of meals served.

These concepts have to be incorporated into cost-volume-profit analysis for a restaurant. If a restaurant serves only three types of meals with food costs per meal of $5.00, $4.00, and $3.00, then the related prices should be $12.50, $10.00, and $7.50 if the 2.5 ratio is used. If 20% of the meals sold were sold for $12.50, 50% were sold for $10.00, and 30% were sold for $7.50, then the average revenue per meal sold would be $9.75 and the average food cost would be $3.90:

$$\$12.50 \times 0.20 = \$2.50$$
$$\$10.00 \times 0.50 = 5.00$$
$$\$ 7.50 \times 0.30 = \underline{2.25}$$
$$\underline{\underline{\$9.75}}$$

$$\$ 5.00 \times 0.20 = \$1.00$$
$$\$ 4.00 \times 0.50 = 2.00$$
$$\$ 3.00 \times 0.30 = \underline{.90}$$
$$\underline{\underline{\$3.90}}$$

The weighted average unit contribution margin, therefore, is $9.75 − $3.90 = $5.85.

If the total fixed costs, including personnel, are $64,350 for a typical 30-day month when the restaurant is open every day for the scheduled hours, the break-even volume would be calculated as follows:

$$\frac{\$64,350}{\$5.85} = 11,000 \text{ meals per month}$$

SITUATION 2 Assume that Johnson Company's managers are considering an advertising campaign that would increase fixed costs by $10,000 and allow a price increase from $20 to $22 per unit. *How would this change affect the break-even point in units?*

$$\text{Break-even Units} = \frac{\text{Total Fixed Cost}}{\text{Unit Contribution Margin}}$$

$$= \frac{\$70,000}{\$22 - \$12}$$

$$= 7,000 \text{ units}$$

The $10,000 advertising campaign and the related $2 price increase would cause the break-even point to decrease from 7,500 units to 7,000 units.

SITUATION 3   Assume that Johnson Company's managers are considering installing robots to replace some of the direct labor plant workers. This change would decrease unit variable cost from $12 to $9 and would increase fixed costs from $60,000 to $83,000. Unit sales price would remain at $20. If the company wants to achieve a net income of $42,000 and if the income tax rate is 30%, *what would the impact be on desired units sold of installing the robots?*

$$\text{Desired Units} = \frac{\text{Total Fixed Cost} + \text{Desired Net Income before Income Tax}}{\text{Unit Contribution Margin}}$$

Without robots,

$$\text{Desired units} = \frac{\$60,000 + \dfrac{\$42,000}{1 - 0.3}}{\$20 - \$12} = 15,000 \text{ units}$$

With robots,

$$\text{Desired units} = \frac{\$83,000 + \dfrac{\$42,000}{1 - 0.3}}{\$20 - \$9} = 13,000 \text{ units}$$

The installation of robots would decrease the desired volume from 15,000 units to 13,000 units. As a result, Johnson Company would be able to sell 2,000 fewer units at the same price and still attain the same desired net income.

Break-even Analysis and Multiple Products

As indicated earlier, we must assume in break-even analysis that only one product is involved or that the product mix (the ratio of units of each product sold to the total units sold) is constant. Break-even sales can be computed for a sales mix of two or more products by calculating the weighted average unit contribution margin.

Assume that a company sells products A and B, has a product sales mix of 75% A and 25% B, and has fixed costs of $88,000. Also assume that the following relationships between selling price and variable cost exist:

	Product A	Product B
Unit selling price	$14.00	$7.00
Unit variable cost	8.00	3.00
Unit contribution margin	$ 6.00	$4.00

The weighted average unit contribution margin can be calculated as follows:

$$\begin{aligned} \text{Product A: } \$6.00 \times 0.75 &= \$4.50 \\ \text{Product B: } \$4.00 \times 0.25 &= \underline{1.00} \\ &\ \underline{\underline{\$5.50}} \end{aligned}$$

The break-even volume can then be calculated:

$$\begin{aligned} \text{Break-even Units} &= \frac{\text{Total Fixed Cost}}{\text{Weighted Average Unit Contribution Margin}} \\ &= \frac{\$88,000}{\$5.50} \\ &= 16,000 \text{ units} \end{aligned}$$

The 16,000 units include units of A and units of B. The exact mix and related contribution margin are calculated as appears on the following page:

Product	Product Mix	Units Sold	Unit Contribution Margin	Total Contribution Margin
A	0.75	12,000	$6	$72,000
B	0.25	4,000	4	16,000
Total		16,000		$88,000

These concepts could be applied to any product mix or number of products.

A Perspective on Cost Analysis

Managing costs is a prevailing concern of management. The concepts introduced in this chapter underlie most efforts to analyze and project cost in a variety of decision situations. In practice, because projections of future costs are subject to many complicating factors, for most companies they are *estimates of probable costs* rather than precise determinations. Properly used—with full recognition of their limitations—cost behavior analyses can be highly useful to management.

KEY POINTS FOR CHAPTER OBJECTIVES

1 DEVELOP an understanding of how specific types of costs change in response to volume changes (pp. 910–913).
- Behavior of total cost in response to volume changes is divided into three basic categories within a relevant range:
  a. Variable, which responds proportionately, with zero cost at zero volume.
  b. Fixed, which is constant.
  c. Semivariable, which responds, but less than proportionately, due to the fixed component.
- Total cost for most entities is best represented by the semivariable cost pattern.
- Semivariable costs may be divided into fixed and variable subelements using graphic plottings, the high-low method, or statistical methods.

2 DEFINE the concept of *relevant range* (pp. 913–914).
- We can assume linearity of cost because it is approximately true within the range of volume relevant to the analysis.
- Within the relevant range, per-unit costs behave as follows when volume is increased:
  a. Variable costs remain constant.
  b. Fixed costs decrease proportionately.
  c. Variable plus fixed cost decreases, but not proportionately.

3 OUTLINE the approach to developing cost formulas (pp. 914–916).
- A general formula for planning total cost follows:
  Total Cost = Total Fixed Cost + (Variable Cost per Unit × Number of Units)

4 PRESENT a discussion of and a formula for calculating the break-even point (pp. 916–918).
- The break-even point (where Revenues = Costs) can be derived by graph, formula, or contribution margin analysis.
- Assumptions underlying break-even analysis include the following:
  a. Total fixed cost and per-unit variable cost are constant over the entire relevant range.
  b. Selling price per unit remains the same regardless of the volume of sales.
  c. When more than one product is involved and sales volume varies, each product's percentage of total sales (sales mix) does not change.

5 DEFINE *contribution margin* and *contribution margin ratio* (pp. 918–919).
- Contribution Margin = Revenue − Variable Cost

- Contribution Margin ratio = $\dfrac{\text{Contribution Margin}}{\text{Sales}}$

  or

  Contribution Margin Ratio = $\dfrac{\text{Unit Contribution Margin}}{\text{Unit Selling Price}}$

6 PRESENT alternate break-even formulas and examples of their application (p. 919).
- Formulas used in break-even analysis include the following:

a. Break-even Units $= \dfrac{\text{Total Fixed Cost}}{\text{Unit Contribution Margin}}$

b. Break-even Sales $= \dfrac{\text{Total Fixed Cost}}{\text{Contribution Margin Ratio}}$

7 **DISCUSS** approaches to planning net income using cost-volume-profit analyses (pp. 919–923).

■ Formulas used in planning net income include the following:

a. Desired Sales = Total Variable Cost + Total Fixed Cost + $\begin{array}{l}\text{Desired Net Income}\\\text{before Income Tax}\end{array}$

b. Desired Units $= \dfrac{\text{Total Fixed Cost} + \text{Desired Net Income before Income Tax}}{\text{Unit Contribution Margin}}$

c. Desired Sales $= \dfrac{\text{Total Fixed Cost} + \text{Desired Net Income before Income Tax}}{\text{Contribution Margin Ratio}}$

■ The relationship between net income before income tax and net income is demonstrated by the formula:

Net Income Before Income Tax $= \dfrac{\text{Net Income}}{1 - \text{Income Tax Rate}}$

■ Margin of Safety = Actual Sales − Break-even Sales
■ Break-even and net income planning computations involving multiple products incorporate the concept of weighted average unit contribution margin.

SELF-TEST QUESTIONS FOR REVIEW

(Answers follow the Solution to Demonstration Problem.)

1. When moving from the low end to the high end of a relevant range, straight-line depreciation expense per unit
   a. Increases.
   b. Decreases.
   c. Remains the same.
   d. Changes unpredictably.

2. In a typical cost formula
   a. Fixed costs are per unit and variable costs are per unit.
   b. Fixed costs are per unit and variable costs are in total.
   c. Fixed costs are in total and variable costs are in total.
   d. Fixed costs are in total and variable costs are per unit.

3. At the break-even point
   a. Contribution margin = fixed costs.
   b. Variable costs = fixed costs.
   c. Sales = contribution margin.
   d. Contribution margin = 0.

4. Contribution margin ratio is
   a. Unit sales price/unit contribution margin.
   b. 1/margin of safety.
   c. Total contribution margin/sales.
   d. Variable cost/fixed cost.

5. Net income before income tax is
   a. Net income/1 − income tax rate.
   b. Income tax rate/net income.
   c. Net income + contribution margin.
   d. Net income/income tax rate.

DEMONSTRATION PROBLEM FOR REVIEW

Maricopa Corporation has developed the budget for its next year of operations. The budget included the following:

Sales of 100,000 units at $5.
Units sold will equal units produced.
Variable costs for 100,000 units:

Direct material	$125,000
Direct labor	100,000

Variable overhead	30,000
Selling and administrative expense	45,000
Total fixed cost	120,000
Income tax rate of 30%.	

REQUIRED

a. What is Maricopa's break-even point, in units and in dollars, for next year?

b. Demonstrate that the units amount reconciles with the dollar amount.

c. What amount of sales revenue would Maricopa need to realize next year so it could generate a net income of $63,000?

d. Demonstrate the correctness of the calculations in requirement (c) by constructing an income statement.

SOLUTION TO DEMONSTRATION PROBLEM

a.

Variable costs:

Direct material	$125,000
Direct labor	100,000
Variable overhead	30,000
Selling and administrative	45,000
Total variable cost at 100,000 units	$300,000

$300,000/100,000 units = $\underline{\$3}$ per unit

Unit contribution margin = $5 − $3 = $2

$$\text{Contribution Margin Ratio} = \frac{\$2}{\$5} = 0.4$$

$$\text{Break-even Units} = \frac{\text{Total Fixed Cost}}{\text{Unit Contribution Margin}}$$

$$= \frac{\$120,000}{\$2}$$

$$= \underline{60,000} \text{ units}$$

$$\text{Break-even Sales} = \frac{\text{Total Fixed Cost}}{\text{Contribution Margin Ratio}}$$

$$= \frac{\$120,000}{0.4}$$

$$= \underline{\$300,000}$$

b.

60,000 units × $5 unit selling price = $300,000

c.

$$\text{Desired Sales} = \frac{\text{Total Fixed Cost} + \dfrac{\text{Net Income}}{1 - \text{Income Tax Rate}}}{\text{Contribution Margin Ratio}}$$

$$= \frac{\$120,000 + \dfrac{\$63,000}{1 - 0.3}}{0.4}$$

$$= \underline{\$525,000}$$

d.

Sales	$525,000
Variable Cost [(1 − 0.4) × $525,000]	315,000
Contribution Margin	$210,000
Fixed Cost	120,000
Net Income before Income Tax	$ 90,000
Income Tax at 30%	27,000
Net Income	$ 63,000

ANSWERS TO SELF-TEST QUESTIONS

1. b, p. 914   **2.** d, p. 915   **3.** a, p. 918   **4.** c, p. 918   **5.** a, p. 920

GLOSSARY OF KEY TERMS USED IN THIS CHAPTER

break-even point   That level of business volume at which total revenue equals total costs or expenses (p. 916).

contribution margin   The excess of revenue over variable costs; the amount contributed toward absorption of fixed costs and eventually the generation of profit (p. 918).

contribution margin ratio   Contribution margin divided by sales; can be calculated in total or per unit (p. 918).

cost behavior analysis   Study of the ways in which specific costs respond to changes in the volume of business activity (p. 910).

fixed costs   Costs whose total remains constant within the relevant range even though the volume of activity changes (p. 911).

high-low method   A method for dividing costs into their variable and fixed components by comparing costs at the highest and lowest levels of activity for which representative cost data are available. The variable cost per activity measure is determined by dividing the difference in costs by the difference in activity (p. 913).

margin of safety   The amount by which the actual sales level exceeds the break-even sales level (p. 920).

relevant range   The range of changes in the volume of activity within which the assumptions made regarding cost behavior patterns are valid (p. 913).

semivariable costs   Costs, sometimes called *mixed costs*, whose total responds, but less than proportionately, to changes in the volume of activity (p. 911).

variable costs   Costs whose total responds proportionately to changes in volume of activity (p. 911).

QUESTIONS

24-1   Define the terms *cost behavior* and *relevant range*.

24-2   Identify some common activity bases in terms of which the volume of a manufacturing operation might be stated. What general criterion might be used in choosing a basis?

24-3   Name and define briefly the three most widely recognized cost behavior patterns.

24-4   Explain (a) how a semivariable cost can be considered "partly fixed and partly variable," and (b) why a firm's total cost is best represented by the semivariable cost pattern.

24-5   Briefly describe two techniques for dividing a semivariable cost into its fixed and variable components.

24-6   "Actual costs often behave in a nonlinear fashion. Therefore, assumptions of linearity invalidate most cost behavior analyses." Do you agree or disagree with this statement? Briefly defend your position.

24-7   Describe how fixed and variable costs per unit respond to volume increases.

24-8   Present a formula based on units for planning total cost, and explain how semivariable costs are incorporated into the formula.

24-9   Define and briefly explain three approaches to break-even analysis.

24-10   Patrick's Bakery Shop has fixed costs per month of $3,600, and variable costs are 55% of sales. What amount of monthly sales allows the shop to break even?

24-11   Quality Car Wash has fixed costs per month of $16,800, and variable costs are 20% of sales. The average amount collected per car washed during the past year has been $5. How many cars must be washed per month to break even?

24-12   You have graphed the cost-volume-profit relationships for a company on a break-even chart after being informed of certain assumptions. Explain how the lines on the chart would change (a) if fixed costs increased over the entire range of activity, (b) if selling price per unit decreased, and (c) if variable costs per unit increased.

24-13   Define *contribution margin*. Is it best expressed as a total amount or as a per-unit amount? In what way is the term descriptive of the concept it represents?

24-14   Explain the approach to break-even analysis that is used for a mix of two or more products.

24-15 Explain how break-even formulas can provide income-planning analyses.

24-16 In planning net income, how can net income be incorporated into the planning formula?

EXERCISES

COST-VOLUME GRAPH
— OBJ. 1 —

24-17 Set up a cost-volume graph similar to those presented in the chapter. Volume should range from zero to 24,000 units (in 4,000-unit increments), and cost should range from zero to $24,000 (in $4,000 increments). Plot each of the following groups of cost data using different marks for each group. After completing the graph, indicate the type of cost behavior exhibited by each group.

Volume (applicable to each group)	Group A Costs	Group B Costs	Group C Costs
2,000	$ 6,600	$ 2,400	$8,000
6,000	9,800	7,200	8,000
10,000	13,000	12,000	8,000
20,000	21,000	24,000	8,000

HIGH-LOW METHOD
— OBJ. 1 —

24-18 Apply the high-low method of cost analysis to the three cost data groups in Exercise 24-17. What cost behavior patterns are apparent? Express each as a cost formula.

HIGH-LOW METHOD
— OBJ. 1 —

24-19 The following selected data relate to the major cost categories experienced by Shaw Company at varying levels of operating volumes. Assuming that all operating volumes are within the relevant range, calculate the appropriate costs in each column in which blanks appear.

	Total Cost (at 3,000 units)	Total Cost (at 4,000 units)	Variable Cost per Unit	Total Fixed Cost	Total Cost (at 5,000 units)
Direct labor (variable)	$60,000	$80,000	_____	_____	_____
Factory supervision (semivariable)	50,000	65,000	_____	_____	_____
Factory depreciation (fixed)	30,000	30,000	_____	_____	_____

COST FORMULA
— OBJ. 3 —

24-20 Davis Company has analyzed its overhead costs and derived a general formula for their behavior: $60,000 + $14 per direct labor hour employed. The company expects to use 50,000 direct labor hours during the next accounting period. What overhead rate per direct labor hour should be applied to jobs worked during the period?

BREAK-EVEN CHART
— OBJ. 4 —

24-21 Set up a break-even chart similar to the one in Exhibit 24-11 with proportional scales from zero to $72,000 (in $12,000 increments) on the vertical axis and from zero to 12,000 units of production (in 2,000-unit increments) on the horizontal axis. Prepare the break-even chart for Morton Company, assuming total fixed costs of $18,000 and unit selling price and unit variable cost for the company's one product of $6 and $4, respectively.

NET INCOME PLANNING
— OBJ. 7 —

24-22 Nolden Company has experienced a unit selling price of $20, unit variable cost of $14, and total fixed cost of $90,000. What unit sales volume is necessary to earn the following related amounts of net income before income tax? (a) $18,000; (b) $27,000; or (c) equal to 20% of sales revenue.

COST-VOLUME-PROFIT
ANALYSIS
— OBJ. 2, 7 —

24-23 Hallstrom Company sells a single product for $22 per unit. Variable costs are $14 per unit and fixed costs are $60,000 at an operating level of 7,000 to 12,000 units.
a. What is Hallstrom Company's break-even point in units?
b. How many units must be sold to earn $12,000 before income tax?
c. How many units must be sold to earn $13,000 after income tax, assuming a 35% tax rate?

MULTIPLE PRODUCT
BREAK-EVEN
— OBJ. 7 —

24-24 Warner Company has $228,000 total fixed cost and sells products A and B with a product mix of 40% A and 60% B. Selling prices and variable costs for A and B result in contribution margins per unit of $10 and $6, respectively. Compute the break-even point.

COST PATTERNS
— OBJ. 1, 3 —

24-25 The graphs below represent approximations of cost behavior patterns. The horizontal axis of each graph represents units and the vertical axis represents dollars of total cost.

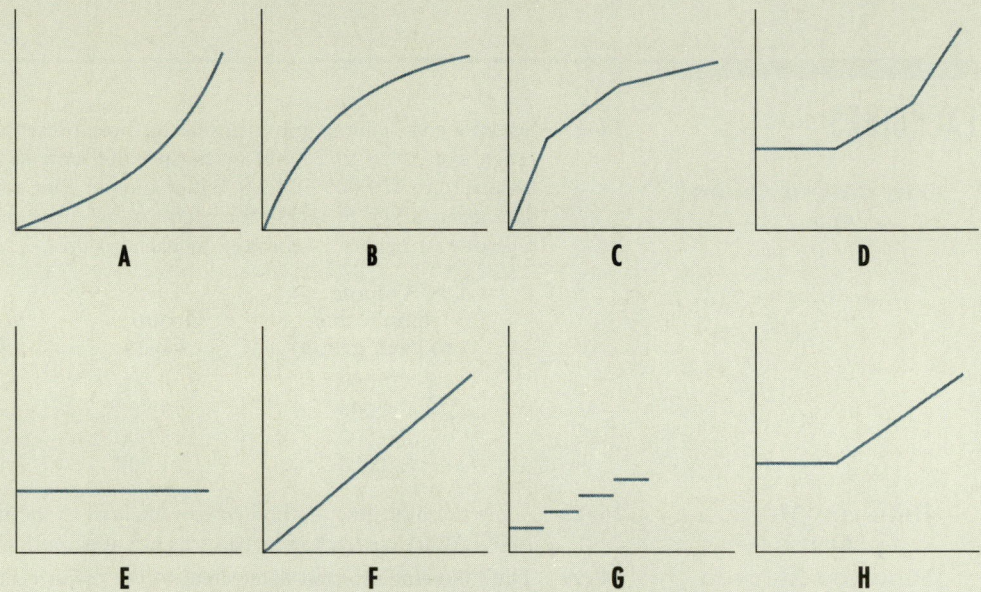

Select the graph that best matches each of the situations described below. Each graph may be selected more than once.

a. Straight-line depreciation of a factory building.

b. Utility bill for electricity that includes a fixed charge per month plus a constant usage rate per hour for hours in excess of 100.

c. Cost of microchip incorporated into a product.

d. Labor cost of machine operators who become more productive as they gain experience.

e. Water bill that includes a flat fee for the first 10,000 gallons used plus an increasing usage charge for each additional 10,000 gallons used.

f. Cost of factory supplies when increasing quantities bring cost discounts as each price break level is attained.

g. Salaries of quality inspectors when one additional inspector is hired for each 20,000 units produced.

h. Cost of an advertising campaign.

PROBLEMS

NET INCOME PLANNING
— OBJ. 5, 7 —

24-26 Selected operating data for Oakbrook Company in four independent situations are shown below.

	A	B	C	D
Sales	$300,000	$____c____	$____e____	$260,000
Variable expense	$____a____	$ 91,000	$____f____	$____g____
Fixed expense	$____b____	$ 62,000	$ 43,200	$ 89,000
Net income before tax (loss)	$ 20,000	$ 15,000	$ 28,800	($ 11,000)
Units sold	30,000	____d____		
Unit contribution margin	$5.20	$7.00		
Contribution margin ratio			0.40	____h____

REQUIRED

Fill in the blanks for each independent situation. Show your calculations.

GRAPHING SEMIVARIABLE
COST
— OBJ. 1 —

24-27 During a recent six-month period, Wade Corporation had the following monthly volume of production and total monthly maintenance expense:

	Units Produced	Maintenance Expense
March	21,000	$140,800
April	15,000	112,000
May	30,000	184,000
June	27,500	172,000
July	35,000	208,000
August	25,000	160,000

REQUIRED

Assume that all volumes are in the relevant range.

a. Explain why the data indicate that the maintenance expense is neither a fixed nor a variable expense.

b. Construct a graph similar to the one in Exhibit 24-6 and plot the above cost observations.

c. Fit a line (by sight) to the cost observation points and estimate the cost formula.

d. Confirm your answer in requirement (c) with high-low analysis.

**COST FORMULAS
— OBJ. 1 —**

24-28 Shorewood Manufacturing produces a single product requiring the following direct material and direct labor:

Description	Cost per Unit of Input	Required Amount per Unit of Product
Material A	$ 8/pound	10 ounces
Material B	5/pound	8 ounces
Material C	20/gallon	0.3 gallon
Cutting labor	9/hour	30 minutes
Shaping labor	11/hour	15 minutes
Finishing labor	12/hour	45 minutes

Factory overhead consists of indirect material, $0.60 per unit of product; indirect labor, $1,000 per month plus $0.70 per unit of product; factory maintenance, $14,000 per year plus $0.55 per unit of product; factory depreciation, $15,000 per year; and annual factory property taxes, $8,000. Selling and administrative expenses include the salaries of a sales manager, $30,000 per year; an office manager, $18,000 per year; and two salespersons, each of whom is paid a base salary of $11,000 per year and a commission of $3 per unit sold. Advertising and promotion of the product are done through a year-round media package program costing $1,000 per week.

REQUIRED

a. Analyze all cost and expense factors to determine a general formula (based on units of production) for total cost.

b. Assuming a relevant range of 10,000 to 20,000 units, what is the estimated unit cost for producing and selling 10,000 units? 20,000 units? Explain the variation in unit cost at the two levels of production.

c. If 15,000 units are produced and sold in a year, what selling price results in a net income before income tax of $60,000?

**HIGH-LOW AND COST
FORMULA
— OBJ. 1 —**

24-29 Harrison Company has accumulated the following total factory overhead costs for two levels of activity (within the relevant range):

	Low	High
Activity (direct labor hours)	80,000	120,000
Total factory overhead	$468,000	$604,000

The total overhead cost includes variable, fixed, and semivariable (mixed) costs. At 120,000 direct labor hours, the total cost breakdown is as follows:

Variable cost	$264,000
Fixed cost	160,000
Semivariable cost	180,000

REQUIRED

a. Using the high-low method of cost analysis, determine the variable portion of the semivariable cost per direct labor hour. Determine the total fixed cost component of the semivariable cost.

b. What should the total planned overhead cost be at 100,000 direct labor hours?

COST FORMULA
— OBJ. 1, 2, 3 —

24-30 The following total cost data are for Princeton Manufacturing Company, which has a normal capacity per period of 25,000 units of product that sell for $40 each. For the foreseeable future, sales volume should equal normal capacity of production.

Direct material	$295,000
Direct labor	165,000
Variable overhead	85,000
Fixed overhead (Note 1)	140,000
Selling expense (Note 2)	80,000
Administrative expense (fixed)	56,000
	$821,000

Notes:

1. Beyond normal capacity, fixed overhead cost increases $6,350 for each 1,000 units *or fraction thereof* until a maximum capacity of 30,000 units is reached.
2. Selling expenses are a 5% sales commission plus shipping costs of $1.20 per unit.

REQUIRED

a. Using the information available, prepare a formula to estimate Princeton's total cost at various production volumes up to normal capacity.
b. Prove your answer in requirement (a) against the above total cost figure at 25,000 units.
c. Calculate the planned total cost at 20,000 units, and explain why total cost did not decrease in proportion to the reduced volume.
d. If Princeton were operating at normal capacity and accepted an order for 500 more units, what would it have to charge for the order to earn a net income before income tax of $8 per unit on the new sale?

NET INCOME PLANNING
— OBJ. 5, 7 —

24-31 Superior Corporation sells a single product for $60 per unit, of which $36 is contribution margin. Total fixed cost is $72,000 and net income before income tax is $28,800.

REQUIRED

Determine the following (show key computations):
a. The present sales volume in dollars.
b. The break-even point in units.
c. The sales volume in units necessary to attain a net income before income tax of $39,600.
d. The sales volume in units necessary to attain a net income before income tax equal to 20% of sales revenue.
e. The sales volume in units necessary to attain a net income of $43,200 if the tax rate is 40%.

BREAK-EVEN AND NET
INCOME PLANNING
— OBJ. 4, 5, 7 —

24-32 The controller of Grafton Company is preparing data for a conference concerning certain *independent* aspects of its operations.

REQUIRED

Prepare answers to the following questions for the controller:
a. Total fixed cost is $1,440,000 and a unit of product is sold for $12 in excess of its unit variable cost. What is the break-even unit volume?
b. The company will sell 60,000 units of product—each having a unit variable cost of $22—at a price that will enable the product to absorb $600,000 of fixed cost. What minimum unit sales price must be charged to break even?
c. Net income before income tax of $320,000 is desired after covering $1,200,000 of fixed cost. What minimum contribution margin ratio must be maintained if total sales revenue is to be $3,800,000?
d. Net income before income tax is 10% of sales revenue, the contribution margin ratio is 30%, and the break-even dollar sales is $640,000. What is the amount of total revenue?
e. Total fixed cost is $1,000,000, variable cost per unit is $30, and unit sales price is $80. What dollar sales volume will generate a net income of $84,000 when the income tax rate is 40%?

BREAK-EVEN AND NET
INCOME PLANNING
— OBJ. 4, 5, 7 —

24-33 Paulson Company has recently leased facilities for the manufacture of a new product. Based on studies made by its accounting personnel, the following data are available:

Estimated annual sales: 40,000 units

Estimated Costs	Amount	Unit Cost
Direct material	$ 696,000	$17.40
Direct labor	584,000	14.60
Factory overhead	376,000	9.40
Administrative expenses	187,200	4.68
	$1,843,200	$46.08

Selling expenses are expected to be 10% of sales, and the selling price is $64 per unit. Ignore income tax in this problem.

REQUIRED

a. Compute a break-even point in dollars and in units. Assume that factory overhead and administrative expenses are fixed but that other costs are variable.
b. What would net income before income tax be if 30,000 units were sold?
c. How many units must be sold to earn a net income before income tax of 10% of sales?

MULTIPLE PRODUCT BREAK-EVEN AND NET INCOME PLANNING
— OBJ. 4, 5, 7 —

24-34 Grand Company manufactures and sells the following three products:

	Economy	Standard	Deluxe
Unit sales	10,000	6,000	4,000
Unit sales price	$48	$56	$68
Unit variable cost	$30	$32	$36

REQUIRED

Assume that total fixed cost is $339,000.
a. Compute the net income before income tax based on the sales volumes shown above.
b. Compute the break-even point in total dollars of revenue and in units for each product.
c. Prove your break-even calculations by computing the total contribution margin related to your answer in requirement (b).

ALTERNATE EXERCISES

HIGH-LOW METHOD
— OBJ. 1 —

24-17A The highest and lowest levels of activity for the Denton Company were 54,000 direct labor hours and 36,000 direct labor hours, respectively. If maintenance costs were $320,000 at the 54,000-hour level and $230,000 at the 36,000-hour level, what cost might we expect at an operating level of 40,000 direct labor hours?

HIGH-LOW METHOD
— OBJ. 1 —

24-18A During the past year, Cutler, Inc., operated within the relevant range of its fixed costs. Monthly production volume during the year ranged from 40,000 to 60,000 units of product and corresponding average manufacturing costs ranged from $4.00 to $3.80 per unit. Determine the total cost behavior pattern experienced by Cutler, Inc.

HIGH-LOW METHOD
— OBJ. 1 —

24-19A The following selected data relate to the major cost categories experienced by Sterling Company at varying levels of operating volumes. Assuming that all operating volumes are within the relevant range, calculate the appropriate costs in each column in which blanks appear:

	Total Cost (at 5,000 units)	Total Cost (at 6,000 units)	Variable Cost per Unit	Total Fixed Cost	Total Cost (at 7,000 units)
Direct labor (variable)	$60,000	$72,000	_____	_____	_____
Factory supervision (semivariable)	20,000	22,000	_____	_____	_____
Factory depreciation (fixed)	18,000	18,000	_____	_____	_____

COST FORMULA
— OBJ. 3 —

24-20A   The following amounts of various cost categories are experienced by Columbia Factories in producing and selling its only product:

Direct material	$8 per unit of product
Direct labor	$10 per direct labor hour*
Factory overhead	$12,000 + $4 per direct labor hour
Selling expenses	$14,000 + $3 per unit of product
Administrative expenses	$7,000 + $0.50 per unit of product

*Each unit of product requires one-half direct labor hour.

Combine the various cost factors into a general total cost formula for Columbia Factories and determine the total cost of producing and selling 20,000 units.

BREAK-EVEN
CALCULATIONS
— OBJ. 4 —

24-21A   Compute the break-even point in units for each of the following independent situations:

	Unit Selling Price	Unit Variable Cost	Total Fixed Cost
a.	$10	$7	$ 90,000
b.	12	9	144,000
c.	5	3	54,000

Confirm each answer using contribution margin ratio analysis.

NET INCOME PLANNING
— OBJ. 7 —

24-22A   Holland Corporation earned a net income of $120,000 last year. Fixed costs were $600,000. The selling price per unit of its product was $120, of which $50 was a contribution to fixed cost and net income. The income tax rate was 40%.
a. How many units of product were sold last year?
b. What was the break-even point in units last year?
c. The company wishes to increase its net income by 20% this year. If selling prices and the income tax rate remain unchanged, how many units must be sold?

COST-VOLUME-PROFIT
ANALYSIS
— OBJ. 2, 7 —

24-23A   Gannon Company sells a single product for $15 per unit. Variable costs are $10 per unit and fixed costs are $90,000 at an operating level of 16,000 to 30,000 units.
a. What is Gannon Company's break-even point in units?
b. How many units must be sold to earn $20,000 before income tax?
c. How many units must be sold to earn $30,000 after income tax, assuming a 40% tax rate?

MULTIPLE PRODUCT
BREAK-EVEN ANALYSIS
— OBJ. 7 —

24-24A   Wynn Company has $142,000 total fixed cost and sells products A and B with a product mix of 70% A and 30% B. Selling prices and variable costs for A and B result in contribution margins per unit of $8 and $5, respectively. Compute the break-even point.

COST PATTERNS
— OBJ. 4 —

24-25A   The following graph depicts cost-volume relationships for Tallmadge Company:

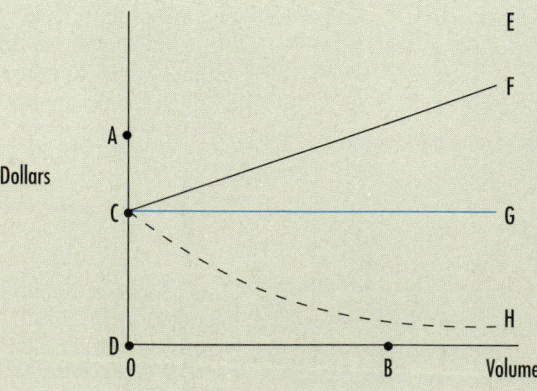

Choose a labeled point *or* line on the graph that *best* represents the behavior of each of the following items as operating volume is increased. Answers may be the same for more than one item. Answer each item independently.

a. Total sales revenue.
b. Total cost for the firm.
c. Variable cost per unit.
d. Total variable cost.

e. Total fixed cost.
f. Fixed cost per unit.
g. Total semivariable cost.
h. Break-even point.

ALTERNATE PROBLEMS

NET INCOME PLANNING
— OBJ. 5, 7 —

24-26A Selected operating data for Verona Company in four independent situations are shown below.

	A	B	C	D
Sales	$320,000	$ ___c___	$ ___e___	$280,000
Variable expense	$ ___a___	$ 48,000	$ ___f___	$ ___g___
Fixed expense	$ ___b___	$ 56,000	$240,000	$120,000
Net income before tax (loss)	$ 40,000	$ 16,000	$ 96,000	($ 8,000)
Units sold	7,000	___d___		
Unit contribution margin	$20	$9		
Contribution margin ratio			0.70	___h___

REQUIRED

Fill in the blanks for each independent situation. Show your calculations.

GRAPHING SEMIVARIABLE
COST
— OBJ. 1 —

24-27A During the past operating year, Davenport Corporation had the following monthly volume of production and total monthly maintenance expense:

	Units Produced	Maintenance Expense		Units Produced	Maintenance Expense
January	120,000	$22,400	July	124,000	$22,800
February	144,000	25,400	August	154,000	26,600
March	156,000	26,800	September	128,000	23,400
April	130,000	23,200	October	160,000	27,200
May	140,000	25,000	November	152,000	26,400
June	150,000	26,400	December	156,000	26,800

REQUIRED

Assume that all volumes are in the relevant range.

a. Explain why the data indicate that the maintenance expense is neither a fixed nor a variable expense.

b. Construct a graph similar to the one in Exhibit 24-6 and plot the above cost observations.

c. Fit a line (by sight) to the cost observation points, and estimate the cost formula.

d. Confirm your answer in requirement (c) with high-low analysis.

COST FORMULAS
— OBJ. 1 —

24-28A Colonial Manufacturing produces a single product requiring the following direct material and direct labor:

Description	Cost per Unit of Input	Required Amount per Unit of Product
Material A	$ 9/pound	24 ounces
Material B	6/pound	12 ounces
Material C	12/gallon	0.5 gallon
Cutting labor	10/hour	45 minutes
Shaping labor	12/hour	15 minutes
Finishing labor	11/hour	30 minutes

Factory overhead consists of indirect materials, $0.80 per unit of product; indirect labor, $10,000 per year plus $1.20 per unit of product; factory maintenance, $1,000 per month plus $0.60 per unit of product; factory depreciation, $22,000 per year;

and annual factory property taxes, $20,000. Selling and administrative expenses include the salaries of a sales manager, $30,000 per year, an office manager, $18,000 per year, and two salespersons, each of whom is paid a base salary of $12,000 per year and a commission of $4 per unit sold. Advertising and promotion of the product are done through a year-round media package program costing $600 per week.

REQUIRED

a. Analyze all cost and expense factors to determine a general formula (based on units of production) for total cost.

b. Assuming a relevant range of 20,000 to 40,000 units, what is the estimated unit cost for producing and selling 20,000 units? 40,000 units? Explain the variation in unit cost at the two levels of production.

c. If 35,000 units are produced and sold in a year, what selling price results in a net income before taxes of $56,800?

HIGH-LOW AND COST FORMULA
— OBJ. 1 —

24-29A Adams Company has accumulated the following total factory overhead costs for two levels of activity (within the relevant range):

	Low	High
Activity (direct labor hours)	30,000	50,000
Total factory overhead	$270,000	$362,000

The total overhead cost includes variable, fixed, and semivariable (mixed) costs. At 50,000 direct labor hours, the total cost breakdown is as follows:

Variable cost	$200,000
Fixed cost	90,000
Semivariable cost	72,000

REQUIRED

a. Using the high-low method of cost analysis, determine the variable portion of the semivariable cost per direct labor hour. Determine the total fixed cost component of the semivariable cost.

b. What should the total planned overhead cost be at 40,000 direct labor hours?

COST FORMULA
— OBJ. 1, 2, 3 —

24-30A The following total cost data are for Phoenix Manufacturing Company, which has a normal capacity per period of 40,000 units of product that sell for $60 each. For the foreseeable future, sales volume should equal normal capacity of production.

Direct material	$ 640,000
Direct labor	400,000
Variable overhead	200,000
Fixed overhead (Note 1)	216,000
Selling expense (Note 2)	280,000
Administrative expense (fixed)	88,000
	$1,824,000

Notes:

1. Beyond normal capacity, fixed overhead cost increases $6,240 for each 2,000 units *or fraction thereof* until a maximum capacity of 50,000 units is reached.

2. Selling expenses are a 10% sales commission plus shipping costs of $1 per unit.

REQUIRED

a. Using the information available, prepare a formula to estimate Phoenix's total cost at various production volumes up to normal capacity.

b. Prove your answer in requirement (a) against the above total cost figure at 40,000 units.

c. Calculate the planned total cost at 30,000 units, and explain why total cost did not decrease in proportion to the reduced volume.

d. If Phoenix were operating at normal capacity and accepted an order for 600 more units, what would it have to charge for the order to earn a net income before tax of $8 per unit on the new sale?

**NET INCOME PLANNING
— OBJ. 5, 7 —**

24-31A Midvale Corporation sells a single product for $100 per unit, of which $40 is contribution margin. Total fixed cost is $120,000, and net income before income tax is $48,000.

REQUIRED

Determine the following (show key computations):

a. The present sales volume in dollars.
b. The break-even point in units.
c. The sales volume in units necessary to attain a net income before income tax of $60,000.
d. The sales volume in units necessary to attain a net income before income tax equal to 10% of sales revenue.
e. The sales volume in units necessary to attain a net income of $54,000 if the tax rate is 40%.

**BREAK-EVEN AND NET INCOME PLANNING
— OBJ. 4, 5, 7 —**

24-32A The controller of Wright Company is preparing data for a conference concerning certain *independent* aspects of its operations.

REQUIRED

Prepare answers to the following questions for the controller:

a. Total fixed cost is $720,000, and a unit of product is sold for $10 in excess of its unit variable cost. What is the break-even unit volume?
b. The company will sell 30,000 units of product—each having a unit variable cost of $14—at a price that will enable the product to absorb $360,000 of fixed cost. What minimum unit sales price must be charged to break even?
c. Net income before income tax of $150,000 is desired after covering $410,000 of fixed cost. What minimum contribution margin ratio must be maintained if total sales revenue is to be $1,600,000?
d. Net income before income tax is 20% of sales revenue, the contribution margin ratio is 60%, and the break-even dollar sales is $200,000. What is the amount of total revenue?
e. Total fixed cost is $350,000, variable cost per unit is $26, and unit sales price is $50. What dollar sales volume will generate a net income of $60,000 when the income tax rate is 40%?

**BREAK-EVEN AND NET INCOME PLANNING
— OBJ. 4, 5, 7 —**

24-33A Venice Company has recently leased facilities for the manufacture of a new product. Based on studies made by its accounting personnel, the following data are available:

Estimated annual sales: 60,000 units

Estimated Costs	Amount	Unit Cost
Direct material	$ 666,000	$11.10
Direct labor	468,000	7.80
Factory overhead	540,000	9.00
Administrative expenses	291,600	4.86
	$1,965,600	$32.76

Selling expenses are expected to be 10% of sales, and the selling price is $42 per unit. Ignore income tax in this problem.

REQUIRED

a. Compute a break-even point in dollars and in units. Assume that factory overhead and administrative expenses are fixed but that other costs are variable.
b. What would net income before income tax be if 50,000 units were sold?
c. How many units must be sold to earn a net income before income tax of 10% of sales?

MULTIPLE PRODUCT BREAK-EVEN AND NET INCOME PLANNING
— OBJ. 4, 5, 7 —

24-34A Madison Company manufactures and sells the following three products:

	Red	Blue	Green
Unit sales	20,000	30,000	50,000
Unit sales price	$30	$62	$18
Unit variable cost	$18	$38	$14

REQUIRED
Assume that total fixed cost is $324,800.
a. Compute the net income before income tax based on the sales volumes shown above.
b. Compute the break-even point in total dollars of revenue and in specific unit sales volume for each product.
c. Prove your break-even calculations by computing the total contribution margin related to your answer in requirement (b).

CASES

Business Decision Case

The following total cost data are for Ralston Manufacturing Company, which has a normal capacity per period of 400,000 units of product that sell for $18 each. For the foreseeable future, regular sales volume should continue at normal capacity of production.

Direct material	$1,720,000
Direct labor	1,120,000
Variable overhead	560,000
Fixed overhead (Note 1)	880,000
Selling expense (Note 2)	720,000
Administrative expense (fixed)	200,000
	$5,200,000

Notes:
1. Beyond normal capacity, fixed overhead cost increases $30,000 for each 20,000 units *or fraction thereof* until a maximum capacity of 640,000 units is reached.
2. Selling expenses are a 10% sales commission plus shipping costs of 60 cents per unit. Ralston pays only one-half of the regular sales commission rate on any sale of 20,000 or more units.

Ralston's sales manager has received a special order for 48,000 units from a large discount chain at a special price of $16 each, F.O.B. factory. The controller's office has furnished the following additional cost data related to the special order:

1. Changes in the product's construction will reduce direct material $1.80 per unit.
2. Special processing will add 25% to the per-unit direct labor costs.
3. Variable overhead will continue at the same proportion of direct labor costs.
4. Other costs should not be affected.

REQUIRED
a. Present an analysis supporting a decision to accept or reject the special order. Assume Ralston's regular sales are not affected by this special order.
b. What is the lowest unit sales price Ralston could receive and still make a before-tax profit of $39,600 on the special order?

Ethics Case

Gina DeMarc, a partner in a large CPA firm, has been approached by Bruce Jonas, a manager, with the following recommendation for incentive bonuses for staff members. Jonas recommends that the firm continue to pay each staff member a straight annual salary (which has been traditionally the only payment made) plus a bonus based on the staff member's ability to achieve a 10% reduction in time spent on each client's work. The firm would also pay a 5% finder's fee for any new client the staff member brings into the firm.

Jonas believes this will motivate the staff to work more efficiently, to sell the firm to new clients, and to service more clients in any given time period. This should also generate more revenue for the firm.

REQUIRED

How would you advise Gina DeMarc? What ethical issues should she consider?

Which information and what forms of analysis are used by management to evaluate performance and analyze new opportunities?

A business may consist of many *different* businesses with a common ownership. ■ For example, General Cinema Corp. owns publisher Harcourt Brace Jovanovich, Inc., specialty retailer The Nieman Marcus Group (Nieman Marcus, Bergdorf Goodman, and Contempo Casuals), and General Cinema Theatres. ■ Management must analyze gross profit, net income, and contribution to gauge each segment's performance. ■ Managers apply differential analysis to special orders, product emphasis, and similar decisions.

25 SPECIAL ANALYSES FOR MANAGEMENT

well-developed accounting system is a continuing source of operational information for management. The quality of information available to management will influence the success of the operating decisions based on that information. In this chapter, we consider the management decision-making process and some cost concepts that are used in managerial analyses.

There are many definitions of *management*. In the broad sense, anyone who directs the activities of others is a manager. For a typical manufacturing firm, this includes shop supervisors, department heads, plant supervisors, division managers, and the company president. A large, complex firm has many management levels.

MANAGEMENT AND THE DECISION-MAKING PROCESS

OBJECTIVE ❶ DESCRIBE *management's use of accounting information in the decision-making process.*

As depicted in Exhibit 25-1, top management is responsible for establishing long-range goals and policies, including major financial arrangements, expansion into foreign markets, and mergers with other firms. Middle-level management may deal with the strategies and tactics related to the automation of a department, the establishment of new product lines, and the direction of the merchandising plan. Such matters as daily production quotas, compliance with planned costs, and other detailed operating concerns are the responsibility of lower-level management. To varying degrees, therefore, all levels of management are involved in decision making.

Decision making requires that a choice be made among alternatives. The business decision process is analogous to the play of a well-organized football team. Virtually all elements of decision making are present in football: the awareness of the objectives and goals that lead to winning; the balancing of such short-run goals as first downs with the long-run goals of winning games and conference championships; the presence of organization, strategy, and tactics in a "hostile" environment in which inaction and poor performance result in losses; the development of plays with the hope of achieving particular results; the moment of commitment in the huddle, immediately followed by the period of execution; and, finally, the informal evaluation of performance on the field followed by a formal evaluation when game films are analyzed.

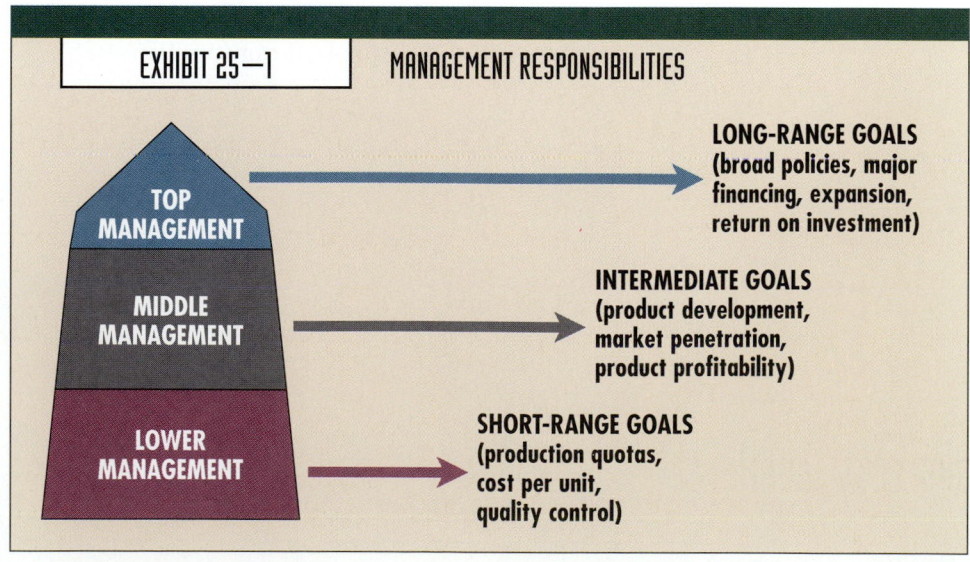

EXHIBIT 25—1   MANAGEMENT RESPONSIBILITIES

TOP MANAGEMENT → **LONG-RANGE GOALS** (broad policies, major financing, expansion, return on investment)

MIDDLE MANAGEMENT → **INTERMEDIATE GOALS** (product development, market penetration, product profitability)

LOWER MANAGEMENT → **SHORT-RANGE GOALS** (production quotas, cost per unit, quality control)

Phases of Decision Making

Decision making may be divided roughly into a planning phase, an execution phase, and an evaluation phase incorporating some form of remedial feedback. The following diagram illustrates the sequential nature of the elements of most decision processes:

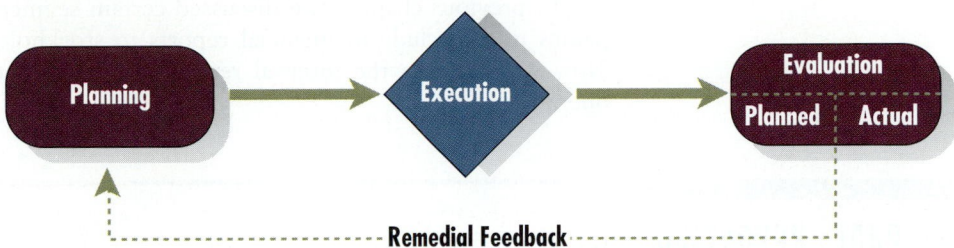

The **planning phase** begins with *goal identification*, the specification of objectives to be sought or accomplished. One of the most common business goals is the long-run optimization of net income. Other goals include target growth rates in sales revenue or total assets and target shares in various markets. Still other goals—such as leadership in product research, innovation, and quality—are difficult to measure. Probably the most widely recognized goal is a specified return on assets.

The next steps in planning are identifying feasible alternative courses of action for achieving desired goals and estimating their qualitative and quantitative effects on the specified goals. All planning involves the future. As a result, data related to the alternative courses of action must be estimated and projected in an environment of uncertainty.

The **execution phase** begins with the actual moment of decision: management commits to a specific plan of action. Because of the complexity of modern industry, some elaborate plans may need lead times of several years. Poor planning, or the absence of planning, may lead to operating crises that carry significant penalties for the firm in terms of extra costs, lost opportunities, and—in extreme cases—bankruptcy.

Once a decision has been made, the plan is implemented, which usually involves the acquisition and commitment of materials, labor, and long-lived assets such as machinery and buildings. Management is kept informed through periodic accounting reports on the acquisition and use of these facilities during the execution phase.

In the **evaluation phase,** steps are taken to control the outcome of a specific plan of action. Virtually every important aspect of business—costs, product quality, inventory levels, and sales revenue—must be reasonably well controlled if a firm is to operate successfully. Measuring performance is an essential element of control. Performance measurement must compare current operations with desired operations to allow management to take remedial action when significant unfavorable variations exist. **Managerial accounting** data and reports play a key role in informing management about performance in various areas during the evaluation phase of decision making.

Decision processes do not, however, fall into three neatly divided phases. Changes in competition, technology, and customer demand must be considered. Furthermore, most management teams are engaged in all three decision-making phases at any given time. They may be planning decisions in one area, executing them in a second, and evaluating them in a third.

BUSINESS SEGMENTS

Many business entities are very complex, with diverse divisions and departments in multiple locations. Management of this type of entity finds it useful to divide the entity into *segments* to enhance managerial planning and control. Segments usually are based on organizational units (divisions or departments) or areas of economic activity (geographic regions or product lines). Many large companies have found that segmentation by organizational unit is the approach that proves most useful. It is important that the managerial accounting systems and procedures that develop information for planning and control decisions be structured to reflect the segmentation.

In previous chapters we discussed certain segment disclosures that public companies must include in financial reports to stockholders and other outside parties. Now we focus on the internal reporting of segment data, including departmental operations.

INTERNAL REPORTING OF SEGMENT OPERATIONS

OBJECTIVE ❷ PRESENT *an overview of reporting operations for segments of a business.*

Internal reporting of segment operations deals primarily with the measurement of operating performance. As a result, segmented reports usually take the format of an income statement or a portion of an income statement. These statements may provide information to answer the following types of questions:

1. What amount does each segment contribute to sales and operating income of the entity as a whole?
2. How do revenues and expenses for each segment compare to planned or budgeted amounts?
3. What is the rate of profitability of each segment? Should any segment be expanded, reduced, or eliminated?
4. Which areas need corrective action and what should be done?
5. Where should promotional effort be directed?

Segments such as divisions or departments are usually classified as either cost centers or profit centers. The manager of a **cost center** is responsible for the costs and expenses of only that segment of the business. He or she has no responsibility for revenue generation. An example of a cost center is the machining department of a manufacturer of consumer products. The output of this department is only a part or an intermediate product that is not sold to consumers outside the company. As a result, no revenue is generated directly by this department.

The manager of a **profit center** is responsible for revenue generation as well as for cost and expense control. An example of a profit center is a division that completely produces a product and sells it to consumers outside the company.

Managerial reports that measure the operating performance of a business entity and its segments reflect whether the segments are profit centers or cost centers. Revenue, expenses, and profitability are reported for segments that are profit centers; only expenses are reported for cost centers. The examples in this chapter are profit centers.

A common principle of segment reporting is that costs are classified as either *controllable* or *noncontrollable*. Under this principle, segment managers should be held responsible *for only costs and expenses that they control*. Frequently, costs are considered controllable at one level of management but not at other levels. For example, the vice president of marketing may be responsible for decisions related to advertising. Even though the cost of advertising is incurred at the division level, the manager of the division should not be held responsible for that expense if a higher-level manager makes all the decisions relative to that cost or expense.

PERFORMANCE REPORTING

Performance reports are usually constructed periodically for each profit center and cost center. They contain different levels of detail for different levels of management. In general, top managers need highly summarized information whereas lower-level managers need specialized reports with greater detail.

OBJECTIVE ③ INTRODUCE *the concept of multiple-level performance reporting.*

Exhibit 25-2 presents three performance reports for three successively higher levels of management. The arrows show how the totals from the lower-level reports flow to and are included in the higher-level reports. Although not all performance reports have the exact format of those in Exhibit 25-2, most will include a comparison of budgeted performance to actual performance.

DEPARTMENTAL OPERATIONS

OBJECTIVE ④ OUTLINE *the procedures for reporting revenue and expense by department and for allocating indirect expenses.*

Departmentalization is a common and logical type of segmentation for many firms. In manufacturing and merchandising firms, departments are generally classified by product sold. The very term *department store* signifies a type of merchandising by product. Food stores are also commonly departmentalized by product groups such as meat, produce, groceries, delicatessen, and so forth. Sometimes departments are classified by type of customer. For example, firms selling such products as floor coverings, lighting fixtures, and heating and air conditioning units may separate commercial sales operations from residential sales operations.

The methods of accounting and reporting for departmental operating activity depend on the performance measures used and the degree of analysis desired by management. Some firms may desire to identify only gross profit by department. In other firms, management may wish to determine a net income figure for each department. Still others may adopt an intermediate performance measure, such as gross profit less only those expenses directly incurred by the department.

Departmental Gross Profit

The main reason for analyzing gross profit by department is that it permits management to review pricing policies and supplier costs. Comparisons can be made among departments to determine areas with high gross profit and in which areas to make major promotional efforts. Comparisons can also be made with gross profit achieved in other periods, or with average percentage statistics for other firms selling the same lines. (These statistics may be obtained from trade association publications and credit agencies.) Often, very low gross profit signals a need to investigate purchasing policies or to revise prices.

To obtain gross profit figures by department, a firm customarily keeps separate departmental accounts for the data used to compute gross profit. Although the specific accounts will vary depending on the inventory system used, the typical departmental accounts include sales and related discounts, returns, and allowances; inventory and cost of goods sold (perpetual inventory system); and inventory, purchases and related discounts, returns, allowances, and transportation in (periodic inventory system).

Exhibit 25-3 is a departmental income statement for Decorator Lighting Company, which uses a periodic inventory system and accumulates gross profit data by department. This firm, segmented into two departments—residential and commercial—sells lighting fixtures to retail residential customers and to builders who purchase fixtures for home construction. In addition, the company supplies lighting fixtures to large-scale contractors engaged in the construction of office buildings and other commercial installations. We will use the data in this income statement in the departmental comparisons that follow.

Departmental Net Income

Ordinarily, it is not difficult to maintain an accounting system in which departmental reporting is carried only to the point of measuring gross profit. A firm that desires a more refined measure of operating performance, however, is faced with the problem of assigning or *allocating* operating expenses to the departments. If a measure of departmental net income is desired, it is necessary to trace *all* expenses to departments.

Some expenses may be readily identified with the operation of particular departments, but others cannot be. To identify expenses with departments, it is helpful to classify them into the two general categories, which appear on the following page:

EXHIBIT 25—2

PERFORMANCE REPORT—SUPERVISOR OF DRILLING DEPARTMENT
FOR THE MONTH OF AUGUST, 1993

	Budgeted Cost	Actual Cost	Over (Under)
Direct material	$16,000	$15,800	$ (200)
Direct labor	18,000	16,700	(1,300)
Factory overhead (listed in detail)	6,200	6,500	300
	$40,200	$39,000	$(1,200)

PERFORMANCE REPORT—MANAGER OF MACHINING OPERATIONS
FOR THE MONTH OF AUGUST, 1993

	Budgeted Cost	Actual Cost	Over (Under)
Lathe department	$ 56,200	$ 51,000	$(5,200)
Drilling department	40,200	39,000	(1,200)
Finishing department	25,900	30,000	4,100
	$122,300	$120,000	$(2,300)

PERFORMANCE REPORT—VICE PRESIDENT OF PRODUCTION
FOR THE MONTH OF AUGUST, 1993

	Budgeted Cost	Actual Cost	Over (Under)
Administration	$ 14,700	$ 19,100	$ 4,400
Machining operations	122,300	120,000	(2,300)
Fabricating operations	118,600	122,300	3,700
Assembly operations	118,400	118,600	200
	$374,000	$380,000	$ 6,000

Direct expenses or costs: Those operating expenses or costs traceable to and incurred for the benefit of a single department and thus ordinarily controllable by the department.

Indirect expenses or costs: Those operating expenses or costs incurred for the benefit of multiple departments and thus neither traceable to nor controllable by a specific department.

For example, payroll expense related to personnel who work exclusively in one department is a direct expense of that department. Payroll expense related to administrative personnel whose work benefits all departments is an indirect expense of the operating departments. A firm usually has many indirect expenses, incurred for the benefit of more than one department. Some examples are heat, light, maintenance, depreciation, and other occupancy expenses, office salaries, executive salaries, and a variety of other administrative expenses. These expenses must be fairly allocated to the operating departments if the measure of departmental net income is to be meaningful. Because it is difficult and cumbersome to allocate indirect expenses at the time

---

EXHIBIT 25—3

DECORATOR LIGHTING COMPANY
DEPARTMENTAL INCOME STATEMENT
FOR THE YEAR ENDED DECEMBER 31, 1993

	Residential Department	Commercial Department	Total
Sales	$330,000	$220,000	$550,000
Less: Sales Returns and Allowances	(4,000)	(5,500)	(9,500)
Sales Discounts	(6,000)	(4,500)	(10,500)
Net Sales	$320,000	$210,000	$530,000
Cost of Goods Sold:			
Inventory, Jan. 1, 1993	$ 88,000	$ 42,000	$130,000
Purchases	194,000	144,000	338,000
Less: Purchases Returns	(4,500)	(2,000)	(6,500)
Purchases Discounts	(3,500)	(3,000)	(6,500)
Transportation In	6,000	4,000	10,000
Cost of Goods Available for Sale	$280,000	$185,000	$465,000
Less: Inventory, Dec. 31, 1993	72,000	38,000	110,000
Cost of Goods Sold	$208,000	$147,000	$355,000
Gross Profit	$112,000	$ 63,000	$175,000
Operating Expenses:			
Selling Expenses			$ 70,000
Administrative Expenses			60,000
Total Operating Expenses			$130,000
Income before Tax			$ 45,000
Income Tax Expense			15,100
Net Income			$ 29,900

they are incurred, they are usually analyzed and allocated to departments at the end of the accounting period.[1]

Assume that the $130,000 operating expenses for Decorator Lighting Company in Exhibit 25-3 consisted of the following:

Sales salaries expense	$ 45,000
Advertising expense	15,000
Delivery expense	10,000
Insurance expense (on merchandise)	6,000
Occupancy expense	16,000
Uncollectible accounts expense	3,000
Office salaries expense	20,000
Other administrative expense	15,000
	$130,000

In preparing a departmental income statement, Decorator Lighting might analyze and allocate these expenses, and the income tax expense of $15,100, as follows.

SALES SALARIES EXPENSE   The sales force for the residential department is separate from that of the commercial department. Therefore, the sales salaries for each department can be directly determined from payroll records, which show $25,000 for the residential department and $20,000 for the commercial department.

---

[1] This approach is consistent with allocation approaches presented in previous chapters (package purchase and service department costs and joint product cost).

ADVERTISING EXPENSE

Of the company's $15,000 advertising expense, $7,000 was spent on newspaper and television advertising of residential lighting products, $3,000 on producing illustrated brochures with price lists for commercial customers, and $5,000 on general newspaper advertising directed at both markets. The latter amount was allocated on the basis of relative sales ($330,000/$550,000 = 60% residential; $220,000/$550,000 = 40% commercial).

	Residential	Commercial	Total
Direct advertising	$ 7,000	$3,000	$10,000
Indirect advertising	3,000	2,000	5,000
	$10,000	$5,000	$15,000

DELIVERY EXPENSE

Products are delivered to all commercial customers via Ace Trucking Service at a cost of $2,000. All residential deliveries are made with the company's own truck or via United Delivery Service and total $8,000. Thus, departmental delivery costs can be determined directly.

INSURANCE EXPENSE (on merchandise)

The cost of insurance is based on the average inventories of the two departments:

Residential ($88,000 + $72,000)/2 =	$ 80,000	80/120 × $6,000 = $4,000
Commercial ($42,000 + $38,000)/2 =	40,000	40/120 × $6,000 = 2,000
	$120,000	$6,000

OCCUPANCY EXPENSE

Rent, maintenance, and utility expenses are included in this item, which is allocated on the basis of square feet of floor space used by each department. Of the total floor space, $\frac{5}{8}$ is occupied by the residential department and $\frac{3}{8}$ by the commercial department. Of the $16,000 total cost, $10,000 is allocated to the residential department and $6,000 to the commercial department.

UNCOLLECTIBLE ACCOUNTS EXPENSE

The firm maintains a separate customers' ledger for each department and determines its expense from uncollectible accounts by aging the accounts. Estimated uncollectible accounts totaled $1,600 for residential customers and $1,400 for commercial customers.

OFFICE SALARIES AND OTHER ADMINISTRATIVE EXPENSE

Often, salaries of office personnel and other administrative expenses are allocated to departments on the basis of the relative sales of each department, since a good share of this cost is related to billings, collections, and customer inquiries. The alternative is to attempt an analysis of time spent by office employees on the affairs of each department and to estimate administrative supplies used, correspondence, and other office expenses by department. Such analysis is liable to be costly and time-consuming, and it may not provide much additional accuracy. Decorator Lighting uses relative sales as a basis, allocating 60% of the expenses to the residential department and 40% to the commercial department:

	Residential 60%	Commercial 40%	Total
Office salaries expense	$12,000	$ 8,000	$20,000
Other administrative expense	9,000	6,000	15,000
	$21,000	$14,000	$35,000

INCOME TAX EXPENSE

Because Decorator Lighting Company is a corporation, it must pay federal income taxes at the appropriate rates on various portions of its taxable income. Here we assume that the total tax on $45,000 income is $15,100. The only realistic way to allocate the tax expense is on the basis of income before taxes. These amounts must be calculated by department (see Exhibit 25-4) before income tax expense can be allocated to the departments. Thus $32,400/$45,000 × $15,100 = $10,872 tax expense for the residential department, and $12,600/$45,000 × $15,100 = $4,228 tax

EXHIBIT 25-4

DECORATOR LIGHTING COMPANY
DEPARTMENTAL INCOME STATEMENT
FOR THE YEAR ENDED DECEMBER 31, 1993

	Residential Department	Commercial Department	Total
Net Sales	$320,000	$210,000	$530,000
Cost of Goods Sold	208,000	147,000	355,000
Gross Profit	$112,000	$ 63,000	$175,000
Operating Expenses:			
Sales Salaries Expense	$ 25,000	$ 20,000	$ 45,000
Advertising Expense	10,000	5,000	15,000
Delivery Expense	8,000	2,000	10,000
Insurance Expense	4,000	2,000	6,000
Occupancy Expense	10,000	6,000	16,000
Uncollectible Accounts Expense	1,600	1,400	3,000
Office Salaries Expense	12,000	8,000	20,000
Other Administrative Expense	9,000	6,000	15,000
Total Operating Expenses	$ 79,600	$ 50,400	$130,000
Income before Tax	$ 32,400	$ 12,600	$ 45,000
Income Tax Expense	10,872	4,228	15,100
Net Income	$ 21,528	$ 8,372	$ 29,900

expense for the commercial department. Some accountants believe that because departments are not taxable entities, allocation of tax expense among them does not result in meaningful performance measures; they would extend the departmental figures only to income before taxes.

A summary of the operating expenses and income tax expense, giving the direct expenses and allocated indirect expenses of each department, follows.

	Residential Department			Commercial Department		
	Direct	Indirect	Total	Direct	Indirect	Total
Sales salaries expense	$25,000		$25,000	$20,000		$20,000
Advertising expense	7,000	$ 3,000	10,000	3,000	$ 2,000	5,000
Delivery expense	8,000		8,000	2,000		2,000
Insurance expense (on merchandise)	4,000		4,000	2,000		2,000
Occupancy expense		10,000	10,000		6,000	6,000
Uncollectible accounts expense	1,600		1,600	1,400		1,400
Office salaries expense		12,000	12,000		8,000	8,000
Other administrative expense		9,000	9,000		6,000	6,000
Total	$45,600	$34,000	$79,600	$28,400	$22,000	$50,400
Income tax expense		$10,872			$ 4,228	

This departmental expense distribution was used to prepare the income statement for Decorator Lighting Company shown in Exhibit 25-4, which extends the departmental operating results through net income.

Departmental Contribution to Indirect Expenses

Operating statements that extend departmental results to net income measures are often criticized on the grounds that the indirect or common expenses are not controllable at the departmental level and therefore should not be assigned to departments when measuring performance. An additional criticism is that the bases for assignment of indirect expenses are frequently arbitrary.

EXHIBIT 25—5

DECORATOR LIGHTING COMPANY
DEPARTMENTAL INCOME STATEMENT
SHOWING CONTRIBUTIONS TO INDIRECT EXPENSES
FOR THE YEAR ENDED DECEMBER 31, 1993

	Residential Department	Commercial Department	Total
Net Sales	$320,000	$210,000	$530,000
Cost of Goods Sold	208,000	147,000	355,000
Gross Profit	$112,000	$ 63,000	$175,000
Direct Operating Expenses:			
Sales Salaries Expense	$ 25,000	$ 20,000	$ 45,000
Advertising Expense	7,000	3,000	10,000
Delivery Expense	8,000	2,000	10,000
Insurance Expense	4,000	2,000	6,000
Uncollectible Accounts Expense	1,600	1,400	3,000
Total Direct Expenses	$ 45,600	$ 28,400	$ 74,000
Contribution to Indirect Expenses	$ 66,400	$ 34,600	$101,000
Indirect Operating Expenses:			
Advertising Expense			$ 5,000
Occupancy Expense			16,000
Office Salaries Expense			20,000
Other Administrative Expense			15,000
Total Indirect Expenses			$ 56,000
Income before Tax			$ 45,000
Income Tax Expense			15,100
Net Income			$ 29,900

Some accountants favor an intermediate type of performance measure as a means of appraising departmental operating results. The **departmental contribution to indirect expenses** is obtained by deducting the direct departmental expenses from departmental gross profit. The resulting amount is a measure of the department's contribution to the firm's pool of common or indirect expenses incurred for the benefit of all operating units. Using this measure eliminates the need for allocating the indirect expenses. Although this approach emphasizes direct expenses, it should not be assumed that all aspects of direct expenses are controllable at the departmental level. Higher management may direct that a certain amount of expense be incurred by a department. The expense is properly described as direct and no allocation is required, but to say it is fully controllable at the departmental level would be incorrect. A departmental income statement showing departmental contributions appears in Exhibit 25-5.

VARIABLE COSTING

OBJECTIVE ⑤ DISCUSS *variable costing and the differences between variable costing and absorption costing.*

In a previous chapter, we defined product costs as all factory costs: direct material, direct labor, and factory overhead. These costs were capitalized as inventory during the production period and recognized as expense (cost of goods sold) only when the related merchandise was sold. This method of attaching all factory costs to the product is known as **absorption costing.**

In contrast, some firms use **variable costing** to determine the cost of their manufactured products.[2] Under variable costing, only variable manufacturing costs are

---

[2] Variable costing is also referred to as *direct costing.* The latter is a misnomer, however, because *variable* costs—not *direct* costs—are capitalized under direct costing. This distinction is readily apparent in Exhibit 25-6.

| EXHIBIT 25—6 | COMPARISON OF ABSORPTION AND VARIABLE COSTING | | | | | |

Typical Manufacturing Cost (or Expense)	Typical Behavior Pattern	Absorption Costing Product Cost	Absorption Costing Period Cost	Variable Costing Product Cost	Variable Costing Period Cost
Direct costs:					
Direct material	Variable	X		X	
Direct labor	Variable	X		X	
Indirect costs:					
Variable factory overhead	Variable	X		X	
Fixed factory overhead	Fixed	X			X
Other expenses:					
Selling	Semivariable		X		X
Nonfactory administrative	Semivariable		X		X

capitalized as inventory. Any fixed manufacturing cost is expensed in the period incurred. Exhibit 25-6 contrasts the two approaches to costing. The only difference between absorption and variable costing is that fixed factory overhead is capitalized under absorption costing and expensed under variable costing.

In general, variable costing (carrying only variable costs in the inventory accounts) is considered a departure from financial accounting standards. These standards require that published financial reports attested to by CPAs be prepared on an absorption costing basis. In these reports, all factory costs should be attributed to products, and inventories of work in process and finished goods should contain their allocable shares of factory costs, both fixed and variable. Likewise, the Internal Revenue Service has generally insisted on the use of absorption costing in determining net income for tax purposes, with some adjustments.

Although variable costing should not be used to prepare financial statements for external use, management may use variable costing statements for internal analytical purposes. A principal benefit is that variable costing usually causes net income figures to move in the same direction as sales. With absorption costing, net income may increase in periods when production volume outstrips sales and decrease when the company outsells production and thus reduces inventory levels.

In Exhibit 25-7, a comparison of partial income statements for Elway Company for three periods, using both absorption costing and variable costing, demonstrates the effects just discussed. For this simple illustration, we assume that a single item is sold for $5 per unit, that variable product costs are $1 per unit, and that fixed manufacturing costs are $300 per period. The following sales and production figures, in units, are given for the three periods:

	Period 1	Period 2	Period 3	Total
Sales (in units)	100	100	100	300
Production (in units)	100	150	50	300

Elway Company normally produces and sells 100 units per period. Note, however, that in period 2 the company produced an additional 50 units for inventory that are sold in period 3 together with the 50 units produced in period 3.

In the absorption costing statement shown in the top half of Exhibit 25-7, the cost of goods manufactured includes fixed product costs of $300 per period and variable product costs of $1 per unit produced. The $150 inventory shown at the end of period 2 consists of $50 variable costs (50 units × $1) and $100 fixed costs. (Because one-third of the units produced remains in inventory, one-third of the $300 fixed costs is assigned to the inventory.)

In the variable costing statement shown in the lower half of Exhibit 25-7, the cost of goods manufactured includes only variable product costs at $1 per unit

MEASUREMENT AND CONTROL OF DIVISIONAL PERFORMANCE

To measure divisional performance by means of a profit figure arrived at after deducting items that are neither controllable at divisional level nor directly related to divisional activity is to use a measure that is arbitrary to the extent that the allocations are arbitrary. It is not independent of conditions outside the division and may lead divisions into courses of action detrimental to the company. It could, moreover, mislead head office executives into thinking that a division was making a loss or a very small profit, and that therefore it should be liquidated. This could happen even though the facts were that, although the division was failing to make an adequate contribution to the head office expenses and profit, it was making *some* contribution, sufficient perhaps to keep it operating in the hope of eventual recovery.

Most company executives are aware of these arguments against expense allocations but are not always convinced by them. The counterargument most commonly used is that divisions must be made aware that there are nondivisional costs to be covered out of their earnings before the company as a whole can show a profit. Unless this awareness is sharpened by showing the central expense allocations on the divisional profit statements each month, the division may, in pricing policies and other marketing decisions, plan to contribute less than its due share of the company's net income. Moreover, it is argued, if the division were an independent company it would have a top administration of its own.

These counterarguments are not convincing. It is true that some methods of overhead allocation (e.g., allocations based on divisional sales) create possibilities for a division to diminish its contribution to the company's over-all profitability while increasing its own apparent net profit. But such aberrations result simply from the fact of allocation itself. Apart from such allocation practices, *so long as corporate (i.e., nondivisional) expenses are independent of divisional activity*, whatever policies maximize divisional net profits will also maximize divisional contributions to corporate profits before the allocation of corporate expenses. In the general case, in other words, corporate net profits will not suffer if corporate fixed expenses are left unallocated.

SOURCE: David Solomons, *Divisional Performance: Measurement and Control*, (New York: Financial Executives Research Foundation, Inc., 1965). Reprinted by permission.

---

produced. Likewise, the inventory at the end of period 2 consists of only $1 variable product cost times the 50 units in the inventory.

A total of $300 gross profit is reported for the three periods under both methods. However, the variable costing method shows the same gross profit figures each period, which are correlated with the constant sales volume over the three periods. On the other hand, under the absorption costing method, gross profit moves up and down with production. The reason, of course, is that the fixed costs are added to the inventory when production outstrips sales and are released when the company sells its entire inventory.

To highlight the effect of variable costing on inventories and income in the foregoing illustration, we considered only manufacturing costs. When detailed income statements are prepared under the variable costing method, fixed and variable costs of all types—including selling and administrative expenses—must be properly segregated. An example of a detailed income statement prepared in accordance with the variable costing concept is shown in Exhibit 25-8.

The term **manufacturing margin,** which appears in Exhibit 25-8, is defined as the difference between revenue and variable cost of goods sold. Contribution margin

EXHIBIT 25—7

ELWAY COMPANY
PARTIAL INCOME STATEMENTS

Absorption Costing

	Period 1	Period 2	Period 3
Sales (100 units @ $5)	$500	$500	$500
Cost of Goods Sold:			
Beginning Inventory	$–0–	$–0–	$150
Cost of Goods Manufactured	400	450	350
	$400	$450	$500
Ending Inventory	–0–	150	–0–
Cost of Goods Sold	400	300	500
Gross Profit	$100	$200	$–0–

Variable Costing

	Period 1	Period 2	Period 3
Sales (100 units @ $5)	$500	$500	$500
Cost of Goods Sold:			
Beginning Inventory	$–0–	$–0–	$ 50
Variable Cost of Goods Manufactured	100	150	50
	$100	$150	$100
Ending Inventory	–0–	50	–0–
Variable Cost of Goods Sold	100	100	100
	$400	$400	$400
Fixed Manufacturing Costs	300	300	300
Gross Profit	$100	$100	$100

EXHIBIT 25—8

ROGERS COMPANY
VARIABLE COSTING INCOME STATEMENT
FOR THE YEAR ENDED DECEMBER 31, 1993

Sales (20,000 units @ $5)		$100,000
Variable Cost of Goods Sold:		
Beginning Inventory (12,000 units @ $3)	$36,000	
Cost of Goods Manufactured (18,000 units @ $3)	54,000	
Goods Available for Sale	$90,000	
Ending Inventory (10,000 units @ $3)	30,000	60,000
Manufacturing Margin		$ 40,000
Variable Selling and Administrative Expenses:		
Variable Selling Expense	$ 8,000	
Variable Administrative Expense	4,000	12,000
Contribution Margin		$ 28,000
Fixed Costs and Expenses:		
Fixed Manufacturing Cost	$12,000	
Fixed Selling Expense	5,000	
Fixed Administrative Expense	3,000	20,000
Net Income		$ 8,000

can be determined by deducting variable selling and administrative expenses from the manufacturing margin. All types of fixed costs and expenses—manufacturing, selling, and administrative—are deducted to arrive at net income.

The following advantages and disadvantages of using variable costing originate in the fact that under variable costing no fixed overhead costs are assigned to inventory carrying values.

Advantages of Variable Costing

1. Management may be more aware of cost behavior in the firm's operations and may be likely to use this information in short-term decision situations in which contribution margin analysis is most appropriate.
2. Reported net income tends to follow sales volume. (This may not be true under absorption costing.)
3. Cost-volume-profit relationships are more easily discerned from variable costing income statements than from conventional absorption costing statements.

Disadvantages of Variable Costing

1. Accounting measures derived under variable costing are not in accord with generally accepted accounting principles, nor are they acceptable for reporting purposes under the Internal Revenue Code.
2. Inventories (and therefore working capital and owners' equity) tend to be understated.
3. Carrying inventories at only their variable costs may lead to long-run pricing decisions that provide for recovery of variable cost only rather than total cost, and thus does not produce net income in the long run.

DIFFERENTIAL ANALYSIS

OBJECTIVE **6** DESCRIBE *the use of differential analysis.*

Differential analysis is based on the widely accepted decision rule that *only the aspects of a choice that differ among alternatives are relevant to a decision.* For example, when you are deciding which theater to attend, the admission price is irrelevant if both theaters charge the same price. However, if the cost to park is $4 at one and $3 at the other, then the $1 differential cost is relevant to the choice. The decision process is simplified by concentrating on only the factors that are different.

Suppose a firm may use certain facilities to produce and sell either product A or product B. The decision is to be in favor of the product promising the higher net income based on the following estimated operating data:

	Alternatives	
	Product A	**Product B**
Units that can be produced and sold	12,000	18,000
Unit selling price	$8	$6
Manufacturing costs:		
Variable (per unit)	$3	$2
Fixed (total)	$32,000	$32,000
Selling and administrative expenses:		
Variable (per unit)	$1.50	$1.50
Fixed (total)	$6,000	$6,000

We may compare the alternatives by preparing comparative income statements from this estimated data:

	Alternatives		
	Product A	**Product B**	**Difference**
Revenue			
(12,000 units @ $8)	$96,000		
(18,000 units @ $6)		$108,000	$12,000

Cost of goods sold (manufacturing costs):			
Variable (12,000 @ $3 per unit)	$36,000		
(18,000 @ $2 per unit)		$ 36,000	$ –0–
Fixed (total)	32,000	32,000	–0–
Selling and administrative expenses:			
Variable (@ $1.50 per unit)	18,000	27,000	9,000
Fixed (total)	6,000	6,000	–0–
Total expenses	$92,000	$101,000	$ 9,000
Net income	$ 4,000	$ 7,000	$ 3,000

This analysis shows a $3,000 increase in net income associated with product B as a result of a $12,000 increase in total revenue that is partially offset by a $9,000 increase in variable selling and administrative expenses.

Differential analysis of the same situation is illustrated below, where consideration is limited to the revenue and expense factors that differ if product B is produced rather than product A.

Differential revenue:		
Revenue forgone on first 12,000 units [($8 − $6) × 12,000]		($24,000)
Additional revenue from increased sales volume ($6 × 6,000)		36,000
Net additional revenue		$12,000
Differential costs:		
Increase in variable selling and administrative expenses ($1.50 × 6,000)		9,000
Net differential income in favor of product B		$ 3,000

Clearly, the differential approach shows the same net advantage for product B as the income statements but does so more concisely. For this reason, management often uses differential analysis in decision making.

ILLUSTRATIONS OF DIFFERENTIAL ANALYSIS

Business firms occasionally receive special orders from purchasers who wish a price concession. The prospective purchaser may suggest a price or ask for a bid. Sometimes the buyer may request that the firm produce a special version of a product to be identified with the buyer's private brand. As long as no overriding qualitative considerations exist, management should evaluate such propositions fully and be receptive to their profit potential.

The Special Order

OBJECTIVE 7 PROVIDE *examples of the use of differential analysis in managerial decision making.*

BUSINESS SITUATION Assume that Oxford Company makes a nationally advertised automobile accessory, which it sells to distributors for $16. A discount firm has proposed that Oxford Company supply 2,000 units of the accessory for $14 per unit. The accessory would carry the brand name of the discount firm. If Oxford Company were to accept the order, a special machine attachment would be needed to differentiate the product and imprint the private brand. This attachment, which costs $1,500, would be discarded after the order was processed. Also assume that Oxford Company has unused production capacity, and thus anticipates no change in fixed capacity costs. The following unit cost data are available for the regular production of the accessory item:

Direct material	$ 5
Direct labor	4
Variable factory overhead	2
Fixed factory overhead (allocated)	3
Total cost per unit	$14

ANALYSIS AND RECOMMENDATION At first glance, the proposal seems unprofitable because the unit cost figure shown here is $14, the same as the buyer's offered price, and an additional cost of $1,500 must be incurred to process the order. However, the fixed overhead of $3 included in the $14 total unit cost is not relevant to the decision and should not be considered, because Oxford Company's total fixed cost will be incurred whether the special order is accepted or not. The following differential cost and revenue analysis reveals that the special order should be accepted:

Increase in revenue (2,000 units × $14)			$28,000
Increase in costs:			
Direct material	$ 5 per unit		
Direct labor	4 per unit		
Variable factory overhead	2 per unit		
	$11 × 2,000 units	$22,000	
Cost of special attachment		1,500	
Total differential cost			23,500
Net advantage in accepting special order			$ 4,500

The differential costs of accepting the order consist of the variable production costs and the additional cost of the attachment needed to differentiate the product. Actually, with any price higher than $11.75 ($23,500 total differential costs ÷ 2,000 units), Oxford Company would earn a profit on the order.

Note that excess production capacity is significant to the special order decision. Without sufficient excess capacity, the additional production would probably cause additional amounts of fixed costs to be incurred. Also observe that although the $1,500 special attachment in this example is a fixed cost, it is relevant to this decision.

ADDITIONAL DECISION FACTORS   Specific qualitative factors that should be considered here include ascertaining that (1) the special price does not constitute unfair price discrimination prohibited under the Robinson-Patman Act, (2) regular sales at regular prices are not unfavorably affected by the sales of the discount store, and (3) the long-term price structure for the product is not adversely affected by the special order. Significant concern in any of these areas might be a basis for rejecting the special order despite the potential $4,500 profit.

Make or Buy?

Many manufacturing situations require the assembly of large numbers of specially designed components and subassemblies. Usually, the manufacturer must choose between making these components and subassemblies or buying them from outside suppliers. In each situation, management should evaluate the relative costs of the two choices. Because making a component uses some portion of the firm's manufacturing capacity, we assume that no more attractive use of that capacity is available.

BUSINESS SITUATION   To illustrate the make-or-buy decision, we assume that Gordon Company has made 10,000 units of a necessary component at the following costs:

Direct material	$10,000
Direct labor	12,000
Variable factory overhead	4,000
Fixed factory overhead	24,000
Total cost	$50,000
Cost per unit ($50,000/10,000)	$5

Investigations by Gordon Company's purchasing department indicate that a comparable component can be purchased in sufficient quantities at a unit price of $4.50, an indicated savings of 50 cents per unit. At first glance, the opportunity to purchase seems most attractive. The analysis of differential costs, however, shows quite the contrary.

ANALYSIS AND RECOMMENDATION   A review of operations indicates that by purchasing the component, Gordon Company can reduce fixed overhead associated with producing the component from $24,000 to $8,000. A differential analysis follows:

	Make Part	Buy Part	Increase (Decrease) in Cost if Part Is Bought
Cost of 10,000 units:			
Direct material	$10,000		($10,000)
Direct labor	12,000		(12,000)
Variable factory overhead	4,000		(4,000)
Fixed factory overhead	24,000	$ 8,000	(16,000)
Purchase price of components		45,000	45,000
	$50,000	$53,000	$ 3,000

The following approach to this analysis confirms the more comprehensive one above.

Cost to purchase component (10,000 × $4.50)		$45,000
Less costs avoided by purchasing:		
Direct material	$10,000	
Direct labor	12,000	
Variable factory overhead	4,000	
Fixed factory overhead	16,000	42,000
Increase in acquisition cost by purchasing		$ 3,000

ADDITIONAL DECISION FACTORS These analyses assume that the manufacturing capacity released by the decision to purchase would not be used. However, should an opportunity arise to use this capacity to generate more than $3,000 of contribution margin, then the opportunity to purchase the components would be attractive.

Dropping Unprofitable Segments

BUSINESS SITUATION Assume that the condensed income statement in Exhibit 25-9 reflects last year's operations of Martin Company. It might seem that the firm's total income could be raised to $125,000 by discontinuing department C and avoiding that segment's $25,000 operating loss.

ANALYSIS AND RECOMMENDATION The following differential analysis, however, indicates that the firm's overall income would decrease, rather than increase, by discontinuing department C (assume fixed manufacturing cost would decrease by $20,000):

Decrease in revenue		$300,000
Decrease in costs and expenses:		
Variable cost of goods sold	$175,000	
Variable operating expense	70,000	
Fixed manufacturing cost	20,000	265,000
Decrease in total contribution margin (and net income) from discontinuing department C		$ 35,000

Even though department C reports a $25,000 annual loss, it does generate a contribution margin of $55,000 toward the absorption of fixed costs and expenses. If department C is discontinued, there would be no contribution margin, although $60,000 of fixed cost would remain. This would result in a loss of $60,000, which is $35,000 worse than the current $25,000 loss.

ADDITIONAL DECISION FACTORS Management must often consider other factors in decisions of this type. Among these are (1) the potential termination of employees and subsequent effects on employee morale and (2) the possible effects on customer patronage (for example, customers of departments A and B may go to other firms for all their purchases if department C's products are no longer available from the same source).

Sell or Process Further?

Firms sometimes face the decision of either selling products at one point in the production sequence or processing them further and selling them at a higher price. Examples are finished versus unfinished furniture, regular versus high-test gasoline,

---

EXHIBIT 25—9

MARTIN COMPANY
CONDENSED INCOME STATEMENT
FOR THE YEAR ENDED JUNE 30, 1993
(THOUSANDS OF DOLLARS)

	Total	A	B	C
Sales	$1,400	$700	$400	$300
Variable Costs:				
Manufacturing	$ 600	$300	$125	$175
Operating	130	40	20	70
Total Variable Costs	$ 730	$340	$145	$245
Contribution Margin	$ 670	$360	$255	$ 55
Fixed Costs:				
Manufacturing	$ 400	$200	$150	$ 50
Operating	170	80	60	30
Total Fixed Costs	$ 570	$280	$210	$ 80
Net Income	$ 100	$ 80	$ 45	$ (25)

---

and unassembled kits versus assembled units of product. These process-further decision situations present another opportunity to apply differential analysis.

BUSINESS SITUATION Assume that Lindar Company makes and sells 50,000 unfinished telephone stands with the following operating figures per unit:

Current sales price		$12.00
Costs:		
Direct material	$4.00	
Direct labor	2.00	
Variable factory overhead	1.50	
Fixed factory overhead*	1.00	8.50
Gross margin per unit		$ 3.50

*Applied at 50% of direct labor costs (total fixed factory overhead is $60,000).

Lindar Company now has excess productive capacity, which should remain available in the foreseeable future. Consequently, management believes that part of this excess capacity could be used to paint and decorate the telephone stands and sell them at $15 per unit in the finished furniture market. A study carried out by the company's production department indicates that the additional processing will add $1.30 to the direct material cost and 80 cents to the direct labor cost of each unit and that variable overhead will continue to be incurred at 75% of direct labor cost.

ANALYSIS AND RECOMMENDATION The following differential analysis supports the proposal to process further:

	Per Unit	Totals for 50,000 Units
Differential revenue ($15 − $12)	$3.00	$150,000
Differential cost:		
Direct material	$1.30	$ 65,000
Direct labor	0.80	40,000
Variable factory overhead (75% of $0.80)	0.60	30,000
Fixed factory overhead	–0–	–0–
Total differential cost	2.70	$135,000
Excess of differential revenue over differential cost	$0.30	$ 15,000

Both the per-unit and total differential analyses indicate the advantage of processing further.

Product Emphasis

Because most firms produce several products, management must continually examine operating data and decide which combination of products offers the greatest total long-term profit potential. The decisions related to product emphasis are seldom as simple as determining the most profitable product and confining production to that one product. Typically, management faces such operational constraints as limited demand for the most profitable products, the competitive necessity of offering a line of products with a variety of qualities and capacities, and, in seeking better utilization of existing capacity, the need to produce other, less profitable products.

In product emphasis analysis, an important and widely accepted generalization is that *the firm optimizes its income when it maximizes the contribution margin earned per unit of constraining resource.* The concept of constraining resource stems from the realization that as a firm increases its volume, some resource is eventually exhausted and thus constrains, or limits, the continued expansion of the firm. Which resources are constraining depends on the firm, the operating conditions, and even the products under consideration. Typical examples are key materials, labor skills, machine capacities, and factory floor space or storage space. Simply stated, management has optimized the firm's product mix when it maximizes the contribution margin earned on each unit of the particular resource that limits increased production.

BUSINESS SITUATION To illustrate product emphasis decisions, assume that Beta Company produces products X, Y, and Z, and that factory machine capacity is its constraining resource. Beta Company operates at 90% capacity, and management wants to devote the unused capacity to one of the products. The following data represent Beta Company's current operations:

	Products		
	X	**Y**	**Z**
Per-unit data:			
Sales price	$20	$22	$6
Variable costs	8	16	2
Contribution margin	$12	$ 6	$4
Fixed costs*	6	2	1
Net income	$ 6	$ 4	$3

*Allocated on basis of machine hours at $1 per hour.

ANALYSIS AND RECOMMENDATION Intuition suggests that the extra capacity should be devoted either to product Y, which has the highest sales price, or to product X, which has the highest per-unit contribution margin and net income. However, an analysis of the *contribution margin of each product per unit of constraining factor* reveals that product Z should receive the added capacity.

Note that fixed costs are allocated among products on the basis of machine hours—the constraining resource in our example. Furthermore, the unit allocations of fixed costs, above, indicate that product X requires three times as many machine hours as product Y and six times as many as product Z. The contribution per unit of machine capacity for each product follows:

	Products		
	X	**Y**	**Z**
Contribution margin per unit	$12	$6	$4
Divided by units of machine capacity required	6	2	1
Contribution margin per unit of machine capacity (the constraining resource)	$ 2	$3	$4

Use of the remaining capacity generates a greater contribution margin if devoted to product Z. As this example illustrates, in deciding product emphasis, management should use contribution margin per unit of constraining resource, rather than the relative sales prices, unit contribution margins, or even unit profit of various products.

KEY POINTS FOR CHAPTER OBJECTIVES

❶ **DESCRIBE** management's use of accounting information in the decision-making process (pp. 940–942).
- Top management establishes long-range goals, middle management deals with intermediate goals, and lower management focuses on short-range goals.
- Decision making, which is essentially choosing among alternatives, usually comprises three phases: planning, execution, and evaluation.

❷ **PRESENT** an overview of reporting operations for segments of a business (p. 942).
- Business segments may consist of organizational units (departments or divisions) or areas of economic activity (product lines or markets).
- A business segment may be a profit center (where management is responsible for both revenues and expenses) or a cost center (where management is responsible for expenses only).
- Accounting and reporting by business segment are indispensible to management and very important to external groups such as investors and creditors.

❸ **INTRODUCE** the concept of multiple-level performance reporting (pp. 942–943).
- A performance report is usually prepared each accounting period for each profit center and each cost center.
- Total amounts from lower-level reports flow to and are included in higher-level reports.

❹ **OUTLINE** the procedures for reporting revenue and expense by department and for allocating indirect expenses (pp. 943–948).
- Expenses incurred by, or for the benefit of, one business segment are called *direct expenses*. Expenses incurred for more than one business segment are called *indirect expenses* and are allocated to segments using appropriate bases of allocation.
- Reporting for segments of a firm is typically extended to one of three operating measures: gross profit, contribution to indirect expenses, or net income. When net income is used, both direct and indirect expenses are deducted from gross profit. When contribution to indirect expenses is used, only direct expenses are deducted.

❺ **DISCUSS** variable costing and the differences between variable costing and absorption costing (pp. 948–952).
- Variable costing does not assign fixed factory overhead as a product cost but expenses it in the period incurred.
- Manufacturing margin describes the difference between revenue and variable cost of goods sold.
- Accounting measures derived under variable costing are not in accord with generally acceptable accounting principles, nor are they acceptable for tax reporting.

❻ **DESCRIBE** the use of differential analysis (pp. 952–953).
- Differential analysis is the study of those amounts that are expected to differ among alternatives.

❼ **PROVIDE** examples of the use of differential analysis in managerial decision making (pp. 953–958).
- The special order at a special price.
- Make or buy needed components for products.
- Dropping unprofitable business segments.
- Sell or process further.
- Product emphasis.

SELF-TEST QUESTIONS FOR REVIEW

(Answers follow the Solution to Demonstration Problem.)

1. The manager of which of the following segments of a business is responsible for revenue generation as well as for cost and expense control?
   - **a.** Cost center.
   - **b.** Accounting department.
   - **c.** Profit center.
   - **d.** Assembly line.

2. Which of the following is not considered in determining contribution to indirect expenses?
   a. Income taxes.
   b. Cost of goods sold.
   c. Direct expenses.
   d. Net sales.

3. In performance reporting (budgeted cost compared to actual cost), which performance report must be prepared first?
   a. Division, consisting of five departments.
   b. Region, consisting of three divisions.
   c. Department, consisting of four cost centers.
   d. Company, consisting of two regions.

4. When using differential analysis to analyze two alternatives to the current operation, what factors should not be considered?
   a. Direct material costs that are different.
   b. Direct labor costs that exist for only one alternative.
   c. Overhead costs that are the same for both alternatives.
   d. Sales commissions that apply to only one alternative.

5. In determining inventory costs, which of the following cost elements is included when using absorption costing but excluded when using variable costing?
   a. Selling costs.
   b. Direct labor cost.
   c. Nonfactory administrative costs.
   d. Fixed overhead.

DEMONSTRATION PROBLEM FOR REVIEW

Tuttle Manufacturing Company produces only one product, which sells for $50. Product costs at the normal level of manufacturing operations (10,000 units) are the following:

Direct material	$14 per unit
Direct labor	$12 per unit
Variable overhead	$ 4 per unit
Fixed overhead	$49,500

Selling expenses (100% variable) are $3 per unit; administrative expenses (100% fixed) are $30,000. During the year, Tuttle produced 11,000 units and sold 9,000 units. Tuttle had no beginning inventory of product.

REQUIRED

a. Determine net income (ignoring income taxes) using
   1. Absorption costing.
   2. Variable costing.
b. Compare the total net income derived under the two methods.

SOLUTION TO DEMONSTRATION PROBLEM

a.   **Absorption Costing**

Sales (9,000 units × $50)			$450,000
Cost of goods sold:			
Direct material (11,000 × $14)		$154,000	
Direct labor (11,000 × $12)		132,000	
Variable overhead (11,000 × $4)		44,000	
Fixed overhead		49,500	
		$379,500	
Less: Ending inventory			
[($379,500/11,000) × 2,000]		69,000	
Cost of goods sold			310,500
Gross profit			$139,500
Selling expense (9,000 units × $3)		$ 27,000	
Administrative expense		30,000	
			57,000
Net income			$ 82,500

Variable Costing

Sales (9,000 units × $50)		$450,000
Variable expenses:		
Direct material (11,000 × $14)	$154,000	
Direct labor (11,000 × $12)	132,000	
Variable overhead (11,000 × $4)	44,000	
	$330,000	
Less: Ending inventory		
[($330,000/11,000) × 2,000]	60,000	
Variable cost of goods sold		270,000
Manufacturing margin		$180,000
Less: Variable selling expense (9,000 × $3)		27,000
Contribution margin		$153,000
Fixed expenses:		
Fixed overhead	$ 49,500	
Administrative expense	30,000	
		79,500
Net income		$ 73,500

b. **Comparison**

Absorption costing net income	$ 82,500
Variable costing net income	73,500
Difference (explained below)	$ 9,000

The following is the amount of fixed overhead contained in the absorption costing ending inventory:

$$[(\$49,500/11,000) \times 2,000] = \$9,000$$

The amount of fixed overhead contained in the variable costing ending inventory is 0. The different treatment of fixed overhead fully explains the difference.

ANSWERS TO SELF-TEST QUESTIONS

1. c, p. 942   **2.** a, p. 948   **3.** c, p. 944   **4.** c, p. 952   **5.** d, p. 949

Management of a large, complex company usually divides the business into a number of *segments*. A segment is a logical portion of a business such as a division or department. A *performance report* is prepared periodically for each business segment. The performance report typically compares actual operating results with budgeted results so the management of the segment can be evaluated.

When a segment is established as a *profit center*, the segment's manager is responsible for revenue generation as well as cost and expense control. If the profit center *receives* products or services from another profit center within the same business *or* *provides* products or services to another profit center within the same business, the two profit center managers must agree on a transfer price for the product or service. The **transfer price** is the price that the selling profit center will charge the buying profit center for the product or service provided.

OBJECTIVES FOR TRANSFER PRICING

Two objectives should be met when establishing transfer prices. First, the transfer price of the product or service transferred should allow both the selling and buying division to make a reasonable gross profit. Second, contribution margin of the entire business should be maximized. We address the first objective in the next section and the second objective in the following section.

REASONABLE GROSS PROFIT

Assume that the Fletcher Company has two operating divisions, the component division and the product division. Top management has decided that the component division should sell a particular component to the product division, which will incorporate the component into a product that it manufactures and sells for $56 per unit. The per-unit product costs incurred in this process are the following:

	Component Division	Product Division
Direct material	$8	$6
Direct labor	4	6
Variable overhead	2	3
Fixed overhead	4	3
Transfer price of component		?

SITUATION 1: Assume that the transfer price is established as $18, the total absorption product cost of the component in the component division ($8 + $4 + $2 + $4 = $18). The resulting gross profit per unit for the two divisions would be calculated as follows:

	Component Division	Product Division
Revenue:		
Transfer price	$18	
Sales price		$56
Cost:		
Transfer price		$18
Direct material	$8	6
Direct labor	4	6
Variable overhead	2	3
Fixed overhead	4	3
	18	36
Gross profit per unit	$ 0	$20

SITUATION 2: Assume that the transfer price is established as $24, the price that the component division would receive from an outside customer and the cost that the product division would incur with an outside supplier. The resulting gross profit per unit for the two divisions would be calculated as follows:

	Component Divison	Product Division
Revenue:		
Transfer price	$24	
Sales price		$56
Cost:		
Transfer price		$24
Direct material	$8	6
Direct labor	4	6
Variable overhead	2	3
Fixed overhead	4	3
	18	42
Gross profit per unit	$ 6	$14

In situation 1, the product division generates a 35.7% gross profit ($20/$56 = 0.357) and the component division generates no gross profit. In situation 2, both divisions generate a 25% gross profit ($6/$24 = 0.25 and $14/$56 = 0.25). Situation 1 illustrates a full absorption product cost transfer price and situation 2 illustrates a market price transfer price. In both situations, total gross profit per unit is $20.

Situation 2 meets the first objective—the transfer price of the product or service transferred should allow both the selling and buying division to make a reasonable gross profit. In general, a transfer price based on market price, not absorption product cost, will satisfy the objective of reasonable gross profits for both the selling and buying profit centers or divisions.

MAXIMIZE CONTRIBUTION MARGIN

The second objective—contribution margin of the entire business should be maximized—can be met by identifying a proper minimum transfer price and allowing the manager of the buying profit center to decide whether to buy from the selling profit center or from an outside supplier. Assume the component division of Fletcher Company is currently manufacturing and selling only product A to outside customers. The product division has proposed that the component division begin manufacturing and selling 2,000 units of product B per year to the product division. The formula for the minimum transfer price for product B is the following:

$$\begin{array}{c} \text{Product B} \\ \text{Minimum Transfer} \\ \text{Price} \end{array} = \begin{array}{c} \text{Variable Cost} \\ \text{of Product B,} \\ \text{Per Unit} \end{array} + \begin{array}{c} \text{Contribution Margin Lost} \\ \text{from Not Selling Product A,} \\ \text{Per Unit of Product B} \end{array}$$

No Excess Capacity

Assume the component division has no excess manufacturing capacity. Therefore, if the component division produces product B for the product division, the component division will have to reduce its production and sale of product A to outside customers. Assume that 5,000 fewer units of product A will have to be produced and sold to allow the manufacture and sale of 2,000 units of product B.

The minimum transfer price that the component division is willing to accept is one that maintains the contribution margin of the component division at its current level. The formula above will generate a transfer price that would allow this to happen. Assume that the variable cost per unit of product A is $16 and its selling price is $30. The variable cost per unit of product B is $42. The total contribution margin that would be given up on 5,000 units of product A is $70,000 [5,000 × ($30 − $16)]. Using the formula, the minimum transfer price for product B is $77 [$42 + ($70,000/2,000 units of B)].

The switch from the production and sale of 5,000 units of product A to 2,000 units of product B would not affect total fixed costs, would create new variable costs of $42 per unit, and would eliminate $70,000 of contribution margin. The $77 transfer price would reimburse the component division for the additional variable costs and the lost contribution margin. As a result, the component division would generate exactly the same contribution margin whether it produced and sold product A or product B.

With the transfer price set at $77, the product division is in a position to make a decision that will maximize its contribution margin and the contribution margin of the entire business. Assume that the product division adds $20 of variable cost and then sells its product for $150. If the product division can buy product B from an outside supplier for a price greater than $77, then it will choose to buy product B from the component division. However, if the product division can buy product B from an outside supplier for a price less than $77, then it will choose to buy the product from the outside supplier. In either case, the contribution margin of the company as a whole has been maximized.

To illustrate, let us assume two situations: (1) the outside supplier's price is $85, and (2) the outside supplier's price is $70. A comparison follows of the impact on contribution margin of the alternatives available to the product division.

Situation 1: Outside supplier's price for product B is $85

Alternative 1: Buy product B for $77 from component division:
Component division contribution margin:

($77 − $42) × 2,000	$ 70,000
Product division contribution margin:	
($150 − $77 − $20) × 2,000	106,000
Total contribution margin	$176,000

Alternative 2: Buy product B for $85 from outside supplier:
Component division contribution margin:

($30 − $16) × 5,000	$ 70,000
Product division contribution margin:	
($150 − $85 − $20) × 2,000	90,000
Total contribution margin	$160,000

■ ANALYSIS: Buying product B from the component division results in $16,000 more total contribution margin.

Situation 2: Outside supplier's price for product B is $70

Alternative 1: Buy product B for $77 from component division:
Component division contribution margin:

($77 − $42) × 2,000	$ 70,000
Product division contribution margin:	
($150 − $77 − $20) × 2,000	106,000
Total contribution margin	$176,000

Alternative 2: Buy product B for $70 from outside supplier:
Component division contribution margin:

($30 − $16) × 5,000	$ 70,000
Product division contribution margin:	
($150 − $70 − $20) × 2,000	120,000
Total contribution margin	$190,000

■ ANALYSIS: Buying product B from the outside supplier results in $14,000 more total contribution margin.

Excess Capacity

In the above example, we assumed that the component division had no excess manufacturing capacity. If we now assume that the component division has sufficient capacity to produce and sell the 2,000 units of product B without reducing the production and sale of product A, we will determine a different minimum transfer price. Applying the above formula, we determine that the minimum transfer price is $42 [$42 + ($0/2,000)].

In this case, the production and sale of 2,000 units of product B would not affect total fixed costs, would create new variable costs of $42 per unit, and would eliminate no contribution margin from the production and sale of product A. The $42 transfer price would reimburse the component division for the additional variable costs. As a result, the component division would generate exactly the same contribution margin whether or not it produced and sold product B.

Negotiated Transfer Prices

The formula that determines minimum transfer price results in a transfer price that is frequently different than the market value of the product or service being transferred. If the minimum transfer price is greater than the market price, then the buying profit center will buy the product or service from an outside supplier and there will be no need for a transfer price.

If the minimum transfer price is less than the market price, however, then the buying profit center will buy the product or service from the other profit center in the same company. The exact transfer price will be negotiated by the two profit centers. The resulting amount will be greater than or equal to the minimum transfer price and less than or equal to the market price. Any negotiated transfer price within this range will result in the same total contribution margin for the firm. For example, with a minimum transfer price of $77 and a market price of $85, any transfer price from $77 to $85 results in a contribution margin of $176,000 for the firm.

INTERNATIONAL TRANSFER PRICING

Transfer pricing becomes more complex if one of the segments is in a different country than the other. When products or services are being transferred between segments in different countries, the two objectives stated above still apply. However, there also are additional objectives that may conflict with the two previously mentioned. The additional objectives include minimization of international income taxes and tariffs and conformance with international trade agreements.

International Income Taxes

International income taxes have a major impact on transfer prices. For example, a company may have segments in three different countries—Country A, Country B, and Country C—with three different income tax rates—1%, 25%, and 45%, respectively. Assume that the company wants to transfer product costing the equivalent of $40 per unit from the segment in Country A to the segment in Country C, where it will be sold to consumers for the equivalent of $120 per unit.

Assume that the transfer price is set at $40 on 10,000 units. The impact on total income tax in the two countries would be calculated as follows:

Country A: ($40 − $40) × 10,000 × 1%	$ –0–
Country B: ($120 − $40) × 10,000 × 45%	360,000
Total	$360,000

Now assume that the transfer price is set at $120 on 10,000 units. The impact on total income tax in the two countries would be calculated as follows:

Country A: ($120 − $40) × 10,000 × 1%	$ 8,000
Country B: ($120 − $120) × 10,000 × 45%	–0–
Total	$ 8,000

The $120 transfer price results in $8,000 of total income tax and the $40 transfer price results in $360,000 of total income tax. In general, when transferring the product from a low income tax country to a high income tax country, a high transfer price will minimize total international income tax. Similarly, when transferring the product from a high income tax country to a low income tax country, a low transfer price will minimize international income tax. These general guidelines frequently conflict with the objective of reasonable gross profits for all segments. Further, some high income tax countries, such as the United States, are trying to defeat the use of unusually high transfer prices under the presumption that the transfer prices were set to avoid paying income tax in the high income tax country.

Tariffs

Tariffs, or import taxes, are often assessed on the value of the product being imported. When tariff rates are high, low transfer prices may result in lower tariffs. Some countries are attempting to determine the real market value of products being imported and assessing the tariffs on the market value rather than the transfer price.

Conformance with Trade Agreements

Conformance with trade agreements can be a very important additional objective when setting international transfer prices. A transfer price that minimizes international income tax may not conform with a trade agreement with the country to which the product is being shipped. This could result in higher tariffs, partial or total restriction on the import of the product, or limitations on the amount of cash that can be transferred from one country to another.

Multinational companies are facing many complex challenges. International transfer pricing is one of those challenges that does not have a set of simple solutions.

Federal, state, and local government are much like businesses in the sense that they need revenue to operate. While the primary purpose of taxation is to raise revenue, taxes also serve many other purposes such as economic control, special interest promotion, and wealth and income redistribution. Various types of taxes lend themselves to each of these purposes.

TYPES OF TAXES THAT AFFECT BUSINESS DECISIONS

Federal, state, and local governing units collect many different types of taxes from businesses. The federal government collects income taxes, payroll taxes, excise taxes, and tariffs. State governments collect income taxes, payroll taxes, excise and sales taxes, and property taxes. Local governments collect income taxes, sales taxes, and property taxes.

Income Taxes

Income taxes are levied on the taxable income of the taxpayer. Income taxes are usually considered progressive taxes because the tax rate typically increases as the income subject to taxation increases. This is based on the theory that as income rises, the taxpayer has a greater ability to pay. Taxable income differs from pretax financial income due to provisions in the tax laws that provide for different methods of computing items such as depreciation and amortization.

Income taxes apply directly to the earnings of corporations but not sole proprietorships and partnerships. The income of sole proprietorships and partnerships is added to the taxable income of the owners and taxed at the income tax rate applicable to the owners. Exhibit J-1 illustrates the tax rate schedule for married individuals who file jointly and the tax rate schedule for corporations.

MARGINAL AND AVERAGE INCOME TAX RATES

The *average income tax rate* is found by dividing the total tax liability by the taxable income of the taxpayer and represents an arithmetic mean tax rate. The *marginal income tax rate* is the tax rate that will be charged on the next dollar of taxable income. The marginal income tax rate is usually higher than the average income tax rate and should be used when evaluating the tax consequences of decisions.

Assume that a corporation has $60,000 of taxable income. The federal income tax liability, the average income tax rate, and the marginal income tax rate are determined as follows (see Exhibit J-1):

	Taxable Income		Tax Rate		Tax Liability
First	$50,000	×	15%	=	$ 7,500
Next	10,000	×	25%	=	2,500
	$60,000				$10,000

Average income tax rate: $10,000/$60,000 = 0.1667 or 16.67%
Marginal income tax rate: 25%

Additional income will not be taxed at the average income tax rate but at the marginal income tax rate. For corporations, the marginal tax rate changes to (1) 34% when taxable income reaches $75,000; (2) 39% when taxable income reaches $100,000; and (3) 34% again when taxable income reaches $335,000.

Payroll Taxes

Payroll taxes are collected for retirement (social security), health care (Medicare), and unemployment benefits. The employee pays half of the social security and Medicare taxes and the employer pays the other half. Unemployment taxes (both federal and state) are usually paid only by the employer. The federal unemployment tax is levied on the first $7,000 of each employee's wages. The rates and salary bases used by states vary widely. These taxes cease to be levied after the salary base for each employee is

EXHIBIT J—1	1991 TAX BRACKETS FOR TAXABLE INCOME					
Individuals				Corporations		
(Married Filing Jointly)						
Over	But Not Over	Rate		Over	But Not Over	Rate
$ 0	$34,000	15%		$ 0	$ 50,000	15%
34,000	82,150	28%		50,000	75,000	25%
82,150	—	31%		75,000	100,000	34%
				100,000	335,000	39%
				335,000	—	34%

reached. The application of these taxes was discussed in the chapter on current liabilities and payroll accounting.

Excise and Sales Taxes

Excise taxes are similar to sales taxes in that both are levied on transfer transactions. While sales taxes are usually state and local taxes levied against all sales, excise taxes are levied on specific transactions. Examples of federal excise taxes are taxes on gasoline and aviation fuel, trucks and trailers, highway use tires, telephone calls, alcohol, tobacco, firearms, air travel, certain motor vehicles, chemicals, ozone-depleting chemicals, and wagering. State and local governments levy excise taxes on items such as tobacco, firearms, alcohol, gasoline and aviation fuel, trucks and trailers, and telephone calls.

Because excise taxes are levied against the sale and use of specific items, the rates are raised and lowered with the political and economic desirability of the items' use. Many excise taxes are levied at the wholesale level so end-consumers are often unaware of these taxes because they are included in the retail price of goods. They are, therefore, referred to as hidden taxes.

Tariffs

Tariffs are charges made on import and export transactions. Tariffs have become an economic and political weapon, and form entry and exit barriers for foreign trade. In our global marketplace, these have become significant costs and often affect the competitiveness of prices.

Property Taxes

Property taxes, sometimes called ad valorem taxes, are usually assessed at the local level annually based upon the ownership of tangible and real property. They are a major source of revenue for local governments. Because they are not derived from income or transfer transactions, these taxes require other income sources for the owner of the property. These taxes are not based on the ability to pay but rather on the evidence of ownership.

AFTER-TAX CONSIDERATIONS IN DECISION MAKING

Whenever decision alternatives are considered by a decision-making body, the after-tax effect should be considered the basis for the decision. This consideration should not be limited to the income tax effects but should include all of the taxes previously discussed.

Purchase of Asset

For example, Roberts Trucking Corporation is considering the purchase of a truck that will require a full-time driver. The 65,000 pound truck will cost $85,000 plus a

12% federal excise tax and a 3% state sales tax. Annual highway motor vehicle tax is $100 per year plus $22 for every one thousand pounds over 55,000 pounds. The vehicle license tag (a personal property tax) will cost $750 per year. The driver will be paid an annual salary of $46,000 per year with a benefits package that is equivalent to 13 percent of salary. The company pays social security tax of 6.2% of the first $53,400 of salary per employee, Medicare tax of 1.45% of the first $125,000 of salary per employee; federal unemployment tax of 0.8% of the first $7,000 of salary per employee; and state unemployment tax of 1.2% of the first $9,000 of salary per employee. The corporation has a marginal federal income tax rate of 34% and a marginal state income tax rate of 5%. Tax-basis depreciation will be 20% of the truck's cost for the first year. The president of the corporation wants to know the after-tax cost of the decision for the next tax year assuming the purchase and hiring occur on January 2. The costs can be summarized as follows:

Purchase cost of the truck:

Cost of the truck	$85,000
12% Federal excise tax	10,200
3% State sales tax	2,550
Total purchase cost of the truck	$97,750

Annual income tax deduction for the truck:

Depreciation (20% × $97,750)	$19,550
Road taxes ($100 + [$22 × 10])	320
License tag	750
Annual deduction for the truck	$20,620

Annual cost of the driver:

Salary	$46,000
Social security (6.2% × $46,000)	2,852
Medicare (1.45% × $46,000)	667
Federal unemployment (0.8% × $7,000)	56
State unemployment (1.2% × $9,000)	108
Benefits package (13% × $46,000)	5,980
Annual cost of the driver	$55,663

Total net annual cost:

Annual deduction for the truck	$20,620
Annual cost of the driver	55,663
Annual cost before income tax	$76,283
Less: Tax savings (0.34 + 0.05) × $76,283	29,750 (rounded)
Net annual after-tax cost	$46,533

To generalize, the after-tax cost of a business expenditure is the total annual tax-basis cost (before income tax) multiplied by one minus the marginal tax rate.

$$AT = \text{After-tax effect}$$
$$AC = \text{Annual cost before income tax}$$
$$MR = \text{Marginal income tax rate (federal and state)}$$

$$AT = AC \times (1 - MR)$$
$$\$46,533 = \$76,283 \times (1 - 0.39)$$

Income Tax Effects of Gains and Losses

Some decisions require the determination of the effect of a gain or loss on the taxes owed by a company. The tax consequences are determined by multiplying the gain or loss for tax purposes by the marginal tax rate. The gain or loss is the difference between the sales price and the tax basis of the asset. The asset's tax basis is often different than the accounting book value due to temporary differences in the amount of depreciation or amortization taken. The income tax effect is always based on the gain or loss as calculated using the asset's tax basis.

To illustrate, assume Roberts Trucking Corporation plans to sell equipment that has a tax basis of $5,000 and an accounting book value of $9,000. The expected selling price is $23,000. The marginal federal income tax rate is 34% and the marginal state rate is 5%. Although the books will show a gain of $14,000 ($23,000 − $9,000) when the asset is sold, the gain for tax purposes is $18,000 ($23,000 − $5,000). The income taxes owed by the company will be based on the $18,000 gain for tax purposes. Should the equipment be sold, the impact on income tax will be $7,020 ($18,000 × 0.39).

Buying versus Leasing

When comparing the costs of alternative courses of action, it is important to compare the costs on an after-tax basis. The difference in after-tax costs will often be smaller than the difference in costs before taxes. Identifying the proper cost differential between alternative actions is important because the decision to select an alternative will consider qualitative factors as well as costs. When assessing whether qualitative factors will outweigh cost differentials, it is important to have identified the proper cost amounts.

For example, assume the president of Roberts Trucking Corporation wants to compare leasing with buying the $85,000 truck described previously. The total purchase cost of the truck was $97,750. Assume the entire $97,750 is borrowed from a bank at 10% interest. Tax-basis depreciation for the first year of $19,550 plus $320 for road taxes and $750 for license tag fees resulted in an annual income tax deduction for the truck of $20,620. Assume the truck will be used for five years and will have no salvage value at the end of five years.

If the truck is leased for five years, the annual lease cost will be $32,000. The leasing company will pay road taxes and license tag fees. An analysis of the annual after-tax costs of buying versus leasing follows:

	Buy	**Lease**
Annual deduction for the truck	$20,620	
Interest deduction ($97,750 × 10%)	9,775	
Annual lease cost		$32,000
Annual cost of the driver	55,663	55,663
Annual cost before income tax	$86,058	$87,663
Less: Tax savings (0.34 + 0.05)	33,563	34,189 (rounded)
Net annual after-tax cost	$52,495	$53,474

Before allowing for income taxes, the annual cost of leasing exceeds the buying alternative by $1,605 ($87,663 − $86,058). Comparing the after-tax costs, the annual leasing cost exceeds the buying alternative by $979 ($53,474 − $52,495). Cost will be one of many factors that the president considers in selecting whether to lease or buy. The proper cost differential for the president to consider in arriving at a decision is the $979.

Hiring versus Leasing

A similar decision situation relates to one of the newer practices: leasing employees from organizations that pay the employee; pay the related payroll taxes and fringe benefits; and prepare the appropriate tax reports to the federal, state, and local governments. This practice has become popular because of the considerable costs beyond salaries and wages of hiring employees, including payroll taxes, benefit packages, and administrative costs of the personnel department.

Assume, for example, that the president of Roberts Trucking Corporation has determined that he can lease a driver for $4,600 per month from a firm that provides many other corporations with drivers. In addition, the corporation is only obligated on a monthly basis, with no severance pay required. The firm has experienced average turnover of similar personnel every 24 months with a severance cost of 10% of annual wages and annual administrative costs of 2% of salaries. An analysis of costs appears on the following page:

	Hire	**Lease**
Annual salary	$46,000	
Annual lease cost ($4,600 × 12)		$55,200
Social security (6.2% × $46,000)	2,852	
Medicare (1.45% × $46,000)	667	
Federal unemployment (0.8% × $7,000)	56	
State unemployment (1.2% × $9,000)	108	
Benefits package (13% × $46,000)	5,980	
Administrative cost (2% × $46,000)	920	
Severance cost (5% × $46,000)	2,300	
Total annual costs	$58,883	$55,200
Less: Tax savings (0.34 + 0.05)	22,964	21,528 (rounded)
Net annual after-tax cost	$35,919	$33,672

Before allowing for income taxes, the hiring alternative cost exceeds the leasing alternative cost by $3,683 ($58,883 − $55,200). Comparing the after-tax costs, the hiring alternative exceeds the leasing alternative by $2,247 ($35,919 − $33,672). Cost will be one of many factors the president considers in selecting whether to lease or buy. The proper cost differential for the president to consider in arriving at a decision is the $2,247. Also note that the corporation could pay up to $58,883 to lease an employee before the costs would equal hiring the employee.

MINIMIZING INCOME TAXES

Taxpayers who deliberately misstate their taxable income, whether by omitting income or claiming fraudulent deductions, are practicing *tax evasion*. This is illegal, and the penalties for such a practice can be severe. However, taxpayers are perfectly within their rights to practice *tax avoidance*—arranging their business affairs to minimize their tax liability. The effectiveness of some methods of tax avoidance, particularly certain tax shelters and deferred methods of income recognition, have been seriously curtailed by the Tax Reform Act of 1986. However, there are still some areas of taxation that permit an informed taxpayer to minimize taxes.

Timing of Transactions

Most of the transactions of a business occur without the ability to preplan their timing. But some decisions, such as the disposal of a business segment or other business asset, can have a planned transaction date. The timing of the sale should consider the tax consequences and the timing of the required payment of those taxes. The difference in the date of a transaction can change the due date for paying the federal and state income taxes by as much as one year. Individuals and corporations must make quarterly tax estimates that approximate the taxes due for income earned that quarter. Special provisions, however, allow the payment to be delayed until the filing of the tax return. For example, a corporation wants to dispose of a business segment on December 14, 1993. If the segment is sold on that date, the tax due on the gain of that sale should be remitted to the Internal Revenue Service by December 15, 1993, or under certain conditions by March 15, 1994. By delaying the disposal until January 2, 1994, the tax payment can be delayed until March 15, 1995 (under certain conditions) or be paid 25% on April 15, 1994, 25% on June 15, 1994, 25% on September 15, 1994, and 25% on December 15, 1994. The corporation would retain the cash for an additional 3 to 15 months. Likewise, if the disposal would generate a tax loss, the corporation normally would want to be sure the disposal took place in December, to reduce the current year tax liability.

Form of Business Organization

Most large businesses operate as corporations to have wider access to capital, limit liability, or enjoy other advantages of incorporation as previously explained. For small businesses, with perhaps a single owner or a few owners, tax considerations may well influence the form of ownership.

Let us examine some general factors in determining the relative tax effects. First, all income of single proprietorships and partnerships is taxable to the *owners* as earned, whether or not it is distributed. Second, corporations must pay a tax on earnings, but may deduct reasonable salaries paid to owners. Furthermore, corporations may pay only a portion of the earnings as dividends (as long as accumulations are not deemed unreasonable). Other relevant factors are the amount of the business earnings and the amount of the owners' other separate income.

For example, consider the comparative tax effects of the corporate and sole proprietorship forms of organization for a married individual whose business is expected to generate $50,000 net income annually. Of this amount, $30,000 is withdrawn each year (as a salary, if the corporate form is used). The owner's other income, less all deductions and exemptions, is $8,000 annually. A comparison of the total tax effect of the two forms of organization is shown in Exhibit J-2. Tax brackets and rates were obtained from Exhibit J-1.

The example assumes no distribution of dividends by the corporation. This policy might require justification if questioned by the IRS. Generally, the IRS may impose a penalty on unreasonable retention of earnings without a genuine business purpose. Of course, the owner will be taxed on the $17,000 earnings retained ($20,000 − $3,000 tax) if distributed in the future. However, it is almost always beneficial to defer taxes to the future.

No general rule or formula can determine the most beneficial form of organization for tax purposes. The type of analysis we have illustrated may be modified in response to changes in the levels of business income, other income, reasonableness of salary levels, dividend policy, and other factors. The addition of owners and increases in the size and scope of the business may be influential. Finally, depending on the nature of the ownership, small corporations can sometimes elect to be taxed as partnerships.

EXHIBIT J—2	COMPARATIVE TAX RESULTS IN TWO FORMS OF ORGANIZATION		

		Corporation	Sole Proprietorship
Income from business		$50,000	$50,000
Less: Owner's salary		30,000	—
Business taxable income		$20,000	$50,000
Corporate tax on $20,000 at 15%		$ 3,000	
Salary	$30,000		
Other income less deductions and exemptions	8,000		8,000
Owner's taxable income	$38,000		$58,000
Tax on $38,000		6,220*	
Tax on $58,000			$11,820†
Total tax		$ 9,220	$11,820

*$34,000	×	15%	=	$5,100		†$34,000	×	15%	=	$ 5,100
4,000	×	28%	=	1,120		24,000	×	28%	=	6,720
$38,000				$6,220		$58,000				$11,820

PRACTICAL GUIDELINES RELATING TO TAX CONSIDERATIONS

There are two practical guidelines to remember when making important business decisions.

1. Business and investment decisions should be made primarily on the merits of the investment, not the tax effects. The tax implications of the investment should improve the desirability of the investment but not create the desirability of the investment. Tax motivated transactions are seldom worthwhile investments. Changes in the income tax regulations can negate the tax advantage of such transactions plus impose substantial monetary penalties.

2. Proposed business decisions should always be thoroughly researched for unknown tax consequences. Many business transactions are completed before the parties examine the tax consequences of the transaction. The wording of a contract or timing of a transaction can have serious tax consequences. Once the transaction is completed, nothing can be done to mitigate these tax consequences. Managers should seek legal and tax advice *before* entering into important decisions that have tax consequences. The various taxing agencies do not always notify businesses of taxes they may be subject to, because the U.S. tax system is for the most part self-assessed. Once the agencies are aware of a tax liability, they can collect back taxes with substantial penalties and interest.

GLOSSARY OF KEY TERMS USED IN THIS CHAPTER

absorption costing A product costing method that treats all manufacturing costs as product costs (p. 948).

cost center A segment of a business with which specific costs can be identified; sometimes called an *expense center* (p. 942).

decision making A process of identifying alternative courses of action and selecting a choice from among the alternatives (p. 940).

departmental contribution to indirect expenses The excess of departmental revenue over direct department expenses; contributed to the absorption of the firm's pool of indirect expenses (p. 948).

differential analysis A concept of limiting consideration in a decision situation to only those factors that differ among alternatives (p. 952).

direct expenses (costs) Expenses (costs) that can be readily identified with a particular department, product, or activity (p. 944).

evaluation phase A phase of decision making that deals with steps taken to control the outcome of a specific plan of action; performance measures are a part of this phase (p. 941).

execution phase A phase of decision making that deals with the steps taken to implement a specific plan of action (p. 941).

indirect expenses (costs) Expenses (costs) that are not readily identified with products or activities; usually allocated by some arbitrary formula to various products and activities (p. 944).

managerial accounting The accounting procedures used by an organization's accounting staff primarily to furnish its management with accounting analyses and reports needed for decision making (p. 941).

manufacturing margin The excess of revenue over variable manufacturing costs; an amount often presented on variable costing income statements (p. 950).

performance reports Documents portraying, for a given operating unit, planned amounts of cost, actual costs incurred, and any related variances (p. 942).

planning phase A phase of decision making that involves specifying goals, identifying alternative courses of action, and estimating the qualitative and quantitative effects of the alternative actions on the specified goals (p. 941).

profit center A segment of a business, such as a division, for which the manager is responsible for revenue generation as well as cost and expense control (p. 942).

transfer price The price that one profit center of a business charges another profit center of the same business for a product or service (p. 961).

variable costing A product costing method that associates only variable manufacturing costs with the product; fixed manufacturing costs are treated as period expenses in the period incurred (p. 948).

QUESTIONS

25-1 Give examples of segments of business firms segmented by (a) organizational unit and (b) economic activity.

25-2 Identify three phases of decision making and briefly discuss the role of each phase in the decision process.

25-3 Distinguish between a *profit center* and a *cost center.*

25-4 Distinguish between *direct expenses* and *indirect expenses.* Which are more likely to be controllable at the department level?

25-5 When a firm wishes to measure gross profit by department, what basic modifications are needed in the chart of accounts?

25-6 Suggest an allocation basis for each of the following common expenses of a departmentalized firm that uses a net income measure to determine the profitability of departments:
  a. Janitorial expense.
  b. Plant manager's salary.
  c. Utilities (heat, light, and air conditioning).
  d. Sales salaries.
  e. Uncollectible accounts.
  f. Property taxes.

25-7 What is meant by departmental contribution to indirect expenses? What advantages does this measure have over net income in measuring departmental performance?

25-8 "The higher the management level receiving reports, the more detailed the reports should be." Comment.

25-9 Although separate phases of decision making are identifiable, management is usually involved in all phases at the same time. Explain.

25-10 List several common aspects of decision making that are often not subject to quantification.

25-11 What is variable costing? List its advantages and disadvantages.

25-12 What generalizations can be made about the difference in income reported under variable and absorption costing?

25-13 Explain what is meant by the term *differential analysis.*

25-14 Explain how differential analysis can be applied to the following types of decisions:
  a. Accepting special orders.
  b. Making or buying product components.
  c. Dropping unprofitable segments of the firm.
  d. Selling or processing further.
  e. Product emphasis.

25-15 Department B of the local Top Value Store shows a contribution to indirect expenses of $22,000 and a net loss of $9,000 (before taxes). The firm believes that discontinuing department B will not affect sales, gross profit, or direct expenses of other departments. If total indirect expenses remain unchanged, what effect will discontinuing department B have on the income before taxes of the Top Value Store?

25-16 Department 2 of Kapp Company has a gross profit of $100,000, representing 40% of net departmental sales. Direct departmental expenses are $75,000. Management believes that an increase of $6,500 in advertising, coupled with a 5% average increase in sales prices, will permit the physical volume of products sold to remain the same next period but will improve the department's contribution to indirect expenses. If management's expectations are correct, what will be the effect on this contribution?

25-17 Department A of Racine Company has a gross profit of $140,000, representing 35% of net departmental sales. Management believes that an increase of $36,000 in advertising will increase volume of product sold by 20%. Other direct departmental expenses are $64,000. What effect will this decision have on department A's contribution to indirect expenses?

25-18 Operating at 80% capacity, Batavia Company produces and sells 16,000 units of its only product for $60. Per-unit costs are direct material, $12; direct labor, $16; variable factory overhead, $8; and fixed factory overhead, $10. A special order is received for 1,000 units. Based on this information, what price should Batavia charge to make a $6,000 gross profit on the special order?

25-19 Delton Company produces unassembled picture frames at the following average per-unit costs: direct material, $X; direct labor, $Y; and factory overhead, $Z. Delton can assemble the frames at a unit cost of $2.50 and raise the selling price from $11 to $15. What is the apparent advantage or disadvantage of assembling the frames?

25-20 Explain the concept of *constraining resource*, and present a general rule for optimizing product mixes.

25-21 "In differential analysis, we can generally count on variable cost being relevant and fixed cost being irrelevant." Comment.

25-22 If both approaches to a decision lead to the same conclusion, why might differential analysis be considered superior to a comprehensive analysis that reflects all revenue and costs?

EXERCISES

ALLOCATING INDIRECT EXPENSES
— OBJ. 4 —

25-23 Selected data for Miller Company, which operates three departments, follow:

	Department A	Department B	Department C
Inventory	$ 80,000	$288,000	$112,000
Equipment (average cost)	720,000	432,000	288,000
Payroll	405,000	360,000	135,000
Square feet of floor space	18,000	9,000	3,000

During the year, the company's indirect expenses included the following:

Depreciation on equipment	$80,000
Real estate taxes	24,000
Personal property taxes (on inventory and equipment)	38,400
Personnel department expenses	40,000

Using the most causally related bases, prepare a schedule allocating the indirect expenses to the three departments.

DROPPING UNPROFITABLE DEPARTMENT
— OBJ. 7 —

25-24 Thomas Corporation has four departments, all of which appear to be profitable except department 4. Operating data for 1993 are as follows:

	Total	Departments 1–3	Department 4
Sales	$950,000	$800,000	$150,000
Cost of goods sold	634,000	520,000	114,000
Gross profit	$316,000	$280,000	$ 36,000
Direct expenses	$144,000	$120,000	$ 24,000
Indirect expenses	123,000	105,000	18,000
Total expenses	$267,000	$225,000	$ 42,000
Net income (Loss)	$ 49,000	$ 55,000	($ 6,000)

a. Calculate the gross profit percentage for departments 1–3 combined and for department 4.
b. What effect would elimination of department 4 have had on total firm net income? (Ignore the effect of income tax.)

ANALYZING OPERATIONAL CHANGES
— OBJ. 4 —

25-25 Operating results for department B of Delta Company during 1993 are as follows:

Sales	$540,000
Cost of goods sold	378,000
Gross profit	$162,000
Direct expenses	$120,000
Indirect expenses	66,000
Total expenses	$186,000
Net loss	($ 24,000)

If department B could maintain the same physical volume of product sold while raising selling prices an average of 15% and making an additional advertising expenditure of $45,000, what would be the effect on the department's net income or net loss? (Ignore income tax in your calculations.)

ANALYZING OPERATIONAL CHANGES
— OBJ. 4 —

25-26 Suppose that department B in Exercise 25-25 could increase physical volume of product sold by 10% if it spent an additional $18,000 on advertising while leaving selling prices unchanged. What effect would this have on the department's net income or net loss? (Ignore income tax in your calculations.)

DIFFERENTIAL ANALYSIS
— OBJ. 6 —

25-27 In each of four independent cases, the amount of differential revenue or differential cost is as follows (parentheses indicate decreases):

	1	2	3	4
Increases (decreases) in:				
Revenue	$18,000	$–0–	?	?
Costs	?	?	($12,000)	$–0–

For each case, determine the missing amount that would be necessary for the net differential amount to be
a. $10,000.
b. ($6,000).
Indicate whether your answers reflect increases or decreases.

SPECIAL ORDER
— OBJ. 7 —

25-28 Carson Manufacturing, Inc., sells a single product for $36 per unit. At an operating level of 8,000 units, variable costs are $18 per unit and fixed costs $10 per unit.

Carson has been offered a price of $20 per unit on a special order of 2,000 units by Big Mart Discount Stores, which would use its own brand name on the item. If Carson accepts the order, material cost will be $3 less per unit than for regular production. However, special stamping equipment costing $4,000 would be needed to process the order; the equipment would then be discarded.

Assuming that volume remains within the relevant range, prepare an analysis of differential revenue and costs to determine whether Carson should accept the special order.

MAKE OR BUY
— OBJ. 7 —

25-29 Eastside Company incurs a total cost of $120,000 in producing 10,000 units of a component needed in the assembly of its major product. The component can be purchased from an outside supplier for $11 per unit. A related cost study indicates that the total cost of the component includes fixed costs equal to 50% of the variable costs involved.
a. Should Eastside buy the component if it cannot otherwise use the released capacity? Present your answer in the form of differential analysis.
b. What would be your answer to requirement (a) if the released capacity could be used in a project that would generate $50,000 of contribution margin?

SELL OR PROCESS FURTHER
— OBJ. 7 —

25-30 Jensen Manufacturing Company makes a partially completed assembly unit that it sells for $36 per unit. Normally, 42,000 units are sold each year. Variable unit cost data on the assembly are as follows:

Direct material	$10
Direct labor	8
Variable factory overhead	4

The company is now using only 70% of its normal capacity; it could fully use its normal capacity by processing the assembly further and selling it for $43 per unit. If the company does this, material and labor costs will each increase by $2 per unit and variable overhead will go up by $1 per unit. Fixed costs will increase from the current level of $160,000 to $220,000.

Prepare an analysis showing whether Jensen should process the assemblies further.

PRODUCT EMPHASIS
— OBJ. 7 —

25-31 The following analysis of selected data is for each of the two products Gates Corporation produces.

	Product A	Product B
Per-unit Data at 10,000 Units		
Sales price	$26	$22
Production costs:		
Variable	9	9
Fixed	6	4

Selling and administrative expenses:		
Variable	5	3
Fixed	3	1

In the Gates operation, machine capacity is the company's constraining resource. Each unit of A requires 3 hours of machine time, and each unit of B requires 2 hours of machine time. Assuming that all production can be sold at a normal price, prepare an analysis showing which of the two products should be produced with any unused productive capacity that Gates might have.

VARIABLE AND ABSORPTION COSTING
— OBJ. 5 —

25-32 Chandler Company sells its product for $100 per unit. Variable manufacturing costs per unit are $40, and fixed manufacturing costs at the normal operating level of 12,000 units are $240,000. Variable selling expenses are $16 per unit sold. Fixed administrative expenses total $104,000. Chandler had no beginning inventory in 1993. During 1993, the company produced 12,000 units and sold 9,000. Would net income for Chandler Company in 1993 be higher if calculated using variable costing or using absorption costing? Calculate reported income using each method (ignore income tax).

PROBLEMS

DEPARTMENTAL INCOME STATEMENT
— OBJ. 4 —

25-33 Elgin Flooring Company sells floor coverings through two departments, carpeting and hard covering (tile and linoleum). Operating information for 1993 appears below.

	Carpeting Department	Hard Covering Department
Inventory, January 1, 1993	$ 60,000	$ 26,000
Inventory, December 31, 1993	50,000	30,000
Net sales	780,000	480,000
Purchases	484,000	362,000
Purchases returns	28,000	8,000
Purchases discounts	16,000	4,000
Transportation in	18,000	14,000
Direct departmental expenses	108,000	56,000

Indirect operating expenses of the firm were $120,000.

REQUIRED

a. Prepare a departmental income statement showing departmental contribution to indirect expenses and net income of the firm. Assume an overall effective income tax rate of 35%. Elgin uses a periodic inventory system.

b. Calculate the gross profit percentage for each department.

c. If the indirect expenses were allocated 60% to the carpeting department and 40% to the hard covering department, what would the net income be for each department?

ALLOCATE INDIRECT EXPENSES
— OBJ. 4 —

25-34 The following information was obtained from the ledger of Woodfield Candies, Inc., at the end of 1993:

WOODFIELD CANDIES, INC.
TRIAL BALANCE
DECEMBER 31, 1993

	Debit	Credit
Cash	$ 42,000	
Accounts Receivable (Net)	156,000	
Inventory, December 31, 1993	180,000	
Equipment and Fixtures (Net)	540,000	
Accounts Payable		$ 108,000
Common Stock		450,000
Retained Earnings		180,000
Sales—Department X		840,000
Sales—Department Y		360,000

Cost of Goods Sold—Department X	420,000	
Cost of Goods Sold—Department Y	216,000	
Sales Salaries Expense	192,000	
Advertising Expense	42,000	
Insurance Expense	24,000	
Uncollectible Accounts Expense	9,000	
Occupancy Expense	36,000	
Office and Other Administrative Expense	81,000	
	$1,938,000	$1,938,000

Woodfield analyzes its operating expenses at the end of each period in order to prepare an income statement that will exhibit net income by department. From payroll records, advertising copy, and other records, the following tabulation was obtained:

	Direct Expense		Indirect Expense	Allocation Basis for Indirect Expense
	Dept. X	Dept. Y		
Sales salaries expense	$147,000	$45,000		
Advertising expense	18,000	6,000	$18,000	Relative sales
Insurance expense	15,000	9,000		
Uncollectible accounts expense	6,000	3,000		
Occupancy expense			36,000	Floor space
Office and other administrative expense	12,000	9,000	60,000	6-to-4 ratio (X to Y)

Department X occupies 10,000 square feet of floor space, department Y, 5,000 square feet. Indirect expenses should be allocated to departments as indicated above.

REQUIRED

Prepare a departmental income statement for Woodfield Candies, Inc., showing net income by department, assuming an overall income tax rate of 35%.

ANALYZE OPERATIONAL CHANGES — OBJ. 4 —

25-35 Richmond's is a retail store with eight departments, including a garden department that has been operating at a loss. The following condensed income statement gives the latest year's operating results:

	Garden Department	All Other Departments
Sales	$336,000	$2,400,000
Cost of goods sold	201,600	1,560,000
Gross profit	$134,400	$ 840,000
Direct expenses	$108,000	$ 273,000
Indirect expenses	48,000	312,000
Total expenses	$156,000	$ 585,000
Net income (Loss)	($ 21,600)	$ 255,000

REQUIRED

a. Calculate the gross profit percentage for the garden department and for the other departments as a group.
b. Suppose that if the garden department were discontinued, the space occupied could be rented to an outside firm for $18,000 per year, and the indirect expenses of the firm would be reduced by $4,500. What effect would this action have on Richmond's net income? (Ignore income tax in your calculations.)
c. It is estimated that if an additional $6,000 were spent on advertising, prices in the garden center could be raised an average of 5% without a change in physical volume of products sold. What effect would this have on operating results of the garden department? (Again, ignore income tax in your calculations.)

DEPARTMENTAL CONTRIBUTION TO INDIRECT EXPENSES — OBJ. 4 —

25-36 Certain operating information is shown below for Palmer Department Store:

	Department A	Department B	All Other Departments
Sales	$600,000	$900,000	$2,100,000
Direct expenses	105,000	165,000	600,000
Indirect expenses	90,000	120,000	300,000
Gross profit percentage	30%	40%	50%

The managers are disappointed with the operating results of department A. They do not believe that competition will permit raising prices; however, they believe that spending $21,000 more for promoting this department's products will increase the physical volume of products sold by 20%.

An alternative is to discontinue department A and use the space to expand department B. It is believed that department B's physical volume of products sold can thus be increased 37.5%. Special sales personnel are needed, however, and department B's direct expenses would increase by $90,000. Neither alternative would appreciably affect the total indirect departmental expense.

REQUIRED

a. Calculate the contribution now being made to indirect expenses by department A, by department B, and by the combination of other departments.

b. Which of the two alternatives should management choose: increase promotional outlays for department A or discontinue department A and expand department B? Support your answer with calculations.

SPECIAL ORDER — OBJ. 7 —

25-37 Total cost data follow for Glendale Manufacturing Company, which has a normal capacity per period of 8,000 units of product that sell for $60 each. For the foreseeable future, regular sales volume should continue to equal normal capacity.

Direct material	$100,800
Direct labor	62,400
Variable factory overhead	46,800
Fixed factory overhead (Note 1)	38,400
Selling expense (Note 2)	35,200
Administrative expense (fixed)	15,000
	$298,600

Notes:

1. Beyond normal capacity, fixed overhead costs increase $1,800 for each 500 units *or fraction thereof* until a maximum capacity of 10,000 units is reached.

2. Selling expenses consist of a 6% sales commission and shipping costs of 80 cents per unit. Glendale pays only three-fourths of the regular sales commission rate on sales totaling 501 to 1,000 units and only two-thirds the regular commission on sales totaling 1,000 units or more.

Glendale's sales manager has received a special order for 1,200 units from a large discount chain at a price of $36 each, F.O.B. factory. The controller's office has furnished the following additional cost data related to the special order:

1. Changes in the product's design will reduce direct material costs $1.50 per unit.

2. Special processing will add 20% to the per-unit direct labor costs.

3. Variable overhead will continue at the same proportion of direct labor costs.

4. Other costs should not be affected.

REQUIRED

a. Present an analysis supporting a decision to accept or reject the special order. (Round computations to the nearest cent.)

b. What is the lowest price Glendale could receive and still make a $3,600 profit before income taxes on the special order?

c. What general qualitative factors should Glendale consider?

MAKE OR BUY — OBJ. 7 —

25-38 Allen Corporation currently makes the nylon convertible top for its main product, a fiberglass boat designed especially for water skiing. The costs of producing the 1,500 tops needed each year follow:

Nylon fabric	$270,000
Aluminum tubing	96,000
Frame fittings	24,000
Direct labor	162,000
Variable factory overhead	30,000
Fixed factory overhead	152,000

Dustin Company, a specialty fabricator of synthetic materials, can make the needed tops of comparable quality for $400 each, F.O.B. shipping point. Allen would furnish its own trademark insignia at a unit cost of $16. Transportation in would be $28 per unit, paid by Allen Corporation.

Allen's chief accountant has prepared a cost analysis that shows that only 20% of fixed overhead could be avoided if the tops are purchased. The tops have been made in a remote section of Allen's factory building, using equipment for which no alternate use is apparent in the foreseeable future.

REQUIRED

a. Prepare a differential analysis showing whether or not you would recommend that the convertible tops be purchased from Dustin Company.

b. Assuming that the production capacity released by purchasing the tops could be devoted to a subcontracting job for another company that netted a contribution margin of $41,600, what maximum purchase price could Allen Corporation pay for the tops?

c. Identify two important qualitative factors that Allen Corporation should consider in deciding whether to purchase the needed tops.

DROPPING UNPROFITABLE DIVISION — OBJ. 7 —

25-39 Based on the following analysis of last year's operations of Bingham, Inc., a financial vice president of the company believes that the firm's total net income could be increased by $200,000 if its soft goods division were discontinued. (Amounts are given in thousands of dollars.)

	Totals	All Other Divisions	Soft Goods Division
Sales	$11,200	$8,000	$3,200
Cost of goods sold:			
Variable	(3,880)	(2,600)	(1,280)
Fixed	(2,120)	(1,400)	(720)
Gross profit	$ 5,200	$4,000	$1,200
Operating expenses:			
Variable	(3,000)	(2,000)	(1,000)
Fixed	(1,600)	(1,200)	(400)
Net income (loss)	$ 600	$ 800	($ 200)

REQUIRED

Provide answers for each of the following independent situations:

a. Assuming that total fixed costs and expenses would not be affected by discontinuing the soft goods division, prepare an analysis showing why you agree or disagree with the vice president.

b. Assume that discontinuance of the soft goods division will enable the company to avoid 20% of the fixed portion of cost of goods sold and 25% of the fixed operating expenses allocated to the soft goods division. Calculate the resulting effect on net income.

c. Assume that in addition to the cost avoidance in requirement (b), the production capacity released by discontinuance of the soft goods division can be used to produce 6,000 units of a new product that would have a variable cost per unit of $36 and would require additional fixed costs totaling $68,000. At what unit price must the new product be sold if Bingham is to increase its total net income by $120,000?

PRODUCT EMPHASIS — OBJ. 7 —

25-40 Lowell Corporation manufactures both a deluxe and a standard model of a household food blender. Because of limited demand, for several years production has been at 80% of estimated capacity, which is thought to be limited by the number of machine hours available. At current operation levels, a profit analysis for each product line shows the following data, which appears on the next page.

	Per-unit Data	
	Deluxe	**Standard**
Sales price	$216	$84
Production costs:		
Direct material	$89	$12
Direct labor	36	23
Variable factory overhead	15	11
Fixed factory overhead*	25 $165	10 $56
Variable operating expenses	18	10
Fixed operating expenses	8	5
Total cost	$191	$71
Operating income	$ 25	$13

*Assigned on the basis of machine hours at normal capacity.

Management wants to utilize the company's current excess capacity by increasing production.

REQUIRED

a. What general decision guideline applies in this situation?

b. Assuming that sufficient units of either product can be sold at current prices to use existing capacity fully and that total fixed cost will not be affected, prepare an analysis showing which product line should be emphasized if net income for the firm is the decision basis.

VARIABLE AND ABSORPTION COSTING — OBJ. 5 —

25-41 Scott Manufacturing makes only one product with total unit manufacturing cost of $54, of which $36 is variable. No units were on hand at the beginning of 1992. During 1992 and 1993, the only product manufactured was sold for $84 per unit, and the cost structure did not change. Scott uses the first-in, first-out inventory method and has the following production and sales for 1992 and 1993:

	Units Manufactured	**Units Sold**
1992	120,000	90,000
1993	120,000	130,000

REQUIRED

a. Prepare gross profit computations for 1992 and 1993 using absorption costing.

b. Prepare gross profit computations for 1992 and 1993 using variable costing.

c. Explain how your answers illustrate the impact of differences between production and sales volumes on the gross profits reported each year under absorption and variable costing.

VARIABLE AND ABSORPTION COSTING — OBJ. 5 —

25-42 Summarized data for 1993 (the first year of operations) for Gorman Products, Inc., follow:

Sales (75,000 units)	$3,000,000
Production costs (80,000 units):	
Direct material	880,000
Direct labor	720,000
Factory overhead:	
Variable	544,000
Fixed	320,000
Operating expenses:	
Variable	168,000
Fixed	240,000

REQUIRED

a. Prepare an income statement based on full absorption costing.

b. Prepare an income statement based on variable costing.

c. Assume that you must decide quickly whether to accept a special one-time order for 1,000 units for $30 per unit. Which income statement presents the most relevant data? Determine the apparent profit or loss on the special order based solely on this data.

d. If the ending inventory is destroyed by fire, which costing approach would you use as a basis for filing an insurance claim for the fire loss? Why?

TRANSFER PRICING
— APPENDIX I —

25-43 Capland Company has three divisions that operate as profit centers—motors, industrial equipment, and residential products. The motors division is trying to determine the transfer price for a model X2J motor that it plans to sell to the residential products division. Motors variable cost per unit of the X2J is $65. Residential products plans to incorporate the X2J into a product that residential products would sell to consumers for $200. Residential products can buy a similar motor from an outside supplier for $80. Residential products would buy 5,000 X2J motors each year.

REQUIRED

a. What is the minimum transfer price that the motors division would be willing to accept from residential products division if motors has no excess capacity and would have to stop manufacturing and selling 3,000 K3J motors ($70 selling price and $30 variable cost) in order to produce and sell the needed X2J motors? Should the residential products division buy the motors from the motors division or the outside supplier? Why?

b. What is the minimum transfer price if the motors division has sufficient excess capacity to produce all the needed X2J motors? Should the residential products division buy the motors from the motors division or the outside supplier?

c. If the conditions in requirement (b) exist, what is the range (minimum and maximum) in which the exact transfer price will be negotiated?

INTERNATIONAL TRANSFER
PRICING
— APPENDIX I —

25-44 Beloti Company has divisions located in the United States and a foreign country. The applicable income tax rates are 38% in the United States, and 4% in the foreign country. Beloti manufactures a component in the foreign country and a finished product (which incorporates the component) in the United States. The component has a product cost of $18. The U.S. division adds $45 of variable product cost to the component when the finished product is produced. The finished product sells to consumers for $125. The component could be purchased from another company for $29. Assume that each year 10,000 components are transferred, incorporated into finished product, and sold to consumers. Also assume that no beginning or ending inventories exist in either division. All amounts are stated in equivalent U.S. dollars.

REQUIRED

a. Calculate the gross profits for the foreign division and the U.S. division for the current year assuming that the foreign division's product cost is used as the transfer price.

b. Calculate the gross profits for the foreign division and the U.S. division for the current year assuming that market price is used as the transfer price.

c. Which alternative—product cost or market price—is the more appropriate choice for transfer price and why?

d. Calculate the impact of the transfer on international income taxes if product cost is used as the transfer price.

e. Calculate the impact of the transfer on international income taxes if market price is used as the transfer price.

TAX CONSIDERATIONS IN
DECISION MAKING
— APPENDIX J —

25-45 The vice-president of production for Jonstone Framing Corporation has proposed that the company invest in a new machine that will increase the output of metal frames. The new machine will cost $120,000 plus 5% state sales tax. The old machine it will replace has a tax-basis book value of $25,000 and can be sold for $14,000. The new machine requires only one worker; the old machine required two workers. These workers earn $25,000 per year and have a benefits package that costs the company 11.5% of their salary. The company's total payroll tax burden is 8% of the gross salary for these employees and the marginal federal and state income tax rate is 39%. Assume that the first year's tax-basis depreciation will be 20% of the depreciable basis.

REQUIRED

Assume the new machine would be purchased at the start of 1993. Compute the effect on 1993 income tax.

TAX CONSIDERATIONS IN
DECISION MAKING
— APPENDIX J —

25-46 Ann Williams Corporation is considering the lease or purchase of automobiles for its sales representatives. The cars can be purchased for $9,000 each plus state sales tax of 5% (which is added to the cost) and an annual license tag fee of $400 (which is a deductible expense). The automobiles will be used for three years and can be sold for $2,000 on the last day of the third year. With a special financing plan, the cars can be purchased with no money down. Interest expense in years 1 through 3 will be $800,

$500, and $300, respectively. The same cars can be leased for 3 years at $4,000 per year. The leasing company will pay the sales tax and the license tag fees. Assume that the tax-basis depreciation will be $3,100 per car per year. The corporation's marginal income tax rate is 38%.

REQUIRED

a. Compute the net after-tax cost of each car for each of the 3 years if the cars are purchased.
b. Compute the net after-tax cost of each car for each of the 3 years if the cars are leased.

ALTERNATE EXERCISES

ALLOCATING INDIRECT EXPENSES
— OBJ. 4 —

25-23A Selected data for Colony Company, which operates three departments, follow:

	Department A	Department B	Department C
Inventory	$ 40,000	$144,000	$ 56,000
Equipment (average cost)	360,000	216,000	144,000
Payroll	607,500	540,000	202,500
Square feet of floor space	27,000	13,500	4,500

During the year, the company's indirect expenses included the following:

Depreciation on equipment	$60,000
Real estate taxes	18,000
Personal property taxes (on inventory and equipment)	28,800
Personnel department expenses	30,000

Using the most causally related bases, prepare a schedule allocating the indirect expenses to the three departments.

DROPPING UNPROFITABLE DEPARTMENT
— OBJ. 7 —

25-24A Penn Corporation has four departments, all of which appear to be profitable except department 4. Operating data for 1993 are as follows:

	Total	Departments 1–3	Department 4
Sales	$1,052,000	$900,000	$152,000
Cost of goods sold	654,000	540,000	114,000
Gross profit	$ 398,000	$360,000	$ 38,000
Direct expenses	$ 177,000	$150,000	$ 27,000
Indirect expenses	140,000	120,000	20,000
Total expenses	$ 317,000	$270,000	$ 47,000
Net income (loss)	$ 81,000	$ 90,000	($ 9,000)

a. Calculate the gross profit percentage for departments 1–3 combined and for department 4.
b. What effect would elimination of department 4 have had on total firm net income? (Ignore the effect of income tax.)

ANALYZING OPERATIONAL CHANGES
— OBJ. 4 —

25-25A Operating results for department B of Shaw Company during 1993 are as follows:

Sales	$800,000
Cost of goods sold	480,000
Gross profit	$320,000
Direct expenses	$215,000
Indirect expenses	123,000
Total expenses	$338,000
Net loss	($ 18,000)

If department B could maintain the same physical volume of product sold while raising selling prices an average of 10% and making an additional advertising expenditure of $50,000, what would be the effect on the department's net income or net loss? (Ignore income tax in your calculations.)

ANALYZING OPERATIONAL CHANGES
— OBJ. 4 —

25-26A Suppose that department B in Exercise 25-25A could increase physical volume of product sold by 10% if it spent an additional $40,000 on advertising while leaving selling prices unchanged. What effect would this have on the department's net income or net loss? (Ignore income tax in your calculations.)

DIFFERENTIAL ANALYSIS
— OBJ. 6 —

25-27A In each of four independent cases, the amount of differential revenue or differential cost is as follows (parentheses indicate decreases):

	1	2	3	4
Increases (decreases) in:				
Revenue	$36,000	$–0–	?	?
Costs	?	?	($20,000)	$–0–

For each case, determine the missing amount that would be necessary for the net differential amount to be

a. $24,000.

b. ($16,000).

Indicate whether your answers reflect increases or decreases.

SPECIAL ORDER
— OBJ. 7 —

25-28A Northern Company regularly sells its only product for $34 per unit and has a 25% profit on each sale. The company has accepted a special order for a number of units, the production of which would use part of its unused capacity. The special order sales price is 50% of the normal price, and the profit margin is only 60% of the regular dollar profit. What, apparently, is

a. Northern's profit per unit on the special order?

b. Northern's variable cost per unit?

c. Northern's average fixed cost per unit on regular sales?

MAKE OR BUY
— OBJ. 7 —

25-29A Harper Company incurs a total cost of $252,000 in producing 20,000 units of a component needed in the assembly of its major product. The component can be purchased from an outside supplier for $6 per unit. A related cost study indicates that the total cost of the component includes fixed costs equal to 80% of the variable costs involved.

a. Should Harper buy the component if it cannot otherwise use the released capacity? Present your answer in the form of differential analysis.

b. What would be your answer to requirement (a) if the released capacity could be used in a project that would generate $15,000 of contribution margin?

SELL OR PROCESS FURTHER
— OBJ. 7 —

25-30A Turner Manufacturing Company makes a partially completed assembly unit that it sells for $50 per unit. Normally, 35,000 units are sold each year. Variable unit cost data on the assembly are as follows:

Direct material	$12
Direct labor	7
Variable factory overhead	9

The company is now using only 75% of its normal capacity; it could fully use its normal capacity by processing the assembly further and selling it for $58 per unit. If the company does this, material and labor costs will each increase by $2 per unit and variable overhead will go up by $1 per unit. Fixed costs will increase from the current level of $125,000 to $165,000.

Prepare an analysis showing whether Turner should process the assemblies further.

PRODUCT EMPHASIS
— OBJ. 7 —

25-31A The following analysis of selected data is for each of the two products Rockville Corporation produces.

	Product G	Product H
Per-unit Data at 10,000 Units		
Sales price	$29	$16
Production costs:		
Variable	9	7
Fixed	6	4
Selling and administrative expenses:		
Variable	5	2
Fixed	3	1

In Rockville's operation, machine capacity is the company's constraining resource. Each unit of G requires 3 hours of machine time, and each unit of H requires 1 hour of machine time. Assuming that all production can be sold at a normal price, prepare an analysis showing which of the two products should be produced with any unused productive capacity that Rockville might have.

VARIABLE AND ABSORPTION COSTING
— OBJ. 5 —

25-32A During its first year, Concord, Inc., showed a $21 per-unit profit under absorption costing but would have reported a total profit $16,800 less under variable costing. If production exceeded sales by 700 units and an average contribution margin of 60% was maintained, what is the apparent
a. Fixed cost per unit?
b. Sales price per unit?
c. Variable cost per unit?
d. Unit sales volume if total profit under absorption costing was $189,000?

ALTERNATE PROBLEMS

25-33A Perkins Appliance & Furniture Company has two departments, appliances and furniture. Operating information for 1993 appears below.

DEPARTMENTAL INCOME STATEMENT
— OBJ. 4 —

	Appliance Department	Furniture Department
Inventory, January 1, 1993	$ 120,000	$ 90,000
Inventory, December 31, 1993	75,600	48,000
Net sales	1,120,000	760,000
Purchases	640,000	480,000
Purchases discounts	8,000	6,000
Transportation in	18,000	16,000
Direct departmental expenses	199,600	82,000

Indirect operating expenses of the firm were $180,000.

REQUIRED

a. Prepare a departmental income statement showing departmental contribution to indirect expenses and net income of the firm. Assume an overall effective income tax rate of 40%. Perkins uses a periodic inventory system.
b. Calculate the gross profit percentage for each department.
c. If the indirect expenses were allocated 70% to the appliance department and 30% to the furniture department, what would the net income be for each department?

ALLOCATE INDIRECT EXPENSES
— OBJ. 4 —

25-34A The following information was obtained from the ledger of Stillwell Emporium, Inc., at the end of 1993:

STILLWELL EMPORIUM, INC.
TRIAL BALANCE
DECEMBER 31, 1993

	Debit	Credit
Cash	$ 18,000	
Accounts Receivable (net)	70,000	
Inventory, December 31, 1993	45,000	
Equipment and Fixtures (Net)	97,000	
Accounts Payable		$34,000
Common Stock		120,000
Retained Earnings		30,000
Sales—Department A		360,000
Sales—Department B		140,000
Cost of Goods Sold—Department A	216,000	
Cost of Goods Sold—Department B	70,000	
Sales Salaries Expense	74,000	
Advertising Expense	31,000	
Insurance Expense (On merchandise)	10,000	
Uncollectible Accounts Expense	3,000	
Occupancy Expense	16,000	
Office and Other Administrative Expense	34,000	
	$684,000	$684,000

Stillwell analyzes its operating expenses at the end of each period in order to prepare an income statement that will exhibit net income by department. From payroll records, advertising copy, and other records, the following tabulation was obtained:

	Direct Expense		Indirect Expense	Allocation Basis for Indirect Expenses
	Dept. A	Dept. B		
Sales salaries expense	$48,000	$20,000	$ 6,000	Equally
Advertising expense	15,000	6,000	10,000	Relative sales
Insurance expense	8,000	2,000		
Occupancy expense			16,000	Floor space
Uncollectible accounts expense	2,000	1,000		
Office and other administrative expense	17,000	9,000	8,000	3-to-1 ratio (A to B)

Department A occupies 5,000 square feet of floor space, department B 3,000 square feet. Indirect expenses should be allocated to departments as indicated above.

REQUIRED

Prepare a departmental income statement for Stillwell Emporium, Inc., showing net income by department, assuming an overall income tax rate of 30%.

ANALYZE OPERATIONAL CHANGES — OBJ. 4 —

25-35A The management of Manchester's Department Store is concerned about the operation of its sporting goods department, which has not been very successful. The following condensed income statement gives the latest year's results:

	Sporting Goods Department	All Other Departments
Sales	$480,000	$2,400,000
Cost of Goods Sold	360,000	1,560,000
Gross Profit	$120,000	$ 840,000
Direct Expenses	$ 67,500	$ 336,000
Indirect Expenses	48,000	240,000
Total Expenses	$115,500	$ 576,000
Net Income	$ 4,500	$ 264,000

REQUIRED

a. Calculate the gross profit percentage for the sporting goods department and for the other departments as a group.
b. It is estimated that if an additional $10,500 were spent on promotion of sporting goods, average prices can be raised 5% without affecting physical volume of goods sold. What effect would this have on operating results of the sporting goods department? (Ignore the effect of income tax.)
c. Alternatively, it is estimated that physical volume of goods sold could be increased 8% if an additional $15,000 were spent on promotion of sporting goods and prices were not increased. Assuming that operating expenses remain the same, what effect would this have on the operating results of the sporting goods department? (Ignore the effect of income tax.)

DEPARTMENTAL CONTRIBUTION TO INDIRECT EXPENSES — OBJ. 4 —

25-36A Certain operating information is shown below for Harris Department Store:

	Department R	Department S	All Other Departments
Sales	$320,000	$480,000	$1,120,000
Direct expenses	56,000	88,000	320,000
Indirect expenses	48,000	64,000	160,000
Gross profit percentage	30%	40%	50%

The managers are disappointed with the operating results of department R. They do not believe that competition will permit raising prices; however, they believe that spending $10,000 more for promoting this department's products will increase the physical volume of products sold by 20%.

An alternative is to discontinue department R and use the space to expand department S. It is believed that department S's physical volume of products sold can thus be increased 35%. Special sales personnel are needed, however, and department S's direct expenses would increase by $48,000. Neither alternative would appreciably affect the total indirect departmental expense.

REQUIRED

a. Calculate the contribution now being made to indirect expenses by department R, by department S, and by the combination of other departments.

b. Which of the two alternatives should management choose: increase promotional outlays for department R, or discontinue department R and expand department S? Support your answer with calculations.

SPECIAL ORDER
— OBJ. 7 —

25-37A Total cost data follow for Greenfield Manufacturing Company, which has a normal capacity per period of 20,000 units of product that sell for $54 each. For the foreseeable future, regular sales volume should continue to equal normal capacity.

Direct material	$266,800
Direct labor	200,000
Variable factory overhead	152,000
Fixed factory overhead (Note 1)	118,800
Selling expense (Note 2)	129,600
Administrative expense (fixed)	50,000
	$917,200

Notes:

1. Beyond normal capacity, fixed overhead costs increase $4,500 for each 1,000 units *or fraction thereof* until a maximum capacity of 24,000 units is reached.

2. Selling expenses consist of a 10% sales commission and shipping costs of $1 per unit. Greenfield pays only one-half of the regular sales commission rate on sales amounting to $3,000 or more.

Greenfield's sales manager has received a special order for 2,500 units from a large discount chain at a price of $44 each, F.O.B. factory. The controller's office has furnished the following additional cost data related to the special order:

1. Changes in the product's design will reduce direct material costs $4 per unit.

2. Special processing will add 10% to the per-unit direct labor costs.

3. Variable overhead will continue at the same proportion of direct labor costs.

4. Other costs should not be affected.

REQUIRED

a. Present an analysis supporting a decision to accept or reject the special order.

b. What is the lowest price Greenfield could receive and still make a profit of $5,000 before income taxes on the special order?

c. What general qualitative factors should Greenfield consider?

MAKE OR BUY
— OBJ. 7 —

25-38A Walsh Corporation currently makes the nylon mooring cover for its main product, a fiberglass boat designed for tournament bass fishing. The costs of producing the 2,000 covers needed each year follow:

Nylon fabric	$320,000
Wood battens	64,000
Brass fittings	32,000
Direct labor	128,000
Variable factory overhead	96,000
Fixed factory overhead	160,000

Calvin Company, a specialty fabricator of synthetic materials, can make the needed tops of comparable quality for $320 each, F.O.B. shipping point. Walsh would furnish its own trademark insignia at a unit cost of $20. Transportation in would be $16 per unit, paid by Walsh Corporation.

Walsh's chief accountant has prepared a cost analysis that shows that only 30% of fixed overhead could be avoided if the covers are purchased. The covers have been made in a remote section of Walsh's factory building, using equipment for which no alternate use is apparent in the foreseeable future.

REQUIRED

a. Prepare a differential analysis showing whether or not you would recommend that the mooring covers be purchased from Calvin Company.

b. Assuming that the production capacity released by purchasing the covers could be devoted to a subcontracting job for another company that netted a contribution margin of $64,000, what maximum purchase price could Walsh pay for the covers?

c. Identify two important qualitative factors that Walsh Corporation should consider in deciding whether to purchase the needed covers.

**DROPPING UNPROFITABLE
DIVISION
— OBJ. 7 —**

25-39A Based on the following analysis of last year's operations of Groves, Inc., a financial vice president of the company believes that the firm's total net income could be increased by $160,000 if its soft goods division were discontinued. (Amounts are given in thousands of dollars.)

	Totals	All Other Divisions	Soft Goods Division
Sales	$18,800	$14,400	$4,400
Cost of goods sold:			
Variable	(7,600)	(5,600)	(2,000)
Fixed	(4,800)	(4,000)	(800)
Gross profit	$ 6,400	$ 4,800	$1,600
Operating expenses:			
Variable	(3,360)	(2,000)	(1,360)
Fixed	(1,600)	(1,200)	(400)
Net income (loss)	$ 1,440	$ 1,600	($ 160)

REQUIRED

Provide answers for each of the following independent situations:

a. Assuming that total fixed costs and expenses would not be affected by discontinuing the soft goods division, prepare an analysis showing why you agree or disagree with the vice president.

b. Assume that discontinuance of the soft goods division will enable the company to avoid 30% of the fixed portion of cost of goods sold and 40% of the fixed operating expenses allocated to the soft goods division. Calculate the resulting effect on net income.

c. Assume that in addition to the cost avoidance in requirement (b), the production capacity released by discontinuance of the soft goods division can be used to produce 6,000 units of a new product that would have a variable cost per unit of $60 and would require additional fixed costs totaling $68,000. At what unit price must the new product be sold if Groves is to increase its total net income by $180,000?

**PRODUCT EMPHASIS
— OBJ. 7 —**

25-40A McDermott Corporation manufactures both automatic and manual residential water treatment units. Because of limited demand, for several years production has been at 90% of estimated capacity, which is thought to be limited by the number of machine hours available. At current operation levels, a profit analysis for each product line shows the following:

	Per-unit Data			
	Automatic		**Manual**	
Sales price		$800		$416
Production costs:				
Direct material	$144		$80	
Direct labor	128		64	
Variable factory overhead	64		32	
Fixed factory overhead*	144	$480	72	$248
Variable operating expenses		80		16
Fixed operating expenses		144		96
Total cost		$704		$360
Operating income		$ 96		$ 56

*Assigned on the basis of machine hours at normal capacity.

Management wants to utilize the company's current excess capacity by increasing production.

REQUIRED

a. What general decision guideline applies in this situation?

b. Assuming that sufficient units of either product can be sold at current prices to use existing capacity fully and that total fixed cost will not be affected, prepare an analysis showing which product line should be emphasized if net income for the firm is the decision basis.

VARIABLE AND ABSORPTION COSTING
— OBJ. 5 —

25-41A Frances Manufacturing makes a product with total unit manufacturing cost of $64, of which $36 is variable. No units were on hand at the beginning of 1992. During 1992 and 1993, the only product manufactured was sold for $96 per unit, and the cost structure did not change. Frances uses the first-in, first-out inventory method and has the following production and sales for 1992 and 1993:

	Units Manufactured	Units Sold
1992	100,000	70,000
1993	100,000	120,000

REQUIRED

a. Prepare gross profit computations for 1992 and 1993 using absorption costing.

b. Prepare gross profit computations for 1992 and 1993 using variable costing.

c. Explain how your answers illustrate the impact of differences between production and sales volumes on the gross profits reported each year under absorption and variable costing.

VARIABLE AND ABSORPTION COSTING
— OBJ. 5 —

25-42A Summarized data for 1993 (the first year of operations) for Trenton Products, Inc., are as follows:

Sales (200,000 units)	$8,000,000
Production costs (210,000 units):	
Direct material	2,100,000
Direct labor	1,680,000
Factory overhead:	
Variable	1,260,000
Fixed	1,050,000
Operating expenses:	
Variable	560,000
Fixed	640,000

REQUIRED

a. Prepare an income statement based on full absorption costing.

b. Prepare an income statement based on variable costing.

c. Assume that you must decide quickly whether to accept a special one-time order for 1,000 units for $28 per unit. Which income statement presents the most relevant data? Determine the apparent profit or loss on the special order based solely on this data.

d. If the ending inventory is destroyed by fire, which costing approach would you use as a basis for filing an insurance claim for the fire loss? Why?

TRANSFER PRICING
— APPENDIX I —

25-43A Trandom Company has three divisions that operate as profit centers—components, industrial products, and agricultural products. The industrial products division is trying to determine the transfer price for a model Q5M part that it plans to sell to the agricultural products division. Industrial's variable cost per unit of the Q5M is $90. Agricultural products plans to incorporate the Q5M into a product that agricultural products would sell to consumers for $280. Agricultural products can buy a similar part from an outside supplier for $110. Agricultural products would buy 4,000 Q5M parts each year.

REQUIRED

a. What is the minimum transfer price that the industrial division would be willing to accept from agricultural products division if industrial has no excess capacity and would have to stop manufacturing and selling 2,400 XXQ motors ($100 selling price and $40 variable cost) in order to produce and sell the needed Q5M parts? Should the agricultural products division buy the parts from the industrial products division or the outside supplier? Why?

b. What is the minimum transfer price if the industrial division has sufficient excess capacity to produce all the needed Q5M parts? Should the agricultural products division buy the parts from the industrial products division or the outside supplier?

c. If the conditions in requirement (b) exist, what is the range (minimum and maximum) in which the exact transfer price will be negotiated?

INTERNATIONAL TRANSFER PRICING
— APPENDIX I —

25-44A Masoni Company has divisions located in the United States and a foreign country. The applicable income tax rates are 36% in the United States and 3% in the foreign country. Masoni manufactures a component in the foreign country and a finished product (which incorporates the component) in the United States. The component has a product cost of $22. The U.S. division adds $55 of variable product cost to the component when the finished product is produced. The finished product sells to consumers for $150. The component could be purchased from another company for $35. Assume that each year 20,000 components are transferred, incorporated into finished product, and sold to consumers. Also assume that no beginning or ending inventories exist in either division. All amounts are stated in equivalent U.S. dollars.

REQUIRED

a. Calculate the gross profits for the foreign division and the U.S. division for the current year assuming that the foreign division's product cost is used as the transfer price.

b. Calculate the gross profits for the foreign division and the U.S. division for the current year assuming that market price is used as the transfer price.

c. Which alternative—product cost or market price—is the more appropriate choice for transfer price and why?

d. Calculate the impact of the transfer on international income taxes if product cost is used as the transfer price.

e. Calculate the impact of the transfer on international income taxes if market price is used as the transfer price.

TAX CONSIDERATIONS IN DECISION MAKING
— APPENDIX J —

25-45A Louis Corporation is currently planning to hire three new employees. Louis Corporation has a benefit package that costs 12.5% of salaries with a maximum cost of $7,500 per employee. Assume that social security is 6.2% of the first $53,400 per employee; Medicare is 1.45% of the first $125,000 per employee; federal unemployment is 0.8% of the first $7,000 per employee; and state unemployment is 2.1% of the first $8,500 per employee. The marginal income tax rate for Louis Corporation is 34% federal and 7% state. Louis Corporation enjoys an average income tax rate of 30% federal and 6% state.

REQUIRED

Compute the annual after-tax cost of each of three employees whose respective salaries are listed below. Round all calculations to the nearest dollar.
a. $25,000.
b. $52,000.
c. $85,000.

TAX CONSIDERATIONS IN DECISION MAKING
— APPENDIX J —

25-46A For each salary level in problem 25-45A, determine at what amount the corporation could lease an employee and incur the same after-tax cost. Round your answers to the nearest dollar.

CASES

Business Decision Case

Marvin Corporation manufactures both an automatic and a manual household dehumidifier. Because of limited demand, for several years production has been at 80% of estimated capacity, which is thought to be limited by the number of machine hours available. At current operation levels, a profit analysis for each product line shows the following:

| | **Per-unit Data** | | | |
	Automatic		**Manual**	
Sales price		$350		$150
Production costs:				
Direct material	$65		$32	
Direct labor	35		25	
Variable factory overhead	68		16	
Fixed factory overhead	50	$218	18	$ 91
Variable operating expenses		52		21
Fixed operating expenses		30		13
Total cost		$300		$125
Operating income		$ 50		$ 25

Management wants to make use of the company's current excess capacity by increasing production. Each unit of the automatic model requires 2.5 machine hours; the manual model requires 1 machine hour per unit.

REQUIRED

Present answers for the following questions in each independent situation:

a. Assume that sufficient units of either product can be sold at current prices to utilize existing capacity fully and that fixed costs will not be affected.
1. To which product should the excess capacity be devoted if the decision basis is maximization of contribution margin per unit of product?
2. Prepare an analysis showing which product line should be emphasized if the firm's net income is the decision basis.
3. What general decision guideline applies in this situation?

b. Suppose the excess capacity represents 10,000 machine hours, which can be used to make 4,000 automatic units or 10,000 manual units or any proportionate combination. The only market available for these extra units is a foreign market in which the sales prices must be reduced by 20% and in which no more than 6,000 units of either model can be sold. All costs will remain the same except that the sales commission of 10% (included in variable operating expenses) will be avoided. Prepare an analysis showing which product should be emphasized and the effect on the firm's net income.

c. Assume that the excess capacity can be used as indicated in requirement (b) and that the firm's market research department believes that the production available from using the excess capacity exclusively on either model can be sold in the domestic market at regular prices if a promotion campaign costing $225,000 is undertaken for the automatic model or $235,000 for the manual model. Prepare an analysis indicating for which product the campaign should be undertaken.

Ethics Case

Swan Sports manufactures golfing equipment. Traditionally, the company has been busy all year but has noticed that over the past few years business has fallen off in October and November. If new business does not come in this year, the company will have to lay off some long-time employees for those two months.

Rob Patell, a sales representative, received an order from Better Equipment Co., a competitor. Better Equipment cannot meet a customer's rush order on time and is willing to subcontract the work to Swan Sports on the condition that the Better Equipment Co. name—not Swan Sports' name—appear on all products. The order is at a price substantially below Swan Sports' usual selling price. The only way this order can be produced is to use lower-quality materials than Swan Sports normally uses in its own products.

Rob Patell has recommended to his supervisor that this order be accepted and that lower-quality materials be used. Patell's reasoning includes the following points:

1. It is clearly a one-time order.
2. Swan Sports' name will not appear on it.
3. Workers will not have to be laid off during October and November.

A differential analysis shows that Swan Sports will lose $1,000 on the order.

REQUIRED

What should the sales supervisor consider before making a decision?

What approach should a business take to plan its future operations?

Most businesses use planning and budgeting procedures to prepare for the future rather than react to it when it arrives. ■ Manufacturers need to understand the relationship of sales revenue to product costs, selling expenses, and administrative expenses as early as possible in product development. ■ For example, Giddings & Lewis, a high-technology manufacturer of machine tools (shown here) typically commits on amount equal to 10% of sales to R&D expenditures.

26

PLANNING AND BUDGETING

anagement has a basic responsibility to plan, control, and measure performance and to make decisions. To carry out these responsibilities, management must develop plans and budgets, determine actual operating results, compare actual results to planned results, evaluate differences, and take corrective action to improve operations. This chapter focuses on managerial planning and budgeting.

Prediction is very difficult, especially about the future.

NIELS BEHR

PLANNING

OBJECTIVE ① DESCRIBE *the planning process, including strategic planning and operational planning, used by businesses and other entities.*

All types of organizations—service organizations, merchandising firms, manufacturing companies, government agencies, and not-for-profit entities—can benefit from formalized planning. A formal planning process usually includes strategic planning and operational planning.

Planning horizon is the future time span, usually expressed in years, for which a particular plan is developed. Different types of plans have different planning horizons. Typically, longer planning horizons are associated with higher-level planning (such as strategic planning) whereas shorter planning horizons are associated with lower-level planning (such as annual operational planning.)

Strategic Planning

Strategic planning is a formal process that addresses and documents the overall mission and long-term goals of the organization. Management must evaluate and decide what directions the organization should go in the future. Issues to be decided include what basic lines of business to pursue, which geographic markets to establish, what organization structure to develop, where to locate facilities, which means of sales and distribution to use, and how aggressively the organization should grow.

Management must accumulate and analyze a great deal of information to properly make these decisions. Many companies use a technique such as **SWOT analysis** to begin this accumulation and analysis process. Management uses SWOT analysis to analyze current and future operations and to document *strengths* of the current operation (S), *weaknesses* of the current operations (W), *opportunities* in the future (O), and *threats* in the future (T). The SWOT analysis will specifically address management, employees, products, services, physical facilities, customers, competitors, distribution channels, and systems. It is very important to recognize and document the current strengths and weaknesses of the firm as well as the future opportunities and threats facing it when formulating the firm's future strategic directions.

Management takes the information accumulated during the SWOT analysis, makes some assumptions about the economy and the future competitive environment, and formulates management strategies for the entity. A 10-year planning horizon is typical. These strategies are documented in the strategic plan, which is typically updated and revised annually for changing conditions.

Operational Planning

Management also prepares operational plans consistent with the strategic plan. **Operational planning** is the process of developing specific goals and objectives for the entity as a whole and its individual departments, formulating a plan of attack to accomplish the goals and objectives, and preparing written documentation of the goals and objectives as well as the plan of attack. Firms frequently develop a long-term operational plan that covers a three- to five-year planning horizon as well as an annual operational plan that covers a one-year planning horizon. The goals, objectives, and plan of attack are more detailed in the annual operational plan than in the long-term operational plan.

The annual operational plan projects some of the current operations as they exist and provides for changes in others to reflect management's desires for improvements in the operations. The annual operational plan reflects the strategies, goals, objectives, and plan of attack documented in the strategic plan and the long-term operational plan. Further, the annual operating plan is usually not in a format that enables management to determine whether the plans are economically feasible. Management tests the economic feasibility of the annual operational plan through the development of the annual operating budget.

BUDGETING

OBJECTIVE **2** DISCUSS *the budgeting process.*

Budgeting is the process of developing a formal, written operational plan that presents management's planned actions in financial terms. Budgeting should reflect the conclusions reached in the strategic plan and the operational plan. Two budgets usually result from the budgeting process: the annual operating budget and the capital expenditures budget. The annual operating budget is presented and discussed in this chapter, and the capital expenditures budget is briefly presented in this chapter and discussed in detail in a later chapter. Exhibit 26-1 presents the sequence for preparing the various types of plans and budgets.

All types of entities can derive benefits from the budgeting process. Although the basic concepts of budgeting apply to all types of entities, the precise budget form will vary among various types of entities. Budgeting typically incorporates many accounting concepts discussed in previous chapters. In fact, some components of the annual operating budget have familiar accounting formats.

ADVANTAGES OF BUDGETING

The annual planning and budgeting process described above forces management to step back from the daily operations of the entity, examine current operations, decide what improvements are necessary, and formulate plans and budgets that implement

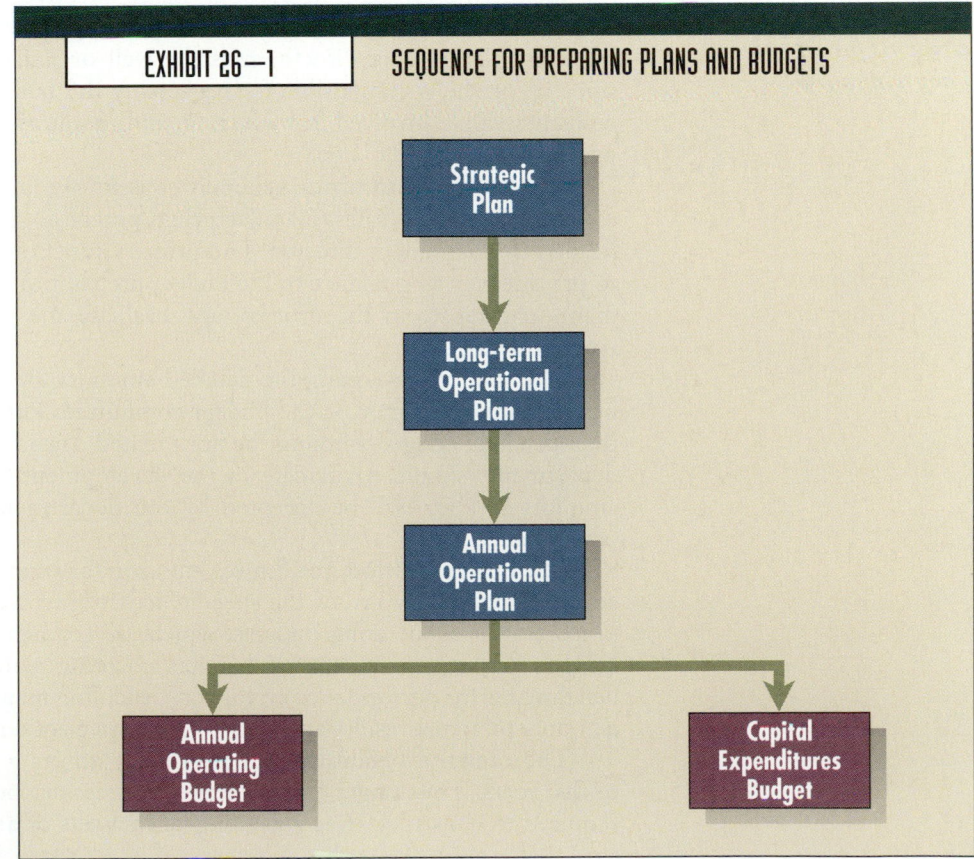

EXHIBIT 26—1   **SEQUENCE FOR PREPARING PLANS AND BUDGETS**

OBJECTIVE ❸ LIST *and* DISCUSS *the advantages of budgeting.* the established goals and objectives for the entity. The annual operating budget represents a specific plan for accomplishing goals and objectives.

A budget can be used to control operations. When a business is large enough to be divided into departments, management needs to ensure that the operation of each department is consistent with the overall plans for the entity as a whole. The budget provides guidance for the departmental managers so their decisions will be consistent with decisions in other departments. For example, the budget provides guidance so the purchasing department buys quantities of material consistent with the factory's budget of units to be manufactured; that budget, in turn, is consistent with the sales department's budget of units to be sold.

One responsibility of top management of any business is to evaluate the performance of the other managers in the organization. The budget provides a sound basis for this type of evaluation; actual results are compared to budgeted results.

Performance evaluations could be based on comparison of actual results to prior period results. However, comparison to prior period results fails to take into account the changes and improvements that have been incorporated into the budget. As a result, the budget is frequently the basis for evaluating performance.

Because the budget is used as a basis for evaluating performance, it can also be a motivating factor for individual managers. Assuming that the budget is realistic, it provides a target that each manager will try to attain.

ELEMENTS OF EFFECTIVE BUDGETING

OBJECTIVE ❹ PRESENT *the elements for effective budgeting.* Even though specific budgeting procedures vary widely among business firms, all entities engaged in comprehensive budgeting should consider the following elements of effective budgeting.

Identifying a **budget director** is vital to effective budgeting. Budget director may be a full-time or part-time position, depending on the size and complexity of the business. The budget director must be well organized and a good communicator, since he or she is responsible for organizing the budgeting process, communicating with the people involved in budgeting, and monitoring the process to ensure that it proceeds on a timely basis.

The **budget committee** generally consists of representatives from all major areas of the firm, such as sales, manufacturing, purchasing, and accounting, and is usually headed by the budget director. The primary functions of the budget committee are to provide central guidance to the budget preparation process, ensure that all departments participate in the process, and evaluate the proposed budget segments for reasonableness.

The task of developing the detailed amounts for the budget is usually not done by the budget director or the budget committee. **Participative budgeting** requires that detailed budget amounts be formulated "from the bottom up." That is, all departments should participate in the development and refinement of the budget amounts so they will be accepted by the departments as reasonable standards of performance.

The **budget period,** the future time span for which the budget is prepared, varies according to the nature of the specific activity involved. Most companies, however, prepare annual operating budgets, which are segmented into quarterly or monthly budgets. Short-term operating budgets covering a month or a quarter are useful benchmarks for performance evaluations, enabling management to compare budgeted amounts to actual results and initiate corrective action as required.

The capital expenditures budget usually covers a multiyear period, often three to five years. This longer budget period is necessary because of the long time period required to construct or acquire long-term assets of a unique nature.

Many businesses use **continuous budgeting** techniques for the operating budget. As each monthly or quarterly budget period passes, the oldest month or quarter is removed from the budget and another month or quarter is added to extend the budget to a full year in the future. With this approach, regardless of the time of the year, the budget always covers 12 months or four quarters. The resulting budget is known as a *continuous budget, perpetual budget,* or *rolling budget.*

The use of budgets to manage and control a firm's activities is known as **budgetary control.** Budgetary control involves the steps taken by management to ensure that the goals and objectives established during the planning stage are attained, and to ensure that all segments of the firm operate in a manner consistent with organizational policies. Budgets serve as guides and targets to managers when they make decisions and as the basis for performance evaluation.

MASTER BUDGET

OBJECTIVE 5 OUTLINE *the components of the master budget and* DISCUSS *the interrelationships of the individual budgets that the master budget comprises.*

Master budget is the name given to the comprehensive annual operating budget. The master budget combines and integrates all the individual, detailed operating budgets for all of the firm's various activities for the year. All amounts in the master budget are usually based on the expected level of operations. The exact structure of the master budget varies according to whether the firm's operations are manufacturing, merchandising, service, or government oriented. In this chapter, we illustrate budgeting and a master budget for a small manufacturing company, Benson Manufacturing Corporation. The following budgets constitute Benson Manufacturing Corporation's master budget:

Sales budget.
Production budget.
Direct material budget.
Direct labor budget.
Factory overhead budget.
Selling and administrative expense budget.
Capital expenditures budget.
Cash budget.
Budgeted income statement.
Budgeted balance sheet.
Budgeted statement of cash flows.

A manufacturing company's master budget includes budgets that are interdependent and must be prepared in a specific sequence. Exhibit 26-2 presents the budgets that Benson Manufacturing Corporation's master budget comprises and the data flows that are necessary between the individual budgets during their preparation.

The *sales budget* is prepared first to establish the quantities of each product that must be available for sale. Then the *production budget* is prepared to identify the number of units of each product to be manufactured. Then the *direct material budget,* the *direct labor budget,* and the *factory overhead budget* determine the levels of product cost to be incurred based on the units to be manufactured. The *selling and administrative expense budget* determines the level of selling and general administrative expense based on the units to be sold.

The *cash budget* receives input from the budgets established previously as well as the *capital expenditures budget* and the *budgeted income statement* (for items such as interest expense). In turn, the cash budget provides inputs to the *budgeted balance sheet* and the *budgeted statement of cash flows.* The budgeted balance sheet also receives input from the budgeted income statement and the capital expenditures budget and supplies input to the budgeted income statement. These interrelationships are illustrated in the following example.

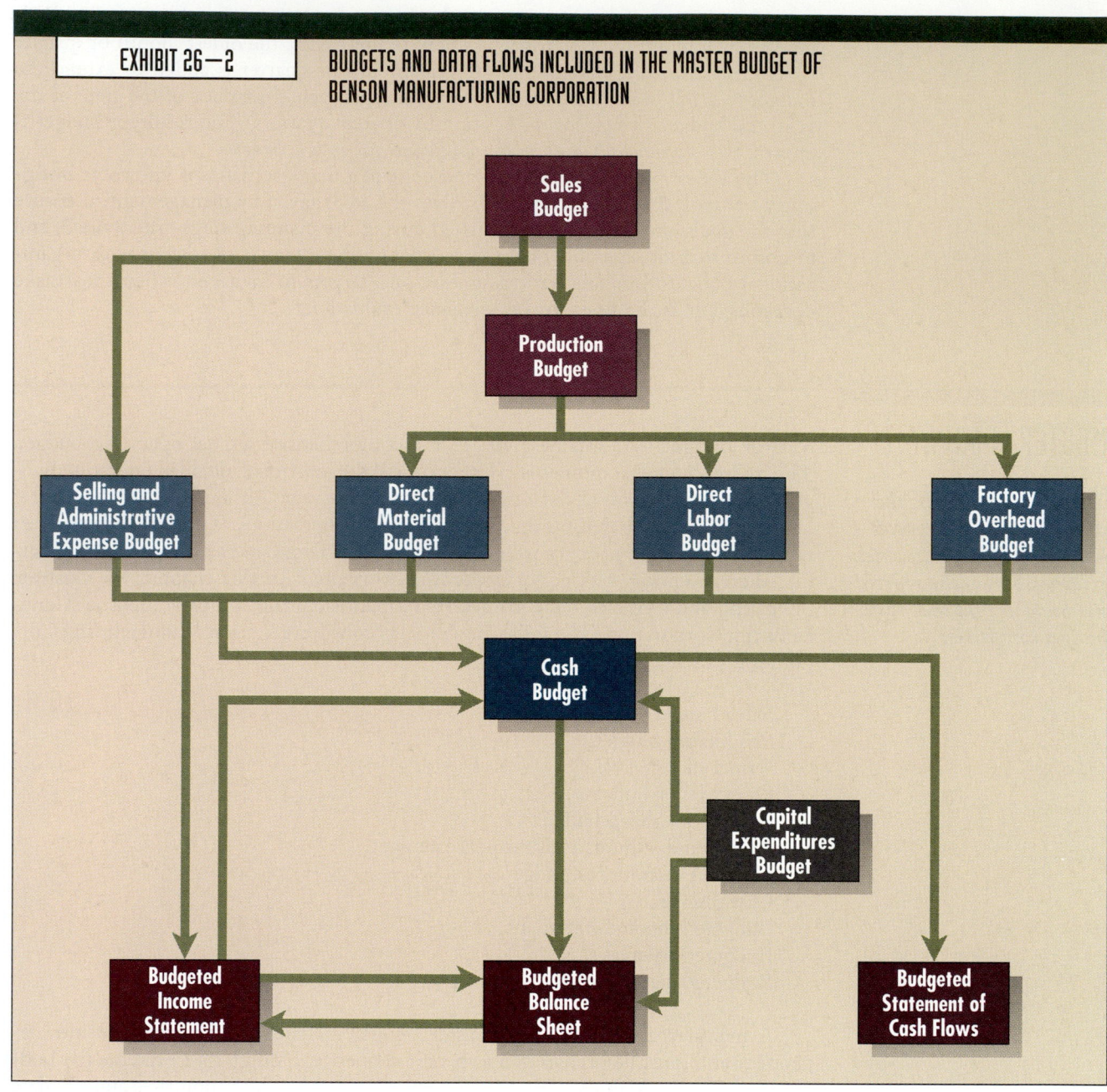

EXHIBIT 26—2 BUDGETS AND DATA FLOWS INCLUDED IN THE MASTER BUDGET OF BENSON MANUFACTURING CORPORATION

ILLUSTRATIONS OF BUDGETS

OBJECTIVE **6** PRESENT *illustrations of individual budgets for a manufacturing company.*

The following illustrations of various budgets outline the development of the master budget for Benson Manufacturing Corporation. The budgets are discussed in the sequence in which they would normally be prepared. The first budget, the sales budget, is based on the sales forecast for the year. The **sales forecast** is the sales department's best guess of what sales will be for the company and the industries in which it operates. Factors that are evaluated in preparing the sales forecast include prior company sales levels, future pricing policies, market research studies, general economic conditions, specific economic indicators, advertising and promotion plans, and anticipated activities of the competition.

Sales Budget

The **sales budget** is prepared first. Anticipated unit sales volume is based on the sales forecast. This forecast must be prepared very carefully. Overestimating sales volume

BENSON MANUFACTURING CORPORATION
SALES BUDGET
FOR THE QUARTER ENDED JUNE 30, 1994

	Forecast Unit Sales Volume	Planned Unit Sales Price	Budgeted Total Sales
Product A: Eastern Sales Region	40,000	$45	$1,800,000
Western Sales Region	28,000	45	1,260,000
Total product A	68,000		$3,060,000
Product B: Eastern Sales Region	20,000	$80	$1,600,000
Western Sales Region	11,000	80	880,000
Total product B	31,000		$2,480,000
Total sales revenue			$5,540,000

can lead to large unwanted inventories, which in turn result in extra storage costs and possibly sales price reductions when liquidating the excess inventory. Underestimating sales can lead to loss of sales revenue and customer ill will stemming from unfilled orders.

The estimated unit sales volume of each product is multiplied by planned unit sales prices to estimate sales revenue. An example of a sales budget is presented in Exhibit 26-3.

Production Budget

The **production budget** reflects the quantity of each product to be produced during the budget period. Scheduled production should specifically provide for anticipated sales and desired ending inventories and, of course, consider the beginning inventories of each product. Assume that Benson Manufacturing Corporation wants to increase its inventory of product A by 20% (from 10,000 to 12,000 units) and decrease its inventory of product B by 20% (from 5,000 to 4,000 units). Benson's production budget appears in Exhibit 26-4. Note that the desired change in inventory of each product is accomplished by scheduling the appropriate production volumes.

Some manufacturing companies have recently experienced a significant change in the way they plan production. These companies use the just-in-time approach for finished goods inventory to reduce their inventory carrying costs. When the **just-in-time inventory** approach is used, finished goods are not produced until they are

BENSON MANUFACTURING CORPORATION
PRODUCTION BUDGET
FOR THE QUARTER ENDED JUNE 30, 1994

	Units of Finished Product	
	A	B
Forecast unit sales	68,000	31,000
Desired ending finished goods inventories	12,000	4,000
Quantities to be available	80,000	35,000
Less: Beginning finished goods inventories	10,000	5,000
Total production to be scheduled	70,000	30,000

needed for shipment to customers. As a result, the planned ending inventory of finished goods is zero or nearly zero.

This approach is practical only for companies that can forecast their sales very accurately, that do not have highly seasonal demand, and that have highly reliable suppliers of the materials and components needed to manufacture the finished goods. Many companies prefer to maintain a safety stock of finished goods inventory so they minimize the risk of running out of stock. **Safety stock** is defined as a quantity of inventory maintained to supply unexpected demand or to provide stock when manufacturing is slowed through delays in receipt of materials and components from suppliers.

Direct Material Budget

The quantities of material to be purchased to meet scheduled production and desired ending materials inventory requirements are presented in the **direct material budget.** Any beginning material inventory must be considered in estimating purchases for the budget period. The quantities to be acquired are multiplied by the anticipated unit prices to calculate the total dollar amounts of material purchases. In the direct material budget illustrated in Exhibit 26-5, we assume that Benson Manufacturing Corporation uses only two direct materials, X and Y, in producing products A and B.

The just-in-time inventory philosophy may also apply to the materials inventory of manufacturing firms. Under this philosophy, materials and components needed to manufacture finished products would not be received from the suppliers until immediately before they are needed for manufacturing. As a result, the material inventory would be zero or nearly zero. Many firms prefer to carry safety stocks of materials and components to ensure that the manufacturing facility is not slowed or stopped by a supplier missing a scheduled delivery.

Direct Labor Budget

The **direct labor budget** presents the number of direct labor hours necessary for the production volume planned for the budget period. These hours are multiplied by the applicable hourly labor rates to determine the total dollar amounts of direct labor costs to be budgeted. In the direct labor budget for Benson Manufacturing Corporation in Exhibit 26-6, we have assumed that both products A and B require manufacturing work in the machining and finishing departments, as appears on the following page.

EXHIBIT 26—5

BENSON MANUFACTURING CORPORATION
DIRECT MATERIAL BUDGET
FOR THE QUARTER ENDED JUNE 30, 1994

	Material X	Material Y
Direct material required:		
Product A: 70,000 × 2.0	140,000	
70,000 × 0.5		35,000
Product B: 30,000 × 3.0	90,000	
30,000 × 2.0		60,000
Desired ending material inventory	40,000	15,000
Total units of material to be available	270,000	110,000
Less: Beginning material inventory	40,000	30,000
Total units of material to be purchased	230,000	80,000
Unit purchase prices	× $4.00	× $5.00
Total material purchases	$920,000	$400,000

EXHIBIT 26—6

BENSON MANUFACTURING CORPORATION
DIRECT LABOR BUDGET
FOR THE QUARTER ENDED JUNE 30, 1994

	Machining Department	Finishing Department
Direct labor hours required for production:		
Product A: 70,000 units × 0.5 hours	35,000	
70,000 units × 0.3 hours		21,000
Product B: 30,000 units × 1.0 hours	30,000	
30,000 units × 0.4 hours		12,000
Total direct labor hours	65,000	33,000
Hourly rate for direct labor	× $12	× $10
Total direct labor cost	$780,000	$330,000

	Machining Department	Finishing Department
Product A	0.5 hours	0.3 hours
Product B	1.0 hours	0.4 hours

Factory Overhead Budget

Recall from earlier chapters that *factory overhead* comprises all factory costs that are not direct material or direct labor. Examples of factory overhead are indirect material, indirect labor, factory supervisory salaries, factory utilities, factory depreciation, factory maintenance, factory taxes, and factory insurance. Because of the variety of cost factors, factory overhead includes both variable and fixed cost elements.

The **factory overhead budget** for the machining department of Benson Manufacturing Corporation is shown in Exhibit 26-7. Note that the format separates variable and fixed overhead cost elements and presents budgeted factory overhead costs

EXHIBIT 26—7

BENSON MANUFACTURING CORPORATION
MACHINING DEPARTMENT
FACTORY OVERHEAD BUDGET
FOR THE QUARTER ENDED JUNE 30, 1994

	Variable Cost per Direct Labor Hour	Overhead Costs at 65,000 Direct Labor Hours
Variable costs:		
Indirect material	$0.60	$ 39,000
Indirect labor	0.80	52,000
Factory utilities	0.40	26,000
Factory maintenance	0.20	13,000
Total variable overhead	$2.00	$130,000
Fixed costs:		
Supervisory salaries		$ 60,000
Depreciation on factory equipment		30,000
Factory utilities		40,000
Factory maintenance		24,000
Factory property taxes and insurance		54,000
Total fixed overhead		$208,000
Total factory overhead		$338,000

EXHIBIT 26—8

BENSON MANUFACTURING CORPORATION
FINISHING DEPARTMENT
FACTORY OVERHEAD BUDGET
FOR THE QUARTER ENDED JUNE 30, 1994

	Variable Cost per Direct Labor Hour	Overhead Costs at 33,000 Direct Labor Hours
Variable costs:		
Indirect material	$0.40	$13,200
Indirect labor	0.30	9,900
Factory utilities	0.10	3,300
Factory maintenance	0.20	6,600
Total variable overhead	$1.00	$33,000
Fixed costs:		
Supervisory salaries		$18,000
Depreciation on factory equipment		10,000
Factory utilities		13,000
Factory maintenance		9,000
Property taxes and insurance		16,000
Total fixed overhead		$66,000
Total factory overhead		$99,000

for the 65,000 direct labor hours level. For the machining department of Benson Manufacturing Corporation for the quarter ended June 30, 1994, the total cost formula for factory overhead at the planned operating volume of 65,000 direct labor hours would be as follows:

$$
\begin{array}{ccccc}
\text{Total} & & \text{Total} & & \left(\begin{array}{ccc} \text{Variable} \\ \text{Overhead} \\ \text{per Direct} \\ \text{Labor Hour} \end{array} \times \begin{array}{c} \text{Production} \\ \text{Volume} \end{array} \right) \\
\text{Factory} & = & \text{Fixed} & + \\
\text{Overhead} & & \text{Overhead} \\
\end{array}
$$

$$
\$338{,}000 = \$208{,}000 + \left(\$2 \times \begin{array}{c} 65{,}000 \text{ direct} \\ \text{labor hours} \end{array} \right)
$$

The factory overhead budget for the finishing department of Benson Manufacturing Corporation is shown in Exhibit 26-8. It is based on 33,000 direct labor hours from Exhibit 26-6.

Selling and Administrative Expense Budget

The **selling and administrative expense budget** will consist of variable and fixed expenses. The variable selling expenses will typically vary with dollars of sales. Exhibit 26-9 presents the selling and administrative expense budget for Benson Manufacturing Corporation.

Capital Expenditures Budget

Expenditures for property, plant, and equipment are among a firm's most important transactions. The type of analysis that is undertaken to determine whether a particular item should be acquired is known as *capital budgeting* and is discussed in detail in a later chapter. The **capital expenditures budget** lists long-term assets that are planned to be acquired over a multiyear period. The illustration for Benson Manufacturing Corporation, presented in Exhibit 26-10, covers only the quarter ended June 30, 1994. We will assume that it was abstracted from the complete capital expenditures budget.

EXHIBIT 26—9

BENSON MANUFACTURING CORPORATION
SELLING AND ADMINISTRATIVE EXPENSE BUDGET
FOR THE QUARTER ENDED JUNE 30, 1994

	Percentage of Sales	Total Cost
Selling expenses:		
Variable costs:		
Sales commissions	10%	$ 554,000
Shipping expense	3%	166,200
Fixed costs:		
Advertising expense		650,000
Administrative expenses:		
Fixed costs:		
Executive salaries expense		225,000
Other administrative expenses		118,700
Total selling and administrative expenses		$1,713,900

The capital expenditures budget has an impact on many other budgets. The plant and equipment available at any point in time determine the productive capacity of the firm. Further, depreciation expense in both the factory overhead budgets and the selling and administrative expense budget is affected by the capital expenditures budget, as are the cash expenditures in the cash budget and the plant assets on the balance sheet.

Cash Budget

OBJECTIVE 7   OUTLINE *the process for preparing the cash budget.*

The **cash budget** presents the projected cash flows during the budget period. The budgeted cash flows are separated into two groups, *cash receipts* (inflows of cash) and *cash disbursements* (outflows of cash). *Cash receipts* include cash sales, collections of accounts receivable, sale of investments and unneeded assets, and proceeds from borrowings and stock sales. *Cash disbursements* include payments for manufacturing costs (direct material, direct labor, and factory overhead), payments for selling and administrative expenses, interest expense, capital expenditures (land, buildings, and equipment), income tax payments, and cash dividends.

Much of the information needed to prepare the cash budget is available in the previously prepared budgets. However, because of the characteristic time lags between transactions and their related effects on cash, cash budgeting often requires the analysis of other data as well. For example, sales precede collections from cus-

EXHIBIT 26—10

BENSON MANUFACTURING CORPORATION
CAPITAL EXPENDITURES BUDGET
FOR THE QUARTER ENDED JUNE 30, 1994

	April	May	June
Machinery	$230,000		$ 25,000
Delivery equipment		$ 40,000	
Computers		80,000	110,000
Total	$230,000	$120,000	$135,000

ZERO-BASE BUDGETING

Traditional budgeting procedures typically use an incremental approach to the development of the annual operating budget. For example, the level of each expense for the prior year is used as the starting point for determining the budgeted level for the next year. The person preparing the budget then either adds to or subtracts from the amount in the previous budget. During the budget process, only the increase or decrease is justified to the managers reviewing the drafts of the budget. The prior year base amount is assumed to be reasonable.

Many organizations—manufacturing companies, merchandising firms, service organizations, governmental agencies, and not-for-profit entities—have experienced increases in their annual operating budgets that they deem to be unacceptable. Some of these organizations have decided to use zero-base budgeting techniques to attack this problem. **Zero-base budgeting** requires budget preparers to start at a zero level for every item in the budget and justify every dollar, not just the increases or decreases. In effect, the budget is prepared "from the ground up" as if the entity had just been formed.

Organizations that have adopted zero-base budgeting use a variety of specific procedures. A common approach is to segment the budget into "decision packages" in which the preparer ranks all of the activities according to their relative importance. For each activity, the preparer might note the consequences of not performing the activity, possible alternative activities, and whether there is an external mandate to perform the activity. This approach enables various levels of management to eliminate low-ranking activities until a desired budget level is reached.

Zero-base budgeting is a time-consuming and costly process. As a result, many entities that employ the technique usually do not apply it to all portions of the operating budget each year. Some use zero-base budgeting every year but apply the technique to only selected segments of the budget so that all segments will be subjected to the technique once during each five-year period. Others apply the technique to all segments periodically (such as every third year). As a result, traditional budgeting techniques might be used to prepare budgets for years 1 and 2 with zero-base budgeting used to prepare the budget for Year 3.

---

tomers, purchases precede payments on account, depreciation does not represent current cash outflows, and prepayments call for cash outlays before the related expenses are recognized.

Assume that Benson Manufacturing Corporation has collected the following actual data for February and March 1994 and developed the following forecasted data for the quarter ended June 30, 1994:

1. Actual sales for February and March, 1994, were the following:

	Actual Cash Sales	Actual Credit Sales
February	$310,000	$1,700,000
March	220,000	1,500,000

2. Forecast sales for the quarter ended June 30, 1994, are as follows:

	Forecast Cash Sales	Forecast Credit Sales
April	$200,000	$1,600,000
May	300,000	1,800,000
June	240,000	1,400,000

3. The collection of cash from credit sales during the quarter ended June 30, 1994, will follow the same pattern as the previous quarter:

a. In the month of sale, 30% is collected subject to a 2% cash discount. (The cash received is calculated as 30% of the credit sales times 98%.)

b. In the month following sale, 50% is collected; no cash discounts are involved.

c. In the second month following sale, 18% is collected. The remaining 2% of accounts receivable are written off as uncollectible.

4. Expected sale of investments during April 1994, should yield $20,000 cash.

5. Forecast cash disbursements for the quarter ended June 30, 1994, are as follows:

Forecast Cash Disbursements

	April	May	June
Manufacturing costs	$950,000	$985,000	$970,000
Selling and administrative expenses	560,000	540,000	575,000
Interest expense (on existing debt)	18,000	18,000	18,000
Income tax payment	–0–	–0–	350,000
Cash dividends	–0–	–0–	100,000

6. Interest expense payments on additional borrowing will be at the rate of $1,000 per month for each $100,000 borrowed.

The collections of cash from customers on accounts receivables during the quarter ended June 30, 1994, can be determined as follows, using data from the first three items above:

Cash Collections from Customers

Month of Credit Sale	April	May	June
February:			
$1,700,000 × 18%	$ 306,000		
March:			
$1,500,000 × 50%	750,000		
$1,500,000 × 18%		$ 270,000	
April:			
$1,600,000 × 30% × 98%	470,400		
$1,600,000 × 50%		800,000	
$1,600,000 × 18%			$ 288,000
May:			
$1,800,000 × 30% × 98%		529,200	
$1,800,000 × 50%			900,000
June:			
$1,400,000 × 30% × 98%			411,600
	$1,526,400	$1,599,200	$1,599,600

The cash budget for Benson Manufacturing Corporation is shown in Exhibit 26-11. A three-column format is used so the cash flow of each month of the quarter can be analyzed separately. The starting point in preparing this cash budget is the beginning cash balance for the first month, April. The cash receipts and cash disbursements for April are then added to the budget. The tentative ending cash balance of $40,900 is then calculated. Assume that Benson Manufacturing Corporation has adopted the rule that the budgeted ending cash balance should never fall below $50,000. As a result, borrowing will be required. Further assume that Benson Manufacturing Corporation borrows in increments of $100,000. This $100,000 is placed on the short-term borrowing line among the cash receipts and the ending cash balance is recalculated to be $140,900.

The budgeted ending cash balance for April becomes the budgeted beginning cash balance for May. The procedure described above is then repeated for May. Note that short-term borrowing is not necessary for May. Also note that interest expense

EXHIBIT 26—11

BENSON MANUFACTURING CORPORATION
CASH BUDGET
FOR THE QUARTER ENDED JUNE 30, 1994

	April	May	June
Beginning cash balance	$ 52,500	$ 140,900	$ 376,100
Cash receipts:			
Cash sales	200,000	300,000	240,000
Collections from customers	1,526,400	1,599,200	1,599,600
Sale of investments	20,000	—	—
Short-term borrowing	100,000	—	—
Cash available	$1,898,900	$2,040,100	$2,215,700
Cash disbursements:			
Manufacturing costs	$ 950,000	$ 985,000	$ 970,000
Selling and			
administrative expenses	560,000	540,000	575,000
Interest expense	18,000	19,000	19,000
Income tax payment	—	—	350,000
Capital expenditures	230,000	120,000	135,000
Cash dividends	—	—	100,000
Total disbursements	$1,758,000	$1,664,000	$2,149,000
Ending cash balance	$ 140,900	$ 376,100	$ 66,700

for May has increased from $18,000 to $19,000 because of the short-term borrowing in April.

The budgeted ending cash balance for May then becomes the budgeted beginning cash balance for June and the process is repeated again. Two additional cash disbursements appear in June: the $350,000 income tax payment and the $100,000 cash dividend.

Budgeted Income Statement

OBJECTIVE **8** ILLUSTRATE *budgeted financial statements.*

The development of the master budget is completed with the preparation of the budgeted financial statements: the budgeted income statement, the budgeted balance sheet, and the budgeted statement of cash flows. The **budgeted income statement** is usually prepared first. In addition to the budgets that were previously prepared, supplemental schedules and worksheets may be needed to prepare the budgeted income statement. In the Benson Manufacturing Corporation example, one of these supplementary schedules is the *schedule of estimated product cost per unit*, which is presented in Exhibit 26-12. The budgeted income statement for Benson Manufacturing Corporation is shown in Exhibit 26-13.

Budgeted Balance Sheet

The preparation of the **budgeted balance sheet** usually follows the preparation of the budgeted income statement. It is important to note that the budgeted balance sheet is dated as of the end of the budget period. The budgeted balance sheet for Benson Manufacturing Corporation, as of June 30, 1994, is shown in Exhibit 26-14.

Budgeted Statement of Cash Flows

The **budgeted statement of cash flows** follows directly from the cash budget. The dollar amounts will be the same, but the grouping and sequence will usually be different. Exhibit 26-15 presents the budgeted statement of cash flows for Benson Manufacturing Corporation. Note that this statement combines the three individual months into one column and groups the cash flows into three sections: cash flows

EXHIBIT 26—12

BENSON MANUFACTURING CORPORATION
SCHEDULE OF ESTIMATED PRODUCT COST PER UNIT
FOR THE QUARTER ENDED JUNE 30, 1994

	Quantity		Cost		Product A	Product B
Direct material:						
Material X:	2.0	×	$4.00	=	$8.00	
	3.0	×	$4.00	=		$12.00
Material Y:	0.5	×	$5.00	=	2.50	
	2.0	×	$5.00	=		10.00
Direct labor:						
Machining	0.5	×	$12.00	=	6.00	
	1.0	×	$12.00	=		12.00
Finishing	0.3	×	$10.00	=	3.00	
	0.4	×	$10.00	=		4.00
Factory overhead:						
Machining	0.5	×	$5.20*	=	2.60	
	1.0	×	$5.20*	=		5.20
Finishing	0.3	×	$3.00†	=	0.90	
	0.4	×	$3.00†	=		1.20
Product cost per unit					$23.00	$44.40

* $338,000/65,000 direct labor hours = $5.20
† $99,000/33,000 direct labor hours = $3

EXHIBIT 26—13

BENSON MANUFACTURING CORPORATION
BUDGETED INCOME STATEMENT
FOR THE QUARTER ENDED JUNE 30, 1994

Sales (*from Sales Budget in Exhibit 26-3*)		$5,540,000
Less: Cost of Goods Sold:		
Product A: 68,000 units × $23.00* = $1,564,000		
Product B: 31,000 units × $44.40* = 1,376,400		
		2,940,400
Gross Profit		$2,599,600
Less: Selling and Administrative Expense (*from Selling and Administrative Expense Budget in Exhibit 26-9*)		1,713,900
Income from Operations		$ 885,700
Less: Interest Expense (*from Cash Budget in Exhibit 26-11*)		56,000
Income before Income Taxes		$ 829,700
Less: Income Taxes (*separate schedule not shown*)		332,500
Net Income		$ 497,200

* *from Schedule of Estimated Product Cost per Unit in Exhibit 26-12*

EXHIBIT 26—14		

BENSON MANUFACTURING CORPORATION
BUDGETED BALANCE SHEET
AS OF JUNE 30, 1994

Assets

Current Assets:		
Cash		$ 66,700
Accounts Receivable		1,276,000
Inventories		1,345,000
Total Current Assets		$ 2,687,700
Plant Assets:		
Land		$ 2,000,000
Buildings and Equipment	$13,000,000	
Less: Accumulated Depreciation	6,000,000	7,000,000
Total Plant Assets		$ 9,000,000
Total Assets		$11,687,700

Liabilities

Current Liabilities:		
Accounts Payable		$ 158,000
Short-term borrowing		100,000
Total Current Liabilities		$ 258,000
Long-term Liabilities:		
Notes Payable		2,500,000
Total Liabilities		$ 2,758,000

Stockholders' Equity

Common Stock		$ 1,000,000
Paid in Capital—Excess of Par-Common Stock		4,000,000
Total Paid-in Capital		$ 5,000,000
Retained Earnings		3,929,700
Total Stockholders' Equity		$ 8,929,700
Total Liabilities and Stockholders' Equity		$11,687,700

from operating activities, cash flows from investing activities, and cash flows from financing activities.

KEY POINTS FOR CHAPTER OBJECTIVES

1 **DESCRIBE** the planning process, including strategic planning and operational planning, used by businesses and other entities (pp. 994–995).
- Strategic planning is a formal process that addresses and documents the mission and long-term goals of the organization. SWOT analysis is used to develop and analyze the data needed for this type of planning.
- Operational planning is the development of specific goals and objectives for the entity as a whole and its individual departments, the formulation of a plan of attack to accomplish the goals and objectives, and the written documentation of the goals and objectives and the plan of attack.

2 **DISCUSS** the budgeting process (p. 995).
- Budgeting is the process of developing a formal, written operational plan that presents management's planned actions in financial terms.
- Two budgets result from the budgeting process: the annual operating budget that covers a one-year budget period and the capital expenditures budget that covers a multiple-year budget period.

EXHIBIT 26—15

BENSON MANUFACTURING CORPORATION
BUDGETED STATEMENT OF CASH FLOWS
FOR THE QUARTER ENDED JUNE 30, 1994

Cash flows from operating activities

Cash receipts:

Cash sales		$ 740,000
Collections from customers		4,725,200
		$5,465,200

Cash disbursements:

Manufacturing costs		$2,905,000
Selling and administrative expenses		1,675,000
Interest expense		56,000
Income tax payment		350,000
		$4,986,000
Net cash provided by operating activities		$ 479,200

Cash flows from investing activities

Sale of investments		$ 20,000
Capital expenditures		(485,000)
Net cash used by investing activities		$ (465,000)

Cash flows from financing activities

Short-term borrowing		$ 100,000
Cash dividends		(100,000)
Net cash provided by financing activities		$ 0
Net increase (decrease) in cash		$ 14,200
Beginning cash balance		52,500
Ending cash balance		$ 66,700

❸ **LIST** and **DISCUSS** the advantages of budgeting (pp. 995–996).
  ■ Budgets represent a plan for accomplishing goals and objectives.
  ■ The budget provides operational guidance to the department mangers so they make decisions that are consistent with decisions made in other departments.
  ■ The budget is the basis for evaluating performance.
  ■ Because the budget is used as a basis for evaluating performance, it serves as a target for individual managers.

❹ **PRESENT** the elements for effective budgeting (pp. 996–997).
  ■ A budget director should be identified to organize the budgeting process, communicate with people involved in budgeting, and monitor the budgeting process.
  ■ A budget committee, consisting of representatives from all major areas of the company, should provide general guidance to the budgeting process and evaluate proposed budget segments for reasonableness.
  ■ Participative budgeting requires that all departments participate in the development and refinement of the budget amounts so that departmental managers will accept the budget as a reasonable standard of performance.
  ■ The future time span for which the budget is prepared, known as the *budget period*, varies according to the activity involved.
  ■ The use of budgets to manage and control a firm's activities is known as *budgetary control*.

❺ **OUTLINE** the components of the master budget and **DISCUSS** the interrelationships of the individual budgets that the master budget comprises (pp. 997–998).
  ■ The master budget for a manufacturing firm consists of at least the following individual budgets:
    Sales budget.
    Production budget.
    Direct material budget.
    Direct labor budget.

Factory overhead budget.
Selling and administrative expense budget.
Capital expenditures budget.
Cash budget.
Budgeted income statement.
Budgeted balance sheet.
Budgeted statement of cash flows.

■ The individual budgets must be prepared in a specific sequence, beginning with the sales budget, to properly reflect the interrelationships among the individual budgets.

6 **PRESENT** illustrations of individual budgets for a manufacturing company (pp. 998–1003).

■ The sales budget is based on the sales forecast.

■ The production budget determines the number of units of each product that should be manufactured during the budget period.

■ The direct material budget displays the amount of each direct material item that should be purchased to supply the budgeted production.

■ The direct labor budget presents the amount of direct labor, by department, that is required to accomplish the budgeted production.

■ The factory overhead budget determines, for each factory department, the amount of variable overhead and the amount of fixed overhead needed to complete the budgeted production.

■ The selling and administrative expense budget accumulates the variable and fixed selling and administrative expenses for the entity. Some of the expenses may vary with sales; others may vary with production.

■ The capital expenditures budget presents the planned expenditures for property, plant, and equipment over an extended budget period, possibly five years.

7 **OUTLINE** the process of preparing the cash budget (pp. 1003–1006).

■ The cash budget, usually segmented by month, presents all the cash receipts and cash disbursements planned for the budget period.

■ Much of the information needed to prepare the cash budget comes from previously prepared budgets. However, additional schedules and worksheets are usually needed to place required information in proper form.

■ Cash collected from customers from prior credit sales needs careful analysis to take into account timing, cash discounts, and uncollectibles.

8 **ILLUSTRATE** budgeted financial statements (pp. 1006–1008).

■ The budgeted income statement is prepared for the budget period.

■ The budgeted balance sheet is prepared as of the ending date of the budget period.

■ The budgeted statement of cash flows is prepared for the budget period, based primarily on data from the cash budget.

SELF-TEST QUESTIONS FOR REVIEW

(Answers follow the Solution to Demonstration Problem.)

1. If a company uses participative budgeting, which group should prepare the initial set of budget dollar amounts?
   a. Budget committee.
   b. Operating department managers.
   c. Top management.
   d. Accounting department.

2. Which of the following budgets will typically have the longest budget period?
   a. Capital expenditures budget.
   b. Cash budget.
   c. Sales budget.
   d. Budgeted income statement.

3. Which of the following budgets should be prepared before all of the others listed below?
   a. Cash budget.
   b. Direct materials budget.
   c. Factory overhead budget.
   d. Production budget.

4. If the beginning inventory of a company that manufactures only one product is 5,000 units, the sales forecast is 34,000 units sold, and the desired ending inventory is 6,000 units, how many units should be produced?
   a. 35,000.
   b. 33,000.
   c. 40,000.
   d. 39,000.

5. Smith Company started business on September 1. Smith had credit sales of $200,000 in September and $300,000 in October. The pattern for collection of cash from customers is expected to be 40% in the month of sale (subject to a 2% cash discount), 50% in the month following the month of sale, and 7% in the second month following the month of sale with 3% uncollectible. How much cash did Smith Company receive from customers on account during October?

a. $120,000.   c. $217,600.
b. $117,600.   d. $220,000.

DEMONSTRATION PROBLEM FOR REVIEW

The sales department of Jackson Manufacturing, Inc., has completed the following sales forecast for the months of January through March 1994 for its only two products: 40,000 units of X1 to be sold at $110 each and 20,000 units of X2 to be sold at $85 each. The desired unit inventories at March 31, 1994, are 10% of the next quarter's unit sales forecast, which are 50,000 units of X1 and 25,000 units of X2. The January 1, 1994, unit inventories were 7,000 units of X1 and 1,500 units of X2.

Each unit of X1 requires 4 pounds of material R and 2 pounds of material S for its manufacture; X2 requires 2 pounds of R and 3 pounds of S. Purchase cost of R is $10 per pound and of S is $5 per pound. Materials on hand at January 1, 1994, were 20,000 pounds of R and 8,000 pounds of S. Desired inventories at March 31, 1994, are 15,000 pounds of R and 6,000 pounds of S.

Each unit of X1 requires 0.5 hour of direct labor in the factory; each unit of X2 requires 1.0 hour of direct labor. The average hourly rate for direct labor is $12 per hour. Estimated factory overhead cost is $8 per direct labor hour plus $100,000 per month. Selling and administrative expenses are estimated to be 10% of sales revenue plus $200,000 per month.

Cash sales in December 1993 were $250,000 and credit sales were $2,000,000. Cash sales for the first quarter are estimated to be $200,000 per month. It is forecast that 40% of the credit sales for the quarter ended March 31, 1994, will occur in January, 30% in February, and 30% in March. Of credit sales (December through March), 40% will be collected as cash in the month of sale and 50% will be collected in the following month. The remainder will be uncollectible.

The January 1, 1994, cash balance was $60,000. The minimum acceptable cash balance at the end of each month is $50,000. Short-term borrowings are made in multiples of $10,000 with interest charged at the rate of 1% per month. The first interest payment is made the month following the borrowing. Cash disbursements (excluding interest on short-term borrowings) are estimated as follows:

	January	February	March
Manufacturing costs	$1,200,000	$1,100,000	$1,000,000
Selling and administrative expenses	380,000	400,000	340,000
Interest expense	100,000	100,000	100,000
Income tax payment	–0–	–0–	200,000
Capital expenditures	100,000	340,000	60,000
Cash dividends	400,000	–0–	–0–

REQUIRED

a. Prepare the sales budget for the quarter ended March 31, 1994.
b. Prepare the production budget for the quarter ended March 31, 1994.
c. Prepare the direct material budget for the quarter ended March 31, 1994.
d. Prepare the direct labor budget for the quarter ended March 31, 1994.
e. Prepare the factory overhead budget for the quarter ended March 31, 1994.
f. Prepare a schedule of estimated product cost per unit for the quarter ended March 31, 1994.
g. Prepare the selling and administrative expense budget for the quarter ended March 31, 1994.
h. Prepare a schedule of cash collected from customers for the quarter ended March 31, 1994.
i. Prepare the cash budget for the quarter ended March 31, 1994.

SOLUTION TO DEMONSTRATION PROBLEM

a.

JACKSON MANUFACTURING, INC.
SALES BUDGET
FOR THE QUARTER ENDED MARCH 31, 1994

Product	Forecast Unit Sales Volume	Planned Unit Sales Price	Budgeted Total Sales
X1	40,000	$110	$4,400,000
X2	20,000	85	1,700,000
Total sales revenue			$6,100,000

b.

JACKSON MANUFACTURING, INC.
PRODUCTION BUDGET
FOR THE QUARTER ENDED MARCH 31, 1994

	Units of Finished Product	
	X1	X2
Forecast unit sales	40,000	20,000
Desired ending inventories:		
10% × 50,000	5,000	
10% × 25,000		2,500
Quantities to be available	45,000	22,500
Less: Beginning inventories	7,000	1,500
Total production to be scheduled	38,000	21,000

c.

JACKSON MANUFACTURING, INC.
DIRECT MATERIAL BUDGET
FOR THE QUARTER ENDED MARCH 31, 1994

	Material R	Material S
Direct material required:		
Product X1: 38,000 × 4	152,000	
38,000 × 2		76,000
Product X2: 21,000 × 2	42,000	
21,000 × 3		63,000
Desired ending material inventories	15,000	6,000
Total pounds of material to be available	209,000	145,000
Less: Beginning material inventories	20,000	8,000
Total pounds of material to be purchased	189,000	137,000
Unit purchase price	× $10	× $5
Total material purchases	$1,890,000	$685,000

d.

JACKSON MANUFACTURING, INC.
DIRECT LABOR BUDGET
FOR THE QUARTER ENDED MARCH 31, 1994

Direct labor hours required for production:	
Product X1: 38,000 × 0.5 hours	19,000
Product X2: 21,000 × 1.0 hours	21,000
Total direct labor hours required	40,000
Hourly rate for direct labor	× $12
Total direct labor cost	$480,000

e.

JACKSON MANUFACTURING, INC.
FACTORY OVERHEAD BUDGET
FOR THE QUARTER ENDED MARCH 31, 1994

Total direct labor hours	40,000
Variable factory overhead rate	× $8
Variable factory overhead cost	$320,000
Fixed factory overhead cost	
$100,000 × 3	300,000
Total factory overhead cost	$620,000

f.

JACKSON MANUFACTURING, INC.
SCHEDULE OF ESTIMATED PRODUCT COST PER UNIT
FOR THE QUARTER ENDED MARCH 31, 1994

	Quantity		Cost	Product X1	Product X2
Direct material:					
Material R:	4	×	$10	$40.00	
	2	×	$10		$20.00
Material S:	2	×	$5	10.00	
	3	×	$5		15.00
Direct labor:	0.5	×	$12	6.00	
	1.0	×	$12		12.00
Factory overhead:	0.5	×	$15.50*	7.75	
	1.0	×	$15.50*		15.50
Product cost per unit				$63.75	$62.50

*$620,000/40,000 = $15.50 per direct labor hour

g.

JACKSON MANUFACTURING, INC.
SELLING AND ADMINISTRATIVE EXPENSE BUDGET
FOR THE QUARTER ENDED MARCH 31, 1994

Total sales revenue	$6,100,000
Variable selling and administrative rate	× 10%
Variable selling and administrative expense	$ 610,000
Fixed selling and administrative expense	
$200,000 × 3	600,000
Total selling and administrative expense	$1,210,000

h.

JACKSON MANUFACTURING, INC.
SCHEDULE OF CASH COLLECTED FROM CUSTOMERS
FOR THE QUARTER ENDED MARCH 31, 1994

	January	February	March
Cash sales:	$200,000	$200,000	$200,000
Credit sales:			
December: $2,000,000 × 50%	$1,000,000		
January: $2,200,000 × 40%	880,000		
$2,200,000 × 50%		$1,100,000	
February: $1,650,000 × 40%		660,000	
$1,650,000 × 50%			$ 825,000
March: $1,650,000 × 40%			660,000
	$1,880,000	$1,760,000	$1,485,000

($6,100,000 − $600,000) × 40% = $2,200,000
($6,100,000 − $600,000) × 30% = $1,650,000

i.

Jackson Manufacturing, Inc.
Cash Budget
For the Quarter Ended March 31, 1994

	January	February	March
Beginning cash balance	$ 60,000	$ 50,000	$ 69,100
Cash receipts:			
Cash sales	200,000	200,000	200,000
Collections from customers	1,880,000	1,760,000	1,485,000
Short-term borrowing	90,000	—	—
Cash available	$2,230,000	$2,010,000	$1,754,100
Cash disbursements:			
Manufacturing costs	$1,200,000	$1,100,000	$1,000,000
Selling and administrative expenses	380,000	400,000	340,000
Interest expense	100,000	100,900*	100,900
Income tax payments	—	—	200,000
Capital expenditures	100,000	340,000	60,000
Cash dividends	400,000	—	—
Total disbursements	$2,180,000	$1,940,900	$1,700,900
Ending cash balance	$ 50,000	$ 69,100	$ 53,200

*$100,000 + ($90,000 × 1%) = $100,900

ANSWERS TO SELF-TEST QUESTIONS   **1.** b, p. 996   **2.** a, p. 1002   **3.** d, p. 997   **4.** a, p. 999   **5.** c, p. 1005

GLOSSARY OF KEY TERMS USED IN THIS CHAPTER

budget committee   A group of representatives from all major areas of the firm whose responsibilities include providing central guidance in the budget preparation process, ensuring that all departments participate in the process, and evaluating the proposed budget segments for reasonableness (p. 996).

budget director   The person within a company who is responsible for organizing the budget process, communicating with people involved in budgeting, and monitoring the process to ensure that it proceeds on a timely basis (p. 996).

budget period   The future time span for which the budget is prepared (p. 996).

budgetary control   The use of budgets to manage and control a firm's activities. The budgets serve as guides and targets to managers when they make decisions and as the basis for performance evaluation (p. 997).

budgeted balance sheet   The planned balance sheet as of the end of the budget period; derived from the other budgets that the master budget comprises (p. 1006).

budgeted income statement   The planned income statement for the budget period; derived from the other budgets that the master budget comprises (p. 1006).

budgeted statement of cash flows   The planned statement of cash flows for the budget period; derived primarily from the cash budget (p. 1006).

budgeting   The process of formal financial planning (p. 995).

capital expenditures budget   A listing of the types of plant assets and the dollar amounts budgeted for their acquisition during a multiple year planning horizon. The portion affecting the current operating year is included in the master budget (p. 1002).

cash budget   The budget that presents the planned cash receipts and cash disbursements for the budgeting period; a component of the master budget (p. 1003).

continuous budgeting   A budgeting process that segments the annual operating budget into months or quarters and adds a new month or quarter as each month or quarter expires (p. 996).

direct labor budget   The budget that presents the amount of direct labor, by department, that is required to accomplish the budgeted production (p. 1000).

direct material budget   The budget that displays the amount of each direct material item that should be purchased to supply the budgeted production (p. 1000).

factory overhead budget   The budget that determines, for each factory department, the amount of variable overhead and the amount of fixed overhead needed to complete the budgeted production (p. 1001).

just-in-time inventory The approach to planning and managing inventory that prescribes that finished goods inventory should not be produced until needed for shipment to customers and that materials and components needed to manufacture the finished products should not be received from suppliers until they are needed for manufacturing (p. 999).

master budget The comprehensive financial plan that includes budgets for sales, production, direct material, direct labor, factory overhead, selling and administrative expenses, capital expenditures, and cash as well as the budgeted income statement for the budget period, the budgeted balance sheet as of the end of the budget period, and the budgeted statement of cash flows for the budget period (p. 997).

operational planning The development of specific goals and objectives for the entity as a whole and its individual departments, the formulation of a plan of attack to accomplish the goals and objectives, and the written documentation of the goals and objectives as well as the plan of attack (p. 994).

participative budgeting Budgeting that involves all departments in the development and refinement of budget amounts so the budget will be accepted by the departments as reasonable standards of performance (p. 996).

planning horizon The future time period, usually expressed in years, for which a particular plan is developed (p. 994).

production budget The budget that determines the number of units of each product that should be manufactured during the budget period (p. 999).

safety stock The quantity of on-hand inventory maintained to supply unexpected demand or to provide stock when manufacturing is slowed through delays in receipt of materials and components from suppliers (p. 1000).

sales budget The budget showing estimated unit sales and sales revenues for the budget period; based on the sales forecast (p. 998).

sales forecast The sales department's estimate of sales for the company and the industries in which it operates (p. 998).

selling and administrative expense budget The budget that accumulates the variable and fixed selling and administrative expenses for the entity. Some of the expenses may vary with sales; others may vary with production (p. 1002).

strategic planning The formal process that addresses and documents the mission and long-term goals of the organization. SWOT analysis is used to develop and analyze the data needed for this type of planning (p. 994).

SWOT analysis A technique used to identify, document, and analyze the current strengths and weaknesses of an organization and its future opportunities and threats (p. 994).

zero-base budgeting A budgeting process that requires each budgetary unit to justify all of its expenditures as if the unit's operations were just starting (p. 1004).

QUESTIONS

26-1 What is a planning horizon? How will it differ between strategic planning and operational planning?

26-2 Describe strategic planning.

26-3 Describe operational planning.

26-4 Define *budgeting*.

26-5 List and briefly explain four advantages of budgeting.

26-6 Describe the budget committee.

26-7 Why is participative budgeting important to the success of the budgeting process?

26-8 What is meant by *continuous budgeting*?

26-9 What is the master budget? List, in the order of preparation, the various budgets that the master budget for a small manufacturing company might comprise.

26-10 Why do most firms prepare the sales budget first?

26-11 Beginning finished goods inventory is 10,000 units, anticipated sales volume is 60,000 units, and the desired ending finished goods inventory is 12,000 units. What number of units should be produced?

26-12 Three pounds of material R (costing $5 per pound) and 4 pounds of material S (costing $7 per pound) are required to make one unit of product T. If management plans to increase the inventory of material R by 500 pounds and reduce the inventory of material S by 800 pounds during a period when 3,000 units of product T are to be produced, what are the budgeted purchase costs of material R and material S?

26-13 Carroll Manufacturing Company has two labor operations in its factory: machining and assembly. Workers in the machining department are paid $14 per hour; workers in the assembly department are paid $12 per hour. During January, 10,000 units of product A and 20,000 units of product B are to be manufactured. Each unit of A requires 1 hour of machining and 2 hours of assembly; each unit of B requires 3 hours of machining and 1 hour of assembly. What is the total direct labor budget for January?

26-14 Johnson Manufacturing Company has budgeted 30,000 direct labor hours for March. The budgeted cost formula for monthly factory overhead is $4 per direct labor hour plus $65,000. What is the factory overhead budget for March?

26-15 A company collects cash from its credit sales in the following pattern: 30% in the month of sale, 50% in the month following the month of sale, and 20% in the second month following the month of sale. What percentage of which months' credit sales will be collected during October?

26-16 What are the three major groupings of cash flows in the budgeted statement of cash flows?

EXERCISES

BUDGETING INVENTORIES
— OBJ. 6 —

26-17 For each independent situation below, determine the amounts indicated by the question marks.

Number of Units	A	B	C	D
Beginning inventory	10,000	?	7,000	?
Produced	40,000	27,000	?	60,000
Available	?	?	26,000	64,000
Sold	45,000	28,000	?	?
Ending inventory	?	10,000	6,000	2,000

BUDGET PREPARATION
— OBJ. 6 —

26-18 Collins Company is preparing its master budget for April. Use the given estimates to determine the amounts required in each requirement below. (Estimates may be related to more than one requirement.)
  a. What should total sales revenue be if territories A and B estimate sales of 10,000 and 12,000 units, respectively, and the unit selling price is $40?
  b. If the beginning finished goods inventory is an estimated 2,000 units and the desired ending inventory is 3,000 units, how many units should be produced?
  c. What dollar amount of material should be purchased at $4 per pound if each unit of product requires 3 pounds and beginning and ending materials inventories should be 5,000 and 4,000 pounds, respectively?
  d. How much direct labor cost should be incurred if each unit produced requires 1.5 hours at an hourly rate of $13?
  e. How much factory overhead should be incurred if fixed factory overhead is $50,000 and variable factory overhead is $2.50 per direct labor hour?

BUDGET PREPARATION
— OBJ. 6 —

26-19 Westport Company is preparing its master budget for May. Use the estimates provided to determine the amounts required in each requirement below. (Estimates may be related to more than one requirement.)
  a. What should total sales revenue be if territories E and W estimate sales of 50,000 and 100,000 units, respectively, and the unit selling price is $27?
  b. If the beginning finished goods inventory is an estimated 7,000 units and the desired ending inventory is 6,000 units, how many units should be produced?
  c. What dollar amount of material should be purchased at $2 per pound if each unit of product requires 2.5 pounds and beginning and ending materials inventories should be 13,500 and 12,000 pounds, respectively?
  d. How much direct labor cost should be incurred if each unit produced requires 0.5 hours at an hourly rate of $11?
  e. How much factory overhead should be incurred if fixed factory overhead is $45,000 and variable factory overhead is $1.30 per direct labor hour?

BUDGETING CASH COLLECTIONS
— OBJ. 7 —

26-20 Spencer Company, which sells on terms 2/10, n/30, had credit sales for May and June of $70,000 and $80,000, respectively. Analysis of Spencer's operations indicates that the pattern of customers' payments on account is as follows (percentages are of total monthly credit sales):

	Receiving Discount	Beyond Discount Period	Totals
In month of sale	50%	20%	70%
In month following sale	15%	10%	25%
Uncollectible accounts, returns, and allowances			5%
			$100%

Determine the estimated cash collected on customers' accounts in June.

BUDGETING CASH FLOW
— OBJ. 7 —

26-21 The following various elements relate to Whitfield, Inc.'s cash budget for April of the current year. For each item, determine the amount of cash that Whitfield should receive or pay in April.

a. At $28 each, unit sales are 5,000 and 6,000 for March and April, respectively. Total sales are typically 40% for cash and 60% on credit; 30% of credit sales are collected in the month of sale, with the balance collected in the following month. Uncollectible accounts are negligible.

b. Merchandise purchases were $45,000 and $78,000 for March and April, respectively. Typically, 20% of total purchases are paid for in the month of purchase with a 5% cash discount. The balance of purchases is paid for (without discount) in the following month.

c. Fixed administrative expenses, which total $11,000 per month, are paid in the month incurred. Variable administrative expenses amount to 20% of total monthly sales revenue, one-half of which is paid in the month incurred, with the balance paid in the following month.

d. A plant asset originally cost $8,000, on which $6,000 depreciation has been taken, is sold for cash at a loss of $400.

PREPARE CASH BUDGET FOR THREE MONTHS
— OBJ. 7 —

26-22 Brewster Corporation expects the following cash receipts and disbursements during the first quarter of 1994 (receipts exclude new borrowings and disbursements exclude interest payments on borrowings since January 1, 1994):

	January	February	March
Cash receipts	$260,000	$280,000	$250,000
Cash disbursements	240,000	320,000	260,000

The expected cash balance at January 1, 1994, is $42,000. Brewster wants to maintain a cash balance at the end of each month of at least $40,000. Short-term borrowings at 1% interest per month will be used to accomplish this, if necessary. Borrowings (in multiples of $1,000) will be made at the beginning of the month in which they are needed, with interest for that month paid at the end of the month.

Prepare a cash budget for the quarter ended March 31, 1994.

PREPARE CASH BUDGET FROM BUDGETED TRANSACTIONS
— OBJ. 7 —

26-23 Cambridge Company anticipates a cash balance of $84,000 on May 1, 1994. The following budgeted transactions for May 1994 present data related to anticipated cash receipts and cash disbursements:

1. For May, budgeted cash sales are $60,000 and budgeted credit sales are $500,000. (Credit sales for April were $450,000.) In the month of sale, 40% of credit sales are collected with the balance collected in the month following sale.

2. Budgeted merchandise purchases for May are $280,000. (Merchandise purchases in April were $240,000.) In the month of purchase, 70% of merchandise purchases are paid for, and the balance is paid for in the following month.

3. Budgeted cash disbursements for salaries and operating expenses for May total $165,000.

4. During May, $25,000 of principal repayment and $4,000 of interest payment are due the bank.

5. A $20,000 income tax deposit is due the federal government during May.

6. A new delivery truck will be purchased during May for $6,000 cash and an $8,000 note payable. Depreciation for May will be $500.

Prepare a cash budget for Cambridge Company for the month of May 1994.

PROBLEMS

Budgeting Cash
— Obj. 7 —

26-24 Whitneys, Inc., sells on terms of 5% discount for "cash and carry" or 2/10, n/30 and estimates its total sales for the second calendar quarter of next year as follows: April, $300,000; May, $240,000; and June, $360,000. An analysis of operations indicates the following customer collection patterns:

	Portions of Total Sales
In month of sale:	
Cash at time of sale	25%
On account, during discount period	15%
On account, after discount period	10%
In month following sale:	
On account, during discount period	20%
On account, after discount period	10%
In second month following sale:	
On account, after discount period	15%
Average portion uncollectible	5%
	100%

REQUIRED

Prepare an estimate of the cash to be collected from customers during June.

Preparation of
Individual Budgets
— Obj. 6, 8 —

26-25 During the first calendar quarter of 1994, Clinton Corporation is planning to manufacture a new product and introduce it in two regions. Market research indicates that sales will be 6,000 units in the urban region at a unit price of $53 and 5,000 units in the rural region at $48 each. Since the sales manager expects the product to catch on, he has asked for production sufficient to generate a 4,000-unit ending inventory. The production manager has furnished the following estimates related to manufacturing costs and operating expenses.

	Variable (per unit)	Fixed (total)
Manufacturing costs:		
Direct material:		
A (4 lbs. @ $3.15/lb.)	$12.60	—
B (2 lbs. @ $4.65/lb.)	9.30	—
Direct labor (0.5 hr. per unit)	7.50	—
Factory overhead:		
Depreciation	—	$ 7,650
Factory supplies	0.90	4,500
Supervisory salaries	—	28,800
Other	0.75	22,950
Operating expenses:		
Selling:		
Advertising	—	22,500
Sales salaries and commissions*	1.50	15,000
Other*	0.90	3,000
Administrative:		
Office salaries	—	2,700
Supplies	0.15	1,050
Other	0.08	1,950

*Varies per unit sold, not per unit produced.

REQUIRED

a. Assuming that the desired ending inventories of materials A and B are 4,000 and 6,000 pounds, respectively, and that work in process inventories are immaterial, prepare budgets for the calendar quarter in which the new product will be introduced for each of the following operating factors:
   1. Total sales.
   2. Production.
   3. Material purchases cost.
   4. Direct labor costs.

5. Factory overhead costs.
6. Selling and administrative expenses.

b. Using data generated in requirement (a), prepare a budgeted income statement for the calendar quarter. Assume an overall effective income tax rate of 30%.

MONTHLY CASH BUDGET
— OBJ. 7 —

26-26 Grove, Inc., is a wholesaler for its only product, a deluxe wireless electric drill, which sells for $90 each and costs Grove $54 each. On December 1, 1994, Grove's management requested a cash budget for December. The following selected account balances at November 30, 1994, were gathered by the accounting department:

Cash	$ 135,000
Marketable securities (at cost)	210,000
Accounts receivable (all trade)	1,710,000
Inventories (15,000 units)	810,000
Operating expenses payable	140,400
Accounts payable (all merchandise)	583,200
Note payable (due 12/31/94)	393,000

Actual sales for the months of October and November were 20,000 and 30,000 units, respectively. Projected unit sales for December and January are 50,000 and 40,000, respectively. Experience indicates that 50% of sales should be collected in the month of sale, 30% in the month following sale, and the balance in the second month following sale. Uncollectibles, returns, and allowances are negligible.

Planned purchases should provide ending inventories equal to 30% of next month's unit sales volume. Approximately 70% of the purchases are paid for in the month of purchase and the balance in the following month.

Monthly operating expenses are budgeted at $8.10 per unit sold plus a fixed amount of $189,000 including depreciation of $81,000. Except for depreciation, 60% of operating expenses are paid in the month incurred and the balance in the following month. Interest expense is included in operating expenses.

Special anticipated year-end transactions include the following:
1. Declaration of a $22,500 cash dividend to be paid two weeks after the December 20 date of record.
2. Sale of one-half of the marketable securities held on November 30; a gain of $21,000 is anticipated.
3. Pay off the note payable due December 31, 1994.
4. Trade-in of an old computer originally costing $675,000 and now having accumulated depreciation of $540,000 at a gain of $157,500 on a new computer costing $1,350,000. Sufficient cash will be paid at the time of trade-in so that only 50% of the total price will have to be financed.
5. Groves's treasurer has a policy of maintaining a minimum month-end cash balance of $135,000 but wants to raise this to $225,000 at December 31. She has a standing arrangement with the bank to borrow any amount up to a limit of $450,000.

REQUIRED
Prepare a cash budget for Grove, Inc., for December 1994.

BUDGETING PRODUCTION
AND PURCHASES AND JUST-
IN-TIME MATERIALS
INVENTORY
— OBJ. 6 —

26-27 Hancock Manufacturing, Inc., is preparing budgets for the third quarter of 1994. Hancock produces only one product in its factory. This product requires 5 pounds of material B, 2 pounds of material G, and a component, K, that is purchased from another manufacturer. Hancock operates on a just-in-time basis for material B. As a result, Hancock maintains no inventory of material B. On July 1, 1994, the inventory of material G is expected to be 2,000 pounds and the inventory of component K is expected to be 500 units. Hancock wants the inventories of G and K at September 30, 1994, to be 20% less than the inventories at July 1, 1994. The inventory of finished products at June 30, 1994, is expected to be 1,000 units; the desired inventory at September 30, 1994, is 3,000 units to allow a buildup for heavy sales in the fourth quarter. The sales forecast for the third quarter is 12,000 units at $300 each. Budgeted purchase costs are $10 per pound for B, $7 per pound for G, and $40 per component for K.

REQUIRED
a. Prepare the production budget for Hancock Manufacturing, Inc., for the third quarter of 1994.

b. Prepare the direct material budget for Hancock Manufacturing, Inc., for the third quarter of 1994.

PREPARE AND EVALUATE BUDGETED INCOME STATEMENT — OBJ. 8 —

26-28　Fairfield Stores, a retailer in a shopping mall, prepared the following income statement for its operations for the month just ended:

FAIRFIELD STORES
INCOME STATEMENT
FOR THE MONTH ENDED APRIL 30, 1994

Sales		$500,000
Cost of Goods Sold		240,000
Gross Profit		$260,000
Operating Expenses:		
Sales Commissions Expense	$25,000	
Advertising Expense	60,000	
Lease Expense	20,000	
Depreciation Expense	10,000	
Salaries Expense	30,000	
Other Operating Expenses	15,000	160,000
Income before Income Taxes		$100,000
Income Tax Expense		30,000
Net Income		$ 70,000

Sales commissions were 5% of sales. Income taxes were 30% of income before income taxes. Both should continue at the same rate for the remainder of the year.

Fairfield Stores is preparing the budget for the month of May 1994. If no basic changes are made, Fairfield management expects that the income statement would be virtually identical to the one for April. However, Fairfield's management has decided to make some changes in the operations. The plans include the following:

1. Increase advertising expense by 40%.
2. Decrease all selling prices by 10%.
3. Increase the number of units sold by 25% as a result of the first two changes.

REQUIRED

a. Prepare a budgeted income statement for the month of May 1994. (Round all amounts on the income statement to the nearest dollar.)
b. Should Fairfield's management make the planned changes?

ALTERNATE EXERCISES

26-17A　For each independent situation below, determine the amounts indicated by the question marks.

BUDGETING INVENTORIES — OBJ. 6 —

Number of Units	A	B	C	D
Beginning inventory	9,000	?	6,000	?
Produced	15,000	27,000	?	75,000
Available	?	?	46,000	85,000
Sold	18,000	28,000	?	?
Ending inventory	?	3,000	8,000	11,000

BUDGET PREPARATION — OBJ. 6 —

26-18A　Reeves Company is preparing its master budget for July. Use the given estimates to determine the amounts required in each requirement below. (Estimates may be related to more than one requirement.)

a. What should total sales revenue be if territories A and B estimate sales of 8,000 and 20,000 units, respectively, and the unit selling price is $50?
b. If the beginning finished goods inventory is an estimated 1,500 units and the desired ending inventory is 2,500 units, how many units should be produced?
c. What dollar amount of material should be purchased at $3 per pound if each unit of product requires 2 pounds and beginning and ending materials inventories should be 4,000 and 3,000 pounds, respectively?

d. How much direct labor cost should be incurred if each unit produced requires 1.5 hours at an hourly rate of $14?

e. How much factory overhead should be incurred if fixed factory overhead is $60,000 and variable factory overhead is $1.50 per direct labor hour?

BUDGET PREPARATION
— OBJ. 6 —

26-19A Tuttle Company is preparing its master budget for November. Use the estimates provided to determine the amounts required in each requirement below. (Estimates may be related to more than one requirement.)

a. What should total sales revenue be if territories N and S estimate sales of 40,000 and 80,000 units, respectively, and the unit selling price is $18?

b. If the beginning finished goods inventory is an estimated 6,000 units and the desired ending inventory is 5,000 units, how many units should be produced?

c. What dollar amount of material should be purchased at $2 per pound if each unit of product requires 3 pounds and beginning and ending materials inventories should be 12,000 and 10,000 pounds, respectively?

d. How much direct labor cost should be incurred if each unit produced requires 0.5 hours at an hourly rate of $10?

e. How much factory overhead should be incurred if fixed factory overhead is $32,000 and variable factory overhead is $1 per direct labor hour?

BUDGETING CASH
COLLECTIONS
— OBJ. 7 —

26-20A Lowell Company, which sells on terms 2/10, n/30, had credit sales for March and April of $60,000 and $50,000, respectively. Analysis of Lowell's operations indicates that the pattern of customers' payments on account is as follows (percentages are of total monthly credit sales):

	Receiving Discount	Beyond Discount Period	Totals
In month of sale	40%	20%	60%
In month following sale	15%	20%	35%
Uncollectible accounts, returns, and allowances			5%
			$100%

Determine the estimated cash collected on customers' accounts in April.

BUDGETING CASH FLOW
— OBJ. 7 —

26-21A The following various elements relate to Murphy, Inc.'s cash budget for October of the current year. For each item, determine the amount of cash that Murphy should receive or pay in October.

a. At $24 each, unit sales are 10,000 and 12,000 for September and October, respectively. Total sales are typically 30% for cash and 70% on credit; 40% of credit sales are collected in the month of sale, with the balance collected in the following month. Uncollectible accounts are negligible.

b. Merchandise purchases were $43,000 and $76,000 for September and October, respectively. Typically, 20% of total purchases are paid for in the month of purchase with a 5% cash discount. The balance of purchases is paid for (without discount) in the following month.

c. Fixed administrative expenses, which total $15,000 per month, are paid in the month incurred. Variable administrative expenses amount to 20% of total monthly sales revenue, 65% of which is paid in the month incurred, with the balance paid in the following month.

d. Fixed selling expenses, which total $4,200 per month, are paid in the month incurred. Variable selling expenses, which are 5% of total sales revenue, are paid in the month following their incurrence.

PREPARE CASH BUDGET
FOR THREE MONTHS
— OBJ. 7 —

26-22A Windsor Corporation expects the following cash receipts and disbursements during the first quarter of 1994 (receipts exclude new borrowings and disbursements exclude interest payments on borrowings since January 1, 1994):

	January	February	March
Cash receipts	$430,000	$440,000	$400,000
Cash disbursements	390,000	520,000	420,000

The expected cash balance at January 1, 1994, is $75,000. Windsor wants to maintain a cash balance at the end of each month of at least $60,000. Short-term borrowings at 1% interest per month will be used to accomplish this, if necessary. Borrowings (in multiples of $1,000) will be made at the beginning of the month in which they are needed, with interest for that month paid at the end of the month.

Prepare a cash budget for the quarter ended March 31, 1994.

PREPARE CASH BUDGET FROM BUDGETED TRANSACTIONS
— OBJ. 7 —

26-23A McCall Company anticipates a cash balance of $100,000 on July 1, 1994. The following budgeted transactions for July 1994 present data related to anticipated cash receipts and cash disbursements:

1. For July, budgeted cash sales are $72,000 and budgeted credit sales are $600,000. (Credit sales for June were $550,000.) In the month of sale, 40% of credit sales are collected with the balance collected in the month following sale.
2. Budgeted merchandise purchases for July are $340,000. (Merchandise purchases in June were $290,000.) In the month of purchase, 70% of merchandise purchases are paid for, and the balance is paid for in the following month.
3. Budgeted cash disbursements for salaries and operating expenses for July total $200,000.
4. During July, $30,000 of principal repayment and $5,000 of interest payment are due the bank.
5. A $25,000 income tax deposit is due the federal government during July.
6. A new delivery truck will be purchased during July for $7,000 cash and a $10,000 note payable. Depreciation for July will be $600.

Prepare a cash budget for McCall Company for the month of July 1994.

ALTERNATE PROBLEMS

BUDGETING CASH
— OBJ. 7 —

26-24A Judson, Inc., sells on terms of 5% discount for "cash and carry" or 2/10, n/30 and estimates its total sales for the second calendar quarter of next year as follows: July, $225,000; August, $150,000; and September, $180,000. An analysis of operations indicates the following customer collection patterns:

	Portions of Total Sales
In month of sale:	
Cash at time of sale	30%
On account, during discount period	20%
On account, after discount period	10%
In month following sale:	
On account, during discount period	20%
On account, after discount period	10%
In second month following sale:	
On account, after discount period	7%
Average portion uncollectible	3%
	100%

REQUIRED

Prepare an estimate of the cash to be collected from customers during September.

PREPARATION OF INDIVIDUAL BUDGETS
— OBJ. 6, 8 —

26-25A During the first calendar quarter of 1994, Williams Corporation is planning to manufacture a new product and introduce it in two regions. Market research indicates that sales will be 8,000 units in the urban region at a unit price of $65 and 6,000 units in the rural region at $55 each. Since the sales manager expects the product to catch on, she has asked for production sufficient to generate a 4,000-unit ending inventory. The production manager has furnished the following estimates related to manufacturing costs and operating expenses.

	Variable (per unit)	Fixed (total)
Manufacturing costs:		
Direct material:		
A (2 lbs. @ $2.50/lb.)	$ 5	—
B (5 lbs. @ $1.40/lb.)	7	—
Direct labor (2 hrs. per unit)	20	—

Factory overhead:		
Depreciation	—	$22,500
Factory supplies	0.55	2,500
Supervisory salaries	—	16,250
Other	0.65	9,200
Operating expenses:		
Selling:		
Advertising	—	12,500
Sales salaries and commissions*	1.25	20,000
Other*	0.50	4,200
Administrative:		
Office salaries	—	15,000
Supplies	0.40	1,200
Other	0.25	5,000

*Varies per unit sold, not per unit produced.

REQUIRED

a. Assuming that the desired ending inventories of materials A and B are 4,000 and 20,000 pounds, respectively, and that work in process inventories are immaterial, prepare budgets for the calendar quarter in which the new product will be introduced for each of the following operating factors:
  1. Total sales.
  2. Production.
  3. Material purchases cost.
  4. Direct labor costs.
  5. Factory overhead costs.
  6. Selling and administrative expenses.
b. Using data generated in requirement (a), prepare a budgeted income statement for the calendar quarter. Assume an overall effective income tax rate of 35%. (Round income statement amounts to nearest dollar.)

MONTHLY CASH BUDGET — OBJ. 7 —

26-26A Sutter, Inc., is a wholesaler for its only product, a deluxe wireless rechargeable electric shaver, which sells for $70 each and costs Sutter $48 each. On June 1, 1994, Sutter's management requested a cash budget for June. The following selected account balances at May 31, 1994, were gathered by the accounting department:

Cash	$ 56,000
Marketable securities (at cost)	160,000
Accounts receivable (all trade)	2,170,000
Inventories (12,000 units)	576,000
Operating expenses payable	196,800
Accounts payable (all merchandise)	902,400
Note payable	600,000

Actual sales for April and May were 30,000 and 50,000 units, respectively. Projected unit sales for June and July are 40,000 and 20,000, respectively. Experience indicates that 50% of sales should be collected in the month of sale, 30% in the month following sale, and the balance in the second month following sale. Uncollectibles, returns, and allowances are negligible.

Planned purchases should provide ending inventories equal to 30% of next month's unit sales volume. Approximately 60% of the purchases are paid for in the month of purchase and the balance in the following month.

Monthly operating expenses are budgeted at $9.60 per unit sold plus a fixed amount of $288,000 including depreciation of $112,000. Except for depreciation, 70% of operating expenses are paid in the month incurred and the balance in the following month. Interest expense is included in operating expenses.

Special anticipated June transactions include the following:
1. Declaration of a $60,000 cash dividend to be paid two weeks after the June 20 date of record.
2. Sale of all but $40,000 of the marketable securities held on May 31; a gain of $18,000 is anticipated.
3. Payment of $50,000 installment on the note payable.
4. Trade-in of an old company plane originally costing $300,000 and now having accumulated depreciation of $200,000 at a gain of $160,000 on a new plane

costing $2,000,000. Sufficient cash will be paid at the time of trade-in so that only 50% of the total price will have to be financed.

5. Sutter's treasurer has a policy of maintaining a minimum month-end cash balance of $40,000 and has a standing arrangement with the bank to borrow any amount up to a limit of $400,000.

REQUIRED

Prepare a cash budget for Sutter, Inc., for June 1994.

BUDGETING PRODUCTION AND PURCHASES AND JUST-IN-TIME MATERIALS INVENTORY — OBJ. 6 —

26-27A   Central Manufacturing, Inc., is preparing budgets for the second quarter of 1994. Central produces only one product in its factory. This product requires 4 pounds of material C, 3 pounds of material H, and a component, M, that is purchased from another manufacturer. Central operates on a just-in-time basis for material C. As a result, Central maintains no inventory of material C. On April 1, 1994, the inventory of material H is expected to be 3,000 pounds and the inventory of component M is expected to be 600 units. Central wants the inventories of H and M at June 30, 1994, to be 20% less than the inventories at April 1, 1994. The inventory of finished products at March 31, 1994, is expected to be 2,000 units; the desired inventory at June 30, 1994, is 4,000 units to allow a buildup for heavy sales in the third quarter. The sales forecast for the second quarter is 14,000 units at $200 each. Budgeted purchase costs are $5 per pound for C, $6 per pound for H, and $50 per component for M.

REQUIRED

a. Prepare the production budget for the third quarter of 1994.
b. Prepare the direct material budget for the third quarter of 1994.

PREPARE AND EVALUATE BUDGETED INCOME STATEMENT — OBJ. 8 —

26-28A   Medford Stores, a retailer in a shopping mall, prepared the following income statement for its operations for the month just ended:

MEDFORD STORES
INCOME STATEMENT
FOR THE MONTH ENDED APRIL 30, 1994

Sales		$700,000
Cost of Goods Sold		330,000
Gross Profit		$370,000
Operating Expenses:		
Sales Commissions Expense	$35,000	
Advertising Expense	90,000	
Lease Expense	50,000	
Depreciation Expense	20,000	
Salaries Expense	40,000	
Other Operating Expenses	25,000	260,000
Income before Income Taxes		$110,000
Income Tax Expense		33,000
Net Income		$ 77,000

Sales commissions were 5% of sales. Income taxes were 30% of income before income taxes. Both should continue at the same rate for the remainder of the year.

Medford Stores is preparing the budget for the month of May 1994. If no basic changes are made, Medford's management expects that the income statement would be virtually identical to the one for April. However, Medford's management has decided to make some changes in the operations. The plans include the following:

1. Increase advertising expense by 30%.
2. Decrease all selling prices by 10%.
3. Increase the number of units sold by 20% as a result of the first two changes.

REQUIRED

a. Prepare a budgeted income statement for the month of May 1994. (Round all amounts on the income statement to the nearest dollar.)
b. Should Medford's management make the planned changes?

CASES

Business Decision Case

The sales department of Donovan Manufacturing, Inc., has completed the following sales forecast for the months of January through March 1994 for its only two products: 50,000 units of J to be sold at $90 each and 30,000 units of K to be sold at $70 each. The desired unit inventories at March 31, 1994, are 10% of the next quarter's unit sales forecast, which are 60,000 units of J and 30,000 units of K. The January 1, 1994, unit inventories were 5,000 units of J and 2,000 units of K.

Each unit of J requires 3 pounds of material A and 2 pounds of material B for its manufacture; K requires 2 pounds of A and 4 pounds of B. Purchase cost of A is $9 per pound and the purchase cost of B is $5 per pound. Materials A and B on hand at January 1, 1994, were 19,000 pounds of A and 7,000 pounds of B. Desired inventories at March 31, 1994, are 14,000 pounds of A and 8,000 pounds of B.

Each unit of J requires 0.5 hour of direct labor in the factory; each unit of K requires 1.0 hour of direct labor. The average hourly rate for direct labor is $12 per hour. Estimated factory overhead cost is $6 per direct labor hour plus $90,000 per month. Selling and administrative expenses are estimated to be 10% of sales revenue plus $180,000 per month.

Cash sales for the first quarter are estimated to be $300,000 per month. It is forecast that 30% of the credit sales for the quarter ended March 31, 1994, will occur in January, 30% in February, and 40% in March. Of credit sales (December through March), 40% will be collected as cash in the month of sale and 55% will be collected in the following month. The remainder will be uncollectible. Cash collected in January 1994 from December 1993 sales will be $1,050,000.

The January 1, 1994, cash balance was $70,000. The minimum acceptable cash balance at the end of each month is $60,000. Short-term borrowings (six month term) are made in multiples of $10,000. Interest is charged at the rate of 1% per month on short-term borrowings. The first interest payment is made the month following the borrowing. Cash disbursements (excluding interest on short-term borrowings) are estimated as follows:

	January	February	March
Manufacturing costs	$1,500,000	$1,300,000	$1,400,000
Selling and administrative expenses	390,000	410,000	400,000
Interest expense	90,000	90,000	90,000
Income tax payment	–0–	–0–	210,000
Capital expenditures	124,000	110,000	50,000
Cash dividends	300,000	–0–	–0–

REQUIRED

a. Prepare the sales budget for the quarter ended March 31, 1994.
b. Prepare the production budget for the quarter ended March 31, 1994.
c. Prepare the direct material budget for the quarter ended March 31, 1994.
d. Prepare the direct labor budget for the quarter ended March 31, 1994.
e. Prepare the factory overhead budget for the quarter ended March 31, 1994.
f. Prepare the selling and administrative expense budget for the quarter ended March 31, 1994.
g. Prepare a schedule of cash collected from customers for the quarter ended March 31, 1994.
h. Prepare the cash budget for the quarter ended March 31, 1994.

Ethics Case

Steve Waller is the corporate accounting manager for Giant Video Stores. As part of the budgeting process for the entire corporation, he has asked the manager of each video store to prepare a store master budget.

The manager of one of the largest stores, Jeff Miller, decides to understate the sales budget and overstate all the budgets related to expenses. Jeff believes this is a more conservative approach than using the estimated numbers he honestly believes will be achieved for the year. He also thinks that the corporate office will look more favorably on his store's actual achievements when they are subsequently compared to this budget.

Jeff has asked Lisa Dorton, his assistant manager, to review the budget before it is submitted. Lisa is aware of the real estimates that Jeff made.

REQUIRED

What is the impact of Jeff Miller's budget for the corporation? What ethical issues face Lisa Dorton?

What techniques do manufacturing firms use to analyze actual product costs so they can acquire and use resources effectively?

Manufacturing firms set up cost accounting systems so they can collect, process, and analyze detailed product costs and variances. ■ *An automobile manufacturer like Chrysler Corporation, a tool manufacturer like Black and Decker, and a chemical manufacturer like DuPont all would use a cost accounting system and variance analysis.* ■ *Many nonmanufacturing firms also use cost accounting systems and modified variance analysis, including hospitals, laboratories, contractors, and professional firms.*

27

FLEXIBLE BUDGETS, STANDARD COSTS, AND COST VARIANCES

CHAPTER OBJECTIVES

1 DESCRIBE a static budget, ILLUSTRATE its use, and PRESENT an example of a static budget performance report (pp. 1028–1029).

2 INTRODUCE the flexible budget, ILLUSTRATE its use, and PRESENT an example of a flexible budget performance report (pp. 1029–1030).

3 DEFINE *standard costs* and DESCRIBE their use in standard cost accounting (pp. 1030–1031).

4 DEVELOP an understanding of the determination of standard costs for direct material, direct labor, variable overhead, and fixed overhead (pp. 1031–1034).

5 OUTLINE the procedures for determining cost variances for direct material, direct labor, variable overhead, and fixed overhead (pp. 1034–1041).

6 DESCRIBE the procedures for calculating total overhead variances (pp. 1041–1043).

7 PRESENT and ILLUSTRATE the use of standard costs in financial statements (pp. 1043–1044).

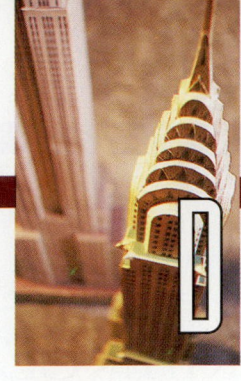

Fortune is the arbiter of half our actions, but she still leaves the control of the other half to us.

MACHIAVELLI

eveloping and using budgets are important parts of the management process of any entity. **Budgetary control** involves the steps taken by management to ensure that the goals and objectives established during the planning stage are attained, and to ensure that all segments of the firm operate in a manner consistent with organizational policies. Budgets should serve as guides and targets to managers when they make decisions since the budget is usually the basis for performance evaluation.

In this context, performance evaluation involves the comparison of actual results to budgeted results, with the differences between actual results and budgeted results known as **variances.** Cost and expense variances are considered to be favorable if actual cost is less than budgeted cost or unfavorable if actual cost is greater than budgeted cost.

In a previous chapter, we presented and discussed the components of the master budget. In this chapter, we present and discuss the concept of *flexible budgeting* and its use in performance reporting. We then examine the nature and use of standard costs and conclude the chapter with an analysis of product cost variances.

STATIC BUDGETS AND FLEXIBLE BUDGETS

OBJECTIVE 1 DESCRIBE *a static budget,* ILLUSTRATE *its use, and* PRESENT *an example of a static budget performance report.*

The master budget is made up of budgets known as *static budgets.* A **static budget** is a financial plan that has been developed for one level of operating activity, typically the expected or most likely level. If actual results are compared to a static budget, the variances that result are of little use to management, because the budget is often based on a different level of activity than the actual operations. The following example illustrates this point.

Exhibit 27-1 presents a simple static budget for Dillard Company for the month ended September 30, 1993, and Exhibit 27-2 presents a static budget performance report for Dillard Company for the same month. Dillard Company manufactures and sells only one product.

The *static budget performance report* in Exhibit 27-2 accurately reveals that actual units of production were 2,000 fewer than budgeted production. In a performance report, **F** identifies a favorable variance and **U** identifies an unfavorable variance. The static budget performance report provides misleading cost variances, however. For example, the direct material variance is $10,000 favorable (actual cost is less than budgeted cost). This comparison is misleading because actual cost to produce 28,000 units is being compared to budgeted cost to produce 30,000 units, not 28,000 units.

EXHIBIT 27—1	
DILLARD COMPANY	
STATIC BUDGET FOR PRODUCT COSTS	
FOR THE MONTH ENDED SEPTEMBER 30, 1993	
Budgeted units of production	30,000
Budgeted costs:	
Direct material	$120,000
Direct labor	75,000
Factory overhead	90,000
Total	$285,000

EXHIBIT 27–2

DILLARD COMPANY
STATIC BUDGET PERFORMANCE REPORT
FOR THE MONTH ENDED SEPTEMBER 30, 1993

Budgeted units of production		30,000
Actual units of production		28,000
Units of production variance		2,000 U

	Actual Cost Incurred for 28,000 units	Budget Based on 30,000 units	Cost Variances
Direct material	$110,000	$120,000	$10,000 F
Direct labor	74,000	75,000	1,000 F
Factory overhead	91,000	90,000	1,000 U
Total	$275,000	$285,000	$10,000 F

OBJECTIVE 2 INTRODUCE *the flexible budget,* ILLUSTRATE *its use, and* PRESENT *an example of a flexible budget performance report.*

A **flexible budget** is a financial plan in the form of a cost formula or a multiple-column presentation that addresses various levels of activity within a relevant range of activity. Exhibit 27-3 presents a flexible budget for Dillard Company that includes both a cost formula and a multiple-column presentation. **1** The first two amount columns represent the *cost formula approach* to flexible budgeting. **2** The last three amount columns represent the *multiple-column approach* to flexible budgeting. One of the columns is a budget for 30,000 units of production that would be comparable to the static budget in Exhibit 27-1. *The formula approach is typically preferred, since it can be used to generate the total budget at any level of activity within the relevant range, not only those levels for which there is a prepared column.*

Exhibit 27-3 demonstrates a number of the characteristics about flexible budgets. First, the flexible budget usually divides costs and expenses into two groups: variable and fixed. Second, the flexible budget typically presents the variable costs and expenses *per unit* and the fixed costs and expenses *in total.* Third, if a columnar format

EXHIBIT 27–3

DILLARD COMPANY
FLEXIBLE BUDGET FOR PRODUCT COSTS
FOR THE MONTH ENDED SEPTEMBER 30, 1993

	1 Cost Formula		**2** Relevant Range Budgets		
	Variable Cost per Unit	Total Fixed Cost	25,000 Units	30,000 Units	35,000 Units
Variable costs					
Direct material	$4.00		$100,000	$120,000	$140,000
Direct labor	2.50		62,500	75,000	87,500
Variable overhead	1.00		25,000	30,000	35,000
	$7.50		$187,500	$225,000	$262,500
Fixed costs					
Fixed overhead		$60,000	$ 60,000	$ 60,000	$ 60,000
Total			$247,500	$285,000	$322,500

EXHIBIT 27—4			

DILLARD COMPANY
FLEXIBLE BUDGET PERFORMANCE REPORT
FOR THE MONTH ENDED SEPTEMBER 30, 1993

Budgeted units of production			30,000
Actual units of production			28,000
Units of production variance			2,000 U

	Actual Costs Incurred for 28,000 Units	Budget Based on 28,000 Units	Cost Variances
Variable costs			
Direct material	$110,000	$112,000	$2,000 F
Direct labor	74,000	70,000	4,000 U
Variable overhead	29,000	28,000	1,000 U
	$213,000	$210,000	$3,000 U
Fixed costs			
Fixed overhead	$ 62,000	$ 60,000	$2,000 U
Total	$275,000	$270,000	$5,000 U

is presented, all of the columns are based on levels of activity within the relevant range. *It is important to remember that the flexible budget formula is valid only for the range of activity for which it was formulated.*

Exhibit 27-4 presents the flexible budget performance report for Dillard Company. This performance report compares budgeted units of production to actual units of production to generate the units of production variance. In addition, actual costs are compared to a budget based on 28,000 units. These budgeted amounts were calculated by inserting 28,000 units into the flexible budget formula. Therefore, the budgeted amounts represent what the various costs should have been at the 28,000-unit level of activity. The resulting variances provide valuable information to management.

A comparison of cost variances in the static budget performance report (Exhibit 27-2) to the cost variances in the flexible budget performance report (Exhibit 27-4) reveals a very different result. The static budget performance report reveals a total cost variance of $10,000 favorable; the flexible budget performance report reveals a total cost variance of $5,000 unfavorable. *The variances from the flexible budget performance report are preferable because they are based on a comparison of what the costs actually were to what the costs should have been at the actual level of activity.*

STANDARD COSTS

OBJECTIVE ③ DEFINE standard costs *and* **DESCRIBE** *their
use in standard cost
accounting.*

Standard costs are the costs that should be incurred under normal conditions to produce specific products or to perform specific services. A complex process, involving engineering specifications, time and motion studies, estimates of supply and demand, and analyses of historical trends, is used to develop standard costs. Standard costs are usually stated per unit of product or service and are useful for a number of purposes, including preparing flexible budgets and master budgets, establishing selling prices, and preparing performance reports.

Standard costs are budgeted costs, the costs that should be incurred during the upcoming year. Reasonably attainable levels of efficiency and productivity are used to establish standard costs, so they can serve as a motivating factor and a standard of performance. Typically, standard costs are revised no more frequently than once each year.

Standard costs are usually established prior to the beginning of each year as part of the budgeting process. They should not be updated during the year unless there are major, unexpected changes in vendor costs, wage rates, technology, or product design. One of the important uses of standard costs is to compare them to actual costs to identify significant differences. This comparison process will be most meaningful when the standards used represent the level of efficiency and productivity that was planned during the budgeting process.

Standard Cost Accounting

Many companies, especially manufacturing firms, adopt **standard cost accounting** for product costs. When this approach is taken, all inventory accounts—material, work in process, and finished goods—and the Cost of Goods Sold account are stated in terms of standard or predetermined costs rather than actual costs incurred. Specifically, standard costs are used for direct material, direct labor, variable overhead, and fixed overhead.

Standard cost accounting can be used with either job order costing or process costing. When standard cost accounting is used, actual product costs are accumulated separately and standard costs are carried in the inventory accounts and the Cost of Goods Sold account.

OBJECTIVE 4 DEVELOP *an understanding of the determination of standard costs for direct material, direct labor, variable overhead, and fixed overhead.*

The development of standard costs per unit of product requires the use of eight components: (1) direct material standard price; (2) direct material standard quantity; (3) direct labor standard rate; (4) direct labor standard time; (5) standard variable overhead rate; (6) variable overhead standard capacity; (7) standard fixed overhead rate; and (8) fixed overhead standard capacity. The cost-related components are developed and updated as part of the budgeting process, and quantity and capacity standards are usually developed as part of the product design and engineering process. The eight components are described in the following sections.

Direct Material Standards

The standard cost of direct material used to make a unit of a particular finished product is determined by multiplying the *direct material standard price* by the *direct material standard quantity*:

$$\begin{array}{c} \text{Standard Cost of} \\ \text{Direct Material} \\ \text{per Unit} \end{array} = \begin{array}{c} \text{Direct Material} \\ \text{Standard Price} \end{array} \times \begin{array}{c} \text{Direct Material} \\ \text{Standard Quantity} \end{array}$$

To illustrate this calculation, assume that Gregg Manufacturing Company produces product X, which requires only one type of direct material, M. The standard purchase price of M is $4 per pound, and the standard quantity of M needed to make one unit of product X is 3 pounds. The standard direct material cost to produce one unit of product X is $12:

$$\begin{array}{c} \text{Standard cost of} \\ \text{direct material} \\ \text{per unit of X} \end{array} = \begin{array}{c} \$4 \text{ per} \\ \text{pound} \\ \text{of M} \end{array} \times \begin{array}{c} 3 \text{ pounds} \\ \text{of M per} \\ \text{unit of X} \end{array} = \begin{array}{c} \$12 \text{ per} \\ \text{unit of} \\ \text{product X} \end{array}$$

A number of factors affect the direct material standard price, including the quality of the material, its availability, and discounts for volume purchases. Factors affecting the direct material standard quantity include material quality, engineering specifications, the skill of the direct labor workers, and the capabilities of the equipment used to process the material.

Direct Labor Standards

The standard cost of direct labor required to produce one unit of a particular product is determined by multiplying the *direct labor standard rate* by the *direct labor standard time*:

$$\begin{array}{c} \text{Standard Cost of} \\ \text{Direct Labor} \\ \text{per Unit} \end{array} = \begin{array}{c} \text{Direct Labor} \\ \text{Standard Rate} \end{array} \times \begin{array}{c} \text{Direct Labor} \\ \text{Standard Time} \end{array}$$

Continuing the Gregg Manufacturing Company illustration, assume that the standard hourly rate for direct labor is $10 and that the standard amount of direct labor needed is 2 hours per unit of product X. The resulting standard direct labor cost per unit of product X is $20:

$$\begin{array}{c} \text{Standard cost of} \\ \text{direct labor} \\ \text{per unit of X} \end{array} = \begin{array}{c} \$10 \text{ per} \\ \text{direct} \\ \text{labor} \\ \text{hour} \end{array} \times \begin{array}{c} 2 \text{ direct} \\ \text{labor hours} \\ \text{per unit of X} \end{array} = \begin{array}{c} \$20 \text{ per} \\ \text{unit of} \\ \text{product X} \end{array}$$

The direct labor standard rate represents the expected weighted average of labor rates for all levels of workers who undertake direct labor tasks on the product. The rates for the various levels of workers are set by the company or prescribed by labor contract. Direct labor standard times are based primarily on prior employee performance and current time and motion studies.

Variable Overhead Standards

The standard cost of variable overhead needed to manufacture one unit of a particular product is determined by multiplying the *standard* (or predetermined) *variable overhead rate* by the *variable overhead standard capacity*:

$$\begin{array}{c} \text{Standard Cost of} \\ \text{Variable Overhead} \\ \text{per Unit} \end{array} = \begin{array}{c} \text{Standard} \\ \text{Variable} \\ \text{Overhead Rate} \end{array} \times \begin{array}{c} \text{Variable} \\ \text{Overhead} \\ \text{Standard} \\ \text{Capacity} \end{array}$$

The basis for determining the standard variable overhead rate (which applies to all products) can be direct labor hours, direct labor dollars, machine hours, or one of the lesser-used bases. The basis selected should be the best common measure of variable overhead capacity utilized during production. The variable overhead capacity standard should also be stated in terms of this basis. If the basis for variable overhead is direct labor hours, then the variable overhead standard capacity will be the same as the direct labor standard time.

In the Gregg Manufacturing Company illustration, assume that the standard variable overhead rate is $3.50 per direct labor hour and that the variable overhead standard capacity is 2 direct labor hours per unit of product X (same as the direct labor standard time). The resulting standard variable overhead cost per unit of product X is $7:

$$\begin{array}{c} \text{Standard cost of} \\ \text{variable overhead} \\ \text{per unit of X} \end{array} = \begin{array}{c} \$3.50 \text{ per} \\ \text{direct labor} \\ \text{hour} \end{array} \times \begin{array}{c} 2 \text{ direct} \\ \text{labor hours} \\ \text{per unit} \\ \text{of X} \end{array} = \begin{array}{c} \$7 \text{ per} \\ \text{unit of} \\ \text{product X} \end{array}$$

The standard variable overhead rate is based on the *expected* level of operations. Since a wide variety of cost items is included in variable overhead, many different factors affect the rate. The variable overhead standard capacity is influenced by such factors as prior employee performance, prior machine performance, and current time and motion studies.

Fixed Overhead Standards

The standard cost of fixed overhead to produce one unit of a particular product is determined by multiplying the *standard fixed overhead rate* by the *fixed overhead standard capacity*:

$$\begin{array}{c} \text{Standard Cost of} \\ \text{Fixed Overhead} \\ \text{per Unit} \end{array} = \begin{array}{c} \text{Standard Fixed} \\ \text{Overhead Rate} \end{array} \times \begin{array}{c} \text{Fixed Overhead} \\ \text{Standard Capacity} \end{array}$$

The basis for determining the standard fixed overhead rate (which applies to all products) can be the same or different than the basis for variable overhead. The basis selected (direct labor hours, machine hours, and so on) for fixed overhead should be the best common measure of fixed overhead capacity used during production. The fixed overhead standard capacity should be stated in terms of this basis. If the basis for fixed overhead is direct labor hours, then the fixed overhead standard capacity will be the same as the direct labor standard time.

Continuing the Gregg Manufacturing Company example, assume that the standard fixed overhead rate is $4.50 per machine hour and that the fixed overhead standard capacity is 1.5 machine hours per unit of product X. The resulting standard fixed overhead cost per unit of X is $6.75:

$$\begin{array}{c} \text{Standard cost of} \\ \text{fixed overhead} \\ \text{per unit of X} \end{array} = \begin{array}{c} \$4.50 \text{ per} \\ \text{machine} \\ \text{hour} \end{array} \times \begin{array}{c} 1.5 \text{ machine} \\ \text{hours per} \\ \text{unit of X} \end{array} = \begin{array}{c} \$6.75 \text{ per} \\ \text{unit of} \\ \text{product X} \end{array}$$

The standard fixed overhead rate is typically based on the *normal* level of operations, usually a multiple-year average. Factors similar to those affecting the variable overhead standards will affect fixed overhead standards.

Total Standard Costs

The relationships described above are summarized in Exhibit 27-5. Most firms that use standard costs prepare a summary of the standard product costs for each product that they produce. Based on the preceding concepts, Gregg Manufacturing Company's standard cost summary for product X would appear as in Exhibit 27-6. If Gregg were to use standard cost accounting, then all units in Gregg's inventories and Cost of Goods Sold would have a product cost of $45.75 per unit, as shown in Exhibit 27-6.

Standard costs are also used in determining product cost variances. The remaining sections of this chapter deal with the calculation and use of product cost variances.

EXHIBIT 27—5 **SUMMARY OF COMPONENTS USED TO DETERMINE STANDARD COST PER UNIT OF PRODUCT**

Standard Cost of Direct Material per Unit

$$\begin{array}{c} \text{Direct Material} \\ \text{Standard Price} \end{array} \times \begin{array}{c} \text{Direct Material} \\ \text{Standard Quantity} \end{array}$$

Standard Cost of Direct Labor per Unit

$$\begin{array}{c} \text{Direct Labor} \\ \text{Standard Rate} \end{array} \times \begin{array}{c} \text{Direct Labor} \\ \text{Standard Time} \end{array}$$

Standard Cost of Variable Overhead per Unit

$$\begin{array}{c} \text{Standard Variable} \\ \text{Overhead Rate} \end{array} \times \begin{array}{c} \text{Variable Overhead} \\ \text{Standard Capacity} \end{array}$$

Standard Cost of Fixed Overhead per Unit

$$\begin{array}{c} \text{Standard Fixed} \\ \text{Overhead Rate} \end{array} \times \begin{array}{c} \text{Fixed Overhead} \\ \text{Standard Capacity} \end{array}$$

EXHIBIT 27–6

GREGG MANUFACTURING COMPANY
STANDARD COST SUMMARY FOR PRODUCT X

Direct material ($4.00/pound × 3 pounds)	$12.00
Direct labor ($10.00/DLH × 2 DLH)	20.00
Variable overhead ($3.50/DLH × 2 DLH)	7.00
Fixed overhead ($4.50/MH × 1.5 MH)	6.75
Total standard product cost per unit of X	$45.75

DLH = Direct labor hour(s)
MH = Machine hour(s)

COST VARIANCES

OBJECTIVE 5 OUTLINE *the procedures for determining cost variances for direct material, direct labor, variable overhead, and fixed overhead.*

Even in well-managed companies with carefully established and currently maintained cost standards, actual costs often differ from standard costs. The differences should be analyzed for indications of their cause so that appropriate action may be taken.

Suppose that during June 1993, Gregg Manufacturing Company produced 9,800 units of product X for which it incurred the following actual costs (assume no beginning or ending work in process inventories):

Direct material ($4.20 × 28,600 pounds)	$120,120
Direct labor ($9.94 × 20,000 direct labor hours)	198,800
Variable overhead	67,000
Fixed overhead	67,500
Total actual production costs	$453,420

In Exhibit 27-7 the actual costs are compared with standard costs for 9,800 units of product, and the differences, or variances, for each cost category are calculated. The standard costs (from our standard cost summary for product X) are multiplied by the actual quantity of 9,800 units produced in June. Note that both favorable and unfavorable variances exist and that the overall net variance of $5,070 is unfavorable. To initiate remedial action, management must analyze the variance for each manufacturing cost element to determine the underlying causal factors related to prices paid, quantities used, and productive capacity used. The following paragraphs present these analyses and the related general journal entries (in summary form) for recording variances.

EXHIBIT 27–7

GREGG MANUFACTURING COMPANY
COMPARISON OF STANDARD AND ACTUAL COSTS OF PRODUCT X
FOR THE MONTH OF JUNE, 1993

	Standard Costs (9,800 units)	Actual Costs (9,800 units)	Total Variances
Direct material	$117,600	$120,120	$2,520 U
Direct labor	196,000	198,800	2,800 U
Variable overhead	68,600	67,000	1,600 F
Fixed overhead	66,150	67,500	1,350 U
	$448,350	$453,420	$5,070 U

Material Variances

Variances for direct material stem primarily from paying more or less than the standard price (the **material price variance**) and from using more or less than the standard quantity (the **material quantity variance**). Gregg Manufacturing Company's material price variance for June would be the following:

$$\begin{array}{ccc} \text{Material} \\ \text{Price} \\ \text{Variance} \end{array} = \left(\begin{array}{c} \text{Actual} \\ \text{Price} \end{array} - \begin{array}{c} \text{Standard} \\ \text{Price} \end{array} \right) \times \begin{array}{c} \text{Actual} \\ \text{Quantity} \end{array}$$

$$= \quad (\$4.20 \quad - \quad \$4.00) \quad \times \quad 28,600$$

$$= \$5,720 \text{ U}$$

The material price variance is unfavorable since actual price is greater than standard price. If actual price had been less than standard price, then the material price variance would have been favorable.

The material quantity variance for Gregg would be the following:

$$\begin{array}{ccc} \text{Material} \\ \text{Quantity} \\ \text{Variance} \end{array} = \left(\begin{array}{c} \text{Actual} \\ \text{Quantity} \end{array} - \begin{array}{c} \text{Standard} \\ \text{Quantity} \end{array} \right) \times \begin{array}{c} \text{Standard} \\ \text{Price} \end{array}$$

$$= \quad (28,600 \quad - \quad 29,400) \quad \times \quad \$4.00$$

$$= \$3,200 \text{ F}$$

The *standard quantity* is the quantity that should have been used to produce 9,800 units (9,800 units × 3 pounds per unit = 29,400 pounds). The material quantity variance is favorable since actual quantity is less than standard quantity. If actual quantity had been higher than standard quantity, then material quantity variance would have been unfavorable.

The total material variance would be as follows:

Material price variance	$5,720	U
Material quantity variance	3,200	F
Total material variance	$2,520	U

Notice that the total material variance agrees with the amount in Exhibit 27-7.

The unfavorable price variance may have been caused by increases in supplier prices, improper purchasing, or other factors. The favorable quantity variance may have been caused by efficient workers, superior-quality material, or other factors.

The general journal entry to record material costs and variances is as follows:

Work in Process Inventory [standard price and quantity]	117,600	
Material Price Variance	5,720	
Material Quantity Variance		3,200
Materials Inventory [actual price and quantity]		120,120
To record direct material costs and related cost variances.		

Note that the journal entry debits Work in Process for standard costs, records the unfavorable variance as a debit, records the favorable variance as a credit, and records the actual cost of material requisitioned during June.[1]

Labor Variances

Variances for direct labor result from paying more or less than the standard wage rates for direct labor (the **labor rate variance**) and from using more or less than the standard amount of direct labor hours (the **labor efficiency variance**). Gregg Manufacturing Company's direct labor variances are computed and recorded as shown below. Note that the basic calculations are the same as for material, but the term *rate* is used instead of *price* and the term *efficiency* is used instead of *quantity*.

---

[1] In our illustration, we recognize and record the material price variance when the materials start into production. Some firms recognize and record the price variance when materials purchases are recorded.

OLD ROSEBUD

*O*ld Rosebud is a 400-acre farm on the outskirts of the Kentucky Bluegrass, specializing in boarding broodmares and their foals. ■ The economic downturn in the thoroughbred industry has led to a decline in breeding activities. As a consequence, the demand for thoroughbred boarding has decreased, making the boarding business extremely competitive. To meet the competition, in 1988 Old Rosebud planned to entertain clients, advertise, and absorb expenses formerly borne by clients—for example, henceforth it would pay for both veterinary and blacksmith's fees.

OLD ROSEBUD'S STATIC BUDGET

Exhibit A presents the variances between Old Rosebud's actual operating results in 1988 and amounts budgeted for that year. Its budget—like those of most service organizations—was a static one; that is, it forecast an expected level of activity. Old Rosebud expected to log 21,900 boarding days, and it budgeted boarding rates at $25 per day per mare. The variable expenses per mare per day were budgeted:

■ Feed: $5.
■ Veterinary fees: $3.
■ Blacksmith fees: $0.30.
■ Supplies: $0.40.

All other budgeted expenses were either semifixed or fixed.

The static budget in Exhibit A can be used to explain only two factors: sales and fixed expenses.

As sales volume problems arose during the year, Old Rosebud decided not to replace a farm worker who quit in March. It also developed a new farm brochure and entertained more potential clients. These strategies generated the fixed-expense variances—that is, the differences between the budgeted and actual line item amounts in the income statement.

No sound conclusions can be drawn about either the effect of price changes on the decrease in net income or the expense variances. When sales volume declines, sales revenue and variable expenses may be expected to decrease proportionately. However, the rate of Old Rosebud's decline in the number of boarding days (13%) differs from the rate of decrease in sales revenue (30%) and the rate of decrease in variable expenses (7%).

A plausible interpretation of the variances in Exhibit A is that the large variance in net income is caused by a decrease in sales volume. This interpretation follows from the huge unfavorable sales revenue variance and the generally favorable expense variances.

Indeed, at first glance, it appears as though expenses are well under control. All variable-expense variances are favorable, and the total of the two unfavorable fixed-expense variances is insignificant in relation to the total sales-revenue variance. The unfavorable advertising and entertainment variances may be interpreted as having prevented the unfavorable net

EXHIBIT A

Old Rosebud
Static Budget Income Statement
Year Ended December 31, 1988

	Actual	Master Budget	Variance
Number of mares	52	60	8*
Number of boarding days	18,980	21,900	2,920*
Sales	$379,600	$547,500	$167,900*
Less variable expenses:			
Feed	$104,390	$109,500	$ 5,110
Veterinary fees	58,838	65,700	6,862
Blacksmith fees	6,074	6,570	496
Supplies	7,402	8,760	1,358
Total variable expenses	$176,704	$190,530	$ 13,826
Contribution margin	$202,896	$356,970	$154,074*
Less fixed expenses:			
Depreciation	$ 45,000	$ 45,000	$ —
Insurance	11,000	11,000	—
Utilities	12,000	14,000	2,000
Repairs and maintenance	10,000	11,000	1,000
Labor	88,000	96,000	8,000
Advertisement	11,000	8,000	3,000*
Entertainment	8,000	5,000	3,000*
Total fixed expenses	$185,000	$190,000	$ 5,000
Net income	$ 17,896	$166,970	$149,074*

*Unfavorable variance.

income variance from being even greater: More business might have been lost had Old Rosebud not overspent its budgeted amounts for those items.

Since sales are down and expenses are well under control, this analysis suggests an obvious *but faulty* remedy: Do more advertising and entertaining.

OLD ROSEBUD'S FLEXIBLE BUDGET

Exhibit B compares Old Rosebud's actual operating results with those in a flexible budget for 1988. The flexible budget takes the same budgeted per-unit amounts for sales and variable expenses and applies them to the actual number of boarding days achieved in 1988. Since, by definition, fixed expenses don't vary with volume, they're the same as in the static budget. A budget constructed in this way removes the distortion in sales-revenue and variable-expense variances of a static budget.

Two surprises immediately jump out. First, when the effect of sales volume is removed from the total sales-revenue variance, the sales-price variance ($94,900) is about double the sales-volume variance ($47,596). Further investigation of the sales-price variance revealed that Old Rosebud lost a major client in 1988. Moreover, because of fierce competition, the farm reduced its boarding charges well below $25 per day per mare as the year progressed. As a result, the average boarding rate declined for the year.

The second surprise in Exhibit B is that expense control was far worse than analysis of the static budget variance had indicated. All variable-expense variances, except supplies,

(CONTINUED)

EXHIBIT B

Old Rosebud
Flexible Budget Income Statement
Year Ended December 31, 1988

	Budget Formula (per mare per day)	Actual	Flexible Budget	Variance
Budgeted number of boarding days		21,900		
Actual number of boarding days		18,980		
Number of mares		52	52	—
Number of boarding days		18,980	18,980	—
Sales	$25.00	$379,600	$474,500	$ 94,900*
Less variable expenses:				
Feed	5.00	$104,390	$ 94,900	$ 9,490*
Veterinary fees	3.00	58,838	56,940	1,898*
Blacksmith fees	.30	6,074	5,694	380*
Supplies	.40	7,402	7,592	190
Total variable expenses	$ 8.70	$176,704	$165,126	$ 11,578*
Contribution margin	$16.30	$202,896	$309,374	$106,478*
Less fixed expenses:				
Depreciation		$ 45,000	$ 45,000	$ —
Insurance		11,000	11,000	—
Utilities		12,000	14,000	2,000
Repairs and maintenance		10,000	11,000	1,000
Labor		88,000	96,000	8,000
Advertisement		11,000	8,000	3,000*
Entertainment		8,000	5,000	3,000*
Total fixed expenses		$185,000	$190,000	$ 5,000
Net income		$ 17,896	$119,374	$101,478*

*Unfavorable variance.

(CONTINUED FROM PAGE 1037)

were *unfavorable*. The feed variance ($9,490) alone accounted for nearly 82% of the total variable-expense variances ($11,578). The large feed variance was explained by the drought that hit Kentucky and most of the rest of the nation in 1988. In addition, several recent studies had indicated that copper feed supplements may be necessary to minimize skeletal bone disease in young horses. Old Rosebud incorporated the supplement at an increased cost and continued to feed first-class hay despite the drought.

COMPARING THE FLEXIBLE AND STATIC RESULTS

Accurate information about what causes the differences between actual and expected results is a precondition for corrective action. Variance analysis can lead to an accurate analysis. In contrast, a static budget can focus only on sales and fixed expenses that differ from budgeted figures. Not realizing this may lead to faulty analysis of the results. Flexible budget variances aren't misleading because they incorporate actual levels of activity if different from those expected.

For Old Rosebud, the main problem is *price*—not volume. Had the farm been able to maintain its boarding rates but not the number of boarding days, its actual net income would have been:

Sales revenue	$474,500
Less total variable expenses	(176,704)
Less total fixed expenses	(185,000)
Net income	$112,796

This amount is six times greater than the net income of $17,896 actually achieved. The farm needs to develop a strategy that *restores boarding rates* more than it needs to replace the eight horses it lost. . . .

SOURCE: Hans Sprohge and John Talbott, "New Applications for Variance Analysis," *Journal of Accountancy*, April 1989, pp. 137, 138, 140, 141. Reprinted with permission from the Journal of Public Accountancy, copyright © 1989 by the American Institute of Certified Public Accountants, Inc. Opinions of the authors are their own and do not necessarily reflect the policies of the AICPA.

$$\begin{array}{l}\text{Labor Rate Variance} = \left(\begin{array}{c}\text{Actual} \\ \text{Rate}\end{array} - \begin{array}{c}\text{Standard} \\ \text{Rate}\end{array} \right) \times \begin{array}{c}\text{Actual} \\ \text{Hours}\end{array} \\ \qquad\qquad = (\$9.94 - \$10.00) \times 20,000 \\ \qquad\qquad = \$1,200 \text{ F}\end{array}$$

$$\begin{array}{l}\text{Labor Efficiency Variance} = \left(\begin{array}{c}\text{Actual} \\ \text{Hours}\end{array} - \begin{array}{c}\text{Standard} \\ \text{Hours}\end{array} \right) \times \begin{array}{c}\text{Standard} \\ \text{Rate}\end{array} \\ \qquad\qquad = (20,000 - 19,600) \times \$10.00 \\ \qquad\qquad = \$4,000 \text{ U}\end{array}$$

Labor rate variance	$1,200	F
Labor efficiency variance	4,000	U
Total labor variance	$2,800	U

Notice that the total labor variance also agrees with the amount in Exhibit 27-7.

The unfavorable labor efficiency variance might be charged to the production supervisor, who presumably oversees the production teams. The favorable labor rate variance could have resulted from assigning lower-paid employees more than specified, using less overtime, or paying decreased labor rates.

The following journal entry records these costs and variances:

Work in Process Inventory [standard rate and hours]	196,000	
Labor Efficiency Variance	4,000	
Labor Rate Variance		1,200
Factory Payroll Payable [actual rates and hours]		198,800
To record direct labor costs and related cost variances.		

The journal entry shown charges Work in Process Inventory with standard direct labor costs, records the unfavorable labor efficiency variance as a debit and the favorable labor rate variance as a credit, and records the liability for direct labor at the amount owed, which is determined using actual hours worked and actual rates paid.

Alternative Calculations

Material and labor variances can also be determined using alternative calculations, as outlined in Exhibit 27-8. The total material variance and the total labor variance are determined by comparing total actual cost to total standard cost. Material price and labor rate variances are calculated by comparing actual quantity times actual price (total actual cost) to actual quantity times standard price. Material quantity and labor efficiency variances are calculated by comparing actual quantity times standard price to standard quantity times standard price (total standard cost). Note that the resulting variances are the same as those previously calculated.

The standard quantity amounts require further explanation. The standard quantity of material required to produce one unit of product X is 3 pounds. Therefore, the standard quantity of material allowed to produce 9,800 units of product X is 29,600 pounds (9,800 × 3). Similarly, the standard quantity of labor required to produce one unit of X is 2 hours, resulting in 19,600 hours (9,800 × 2) allowed to produce 9,800 units of product X.

Variable Overhead Variances

Variances for variable overhead result from paying more or less than planned for items that comprise variable overhead (the **variable overhead spending variance**) and from using more or less than the standard amount of capacity (the **variable over-**

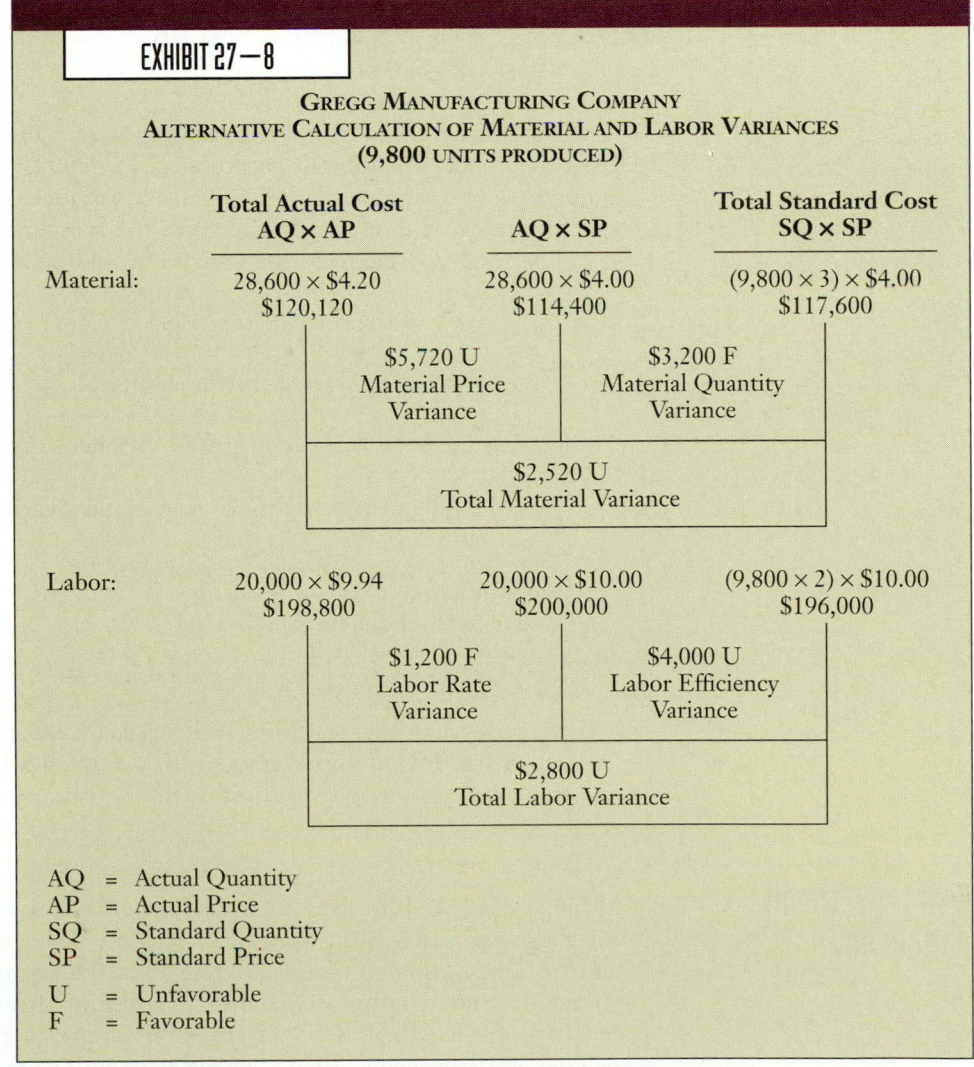

EXHIBIT 27—8

GREGG MANUFACTURING COMPANY
ALTERNATIVE CALCULATION OF MATERIAL AND LABOR VARIANCES
(9,800 UNITS PRODUCED)

	Total Actual Cost AQ × AP	AQ × SP	Total Standard Cost SQ × SP
Material:	28,600 × $4.20 $120,120	28,600 × $4.00 $114,400	(9,800 × 3) × $4.00 $117,600

$5,720 U
Material Price
Variance

$3,200 F
Material Quantity
Variance

$2,520 U
Total Material Variance

| Labor: | 20,000 × $9.94 $198,800 | 20,000 × $10.00 $200,000 | (9,800 × 2) × $10.00 $196,000 |

$1,200 F
Labor Rate
Variance

$4,000 U
Labor Efficiency
Variance

$2,800 U
Total Labor Variance

AQ = Actual Quantity
AP = Actual Price
SQ = Standard Quantity
SP = Standard Price

U = Unfavorable
F = Favorable

head efficiency variance). The variable overhead variances for Gregg Manufacturing Company are computed and recorded as shown below. The calculations are similar to those for material and labor, which, like variable overhead, are variable product cost components. The variable overhead spending variance for Gregg would be as follows:

$$\begin{array}{c}\text{Variable}\\\text{Overhead}\\\text{Spending}\\\text{Variance}\end{array} = \begin{array}{c}\text{Actual}\\\text{Variable}\\\text{Overhead}\\\text{Cost}\end{array} - \left(\begin{array}{c}\text{Variable}\\\text{Overhead}\\\text{Actual}\\\text{Capacity}\\\text{Used}\end{array} \times \begin{array}{c}\text{Standard}\\\text{Variable}\\\text{Overhead}\\\text{Rate}\end{array}\right)$$

$$= \quad \$67{,}000 \quad - \quad (20{,}000 \quad \times \quad \$3.50)$$
$$= \$3{,}000 \text{ F}$$

The variable overhead spending variance is favorable since actual variable overhead cost ($67,000) is less than actual capacity used times standard price ($70,000).

The variable overhead efficiency variance for Gregg would be the following:

$$\begin{array}{c}\text{Variable}\\\text{Overhead}\\\text{Efficiency}\\\text{Variance}\end{array} = \left(\begin{array}{c}\text{Variable}\\\text{Overhead}\\\text{Actual}\\\text{Capacity}\\\text{Used}\end{array} \times \begin{array}{c}\text{Standard}\\\text{Variable}\\\text{Overhead}\\\text{Rate}\end{array}\right) - \left(\begin{array}{c}\text{Variable}\\\text{Overhead}\\\text{Standard}\\\text{Capacity}\\\text{Allowed}\end{array} \times \begin{array}{c}\text{Standard}\\\text{Variable}\\\text{Overhead}\\\text{Rate}\end{array}\right)$$

$$= \quad (20{,}000 \quad \times \quad \$3.50) \quad - \quad [(9{,}800 \times 2) \times \quad \$3.50]$$
$$= \$1{,}400 \text{ U}$$

The variable overhead standard capacity allowed is the capacity that should have been used to produce 9,800 units of product X (9,800 units × 2 direct labor hours per unit of X). The variable overhead efficiency variance is unfavorable because the actual quantity of capacity used is greater than the standard capacity allowed.

The total variable overhead variance would be as follows:

Variable overhead spending variance	$3,000	F
Variable overhead efficiency variance	1,400	U
Total variable overhead variance	$1,600	F

Notice that the total variable overhead variance agrees with the amount in Exhibit 27-7.

The general journal entry to record variable overhead costs and variances follows:

Work in Process Inventory [at standard rate]	68,600	
Variable Overhead Efficiency Variance	1,400	
Variable Overhead Spending Variance		3,000
[Various accounts]		67,000
To record variable overhead costs and related cost variances.		

This journal entry charges Work in Process Inventory with standard variable overhead costs, records the unfavorable variable overhead efficiency variance as a debit and the favorable variable overhead spending variance as a credit.

Fixed Overhead Variances

Variances for fixed overhead stem primarily from paying more or less than planned for the items included in fixed overhead (the **fixed overhead spending variance**) and from operating at a level different than the normal level of capacity utilization (**fixed overhead volume variance**). Assuming fixed overhead was budgeted at $67,050, the fixed overhead variances for Gregg Manufacturing Company are calculated and recorded as shown on the following page.

$$\begin{array}{c} \text{Fixed} \\ \text{Overhead} \\ \text{Spending} \\ \text{Variance} \end{array} = \begin{array}{c} \text{Actual} \\ \text{Fixed} \\ \text{Overhead} \\ \text{Cost} \end{array} - \begin{array}{c} \text{Budgeted} \\ \text{Fixed} \\ \text{Overhead} \\ \text{Cost} \end{array}$$

$$= \$67,500 - \$67,050$$
$$= \$450 \text{ U}$$

$$\begin{array}{c} \text{Fixed} \\ \text{Overhead} \\ \text{Volume} \\ \text{Variance} \end{array} = \begin{array}{c} \text{Budgeted} \\ \text{Fixed} \\ \text{Overhead} \\ \text{Cost} \end{array} - \left(\begin{array}{c} \text{Fixed} \\ \text{Overhead} \\ \text{Standard} \\ \text{Capacity} \\ \text{Allowed} \end{array} \times \begin{array}{c} \text{Standard} \\ \text{Fixed} \\ \text{Overhead} \\ \text{Rate} \end{array} \right)$$

$$= \$67,050 - [(9,800 \times 1.5) \times \$4.50]$$
$$= \$900 \text{ U}$$

Fixed overhead spending variance	$ 450 U
Fixed overhead volume variance	900 U
Total fixed overhead variance	$1,350 U

Notice that the total fixed overhead variance agrees with the amount in Exhibit 27-7.

The standard quantity of capacity allowed is the capacity that should have been used to produce 9,800 units of product X (9,800 units × 1.5 machine hours per unit). The fixed overhead volume variance is unfavorable since the amount of fixed overhead applied to product X (standard quantity of capacity allowed × standard fixed overhead rate) is less than the total budgeted fixed overhead cost.

The general journal entry to record fixed overhead costs and variances follows:

Work in Process Inventory [at standard rate]	66,150	
Fixed Overhead Spending Variance	450	
Fixed Overhead Volume Variance	900	
[Various accounts]		67,500
To record fixed overhead costs and related cost variances.		

Exhibit 27-9 presents a summary of the product cost variances presented in the previous sections of this chapter. These eight variances are important management tools for controlling and analyzing manufacturing operations.

Total Overhead Variances

OBJECTIVE 6 DESCRIBE *the procedures for calculating total overhead variances.*

Some companies choose to analyze variances related only to total overhead rather than analyze separate variances for variable overhead and fixed overhead. It is important to note, however, that separate variances for variable overhead and fixed overhead are generally considered to be superior.

There are two primary approaches to developing total overhead variances: the *three-overhead-variance system* and the *two-overhead-variance system*. Total overhead variances can be determined by combining or relabeling the variances previously determined for variable overhead and fixed overhead. Exhibit 27-10 outlines how the total overhead variances can be determined.

In the Gregg Manufacturing Company illustration, total overhead variances would be calculated as follows:

Three-Overhead-Variance System

$$\begin{array}{c} \text{Overhead} \\ \text{Spending} \\ \text{Variance} \end{array} = \begin{array}{c} \text{Variable} \\ \text{Overhead} \\ \text{Spending} \\ \text{Variance} \end{array} + \begin{array}{c} \text{Fixed} \\ \text{Overhead} \\ \text{Spending} \\ \text{Variance} \end{array}$$

$$= \$3,000 \text{ F} + \$450 \text{ U}$$
$$= \$2,550 \text{ F}$$

EXHIBIT 27—9	SUMMARY OF PRODUCT COST VARIANCES

Direct Material Variances

$$\text{Material Price Variance} = \left(\text{Actual Price} - \text{Standard Price}\right) \times \text{Actual Quantity}$$

$$\text{Material Quantity Variance} = \left(\text{Actual Quantity} - \text{Standard Quantity}\right) \times \text{Standard Price}$$

Direct Labor Variances

$$\text{Labor Rate Variance} = \left(\text{Actual Rate} - \text{Standard Rate}\right) \times \text{Actual Hours}$$

$$\text{Labor Efficiency Variance} = \left(\text{Actual Hours} - \text{Standard Hours}\right) \times \text{Standard Rate}$$

Variable Overhead Variances

$$\text{Variable Overhead Spending Variance} = \text{Actual Variable Overhead Cost} - \left(\begin{array}{c}\text{Variable Overhead Actual Capacity Used}\end{array} \times \begin{array}{c}\text{Standard Variable Overhead Rate}\end{array}\right)$$

$$\text{Variable Overhead Efficiency Variance} = \left(\begin{array}{c}\text{Variable Overhead Actual Capacity Used}\end{array} \times \begin{array}{c}\text{Standard Variable Overhead Rate}\end{array}\right) - \left(\begin{array}{c}\text{Variable Overhead Standard Capacity Allowed}\end{array} \times \begin{array}{c}\text{Standard Variable Overhead Rate}\end{array}\right)$$

Fixed Overhead Variances

$$\text{Fixed Overhead Spending Variance} = \text{Actual Fixed Overhead Cost} - \text{Budgeted Fixed Overhead Cost}$$

$$\text{Fixed Overhead Volume Variance} = \text{Budgeted Fixed Overhead Cost} - \left(\begin{array}{c}\text{Fixed Overhead Standard Capacity Allowed}\end{array} \times \begin{array}{c}\text{Standard Fixed Overhead Rate}\end{array}\right)$$

$$\text{Overhead Efficiency Variance} = \text{Variable Overhead Efficiency Variance} = \$1,400 \text{ U}$$

$$\text{Overhead Volume Variance} = \text{Fixed Overhead Volume Variance} = \$900 \text{ U}$$

Two-Overhead-Variance System

$$\text{Overhead Controllable Variance} = \text{Variable Overhead Spending Variance} + \text{Fixed Overhead Spending Variance} + \text{Variable Overhead Efficiency Variance}$$

$$= \$3,000 \text{ F} + \$450 \text{ U} + \$1,400 \text{ U}$$
$$= \$1,150 \text{ F}$$

| EXHIBIT 27–10 | TOTAL OVERHEAD VARIANCES |

Three-Variance Approach

| Overhead Spending Variance | = | Variable Overhead Spending Variance | + | Fixed Overhead Spending Variance |

| Overhead Efficiency Variance | = | Variable Overhead Efficiency Variance |

| Overhead Volume Variance | = | Fixed Overhead Volume Variance |

Two-Variance Approach

| Overhead Controllable Variance | = | Variable Overhead Spending Variance | + | Fixed Overhead Spending Variance | + | Variable Overhead Efficiency Variance |

| Overhead Volume Variance | = | Fixed Overhead Volume Variance |

| *Note:* | | Overhead Controllable Variance | = | Overhead Spending Variance | + | Overhead Efficiency Variance |

$$\text{Overhead Volume Variance} = \text{Fixed Overhead Volume Variance} = \$900 \text{ U}$$

In the three-overhead-variance system, the **overhead spending variance** reflects how much more (unfavorable) or less (favorable) was spent on factory overhead than the budget allowed for the actual work completed. The **overhead efficiency variance** shows how much overhead cost was either added or saved as a result of operating above or below the standard level of efficiency. Note that no part of fixed overhead enters into this variance, since fixed overhead should remain constant regardless of the level of efficiency. The **overhead volume variance** reflects the costs associated with using factory capacity at more or less than the normal level. Note that variable overhead costs play no role in the volume variance since variable overhead costs respond to the level of production.

In the two-overhead-variance system, the **overhead controllable variance** measures how well the actual factory overhead costs have been kept within the budgetary limits. Both spending and efficiency factors are considered, since these are the factors controllable by management. The overhead volume variance is identical to the overhead volume variance described above.

STANDARD COSTS IN FINANCIAL STATEMENTS

When the standard costs and related variances for direct material, direct labor, variable overhead, and fixed overhead are recorded as previously illustrated, the Work in Process account is debited for each in amounts representing standard quantities and

OBJECTIVE 7 PRESENT *and* ILLUSTRATE *the use of standard costs in financial statements.*

standard prices. All variances—favorable or unfavorable—are carried in separate accounts with appropriate titles. Gregg Manufacturing Company records completed production for June in the following entry (assume no beginning or ending work in process inventories):

Finished Goods Inventory [at standard cost]	448,350	
Work in Process Inventory [at standard cost]		448,350

To record completion of June's production of 9,800 units at a standard unit cost of $45.75 ($117,600 material, $196,000 labor, $68,600 variable overhead, and $66,150 fixed overhead).

As each month's production is sold, the related amounts of standard costs are transferred from Finished Goods Inventory to Cost of Goods Sold.

Standard costs and related variances are usually reported in financial reports intended only for management's use. The following partial income statement illustrates how variances often appear on interim financial statements for internal use (amounts are assumed).

GREGG MANUFACTURING COMPANY
PARTIAL INCOME STATEMENT
FOR THE MONTH ENDED JUNE 30, 1993

Sales	$600,000
Cost of Goods Sold at Standard Cost	400,000
Gross Profit at Standard Cost	$200,000
Less: Net Unfavorable Cost Variance	5,070
Gross Profit	$194,930

The total net variance could be broken down into subvariances or possibly detailed in a schedule of variances accompanying the financial statements.

At year-end, firms commonly close the variance accounts by transferring their balances to Cost of Goods Sold. In effect, this transfer converts the Cost of Goods Sold account from standard costs to actual costs. If large variances exist at year-end and there is evidence that the standards may not apply, a firm may be justified in allocating all or part of the variances to Work in Process Inventory, Finished Goods Inventory, and Cost of Goods Sold.

KEY POINTS FOR CHAPTER OBJECTIVES

1 DESCRIBE a static budget, ILLUSTRATE its use, and PRESENT an example of a static budget performance report (pp. 1028–1029).
- A static budget is a financial plan that has been developed for one level of operating activity, usually the expected level.
- The static budget performance report accurately displays the units of production variance but provides misleading cost variances.

2 INTRODUCE the flexible budget, ILLUSTRATE its use, and PRESENT an example of a flexible budget performance report (pp. 1029–1030).
- A flexible budget is a financial plan in the form of a cost formula or a multiple-column presentation that addresses various levels of activity within a relevant range of activity.
- The flexible budget performance report, the preferred format, not only displays the units of production variance accurately but also properly presents the cost variances. Actual costs are compared to what the costs should have been at the actual level of activity.

3 DEFINE *standard costs* and DESCRIBE their use in standard cost accounting (pp. 1030–1031).
- Standard costs represent the costs per unit that should be incurred during the upcoming year. They are established as part of the budgeting process.
- When standard cost accounting is used, all inventory accounts—material, work in process, and finished goods—and the Cost of Goods Sold account are stated in terms of standard costs. Actual costs are accumulated separately.

④ **DEVELOP** an understanding of the determination of standard costs for direct material, direct labor, variable overhead, and fixed overhead (pp. 1031–1034).
  ■ Eight components are required to develop standard product costs:

> Direct material standard price.
> Direct material standard quantity.
> Direct labor standard rate.
> Direct labor standard time.
> Standard variable overhead rate.
> Variable overhead standard capacity.
> Standard fixed overhead rate.
> Fixed overhead standard capacity.

  ■ A standard cost summary is usually prepared for each product that is manufactured.

⑤ **OUTLINE** the procedures for determining cost variances for direct material, direct labor, variable overhead, and fixed overhead (pp. 1034–1041).
  ■ The following product cost variances are calculated:

> Material price variance.
> Material quantity variance.
> Labor rate variance.
> Labor efficiency variance.
> Variable overhead spending variance.
> Variable overhead efficiency variance.
> Fixed overhead spending variance.
> Fixed overhead volume variance.

  ■ Each variance can be either favorable or unfavorable.

⑥ **DESCRIBE** the procedures for calculating total overhead variances (pp. 1041–1043).
  ■ There are two schemes for total overhead variances: a three-variance system and a two-variance system.
  ■ Total overhead variances are determined by combining variances calculated individually for variable overhead and fixed overhead.

⑦ **PRESENT** and **ILLUSTRATE** the use of standard costs in financial statements (pp. 1043–1044).
  ■ Standard costs are typically used in financial statements for internal use only by management.
  ■ Both gross profit at standard cost and gross profit (net of product cost variances) will appear on the income statement.

SELF-TEST QUESTIONS FOR REVIEW

(Answers follow the Solution to Demonstration Problem.)

1. Which type of performance report is the preferred type?
   a. Static budget.
   b. Master budget.
   c. Flexible budget.
   d. Production budget.

2. In what terms are standard overhead rates usually stated?
   a. Per dollar.
   b. Per direct labor hour.
   c. Per unit of product.
   d. Per month.

3. The formula [(Actual Price − Standard Price) × Actual Quantity] can be used to calculate which cost variance?
   a. Fixed overhead volume.
   b. Labor efficiency.
   c. Material quantity.
   d. Material price.

4. Which variance considers production capacity not used?
   a. Fixed overhead volume.
   b. Labor efficiency.
   c. Variable overhead spending.
   d. Material quantity.

5. The gross profit on the interim income statement of a firm using standard costs is computed as follows:
   a. Sales less cost of goods sold at standard.
   b. Sales less cost of goods sold at standard plus net unfavorable variances.
   c. Sales less cost of goods sold at standard less net unfavorable variances.
   d. Sales less cost of goods sold at actual.

DEMONSTRATION PROBLEM FOR REVIEW

Crenshaw Manufacturing, Inc., planned to produce 25,000 units of its only product during the year. The standard cost data for this product follow:

	Per Unit
Direct material (3 lbs. at $2 per lb.)	$ 6
Direct labor (0.5 hr. at $8 per hr.)	4
Variable overhead (0.5 hr. at $4 per hr.)	2
Fixed overhead (0.5 hr. at $6* per hr.)	3
Total standard cost per unit	$15

*Standard fixed overhead rate is computed by dividing total budgeted fixed overhead of $81,000 by normal hours of 13,500 to yield a rate of $6 per hour.

The actual level of production was 24,000 units, with the following actual total costs incurred:

	Total Cost
Direct material (74,000 lbs. at $1.80)	$133,200
Direct labor (13,000 hrs. at $8.10)	105,300
Variable overhead	50,200
Fixed overhead	80,100
Total actual cost	$368,800

REQUIRED

a. Calculate the variances for material, labor, variable overhead, and fixed overhead.
b. Show that the difference between total actual cost and total standard cost equals the sum of all the variances.
c. Determine the total overhead variances if a three-variance system is used.

SOLUTION TO DEMONSTRATION PROBLEM

a. Material Price Variance

$$\text{Material Price Variance} = \left(\text{Actual Price} - \text{Standard Price} \right) \times \text{Actual Quantity}$$

$$= (\$1.80 - \$2.00) \times 74,000$$
$$= \underline{\$14,800} \text{ F}$$

$$\text{Material Quantity Variance} = \left(\text{Actual Quantity} - \text{Standard Quantity} \right) \times \text{Standard Price}$$

$$= [74,000 - (3 \times 24,000)] \times \$2.00$$
$$= \underline{\$4,000} \text{ U}$$

$$\text{Labor Rate Variance} = \left(\text{Actual Rate} - \text{Standard Rate} \right) \times \text{Actual Hours}$$

$$= (\$8.10 - \$8.00) \times 13,000$$
$$= \underline{\$1,300} \text{ U}$$

$$\text{Labor Efficiency Variance} = \left(\text{Actual Hours} - \text{Standard Hours} \right) \times \text{Standard Rate}$$

$$= [13,000 - (0.5 \times 24,000)] \times \$8.00$$
$$= \underline{\$8,000} \text{ U}$$

$$\begin{array}{c}\text{Variable} \\ \text{Overhead} \\ \text{Spending} \\ \text{Variance}\end{array} = \begin{array}{c}\text{Actual} \\ \text{Variable} \\ \text{Overhead} \\ \text{Cost}\end{array} - \left(\begin{array}{c}\text{Variable} \\ \text{Overhead} \\ \text{Actual} \\ \text{Capacity} \\ \text{Used}\end{array} \times \begin{array}{c}\text{Standard} \\ \text{Variable} \\ \text{Overhead} \\ \text{Rate}\end{array}\right)$$

$$= \$50,200 - (13,000 \times \$4.00)$$
$$= \underline{\underline{\$1,800}} \text{ F}$$

$$\begin{array}{c}\text{Variable} \\ \text{Overhead} \\ \text{Efficiency} \\ \text{Variance}\end{array} = \left(\begin{array}{c}\text{Variable} \\ \text{Overhead} \\ \text{Actual} \\ \text{Capacity} \\ \text{Used}\end{array} \times \begin{array}{c}\text{Standard} \\ \text{Variable} \\ \text{Overhead} \\ \text{Rate}\end{array}\right) - \left(\begin{array}{c}\text{Variable} \\ \text{Overhead} \\ \text{Standard} \\ \text{Capacity} \\ \text{Allowed}\end{array} \times \begin{array}{c}\text{Standard} \\ \text{Variable} \\ \text{Overhead} \\ \text{Rate}\end{array}\right)$$

$$= (13,000 \times \$4.00) - [(0.5 \times 24,000) \times \$4.00]$$
$$= \underline{\underline{\$4,000}} \text{ U}$$

$$\begin{array}{c}\text{Fixed} \\ \text{Overhead} \\ \text{Spending} \\ \text{Variance}\end{array} = \begin{array}{c}\text{Actual} \\ \text{Fixed} \\ \text{Overhead} \\ \text{Cost}\end{array} - \begin{array}{c}\text{Budgeted} \\ \text{Fixed} \\ \text{Overhead} \\ \text{Cost}\end{array}$$

$$= \$80,100 - \$81,000$$
$$= \underline{\underline{\$900}} \text{ F}$$

$$\begin{array}{c}\text{Fixed} \\ \text{Overhead} \\ \text{Volume} \\ \text{Variance}\end{array} = \begin{array}{c}\text{Budgeted} \\ \text{Fixed} \\ \text{Overhead} \\ \text{Cost}\end{array} - \left(\begin{array}{c}\text{Fixed} \\ \text{Overhead} \\ \text{Standard} \\ \text{Capacity} \\ \text{Allowed}\end{array} \times \begin{array}{c}\text{Standard} \\ \text{Fixed} \\ \text{Overhead} \\ \text{Rate}\end{array}\right)$$

$$= \$81,000 - [(0.5 \times 24,000) \times \$6.00]$$
$$= \underline{\underline{\$9,000}} \text{ U}$$

b.

Total standard cost ($15 × 24,000)	$360,000
Total actual cost	368,800
Total variance	$ 8,800 U
Material price variance	$ 14,800 F
Material quantity variance	4,000 U
Labor rate variance	1,300 U
Labor efficiency variance	8,000 U
Variable overhead spending variance	1,800 F
Variable overhead efficiency variance	4,000 U
Fixed overhead spending variance	900 F
Fixed overhead volume variance	9,000 U
Sum of all variances	$ 8,800 U

c.

$$\begin{array}{c}\text{Overhead} \\ \text{Spending} \\ \text{Variance}\end{array} = \begin{array}{c}\text{Variable} \\ \text{Overhead} \\ \text{Spending} \\ \text{Variance}\end{array} + \begin{array}{c}\text{Fixed} \\ \text{Overhead} \\ \text{Spending} \\ \text{Variance}\end{array}$$

$$= \$1,800 \text{ F} + \$900 \text{ F}$$
$$= \underline{\underline{\$2,700}} \text{ F}$$

$$\begin{array}{c}\text{Overhead} \\ \text{Efficiency} \\ \text{Variance}\end{array} = \begin{array}{c}\text{Variable} \\ \text{Overhead} \\ \text{Efficiency} \\ \text{Variance}\end{array} = \underline{\underline{\$4,000}} \text{ U}$$

$$\begin{array}{c}\text{Overhead} \\ \text{Volume} \\ \text{Variance}\end{array} = \begin{array}{c}\text{Fixed} \\ \text{Overhead} \\ \text{Volume} \\ \text{Variance}\end{array} = \underline{\underline{\$9{,}000 \text{ U}}}$$

ANSWERS TO SELF-TEST QUESTIONS   **1.** c, p. 1030   **2.** b, p. 1032   **3.** d, p. 1035   **4.** a, p. 1041   **5.** c, p. 1044

GLOSSARY OF KEY TERMS USED IN THIS CHAPTER

budgetary control   The steps taken by management to ensure that the goals and objectives established during the budget planning stage are attained, and to ensure that all segments of the firm operate in a manner consistent with organizational policies (p. 1028).

fixed overhead spending variance   A fixed overhead variance computed as Actual Fixed Overhead Cost − Budgeted Fixed Overhead Cost (p. 1040).

fixed overhead volume variance   A fixed overhead variance as Budgeted Fixed Overhead − (Fixed Overhead Standard Capacity Allowed × Standard Fixed Overhead Rate). Called *overhead volume variance* in two-variance and three-variance systems (p. 1040).

flexible budget   A financial plan in the form of a cost formula or a multiple-column presentation that addresses various levels of activity within a relevant range (p. 1029).

labor efficiency variance   A labor variance computed as (Actual Labor Hours − Standard Labor Hours) × (Standard Labor Rate) (p. 1035).

labor rate variance   A labor variance computed as (Actual Labor Rate − Standard Labor Rate) × (Actual Labor Hours) (p. 1035).

material price variance   A material variance computed as (Actual Material Price − Standard Material Price) × (Actual Material Quantity) (p. 1035).

material quantity variance   A material variance computed as (Actual Material Quantity − Standard Material Quantity) × (Standard Material Price) (p. 1035).

overhead controllable variance   An overhead variance computed as Variable Overhead Spending Variance + Fixed Overhead Spending Variance + Variable Overhead Efficiency Variance (p. 1043).

overhead efficiency variance   An overhead variance that is the same as the variable overhead efficiency variance (p. 1043).

overhead spending variance   An overhead variance computed as Variable Overhead Spending Variance + Fixed Overhead Spending Variance (p. 1043).

overhead volume variance   An overhead variance that is the same as the fixed overhead volume variance (p. 1043).

standard cost accounting   A system of using standard costs in accounting for manufactured products (p. 1031).

standard costs   Those costs, usually expressed on a per-unit basis, that should be incurred for direct material, direct labor, and factory overhead (p. 1030).

static budget   A financial plan that has been developed for one level of operating activity, typically the expected level of activity (p. 1028).

variable overhead efficiency variance   A variable overhead variance computed as (Variable Overhead Actual Capacity Used × Standard Variable Overhead Rate) − (Variable Overhead Standard Capacity Allowed × Standard Variable Overhead Rate) (p. 1039).

variable overhead spending variance   A variable overhead variance computed as Actual Variable Overhead Cost − (Variable Overhead Actual Capacity Used × Standard Variable Overhead Rate) (p. 1039).

variances   Favorable or unfavorable differences between budgeted or standard costs and actual amounts. A variance is considered favorable if actual cost is less than budgeted or standard cost. A variance is considered unfavorable if actual cost is larger than budgeted or standard (p. 1028).

QUESTIONS

27-1   What is the difference between budgeted costs and standard costs?

27-2   What is flexible budgeting? Describe the two formats used for a flexible budget.

27-3   Why is a flexible budget performance report preferred over a static budget performance report?

27-4 Define *standard costs* and describe how they are developed.

27-5 When should standard costs be established and how often should such standards be changed?

27-6 "Standard costs can be set too high or too low for motivational purposes." Comment.

27-7 What is standard cost accounting?

27-8 A finished product requires 2 pounds of a material costing $6 per pound. What is the standard cost of direct material per unit of product?

27-9 A finished product requires 20 minutes of direct labor to complete each unit. Factory workers are paid $12 per hour. What is the standard cost of direct labor per unit of product?

27-10 Assume that the variable overhead rate for the product described in Question 27-9 is $9 per hour. What is the standard cost of variable overhead per unit of product?

27-11 Name and briefly describe the two direct material variances.

27-12 Garcia Company used 6,300 pounds of direct material costing $7.80 per pound for a batch of products that should have consumed 6,000 pounds costing $8 per pound. What are the material variances?

27-13 Name and briefly describe the two direct labor variances.

27-14 Wong Lee used 1,200 direct labor hours at an average wage rate of $8.70 to manufacture products that should have used 1,300 direct labor hours at an average wage rate of $8.50 per hour. What are the labor variances?

27-15 Name and describe the total overhead variances calculated in a three-variance system.

27-16 "Total actual cost exactly equals total standard cost, so everything must be okay." Comment.

27-17 The variable overhead rate is $5 per direct labor hour; 31,000 direct labor hours were used to produce 7,500 units of product. The standard is 4 direct labor hours per unit. Actual variable overhead cost was $153,000. Determine the variable overhead variances.

27-18 Who in the firm might be responsible for each of the following variances?
 a. Material price and quantity variances.
 b. Labor rate and efficiency variances.
 c. Variable overhead spending and efficiency variances.

27-19 Briefly explain how standard cost variances are reported on financial statements.

EXERCISES

USING FLEXIBLE BUDGETS
— OBJ. 2 —

27-20 The following summary data are from a performance report for Sterling Company for May, during which 9,600 units were produced. The budget reflects the company's normal capacity of 10,000 units.

	Budget (10,000 units)	Actual Costs (9,600 units)	Variances
Direct material	$140,000	$136,800	$3,200 F
Direct labor	280,000	277,200	2,800 F
Variable overhead	96,000	98,400	2,400 U
Fixed overhead	72,000	72,400	400 U
Total	$588,000	$584,800	$3,200 F

a. What is the general implication of the performance report? Why might Sterling question the significance of the report?

b. Revise the performance report using flexible budgeting, and comment on the general implication of the revised report.

STANDARD PRODUCT COSTS
— OBJ. 4 —

27-21 Deerfield Company manufactures product M in its factory. To make product M, 2 pounds of material P costing $4 per pound and 0.5 hour of direct labor costing $10 per hour are required. The variable overhead rate is $8 per direct labor hour, and the fixed overhead rate is $12 per direct labor hour. What is the standard product cost for product M?

MATERIAL AND LABOR VARIANCES
— OBJ. 5 —

27-22 The following actual and standard cost data for direct material and direct labor relate to the production of 2,000 units of a product:

	Actual Costs	Standard Costs
Direct material	3,900 lbs. @ $5.30	4,000 lbs. @ $5.10
Direct labor	6,200 hrs. @ $8.40	6,000 hrs. @ $8.70

Determine the following variances:
a. Material price.
b. Material quantity.
c. Labor rate.
d. Labor efficiency.

FIXED AND VARIABLE OVERHEAD VARIANCES
— OBJ. 5 —

27-23 Morgan Company considers 6,000 direct labor hours or 3,000 units of product its normal monthly capacity. Its standard variable and fixed factory overhead rates are $5 and $9, respectively, per direct labor hour. During the current month, $25,400 of variable overhead cost and $48,400 of fixed overhead cost were incurred in working 5,600 direct labor hours to produce 2,700 units of product. The fixed overhead budget was $49,000. Determine the following variances, and indicate whether each is favorable or unfavorable:
a. Variable overhead spending.
b. Variable overhead efficiency.
c. Fixed overhead spending.
d. Fixed overhead volume.

MATERIAL, LABOR, VARIABLE OVERHEAD, AND FIXED OVERHEAD VARIANCES
— OBJ. 5 —

27-24 The following summarized manufacturing data relate to Thomas Corporation's April operations, during which 2,000 finished units of product were produced. Normal monthly capacity is 1,100 direct labor hours and the fixed overhead budget is $13,200.

	Standard Unit Costs	Total Actual Costs
Direct material:		
Standard (2 lbs. @ $9/lb.)	$18	
Actual (4,200 lbs. @ $10.20/lb.)		$42,840
Direct labor:		
Standard (0.5 hr. @ $24/hr.)	12	
Actual (950 hrs. @ $23.40/hr.)		22,230
Variable overhead:		
Standard (0.5 hr. @ $6/hr.)	3	
Actual		6,450
Fixed overhead:		
Standard (0.5 hr. @ $12/hr.)	6	
Actual		13,650
Total	$39	$85,170

Determine the material price and quantity variances, labor rate and efficiency variances, variable overhead spending and efficiency variances, and fixed overhead spending and volume variances.

WORKING WITH VARIANCES
— OBJ. 5 —

27-25 From the following data, determine the total actual costs incurred for direct material, direct labor, and variable overhead.

	Standard Costs	Variances
Direct material	$120,000	
Price variance		$3,000 U
Quantity variance		4,000 F
Direct labor	100,000	
Rate variance		1,400 U
Efficiency variance		1,800 U
Variable overhead	44,000	
Spending variance		1,000 F
Efficiency variance		600 U

STANDARD COSTS IN FINANCIAL STATEMENTS
— OBJ. 7 —

27-26 For producing and selling 3,500 units of its only product for the month ended April 30, 1993, Concord Company's records reflect the following selected data:

	Standard Unit Costs	Total Actual Costs
Direct material	$12	$45,000
Direct labor	20	67,600
Variable overhead	4	13,200
Fixed overhead	10	36,600

Assuming that the product sells for $96 per unit and that Concord Company uses standard costs in its general ledger accounts, prepare a partial summary income statement (through gross profit) including total net variances.

PROBLEMS

27-27 The polishing department of Taylor Manufacturing Company operated during April 1993 with the following factory overhead cost budget based on 5,000 hours of monthly productive capacity:

TAYLOR MANUFACTURING COMPANY
POLISHING DEPARTMENT
OVERHEAD BUDGET (5,000 HOURS)
FOR THE MONTH OF APRIL, 1993

Variable costs:		
Factory supplies	$100,000	
Indirect labor	152,000	
Utilities (usage charge)	68,000	
Patent royalties on secret process	296,000	
Total variable overhead		$ 616,000
Fixed costs:		
Supervisory salaries	$160,000	
Depreciation on factory equipment	144,000	
Factory taxes	48,000	
Factory insurance	32,000	
Utilities (base charge)	80,000	
Total fixed overhead		464,000
Total factory overhead		$1,080,000

The polishing department was operated for 4,600 hours during April and incurred the following factory overhead costs:

Factory supplies	$ 97,520
Indirect labor	136,160
Utilities (usage factor)	82,800
Utilities (base factor)	96,000
Patent royalties	280,416
Supervisory salaries	168,000
Depreciation on factory equipment	144,000
Factory taxes	56,000
Factory insurance	32,000
Total factory overhead incurred	$1,092,896

REQUIRED

Using a flexible budgeting approach, prepare a performance report for the polishing department for April 1993, comparing actual overhead costs with budgeted overhead costs for 4,600 hours. Separate overhead costs into variable and fixed components and show the amounts of any variances between actual and budgeted amounts.

CALCULATE VARIANCES
— OBJ. 5 —

27-28 The following summary data relate to the operations of Dobson Company for April, during which 9,000 finished units were produced. Normal monthly capacity was 20,000 direct labor hours and the fixed overhead budget for April was $50,000.

	Standard Unit Costs	Actual Total Costs
Direct material:		
Standard (4 lbs. @ $2.20/lb.)	$ 8.80	
Actual (38,000 lbs. @ $2.00/lb.)		$ 76,000
Direct labor:		
Standard (2 hrs. @ $11.00/hr.)	22.00	
Actual (18,500 hrs. @ $11.30/hr.)		209,050
Variable overhead:		
Standard (2 hrs. @ $3.00/hr.)	6.00	
Actual		54,900
Fixed overhead:		
Standard (2 hrs. @ $2.50/hr.)	5.00	
Actual		52,000
Total	$41.80	$391,950

REQUIRED

Determine the following variances and indicate whether each is favorable or unfavorable:

a. Material price and quantity variances.
b. Labor rate and efficiency variances.
c. Variable overhead spending and efficiency variances.
d. Fixed overhead spending and volume variances.

VARIANCES, ENTRIES, AND INCOME STATEMENT — OBJ. 5, 7 —

27-29 A summary of Glendale Company's manufacturing variance report for May 1993 follows.

	Total Standard Costs (9,200 units)	Total Actual Costs (9,200 units)	Variances
Direct material	$ 38,640	$ 42,630	$3,990 U
Direct labor	193,200	193,120	80 F
Variable overhead	23,460	23,230	230 F
Fixed overhead	9,660	10,640	980 U
	$264,960	$269,620	$4,660 U

Standard material cost per unit of product is 0.5 pounds at $8.40 per pound, and standard direct labor cost is 1.5 hours at $14.00 per hour. The total actual material cost represents 4,900 pounds purchased at $8.70 per pound; total actual labor cost represents 14,200 hours at $13.60 per hour. Standard variable and fixed overhead rates are $1.70 and 70 cents, respectively, per direct labor hour (based on a normal capacity of 15,000 direct labor hours or 10,000 units of product).

REQUIRED

a. Calculate variances for material price and quantity, labor rate and efficiency, variable overhead spending and efficiency, and fixed overhead spending and volume.
b. Prepare compound general journal entries to record standard costs, actual costs, and related variances for material, labor, and overhead.
c. Prepare journal entries to record the transfer of all completed units to Finished Goods Inventory and the subsequent sale of 8,400 units on account at $54 each (assume no beginning finished goods inventory).
d. Prepare a partial income statement (through gross profit on sales) showing gross profit based on standard costs, the incorporation of variances, and gross profit based on actual costs.

VARIANCES AND JOURNAL ENTRIES — OBJ. 5 —

27-30 Jacobs Company manufactures a single product and uses a standard costing system. The nature of its product dictates that material is used as purchased and no ending material or work in process inventories occur. Per-unit standard product costs are material, $8 (4 pounds); labor, $6 (0.5 hour); variable overhead, $4 (based on direct labor hours); and fixed overhead, $3 (based on a normal monthly capacity of 9,000 direct labor hours and a fixed overhead budget of $54,000).

Jacobs accounts for work in process and finished goods inventories and cost of goods sold at standard cost and records each variance in a separate account. The following data relate to May, when 17,700 finished units were produced.

REQUIRED

a. Assuming that 67,000 pounds of material purchased on account at $2.20 per pound were used in May's production, prepare a compound journal entry to record actual costs, standard costs, and any material variances.

b. Assuming that 8,900 direct labor hours were worked at an average hourly rate of $11.70, prepare a compound journal entry to record actual costs, standard costs, and any labor variances.

c. Assuming that actual variable overhead incurred was $74,200 and that fixed overhead incurred was $54,700, prepare a compound journal entry to record actual and standard overhead costs and any overhead variances.

d. Set up T accounts for Work in Process Inventory, Finished Goods Inventory, and Cost of Goods Sold, and enter the amounts for requirements (a), (b), and (c). Assume that no beginning inventories exist, that all production was completed, and that all but 500 units produced were sold. Prepare and post journal entries to (1) record production completed and (2) record cost of goods sold at standard costs.

VARIANCES, TOTAL OVERHEAD VARIANCES, AND VARIANCE RECONCILIATION
— OBJ. 5, 6 —

27-31 Milton Company planned to produce 21,000 units of its only product during the year. Milton established the following standard cost data for this product prior to the beginning of the year:

	Per Unit
Direct material (3 lbs. at $5.00 per lb.)	$15.00
Direct labor (2 hrs. at $17.50 per hr.)	35.00
Variable overhead (2 hrs. at $6 per hr.)	12.00
Fixed overhead (2 hrs. at $10* per hr.)	20.00
Total standard cost per unit	$82.00

*Standard fixed overhead rate is computed by dividing total budgeted fixed overhead of $400,000 by 40,000 normal hours to yield a rate of $10 per hour.

The actual level of production was 22,000 units, with the following actual total costs incurred:

	Total Cost
Direct material (68,000 lbs. at $4.80)	$ 326,400
Direct labor (43,000 hrs. at $18.00)	774,000
Variable overhead	262,320
Fixed overhead	409,600
Total actual cost	$1,772,320

REQUIRED

a. Calculate the variances for material, labor, variable overhead, and fixed overhead.

b. Show that the difference between total actual cost and total standard cost equals the sum of all the variances.

c. Determine the total overhead variances if a three-variance system is used.

ALTERNATE EXERCISES

USING FLEXIBLE BUDGETS
— OBJ. 2 —

27-20A The following summary data are from a performance report for Hyland Company for June, during which 9,600 units were produced. The budget reflects the company's normal capacity of 10,000 units.

	Budget (10,000 units)	Actual Costs (9,600 units)	Variances
Direct material	$105,000	$102,600	$2,400 F
Direct labor	210,000	207,900	2,100 F
Variable overhead	72,000	73,800	1,800 U
Fixed overhead	54,000	54,300	300 U
Total	$441,000	$438,600	$2,400 F

a. What is the general implication of the performance report? Why might Hyland question the significance of the report?

b. Revise the performance report using flexible budgeting, and comment on the general implication of the revised report.

STANDARD PRODUCT COSTS
— OBJ. 4 —

27-21A Harrison Company manufactures product Q in its factory. To make product Q, 3 pounds of material T costing $7 per pound and 2 hours of direct labor costing $10 per hour are required. The variable overhead rate is $6 per direct labor hour, and the fixed overhead rate is $9 per direct labor hour. What is the standard product cost for product Q?

MATERIAL AND LABOR
VARIANCES
— OBJ. 5 —

27-22A The following actual and standard cost data for direct material and direct labor relate to the production of 2,000 units of a product:

	Actual Costs	Standard Costs
Direct material	4,200 lbs. @ $4.90	4,000 lbs. @ $5.20
Direct labor	5,700 hrs. @ $9.30	6,000 hrs. @ $9.50

Determine the following variances:

a. Material price.   c. Labor rate.
b. Material quantity.   d. Labor efficiency.

FIXED AND VARIABLE
OVERHEAD VARIANCES
— OBJ. 5 —

27-23A Marshfield Company considers 8,000 direct labor hours or 4,000 units of product its normal monthly capacity. Its standard variable and fixed factory overhead rates are $4 and $7, respectively, per direct labor hour. During the current month, $31,500 of variable overhead cost and $51,600 of fixed overhead cost were incurred in working 7,500 direct labor hours to produce 3,600 units of product. The fixed overhead budget was $52,000. Determine the following variances, and indicate whether each is favorable or unfavorable:

a. Variable overhead spending.   c. Fixed overhead spending.
b. Variable overhead efficiency.   d. Fixed overhead volume.

MATERIAL, LABOR,
VARIABLE OVERHEAD, AND
FIXED OVERHEAD
VARIANCES
— OBJ. 5 —

27-24A The following summarized manufacturing data relate to Brown Corporation's May operations, during which 2,000 finished units of product were produced. Normal monthly capacity is 1,100 direct labor hours and the fixed overhead budget is $6,600.

	Standard Unit Costs	Total Actual Costs
Direct material:		
Standard (3 lbs. @ $2/lb.)	$ 6	
Actual (6,400 lbs. @ $2.20/lb.)		$14,080
Direct labor:		
Standard (0.5 hr. @ $14/hr.)	7	
Actual (950 hrs. @ $13.70/hr.)		13,015
Variable overhead:		
Standard (0.5 hr. @ $4/hr.)	2	
Actual		4,300
Fixed overhead:		
Standard (0.5 hr. @ $6/hr.)	3	
Actual		6,820
Total	$18	$38,215

Determine the material price and quantity variances, labor rate and efficiency variances, variable overhead spending and efficiency variances, and fixed overhead spending and volume variances.

WORKING WITH VARIANCES
— OBJ. 5 —

27-25A From the following data, determine the total actual costs incurred for direct material, direct labor, and variable overhead.

	Standard Costs	Variances
Direct material	$55,000	
Price variance		$1,200 U
Quantity variance		2,200 F
Direct labor	46,000	
Rate variance		500 U
Efficiency variance		800 U
Variable overhead	18,000	
Spending variance		400 F
Efficiency variance		700 U

STANDARD COSTS IN FINANCIAL STATEMENTS — OBJ. 7 —

27-26A For producing and selling 5,000 units of its only product for the month ended October 31, 1993, Redding Company's records reflect the following selected data:

	Standard Unit Costs	Total Actual Costs
Direct material	$5	$26,400
Direct labor	8	38,500
Variable overhead	3	14,400
Fixed overhead	4	21,100

Assuming that the product sells for $48 per unit and that Redding Company uses standard costs in its general ledger accounts, prepare a partial summary income statement (through gross profit) including total net variances.

ALTERNATE PROBLEMS

FLEXIBLE BUDGET APPLICATION — OBJ. 2 —

27-27A The cutting department of Liberty Manufacturing Company operated during September 1993 with the following factory overhead cost budget based on 6,000 hours of monthly productive capacity:

LIBERTY MANUFACTURING COMPANY
CUTTING DEPARTMENT
OVERHEAD BUDGET (6,000 HOURS)
FOR THE MONTH OF SEPTEMBER, 1993

Variable costs:		
Factory supplies	$ 48,000	
Indirect labor	72,000	
Utilities (usage charge)	36,000	
Patent royalties on secret process	144,000	
Total variable overhead		$300,000
Fixed costs:		
Supervisory salaries	$ 96,000	
Depreciation on factory equipment	140,000	
Factory taxes	40,000	
Factory insurance	24,000	
Utilities (base charge)	32,000	
Total fixed overhead		332,000
Total factory overhead		$632,000

The cutting department was operated for 5,500 hours during September and incurred the following factory overhead costs:

Factory supplies	$ 40,400
Indirect labor	67,200
Utilities (usage factor)	38,100
Utilities (base factor)	32,000
Patent royalties	134,000
Supervisory salaries	96,000
Depreciation on factory equipment	140,000
Factory taxes	43,400
Factory insurance	27,000
Total factory overhead incurred	$618,100

REQUIRED

Using a flexible budgeting approach, prepare a performance report for the cutting department for September 1993, comparing actual overhead costs with budgeted overhead costs for 5,500 hours. Separate overhead costs into variable and fixed components and show the amounts of any variances between actual and budgeted amounts.

CALCULATE VARIANCES — OBJ. 5 —

27-28A The following summary data relate to the operations of Randolph Company for July, during which 4,500 finished units were produced:

	Standard Unit Costs	Total Actual Costs
Direct material:		
Standard (0.6 lb. @ $9.00/lb.)	$ 5.40	
Actual (3,000 lbs. @ $9.40/lb.)		$ 28,200
Direct labor:		
Standard (0.8 hr. @ $12.80/hr.)	10.24	
Actual (3,800 hrs. @ $12.50/hr.)		47,500
Variable overhead:		
Standard (0.8 hr. @ $7.50/hr.)	6.00	
Actual		30,100
Fixed overhead*:		
Standard (0.8 hr. @ $22.50/hr.)	18.00	
Actual		88,700
Total	$39.64	$194,500

*Fixed overhead budget is $90,000 at normal monthly capacity of 4,000 direct labor hours.

REQUIRED

Determine the following variances and indicate whether each is favorable or unfavorable:

a. Material price variance and quantity variance.
b. Labor rate variance and efficiency variance.
c. Variable overhead spending variance and efficiency variance.
d. Fixed overhead spending variance and volume variance.

VARIANCES, ENTRIES, AND INCOME STATEMENT — OBJ. 5, 7 —

27-29A A summary of Blake Company's manufacturing variance report for June 1993 follows.

	Total Standard Costs (7,600 units)	Total Actual Costs (7,600 units)	Variances
Direct material	$ 66,880	$ 65,100	$1,780 F
Direct labor	77,520	82,800	5,280 U
Variable overhead	34,200	33,000	1,200 F
Fixed overhead	102,600	109,500	6,900 U
	$281,200	$290,400	$9,200 U

Standard material cost per unit of product is 4 pounds at $2.20 per pound, and standard direct labor cost is 0.75 hours at $13.60 per hour. Total actual material cost represents 31,000 pounds purchased at $2.10 per pound; total actual labor cost represents 6,000 hours at $13.80 per hour. Variable and fixed factory overhead rates are $6 and $18, respectively, per direct labor hour (based on a normal capacity of 6,000 direct labor hours or 8,000 units of product).

REQUIRED

a. Calculate variances for material price and quantity, labor rate and efficiency, variable overhead spending and efficiency, and fixed overhead spending and volume.
b. Prepare compound general journal entries to record standard costs, actual costs, and related variances for material, labor, and overhead.
c. Prepare journal entries to record the transfer of all completed units to Finished Goods Inventory and the subsequent sale of 6,400 units on account at $60 each (assume no beginning finished goods inventory).
d. Prepare a partial income statement (through gross profit on sales) showing gross profit based on standard costs, the incorporation of variances, and gross profit based on actual costs.

VARIANCES AND JOURNAL ENTRIES — OBJ. 5 —

27-30A Kent Company manufactures a single product and uses a standard costing system. The nature of its product dictates that material is used as purchased and no ending material or work in process inventories occur. Per-unit standard product costs are material, $6 (0.5 pound); labor, $15 (1.5 hours); variable overhead, $3 (based on direct labor hours); and fixed overhead, $12 (based on a normal monthly capacity of 12,000 direct labor hours and a fixed overhead budget of $96,000).

Kent Company accounts for work in process and finished goods inventories and cost of goods sold at standard cost and records each variance in a separate account. The following data relate to June, when 7,800 finished units were produced.

REQUIRED

a. Assuming that 4,200 pounds of material purchased on account at $11.60 per pound were used in June's production, prepare a compound journal entry to record actual costs, standard costs, and any material variances.

b. Assuming that 12,000 direct labor hours were worked at an average hourly rate of $10.50, prepare a compound journal entry to record actual costs, standard costs, and any labor variances.

c. Assuming that actual variable overhead incurred was $23,100 and that actual fixed overhead was $97,100, prepare a compound journal entry to record actual and standard overhead costs and any overhead variances.

d. Set up T accounts for Work in Process Inventory, Finished Goods Inventory, and Cost of Goods Sold, and enter the amounts for requirements (a), (b), and (c). Assume that no beginning inventories exist, that all production was completed, and that all but 900 units produced were sold. Prepare and post journal entries to (1) record production completed and (2) record cost of goods sold at standard costs.

VARIANCES, TOTAL OVERHEAD VARIANCES, AND VARIANCE RECONCILIATION — OBJ. 5, 6 —

27-31A Sanchez Company planned to produce 10,000 units of its only product during the year. Sanchez established the following standard cost data for this product prior to the beginning of the year:

	Per Unit
Direct material (2 lbs. at $7.50 per lb.)	$15.00
Direct labor (1.5 hrs. at $13.50 per hr.)	20.25
Variable overhead (1.5 hrs. at $6 per hr.)	9.00
Fixed overhead (1.5 hrs. at $9* per hr.)	13.50
Total standard cost per unit	$57.75

*Standard fixed overhead rate is computed by dividing total budgeted fixed overhead of $144,000 by 16,000 normal hours to yield a rate of $9 per hour.

The actual level of production was 9,000 units, with the following actual total costs incurred:

	Total Cost
Direct material (17,000 lbs. at $7.80)	$132,600
Direct labor (14,000 hrs. at $13.35)	186,900
Variable overhead	80,250
Fixed overhead	145,650
Total actual cost	$545,400

REQUIRED

a. Calculate the variances for material, labor, variable overhead, and fixed overhead.

b. Show that the difference between total actual cost and total standard cost equals the sum of all the variances.

c. Determine the total overhead variances if a three-variance system is used.

CASES

Business Decision Case

Porter Corporation has just hired Bill Harlow as its new controller. Although Harlow has had little formal accounting training, he professes to be highly experienced, having learned accounting "the hard way" in the field. At the end of his first month's work, Harlow prepared the following performance report, which appears on the next page:

PORTER CORPORATION
PERFORMANCE REPORT
FOR THE MONTH OF JUNE, 1993

	Total Actual Costs	Total Budgeted Costs	Variances
Direct material	$216,630	$237,600	$20,970 F
Direct labor	119,340	132,000	12,660 F
Variable overhead	63,000	66,000	3,000 F
Fixed overhead	184,000	187,000	3,000 F
	$582,970	$622,600	$39,630 F

In his presentation at Porter's month-end management meeting, Harlow indicated that things were going "fantastically." "The figures indicate," he said, "that the firm is beating its budget in all cost categories." This good news made everyone at the meeting happy and furthered Harlow's acceptance as a member of the management team.

After the management meeting, Susan Jones, Porter's general manager, asked you, as an independent consultant, to review Harlow's report. Jones' concern stemmed from the fact that Porter has never operated as favorably as Harlow's report seems to imply, and she cannot explain the apparent significant improvement.

While reviewing Harlow's report, you are provided the following cost and operating data for June: Porter has a monthly normal capacity of 11,000 direct labor hours or 8,800 units of product. Standard costs per unit for its only product are direct material, 3 pounds at $9 per pound; direct labor, 1.25 hours at $12 per hour; and variable and fixed overhead rates per direct labor hour of $6 and $17, respectively. During June, Porter produced 8,000 units of product using 24,900 pounds of material costing $8.70 each, 10,200 direct labor hours at an average rate of $11.70 each, and incurred variable overhead costs of $63,000 and fixed overhead costs of $184,000.

After reviewing Porter's June cost data, you tell Harlow that his cost report contains a classic budgeting error, and you explain how he can remedy it. In response to your suggestion, Harlow revises his report as follows:

	Total Actual Costs	Total Budgeted Costs	Variances
Direct material	$216,630	$216,000	$ 630 U
Direct labor	119,340	120,000	660 F
Variable overhead	63,000	60,000	3,000 U
Fixed overhead	184,000	187,000	3,000 F
	$582,970	$583,000	$ 30 F

Harlow's revised report is accompanied by remarks expressing regret at the oversight in the original report.

REQUIRED

In your role as consultant,
a. Verify that Harlow's actual cost figures are correct.
b. Identify and explain the classic budgeting error that Harlow apparently incorporated into his original cost report.
c. Explain why Harlow's revised figures could be considered deficient.
d. Further analyze Harlow's revised variances, isolating underlying potential causal factors. How do your analyses indicate bases for concern to management?

Ethics Case

Custom Furniture, manufacturer of handmade furniture, uses standard cost accounting for the company. Standards are developed annually based on input from production workers and supervisors.

The supervisor of the table department has approached several employees that work for him and suggested that the employees overestimate the amount of material (by 20%) and labor (by 30%) involved in producing certain new tables. He states that it is better to overestimate than underestimate costs as the product has never been manufactured in quantity before and

CASES   1059

it is uncertain what the actual materials and labor will be. In addition, he states that this would result in any variances being favorable to the department.

The employees are not sure what estimates they should discuss with the accounting department. The accounting department wants accurate input that it will adjust for uncertainty.

REQUIRED

How would you advise the employees? What ethical issues are involved?

What techniques should a manager use to decide whether to acquire a particular plant asset or office asset?

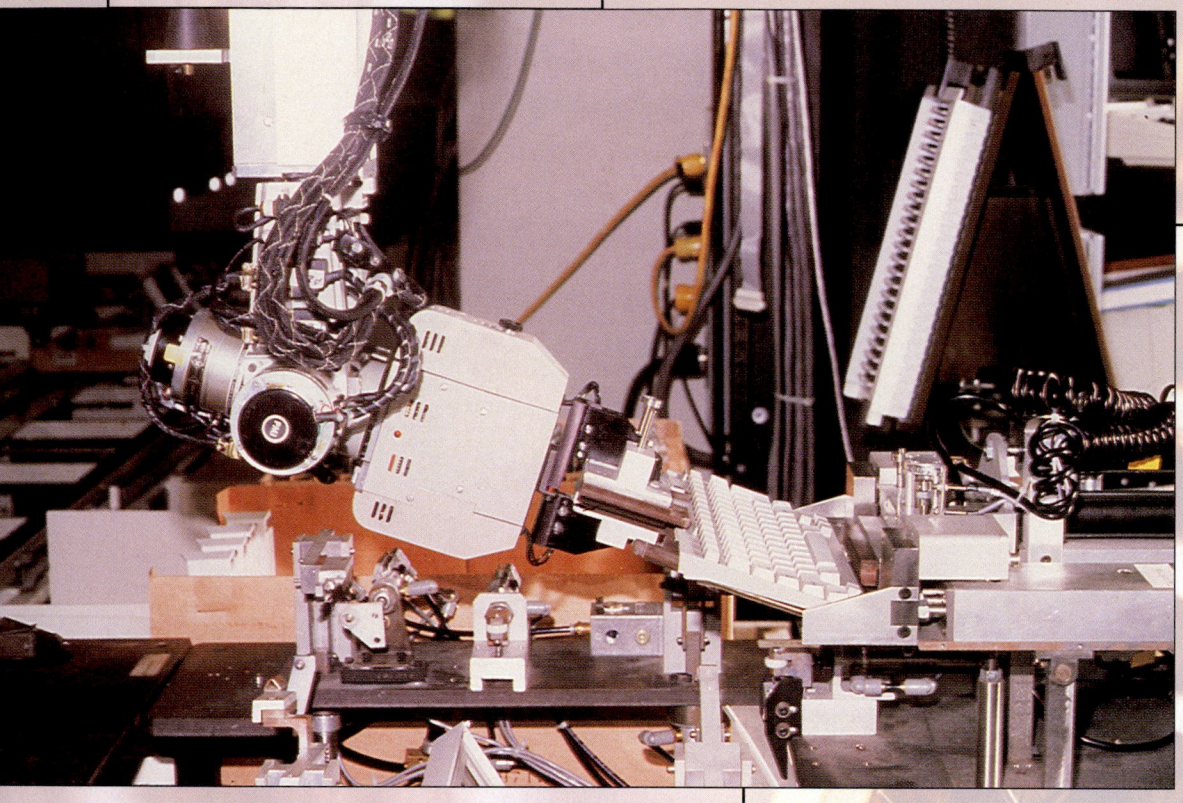

The analysis made prior to acquiring a physical asset can be complex, as this chapter shows. ■ *Manufacturers are faced with many decisions such as replacing a five-year-old paint sprayer with a new one or replacing two human welders with a robotic welder.* ■ *U.S. companies that have invested heavily in factory automation after careful analysis include IBM, Apple Computer, General Electric, and Allen-Bradley.* ■ *Non-manufacturing conpanies can also benefit from careful analysis of asset acquisition.*

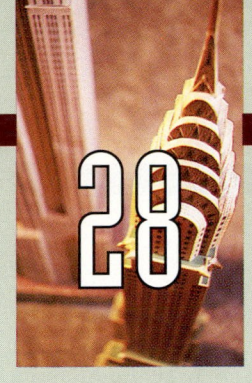

28 CAPITAL BUDGETING

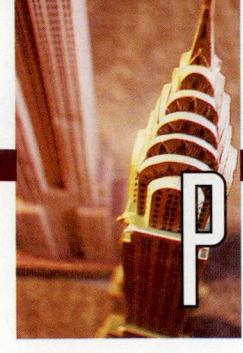

lanning long-term investments in plant assets is known as **capital budgeting.** The term reflects the fact that for most firms the total cost of all attractive investment opportunities exceeds the available investment capital. Thus, management must ration, or budget, investment capital among competing investment proposals. In deciding which new long-term assets to acquire, management must seek investments that promise to optimize return on the funds employed.

Capital budgeting is most valuable for organizations in which managers are responsible for the long-term profitability of their area of concern and are therefore encouraged to develop new products and more efficient production processes. Firms often make their most capable employees responsible for capital budgeting decisions, because such decisions determine how large sums of money are invested and commit the firm for extended future periods. Furthermore, investment decision errors are often difficult and costly to remedy or abandon.

Managers as well as accountants should be familiar with the special analytical techniques that evaluate the relative attractiveness of alternative uses of available capital. In this chapter, we first discuss the nature and procedures of capital budgeting, how required investment earning rates are determined, the time value of money, and the effect of income taxes on capital expenditure decisions. We conclude by illustrating three approaches to capital expenditure analysis: the *net present value method*, the *cash payback method*, and the *average rate of return method*.

ELEMENTS OF CAPITAL BUDGETING

OBJECTIVE ❶ INTRODUCE *and* ILLUSTRATE *the elements of capital budgeting*.

Many firms have a capital budgeting calendar calling for consideration of capital expenditure proposals at regular intervals, for example, every six months or a year. Proposals are usually examined with respect to (1) compliance with capital budget policies and procedures; (2) aspects of operational urgency, such as the need to replace critical equipment; (3) established criteria for minimum return on capital investments; and (4) consistency with the firm's operating policies and long-term goals. Proposals for relatively small cash outlays may require the approval of low-level management only, whereas comprehensive proposals are subject to approval at high management levels, perhaps including the board of directors. These comprehensive proposals and the decisions based on them profoundly affect a firm's long-term success.

Once approved, capital expenditures should be monitored to ensure that amounts and purposes are consistent with the original proposal. At appropriate intervals, the actual rates of return earned on important expenditures should be compared with projected rates. These periodic reviews encourage those responsible to formulate thorough and realistic proposals, and often provide an incentive for improving overall capital budgeting procedures.

CAPITAL EXPENDITURE ANALYSIS

The scope of capital expenditures varies widely, ranging from the routine replacement of production equipment to the construction of entire factory complexes. Whatever their size, most capital expenditure projects have the following three recognizable stages:

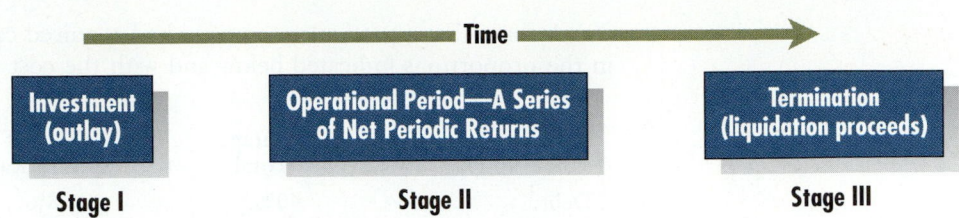

Time

Investment (outlay)	Operational Period—A Series of Net Periodic Returns	Termination (liquidation proceeds)
Stage I	Stage II	Stage III

Investment (stage I) consists of the net cash outlay for a project or an asset. Net periodic returns during the life of the project (stage II) may result from either an excess of periodic revenue over related expenses or a periodic saving in some expense. Finally, because most efficient firms replace capital equipment before it becomes worthless, the termination of a project (stage III) often results in some amount of liquidation proceeds.

The attractiveness of a particular investment is determined in large part by the quantitative relationship between the investment in stage I and the receipts expected in stages II and III. This relationship is usually expressed as a ratio known as the *rate of return*:

$$\text{Rate of Return} = \frac{\text{Returns}}{\text{Investment}}$$

All other things being equal, the higher the expected rate of return, the more attractive the investment opportunity. Proposed investments can be ranked according to their expected rates of return, and capital outlays can be allocated among the most attractive investments. In its simplest terms, capital expenditure analysis consists of judging the attractiveness of income-producing or cost-saving opportunities in relation to required investments. The results of this analysis are among the most important input data in capital budgeting decisions.

Three questions are of considerable concern in capital budgeting:

1. How do we determine an acceptable rate of return for a given project?
2. How can we meaningfully compare investments made now with returns to be received in the future?
3. In what terms should investments and returns be measured?

These challenging problems are considered in the following sections of this chapter.

REQUIRED RATES OF RETURN

OBJECTIVE ② DISCUSS *required rates of return and the time value of money.*

In determining an acceptable rate of return for a given project, we must consider not only the required capital outlay, but also the costs associated with the acquisition of that capital. The parties providing the funds expect to be reasonably compensated for their use. When the money is borrowed (usually through a bond issue), the interest paid by the firm is a cost of using the funds. When stockholder funds are used, we assume that some combination of dividend payments and increase in the value of the capital stock compensates stockholders for furnishing the investment capital. The cost to the firm of acquiring the funds used in capital investment projects—typically expressed as an annual percentage rate—is called the **cost of capital.**

Determining the actual cost of capital for a firm may require complex calculations, and even well-informed authorities in finance disagree about certain aspects of these calculations. Many firms use an approach that distinguishes among the various sources of financing.

A firm may acquire capital by issuing preferred or common stock, using retained earnings, borrowing, or some combination of these. Consequently, the overall cost of capital for a given project may reflect the cost rates of the several sources of funds in proportion to the amounts obtained from each source. This situation has led to the concept of the **weighted average cost of capital,** illustrated as follows.

Assume that a particular company had acquired capital through all four sources, in the proportions indicated below and with the cost of capital rates as shown.

Source of Capital	Percentage of Total	×	Cost of Capital Rate	=	Weighted Average Cost of Capital Component
Debt	40%		8%		3.2%
Preferred stock	10		9		0.9
Common stock	20		12		2.4
Retained earnings	30		12		3.6
Weighted average cost of capital					10.1%

Multiplying the percentage of each capital source by its cost of capital rate provides weighted cost factors whose sum is the weighted average cost of capital. This percentage (in this case, 10.1%) can then be used to compare the attractiveness of proposed investments.

Logically, for a capital investment to be considered favorably by a firm, its expected rate of return must be *at least as high* as the cost of capital. Therefore, *the cost of capital represents a minimum required rate of return*. In other words, a firm whose cost of capital is 10% will ordinarily want to invest in only an asset or project whose expected rate of return is more than 10%. An investment whose return is less than the cost of capital would be economically detrimental, although firms sometimes disregard their cost of capital if qualitative considerations override the quantitative aspects of the decision. Qualitative considerations might include the desire to achieve certain environmental goals, the desire to maintain research leadership in the field, and the need to maintain full employment of the work force during a business slowdown.

Some firms consider only investments whose rates of return are at least a certain number of percentage points higher than the cost of capital. This **buffer margin** acts as a safety factor, because proposals, which rely heavily on estimates of costs and future returns, may involve what will prove to be an erroneous estimated rate of return. Of course, even proposals whose expected rate of return is higher than the **cutoff** or **hurdle rate** (Cost of Capital + Buffer Margin) may be rejected if other investment opportunities offer still higher returns.

TIME VALUE OF MONEY

We have seen that in determining the desirability of a proposed capital investment, management compares the amount of investment required at the beginning of a project with its expected returns—typically a series of returns extending several years into the future. This comparison, which is so important in capital outlay decisions, cannot be made properly using the absolute amounts of the future returns because *money has a time value*. The **time value of money** means that the right to receive an amount of money today is worth more than the right to receive the same amount at some future date, because a current receipt can be invested to earn interest over the intervening period. Thus, if 10% annual interest can be obtained on investments, $100 received today is equal in value to $110 received one year from now. Today's $100 has a *future value* of $110 one year from now; conversely, the *present value* of a $110 receipt expected one year from today is $100.

The difference between present and future values is a function of interest rates and time periods. The higher the interest rate or longer the time period involved, the higher the amount by which a future value is reduced, or *discounted*, in deriving its present value. For example, Exhibit 28-1 shows just how significant the time value of money can be at various interest rates and time periods. As the table indicates, $100 five years from now has a present value of $78, $62, or $40 if the applicable interest rates are 5%, 10%, and 20%, respectively. Note also that the higher the time

EXHIBIT 28—1	PRESENT VALUE OF $100 DISCOUNTED FOR YEARS AND INTEREST RATES SHOWN (ROUNDED TO NEAREST DOLLAR)		
Years Discounted	**5%**	**10%**	**20%**
1	$95	$91	$83
2	91	83	69
3	86	75	58
4	82	68	48
5	78	62	40
10	61	39	16
20	38	15	3
30	23	6	—
40	14	2	—
50	9	1	—

period or the interest rate, the larger the difference between the future value of $100 and its present value. Comparing a current investment with its future returns without discounting the returns to their present value would substantially overstate the economic significance of the returns. We must, therefore, recognize the time value of money in capital budgeting procedures.

We should also recognize that techniques for discounting future cash flows to their present values apply to both cash receipts and cash outlays. In other words, the current value of the *right to receive*—or the current value of the *obligation to pay*—a sum in the future is its present value computed at an appropriate interest rate. We maximize our economic position by arranging to receive amounts as early as possible and postponing amounts to be paid as long as possible. The intrinsic role of these generalizations is apparent in the capital budgeting illustrations later in the chapter.

USING PRESENT VALUE TABLES

Widely available present value tables simplify our work considerably in computing present values. Tables I and II give the present values of $1 for a number of rates and time periods. The amounts in these tables are called **present value factors,** or **discount factors,** because we convert any given cash flow to its present value by multiplying the amount of the cash flow by the appropriate factor.

Single-Sum Flows

OBJECTIVE ❸ ILLUSTRATE *the use of present value tables.*

Table I gives present value factors for amounts received in a single sum at the end of a specified number of periods. We use Table I to determine the present value of sporadic cash flows—when the returns expected on an investment, or the expenditures it requires, are unequal amounts or are expected at irregular intervals during or at the end of the life of the investment.

To illustrate the use of Table I, we assume that an investment project promises a return of $2,000 at the end of two years and another $1,000 at the end of five years. The desired rate of return is 10%. The factor in the 10% column of the table for two periods from now is 0.826; the factor for five periods from now is 0.621. The total present value of the combined flows is $2,273, calculated as follows:

Future Receipts			PV Factor		Present Value
2 years from now	$2,000	×	0.826	=	$1,652
5 years from now	1,000	×	0.621	=	621
					$2,273

TABLE I	PRESENT VALUE OF $1

Periods Hence	Rate per Compounding Period						
	5%	6%	8%	10%	12%	15%	20%
1	0.952	0.943	0.926	0.909	0.893	0.870	0.833
2	0.907	0.890	0.857	0.826	0.797	0.756	0.694
3	0.864	0.840	0.794	0.751	0.712	0.658	0.579
4	0.823	0.792	0.735	0.683	0.636	0.572	0.482
5	0.784	0.747	0.681	0.621	0.567	0.497	0.402
6	0.746	0.705	0.630	0.564	0.507	0.432	0.335
7	0.711	0.665	0.583	0.513	0.452	0.376	0.279
8	0.677	0.627	0.540	0.467	0.404	0.327	0.233
9	0.645	0.592	0.500	0.424	0.361	0.284	0.194
10	0.614	0.558	0.463	0.386	0.322	0.247	0.162
11	0.585	0.527	0.429	0.350	0.287	0.215	0.135
12	0.557	0.497	0.397	0.319	0.257	0.187	0.112
13	0.530	0.469	0.368	0.290	0.229	0.163	0.093
14	0.505	0.442	0.340	0.263	0.205	0.141	0.078
15	0.481	0.417	0.315	0.239	0.183	0.123	0.065

Annuity Flows

We can compute the present value of a single cash flow sum—or any combinations of single sums—using Table I. Cash flows that are the same each period over two or more periods are an annuity, and using an annuity table is more convenient. Generally, annuity tables are cumulative versions of single-sum tables. Table II, for example, is an annuity table based on present value factors from Table I.

To illustrate, we assume that a project has expected cash inflows of $1,000 at the end of each of the next three periods, and 8% is the appropriate interest rate. Using Table I, we compute the total present value as the sum of three individual amounts, as shown below:

Periods Hence	Cash Inflows		PV Factor (Table I @ 8%)		Present Value
1	$1,000	×	0.926	=	$ 926
2	1,000	×	0.857	=	857
3	1,000	×	0.794	=	794
			2.577		$2,577

Alternatively, using Table II, we need only multiply the periodic cash flow by a single present value factor for three periods at 8%.

Periods Hence (in annuity)	Periodic Cash Inflow		PV Factor (Table II @ 8%)		Present Value
3	$1,000	×	2.577	=	$2,577

Note that the present value factor for Table II is applied to the periodic cash flow of $1,000, not to the $3,000 total amount of cash flows in the annuity.

The advantage of Table II is that a single present value factor is provided for two or more equal amounts occurring evenly throughout a series of periods. When analyzing investments involving extended series of equal cash flows, the savings in computational effort can be significant.

	TABLE II			PRESENT VALUE OF AN ORDINARY ANNUITY OF $1 PER PERIOD			

Periods Hence	Rate per Compounding Period						
	5%	6%	8%	10%	12%	15%	20%
1	0.952	0.943	0.926	0.909	0.893	0.870	0.833
2	1.859	1.833	1.783	1.736	1.690	1.626	1.528
3	2.723	2.673	2.577	2.487	2.402	2.283	2.106
4	3.546	3.465	3.312	3.170	3.037	2.855	2.589
5	4.330	4.212	3.993	3.791	3.605	3.352	2.991
6	5.076	4.917	4.623	4.355	4.111	3.784	3.326
7	5.786	5.582	5.206	4.868	4.564	4.160	3.605
8	6.463	6.210	5.747	5.335	4.968	4.487	3.837
9	7.108	6.802	6.247	5.760	5.328	4.772	4.031
10	7.722	7.360	6.710	6.145	5.650	5.019	4.192
11	8.306	7.887	7.139	6.495	5.988	5.234	4.327
12	8.863	8.384	7.536	6.814	6.194	5.421	4.439
13	9.394	8.853	7.904	7.103	6.424	5.583	4.533
14	9.899	9.295	8.244	7.367	6.628	5.724	4.611
15	10.380	9.712	8.560	7.606	6.811	5.847	4.675

Tables I and II both assume that all cash flows occur at the end of the periods shown. This assumption is somewhat simplistic, because cash receipts or cost savings from most industrial investments occur in a steady stream throughout the operating period. Nevertheless, businesses use such tables principally because of their availability and ease of use. These tables will understate present values of flows that are gradual throughout the period, because the present values of cash flows early in the period are higher than similar inflows or outlays at the end of the period. The difference in the factors, however, is normally not material.

MEASUREMENT OF INVESTMENTS AND RETURNS

OBJECTIVE **4** EXPLAIN *and* ILLUSTRATE *the determination of after-tax cash flows.*

When present value analysis is used to make investment decisions, investments and returns must be stated in the form of *cash* flows. Present value determinations are basically interest calculations, and therefore only money amounts—cash flows—are properly used in interest calculations. Furthermore, only the *incremental cash flows* that will occur if the project is accepted should be considered in the analysis.

Typically, financial data available in the accounts are not stated in terms of cash flows because accrual-basis accounting is used. Amounts compiled on the accrual basis must be restated to the appropriate cash flows for capital budgeting purposes. For example, apportioning the cost of an asset over its life through depreciation accounting is an important feature of accrual accounting. When present value analysis is used, the cost of an asset is treated as a cash outlay when the asset is paid for. In measuring future returns related to the asset, depreciation expense does not represent a cash outlay. However, depreciation expense affects cash flows indirectly by reducing cash outlays for income tax payments.

Likewise, earnings from projects should reflect the cash inflows rather than the revenue amounts computed using accrual accounting. The timing of the cash collections is important, too, because the essence of present value analysis is that cash received can be reinvested.

If specific accruals or deferrals are not material in amount, or if their amounts at the beginning and end of the period are roughly the same, they are often ignored in restating accrual-basis amounts to cash flows. Ignoring the impact of accruals and deferrals in these instances will not adversely affect the capital budgeting analysis.

After-tax Cash Flows

Both federal and state income taxes are important to investment decisions; for some companies, the combined federal and state income tax rate may approach 40%. Generally, income taxes reduce the economic significance of taxable receipts and deductible outlays. For example, assuming a 40% tax rate, a $40,000 before-tax gain would increase taxable income by $40,000 and income taxes by $16,000 (40% × $40,000), resulting in a $24,000 after-tax gain. A $15,000 before-tax expense would reduce taxable income by $15,000 and income taxes by $6,000 (40% × $15,000), resulting in a $9,000 after-tax expense. Because income tax rates can be substantial, management has a continuing responsibility to minimize the firm's income tax. After-tax cash flows are more relevant than before-tax cash flows because they represent the amounts available to retire debt, finance expansions, or pay dividends. For these reasons, investment decision analyses must be formulated in terms of after-tax cash flows.

Illustration of After-tax Cash Flows

Thinking in terms of after-tax cash flows represents a significant departure from the accrual-based accounting for revenue and expenses that dominates much of our earlier study of accounting. Exhibit 28-2 builds on the traditional income statement to illustrate (1) the conversion of net income to after-tax cash flows, (2) the confirmation of that amount as actual cash flows, and (3) the determination of the individual after-tax cash flow effects of receiving revenue, incurring cash expenses, and recording depreciation. An understanding of Exhibit 28-2 provides a basis for studying the comprehensive illustration of capital budgeting later in the chapter.

The highlighted area in Exhibit 28-2 is the traditional income statement, showing that revenue minus operating expenses and income taxes results in a net income of $18,000. For simplicity, we assume that revenue and cash expenses involve no significant accruals and that depreciation is the same on both the books and the tax return. Ordinarily, net income does not represent after-tax cash flows because depreciation expense—a noncash expense—is deducted to derive net income. As indicated in column **A** of Exhibit 28-2, to convert the $18,000 net income to an after-tax cash

---

EXHIBIT 28—2   ILLUSTRATION OF DETERMINING AFTER-TAX CASH FLOWS

		A Traditional Income Statement	**B** Income Statement Cash Inflows (Outflows)	**C** Individual After-tax Cash Inflow (Outflow) Effects
Cash revenue (sales)		$100,000	$100,000	$60,000
Cash operating expenses	$60,000		(60,000)	(36,000)
Depreciation expense	10,000			4,000
Total operating expenses		70,000		
Income before tax		$ 30,000		
Income tax expense at 40%		12,000	(12,000)	
Net income		$ 18,000		
Add back depreciation expense		10,000		
After-tax cash flow		$ 28,000	$ 28,000	$28,000

flow, we must add back the depreciation of $10,000, resulting in $28,000 of after-tax cash flow.[1] Present value computations are properly applied to this amount.

Column **B** of Exhibit 28-2 confirms the $28,000 amount of after-tax cash flow determined in column **A**. This is accomplished by simply listing the amounts in column **A** that constitute cash inflows (revenue of $100,000) and cash outflows (cash expenses of $60,000 and income tax payments of $12,000). Depreciation is excluded because it does not represent a cash payment.

Column **C** in Exhibit 28-2 illustrates the determination of the individual amounts of after-tax cash flows for each item on the income statement. We use this approach in the comprehensive illustration of capital budgeting appearing later in the chapter. Amounts in column **C** are determined as follows (again, a 40% income tax rate is assumed):

Receipt of $100,000 cash revenue: Receipt of $100,000 cash revenue would, by itself, increase taxable income by $100,000, adding $40,000 ($100,000 × 40%) to income taxes. The $60,000 after-tax cash inflow is the difference between the $100,000 cash revenue received and the related $40,000 increase in income taxes (a cash outflow).

Payment of $60,000 in cash operating expenses: Payment of $60,000 in cash operating expenses represents a deductible cash outflow that reduces taxable income by $60,000 and thus reduces income taxes by $24,000 ($60,000 × 40%). The $36,000 net cash outflow is the difference between the $60,000 actually paid out for expenses and the $24,000 of income tax payments avoided by virtue of the tax deductibility of the expenses.

Notice that *avoiding a cash outflow* has the same effect on net cash flows as a cash inflow. In other words, total net cash inflows can be increased by adding to cash inflows or by avoiding cash outflows.

Recording $10,000 of depreciation expense: Although depreciation expense is tax deductible, no related cash expenditure occurs during the period. The $10,000 deduction reduces taxable income $10,000 and income taxes $4,000 ($10,000 × 40%). Because the depreciation deduction results in avoidance of an outflow, its after-tax cash flow effect is that of a cash inflow. Depreciation expense and similar noncash expense deductions are often referred to as *tax shields* because they shield an equal amount of income from whatever income tax rate is applicable.

The depreciation amount that provides a tax shield is the depreciation deduction on the tax return. Tax depreciation deductions are governed by tax regulations, not by generally accepted accounting principles. Often the periodic tax depreciation will differ from depreciation expense on the income statement (in Exhibit 28-2 we assume that the amounts are equal). When identifying the depreciation tax shield in capital budgeting analysis, then, it is important to use the depreciation amount from the tax return.

Combining the after-tax cash flow effect of each individual amount in column **C** again confirms that net cash inflows total $28,000. It is helpful to realize that the after-tax cash flow effect of cash receipts and cash expenses is derived by multiplying the before-tax amounts by (1 − income tax rate). In contrast, the after-tax cash flow effect of depreciation expense is derived by multiplying the before-tax amounts by the tax rate. In our example,

Cash revenue [$100,000 × (1 − 40%)]	$60,000
Cash expenses [$60,000 × (1 − 40%)]	(36,000)
Depreciation expense ($10,000 × 40%)	4,000
Net cash flow	$28,000

---

[1] If present, other amounts of noncash expense—such as amortization of intangible assets and depletion of natural resources—are also added back.

SUMMARY OF CONCERNS UNDERLYING CAPITAL BUDGETING

1. The typical investment pattern involves a present investment of funds resulting in anticipated returns, often extending years into the future.
2. The basic question in capital budgeting is whether present investments are justified by related future returns.
3. Because money has a time value, returns that occur in the future must be discounted to their present values for a proper comparison with present investments.
4. To use discounting (interest) calculations properly, we must state amounts in capital budgeting analyses in terms of cash flows.
5. Because income tax rates are substantial, capital budgeting analyses should be formulated in terms of after-tax cash flows.

In this chapter, we have presented a number of important aspects of capital budgeting as background for the review of several approaches to capital expenditure analysis. These background materials have focused on the analytical concept known as *net present value*. Accountants generally concede that the net present value approach is conceptually and analytically superior to the other two approaches that we illustrate: *cash payback* and *average rate of return*.

NET PRESENT VALUE ANALYSIS

OBJECTIVE 5 DESCRIBE *the net present value method of capital expenditure analysis.*

The basic considerations of the **net present value method** are shown schematically in Exhibit 28-3. Referring to the items in the diagram, we can explain the steps in the net present value approach as follows:

1 Determine in terms of incremental after-tax cash flows the amount of the investment outlay required.

2 Estimate in terms of incremental after-tax cash flows the amounts and timing of future operating receipts or cost savings.

3 Estimate any incremental after-tax liquidation proceeds to be received on termination of the project.

4 Discount all future cash flows to their present value at an appropriate interest rate, usually the minimum desired rate of return on capital.

5 Subtract the investment outlay from the total present value of future cash flows to determine *net* present value. If net present value is zero or positive (returns equal or exceed investment), then the project's rate of return equals or exceeds the minimum desired rate and should be accepted. Negative net present values indicate that the project's return is less than desired, and the project should be rejected.

To illustrate net present value analysis, assume that, with a minimum desired return of 10%, a glass manufacturer is considering the purchase of a $12,000 special shipping rack that will save $5,000 annually in cash operating expenses; will have a useful life of three years; will be depreciated over three years on the tax return—$2,400 in Year 1, $4,800 in Year 2, and $4,800 in Year 3; and will be sold for $2,000 at the end of the third year. Also assume that all income and gains are taxed at 40%.

Exhibit 28-4 presents a net present value analysis of the shipping rack as an investment project. Note that the format follows the schematic analysis presented in Exhibit 28-3: future returns are stated in terms of after-tax cash flows; then, from Tables I and II, the present values of future cash flows are determined and compared with the investment. The computations shown in Exhibit 28-4 are explained below.

Annual cash expense savings: Cash savings or expense reductions have the same effects as cash revenue, income, or gains. They also have the same consequence of increasing income taxes. In our example, saving $5,000 in cash expenses each year

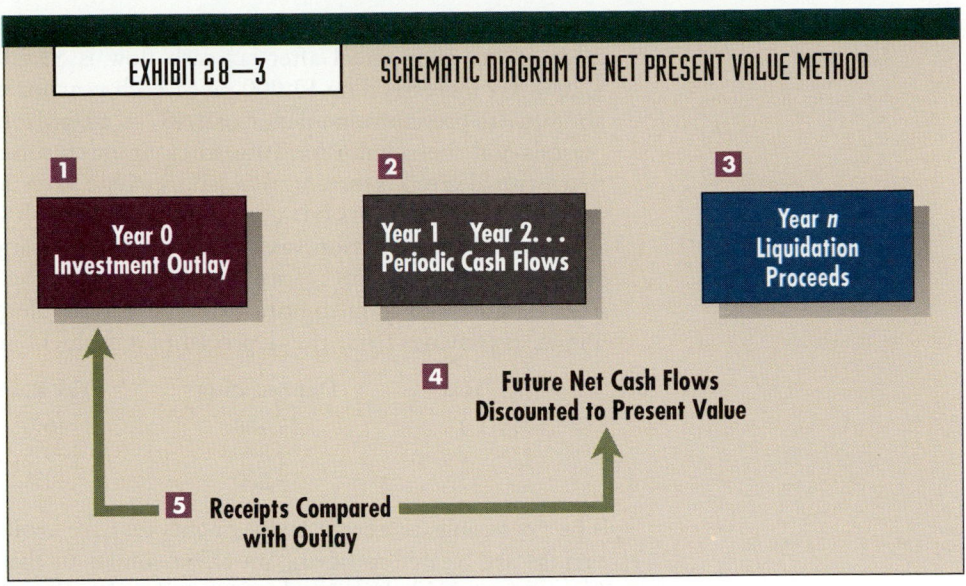

EXHIBIT 28–3 — SCHEMATIC DIAGRAM OF NET PRESENT VALUE METHOD

1. Year 0 Investment Outlay
2. Year 1 Year 2... Periodic Cash Flows
3. Year n Liquidation Proceeds
4. Future Net Cash Flows Discounted to Present Value
5. Receipts Compared with Outlay

EXHIBIT 28–4 — ILLUSTRATION OF NET PRESENT VALUE ANALYSIS: AFTER-TAX CASH FLOWS [ROUNDED TO NEAREST DOLLAR]

Analysis of After-tax Cash Flows		Present Value Factors at 10% (Table I or II)	Total Present Value	Projected After-tax Cash Flows			
				Year 0	Year 1	Year 2	Year 3
Annual cash expense savings:							
Annual cash expense saving	$5,000						
Less income tax @ 40%	2,000						
After-tax expense savings	$3,000	(II) 2.487	$ 7,461		$3,000	$3,000	$3,000
Tax savings from depreciation tax shield:							
Year 1: $2,400 × 40%	$ 960	(I) 0.909	873		960		
Year 2: $4,800 × 40%	$1,920	(I) 0.826	1,586			1,920	
Year 3: $4,800 × 40%	$1,920	(I) 0.751	1,442				1,920
Liquidation proceeds:							
Sales price of rack	$2,000						
Tax book value (original cost of $12,000 less accumulated depreciation of $12,000)	–0–						
Gain on sale	$2,000						
Sales price of rack	$2,000						
Income tax on gain @ 40%	800						
After-tax proceeds of sale	$1,200	(I) 0.751	901				1,200
Total present value of future cash flows			$12,263				
Investment required in rack			(12,000)	($12,000)*			
Net positive present value			$ 263				

*Outflow

raises taxable income by $5,000, which leads to a $2,000 ($5,000 × 40%) increase in taxes. Thus, the annual after-tax cash flow is $3,000—the $5,000 savings less the $2,000 tax increase. The $3,000 saved each year for three years can be treated as an annuity. Its present value factor of 2.487 is taken from Table II on the line for three periods and the column for 10% (the minimum return desired). The analysis shows that, with desired return at 10% and income taxes at 40%, saving $5,000 annually for the next three years has a present value of $7,461.

Annual depreciation tax shield: The depreciation deduction on the tax return shields an equal amount of income from taxes. The avoided taxes are equal to the depreciation deduction multiplied by the applicable tax rate. In our illustration, the annual tax savings from the depreciation tax shield are as follows:

Year	Depreciation		Tax Rate		Tax Savings
1	$2,400	×	40%	=	$ 960
2	4,800	×	40%	=	1,920
3	4,800	×	40%	=	1,920

The tax savings represent tax payments that are avoided. In analyzing cash flows, tax savings are treated as having an effect similar to that of cash inflows. Present value factors from Table I are used to determine that the present values of these tax savings are $873, $1,586, and $1,442, respectively, for each of the three years.

Liquidation proceeds: The amount realized when an asset is liquidated contributes to the relative attractiveness of an investment in capital equipment. Liquidation proceeds on long-lived assets are sometimes disregarded because their occurrence is so far in the future that the amounts are difficult to predict, and their present values tend to be small. When useful lives are short, however, liquidation proceeds may be a deciding factor in the analysis. In our illustration, the shipping rack costing $12,000 is sold after three years for $2,000. For tax purposes, salvage value may be ignored in computing depreciation, so the machine is fully depreciated over the three years to a zero book value. The rack's sale for $2,000, then, creates a $2,000 gain on the tax return ($2,000 sales price − $0 tax book value). The $2,000 gain increases income taxes by $800, which is deducted from the sales price of $2,000 to produce a net after-tax cash flow of $1,200. Because the $1,200 is a single sum received at the end of Year 3, its present value of $901 is derived by multiplying the $1,200 by the 0.751 factor from Table I (three periods hence at 10%).

If an asset is sold before the end of its tax depreciation period, a loss may be generated for tax purposes. The loss operates as a tax shield because it shields an equal amount of income from taxes. To illustrate the calculation of cash flows related to a loss sale, assume that the machine was sold after two years for $3,200. The total after-tax cash flow is computed as follows:

Tax book value of machine ($12,000 original cost − $7,200 accumulated depreciation)	$4,800
Less sales price of machine	3,200
Loss on sale	$1,600
Income tax rate	× 0.40
Income tax savings from loss	$ 640
Plus sales price of machine	3,200
Total after-tax cash flow from sale	$3,840

Required investment: Proper consideration of the required investment involves neither an income tax nor a present value calculation. The $12,000 investment itself is not tax deductible; the related depreciation deductions are tax deductible, and are, of course, incorporated into our analysis. Since the investment expenditure is immediate, no discounting for present value is required. Thus, $12,000 represents the after-tax present value of the required investment outflow.

DECISION RULE   With its annual savings of cash expense, tax savings from the depreciation tax shield and liquidation proceeds, the $12,000 investment results in future cash flows with a total present value of $12,263 and therefore a net present value of $263. This return on the capital invested, adjusted for the time value of money, exceeds the 10% return rate sought, and the investment is acceptable.

Another interpretation of our analysis is that as much as $12,263 could be paid for the machine and still attain the desired 10% rate of return. Paying more than $12,263 for the machine results in a return of less than 10%.

Excess Present Value Index

Alternative capital expenditure proposals may be compared in terms of their **excess present value index**, defined as

$$\text{Excess Present Value Index} = \frac{\text{Total Present Value of Future Cash Flows}}{\text{Initial Investment}}$$

For the investment presented in Exhibit 28-4, the excess present value index would be

$$\frac{\$12,263}{\$12,000} = 1.022$$

The higher the ratio of return on investment, the more attractive the proposal. Although the excess present value index may be a convenient measure for ranking various proposals, it does not reflect the amount of the investment. Two proposals, requiring initial cash investments of $5,000 and $5,000,000, respectively, could have identical excess present value indexes but could hardly be considered equal investment opportunities.

CASH PAYBACK ANALYSIS

OBJECTIVE ⑥ PRESENT *the cash payback and average rate of return methods of capital expenditure analysis.*

The **cash payback method** is a form of capital expenditure analysis that evaluates investment proposals in terms of the cash payback period. The **cash payback period** is *the time in years that it takes net future after-tax cash inflows to equal the original investment.*

Assume that a firm is considering purchasing either machine A or machine B, for which the following data are given:

Machine	Investment Required	Estimated Annual Net After-tax Cash Inflows	Useful Life
A	$10,000	$2,500	8 years
B	15,000	5,000	3 years

If annual net cash inflows are *equal*, the cash payback period is computed as

$$\frac{\text{Original Investment}}{\text{Annual Net Cash Inflows}} = \text{Cash Payback in Years}$$

Thus, for the two machines, we obtain

$$\text{Machine A:} \quad \frac{\$10,000}{\$2,500} = \text{4-year cash payback}$$

$$\text{Machine B:} \quad \frac{\$15,000}{\$5,000} = \text{3-year cash payback}$$

This analysis shows that machine A will pay back its required investment in four years, and machine B will take only three years. Because the decision rule in cash payback analysis states that *the shorter the payback period the better,* machine B would be considered the better investment.

If annual net cash inflows are *not equal,* the cash payback period is computed by summing the annual cash inflows until the cumulative amount equals the initial investment. For example, assume that a $14,000 investment in machine C is also being considered. The investment is expected to generate annual net after-tax cash inflows for six years, as follows:

Year	Estimated Annual Net After-tax Cash Inflows	Cumulative Cash Payback	
1	$3,000	$ 3,000	
2	4,000	7,000	
3	5,500	12,500	
4	6,000	14,000	(requires $\frac{1}{4}$ of $6,000
5	4,000		to reach $14,000)
6	2,500		

As shown in the cumulative cash payback column, the original investment in machine C will be recovered in cash one-fourth of the way through Year 4. The cash payback period, then, is $3\frac{1}{4}$ years.

Concern for the payback of investments is quite natural because the shorter a project's payback period, the more quickly the funds invested in that project are recovered and available for other investments. In high-risk investments, the payback period indicates how soon a firm is "bailed out" of an investment should it prove unattractive.

The cash payback method is considered less sophisticated than net present value analysis. A primary limitation to cash payback analysis is that the *relative profitability of various investments is not specifically considered*. Note, for example, that in the foregoing illustration, machine B has the better (shorter) cash payback period. However, its useful life, which is ignored in cash payback analysis, indicates that machine B will stop generating cash inflows just when payback is completed. Consequently, there will be no opportunity to generate profit. In contrast, although machines A and C have longer payback periods, they will generate future cash inflows for several years beyond payback and therefore promise to be profitable.

Regardless of its failure to consider profitability, cash payback analysis is widely used in industry, probably because of its relative simplicity. It can be useful in conjunction with other analyses or as a preliminary screening device for investment projects under consideration.

AVERAGE RATE OF RETURN ANALYSIS

Another approach to capital outlay analysis, the **average rate of return method,** relies heavily on accounting determinations of net income. This measure is calculated as follows:

$$\text{Average Rate of Return} = \frac{\text{Average Annual Net Income from Investment}}{\text{Average Investment}}$$

Note that the focus here is not on after-tax cash flows but on traditional accounting net income (with depreciation deducted).

Assume that machine D requires an initial investment of $48,000, provides $12,000 annual cash inflows from operations, and has a useful life of 12 years. Assuming no salvage value, annual straight-line depreciation on machine D would be ($48,000/12), or $4,000. With an income tax rate of 40%, the average annual net income from the investment would be $4,800, computed as follows:

Cash inflow from operations	$12,000
Depreciation expense	4,000
Pretax income from investment	$ 8,000
Income tax expense	3,200
Net income from investment	$ 4,800

If the annual net incomes from investment are unequal, we would compute the average annual net income from investment by (1) summing the annual net incomes and (2) dividing by the number of such incomes.

CAPITAL INVESTMENT A PRIORITY FOR MOST FIRMS

What are U.S. industrial companies doing to keep up with their foreign rivals? According to the Grant Thornton Survey of American Manufacturers, more than a third of all mid-sized manufacturers plan to increase capital spending in 1991, while another 42% intend to invest at least as much in plant and equipment in 1991 as they did in 1990. Only one manufacturer in five plans to spend less on facilities and equipment in 1991.... ■ When asked why they plan for either consistent or higher levels of capital expenditures, the most common reason

manufacturers cite is to "increase productivity."...

"Increasing capacity" is the second most common reason manufacturers give for maintaining or raising capital investment levels. New-product development and general growth or expansion are also motivating factors.

Among manufacturers who plan to spend less on capital investment, more than a third say they have invested enough in facilities or equipment or have just made capital investments. One-fifth cite poor earnings or insufficient funds....

AUTOMATION A FAVORITE GOAL

Approximately one-third of all manufacturers' capital expenditures will go toward automation, with one company in five allocating more than half of its planned investment in automation. At the same time, one-fifth of all

companies surveyed say they will spend nothing on automation....

MOST PREFER TO PAY WITH CASH

Nearly three-fourths of all manufacturers prefer to purchase rather than lease production equipment.

Of those who favor purchasing over leasing, nearly three-quarters would prefer to pay cash, because they either have the funds, don't like to borrow or owe, or believe they can obtain a better price by paying cash. Those who favor leasing cite cash flow considerations as their primary reason.

Only one company in five prefers to finance the purchase of new equipment. More than three-fourths of those who favor borrowing would go to a commercial bank for a term loan.

Fewer than one in five say they would seek a term loan from an asset-based lender....

PAYBACK, ROI MOST COMMON METHODS

Nearly all manufacturers use at least one formal cost-justification model to evaluate capital expenditures, and more than a fifth use two or more.

Almost half use the familiar payback method, which calculates the time it takes to "earn back" their capital outlay, either through new efficiencies or direct revenue. Two in five use return on investment (ROI). Less common: internal rate of return and net present value, which only one-fifth of all firms employ.

While it is encouraging that most manufacturers employ at least one method to evaluate proposed capital expenditures, it is important to recognize that all of these traditional analytical methods have their limitations, particularly in their ability (or inability) to accurately reflect cost savings resulting from the reduction of time that automation can generate....

SOURCE: *Grant Thornton Survey of American Manufacturers 1990*, "Capital Investment." Grant Thornton—Accountants and Management Consultants, 1990, pp. 14–19. Reprinted with permission from The Grant Thornton Survey of American Manufacturers, 1990.

We may calculate average investment simply by adding the beginning and ending investments and dividing by 2. The ending investment is the expected salvage value. In our illustration, machine D has no salvage value, so the ending investment is zero. Average investment is therefore ($48,000 + $0)/2 = $24,000.

The average rate of return on machine D is

$$\frac{\$4,800}{\$24,000} = 20\%$$

The decision rule for average rate of return analyses states that *the higher the return, the more attractive the investment.*

As an approach to capital expenditure analysis, the average rate of return method is often defended as being most easily understood by management personnel who are accustomed to thinking in accounting terms and concepts. It has two major limitations, however. First, the calculations rely heavily on accounting computations of net income and depreciation, and are thus subject to arbitrary choices, such as the selection of a depreciation method. Second, average rate of return calculations do not consider the time value of money. Future cash flows are treated the same as current cash flows. Our discussion of net present value analysis amply illustrates the often substantial differences between future values and related present values discounted by even moderate interest rates.

As an example of how deceptive the average annual income figures used in average rate of return computations can be, consider three investment proposals, each of which requires a $40,000 initial investment (with a zero salvage value) and promises the annual cash inflows shown in Exhibit 28-5. Note that cash flows are concentrated in Year 1 in proposal A, are uniform in proposal B, and are concentrated in Year 5 in proposal C. Because average rate of return calculations fail to consider the timing of cash flows from operations, these three proposals would have identical 10% average rates of return and therefore would be considered equally attractive. Such an implication is hardly defensible in view of the substantial differences in the relative net present values of the operating cash flows. In our illustration, the difference between the present values of A and C is $12,960, an amount equal to 41% of the present value of C.

EXHIBIT 28−5	PRESENT VALUE COMPARISON OF EQUAL ANNUAL AVERAGE INCOMES		

| | Proposals | | |
	A	B	C
Annual net cash inflows			
Year 1	$46,000	$10,000	$ 1,000
2	1,000	10,000	1,000
3	1,000	10,000	1,000
4	1,000	10,000	1,000
5	1,000	10,000	46,000
Aggregate net cash inflows	$50,000	$50,000	$50,000
Average annual net cash inflows	$10,000	$10,000	$10,000
Less depreciation ($40,000/5)	8,000	8,000	8,000
Average annual net income	$ 2,000	$ 2,000	$ 2,000
Average rate of return on investment $2,000/[($40,000 + $0)/2]	10%	10%	10%
Present value of net cash inflows at 10%:			
(A) One year hence, $45,000 × 0.909	$40,905		
5-year annuity of $1,000 × 3.791	3,791		
	$44,696		
(B) 5-year annuity of $10,000 × 3.791		$37,910	
(C) 5-year annuity of $1,000 × 3.791			$ 3,791
5 years hence, $45,000 × 0.621			27,945
			$31,736

CAPITAL BUDGETING: A COMPLEX SUBJECT

Because it incorporates aspects of such fields as economics, finance, business management, and accounting, the subject of capital budgeting is too complex to treat comprehensively in an introductory accounting book. In this chapter, we have simply provided some insight into problem-solving techniques in capital budgeting by stating decision rules in their simplest form, showing the relevance of present value concepts and after-tax cash flows, and creating an awareness of the potentials and limitations of several widely used approaches to capital expenditure analysis. The illustrations have highlighted key relationships. The rudiments presented here should serve as a basis for further study in finance and economics courses.

KEY POINTS FOR CHAPTER OBJECTIVES

❶ INTRODUCE and ILLUSTRATE the elements of capital budgeting (pp. 1062–1063).
- Capital budgeting is the planning of long-lived asset investments. Capital expenditure analysis basically examines how well prospective future returns justify related current investments.

❷ DISCUSS required rates of return and the time value of money (pp. 1063–1065).
- Cost of capital is a measure of the firm's cost for investment capital; it usually represents the minimum acceptable return for investment opportunities.
- The time value of money concept recognizes that the further into the future cash flows occur, the less current economic worth they have.

❸ ILLUSTRATE the use of present value tables (pp. 1065–1067).
- Present value tables enable us conveniently to convert future cash flows to their present values at appropriate interest rates.
- The present value tables used most frequently in capital budgeting are those for future single sum flows and end-of-period annuity flows.

❹ EXPLAIN and ILLUSTRATE the determination of after-tax cash flows (pp. 1067–1070).
- After-tax cash flows probably represent the most relevant measure of the prospective returns of proposed investments.
- We convert cash flows from revenues and expenses into after-tax amounts by multiplying them by (1 − income tax rate). We convert depreciation deductions into their after-tax cash flow effect by multiplying the deduction by the applicable income tax rate.

❺ DESCRIBE the net present value method of capital expenditure analysis (pp. 1070–1073).
- Net present value analysis compares the present value of net future cash flow returns with the investment. Projects having zero or positive net present value are acceptable.
- Alternative investment proposals may be compared in terms of their excess present value index; the higher the index, the more attractive the proposal.

❻ PRESENT the cash payback and average rate of return methods of capital expenditure analysis (pp. 1073–1077).
- Cash payback analysis measures the time in years necessary for the net future after-tax cash flows to equal the original investment. In this type of analysis, the shorter the payback period, the more attractive the investment.
- Average rate of return analysis compares the annual average net income with the average investment. The higher this ratio, the more attractive the investment.
- Cash payback analysis fails to consider the relative profitability of alternative projects. Average rate of return analysis fails to consider the time value of money.

SELF-TEST QUESTIONS FOR REVIEW

(Answers follow the Solution to Demonstration Problem.)

1. A firm's cost of acquiring the funds for capital investment projects is known as the
   - **a.** Payback period.
   - **b.** Rate of return.
   - **c.** Cost of capital.
   - **d.** Time value of money.

2. All other things remaining the same, when the interest rate used to discount future values increases, the present value amount will
   a. Decrease.
   b. Increase in proportion to the interest rate increase.
   c. Remain the same.
   d. Increase but not in proportion to the interest rate increase.

3. Although depreciation is a noncash expense, it does have an indirect effect on cash flows because it shelters an equal amount of income from income taxes. This feature is known as a
   a. Buffer margin.   c. Depreciation flow.
   b. Cash payback.   d. Tax shield.

4. Blaine Company is considering four investment proposals, each requiring the same amount of initial cash investment. The excess present value index for each proposal is listed below. Using the index as a selection criterion, identify the index of the most attractive proposal.
   a. 90   b. 100   c. 110   d. 115

5. The primary limitation of the cash payback method is that it
   a. Uses before-tax cash flows.
   b. Identifies the length of time it will take to recover the investment outlay in cash.
   c. Ignores the profitability of one investment project as compared to another.
   d. Involves a more sophisticated analysis than the net present value method.

DEMONSTRATION PROBLEM FOR REVIEW

Carolina Company is evaluating a possible $150,000 investment in equipment that would increase cash flows from operations for four years. The equipment will have no salvage value. The income tax rate is 30%. Carolina uses a 15% cutoff rate when using net present value analysis. Other information regarding the proposal is as follows:

	Year 1	Year 2	Year 3	Year 4
Cash inflow from operations (pretax)	$60,000	$87,000	$42,000	$40,000
Depreciation on tax return	50,000	67,000	22,000	11,000
Depreciation in financial statements	37,500	37,500	37,500	37,500
Net income from investment	15,750	34,650	3,150	1,750

REQUIRED

a. What are the annual net after-tax cash inflows from this proposal?
b. Compute the net present value and indicate whether it is positive or negative (round amounts to nearest dollar).
c. Compute the cash payback period.
d. Compute the average rate of return.

SOLUTION TO DEMONSTRATION PROBLEM

a. We may compute the individual after-tax cash effects by multiplying (1) the cash inflow from operations by 70% (that is, 1 − income tax rate) and (2) the tax return depreciation by 30% (that is, the income tax rate). Combining the individual after-tax cash effects gives the annual net after-tax cash inflows.

Year 1:	$60,000 × 70%	$42,000	Year 3:	$42,000 × 70%	$29,400
	50,000 × 30%	15,000		22,000 × 30%	6,600
	After-tax cash flow	$57,000		After-tax cash flow	$36,000
Year 2:	$87,000 × 70%	$60,900	Year 4:	$40,000 × 70%	$28,000
	67,000 × 30%	20,100		11,000 × 30%	3,300
	After-tax cash flow	$81,000		After-tax cash flow	$31,300

Alternatively, we may compute the net after-tax cash inflows by subtracting the cash income tax payments from the cash inflows from operations. The annual cash income tax payments are 30% of the cash inflow from operations less the tax return depreciation.

	Year 1	Year 2	Year 3	Year 4
Cash inflow from operations	$60,000	$87,000	$42,000	$40,000
Cash payment for income taxes	3,000	6,000	6,000	8,700
After-tax cash flows	$57,000	$81,000	$36,000	$31,300

b.

Year	Annual Net After-tax Cash Inflows		Table I Present Value Factors		Present Value
1	$57,000	×	0.870	=	$ 49,590
2	81,000	×	0.756	=	61,236
3	36,000	×	0.658	=	23,688
4	31,300	×	0.572	=	17,904

Total present value	$152,418
Investment required in equipment	150,000
Net positive present value	$ 2,418

c. The cash payback period is $2\frac{1}{3}$ years, computed as follows:

Year	Annual Net After-tax Cash Inflows	Cumulative Cash Payback	
1	$57,000	$ 57,000	
2	81,000	138,000	
3	36,000	150,000	(requires $\frac{1}{3}$ of $36,000 to
4	31,300		reach $150,000)

d. Annual net income from investment:

Year 1	$15,750
Year 2	34,650
Year 3	3,150
Year 4	1,750
Total	$55,300

Average annual net income from investment: $55,300/4 = $13,825.

Average investment: ($150,000 + $0)/2 = $75,000.

Average rate of return: $13,825/$75,000 = 18.4%.

ANSWERS TO SELF-TEST QUESTIONS

1. c, p. 1063   **2.** a, p. 1066   **3.** d, p. 1069   **4.** d, p. 1073   **5.** c, p. 1074

GLOSSARY OF KEY TERMS USED IN THIS CHAPTER

average rate of return method   A method of capital outlay analysis that focuses on the ratio of expected average annual net income to the related average investment (p. 1074).

buffer margin   The number of percentage points added to a firm's cost of capital to derive a cutoff rate for evaluating and selecting capital investment proposals (p. 1064).

capital budgeting   Planning long-term investments in property, plant, and equipment (p. 1062).

cash payback method   A form of capital expenditure analysis that evaluates investment proposals in terms of the cash payback period (p. 1073).

cash payback period   The time in years that it takes net future cash inflows to equal the original investment amount; used in evaluating investment proposals by the payback method (p. 1073).

cost of capital   Expressed as a percentage, the cost to the firm to acquire investment capital from sources such as equity securities, debt, and internally generated funds (p. 1063).

cutoff rate   The minimum acceptable rate of return for an investment proposal; the cutoff rate is equal to the cost of capital plus the buffer margin. Also known as the *hurdle rate* (p. 1064).

discount factors   Multipliers found in present value tables formulated to show the present value of $1 (or a $1 annuity) discounted at various interest rates and for various periods of time. Also known as *present value factors* (p. 1065).

excess present value index   Ratio of the total present value of net future cash flows to the related cash investment (p. 1073).

hurdle rate The minimum acceptable rate of return for an investment proposal; the hurdle rate is equal to the cost of capital plus the buffer margin. Also known as the *cutoff rate* (p. 1064).

net present value method A method of capital outlay analysis that compares a required investment amount with the present value of resulting net future cash flows discounted at the minimum desired rate of return (p. 1070).

present value factors Multipliers found in present value tables formulated to show the present value of $1 (or a $1 annuity) discounted at various interest rates and for various periods of time. Also known as *discount factors* (p. 1065).

time value of money An expression stating the ability of money to earn interest, the total potential for which is a function of the principal amount, the applicable interest rate, and the time period involved (p. 1064).

weighted average cost of capital Expressed as a percentage, the cost to the firm to acquire investment capital, weighted to reflect the specific cost rates associated with and the proportions used from specific sources such as equity securities, debt, and internally generated funds (p. 1063).

QUESTIONS

28-1 What is capital budgeting?

28-2 List three reasons why capital budgeting decisions are often important.

28-3 What are the three stages typical of most investments in plant and equipment?

28-4 Briefly describe the concept of *weighted average cost of capital*.

28-5 In what sense does the cost of capital limit a firm's investment considerations?

28-6 A company plans to accumulate 75% of its needed investment capital by issuing bonds having a capital cost percentage of 12%; the balance will be raised by issuing stock having a capital cost percentage of 16%. What would be the weighted average cost of capital for the total amount of capital?

28-7 Briefly describe the concept of the *time value of money*.

28-8 In which interest rate columns and periods hence lines in a table showing the present values of $1 received in the future would you expect the smallest factors? Why?

28-9 In which interest rate columns and periods hence lines in a table showing the present values of a $1 annuity would you expect the largest factors? Why?

28-10 What is the relationship between a table showing the present values of $1 and a table showing the present values of a $1 annuity, when both tables use the same interest rates and time periods?

28-11 You have the right to receive $30,000 at the end of each of the next four years, and money is worth 8%. Using Table II, compute the present value involved. Illustrate how Table I can be used to confirm your answer.

28-12 A rich uncle allows you to stipulate which of two ways you receive your inheritance: (a) $850,000 one year after his death or (b) $250,000 on his death and $200,000 each year at the end of the first, second, and third years following his death. If money is worth 10%, what is the relative advantage of the more attractive alternative?

28-13 You can settle a debt with either a single payment now of $30,000 or with payments of $8,000 at the end of each of the next five years. If money is worth 10%, what is the relative advantage of the most attractive alternative? If money is worth 12%, would your answer change? Why?

28-14 Explain how to convert before-tax cash operating expenses and depreciation deductions into after-tax amounts.

28-15 What is meant by the term *depreciation tax shield*?

28-16 What amounts are compared in net present value analysis? State the related decision rule.

28-17 What is an excess present value index?

28-18 Define *cash payback period*, state the related decision rule, and specify an important limitation of this analysis.

28-19 Define *average rate of return*, state the related decision rule, and specify an important limitation of this analysis.

EXERCISES

WEIGHTED AVERAGE COST OF CAPITAL
— OBJ. 2 —

28-20 Gardner, Inc., plans to finance its expansion by raising the needed investment capital from the following sources in the indicated proportions and respective capital cost rates:

Source	Proportion	Capital Cost Rate
Bonds	40%	13%
Preferred stock	20	9
Common stock	30	12
Retained earnings	10	9
	100%	

Calculate the weighted average cost of capital.

PRESENT VALUE COMPUTATIONS
— OBJ. 3 —

28-21 **a.** Assuming that money is worth 10%, compute the present value of
1. $7,000 received 15 years from today.
2. The right to inherit $1,000,000 14 years from now.
3. The right to receive $1,000 at the end of each of the next six years.
4. The obligation to pay $3,000 at the end of each of the next 10 years.
5. The right to receive $5,000 at the end of the 7th, 8th, 9th, and 10th years from today.
b. Confirm your answer to part (a)(5) by using Table II and subtracting the present value of a 6-year annuity from a 10-year annuity (isolating the 4 relevant years).

AFTER-TAX CASH FLOWS
— OBJ. 4 —

28-22 For each of the following independent situations, compute the net after-tax cash flow amount by subtracting cash outlays for operating expenses and income taxes from cash revenue. The cash outlay for income taxes is determined by applying the income tax rate to the cash revenue received less the cash and noncash (depreciation) expenses.

	A	B	C
Cash revenue received	$90,000	$450,000	$220,000
Cash operating expenses paid	54,000	315,000	145,000
Depreciation on tax return	12,000	30,000	20,000
Income tax rate	40%	30%	20%

AFTER-TAX CASH FLOWS
— OBJ. 4 —

28-23 Using the data in Exercise 28-22, (a) calculate—as shown in column **C** of Exhibit 28-2—the individual after-tax cash flow effect of each relevant item in each independent situation, and (b) sum the individual after-tax cash flows in each situation to determine the overall net after-tax cash flow.

DEPRECIATION TAX SHIELDS
— OBJ. 4 —

28-24 Lincoln Company has purchased equipment for $200,000. After it is fully depreciated, the equipment will have no salvage value. Lincoln may select either of the following depreciation schedules for tax purposes:

Year	Option 1 Depreciation	Option 2 Depreciation
1	$40,000	$20,000
2	64,000	40,000
3	38,400	40,000
4	23,040	40,000
5	23,040	40,000
6	11,520	20,000

 Assuming a 40% tax rate and a 12% desired annual return, compute the total present value of the tax savings provided by these alternative depreciation tax shields. Which depreciation schedule would be more attractive to Lincoln?

NET PRESENT VALUE ANALYSIS
— OBJ. 5 —

28-25 Anderson Company must evaluate two capital expenditure proposals. Anderson's cut-off rate is 15%. Data for the two proposals follow.

	Proposal X	Proposal Y
Required investment	$120,000	$120,000
Annual after-tax cash inflows	24,000	
After-tax cash inflows at the end of years 3, 6, 9, and 12		72,000
Life of project	12 years	12 years

Using net present value analysis, which proposal is the more attractive? If Anderson has sufficient funds available, should both proposals be accepted?

CASH PAYBACK
— OBJ. 6 —

28-26 Refer to the data in Exercise 28-25. What is the cash payback period for proposal X? for proposal Y?

AVERAGE RATE OF RETURN
— OBJ. 6 —

28-27 Lakeland Company is considering the purchase of equipment for $150,000. The equipment will expand the company's production and increase revenue by $40,000 per year. Annual cash operating expenses will increase by $10,000. The equipment's useful life is 10 years with no salvage value. Lakeland uses straight-line depreciation. The income tax rate is 35%. What is the average rate of return on the investment?

PROBLEMS

**AFTER-TAX CASH FLOWS
AND PRESENT VALUE
FACTORS
— OBJ. 4, 5 —**

28-28 Below is a list of aspects of various capital expenditure proposals that the capital budgeting team of Anchor, Inc., has incorporated into its net present value analyses during the past year. Unless otherwise noted, the items listed are unrelated to each other. All situations assume a 40% income tax rate and a 15% minimum desired rate of return.

1. Pretax savings of $4,000 in cash expenses will occur in each of the next three years.
2. A machine is purchased now for $37,000 cash.
3. A long-haul tractor costing $27,000 will be depreciated $9,000, $12,000, $4,050, and $1,950, respectively, on the tax return over four years.
4. Equipment costing $200,000 will be depreciated over five years on the tax return in the following amounts: $25,000; $50,000; $50,000; $50,000; and $25,000.
5. Pretax savings of $8,800 in cash expenses will occur in each of the next six years.
6. Pretax savings of $7,000 in cash expenses will occur in the first, third, and fifth years from now.
7. The tractor described in aspect 3 will be sold after four years for $5,000 cash.
8. The equipment described in aspect 4 will be sold after four years for $20,000 cash.

REQUIRED

Set up an answer form with the four column headings as shown below. Answer each investment aspect separately. Prepare your calculations on a separate paper and key them to each item. The answer to investment aspect 1 is presented as an example.

Investment Aspect	A After-tax Cash Flow Effect(s) Inflows (Outflows)	B Year(s) of Cash Flow	C Applicable Present Value Multiple
1	$2,400	1, 2, 3	(II) 2.283

Calculations:

1. Pretax cash savings	$4,000	
Less income tax at 40%	1,600	
After-tax cash inflow	$2,400	

a. Calculate and record in column A the related after-tax cash flow effect(s). Place parentheses around outflows.
b. Indicate in column B the timing of each cash flow shown in column A. Use 0 to indicate immediately and 1, 2, 3, 4, and so on for each year involved.
c. When relevant, record in column C the present value multiple from Table I or II that you would apply to the cash flow amount shown in column A.

**NET PRESENT VALUE
ANALYSIS
— OBJ. 4, 5 —**

28-29 Champion Company is considering a contract that would require an expansion of its food processing capabilities. The contract covers five years. To provide the required products, Champion would have to purchase additional equipment for $64,000. Champion estimates the contract will provide annual net cash inflows (before taxes) of $26,000. For tax purposes, the equipment will be depreciated as follows:

Year 1	$ 8,000
Year 2	16,000
Year 3	16,000
Year 4	16,000
Year 5	8,000

Although salvage value is ignored in the tax depreciation calculations, Champion estimates the equipment will be sold for $8,000 after five years.

REQUIRED

Assuming a 35% income tax rate and a 15% cutoff rate, compute the net present value of this contract proposal. Using net present value analysis, should Champion accept the contract? (Round amounts to the nearest dollar.)

NET PRESENT VALUE, CASH PAYBACK, AND AVERAGE RATE OF RETURN METHODS — OBJ. 4, 5, 6 —

28-30 Western Company is evaluating a possible $42,000 investment in special tools that would increase cash flows from operations for four years. The tools will have no salvage value. The income tax rate is 40%. Western uses a 12% cutoff rate when using present value analysis. Other information regarding the proposal is as follows:

	Year 1	Year 2	Year 3	Year 4
Cash inflow from operations (pretax)	$15,000	$20,000	$16,500	$12,000
Depreciation on tax return	14,000	18,500	6,500	3,000
Depreciation in financial statements	10,500	10,500	10,500	10,500
Net income from investment	2,700	5,700	3,600	900

REQUIRED

a. What are the annual net after-tax cash inflows from this proposal?
b. Compute the net present value and indicate whether it is positive or negative (round amounts to nearest dollar).
c. Compute the excess present value index.
d. Compute the cash payback period.
e. Compute the average rate of return.

EXCESS PRESENT VALUE INDEX AND AVERAGE RATE OF RETURN — OBJ. 5, 6 —

28-31 Highpoint Company is evaluating five different capital expenditure proposals. The company's cutoff rate for net present value analyses is 12%. A 10% salvage value is expected from each of the investments. Information on the five proposals is as follows:

Proposal	Required Investment	Present Value at 12% of After-tax Cash Flows	Average Annual Net Income from Investment
A	$270,000	$310,030	$37,400
B	200,000	236,780	26,000
C	160,000	173,040	19,200
D	180,000	216,300	27,600
E	128,000	136,990	14,960

REQUIRED

a. Compute the excess present value index for each of the five proposals.
b. Compute the average rate of return for each of the five proposals.
c. Assume that Highpoint will commit no more than $500,000 to new capital expenditure proposals. Using the excess present value index, which proposals would be accepted? Using the average rate of return, which proposals would be accepted?

CASH PAYBACK, AVERAGE RATE OF RETURN, AND NET PRESENT VALUE METHODS — OBJ. 5, 6 —

28-32 Landover Amusement Park is considering the construction of a new facility to house a curved, multistory movie screen. The facility will cost $400,000 and be useful for 10 years, with no salvage value. The facility will be depreciated on a straight-line basis over 10 years on both the books and the tax return. The following annual results are expected if the facility is constructed:

Increase in annual cash revenue		$200,000
Increase in expenses:		
Cash operating expenses	$80,000	
Depreciation	40,000	120,000
Pretax income		$ 80,000
Income tax expense (40%)		32,000
Net income		$ 48,000

Landover uses a 15% cutoff rate when analyzing capital expenditure proposals using net present value.

REQUIRED

a. What are the annual net cash flows (net inflows) from this project?
b. Compute the cash payback period.

c. Compute the average rate of return.

d. Compute the net present value and indicate whether it is positive or negative.

e. Assume that Landover decides to use a 20% cutoff rate when using net present value analysis. Compute the net present value using a 20% cutoff rate and indicate whether it is positive or negative.

WEIGHTED AVERAGE COST OF CAPITAL AND NET PRESENT VALUE ANALYSIS — OBJ. 2, 5 —

28-33 Tate Company is considering a proposal to acquire new equipment for its manufacturing division. The equipment will cost $192,000, be useful for four years, and have a $12,000 salvage value. Tate expects annual savings in cash operating expenses (before taxes) of $68,000. For tax purposes, the annual depreciation deduction will be $64,000, $86,000, $28,000, and $14,000, respectively, for the four years (the salvage value is ignored on the tax return). The income tax rate is 40%.

Tate establishes a cutoff rate for a net present value analysis at the company's weighted average cost of capital plus 1 percentage point. Tate's capital is provided in the following proportions: debt, 60%; common stock, 20%; and retained earnings, 20%. The cost rates for these capital sources are debt, 10%; common stock, 12%; and retained earnings, 13%.

REQUIRED

a. Compute Tate's (1) weighted average cost of capital and (2) cutoff rate.

b. Using Tate's cutoff rate, compute the net present value of this capital expenditure proposal. Under net present value analysis, should Tate accept the proposal? (Round amounts to the nearest dollar.)

ALTERNATE EXERCISES

WEIGHTED AVERAGE COST OF CAPITAL — OBJ. 2 —

28-20A Austin, Inc., plans to finance its expansion by raising the needed investment capital from the following sources in the indicated proportions and respective capital cost rates:

Source	Proportion	Capital Cost Rate
Bonds	45%	10%
Preferred stock	10	8
Common stock	25	14
Retained earnings	20	12
	100%	

Calculate the weighted average cost of capital.

PRESENT VALUE COMPUTATIONS — OBJ. 3 —

28-21A **a.** Assuming that money is worth 10%, compute the present value of

1. $6,000 received 15 years from today.
2. The right to inherit $2,000,000 14 years from now.
3. The right to receive $2,000 at the end of each of the next six years.
4. The obligation to pay $1,000 at the end of each of the next 10 years.
5. The right to receive $10,000 at the end of the 7th, 8th, 9th, and 10th years from today.

b. Confirm your answer to requirement (a)(5) by using Table II and subtracting the present value of a 6-year annuity from a 10-year annuity (isolating the 4 relevant years).

AFTER-TAX CASH FLOWS — OBJ. 4 —

28-22A For each of the following independent situations, compute the net after-tax cash flow amount by subtracting cash outlays for operating expenses and income taxes from cash revenue. The cash outlay for income taxes is determined by applying the income tax rate to the cash revenue received less the cash and noncash (depreciation) expenses.

	A	B	C
Cash revenue received	$80,000	$400,000	$200,000
Cash operating expenses paid	45,000	260,000	120,000
Depreciation on tax return	10,000	25,000	15,000
Income tax rate	30%	40%	20%

AFTER-TAX CASH FLOWS
— OBJ. 4 —

28-23A Using the data in Exercise 28-22A, (a) calculate—as shown in column C of Exhibit 28-2—the individual after-tax cash flow effect of each relevant item in each independent situation, and (b) sum the individual after-tax cash flows in each situation to determine the overall net after-tax cash flow.

DEPRECIATION TAX
SHIELDS
— OBJ. 4 —

28-24A Mendota Company has purchased equipment for $100,000. After it is fully depreciated, the equipment will have no salvage value. Mendota may select either of the following depreciation schedules for tax purposes:

Year	Option 1 Depreciation	Option 2 Depreciation
1	$20,000	$10,000
2	32,000	20,000
3	19,200	20,000
4	11,520	20,000
5	11,520	20,000
6	5,760	10,000

Assuming a 40% tax rate and a 12% desired annual return, compute the total present value of the tax savings provided by these alternative depreciation tax shields. Which depreciation schedule would be more attractive to Mendota?

NET PRESENT VALUE
ANALYSIS
— OBJ. 5 —

28-25A Hermson Company must evaluate two capital expenditure proposals. Hermson's cutoff rate is 20%. Data for the two proposals follow.

	Proposal X	Proposal Y
Required investment	$140,000	$140,000
Annual after-tax cash inflows	33,000	
After-tax cash inflows at the end of years 3, 6, 9, and 12		99,000
Life of project	12 years	12 years

Using net present value analysis, which proposal do you find to be the more attractive? If Hermson has sufficient funds available, should both proposals be accepted?

CASH PAYBACK
— OBJ. 6 —

28-26A Refer to the data in Exercise 28-25A. What is the cash payback period for proposal X? for proposal Y?

AVERAGE RATE OF RETURN
— OBJ. 6 —

28-27A Clancy Company is considering the purchase of equipment for $100,000. The equipment will expand the company's production and increase revenue by $30,000 per year. Annual cash operating expenses will increase by $8,000. The equipment's useful life is 10 years with no salvage value. Clancy uses straight-line depreciation. The income tax rate is 35%. What is the average rate of return on the investment?

ALTERNATE PROBLEMS

AFTER-TAX CASH FLOWS
AND PRESENT VALUE
FACTORS
— OBJ. 4, 5 —

28-28A Below is a list of aspects of various capital expenditure proposals that the capital budgeting team of Modern Systems, Inc., has incorporated into its net present value analyses during the past year. Unless otherwise noted, the items listed are unrelated to each other. All situations assume a 30% income tax rate and a 20% minimum desired rate of return.

1. Pretax savings of $5,000 in cash expenses will occur in each of the next three years.
2. A machine is purchased now for $82,000.
3. Special tools costing $45,000 will be depreciated $9,000, $18,000, and $18,000, respectively, on the tax return over a three-year life.
4. A patent purchased for $330,000 will be amortized on a straight-line basis over 15 years on the tax return. No salvage value is expected.
5. Pretax savings of $8,000 in cash expenses will occur in each of the next seven years.
6. Pretax savings of $5,500 in cash expenses will occur in the first, fourth, and seventh years from now.
7. The special tools described in aspect 3 will be sold after three years for $10,000 cash.
8. A truck with a tax book value of $7,200 after two years will be sold at that time for $4,600.

REQUIRED

Set up an answer form with the four column headings as shown below. Answer each investment aspect separately. Prepare your calculations on a separate paper and key them to each item. The answer to investment aspect 1 is presented as an example.

	A After-tax Cash Flow Effect(s) Inflows (Outflows)	B Year(s) of Cash Flow	C Applicable Present Value Multiple
Investment Aspect			
1	$3,500	1, 2, 3	(II) 2.106

Calculations:

1. Pretax cash savings	$5,000	
Less income tax at 30%	1,500	
After-tax cash inflow	$3,500	

a. Calculate and record in column A the related after-tax cash flow effect(s). Place parentheses around outflows.

b. Indicate in column B the timing of each cash flow shown in column A. Use 0 to indicate immediately and 1, 2, 3, 4, and so on for each year involved.

c. When relevant, record in column C the present value multiple from Table I or II that you would apply to the cash flow amount shown in column A.

NET PRESENT VALUE ANALYSIS — OBJ. 4, 5 —

28-29A You have an opportunity to invest in a concession at a world exposition. To use the building and exhibits more fully, the venture is expected to cover a six-year period consisting of a preliminary year, the two years of formal exposition, and a three-year period of reduced operation as a regional exposition.

The terms of the concession agreement specify the following:

1. At inception, a $60,000 deposit is paid to Global Expo, Inc., the promoting organization. This amount is returned in full at the end of the six years if the operator maintains the concession in order and keeps it open during scheduled hours. The deposit is not tax deductible, nor is its return subject to income taxes.

2. The operator must install certain fixtures that will cost $240,000. The fixtures become the property of Global Expo, Inc., at the end of the six years.

After careful investigation and consultation with local experts, you conclude that the following schedule reflects the estimated pretax income of the concession (amounts in thousands of dollars):

	Year 1	Year 2	Year 3	Year 4	Year 5	Year 6
Sales (all cash)	$150	$435	$488	$300	$240	$180
Operating expenses:						
Cash	$ 75	$228	$279	$170	$140	$106
Tax depreciation	48	77	46	28	28	13
Total expenses	$123	$305	$325	$198	$168	$119
Pretax income	$ 27	$130	$163	$102	$ 72	$ 61

REQUIRED

Assuming an income tax rate of 40% and a desired annual return of 15%, what is the net present value of this investment opportunity? What is the maximum amount that could be invested and still earn a 15% annual return? (Round amounts to the nearest dollar.)

CASH PAYBACK, AVERAGE RATE OF RETURN, AND NET PRESENT VALUE METHODS — OBJ. 4, 5, 6 —

28-30A At a cash cost of $330,000, Monona, Inc., can acquire equipment that will save $100,000 in annual cash operating expenses. No salvage value is expected at the end of its five-year useful life. Assume the machine will be depreciated over five years on a straight-line basis on both the books and the tax return. The income tax rate is 30% and Monona has a 10% cutoff rate when using a net present value analysis.

REQUIRED

a. What are the annual after-tax cash savings in operating expenses?

b. What are the annual tax savings from the depreciation tax shield?

c. Compute the cash payback period.

d. Compute the average rate of return.

e. Compute the net present value and indicate whether it is positive or negative (round amounts to nearest dollar).

f. Compute the excess present value index.

EXCESS PRESENT VALUE INDEX AND AVERAGE RATE OF RETURN — OBJ. 5, 6 —

28-31A Swanson Corporation is evaluating five different capital expenditure proposals. The company's cutoff rate for net present value analysis is 15%. A 15% salvage value is expected from each of the investments. Information on the five proposals is as follows:

Proposal	Required Investment	Net Present Value	Average Annual Net Income from Investment
A	$50,000	$ 8,996	$ 9,100
B	80,000	5,812	12,000
C	110,000	27,034	18,300
D	150,000	7,544	21,500
E	72,000	15,822	13,960

REQUIRED

a. Compute the excess present value index for each of the five proposals.

b. Compute the average rate of return for each of the five proposals.

c. Assume that Swanson will commit no more than $200,000 to new capital expenditure proposals. Using the excess present value index, which proposals would be accepted? Using the average rate of return, which proposals would be accepted?

CASH PAYBACK, AVERAGE RATE OF RETURN, AND NET PRESENT VALUE METHODS — OBJ. 5, 6 —

28-32A Lyle Company is considering whether to enter into a franchise agreement that would give the company exclusive distribution rights in a three-state region to a quality line of leisure spas. The franchise agreement will extend eight years and cost $600,000. There is no salvage value. The franchise cost will be amortized on a straight-line basis over eight years on both the books and the tax return. The following annual results are expected if the franchise is acquired:

Increase in annual cash revenue		$230,000
Increases in expenses:		
Cash operating expenses	$95,000	
Amortization	75,000	170,000
Pretax income		$ 60,000
Income tax expense (35%)		21,000
Net income		$ 39,000

Lyle uses a 12% cutoff rate when analyzing capital expenditure proposals using net present value.

REQUIRED

a. What are the annual net cash flows (net inflows) from this proposal?

b. Compute the cash payback period.

c. Compute the average rate of return.

d. Compute the net present value and indicate whether it is positive or negative.

e. Assume that Lyle decides to use a 10% cutoff rate when using net present value analysis. Compute the net present value using a 10% cutoff rate and indicate whether it is positive or negative.

WEIGHTED AVERAGE COST OF CAPITAL AND NET PRESENT VALUE ANALYSIS — OBJ. 2, 5 —

28-33A Manchester Company is considering a proposal to purchase special equipment at a cost of $640,000. The equipment will be useful for five years and has an expected $60,000 salvage value. Manchester expects annual savings in cash operating expenses (before taxes) of $230,000. For tax purposes, the annual depreciation deduction will be as follows (salvage value is ignored on the tax return):

Year 1	$80,000
Year 2	160,000
Year 3	160,000
Year 4	160,000
Year 5	80,000

The income tax rate is 40%.

Manchester establishes a cutoff rate for a net present value analysis at the company's weighted average cost of capital plus 2 percentage points. Manchester's capital is provided in the following proportions: debt, 70%; common stock, 20%; and retained earnings, 10%. The cost rates for these capital sources are debt, 12%; common stock, 16%; and retained earnings, 14%.

REQUIRED

a. Compute Manchester's (1) weighted average cost of capital and (2) cutoff rate.
b. Using Manchester's cutoff rate, compute the net present value of this capital expenditure proposal. Under net present value analysis, should Manchester accept the proposal?

CASES

Business Decision Case

New Haven Corporation recently identified an investment opportunity involving the purchase of a patent that will permit the company to modify its line of videocassette recorders. The patent's purchase price is $720,000 and the legal protection it provides will last for five more years. There is no salvage value. However, after preparing the capital expenditure analysis below, New Haven's treasurer has recommended to the company's capital budgeting committee that the investment be rejected. Brad Decker, chairperson of the capital budgeting committee, finds it difficult to accept the treasurer's analysis because he "feels intuitively" that the investment is attractive. For this reason, he has retained you to review the treasurer's analysis and recommendation. You are provided with the following data and summary of the treasurer's analysis:

1. Required investment: $720,000 cash for the patent to be amortized on a straight-line basis, five-year useful life, with a zero salvage value.

2. Projected cash revenue and operating expenses:

Year	Cash Revenue	Cash Expenses
1	$ 620,000	$240,000
2	560,000	200,000
3	400,000	170,000
4	250,000	80,000
5	200,000	50,000
	$2,030,000	$740,000

3. Source of capital: New Haven plans to raise 10% of the needed capital by issuing bonds, 30% by issuing stock, and the balance from retained earnings. For these sources, the capital cost rates are 11%, 12%, and 13%, respectively. New Haven has a policy of seeking a return equal to the weighted average cost of capital plus 2.5 percentage points as a "buffer margin" for the uncertainties involved.

4. Income taxes: New Haven has an overall income tax rate of 30%.

5. Treasurer's analysis:

Average cost of capital (11% + 12% + 13%) ÷ 3 = 12%

Total cash revenue		$2,030,000
Total cash expenses	$740,000	
Total amortization	720,000	
Total operating expenses		1,460,000
Projected net income over five years		$ 570,000
Average annual income ($570,000 ÷ 5)		$ 114,000
Present value factor of five-year annuity at 12%		× 3.605
Present value of future returns		$ 410,970
Required investment		720,000
Negative net present value		$ 309,030

Recommendation: Reject investment because of insufficient net present value.

REQUIRED

a. Review the treasurer's analysis, identifying any questionable aspects and briefly commenting on the apparent effect of each such item on the treasurer's analysis.

b. Prepare your own analysis of the investment, including a calculation of the proper cost of capital and cutoff rates, a net present value analysis of the project, and a brief recommendation to Decker regarding the investment (round amounts to nearest dollar).

c. Because of his concern for the uncertainties of the videocassette recorder business, Decker also has asked you to provide analyses supporting whether or not your recommendation would change

   1. If estimates of projected cash revenue were reduced by 10%.

   2. If the "buffer margin" were tripled from 2.5% to 7.5%.

Ethics Case

Sandy Williams is the manager of General Company's cutting department, which employs 70 people. The cutting department desperately needs new equipment to increase productivity and thus avoid the layoff of 25 people. This department is one of four departments being considered for new equipment. The budget committee has announced that only one department's capital request will be approved this year.

Williams works up the cost savings from the new machinery and contacts suppliers to learn the equipment's estimated cost. Williams knows that General Company uses the payback method to evaluate capital projects. The estimated costs for the equipment are extremely high, particularly with all the safety shields recommended by the manufacturer. If one of these recommended safety features, electronic safety sensors not on the current equipment, were left off, the cost would be $200,000 less and the payback period would decrease by three years. If only minimum electronic safety sensors required by the union contract were included, the cost would be $70,000 less and the payback period would decrease by one year.

REQUIRED

What are the ethical considerations Sandy Williams faces as he prepares the equipment proposal?

The primary purpose of the federal income tax laws is raising revenue to pay for the operations of the government. In addition to the primary revenue-producing purpose, many amendments to the Internal Revenue Code have been enacted for other purposes. Federal taxation has changed since its inception in 1913 in both purpose and magnitude. The income tax system has become an instrument of the government for economic and social policy.

Through its taxing powers, the government can attempt to distribute income more equitably, stimulate economic growth, combat inflation and unemployment, and finance projects it considers socially desirable. In addition, a number of changes in the tax laws are the result of political influences on Congress, which formulates tax laws. Thus, multidimensional influences have contributed to the complexity of rapidly changing income tax laws.

The main entities that are recognized for purposes of federal income taxation are individuals, partnerships, corporations, and estates or trusts. Our focus in this appendix is on the taxation of individuals.

Although they are business entities, *sole proprietorships and partnerships are not taxable entities.* The owners of such firms must include their shares of business income along with income from other sources in their respective individual tax returns. The allocable shares of their business income are taxed directly to them whether or not they have withdrawn such amounts.

DETERMINING INDIVIDUAL TAXABLE INCOME

Generally, individuals who are citizens of the United States are taxed on all income from whatever source, unless it is specifically excluded by law. Thus, the gross income reported in an individual's federal income tax return consists of total income and gains *less exclusions.* Various deductions and exemptions are permitted to convert gross income to taxable income. Deductions and exemptions must be enumerated in the individual's federal return (Form 1040) or in supporting schedules.

Although the manner in which this information is detailed in the return varies, a basic, logical format guides the computation of taxable income and the related tax liability. This format, illustrated in Exhibit K-1, describes the classifications used in the tax laws and is a useful frame of reference in compiling the information needed to prepare an individual's tax return.

Filing Status

There are basically five possible ways in which individuals may file federal income tax returns: single taxpayer, married taxpayers filing jointly, married taxpayers filing separately, unmarried head of a household, and qualifying surviving spouse with a dependent child. When we refer to *individual* taxpayers, we are referring to tax returns filed under these various categories. Tax rates, exemption amounts, and other provisions of the tax laws differ, depending on filing status. Keep in mind that the provisions of the tax laws relating to tax rates, exemption amounts, various prescribed limits, and other details have been changing rapidly and will continue to change.

Gross Income

As shown in Exhibit K-1, **gross income** is income from all sources, less allowable exclusions. Some of the most common types of income are wages, salaries, unemployment compensation, bonuses, fees, tips, interest, dividends, profits or shares of profits from business, pensions, annuities, rents, royalties, prizes, taxable gains on sales of property or securities, fellowships, and scholarships. The list also includes income from gambling and even illegal income. (Racketeers and other criminals have often been more easily apprehended through income tax investigations than through regular criminal investigations.) Special rules and procedures apply to certain of these sources of gross income in determining the portion to be included.

| EXHIBIT H—1 | FORMAT FOR DETERMINING TAX LIABILITY OF INDIVIDUALS |

Steps		Explanation
Determine:	Total income	All income from whatever source
Less:	Exclusions	Items of income excluded by law (p. 1091)
Equals:	Gross income	Income subject to tax (before deductions and exemptions)
Less:	Deductions from gross income	Business-related expenses, losses, and specific deductions from gross income (p. 1091)
Equals:	Adjusted gross income	Base for computation of limitations on some personal (itemized) deductions
Less:	Itemized deductions or standard deduction	Itemized deductions permitted by law or standard deduction stipulated by law in lieu of itemized deductions (p. 1091)
	Personal exemptions	An amount stipulated by law for taxpayer, spouse, and each dependent. The amount depends on filing status, and it is phased out at certain income levels (p. 1094)
Equals:	Taxable income	Amount used to compute the tax from the appropriate tax rate schedule
Results in:	Income tax	Taxable income multiplied by appropriate tax rate
Less:	Tax credits	Specified credits against the tax (p. 1094)
Equals:	Tax liability	Amount of tax owed by the taxpayer

Exclusions from Gross Income

Some items excluded by law from gross income include interest on certain state and municipal bonds; Social Security receipts[1]; gifts, bequests, and inheritances; worker's compensation for sickness or injury; certain disability benefits; life insurance proceeds received at the death of the insured; and the portion of scholarships or fellowships for degree candidates that is spent for tuition and course-required materials. (Amounts for room, board, or incidental expenses are not excludable.) The exclusions also exempt amounts of pensions and annuities that are returns of capital invested in them.

Deductions from Gross Income

Individual taxpayers are generally permitted two types of deductions—deductions from gross income to arrive at *adjusted gross income* and deductions from adjusted gross income. The first type is widely characterized as most business expenses and expenses incurred in the production of rents and royalties, whereas the second is generally described as allowable personal deductions.

The calculation of **adjusted gross income** is important in the taxation of individuals because it may affect the amount of certain personal deductions. Generally, we determine adjusted gross income to provide a more equitable base for certain other calculations than that provided by a gross income measure. Thus, a person who generates a large amount of gross income by incurring large amounts of business expenses or other related costs of producing such income is provided a base for determining personal deductions that is fairly comparable to the income of a wage earner or salaried taxpayer who does not have such business expenses.

Deductions permitted the individual taxpayer in arriving at adjusted gross income appear on the following page. (Remember these are subject to change.)

---

[1]However, taxpayers with "modified" adjusted gross income in excess of certain specified base amounts may have as much as 50% of their Social Security benefits included in taxable income.

1. *Trade and business deductions*—Ordinary and necessary expenses attributable to a trade or business carried on by the taxpayer may be deducted, provided such activity does not consist of performance of services by an employee. (However, if an employee has reimbursed expenses in gross income, they can be deducted.) Only 80% of business meals and entertainment may be included with trade and business deductions, and certain kinds of entertainment expenses are not deductible.

2. *Losses from sales or exchanges of property*—Losses from the sale or exchange of business or investment property are deductible in arriving at adjusted gross income. However, losses on the sale or exchange of "personal use" property are not deductible.

3. *Net operating loss deduction*—Generally, a business's operating loss in a particular year, which is of no tax benefit for that year, may be carried back to the three preceding years and forward to the next 15 years to reduce the tax liability for those years. After certain adjustments, the loss is carried back to the earliest preceding year first, then successively to each succeeding period, if unused. A taxpayer may forgo the carryback and carry the loss forward only 15 years.

4. *Other deductions*—Certain other deductions, relating to rents, royalties, pensions, profit sharing, bond purchase plans of self-employed individuals, and individual retirement accounts (IRAs) are allowed. Individuals not covered by employer-sponsored qualified pension plans can fully deduct IRA contributions. However, the deduction for IRA contributions is either limited or completely denied to individuals covered by employer plans. For these individuals, the maximum deduction is reduced between $40,000 and $50,000 of adjusted gross income, if married, and between $25,000 and $35,000, if single.

Itemized Deductions and Standard Deduction

An individual taxpayer may deduct from adjusted gross income certain itemized personal and other expenses specified by the tax law, or may, in lieu of itemizing expenses, take advantage of a **standard deduction.** The amount of the standard deduction for 1991 is given below for single taxpayers and married taxpayers filing jointly.

Single taxpayer	$3,400
Married taxpayers filing jointly	5,700

The above amounts are increased for married individuals if they are elderly or blind by $650 for each condition; for single taxpayers the corresponding amount is $850. In our illustrations, exercises, and problems, we use the 1991 standard deduction amount.

Personal expenses that may be itemized and deducted from adjusted gross income are classified as follows:

1. *Medical expenses*—With certain limitations, a taxpayer may deduct his or her medical and dental expenses, and those for dependents, not compensated for by insurance or otherwise. The total medical and dental expenses are deductible to the extent that they exceed 7.5% of adjusted gross income. Prescription drugs and insulin are the only drugs that are considered medical expenses.

    For example, a taxpayer with an adjusted gross income of $30,000 has the following medical expenses: health insurance premiums, $900; prescription drugs, $620; and other medical expenses not compensated for by insurance, $1,400. The deduction is calculated as follows:

Insurance premiums	$ 900
Prescription drugs	620
Other medical expenses	1,400
	$2,920
Less 7.5% of $30,000 adjusted gross income	2,250
Medical deduction	$ 670

2. *Taxes*—State and local income taxes, real estate taxes, and personal property taxes are deductible. Sales taxes are not deductible. Federal taxes do not qualify as itemized deductions, nor do flat fees paid for most types of licenses (auto, driver's, pet, and so on). Variable auto license fees required by some states may be deductible. State and local gasoline taxes are not deductible.

3. *Interest*—Interest on indebtedness incurred to purchase a principal or second home is deductible. However, with certain exceptions, mortgage interest is not deductible on the excess of loans over the purchase price plus improvement costs. Consumer interest, such as amounts paid for credit card balances and automobile installment loans, is not deductible. Interest on a federal tax deficiency is considered consumer interest.

4. *Charitable contributions*—The amount of gifts made to religious, scientific, educational, and other charitable organizations officially recognized by the Internal Revenue Service can be deducted. Limitations apply to total contributions, noncash contributions, and gifts to foundations. Gifts to individuals or labor unions and donations to organizations whose major activity is to influence legislation are not deductible.

5. *Casualty losses*—To the extent that they exceed $100 for each casualty loss *and* 10% of adjusted gross income in total, certain casualty and theft losses are deductible unless compensated by insurance. Casualty losses must be sudden and unexpected: losses from fire, accident, windstorm, and so forth qualify as deductions. Certain "gradual" losses, such as termite damage, usually do not qualify.

6. *Moving expenses*—Employees and self-employed persons can deduct certain moving expenses if the move was in connection with a job or business. Certain restrictions apply.

7. *Miscellaneous deductions*—Certain itemized miscellaneous deductions are allowed to the extent that they aggregate more than 2% of the taxpayer's adjusted gross income. There are some expenses, however, to which the 2% floor does not apply. For example, gambling losses can be deducted to the extent of gambling winnings, which must be included in income. Some of the most common miscellaneous deductions are

Unreimbursed employee business expenses	Employment agency fees
Professional dues	Required protective clothing
Subscriptions to professional publications	Certain educational expenses related to present job, incurred to improve or maintain skills, or to meet employer's requirements
Union dues	Fees paid for income tax assistance
Uniforms and tools	
Safe-deposit box rental	

Capital Gains and Losses

Capital gains and losses are those gains and losses that result from the sale or exchange of capital assets. Although they are sometimes difficult to define, capital assets generally include any of the taxpayer's business and investment property except receivables, inventories, real and depreciable business property, certain governmental obligations, and rights to literary and other artistic works. Under certain conditions, however, business real estate and depreciable assets may be treated as capital assets when gains from sales of such assets exceed losses.

Gains or losses on capital assets sold or exchanged are classified as long term if the assets have been held longer than one year. If the assets have been held for one year or less, disposition results in short-term gains or losses.

If a taxpayer has both long-term and short-term transactions during the year, each type is reported separately and gains and losses from each type are netted separately. After this netting process has been achieved, the net long-term capital gain or loss for the year is combined with the net short-term capital gain or loss for the year to arrive at an overall (net) capital gain or loss for the year. If capital gains exceed capital losses, the overall gain is included with the taxpayer's other taxable income and is taxed at the regular tax rates. For many taxpayers, the maximum rate of tax on net capital gains is 28%.

If the net amount from capital transactions is a loss, individuals and other non-corporate taxpayers may offset the loss against ordinary income up to $3,000 in any year. The amount of the losses that are not offset may be carried forward indefinitely to offset capital gains or $3,000 of ordinary income in any year.

Personal Exemptions

In arriving at taxable income, the individual taxpayer may deduct an amount for each **personal exemption** he or she may legally claim. Married taxpayers filing jointly are allowed an exemption for each spouse and one for each dependent. To qualify for a dependency exemption, a person must (1) be closely related to the taxpayer or live in the taxpayer's household for the entire year as a member of the family; (2) have received more than one-half of his or her support from the taxpayer; (3) if married, not file a joint return with the spouse; (4) have, with certain exceptions, income less than the exemption amount; and (5) be a U.S. citizen or a resident of the United States, Canada, or Mexico.

The personal exemption amount for 1991 was $2,150 per exemption. This amount will be indexed for inflation in the future. The total amount for exemptions is reduced for high-income taxpayers. For example, a married taxpayer filing jointly in 1991, with adjusted gross income of $200,000 and two exemptions, received a total personal exemption of $2,580, rather than $4,300 (2 × $2,150).

DETERMINING INDIVIDUAL TAX LIABILITY

Applying the appropriate tax rate to taxable income results in the tax liability, unless there are tax credits (discussed later). Individual taxpayers with taxable incomes less than $50,000 use simplified **tax tables** to determine their tax liability. All other taxpayers use **tax schedules.** Schedules are provided by the IRS for (1) single taxpayers, (2) married taxpayers filing a joint return (and surviving spouses), (3) married taxpayers filing separately, and (4) unmarried taxpayers who qualify as heads of households. Exhibit K-2 illustrates the tax rate schedules for 1991.

Unmarried taxpayers who qualify as **heads of households** determine their tax liability from tables or schedules that generally determine a tax liability falling between that of single taxpayers and married taxpayers filing jointly. Generally, the qualification can be met by unmarried taxpayers who pay more than one-half the cost of maintaining a home in which a parent resides, if the parent qualifies as a dependent. A taxpayer who pays more than one-half of the cost of maintaining his or her own home where a dependent relative or where unmarried children, adopted stepchildren, or grandchildren reside may also qualify as a head of household.

CREDITS AGAINST THE TAX

Once the income tax has been calculated, certain credits specified in the tax law may reduce the amount owed. Two of the most important of these credits for individual taxpayers are the earned income credit and the child and dependent care credit.

Earned Income Credit

The **earned income credit** provides tax relief to lower-income workers with children who live with them. The earned income credit consists of three component credits: a basic credit, a health insurance credit, and an extra credit for a child born during the tax year. The basic credit is based on the number of qualifying children living with the taxpayer and may reach as much as $1,235. The health insurance credit is available if the taxpayer paid health insurance premiums covering one or more qualifying children and may be as much as $428. The extra credit for a newborn child could be as high as $357. The taxpayer may take this extra credit or the child and

EXHIBIT H—2	1991 TAX RATE SCHEDULES*

Schedule X: Single Individual

If Taxable Income Is

Over	But Not Over	Tax Is		Of the Amount Over
$ –0–	$20,350	—	15%	$ –0–
20,350	49,300	$ 3,052.50 +	28%	20,350
49,300	—	11,158.50 +	31%	49,300

Schedule Z: Head of Household

If Taxable Income Is

Over	But Not Over	Tax Is		Of the Amount Over
$ –0–	$27,300	—	15%	$ –0–
27,300	70,450	$ 4,095.00 +	28%	27,300
70,450	—	16,177.00 +	31%	70,450

Schedule Y-1: Married Filing Jointly or Qualifying Widow(er)

If Taxable Income Is

Over	But Not Over	Tax Is		Of the Amount Over
$ –0–	$34,000	—	15%	$ –0–
34,000	82,150	$ 5,100.00 +	28%	34,000
82,150	—	18,582.00 +	31%	82,150

Schedule Y-2: Married Filing Separately

If Taxable Income Is

Over	But Not Over	Tax Is		Of the Amount Over
$ –0–	$17,000	—	15%	$ –0–
17,000	41,075	$2,550.00 +	28%	17,000
41,075	—	9,291.00 +	31%	41,075

* Taxpayers can use these schedules only if taxable income is $50,000 or more. If less than $50,000, taxpayers must use tax tables provided by the Internal Revenue Service.

dependent care credit for the child (discussed in the next section), but may not take both of these credits. No earned income credit is available for taxpayers whose earned income or adjusted gross income is $21,250 or more.

Child and Dependent Care Credit

A tax credit is available for taxpayers who maintain a household and incur expenses in caring for a child under 13 years or an incapacitated dependent or spouse, if the expenses incurred permitted the taxpayer to be gainfully employed. The amount of this **child and dependent care credit** is determined by multiplying a decimal ranging from 0.2 to 0.3 (depending on the level of adjusted gross income) times the employment-related expenses (up to a maximum of $2,400 for one qualifying individual and $4,800 for two or more qualifying individuals).

WITHHOLDING AND ESTIMATED TAX

Ordinarily, tax returns must be filed within $3\frac{1}{2}$ months of the close of the individual's taxable year. Because most taxpayers are on a calendar-year basis, they must file their returns by April 15 following the end of the taxable year. During the taxable year, employers of wage earners and salaried employees have withheld tax payments based on the employees' estimated earnings and the number of withholding allowances claimed. Taxpayers who have income not subject to withholding (beyond a certain amount) must estimate income for the current year and file a Declaration of Estimated Tax. The estimated tax, less the amounts expected to be withheld, is usually paid in four installments. Therefore, when the tax return is filed, the amounts paid through the withholding and declaration process are credits that offset the total tax liability.

INDIVIDUAL TAX COMPUTATION: TWO EXAMPLES

We present two examples of the common elements of individual tax computations. Exhibit K-3 shows the relevant tax data for the joint return of Brian and Mary Fleming, and Exhibit K-4 shows data for the single-taxpayer return of James Malone. Although some of this information would be shown in separate schedules that reveal more detail, we have condensed the data into single schedules to conserve space. Both returns are for the 1991 calendar year.

Brian and Mary Fleming have one child who qualifies as a dependency exemption. Brian operates a tax service and has paid $600 in estimated tax quarterly. Mary works part-time as a nurse and has tax withheld from her salary. During the year, Brian sold at a $1,200 gain securities purchased two years ago. The couple has been contributing $4,000 each year to an individual retirement account (IRA). Neither Brian nor Mary is covered by an employer-sponsored retirement plan. The Fleming family's medical expenses were not significant during the year. Notice that the Flemings can deduct their $4,000 contribution to an IRA because they are not covered by an employer retirement plan and they fall below the income levels at which these contributions are not deductible. Brian and Mary are each allowed a $2,000 deductible contribution because both are working. Also notice that their miscellaneous deductions are slightly higher than 2% of adjusted gross income, so that they can deduct a small amount of this expense.

EXHIBIT K-3	BRIAN AND MARY FLEMING'S 1991 JOINT FEDERAL INCOME TAX RETURN INFORMATION		
Net income from Fleming Tax Service:			
Fees collected		$48,000	
Ordinary and necessary expenses		18,000	$30,000
Salary (Mary's)			5,600
Interest on savings accounts (excluding IRA interest)			1,400
Dividend income			650
Net capital gain on sale of securities			1,200
Contribution to individual retirement account			(4,000)
Adjusted gross income			$34,850
Deductions from adjusted gross income:			
Taxes:			
Property tax on home	$2,200		
State income tax	1,530	$3,730	
Interest on home mortgage		1,620	
Charitable contributions		950	
Professional dues, nurse's uniforms, and other miscellaneous deductions	$ 775		
Less 2% of $34,850 adjusted gross income not deductible	697	78	
Total itemized deductions			6,378
			$28,472
Less exemptions (3 × $2,150)			6,450
Taxable income			$22,022
Tax: 15% of $22,022 (rounded)			$ 3,303
Less prepayments:			
Tax withheld from salary		$ 680	
Estimated taxes paid quarterly		2,400	
Total tax withheld or prepaid			3,080
Balance of tax due with return			$ 223

EXHIBIT K—4   JAMES MALONE'S 1991 FEDERAL INCOME TAX RETURN INFORMATION

Salary			$56,480
Interest (excluding interest on individual retirement account)			2,410
Dividends			2,190
Net capital gain on sale of securities			1,600
Adjusted gross income			$62,680
Deductions from adjusted gross income:			
Taxes:			
Property taxes on home and vacation home	$2,250		
State income tax	3,070	$5,320	
Interest:			
On home mortgage	$2,560		
On vacation home mortgage	200	2,760	
Charitable contributions		1,550	
Employee moving expense		650	
Miscellaneous expenses	$ 960		
Less 2% of adjusted gross income	1,254	–0–	
Total itemized deductions			10,280
			$52,400
Less one exemption ($2,150)			2,150
Taxable income			$50,250
Tax: $11,158.50 + 31% ($50,250 – $49,300)			$11,453
Less prepayments:			
Tax withheld from salary		$7,100	
Estimated taxes paid quarterly		5,200	12,300
Overpayment of tax			$ 847

James Malone, whose 1991 federal income tax data are given in Exhibit K-4, is single and is covered by an employer-sponsored retirement program. Malone contributed $2,000 to an IRA as he has done for several years. This amount is not deductible in calculating adjusted gross income (both because he is in a retirement program and because of his income level). However, the interest on his IRA is deferred for tax purposes and is not included in adjusted gross income. Malone was transferred by his employer in 1991 and had unreimbursed moving expenses of $650, which are fully deductible. Malone's miscellaneous expenses are not deductible because they fall below 2% of adjusted gross income. During the year Malone paid estimated tax of $1,300 each quarter (total, $5,200) and had $7,100 withheld from his salary.

GLOSSARY OF KEY TERMS USED IN THIS APPENDIX

adjusted gross income A federal income tax term denoting the amount obtained by subtracting from gross income certain business expenses and expenses incurred in producing rents and royalties (p. 1091).

capital gains and losses Gains and losses from the sale or exchange of certain assets qualifying as capital assets (p. 1093).

child and dependent care credit A credit against federal income tax that provides relief to lower-income working individuals who care for a child under 13 years old or an incapacitated dependent or spouse (p. 1095).

earned income credit A credit against federal income tax which provides relief to lower-income working individuals with children (p. 1094).

gross income In the context of preparing federal income tax returns, gross income is income from all sources less allowable exclusions (p. 1090).

head of household A federal income tax category of unmarried taxpayers who pay more than one-half the cost of maintaining a home for qualified dependents and whose tax liability generally falls between that of single taxpayers and married taxpayers filing jointly (p. 1094).

personal exemption A prescribed amount that a taxpayer may deduct for himself or herself and each qualified dependent in computing taxable income (p. 1094).

standard deduction A fixed dollar amount that individual taxpayers are allowed to deduct from adjusted gross income on their federal income tax returns in lieu of itemizing expenses (p. 1092).

tax schedules Schedules available for individual taxpayers to compute their federal income tax liabilities when they are not eligible to use the simplified tax tables (p. 1094).

tax tables Simplified tables available for individual taxpayers to compute their federal income tax liabilities (p. 1094).

EXERCISES

ADJUSTED GROSS INCOME CALCULATION

K-1 Calculate the adjusted gross income for the joint return of Arthur and Mary Thompson from the following 1991 data:

Share of partnership net income	$46,200
Interest on municipal bonds	1,200
Dividend income	700
Interest income	430
Lottery prize	500
Gift from relative	1,500
Net capital gain on sale of securities	2,000
Qualified contributions to individual retirement account	2,100

TAXABLE INCOME CALCULATION

K-2 According to their 1991 joint return, Bart and Irene Lopez have two dependents, and their adjusted gross income is $36,000. Using the relevant data from the items shown below, calculate their taxable income.

Real estate taxes	$1,400	State gasoline taxes	$ 150
Interest on home mortgage	2,400	Health insurance premiums	900
Charitable contributions	650	Other medical expenses	2,100
Gift to relative	200	Automobile licenses	36
State income taxes	700	Employee moving expense	400
State sales taxes	280	Union dues	150
Interest on car payments	300	Income tax return preparation	180

INDIVIDUAL TAX LIABILITY

K-3 Using the appropriate schedule in Exhibit K-2, calculate the amount of tax due (or over-payment) for Ellen Wade, a single taxpayer (with no dependents) who has given you the following information:

Gross income	$29,500
Deductions to determine adjusted gross income	1,450
Allowable itemized personal expenses	3,500
Tax withheld from salary	3,250
Payments of estimated tax	250

PROBLEMS

JOINT TAX RETURN

K-4 Vincent and Sharon Wang, who have three school-age children, are filing a joint federal income tax return. Vincent, whose annual salary is $40,000 as an accountant for Byrd Corporation, operates a tax service in his spare time. During 1991, he had $7,200 gross income and $1,600 business expenses in his tax service. He received $120 in dividends from his investments and $600 interest on municipal bonds. Sharon had $250 in dividend income on her stocks. In addition, Vincent sold for $45 per share 100 shares of stock purchased five years ago for $30 per share. Income taxes deducted from Vincent's salary during 1991 amounted to $4,900, and his payments of estimated tax were $540. Personal expenses of the Wang family for 1991 included the following:

Mortgage payments (of which $2,800 was interest)	$3,600
Real estate taxes	1,800
State income taxes	1,400
State sales taxes	360
Charitable contributions	560
Medical and dental expenses (unreimbursed)	1,920
License fees for auto, pets, etc.	52
Interest on charge accounts	250

REQUIRED

Calculate the amount of tax due (or overpayment) shown on the Wang's 1991 joint income tax return. Use the appropriate schedule in Exhibit K-2. Round computations to the nearest dollar.

TYPES OF DEDUCTIONS   **K-5**   The following items relate to the federal income taxes of individuals who itemize their deductions in computing their tax. Consider each item independently.

1. Fee paid employment agency for obtaining employment.
2. Payment of $150 repair bill for damage to pleasure automobile from skid on icy road (not compensated for by insurance).
3. Labor union dues.
4. Contribution to Empty Stocking Fund formed by neighbors for children of a needy family.
5. State income tax paid.
6. Federal cigarette tax.
7. State gasoline tax for pleasure car.
8. State fishing license.
9. Gambling losses in excess of gambling gains.
10. Fee paid by unemployed student to take the CPA examination.
11. Fee paid to Smith & Brown, CPAs, for preparation of personal tax return.
12. Cost of cleaning uniform paid by train conductor.
13. Fair market value of furniture given to the Salvation Army.
14. Entertainment expenses of a salesperson, not reimbursed.
15. Life insurance premiums paid.
16. Trade and business expenses of sole proprietorship.
17. Net capital loss of $1,200 on sale of securities.

REQUIRED

Indicate whether each of the above items is (a) nondeductible, (b) deductible in determining adjusted gross income, or (c) deductible from adjusted gross income. If answer (c) is given, indicate whether there are limitations on the amount of the deduction.

JOINT TAX RETURN   **K-6**   Kevin and Lisa Todd are married and are both under 65 years of age. Their one child, Sally, is 18 years old and a full-time student at a university; they contribute over one-half of her support, and Sally earned $1,500 from part-time work during the year.

Lisa Todd operates a retail dress shop as a sole proprietorship. The following information is available for 1991 operations:

Sales	$86,500
Merchandise inventory, January 1	22,600
Merchandise purchases	48,200
Rent expense	5,400
Utilities and supplies expense	800
Salaries of part-time help	4,600
Insurance expense	700
Merchandise inventory, December 31	24,500

Kevin Todd's annual salary as a purchasing agent for a local firm was $45,000 and income tax withheld was $9,600. Quarterly payments of estimated tax totaled $4,500. The following information for the year was compiled from Todd's checkbook and other sources:

Dividends received	$1,150
Interest income:	
Savings account	900
Municipal bonds	600
Real estate taxes on home	2,000
State sales taxes	380
Medical expenses (unreimbursed)	1,850
State income taxes paid	1,760
Contribution to Salvation Army	400
Accountant's services (preparing last year's income tax return)	200
Auto license on personal car	24
Safe-deposit box rental (used for jewelry)	32
Subscriptions to professional journals	120
Country club dues	450
Interest expense on home mortgage	3,200
Interest paid on personal loans	500

During the year, Kevin sold the following corporate stock:

Security	Holding Period	Cost	Proceeds
Xerox	26 months	$5,100	$6,300
Reebok	24 months	2,100	1,800
Tenneco	4 months	3,850	5,050
Genentech	3 months	2,450	1,750

REQUIRED

Compute the amount of tax due (or any overpayment) reported in the Todd's 1991 joint income tax return. Use the appropriate schedule in Exhibit K-2. (Round computations to the nearest dollar.)

JOINT TAX RETURN

K-7 Rod and Katy Barker are both under 65 years of age and have two dependent children. Rod furnished over one-half the support for his mother-in-law, who lives with them. Her total income during 1991 consists of $800 interest on a savings account. Katy has no outside employment. Rod owns an office building from which rentals for 1991 totaled $42,000. During 1991, he had the following items related to the building:

Heat	$3,700
Janitor service	2,200
Depreciation	2,500
Interest on mortgage	3,600
Real estate taxes	4,800
Insurance premium	400

Rod's annual salary as sales manager for an insurance firm was $45,000, from which $6,800 was withheld for federal income taxes during 1991. He also paid $4,200 in estimated tax during 1991. The following information for 1991 was compiled from the family's checkbook and other sources:

Dividends received	$1,620
Interest income:	
Savings account	840
Municipal bonds	1,200
Real estate taxes on home	2,200
State sales taxes	480
Medical expenses (unreimbursed)	4,200
State income taxes paid	3,100
Contributions to United Fund	750
Accountant's services (preparing last year's income tax return)	200
Athletic club dues	450
Auto licenses on personal cars	48
Safe deposit box rental (used for jewelry)	40
Subscriptions to professional journals	180
Lottery winnings	200
Interest expense on mortgage	5,000

During 1991, Rod sold the following corporate stock:

Security	Holding Period	Cost	Proceeds
Heinz	24 months	$2,200	$3,400
Olin	28 months	1,600	1,300
Chrysler	3 months	2,800	2,200
Syntex	5 months	3,600	4,100

REQUIRED

Compute the amount of tax due (or any overpayment) reported in the Barkers' joint income tax return. Use the appropriate schedule in Exhibit K-2. (Round computations to the nearest dollar.)

The financial statements and related disclosures from the 1991 annual report of Donnelly Corporation are presented in this appendix. Donnelly Corporation is headquartered in Holland, Michigan. Approximately 85–90% of Donnelly's business is the manufacture of automotive vision systems (such as interior and exterior rearview mirrors) and automotive modular window systems; other operations focus on the manufacture of solid-state glass coatings for products used in the computer and electronics industries.

The information presented consists of management's discussion and analysis of results of operations and financial condition, combined consolidated financial statements, notes to the financial statements, management's responsibility for financial reporting, report of the independent certified public accountants, and selected financial data for a ten-year period.

DONNELLY CORPORATION
AND SUBSIDIARIES
FINANCIAL REVIEW

RESULTS OF OPERATIONS

COMPARISON OF 1991 TO 1990

Donnelly sales continued to set new records in 1991, increasing 9.3% to $232,841,000, despite a 9.5% decrease in U.S. automobile production. Automotive Products net sales increased 7.1% to $202,514,000. Fortunately, the Company's new programs in both Modular Window Systems and Automotive Vision Systems, along with being a supplier to most of the "transplant" manufacturers (foreign companies operating in the U.S.), has softened the impact of the current industry downturn. Automotive gross profit margin increased to 20.8% from 20.3% last year. This increase occurred despite heavy start-up costs in compass mirrors and at D&A Technology, Inc. (D&A), the Company's new joint venture in Tennessee. The depressed automotive market also put significant pressure on gross profit margins. These negative influences however, were more than offset by operating and mix improvements in modular windows, lighted mirrors and the complete exterior mirror business.

Coated Products net sales increased 26.0% to $30,327,000 in 1991. Gross profit margin also increased to 21.8% in 1991, from a depressed 17.1% last year. Sales volume increases, some relief through price increases and improvements in operational efficiency have helped improve gross profit margin. However, glass price increases of 15-20% and continued sales price pressures continue to hurt performance in this area.

Selling, administrative, and general expenses increased to $28,698,000 or 12.3% of sales from 11.6% last year. The increased expenses included higher litigation expenditures, a reinstatement of management pay reductions from a year ago and the annual pay package increase. The litigation expenses are expected to continue into 1992.

Research and development expenditures increased to $12,499,000 but decreased to 5.4% of sales from 5.6% last year.

Interest expense decreased to $3,914,000 in 1991 from $4,273,000 in 1990. The decrease was primarily the result of lower long-term debt as working capital decreased and capital spending was reduced.

Royalties increased to $1,484,000 in 1991, from $788,000 in 1990. This increase resulted from licensees increasing their output of related products.

Other income of $561,000 in 1991 consisted primarily of interest income of $440,000 earned primarily from trust balances of industrial revenue bonds and $100,000 of foreign currency transaction gains. This is an increase over other expense of $471,000 last year. Last year's expense included a foreign currency transaction loss of $728,000 and $401,000 of interest income.

Net income increased to $4,168,000 in 1991. Although this represents an increase over 1990, it is well short of 1989 record earnings. The Company was faced with a very depressed automotive market and continued price pressures in coated products during 1991, restricting sales growth and hampering profitability. Significant start-up losses at D&A and new development programs also negatively impacted earnings during the year.

The Company's effective tax rate is higher than the Federal Statutory rate due to losses at D&A which currently provide no tax benefit. This situation is expected to begin reversing itself in the future as D&A begins earning a profit.

COMPARISON OF 1990 TO 1989

Donnelly's sales set new records in 1990, increasing 7.4% to $213,086,000. Automotive Products net sales increased 14.2% to $189,024,000. During this same period, U.S. automobile production decreased 14.5%. Sales of complete exterior mirror assemblies increased over 100% during 1990, due to production of additional models and increased production of heavy duty truck mirrors. Greater market penetration for both modular windows and lighted mirrors allowed sales of these products to increase, while automobile production decreased. Automotive gross profit margin remained flat at 20.3% in both 1990 and 1989. Improvements in the gross profit margins of complete exterior mirror assemblies and modular windows helped offset product mix effects and start-up costs for compass mirrors and at D&A.

Coated Products net sales decreased 26.8% to $24,062,000 in 1990. This business segment experienced a severe business downturn in the market for liquid crystal displays used in watches, calculators and games. The market decline, along with increased capacity in the industry, resulted in lower prices for coated glass. Gross profit margin in Coated Products was 17.1% in 1990, down from 25.5% in 1989. This decrease was directly attributable to the overall effects of the market decline. Profit margin was also affected by the cost of developing new business in the larger Japanese market and depreciation and other costs associated with the coating capacity added late in 1989.

Selling, administrative and general expenses increased to $24,699,000 or 11.6% of sales from 10.6% in 1989. This increase resulted from additional overhead to support start-up activities without correspondingly higher sales levels being achieved.

Research and development increased to $11,861,000 or 5.6% of sales from 5.4% of sales in 1989. Development work began at the Company's new Advanced Technology Center in Tucson, Arizona during 1990.

Interest expense increased to $4,273,000 in 1990 from $2,648,000 in 1989. The increase resulted from higher debt levels associated with increased capital spending and higher working capital throughout the year.

Royalties increased to $788,000 in 1990, from $171,000 in 1989. Licensed companies began to increase their production levels of related products.

Other expense of $471,000 in 1990 included $728,000 of foreign currency transaction losses occurring at the Company's wholly owned foreign subsidiary as the Japanese yen weakened against the Irish punt, and $401,000 of interest income.

Net income decreased to $2,337,000 in 1990. The downturns in each of the Company's major markets restricted sales growth and placed significant pressure on profitability. Start-up costs for compass mirrors and at D&A also hurt profitability in 1990.

To ensure profitability in 1990, the Company aggressively implemented a profitability improvement plan to reduce and contain costs at all levels of the organization. Actions taken included: 1) a reduction of and/or delay of major capital spending programs; 2) office staff reductions of 10% (on average) throughout the Company; 3) salary reductions for selected managerial groups; and 4) focusing development efforts more intensely on highly strategic programs and postponing work in nonstrategic areas.

JOINT VENTURES

The Company entered into two new joint ventures in 1991. On December 11, 1990 the Company formed a joint venture, OSD Envizion Company, with Surface Mode Eye Protection, Ltd, an affiliate of Optical Shields, Inc. of Menlo Park, California to commercialize surface mode liquid crystal technology for eye protection. It is initially being operated in Optical Shield's facility in Menlo Park and the arrangement ultimately provides for equal ownership by the partners. Initial capitalization is being provided by the Company through equity and loans aggregating up to $1,000,000.

On December 20, 1990 the Company also entered into a joint venture, Electrochromic Technology Company, with Optical Coating Laboratory, Inc. (OCLI) of Santa Rosa, California for the commercialization of high technology, thin film, solid-state, electrochromic coatings. Initial production will take place at OCLI facilities in Santa Rosa. Ownership is split equally by the partners. No financial funding was initially required, or is expected in fiscal 1992.

LIQUIDITY AND CAPITAL RESOURCES

The Company's current ratio was 1.8 at June 30, 1991 and 1.9 at June 30, 1990. Working capital was $26,056,000 at June 30, 1991 compared to $28,433,000 at June 30, 1990. This decrease resulted from the use of cash to pay down long term debt and lower prepaid expenses and refundable income taxes.

Capital spending levels decreased significantly to $8,154,000 in 1991 compared to $21,541,000 in 1990. In keeping with the profitability improvement plan implemented last year, serious efforts were made to reduce capital spending so that the Company's debt position could be improved. The major additions to capital occurred in the Modular Window Systems area, where equipment was added to increase capacity. Other assets decreased as industrial revenue bond trust funds were used to pay for $3,321,000 of capital expenditures. Capital expenditures are expected to increase to more historical levels in the future.

The funded status of the retirement plan did not require a contribution for 1991, and therefore no retirement plan accrual existed at year-end. It is expected that funding requirements will be required in 1992.

In March 1991, the Company renegotiated its $50,000,000 bank revolving credit and term loan agreement. The new agreement expires March 31, 1995 and has more favorable rates and covenant restrictions than the prior agreement. This agreement had borrowings against it of $16,000,000 at June 30, 1991.

In April 1991, the Company entered into two interest rate swap transactions to lock in favorable fixed interest rate levels and reduce the Company's interest rate risk. One transaction effectively changes a $5 million portion of the current borrowing to a fixed rate of 8.8% for 5 years. The other effectively changes a $5 million portion to a fixed rate of 9.01% for 7 years.

ACCOUNTING FOR POSTRETIREMENT BENEFITS OTHER THAN PENSIONS

In December 1990, the FASB issued Statement No. 106 "Employers' Accounting for Postretirement Benefits Other Than Pensions". This statement will significantly change the prevalent current practice of accounting for postretirement benefits on a cash basis by requiring accrual of the expected costs of providing these benefits during the years that the employee renders service. When adopted, this statement also requires recognition of the accumulated benefits that arose in prior periods. The statement allows for immediate recognition of this transition obligation or delayed recognition over the employee's future service periods.

Although early application is permitted, this statement is not effective until the Company's fiscal year beginning July 1, 1993. When adopted, the statement is expected to have a significant effect on the Company's financial statements. The Company is currently in the process of estimating these effects and, therefore, has not determined when to adopt this statement or when to recognize the transition obligation. In addition, these benefit plans are currently being reviewed for possible benefit modifications.

COMBINED CONSOLIDATED
STATEMENTS OF INCOME

(in thousands, except per share data) Year ended June 30,	1991	1990	1989
Net sales..	$232,841	$ 213,086	$ 198,323
Cost of sales	184,029	170,675	156,275
Gross profit	48,812	42,411	42,048
Operating expenses:			
Selling	4,938	3,743	3,628
Administrative and general	23,760	20,956	17,460
Research and development............................	12,499	11,861	10,776
Total operating expenses	41,197	36,560	31,864
Operating income	7,615	5,851	10,184
Non-operating expenses (income):			
Interest expense...	3,914	4,273	2,648
Royalty income...	(1,484)	(788)	(171)
Other expense (income), net	(561)	471	(657)
Non-operating expense................................	1,869	3,956	1,820
Income before taxes on income and minority interest..	5,746	1,895	8,364
Taxes on income...	2,465	71	2,148
Income before minority interest.....................	3,281	1,824	6,216
Minority interest in loss of subsidiary	887	513	
Net income	$ 4,168	$ 2,337	$ 6,216
Income per share of common stock	$ 0.74	$ 0.41	$ 1.11

The accompanying notes are an integral part of these statements.

Donnelly Corporation and Subsidiaries

COMBINED CONSOLIDATED BALANCE SHEETS

(in thousands) June 30,	1991	1990
ASSETS		
Current assets:		
Cash and cash equivalents	$ 1,037	$ 2,273
Accounts receivable, less allowances of $658 and $457	36,301	34,784
Inventories	16,641	15,871
Prepaid expenses	3,819	6,623
Refundable and deferred income taxes	568	1,698
Total current assets	58,366	61,249
Property, plant and equipment:		
Land	1,132	1,134
Buildings	21,379	21,651
Machinery and equipment	69,806	65,003
Construction in progress	2,045	538
	94,362	88,326
Less accumulated depreciation	35,240	29,078
Net property, plant and equipment	59,122	59,248
Other assets	3,916	8,173
	$121,404	$ 128,670
LIABILITIES AND SHAREHOLDERS' EQUITY		
Current liabilities:		
Accounts payable	$ 23,068	$ 23,149
Current maturities of long-term debt	78	117
Accruals:		
Compensation	5,335	4,005
Taxes	2,491	1,645
Retirement plans		2,108
Other	1,338	1,792
Total current liabilities	32,310	32,816
Long-term debt, less current maturities	41,265	48,568
Deferred income taxes and other	4,899	6,203
Total liabilities	78,474	87,587
Shareholders' equity:		
Preferred stock	531	531
Common stock	561	560
Additional paid-in capital	8,644	8,523
Foreign currency translation adjustment	(494)	352
Retained earnings	33,688	31,117
Total shareholders' equity	42,930	41,083
	$121,404	$ 128,670

The accompanying notes are an integral part of these statements.

COMBINED CONSOLIDATED
STATEMENTS OF CASH FLOWS

(in thousands) Year ended June 30,	1991	1990	1989
OPERATING ACTIVITIES:			
Net income..	$ 4,168	$ 2,337	$ 6,216
Depreciation and amortization...	8,099	8,130	6,688
Deferred pension cost...	1,794	(847)	(999)
Deferred income taxes..	(496)	1,473	921
Minority interest...	(887)	(513)	
Changes in operating assets and liabilities:			
Accounts receivable	(1,517)	(5,798)	(3,343)
Inventories, prepaid expenses and other current assets	3,255	(3,137)	(3,632)
Accounts payable and other current liabilities....................	(506)	6,434	(415)
Other...	16	300	36
Net cash from operating activities	13,926	8,379	5,472
INVESTING ACTIVITIES:			
Capital expenditures...	(8,154)	(21,541)	(18,805)
Change in unexpended bond proceeds	3,321	(2,754)	1,109
Proceeds from sale-lease back		2,800	
Other...	(1,551)	1,239	(463)
Net cash for investing activities	(6,384)	(20,256)	(18,159)
FINANCING ACTIVITIES:			
Proceeds from long-term debt	2,297	13,795	14,500
Repayments on long-term debt	(9,600)		(94)
Resources provided by minority interest		400	
Common stock issuance	122		
Dividends paid..	(1,597)	(1,596)	(1,596)
Net cash from (for) financing activities.......................	(8,778)	12,599	12,810
Increase (decrease) in cash and cash equivalents	(1,236)	722	123
Cash and cash equivalents at beginning of year	2,273	1,551	1,428
Cash and cash equivalents at end of year........................	$ 1,037	$ 2,273	$ 1,551

The accompanying notes are an integral part of these statements.

Donnelly Corporation and Subsidiaries

COMBINED CONSOLIDATED STATEMENTS OF SHAREHOLDERS' EQUITY

(in thousands, except per share data)	Preferred stock	Common stock Class A	Common stock Class B	Donnelly Export Corporation	Additional paid-in capital	Foreign currency translation adjustment	Retained earnings
Balance, July 1, 1988	$ 531	$ 268	$ 288	$ 4	$ 8,837	$ (482)	$ 25,448
Net income							6,216
Foreign currency translation adjustment						(626)	
Cash dividends declared:							
Preferred stock-$.75 per share							(40)
Common stock:							
Class A-$.28 per share							(750)
Class B-$.28 per share							(806)
Other					(6)		
Balance, June 30, 1989	531	268	288	4	8,831	(1,108)	30,068
Net income							2,337
Foreign currency translation adjustment						1,460	
Cash dividends declared:							
Preferred stock-$.75 per share							(40)
Common stock:							
Class A-$.28 per share							(750)
Class B-$.28 per share							(806)
Other					(308)		308
Balance, June 30, 1990	531	268	288	4	8,523	352	31,117
Net income							4,168
Foreign currency translation adjustment						(846)	
Cash dividends declared:							
Preferred stock-$.75 per share							(40)
Common stock:							
Class A-$.28 per share							(752)
Class B-$.28 per share							(805)
Common stock issued under employee benefit plan		1			121		
Other		1	(1)				
Balance, June 30, 1991	$ 531	$ 270	$ 287	$ 4	$ 8,644	$ (494)	$ 33,688

The accompanying notes are an integral part of these statements.

NOTES TO THE COMBINED CONSOLIDATED FINANCIAL STATEMENTS

1. SUMMARY OF SIGNIFICANT ACCOUNTING POLICIES

PRINCIPLES OF COMBINATION AND CONSOLIDATION

The combined consolidated financial statements include the accounts of Donnelly Corporation, Donnelly Export Corporation and all majority owned subsidiaries (the Company) after all significant intercompany balances, transactions and shareholdings have been eliminated.

Voting control of Donnelly Corporation and Donnelly Export Corporation is vested in the same shareholders and the corporations are under common management. Because of these relationships the accounts of the two corporations are included in the financial statements as if they were a single entity.

FOREIGN CURRENCY TRANSLATION

Assets and liabilities of the Company's foreign consolidated subsidiary are translated into U.S. dollars at the current exchange rates, while income and expenses are translated at the average rates of exchange during the period. Translation adjustments are reported in a separate component of shareholders' equity. Other foreign currency transaction gains or (losses) are included in net income and were $100,000, ($728,000) and $36,000 for 1991, 1990, and 1989, respectively.

CASH EQUIVALENTS

Cash equivalents include all highly liquid investments with a maturity of three months or less when purchased.

INVENTORIES

Inventories are stated at the lower of cost or market. Cost is determined by the last-in, first-out (LIFO) method, except for inventories of the subsidiaries which are valued at the first-in, first-out (FIFO) method.

PROPERTY, PLANT AND EQUIPMENT

Property, plant and equipment are stated at cost. Depreciation is provided primarily by the sum-of-the-years-digits accelerated method for property acquired prior to July 1, 1989 and the straight-line method for property acquired after June 30, 1989. Depreciation is computed over the estimated useful lives of the assets as follows:

	Years
Buildings	10 to 40
Machinery and equipment	3 to 12

For tax purposes, useful lives and accelerated methods are used as permitted by the taxing authorities.

RETIREMENT AND BENEFIT PLANS

The Company sponsors defined benefit pension plans covering substantially all employees. Pension costs for the plans are funded in amounts which equal or exceed regulatory requirements. Benefits under these plans are based primarily on years of service and the highest average level of compensation.

In addition to providing pension benefits, the Company provides certain health care and life insurance benefits for its active and eligible retired employees. The cost of retiree health care and life insurance benefits is recognized as expense as claims are paid. In December 1990, the FASB issued Statement No. 106 which requires the Company to record the liability for postretirement benefits other than pensions beginning in 1994. When adopted, the statement is expected to have a significant effect on the Company's financial statements. The Company is currently in the process of estimating the effects and therefore has not determined when to adopt this statement or when to recognize the transition obligation. In addition, the benefit plans are currently being reviewed for possible modifications.

INCOME TAXES

Deferred income taxes are provided on the difference in income determined for tax and financial statement purposes, which is caused primarily by timing differences relating to depreciation and pension cost.

Available tax credits are taken into income as reductions of current income tax provisions.

In December 1987, the FASB issued a new standard covering accounting for income taxes. The FASB subsequently delayed implementation of this new standard and is currently considering amendments to it. Accordingly, the Company is not in a position to evaluate the effect of any amendments to the standard. Based on its initial issuance, the application of the standard would not have a material effect on the Company.

INCOME PER SHARE OF COMMON STOCK

Income per share is computed by dividing net income, adjusted for preferred stock dividends, by the weighted average number of shares of Donnelly Corporation common stock outstanding (5,563,115 in 1991, and 5,558,087 shares in 1990 and 1989).

RECLASSIFICATIONS

Certain reclassifications have been made to prior year data to conform to the current year presentation.

2. INVENTORIES

Inventories consist of:

(in thousands) June 30,	1991	1990
LIFO cost:		
Finished products and work in process	$ 7,228	$ 7,291
Raw materials	8,169	7,222
	15,397	14,513
FIFO cost:		
Finished products and work in process	595	764
Raw materials	649	594
	1,244	1,358
	$16,641	$15,871

If only the first-in, first-out method of inventory valuation had been used, inventories would have been $413,000 and $826,000 higher than reported at June 30, 1991 and 1990, respectively, and would have approximated replacement cost.

3. LONG-TERM DEBT

Long-term debt consists of:

(in thousands) June 30,	1991	1990
Revolving credit agreements	$18,348	$25,600
Industrial revenue bonds	14,000	14,000
Insurance company note payable	8,000	8,000
Economic Development Corporation note payable	781	781
Other	214	304
Total	41,343	48,685
Less current maturities	78	117
	$41,265	$48,568

The Company has a revolving credit agreement in the amount of $50,000,000. The agreement expires March 31, 1995, at which time existing borrowings may be converted to a term loan payable in 16 equal, quarterly installments. Commitment fees range from .1875% to .375% of the unused portion of the credit line. Under the agreement, borrowings bear interest at prime unless one of three alternate elections are made by the Company. At June 30, 1991, borrowings of $16,000,000 were outstanding at an average rate of 7.1%.

The Company also has a revolving credit agreement in the amount of $2,500,000. The agreement expires September 1, 1992. Borrowings bear interest at 1.25% under prime unless one of two alternative elections are made by the Company. At June 30, 1991 borrowings of $2,348,000 were outstanding at a rate of 7.25%.

The industrial revenue bonds bear interest at adjustable rates, currently 4.95% to 5.00%. The bonds mature in fiscal years 2008-2010, provided letters of credit securing the bonds are renewed yearly. Maturity of the bonds may be accelerated under certain conditions as specified under the agreement. Unexpended proceeds from the bonds are held by trustees and are available only for property purchases on specified projects.

The insurance company note bears a fixed interest rate of 9.01%. Principal payments of $727,272 are due semiannually beginning September 30, 1991 until maturity on September 30, 1996. These amounts are classified as long-term as it is the Company's intent to refinance these borrowings on a long-term basis.

The Economic Development Corporation note bears interest at a rate equal to 76% of the prime interest rate. The note becomes due on June 1, 1995.

The various borrowings subject the Company to certain restrictions relating to, among other things, minimum net worth, payment of dividends and maintenance of certain financial ratios. Retained earnings available for dividends at June 30, 1991 are $4,201,000.

Annual principal maturities (in thousands) consist of:

Year ending June 30,	Amount
1992	$ 78
1993	2,389
1994	
1995	4,824
1996	6,561
1997 and thereafter	27,491
	$ 41,343

In 1991, the Company entered into interest rate swap agreements ranging from 5 to 7 years. These agreements convert $10 million of variable interest rate debt to fixed interest rates averaging 8.9%.

Interest payments of $4,190,000, $4,127,000, and $2,215,000 were made in 1991, 1990, and 1989 respectively.

NOTES TO THE COMBINED CONSOLIDATED FINANCIAL STATEMENTS (Continued)

4. PREFERRED STOCK AND COMMON STOCK

Preferred stock consists of:

(in thousands) June 30,	1991	1990
7 1/2% cumulative, $10 par-shares authorized 250; outstanding 53	$ 531	$ 531
Series preferred, no par-shares authorized 1,000; outstanding none		
	$ 531	$ 531

Common stock consists of:

(in thousands) June 30,	1991	1990
Class A, $.10 par-shares authorized 10,000; outstanding 2,697 and 2,682	$ 270	$ 268
Class B, $.10 par-shares authorized 6,000; outstanding 2,875, and 2,876	287	288
Donnelly Export Corporation, $.01 par-shares authorized 600; outstanding 411	4	4
	$ 561	$ 560

Each share of 7 1/2% cumulative preferred stock is entitled to one vote for the election of the members of the Board of Directors not elected by the holders of Class A Common Stock, and all other matters at all shareholders' meetings whenever dividend payments are in arrears for four cumulative quarters. No arrearage existed at June 30, 1991. The preferred stock is redeemable in whole or in part, if called by the Company, at $10.50 per share.

Each share of Class A Common Stock and Class B Common Stock is entitled to one vote and ten votes, respectively, at all shareholders' meetings. The holders of Class A Common Stock are entitled to elect one-quarter of the members of the Board of Directors. The remaining directors are elected by the holders of Class B Common Stock and any preferred stock entitled to vote.

5. STOCK PURCHASE AND OPTION PLANS

The Company's Employees' Stock Purchase Plan permits the purchase in an aggregate amount of up to 350,000 shares of Class A Common Stock. Eligible employees may purchase stock at market value, or 90% of market value if the price is $10 per share or higher, up to a maximum of $5,000 per employee in any fiscal year. This plan became effective July 1, 1990 and during 1991 the Company issued 12, 598 shares under this plan.

The Company's Stock Option Plan permits the granting of either nonqualified or incentive stock options to certain key employees and directors to purchase in an aggregate amount of up to 250,000 shares of the Corporation's Class A Common Stock. The options, which become exercisable twelve months after date of grant, expire after ten years from date of grant. Although the plan administrator may establish the nonqualified option price at below market value at date of grant, incentive stock options may be granted only at prices not less than the market value.

Options have been granted to purchase common stock at prices ranging from $11.50 to $13.00 per share. A summary of option transactions follows:

(in thousands) Year ended June 30,	1991	1990	1989
Options outstanding, beginning of year	149	149	94
Options granted			55
Options exercised			
Options outstanding, end of year	149	149	149
Exercisable at June 30,	149	149	94

The Company has reserved 100,900 shares for future grants at June 30, 1991.

6. RETIREMENT PLANS

Assumptions and net periodic pension costs are as follows:

(in thousands) Year ended June 30,	1991	1990	1989
Discount rate	9%	9%	9%
Compensation increase	5%	5%	5%
Expected return on plan assets	10%	10%	10%
Service cost	$1,848	$1,612	$1,209
Interest cost	2,558	2,200	1,868
Actual return on plan assets	(1,554)	(2,052)	(2,285)
Net amortization and deferral	(887)	217	582
	$1,965	$1,977	$1,374

The funded status of the defined benefit plans is summarized below.

(in thousands) June 30,	1991	1990
Accumulated benefit obligation, including vested benefits of $17,752 and $15,217	$ (18,608)	$ (15,896)
Effect of projected compensation increases..........	(12,085)	(11,138)
Projected benefit obligation for service rendered to date.......................	(30,693)	(27,034)
Plan assets at fair value, primarily corporate equity and debt securities..................	29,622	26,764
Projected benefit obligation in excess of plan assets...........	(1,071)	(270)
Unrecognized net transition obligation..................................	854	926
Unrecognized prior service cost	217	234
Unrecognized net (gain) loss...	1,106	(125)
Net pension asset	$ 1,106	$ 765

7. TAXES ON INCOME

(in thousands) Year ended June 30,	1991	1990	1989
Income before taxes on income consists of:			
Domestic	$5,043	$ 891	$6,699
Foreign	703	1,004	1,665
	$5,746	$1,895	$8,364
Tax expense (benefits) consist of:			
Current:			
Domestic	$2,816	$(1,495)	$1,038
Foreign	145	93	189
	2,961	(1,402)	1,227
Deferred:			
Domestic	(496)	1,325	929
Foreign		148	(8)
	(496)	1,473	921
	$2,465	$ 71	$2,148

Deferred income taxes resulted from the following timing differences:	1991	1990	1989
Depreciation	$ 567	$ 1,169	$ 714
Pension cost	(840)	519	340
Dividend from foreign subsidiary	(250)		(50)
Undistributed earnings of foreign subsidiary...............	(5)	(40)	152
Other	32	(175)	(235)
	$ (496)	$ 1,473	$ 921

The difference from the amount that would be computed by applying the federal statutory income tax rate to income before taxes on income is reconciled as follows:

(in thousands) Year ended June 30,	1991	1990	1989
Income taxes at federal statutory rate	34%	34%	34%
Impact of:			
Available tax credits................	(6)	(21)	(5)
Foreign subsidiary earnings..................................	(2)	(7)	(3)
DISC earnings..........................	(5)	(10)	(2)
Joint venture losses with no current tax benefit	16	23	
Tax benefit of net operating loss		(18)	
Other	6	3	2
Effective tax rate....................	43%	4%	26%
Income taxes paid..................	$1,439	$ 238	$1,522

Cumulative undistributed earnings of the foreign subsidiary amounted to $6,892,000 and $7,334,000 at June 30, 1991 and 1990, respectively, of which approximately $5,516,000 and $5,249,000 respectively, is intended to be permanently reinvested. Deferred federal income taxes of $456,000 and $711,000, respectively, have been provided against future expected distributions to the Company.

8. COMMITMENTS AND CONTINGENCIES

In May, 1990 the Company brought a patent-related suit to seek Court resolution to what were considered unfounded charges by a competitor against its electrochromic mirror. The Company is seeking a declaration that its electrochromic mirror does not infringe the competitor's U.S. patent and that the patent is invalid and unenforceable.

On the same day the above action was initiated, the competitor brought suit charging that the Company's mirror infringed a different U.S. patent. Subsequently the competitor has also charged that the Company's mirror infringes another U.S. patent. These actions have been consolidated and are now at the stage of discovery and other pretrial proceedings.

The Company's management believes the competitors charges are without merit and the Company intends to vigorously litigate the asserted claims.

9. LEASES

The Company leases various facilities and equipment. Rental expense charged to operations amounted to approximately $1,816,000 for 1991, $1,310,000 for 1990, and $937,000 for 1989.

Future minimum lease payments (in thousands) consist of:

Year ending June 30,	Amount
1992	$ 2,162
1993	1,718
1994	1,242
1995	1,088
1996	998
1997 and thereafter	377
	$ 7,585

10. SEGMENT REPORTING

The operations of the Company are divided into the following business segments for financial reporting purposes:

Automotive Products

The manufacture of interior and exterior rearview mirrors for world automotive markets and manufacture of modular windows for domestic automotive markets.

Coated Products

The manufacture of highly technical solid-state glass coatings for products used primarily in the electronics and computer industries worldwide.

Information by business segments is as follows:

(in thousands) Year ended June 30,	1991	1990	1989
Net Sales:			
Automotive Products	$202,514	$189,024	$165,462
Coated Products	30,327	24,062	32,861
	$232,841	$213,086	$198,323
Operating Income (Loss):			
Automotive Products	$ 6,906	$ 8,558	$ 8,432
Coated Products	709	(2,707)	1,752
	$ 7,615	$ 5,851	$ 10,184
Identifiable Assets:			
Automotive Products	$ 96,463	$103,755	$ 78,844
Coated Products	24,941	24,915	25,381
	$121,404	$128,670	$104,225
Depreciation Expense:			
Automotive Products	$ 5,978	$ 5,885	$ 4,724
Coated Products	2,121	2,245	1,964
	$ 8,099	$ 8,130	$ 6,688
Capital Expenditures:			
Automotive Products	$ 7,476	$ 20,135	$ 9,666
Coated Products	678	1,406	9,139
	$ 8,154	$ 21,541	$ 18,805

The Company derived approximately 28% of its consolidated revenues from markets outside the United States in 1991, 29% in 1990 and 30% in 1989.

Export revenues are foreign revenues produced by identifiable assets located in the United States. Foreign revenues are generated by identifiable assets located at the Company's Irish subsidiary which produces automotive products.

A summary of the Company's operations by geographic area follows:

(in thousands) Year ended June 30,	1991	1990	1989
Revenues:			
United States	$167,717	$151,606	$139,491
Foreign	19,504	19,668	18,391
Export:			
Americas	22,242	19,369	14,377
Asia	19,847	16,605	23,267
Europe	2,683	4,361	2,243
Other	848	1,477	554
	$232,841	$213,086	$198,323
Operating Income:			
United States	$ 6,925	$ 4,094	$ 8,668
Foreign	690	1,757	1,516
	$ 7,615	$ 5,851	$ 10,184
Identifiable Assets:			
United States	$108,681	$114,650	$ 93,220
Foreign	12,723	14,020	11,005
	$121,404	$128,670	$104,225

Sales to major U.S. automobile manufacturers as a percent of the Company's net sales follows:

Year ended June 30,	1991	1990	1989
General Motors Corporation	22%	22%	16%
Ford Motor Company	19	27	32
Honda of America Mfg., Inc.	16	12	7
Chrysler Corporation	11	12	13
	68%	73%	68%

11. COMMON STOCK PRICE PER SHARE - UNAUDITED

Fiscal Quarter	1991 High	1991 Low	1990 High	1990 Low
First	$ 10⁵/₈	$ 7³/₄	$ 13¹/₄	$ 11¹/₈
Second	9⁵/₈	8	12¹/₈	8¹/₂
Third	12⁷/₈	8³/₄	9³/₈	8
Fourth	13¹/₈	11	10⁷/₈	9³/₈

As of August 2, 1991, the Company had approximately 2,500 holders of record.

12. QUARTERLY FINANCIAL DATA - UNAUDITED

(in thousands, except per share data) Three months ended,	September 30	December 31	March 31	June 30	Total Year
1991					
Net sales	$ 58,447	$ 57,769	$ 52,189	$ 64,436	$ 232,841
Gross profit	12,043	11,379	10,495	14,895	48,812
Operating income	2,640	1,642	428	2,905	7,615
Net income	1,646	1,041	160	1,321	4,168
Income per share of common stock	.29	.19	.03	.23	.74
Dividends declared per share of common stock	.07	.07	.07	.07	.28
1990					
Net sales	$ 44,730	$ 50,952	$ 55,084	$ 62,320	$ 213,086
Gross profit	7,272	10,963	10,823	13,353	42,411
Operating income (loss)	(1,405)	2,006	2,331	2,919	5,851
Net income (loss)	(1,347)	610	1,055	2,019	2,337
Income (loss) per share of common stock	(.24)	.11	.19	.35	.41
Dividends declared per share of common stock	.07	.07	.07	.07	.28

REPORT OF INDEPENDENT CERTIFIED PUBLIC ACCOUNTANTS

We have audited the combined consolidated balance sheets of Donnelly Corporation and subsidiaries as of June 30, 1991 and 1990, and the related combined consolidated statements of income, shareholders' equity, and cash flows for each of the three years in the period ended June 30, 1991. These financial statements are the responsibility of the Company's management. Our responsibility is to express an opinion on these financial statements based on our audits. We did not audit the financial statements of Donnelly Mirrors Limited, the foreign subsidiary, which statements reflect total assets, net sales and net income constituting 10%, 8%, and 13% respectively for 1991, 11%, 9%, and 33% for 1990, and 9% and 24% of net sales and net income, respectively, for 1989, of related combined consolidated totals. Those statements were audited by other auditors whose reports thereon have been furnished to us, and our opinion expressed herein, insofar as it relates to the amounts included for Donnelly Mirrors Limited, is based solely upon the reports of the other auditors.

We conducted our audits in accordance with generally accepted auditing standards. Those standards require that we plan and perform the audit to obtain reasonable assurance about whether the financial statements are free of material misstatement. An audit includes examining, on a test basis, evidence supporting the amounts and disclosures in the financial statements. An audit also includes assessing the accounting principles used and significant estimates made by management, as well as evaluating the overall financial statement presentation. We believe that our audits and the reports of the other auditors provide a reasonable basis for our opinion.

In our opinion, based on our audits and the reports of the other auditors, the combined consolidated financial statements referred to above present fairly, in all material respects, the financial position of Donnelly Corporation and subsidiaries as of June 30, 1991 and 1990, and the results of their operations and cash flows for each of the three years in the period ended June 30, 1991, in conformity with generally accepted accounting principles.

BDO Seidman
Certified Public Accountants
Grand Rapids, Michigan
July 29, 1991

Donnelly Corporation and Subsidiaries

SELECTED FINANCIAL DATA

(in thousands, except per share and employee data) Year ended June 30,	1991	1990
SUMMARY OF OPERATIONS		
Automotive Products net sales	$202,514	$189,024
Coated Products net sales	30,327	24,062
Total net sales	232,841	213,086
Cost of sales	184,029	170,675
Gross profit	48,812	42,411
Selling, administrative and general expenses	28,698	24,699
Research and development expenses	12,499	11,861
Operating income	7,615	5,851
Interest expense	3,914	4,273
Royalty income	(1,484)	(788)
Non-operating expense (income)	(561)	471
Income before taxes on income	5,746	1,895
Taxes on income	2,465	71
Income before minority interest	3,281	1,824
Minority interest in loss of subsidiary	887	513
Net income	$ 4,168	$ 2,337
PER SHARE OF COMMON STOCK		
Net income	$ 0.74	$ 0.41
Dividends	0.28	0.28
Book value	7.61	7.29
FINANCIAL POSITION		
Current assets	$ 58,366	$ 61,249
Current liabilities	32,310	32,816
Working capital	26,056	28,433
Property, plant and equipment - net	59,122	59,248
Total assets	121,404	128,670
Debt including current maturities	41,343	48,685
Redeemable preferred stock	531	531
Shareholders' equity (common)	42,372	40,525
Shareholders' equity (total)	42,930	41,083
ADDITIONAL INFORMATION		
Capital expenditures	$ 8,154	$ 21,541
Depreciation and amortization	8,099	8,130
Average number of employees	2,319	2,157
Return on average shareholders' equity	9.9	5.8
Dividends as a percent of net income	38.3	68.3
Weighted average common shares outstanding	5,563	5,558

1989	1988	1987	1986	1985	1984	1983	1982
$ 165,462	$131,811	$ 108,188	$ 94,254	$ 66,844	$ 60,389	$ 37,389	$ 36,984
32,861	25,314	17,756	10,870	10,192	8,255	8,477	5,434
198,323	157,125	125,944	105,124	77,036	68,644	45,866	42,418
156,275	122,087	95,115	81,800	58,010	52,765	33,500	32,138
42,048	35,038	30,829	23,324	19,026	15,879	12,366	10,280
21,088	18,111	16,028	11,957	10,179	8,114	6,639	5,660
10,776	9,475	7,093	5,029	4,014	3,073	2,649	1,862
10,184	7,452	7,708	6,338	4,833	4,692	3,078	2,758
2,648	1,341	1,012	784	650	491	284	791
(171)	(96)						
(657)	(948)	(460)	(521)	(88)	(126)	(456)	(177)
8,364	7,155	7,156	6,075	4,271	4,327	3,250	2,144
2,148	1,746	2,132	1,667	1,053	1,271	1,148	842
6,216	5,409	5,024	4,408	3,218	3,056	2,102	1,302
$ 6,216	$ 5,409	$ 5,024	$ 4,408	$ 3,218	$ 3,056	$ 2,102	$ 1,302
$ 1.11	$ 1.06	$ 1.01	$ 0.88	$ 0.64	$ 0.61	$ 0.41	$ 0.25
0.28	0.23	0.21	0.20	0.15	0.14	0.05	0.03
6.90	6.18	4.88	4.01	3.10	2.66	2.30	2.12
$ 51,553	$ 44,312	$ 29,580	$ 26,268	$ 20,204	$ 17,948	$ 15,685	$ 12,630
26,382	26,797	16,154	14,268	12,251	8,350	7,823	6,143
25,171	17,515	13,426	12,000	7,953	9,598	7,862	6,487
48,415	36,467	26,011	20,615	15,764	10,395	7,923	8,526
104,225	85,182	57,557	47,096	36,113	28,469	23,943	21,451
34,855	20,568	14,150	10,500	7,003	5,346	3,072	2,647
531	531	531	678	678	698	698	698
38,324	34,336	24,077	19,802	15,291	13,118	11,338	10,487
38,882	34,894	24,635	20,514	16,003	13,851	12,071	11,220
$ 18,805	$ 16,281	$ 9,751	$ 8,071	$ 7,789	$ 4,238	$ 1,206	$ 329
6,688	5,711	4,272	3,123	2,216	1,557	1,289	1,262
1,969	1,598	1,364	1,262	1,051	959	744	703
16.9	17.3	22.3	24.1	21.6	23.6	18.0	11.4
25.7	22.7	22.6	25.0	26.0	26.1	19.4	24.0
5,558	5,077	4,937	4,937	4,937	4,937	4,937	4,940

MANAGEMENT'S RESPONSIBILITY FOR FINANCIAL REPORTING

The management of Donnelly Corporation is responsible for the preparation and integrity of the combined consolidated financial statements and all other information contained in this Annual Report. The financial statements were prepared in accordance with generally accepted accounting principles and include amounts that are based on management's informed estimates and judgements.

In fulfilling its responsibility for the integrity of financial information, management has established a system of internal accounting control which provides reasonable assurance that assets are properly safeguarded and accounted for and that transactions are executed in accordance with management's authorization and recorded and reported properly.

The financial statements have been audited by our independent public accountants, BDO Seidman, whose unqualified report is presented on the next page. The independent accountants provide an objective assessment of the degree to which management meets its responsibility for fairness of financial reporting. They regularly evaluate the control structure and perform such tests and other procedures as they deem necessary to reach and express an opinion on the fairness of the financial statements.

The Audit Committee of the Board of Directors, consisting solely of outside directors, meets regularly with the independent public accountants and management to review and discuss the major audit findings, the adequacy of the system of internal accounting control, and quality of financial reporting. The independent accountants also have free access to the Audit Committee to discuss auditing and financial reporting matters with or without management present.

J. Dwane Baumgardner, Ph.D.
*Chief Executive Officer and
Chairman of the Board*

Paul G. Kalkman
President

James A. Knister
*Senior Vice President of Administration
and Chief Financial Officer*

William R. Jellison
*Treasurer and
Corporate Controller*

APPENDIX

M

MICROSTUDY+® can help you learn a great deal more about accounting through computer interaction. Special care has been taken to make the program as flexible and as comprehensive as possible to speed the learning process.

Please study the chapters in your textbook prior to reviewing them. Otherwise, you will be guessing at most of the answers to the questions. Remember, the overall purpose of MICROSTUDY+ is to reinforce the content, rather than to teach you new materials from scratch.

STARTING MICROSTUDY+

Hard-Disk Users

A batch program will simplify installation onto the hard disk drive. Insert the program disk into Drive A and obtain an A> prompt. Then enter the following command:

```
install c
```

Assuming that C:\ is the default hard drive, INSTALL will copy the software to the hard disk subdirectory\study\hanson. Follow all the instructions as they appear on the screen, transferring one disk after the other. When INSTALL finishes, start the program by entering STUDY in response to the DOS prompt.

Twin-Floppy Users

Boot the PC and obtain an A> prompt. Insert the Program Disk into Drive A. Insert the data disk into Drive B. Enter STUDY in response to the A> prompt.

THE MAIN MENU OPTIONS

When the Main Menu appears; you may use the up or down arrow keys or Tab to adjust Main Menu options. As you move from one option to the next, the new option will be highlighted.

To select the highlighted option, press the ↵ key to accept it. The numeric keys are "hot keys" that will immediately invoke an option without pressing ↵.

Initially, you will want to select a chapter from your textbook for review. To do this, simply press ↵ or <1>. A window will appear containing chapter numbers and titles. Use your cursor control keys to scroll through the list. Select the highlighted chapter by pressing ↵, and the Main Menu will reappear. The chapter you select will be retained by the program even after you turn it off.

Learning Objectives

The Chapter Objectives will be presented after selecting Option 2. Study them carefully to provide direction for your study of the various topics covered in the chapter. The learning objectives establish a setting and provide a conceptual framework for what you should learn.

Key Terms

Option 3 initiates a list of key terms that you should be able to define and understand. Study the list carefully. If you are unfamiliar with any of them, look them up in your textbook before moving on to the rest of the learning modules. The terms are shown first in the order that they appear in the chapter. You can alphabetize the list by pressing the F1 function key.

Matching

Option 4 starts a matching quiz to test your vocabulary. Some chapters have two or more sets of questions for you. A list of terms will appear in a window at the top of the screen. It is your job to pair one of these terms up with a sentence containing

```
┌──────────────────────────────────────────────────────────────┐
│ ◄    MICROSTUDY MAIN MENU   ►                                 │
├──────────────────────────────────────────────────────────────┤
│ OPTIONS                                                        │
│                                                                │
│ 1 ═►Select Chapter in Textbook for Review                      │
│                                                                │
│ 2 ═►Study Chapter Learning Objectives                          │
│                                           ┌──────────────────┐ │
│ 3 ═►List Key Terms in the Chapter         │ Studying Chapter 1│ │
│                                           │                  │ │
│ 4 ═►Vocabulary Building with Matching Exercises               │ │
│                                           │                  │ │
│ 5 ═►True/False Statement Drill            │                  │ │
│                                           │                  │ │
│ 6 ═►Multiple Choice Question Drill        │                  │ │
│                                           │                  │ │
│ 7 ═►Review Instructions for Using MICROSTUDY                  │ │
│                                           └──────────────────┘ │
│ 8 ═►Set or Change the Operating Environment                    │
│                                                                │
│ Hanson / Hamre / Walgenbach        Select Your Option (1 - 8)  │
├──────────────────────────────────────────────────────────────┤
│ PRINCIPLES OF ACCOUNTING, 6/e                  <Esc> to Exit   │
└──────────────────────────────────────────────────────────────┘
```

the term. This sentence may actually define the term, or it may require the term to complete the underlying thought. If you select the right corresponding term, it will flash momentarily in the top window. Some of the terms in a set may not have an accompanying definition or description.

Scoring

MICROSTUDY+ will track your scores of rights, wrongs, and attempts (tries). If you miss the term more than once, your percent score will not decrease, but the number of tries will increase. Always try to find the correct term on your first attempt.

Timer

A timer will be set the instant you are prompted for an answer to each item in a quiz. The watch stops when you supply the correct answer and is reset to zero until the next item appears. The elapsed testing time is recorded, and it will appear whenever you return to the Main Menu. By using the timer coupled with a preset number of questions, you can use MICROSTUDY+ to practice for in-class tests and know precisely whether you will be able to finish on time.

By pressing the F1 function key from the Main Menu screen you may reset the scoring tallies to zero. Pressing the F2 function key resets the timer for a fresh start. The F1 and F2 keys are independent toggle switches that restore the scores or the timer in case you clear them unintentionally. However, once you depart from the Main Menu to perform some other activity, you will not be able to restore values that have been cleared.

True/False

Option 5 invokes a true/false statement quiz. As soon as you supply an answer, you will see a rejoinder response on the screen, indicating whether you were right or wrong. Additional discussion is provided for each of the false statements to explain why the statement is false. Once again, your score of rights, wrongs, and attempts (tries) will be tallied as you move along.

Multiple Choice

Option 6 launches a multiple-choice question quiz to test further your knowledge of the chapter material. As soon as you choose the correct answer, a rejoinder will appear to reinforce your decision. Study it carefully to be sure that your reasoning for selecting the correct answer was similar to the authors'.

Whenever a long question appears that exceeds the boundary of the text window, use the arrow keys or the <PgDn> and <PgUp> keys to scroll through the text. Vertical arrows let you know which direction you can scroll. The window that is ready for scrolling will be framed with a double line and a <down arrow> will appear in the corner the instant a question or a discussion larger than the window is detected. You can toggle between scrollable text windows using the left and right arrow keys.

Printing

When you have completed all of the multiple-choice questions available for a given chapter, you have the opportunity to print each item and the accompanying answers that relate to each. If a printer is connected to the computer, be sure it is on line and ready with paper before you begin. The program will issue a form feed before starting. After you position the printer head at the perforation of the paper, pagination will be correct once the printing commences. Each chapter will require several pages to finish.

OPERATING ENVIRONMENT

The operating environment can be adjusted by selecting Option 8. Use this screen to change the audio and video alternatives, switch disk drive letters, or turn off the timer display. Your instructor may request that the speaker be silenced while you are using MICROSTUDY+ in the laboratory so that other students are not disturbed. Note that once you have configured the operating environment correctly, you will seldom if ever have to change it in order to use the program.

You may also review these instructions by selecting Option 7, just in case you get lost and need a little help to get back on track. When you are finished or want to take a break, press the <Esc> key.

USING MICROSTUDY+ ON THE MACINTOSH

The minimum hardware requirements for the Macintosh version of MICROSTUDY+ are 512 KB RAM and a single 800 KB disk drive. Complete operating instructions for the Macintosh version of MICROSTUDY+ are available in the form of a MacWrite file on the Macintosh diskette.

1-29 a. Total assets, $17,840
1-30 b. Total assets, $26,360
1-31 b. Total assets, $72,200
1-32 a. Net income, $8,400
     c. Total assets, $25,800
1-33 a. Total assets, $64,300 for 1993
1-34 a. Total assets, $85,900
1-29A a. Total assets, $19,620
1-30A b. Total assets, $13,650
1-31A b. Total assets, $28,060
1-32A a. Net income, $13,000
     c. Total assets, $22,500
1-33A a. Total assets, $259,000 for 1993
1-34A a. Total assets, $178,900
Business Decision Case a. Seale's return, 28%
Analytical Application Case a. Year 1, 1.10

2-29 b. Trial balance total, $40,870
2-30 a. Trial balance total, $37,050
2-31 b. Corrected trial balance total, $21,420
2-32 b. Trial balance total, $33,460
2-33 b. Trial balance total, $118,650
2-34 No key figure
2-29A b. Trial balance total, $31,200
2-30A a. Trial balance total, $23,200
2-31A b. Corrected trial balance total, $43,140
2-32A b. Trial balance total, $17,700
2-33A b. Trial balance total, $53,440
2-34A No key figure
Business Decision Case a. Net income, $19,490
Analytical Application Case a. Year 2, 0.26

3-26 d. Trial balance total, $20,200
3-27 c. Trial balance total, $23,100
3-28 a. Trial balance total, $44,930
3-29 No key figure
3-30 No key figure
3-31 b. Ticket revenue, $13,600
3-26A d. Trial balance total, $12,925
3-27A c. Trial balance total, $43,700
3-28A a. Trial balance total, $99,250
3-29A No key figure
3-30A No key figure
3-31A b. Rent revenue, $34,500
Business Decision Case Revised owner's equity, $30,650
Analytical Application Case a. Year 3, Net income, 158.7

4-28 a. Net income, $16,060
4-29 a. Net income, $8,795
4-30 No key figure
4-31 a. Net income, $9,900
4-32 No key figure
4-33 No key figure
4-28A a. Net income, $24,300
4-29A a. Net income, $41,900
4-30A b. Net income, $4,350
4-31A a. Net income, $7,940
4-32A a. Net income, $23,140
4-33A No key figure
Business Decision Case L. Hart, Capital, Aug. 31, $6,345
Analytical Application Case b. 1988, 1.03
Mini Practice Set—Howe c. Net income, $5,290
Mini Practice Set—Fero c. Net income, $3,540

5-31 No key figure
5-32 No key figure
5-33 Net income, $77,920
5-34 a. Net income, $15,000
5-35 a. Net income, $27,000
5-36 Net income, $48,000
5-37 b. Net income, $38,800
5-38 No key figure
5-39 No key figure
5-40 Net income, $77,920
5-41 Net income, $77,920
5-42 a. Net income, $27,000
5-31A No key figure
5-32A No key figure
5-33A Net loss, $6,440
5-34A a. Net income, $31,200
5-35A a. Net income, $29,800
5-36A Net income, $28,800
5-37A b. Net income, $34,000
5-38A No key figure
5-39A No key figure
5-40A Net loss, $6,440
5-41A Net loss, $6,440
5-42A a. Net income, $29,800
Business Decision Case December ending inventory, $110,000
Analytical Application Case Year 3, 39.9%

6-24 a. Cash receipts, $9,202
6-25 a. Cash disbursements, $8,500
6-26 a. Cash receipts, $24,224; cash disbursements, $5,040
6-27 c. Cash receipts, $3,511; cash disbursements, $6,022
     e. Trial balance total, $67,418
6-28 Trial balance total, $246,960

6-29 b. Vouchers payable credit in voucher register, $6,406; cash credit in check register, $5,024

6-30 Vouchers payable credit in voucher register, $4,377; cash credit in check register, $2,296

6-24A a. Cash receipts, $6,628

6-25A a. Cash disbursements, $6,684

6-26A a. Cash receipts, $33,235; cash disbursements, $5,044

6-27A c. Cash receipts, $3,664; cash disbursements, $7,079
       e. Trial balance total, $79,936

6-28A Trial balance total $251,330

6-29A b. Vouchers payable credit in voucher register, $7,947; cash credit in check register, $7,243

6-30A Vouchers payable credit in voucher register, $5,172; cash credit in check register, $2,806

Business Decision Case No key figure
Analytical Application Case Year 3, 4.1%

7-28 No key figure
7-29 No key figure
7-30 a. Adjusted balance, $11,532.60
7-31 a. Adjusted balance, $14,008
7-32 No key figure
7-33 a. Dec. 31, 1992 Unrealized loss, $8,298
7-34 a. Dec. 31, 1992 Unrealized loss, $9,000
7-28A No key figure
7-29A No key figure
7-30A a. Adjusted balance, $7,554.30
7-31A a. Adjusted balance, $13,446
7-32A No key figure
7-33A a. Dec. 31, 1991 Unrealized loss, $5,520
7-34A No key figure

Business Decision Case
a. Discrepancy, $5,000
Analytical Application Case
a. Phillips, 0.78

8-27 Total uncollectible accounts expense: a. $18,200; b. $27,625
8-28 b. Net accounts receivable, $126,655
8-29 b. Net accounts receivable, $353,960
8-30 No key figure
8-31 b. 1. 8.16%
8-32 b. Interest income adjustment, $25
8-33 Dec. 31 interest expense adjustment, $108

8-34 c. Dec. 31 interest expense adjustment, $50
8-27A Total uncollectible accounts expense: a. $17,300; b. $25,920
8-28A b. Net accounts receivable, $126,640
8-29A b. Net accounts receivable, $298,880
8-30A No key figure
8-31A No key figure
8-32A b. Interest income adjustment, $36
8-33A Dec. 31 interest expense adjustment, $135
8-34A c. Dec. 31 Interest expense adjustment, $120

Business Decision Case Net income, $37,483
Analytical Application Case Accounts receivable turnover, Snap-on Tools, Year 2, 2.16

9-28 a. Ending inventory: LIFO, $21,000; weighted average, $24,000
9-29 b. Ending inventory, $9,750
9-30 a. $83,000
9-31 a. 1. $46,380
9-32 No key figure
9-33 a. Cost-to-retail percentage, 64%
9-34 No key figure
9-28A a. Ending inventory: FIFO, $57,400
9-29A a. Ending inventory, $1,530
9-30A a. $98,000
9-31A a. 2. $53,920
9-32A a. 1991, 35%
9-33A a. Cost-to-retail percentage, 66%
9-34A No key figure

Business Decision Case No key figure
Analytical Application Case
a. Grainger turnover: Yr 1, 3.03

10-28 Building, $4,389,800
10-29 a. $97,500 allocated to Land
10-30 b. Year 2, $20,250; c. Year 2, $18,000
10-31 No key figure
10-32 1995 depreciation, $2,430
10-33 a. 1994 depreciation, $3,750
10-34 No key figure
10-28A Land, $183,800
10-29A a. $22,000 allocated to Trucks
10-30A b. 2. 1995, $21,700; 3. 1995, $21,600
10-31A No key figure
10-32A 1994 depreciation, $2,540
10-33A b. $18,050
10-34A No key figure

Business Decision Case No key figure
Analytical Application Case a. Year 1, 12.1%

11-29 d. Loss on sale of plant assets,
       $10,000
11-30 No key figure
11-31 b. $78,000
11-32 No key figure
11-33 b. Depreciation on truck,
       $150
11-34 Total assets, $1,276,000
11-29A f. Theft loss, $6,600
11-30A No key figure
11-31A c. $100,000
11-32A No key figure
11-33A b. Depreciation on printing
       equipment, $2,750
11-34A Total assets, $910,000
Business Decision Case No key figure
Analytical Application Case a. Year 1,
1.45

12-25 a. $2,625
12-26 a. Sales tax payable, $10,080
12-27 a. Payroll payable, $70,000
12-28 a. Payroll payable, $63,436
12-29 a. Total net earnings,
       $1,520.27
12-25A a. $4,240
12-26A a. Sales tax payable, $12,000
12-27A a. Payroll payable, $72,900
12-28A a. Payroll payable, $65,862
12-29A a. Total net earnings,
       $1,591.84
Business Decision Case Annual
savings, $33,201.50
Analytical Application Case b. Year 3,
0.28

13-26 No key figure
13-27 b. 2. 1994, $70,560
13-28 b. 2. 1994, $4,480,000
13-29 No key figure
13-30 a. Total assets, $2,168,500
13-31 a. Net income, $50,000
13-26A No key figure
13-27A b. 1993, $118,000
13-28A b 2. 1995, $1,000,000
13-29A No key figure
13-30A b. 1994, $5,000,000
13-31A a. Net income, $13,000
Business Decision Case No key
figure
Analytical Application Case a. Year 1,
2.36

14-26 a. 3. Credits to capital:
       Gordon, $26,000;
       Madden, $22,000
14-27 a. 3. Credits to capital:
       Dole, $30,000; Fine,
       $30,000; Thomas,
       $60,000
14-28 c. Credits to capital:
       Brady, $4,000; Dalton,
       $4,000; Felton, $38,000
14-29 c. Debits to capital:
       Klein, $100,000; Bower,
       $8,000; Green, $8,000

14-30 b. Capital balances:
       Fletcher, $60,000;
       Marshall, $96,000
14-31 Ending capital balance for
       Litton, $68,000
14-32 a. Cash distribution:
       Frain, $30,000; Hawk,
       $102,000; Lund, $88,000
14-33 b. Cash distribution:
       Boyd, $78,000; Dunn,
       $90,000
14-26A a. 3. Credits to capital: Ritter,
       $24,000; Varney, $18,000
14-27A a. 3. Credits to capital:
       Baker, $40,000; Kane,
       $20,000; Quinn, $12,000
14-28A c. Credits to capital:
       Curtis, $8,000; James,
       $8,000; Pierce, $52,000
14-29A c. Debits to capital: Warren,
       $80,000; Anderson, $6,000;
       Carroll, $6,000
14-30A b. Capital balances: Allen,
       $80,000; Kohl, $90,000
14-31A Ending capital balance for
       Arnold, $61,600
14-32A a. Cash distribution: Cody,
       $17,000; Lyon, $51,000;
       Parker, $82,000
14-33A b. Cash distribution: Gregg,
       $94,000; Ritt, $46,000
Business Decision Case Cash
distribution: Campbell, $230,000;
Miller, $330,000
Analytical Application Case Net
Income: Year 2, 5.9%; Year 1, 10.8%

15-26 b. Total: preferred, $420,000;
       common, $340,000
15-27 b. Total stockholders' equity,
       $1,384,500
15-28 c. Total stockholders' equity,
       $2,103,200
15-29 c. Total stockholders' equity,
       $2,708,700
15-30 No key figure
15-31 a. Preferred stock, $103;
       common stock, $16.20
15-26A b. Total: preferred, $81,000;
       common, $108,000
15-27A b. Total stockholders' equity,
       $2,034,000
15-28A c. Total stockholders' equity,
       $1,695,600
15-29A c. Total stockholders' equity,
       $2,760,700
15-30A No key figure
15-31A a. Preferred stock, $77;
       common stock, $9.40
Business Decision Case a. Total assets,
$483,100
Analytical Application Case b. 3.
Northrop's return, 22.1%

16-28 b. Total year-end retained
       earnings, $339,000

16-29 b. Total year-end retained earnings, $566,500

16-30 b. Total stockholders' equity, $1,176,400

16-31 a. Net income, $75,000

16-32 a. $3.00

16-33 Net income, $93,000

16-28A b. Total year-end retained earnings, $320,850

16-29A b. Total year-end retained earnings, $321,300

16-30A b. 277,500

16-31A a. Net income, $135,000

16-32A a. $3.00

16-33A Net income, $279,000

Business Decision Case b. 1993, $38.80; 1994, $37.00

Analytical Application Case a. $1.35

17-29 b. Loss on bond retirement, $1,800

17-30 a. 5. Loss on bond retirement, $9,000

17-31 a. Book value, end of period 2, $529,930

17-32 a. Book value, end of period 2, $438,615

17-33 No key figure

17-34 No key figure

17-35 No key figure

17-36 a. 1994, $1,600

17-37 a. 1. $32,410; c. $8,646; e. $46,340

17-29A b. Gain on bond retirement, $800

17-30A a. 5. Loss on bond retirement, $3,875

17-31A a. Book value, end of period 2, $662,261

17-32A a. Book value, end of period 2, $349,885

17-33A No key figure

17-34A No key figure

17-35A No key figure

17-36A c. 1993, $3,750

17-37A a. $34,506.56; c. $25,932

Business Decision Case No key figure

Analytical Application Case a. Year 1, 75.9

18-29 No key figure

18-30 December 31, 1993 adjustment, $7,000

18-31 No key figure

18-32 a. Goodwill from consolidation, $35,000

18-33 c. $1,025,000

18-34 Total consolidated assets, $1,875,000

18-35 Consolidated net income $131,500

18-36 No key figure

18-37 d. $153,800

18-38 Total assets, $557,600

18-29A No key figure

18-30A December 31, 1993 adjustment, $19,500

18-31A No key figure

18-32A a. Goodwill from consolidation, $75,000

18-33A c. $1,143,000

18-34A Total consolidated assets, $1,910,000

18-35A Consolidated net income, $63,000

18-36A No key figure

18-37A d. $150,500

18-38A Total assets, $583,400

Business Decision Case No key figure

Analytical Application Case a. Ball Corporation, 4.2%

19-30 b. Net cash provided by operating activities, $16,000

19-31 b. Net cash used by operating activities, $28,000

19-32 b. Net cash provided by operating activities, $143,000

19-33 b. Net cash provided by operating activities, $86,000

19-34 b. Net cash provided by operating activities, $16,000

19-35 b. Net cash used by operating activities, $28,000

19-36 b. Net cash provided by operating activities, $143,000

19-37 b. Net cash provided by operating activities, $86,000

19-38 b. Net cash provided by operating activities, $16,000

19-39 b. Net cash used by operating activities, $28,000

19-40 b. Net cash provided by operating activities, $143,000

19-41 b. Net cash provided by operating activities, $86,000

19-30A b. Net cash provided by operating activities, $67,000

19-31A b. Net cash provided by operating activities, $72,000

19-32A b. Net cash provided by operating activities, $35,000

19-33A b. Net cash provided by operating activities, $39,000

19-34A b. Net cash provided by operating activities, $67,000

19-35A b. Net cash provided by operating activities, $72,000

19-36A b. Net cash provided by operating activities, $35,000

19-37A b. Net cash provided by operating activities, $39,000

19-38A b. Net cash provided by operating activities, $67,000

19-39A b. Net cash provided by operating activities, $72,000

19-40A b. Net cash provided by operating activities, $39,000

19-41A b. Net cash provided by operating activities, $35,000

Business Decision Case No key figure
Analytical Application Case a. Year 1, Grumman Corp., 43.1%

20-26 a. 1994, net sales, 133.0%
20-27 a. 2. 8.6%
20-28 a. 1994 quick ratio, 0.86
20-29 Gross profit, $1,600,000; inventory, $910,000
20-30 a. 3. 18.5%
20-31 a. 4. 3.11
20-26A a. 1990, Ford Motor Company, 130.2%
20-27A a. 5. 4.64
20-28A a. 1994 debt-to-equity ratio, 0.72
20-29A Gross profit, $234,000; inventory, $90,000
20-30A a. 1. 7.8%
20-31A a. 2. 2.30
Business Decision Case 1993: current ratio, 2.07; return on sales, 2.1%
Analytical Application Case a. 1. 1991, 21.0%; a. 6. 1991, 1.81

21-24 Cost of goods sold, $403,000
21-25 Period C cost of goods sold, $1,840
21-26 No key figure
21-27 b. Work in process inventory ending balance, $47,500
21-28 b. Net income, $60,000
21-29 b. Net income, $103,600
21-30 c. Cost of goods sold, $414,000
21-31 b. Finished goods, $11,500
21-24A Cost of goods sold, $814,000
21-25A Period C cost of goods sold, $3,680
21-26A No key figure
21-27A b. Work in process inventory ending balance, $49,600
21-28A b. Net income, $50,000
21-29A b. Net income, $144,000
21-30A c. Cost of goods sold, $1,294,400

21-31A b. Finished goods, $13,600
Business Decision Case b. Net income, $80,150

22-27 c. Overhead assigned, $160
22-28 b. Indirect labor cost incurred, $25,500
22-29 b. Underapplied overhead, $8,800
22-30 b. Overapplied overhead, $2,000
22-31 b. Cost of goods manufactured, $1,053,000
22-32 c. Ending work in process inventory, $30,800
22-33 d. Ending work in process inventory, $53,040
22-34 d. Activity-based product cost, $32,610
22-27A c. Overhead assigned, $342
22-28A b. Indirect labor cost incurred, $16,000
22-29A b. Underapplied overhead, $8,000
22-30A h. Overapplied overhead, $1,100
22-31A b. Cost of goods manufactured, $1,176,000
22-32A c. Ending work in process inventory, $52,400
22-33A d. Ending work in process inventory, $90,800
22-34A d. Activity-based product cost, $45,361
Business Decision Case a. Total amount billed, $11,996.60

23-26 a. Units transferred into printing, 59,000
23-27 b. Phase I equivalent units for material and conversion, 202,000
23-28 b. Equivalent units: material, 61,000; conversion, 61,200
23-29 c. Unit cost transferred out, $5.50
23-30 b. Finished goods inventory, $122,000
23-31 Cost of units transferred out, $770,250
23-32 b. Department 1, $14.20 per machine hour
23-33 a. Allocated to R, $59,500
23-34 b. Equivalent units: Cutting: material, 66,000; conversion, 61,800
23-35 a. Cost of units transferred out, $887,800
23-26A a. Units transferred into painting, 74,000
23-27A b. Phase I equivalent units for material and coversion, 118,000
23-28A b. Equivalent units: material, 71,000; conversion, 70,000

23-29A c. Unit cost transferred out, $3.70

23-30A b. Finished goods inventory, $76,800

23-31A Cost of goods transferred out, $740,600

23-32A b. Department 1, $4 per machine hour

23-33A a. Allocated to F, $42,400

23-34A b. Equivalent units: Blending: material, 66,000; conversion, 64,200

23-35A a. Cost of units transferred out, $5,070,000

Business Decision Case Plan A, $55,500

24-26 a. $144,000; b. $136,000

24-27 d. Variable cost per unit, $4.80

24-28 a. Total cost = $171,000 + ($34.60 × units)

24-29 b. $536,000

24-30 b. $821,000

24-31 d. 3,000 units

24-32 c. 40%

24-33 a. Break-even units, 22,000

24-34 b. 15,000 units

24-26A a. $180,000; b. $100,000

24-27A d. Variable cost per unit, $0.12

24-28A a. Total cost = $167,200 + ($46.60 × units)

24-29A b. $316,000

24-30A b. $1,824,000

24-31A d. 4,000 units

24-32A c. 35%

24-33A a. Break-even units, 44,000

24-34A b. 28,000 units

Business Decision Case b. $11 minimum price per unit

25-33 b. Carpeting department, 40%

25-34 Department Y net income, $19,890

25-35 b. Net income, $229,500

25-36 a. Department A, $75,000

25-37 b. $36.44

25-38 b. $392

25-39 b. Net decrease, $676,000

25-40 b. Deluxe, $23.20

25-41 b. 1993, $4,080

25-42 b. Net income, $262,000

25-43 a. $89

25-44 d. $235,600

25-45 Reduction in 1993 income tax, $2,467

25-46 b. Year 1, $2,480

25-33A b. Appliance department, 38%

25-34A Department B net income, $12,740

25-35A b. Net income, $18,000

25-36A a. Department R, $40,000

25-37A b. $36.10

25-38A b. $340

25-39A b. Net decrease, $640,000

25-40A b. Automatic, $192

25-41A b. 1993, $4,400

25-42A b. Net increase, $950,000

25-43A a. $126

25-44A d. $525,600

25-45A a. $17,861

25-46A a. $30,273

Business Decision Case
a. 1. Automatic, $130

26-24 $290,460

26-25 b. Net income, $65,478

26-26 Ending cash balance, $225,000

26-27 b. Purchases of component K, $556,000

26-28 a. Net income, $52,762

26-24A $164,730

26-25A b. Net income, $163,710

26-26A Ending cash balance, $40,000

26-27A b. Purchases of component M, $794,000

26-28A a. Net income, $49,140

Business Decision Case h. March ending cash balance, $69,800

27-27 Total variance, $62,176 U

27-28 c. Variable overhead efficiency variance, $1,500 U

27-29 a. Fixed overhead volume variance, $840 U; d. Gross profit, $207,020

27-30 b. Labor efficiency variance, $600 U; c. Variable overhead efficiency variance, $400 U

27-31 b. Total variance, $31,680 F

27-27A Total variance, $11,100 U

27-28A c. Variable overhead efficiency variance, $1,500 U

27-29A a. Fixed overhead volume variance, $5,400 U; d. Gross profit, $138,000

27-30A b. Labor efficiency variance, $3,000 U; c. Variable overhead efficiency variance, $600 U

27-31A b. Total variance, $25,650 U

Business Decision Case Total variance, $16,970 U

28-28 No key figure

28-29 Net positive present value, $10,183

28-30 c. 1.018

28-31 Proposal A: a. 1.148; b. 25.2%

28-32 d. Net positive present value, $41,672

28-33 b. Net present value (negative), $1,697

28-28A No key figure

28-29A Net positive present value, $101,409

28-30A   c. 1.032
28-31A   Proposal A: a. 1.180;
          b. 31.7%
28-32A   d. Net present value
              (negative), $33,648
28-33A   b. Net present value
              (positive), $11,316
Business Decision Case b. Cutoff rate,
15%

K-4   Overpayment, $916
K-5   No key figure
K-6   Overpayment, $785
K-7   Overpayment, $1,011

REAL COMPANY
INDEX

SUBJECT INDEX

Note: Numbers that appear in **boldface type** indicate terms that appear in end-of-chapter glossaries.